SYNOPSIS

OF THE

PAULINE LETTERS

IN GREEK AND ENGLISH

SYNOPSIS

OF THE

PAULINE LETTERS

IN GREEK AND ENGLISH

EDITED BY

JAMES P. WARE

incorporating the thirteen Pauline letters
and passages of the Acts of the Apostles pertaining to Paul

from the Nestle-Aland *Novum Testamentum Graece*
and the New Revised Standard Version

arranged topically, with a critical apparatus

Baker Academic
a division of Baker Publishing Group
Grand Rapids, Michigan

Published by Baker Academic
a division of Baker Publishing Group
P.O. Box 6287, Grand Rapids, MI 49516-6287
www.bakeracademic.com

Paperback edition published 2020
ISBN 978-1-5409-6445-8

Printed in the United States of America

The Library of Congress has cataloged the hardcover edition as follows:
Synopsis of the Pauline letters in Greek and English / edited by James P. Ware.
p. cm.
"Incorporating the thirteen Pauline letters and passages of the Acts of the Apostles pertaining to Paul from the Nestle-Aland Novum Testamentum Graece and the New Revised Standard Version arranged topically, with a critical apparatus."
Includes bibliographical references.
ISBN 978-0-8010-3889-1 (cloth)
1. Bible. N.T. Epistles of Paul—Outlines, syllabi, etc. 2. Bible. N.T. Greek—Versions—Nestle-Aland—Outlines, syllabi, etc. I. Ware, James P. (James Patrick), 1957– II. Bible. N.T. Greek. Nestle-Aland. Selections. 1993. III. Bible. N.T. English. New Revised Standard. Selections. 1989.
BS2650.55.S96 2010
227'.048—dc22 2010024317

To
Andrew James Ware

Table of Contents

Preface

I wish to express my thanks to Charles Puskas, who first suggested to me the need for a Greek-English synopsis of Paul's letters and encouraged me to take up this task. In the course of this work I became convinced that the scholarly study of parallel passages in the Pauline epistles required not only the collection of parallels in Greek as well as English but also an entirely new approach that would permit the systematic study of the multiple themes and motifs that cluster in each passage within these letters. The present work, a labor of love over several years, is the result. I also wish to express my thanks to Brian Bolger and James Ernest, editors at Baker Academic, not only for their fine editorial skills but also for their fruitful ideas and suggestions that have enhanced the usefulness of this volume. I am also grateful to Dan Malda for the design and layout of the text. I owe a special debt of thanks to James Ernest, who saw the potential of this work as a scholarly tool and recommended its publication by Baker Academic. My work on this volume has served as a constant reminder of the debt I owe to many scholars but especially of how much I continue to owe my teachers in New Testament at Yale, Abraham J. Malherbe and Wayne A. Meeks. I am also grateful to Christopher Hutson, Robert Mowery, and Jeffrey Peterson, who examined the work at various stages and made helpful comments and suggestions. I also wish to thank students Allen Armstrong, Traci Hoehn, Sierra Ryan, and Alex Thompson, as well as my son Andrew, for their assistance with various aspects of the project. Above all, I am grateful for the love, support, and encouragement of my wife, Jan, and our son, Andrew. It is to Andrew that this work is dedicated.

Introduction

The *Synopsis of the Pauline Letters* is a new resource for the study of Paul. This work brings together passages in the Pauline letters that are related or parallel, whether by epistolary structure, literary form, or content, thus providing an effective tool for close comparison of related passages. It is designed to provide a helpful resource for all serious students of Paul's letters, whether scholars, students, clergy, or laypeople.

The Scope of the Synopsis

In both scope and format the *Synopsis of the Pauline Letters* is a marked advance over previous tools for the comparative study of Paul.[1] The present work is the first synopsis of related passages in Paul's letters in the original Greek. Each set of parallel passages is given both in Greek and in English translation, on facing pages. The Greek text provided is that of the Nestle-Aland 27th edition, and the English translation is the New Revised Standard Version (NRSV). In addition, a working textual apparatus is furnished for both the Greek text and the English translation, enabling the user to examine the most crucial textual variants in Paul's letters and weigh the essential manuscript evidence for each reading.

This synopsis includes the entire corpus of the Pauline letters in the New Testament. Among the Pauline epistles are some letters whose direct authorship by Paul himself is undisputed; in the case of other letters it is debated whether they are authored by Paul or by one of his disciples. The plan of the synopsis involves no prejudgment on such questions. Both the letters whose Pauline authorship is uncontested (Romans, 1 Corinthians, 2 Corinthians, Galatians, Philippians, 1 Thessalonians, Philemon) and those whose authorship is debated (Ephesians, Colossians, 2 Thessalonians, 1 Timothy, 2 Timothy, Titus) are included in the present work, enabling users to work with the entire canonical corpus of Paul's letters. Another important feature of the present work is the inclusion of relevant passages from the portrayal of Paul's teaching and ministry in the book of Acts. The inclusion of all the Pauline letters together with related passages from Acts thus permits the user to do comparative study of any passage within the Pauline corpus in light of the entire canonical witness to Paul's teaching and mission within the New Testament.

The Format of the Synopsis

The innovative format of this synopsis enables users to work with the multiple and many-faceted parallels to any passage in Paul easily, systematically, and comprehensively.

1. Previous efforts to bring together related passages in Paul's letters include the groundbreaking work of J. Paul Sampley and Fred O. Francis (*Pauline Parallels* [2nd ed.; Philadelphia: Fortress, 1984]), and the more recent volumes by Walter Wilson (*Pauline Parallels: A Comprehensive Guide* [Louisville: Westminster/John Knox, 2009]) and Patricia Elyse Terrell (*Paul's Parallels: An Echoes Synopsis* [London: T&T Clark, 2009]).

The Body of the Work

The body of the work consists of 177 groups of related passages. Each set of parallels is given a *number* and a *topic* label, identifying the structural, formal, or thematic relationship connecting the passages (e.g., "1. Salutation"). Of course, the selection and labeling of topics necessarily introduces a subjective element into the enterprise, a difficulty compounded by the well-known density and richness of the apostle's thought. The whirlwind can hardly be captured in a bottle! However, the choice of thematic topics reflects, as far as possible, Paul's own categories of thought, as informed by current scholarship on Paul, while avoiding the imposition of any particular view of Paul's theology.[2] Within the body of the work the topics are arranged in the following order: epistolary structure (1–8), epistolary forms (9–14), literary forms (15–22), content or theme (23–161), key events of the Pauline mission (162–66), and Paul's co-workers (167–77). The order of thematic topics roughly follows the general order in which Paul addresses themes in Romans. Related topics are grouped together whenever possible. Cross-references to related topics are also provided at the close of many topics.

The choice of passages within each topic includes debatable as well as obvious parallels, leaving to the user the final decision as to the relevance of any parallel passage. Whole sense units have been given as often as possible, within allowable space. A list of additional passages for comparison, which space precludes giving in full text, is provided at the close of many topics. This feature allows the collection of parallel passages within each topic to be of a manageable size, while at the same time permitting a level of comprehensiveness. Users desiring a full presentation of the relevant evidence will always wish to examine both the passages given in full text, and the list of additional passages.

The Table of Parallels

The key to using the *Synopsis of the Pauline Letters* is the Table of Parallels at the front of the work, immediately following this introduction. Arranged in the canonical order of Paul's letters, the Table of Parallels lists every passage from Paul's letters, as well as the book of Acts, found in the body of the work. When studying any passage in Paul, the user simply looks up the passage in the Table of Parallels to find the topic number or numbers in which the passage is found in the body of the work. This will lead the user to the topic or topics in the synopsis where there are collections of passages parallel to the text under study. The abbreviation "cf." in the Table of Parallels indicates that the text is one of the additional passages for comparison given under the indicated topic or topics.

The texts listed in the Table of Parallels are arranged according to the standard sense divisions of Paul's letters, with smaller sense units indented under the larger passage, and topic numbers listed for both the larger passage and its subsections. This feature allows the user, when working with any passage in Paul, to examine all relevant parallels, both to the passage as a whole, and to individual units and elements within it. Therefore when working with any passage, the user should always consult not only the topics listed for the passage as a whole but also the topics listed for smaller sense units within the passage.

2. In my endeavor to frame the thematic topics within Paul's own lines of thought, I have been helped by the work of Pauline scholars too numerous to mention. The following interpreters I have found especially helpful, and their insights into Pauline theology are evident at various points throughout this work: Abraham J. Malherbe, Wayne Meeks, Richard Hays, N. T. Wright, Joseph A. Fitzmyer, J. Paul Sampley, James D. G. Dunn, David Wenham, Robert C. Tannehill, and Stephen E. Fowl. Special mention should be made of Robert C. Tannehill's seminal essay "Participation in Christ: A Central Theme in Pauline Soteriology" in *The Shape of the Gospel* (Eugene, OR: Wipf & Stock, 2007), 225-39, which illumines a key but often neglected feature of Paul's thought reflected in topic 30 ("The Son of God's Redemptive Sharing in the Human Plight").

Both the larger passages and the smaller sense units in the Table of Parallels often have more than one topic number, and in many cases several. This reflects the fact that passages in Paul are generally related or parallel to other passages in several distinct respects. In previous tools, the user could only work with these various parallels at best partially and haphazardly. In the *Synopsis of the Pauline Letters*, by contrast, the parallels are arranged in the body of the work by topic, corresponding to the various themes, facets, and motifs of Paul's letters, and the Table of Parallels directs the user to each of the various topics in which the passage under study is found. By turning in the body of the work to each of these topics in turn, the user is thus able to work with the relevant parallels to each of the various themes, facets, and motifs of any passage under study.

The Table of Parallels is the indispensable key to the effective use of this scholarly tool. Users should normally begin their work in the synopsis with the Table of Parallels. By first consulting the Table of Parallels to discover the relevant topics for any given passage, then turning to the body of the work to closely examine the parallel passages within each of these topics (including the passages for comparison) and also turning to any related topics listed in the cross-references, users will as a rule gain a remarkably comprehensive overview of passages parallel or related to the passage under study.

The Greek Text and Apparatus

The Greek text used in this work is that of the Nestle-Aland *Novum Testamentum Graece*, 27th edition, the standard manual critical edition of the Greek New Testament used by New Testament scholars today. A streamlined textual apparatus in the synopsis provides the most essential manuscript evidence for a select number of the more important textual variants within Paul's letters and Acts. The variants were selected based on their importance for exegesis and include over 175 of the most significant points of textual variation within the Pauline epistles and the book of Acts. The apparatus exhibits for each variant the evidence of all available papyri, the most critical uncials, and a handful of essential minuscules. The manuscript evidence for the reading of the text appears first, followed by the variant reading or readings and their textual support. Of course, for a full presentation of the manuscript, versional, and patristic evidence, one should consult a standard critical edition of the Greek New Testament. But as a working tool, the streamlined apparatus provided here enables the user to examine and assess the most important variant readings found in the manuscripts of both Paul's letters and Acts. For a brief guide to using the apparatus, see "Using the Greek Textual Apparatus" below.

The English Translation and Apparatus

The English translation used, except where noted, is that of the New Revised Standard Version (NRSV), one of the most elegant and widely used translations published today. A working textual apparatus is also provided, alerting the user to the key alternate readings exhibited in the apparatus of the corresponding Greek text. The English apparatus includes all of the NRSV's text critical notes, supplemented or corrected where necessary, together with a substantial number of additional notes created for this volume. This apparatus explains the content of the variants and provides a general description of the weight of the manuscript evidence; for a presentation of the most important manuscript evidence in support of each reading, the user should consult the Greek textual apparatus.

Unlike previous tools, the *Synopsis of the Pauline Letters* displays parallel passages selected entirely on the basis of the Greek text of Paul's letters. As a result, the varied connections between parallel passages in this work are often only fully evident in the original Greek, not English translation. However, the present work contains features that serve to bridge the gap between original and translation for the English reader. Notes are included at the close of a number of topics to provide guidance regarding relevant translation issues or to explain common Greek terms underlying varied words in the NRSV translation. In a very few verses, where the NRSV translation obscures the parallels or their connections for the English reader, an alternative translation differing from the NRSV has been provided. In such cases, the departure from the NRSV is carefully indicated by a note within the English apparatus.

The Table of Topics, the Index of Subjects, and the Glossary

The format of the synopsis assumes that users will normally employ it to explore a particular passage, as guided by the Table of Parallels. However, users may also wish to explore a particular topic or subject within the Pauline letters, and the present work includes features designed to facilitate this kind of study as well. Immediately preceding the body of the work, the Table of Topics provides a list of the numbered topics. At the back of the work, the Index of Subjects supplies a summary of subjects within the Pauline passages collected in the synopsis, in alphabetical order. The Glossary provides a brief, working definition of selected terms used in the topic titles and in the notes.

Illumining Paul's Letters through Comparative Study

The *Synopsis of the Pauline Letters* is designed as a working tool to enrich the study of these letters within their distinctive historical contexts. Close study of any passage using the synopsis should therefore always be accompanied by study of the larger letter of which it is a part. And when working through the various parallels to the passage under study it is crucial for the user to remain in constant engagement with Paul's letters as whole documents, situating each passage in its literary, logical, and rhetorical context within the letter. Moreover, it is important that users employ this resource as part of an integrated approach to the interpretation of Paul's letters, complementing their work with the synopsis by the use of concordances, commentaries, and other exegetical tools. When used as part of such an integrated approach, the synopsis can be an invaluable addition to other exegetical aids for the close study of Paul.

The possibilities for illumining Paul's letters through comparative study are limitless, and can hardly be confined to a single formula. Tracing a theme or motif throughout Paul's letters will almost always yield fresh insights, new connections, and an enriched grasp of Paul's thought. Moreover, examining passages where Paul treats the same topic or theme helps one to see Paul's thought on that theme in its wholeness and depth, thus avoiding the shallow or mistaken understandings that arise when a given passage is studied in isolation from his thought as a whole.

One of the exciting (and sometimes daunting) aspects of interpreting Paul's letters is the rich and kaleidoscopic character of his thought. A given passage in Paul rarely has a single theme; rather, in most passages, thoughts, themes, and motifs cascade one upon another. The distinctive format of the *Synopsis of the Pauline Letters* allows the interpreter to unpack each of these various themes and motifs and trace them throughout the letters, in order to gain a fuller, richer understanding of the passage.

Comparative study of Paul's letters is invaluable in many other ways. The importance or development of a given theme in the letter under study, which might otherwise be missed, is often brought out clearly by study of related passages from the same letter. The synopsis therefore brings to life connections, inclusions, and recurrences within the same letter hitherto unrecognized. Through the synopsis, the interpreter is also able to compare and contrast the ways the same topic may be treated from letter to letter. Interpreters wishing to examine the use of a particular epistolary convention or literary device have all of the relevant passages at their fingertips. In short, the possible uses of the *Synopsis of the Pauline Letters* for enriching the study of Paul are manifold, depending on the purposes and creativity of the user. Anyone who works closely with this resource will find it an indispensable aid to unlocking the riches of Paul's letters.

Using the Greek Textual Apparatus

The letters of Paul began to be copied shortly after they were composed and were transmitted over the centuries by handwritten copies, or manuscripts. Although copyists normally worked with great care, from early on variations began to creep into the manuscripts, the result of unintended slips of the eye or pen, as well as intentional additions, omissions, or alterations. Close analysis of the textual witnesses that support each reading, or textual criticism, seeks to determine the original text of a passage when differences occur in the manuscripts.

The vast majority of variants within the Pauline letters are, as a result of the fidelity and quality of the New Testament manuscript tradition, relatively minor. But while one's decision as to the original text is accordingly rarely *crucial* for the meaning of a passage, it can often be *significant*. In these cases, the wealth of the New Testament manuscript tradition enables the student of Paul to weigh the various readings and come to a sound decision regarding the original text. Close study of any passage should therefore always include the study and assessment of significant variant readings that occur in the passage.

In arriving at a decision concerning the original reading, sound methods of textual criticism consider both the external evidence of the age, character, and distribution of the manuscript witnesses in support of each reading, and the internal evidence of each reading's transcriptional and intrinsic probability. Of these manuscript witnesses, within Paul's letters the great uncials are perhaps of supreme value. But the papyri, especially those predating the uncials, are also of significant weight. A select number of minuscules also preserve a text of great antiquity. The science of textual criticism has identified at least three major text types, or manuscript families, among the manuscript witnesses to Paul's letters and Acts. The Byzantine text type, which eventually became the predominant text form in the Greek-speaking East, is marked by systematic polishing, conflation and harmonization, and is generally inferior. The Western text type preserves an early text but is marked by freedom of editorial activity. The manuscripts of this text type are thus valuable, but generally only when they stand in agreement with other important witnesses. The Alexandrian text type is generally recognized as the most reliable of the text types and closest to the original text. The combined witness of the Alexandrian and Western, or Alexandrian and Byzantine, text types provides especially strong evidence of the originality of a given reading. The most convincing evidence for the originality of a reading arises from a convergence of both the external and internal evidence in support of that reading.

The condensed apparatus furnished in the present work is designed to facilitate such text critical assessment by permitting the user to note major textual variants and the evidence of the key manuscript witnesses for each. The apparatus provides the evidence of all extant papyri, the most important uncials, and a small group of essential minuscules for a substantial number of the most exegetically significant instances of textual variation within the Pauline corpus and Acts. A descriptive list of the manuscripts cited within the apparatus is given below, providing each manuscript's symbol, name, date, text type, and current location. This list is designed to function as a handy reference tool as the user works through the manuscript evidence in the apparatus. This is followed by a complete list of sigla and abbreviations used within the apparatus.

Manuscripts Cited within the Apparatus

Papyri

Symbol	Name	Date	Text Type*	Location
$\mathfrak{P}^{10}$	P. Oxy. 209	4th cent.	Alexandrian	Cambridge, MA
$\mathfrak{P}^{11}$		6th cent.	Alexandrian	St. Petersburg
$\mathfrak{P}^{26}$	P. Oxy. 1354	c. 600	Alexandrian	Dallas
$\mathfrak{P}^{27}$	P. Oxy. 1355	3rd cent.	mixed	Cambridge
$\mathfrak{P}^{30}$	P. Oxy. 1598	3rd cent.	mixed	Ghent
$\mathfrak{P}^{33}$		6th cent.	Alexandrian	Vienna
$\mathfrak{P}^{45}$	P. Chester Beatty I	3rd cent.	Alexandrian	Dublin/Vienna
$\mathfrak{P}^{46}$	P. Chester Beatty II	c. 200	Alexandrian	Dublin/Ann Arbor
$\mathfrak{P}^{49}$	P. Yale 415	3rd cent.	Alexandrian	New Haven
$\mathfrak{P}^{61}$	P. Colt 5	c. 700	Alexandrian	New York
$\mathfrak{P}^{65}$		3rd cent.	Alexandrian	Florence
$\mathfrak{P}^{74}$	P. Bodmer XVII	7th cent.	Alexandrian	Cologny
$\mathfrak{P}^{87}$		3rd cent.	Alexandrian	Cologne

*Indicates the manuscript's text type within Paul's letters or Acts, not necessarily elsewhere in the New Testament.

Uncials

Symbol	Name	Date	Text Type*	Location
$\aleph$	Sinaiticus	4th cent.	Alexandrian	London
$\aleph^{1}$	first corrector	4th cent.–6th. cent.		
$\aleph^{2}$	second corrector	c. 7th cent.		
$\aleph^{c}$	third corrector	12th cent.		
A	Alexandrinus	5th cent.	Alexandrian	London
B	Vaticanus	4th cent.	Alexandrian	Rome
B^{1}	first corrector	4th cent.		
B^{2}	second corrector	6th/7th cent.		
C	Ephraemi Rescriptus	5th cent.	Alexandrian	Paris
C^{1}	first corrector	5th cent.		
C^{2}	second corrector	c. 6th cent.		
C^{3}	third corrector	c. 9th cent.		
D (05)	Bezae Cantabrigiensis	5th cent.	Western	Cambridge
D^{1}	first corrector	6th cent.–7th cent.		
D^{2}	second corrector	c. 9th cent.		
D^{c}	third corrector	12th cent.		
D (06)	Claromontanus	6th cent.	Western	Paris
D^{1}	first corrector	c. 7th cent.		
D^{2}	second corrector	c. 9th cent.		
D^{c}	third corrector			
E (08)	Laudianus	6th cent.	mixed	Oxford
I	Freerianus (Washingtonensis)	5th cent.	Alexandrian	Washington
048		5th cent.		Rome
088		5th/6th cent.	Alexandrian	St. Petersburg
0111		7th cent.	Alexandrian	Berlin
0220		3rd cent.	Alexandrian	Oslo/London
0223		6th cent.	Alexandrian	Vienna

*Indicates the manuscript's text type within Paul's letters and/or Acts, not necessarily elsewhere in the New Testament.

Minuscules

Symbol	Date	Text Type	Location
33	9th cent.	Alexandrian	Paris
1739	10th cent.	Alexandrian	Athos
1881	14th cent.	Alexandrian	Sinai

Manuscript Groups

Symbol	Description	Date	Text Type
Byz	manuscripts of the Byzantine text type	5th cent.–16th cent.	Byzantine
Byz[pt]	one portion of Byzantine manuscripts when their testimony is divided		Byzantine
omnes	(= *omnes codices*) all manuscripts		
pc	(= *pauci codices*) a few manuscripts		

Sigla and Abbreviations Used in the Apparatus and the Greek Text

⸀	identifies a single word within the text for which a variant is given in the apparatus
⸂ ⸃	identifies two or more words within the text for which a variant is given in the apparatus
[ ]	encloses words within the text identified by the Nestle-Aland editors as subject to some doubt regarding their originality. Only a select number of such instances are treated in the apparatus; in all other cases the user may consult the apparatus of the Nestle-Aland edition for more information
]	placed at the close of the text reading and its supporting witnesses
¦	separates alternate readings together with their supporting witnesses
•	separates multiple cases of textual variation within the same verse
*	the original reading of a manuscript when a correction or alternate reading is also supplied
1,2,3	the various correctors of the great uncials (see manuscript list for details)
c	a corrector of a manuscript
mg	an alternate reading given in the margin of the manuscript
vid	(= *videtur*) the reading of the manuscript is uncertain
v.l.	(= *varia lectio*) the reading is identified as a variant reading within the manuscript
( )	the manuscript supports the reading in question despite negligible variations
acc.	(= *accentus*) accentuation
add.	(= *addit/-unt*) add(s)
cj	(= *conjectura*) a reading not found in the manuscripts but conjectured as original by modern scholars
om.	(= *omittit/-unt*) omit(s)
om. hic et pon. p.	(= *omittit/-unt hic et ponit/-unt post*) omit(s) here and place(s) after
pon. hic	(= *ponit/-unt hic*) place(s) here
pon. hic et p.	(= *ponit/-unt hic et post*) place(s) here and after
pon. p.	(= *ponit/-unt post*) place(s) after
sine acc.	(= *sine accentu*) without accentuation

Table of Parallels

Note: Numbers following Scripture references refer to section numbers within the synopsis *not* to page numbers.

1 Corinthians

2 Corinthians

Galatians

Ephesians

Philippians

2 Thessalonians

1 Timothy

2 Timothy

Titus

Philemon

Acts

Table of Topics

SYNOPSIS

OF THE

PAULINE LETTERS

IN GREEK AND ENGLISH

Synopsis

1. Salutation

Rom 1:1–7

Παῦλος δοῦλος ⸂Χριστοῦ Ἰησοῦ⸃, κλητὸς
ἀπόστολος ἀφωρισμένος εἰς εὐαγγέλιον
θεοῦ, 2 ὃ προεπηγγείλατο διὰ τῶν προ-
φητῶν αὐτοῦ ἐν γραφαῖς ἁγίαις 3 περὶ τοῦ
υἱοῦ αὐτοῦ τοῦ γενομένου ἐκ σπέρματος
Δαυὶδ κατὰ σάρκα, 4 τοῦ ὁρισθέντος υἱοῦ
θεοῦ ἐν δυνάμει κατὰ πνεῦμα ἁγιωσύνης
ἐξ ἀναστάσεως νεκρῶν, Ἰησοῦ Χριστοῦ
τοῦ κυρίου ἡμῶν, 5 δι' οὗ ἐλάβομεν χάριν
καὶ ἀποστολὴν εἰς ὑπακοὴν πίστεως ἐν
πᾶσιν τοῖς ἔθνεσιν ὑπὲρ τοῦ ὀνόματος
αὐτοῦ, 6 ἐν οἷς ἐστε καὶ ὑμεῖς κλητοὶ
Ἰησοῦ Χριστοῦ, 7 πᾶσιν τοῖς οὖσιν ἐν
Ῥώμῃ ἀγαπητοῖς θεοῦ, κλητοῖς ἁγίοις,
χάρις ὑμῖν καὶ εἰρήνη ἀπὸ θεοῦ πατρὸς
ἡμῶν καὶ κυρίου Ἰησοῦ Χριστοῦ.

1 Cor 1:1–3

Παῦλος κλητὸς ἀπόστολος Χριστοῦ Ἰη-
σοῦ διὰ θελήματος θεοῦ καὶ Σωσθένης
ὁ ἀδελφὸς 2 τῇ ἐκκλησίᾳ τοῦ θεοῦ τῇ
οὔσῃ ἐν Κορίνθῳ, ἡγιασμένοις ἐν Χριστῷ
Ἰησοῦ, κλητοῖς ἁγίοις, σὺν πᾶσιν τοῖς
ἐπικαλουμένοις τὸ ὄνομα τοῦ κυρίου
ἡμῶν Ἰησοῦ Χριστοῦ ἐν παντὶ τόπῳ,
αὐτῶν καὶ ἡμῶν· 3 χάρις ὑμῖν καὶ εἰρήνη
ἀπὸ θεοῦ πατρὸς ἡμῶν καὶ κυρίου Ἰη-
σοῦ Χριστοῦ.

2 Cor 1:1–2

Παῦλος ἀπόστολος Χριστοῦ Ἰησοῦ διὰ
θελήματος θεοῦ καὶ Τιμόθεος ὁ ἀδελ-
φὸς τῇ ἐκκλησίᾳ τοῦ θεοῦ τῇ οὔσῃ ἐν
Κορίνθῳ σὺν τοῖς ἁγίοις πᾶσιν τοῖς οὖσιν
ἐν ὅλῃ τῇ Ἀχαΐᾳ, 2 χάρις ὑμῖν καὶ εἰρήνη
ἀπὸ θεοῦ πατρὸς ἡμῶν καὶ κυρίου Ἰη-
σοῦ Χριστοῦ.

Gal 1:1–5

Παῦλος ἀπόστολος οὐκ ἀπ' ἀνθρώπων
οὐδὲ δι' ἀνθρώπου ἀλλὰ διὰ Ἰησοῦ Χρι-
στοῦ καὶ θεοῦ πατρὸς τοῦ ἐγείραντος
αὐτὸν ἐκ νεκρῶν, 2 καὶ οἱ σὺν ἐμοὶ πάντες
ἀδελφοὶ ταῖς ἐκκλησίαις τῆς Γαλατίας,
3 χάρις ὑμῖν καὶ εἰρήνη ἀπὸ θεοῦ πατρὸς
ἡμῶν καὶ κυρίου Ἰησοῦ Χριστοῦ 4 τοῦ
δόντος ἑαυτὸν ὑπὲρ τῶν ἁμαρτιῶν ἡμῶν,
ὅπως ἐξέληται ἡμᾶς ἐκ τοῦ αἰῶνος τοῦ
ἐνεστῶτος πονηροῦ κατὰ τὸ θέλημα τοῦ
θεοῦ καὶ πατρὸς ἡμῶν, 5 ᾧ ἡ δόξα εἰς
τοὺς αἰῶνας τῶν αἰώνων, ἀμήν.

Eph 1:1–2

Παῦλος ἀπόστολος Χριστοῦ Ἰησοῦ διὰ
θελήματος θεοῦ τοῖς ἁγίοις τοῖς οὖσιν ⸂[ἐν
Ἐφέσῳ]⸃ καὶ πιστοῖς ἐν Χριστῷ Ἰησοῦ,
2 χάρις ὑμῖν καὶ εἰρήνη ἀπὸ θεοῦ πατρὸς
ἡμῶν καὶ κυρίου Ἰησοῦ Χριστοῦ.

Phil 1:1–2

Παῦλος καὶ Τιμόθεος δοῦλοι Χριστοῦ
Ἰησοῦ πᾶσιν τοῖς ἁγίοις ἐν Χριστῷ Ἰησοῦ
τοῖς οὖσιν ἐν Φιλίπποις σὺν ἐπισκόποις
καὶ διακόνοις, 2 χάρις ὑμῖν καὶ εἰρήνη
ἀπὸ θεοῦ πατρὸς ἡμῶν καὶ κυρίου Ἰη-
σοῦ Χριστοῦ.

Col 1:1–2

Παῦλος ἀπόστολος Χριστοῦ Ἰησοῦ διὰ
θελήματος θεοῦ καὶ Τιμόθεος ὁ ἀδελφὸς
2 τοῖς ἐν Κολοσσαῖς ἁγίοις καὶ πιστοῖς
ἀδελφοῖς ἐν Χριστῷ, χάρις ὑμῖν καὶ
εἰρήνη ἀπὸ θεοῦ πατρὸς ἡμῶν.

1 Thess 1:1

Παῦλος καὶ Σιλουανὸς καὶ Τιμόθεος
τῇ ἐκκλησίᾳ Θεσσαλονικέων ἐν θεῷ
πατρὶ καὶ κυρίῳ Ἰησοῦ Χριστῷ, χάρις
ὑμῖν καὶ ⸀εἰρήνη.

2 Thess 1:1–2

Παῦλος καὶ Σιλουανὸς καὶ Τιμόθεος τῇ
ἐκκλησίᾳ Θεσσαλονικέων ἐν θεῷ πατρὶ
ἡμῶν καὶ κυρίῳ Ἰησοῦ Χριστῷ, 2 χάρις
ὑμῖν καὶ εἰρήνη ἀπὸ θεοῦ πατρὸς ⸀[ἡμῶν]
καὶ κυρίου Ἰησοῦ Χριστοῦ.

1 Tim 1:1–2

Παῦλος ἀπόστολος Χριστοῦ Ἰησοῦ κατ'
ἐπιταγὴν θεοῦ σωτῆρος ἡμῶν καὶ Χρι-
στοῦ Ἰησοῦ τῆς ἐλπίδος ἡμῶν 2 Τιμοθέῳ
γνησίῳ τέκνῳ ἐν πίστει, χάρις ἔλεος
εἰρήνη ἀπὸ θεοῦ πατρὸς καὶ Χριστοῦ
Ἰησοῦ τοῦ κυρίου ἡμῶν.

2 Tim 1:1–2

Παῦλος ἀπόστολος Χριστοῦ Ἰησοῦ διὰ
θελήματος θεοῦ κατ' ἐπαγγελίαν ζωῆς
τῆς ἐν Χριστῷ Ἰησοῦ 2 Τιμοθέῳ ἀγα-
πητῷ τέκνῳ, χάρις ἔλεος εἰρήνη ἀπὸ
θεοῦ πατρὸς καὶ Χριστοῦ Ἰησοῦ τοῦ
κυρίου ἡμῶν.

Titus 1:1–4

Παῦλος δοῦλος θεοῦ, ἀπόστολος δὲ
Ἰησοῦ Χριστοῦ κατὰ πίστιν ἐκλεκτῶν
θεοῦ καὶ ἐπίγνωσιν ἀληθείας τῆς κατ'
εὐσέβειαν 2 ἐπ' ἐλπίδι ζωῆς αἰωνίου, ἣν
ἐπηγγείλατο ὁ ἀψευδὴς θεὸς πρὸ χρό-
νων αἰωνίων, 3 ἐφανέρωσεν δὲ καιροῖς
ἰδίοις τὸν λόγον αὐτοῦ ἐν κηρύγματι, ὃ
ἐπιστεύθην ἐγὼ κατ' ἐπιταγὴν τοῦ σω-
τῆρος ἡμῶν θεοῦ, 4 Τίτῳ γνησίῳ τέκνῳ
κατὰ κοινὴν πίστιν, χάρις ⸀καὶ εἰρήνη
ἀπὸ θεοῦ πατρὸς καὶ Χριστοῦ Ἰησοῦ τοῦ
σωτῆρος ἡμῶν.

Phlm 1–3

Παῦλος δέσμιος Χριστοῦ Ἰησοῦ καὶ Τι-
μόθεος ὁ ἀδελφὸς Φιλήμονι τῷ ἀγαπητῷ
καὶ συνεργῷ ἡμῶν 2 καὶ Ἀπφίᾳ τῇ ἀδελφῇ

§ 1 **Rom 1:1** ***Χριστου Ιησου*** 𝔓10 B] Ιησου Χριστου 𝔓26 א A 33. 1739. 1881 *Byz* **Eph 1:1** ***εν Εφεσω*** א2 A B2 D 33. 1881 *Byz*] *om.* 𝔓46 א* B* 1739 **1 Thess 1:1** ***ειρηνη*** B 1739. 1881] *add.* απο θεου πατρος ημων και κυριου Ιησου Χριστου א A (D) I 33 *Byz* **2 Thess 1:2** ***ημων*** א A I *Byz*] *om.* B D 0111vid. 33. 1739. 1881 **Titus 1:4** ***και*** א C* D 088] ελεος A C2 *Byz* ¦ *om.* 1739. 1881 ¦ υμιν και 33

1. Salutation

Rom 1:1–7

Paul, a servant of Jesus Christ,[a] called to be an apostle, set apart for the gospel of God, **2** which he promised beforehand through his prophets in the holy scriptures, **3** the gospel concerning his Son, who was descended from David according to the flesh **4** and was declared to be Son of God with power according to the Spirit[b] of holiness by resurrection from the dead, Jesus Christ our Lord, **5** through whom we have received grace and apostleship to bring about the obedience of faith among all the Gentiles for the sake of his name, **6** including yourselves who are called to belong to Jesus Christ, **7** To all God's beloved in Rome, who are called to be saints: Grace to you and peace from God our Father and the Lord Jesus Christ.

1 Cor 1:1–3

Paul, called to be an apostle of Christ Jesus by the will of God, and our brother Sosthenes, **2** To the church of God that is in Corinth, to those who are sanctified in Christ Jesus, called to be saints, together with all those who in every place call on the name of our Lord Jesus Christ, both their Lord and ours: **3** Grace to you and peace from God our Father and the Lord Jesus Christ.

2 Cor 1:1–2

Paul, an apostle of Christ Jesus by the will of God, and Timothy our brother, to the church of God that is in Corinth, including all the saints throughout Achaia: **2** Grace to you and peace from God our Father and the Lord Jesus Christ.

Gal 1:1–5

Paul an apostle—sent neither by human commission nor from human authorities, but through Jesus Christ and God the Father, who raised him from the dead— **2** and all the members of God's family who are with me, To the churches of Galatia: **3** Grace to you and peace from God our Father and the Lord Jesus Christ, **4** who gave himself for our sins to set us free from the present evil age, according to the will of our God and Father, **5** to whom be the glory forever and ever. Amen.

Eph 1:1–2

Paul, an apostle of Christ Jesus by the will of God, To the saints who are in Ephesus and are faithful[c] in Christ Jesus: **2** Grace to you and peace from God our Father and the Lord Jesus Christ.

Phil 1:1–2

Paul and Timothy, servants of Christ Jesus, To all the saints in Christ Jesus who are in Philippi, with the bishops and deacons: **2** Grace to you and peace from God our Father and the Lord Jesus Christ.

Col 1:1–2

Paul, an apostle of Christ Jesus by the will of God, and Timothy our brother, **2** To the saints and faithful brothers and sisters in Christ in Colossae: Grace to you and peace from God our Father.

1 Thess 1:1

Paul, Silvanus, and Timothy, To the church of the Thessalonians in God the Father and the Lord Jesus Christ: Grace to you and peace.[d]

2 Thess 1:1–2

Paul, Silvanus, and Timothy, To the church of the Thessalonians in God our Father and the Lord Jesus Christ: **2** Grace to you and peace from God our[e] Father and the Lord Jesus Christ.

1 Tim 1:1–2

Paul, an apostle of Christ Jesus by the command of God our Savior and of Christ Jesus our hope, **2** To Timothy, my loyal child in the faith: Grace, mercy, and peace from God the Father and Christ Jesus our Lord.

2 Tim 1:1–2

Paul, an apostle of Christ Jesus by the will of God, for the sake of the promise of life that is in Christ Jesus, **2** To Timothy, my beloved child: Grace, mercy, and peace from God the Father and Christ Jesus our Lord.

Titus 1:1–4

Paul, a servant of God and an apostle of Jesus Christ, for the sake of the faith of God's elect and the knowledge of the truth that is in accordance with godliness, **2** in the hope of eternal life that God, who never lies, promised before the ages began— **3** in due time he revealed his word through the proclamation with which I have been entrusted by the command of God our Savior, **4** To Titus, my loyal child in the faith we share: Grace and[f] peace from God the Father and Christ Jesus our Savior.

Phlm 1–3

Paul, a prisoner of Christ Jesus, and Timothy our brother, to Philemon our dear friend and co-worker, **2** to Apphia

§ 1 [a] **Rom 1:1** *Jesus Christ* Other ancient authorities read *Christ Jesus* [b] **Rom 1:4** *Spirit* NRSV alternate translation [c] **Eph 1:1** *saints who are in Ephesus and are faithful* Other ancient authorities lack *in Ephesus*, reading *saints who are also faithful* or possibly revealing evidence of a circular letter [d] **1 Thess 1:1** *peace* Other ancient authorities add *from God our Father and the Lord Jesus Christ* [e] **2 Thess 1:2** *our* Other ancient authorities read *the* [f] **Titus 1:4** *Grace and* Other ancient authorities read *Grace, mercy*

καὶ Ἀρχίππῳ τῷ συστρατιώτῃ ἡμῶν καὶ τῇ κατʼ οἶκόν σου ἐκκλησίᾳ, 3 χάρις ὑμῖν καὶ εἰρήνη ἀπὸ θεοῦ πατρὸς ἡμῶν καὶ κυρίου Ἰησοῦ Χριστοῦ.

2. *Thanksgiving*

Rom 1:8–12

Πρῶτον μὲν εὐχαριστῶ τῷ θεῷ μου διὰ Ἰησοῦ Χριστοῦ περὶ πάντων ὑμῶν ὅτι ἡ πίστις ὑμῶν καταγγέλλεται ἐν ὅλῳ τῷ κόσμῳ. 9 μάρτυς γάρ μού ἐστιν ὁ θεός, ᾧ λατρεύω ἐν τῷ πνεύματί μου ἐν τῷ εὐαγγελίῳ τοῦ υἱοῦ αὐτοῦ, ὡς ἀδιαλείπτως μνείαν ὑμῶν ποιοῦμαι 10 πάντοτε ἐπὶ τῶν προσευχῶν μου δεόμενος εἴ πως ἤδη ποτὲ εὐοδωθήσομαι ἐν τῷ θελήματι τοῦ θεοῦ ἐλθεῖν πρὸς ὑμᾶς. 11 ἐπιποθῶ γὰρ ἰδεῖν ὑμᾶς, ἵνα τι μεταδῶ χάρισμα ὑμῖν πνευματικὸν εἰς τὸ στηριχθῆναι ὑμᾶς, 12 τοῦτο δέ ἐστιν συμπαρακληθῆναι ἐν ὑμῖν διὰ τῆς ἐν ἀλλήλοις πίστεως ὑμῶν τε καὶ ἐμοῦ.

1 Cor 1:4–9

Εὐχαριστῶ τῷ θεῷ ⸀μου πάντοτε περὶ ὑμῶν ἐπὶ τῇ χάριτι τοῦ θεοῦ τῇ δοθείσῃ ὑμῖν ἐν Χριστῷ Ἰησοῦ, 5 ὅτι ἐν παντὶ ἐπλουτίσθητε ἐν αὐτῷ, ἐν παντὶ λόγῳ καὶ πάσῃ γνώσει, 6 καθὼς τὸ μαρτύριον τοῦ Χριστοῦ ἐβεβαιώθη ἐν ὑμῖν, 7 ὥστε ὑμᾶς μὴ ὑστερεῖσθαι ἐν μηδενὶ χαρίσματι ἀπεκδεχομένους τὴν ἀποκάλυψιν τοῦ κυρίου ἡμῶν Ἰησοῦ Χριστοῦ· 8 ὃς καὶ βεβαιώσει ὑμᾶς ἕως τέλους ἀνεγκλήτους ἐν τῇ ἡμέρᾳ τοῦ κυρίου ἡμῶν Ἰησοῦ [Χριστοῦ]. 9 πιστὸς ὁ θεός, διʼ οὗ ἐκλήθητε εἰς κοινωνίαν τοῦ υἱοῦ αὐτοῦ Ἰησοῦ Χριστοῦ τοῦ κυρίου ἡμῶν.

Phil 1:3–11

Εὐχαριστῶ τῷ θεῷ μου ἐπὶ πάσῃ τῇ μνείᾳ ὑμῶν 4 πάντοτε ἐν πάσῃ δεήσει μου ὑπὲρ πάντων ὑμῶν, μετὰ χαρᾶς τὴν δέησιν ποιούμενος, 5 ἐπὶ τῇ κοινωνίᾳ ὑμῶν εἰς τὸ εὐαγγέλιον ἀπὸ τῆς πρώτης ἡμέρας ἄχρι τοῦ νῦν, 6 πεποιθὼς αὐτὸ τοῦτο, ὅτι ὁ ἐναρξάμενος ἐν ὑμῖν ἔργον ἀγαθὸν ἐπιτελέσει ἄχρι ἡμέρας ⸂Χριστοῦ Ἰησοῦ⸃· 7 Καθώς ἐστιν δίκαιον ἐμοὶ τοῦτο φρονεῖν ὑπὲρ πάντων ὑμῶν διὰ τὸ ἔχειν με ἐν τῇ καρδίᾳ ὑμᾶς, ἔν τε τοῖς δεσμοῖς μου καὶ ἐν τῇ ἀπολογίᾳ καὶ βεβαιώσει τοῦ εὐαγγελίου συγκοινωνούς μου τῆς χάριτος πάντας ὑμᾶς ὄντας. 8 μάρτυς γάρ μου ὁ θεὸς ὡς ἐπιποθῶ πάντας ὑμᾶς ἐν σπλάγχνοις Χριστοῦ Ἰησοῦ. 9 Καὶ τοῦτο προσεύχομαι, ἵνα ἡ ἀγάπη ὑμῶν ἔτι μᾶλλον καὶ μᾶλλον περισσεύῃ ἐν ἐπιγνώσει καὶ πάσῃ αἰσθήσει 10 εἰς τὸ δοκιμάζειν ὑμᾶς τὰ διαφέροντα, ἵνα ἦτε εἰλικρινεῖς καὶ ἀπρόσκοποι εἰς ἡμέραν Χριστοῦ, 11 πεπληρωμένοι καρπὸν δικαιοσύνης τὸν διὰ Ἰησοῦ Χριστοῦ εἰς δόξαν καὶ ἔπαινον θεοῦ.

Col 1:3–12 (or 29)

Εὐχαριστοῦμεν τῷ θεῷ πατρὶ τοῦ κυρίου ἡμῶν Ἰησοῦ Χριστοῦ πάντοτε περὶ ὑμῶν προσευχόμενοι, 4 ἀκούσαντες τὴν πίστιν ὑμῶν ἐν Χριστῷ Ἰησοῦ καὶ τὴν ἀγάπην ἣν ἔχετε εἰς πάντας τοὺς ἁγίους 5 διὰ τὴν ἐλπίδα τὴν ἀποκειμένην ὑμῖν ἐν τοῖς οὐρανοῖς, ἣν προηκούσατε ἐν τῷ λόγῳ τῆς ἀληθείας τοῦ εὐαγγελίου 6 τοῦ παρόντος εἰς ὑμᾶς, καθὼς καὶ ἐν παντὶ τῷ κόσμῳ ἐστὶν καρποφορούμενον καὶ αὐξανόμενον καθὼς καὶ ἐν ὑμῖν, ἀφʼ ἧς ἡμέρας ἠκούσατε καὶ ἐπέγνωτε τὴν χάριν τοῦ θεοῦ ἐν ἀληθείᾳ· 7 καθὼς ἐμάθετε ἀπὸ Ἐπαφρᾶ τοῦ ἀγαπητοῦ συνδούλου ἡμῶν, ὅς ἐστιν πιστὸς ὑπὲρ ⸀ὑμῶν διάκονος τοῦ Χριστοῦ, 8 ὁ καὶ δηλώσας ἡμῖν τὴν ὑμῶν ἀγάπην ἐν πνεύματι. 9 Διὰ τοῦτο καὶ ἡμεῖς, ἀφʼ ἧς ἡμέρας ἠκούσαμεν, οὐ παυόμεθα ὑπὲρ ὑμῶν προσευχόμενοι καὶ αἰτούμενοι, ἵνα πληρωθῆτε τὴν ἐπίγνωσιν τοῦ θελήματος αὐτοῦ ἐν πάσῃ σοφίᾳ καὶ συνέσει πνευματικῇ, 10 περιπατῆσαι ἀξίως τοῦ κυρίου εἰς πᾶσαν ἀρεσκείαν, ἐν παντὶ ἔργῳ ἀγαθῷ καρποφοροῦντες καὶ αὐξανόμενοι τῇ ἐπιγνώσει τοῦ θεοῦ, 11 ἐν πάσῃ δυνάμει δυναμούμενοι κατὰ τὸ κράτος τῆς δόξης αὐτοῦ εἰς πᾶσαν ὑπομονὴν καὶ μακροθυμίαν. Μετὰ χαρᾶς 12 εὐχαριστοῦντες τῷ πατρὶ τῷ ⸀ἱκανώσαντι ⸀ὑμᾶς εἰς τὴν μερίδα τοῦ κλήρου τῶν ἁγίων ἐν τῷ φωτί

1 Thess 1:2–10 (or 1:2–3:13)

Εὐχαριστοῦμεν τῷ θεῷ πάντοτε περὶ πάντων ὑμῶν μνείαν ποιούμενοι ἐπὶ τῶν προσευχῶν ἡμῶν, ἀδιαλείπτως 3 μνημονεύοντες ὑμῶν τοῦ ἔργου τῆς πίστεως καὶ τοῦ κόπου τῆς ἀγάπης καὶ τῆς ὑπομονῆς τῆς ἐλπίδος τοῦ κυρίου ἡμῶν Ἰησοῦ Χριστοῦ ἔμπροσθεν τοῦ θεοῦ καὶ πατρὸς ἡμῶν, 4 εἰδότες, ἀδελφοὶ ἠγαπημένοι ὑπὸ [τοῦ] θεοῦ, τὴν ἐκλογὴν ὑμῶν, 5 ὅτι τὸ εὐαγγέλιον ἡμῶν οὐκ ἐγενήθη εἰς ὑμᾶς ἐν λόγῳ μόνον ἀλλὰ καὶ ἐν δυνάμει καὶ ἐν πνεύματι ἁγίῳ καὶ [ἐν] πληροφορίᾳ πολλῇ, καθὼς οἴδατε οἷοι ἐγενήθημεν [ἐν] ὑμῖν διʼ ὑμᾶς. 6 Καὶ ὑμεῖς μιμηταὶ ἡμῶν ἐγενήθητε καὶ τοῦ κυρίου, δεξάμενοι τὸν λόγον ἐν θλίψει πολλῇ μετὰ χαρᾶς πνεύματος ἁγίου, 7 ὥστε γενέσθαι ὑμᾶς τύπον πᾶσιν τοῖς πιστεύουσιν ἐν τῇ Μακεδονίᾳ καὶ ἐν τῇ Ἀχαΐᾳ. 8 ἀφʼ ὑμῶν γὰρ ἐξήχηται ὁ λόγος τοῦ κυρίου οὐ μόνον ἐν τῇ Μακεδονίᾳ καὶ [ἐν τῇ] Ἀχαΐᾳ, ἀλλʼ ἐν παντὶ τόπῳ ἡ πίστις ὑμῶν ἡ πρὸς τὸν θεὸν ἐξελήλυθεν, ὥστε μὴ χρείαν ἔχειν ἡμᾶς λαλεῖν τι. 9 αὐτοὶ γὰρ περὶ ἡμῶν ἀπαγγέλλουσιν ὁποίαν εἴσοδον ἔσχομεν πρὸς ὑμᾶς, καὶ πῶς ἐπεστρέψατε πρὸς τὸν θεὸν ἀπὸ τῶν εἰδώλων δουλεύειν θεῷ ζῶντι καὶ ἀληθινῷ 10 καὶ ἀναμένειν τὸν υἱὸν αὐτοῦ ἐκ τῶν οὐρανῶν, ὃν ἤγειρεν ἐκ [τῶν] νεκρῶν, Ἰησοῦν τὸν ῥυόμενον ἡμᾶς ἐκ τῆς ὀργῆς τῆς ἐρχομένης.

2 Thess 1:3–12

Εὐχαριστεῖν ὀφείλομεν τῷ θεῷ πάντοτε περὶ ὑμῶν, ἀδελφοί, καθὼς ἄξιόν ἐστιν, ὅτι ὑπεραυξάνει ἡ πίστις ὑμῶν καὶ πλεονάζει ἡ ἀγάπη ἑνὸς ἑκάστου πάντων ὑμῶν εἰς ἀλλήλους, 4 ὥστε αὐτοὺς ἡμᾶς ἐν ὑμῖν ἐγκαυχᾶσθαι ἐν ταῖς ἐκκλησίαις τοῦ θεοῦ ὑπὲρ τῆς ὑπομονῆς ὑμῶν καὶ πίστεως ἐν πᾶσιν τοῖς διωγμοῖς ὑμῶν καὶ ταῖς θλίψεσιν αἷς ἀνέχεσθε, 5 ἔνδειγμα τῆς δικαίας κρίσεως τοῦ θεοῦ εἰς τὸ καταξιωθῆναι ὑμᾶς τῆς βασιλείας

§ 2 1 Cor 1:4 ***μου*** ℵ^{2} A C D 33. 1739. 1881 *Byz*] *om.* ℵ* B **Phil 1:6** ***Χριστου Ιησου*** 𝔓^{46} B D *Byz*] Ιησου Χριστου ℵ A 33. 1739. 1881 **Col 1:7** ***υμων*** ℵ^{2} C D^{1} 33. 1739. 1881 *Byz*] ημων 𝔓^{46} ℵ* A B D* **Col 1:12** ***ικανωσαντι*** 𝔓^{46} 𝔓^{61vid} ℵ A C D^{2} I 1739. 1881 *Byz*] καλεσαντι D* 33 ¦ καλεσαντι και ικανωσαντι B • ***υμας*** ℵ B 1739. 1881] ημας A C D 33 *Byz*

our sister, to Archippus our fellow soldier, and to the church in your house: **3** Grace to you and peace from God our Father and the Lord Jesus Christ.

2. Thanksgiving

Rom 1:8–12

First, I thank my God through Jesus Christ for all of you, because your faith is proclaimed throughout the world. **9** For God, whom I serve with my spirit by announcing the gospel of his Son, is my witness that without ceasing I remember you always in my prayers, **10** asking that by God's will I may somehow at last succeed in coming to you. **11** For I am longing to see you so that I may share with you some spiritual gift to strengthen you— **12** or rather so that we may be mutually encouraged by each other's faith, both yours and mine.

1 Cor 1:4–9

I give thanks to my[a] God always for you because of the grace of God that has been given you in Christ Jesus, **5** for in every way you have been enriched in him, in speech and knowledge of every kind— **6** just as the testimony of Christ has been strengthened among you— **7** so that you are not lacking in any spiritual gift as you wait for the revealing of our Lord Jesus Christ. **8** He will also strengthen you to the end, so that you may be blameless on the day of our Lord Jesus Christ. **9** God is faithful; by him you were called into the fellowship of his Son, Jesus Christ our Lord.

Phil 1:3–11

I thank my God every time I remember you, **4** constantly praying with joy in every one of my prayers for all of you, **5** because of your sharing in the gospel proclamation[b] from the first day until now. **6** I am confident of this, that the one who began a good work among you will bring it to completion by the day of Jesus Christ.[c] **7** It is right for me to think this way about all of you, because you hold me in your heart, for all of you share in God's grace with me, both in my imprisonment and in the defense and confirmation of the gospel. **8** For God is my witness, how I long for all of you with the compassion of Christ Jesus. **9** And this is my prayer, that your love may overflow more and more with knowledge and full insight **10** to help you to determine what is best, so that in the day of Christ you may be pure and blameless, **11** having produced the harvest of righteousness that comes through Jesus Christ for the glory and praise of God.

Col 1:3–12 (or 29)

In our prayers for you we always thank God, the Father of our Lord Jesus Christ, **4** for we have heard of your faith in Christ Jesus and of the love that you have for all the saints, **5** because of the hope laid up for you in heaven. You have heard of this hope before in the word of the truth, the gospel **6** that has come to you. Just as it is bearing fruit and growing in the whole world, so it has been bearing fruit among yourselves from the day you heard it and truly comprehended the grace of God. **7** This you learned from Epaphras, our beloved fellow servant. He is a faithful minister of Christ on your[d] behalf, **8** and he has made known to us your love in the Spirit. **9** For this reason, since the day we heard it, we have not ceased praying for you and asking that you may be filled with the knowledge of God's will in all spiritual wisdom and understanding, **10** so that you may lead lives worthy of the Lord, fully pleasing to him, as you bear fruit in every good work and as you grow in the knowledge of God. **11** May you be made strong with all the strength that comes from his glorious power, and may you be prepared to endure everything with patience, while joyfully **12** giving thanks to the Father, who has enabled[e] you[f] to share in the inheritance of the saints in the light.

1 Thess 1:2–10 (or 1:2–3:13)

We always give thanks to God for all of you and mention you in our prayers, constantly **3** remembering before our God and Father your work of faith and labor of love and steadfastness of hope in our Lord Jesus Christ. **4** For we know, brothers and sisters beloved by God, that he has chosen you, **5** because our message of the gospel came to you not in word only, but also in power and in the Holy Spirit and with full conviction; just as you know what kind of persons we proved to be among you for your sake. **6** And you became imitators of us and of the Lord, for in spite of persecution you received the word with joy inspired by the Holy Spirit, **7** so that you became an example to all the believers in Macedonia and in Achaia. **8** For the word of the Lord has sounded forth from you not only in Macedonia and Achaia, but in every place your faith in God has become known, so that we have no need to speak about it. **9** For the people of those regions report about us what kind of welcome we had among you, and how you turned to God from idols, to serve a living and true God, **10** and to wait for his Son from heaven, whom he raised from the dead—Jesus, who rescues us from the wrath that is coming.

2 Thess 1:3–12

We must always give thanks to God for you, brothers and sisters, as is right, because your faith is growing abundantly, and the love of every one of you for one another is increasing. **4** Therefore we ourselves boast of you among the churches of God for your steadfastness and faith during all your persecutions and the afflictions that you are enduring. **5** This is evidence of the righteous judgment of God, and is intended to make you worthy of the kingdom of God, for which you are also suffering.

§ 2 [a] **1 Cor 1:4** ***my*** Other ancient authorities lack *my* [b] **Phil 1:5** ***gospel proclamation*** NRSV translates *gospel* [c] **Phil 1:6** ***Jesus Christ*** Other ancient authorities read *Christ Jesus* [d] **Col 1:7** ***your*** Other ancient authorities read *our* [e] **Col 1:12** ***enabled*** Other ancient authorities read *called* [f] **Col 1:12** ***you*** Other ancient authorities read *us*

τοῦ θεοῦ, ὑπὲρ ἧς καὶ πάσχετε, 6 εἴπερ δίκαιον παρὰ θεῷ ἀνταποδοῦναι τοῖς θλίβουσιν ὑμᾶς θλῖψιν 7 καὶ ὑμῖν τοῖς θλιβομένοις ἄνεσιν μεθ᾽ ἡμῶν, ἐν τῇ ἀποκαλύψει τοῦ κυρίου Ἰησοῦ ἀπ᾽ οὐρανοῦ μετ᾽ ἀγγέλων δυνάμεως αὐτοῦ 8 ἐν πυρὶ φλογός, διδόντος ἐκδίκησιν τοῖς μὴ εἰδόσιν θεὸν καὶ τοῖς μὴ ὑπακούουσιν τῷ εὐαγγελίῳ τοῦ κυρίου ἡμῶν Ἰησοῦ, 9 οἵτινες δίκην τίσουσιν ὄλεθρον αἰώνιον ἀπὸ προσώπου τοῦ κυρίου καὶ ἀπὸ τῆς δόξης τῆς ἰσχύος αὐτοῦ, 10 ὅταν ἔλθῃ ἐνδοξασθῆναι ἐν τοῖς ἁγίοις αὐτοῦ καὶ θαυμασθῆναι ἐν πᾶσιν τοῖς πιστεύσασιν, ὅτι ἐπιστεύθη τὸ μαρτύριον ἡμῶν ἐφ᾽ ὑμᾶς, ἐν τῇ ἡμέρᾳ ἐκείνῃ. 11 Εἰς ὃ καὶ προσευχόμεθα πάντοτε περὶ ὑμῶν, ἵνα ὑμᾶς ἀξιώσῃ τῆς κλήσεως ὁ θεὸς ἡμῶν καὶ πληρώσῃ πᾶσαν εὐδοκίαν ἀγαθωσύνης καὶ ἔργον πίστεως ἐν δυνάμει, 12 ὅπως ἐνδοξασθῇ τὸ ὄνομα τοῦ κυρίου ἡμῶν Ἰησοῦ ἐν ὑμῖν, καὶ ὑμεῖς ἐν αὐτῷ, κατὰ τὴν χάριν τοῦ θεοῦ ἡμῶν καὶ κυρίου Ἰησοῦ Χριστοῦ.

1 Tim 1:12–17

Χάριν ἔχω τῷ ἐνδυναμώσαντί με Χριστῷ Ἰησοῦ τῷ κυρίῳ ἡμῶν, ὅτι πιστόν με ἡγήσατο θέμενος εἰς διακονίαν 13 τὸ πρότερον ὄντα βλάσφημον καὶ διώκτην καὶ ὑβριστήν, ἀλλὰ ἠλεήθην, ὅτι ἀγνοῶν ἐποίησα ἐν ἀπιστίᾳ· 14 ὑπερεπλεόνασεν δὲ ἡ χάρις τοῦ κυρίου ἡμῶν μετὰ πίστεως καὶ ἀγάπης τῆς ἐν Χριστῷ Ἰησοῦ. 15 πιστὸς ὁ λόγος καὶ πάσης ἀποδοχῆς ἄξιος, ὅτι Χριστὸς Ἰησοῦς ἦλθεν εἰς τὸν κόσμον ἁμαρτωλοὺς σῶσαι, ὧν πρῶτός εἰμι ἐγώ. 16 ἀλλὰ διὰ τοῦτο ἠλεήθην, ἵνα ἐν ἐμοὶ πρώτῳ ἐνδείξηται Χριστὸς Ἰησοῦς τὴν ἅπασαν μακροθυμίαν πρὸς ὑποτύπωσιν τῶν μελλόντων πιστεύειν ἐπ᾽ αὐτῷ εἰς ζωὴν αἰώνιον. 17 Τῷ δὲ βασιλεῖ τῶν αἰώνων, ἀφθάρτῳ ἀοράτῳ μόνῳ θεῷ, τιμὴ καὶ δόξα εἰς τοὺς αἰῶνας τῶν αἰώνων, ἀμήν.

2 Tim 1:3–5

Χάριν ἔχω τῷ θεῷ, ᾧ λατρεύω ἀπὸ προγόνων ἐν καθαρᾷ συνειδήσει, ὡς ἀδιάλειπτον ἔχω τὴν περὶ σοῦ μνείαν ἐν ταῖς δεήσεσίν μου νυκτὸς καὶ ἡμέρας, 4 ἐπιποθῶν σε ἰδεῖν, μεμνημένος σου τῶν δακρύων, ἵνα χαρᾶς πληρωθῶ, 5 ὑπόμνησιν λαβὼν τῆς ἐν σοὶ ἀνυποκρίτου πίστεως, ἥτις ἐνῴκησεν πρῶτον ἐν τῇ μάμμῃ σου Λωΐδι καὶ τῇ μητρί σου Εὐνίκῃ, πέπεισμαι δὲ ὅτι καὶ ἐν σοί.

Phlm 4–7

Εὐχαριστῶ τῷ θεῷ μου πάντοτε μνείαν σου ποιούμενος ἐπὶ τῶν προσευχῶν μου, 5 ἀκούων σου τὴν ἀγάπην καὶ τὴν πίστιν, ἣν ἔχεις πρὸς τὸν κύριον Ἰησοῦν καὶ εἰς πάντας τοὺς ἁγίους, 6 ὅπως ἡ κοινωνία τῆς πίστεώς σου ἐνεργὴς γένηται ἐν ἐπιγνώσει παντὸς ἀγαθοῦ τοῦ ἐν ⸀ἡμῖν εἰς Χριστόν. 7 χαρὰν γὰρ πολλὴν ἔσχον καὶ παράκλησιν ἐπὶ τῇ ἀγάπῃ σου, ὅτι τὰ σπλάγχνα τῶν ἁγίων ἀναπέπαυται διὰ σοῦ, ἀδελφέ.

The reference at the head of some excerpts above is followed by a different reference in parentheses in cases where scholars disagree as to the extent of the unit within the structure of the letter.

See also § 3 Blessing.

3. Blessing

2 Cor 1:3–7

Εὐλογητὸς ὁ θεὸς καὶ πατὴρ τοῦ κυρίου ἡμῶν Ἰησοῦ Χριστοῦ, ὁ πατὴρ τῶν οἰκτιρμῶν καὶ θεὸς πάσης παρακλήσεως, 4 ὁ παρακαλῶν ἡμᾶς ἐπὶ πάσῃ τῇ θλίψει ἡμῶν εἰς τὸ δύνασθαι ἡμᾶς παρακαλεῖν τοὺς ἐν πάσῃ θλίψει διὰ τῆς παρακλήσεως ἧς παρακαλούμεθα αὐτοὶ ὑπὸ τοῦ θεοῦ. 5 ὅτι καθὼς περισσεύει τὰ παθήματα τοῦ Χριστοῦ εἰς ἡμᾶς, οὕτως διὰ τοῦ Χριστοῦ περισσεύει καὶ ἡ παράκλησις ἡμῶν. 6 εἴτε δὲ θλιβόμεθα, ὑπὲρ τῆς ὑμῶν παρακλήσεως καὶ σωτηρίας· εἴτε παρακαλούμεθα, ὑπὲρ τῆς ὑμῶν παρακλήσεως τῆς ἐνεργουμένης ἐν ὑπομονῇ τῶν αὐτῶν παθημάτων ὧν καὶ ἡμεῖς πάσχομεν. 7 καὶ ἡ ἐλπὶς ἡμῶν βεβαία ὑπὲρ ὑμῶν εἰδότες ὅτι ὡς κοινωνοί ἐστε τῶν παθημάτων, οὕτως καὶ τῆς παρακλήσεως.

Eph 1:3–23 (or 1:3–3:21)

Εὐλογητὸς ὁ θεὸς καὶ πατὴρ τοῦ κυρίου ἡμῶν Ἰησοῦ Χριστοῦ, ὁ εὐλογήσας ἡμᾶς ἐν πάσῃ εὐλογίᾳ πνευματικῇ ἐν τοῖς ἐπουρανίοις ἐν Χριστῷ, 4 καθὼς ἐξελέξατο ἡμᾶς ἐν αὐτῷ πρὸ καταβολῆς κόσμου εἶναι ἡμᾶς ἁγίους καὶ ἀμώμους κατενώπιον αὐτοῦ ἐν ἀγάπῃ, 5 προορίσας ἡμᾶς εἰς υἱοθεσίαν διὰ Ἰησοῦ Χριστοῦ εἰς αὐτόν, κατὰ τὴν εὐδοκίαν τοῦ θελήματος αὐτοῦ, 6 εἰς ἔπαινον δόξης τῆς χάριτος αὐτοῦ ἧς ἐχαρίτωσεν ἡμᾶς ἐν τῷ ἠγαπημένῳ. 7 Ἐν ᾧ ἔχομεν τὴν ἀπολύτρωσιν διὰ τοῦ αἵματος αὐτοῦ, τὴν ἄφεσιν τῶν παραπτωμάτων, κατὰ τὸ πλοῦτος τῆς χάριτος αὐτοῦ 8 ἧς ἐπερίσσευσεν εἰς ἡμᾶς, ἐν πάσῃ σοφίᾳ καὶ φρονήσει, 9 γνωρίσας ἡμῖν τὸ μυστήριον τοῦ θελήματος αὐτοῦ, κατὰ τὴν εὐδοκίαν αὐτοῦ ἣν προέθετο ἐν αὐτῷ 10 εἰς οἰκονομίαν τοῦ πληρώματος τῶν καιρῶν, ἀνακεφαλαιώσασθαι τὰ πάντα ἐν τῷ Χριστῷ, τὰ ἐπὶ τοῖς οὐρανοῖς καὶ τὰ ἐπὶ τῆς γῆς ἐν αὐτῷ. 11 Ἐν ᾧ καὶ ἐκληρώθημεν προορισθέντες κατὰ πρόθεσιν τοῦ τὰ πάντα ἐνεργοῦντος κατὰ τὴν βουλὴν τοῦ θελήματος αὐτοῦ 12 εἰς τὸ εἶναι ἡμᾶς εἰς ἔπαινον δόξης αὐτοῦ τοὺς προηλπικότας ἐν τῷ Χριστῷ. 13 Ἐν ᾧ καὶ ὑμεῖς ἀκούσαντες τὸν λόγον τῆς ἀληθείας, τὸ εὐαγγέλιον τῆς σωτηρίας ὑμῶν, ἐν ᾧ καὶ πιστεύσαντες ἐσφραγίσθητε τῷ πνεύματι τῆς ἐπαγγελίας τῷ ἁγίῳ, 14 ⸀ὅ ἐστιν ἀρραβὼν τῆς κληρονομίας ἡμῶν, εἰς ἀπολύτρωσιν τῆς περιποιήσεως, εἰς ἔπαινον τῆς δόξης αὐτοῦ. 15 Διὰ τοῦτο κἀγὼ ἀκούσας τὴν καθ᾽ ὑμᾶς πίστιν ἐν τῷ κυρίῳ Ἰησοῦ καὶ ⸂τὴν ἀγάπην τὴν⸃ εἰς πάντας τοὺς ἁγίους 16 οὐ παύομαι εὐχαριστῶν ὑπὲρ ὑμῶν μνείαν ποιούμενος ἐπὶ τῶν προσευχῶν μου, 17 ἵνα ὁ θεὸς τοῦ κυρίου ἡμῶν Ἰησοῦ Χριστοῦ, ὁ πατὴρ τῆς δόξης, δώῃ ὑμῖν πνεῦμα σοφίας καὶ ἀποκαλύψεως ἐν ἐπιγνώσει αὐτοῦ, 18 πεφωτισμένους τοὺς ὀφθαλμοὺς τῆς καρδίας [ὑμῶν] εἰς τὸ εἰδέναι ὑμᾶς τίς ἐστιν ἡ ἐλπὶς τῆς κλήσεως αὐτοῦ, τίς ὁ πλοῦτος τῆς δόξης τῆς κληρονομίας αὐτοῦ ἐν τοῖς ἁγίοις, 19 καὶ τί τὸ ὑπερβάλλον μέγεθος τῆς δυνάμεως αὐτοῦ εἰς ἡμᾶς τοὺς πιστεύοντας κατὰ τὴν

Phlm 6 ***ημιν*** A C D 048^{vid} *Byz*] υμιν $\mathfrak{P}^{61}$ ℵ 33. 1739. 1881 **§ 3** **Eph 1:14** ***ὅ*** $\mathfrak{P}^{46}$ A B 1739. 1881] ος ℵ D 33 *Byz* **Eph 1:15** ***την αγαπην την*** ℵ^{2} D^{1} *Byz*] την $\mathfrak{P}^{46}$ ℵ* A B 33. 1739. 1881 ¦ την αγαπην D*

6 For it is indeed just of God to repay with affliction those who afflict you, 7 and to give relief to the afflicted as well as to us, when the Lord Jesus is revealed from heaven with his mighty angels 8 in flaming fire, inflicting vengeance on those who do not know God and on those who do not obey the gospel of our Lord Jesus. 9 These will suffer the punishment of eternal destruction, separated from the presence of the Lord and from the glory of his might, 10 when he comes to be glorified by his saints and to be marveled at on that day among all who have believed, because our testimony to you was believed. 11 To this end we always pray for you, asking that our God will make you worthy of his call and will fulfill by his power every good resolve and work of faith, 12 so that the name of our Lord Jesus may be glorified in you, and you in him, according to the grace of our God and the Lord Jesus Christ.

1 Tim 1:12–17

I am grateful to Christ Jesus our Lord, who has strengthened me, because he judged me faithful and appointed me to his service, 13 even though I was formerly a blasphemer, a persecutor, and a man of violence. But I received mercy because I had acted ignorantly in unbelief, 14 and the grace of our Lord overflowed for me with the faith and love that are in Christ Jesus. 15 The saying is sure and worthy of full acceptance, that Christ Jesus came into the world to save sinners—of whom I am the foremost. 16 But for that very reason I received mercy, so that in me, as the foremost, Jesus Christ might display the utmost patience, making me an example to those who would come to believe in him for eternal life. 17 To the King of the ages, immortal, invisible, the only God, be honor and glory forever and ever. Amen.

2 Tim 1:3–5

I am grateful to God—whom I worship with a clear conscience, as my ancestors did—when I remember you constantly in my prayers night and day. 4 Recalling your tears, I long to see you so that I may be filled with joy. 5 I am reminded of your sincere faith, a faith that lived first in your grandmother Lois and your mother Eunice and now, I am sure, lives in you.

Phlm 4–7

When I remember you in my prayers, I always thank my God 5 because I hear of your love for all the saints and your faith toward the Lord Jesus. 6 I pray that the sharing of your faith may become effective when you perceive all the good that we[g] may do for Christ. 7 I have indeed received much joy and encouragement from your love, because the hearts of the saints have been refreshed through you, my brother.

The reference at the head of some excerpts above is followed by a different reference in parentheses in cases where scholars disagree as to the extent of the unit within the structure of the letter.

See also § 3 Blessing.

3. Blessing

2 Cor 1:3–7

Blessed be the God and Father of our Lord Jesus Christ, the Father of mercies and the God of all consolation, 4 who consoles us in all our affliction, so that we may be able to console those who are in any affliction with the consolation with which we ourselves are consoled by God. 5 For just as the sufferings of Christ are abundant for us, so also our consolation is abundant through Christ. 6 If we are being afflicted, it is for your consolation and salvation; if we are being consoled, it is for your consolation, which you experience when you patiently endure the same sufferings that we are also suffering. 7 Our hope for you is unshaken; for we know that as you share in our sufferings, so also you share in our consolation.

Eph 1:3–23 (or 1:3–3:21)

Blessed be the God and Father of our Lord Jesus Christ, who has blessed us in Christ with every spiritual blessing in the heavenly places, 4 just as he chose us in Christ before the foundation of the world to be holy and blameless before him in love. 5 He destined us for adoption as his children through Jesus Christ, according to the good pleasure of his will, 6 to the praise of his glorious grace that he freely bestowed on us in the Beloved. 7 In him we have redemption through his blood, the forgiveness of our trespasses, according to the riches of his grace 8 that he lavished on us. With all wisdom and insight 9 he has made known to us the mystery of his will, according to his good pleasure that he set forth in Christ, 10 as a plan for the fullness of time, to gather up all things in him, things in heaven and things on earth. 11 In Christ we have also obtained an inheritance, having been destined according to the purpose of him who accomplishes all things according to his counsel and will, 12 so that we, who were the first to set our hope on Christ, might live for the praise of his glory. 13 In him you also, when you had heard the word of truth, the gospel of your salvation, and had believed in him, were marked with the seal of the promised Holy Spirit; 14 this[a] is the pledge of our inheritance toward redemption as God's own people, to the praise of his glory. 15 I have heard of your faith in the Lord Jesus and your love[b] toward all the saints, and for this reason 16 I do not cease to give thanks for you as I remember you in my prayers. 17 I pray that the God of our Lord Jesus Christ, the Father of glory, may give you a spirit of wisdom and revelation as you come to know him, 18 so that, with the eyes of your heart enlightened, you may know what is the hope to which he has called you, what are the riches of his glorious inheritance among the saints, 19 and what is the immeasurable greatness of his power for us who believe,

[g] **Phlm 6** *we* Other ancient authorities read *you* (plural) **§ 3** [a] **Eph 1:14** *this* Other ancient authorities read *who* [b] **Eph 1:15** *and your love* Other ancient authorities lack *and your love*

ἐνέργειαν τοῦ κράτους τῆς ἰσχύος αὐτοῦ. **20** Ἣν ⸀ἐνήργησεν ἐν τῷ Χριστῷ ἐγείρας αὐτὸν ἐκ νεκρῶν καὶ καθίσας ἐν δεξιᾷ αὐτοῦ ἐν τοῖς ἐπουρανίοις **21** ὑπεράνω πάσης ἀρχῆς καὶ ἐξουσίας καὶ δυνάμεως καὶ κυριότητος καὶ παντὸς ὀνόματος ὀνομαζομένου, οὐ μόνον ἐν τῷ αἰῶνι τούτῳ ἀλλὰ καὶ ἐν τῷ μέλλοντι· **22** καὶ πάντα ὑπέταξεν ὑπὸ τοὺς πόδας αὐτοῦ καὶ αὐτὸν ἔδωκεν κεφαλὴν ὑπὲρ πάντα τῇ ἐκκλησίᾳ, **23** ἥτις ἐστὶν τὸ σῶμα αὐτοῦ, τὸ πλήρωμα τοῦ τὰ πάντα ἐν πᾶσιν πληρουμένου.

The reference at the head of one excerpt above is followed by a different reference in parentheses, reflecting scholarly disagreement as to the extent of the unit within the structure of the letter.

See also § 2 Thanksgiving.

4. Opening of the Body of the Letter

Rom 1:13–17

οὐ θέλω δὲ ὑμᾶς ἀγνοεῖν, ἀδελφοί, ὅτι πολλάκις προεθέμην ἐλθεῖν πρὸς ὑμᾶς, καὶ ἐκωλύθην ἄχρι τοῦ δεῦρο, ἵνα τινὰ καρπὸν σχῶ καὶ ἐν ὑμῖν καθὼς καὶ ἐν τοῖς λοιποῖς ἔθνεσιν. **14** Ἕλλησίν τε καὶ βαρβάροις, σοφοῖς τε καὶ ἀνοήτοις ὀφειλέτης εἰμί, **15** οὕτως τὸ κατ᾽ ἐμὲ πρόθυμον καὶ ὑμῖν τοῖς ἐν Ῥώμῃ εὐαγγελίσασθαι. **16** Οὐ γὰρ ἐπαισχύνομαι τὸ εὐαγγέλιον, δύναμις γὰρ θεοῦ ἐστιν εἰς σωτηρίαν παντὶ τῷ πιστεύοντι, Ἰουδαίῳ τε πρῶτον καὶ Ἕλληνι. **17** δικαιοσύνη γὰρ θεοῦ ἐν αὐτῷ ἀποκαλύπτεται ἐκ πίστεως εἰς πίστιν, καθὼς γέγραπται· ὁ δὲ δίκαιος ἐκ πίστεως ζήσεται.

1 Cor 1:10–17

Παρακαλῶ δὲ ὑμᾶς, ἀδελφοί, διὰ τοῦ ὀνόματος τοῦ κυρίου ἡμῶν Ἰησοῦ Χριστοῦ, ἵνα τὸ αὐτὸ λέγητε πάντες καὶ μὴ ᾖ ἐν ὑμῖν σχίσματα, ἦτε δὲ κατηρτισμένοι ἐν τῷ αὐτῷ νοῒ καὶ ἐν τῇ αὐτῇ γνώμῃ. **11** ἐδηλώθη γάρ μοι περὶ ὑμῶν, ἀδελφοί μου, ὑπὸ τῶν Χλόης ὅτι ἔριδες ἐν ὑμῖν εἰσιν. **12** λέγω δὲ τοῦτο ὅτι ἕκαστος ὑμῶν λέγει· ἐγὼ μέν εἰμι Παύλου, ἐγὼ δὲ Ἀπολλῶ, ἐγὼ δὲ Κηφᾶ, ἐγὼ δὲ Χριστοῦ. **13** μεμέρισται ὁ Χριστός; μὴ Παῦλος ἐσταυρώθη ὑπὲρ ὑμῶν, ἢ εἰς τὸ ὄνομα Παύλου ἐβαπτίσθητε; **14** εὐχαριστῶ ⸂[τῷ θεῷ]⸃ ὅτι οὐδένα ὑμῶν ἐβάπτισα εἰ μὴ Κρίσπον καὶ Γάϊον, **15** ἵνα μή τις εἴπῃ ὅτι εἰς τὸ ἐμὸν ὄνομα ἐβαπτίσθητε. **16** ἐβάπτισα δὲ καὶ τὸν Στεφανᾶ οἶκον, λοιπὸν οὐκ οἶδα εἴ τινα ἄλλον ἐβάπτισα. **17** οὐ γὰρ ἀπέστειλέν με Χριστὸς βαπτίζειν ἀλλὰ εὐαγγελίζεσθαι, οὐκ ἐν σοφίᾳ λόγου, ἵνα μὴ κενωθῇ ὁ σταυρὸς τοῦ Χριστοῦ.

2 Cor 1:8–11

Οὐ γὰρ θέλομεν ὑμᾶς ἀγνοεῖν, ἀδελφοί, ὑπὲρ τῆς θλίψεως ἡμῶν τῆς γενομένης ἐν τῇ Ἀσίᾳ, ὅτι καθ᾽ ὑπερβολὴν ὑπὲρ δύναμιν ἐβαρήθημεν ὥστε ἐξαπορηθῆναι ἡμᾶς καὶ τοῦ ζῆν· **9** ἀλλὰ αὐτοὶ ἐν ἑαυτοῖς τὸ ἀπόκριμα τοῦ θανάτου ἐσχήκαμεν, ἵνα μὴ πεποιθότες ὦμεν ἐφ᾽ ἑαυτοῖς ἀλλ᾽ ἐπὶ τῷ θεῷ τῷ ἐγείροντι τοὺς νεκρούς· **10** ὃς ἐκ ⸂τηλικούτου θανάτου⸃ ἐρρύσατο ἡμᾶς καὶ ῥύσεται, εἰς ὃν ἠλπίκαμεν [ὅτι] καὶ ἔτι ῥύσεται, **11** συνυπουργούντων καὶ ὑμῶν ὑπὲρ ἡμῶν τῇ δεήσει, ἵνα ἐκ πολλῶν προσώπων τὸ εἰς ἡμᾶς χάρισμα διὰ πολλῶν εὐχαριστηθῇ ὑπὲρ ⸀ἡμῶν.

Gal 1:6–9 (or 12)

Θαυμάζω ὅτι οὕτως ταχέως μετατίθεσθε ἀπὸ τοῦ καλέσαντος ὑμᾶς ἐν χάριτι [Χριστοῦ] εἰς ἕτερον εὐαγγέλιον, **7** ὃ οὐκ ἔστιν ἄλλο, εἰ μή τινές εἰσιν οἱ ταράσσοντες ὑμᾶς καὶ θέλοντες μεταστρέψαι τὸ εὐαγγέλιον τοῦ Χριστοῦ. **8** ἀλλὰ καὶ ἐὰν ἡμεῖς ἢ ἄγγελος ἐξ οὐρανοῦ εὐαγγελίζηται [ὑμῖν] παρ᾽ ὃ εὐηγγελισάμεθα ὑμῖν, ἀνάθεμα ἔστω. **9** ὡς προειρήκαμεν καὶ ἄρτι πάλιν λέγω· εἴ τις ὑμᾶς εὐαγγελίζεται παρ᾽ ὃ παρελάβετε, ἀνάθεμα ἔστω.

Eph 4:1–3 (or 2:1–10)

Παρακαλῶ οὖν ὑμᾶς ἐγὼ ὁ δέσμιος ἐν κυρίῳ ἀξίως περιπατῆσαι τῆς κλήσεως ἧς ἐκλήθητε, **2** μετὰ πάσης ταπεινοφροσύνης καὶ πραΰτητος, μετὰ μακροθυμίας, ἀνεχόμενοι ἀλλήλων ἐν ἀγάπῃ, **3** σπουδάζοντες τηρεῖν τὴν ἑνότητα τοῦ πνεύματος ἐν τῷ συνδέσμῳ τῆς εἰρήνης

Phil 1:12–14 (or 26)

Γινώσκειν δὲ ὑμᾶς βούλομαι, ἀδελφοί, ὅτι τὰ κατ᾽ ἐμὲ μᾶλλον εἰς προκοπὴν τοῦ εὐαγγελίου ἐλήλυθεν, **13** ὥστε τοὺς δεσμούς μου φανεροὺς ἐν Χριστῷ γενέσθαι ἐν ὅλῳ τῷ πραιτωρίῳ καὶ τοῖς λοιποῖς πᾶσιν, **14** καὶ τοὺς πλείονας τῶν ἀδελφῶν ἐν κυρίῳ πεποιθότας τοῖς δεσμοῖς μου περισσοτέρως τολμᾶν ἀφόβως τὸν ⸀λόγον λαλεῖν.

Col 2:1–3 (or possibly 2:4–7)

Θέλω γὰρ ὑμᾶς εἰδέναι ἡλίκον ἀγῶνα ἔχω ὑπὲρ ὑμῶν καὶ τῶν ἐν Λαοδικείᾳ καὶ ὅσοι οὐχ ἑόρακαν τὸ πρόσωπόν μου ἐν σαρκί, **2** ἵνα παρακληθῶσιν αἱ καρδίαι αὐτῶν συμβιβασθέντες ἐν ἀγάπῃ καὶ εἰς πᾶν πλοῦτος τῆς πληροφορίας τῆς συνέσεως, εἰς ἐπίγνωσιν τοῦ μυστηρίου ⸂τοῦ θεοῦ, Χριστοῦ⸃, **3** ἐν ᾧ εἰσιν πάντες οἱ θησαυροὶ τῆς σοφίας καὶ γνώσεως ἀπόκρυφοι.

1 Thess 2:1–2 (or 4:1–2)

Αὐτοὶ γὰρ οἴδατε, ἀδελφοί, τὴν εἴσοδον ἡμῶν τὴν πρὸς ὑμᾶς ὅτι οὐ κενὴ γέγονεν, **2** ἀλλὰ προπαθόντες καὶ ὑβρισθέντες, καθὼς οἴδατε, ἐν Φιλίπποις ἐπαρρησιασάμεθα ἐν τῷ θεῷ ἡμῶν λαλῆσαι πρὸς ὑμᾶς τὸ εὐαγγέλιον τοῦ θεοῦ ἐν πολλῷ ἀγῶνι.

Eph 1:20 ***ενηργησεν*** **א** D 33. 1739. 1881 *Byz*] ενηργηκεν A B **§ 4** **1 Cor 1:14** ***τω θεω*** **א**^{2} C D 1881 *Byz*] τω θεω μου A 33 ¦ *om.* **א*** B 1739 **2 Cor 1:10** ***τηλικουτου θανατου*** **א** A B C D 33. 1739*. 1881 *Byz*] τηλικουτων θανατων 𝔓^{46} 1739^{mg} **2 Cor 1:11** ***ημων*** 𝔓^{46c} **א** A C D* 33. 1739. 1881 *Byz*^{pt}] υμων 𝔓^{46*} B D^{2} *Byz*^{pt} **Phil 1:14** ***λογον*** 𝔓^{46} D^{2} 1739. 1881 *Byz*] *add.* του θεου **א** A B (D*) 048^{vid}. 33 **Col 2:2** ***του θεου, Χριστου*** 𝔓^{46} B] του θεου πατρος (+ του A C) Χριστου **א*** A C 048^{vid} ¦ του θεου και πατρος του Χριστου **א**^{2} ¦ του θεου και πατρος και του Χριστου D^{2} *Byz* ¦ του θεου ὅ εστιν Χριστος D* ¦ του θεου του εν Χριστω 33 ¦ του θεου D^{1} 1881 ¦ του Χριστου (1739)

according to the working of his great power. 20 God put this power to work[c] in Christ when he raised him from the dead and seated him at his right hand in the heavenly places, 21 far above all rule and authority and power and dominion, and above every name that is named, not only in this age but also in the age to come. 22 And he has put all things under his feet and has made him the head over all things for the church, 23 which is his body, the fullness of him who fills all in all.

The reference at the head of one excerpt above is followed by a different reference in parentheses, reflecting scholarly disagreement as to the extent of the unit within the structure of the letter.

See also § 2 Thanksgiving.

4. *Opening of the Body of the Letter*

Rom 1:13–17

I want you to know, brothers and sisters, that I have often intended to come to you (but thus far have been prevented), in order that I may reap some harvest among you as I have among the rest of the Gentiles. 14 I am a debtor both to Greeks and to barbarians, both to the wise and to the foolish 15—hence my eagerness to proclaim the gospel to you also who are in Rome. 16 For I am not ashamed of the gospel; it is the power of God for salvation to everyone who has faith, to the Jew first and also to the Greek. 17 For in it the righteousness of God is revealed through faith for faith; as it is written, "The one who is righteous will live by faith."

1 Cor 1:10–17

Now I appeal to you, brothers and sisters, by the name of our Lord Jesus Christ, that all of you be in agreement and that there be no divisions among you, but that you be united in the same mind and the same purpose. 11 For it has been reported to me by Chloe's people that there are quarrels among you, my brothers and sisters. 12 What I mean is that each of you says, "I belong to Paul," or "I belong to Apollos," or "I belong to Cephas," or "I belong to Christ." 13 Has Christ been divided? Was Paul crucified for you? Or were you baptized in the name of Paul? 14 I thank God[a] that I baptized none of you except Crispus and Gaius, 15 so that no one can say that you were baptized in my name. 16 (I did baptize also the household of Stephanas; beyond that, I do not know whether I baptized anyone else.) 17 For Christ did not send me to baptize but to proclaim the gospel, and not with eloquent wisdom, so that the cross of Christ might not be emptied of its power.

2 Cor 1:8–11

We do not want you to be unaware, brothers and sisters, of the affliction we experienced in Asia; for we were so utterly, unbearably crushed that we despaired of life itself. 9 Indeed, we felt that we had received the sentence of death so that we would rely not on ourselves but on God who raises the dead. 10 He who rescued us from so deadly a peril[b] will continue to rescue us; on him we have set our hope that he will rescue us again, 11 as you also join in helping us by your prayers, so that many will give thanks on our[c] behalf for the blessing granted us through the prayers of many.

Gal 1:6–9 (or 12)

I am astonished that you are so quickly deserting the one who called you in the grace of Christ and are turning to a different gospel— 7 not that there is another gospel, but there are some who are confusing you and want to pervert the gospel of Christ. 8 But even if we or an angel from heaven should proclaim to you a gospel contrary to what we proclaimed to you, let that one be accursed! 9 As we have said before, so now I repeat, if anyone proclaims to you a gospel contrary to what you received, let that one be accursed!

Eph 4:1–3 (or 2:1–10)

I therefore, the prisoner in the Lord, beg you to lead a life worthy of the calling to which you have been called, 2 with all humility and gentleness, with patience, bearing with one another in love, 3 making every effort to maintain the unity of the Spirit in the bond of peace.

Phil 1:12–14 (or 26)

I want you to know, beloved, that what has happened to me has actually helped to spread the gospel, 13 so that it has become known throughout the whole imperial guard and to everyone else that my imprisonment is for Christ; 14 and most of the brothers and sisters, having been made confident in the Lord by my imprisonment, dare to speak the word[d] with greater boldness and without fear.

Col 2:1–3 (or possibly 2:4–7)

For I want you to know how much I am struggling for you, and for those in Laodicea, and for all who have not seen me face to face. 2 I want their hearts to be encouraged and united in love, so that they may have all the riches of assured understanding and have the knowledge of God's mystery, that is, Christ himself,[e] 3 in whom are hidden all the treasures of wisdom and knowledge.

1 Thess 2:1–2 (or 4:1–2)

You yourselves know, brothers and sisters, that our coming to you was not in vain, 2 but though we had already suffered and been shamefully mistreated at Philippi, as you know, we had courage in our God to declare to you the gospel of God in spite of great opposition.

[c] **Eph 1:20** ***put this power to work*** Other ancient authorities read *has put this power to work* **§ 4** [a] **1 Cor 1:14** ***I thank God*** Other ancient authorities read *I am thankful* or *I thank my God* [b] **2 Cor 1:10** ***so deadly a peril*** lit. *so great a death* Other ancient authorities read *perils so deadly* lit. *such great deaths* [c] **2 Cor 1:11** ***our*** Other ancient authorities read *your* [d] **Phil 1:14** ***word*** Other ancient authorities read *word of God* [e] **Col 2:2** ***of God's mystery, that is, Christ himself*** Other ancient authorities read *of the mystery of God, the Father of Christ* or *of the mystery of God, both of the Father and of Christ*

2 Thess 2:1–2 (or 12)

Ἐρωτῶμεν δὲ ὑμᾶς, ἀδελφοί, ὑπὲρ τῆς
παρουσίας τοῦ κυρίου ἡμῶν Ἰησοῦ Χρι-
στοῦ καὶ ἡμῶν ἐπισυναγωγῆς ἐπ' αὐτὸν
2 εἰς τὸ μὴ ταχέως σαλευθῆναι ὑμᾶς
ἀπὸ τοῦ νοὸς μηδὲ θροεῖσθαι, μήτε διὰ
πνεύματος μήτε διὰ λόγου μήτε δι' ἐπι-
στολῆς ὡς δι' ἡμῶν, ὡς ὅτι ἐνέστηκεν
ἡ ἡμέρα τοῦ κυρίου

1 Tim 1:3–7 (or 11)

Καθὼς παρεκάλεσά σε προσμεῖναι ἐν
Ἐφέσῳ πορευόμενος εἰς Μακεδονίαν,
ἵνα παραγγείλῃς τισὶν μὴ ἑτεροδιδα-
σκαλεῖν 4 μηδὲ προσέχειν μύθοις καὶ
γενεαλογίαις ἀπεράντοις, αἵτινες ἐκζη-
τήσεις παρέχουσιν μᾶλλον ἢ οἰκονομίαν
θεοῦ τὴν ἐν πίστει. 5 τὸ δὲ τέλος τῆς
παραγγελίας ἐστὶν ἀγάπη ἐκ καθαρᾶς
καρδίας καὶ συνειδήσεως ἀγαθῆς καὶ
πίστεως ἀνυποκρίτου, 6 ὧν τινες ἀστο-
χήσαντες ἐξετράπησαν εἰς ματαιολογίαν
7 θέλοντες εἶναι νομοδιδάσκαλοι, μὴ
νοοῦντες μήτε ἃ λέγουσιν μήτε περὶ
τίνων διαβεβαιοῦνται.

2 Tim 1:6–14

Δι' ἣν αἰτίαν ἀναμιμνῄσκω σε ἀναζωπυ-
ρεῖν τὸ χάρισμα τοῦ θεοῦ, ὅ ἐστιν ἐν
σοὶ διὰ τῆς ἐπιθέσεως τῶν χειρῶν μου.
7 οὐ γὰρ ἔδωκεν ἡμῖν ὁ θεὸς πνεῦμα
δειλίας ἀλλὰ δυνάμεως καὶ ἀγάπης καὶ
σωφρονισμοῦ. 8 μὴ οὖν ἐπαισχυνθῇς τὸ
μαρτύριον τοῦ κυρίου ἡμῶν μηδὲ ἐμὲ τὸν
δέσμιον αὐτοῦ, ἀλλὰ συγκακοπάθησον
τῷ εὐαγγελίῳ κατὰ δύναμιν θεοῦ, 9 τοῦ
σώσαντος ἡμᾶς καὶ καλέσαντος κλήσει
ἁγίᾳ, οὐ κατὰ τὰ ἔργα ἡμῶν ἀλλὰ κατὰ
ἰδίαν πρόθεσιν καὶ χάριν, τὴν δοθεῖσαν
ἡμῖν ἐν Χριστῷ Ἰησοῦ πρὸ χρόνων αἰω-
νίων, 10 φανερωθεῖσαν δὲ νῦν διὰ τῆς
ἐπιφανείας τοῦ σωτῆρος ἡμῶν Χριστοῦ
Ἰησοῦ, καταργήσαντος μὲν τὸν θάνατον
φωτίσαντος δὲ ζωὴν καὶ ἀφθαρσίαν διὰ
τοῦ εὐαγγελίου 11 εἰς ὃ ἐτέθην ἐγὼ κῆρυξ
καὶ ἀπόστολος καὶ ⸀διδάσκαλος, 12 δι'
ἣν αἰτίαν καὶ ταῦτα πάσχω· ἀλλ' οὐκ
ἐπαισχύνομαι, οἶδα γὰρ ᾧ πεπίστευκα
καὶ πέπεισμαι ὅτι δυνατός ἐστιν τὴν πα-
ραθήκην μου φυλάξαι εἰς ἐκείνην τὴν
ἡμέραν. 13 Ὑποτύπωσιν ἔχε ὑγιαινόντων
λόγων ὧν παρ' ἐμοῦ ἤκουσας ἐν πίστει
καὶ ἀγάπῃ τῇ ἐν Χριστῷ Ἰησοῦ· 14 τὴν
καλὴν παραθήκην φύλαξον διὰ πνεύματος
ἁγίου τοῦ ἐνοικοῦντος ἐν ἡμῖν.

Titus 1:5–9

Τούτου χάριν ἀπέλιπόν σε ἐν Κρήτῃ, ἵνα
τὰ λείποντα ἐπιδιορθώσῃ καὶ καταστήσῃς
κατὰ πόλιν πρεσβυτέρους, ὡς ἐγώ σοι
διεταξάμην, 6 εἴ τίς ἐστιν ἀνέγκλητος,
μιᾶς γυναικὸς ἀνήρ, τέκνα ἔχων πιστά,
μὴ ἐν κατηγορίᾳ ἀσωτίας ἢ ἀνυπότακτα.
7 δεῖ γὰρ τὸν ἐπίσκοπον ἀνέγκλητον
εἶναι ὡς θεοῦ οἰκονόμον, μὴ αὐθάδη, μὴ
ὀργίλον, μὴ πάροινον, μὴ πλήκτην, μὴ
αἰσχροκερδῆ, 8 ἀλλὰ φιλόξενον φιλάγαθον
σώφρονα δίκαιον ὅσιον ἐγκρατῆ, 9 ἀντε-
χόμενον τοῦ κατὰ τὴν διδαχὴν πιστοῦ
λόγου, ἵνα δυνατὸς ᾖ καὶ παρακαλεῖν ἐν
τῇ διδασκαλίᾳ τῇ ὑγιαινούσῃ καὶ τοὺς
ἀντιλέγοντας ἐλέγχειν.

Phlm 8–14

Διὸ πολλὴν ἐν Χριστῷ παρρησίαν ἔχων
ἐπιτάσσειν σοι τὸ ἀνῆκον 9 διὰ τὴν ἀγά-
πην μᾶλλον παρακαλῶ, τοιοῦτος ὢν
ὡς Παῦλος ⸀πρεσβύτης νυνὶ δὲ καὶ δέ-
σμιος Χριστοῦ Ἰησοῦ· 10 παρακαλῶ σε
περὶ τοῦ ἐμοῦ τέκνου, ὃν ἐγέννησα ἐν
τοῖς δεσμοῖς, Ὀνήσιμον, 11 τόν ποτέ
σοι ἄχρηστον νυνὶ δὲ [καὶ] σοὶ καὶ ἐμοὶ
εὔχρηστον, 12 ὃν ἀνέπεμψά σοι, αὐτόν,
τοῦτ' ἔστιν τὰ ἐμὰ σπλάγχνα· 13 ὃν ἐγὼ
ἐβουλόμην πρὸς ἐμαυτὸν κατέχειν, ἵνα
ὑπὲρ σοῦ μοι διακονῇ ἐν τοῖς δεσμοῖς
τοῦ εὐαγγελίου, 14 χωρὶς δὲ τῆς σῆς
γνώμης οὐδὲν ἠθέλησα ποιῆσαι, ἵνα
μὴ ὡς κατὰ ἀνάγκην τὸ ἀγαθόν σου ᾖ
ἀλλὰ κατὰ ἑκούσιον.

The reference at the head of some excerpts above is followed by a different reference in parentheses in cases where scholars disagree as to the extent or placement of the unit within the structure of the letter.

5. *Closing of the Body of the Letter*

Rom 15:14–29 (or 33)

Πέπεισμαι δέ, ἀδελφοί μου, καὶ αὐτὸς
ἐγὼ περὶ ὑμῶν ὅτι καὶ αὐτοὶ μεστοί ἐστε
ἀγαθωσύνης, πεπληρωμένοι πάσης [τῆς]
γνώσεως, δυνάμενοι καὶ ἀλλήλους νου-
θετεῖν. 15 τολμηρότερον δὲ ἔγραψα ὑμῖν
ἀπὸ μέρους ὡς ἐπαναμιμνῄσκων ὑμᾶς
διὰ τὴν χάριν τὴν δοθεῖσάν μοι ὑπὸ τοῦ
θεοῦ 16 εἰς τὸ εἶναί με λειτουργὸν Χρι-
στοῦ Ἰησοῦ εἰς τὰ ἔθνη, ἱερουργοῦντα
τὸ εὐαγγέλιον τοῦ θεοῦ, ἵνα γένηται ἡ
προσφορὰ τῶν ἐθνῶν εὐπρόσδεκτος,
ἡγιασμένη ἐν πνεύματι ἁγίῳ. 17 ἔχω
οὖν [τὴν] καύχησιν ἐν Χριστῷ Ἰησοῦ
τὰ πρὸς τὸν θεόν· 18 οὐ γὰρ τολμήσω
τι λαλεῖν ὧν οὐ κατειργάσατο Χριστὸς
δι' ἐμοῦ εἰς ὑπακοὴν ἐθνῶν, λόγῳ καὶ
ἔργῳ, 19 ἐν δυνάμει σημείων καὶ τε-
ράτων, ἐν δυνάμει πνεύματος ⸀[θεοῦ]·
ὥστε με ἀπὸ Ἰερουσαλὴμ καὶ κύκλῳ
μέχρι τοῦ Ἰλλυρικοῦ πεπληρωκέναι τὸ
εὐαγγέλιον τοῦ Χριστοῦ, 20 οὕτως δὲ
φιλοτιμούμενον εὐαγγελίζεσθαι οὐχ
ὅπου ὠνομάσθη Χριστός, ἵνα μὴ ἐπ'
ἀλλότριον θεμέλιον οἰκοδομῶ, 21 ἀλλὰ
καθὼς γέγραπται· οἷς οὐκ ἀνηγγέλη περὶ
αὐτοῦ ὄψονται, καὶ οἳ οὐκ ἀκηκόασιν
συνήσουσιν. 22 Διὸ καὶ ἐνεκοπτόμην
τὰ πολλὰ τοῦ ἐλθεῖν πρὸς ὑμᾶς· 23 νυνὶ
δὲ μηκέτι τόπον ἔχων ἐν τοῖς κλίμασι
τούτοις, ἐπιποθίαν δὲ ἔχων τοῦ ἐλθεῖν
πρὸς ὑμᾶς ἀπὸ πολλῶν ἐτῶν, 24 ὡς ἂν
πορεύωμαι εἰς τὴν Σπανίαν· ἐλπίζω
γὰρ διαπορευόμενος θεάσασθαι ὑμᾶς

2 Tim 1:11 ***διδασκαλος*** א* A I] *add.* εθνων א² C D 1739. 1881 *Byz* ¦ διακονος 33 **Phlm 9** ***πρεσβυτης*** *omnes*] πρεσβευτης *cj* **§ 5 Rom 15:19** ***θεου*** 𝔓⁴⁶ א D¹ *Byz*] *om.* B ¦ αγιου A D*,² 33. 1739. 1881

2 Thess 2:1–2 (or 12)

As to the coming of our Lord Jesus Christ and our being gathered together to him, we beg you, brothers and sisters, **2** not to be quickly shaken in mind or alarmed, either by spirit or by word or by letter, as though from us, to the effect that the day of the Lord is already here.

1 Tim 1:3–7 (or 11)

I urge you, as I did when I was on my way to Macedonia, to remain in Ephesus so that you may instruct certain people not to teach any different doctrine, **4** and not to occupy themselves with myths and endless genealogies that promote speculations rather than the divine training that is known by faith. **5** But the aim of such instruction is love that comes from a pure heart, a good conscience, and sincere faith. **6** Some people have deviated from these and turned to meaningless talk, **7** desiring to be teachers of the law, without understanding either what they are saying or the things about which they make assertions.

2 Tim 1:6–14

For this reason I remind you to rekindle the gift of God that is within you through the laying on of my hands; **7** for God did not give us a spirit of cowardice, but rather a spirit of power and of love and of self-discipline. **8** Do not be ashamed, then, of the testimony about our Lord or of me his prisoner, but join with me in suffering for the gospel, relying on the power of God, **9** who saved us and called us with a holy calling, not according to our works but according to his own purpose and grace. This grace was given to us in Christ Jesus before the ages began, **10** but it has now been revealed through the appearing of our Savior Christ Jesus, who abolished death and brought life and immortality to light through the gospel. **11** For this gospel I was appointed a herald and an apostle and a teacher,[f] **12** and for this reason I suffer as I do. But I am not ashamed, for I know the one in whom I have put my trust, and I am sure that he is able to guard until that day what I have entrusted to him. **13** Hold to the standard of sound teaching that you have heard from me, in the faith and love that are in Christ Jesus. **14** Guard the good treasure entrusted to you, with the help of the Holy Spirit living in us.

Titus 1:5–9

I left you behind in Crete for this reason, so that you should put in order what remained to be done, and should appoint elders in every town, as I directed you: **6** someone who is blameless, married only once, whose children are believers, not accused of debauchery and not rebellious. **7** For a bishop, as God's steward, must be blameless; he must not be arrogant or quick-tempered or addicted to wine or violent or greedy for gain; **8** but he must be hospitable, a lover of goodness, prudent, upright, devout, and self-controlled. **9** He must have a firm grasp of the word that is trustworthy in accordance with the teaching, so that he may be able both to preach with sound doctrine and to refute those who contradict it.

Phlm 8–14

For this reason, though I am bold enough in Christ to command you to do your duty, **9** yet I would rather appeal to you on the basis of love—and I, Paul, do this as an old man,[g] and now also as a prisoner of Christ Jesus. **10** I am appealing to you for my child, Onesimus, whose father I have become during my imprisonment. **11** Formerly he was useless to you, but now he is indeed useful both to you and to me. **12** I am sending him, that is, my own heart, back to you. **13** I wanted to keep him with me, so that he might be of service to me in your place during my imprisonment for the gospel; **14** but I preferred to do nothing without your consent, in order that your good deed might be voluntary and not something forced.

The reference at the head of some excerpts above is followed by a different reference in parentheses in cases where scholars disagree as to the extent or placement of the unit within the structure of the letter.

5. *Closing of the Body of the Letter*

Rom 15:14–29 (or 33)

I myself feel confident about you, my brothers and sisters, that you yourselves are full of goodness, filled with all knowledge, and able to instruct one another. **15** Nevertheless on some points I have written to you rather boldly by way of reminder, because of the grace given me by God **16** to be a minister of Christ Jesus to the Gentiles in the priestly service of the gospel of God, so that the offering of the Gentiles may be acceptable, sanctified by the Holy Spirit. **17** In Christ Jesus, then, I have reason to boast of my work for God. **18** For I will not venture to speak of anything except what Christ has accomplished through me to win obedience from the Gentiles, by word and deed, **19** by the power of signs and wonders, by the power of the Spirit of God,[a] so that from Jerusalem and as far around as Illyricum I have fully proclaimed the good news of Christ. **20** Thus I make it my ambition to proclaim the good news, not where Christ has already been named, so that I do not build on someone else's foundation, **21** but as it is written, "Those who have never been told of him shall see, and those who have never heard of him shall understand." **22** This is the reason that I have so often been hindered from coming to you. **23** But now, with no further place for me in these regions, I desire, as I have for many years, to come to you **24** when I go to Spain. For I do hope to see you on my journey and to be sent on by you, once I have

[f] **2 Tim 1:11** *teacher* Other ancient authorities add *of the Gentiles* [g] **Phlm 9** *old man* Some scholars conjecture that the original text read *ambassador*, or that the reading in the manuscripts is a spelling variant for *ambassador* **§ 5** [a] **Rom 15:19** *of the Spirit of God* Other ancient authorities read *of the Spirit* or *of the Holy Spirit*

καὶ ὑφ᾽ ὑμῶν προπεμφθῆναι ἐκεῖ ἐὰν ὑμῶν πρῶτον ἀπὸ μέρους ἐμπλησθῶ. 25 Νυνὶ δὲ πορεύομαι εἰς Ἰερουσαλὴμ διακονῶν τοῖς ἁγίοις. 26 εὐδόκησαν γὰρ Μακεδονία καὶ Ἀχαΐα κοινωνίαν τινὰ ποιήσασθαι εἰς τοὺς πτωχοὺς τῶν ἁγίων τῶν ἐν Ἰερουσαλήμ. 27 εὐδόκησαν γὰρ καὶ ὀφειλέται εἰσὶν αὐτῶν· εἰ γὰρ τοῖς πνευματικοῖς αὐτῶν ἐκοινώνησαν τὰ ἔθνη, ὀφείλουσιν καὶ ἐν τοῖς σαρκικοῖς λειτουργῆσαι αὐτοῖς. 28 τοῦτο οὖν ἐπιτελέσας καὶ σφραγισάμενος αὐτοῖς τὸν καρπὸν τοῦτον, ἀπελεύσομαι δι᾽ ὑμῶν εἰς Σπανίαν· 29 οἶδα δὲ ὅτι ἐρχόμενος πρὸς ὑμᾶς ἐν πληρώματι ⸀εὐλογίας Χριστοῦ ἐλεύσομαι.

1 Cor 16:5–14 (or 1–14)

Ἐλεύσομαι δὲ πρὸς ὑμᾶς ὅταν Μακεδονίαν διέλθω· Μακεδονίαν γὰρ διέρχομαι, 6 πρὸς ὑμᾶς δὲ τυχὸν παραμενῶ ἢ καὶ παραχειμάσω, ἵνα ὑμεῖς με προπέμψητε οὗ ἐὰν πορεύωμαι. 7 οὐ θέλω γὰρ ὑμᾶς ἄρτι ἐν παρόδῳ ἰδεῖν, ἐλπίζω γὰρ χρόνον τινὰ ἐπιμεῖναι πρὸς ὑμᾶς ἐὰν ὁ κύριος ἐπιτρέψῃ. 8 ἐπιμενῶ δὲ ἐν Ἐφέσῳ ἕως τῆς πεντηκοστῆς· 9 θύρα γάρ μοι ἀνέῳγεν μεγάλη καὶ ἐνεργής, καὶ ἀντικείμενοι πολλοί. 10 Ἐὰν δὲ ἔλθῃ Τιμόθεος, βλέπετε, ἵνα ἀφόβως γένηται πρὸς ὑμᾶς· τὸ γὰρ ἔργον κυρίου ἐργάζεται ὡς κἀγώ· 11 μή τις οὖν αὐτὸν ἐξουθενήσῃ. προπέμψατε δὲ αὐτὸν ἐν εἰρήνῃ, ἵνα ἔλθῃ πρός με· ἐκδέχομαι γὰρ αὐτὸν μετὰ τῶν ἀδελφῶν. 12 Περὶ δὲ Ἀπολλῶ τοῦ ἀδελφοῦ, πολλὰ παρεκάλεσα αὐτόν, ἵνα ἔλθῃ πρὸς ὑμᾶς μετὰ τῶν ἀδελφῶν· καὶ πάντως οὐκ ἦν θέλημα ἵνα νῦν ἔλθῃ· ἐλεύσεται δὲ ὅταν εὐκαιρήσῃ. 13 Γρηγορεῖτε, στήκετε ἐν τῇ πίστει, ἀνδρίζεσθε, κραταιοῦσθε. 14 πάντα ὑμῶν ἐν ἀγάπῃ γινέσθω.

2 Cor 13:1–11 (or 12:14–13:11)

Τρίτον τοῦτο ἔρχομαι πρὸς ὑμᾶς· ἐπὶ στόματος δύο μαρτύρων καὶ τριῶν σταθήσεται πᾶν ῥῆμα. 2 προείρηκα καὶ προλέγω, ὡς παρὼν τὸ δεύτερον καὶ ἀπὼν νῦν, τοῖς προημαρτηκόσιν καὶ τοῖς λοιποῖς πᾶσιν, ὅτι ἐὰν ἔλθω εἰς τὸ πάλιν οὐ φείσομαι, 3 ἐπεὶ δοκιμὴν ζητεῖτε τοῦ ἐν ἐμοὶ λαλοῦντος Χριστοῦ, ὃς εἰς ὑμᾶς οὐκ ἀσθενεῖ ἀλλὰ δυνατεῖ ἐν ὑμῖν. 4 καὶ γὰρ ἐσταυρώθη ἐξ ἀσθενείας, ἀλλὰ ζῇ ἐκ δυνάμεως θεοῦ. καὶ γὰρ ἡμεῖς ἀσθενοῦμεν ⸀ἐν αὐτῷ, ἀλλὰ ζήσομεν σὺν αὐτῷ ἐκ δυνάμεως θεοῦ εἰς ὑμᾶς. 5 Ἑαυτοὺς πειράζετε εἰ ἐστὲ ἐν τῇ πίστει, ἑαυτοὺς δοκιμάζετε· ἢ οὐκ ἐπιγινώσκετε ἑαυτοὺς ὅτι Ἰησοῦς Χριστὸς ἐν ὑμῖν; εἰ μήτι ἀδόκιμοί ἐστε. 6 ἐλπίζω δὲ ὅτι γνώσεσθε ὅτι ἡμεῖς οὐκ ἐσμὲν ἀδόκιμοι. 7 εὐχόμεθα δὲ πρὸς τὸν θεὸν μὴ ποιῆσαι ὑμᾶς κακὸν μηδέν, οὐχ ἵνα ἡμεῖς δόκιμοι φανῶμεν, ἀλλ᾽ ἵνα ὑμεῖς τὸ καλὸν ποιῆτε, ἡμεῖς δὲ ὡς ἀδόκιμοι ὦμεν. 8 οὐ γὰρ δυνάμεθά τι κατὰ τῆς ἀληθείας ἀλλὰ ὑπὲρ τῆς ἀληθείας. 9 χαίρομεν γὰρ ὅταν ἡμεῖς ἀσθενῶμεν, ὑμεῖς δὲ δυνατοὶ ἦτε· τοῦτο καὶ εὐχόμεθα, τὴν ὑμῶν κατάρτισιν. 10 Διὰ τοῦτο ταῦτα ἀπὼν γράφω, ἵνα παρὼν μὴ ἀποτόμως χρήσωμαι κατὰ τὴν ἐξουσίαν ἣν ὁ κύριος ἔδωκέν μοι εἰς οἰκοδομὴν καὶ οὐκ εἰς καθαίρεσιν. 11 Λοιπόν, ἀδελφοί, χαίρετε, καταρτίζεσθε, παρακαλεῖσθε, τὸ αὐτὸ φρονεῖτε, εἰρηνεύετε, καὶ ὁ θεὸς τῆς ἀγάπης καὶ εἰρήνης ἔσται μεθ᾽ ὑμῶν.

Gal 6:11–17

Ἴδετε πηλίκοις ὑμῖν γράμμασιν ἔγραψα τῇ ἐμῇ χειρί. 12 Ὅσοι θέλουσιν εὐπροσωπῆσαι ἐν σαρκί, οὗτοι ἀναγκάζουσιν ὑμᾶς περιτέμνεσθαι, μόνον ἵνα τῷ σταυρῷ τοῦ Χριστοῦ μὴ διώκωνται. 13 οὐδὲ γὰρ οἱ περιτεμνόμενοι αὐτοὶ νόμον φυλάσσουσιν ἀλλὰ θέλουσιν ὑμᾶς περιτέμνεσθαι, ἵνα ἐν τῇ ὑμετέρᾳ σαρκὶ καυχήσωνται. 14 Ἐμοὶ δὲ μὴ γένοιτο καυχᾶσθαι εἰ μὴ ἐν τῷ σταυρῷ τοῦ κυρίου ἡμῶν Ἰησοῦ Χριστοῦ, δι᾽ οὗ ἐμοὶ κόσμος ἐσταύρωται κἀγὼ κόσμῳ. 15 ⸂οὔτε γὰρ⸃ περιτομή τί ἐστιν οὔτε ἀκροβυστία ἀλλὰ καινὴ κτίσις. 16 καὶ ὅσοι τῷ κανόνι τούτῳ ⸀στοιχήσουσιν, εἰρήνη ἐπ᾽ αὐτοὺς καὶ ἔλεος καὶ ἐπὶ τὸν Ἰσραὴλ τοῦ θεοῦ. 17 Τοῦ λοιποῦ κόπους μοι μηδεὶς παρεχέτω· ἐγὼ γὰρ τὰ στίγματα τοῦ Ἰησοῦ ἐν τῷ σώματί μου βαστάζω.

Phil 4:10–20

Ἐχάρην δὲ ἐν κυρίῳ μεγάλως ὅτι ἤδη ποτὲ ἀνεθάλετε τὸ ὑπὲρ ἐμοῦ φρονεῖν, ἐφ᾽ ᾧ καὶ ἐφρονεῖτε, ἠκαιρεῖσθε δέ. 11 οὐχ ὅτι καθ᾽ ὑστέρησιν λέγω, ἐγὼ γὰρ ἔμαθον ἐν οἷς εἰμι αὐτάρκης εἶναι. 12 οἶδα καὶ ταπεινοῦσθαι, οἶδα καὶ περισσεύειν· ἐν παντὶ καὶ ἐν πᾶσιν μεμύημαι, καὶ χορτάζεσθαι καὶ πεινᾶν καὶ περισσεύειν καὶ ὑστερεῖσθαι· 13 πάντα ἰσχύω ἐν τῷ ἐνδυναμοῦντί με. 14 πλὴν καλῶς ἐποιήσατε συγκοινωνήσαντές μου τῇ θλίψει. 15 οἴδατε δὲ καὶ ὑμεῖς, Φιλιππήσιοι, ὅτι ἐν ἀρχῇ τοῦ εὐαγγελίου, ὅτε ἐξῆλθον ἀπὸ Μακεδονίας, οὐδεμία μοι ἐκκλησία ἐκοινώνησεν εἰς λόγον δόσεως καὶ λήμψεως εἰ μὴ ὑμεῖς μόνοι, 16 ὅτι καὶ ἐν Θεσσαλονίκῃ καὶ ἅπαξ καὶ δὶς εἰς τὴν χρείαν μοι ἐπέμψατε. 17 οὐχ ὅτι ἐπιζητῶ τὸ δόμα, ἀλλὰ ἐπιζητῶ τὸν καρπὸν τὸν πλεονάζοντα εἰς λόγον ὑμῶν. 18 ἀπέχω δὲ πάντα καὶ περισσεύω· πεπλήρωμαι δεξάμενος παρὰ Ἐπαφροδίτου τὰ παρ᾽ ὑμῶν, ὀσμὴν εὐωδίας, θυσίαν δεκτήν, εὐάρεστον τῷ θεῷ. 19 ὁ δὲ θεός μου πληρώσει πᾶσαν χρείαν ὑμῶν κατὰ τὸ πλοῦτος αὐτοῦ ἐν δόξῃ ἐν Χριστῷ Ἰησοῦ. 20 τῷ δὲ θεῷ καὶ πατρὶ ἡμῶν ἡ δόξα εἰς τοὺς αἰῶνας τῶν αἰώνων, ἀμήν.

2 Thess 3:13–15 (or 16)

Ὑμεῖς δέ, ἀδελφοί, μὴ ἐγκακήσητε καλοποιοῦντες. 14 Εἰ δέ τις οὐχ ὑπακούει τῷ λόγῳ ἡμῶν διὰ τῆς ἐπιστολῆς, τοῦτον σημειοῦσθε μὴ συναναμίγνυσθαι αὐτῷ, ἵνα ἐντραπῇ· 15 καὶ μὴ ὡς ἐχθρὸν ἡγεῖσθε, ἀλλὰ νουθετεῖτε ὡς ἀδελφόν.

2 Tim 4:9–18

Σπούδασον ἐλθεῖν πρός με ταχέως· 10 Δημᾶς γάρ με ἐγκατέλιπεν ἀγαπήσας τὸν νῦν αἰῶνα καὶ ἐπορεύθη εἰς Θεσσαλονίκην, Κρήσκης εἰς ⸀Γαλατίαν, Τίτος εἰς Δαλματίαν· 11 Λουκᾶς ἐστιν μόνος μετ᾽ ἐμοῦ. Μᾶρκον ἀναλαβὼν ἄγε μετὰ σεαυτοῦ, ἔστιν γάρ μοι εὔχρηστος εἰς διακονίαν. 12 Τύχικον δὲ ἀπέστειλα εἰς Ἔφεσον. 13 τὸν φαιλόνην ὃν ἀπέλιπον ἐν Τρῳάδι παρὰ Κάρπῳ ἐρχόμενος φέρε, καὶ τὰ βιβλία

Rom 15:29 ***ευλογιας*** 𝔓[46] ℵ* A B C D 1739. 1881] *add.* του ευαγγελιου του ℵ[2] 33 *Byz* **2 Cor 13:4** ***εν*** B D 33. 1739. 1881 *Byz*] συν ℵ A **Gal 6:15** ***ουτε γαρ*** 𝔓[46] B 33. 1739*] εν γαρ Χριστω Ιησου ουτε ℵ A C D (1739[c]). 1881 *Byz* **Gal 6:16** ***στοιχησουσιν*** ℵ B C[2] 33 *Byz*] στοιχουσιν A C* D 1739. 1881 ¦ στοιχησωσιν 𝔓[46] **2 Tim 4:10** ***Γαλατιαν*** A D 33. 1739. 1881 *Byz*] Γαλλιαν ℵ C

enjoyed your company for a little while. **25** At present, however, I am going to Jerusalem in a ministry to the saints; **26** for Macedonia and Achaia have been pleased to share their resources with the poor among the saints at Jerusalem. **27** They were pleased to do this, and indeed they owe it to them; for if the Gentiles have come to share in their spiritual blessings, they ought also to be of service to them in material things. **28** So, when I have completed this, and have delivered to them what has been collected, I will set out by way of you to Spain; **29** and I know that when I come to you, I will come in the fullness of the blessing[b] of Christ.

1 Cor 16:5–14 (or 1–14)

I will visit you after passing through Macedonia—for I intend to pass through Macedonia— **6** and perhaps I will stay with you or even spend the winter, so that you may send me on my way, wherever I go. **7** I do not want to see you now just in passing, for I hope to spend some time with you, if the Lord permits. **8** But I will stay in Ephesus until Pentecost, **9** for a wide door for effective work has opened to me, and there are many adversaries. **10** If Timothy comes, see that he has nothing to fear among you, for he is doing the work of the Lord just as I am; **11** therefore let no one despise him. Send him on his way in peace, so that he may come to me; for I am expecting him with the brothers. **12** Now concerning our brother Apollos, I strongly urged him to visit you with the other brothers, but he was not at all willing to come now. He will come when he has the opportunity. **13** Keep alert, stand firm in your faith, be courageous, be strong. **14** Let all that you do be done in love.

2 Cor 13:1–11 (or 12:14–13:11)

This is the third time I am coming to you. "Any charge must be sustained by the evidence of two or three witnesses." **2** I warned those who sinned previously and all the others, and I warn them now while absent, as I did when present on my second visit, that if I come again, I will not be lenient— **3** since you desire proof that Christ is speaking in me. He is not weak in dealing with you, but is powerful in you. **4** For he was crucified in weakness, but lives by the power of God. For we are weak in him,[c] but in dealing with you we will live with him by the power of God. **5** Examine yourselves to see whether you are living in the faith. Test yourselves. Do you not realize that Jesus Christ is in you?—unless, indeed, you fail to meet the test! **6** I hope you will find out that we have not failed. **7** But we pray to God that you may not do anything wrong—not that we may appear to have met the test, but that you may do what is right, though we may seem to have failed. **8** For we cannot do anything against the truth, but only for the truth. **9** For we rejoice when we are weak and you are strong. This is what we pray for, that you may become perfect. **10** So I write these things while I am away from you, so that when I come, I may not have to be severe in using the authority that the Lord has given me for building up and not for tearing down. **11** Finally, brothers and sisters, farewell. Put things in order, listen to my appeal, agree with one another, live in peace; and the God of love and peace will be with you.

Gal 6:11–17

See what large letters I make when I am writing in my own hand! **12** It is those who want to make a good showing in the flesh that try to compel you to be circumcised—only that they may not be persecuted for the cross of Christ. **13** Even the circumcised do not themselves obey the law, but they want you to be circumcised so that they may boast about your flesh. **14** May I never boast of anything except the cross of our Lord Jesus Christ, by which the world has been crucified to me, and I to the world. **15** For[d] neither circumcision nor uncircumcision is anything; but a new creation is everything! **16** As for those who will follow[e] this rule—peace be upon them, and mercy, and upon the Israel of God. **17** From now on, let no one make trouble for me; for I carry the marks of Jesus branded on my body.

Phil 4:10–20

I rejoice in the Lord greatly that now at last you have revived your concern for me; indeed, you were concerned for me, but had no opportunity to show it. **11** Not that I am referring to being in need; for I have learned to be content with whatever I have. **12** I know what it is to have little, and I know what it is to have plenty. In any and all circumstances I have learned the secret of being well-fed and of going hungry, of having plenty and of being in need. **13** I can do all things through him who strengthens me. **14** In any case, it was kind of you to share my distress. **15** You Philippians indeed know that in the early days of the gospel, when I left Macedonia, no church shared with me in the matter of giving and receiving, except you alone. **16** For even when I was in Thessalonica, you sent me help for my needs more than once. **17** Not that I seek the gift, but I seek the profit that accumulates to your account. **18** I have been paid in full and have more than enough; I am fully satisfied, now that I have received from Epaphroditus the gifts you sent, a fragrant offering, a sacrifice acceptable and pleasing to God. **19** And my God will fully satisfy every need of yours according to his riches in glory in Christ Jesus. **20** To our God and Father be glory forever and ever. Amen.

2 Thess 3:13–15 (or 16)

Brothers and sisters, do not be weary in doing what is right. **14** Take note of those who do not obey what we say in this letter; have nothing to do with them, so that they may be ashamed. **15** Do not regard them as enemies, but warn them as believers.

2 Tim 4:9–18

Do your best to come to me soon, **10** for Demas, in love with this present world, has deserted me and gone to Thessalonica; Crescens has gone to Galatia,[f] Titus to Dalmatia. **11** Only Luke is with me. Get Mark and bring him with you, for he is useful in my ministry. **12** I have sent Tychicus to Ephesus. **13** When you come, bring the cloak that I left with

[b] **Rom 15:29** ***blessing*** Other ancient authorities add *of the gospel* [c] **2 Cor 13:4** ***in him*** Other ancient authorities read *with him* [d] **Gal 6:15** ***For*** Other ancient authorities add *in Christ Jesus* [e] **Gal 6:16** ***will follow*** Other ancient authorities read *follow* [f] **2 Tim 4:10** ***Galatia*** Other ancient authorities read *Gaul*

μάλιστα τὰς μεμβράνας. **14** Ἀλέξανδρος ὁ χαλκεὺς πολλά μοι κακὰ ἐνεδείξατο· ἀποδώσει αὐτῷ ὁ κύριος κατὰ τὰ ἔργα αὐτοῦ· **15** ὃν καὶ σὺ φυλάσσου, λίαν γὰρ ἀντέστη τοῖς ἡμετέροις λόγοις. **16** Ἐν τῇ πρώτῃ μου ἀπολογίᾳ οὐδείς μοι παρεγένετο, ἀλλὰ πάντες με ἐγκατέλιπον· μὴ αὐτοῖς λογισθείη· **17** ὁ δὲ κύριός μοι παρέστη καὶ ἐνεδυνάμωσέν με, ἵνα δι᾽ ἐμοῦ τὸ κήρυγμα πληροφορηθῇ καὶ ἀκούσωσιν πάντα τὰ ἔθνη, καὶ ἐρρύσθην ἐκ στόματος λέοντος. **18** ῥύσεταί με ὁ κύριος ἀπὸ παντὸς ἔργου πονηροῦ καὶ σώσει εἰς τὴν βασιλείαν αὐτοῦ τὴν ἐπουράνιον· ᾧ ἡ δόξα εἰς τοὺς αἰῶνας τῶν αἰώνων, ἀμήν.

Titus 3:12–14

Ὅταν πέμψω Ἀρτεμᾶν πρὸς σὲ ἢ Τύχικον, σπούδασον ἐλθεῖν πρός με εἰς Νικόπολιν, ἐκεῖ γὰρ κέκρικα παραχειμάσαι. **13** Ζηνᾶν τὸν νομικὸν καὶ Ἀπολλῶν σπουδαίως πρόπεμψον, ἵνα μηδὲν αὐτοῖς λείπῃ. **14** μανθανέτωσαν δὲ καὶ οἱ ἡμέτεροι καλῶν ἔργων προΐστασθαι εἰς τὰς ἀναγκαίας χρείας, ἵνα μὴ ὦσιν ἄκαρποι.

Phlm 21–22

Πεποιθὼς τῇ ὑπακοῇ σου ἔγραψά σοι, εἰδὼς ὅτι καὶ ὑπὲρ ἃ λέγω ποιήσεις. **22** ἅμα δὲ καὶ ἑτοίμαζέ μοι ξενίαν· ἐλπίζω γὰρ ὅτι διὰ τῶν προσευχῶν ὑμῶν χαρισθήσομαι ὑμῖν.

Note: The nature and extent of this segment of the Pauline letter structure is debated. Eph, Col, 1 Thess, and 1 Tim appear to lack a distinct closing of the body such as is found in the other Pauline letters.

The reference at the head of some excerpts above is followed by a different reference in parentheses in cases where scholars disagree as to the extent of the unit within the structure of the letter.

See also § 11 Apostolic Parousia.

6. Greetings

Rom 16:3–23

Ἀσπάσασθε Πρίσκαν καὶ Ἀκύλαν τοὺς συνεργούς μου ἐν Χριστῷ Ἰησοῦ, **4** οἵτινες ὑπὲρ τῆς ψυχῆς μου τὸν ἑαυτῶν τράχηλον ὑπέθηκαν, οἷς οὐκ ἐγὼ μόνος εὐχαριστῶ ἀλλὰ καὶ πᾶσαι αἱ ἐκκλησίαι τῶν ἐθνῶν, **5** καὶ τὴν κατ᾽ οἶκον αὐτῶν ἐκκλησίαν. ἀσπάσασθε Ἐπαίνετον τὸν ἀγαπητόν μου, ὅς ἐστιν ἀπαρχὴ τῆς Ἀσίας εἰς Χριστόν. **6** ἀσπάσασθε Μαρίαν, ἥτις πολλὰ ἐκοπίασεν εἰς ὑμᾶς. **7** ἀσπάσασθε Ἀνδρόνικον καὶ ⸀Ἰουνίαν τοὺς συγγενεῖς μου καὶ συναιχμαλώτους μου, οἵτινές εἰσιν ἐπίσημοι ἐν τοῖς ἀποστόλοις, οἳ καὶ πρὸ ἐμοῦ γέγοναν ἐν Χριστῷ. **8** ἀσπάσασθε Ἀμπλιᾶτον τὸν ἀγαπητόν μου ἐν κυρίῳ. **9** ἀσπάσασθε Οὐρβανὸν τὸν συνεργὸν ἡμῶν ἐν Χριστῷ καὶ Στάχυν τὸν ἀγαπητόν μου. **10** ἀσπάσασθε Ἀπελλῆν τὸν δόκιμον ἐν Χριστῷ. ἀσπάσασθε τοὺς ἐκ τῶν Ἀριστοβούλου. **11** ἀσπάσασθε Ἡρῳδίωνα τὸν συγγενῆ μου. ἀσπάσασθε τοὺς ἐκ τῶν Ναρκίσσου τοὺς ὄντας ἐν κυρίῳ. **12** ἀσπάσασθε Τρύφαιναν καὶ Τρυφῶσαν τὰς κοπιώσας ἐν κυρίῳ. ἀσπάσασθε Περσίδα τὴν ἀγαπητήν, ἥτις πολλὰ ἐκοπίασεν ἐν κυρίῳ. **13** ἀσπάσασθε Ῥοῦφον τὸν ἐκλεκτὸν ἐν κυρίῳ καὶ τὴν μητέρα αὐτοῦ καὶ ἐμοῦ. **14** ἀσπάσασθε Ἀσύγκριτον, Φλέγοντα, Ἑρμῆν, Πατροβᾶν, Ἑρμᾶν καὶ τοὺς σὺν αὐτοῖς ἀδελφούς. **15** ἀσπάσασθε Φιλόλογον καὶ Ἰουλίαν, Νηρέα καὶ τὴν ἀδελφὴν αὐτοῦ, καὶ Ὀλυμπᾶν καὶ τοὺς σὺν αὐτοῖς πάντας ἁγίους. **16** ἀσπάσασθε ἀλλήλους ἐν φιλήματι ἁγίῳ. ἀσπάζονται ὑμᾶς αἱ ἐκκλησίαι πᾶσαι τοῦ Χριστοῦ. **17** Παρακαλῶ δὲ ὑμᾶς, ἀδελφοί, σκοπεῖν τοὺς τὰς διχοστασίας καὶ τὰ σκάνδαλα παρὰ τὴν διδαχὴν ἣν ὑμεῖς ἐμάθετε ποιοῦντας, καὶ ἐκκλίνετε ἀπ᾽ αὐτῶν· **18** οἱ γὰρ τοιοῦτοι τῷ κυρίῳ ἡμῶν Χριστῷ οὐ δουλεύουσιν ἀλλὰ τῇ ἑαυτῶν κοιλίᾳ, καὶ διὰ τῆς χρηστολογίας καὶ εὐλογίας ἐξαπατῶσιν τὰς καρδίας τῶν ἀκάκων. **19** ἡ γὰρ ὑμῶν ὑπακοὴ εἰς πάντας ἀφίκετο· ἐφ᾽ ὑμῖν οὖν χαίρω, θέλω δὲ ὑμᾶς σοφοὺς εἶναι εἰς τὸ ἀγαθόν, ἀκεραίους δὲ εἰς τὸ κακόν. **20** ὁ δὲ θεὸς τῆς εἰρήνης συντρίψει τὸν σατανᾶν ὑπὸ τοὺς πόδας ὑμῶν ἐν τάχει. ⸂Ἡ χάρις τοῦ κυρίου ἡμῶν Ἰησοῦ μεθ᾽ ὑμῶν.⸃ **21** Ἀσπάζεται ὑμᾶς Τιμόθεος ὁ συνεργός μου καὶ Λούκιος καὶ Ἰάσων καὶ Σωσίπατρος οἱ συγγενεῖς μου. **22** ἀσπάζομαι ὑμᾶς ἐγὼ Τέρτιος ὁ γράψας τὴν ἐπιστολὴν ἐν κυρίῳ. **23** ἀσπάζεται ὑμᾶς Γάϊος ὁ ξένος μου καὶ ὅλης τῆς ἐκκλησίας. ἀσπάζεται ὑμᾶς Ἔραστος ὁ οἰκονόμος τῆς πόλεως καὶ Κούαρτος ὁ ἀδελφός.

1 Cor 16:19–20

Ἀσπάζονται ὑμᾶς αἱ ἐκκλησίαι τῆς Ἀσίας. ἀσπάζεται ὑμᾶς ἐν κυρίῳ πολλὰ Ἀκύλας καὶ Πρίσκα σὺν τῇ κατ᾽ οἶκον αὐτῶν ἐκκλησίᾳ. **20** ἀσπάζονται ὑμᾶς οἱ ἀδελφοὶ πάντες. Ἀσπάσασθε ἀλλήλους ἐν φιλήματι ἁγίῳ.

2 Cor 13:12

Ἀσπάσασθε ἀλλήλους ἐν ἁγίῳ φιλήματι. Ἀσπάζονται ὑμᾶς οἱ ἅγιοι πάντες.

Phil 4:21–22

Ἀσπάσασθε πάντα ἅγιον ἐν Χριστῷ Ἰησοῦ. ἀσπάζονται ὑμᾶς οἱ σὺν ἐμοὶ ἀδελφοί. **22** ἀσπάζονται ὑμᾶς πάντες οἱ ἅγιοι, μάλιστα δὲ οἱ ἐκ τῆς Καίσαρος οἰκίας.

Col 4:10–17

Ἀσπάζεται ὑμᾶς Ἀρίσταρχος ὁ συναιχμάλωτός μου καὶ Μᾶρκος ὁ ἀνεψιὸς Βαρναβᾶ (περὶ οὗ ἐλάβετε ἐντολάς, ἐὰν ἔλθῃ πρὸς ὑμᾶς, δέξασθε αὐτόν) **11** καὶ Ἰησοῦς ὁ λεγόμενος Ἰοῦστος, οἱ ὄντες ἐκ περιτομῆς, οὗτοι μόνοι συνεργοὶ εἰς τὴν βασιλείαν τοῦ θεοῦ, οἵτινες ἐγενήθησάν μοι παρηγορία. **12** ἀσπάζεται ὑμᾶς Ἐπαφρᾶς ὁ ἐξ ὑμῶν, δοῦλος Χριστοῦ [Ἰησοῦ], πάντοτε ἀγωνιζόμενος ὑπὲρ ὑμῶν ἐν ταῖς προσευχαῖς, ἵνα σταθῆτε τέλειοι καὶ πεπληροφορημένοι ἐν παντὶ θελήματι τοῦ θεοῦ. **13** μαρτυρῶ γὰρ αὐτῷ ὅτι ἔχει πολὺν πόνον ὑπὲρ ὑμῶν καὶ τῶν ἐν Λαοδικείᾳ καὶ τῶν ἐν Ἱεραπόλει. **14** ἀσπάζεται ὑμᾶς Λουκᾶς ὁ ἰατρὸς ὁ ἀγαπητὸς καὶ Δημᾶς. **15** Ἀσπάσασθε τοὺς ἐν Λαοδικείᾳ ἀδελφοὺς καὶ Νύμφαν καὶ τὴν κατ᾽ οἶκον ⸀αὐτῆς ἐκκλησίαν. **16** καὶ ὅταν ἀναγνωσθῇ παρ᾽ ὑμῖν ἡ ἐπιστολή,

§ 6 **Rom 16:7** ***Ιουνιαν*** ℵ A B C D 33. 1739. 1881 *Byz* (*acc.* Ἰουνίαν B² D² 33. 1739. 1881 *Byz*; *sine acc.* ℵ A B* C D*)] Ιουλιαν 𝔓⁴⁶ **Rom 16:20** ***η χαρις του κυριου ημων Ιησου μεθ υμων*** 𝔓⁴⁶ ℵ B 1881] η χαρις του κυριου ημων Ιησου Χριστου μεθ υμων A C 33. 1739 *Byz* ¦ *om. hic et pon. p.* 16:23 D **Col 4:15** ***αυτης*** B 1739⁽*⁾. 1881] αυτου D *Byz* ¦ αυτων ℵ A C 33

Carpus at Troas, also the books, and above all the parchments. **14** Alexander the coppersmith did me great harm; the Lord will pay him back for his deeds. **15** You also must beware of him, for he strongly opposed our message. **16** At my first defense no one came to my support, but all deserted me. May it not be counted against them! **17** But the Lord stood by me and gave me strength, so that through me the message might be fully proclaimed and all the Gentiles might hear it. So I was rescued from the lion's mouth. **18** The Lord will rescue me from every evil attack and save me for his heavenly kingdom. To him be the glory forever and ever. Amen.

Titus 3:12–14

When I send Artemas to you, or Tychicus, do your best to come to me at Nicopolis, for I have decided to spend the winter there. **13** Make every effort to send Zenas the lawyer and Apollos on their way, and see that they lack nothing. **14** And let people learn to devote themselves to good works in order to meet urgent needs, so that they may not be unproductive.

Phlm 21–22

Confident of your obedience, I am writing to you, knowing that you will do even more than I say. **22** One thing more—prepare a guest room for me, for I am hoping through your prayers to be restored to you.

Note: The nature and extent of this segment of the Pauline letter structure is debated. Eph, Col, 1 Thess, and 1 Tim appear to lack a distinct closing of the body such as is found in the other Pauline letters.

The reference at the head of some excerpts above is followed by a different reference in parentheses in cases where scholars disagree as to the extent of the unit within the structure of the letter.

See also § 11 Apostolic Parousia.

6. *Greetings*

Rom 16:3–23

Greet Prisca and Aquila, who work with me in Christ Jesus, **4** and who risked their necks for my life, to whom not only I give thanks, but also all the churches of the Gentiles. **5** Greet also the church in their house. Greet my beloved Epaenetus, who was the first convert in Asia for Christ. **6** Greet Mary, who has worked very hard among you. **7** Greet Andronicus and Junia,[a] my relatives who were in prison with me; they are prominent among the apostles, and they were in Christ before I was. **8** Greet Ampliatus, my beloved in the Lord. **9** Greet Urbanus, our co-worker in Christ, and my beloved Stachys. **10** Greet Apelles, who is approved in Christ. Greet those who belong to the family of Aristobulus. **11** Greet my relative Herodion. Greet those in the Lord who belong to the family of Narcissus. **12** Greet those workers in the Lord, Tryphaena and Tryphosa. Greet the beloved Persis, who has worked hard in the Lord. **13** Greet Rufus, chosen in the Lord; and greet his mother—a mother to me also. **14** Greet Asyncritus, Phlegon, Hermes, Patrobas, Hermas, and the brothers and sisters who are with them. **15** Greet Philologus, Julia, Nereus and his sister, and Olympas, and all the saints who are with them. **16** Greet one another with a holy kiss. All the churches of Christ greet you. **17** I urge you, brothers and sisters, to keep an eye on those who cause dissensions and offenses, in opposition to the teaching that you have learned; avoid them. **18** For such people do not serve our Lord Christ, but their own appetites, and by smooth talk and flattery they deceive the hearts of the simple-minded. **19** For while your obedience is known to all, so that I rejoice over you, I want you to be wise in what is good and guileless in what is evil. **20** The God of peace will shortly crush Satan under your feet. The grace of our Lord Jesus Christ be with you.[b] **21** Timothy, my co-worker, greets you; so do Lucius and Jason and Sosipater, my relatives. **22** I Tertius, the writer of this letter, greet you in the Lord. **23** Gaius, who is host to me and to the whole church, greets you. Erastus, the city treasurer, and our brother Quartus, greet you.

1 Cor 16:19–20

The churches of Asia send greetings. Aquila and Prisca, together with the church in their house, greet you warmly in the Lord. **20** All the brothers and sisters send greetings. Greet one another with a holy kiss.

2 Cor 13:12 (Eng 12–13)

Greet one another with a holy kiss. All the saints greet you.

Phil 4:21–22

Greet every saint in Christ Jesus. The friends who are with me greet you. **22** All the saints greet you, especially those of the emperor's household.

Col 4:10–17

Aristarchus my fellow prisoner greets you, as does Mark the cousin of Barnabas, concerning whom you have received instructions—if he comes to you, welcome him. **11** And Jesus who is called Justus greets you. These are the only ones of the circumcision among my co-workers for the kingdom of God, and they have been a comfort to me. **12** Epaphras, who is one of you, a servant of Christ Jesus, greets you. He is always wrestling in his prayers on your behalf, so that you may stand mature and fully assured in everything that God wills. **13** For I testify for him that he has worked hard for you and for those in Laodicea and in Hierapolis. **14** Luke, the beloved physician, and Demas greet you. **15** Give my greetings to the brothers and sisters in Laodicea, and to Nympha and the church in her[c] house. **16** And when this letter has been read among you, have it read also in the

§ 6 [a] **Rom 16:7** ***Junia*** Or possibly *Junias*; a few ancient authorities read *Julia* [b] **Rom 16:20** ***you*** A few ancient authorities omit this sentence here and place it after verse 23 [c] **Col 4:15** ***her*** Other ancient authorities read *his* (implying the masculine name *Nymphas*) or *their*

ποιήσατε ἵνα καὶ ἐν τῇ Λαοδικέων ἐκκλησίᾳ
ἀναγνωσθῇ, καὶ τὴν ἐκ Λαοδικείας ἵνα καὶ
ὑμεῖς ἀναγνῶτε. 17 καὶ εἴπατε Ἀρχίππῳ·
βλέπε τὴν διακονίαν ἣν παρέλαβες ἐν
κυρίῳ, ἵνα αὐτὴν πληροῖς.

1 Thess 5:26

Ἀσπάσασθε τοὺς ἀδελφοὺς πάντας ἐν
φιλήματι ἁγίῳ.

2 Tim 4:19–21

Ἄσπασαι Πρίσκαν καὶ Ἀκύλαν καὶ τὸν
Ὀνησιφόρου οἶκον. 20 Ἔραστος ἔμεινεν
ἐν Κορίνθῳ, Τρόφιμον δὲ ἀπέλιπον ἐν
Μιλήτῳ ἀσθενοῦντα. 21 Σπούδασον πρὸ
χειμῶνος ἐλθεῖν. Ἀσπάζεταί σε Εὔβουλος
καὶ Πούδης καὶ Λίνος καὶ Κλαυδία καὶ
οἱ ἀδελφοὶ πάντες.

Titus 3:15

Ἀσπάζονταί σε οἱ μετ' ἐμοῦ πάντες. ἄσπα-
σαι τοὺς φιλοῦντας ἡμᾶς ἐν πίστει. Ἡ
χάρις μετὰ πάντων ⸀ὑμῶν.

Phlm 23–24

Ἀσπάζεταί σε Ἐπαφρᾶς ὁ συναιχμά-
λωτός μου ἐν Χριστῷ Ἰησοῦ, 24 Μᾶρκος,
Ἀρίσταρχος, Δημᾶς, Λουκᾶς, οἱ συνερ-
γοί μου.

For greeting with a holy kiss, see above specifically Rom 16:16; 1 Cor 16:20; 2 Cor 13:12; and 1 Thess 5:26.

7. Signature

1 Cor 16:21–22

Ὁ ἀσπασμὸς τῇ ἐμῇ χειρὶ Παύλου. 22 εἴ
τις οὐ φιλεῖ τὸν κύριον, ἤτω ἀνάθεμα.
μαράνα θά.

Gal 6:11–17

Ἴδετε πηλίκοις ὑμῖν γράμμασιν ἔγραψα
τῇ ἐμῇ χειρί. 12 Ὅσοι θέλουσιν εὐπροσω-
πῆσαι ἐν σαρκί, οὗτοι ἀναγκάζουσιν ὑμᾶς
περιτέμνεσθαι, μόνον ἵνα τῷ σταυρῷ τοῦ
Χριστοῦ μὴ διώκωνται. 13 οὐδὲ γὰρ οἱ
περιτεμνόμενοι αὐτοὶ νόμον φυλάσσου-
σιν ἀλλὰ θέλουσιν ὑμᾶς περιτέμνεσθαι,
ἵνα ἐν τῇ ὑμετέρᾳ σαρκὶ καυχήσωνται.
14 Ἐμοὶ δὲ μὴ γένοιτο καυχᾶσθαι εἰ μὴ
ἐν τῷ σταυρῷ τοῦ κυρίου ἡμῶν Ἰησοῦ
Χριστοῦ, δι' οὗ ἐμοὶ κόσμος ἐσταύρωται
κἀγὼ κόσμῳ. 15 ⸂οὔτε γὰρ⸃ περιτομή τί
ἐστιν οὔτε ἀκροβυστία ἀλλὰ καινὴ κτίσις.
16 καὶ ὅσοι τῷ κανόνι τούτῳ ⸀στοιχήσου-
σιν, εἰρήνη ἐπ' αὐτοὺς καὶ ἔλεος καὶ ἐπὶ
τὸν Ἰσραὴλ τοῦ θεοῦ. 17 Τοῦ λοιποῦ
κόπους μοι μηδεὶς παρεχέτω· ἐγὼ γὰρ
τὰ στίγματα τοῦ Ἰησοῦ ἐν τῷ σώματί
μου βαστάζω.

Col 4:18

Ὁ ἀσπασμὸς τῇ ἐμῇ χειρὶ Παύλου. μνη-
μονεύετέ μου τῶν δεσμῶν. ἡ χάρις μεθ'
⸀ὑμῶν.

2 Thess 3:17

Ὁ ἀσπασμὸς τῇ ἐμῇ χειρὶ Παύλου, ὅ
ἐστιν σημεῖον ἐν πάσῃ ἐπιστολῇ· οὕτως
γράφω.

Phlm 19–20

ἐγὼ Παῦλος ἔγραψα τῇ ἐμῇ χειρί, ἐγὼ
ἀποτίσω· ἵνα μὴ λέγω σοι ὅτι καὶ σεαυ-
τόν μοι προσοφείλεις. 20 ναὶ ἀδελφέ,
ἐγώ σου ὀναίμην ἐν κυρίῳ· ἀνάπαυσόν
μου τὰ σπλάγχνα ἐν Χριστῷ.

8. Closing Benediction

1 Cor 16:23–24

ἡ χάρις τοῦ κυρίου ⸀Ἰησοῦ μεθ' ὑμῶν.
24 ἡ ἀγάπη μου μετὰ πάντων ὑμῶν ἐν
Χριστῷ ⸀Ἰησοῦ.

2 Cor 13:13

Ἡ χάρις τοῦ κυρίου Ἰησοῦ Χριστοῦ καὶ ἡ
ἀγάπη τοῦ θεοῦ καὶ ἡ κοινωνία τοῦ ἁγίου
πνεύματος μετὰ πάντων ὑμῶν.

Gal 6:18

Ἡ χάρις τοῦ κυρίου ἡμῶν Ἰησοῦ Χρι-
στοῦ μετὰ τοῦ πνεύματος ὑμῶν, ἀδελ-
φοί· ἀμήν.

Eph 6:23–24

Εἰρήνη τοῖς ἀδελφοῖς καὶ ἀγάπη μετὰ
πίστεως ἀπὸ θεοῦ πατρὸς καὶ κυρίου
Ἰησοῦ Χριστοῦ. 24 ἡ χάρις μετὰ πάντων
τῶν ἀγαπώντων τὸν κύριον ἡμῶν Ἰη-
σοῦν Χριστὸν ἐν ⸀ἀφθαρσίᾳ.

Phil 4:23

Ἡ χάρις τοῦ κυρίου Ἰησοῦ Χριστοῦ μετὰ
τοῦ πνεύματος ⸀ὑμῶν.

Col 4:18b

ἡ χάρις μεθ' ⸀ὑμῶν.

1 Thess 5:28

Ἡ χάρις τοῦ κυρίου ἡμῶν Ἰησοῦ Χριστοῦ
μεθ' ⸀ὑμῶν.

2 Thess 3:18

Ἡ χάρις τοῦ κυρίου ἡμῶν Ἰησοῦ Χριστοῦ
μετὰ πάντων ⸀ὑμῶν.

Titus 3:15 ***υμων*** ℵ* A C D* 048. 33. 1739. 1881] *add.* αμην ℵ^{2} D^{1} *Byz* **§ 7** **Gal 6:15** ***ουτε γαρ*** 𝔓^{46} B 33. 1739*] εν γαρ Χριστω Ιησου ουτε ℵ A C D (1739^{c}). 1881 *Byz* **Gal 6:16** ***στοιχησουσιν*** ℵ B C^{2} 33 *Byz*] στοιχουσιν A C* D 1739. 1881 ¦ στοιχησωσιν 𝔓^{46} **Col 4:18** ***υμων*** ℵ* A B C 048. 33. 1739*. 1881] *add.* αμην ℵ^{2} D 1739^{c} *Byz* **§ 8** **1 Cor 16:23** ***Ιησου*** ℵ* B 33] *add.* Χριστου ℵ^{2} A C D 1739. 1881 *Byz* **1 Cor 16:24** ***Ιησου*** B 33. 1739*. 1881] *add.* αμην ℵ A C D 1739^{c} *Byz* **Eph 6:24** ***αφθαρσια*** 𝔓^{46} ℵ* A B 33. 1739*. 1881] *add.* αμην ℵ^{2} D 1739^{c} *Byz* **Phil 4:23** ***υμων*** B 1739*. 1881] *add.* αμην 𝔓^{46} ℵ A D 33. 1739^{c} *Byz* **Col 4:18** ***υμων*** ℵ* A B C 048. 33. 1739*. 1881] *add.* αμην ℵ^{2} D 1739^{c} *Byz* **1 Thess 5:28** ***υμων*** B D* 33. 1739*. 1881] *add.* αμην ℵ A D^{1} 1739^{c} *Byz* **2 Thess 3:18** ***υμων*** ℵ* B 33. 1739. 1881*] *add.* αμην ℵ^{2} A D 1881^{c} *Byz*

church of the Laodiceans; and see that you read also the letter from Laodicea. 17 And say to Archippus, "See that you complete the task that you have received in the Lord."

1 Thess 5:26

Greet all the brothers and sisters with a holy kiss.

2 Tim 4:19–21

Greet Prisca and Aquila, and the household of Onesiphorus. 20 Erastus remained in Corinth; Trophimus I left ill in Miletus. 21 Do your best to come before winter. Eubulus sends greetings to you, as do Pudens and Linus and Claudia and all the brothers and sisters.

Titus 3:15

All who are with me send greetings to you. Greet those who love us in the faith. Grace be with all of you.[d]

Phlm 23–24

Epaphras, my fellow prisoner in Christ Jesus, sends greetings to you, 24 and so do Mark, Aristarchus, Demas, and Luke, my fellow workers.

For greeting with a holy kiss, see above specifically Rom 16:16; 1 Cor 16:20; 2 Cor 13:12; and 1 Thess 5:26.

7. Signature

1 Cor 16:21–22

I, Paul, write this greeting with my own hand. 22 Let anyone be accursed who has no love for the Lord. Our Lord, come!

Gal 6:11–17

See what large letters I make when I am writing in my own hand! 12 It is those who want to make a good showing in the flesh that try to compel you to be circumcised—only that they may not be persecuted for the cross of Christ. 13 Even the circumcised do not themselves obey the law, but they want you to be circumcised so that they may boast about your flesh. 14 May I never boast of anything except the cross of our Lord Jesus Christ, by which the world has been crucified to me, and I to the world. 15 For[a] neither circumcision nor uncircumcision is anything; but a new creation is everything! 16 As for those who will follow[b] this rule—peace be upon them, and mercy, and upon the Israel of God. 17 From now on, let no one make trouble for me; for I carry the marks of Jesus branded on my body.

Col 4:18

I, Paul, write this greeting with my own hand. Remember my chains. Grace be with you.[c]

2 Thess 3:17

I, Paul, write this greeting with my own hand. This is the mark in every letter of mine; it is the way I write.

Phlm 19–20

I, Paul, am writing this with my own hand: I will repay it. I say nothing about your owing me even your own self. 20 Yes, brother, let me have this benefit from you in the Lord! Refresh my heart in Christ.

8. Closing Benediction

1 Cor 16:23–24

The grace of the Lord Jesus[a] be with you. 24 My love be with all of you in Christ Jesus.[b]

2 Cor 13:13 (Eng 14)

The grace of the Lord Jesus Christ, the love of God, and the communion of the Holy Spirit be with all of you.

Gal 6:18

May the grace of our Lord Jesus Christ be with your spirit, brothers and sisters. Amen.

Eph 6:23–24

Peace be to the whole community, and love with faith, from God the Father and the Lord Jesus Christ. 24 Grace be with all who have an undying love for our Lord Jesus Christ.[c]

Phil 4:23

The grace of the Lord Jesus Christ be with your spirit.[d]

Col 4:18b

Grace be with you.[e]

1 Thess 5:28

The grace of our Lord Jesus Christ be with you.[f]

2 Thess 3:18

The grace of our Lord Jesus Christ be with all of you.[g]

[d] **Titus 3:15** *you* Other ancient authorities add *Amen* **§ 7** [a] **Gal 6:15** *For* Other ancient authorities add *in Christ Jesus* [b] **Gal 6:16** *will follow* Other ancient authorities read *follow* [c] **Col 4:18** *you* Other ancient authorities add *Amen* **§ 8** [a] **1 Cor 16:23** *Jesus* Other ancient authorities add *Christ* [b] **1 Cor 16:24** *Jesus* Other ancient authorities add *Amen* [c] **Eph 6:24** *Christ* Other ancient authorities add *Amen* [d] **Phil 4:23** *spirit* Other ancient authorities add *Amen* [e] **Col 4:18b** *you* Other ancient authorities add *Amen* [f] **1 Thess 5:28** *you* Other ancient authorities add *Amen* [g] **2 Thess 3:18** *you* Other ancient authorities add *Amen*

1 Tim 6:21b
Ἡ χάρις ⸂μεθʼ ὑμῶν⸃.

2 Tim 4:22
Ὁ κύριος μετὰ τοῦ πνεύματός σου. ἡ χάρις μεθʼ ⸀ὑμῶν.

Titus 3:15b
Ἡ χάρις μετὰ πάντων ⸀ὑμῶν.

Phlm 25
Ἡ χάρις τοῦ κυρίου Ἰησοῦ Χριστοῦ μετὰ τοῦ πνεύματος ⸀ὑμῶν.

Cf. Rom 16:20; 16:24 (v.l.).

9. *Commendation*

Rom 16:1–2
Συνίστημι δὲ ὑμῖν Φοίβην τὴν ἀδελφὴν ἡμῶν, οὖσαν [καὶ] διάκονον τῆς ἐκκλησίας τῆς ἐν Κεγχρεαῖς, **2** ἵνα αὐτὴν προσδέξησθε ἐν κυρίῳ ἀξίως τῶν ἁγίων καὶ παραστῆτε αὐτῇ ἐν ᾧ ἂν ὑμῶν χρῄζῃ πράγματι· καὶ γὰρ αὐτὴ προστάτις πολλῶν ἐγενήθη καὶ ἐμοῦ αὐτοῦ.

1 Cor 16:15–18
Παρακαλῶ δὲ ὑμᾶς, ἀδελφοί· οἴδατε τὴν οἰκίαν Στεφανᾶ, ὅτι ἐστὶν ἀπαρχὴ τῆς Ἀχαΐας καὶ εἰς διακονίαν τοῖς ἁγίοις ἔταξαν ἑαυτούς· **16** ἵνα καὶ ὑμεῖς ὑποτάσσησθε τοῖς τοιούτοις καὶ παντὶ τῷ συνεργοῦντι καὶ κοπιῶντι. **17** χαίρω δὲ ἐπὶ τῇ παρουσίᾳ Στεφανᾶ καὶ Φορτουνάτου καὶ Ἀχαϊκοῦ, ὅτι τὸ ὑμέτερον ὑστέρημα οὗτοι ἀνεπλήρωσαν· **18** ἀνέπαυσαν γὰρ τὸ ἐμὸν πνεῦμα καὶ τὸ ὑμῶν. ἐπιγινώσκετε οὖν τοὺς τοιούτους.

2 Cor 8:16–24
Χάρις δὲ τῷ θεῷ τῷ ⸀δόντι τὴν αὐτὴν σπουδὴν ὑπὲρ ὑμῶν ἐν τῇ καρδίᾳ Τίτου, **17** ὅτι τὴν μὲν παράκλησιν ἐδέξατο, σπουδαιότερος δὲ ὑπάρχων αὐθαίρετος ἐξῆλθεν πρὸς ὑμᾶς. **18** συνεπέμψαμεν δὲ μετʼ αὐτοῦ τὸν ἀδελφὸν οὗ ὁ ἔπαινος ἐν τῷ εὐαγγελίῳ διὰ πασῶν τῶν ἐκκλησιῶν, **19** οὐ μόνον δέ, ἀλλὰ καὶ χειροτονηθεὶς ὑπὸ τῶν ἐκκλησιῶν συνέκδημος ἡμῶν σὺν τῇ χάριτι ταύτῃ τῇ διακονουμένῃ ὑφʼ ἡμῶν πρὸς τὴν ⸀[αὐτοῦ] τοῦ κυρίου δόξαν καὶ προθυμίαν ἡμῶν, **20** στελλόμενοι τοῦτο, μή τις ἡμᾶς μωμήσηται ἐν τῇ ἁδρότητι ταύτῃ τῇ διακονουμένῃ ὑφʼ ἡμῶν· **21** προνοοῦμεν γὰρ καλὰ οὐ μόνον ἐνώπιον κυρίου ἀλλὰ καὶ ἐνώπιον ἀνθρώπων. **22** συνεπέμψαμεν δὲ αὐτοῖς τὸν ἀδελφὸν ἡμῶν ὃν ἐδοκιμάσαμεν ἐν πολλοῖς πολλάκις σπουδαῖον ὄντα, νυνὶ δὲ πολὺ σπουδαιότερον πεποιθήσει πολλῇ τῇ εἰς ὑμᾶς. **23** εἴτε ὑπὲρ Τίτου, κοινωνὸς ἐμὸς καὶ εἰς ὑμᾶς συνεργός· εἴτε ἀδελφοὶ ἡμῶν, ἀπόστολοι ἐκκλησιῶν, δόξα Χριστοῦ. **24** τὴν οὖν ἔνδειξιν τῆς ἀγάπης ὑμῶν καὶ ἡμῶν καυχήσεως ὑπὲρ ὑμῶν εἰς αὐτοὺς ἐνδεικνύμενοι εἰς πρόσωπον τῶν ἐκκλησιῶν.

Eph 6:21–22
Ἵνα δὲ εἰδῆτε καὶ ὑμεῖς τὰ κατʼ ἐμέ, τί πράσσω, πάντα γνωρίσει ὑμῖν Τύχικος ὁ ἀγαπητὸς ἀδελφὸς καὶ πιστὸς διάκονος ἐν κυρίῳ, **22** ὃν ἔπεμψα πρὸς ὑμᾶς εἰς αὐτὸ τοῦτο, ἵνα γνῶτε τὰ περὶ ἡμῶν καὶ παρακαλέσῃ τὰς καρδίας ὑμῶν.

Phil 2:25–30
Ἀναγκαῖον δὲ ἡγησάμην Ἐπαφρόδιτον τὸν ἀδελφὸν καὶ συνεργὸν καὶ συστρατιώτην μου, ὑμῶν δὲ ἀπόστολον καὶ λειτουργὸν τῆς χρείας μου, πέμψαι πρὸς ὑμᾶς, **26** ἐπειδὴ ἐπιποθῶν ἦν ⸂πάντας ὑμᾶς⸃ καὶ ἀδημονῶν, διότι ἠκούσατε ὅτι ἠσθένησεν. **27** καὶ γὰρ ἠσθένησεν παραπλήσιον θανάτῳ· ἀλλὰ ὁ θεὸς ἠλέησεν αὐτόν, οὐκ αὐτὸν δὲ μόνον ἀλλὰ καὶ ἐμέ, ἵνα μὴ λύπην ἐπὶ λύπην σχῶ. **28** σπουδαιοτέρως οὖν ἔπεμψα αὐτόν, ἵνα ἰδόντες αὐτὸν πάλιν χαρῆτε κἀγὼ ἀλυπότερος ὦ. **29** προσδέχεσθε οὖν αὐτὸν ἐν κυρίῳ μετὰ πάσης χαρᾶς καὶ τοὺς τοιούτους ἐντίμους ἔχετε, **30** ὅτι διὰ τὸ ἔργον ⸀Χριστοῦ μέχρι θανάτου ἤγγισεν παραβολευσάμενος τῇ ψυχῇ, ἵνα ἀναπληρώσῃ τὸ ὑμῶν ὑστέρημα τῆς πρός με λειτουργίας.

Col 4:7–9
Τὰ κατʼ ἐμὲ πάντα γνωρίσει ὑμῖν Τύχικος ὁ ἀγαπητὸς ἀδελφὸς καὶ πιστὸς διάκονος καὶ σύνδουλος ἐν κυρίῳ, **8** ὃν ἔπεμψα πρὸς ὑμᾶς εἰς αὐτὸ τοῦτο, ἵνα ⸂γνῶτε τὰ περὶ ἡμῶν⸃ καὶ παρακαλέσῃ τὰς καρδίας ὑμῶν, **9** σὺν Ὀνησίμῳ τῷ πιστῷ καὶ ἀγαπητῷ ἀδελφῷ, ὅς ἐστιν ἐξ ὑμῶν· πάντα ὑμῖν γνωρίσουσιν τὰ ὧδε.

Phlm 8–14
Διὸ πολλὴν ἐν Χριστῷ παρρησίαν ἔχων ἐπιτάσσειν σοι τὸ ἀνῆκον **9** διὰ τὴν ἀγάπην μᾶλλον παρακαλῶ, τοιοῦτος ὢν ὡς Παῦλος ⸀πρεσβύτης νυνὶ δὲ καὶ δέσμιος Χριστοῦ Ἰησοῦ· **10** παρακαλῶ σε περὶ τοῦ ἐμοῦ τέκνου, ὃν ἐγέννησα ἐν τοῖς δεσμοῖς, Ὀνήσιμον, **11** τόν ποτέ σοι ἄχρηστον νυνὶ δὲ [καὶ] σοὶ καὶ ἐμοὶ εὔχρηστον, **12** ὃν ἀνέπεμψά σοι, αὐτόν, τοῦτʼ ἔστιν τὰ ἐμὰ σπλάγχνα· **13** ὃν ἐγὼ ἐβουλόμην πρὸς ἐμαυτὸν κατέχειν, ἵνα ὑπὲρ σοῦ μοι διακονῇ ἐν τοῖς δεσμοῖς τοῦ εὐαγγελίου, **14** χωρὶς δὲ τῆς σῆς γνώμης οὐδὲν ἠθέλησα ποιῆσαι, ἵνα μὴ ὡς κατὰ ἀνάγκην τὸ ἀγαθόν σου ᾖ ἀλλὰ κατὰ ἑκούσιον.

Cf. 2 Cor 3:1–3.

1 Tim 6:21 ***μεθ υμων*** ℵ* A 33] μετα σου D* 048^{vid}. 1739*. 1881 ¦ μεθ υμων, αμην ℵ^{2} ¦ μετα σου, αμην D^{1} 1739^{c} *Byz* **2 Tim 4:22** ***υμων*** ℵ* A C 33. 1739*. 1881] αμην ℵ^{2} D 1739^{c} *Byz* **Titus 3:15** ***υμων*** ℵ* A C D* 048. 33. 1739. 1881] *add.* αμην ℵ^{2} D^{1} *Byz* **Phlm 25** ***υμων*** (𝔓^{87}) A D* 048^{vid}. 33. 1739*. 1881] *add.* αμην ℵ C D^{1} 1739^{c} *Byz* **§ 9** **2 Cor 8:16** ***δοντι*** 𝔓^{46} ℵ^{2} D] διδοντι ℵ* B C I^{vid} (33). 1739. 1881 *Byz* **2 Cor 8:19** ***αυτου*** ℵ D^{1} 1881* *Byz*] *om.* B C D* ¦ αυτην 1739. 1881^{c} **Phil 2:26** ***παντας υμας*** ℵ^{2} 1739. 1881 *Byz*] υμας παντας B ¦ παντας υμας ιδειν ℵ* A C D I^{vid} 33 ¦ πεμψαι προς υμας 𝔓^{46vid} **Phil 2:30** ***Χριστου*** 𝔓^{46} B 1739. 1881] κυριου ℵ A 33 ¦ του Χριστου D *Byz* ¦ *om.* C **Col 4:8** ***γνωτε τα περι ημων*** (ℵ*) A B D$^{*.c}$ 048. 33] γνω τα περι υμων 𝔓^{46} ℵ$^{(2).c}$ C D^{1} 1739. 1881 *Byz* **Phlm 9** ***πρεσβυτης*** *omnes*] πρεσβευτης *cj*

1 Tim 6:21b
Grace be with you.[b]

2 Tim 4:22
The Lord be with your spirit. Grace be with you.[i]

Titus 3:15b
Grace be with all of you.[j]

Phlm 25
The grace of the Lord Jesus Christ be with your spirit.[k]

Cf. Rom 16:20; 16:24 (v.l.).

9. *Commendation*

Rom 16:1–2
I commend to you our sister Phoebe, a deacon of the church at Cenchreae, **2** so that you may welcome her in the Lord as is fitting for the saints, and help her in whatever she may require from you, for she has been a benefactor of many and of myself as well.

1 Cor 16:15–18
Now, brothers and sisters, you know that members of the household of Stephanas were the first converts in Achaia, and they have devoted themselves to the service of the saints; **16** I
urge you to put yourselves at the service of such people, and of everyone who works and toils with them. **17** I rejoice
at the coming of Stephanas and Fortunatus and Achaicus, because they have made up for your absence; **18** for they
refreshed my spirit as well as yours. So give recognition to such persons.

2 Cor 8:16–24
But thanks be to God who put[a] in the heart of Titus the same eagerness for you that I myself have. **17** For he not
only accepted our appeal, but since he is more eager than ever, he is going to you of his own accord. **18** With him we
are sending the brother who is famous among all the churches for his proclaiming the good news; **19** and not only that,
but he has also been appointed by the churches to travel with us while we are administering this generous undertaking for the glory of the Lord himself[b] and to show our goodwill. **20** We intend
that no one should blame us about this generous gift that we are administering, **21** for we intend to do what is right
not only in the Lord's sight but also in the sight of others. **22** And with them
we are sending our brother whom we have often tested and found eager in many matters, but who is now more eager than ever because of his great confidence in you. **23** As for Titus, he
is my partner and co-worker in your service; as for our brothers, they are messengers of the churches, the glory of Christ. **24** Therefore openly before
the churches, show them the proof of your love and of our reason for boasting about you.

Eph 6:21–22
So that you also may know how I am and what I am doing, Tychicus will tell you everything. He is a dear brother and a faithful minister in the Lord. **22** I
am sending him to you for this very purpose, to let you know how we are, and to encourage your hearts.

Phil 2:25–30
Still, I think it necessary to send to you Epaphroditus—my brother and co-worker and fellow soldier, your messenger and minister to my need; **26** for he
has been longing for[c] all of you, and has been distressed because you heard that he was ill. **27** He was indeed so ill that he
nearly died. But God had mercy on him, and not only on him but on me also, so that I would not have one sorrow after another. **28** I am the more eager to send
him, therefore, in order that you may rejoice at seeing him again, and that I may be less anxious. **29** Welcome him
then in the Lord with all joy, and honor such people, **30** because he came close to
death for the work of Christ,[d] risking his life to make up for those services that you could not give me.

Col 4:7–9
Tychicus will tell you all the news about me; he is a beloved brother, a faithful minister, and a fellow servant in the Lord. **8** I have sent him to you for this
very purpose, so that you may know how we are[e] and that he may encourage your hearts; **9** he is coming with Onesi-
mus, the faithful and beloved brother, who is one of you. They will tell you about everything here.

Phlm 8–14
For this reason, though I am bold enough in Christ to command you to do your duty, **9** yet I would rather appeal
to you on the basis of love—and I, Paul, do this as an old man,[f] and now also as a prisoner of Christ Jesus. **10** I am ap-
pealing to you for my child, Onesimus, whose father I have become during my imprisonment. **11** Formerly he was use-
less to you, but now he is indeed useful both to you and to me. **12** I am sending
him, that is, my own heart, back to you.
13 I wanted to keep him with me, so
that he might be of service to me in your place during my imprisonment for the gospel; **14** but I preferred to do
nothing without your consent, in order that your good deed might be voluntary and not something forced.

Cf. 2 Cor 3:1–3.

[b] **1 Tim 6:21b** ***you*** The Greek word for *you* here is plural; in other ancient authorities it is singular. Other ancient authorities add *Amen* [i] **2 Tim 4:22** ***you*** Other ancient authorities add *Amen* [j] **Titus 3:15b** ***you*** Other ancient authorities add *Amen* [k] **Phlm 25** ***spirit*** Other ancient authorities add *Amen* **§ 9** [a] **2 Cor 8:16** ***put*** Other ancient authorities read *puts* [b] **2 Cor 8:19** ***himself*** Other ancient authorities lack *himself* [c] **Phil 2:26** ***longing for*** Other ancient authorities read *longing to see* [d] **Phil 2:30** ***of Christ*** Other ancient authorities read *of the Lord* [e] **Col 4:8** ***that you may know how we are*** Other ancient authorities read *that I may know how you are* [f] **Phlm 9** ***old man*** Some scholars conjecture that the original text read *ambassador*, or that the reading in the manuscripts is a spelling variant for *ambassador*

10. *Appeal*

Rom 12:1–2

Παρακαλῶ οὖν ὑμᾶς, ἀδελφοί, διὰ τῶν οἰκτιρμῶν τοῦ θεοῦ παραστῆσαι τὰ σώματα ὑμῶν θυσίαν ζῶσαν ἁγίαν εὐάρεστον τῷ θεῷ, τὴν λογικὴν λατρείαν ὑμῶν· **2** καὶ μὴ συσχηματίζεσθε τῷ αἰῶνι τούτῳ, ἀλλὰ μεταμορφοῦσθε τῇ ἀνακαινώσει τοῦ νοὸς εἰς τὸ δοκιμάζειν ὑμᾶς τί τὸ θέλημα τοῦ θεοῦ, τὸ ἀγαθὸν καὶ εὐάρεστον καὶ τέλειον.

Rom 15:30–32

Παρακαλῶ δὲ ὑμᾶς[, ἀδελφοί,] διὰ τοῦ κυρίου ἡμῶν Ἰησοῦ Χριστοῦ καὶ διὰ τῆς ἀγάπης τοῦ πνεύματος συναγωνίσασθαί μοι ἐν ταῖς προσευχαῖς ὑπὲρ ἐμοῦ πρὸς τὸν θεόν, **31** ἵνα ῥυσθῶ ἀπὸ τῶν ἀπειθούντων ἐν τῇ Ἰουδαίᾳ καὶ ἡ ⸀διακονία μου ἡ εἰς Ἰερουσαλὴμ εὐπρόσδεκτος τοῖς ἁγίοις γένηται, **32** ἵνα ἐν χαρᾷ ἐλθὼν πρὸς ὑμᾶς διὰ θελήματος θεοῦ συναναπαύσωμαι ὑμῖν.

1 Cor 1:10–11

Παρακαλῶ δὲ ὑμᾶς, ἀδελφοί, διὰ τοῦ ὀνόματος τοῦ κυρίου ἡμῶν Ἰησοῦ Χριστοῦ, ἵνα τὸ αὐτὸ λέγητε πάντες καὶ μὴ ᾖ ἐν ὑμῖν σχίσματα, ἦτε δὲ κατηρτισμένοι ἐν τῷ αὐτῷ νοῒ καὶ ἐν τῇ αὐτῇ γνώμῃ. **11** ἐδηλώθη γάρ μοι περὶ ὑμῶν, ἀδελφοί μου, ὑπὸ τῶν Χλόης ὅτι ἔριδες ἐν ὑμῖν εἰσιν.

1 Cor 16:15–18

Παρακαλῶ δὲ ὑμᾶς, ἀδελφοί· οἴδατε τὴν οἰκίαν Στεφανᾶ, ὅτι ἐστὶν ἀπαρχὴ τῆς Ἀχαΐας καὶ εἰς διακονίαν τοῖς ἁγίοις ἔταξαν ἑαυτούς· **16** ἵνα καὶ ὑμεῖς ὑποτάσσησθε τοῖς τοιούτοις καὶ παντὶ τῷ συνεργοῦντι καὶ κοπιῶντι. **17** χαίρω δὲ ἐπὶ τῇ παρουσίᾳ Στεφανᾶ καὶ Φορτουνάτου καὶ Ἀχαϊκοῦ, ὅτι τὸ ὑμέτερον ὑστέρημα οὗτοι ἀνεπλήρωσαν· **18** ἀνέπαυσαν γὰρ τὸ ἐμὸν πνεῦμα καὶ τὸ ὑμῶν. ἐπιγινώσκετε οὖν τοὺς τοιούτους.

2 Cor 10:1–2

Αὐτὸς δὲ ἐγὼ Παῦλος παρακαλῶ ὑμᾶς διὰ τῆς πραΰτητος καὶ ἐπιεικείας τοῦ Χριστοῦ, ὃς κατὰ πρόσωπον μὲν ταπεινὸς ἐν ὑμῖν, ἀπὼν δὲ θαρρῶ εἰς ὑμᾶς· **2** δέομαι δὲ τὸ μὴ παρὼν θαρρῆσαι τῇ πεποιθήσει ᾗ λογίζομαι τολμῆσαι ἐπί τινας τοὺς λογιζομένους ἡμᾶς ὡς κατὰ σάρκα περιπατοῦντας.

Eph 4:1–3

Παρακαλῶ οὖν ὑμᾶς ἐγὼ ὁ δέσμιος ἐν κυρίῳ ἀξίως περιπατῆσαι τῆς κλήσεως ἧς ἐκλήθητε, **2** μετὰ πάσης ταπεινοφροσύνης καὶ πραΰτητος, μετὰ μακροθυμίας, ἀνεχόμενοι ἀλλήλων ἐν ἀγάπῃ, **3** σπουδάζοντες τηρεῖν τὴν ἑνότητα τοῦ πνεύματος ἐν τῷ συνδέσμῳ τῆς εἰρήνης

Phil 4:2–3

Εὐοδίαν παρακαλῶ καὶ Συντύχην παρακαλῶ τὸ αὐτὸ φρονεῖν ἐν κυρίῳ. **3** ναὶ ἐρωτῶ καὶ σέ, γνήσιε σύζυγε, συλλαμβάνου αὐταῖς, αἵτινες ἐν τῷ εὐαγγελίῳ συνήθλησάν μοι μετὰ καὶ Κλήμεντος καὶ τῶν λοιπῶν συνεργῶν μου, ὧν τὰ ὀνόματα ἐν βίβλῳ ζωῆς.

1 Thess 4:1–2

Λοιπὸν οὖν, ἀδελφοί, ἐρωτῶμεν ὑμᾶς καὶ παρακαλοῦμεν ἐν κυρίῳ Ἰησοῦ, ἵνα καθὼς παρελάβετε παρ᾽ ἡμῶν τὸ πῶς δεῖ ὑμᾶς περιπατεῖν καὶ ἀρέσκειν θεῷ, καθὼς καὶ περιπατεῖτε, ἵνα περισσεύητε μᾶλλον. **2** οἴδατε γὰρ τίνας παραγγελίας ἐδώκαμεν ὑμῖν διὰ τοῦ κυρίου Ἰησοῦ.

1 Thess 5:12–15

Ἐρωτῶμεν δὲ ὑμᾶς, ἀδελφοί, εἰδέναι τοὺς κοπιῶντας ἐν ὑμῖν καὶ προϊσταμένους ὑμῶν ἐν κυρίῳ καὶ νουθετοῦντας ὑμᾶς **13** καὶ ἡγεῖσθαι αὐτοὺς ὑπερεκπερισσοῦ ἐν ἀγάπῃ διὰ τὸ ἔργον αὐτῶν. εἰρηνεύετε ἐν ἑαυτοῖς. **14** Παρακαλοῦμεν δὲ ὑμᾶς, ἀδελφοί, νουθετεῖτε τοὺς ἀτάκτους, παραμυθεῖσθε τοὺς ὀλιγοψύχους, ἀντέχεσθε τῶν ἀσθενῶν, μακροθυμεῖτε πρὸς πάντας. **15** ὁρᾶτε μή τις κακὸν ἀντὶ κακοῦ τινι ἀποδῷ, ἀλλὰ πάντοτε τὸ ἀγαθὸν διώκετε [καὶ] εἰς ἀλλήλους καὶ εἰς πάντας.

2 Thess 2:1–2

Ἐρωτῶμεν δὲ ὑμᾶς, ἀδελφοί, ὑπὲρ τῆς παρουσίας τοῦ κυρίου ἡμῶν Ἰησοῦ Χριστοῦ καὶ ἡμῶν ἐπισυναγωγῆς ἐπ᾽ αὐτὸν **2** εἰς τὸ μὴ ταχέως σαλευθῆναι ὑμᾶς ἀπὸ τοῦ νοὸς μηδὲ θροεῖσθαι, μήτε διὰ πνεύματος μήτε διὰ λόγου μήτε δι᾽ ἐπιστολῆς ὡς δι᾽ ἡμῶν, ὡς ὅτι ἐνέστηκεν ἡ ἡμέρα τοῦ κυρίου

Phlm 8–14

Διὸ πολλὴν ἐν Χριστῷ παρρησίαν ἔχων ἐπιτάσσειν σοι τὸ ἀνῆκον **9** διὰ τὴν ἀγάπην μᾶλλον παρακαλῶ, τοιοῦτος ὢν ὡς Παῦλος ⸀πρεσβύτης νυνὶ δὲ καὶ δέσμιος Χριστοῦ Ἰησοῦ· **10** παρακαλῶ σε περὶ τοῦ ἐμοῦ τέκνου, ὃν ἐγέννησα ἐν τοῖς δεσμοῖς, Ὀνήσιμον, **11** τόν ποτέ σοι ἄχρηστον νυνὶ δὲ [καὶ] σοὶ καὶ ἐμοὶ εὔχρηστον, **12** ὃν ἀνέπεμψά σοι, αὐτόν, τοῦτ᾽ ἔστιν τὰ ἐμὰ σπλάγχνα· **13** ὃν ἐγὼ ἐβουλόμην πρὸς ἐμαυτὸν κατέχειν, ἵνα ὑπὲρ σοῦ μοι διακονῇ ἐν τοῖς δεσμοῖς τοῦ εὐαγγελίου, **14** χωρὶς δὲ τῆς σῆς γνώμης οὐδὲν ἠθέλησα ποιῆσαι, ἵνα μὴ ὡς κατὰ ἀνάγκην τὸ ἀγαθόν σου ᾖ ἀλλὰ κατὰ ἑκούσιον.

Cf. 1 Cor 4:16–17; 2 Cor 2:5–11; 6:11–13; 7:2–4; 1 Thess 4:9–12; 2 Thess 3:11–12; 1 Tim 1:3–4; 2:1–2.

11. *Apostolic Parousia*

Rom 1:8–12 (or 15)

Πρῶτον μὲν εὐχαριστῶ τῷ θεῷ μου διὰ Ἰησοῦ Χριστοῦ περὶ πάντων ὑμῶν ὅτι ἡ πίστις ὑμῶν καταγγέλλεται ἐν ὅλῳ τῷ κόσμῳ. **9** μάρτυς γάρ μού ἐστιν ὁ θεός, ᾧ λατρεύω ἐν τῷ πνεύματί μου ἐν τῷ εὐαγγελίῳ τοῦ υἱοῦ αὐτοῦ, ὡς ἀδιαλείπτως μνείαν ὑμῶν ποιοῦμαι **10** πάντοτε ἐπὶ τῶν προσευχῶν μου δεόμενος εἴ πως ἤδη ποτὲ εὐοδωθήσομαι ἐν τῷ θελήματι τοῦ θεοῦ ἐλθεῖν πρὸς ὑμᾶς. **11** ἐπιποθῶ γὰρ ἰδεῖν ὑμᾶς, ἵνα τι μεταδῶ χάρισμα

§ 10 **Rom 15:31** ***διακονια*** 𝔓[46] ℵ A C D[1] 33. 1739. 1881 *Byz*] δωροφορια B D* **Phlm 9** ***πρεσβυτης*** *omnes*] πρεσβευτης *cj*

10. Appeal

Rom 12:1–2

I appeal to you therefore, brothers and sisters, by the mercies of God, to present your bodies as a living sacrifice, holy and acceptable to God, which is your spiritual worship. **2** Do not be conformed to this world, but be transformed by the renewing of your minds, so that you may discern what is the will of God—what is good and acceptable and perfect.

Rom 15:30–32

I appeal to you, brothers and sisters, by our Lord Jesus Christ and by the love of the Spirit, to join me in earnest prayer to God on my behalf, **31** that I may be rescued from the unbelievers in Judea, and that my ministry[a] to Jerusalem may be acceptable to the saints, **32** so that by God's will I may come to you with joy and be refreshed in your company.

1 Cor 1:10–11

Now I appeal to you, brothers and sisters, by the name of our Lord Jesus Christ, that all of you be in agreement and that there be no divisions among you, but that you be united in the same mind and the same purpose. **11** For it has been reported to me by Chloe's people that there are quarrels among you, my brothers and sisters.

1 Cor 16:15–18

Now, brothers and sisters, you know that members of the household of Stephanas were the first converts in Achaia, and they have devoted themselves to the service of the saints; **16** I urge you to put yourselves at the service of such people, and of everyone who works and toils with them. **17** I rejoice at the coming of Stephanas and Fortunatus and Achaicus, because they have made up for your absence; **18** for they refreshed my spirit as well as yours. So give recognition to such persons.

2 Cor 10:1–2

I myself, Paul, appeal to you by the meekness and gentleness of Christ—I who am humble when face to face with you, but bold toward you when I am away!— **2** I ask that when I am present I need not show boldness by daring to oppose those who think we are acting according to human standards.

Eph 4:1–3

I therefore, the prisoner in the Lord, beg you to lead a life worthy of the calling to which you have been called, **2** with all humility and gentleness, with patience, bearing with one another in love, **3** making every effort to maintain the unity of the Spirit in the bond of peace.

Phil 4:2–3

I urge Euodia and I urge Syntyche to be of the same mind in the Lord. **3** Yes, and I ask you also, my loyal companion, help these women, for they have struggled beside me in the work of the gospel, together with Clement and the rest of my co-workers, whose names are in the book of life.

1 Thess 4:1–2

Finally, brothers and sisters, we ask and urge you in the Lord Jesus that, as you learned from us how you ought to live and to please God (as, in fact, you are doing), you should do so more and more. **2** For you know what instructions we gave you through the Lord Jesus.

1 Thess 5:12–15

But we appeal to you, brothers and sisters, to respect those who labor among you, and have charge of you in the Lord and admonish you; **13** esteem them very highly in love because of their work. Be at peace among yourselves. **14** And we urge you, beloved, to admonish the idlers, encourage the fainthearted, help the weak, be patient with all of them. **15** See that none of you repays evil for evil, but always seek to do good to one another and to all.

2 Thess 2:1–2

As to the coming of our Lord Jesus Christ and our being gathered together to him, we beg you, brothers and sisters, **2** not to be quickly shaken in mind or alarmed, either by spirit or by word or by letter, as though from us, to the effect that the day of the Lord is already here.

Phlm 8–14

For this reason, though I am bold enough in Christ to command you to do your duty, **9** yet I would rather appeal to you on the basis of love—and I, Paul, do this as an old man,[b] and now also as a prisoner of Christ Jesus. **10** I am appealing to you for my child, Onesimus, whose father I have become during my imprisonment. **11** Formerly he was useless to you, but now he is indeed useful both to you and to me. **12** I am sending him, that is, my own heart, back to you. **13** I wanted to keep him with me, so that he might be of service to me in your place during my imprisonment for the gospel; **14** but I preferred to do nothing without your consent, in order that your good deed might be voluntary and not something forced.

Cf. 1 Cor 4:16–17; 2 Cor 2:5–11; 6:11–13; 7:2–4; 1 Thess 4:9–12; 2 Thess 3:11–12; 1 Tim 1:3–4; 2:1–2.

11. Apostolic Parousia

Rom 1:8–12 (or 15)

First, I thank my God through Jesus Christ for all of you, because your faith is proclaimed throughout the world. **9** For God, whom I serve with my spirit by announcing the gospel of his Son, is my witness that without ceasing I remember you always in my prayers, **10** asking that by God's will I may somehow at last succeed in coming to you. **11** For I am longing to see you so that I may share with you some spiritual gift

§ 10 [a] **Rom 15:31** *my ministry* Other ancient authorities read *my bringing of a gift* [b] **Phlm 9** *old man* Some scholars conjecture that the original text read *ambassador*, or that the reading in the manuscripts is a spelling variant for *ambassador*

ὑμῖν πνευματικὸν εἰς τὸ στηριχθῆναι ὑμᾶς, 12 τοῦτο δέ ἐστιν συμπαρακληθῆναι ἐν ὑμῖν διὰ τῆς ἐν ἀλλήλοις πίστεως ὑμῶν τε καὶ ἐμοῦ.

Rom 15:14–33

Πέπεισμαι δέ, ἀδελφοί μου, καὶ αὐτὸς ἐγὼ περὶ ὑμῶν ὅτι καὶ αὐτοὶ μεστοί ἐστε ἀγαθωσύνης, πεπληρωμένοι πάσης [τῆς] γνώσεως, δυνάμενοι καὶ ἀλλήλους νουθετεῖν. 15 τολμηρότερον δὲ ἔγραψα ὑμῖν ἀπὸ μέρους ὡς ἐπαναμιμνῄσκων ὑμᾶς διὰ τὴν χάριν τὴν δοθεῖσάν μοι ὑπὸ τοῦ θεοῦ 16 εἰς τὸ εἶναί με λειτουργὸν Χριστοῦ Ἰησοῦ εἰς τὰ ἔθνη, ἱερουργοῦντα τὸ εὐαγγέλιον τοῦ θεοῦ, ἵνα γένηται ἡ προσφορὰ τῶν ἐθνῶν εὐπρόσδεκτος, ἡγιασμένη ἐν πνεύματι ἁγίῳ. 17 ἔχω οὖν [τὴν] καύχησιν ἐν Χριστῷ Ἰησοῦ τὰ πρὸς τὸν θεόν· 18 οὐ γὰρ τολμήσω τι λαλεῖν ὧν οὐ κατειργάσατο Χριστὸς δι᾽ ἐμοῦ εἰς ὑπακοὴν ἐθνῶν, λόγῳ καὶ ἔργῳ, 19 ἐν δυνάμει σημείων καὶ τεράτων, ἐν δυνάμει πνεύματος ⸀[θεοῦ]· ὥστε με ἀπὸ Ἰερουσαλὴμ καὶ κύκλῳ μέχρι τοῦ Ἰλλυρικοῦ πεπληρωκέναι τὸ εὐαγγέλιον τοῦ Χριστοῦ, 20 οὕτως δὲ φιλοτιμούμενον εὐαγγελίζεσθαι οὐχ ὅπου ὠνομάσθη Χριστός, ἵνα μὴ ἐπ᾽ ἀλλότριον θεμέλιον οἰκοδομῶ, 21 ἀλλὰ καθὼς γέγραπται· οἷς οὐκ ἀνηγγέλη περὶ αὐτοῦ ὄψονται, καὶ οἳ οὐκ ἀκηκόασιν συνήσουσιν. 22 Διὸ καὶ ἐνεκοπτόμην τὰ πολλὰ τοῦ ἐλθεῖν πρὸς ὑμᾶς· 23 νυνὶ δὲ μηκέτι τόπον ἔχων ἐν τοῖς κλίμασι τούτοις, ἐπιποθίαν δὲ ἔχων τοῦ ἐλθεῖν πρὸς ὑμᾶς ἀπὸ πολλῶν ἐτῶν, 24 ὡς ἂν πορεύωμαι εἰς τὴν Σπανίαν· ἐλπίζω γὰρ διαπορευόμενος θεάσασθαι ὑμᾶς καὶ ὑφ᾽ ὑμῶν προπεμφθῆναι ἐκεῖ ἐὰν ὑμῶν πρῶτον ἀπὸ μέρους ἐμπλησθῶ. 25 Νυνὶ δὲ πορεύομαι εἰς Ἰερουσαλὴμ διακονῶν τοῖς ἁγίοις. 26 εὐδόκησαν γὰρ Μακεδονία καὶ Ἀχαΐα κοινωνίαν τινὰ ποιήσασθαι εἰς τοὺς πτωχοὺς τῶν ἁγίων τῶν ἐν Ἰερουσαλήμ. 27 εὐδόκησαν γὰρ καὶ ὀφειλέται εἰσὶν αὐτῶν· εἰ γὰρ τοῖς πνευματικοῖς αὐτῶν ἐκοινώνησαν τὰ ἔθνη, ὀφείλουσιν καὶ ἐν τοῖς σαρκικοῖς λειτουργῆσαι αὐτοῖς. 28 τοῦτο οὖν ἐπιτελέσας καὶ σφραγισάμενος αὐτοῖς τὸν καρπὸν τοῦτον, ἀπελεύσομαι δι᾽ ὑμῶν εἰς Σπανίαν· 29 οἶδα δὲ ὅτι ἐρχόμενος πρὸς ὑμᾶς ἐν πληρώματι ⸀εὐλογίας Χριστοῦ ἐλεύσομαι. 30 Παρακαλῶ δὲ ὑμᾶς[, ἀδελφοί,] διὰ τοῦ κυρίου ἡμῶν Ἰησοῦ Χριστοῦ καὶ διὰ τῆς ἀγάπης τοῦ πνεύματος συναγωνίσασθαί μοι ἐν ταῖς προσευχαῖς ὑπὲρ ἐμοῦ πρὸς τὸν θεόν, 31 ἵνα ῥυσθῶ ἀπὸ τῶν ἀπειθούντων ἐν τῇ Ἰουδαίᾳ καὶ ἡ ⸀διακονία μου ἡ εἰς Ἰερουσαλὴμ εὐπρόσδεκτος τοῖς ἁγίοις γένηται, 32 ἵνα ἐν χαρᾷ ἐλθὼν πρὸς ὑμᾶς διὰ θελήματος θεοῦ συναναπαύσωμαι ὑμῖν. 33 Ὁ δὲ θεὸς τῆς εἰρήνης μετὰ πάντων ὑμῶν, ἀμήν.

1 Cor 4:14–21

Οὐκ ἐντρέπων ὑμᾶς γράφω ταῦτα ἀλλ᾽ ὡς τέκνα μου ἀγαπητὰ νουθετῶ[ν]. 15 ἐὰν γὰρ μυρίους παιδαγωγοὺς ἔχητε ἐν Χριστῷ ἀλλ᾽ οὐ πολλοὺς πατέρας· ἐν γὰρ Χριστῷ Ἰησοῦ διὰ τοῦ εὐαγγελίου ἐγὼ ὑμᾶς ἐγέννησα. 16 Παρακαλῶ οὖν ὑμᾶς, μιμηταί μου γίνεσθε. 17 Διὰ τοῦτο ἔπεμψα ὑμῖν Τιμόθεον, ὅς ἐστίν μου τέκνον ἀγαπητὸν καὶ πιστὸν ἐν κυρίῳ, ὃς ὑμᾶς ἀναμνήσει τὰς ὁδούς μου τὰς ἐν Χριστῷ [Ἰησοῦ], καθὼς πανταχοῦ ἐν πάσῃ ἐκκλησίᾳ διδάσκω. 18 Ὡς μὴ ἐρχομένου δέ μου πρὸς ὑμᾶς ἐφυσιώθησάν τινες· 19 ἐλεύσομαι δὲ ταχέως πρὸς ὑμᾶς ἐὰν ὁ κύριος θελήσῃ, καὶ γνώσομαι οὐ τὸν λόγον τῶν πεφυσιωμένων ἀλλὰ τὴν δύναμιν· 20 οὐ γὰρ ἐν λόγῳ ἡ βασιλεία τοῦ θεοῦ ἀλλ᾽ ἐν δυνάμει. 21 τί θέλετε; ἐν ῥάβδῳ ἔλθω πρὸς ὑμᾶς ἢ ἐν ἀγάπῃ πνεύματί τε πραΰτητος;

2 Cor 12:14–13:13

Ἰδοὺ τρίτον τοῦτο ἑτοίμως ἔχω ἐλθεῖν πρὸς ὑμᾶς, καὶ οὐ καταναρκήσω· οὐ γὰρ ζητῶ τὰ ὑμῶν ἀλλὰ ὑμᾶς. οὐ γὰρ ὀφείλει τὰ τέκνα τοῖς γονεῦσιν θησαυρίζειν ἀλλὰ οἱ γονεῖς τοῖς τέκνοις. 15 ἐγὼ δὲ ἥδιστα δαπανήσω καὶ ἐκδαπανηθήσομαι ὑπὲρ τῶν ψυχῶν ὑμῶν. εἰ περισσοτέρως ὑμᾶς ἀγαπῶ[ν], ἧσσον ἀγαπῶμαι; 16 Ἔστω δέ, ἐγὼ οὐ κατεβάρησα ὑμᾶς· ἀλλὰ ὑπάρχων πανοῦργος δόλῳ ὑμᾶς ἔλαβον. 17 μή τινα ὧν ἀπέσταλκα πρὸς ὑμᾶς, δι᾽ αὐτοῦ ἐπλεονέκτησα ὑμᾶς; 18 παρεκάλεσα Τίτον καὶ συναπέστειλα τὸν ἀδελφόν· μήτι ἐπλεονέκτησεν ὑμᾶς Τίτος; οὐ τῷ αὐτῷ πνεύματι περιεπατήσαμεν; οὐ τοῖς αὐτοῖς ἴχνεσιν; 19 Πάλαι δοκεῖτε ὅτι ὑμῖν ἀπολογούμεθα. κατέναντι θεοῦ ἐν Χριστῷ λαλοῦμεν· τὰ δὲ πάντα, ἀγαπητοί, ὑπὲρ τῆς ὑμῶν οἰκοδομῆς. 20 φοβοῦμαι γὰρ μή πως ἐλθὼν οὐχ οἵους θέλω εὕρω ὑμᾶς κἀγὼ εὑρεθῶ ὑμῖν οἷον οὐ θέλετε· μή πως ἔρις, ζῆλος, θυμοί, ἐριθεῖαι, καταλαλιαί, ψιθυρισμοί, φυσιώσεις, ἀκαταστασίαι· 21 μὴ πάλιν ἐλθόντος μου ταπεινώσῃ με ὁ θεός μου πρὸς ὑμᾶς καὶ πενθήσω πολλοὺς τῶν προημαρτηκότων καὶ μὴ μετανοησάντων ἐπὶ τῇ ἀκαθαρσίᾳ καὶ πορνείᾳ καὶ ἀσελγείᾳ ᾗ ἔπραξαν. **13** Τρίτον τοῦτο ἔρχομαι πρὸς ὑμᾶς· ἐπὶ στόματος δύο μαρτύρων καὶ τριῶν σταθήσεται πᾶν ῥῆμα. 2 προείρηκα καὶ προλέγω, ὡς παρὼν τὸ δεύτερον καὶ ἀπὼν νῦν, τοῖς προημαρτηκόσιν καὶ τοῖς λοιποῖς πᾶσιν, ὅτι ἐὰν ἔλθω εἰς τὸ πάλιν οὐ φείσομαι, 3 ἐπεὶ δοκιμὴν ζητεῖτε τοῦ ἐν ἐμοὶ λαλοῦντος Χριστοῦ, ὃς εἰς ὑμᾶς οὐκ ἀσθενεῖ ἀλλὰ δυνατεῖ ἐν ὑμῖν. 4 καὶ γὰρ ἐσταυρώθη ἐξ ἀσθενείας, ἀλλὰ ζῇ ἐκ δυνάμεως θεοῦ. καὶ γὰρ ἡμεῖς ἀσθενοῦμεν ⸀ἐν αὐτῷ, ἀλλὰ ζήσομεν σὺν αὐτῷ ἐκ δυνάμεως θεοῦ εἰς ὑμᾶς. 5 Ἑαυτοὺς πειράζετε εἰ ἐστὲ ἐν τῇ πίστει, ἑαυτοὺς δοκιμάζετε· ἢ οὐκ ἐπιγινώσκετε ἑαυτοὺς ὅτι Ἰησοῦς Χριστὸς ἐν ὑμῖν; εἰ μήτι ἀδόκιμοί ἐστε. 6 ἐλπίζω δὲ ὅτι γνώσεσθε ὅτι ἡμεῖς οὐκ ἐσμὲν ἀδόκιμοι. 7 εὐχόμεθα δὲ πρὸς τὸν θεὸν μὴ ποιῆσαι ὑμᾶς κακὸν μηδέν, οὐχ ἵνα ἡμεῖς δόκιμοι φανῶμεν, ἀλλ᾽ ἵνα ὑμεῖς τὸ καλὸν ποιῆτε, ἡμεῖς δὲ ὡς ἀδόκιμοι ὦμεν. 8 οὐ γὰρ δυνάμεθά τι κατὰ τῆς ἀληθείας ἀλλὰ ὑπὲρ τῆς ἀληθείας. 9 χαίρομεν γὰρ ὅταν ἡμεῖς ἀσθενῶμεν, ὑμεῖς δὲ δυνατοὶ ἦτε· τοῦτο καὶ εὐχόμεθα, τὴν ὑμῶν κατάρτισιν. 10 Διὰ τοῦτο ταῦτα ἀπὼν γράφω, ἵνα παρὼν μὴ ἀποτόμως χρήσωμαι κατὰ τὴν ἐξουσίαν ἣν ὁ κύριος ἔδωκέν μοι εἰς οἰκοδομὴν καὶ οὐκ εἰς καθαίρεσιν. 11 Λοιπόν, ἀδελφοί, χαίρετε, καταρτίζεσθε,

§ 11 **Rom 15:19** ***θεου*** 𝔓^{46} ℵ D^{1} *Byz*] *om.* B ¦ αγιου A D^{*,2} 33. 1739. 1881 **Rom 15:29** ***ευλογιας*** 𝔓^{46} ℵ* A B C D 1739. 1881] *add.* του ευαγγελιου του ℵ^{2} 33 *Byz* **Rom 15:31** ***διακονια*** 𝔓^{46} ℵ A C D^{1} 33. 1739. 1881 *Byz*] δωροφορια B D* **2 Cor 13:4** ***εν*** B D 33. 1739. 1881 *Byz*] συν ℵ A

to strengthen you— **12** or rather so that we may be mutually encouraged by each other's faith, both yours and mine.

Rom 15:14–33

I myself feel confident about you, my brothers and sisters, that you yourselves are full of goodness, filled with all knowledge, and able to instruct one another. **15** Nevertheless on some points I have written to you rather boldly by way of reminder, because of the grace given me by God **16** to be a minister of Christ Jesus to the Gentiles in the priestly service of the gospel of God, so that the offering of the Gentiles may be acceptable, sanctified by the Holy Spirit. **17** In Christ Jesus, then, I have reason to boast of my work for God. **18** For I will not venture to speak of anything except what Christ has accomplished through me to win obedience from the Gentiles, by word and deed, **19** by the power of signs and wonders, by the power of the Spirit of God,[a] so that from Jerusalem and as far around as Illyricum I have fully proclaimed the good news of Christ. **20** Thus I make it my ambition to proclaim the good news, not where Christ has already been named, so that I do not build on someone else's foundation, **21** but as it is written, "Those who have never been told of him shall see, and those who have never heard of him shall understand." **22** This is the reason that I have so often been hindered from coming to you. **23** But now, with no further place for me in these regions, I desire, as I have for many years, to come to you **24** when I go to Spain. For I do hope to see you on my journey and to be sent on by you, once I have enjoyed your company for a little while. **25** At present, however, I am going to Jerusalem in a ministry to the saints; **26** for Macedonia and Achaia have been pleased to share their resources with the poor among the saints at Jerusalem. **27** They were pleased to do this, and indeed they owe it to them; for if the Gentiles have come to share in their spiritual blessings, they ought also to be of service to them in material things. **28** So, when I have completed this, and have delivered to them what has been collected, I will set out by way of you to Spain; **29** and I know that when I come to you, I will come in the fullness of the blessing[b] of Christ. **30** I appeal to you, brothers and sisters, by our Lord Jesus Christ and by the love of the Spirit, to join me in earnest prayer to God on my behalf, **31** that I may be rescued from the unbelievers in Judea, and that my ministry[c] to Jerusalem may be acceptable to the saints, **32** so that by God's will I may come to you with joy and be refreshed in your company. **33** The God of peace be with all of you. Amen.

1 Cor 4:14–21

I am not writing this to make you ashamed, but to admonish you as my beloved children. **15** For though you might have ten thousand guardians in Christ, you do not have many fathers. Indeed, in Christ Jesus I became your father through the gospel. **16** I appeal to you, then, be imitators of me. **17** For this reason I sent you Timothy, who is my beloved and faithful child in the Lord, to remind you of my ways in Christ Jesus, as I teach them everywhere in every church. **18** But some of you, thinking that I am not coming to you, have become arrogant. **19** But I will come to you soon, if the Lord wills, and I will find out not the talk of these arrogant people but their power. **20** For the kingdom of God depends not on talk but on power. **21** What would you prefer? Am I to come to you with a stick, or with love in a spirit of gentleness?

2 Cor 12:14–13:13

Here I am, ready to come to you this third time. And I will not be a burden, because I do not want what is yours but you; for children ought not to lay up for their parents, but parents for their children. **15** I will most gladly spend and be spent for you. If I love you more, am I to be loved less? **16** Let it be assumed that I did not burden you. Nevertheless (you say) since I was crafty, I took you in by deceit. **17** Did I take advantage of you through any of those whom I sent to you? **18** I urged Titus to go, and sent the brother with him. Titus did not take advantage of you, did he? Did we not conduct ourselves with the same spirit? Did we not take the same steps? **19** Have you been thinking all along that we have been defending ourselves before you? We are speaking in Christ before God. Everything we do, beloved, is for the sake of building you up. **20** For I fear that when I come, I may find you not as I wish, and that you may find me not as you wish; I fear that there may perhaps be quarreling, jealousy, anger, selfishness, slander, gossip, conceit, and disorder. **21** I fear that when I come again, my God may humble me before you, and that I may have to mourn over many who previously sinned and have not repented of the impurity, sexual immorality, and licentiousness that they have practiced. **13** This is the third time I am coming to you. "Any charge must be sustained by the evidence of two or three witnesses." **2** I warned those who sinned previously and all the others, and I warn them now while absent, as I did when present on my second visit, that if I come again, I will not be lenient— **3** since you desire proof that Christ is speaking in me. He is not weak in dealing with you, but is powerful in you. **4** For he was crucified in weakness, but lives by the power of God. For we are weak in him,[d] but in dealing with you we will live with him by the power of God. **5** Examine yourselves to see whether you are living in the faith. Test yourselves. Do you not realize that Jesus Christ is in you?—unless, indeed, you fail to meet the test! **6** I hope you will find out that we have not failed. **7** But we pray to God that you may not do anything wrong—not that we may appear to have met the test, but that you may do what is right, though we may seem to have failed. **8** For we cannot do anything against the truth, but only for the truth. **9** For we rejoice when we are weak and you are strong. This is what we pray for, that you may become perfect. **10** So I write these things while I am away from you, so that when I come, I may not have to be severe in using the authority that the Lord has given me for building up and not for tearing down. **11** Finally, brothers and sisters,

§ 11 [a] **Rom 15:19** ***of the Spirit of God*** Other ancient authorities read *of the Spirit* or *of the Holy Spirit* [b] **Rom 15:29** ***blessing*** Other ancient authorities add *of the gospel* [c] **Rom 15:31** ***my ministry*** Other ancient authorities read *my bringing of a gift* [d] **2 Cor 13:4** ***in him*** Other ancient authorities read *with him*

παρακαλεῖσθε, τὸ αὐτὸ φρονεῖτε, εἰρη-
νεύετε, καὶ ὁ θεὸς τῆς ἀγάπης καὶ εἰρήνης
ἔσται μεθ' ὑμῶν. 12 Ἀσπάσασθε ἀλλήλους
ἐν ἁγίῳ φιλήματι. Ἀσπάζονται ὑμᾶς οἱ
ἅγιοι πάντες. 13 Ἡ χάρις τοῦ κυρίου Ἰη-
σοῦ Χριστοῦ καὶ ἡ ἀγάπη τοῦ θεοῦ καὶ
ἡ κοινωνία τοῦ ἁγίου πνεύματος μετὰ
πάντων ὑμῶν.

Phil 2:19–24

Ἐλπίζω δὲ ἐν κυρίῳ Ἰησοῦ Τιμόθεον
ταχέως πέμψαι ὑμῖν, ἵνα κἀγὼ εὐψυχῶ
γνοὺς τὰ περὶ ὑμῶν. 20 οὐδένα γὰρ ἔχω
ἰσόψυχον, ὅστις γνησίως τὰ περὶ ὑμῶν
μεριμνήσει· 21 οἱ πάντες γὰρ τὰ ἑαυτῶν
ζητοῦσιν, οὐ τὰ Ἰησοῦ Χριστοῦ. 22 τὴν
δὲ δοκιμὴν αὐτοῦ γινώσκετε, ὅτι ὡς
πατρὶ τέκνον σὺν ἐμοὶ ἐδούλευσεν εἰς
τὸ εὐαγγέλιον. 23 τοῦτον μὲν οὖν ἐλπίζω
πέμψαι ὡς ἂν ἀφίδω τὰ περὶ ἐμὲ ἐξαυτῆς·
24 πέποιθα δὲ ἐν κυρίῳ ὅτι καὶ αὐτὸς
ταχέως ἐλεύσομαι.

1 Thess 2:17–3:13

Ἡμεῖς δέ, ἀδελφοί, ἀπορφανισθέντες
ἀφ' ὑμῶν πρὸς καιρὸν ὥρας, προσώπῳ
οὐ καρδίᾳ, περισσοτέρως ἐσπουδάσα-
μεν τὸ πρόσωπον ὑμῶν ἰδεῖν ἐν πολλῇ
ἐπιθυμίᾳ. 18 διότι ἠθελήσαμεν ἐλθεῖν
πρὸς ὑμᾶς, ἐγὼ μὲν Παῦλος καὶ ἅπαξ
καὶ δίς, καὶ ἐνέκοψεν ἡμᾶς ὁ σατανᾶς.
19 τίς γὰρ ἡμῶν ἐλπὶς ἢ χαρὰ ἢ στέφανος
καυχήσεως—ἢ οὐχὶ καὶ ὑμεῖς—ἔμπροσ-
θεν τοῦ κυρίου ἡμῶν Ἰησοῦ ἐν τῇ αὐτοῦ
παρουσίᾳ; 20 ὑμεῖς γάρ ἐστε ἡ δόξα ἡμῶν
καὶ ἡ χαρά. **3** Διὸ μηκέτι στέγοντες εὐδο-
κήσαμεν καταλειφθῆναι ἐν Ἀθήναις
μόνοι 2 καὶ ἐπέμψαμεν Τιμόθεον, τὸν
ἀδελφὸν ἡμῶν καὶ ⸀συνεργὸν τοῦ θε-
οῦ⸀ ἐν τῷ εὐαγγελίῳ τοῦ Χριστοῦ, εἰς τὸ
στηρίξαι ὑμᾶς καὶ παρακαλέσαι ὑπὲρ τῆς
πίστεως ὑμῶν 3 τὸ μηδένα σαίνεσθαι ἐν
ταῖς θλίψεσιν ταύταις. αὐτοὶ γὰρ οἴδατε
ὅτι εἰς τοῦτο κείμεθα· 4 καὶ γὰρ ὅτε πρὸς
ὑμᾶς ἦμεν, προελέγομεν ὑμῖν ὅτι μέλ-
λομεν θλίβεσθαι, καθὼς καὶ ἐγένετο καὶ
οἴδατε. 5 διὰ τοῦτο κἀγὼ μηκέτι στέγων
ἔπεμψα εἰς τὸ γνῶναι τὴν πίστιν ὑμῶν,
μή πως ἐπείρασεν ὑμᾶς ὁ πειράζων καὶ
εἰς κενὸν γένηται ὁ κόπος ἡμῶν. 6 Ἄρτι
δὲ ἐλθόντος Τιμοθέου πρὸς ἡμᾶς ἀφ'
ὑμῶν καὶ εὐαγγελισαμένου ἡμῖν τὴν
πίστιν καὶ τὴν ἀγάπην ὑμῶν καὶ ὅτι
ἔχετε μνείαν ἡμῶν ἀγαθὴν πάντοτε,
ἐπιποθοῦντες ἡμᾶς ἰδεῖν καθάπερ καὶ
ἡμεῖς ὑμᾶς, 7 διὰ τοῦτο παρεκλήθημεν,
ἀδελφοί, ἐφ' ὑμῖν ἐπὶ πάσῃ τῇ ἀνάγκῃ καὶ
θλίψει ἡμῶν διὰ τῆς ὑμῶν πίστεως, 8 ὅτι
νῦν ζῶμεν ἐὰν ὑμεῖς στήκετε ἐν κυρίῳ.
9 τίνα γὰρ εὐχαριστίαν δυνάμεθα τῷ
θεῷ ἀνταποδοῦναι περὶ ὑμῶν ἐπὶ πάσῃ
τῇ χαρᾷ ᾗ χαίρομεν δι' ὑμᾶς ἔμπροσθεν
τοῦ θεοῦ ἡμῶν, 10 νυκτὸς καὶ ἡμέρας
ὑπερεκπερισσοῦ δεόμενοι εἰς τὸ ἰδεῖν
ὑμῶν τὸ πρόσωπον καὶ καταρτίσαι τὰ
ὑστερήματα τῆς πίστεως ὑμῶν; 11 Αὐτὸς
δὲ ὁ θεὸς καὶ πατὴρ ἡμῶν καὶ ὁ κύριος
ἡμῶν Ἰησοῦς κατευθύναι τὴν ὁδὸν ἡμῶν
πρὸς ὑμᾶς· 12 ὑμᾶς δὲ ὁ κύριος πλεονάσαι
καὶ περισσεύσαι τῇ ἀγάπῃ εἰς ἀλλήλους
καὶ εἰς πάντας καθάπερ καὶ ἡμεῖς εἰς
ὑμᾶς, 13 εἰς τὸ στηρίξαι ὑμῶν τὰς καρδίας
ἀμέμπτους ἐν ἁγιωσύνῃ ἔμπροσθεν τοῦ
θεοῦ καὶ πατρὸς ἡμῶν ἐν τῇ παρουσίᾳ
τοῦ κυρίου ἡμῶν Ἰησοῦ μετὰ πάντων
τῶν ἁγίων αὐτοῦ, [ἀμήν].

1 Tim 3:14–15

Ταῦτά σοι γράφω ἐλπίζων ἐλθεῖν πρὸς
σὲ ἐν τάχει· 15 ἐὰν δὲ βραδύνω, ἵνα εἰδῇς
πῶς δεῖ ἐν οἴκῳ θεοῦ ἀναστρέφεσθαι,
ἥτις ἐστὶν ἐκκλησία θεοῦ ζῶντος, στῦλος
καὶ ἑδραίωμα τῆς ἀληθείας.

Phlm 21–22

Πεποιθὼς τῇ ὑπακοῇ σου ἔγραψά σοι,
εἰδὼς ὅτι καὶ ὑπὲρ ἃ λέγω ποιήσεις.
22 ἅμα δὲ καὶ ἑτοίμαζέ μοι ξενίαν· ἐλπίζω
γὰρ ὅτι διὰ τῶν προσευχῶν ὑμῶν χαρι-
σθήσομαι ὑμῖν.

Cf. 1 Cor 5:1–13; 16:5–14; 2 Cor 1:15–2:4; 10:1–6; Gal 4:12–20; Phil 1:18b–26; 1:27; 2:12–13; Col 2:1–5; 1 Tim 4:13.

The reference at the head of one excerpt above is followed by a different reference in parentheses, reflecting scholarly disagreement as to the extent of the unit within the structure of the letter.

This portion of the Pauline letters is sometimes identified as Paul's "travelogue" or "travel plans." For the classification "apostolic parousia," which perhaps best describes the function of this feature of Paul's letters, see the glossary.

12. Prayer

Rom 15:5–6

ὁ δὲ θεὸς τῆς ὑπομονῆς καὶ τῆς παρα-
κλήσεως δῴη ὑμῖν τὸ αὐτὸ φρονεῖν ἐν
ἀλλήλοις κατὰ Χριστὸν Ἰησοῦν, 6 ἵνα
ὁμοθυμαδὸν ἐν ἑνὶ στόματι δοξάζητε
τὸν θεὸν καὶ πατέρα τοῦ κυρίου ἡμῶν
Ἰησοῦ Χριστοῦ.

Rom 15:13

Ὁ δὲ θεὸς τῆς ἐλπίδος πληρώσαι ὑμᾶς
πάσης χαρᾶς καὶ εἰρήνης ἐν τῷ πιστεύειν,
εἰς τὸ περισσεύειν ὑμᾶς ἐν τῇ ἐλπίδι ἐν
δυνάμει πνεύματος ἁγίου.

Rom 15:33

Ὁ δὲ θεὸς τῆς εἰρήνης μετὰ πάντων
ὑμῶν, ἀμήν.

Eph 3:14–19

Τούτου χάριν κάμπτω τὰ γόνατά μου
πρὸς τὸν ⸀πατέρα, 15 ἐξ οὗ πᾶσα πα-
τριὰ ἐν οὐρανοῖς καὶ ἐπὶ γῆς ὀνομάζε-
ται, 16 ἵνα δῷ ὑμῖν κατὰ τὸ πλοῦτος τῆς
δόξης αὐτοῦ δυνάμει κραταιωθῆναι
διὰ τοῦ πνεύματος αὐτοῦ εἰς τὸν ἔσω
ἄνθρωπον, 17 κατοικῆσαι τὸν Χριστὸν
διὰ τῆς πίστεως ἐν ταῖς καρδίαις ὑμῶν,
ἐν ἀγάπῃ ἐρριζωμένοι καὶ τεθεμελιω-
μένοι, 18 ἵνα ἐξισχύσητε καταλαβέσθαι
σὺν πᾶσιν τοῖς ἁγίοις τί τὸ πλάτος καὶ
μῆκος καὶ ὕψος καὶ βάθος, 19 γνῶναί
τε τὴν ὑπερβάλλουσαν τῆς γνώσεως
ἀγάπην τοῦ Χριστοῦ, ἵνα πληρωθῆτε
εἰς πᾶν τὸ πλήρωμα τοῦ θεοῦ.

1 Thess 3:11–13

Αὐτὸς δὲ ὁ θεὸς καὶ πατὴρ ἡμῶν καὶ ὁ
κύριος ἡμῶν Ἰησοῦς κατευθύναι τὴν
ὁδὸν ἡμῶν πρὸς ὑμᾶς· 12 ὑμᾶς δὲ ὁ κύριος
πλεονάσαι καὶ περισσεύσαι τῇ ἀγάπῃ εἰς

1 Thess 3:2 ***συνεργον του θεου*** D* 33] συνεργον B ¦ διακονον του θεου ℵ A 1739. 1881 ¦ διακονον του θεου και συνεργον ημων D² *Byz* **§ 12** **Eph 3:14** ***πατερα*** 𝔓⁴⁶ ℵ* A B C 33. 1739] *add.* του κυριου ημων Ιησου Χριστου ℵ² D 1881 *Byz*

farewell. Put things in order, listen to my appeal, agree with one another, live in peace; and the God of love and peace will be with you. **12** Greet one another with a holy kiss. All the saints greet you. **13** The grace of the Lord Jesus Christ, the love of God, and the communion of the Holy Spirit be with all of you.

Phil 2:19–24

I hope in the Lord Jesus to send Timothy to you soon, so that I may be cheered by news of you. **20** I have no one like him who will be genuinely concerned for your welfare. **21** All of them are seeking their own interests, not those of Jesus Christ. **22** But Timothy's worth you know, how like a son with a father he has served with me in the work of the gospel. **23** I hope therefore to send him as soon as I see how things go with me; **24** and I trust in the Lord that I will also come soon.

1 Thess 2:17–3:13

As for us, brothers and sisters, when, for a short time, we were made orphans by being separated from you—in person, not in heart—we longed with great eagerness to see you face to face. **18** For we wanted to come to you—certainly I, Paul, wanted to again and again—but Satan blocked our way. **19** For what is our hope or joy or crown of boasting before our Lord Jesus at his coming? Is it not you? **20** Yes, you are our glory and joy! **3** Therefore when we could bear it no longer, we decided to be left alone in Athens; **2** and we sent Timothy, our brother and co-worker for God[e] in proclaiming the gospel of Christ, to strengthen and encourage you for the sake of your faith, **3** so that no one would be shaken by these persecutions. Indeed, you yourselves know that this is what we are destined for. **4** In fact, when we were with you, we told you beforehand that we were to suffer persecution; so it turned out, as you know. **5** For this reason, when I could bear it no longer, I sent to find out about your faith; I was afraid that somehow the tempter had tempted you and that our labor had been in vain. **6** But Timothy has just now come to us from you, and has brought us the good news of your faith and love. He has told us also that you always remember us kindly and long to see us—just as we long to see you. **7** For this reason, brothers and sisters, during all our distress and persecution we have been encouraged about you through your faith. **8** For we now live, if you continue to stand firm in the Lord. **9** How can we thank God enough for you in return for all the joy that we feel before our God because of you? **10** Night and day we pray most earnestly that we may see you face to face and restore whatever is lacking in your faith. **11** Now may our God and Father himself and our Lord Jesus direct our way to you. **12** And may the Lord make you increase and abound in love for one another and for all, just as we abound in love for you. **13** And may he so strengthen your hearts in holiness that you may be blameless before our God and Father at the coming of our Lord Jesus with all his saints.

1 Tim 3:14–15

I hope to come to you soon, but I am writing these instructions to you so that, **15** if I am delayed, you may know how one ought to behave in the household of God, which is the church of the living God, the pillar and bulwark of the truth.

Phlm 21–22

Confident of your obedience, I am writing to you, knowing that you will do even more than I say. **22** One thing more—prepare a guest room for me, for I am hoping through your prayers to be restored to you.

Cf. 1 Cor 5:1–13; 16:5–14; 2 Cor 1:15–2:4; 10:1–6; Gal 4:12–20; Phil 1:18b–26; 1:27; 2:12–13; Col 2:1–5; 1 Tim 4:13.

The reference at the head of one excerpt above is followed by a different reference in parentheses, reflecting scholarly disagreement as to the extent of the unit within the structure of the letter.

This portion of the Pauline letters is sometimes identified as Paul's "travelogue" or "travel plans." For the classification "apostolic parousia," which perhaps best describes the function of this feature of Paul's letters, see the glossary.

12. Prayer

Rom 15:5–6

May the God of steadfastness and encouragement grant you to live in harmony with one another, in accordance with Christ Jesus, **6** so that together you may with one voice glorify the God and Father of our Lord Jesus Christ.

Rom 15:13

May the God of hope fill you with all joy and peace in believing, so that you may abound in hope by the power of the Holy Spirit.

Rom 15:33

The God of peace be with all of you. Amen.

Eph 3:14–19

For this reason I bow my knees before the Father,[a] **15** from whom the whole family[b] in heaven and on earth takes its name. **16** I pray that, according to the riches of his glory, he may grant that you may be strengthened in your inner being with power through his Spirit, **17** and that Christ may dwell in your hearts through faith, as you are being rooted and grounded in love. **18** I pray that you may have the power to comprehend, with all the saints, what is the breadth and length and height and depth, **19** and to know the love of Christ that surpasses knowledge, so that you may be filled with all the fullness of God.

1 Thess 3:11–13

Now may our God and Father himself and our Lord Jesus direct our way to you. **12** And may the Lord make you increase and abound in love for one

[e] **1 Thess 3:2** *co-worker for God* lit. *God's co-worker* Other ancient authorities read *God's minister* or *God's minister and our co-worker* **§ 12** [a] **Eph 3:14** *the Father* Other ancient authorities add *of our Lord Jesus Christ* [b] **Eph 3:15** *the whole family* Or *every family* (so NRSV)

ἀλλήλους καὶ εἰς πάντας καθάπερ καὶ
ἡμεῖς εἰς ὑμᾶς, **13** εἰς τὸ στηρίξαι ὑμῶν
τὰς καρδίας ἀμέμπτους ἐν ἁγιωσύνῃ
ἔμπροσθεν τοῦ θεοῦ καὶ πατρὸς ἡμῶν ἐν
τῇ παρουσίᾳ τοῦ κυρίου ἡμῶν Ἰησοῦ μετὰ
πάντων τῶν ἁγίων αὐτοῦ, [ἀμήν].

1 Thess 5:23–24

Αὐτὸς δὲ ὁ θεὸς τῆς εἰρήνης ἁγιάσαι
ὑμᾶς ὁλοτελεῖς, καὶ ὁλόκληρον ὑμῶν τὸ
πνεῦμα καὶ ἡ ψυχὴ καὶ τὸ σῶμα ἀμέμ-
πτως ἐν τῇ παρουσίᾳ τοῦ κυρίου ἡμῶν
Ἰησοῦ Χριστοῦ τηρηθείη. **24** πιστὸς ὁ
καλῶν ὑμᾶς, ὃς καὶ ποιήσει.

2 Thess 2:16–17

Αὐτὸς δὲ ὁ κύριος ἡμῶν Ἰησοῦς Χριστὸς
καὶ [ὁ] θεὸς ὁ πατὴρ ἡμῶν ὁ ἀγαπήσας
ἡμᾶς καὶ δοὺς παράκλησιν αἰωνίαν καὶ
ἐλπίδα ἀγαθὴν ἐν χάριτι, **17** παρακαλέσαι
ὑμῶν τὰς καρδίας καὶ στηρίξαι ἐν παντὶ
ἔργῳ καὶ λόγῳ ἀγαθῷ.

2 Thess 3:5

Ὁ δὲ κύριος κατευθύναι ὑμῶν τὰς καρδίας εἰς τὴν ἀγάπην τοῦ θεοῦ καὶ εἰς τὴν ὑπομονὴν τοῦ Χριστοῦ.

2 Thess 3:16

Αὐτὸς δὲ ὁ κύριος τῆς εἰρήνης δῴη ὑμῖν τὴν εἰρήνην διὰ παντὸς ἐν παντὶ ⸀τρόπῳ. ὁ κύριος μετὰ πάντων ὑμῶν.

Cf. Rom 16:20; Gal 6:16; 2 Tim 1:16–18. See also the prayers that frequently make up part of the Pauline thanksgiving periods, in § 2 Thanksgiving and § 3 Blessing.

13. Request for Prayer

Rom 15:30–33

Παρακαλῶ δὲ ὑμᾶς[, ἀδελφοί,] διὰ τοῦ
κυρίου ἡμῶν Ἰησοῦ Χριστοῦ καὶ διὰ τῆς
ἀγάπης τοῦ πνεύματος συναγωνίσασθαί
μοι ἐν ταῖς προσευχαῖς ὑπὲρ ἐμοῦ πρὸς τὸν
θεόν, **31** ἵνα ῥυσθῶ ἀπὸ τῶν ἀπειθούντων
ἐν τῇ Ἰουδαίᾳ καὶ ἡ ⸀διακονία μου ἡ εἰς
Ἰερουσαλὴμ εὐπρόσδεκτος τοῖς ἁγίοις
γένηται, **32** ἵνα ἐν χαρᾷ ἐλθὼν πρὸς ὑμᾶς
διὰ θελήματος θεοῦ συναναπαύσωμαι
ὑμῖν. **33** Ὁ δὲ θεὸς τῆς εἰρήνης μετὰ πάν-
των ὑμῶν, ἀμήν.

2 Cor 1:11

συνυπουργούντων καὶ ὑμῶν ὑπὲρ ἡμῶν τῇ δεήσει, ἵνα ἐκ πολλῶν προσώπων τὸ εἰς ἡμᾶς χάρισμα διὰ πολλῶν εὐχαριστηθῇ ὑπὲρ ⸀ἡμῶν.

Eph 6:18–20

Διὰ πάσης προσευχῆς καὶ δεήσεως προσ-
ευχόμενοι ἐν παντὶ καιρῷ ἐν πνεύματι,
καὶ εἰς αὐτὸ ἀγρυπνοῦντες ἐν πάσῃ προσ-
καρτερήσει καὶ δεήσει περὶ πάντων τῶν
ἁγίων **19** καὶ ὑπὲρ ἐμοῦ, ἵνα μοι δοθῇ
λόγος ἐν ἀνοίξει τοῦ στόματός μου, ἐν
παρρησίᾳ γνωρίσαι τὸ μυστήριον ⸂τοῦ
εὐαγγελίου⸃, **20** ὑπὲρ οὗ πρεσβεύω ἐν
ἁλύσει, ἵνα ἐν αὐτῷ παρρησιάσωμαι ὡς
δεῖ με λαλῆσαι.

Phil 1:19–20

οἶδα γὰρ ὅτι τοῦτό μοι ἀποβήσεται εἰς
σωτηρίαν διὰ τῆς ὑμῶν δεήσεως καὶ ἐπι-
χορηγίας τοῦ πνεύματος Ἰησοῦ Χριστοῦ
20 κατὰ τὴν ἀποκαραδοκίαν καὶ ἐλπίδα
μου, ὅτι ἐν οὐδενὶ αἰσχυνθήσομαι ἀλλ᾽
ἐν πάσῃ παρρησίᾳ ὡς πάντοτε καὶ νῦν
μεγαλυνθήσεται Χριστὸς ἐν τῷ σώματί
μου, εἴτε διὰ ζωῆς εἴτε διὰ θανάτου.

Col 4:3–4

προσευχόμενοι ἅμα καὶ περὶ ἡμῶν, ἵνα
ὁ θεὸς ἀνοίξῃ ἡμῖν θύραν τοῦ λόγου
λαλῆσαι τὸ μυστήριον τοῦ Χριστοῦ, δι᾽
ὃ καὶ δέδεμαι, **4** ἵνα φανερώσω αὐτὸ ὡς
δεῖ με λαλῆσαι.

1 Thess 5:25

Ἀδελφοί, προσεύχεσθε ⸀[καὶ] περὶ ἡμῶν.

2 Thess 3:1–2

Τὸ λοιπὸν προσεύχεσθε, ἀδελφοί, περὶ
ἡμῶν, ἵνα ὁ λόγος τοῦ κυρίου τρέχῃ
καὶ δοξάζηται καθὼς καὶ πρὸς ὑμᾶς,
2 καὶ ἵνα ῥυσθῶμεν ἀπὸ τῶν ἀτόπων
καὶ πονηρῶν ἀνθρώπων· οὐ γὰρ πάν-
των ἡ πίστις.

Phlm 22

ἅμα δὲ καὶ ἑτοίμαζέ μοι ξενίαν· ἐλπίζω γὰρ ὅτι διὰ τῶν προσευχῶν ὑμῶν χαρισθήσομαι ὑμῖν.

14. Command for Public Reading

Col 4:16

καὶ ὅταν ἀναγνωσθῇ παρ᾽ ὑμῖν ἡ ἐπιστολή, ποιήσατε ἵνα καὶ ἐν τῇ Λαοδικέων ἐκκλησίᾳ ἀναγνωσθῇ, καὶ τὴν ἐκ Λαοδικείας ἵνα καὶ ὑμεῖς ἀναγνῶτε.

1 Thess 5:27

Ἐνορκίζω ὑμᾶς τὸν κύριον ἀναγνωσθῆναι τὴν ἐπιστολὴν πᾶσιν τοῖς ἀδελφοῖς.

Cf. 1 Tim 4:13.

2 Thess 3:16 ***τροπω*** א A^{c} B D^{2} 1739. 1881 *Byz*] τοπω A* D* 33 **§ 13** **Rom 15:31** ***διακονια*** 𝔓^{46} א A C D^{1} 33. 1739. 1881 *Byz*] δωροφορια B D* **2 Cor 1:11** ***ημων*** 𝔓^{46c} א A C D* 33. 1739. 1881 *Byz*^{pt}] υμων 𝔓^{46*} B D^{2} *Byz*^{pt} **Eph 6:19** ***του ευαγγελιου*** א A D I 33. 1739. 1881 *Byz*] *om.* B **1 Thess 5:25** ***και*** 𝔓^{30} B D* 33. 1739. 1881] *om.* א A D^{1} I^{vid} *Byz*

another and for all, just as we abound in love for you. 13 And may he so strengthen your hearts in holiness that you may be blameless before our God and Father at the coming of our Lord Jesus with all his saints.

1 Thess 5:23–24

May the God of peace himself sanctify you entirely; and may your spirit and soul and body be kept sound and blameless at the coming of our Lord Jesus Christ. 24 The one who calls you is faithful, and he will do this.

2 Thess 2:16–17

Now may our Lord Jesus Christ himself and God our Father, who loved us and through grace gave us eternal comfort and good hope, 17 comfort your hearts and strengthen them in every good work and word.

2 Thess 3:5

May the Lord direct your hearts to the love of God and to the steadfastness of Christ.

2 Thess 3:16

Now may the Lord of peace himself give you peace at all times in all ways.[c] The Lord be with all of you.

Cf. Rom 16:20; Gal 6:16; 2 Tim 1:16–18. See also the prayers that frequently make up part of the Pauline thanksgiving periods, in § 2 Thanksgiving and § 3 Blessing.

13. *Request for Prayer*

Rom 15:30–33

I appeal to you, brothers and sisters, by our Lord Jesus Christ and by the love of the Spirit, to join me in earnest prayer to God on my behalf, 31 that I may be rescued from the unbelievers in Judea, and that my ministry[a] to Jerusalem may be acceptable to the saints, 32 so that by God's will I may come to you with joy and be refreshed in your company. 33 The God of peace be with all of you. Amen.

2 Cor 1:11

as you also join in helping us by your prayers, so that many will give thanks on our[b] behalf for the blessing granted us through the prayers of many.

Eph 6:18–20

Pray in the Spirit at all times in every prayer and supplication. To that end keep alert and always persevere in supplication for all the saints. 19 Pray also for me, so that when I speak, a message may be given to me to make known with boldness the mystery of the gospel,[c] 20 for which I am an ambassador in chains. Pray that I may declare it boldly, as I must speak.

Phil 1:19–20

for I know that through your prayers and the supply of the Spirit of Jesus Christ this will turn out for my deliverance.[d] 20 It is my eager expectation and hope that I will not be put to shame in any way, but that by my speaking with all boldness, Christ will be exalted now as always in my body, whether by life or by death.

Col 4:3–4

At the same time pray for us as well that God will open to us a door for the word, that we may declare the mystery of Christ, for which I am in prison, 4 so that I may reveal it clearly, as I should.

1 Thess 5:25

Beloved, pray[e] for us.

2 Thess 3:1–2

Finally, brothers and sisters, pray for us, so that the word of the Lord may spread rapidly and be glorified everywhere, just as it is among you, 2 and that we may be rescued from wicked and evil people; for not all have faith.

Phlm 22

One thing more—prepare a guest room for me, for I am hoping through your prayers to be restored to you.

14. *Command for Public Reading*

Col 4:16

And when this letter has been read among you, have it read also in the church of the Laodiceans; and see that you read also the letter from Laodicea.

1 Thess 5:27

I solemnly command you by the Lord that this letter be read to all of them.

Cf. 1 Tim 4:13.

[c] **2 Thess 3:16** *ways* Other ancient authorities read *places* **§ 13** [a] **Rom 15:31** *my ministry* Other ancient authorities read *my bringing of a gift* [b] **2 Cor 1:11** *our* Other ancient authorities read *your* [c] **Eph 6:19** *of the gospel* Other ancient authorities lack *of the gospel* [d] **Phil 1:19** Translation differs from NRSV [e] **1 Thess 5:25** *pray* Other ancient authorities add *also*

15. Virtue List

2 Cor 6:6–7

ἐν ἁγνότητι, ἐν γνώσει, ἐν μακροθυμίᾳ, ἐν χρηστότητι, ἐν πνεύματι ἁγίῳ, ἐν ἀγάπῃ ἀνυποκρίτῳ, 7 ἐν λόγῳ ἀληθείας, ἐν δυνάμει θεοῦ· διὰ τῶν ὅπλων τῆς δικαιοσύνης τῶν δεξιῶν καὶ ἀριστερῶν

2 Cor 8:7

Ἀλλ᾽ ὥσπερ ἐν παντὶ περισσεύετε, πίστει καὶ λόγῳ καὶ γνώσει καὶ πάσῃ σπουδῇ καὶ τῇ ἐξ ⸂ἡμῶν ἐν ὑμῖν⸃ ἀγάπῃ, ἵνα καὶ ἐν ταύτῃ τῇ χάριτι περισσεύητε.

Gal 5:22–23

ὁ δὲ καρπὸς τοῦ πνεύματός ἐστιν ἀγάπη χαρὰ εἰρήνη, μακροθυμία χρηστότης ἀγαθωσύνη, πίστις 23 πραΰτης ἐγκράτεια· κατὰ τῶν τοιούτων οὐκ ἔστιν νόμος.

Phil 4:8–9

Τὸ λοιπόν, ἀδελφοί, ὅσα ἐστὶν ἀληθῆ, ὅσα σεμνά, ὅσα δίκαια, ὅσα ἁγνά, ὅσα προσφιλῆ, ὅσα εὔφημα, εἴ τις ἀρετὴ καὶ εἴ τις ἔπαινος, ταῦτα λογίζεσθε· 9 ἃ καὶ ἐμάθετε καὶ παρελάβετε καὶ ἠκούσατε καὶ εἴδετε ἐν ἐμοί, ταῦτα πράσσετε· καὶ ὁ θεὸς τῆς εἰρήνης ἔσται μεθ᾽ ὑμῶν.

Col 3:12–15

Ἐνδύσασθε οὖν, ὡς ἐκλεκτοὶ τοῦ θεοῦ ἅγιοι καὶ ἠγαπημένοι, σπλάγχνα οἰκτιρμοῦ χρηστότητα ταπεινοφροσύνην πραΰτητα μακροθυμίαν, 13 ἀνεχόμενοι ἀλλήλων καὶ χαριζόμενοι ἑαυτοῖς ἐάν τις πρός τινα ἔχῃ μομφήν· καθὼς καὶ ὁ ⸀κύριος ἐχαρίσατο ὑμῖν, οὕτως καὶ ὑμεῖς· 14 ἐπὶ πᾶσιν δὲ τούτοις τὴν ἀγάπην, ὅ ἐστιν σύνδεσμος τῆς τελειότητος. 15 καὶ ἡ εἰρήνη τοῦ Χριστοῦ βραβευέτω ἐν ταῖς καρδίαις ὑμῶν, εἰς ἣν καὶ ἐκλήθητε ἐν ἑνὶ σώματι· καὶ εὐχάριστοι γίνεσθε.

1 Tim 3:1–13

⸀πιστὸς ὁ λόγος. Εἴ τις ἐπισκοπῆς ὀρέγεται, καλοῦ ἔργου ἐπιθυμεῖ. 2 δεῖ οὖν τὸν ἐπίσκοπον ἀνεπίλημπτον εἶναι, μιᾶς γυναικὸς ἄνδρα, νηφάλιον σώφρονα κόσμιον φιλόξενον διδακτικόν, 3 μὴ πάροινον μὴ πλήκτην, ἀλλὰ ἐπιεικῆ ἄμαχον ἀφιλάργυρον, 4 τοῦ ἰδίου οἴκου καλῶς προϊστάμενον, τέκνα ἔχοντα ἐν ὑποταγῇ, μετὰ πάσης σεμνότητος 5 (εἰ δέ τις τοῦ ἰδίου οἴκου προστῆναι οὐκ οἶδεν, πῶς ἐκκλησίας θεοῦ ἐπιμελήσεται;), 6 μὴ νεόφυτον, ἵνα μὴ τυφωθεὶς εἰς κρίμα ἐμπέσῃ τοῦ διαβόλου. 7 δεῖ δὲ καὶ μαρτυρίαν καλὴν ἔχειν ἀπὸ τῶν ἔξωθεν, ἵνα μὴ εἰς ὀνειδισμὸν ἐμπέσῃ καὶ παγίδα τοῦ διαβόλου. 8 Διακόνους ὡσαύτως σεμνούς, μὴ διλόγους, μὴ οἴνῳ πολλῷ προσέχοντας, μὴ αἰσχροκερδεῖς, 9 ἔχοντας τὸ μυστήριον τῆς πίστεως ἐν καθαρᾷ συνειδήσει. 10 καὶ οὗτοι δὲ δοκιμαζέσθωσαν πρῶτον, εἶτα διακονείτωσαν ἀνέγκλητοι ὄντες. 11 Γυναῖκας ὡσαύτως σεμνάς, μὴ διαβόλους, νηφαλίους, πιστὰς ἐν πᾶσιν. 12 διάκονοι ἔστωσαν μιᾶς γυναικὸς ἄνδρες, τέκνων καλῶς προϊστάμενοι καὶ τῶν ἰδίων οἴκων. 13 οἱ γὰρ καλῶς διακονήσαντες βαθμὸν ἑαυτοῖς καλὸν περιποιοῦνται καὶ πολλὴν παρρησίαν ἐν πίστει τῇ ἐν Χριστῷ Ἰησοῦ.

1 Tim 4:12

Μηδείς σου τῆς νεότητος καταφρονείτω, ἀλλὰ τύπος γίνου τῶν πιστῶν ἐν λόγῳ, ἐν ἀναστροφῇ, ἐν ἀγάπῃ, ἐν πίστει, ἐν ἁγνείᾳ.

1 Tim 5:9–10

Χήρα καταλεγέσθω μὴ ἔλαττον ἐτῶν ἑξήκοντα γεγονυῖα, ἑνὸς ἀνδρὸς γυνή, 10 ἐν ἔργοις καλοῖς μαρτυρουμένη, εἰ ἐτεκνοτρόφησεν, εἰ ἐξενοδόχησεν, εἰ ἁγίων πόδας ἔνιψεν, εἰ θλιβομένοις ἐπήρκεσεν, εἰ παντὶ ἔργῳ ἀγαθῷ ἐπηκολούθησεν.

1 Tim 6:11

Σὺ δέ, ὦ ἄνθρωπε θεοῦ, ταῦτα φεῦγε· δίωκε δὲ δικαιοσύνην εὐσέβειαν πίστιν, ἀγάπην ὑπομονὴν πραϋπαθίαν.

2 Tim 2:22

Τὰς δὲ νεωτερικὰς ἐπιθυμίας φεῦγε, δίωκε δὲ δικαιοσύνην πίστιν ἀγάπην εἰρήνην μετὰ τῶν ἐπικαλουμένων τὸν κύριον ἐκ καθαρᾶς καρδίας.

2 Tim 3:10–11

Σὺ δὲ παρηκολούθησάς μου τῇ διδασκαλίᾳ, τῇ ἀγωγῇ, τῇ προθέσει, τῇ πίστει, τῇ μακροθυμίᾳ, τῇ ἀγάπῃ, τῇ ὑπομονῇ, 11 τοῖς διωγμοῖς, τοῖς παθήμασιν, οἷά μοι ἐγένετο ἐν Ἀντιοχείᾳ, ἐν Ἰκονίῳ, ἐν Λύστροις, οἵους διωγμοὺς ὑπήνεγκα καὶ ἐκ πάντων με ἐρρύσατο ὁ κύριος.

Titus 1:5–9

Τούτου χάριν ἀπέλιπόν σε ἐν Κρήτῃ, ἵνα τὰ λείποντα ἐπιδιορθώσῃ καὶ καταστήσῃς κατὰ πόλιν πρεσβυτέρους, ὡς ἐγώ σοι διεταξάμην, 6 εἴ τίς ἐστιν ἀνέγκλητος, μιᾶς γυναικὸς ἀνήρ, τέκνα ἔχων πιστά, μὴ ἐν κατηγορίᾳ ἀσωτίας ἢ ἀνυπότακτα. 7 δεῖ γὰρ τὸν ἐπίσκοπον ἀνέγκλητον εἶναι ὡς θεοῦ οἰκονόμον, μὴ αὐθάδη, μὴ ὀργίλον, μὴ πάροινον, μὴ πλήκτην, μὴ αἰσχροκερδῆ, 8 ἀλλὰ φιλόξενον φιλάγαθον σώφρονα δίκαιον ὅσιον ἐγκρατῆ, 9 ἀντεχόμενον τοῦ κατὰ τὴν διδαχὴν πιστοῦ λόγου, ἵνα δυνατὸς ᾖ καὶ παρακαλεῖν ἐν τῇ διδασκαλίᾳ τῇ ὑγιαινούσῃ καὶ τοὺς ἀντιλέγοντας ἐλέγχειν.

Titus 2:2–10

Πρεσβύτας νηφαλίους εἶναι, σεμνούς, σώφρονας, ὑγιαίνοντας τῇ πίστει, τῇ ἀγάπῃ, τῇ ὑπομονῇ· 3 πρεσβύτιδας ὡσαύτως ἐν καταστήματι ἱεροπρεπεῖς, μὴ διαβόλους μὴ οἴνῳ πολλῷ δεδουλωμένας, καλοδιδασκάλους, 4 ἵνα σωφρονίζωσιν τὰς νέας φιλάνδρους εἶναι, φιλοτέκνους 5 σώφρονας ἁγνὰς οἰκουργοὺς ἀγαθάς, ὑποτασσομένας τοῖς ἰδίοις ἀνδράσιν, ἵνα μὴ ὁ λόγος τοῦ θεοῦ βλασφημῆται. 6 Τοὺς νεωτέρους ὡσαύτως παρακάλει σωφρονεῖν 7 περὶ πάντα, σεαυτὸν παρεχόμενος τύπον καλῶν ἔργων, ἐν τῇ διδασκαλίᾳ ἀφθορίαν, σεμνότητα, 8 λόγον ὑγιῆ ἀκατάγνωστον, ἵνα ὁ ἐξ ἐναντίας ἐντραπῇ μηδὲν ἔχων λέγειν

§ 15 **2 Cor 8:7** ***ημων εν υμιν*** $\mathfrak{P}^{46}$ B 1739. 1881] υμων εν ημιν ℵ C D (33) *Byz* **Col 3:13** ***κυριος*** $\mathfrak{P}^{46}$ A B D*] Χριστος ℵ^{2} C D^{1} 1739. 1881 *Byz* ¦ θεος ℵ* ¦ θεος εν Χριστω 33 **1 Tim 3:1** ***πιστος*** ℵ A D^{2} 33. 1739. 1881 *Byz*] ανθρωπινος D*

15. *Virtue List*

2 Cor 6:6–7

by purity, knowledge, patience, kindness, holiness of spirit, genuine love, **7** truthful speech, and the power of God; with the weapons of righteousness for the right hand and for the left

2 Cor 8:7

Now as you excel in everything—in faith, in speech, in knowledge, in utmost eagerness, and in our love for you[a]—so we want you to excel also in this generous undertaking.

Gal 5:22–23

By contrast, the fruit of the Spirit is love, joy, peace, patience, kindness, generosity, faithfulness, **23** gentleness, and self-control. There is no law against such things.

Phil 4:8–9

Finally, beloved, whatever is true, whatever is honorable, whatever is just, whatever is pure, whatever is pleasing, whatever is commendable, if there is any excellence and if there is anything worthy of praise, think about these things. **9** Keep on doing the things that you have learned and received and heard and seen in me, and the God of peace will be with you.

Col 3:12–15

As God's chosen ones, holy and beloved, clothe yourselves with compassion, kindness, humility, meekness, and patience. **13** Bear with one another and, if anyone has a complaint against another, forgive each other; just as the Lord[b] has forgiven you, so you also must forgive. **14** Above all, clothe yourselves with love, which binds everything together in perfect harmony. **15** And let the peace of Christ rule in your hearts, to which indeed you were called in the one body. And be thankful.

1 Tim 3:1–13

The saying is sure:[c] whoever aspires to the office of bishop desires a noble task. **2** Now a bishop must be above reproach, married only once, temperate, sensible, respectable, hospitable, an apt teacher, **3** not a drunkard, not violent but gentle, not quarrelsome, and not a lover of money. **4** He must manage his own household well, keeping his children submissive and respectful in every way— **5** for if someone does not know how to manage his own household, how can he take care of God's church? **6** He must not be a recent convert, or he may be puffed up with conceit and fall into the condemnation of the devil. **7** Moreover, he must be well thought of by outsiders, so that he may not fall into disgrace and the snare of the devil. **8** Deacons likewise must be serious, not double-tongued, not indulging in much wine, not greedy for money; **9** they must hold fast to the mystery of the faith with a clear conscience. **10** And let them first be tested; then, if they prove themselves blameless, let them serve as deacons. **11** Women likewise must be serious, not slanderers, but temperate, faithful in all things. **12** Let deacons be married only once, and let them manage their children and their households well; **13** for those who serve well as deacons gain a good standing for themselves and great boldness in the faith that is in Christ Jesus.

1 Tim 4:12

Let no one despise your youth, but set the believers an example in speech and conduct, in love, in faith, in purity.

1 Tim 5:9–10

Let a widow be put on the list if she is not less than sixty years old and has been married only once; **10** she must be well attested for her good works, as one who has brought up children, shown hospitality, washed the saints' feet, helped the afflicted, and devoted herself to doing good in every way.

1 Tim 6:11

But as for you, man of God, shun all this; pursue righteousness, godliness, faith, love, endurance, gentleness.

2 Tim 2:22

Shun youthful passions and pursue righteousness, faith, love, and peace, along with those who call on the Lord from a pure heart.

2 Tim 3:10–11

Now you have observed my teaching, my conduct, my aim in life, my faith, my patience, my love, my steadfastness, **11** my persecutions, and my suffering the things that happened to me in Antioch, Iconium, and Lystra. What persecutions I endured! Yet the Lord rescued me from all of them.

Titus 1:5–9

I left you behind in Crete for this reason, so that you should put in order what remained to be done, and should appoint elders in every town, as I directed you: **6** someone who is blameless, married only once, whose children are believers, not accused of debauchery and not rebellious. **7** For a bishop, as God's steward, must be blameless; he must not be arrogant or quick-tempered or addicted to wine or violent or greedy for gain; **8** but he must be hospitable, a lover of goodness, prudent, upright, devout, and self-controlled. **9** He must have a firm grasp of the word that is trustworthy in accordance with the teaching, so that he may be able both to preach with sound doctrine and to refute those who contradict it.

Titus 2:2–10

Tell the older men to be temperate, serious, prudent, and sound in faith, in love, and in endurance. **3** Likewise, tell the older women to be reverent in behavior, not to be slanderers or slaves to drink; they are to teach what is good, **4** so that they may encourage the young women to love their husbands, to love their children, **5** to be self-controlled, chaste, good managers of the household, kind, being submissive to their husbands, so that the word of God may not be discredited. **6** Likewise, urge the younger men to be self-controlled. **7** Show yourself in all respects a model of good works, and in your teaching show integrity, gravity, **8** and sound speech that cannot be censured; then

§ 15 [a] **2 Cor 8:7** ***our love for you*** Other ancient authorities read *your love for us* [b] **Col 3:13** ***just as the Lord*** Other ancient authorities read *just as Christ* [c] **1 Tim 3:1** ***The saying is sure*** A few ancient authorities read *The saying is commonly accepted*

περὶ ἡμῶν φαῦλον. 9 Δούλους ἰδίοις δεσπόταις ὑποτάσσεσθαι ἐν πᾶσιν, εὐαρέστους εἶναι, μὴ ἀντιλέγοντας, 10 μὴ νοσφιζομένους, ἀλλὰ πᾶσαν πίστιν ἐνδεικνυμένους ἀγαθήν, ἵνα τὴν διδασκαλίαν τὴν τοῦ σωτῆρος ἡμῶν θεοῦ κοσμῶσιν ἐν πᾶσιν.

Titus 3:1–2

Ὑπομίμνῃσκε αὐτοὺς ἀρχαῖς ἐξουσίαις ὑποτάσσεσθαι, πειθαρχεῖν, πρὸς πᾶν ἔργον ἀγαθὸν ἑτοίμους εἶναι, 2 μηδένα βλασφημεῖν, ἀμάχους εἶναι, ἐπιεικεῖς, πᾶσαν ἐνδεικνυμένους πραΰτητα πρὸς πάντας ἀνθρώπους.

Cf. Rom 5:3–5; 12:9–13; Eph 4:1–3; 6:14–17; 1 Thess 2:7–12; 1 Tim 2:15.

16. Vice List

Rom 1:29–32

πεπληρωμένους πάσῃ ἀδικίᾳ πονηρίᾳ πλεονεξίᾳ κακίᾳ, μεστοὺς φθόνου φόνου ἔριδος δόλου κακοηθείας, ψιθυριστὰς 30 καταλάλους θεοστυγεῖς ὑβριστὰς ὑπερηφάνους ἀλαζόνας, ἐφευρετὰς κακῶν, γονεῦσιν ἀπειθεῖς, 31 ἀσυνέτους ἀσυνθέτους ἀστόργους ἀνελεήμονας· 32 οἵτινες τὸ δικαίωμα τοῦ θεοῦ ἐπιγνόντες ὅτι οἱ τὰ τοιαῦτα πράσσοντες ἄξιοι θανάτου εἰσίν, οὐ μόνον αὐτὰ ποιοῦσιν ἀλλὰ καὶ συνευδοκοῦσιν τοῖς πράσσουσιν.

Rom 13:13–14

ὡς ἐν ἡμέρᾳ εὐσχημόνως περιπατήσωμεν, μὴ κώμοις καὶ μέθαις, μὴ κοίταις καὶ ἀσελγείαις, μὴ ἔριδι καὶ ζήλῳ, 14 ἀλλὰ ἐνδύσασθε τὸν κύριον Ἰησοῦν Χριστὸν καὶ τῆς σαρκὸς πρόνοιαν μὴ ποιεῖσθε εἰς ἐπιθυμίας.

1 Cor 5:9–13

Ἔγραψα ὑμῖν ἐν τῇ ἐπιστολῇ μὴ συναναμίγνυσθαι πόρνοις, 10 οὐ πάντως τοῖς πόρνοις τοῦ κόσμου τούτου ἢ τοῖς πλεονέκταις καὶ ἅρπαξιν ἢ εἰδωλολάτραις, ἐπεὶ ὠφείλετε ἄρα ἐκ τοῦ κόσμου ἐξελθεῖν. 11 νῦν δὲ ἔγραψα ὑμῖν μὴ συναναμίγνυσθαι ἐάν τις ἀδελφὸς ὀνομαζόμενος ᾖ πόρνος ἢ πλεονέκτης ἢ εἰδωλολάτρης ἢ λοίδορος ἢ μέθυσος ἢ ἅρπαξ, τῷ τοιούτῳ μηδὲ συνεσθίειν. 12 τί γάρ μοι τοὺς ἔξω κρίνειν; οὐχὶ τοὺς ἔσω ὑμεῖς κρίνετε; 13 τοὺς δὲ ἔξω ὁ θεὸς κρινεῖ. ἐξάρατε τὸν πονηρὸν ἐξ ὑμῶν αὐτῶν.

1 Cor 6:9–11

Ἢ οὐκ οἴδατε ὅτι ἄδικοι θεοῦ βασιλείαν οὐ κληρονομήσουσιν; μὴ πλανᾶσθε· οὔτε πόρνοι οὔτε εἰδωλολάτραι οὔτε μοιχοὶ οὔτε μαλακοὶ οὔτε ἀρσενοκοῖται 10 οὔτε κλέπται οὔτε πλεονέκται, οὐ μέθυσοι, οὐ λοίδοροι, οὐχ ἅρπαγες βασιλείαν θεοῦ κληρονομήσουσιν. 11 καὶ ταῦτά τινες ἦτε· ἀλλὰ ἀπελούσασθε, ἀλλὰ ἡγιάσθητε, ἀλλὰ ἐδικαιώθητε ἐν τῷ ὀνόματι τοῦ κυρίου ⸀Ἰησοῦ Χριστοῦ⸁ καὶ ἐν τῷ πνεύματι τοῦ θεοῦ ἡμῶν.

2 Cor 12:20–21

φοβοῦμαι γὰρ μή πως ἐλθὼν οὐχ οἵους θέλω εὕρω ὑμᾶς κἀγὼ εὑρεθῶ ὑμῖν οἷον οὐ θέλετε· μή πως ἔρις, ζῆλος, θυμοί, ἐριθεῖαι, καταλαλιαί, ψιθυρισμοί, φυσιώσεις, ἀκαταστασίαι· 21 μὴ πάλιν ἐλθόντος μου ταπεινώσῃ με ὁ θεός μου πρὸς ὑμᾶς καὶ πενθήσω πολλοὺς τῶν προημαρτηκότων καὶ μὴ μετανοησάντων ἐπὶ τῇ ἀκαθαρσίᾳ καὶ πορνείᾳ καὶ ἀσελγείᾳ ᾗ ἔπραξαν.

Gal 5:19–21

φανερὰ δέ ἐστιν τὰ ἔργα τῆς σαρκός, ἅτινά ἐστιν πορνεία, ἀκαθαρσία, ἀσέλγεια, 20 εἰδωλολατρία, φαρμακεία, ἔχθραι, ἔρις, ζῆλος, θυμοί, ἐριθεῖαι, διχοστασίαι, αἱρέσεις, 21 ⸀φθόνοι, μέθαι, κῶμοι καὶ τὰ ὅμοια τούτοις, ἃ προλέγω ὑμῖν, καθὼς προεῖπον ὅτι οἱ τὰ τοιαῦτα πράσσοντες βασιλείαν θεοῦ οὐ κληρονομήσουσιν.

Eph 4:17–19

Τοῦτο οὖν λέγω καὶ μαρτύρομαι ἐν κυρίῳ, μηκέτι ὑμᾶς περιπατεῖν, καθὼς καὶ τὰ ἔθνη περιπατεῖ ἐν ματαιότητι τοῦ νοὸς αὐτῶν, 18 ἐσκοτωμένοι τῇ διανοίᾳ ὄντες, ἀπηλλοτριωμένοι τῆς ζωῆς τοῦ θεοῦ διὰ τὴν ἄγνοιαν τὴν οὖσαν ἐν αὐτοῖς, διὰ τὴν πώρωσιν τῆς καρδίας αὐτῶν, 19 οἵτινες ἀπηλγηκότες ἑαυτοὺς παρέδωκαν τῇ ἀσελγείᾳ εἰς ἐργασίαν ἀκαθαρσίας πάσης ἐν πλεονεξίᾳ.

Eph 4:31

πᾶσα πικρία καὶ θυμὸς καὶ ὀργὴ καὶ κραυγὴ καὶ βλασφημία ἀρθήτω ἀφ᾽ ὑμῶν σὺν πάσῃ κακίᾳ.

Eph 5:3–5

Πορνεία δὲ καὶ ἀκαθαρσία πᾶσα ἢ πλεονεξία μηδὲ ὀνομαζέσθω ἐν ὑμῖν, καθὼς πρέπει ἁγίοις, 4 καὶ αἰσχρότης καὶ μωρολογία ἢ εὐτραπελία, ἃ οὐκ ἀνῆκεν, ἀλλὰ μᾶλλον εὐχαριστία. 5 τοῦτο γὰρ ἴστε γινώσκοντες, ὅτι πᾶς πόρνος ἢ ἀκάθαρτος ἢ πλεονέκτης, ὅ ἐστιν εἰδωλολάτρης, οὐκ ἔχει κληρονομίαν ἐν τῇ βασιλείᾳ τοῦ Χριστοῦ καὶ θεοῦ.

Col 3:5–8

Νεκρώσατε οὖν τὰ μέλη τὰ ἐπὶ τῆς γῆς, πορνείαν ἀκαθαρσίαν πάθος ἐπιθυμίαν κακήν, καὶ τὴν πλεονεξίαν, ἥτις ἐστὶν εἰδωλολατρία, 6 δι᾽ ἃ ἔρχεται ἡ ὀργὴ τοῦ θεοῦ ⸀[ἐπὶ τοὺς υἱοὺς τῆς ἀπειθείας]⸁. 7 ἐν οἷς καὶ ὑμεῖς περιεπατήσατέ ποτε, ὅτε ἐζῆτε ἐν τούτοις· 8 νυνὶ δὲ ἀπόθεσθε καὶ ὑμεῖς τὰ πάντα, ὀργήν, θυμόν, κακίαν, βλασφημίαν, αἰσχρολογίαν ἐκ τοῦ στόματος ὑμῶν

1 Tim 1:8–11

Οἴδαμεν δὲ ὅτι καλὸς ὁ νόμος, ἐάν τις αὐτῷ νομίμως χρῆται, 9 εἰδὼς τοῦτο, ὅτι δικαίῳ νόμος οὐ κεῖται, ἀνόμοις δὲ καὶ ἀνυποτάκτοις, ἀσεβέσι καὶ ἁμαρτωλοῖς,

§ 16 **1 Cor 6:11** ***Ιησου Χριστου*** 𝔓^{11vid} 𝔓^{46} ℵ D*] Ιησου A D^{2} *Byz* ¦ ημων Ιησου Χριστου B C^{vid} 33. 1739. 1881 **Gal 5:21** ***φθονοι*** 𝔓^{46} ℵ B 33] *add.* φονοι A C D 1739. 1881 *Byz* **Col 3:6** ***επι τους υιους της απειθειας*** ℵ A C D I 33. 1739. 1881 *Byz*] *om.* 𝔓^{46} B

any opponent will be put to shame, having nothing evil to say of us. [9] Tell slaves to be submissive to their masters and to give satisfaction in every respect; they are not to talk back, [10] not to pilfer, but to show complete and perfect fidelity, so that in everything they may be an ornament to the doctrine of God our Savior.

Titus 3:1–2

Remind them to be subject to rulers and authorities, to be obedient, to be ready for every good work, [2] to speak evil of no one, to avoid quarreling, to be gentle, and to show every courtesy to everyone.

Cf. Rom 5:3–5; 12:9–13; Eph 4:1–3; 6:14–17; 1 Thess 2:7–12; 1 Tim 2:15.

16. Vice List

Rom 1:29–32

They were filled with every kind of wickedness, evil, covetousness, malice. Full of envy, murder, strife, deceit, craftiness, they are gossips, [30] slanderers, God-haters, insolent, haughty, boastful, inventors of evil, rebellious toward parents, [31] foolish, faithless, heartless, ruthless. [32] They know God's decree, that those who practice such things deserve to die—yet they not only do them but even applaud others who practice them.

Rom 13:13–14

let us walk[a] honorably as in the day, not in reveling and drunkenness, not in debauchery and licentiousness, not in quarreling and jealousy. [14] Instead, put on the Lord Jesus Christ, and make no provision for the flesh, to gratify its desires.

1 Cor 5:9–13

I wrote to you in my letter not to associate with sexually immoral persons—[10] not at all meaning the immoral of this world, or the greedy and robbers, or idolaters, since you would then need to go out of the world. [11] But now I am writing to you not to associate with anyone who bears the name of brother or sister who is sexually immoral or greedy, or is an idolater, reviler, drunkard, or robber. Do not even eat with such a one. [12] For what have I to do with judging those outside? Is it not those who are inside that you are to judge? [13] God will judge those outside. "Drive out the wicked person from among you."

1 Cor 6:9–11

Do you not know that wrongdoers will not inherit the kingdom of God? Do not be deceived! Fornicators, idolaters, adulterers, male prostitutes, sodomites, [10] thieves, the greedy, drunkards, revilers, robbers—none of these will inherit the kingdom of God. [11] And this is what some of you used to be. But you were washed, you were sanctified, you were justified in the name of the Lord Jesus Christ[b] and in the Spirit of our God.

2 Cor 12:20–21

For I fear that when I come, I may find you not as I wish, and that you may find me not as you wish; I fear that there may perhaps be quarreling, jealousy, anger, selfishness, slander, gossip, conceit, and disorder. [21] I fear that when I come again, my God may humble me before you, and that I may have to mourn over many who previously sinned and have not repented of the impurity, sexual immorality, and licentiousness that they have practiced.

Gal 5:19–21

Now the works of the flesh are obvious: fornication, impurity, licentiousness, [20] idolatry, sorcery, enmities, strife, jealousy, anger, quarrels, dissensions, factions, [21] envy,[c] drunkenness, carousing, and things like these. I am warning you, as I warned you before: those who do such things will not inherit the kingdom of God.

Eph 4:17–19

Now this I affirm and insist on in the Lord: you must no longer live as the Gentiles live, in the futility of their minds. [18] They are darkened in their understanding, alienated from the life of God because of their ignorance and hardness of heart. [19] They have lost all sensitivity and have abandoned themselves to licentiousness, greedy to practice every kind of impurity.

Eph 4:31

Put away from you all bitterness and wrath and anger and wrangling and slander, together with all malice

Eph 5:3–5

But fornication and impurity of any kind, or greed, must not even be mentioned among you, as is proper among saints. [4] Entirely out of place is obscene, silly, and vulgar talk; but instead, let there be thanksgiving. [5] Be sure of this, that no fornicator or impure person, or one who is greedy (that is, an idolater), has any inheritance in the kingdom of Christ and of God.

Col 3:5–8

Put to death, therefore, whatever in you is earthly: fornication, impurity, passion, evil desire, and greed (which is idolatry). [6] On account of these the wrath of God is coming on those who are disobedient.[d] [7] These are the ways you also once followed, when you were living that life. [8] But now you must get rid of all such things—anger, wrath, malice, slander, and abusive language from your mouth.

1 Tim 1:8–11

Now we know that the law is good, if one uses it legitimately. [9] This means understanding that the law is laid down not for the innocent but for the lawless and disobedient, for the godless

§ 16 [a] **Rom 13:13** ***walk*** NRSV translates *live* [b] **1 Cor 6:11** ***the Lord Jesus Christ*** Other ancient authorities read *the Lord Jesus* or *our Lord Jesus Christ* [c] **Gal 5:21** ***envy,*** Other ancient authorities add *murder* [d] **Col 3:6** ***on those who are disobedient*** Other ancient authorities lack *on those who are disobedient*

ἀνοσίοις καὶ βεβήλοις, πατρολῴαις καὶ μητρολῴαις, ἀνδροφόνοις 10 πόρνοις ἀρσενοκοίταις ἀνδραποδισταῖς ψεύσταις ἐπιόρκοις, καὶ εἴ τι ἕτερον τῇ ὑγιαινούσῃ διδασκαλίᾳ ἀντίκειται 11 κατὰ τὸ εὐαγγέλιον τῆς δόξης τοῦ μακαρίου θεοῦ, ὃ ἐπιστεύθην ἐγώ.

1 Tim 6:3–5

εἴ τις ἑτεροδιδασκαλεῖ καὶ μὴ προσέρχεται ὑγιαίνουσιν λόγοις τοῖς τοῦ κυρίου ἡμῶν Ἰησοῦ Χριστοῦ καὶ τῇ κατ᾽ εὐσέβειαν διδασκαλίᾳ, 4 τετύφωται, μηδὲν ἐπιστάμενος, ἀλλὰ νοσῶν περὶ ζητήσεις καὶ λογομαχίας, ἐξ ὧν γίνεται φθόνος ἔρις βλασφημίαι, ὑπόνοιαι πονηραί, 5 διαπαρατριβαὶ διεφθαρμένων ἀνθρώπων τὸν νοῦν καὶ ἀπεστερημένων τῆς ἀληθείας, νομιζόντων πορισμὸν εἶναι τὴν ⸀εὐσέβειαν.

2 Tim 3:2–5

ἔσονται γὰρ οἱ ἄνθρωποι φίλαυτοι φιλάργυροι ἀλαζόνες ὑπερήφανοι βλάσφημοι, γονεῦσιν ἀπειθεῖς, ἀχάριστοι ἀνόσιοι 3 ἄστοργοι ἄσπονδοι διάβολοι ἀκρατεῖς ἀνήμεροι ἀφιλάγαθοι 4 προδόται προπετεῖς τετυφωμένοι, φιλήδονοι μᾶλλον ἢ φιλόθεοι, 5 ἔχοντες μόρφωσιν εὐσεβείας τὴν δὲ δύναμιν αὐτῆς ἠρνημένοι· καὶ τούτους ἀποτρέπου.

Titus 3:3

Ἦμεν γάρ ποτε καὶ ἡμεῖς ἀνόητοι, ἀπειθεῖς, πλανώμενοι, δουλεύοντες ἐπιθυμίαις καὶ ἡδοναῖς ποικίλαις, ἐν κακίᾳ καὶ φθόνῳ διάγοντες, στυγητοί, μισοῦντες ἀλλήλους.

Cf. Rom 2:21–24; 2 Cor 11:19–21a; 1 Thess 2:3–6.

17. Hardship Catalogue

Rom 8:35–39

τίς ἡμᾶς χωρίσει ἀπὸ τῆς ἀγάπης τοῦ Χριστοῦ; θλῖψις ἢ στενοχωρία ἢ διωγμὸς ἢ λιμὸς ἢ γυμνότης ἢ κίνδυνος ἢ μάχαιρα; 36 καθὼς γέγραπται ὅτι ἕνεκεν σοῦ θανατούμεθα ὅλην τὴν ἡμέραν, ἐλογίσθημεν ὡς πρόβατα σφαγῆς. 37 ἀλλ᾽ ἐν τούτοις πᾶσιν ὑπερνικῶμεν διὰ τοῦ ἀγαπήσαντος ἡμᾶς. 38 πέπεισμαι γὰρ ὅτι οὔτε θάνατος οὔτε ζωὴ οὔτε ἄγγελοι οὔτε ἀρχαὶ οὔτε ἐνεστῶτα οὔτε μέλλοντα οὔτε δυνάμεις 39 οὔτε ὕψωμα οὔτε βάθος οὔτε τις κτίσις ἑτέρα δυνήσεται ἡμᾶς χωρίσαι ἀπὸ τῆς ἀγάπης τοῦ θεοῦ τῆς ἐν Χριστῷ Ἰησοῦ τῷ κυρίῳ ἡμῶν.

1 Cor 4:9–13

δοκῶ γάρ, ὁ θεὸς ἡμᾶς τοὺς ἀποστόλους ἐσχάτους ἀπέδειξεν ὡς ἐπιθανατίους, ὅτι θέατρον ἐγενήθημεν τῷ κόσμῳ καὶ ἀγγέλοις καὶ ἀνθρώποις. 10 ἡμεῖς μωροὶ διὰ Χριστόν, ὑμεῖς δὲ φρόνιμοι ἐν Χριστῷ· ἡμεῖς ἀσθενεῖς, ὑμεῖς δὲ ἰσχυροί· ὑμεῖς ἔνδοξοι, ἡμεῖς δὲ ἄτιμοι. 11 ἄχρι τῆς ἄρτι ὥρας καὶ πεινῶμεν καὶ διψῶμεν καὶ γυμνιτεύομεν καὶ κολαφιζόμεθα καὶ ἀστατοῦμεν 12 καὶ κοπιῶμεν ἐργαζόμενοι ταῖς ἰδίαις χερσίν· λοιδορούμενοι εὐλογοῦμεν, διωκόμενοι ἀνεχόμεθα, 13 δυσφημούμενοι παρακαλοῦμεν· ὡς περικαθάρματα τοῦ κόσμου ἐγενήθημεν, πάντων περίψημα ἕως ἄρτι.

2 Cor 4:7–12

Ἔχομεν δὲ τὸν θησαυρὸν τοῦτον ἐν ὀστρακίνοις σκεύεσιν, ἵνα ἡ ὑπερβολὴ τῆς δυνάμεως ᾖ τοῦ θεοῦ καὶ μὴ ἐξ ἡμῶν· 8 ἐν παντὶ θλιβόμενοι ἀλλ᾽ οὐ στενοχωρούμενοι, ἀπορούμενοι ἀλλ᾽ οὐκ ἐξαπορούμενοι, 9 διωκόμενοι ἀλλ᾽ οὐκ ἐγκαταλειπόμενοι, καταβαλλόμενοι ἀλλ᾽ οὐκ ἀπολλύμενοι, 10 πάντοτε τὴν νέκρωσιν τοῦ Ἰησοῦ ἐν τῷ σώματι περιφέροντες, ἵνα καὶ ἡ ζωὴ τοῦ Ἰησοῦ ἐν τῷ σώματι ἡμῶν φανερωθῇ. 11 ἀεὶ γὰρ ἡμεῖς οἱ ζῶντες εἰς θάνατον παραδιδόμεθα διὰ Ἰησοῦν, ἵνα καὶ ἡ ζωὴ τοῦ Ἰησοῦ φανερωθῇ ἐν τῇ θνητῇ σαρκὶ ἡμῶν. 12 ὥστε ὁ θάνατος ἐν ἡμῖν ἐνεργεῖται, ἡ δὲ ζωὴ ἐν ὑμῖν.

2 Cor 6:3–10

Μηδεμίαν ἐν μηδενὶ διδόντες προσκοπήν, ἵνα μὴ μωμηθῇ ἡ διακονία, 4 ἀλλ᾽ ἐν παντὶ συνιστάντες ἑαυτοὺς ὡς θεοῦ διάκονοι, ἐν ὑπομονῇ πολλῇ, ἐν θλίψεσιν, ἐν ἀνάγκαις, ἐν στενοχωρίαις, 5 ἐν πληγαῖς, ἐν φυλακαῖς, ἐν ἀκαταστασίαις, ἐν κόποις, ἐν ἀγρυπνίαις, ἐν νηστείαις, 6 ἐν ἁγνότητι, ἐν γνώσει, ἐν μακροθυμίᾳ, ἐν χρηστότητι, ἐν πνεύματι ἁγίῳ, ἐν ἀγάπῃ ἀνυποκρίτῳ, 7 ἐν λόγῳ ἀληθείας, ἐν δυνάμει θεοῦ· διὰ τῶν ὅπλων τῆς δικαιοσύνης τῶν δεξιῶν καὶ ἀριστερῶν, 8 διὰ δόξης καὶ ἀτιμίας, διὰ δυσφημίας καὶ εὐφημίας· ὡς πλάνοι καὶ ἀληθεῖς, 9 ὡς ἀγνοούμενοι καὶ ἐπιγινωσκόμενοι, ὡς ἀποθνῄσκοντες καὶ ἰδοὺ ζῶμεν, ὡς παιδευόμενοι καὶ μὴ θανατούμενοι, 10 ὡς λυπούμενοι ἀεὶ δὲ χαίροντες, ὡς πτωχοὶ πολλοὺς δὲ πλουτίζοντες, ὡς μηδὲν ἔχοντες καὶ πάντα κατέχοντες.

2 Cor 11:21b–33

Ἐν ᾧ δ᾽ ἄν τις τολμᾷ, ἐν ἀφροσύνῃ λέγω, τολμῶ κἀγώ. 22 Ἑβραῖοί εἰσιν; κἀγώ. Ἰσραηλῖταί εἰσιν; κἀγώ. σπέρμα Ἀβραάμ εἰσιν; κἀγώ. 23 διάκονοι Χριστοῦ εἰσιν; παραφρονῶν λαλῶ, ὑπὲρ ἐγώ· ἐν κόποις περισσοτέρως, ἐν φυλακαῖς περισσοτέρως, ἐν πληγαῖς ὑπερβαλλόντως, ἐν θανάτοις πολλάκις. 24 Ὑπὸ Ἰουδαίων πεντάκις τεσσεράκοντα παρὰ μίαν ἔλαβον, 25 τρὶς ἐρραβδίσθην, ἅπαξ ἐλιθάσθην, τρὶς ἐναυάγησα, νυχθήμερον ἐν τῷ βυθῷ πεποίηκα· 26 ὁδοιπορίαις πολλάκις, κινδύνοις ποταμῶν, κινδύνοις λῃστῶν, κινδύνοις ἐκ γένους, κινδύνοις ἐξ ἐθνῶν, κινδύνοις ἐν πόλει, κινδύνοις ἐν ἐρημίᾳ, κινδύνοις ἐν θαλάσσῃ, κινδύνοις ἐν ψευδαδέλφοις, 27 κόπῳ καὶ μόχθῳ, ἐν ἀγρυπνίαις πολλάκις, ἐν λιμῷ καὶ δίψει, ἐν νηστείαις πολλάκις, ἐν ψύχει καὶ γυμνότητι· 28 χωρὶς τῶν παρεκτὸς ἡ ἐπίστασίς μοι ἡ καθ᾽ ἡμέραν, ἡ μέριμνα πασῶν τῶν ἐκκλησιῶν. 29 τίς ἀσθενεῖ καὶ οὐκ ἀσθενῶ; τίς σκανδαλίζεται καὶ οὐκ ἐγὼ πυροῦμαι; 30 Εἰ καυχᾶσθαι δεῖ, τὰ τῆς ἀσθενείας μου καυχήσομαι. 31 ὁ θεὸς καὶ πατὴρ τοῦ κυρίου Ἰησοῦ οἶδεν,

1 Tim 6:5 *ευσεβειαν* ℵ A D* 048. 33. 1739. 1881] *add.* αφιστασο απο των τοιουτων D^2 *Byz*

and sinful, for the unholy and profane, for those who kill their father or mother, for murderers, 10 fornicators, sodomites, slave traders, liars, perjurers, and whatever else is contrary to the sound teaching 11 that conforms to the glorious gospel of the blessed God, which he entrusted to me.

1 Tim 6:3–5

Whoever teaches otherwise and does not agree with the sound words of our Lord Jesus Christ and the teaching that is in accordance with godliness, 4 is conceited, understanding nothing, and has a morbid craving for controversy and for disputes about words. From these come envy, dissension, slander, base suspicions, 5 and wrangling among those who are depraved in mind and bereft of the truth, imagining that godliness is a means of gain.[e]

2 Tim 3:2–5

For people will be lovers of themselves, lovers of money, boasters, arrogant, abusive, disobedient to their parents, ungrateful, unholy, 3 inhuman, implacable, slanderers, profligates, brutes, haters of good, 4 treacherous, reckless, swollen with conceit, lovers of pleasure rather than lovers of God, 5 holding to the outward form of godliness but denying its power. Avoid them!

Titus 3:3

For we ourselves were once foolish, disobedient, led astray, slaves to various passions and pleasures, passing our days in malice and envy, despicable, hating one another.

Cf. Rom 2:21–24; 2 Cor 11:19–21a; 1 Thess 2:3–6.

17. Hardship Catalogue

Rom 8:35–39

Who will separate us from the love of Christ? Will hardship, or distress, or persecution, or famine, or nakedness, or peril, or sword? 36 As it is written, "For your sake we are being killed all day long; we are accounted as sheep to be slaughtered." 37 No, in all these things we are more than conquerors through him who loved us. 38 For I am convinced that neither death, nor life, nor angels, nor rulers, nor things present, nor things to come, nor powers, 39 nor height, nor depth, nor anything else in all creation, will be able to separate us from the love of God in Christ Jesus our Lord.

1 Cor 4:9–13

For I think that God has exhibited us apostles as last of all, as though sentenced to death, because we have become a spectacle to the world, to angels and to mortals. 10 We are fools for the sake of Christ, but you are wise in Christ. We are weak, but you are strong. You are held in honor, but we in disrepute. 11 To the present hour we are hungry and thirsty, we are poorly clothed and beaten and homeless, 12 and we grow weary from the work of our own hands. When reviled, we bless; when persecuted, we endure; 13 when slandered, we speak kindly. We have become like the rubbish of the world, the dregs of all things, to this very day.

2 Cor 4:7–12

But we have this treasure in clay jars, so that it may be made clear that this extraordinary power belongs to God and does not come from us. 8 We are afflicted in every way, but not crushed; perplexed, but not driven to despair; 9 persecuted, but not forsaken; struck down, but not destroyed; 10 always carrying in the body the death of Jesus, so that the life of Jesus may also be made visible in our bodies. 11 For while we live, we are always being given up to death for Jesus' sake, so that the life of Jesus may be made visible in our mortal flesh. 12 So death is at work in us, but life in you.

2 Cor 6:3–10

We are putting no obstacle in anyone's way, so that no fault may be found with our ministry, 4 but as servants of God we have commended ourselves in every way: through great endurance, in afflictions, hardships, calamities, 5 beatings, imprisonments, riots, labors, sleepless nights, hunger; 6 by purity, knowledge, patience, kindness, holiness of spirit, genuine love, 7 truthful speech, and the power of God; with the weapons of righteousness for the right hand and for the left; 8 in honor and dishonor, in ill repute and good repute. We are treated as impostors, and yet are true; 9 as unknown, and yet are well known; as dying, and see—we are alive; as punished, and yet not killed; 10 as sorrowful, yet always rejoicing; as poor, yet making many rich; as having nothing, and yet possessing everything.

2 Cor 11:21b–33

But whatever anyone dares to boast of—I am speaking as a fool—I also dare to boast of that. 22 Are they Hebrews? So am I. Are they Israelites? So am I. Are they descendants of Abraham? So am I. 23 Are they ministers of Christ? I am talking like a madman—I am a better one: with far greater labors, far more imprisonments, with countless floggings, and often near death. 24 Five times I have received from the Jews the forty lashes minus one. 25 Three times I was beaten with rods. Once I received a stoning. Three times I was shipwrecked; for a night and a day I was adrift at sea; 26 on frequent journeys, in danger from rivers, danger from bandits, danger from my own people, danger from Gentiles, danger in the city, danger in the wilderness, danger at sea, danger from false brothers and sisters; 27 in toil and hardship, through many a sleepless night, hungry and thirsty, often without food, cold and naked. 28 And, besides other things, I am under daily pressure because of my anxiety for all the churches. 29 Who is weak, and I am not weak? Who is made to stumble, and I am not indignant? 30 If I must boast, I will boast of the things that show my weakness. 31 The God and Father of the Lord Jesus (blessed be he forever!)

[e] **1 Tim 6:5** *gain* Other ancient authorities add *Withdraw yourself from such people*

ὁ ὢν εὐλογητὸς εἰς τοὺς αἰῶνας, ὅτι οὐ
ψεύδομαι. 32 ἐν Δαμασκῷ ὁ ἐθνάρχης
Ἀρέτα τοῦ βασιλέως ἐφρούρει τὴν πόλιν
Δαμασκηνῶν πιάσαι ⸀με, 33 καὶ διὰ θυρίδος
ἐν σαργάνῃ ἐχαλάσθην διὰ τοῦ τείχους
καὶ ἐξέφυγον τὰς χεῖρας αὐτοῦ.

2 Cor 12:7–10

καὶ τῇ ὑπερβολῇ τῶν ἀποκαλύψεων.
⸀διὸ ἵνα μὴ ὑπεραίρωμαι, ἐδόθη μοι
σκόλοψ τῇ σαρκί, ἄγγελος σατανᾶ, ἵνα
με κολαφίζῃ, ⸂ἵνα μὴ ὑπεραίρωμαι⸃.
8 ὑπὲρ τούτου τρὶς τὸν κύριον παρεκάλεσα
ἵνα ἀποστῇ ἀπ᾽ ἐμοῦ. 9 καὶ εἴρηκέν μοι·
ἀρκεῖ σοι ἡ χάρις μου, ἡ γὰρ ⸀δύναμις
ἐν ἀσθενείᾳ τελεῖται. Ἥδιστα οὖν μᾶλ-
λον καυχήσομαι ἐν ταῖς ἀσθενείαις μου,
ἵνα ἐπισκηνώσῃ ἐπ᾽ ἐμὲ ἡ δύναμις τοῦ
Χριστοῦ. 10 διὸ εὐδοκῶ ἐν ἀσθενείαις,
ἐν ὕβρεσιν, ἐν ἀνάγκαις, ἐν διωγμοῖς
καὶ στενοχωρίαις, ὑπὲρ Χριστοῦ· ὅταν
γὰρ ἀσθενῶ, τότε δυνατός εἰμι.

2 Tim 3:10–11

Σὺ δὲ παρηκολούθησάς μου τῇ διδασκα-
λίᾳ, τῇ ἀγωγῇ, τῇ προθέσει, τῇ πίστει,
τῇ μακροθυμίᾳ, τῇ ἀγάπῃ, τῇ ὑπομονῇ,
11 τοῖς διωγμοῖς, τοῖς παθήμασιν, οἷά
μοι ἐγένετο ἐν Ἀντιοχείᾳ, ἐν Ἰκονίῳ, ἐν
Λύστροις, οἵους διωγμοὺς ὑπήνεγκα καὶ
ἐκ πάντων με ἐρρύσατο ὁ κύριος.

18. *Household Code* (Haustafel)

Eph 5:22–6:9

αἱ γυναῖκες τοῖς ἰδίοις ⸀ἀνδράσιν ὡς
τῷ κυρίῳ, 23 ὅτι ἀνήρ ἐστιν κεφαλὴ τῆς
γυναικὸς ὡς καὶ ὁ Χριστὸς κεφαλὴ τῆς
ἐκκλησίας, αὐτὸς σωτὴρ τοῦ σώματος·
24 ἀλλὰ ὡς ἡ ἐκκλησία ὑποτάσσεται τῷ
Χριστῷ, οὕτως καὶ αἱ γυναῖκες τοῖς ἀνδρά-
σιν ἐν παντί. 25 Οἱ ἄνδρες, ἀγαπᾶτε τὰς
γυναῖκας, καθὼς καὶ ὁ Χριστὸς ἠγάπησεν
τὴν ἐκκλησίαν καὶ ἑαυτὸν παρέδωκεν
ὑπὲρ αὐτῆς, 26 ἵνα αὐτὴν ἁγιάσῃ καθαρίσας
τῷ λουτρῷ τοῦ ὕδατος ἐν ῥήματι, 27 ἵνα
παραστήσῃ αὐτὸς ἑαυτῷ ἔνδοξον τὴν
ἐκκλησίαν, μὴ ἔχουσαν σπίλον ἢ ῥυτίδα
ἤ τι τῶν τοιούτων, ἀλλ᾽ ἵνα ᾖ ἁγία καὶ
ἄμωμος. 28 οὕτως ὀφείλουσιν [καὶ] οἱ
ἄνδρες ἀγαπᾶν τὰς ἑαυτῶν γυναῖκας ὡς
τὰ ἑαυτῶν σώματα. ὁ ἀγαπῶν τὴν ἑαυτοῦ
γυναῖκα ἑαυτὸν ἀγαπᾷ. 29 Οὐδεὶς γάρ
ποτε τὴν ἑαυτοῦ σάρκα ἐμίσησεν ἀλλὰ
ἐκτρέφει καὶ θάλπει αὐτήν, καθὼς καὶ
ὁ Χριστὸς τὴν ἐκκλησίαν, 30 ὅτι μέλη
ἐσμὲν τοῦ σώματος ⸀αὐτοῦ. 31 ἀντὶ τού-
του καταλείψει ἄνθρωπος [τὸν] πατέρα
καὶ [τὴν] μητέρα καὶ προσκολληθήσεται
πρὸς τὴν γυναῖκα αὐτοῦ, καὶ ἔσονται
οἱ δύο εἰς σάρκα μίαν. 32 τὸ μυστήριον
τοῦτο μέγα ἐστίν· ἐγὼ δὲ λέγω εἰς Χρι-
στὸν καὶ εἰς τὴν ἐκκλησίαν. 33 πλὴν καὶ
ὑμεῖς οἱ καθ᾽ ἕνα, ἕκαστος τὴν ἑαυτοῦ
γυναῖκα οὕτως ἀγαπάτω ὡς ἑαυτόν, ἡ
δὲ γυνὴ ἵνα φοβῆται τὸν ἄνδρα. **6** Τὰ
τέκνα, ὑπακούετε τοῖς γονεῦσιν ὑμῶν
⸂[ἐν κυρίῳ]⸃· τοῦτο γάρ ἐστιν δίκαιον.
2 τίμα τὸν πατέρα σου καὶ τὴν μητέρα, ἥτις
ἐστὶν ἐντολὴ πρώτη ἐν ἐπαγγελίᾳ, 3 ἵνα
εὖ σοι γένηται καὶ ἔσῃ μακροχρόνιος ἐπὶ
τῆς γῆς. 4 Καὶ οἱ πατέρες, μὴ παροργίζετε
τὰ τέκνα ὑμῶν ἀλλὰ ἐκτρέφετε αὐτὰ ἐν
παιδείᾳ καὶ νουθεσίᾳ κυρίου. 5 Οἱ δοῦ-
λοι, ὑπακούετε τοῖς κατὰ σάρκα κυρίοις
μετὰ φόβου καὶ τρόμου ἐν ἁπλότητι
τῆς καρδίας ὑμῶν ὡς τῷ Χριστῷ, 6 μὴ
κατ᾽ ὀφθαλμοδουλίαν ὡς ἀνθρωπάρε-
σκοι ἀλλ᾽ ὡς δοῦλοι Χριστοῦ ποιοῦντες
τὸ θέλημα τοῦ θεοῦ ἐκ ψυχῆς, 7 μετ᾽
εὐνοίας δουλεύοντες ὡς τῷ κυρίῳ καὶ
οὐκ ἀνθρώποις, 8 εἰδότες ὅτι ἕκαστος
ἐάν τι ποιήσῃ ἀγαθόν, τοῦτο κομίσεται
παρὰ κυρίου εἴτε δοῦλος εἴτε ἐλεύθερος.
9 Καὶ οἱ κύριοι, τὰ αὐτὰ ποιεῖτε πρὸς
αὐτούς, ἀνιέντες τὴν ἀπειλήν, εἰδότες
ὅτι καὶ αὐτῶν καὶ ὑμῶν ὁ κύριός ἐστιν
ἐν οὐρανοῖς καὶ προσωπολημψία οὐκ
ἔστιν παρ᾽ αὐτῷ.

Col 3:18–4:1

Αἱ γυναῖκες, ὑποτάσσεσθε τοῖς ἀνδράσιν
ὡς ἀνῆκεν ἐν κυρίῳ. 19 Οἱ ἄνδρες, ἀγα-
πᾶτε τὰς γυναῖκας καὶ μὴ πικραίνεσθε
πρὸς αὐτάς. 20 Τὰ τέκνα, ὑπακούετε τοῖς
γονεῦσιν κατὰ πάντα, τοῦτο γὰρ εὐάρεστόν
ἐστιν ἐν κυρίῳ. 21 Οἱ πατέρες, μὴ ἐρεθίζετε
τὰ τέκνα ὑμῶν, ἵνα μὴ ἀθυμῶσιν. 22 Οἱ
δοῦλοι, ὑπακούετε κατὰ πάντα τοῖς κατὰ
σάρκα κυρίοις, μὴ ἐν ὀφθαλμοδουλίᾳ
ὡς ἀνθρωπάρεσκοι, ἀλλ᾽ ἐν ἁπλότητι
καρδίας φοβούμενοι τὸν κύριον. 23 ὃ
ἐὰν ποιῆτε, ἐκ ψυχῆς ἐργάζεσθε ὡς τῷ
κυρίῳ καὶ οὐκ ἀνθρώποις, 24 εἰδότες ὅτι
ἀπὸ κυρίου ἀπολήμψεσθε τὴν ἀνταπόδο-
σιν τῆς κληρονομίας. τῷ κυρίῳ Χριστῷ
δουλεύετε· 25 ὁ γὰρ ἀδικῶν κομίσεται ὃ
ἠδίκησεν, καὶ οὐκ ἔστιν προσωπολημψία.
4 Οἱ κύριοι, τὸ δίκαιον καὶ τὴν ἰσότητα
τοῖς δούλοις παρέχεσθε, εἰδότες ὅτι καὶ
ὑμεῖς ἔχετε κύριον ἐν οὐρανῷ.

Titus 2:2–10

Πρεσβύτας νηφαλίους εἶναι, σεμνούς,
σώφρονας, ὑγιαίνοντας τῇ πίστει, τῇ
ἀγάπῃ, τῇ ὑπομονῇ· 3 πρεσβύτιδας ὡσαύ-
τως ἐν καταστήματι ἱεροπρεπεῖς, μὴ δι-
αβόλους μὴ οἴνῳ πολλῷ δεδουλωμένας,
καλοδιδασκάλους, 4 ἵνα σωφρονίζωσιν
τὰς νέας φιλάνδρους εἶναι, φιλοτέκνους
5 σώφρονας ἁγνὰς οἰκουργοὺς ἀγαθάς,
ὑποτασσομένας τοῖς ἰδίοις ἀνδράσιν, ἵνα
μὴ ὁ λόγος τοῦ θεοῦ βλασφημῆται. 6 Τοὺς
νεωτέρους ὡσαύτως παρακάλει σωφρο-
νεῖν 7 περὶ πάντα, σεαυτὸν παρεχόμενος
τύπον καλῶν ἔργων, ἐν τῇ διδασκαλίᾳ
ἀφθορίαν, σεμνότητα, 8 λόγον ὑγιῆ ἀκα-
τάγνωστον, ἵνα ὁ ἐξ ἐναντίας ἐντραπῇ
μηδὲν ἔχων λέγειν περὶ ἡμῶν φαῦλον.
9 Δούλους ἰδίοις δεσπόταις ὑποτάσσεσθαι
ἐν πᾶσιν, εὐαρέστους εἶναι, μὴ ἀντι-
λέγοντας, 10 μὴ νοσφιζομένους, ἀλλὰ
πᾶσαν πίστιν ἐνδεικνυμένους ἀγαθήν,
ἵνα τὴν διδασκαλίαν τὴν τοῦ σωτῆρος
ἡμῶν θεοῦ κοσμῶσιν ἐν πᾶσιν.

§ 17 **2 Cor 11:32** ***με*** B D*] *add.* θελων ℵ D^{2} 33. (1739). 1881 *Byz* **2 Cor 12:7** ***διο*** ℵ A B 33. 1739] *om.* 𝔓^{46} D 1881 *Byz* **•** ***ινα μη υπεραιρωμαι*** 𝔓^{46} ℵ^{2} B I^{vid} 1739. (1881) *Byz*] *om.* ℵ* A D 33 **2 Cor 12:9** ***δυναμις*** 𝔓^{46vid} ℵ* A* B D*] *add.* μου ℵ^{2} A^{c} D^{1} 33. 1739. 1881 *Byz* **§ 18** **Eph 5:22** ***ανδρασιν*** 𝔓^{46} B] *add.* υποτασσεσθωσαν ℵ A I 33. 1739. 1881 ¦ *add.* υποτασσεσθε (D) *Byz* **Eph 5:30** ***αυτου*** 𝔓^{46} ℵ* A B 048. 33. 1739*. 1881] *add.* εκ της σαρκος αυτου και εκ των οστεων αυτου ℵ^{2} D 1739^{mg} *Byz* **Eph 6:1** ***εν κυριω*** 𝔓^{46} ℵ A D^{1} I^{vid} 33. 1739. 1881 *Byz*] *om.* B D*

knows that I do not lie. **32** In Damascus, the governor under King Aretas guarded the city of Damascus in order to[a] seize me, **33** but I was let down in a basket through a window in the wall, and escaped from his hands.

2 Cor 12:7–10

even considering the exceptional character of the revelations. Therefore, to keep[b] me from being too elated, a thorn was given me in the flesh, a messenger of Satan to torment me, to keep me from being too elated.[c] **8** Three times I appealed to the Lord about this, that it would leave me, **9** but he said to me, "My grace is sufficient for you, for power[d] is made perfect in weakness." So, I will boast all the more gladly of my weaknesses, so that the power of Christ may dwell in me. **10** Therefore I am content with weaknesses, insults, hardships, persecutions, and calamities for the sake of Christ; for whenever I am weak, then I am strong.

2 Tim 3:10–11

Now you have observed my teaching, my conduct, my aim in life, my faith, my patience, my love, my steadfastness, **11** my persecutions, and my suffering the things that happened to me in Antioch, Iconium, and Lystra. What persecutions I endured! Yet the Lord rescued me from all of them.

18. Household Code (Haustafel)

Eph 5:22–6:9

Wives, be subject[a] to your husbands as you are to the Lord. **23** For the husband is the head of the wife just as Christ is the head of the church, the body of which he is the Savior. **24** Just as the church is subject to Christ, so also wives ought to be, in everything, to their husbands. **25** Husbands, love your wives, just as Christ loved the church and gave himself up for her, **26** in order to make her holy by cleansing her with the washing of water by the word, **27** so as to present the church to himself in splendor, without a spot or wrinkle or anything of the kind—yes, so that she may be holy and without blemish. **28** In the same way, husbands should love their wives as they do their own bodies. He who loves his wife loves himself. **29** For no one ever hates his own body, but he nourishes and tenderly cares for it, just as Christ does for the church, **30** because we are members of his body.[b] **31** "For this reason a man will leave his father and mother and be joined to his wife, and the two will become one flesh." **32** This is a great mystery, and I am applying it to Christ and the church. **33** Each of you, however, should love his wife as himself, and a wife should respect her husband. **6** Children, obey your parents in the Lord,[c] for this is right. **2** "Honor your father and mother"—this is the first commandment with a promise: **3** "so that it may be well with you and you may live long on the earth." **4** And, fathers, do not provoke your children to anger, but bring them up in the discipline and instruction of the Lord. **5** Slaves, obey your earthly masters with fear and trembling, in singleness of heart, as you obey Christ; **6** not only while being watched, and in order to please them, but as slaves of Christ, doing the will of God from the heart. **7** Render service with enthusiasm, as to the Lord and not to men and women, **8** knowing that whatever good we do, we will receive the same again from the Lord, whether we are slaves or free. **9** And, masters, do the same to them. Stop threatening them, for you know that both of you have the same Master in heaven, and with him there is no partiality.

Col 3:18–4:1

Wives, be subject to your husbands, as is fitting in the Lord. **19** Husbands, love your wives and never treat them harshly. **20** Children, obey your parents in everything, for this is your acceptable duty in the Lord. **21** Fathers, do not provoke your children, or they may lose heart. **22** Slaves, obey your earthly masters in everything, not only while being watched and in order to please them, but wholeheartedly, fearing the Lord. **23** Whatever your task, put yourselves into it, as done for the Lord and not for your masters, **24** since you know that from the Lord you will receive the inheritance as your reward; you serve the Lord Christ. **25** For the wrongdoer will be paid back for whatever wrong has been done, and there is no partiality. **4** Masters, treat your slaves justly and fairly, for you know that you also have a Master in heaven.

Titus 2:2–10

Tell the older men to be temperate, serious, prudent, and sound in faith, in love, and in endurance. **3** Likewise, tell the older women to be reverent in behavior, not to be slanderers or slaves to drink; they are to teach what is good, **4** so that they may encourage the young women to love their husbands, to love their children, **5** to be self-controlled, chaste, good managers of the household, kind, being submissive to their husbands, so that the word of God may not be discredited. **6** Likewise, urge the younger men to be self-controlled. **7** Show yourself in all respects a model of good works, and in your teaching show integrity, gravity, **8** and sound speech that cannot be censured; then any opponent will be put to shame, having nothing evil to say of us. **9** Tell slaves to be submissive to their masters and to give satisfaction in every respect; they are not to talk back, **10** not to pilfer, but to show complete and perfect fidelity, so that in everything they may be an ornament to the doctrine of God our Savior.

§ 17 [a] **2 Cor 11:32** ***in order to*** Other ancient authorities read *and wanted to* [b] **2 Cor 12:7** ***Therefore, to keep*** Other ancient authorities read *To keep* [c] **2 Cor 12:7** ***to keep me from being too elated*** Other ancient authorities lack *to keep me from being too elated* [d] **2 Cor 12:9** ***power*** Other ancient authorities read *my power* **§ 18** [a] **Eph 5:22** ***Wives, be subject*** Other ancient authorities read *Wives should be subject* [b] **Eph 5:30** ***of his body*** Other ancient authorities add *of his flesh and of his bones* [c] **Eph 6:1** ***in the Lord*** Other ancient authorities lack *in the Lord*

19. Doxology

Rom 1:25

οἵτινες μετήλλαξαν τὴν ἀλήθειαν τοῦ θεοῦ ἐν τῷ ψεύδει καὶ ἐσεβάσθησαν καὶ ἐλάτρευσαν τῇ κτίσει παρὰ τὸν κτίσαντα, ὅς ἐστιν εὐλογητὸς εἰς τοὺς αἰῶνας, ἀμήν.

Rom 9:4–5

οἵτινές εἰσιν Ἰσραηλῖται, ὧν ἡ υἱοθεσία
καὶ ἡ δόξα καὶ ⸂αἱ διαθῆκαι⸃ καὶ ἡ νο-
μοθεσία καὶ ἡ λατρεία καὶ αἱ ἐπαγγελίαι,
5 ὧν οἱ πατέρες καὶ ἐξ ὧν ὁ Χριστὸς τὸ
κατὰ σάρκα, ὁ ὢν ἐπὶ πάντων θεὸς εὐλο-
γητὸς εἰς τοὺς αἰῶνας, ἀμήν.

Rom 11:33–36

Ὦ βάθος πλούτου καὶ σοφίας καὶ γνώ-
σεως θεοῦ· ὡς ἀνεξεραύνητα τὰ κρί-
ματα αὐτοῦ καὶ ἀνεξιχνίαστοι αἱ ὁδοὶ
αὐτοῦ. **34** τίς γὰρ ἔγνω νοῦν κυρίου; ἢ
τίς σύμβουλος αὐτοῦ ἐγένετο; **35** ἢ τίς
προέδωκεν αὐτῷ, καὶ ἀνταποδοθήσε-
ται αὐτῷ; **36** ὅτι ἐξ αὐτοῦ καὶ δι᾽ αὐτοῦ
καὶ εἰς αὐτὸν τὰ πάντα· αὐτῷ ἡ δόξα εἰς
τοὺς αἰῶνας, ἀμήν.

Rom 16:25–27

⸂[Τῷ δὲ δυναμένῳ ὑμᾶς στηρίξαι κατὰ
τὸ εὐαγγέλιόν μου καὶ τὸ κήρυγμα Ἰη-
σοῦ Χριστοῦ, κατὰ ἀποκάλυψιν μυστη-
ρίου χρόνοις αἰωνίοις σεσιγημένου,
26 φανερωθέντος δὲ νῦν διά τε γραφῶν
προφητικῶν κατ᾽ ἐπιταγὴν τοῦ αἰωνίου
θεοῦ εἰς ὑπακοὴν πίστεως εἰς πάντα τὰ
ἔθνη γνωρισθέντος, **27** μόνῳ σοφῷ θεῷ,
διὰ Ἰησοῦ Χριστοῦ, ⸀ᾧ ἡ δόξα εἰς τοὺς
⸀αἰῶνας, ἀμήν.]⸃

2 Cor 11:31

ὁ θεὸς καὶ πατὴρ τοῦ κυρίου Ἰησοῦ οἶδεν, ὁ ὢν εὐλογητὸς εἰς τοὺς αἰῶνας, ὅτι οὐ ψεύδομαι.

Gal 1:3–5

χάρις ὑμῖν καὶ εἰρήνη ἀπὸ θεοῦ πατρὸς
ἡμῶν καὶ κυρίου Ἰησοῦ Χριστοῦ **4** τοῦ
δόντος ἑαυτὸν ὑπὲρ τῶν ἁμαρτιῶν ἡμῶν,
ὅπως ἐξέληται ἡμᾶς ἐκ τοῦ αἰῶνος τοῦ
ἐνεστῶτος πονηροῦ κατὰ τὸ θέλημα τοῦ
θεοῦ καὶ πατρὸς ἡμῶν, **5** ᾧ ἡ δόξα εἰς
τοὺς αἰῶνας τῶν αἰώνων, ἀμήν.

Eph 3:20–21

Τῷ δὲ δυναμένῳ ὑπὲρ πάντα ποιῆσαι
ὑπερεκπερισσοῦ ὧν αἰτούμεθα ἢ νοοῦμεν
κατὰ τὴν δύναμιν τὴν ἐνεργουμένην ἐν
ἡμῖν, **21** αὐτῷ ἡ δόξα ἐν τῇ ἐκκλησίᾳ καὶ
ἐν Χριστῷ Ἰησοῦ εἰς πάσας τὰς γενεὰς
τοῦ αἰῶνος τῶν αἰώνων, ἀμήν.

Eph 4:4–6

Ἓν σῶμα καὶ ἓν πνεῦμα, καθὼς καὶ ἐκλή-
θητε ἐν μιᾷ ἐλπίδι τῆς κλήσεως ὑμῶν·
5 εἷς κύριος, μία πίστις, ἓν βάπτισμα, **6** εἷς
θεὸς καὶ πατὴρ πάντων, ὁ ἐπὶ πάντων
καὶ διὰ πάντων καὶ ἐν πᾶσιν.

Phil 4:20

τῷ δὲ θεῷ καὶ πατρὶ ἡμῶν ἡ δόξα εἰς τοὺς αἰῶνας τῶν αἰώνων, ἀμήν.

1 Tim 1:17

Τῷ δὲ βασιλεῖ τῶν αἰώνων, ἀφθάρτῳ ἀοράτῳ μόνῳ θεῷ, τιμὴ καὶ δόξα εἰς τοὺς αἰῶνας τῶν αἰώνων, ἀμήν.

1 Tim 6:13–16

παραγγέλλω [σοι] ἐνώπιον τοῦ θεοῦ τοῦ
ζῳογονοῦντος τὰ πάντα καὶ Χριστοῦ
Ἰησοῦ τοῦ μαρτυρήσαντος ἐπὶ Ποντίου
Πιλάτου τὴν καλὴν ὁμολογίαν, **14** τηρῆσαί
σε τὴν ἐντολὴν ἄσπιλον ἀνεπίλημπτον
μέχρι τῆς ἐπιφανείας τοῦ κυρίου ἡμῶν
Ἰησοῦ Χριστοῦ, **15** ἣν καιροῖς ἰδίοις δεί-
ξει ὁ μακάριος καὶ μόνος δυνάστης, ὁ
βασιλεὺς τῶν βασιλευόντων καὶ κύριος
τῶν κυριευόντων, **16** ὁ μόνος ἔχων ἀθα-
νασίαν, φῶς οἰκῶν ἀπρόσιτον, ὃν εἶδεν
οὐδεὶς ἀνθρώπων οὐδὲ ἰδεῖν δύναται· ᾧ
τιμὴ καὶ κράτος αἰώνιον, ἀμήν.

2 Tim 4:18

ῥύσεταί με ὁ κύριος ἀπὸ παντὸς ἔργου πονηροῦ καὶ σώσει εἰς τὴν βασιλείαν αὐτοῦ τὴν ἐπουράνιον· ᾧ ἡ δόξα εἰς τοὺς αἰῶνας τῶν αἰώνων, ἀμήν.

20. Summaries of the Faith

Rom 1:3–4

περὶ τοῦ υἱοῦ αὐτοῦ τοῦ γενομένου ἐκ
σπέρματος Δαυὶδ κατὰ σάρκα, **4** τοῦ ὁρι-
σθέντος υἱοῦ θεοῦ ἐν δυνάμει κατὰ πνεῦμα
ἁγιωσύνης ἐξ ἀναστάσεως νεκρῶν, Ἰησοῦ
Χριστοῦ τοῦ κυρίου ἡμῶν

Rom 4:24–25

ἀλλὰ καὶ δι᾽ ἡμᾶς, οἷς μέλλει λογίζεσθαι,
τοῖς πιστεύουσιν ἐπὶ τὸν ἐγείραντα Ἰη-
σοῦν τὸν κύριον ἡμῶν ἐκ νεκρῶν, **25** ὃς
παρεδόθη διὰ τὰ παραπτώματα ἡμῶν καὶ
ἠγέρθη διὰ τὴν δικαίωσιν ἡμῶν.

Rom 8:34

τίς ὁ κατακρινῶν; Χριστὸς [Ἰησοῦς] ὁ ἀποθανών, μᾶλλον δὲ ⸀ἐγερθείς, ὅς καί ἐστιν ἐν δεξιᾷ τοῦ θεοῦ, ὃς καὶ ἐντυγχάνει ὑπὲρ ἡμῶν.

1 Cor 8:6

ἀλλ᾽ ἡμῖν εἷς θεὸς ὁ πατὴρ ἐξ οὗ τὰ πάντα καὶ ἡμεῖς εἰς αὐτόν, καὶ εἷς κύριος Ἰησοῦς Χριστὸς δι᾽ οὗ τὰ πάντα καὶ ἡμεῖς δι᾽ αὐτοῦ.

1 Cor 11:23–25

Ἐγὼ γὰρ παρέλαβον ἀπὸ τοῦ κυρίου, ὃ
καὶ παρέδωκα ὑμῖν, ὅτι ὁ κύριος Ἰησοῦς
ἐν τῇ νυκτὶ ᾗ παρεδίδετο ἔλαβεν ἄρτον
24 καὶ εὐχαριστήσας ἔκλασεν καὶ εἶπεν·
τοῦτό μού ἐστιν τὸ σῶμα τὸ ὑπὲρ ⸀ὑμῶν·
τοῦτο ποιεῖτε εἰς τὴν ἐμὴν ἀνάμνησιν.
25 ὡσαύτως καὶ τὸ ποτήριον μετὰ τὸ
δειπνῆσαι λέγων· τοῦτο τὸ ποτήριον ἡ

§ 19 **Rom 9:4** ***αι διαθηκαι*** ℵ C 33. 1739. 1881 *Byz*] η διαθηκη 𝔓^{46} B D **Rom 16:25–27** *pon. hic* 𝔓^{61} ℵ B C D 1739] *pon. hic et p.* 14:23 A 33 ¦ *pon. p.* 14:23 *Byz* ¦ *pon. p.* 15:33 𝔓^{46} ¦ *om. pc* **Rom 16:27** ***ω*** 𝔓^{46} ℵ A C D 33. 1739. 1881 *Byz*] *om.* B • ***αιωνας*** 𝔓^{46} B C 33. 1739. 1881 *Byz*] *add.* των αιωνων 𝔓^{61} ℵ A D **§ 20** **Rom 8:34** ***εγερθεις*** 𝔓^{27vid} 𝔓^{46} ℵ^{2} B D 1739. 1881 *Byz*] *add.* εκ νεκρων ℵ* A C 33 **1 Cor 11:24** ***υμων*** 𝔓^{46} ℵ* A B C* 33. 1739*] *add.* κλωμενον ℵ^{2} C^{3} D^{2} 1739^{mg}. 1881 *Byz* ¦ *add.* θρυπτομενον D*

19. Doxology

Rom 1:25

because they exchanged the truth about God for a lie and worshiped and served the creature rather than the Creator, who is blessed forever! Amen.

Rom 9:4–5

They are Israelites, and to them belong the adoption, the glory, the covenants,[a] the giving of the law, the worship, and the promises; **5** to them belong the patriarchs, and from them, according to the flesh, comes the Messiah, who is over all, God blessed forever. Amen.

Rom 11:33–36

O the depth of the riches and wisdom and knowledge of God! How unsearchable are his judgments and how inscrutable his ways! **34** "For who has known the mind of the Lord? Or who has been his counselor?" **35** "Or who has given a gift to him, to receive a gift in return?" **36** For from him and through him and to him are all things. To him be the glory forever. Amen.

Rom 16:25–27

Now to God who is able to strengthen you according to my gospel and the proclamation of Jesus Christ, according to the revelation of the mystery that was kept secret for long ages **26** but is now disclosed, and through the prophetic writings is made known to all the Gentiles, according to the command of the eternal God, to bring about the obedience of faith— **27** to the only wise God, through Jesus Christ, to whom[b] be the glory forever![c] Amen.[d]

2 Cor 11:31

The God and Father of the Lord Jesus (blessed be he forever!) knows that I do not lie.

Gal 1:3–5

Grace to you and peace from God our Father and the Lord Jesus Christ, **4** who gave himself for our sins to set us free from the present evil age, according to the will of our God and Father, **5** to whom be the glory forever and ever. Amen.

Eph 3:20–21

Now to him who by the power at work within us is able to accomplish abundantly far more than all we can ask or imagine, **21** to him be glory in the church and in Christ Jesus to all generations, forever and ever. Amen.

Eph 4:4–6

There is one body and one Spirit, just as you were called to the one hope of your calling, **5** one Lord, one faith, one baptism, **6** one God and Father of all, who is above all and through all and in all.

Phil 4:20

To our God and Father be glory forever and ever. Amen.

1 Tim 1:17

To the King of the ages, immortal, invisible, the only God, be honor and glory forever and ever. Amen.

1 Tim 6:13–16

In the presence of God, who gives life to all things, and of Christ Jesus, who in his testimony before Pontius Pilate made the good confession, I charge you **14** to keep the commandment without spot or blame until the manifestation of our Lord Jesus Christ, **15** which he will bring about at the right time—he who is the blessed and only Sovereign, the King of kings and Lord of lords. **16** It is he alone who has immortality and dwells in unapproachable light, whom no one has ever seen or can see; to him be honor and eternal dominion. Amen.

2 Tim 4:18

The Lord will rescue me from every evil attack and save me for his heavenly kingdom. To him be the glory forever and ever. Amen.

20. Summaries of the Faith

Rom 1:3–4

the gospel concerning his Son, who was descended from David according to the flesh **4** and was declared to be Son of God with power according to the Spirit[a] of holiness by resurrection from the dead, Jesus Christ our Lord

Rom 4:24–25

but for ours also. It will be reckoned to us who believe in him who raised Jesus our Lord from the dead, **25** who was handed over to death for our trespasses and was raised for our justification.

Rom 8:34

Who is to condemn? It is Christ Jesus, who died, yes, who was raised,[b] who is at the right hand of God, who indeed intercedes for us.

1 Cor 8:6

yet for us there is one God, the Father, from whom are all things and for whom we exist, and one Lord, Jesus Christ, through whom are all things and through whom we exist.

1 Cor 11:23–25

For I received from the Lord what I also handed on to you, that the Lord Jesus on the night when he was betrayed took a loaf of bread, **24** and when he had given thanks, he broke it and said, "This is my body that is for[c] you. Do this in remembrance of me." **25** In the same way he took the cup also, after supper,

§ 19 [a] **Rom 9:4** ***the covenants*** Other ancient authorities read *the covenant* [b] **Rom 16:27** ***to whom*** A few ancient authorities lack *to whom*. The verse then reads, *to the only wise God be the glory through Jesus Christ forever. Amen.* [c] **Rom 16:27** ***forever*** Other ancient authorities read *forever and ever* [d] **Rom 16:27** ***Amen*** Other ancient authorities include 16:25–27 after 14:23 or 15:33; a few lack these verses altogether **§ 20** [a] **Rom 1:4** ***Spirit*** NRSV alternate translation [b] **Rom 8:34** ***raised*** Other ancient authorities add *from the dead* [c] **1 Cor 11:24** ***is for*** Other ancient authorities read *is broken for*

καινὴ διαθήκη ἐστὶν ἐν τῷ ἐμῷ αἵματι· τοῦτο ποιεῖτε, ὁσάκις ἐὰν πίνητε, εἰς τὴν ἐμὴν ἀνάμνησιν.

1 Cor 15:1–11

Γνωρίζω δὲ ὑμῖν, ἀδελφοί, τὸ εὐαγγέλιον ὃ εὐηγγελισάμην ὑμῖν, ὃ καὶ παρελάβετε, ἐν ᾧ καὶ ἑστήκατε, 2 δι’ οὗ καὶ σῴζεσθε, τίνι λόγῳ εὐηγγελισάμην ὑμῖν εἰ κατέχετε, ἐκτὸς εἰ μὴ εἰκῇ ἐπιστεύσατε. 3 παρέδωκα γὰρ ὑμῖν ἐν πρώτοις, ὃ καὶ παρέλαβον, ὅτι Χριστὸς ἀπέθανεν ὑπὲρ τῶν ἁμαρτιῶν ἡμῶν κατὰ τὰς γραφὰς 4 καὶ ὅτι ἐτάφη καὶ ὅτι ἐγήγερται τῇ ἡμέρᾳ τῇ τρίτῃ κατὰ τὰς γραφὰς 5 καὶ ὅτι ὤφθη Κηφᾷ εἶτα τοῖς δώδεκα· 6 ἔπειτα ὤφθη ἐπάνω πεντακοσίοις ἀδελφοῖς ἐφάπαξ, ἐξ ὧν οἱ πλείονες μένουσιν ἕως ἄρτι, τινὲς δὲ ἐκοιμήθησαν· 7 ἔπειτα ὤφθη Ἰακώβῳ εἶτα τοῖς ἀποστόλοις πᾶσιν· 8 ἔσχατον δὲ πάντων ὡσπερεὶ τῷ ἐκτρώματι ὤφθη κἀμοί. 9 Ἐγὼ γάρ εἰμι ὁ ἐλάχιστος τῶν ἀποστόλων ὃς οὐκ εἰμὶ ἱκανὸς καλεῖσθαι ἀπόστολος, διότι ἐδίωξα τὴν ἐκκλησίαν τοῦ θεοῦ· 10 χάριτι δὲ θεοῦ εἰμι ὅ εἰμι, καὶ ἡ χάρις αὐτοῦ ἡ εἰς ἐμὲ οὐ κενὴ ἐγενήθη, ἀλλὰ περισσότερον αὐτῶν πάντων ἐκοπίασα, οὐκ ἐγὼ δὲ ἀλλὰ ἡ χάρις τοῦ θεοῦ [ἡ] σὺν ἐμοί. 11 εἴτε οὖν ἐγὼ εἴτε ἐκεῖνοι, οὕτως κηρύσσομεν καὶ οὕτως ἐπιστεύσατε.

1 Thess 1:9–10

αὐτοὶ γὰρ περὶ ἡμῶν ἀπαγγέλλουσιν ὁποίαν εἴσοδον ἔσχομεν πρὸς ὑμᾶς, καὶ πῶς ἐπεστρέψατε πρὸς τὸν θεὸν ἀπὸ τῶν εἰδώλων δουλεύειν θεῷ ζῶντι καὶ ἀληθινῷ 10 καὶ ἀναμένειν τὸν υἱὸν αὐτοῦ ἐκ τῶν οὐρανῶν, ὃν ἤγειρεν ἐκ [τῶν] νεκρῶν, Ἰησοῦν τὸν ῥυόμενον ἡμᾶς ἐκ τῆς ὀργῆς τῆς ἐρχομένης.

1 Thess 4:14

εἰ γὰρ πιστεύομεν ὅτι Ἰησοῦς ἀπέθανεν καὶ ἀνέστη, οὕτως καὶ ὁ θεὸς τοὺς κοιμηθέντας διὰ τοῦ Ἰησοῦ ἄξει σὺν αὐτῷ.

1 Tim 2:5–6

Εἷς γὰρ θεός, εἷς καὶ μεσίτης θεοῦ καὶ ἀνθρώπων, ἄνθρωπος Χριστὸς Ἰησοῦς, 6 ὁ δοὺς ἑαυτὸν ἀντίλυτρον ὑπὲρ πάντων, τὸ μαρτύριον καιροῖς ἰδίοις.

1 Tim 3:16

καὶ ὁμολογουμένως μέγα ἐστὶν τὸ τῆς εὐσεβείας μυστήριον· ⸀ὃς ἐφανερώθη ἐν σαρκί, ἐδικαιώθη ἐν πνεύματι, ὤφθη ἀγγέλοις, ἐκηρύχθη ἐν ἔθνεσιν, ἐπιστεύθη ἐν κόσμῳ, ἀνελήμφθη ἐν δόξῃ.

2 Tim 2:8

Μνημόνευε Ἰησοῦν Χριστὸν ἐγηγερμένον ἐκ νεκρῶν, ἐκ σπέρματος Δαυίδ, κατὰ τὸ εὐαγγέλιόν μου

Cf. Rom 10:8–10; 14:9; 1 Cor 12:3; Eph 4:4–6; Phil 2:5–11; Col 1:15–20; 1 Thess 5:9–10; 1 Tim 6:13–14; 2 Tim 1:9–10; 4:1; Titus 2:11–14; 3:4–7; Acts 13:27–33.

In § 20 above are given the explicit confessional formulas identified in the Pauline corpus; for proposed tacit quotations, full or partial, of early Christian creeds and liturgical materials, see § 21 Proposed Creedal Fragments and § 22 Proposed Hymn Fragments. For references in the Pauline letters to the body of Christian teaching, see § 108 The Pattern of Teaching.

21. Proposed Creedal Fragments

Rom 1:3–4

περὶ τοῦ υἱοῦ αὐτοῦ τοῦ γενομένου ἐκ σπέρματος Δαυὶδ κατὰ σάρκα, 4 τοῦ ὁρισθέντος υἱοῦ θεοῦ ἐν δυνάμει κατὰ πνεῦμα ἁγιωσύνης ἐξ ἀναστάσεως νεκρῶν, Ἰησοῦ Χριστοῦ τοῦ κυρίου ἡμῶν

Rom 4:24–25

ἀλλὰ καὶ δι’ ἡμᾶς, οἷς μέλλει λογίζεσθαι, τοῖς πιστεύουσιν ἐπὶ τὸν ἐγείραντα Ἰησοῦν τὸν κύριον ἡμῶν ἐκ νεκρῶν, 25 ὃς παρεδόθη διὰ τὰ παραπτώματα ἡμῶν καὶ ἠγέρθη διὰ τὴν δικαίωσιν ἡμῶν.

Rom 8:34

τίς ὁ κατακρινῶν; Χριστὸς [Ἰησοῦς] ὁ ἀποθανών, μᾶλλον δὲ ⸀ἐγερθείς, ὃς καί ἐστιν ἐν δεξιᾷ τοῦ θεοῦ, ὃς καὶ ἐντυγχάνει ὑπὲρ ἡμῶν.

Rom 10:8–10

ἀλλὰ τί λέγει; ἐγγύς σου τὸ ῥῆμά ἐστιν ἐν τῷ στόματί σου καὶ ἐν τῇ καρδίᾳ σου, τοῦτ’ ἔστιν τὸ ῥῆμα τῆς πίστεως ὃ κηρύσσομεν. 9 ὅτι ἐὰν ὁμολογήσῃς ἐν τῷ στόματί σου κύριον Ἰησοῦν καὶ πιστεύσῃς ἐν τῇ καρδίᾳ σου ὅτι ὁ θεὸς αὐτὸν ἤγειρεν ἐκ νεκρῶν, σωθήσῃ· 10 καρδίᾳ γὰρ πιστεύεται εἰς δικαιοσύνην, στόματι δὲ ὁμολογεῖται εἰς σωτηρίαν.

1 Cor 8:6

ἀλλ’ ἡμῖν εἷς θεὸς ὁ πατὴρ ἐξ οὗ τὰ πάντα καὶ ἡμεῖς εἰς αὐτόν, καὶ εἷς κύριος Ἰησοῦς Χριστὸς δι’ οὗ τὰ πάντα καὶ ἡμεῖς δι’ αὐτοῦ.

1 Cor 12:3

διὸ γνωρίζω ὑμῖν ὅτι οὐδεὶς ἐν πνεύματι θεοῦ λαλῶν λέγει· Ἀνάθεμα Ἰησοῦς, καὶ οὐδεὶς δύναται εἰπεῖν· Κύριος Ἰησοῦς, εἰ μὴ ἐν πνεύματι ἁγίῳ.

Eph 4:4–6

Ἓν σῶμα καὶ ἓν πνεῦμα, καθὼς καὶ ἐκλήθητε ἐν μιᾷ ἐλπίδι τῆς κλήσεως ὑμῶν· 5 εἷς κύριος, μία πίστις, ἓν βάπτισμα, 6 εἷς θεὸς καὶ πατὴρ πάντων, ὁ ἐπὶ πάντων καὶ διὰ πάντων καὶ ἐν πᾶσιν.

1 Thess 4:14

εἰ γὰρ πιστεύομεν ὅτι Ἰησοῦς ἀπέθανεν καὶ ἀνέστη, οὕτως καὶ ὁ θεὸς τοὺς κοιμηθέντας διὰ τοῦ Ἰησοῦ ἄξει σὺν αὐτῷ.

1 Thess 5:9–10

ὅτι οὐκ ἔθετο ἡμᾶς ὁ θεὸς εἰς ὀργὴν ἀλλὰ εἰς περιποίησιν σωτηρίας διὰ τοῦ κυρίου ἡμῶν Ἰησοῦ Χριστοῦ 10 τοῦ ἀποθανόντος ὑπὲρ ἡμῶν, ἵνα εἴτε γρηγορῶμεν εἴτε καθεύδωμεν ἅμα σὺν αὐτῷ ζήσωμεν.

1 Tim 3:16 ***ος*** ℵ* A* C* 33] ὃ D* ¦ θεος ℵ^{c} A^{c} C^{2} D^{2} 1739. 1881 *Byz*] *add.* εκ νεκρων ℵ* A C 33   **§ 21** **Rom 8:34** ***εγερθεις*** 𝔓^{27vid} 𝔓^{46} ℵ^{2} B D 1739. 1881 *Byz*

saying, "This cup is the new covenant in my blood. Do this, as often as you drink it, in remembrance of me."

1 Cor 15:1–11

Now I would remind you, brothers and sisters, of the good news that I proclaimed to you, which you in turn received, in which also you stand, **2** through which also you are being saved, if you hold firmly to the message that I proclaimed to you—unless you have come to believe in vain. **3** For I handed on to you as of first importance what I in turn had received: that Christ died for our sins in accordance with the scriptures, **4** and that he was buried, and that he was raised on the third day in accordance with the scriptures, **5** and that he appeared to Cephas, then to the twelve. **6** Then he appeared to more than five hundred brothers and sisters at one time, most of whom are still alive, though some have died. **7** Then he appeared to James, then to all the apostles. **8** Last of all, as to one untimely born, he appeared also to me. **9** For I am the least of the apostles, unfit to be called an apostle, because I persecuted the church of God. **10** But by the grace of God I am what I am, and his grace toward me has not been in vain. On the contrary, I worked harder than any of them—though it was not I, but the grace of God that is with me. **11** Whether then it was I or they, so we proclaim and so you have come to believe.

1 Thess 1:9–10

For the people of those regions report about us what kind of welcome we had among you, and how you turned to God from idols, to serve a living and true God, **10** and to wait for his Son from heaven, whom he raised from the dead—Jesus, who rescues us from the wrath that is coming.

1 Thess 4:14

For since we believe that Jesus died and rose again, even so, through Jesus, God will bring with him those who have died.

1 Tim 2:5–6

For there is one God; there is also one mediator between God and humankind, Christ Jesus, himself human, **6** who gave himself a ransom for all—this was attested at the right time.

1 Tim 3:16

Without any doubt, the mystery of our religion is great: Who[d] was revealed in flesh, vindicated by the Spirit,[e] seen by angels, proclaimed among Gentiles, believed in throughout the world, taken up in glory.

2 Tim 2:8

Remember Jesus Christ, raised from the dead, a descendant of David—that is my gospel

Cf. Rom 10:8–10; 14:9; 1 Cor 12:3; Eph 4:4–6; Phil 2:5–11; Col 1:15–20; 1 Thess 5:9–10; 1 Tim 6:13–14; 2 Tim 1:9–10; 4:1; Titus 2:11–14; 3:4–7; Acts 13:27–33.

In § 20 above are given the explicit confessional formulas identified in the Pauline corpus; for proposed tacit quotations, full or partial, of early Christian creeds and liturgical materials, see § 21 Proposed Creedal Fragments and § 22 Proposed Hymn Fragments. For references in the Pauline letters to the body of Christian Teaching, see § 108 The Pattern of Teaching.

21. Proposed Creedal Fragments

Rom 1:3–4

the gospel concerning his Son, who was descended from David according to the flesh **4** and was declared to be Son of God with power according to the Spirit[a] of holiness by resurrection from the dead, Jesus Christ our Lord

Rom 4:24–25

but for ours also. It will be reckoned to us who believe in him who raised Jesus our Lord from the dead, **25** who was handed over to death for our trespasses and was raised for our justification.

Rom 8:34

Who is to condemn? It is Christ Jesus, who died, yes, who was raised,[b] who is at the right hand of God, who indeed intercedes for us.

Rom 10:8–10

But what does it say? "The word is near you, on your lips and in your heart" (that is, the word of faith that we proclaim); **9** because if you confess with your lips that Jesus is Lord and believe in your heart that God raised him from the dead, you will be saved. **10** For one believes with the heart and so is justified, and one confesses with the mouth and so is saved.

1 Cor 8:6

yet for us there is one God, the Father, from whom are all things and for whom we exist, and one Lord, Jesus Christ, through whom are all things and through whom we exist.

1 Cor 12:3

Therefore I want you to understand that no one speaking by the Spirit of God ever says "Let Jesus be cursed!" and no one can say "Jesus is Lord" except by the Holy Spirit.

Eph 4:4–6

There is one body and one Spirit, just as you were called to the one hope of your calling, **5** one Lord, one faith, one baptism, **6** one God and Father of all, who is above all and through all and in all.

1 Thess 4:14

For since we believe that Jesus died and rose again, even so, through Jesus, God will bring with him those who have died.

1 Thess 5:9–10

For God has destined us not for wrath but for obtaining salvation through our Lord Jesus Christ, **10** who died for us, so that whether we are awake or asleep we may live with him.

[d] **1 Tim 3:16** *Who* Other ancient authorities read *God*; others, *Which*. NRSV translates Gk *Who* as He [e] **1 Tim 3:16** *by the Spirit* NRSV alternate translation **§ 21** [a] **Rom 1:4** *Spirit* NRSV alternate translation [b] **Rom 8:34** *raised* Other ancient authorities add *from the dead*

1 Tim 2:5–6

Εἷς γὰρ θεός, εἷς καὶ μεσίτης θεοῦ καὶ ἀνθρώπων, ἄνθρωπος Χριστὸς Ἰησοῦς, 6 ὁ δοὺς ἑαυτὸν ἀντίλυτρον ὑπὲρ πάντων, τὸ μαρτύριον καιροῖς ἰδίοις.

1 Tim 6:13–14

παραγγέλλω [σοι] ἐνώπιον τοῦ θεοῦ τοῦ ζῳογονοῦντος τὰ πάντα καὶ Χριστοῦ Ἰησοῦ τοῦ μαρτυρήσαντος ἐπὶ Ποντίου Πιλάτου τὴν καλὴν ὁμολογίαν, 14 τηρῆσαί σε τὴν ἐντολὴν ἄσπιλον ἀνεπίλημπτον μέχρι τῆς ἐπιφανείας τοῦ κυρίου ἡμῶν Ἰησοῦ Χριστοῦ

2 Tim 2:8

Μνημόνευε Ἰησοῦν Χριστὸν ἐγηγερμένον ἐκ νεκρῶν, ἐκ σπέρματος Δαυίδ, κατὰ τὸ εὐαγγέλιόν μου

2 Tim 4:1

Διαμαρτύρομαι ἐνώπιον τοῦ θεοῦ καὶ Χριστοῦ Ἰησοῦ τοῦ μέλλοντος κρίνειν ζῶντας καὶ νεκρούς, καὶ τὴν ἐπιφάνειαν αὐτοῦ καὶ τὴν βασιλείαν αὐτοῦ

Cf. Rom 3:24–26; 14:9; Gal 3:28; Phil 2:5–11; Col 1:15–20; 1 Tim 3:16; 2 Tim 1:9–10; Titus 2:11–14; 3:4–7.

See also § 20 Summaries of the Faith.

22. *Proposed Hymn Fragments*

Eph 5:14

πᾶν γὰρ τὸ φανερούμενον φῶς ἐστιν. διὸ λέγει· ἔγειρε, ὁ καθεύδων, καὶ ἀνάστα ἐκ τῶν νεκρῶν, καὶ ἐπιφαύσει σοι ὁ Χριστός.

Phil 2:5–11

Τοῦτο φρονεῖτε ἐν ὑμῖν ὃ καὶ ἐν Χριστῷ
Ἰησοῦ, 6 ὃς ἐν μορφῇ θεοῦ ὑπάρχων οὐχ
ἁρπαγμὸν ἡγήσατο τὸ εἶναι ἴσα θεῷ,
7 ἀλλὰ ἑαυτὸν ἐκένωσεν μορφὴν δούλου
λαβών, ἐν ὁμοιώματι ἀνθρώπων γενόμενος· καὶ σχήματι εὑρεθεὶς ὡς ἄνθρωπος
8 ἐταπείνωσεν ἑαυτὸν γενόμενος ὑπήκοος
μέχρι θανάτου, θανάτου δὲ σταυροῦ.
9 διὸ καὶ ὁ θεὸς αὐτὸν ὑπερύψωσεν καὶ
ἐχαρίσατο αὐτῷ τὸ ὄνομα τὸ ὑπὲρ πᾶν
ὄνομα, 10 ἵνα ἐν τῷ ὀνόματι Ἰησοῦ πᾶν
γόνυ κάμψῃ ἐπουρανίων καὶ ἐπιγείων
καὶ καταχθονίων 11 καὶ πᾶσα γλῶσσα
ἐξομολογήσηται ὅτι κύριος Ἰησοῦς Χριστὸς εἰς δόξαν θεοῦ πατρός.

Col 1:15–20

ὅς ἐστιν εἰκὼν τοῦ θεοῦ τοῦ ἀοράτου,
πρωτότοκος πάσης κτίσεως, 16 ὅτι ἐν
αὐτῷ ἐκτίσθη τὰ πάντα ἐν τοῖς οὐρανοῖς καὶ ἐπὶ τῆς γῆς, τὰ ὁρατὰ καὶ τὰ ἀόρατα, εἴτε θρόνοι εἴτε κυριότητες εἴτε ἀρχαὶ εἴτε ἐξουσίαι· τὰ πάντα δι᾽ αὐτοῦ καὶ εἰς
αὐτὸν ἔκτισται· 17 καὶ αὐτός ἐστιν πρὸ
πάντων καὶ τὰ πάντα ἐν αὐτῷ συνέστηκεν, 18 καὶ αὐτός ἐστιν ἡ κεφαλὴ τοῦ σώματος τῆς ἐκκλησίας· ὅς ἐστιν ἀρχή, πρωτότοκος ἐκ τῶν νεκρῶν, ἵνα γένηται
ἐν πᾶσιν αὐτὸς πρωτεύων, 19 ὅτι ἐν αὐτῷ
εὐδόκησεν πᾶν τὸ πλήρωμα κατοικῆσαι
20 καὶ δι᾽ αὐτοῦ ἀποκαταλλάξαι τὰ πάντα εἰς αὐτόν, εἰρηνοποιήσας διὰ τοῦ αἵματος τοῦ σταυροῦ αὐτοῦ, [δι᾽ αὐτοῦ] εἴτε τὰ ἐπὶ τῆς γῆς εἴτε τὰ ἐν τοῖς οὐρανοῖς.

1 Tim 3:16

καὶ ὁμολογουμένως μέγα ἐστὶν τὸ τῆς εὐσεβείας μυστήριον· ⸀ὃς ἐφανερώθη ἐν σαρκί, ἐδικαιώθη ἐν πνεύματι, ὤφθη ἀγγέλοις, ἐκηρύχθη ἐν ἔθνεσιν, ἐπιστεύθη ἐν κόσμῳ, ἀνελήμφθη ἐν δόξῃ.

2 Tim 2:11–13

πιστὸς ὁ λόγος· εἰ γὰρ συναπεθάνομεν,
καὶ συζήσομεν· 12 εἰ ὑπομένομεν, καὶ
συμβασιλεύσομεν· εἰ ἀρνησόμεθα, κἀκεῖνος ἀρνήσεται ἡμᾶς· 13 εἰ ἀπιστοῦμεν,
ἐκεῖνος πιστὸς μένει, ἀρνήσασθαι γὰρ ἑαυτὸν οὐ δύναται.

Titus 3:4–7

ὅτε δὲ ἡ χρηστότης καὶ ἡ φιλανθρωπία ἐπεφάνη τοῦ σωτῆρος ἡμῶν θεοῦ,
5 οὐκ ἐξ ἔργων τῶν ἐν δικαιοσύνῃ ἃ ἐποιήσαμεν ἡμεῖς ἀλλὰ κατὰ τὸ αὐτοῦ ἔλεος ἔσωσεν ἡμᾶς διὰ λουτροῦ παλιγγενεσίας καὶ ἀνακαινώσεως πνεύματος
ἁγίου, 6 οὗ ἐξέχεεν ἐφ᾽ ἡμᾶς πλουσίως
διὰ Ἰησοῦ Χριστοῦ τοῦ σωτῆρος ἡμῶν,
7 ἵνα δικαιωθέντες τῇ ἐκείνου χάριτι κληρονόμοι γενηθῶμεν κατ᾽ ἐλπίδα ζωῆς αἰωνίου.

Cf. Rom 11:33–36; 1 Cor 16:22; Phil 3:20–21; 1 Tim 6:15–16; 2 Tim 1:9–10.

See also § 20 Summaries of the Faith; § 21 Proposed Creedal Fragments; § 149 Hymns and Psalms.

23. *The Living Creator God*

Rom 1:18–20

Ἀποκαλύπτεται γὰρ ὀργὴ θεοῦ ἀπ᾽ οὐρανοῦ ἐπὶ πᾶσαν ἀσέβειαν καὶ ἀδικίαν ἀνθρώπων τῶν τὴν ἀλήθειαν ἐν ἀδικίᾳ
κατεχόντων, 19 διότι τὸ γνωστὸν τοῦ
θεοῦ φανερόν ἐστιν ἐν αὐτοῖς· ὁ θεὸς
γὰρ αὐτοῖς ἐφανέρωσεν. 20 τὰ γὰρ ἀόρατα αὐτοῦ ἀπὸ κτίσεως κόσμου τοῖς ποιήμασιν νοούμενα καθορᾶται, ἥ τε ἀΐδιος αὐτοῦ δύναμις καὶ θειότης, εἰς τὸ εἶναι αὐτοὺς ἀναπολογήτους

Rom 4:17

καθὼς γέγραπται ὅτι πατέρα πολλῶν ἐθνῶν τέθεικά σε, κατέναντι οὗ ἐπίστευσεν θεοῦ τοῦ ζῳοποιοῦντος τοὺς νεκροὺς καὶ καλοῦντος τὰ μὴ ὄντα ὡς ὄντα.

Rom 11:33–36

Ὦ βάθος πλούτου καὶ σοφίας καὶ γνώσεως θεοῦ· ὡς ἀνεξεραύνητα τὰ κρίματα αὐτοῦ καὶ ἀνεξιχνίαστοι αἱ ὁδοὶ
αὐτοῦ. 34 τίς γὰρ ἔγνω νοῦν κυρίου; ἢ

§ 22 **1 Tim 3:16** **ος** א* A* C* 33] ὃ D* ¦ θεος א^c A^c C² D² 1739. 1881 *Byz*

1 Tim 2:5–6
For there is one God; there is also one mediator between God and humankind, Christ Jesus, himself human, 6 who gave himself a ransom for all —this was attested at the right time.

1 Tim 6:13–14
In the presence of God, who gives life to all things, and of Christ Jesus, who in his testimony before Pontius Pilate made the good confession, I charge you 14 to keep the commandment without spot or blame until the manifestation of our Lord Jesus Christ

2 Tim 2:8
Remember Jesus Christ, raised from the dead, a descendant of David—that is my gospel

2 Tim 4:1
In the presence of God and of Christ Jesus, who is to judge the living and the dead, and in view of his appearing and his kingdom, I solemnly urge you

Cf. Rom 3:24–26; 14:9; Gal 3:28; Phil 2:5–11; Col 1:15–20; 1 Tim 3:16; 2 Tim 1:9–10; Titus 2:11–14; 3:4–7.

See also § 20 Summaries of the Faith.

22. *Proposed Hymn Fragments*

Eph 5:14
for everything that becomes visible is light. Therefore it says, "Sleeper, awake! Rise from the dead, and Christ will shine on you."

Phil 2:5–11
Let the same mind be in you that was in Christ Jesus, 6 who, though he was in the form of God, did not regard equality with God as something to be exploited, 7 but emptied himself, taking the form of a slave, being born in human likeness. And being found in human form, 8 he humbled himself and became obedient to the point of death— even death on a cross. 9 Therefore God also highly exalted him and gave him the name that is above every name, 10 so that at the name of Jesus every knee should bend, in heaven and on earth and under the earth, 11 and every tongue should confess that Jesus Christ is Lord, to the glory of God the Father.

Col 1:15–20
Who[a] is the image of the invisible God, the firstborn of all creation; 16 for in him all things in heaven and on earth were created, things visible and invisible, whether thrones or dominions or rulers or powers—all things have been created through him and for him. 17 He himself is before all things, and in him all things hold together. 18 He is the head of the body, the church; he is the beginning, the firstborn from the dead, so that he might come to have first place in everything. 19 For in him all the fullness of God was pleased to dwell, 20 and through him God was pleased to reconcile to himself all things, whether on earth or in heaven, by making peace through the blood of his cross.

1 Tim 3:16
Without any doubt, the mystery of our religion is great: Who[b] was revealed in flesh, vindicated by the Spirit,[c] seen by angels, proclaimed among Gentiles, believed in throughout the world, taken up in glory.

2 Tim 2:11–13
The saying is sure: If we have died with him, we will also live with him; 12 if we endure, we will also reign with him; if we deny him, he will also deny us; 13 if we are faithless, he remains faithful— for he cannot deny himself.

Titus 3:4–7
But when the goodness and loving kindness of God our Savior appeared, 5 he saved us, not because of any works of righteousness that we had done, but according to his mercy, through the water of rebirth and renewal by the Holy Spirit. 6 This Spirit he poured out on us richly through Jesus Christ our Savior, 7 so that, having been justified by his grace, we might become heirs according to the hope of eternal life.

Cf. Rom 11:33–36; 1 Cor 16:22; Phil 3:20–21; 1 Tim 6:15–16; 2 Tim 1:9–10.

See also § 20 Summaries of the Faith; § 21 Proposed Creedal Fragments; § 149 Hymns and Psalms.

23. *The Living Creator God*

Rom 1:18–20
For the wrath of God is revealed from heaven against all ungodliness and wickedness of those who by their wickedness suppress the truth. 19 For what can be known about God is plain to them, because God has shown it to them. 20 Ever since the creation of the world his eternal power and divine nature, invisible though they are, have been understood and seen through the things he has made. So they are without excuse

Rom 4:17
as it is written, "I have made you the father of many nations")—in the presence of the God in whom he believed, who gives life to the dead and calls into existence the things that do not exist.

Rom 11:33–36
O the depth of the riches and wisdom and knowledge of God! How unsearchable are his judgments and how inscrutable his ways! 34 "For who has known the mind of the Lord? Or who has been

§ 22 [a] **Col 1:15** *Who* NRSV translates *He* [b] **1 Tim 3:16** *Who* Other ancient authorities read *God*; others, *Which*. NRSV translates Gk *Who* as *He* [c] **1 Tim 3:16** *by the Spirit* NRSV alternate translation

τίς σύμβουλος αὐτοῦ ἐγένετο; **35** ἢ τίς
προέδωκεν αὐτῷ, καὶ ἀνταποδοθήσε-
ται αὐτῷ; **36** ὅτι ἐξ αὐτοῦ καὶ δι' αὐτοῦ
καὶ εἰς αὐτὸν τὰ πάντα· αὐτῷ ἡ δόξα εἰς
τοὺς αἰῶνας, ἀμήν.

1 Cor 8:4–6

Περὶ τῆς βρώσεως οὖν τῶν εἰδωλοθύτων,
οἴδαμεν ὅτι οὐδὲν εἴδωλον ἐν κόσμῳ καὶ
ὅτι οὐδεὶς θεὸς εἰ μὴ εἷς. **5** καὶ γὰρ εἴπερ
εἰσὶν λεγόμενοι θεοὶ εἴτε ἐν οὐρανῷ
εἴτε ἐπὶ γῆς, ὥσπερ εἰσὶν θεοὶ πολλοὶ
καὶ κύριοι πολλοί, **6** ἀλλ' ἡμῖν εἷς θεὸς
ὁ πατὴρ ἐξ οὗ τὰ πάντα καὶ ἡμεῖς εἰς
αὐτόν, καὶ εἷς κύριος Ἰησοῦς Χριστὸς δι'
οὗ τὰ πάντα καὶ ἡμεῖς δι' αὐτοῦ.

1 Cor 12:2–6

Οἴδατε ὅτι ὅτε ἔθνη ἦτε πρὸς τὰ εἴδωλα
τὰ ἄφωνα ὡς ἂν ἤγεσθε ἀπαγόμενοι. **3** διὸ
γνωρίζω ὑμῖν ὅτι οὐδεὶς ἐν πνεύματι
θεοῦ λαλῶν λέγει· Ἀνάθεμα Ἰησοῦς, καὶ
οὐδεὶς δύναται εἰπεῖν· Κύριος Ἰησοῦς,
εἰ μὴ ἐν πνεύματι ἁγίῳ. **4** Διαιρέσεις δὲ
χαρισμάτων εἰσίν, τὸ δὲ αὐτὸ πνεῦμα·
5 καὶ διαιρέσεις διακονιῶν εἰσιν, καὶ ὁ
αὐτὸς κύριος· **6** καὶ διαιρέσεις ἐνεργη-
μάτων εἰσίν, ὁ δὲ αὐτὸς θεὸς ὁ ἐνεργῶν
τὰ πάντα ἐν πᾶσιν.

Eph 3:8–9

Ἐμοὶ τῷ ἐλαχιστοτέρῳ πάντων ἁγίων
ἐδόθη ἡ χάρις αὕτη, τοῖς ἔθνεσιν εὐαγ-
γελίσασθαι τὸ ἀνεξιχνίαστον πλοῦτος
τοῦ Χριστοῦ **9** καὶ φωτίσαι ⸀[πάντας] τίς
ἡ οἰκονομία τοῦ μυστηρίου τοῦ ἀποκε-
κρυμμένου ἀπὸ τῶν αἰώνων ἐν τῷ θεῷ
τῷ τὰ πάντα κτίσαντι

Eph 4:4–6

Ἓν σῶμα καὶ ἓν πνεῦμα, καθὼς καὶ ἐκλή-
θητε ἐν μιᾷ ἐλπίδι τῆς κλήσεως ὑμῶν·
5 εἷς κύριος, μία πίστις, ἓν βάπτισμα, **6** εἷς
θεὸς καὶ πατὴρ πάντων, ὁ ἐπὶ πάντων
καὶ διὰ πάντων καὶ ἐν πᾶσιν.

Col 1:15–17

ὅς ἐστιν εἰκὼν τοῦ θεοῦ τοῦ ἀοράτου,
πρωτότοκος πάσης κτίσεως, **16** ὅτι ἐν
αὐτῷ ἐκτίσθη τὰ πάντα ἐν τοῖς οὐρα-
νοῖς καὶ ἐπὶ τῆς γῆς, τὰ ὁρατὰ καὶ τὰ
ἀόρατα, εἴτε θρόνοι εἴτε κυριότητες
εἴτε ἀρχαὶ εἴτε ἐξουσίαι· τὰ πάντα δι'
αὐτοῦ καὶ εἰς αὐτὸν ἔκτισται· **17** καὶ αὐτός
ἐστιν πρὸ πάντων καὶ τὰ πάντα ἐν αὐτῷ
συνέστηκεν.

1 Thess 1:9–10

αὐτοὶ γὰρ περὶ ἡμῶν ἀπαγγέλλουσιν
ὁποίαν εἴσοδον ἔσχομεν πρὸς ὑμᾶς, καὶ
πῶς ἐπεστρέψατε πρὸς τὸν θεὸν ἀπὸ τῶν
εἰδώλων δουλεύειν θεῷ ζῶντι καὶ ἀλη-
θινῷ **10** καὶ ἀναμένειν τὸν υἱὸν αὐτοῦ
ἐκ τῶν οὐρανῶν, ὃν ἤγειρεν ἐκ [τῶν]
νεκρῶν, Ἰησοῦν τὸν ῥυόμενον ἡμᾶς ἐκ
τῆς ὀργῆς τῆς ἐρχομένης.

1 Tim 1:17

Τῷ δὲ βασιλεῖ τῶν αἰώνων, ἀφθάρτῳ
ἀοράτῳ μόνῳ θεῷ, τιμὴ καὶ δόξα εἰς
τοὺς αἰῶνας τῶν αἰώνων, ἀμήν.

1 Tim 6:13–16

παραγγέλλω [σοι] ἐνώπιον τοῦ θεοῦ τοῦ
ζῳογονοῦντος τὰ πάντα καὶ Χριστοῦ
Ἰησοῦ τοῦ μαρτυρήσαντος ἐπὶ Ποντίου
Πιλάτου τὴν καλὴν ὁμολογίαν, **14** τηρῆσαί
σε τὴν ἐντολὴν ἄσπιλον ἀνεπίλημπτον
μέχρι τῆς ἐπιφανείας τοῦ κυρίου ἡμῶν
Ἰησοῦ Χριστοῦ, **15** ἣν καιροῖς ἰδίοις δεί-
ξει ὁ μακάριος καὶ μόνος δυνάστης, ὁ
βασιλεὺς τῶν βασιλευόντων καὶ κύριος
τῶν κυριευόντων, **16** ὁ μόνος ἔχων ἀθα-
νασίαν, φῶς οἰκῶν ἀπρόσιτον, ὃν εἶδεν
οὐδεὶς ἀνθρώπων οὐδὲ ἰδεῖν δύναται· ᾧ
τιμὴ καὶ κράτος αἰώνιον, ἀμήν.

Acts 14:14–17

Ἀκούσαντες δὲ οἱ ἀπόστολοι Βαρναβᾶς
καὶ Παῦλος διαρρήξαντες τὰ ἱμάτια αὐτῶν
ἐξεπήδησαν εἰς τὸν ὄχλον κράζοντες **15** καὶ
λέγοντες· ἄνδρες, τί ταῦτα ποιεῖτε; καὶ
ἡμεῖς ὁμοιοπαθεῖς ἐσμεν ὑμῖν ἄνθρωποι
εὐαγγελιζόμενοι ὑμᾶς ἀπὸ τούτων τῶν
ματαίων ἐπιστρέφειν ἐπὶ θεὸν ζῶντα, ὃς
ἐποίησεν τὸν οὐρανὸν καὶ τὴν γῆν καὶ
τὴν θάλασσαν καὶ πάντα τὰ ἐν αὐτοῖς·
16 ὃς ἐν ταῖς παρῳχημέναις γενεαῖς εἴα-
σεν πάντα τὰ ἔθνη πορεύεσθαι ταῖς ὁδοῖς
αὐτῶν· **17** καίτοι οὐκ ἀμάρτυρον αὐτὸν
ἀφῆκεν ἀγαθουργῶν, οὐρανόθεν ὑμῖν
ὑετοὺς διδοὺς καὶ καιροὺς καρποφόρους,
ἐμπιπλῶν τροφῆς καὶ εὐφροσύνης τὰς
καρδίας ὑμῶν.

Acts 17:22–28

Σταθεὶς δὲ [ὁ] Παῦλος ἐν μέσῳ τοῦ Ἀρείου
πάγου ἔφη· ἄνδρες Ἀθηναῖοι, κατὰ πάντα
ὡς δεισιδαιμονεστέρους ὑμᾶς θεωρῶ.
23 διερχόμενος γὰρ καὶ ἀναθεωρῶν τὰ
σεβάσματα ὑμῶν εὗρον καὶ βωμὸν ἐν
ᾧ ἐπεγέγραπτο· Ἀγνώστῳ θεῷ. ὃ οὖν
ἀγνοοῦντες εὐσεβεῖτε, τοῦτο ἐγὼ κα-
ταγγέλλω ὑμῖν. **24** ὁ θεὸς ὁ ποιήσας τὸν
κόσμον καὶ πάντα τὰ ἐν αὐτῷ, οὗτος
οὐρανοῦ καὶ γῆς ὑπάρχων κύριος οὐκ
ἐν χειροποιήτοις ναοῖς κατοικεῖ **25** οὐδὲ
ὑπὸ χειρῶν ἀνθρωπίνων θεραπεύεται
προσδεόμενός τινος, αὐτὸς διδοὺς πᾶσι
ζωὴν καὶ πνοὴν καὶ τὰ πάντα· **26** ἐποί-
ησέν τε ἐξ ⸀ἑνὸς πᾶν ἔθνος ἀνθρώπων
κατοικεῖν ἐπὶ παντὸς προσώπου τῆς γῆς,
ὁρίσας προστεταγμένους καιροὺς καὶ τὰς
ὁροθεσίας τῆς κατοικίας αὐτῶν **27** ζητεῖν
⸂τὸν θεόν⸃, εἰ ἄρα γε ψηλαφήσειαν αὐτὸν
καὶ εὕροιεν, καί γε οὐ μακρὰν ἀπὸ ἑνὸς
ἑκάστου ἡμῶν ὑπάρχοντα. **28** ἐν αὐτῷ γὰρ
ζῶμεν καὶ κινούμεθα καὶ ἐσμέν, ὡς καί
τινες τῶν καθ' ὑμᾶς ποιητῶν εἰρήκασιν·
τοῦ γὰρ καὶ γένος ἐσμέν.

Cf. Rom 3:29–30; 16:25–27; 1 Cor 10:14–22; 2 Cor 6:14–7:1; Gal 3:19–22; 1 Tim 2:5–7; 4:3–5; 4:8–10; Acts 19:23–27.

24. Idolatry and Dehumanization

Rom 1:18–32

Ἀποκαλύπτεται γὰρ ὀργὴ θεοῦ ἀπ' οὐρα-
νοῦ ἐπὶ πᾶσαν ἀσέβειαν καὶ ἀδικίαν
ἀνθρώπων τῶν τὴν ἀλήθειαν ἐν ἀδικίᾳ
κατεχόντων, **19** διότι τὸ γνωστὸν τοῦ
θεοῦ φανερόν ἐστιν ἐν αὐτοῖς· ὁ θεὸς

§ 23 **Eph 3:9** ***παντας*** 𝔓46 א2 B C D 33 *Byz*] *om.* א* A 1739. 1881 **Acts 17:26** ***ενος*** 𝔓74 א A B 33. 1739] *add.* αιματος D E *Byz* **Acts 17:27** ***τον θεον*** 𝔓74 א A B 33vid. 1739] τον κυριον E *Byz* ¦ το θειον D

his counselor?" 35 "Or who has given a gift to him, to receive a gift in return?" 36 For from him and through him and to him are all things. To him be the glory forever. Amen.

1 Cor 8:4–6

Hence, as to the eating of food offered to idols, we know that "no idol in the world really exists," and that "there is no God but one." 5 Indeed, even though there may be so-called gods in heaven or on earth—as in fact there are many gods and many lords— 6 yet for us there is one God, the Father, from whom are all things and for whom we exist, and one Lord, Jesus Christ, through whom are all things and through whom we exist.

1 Cor 12:2–6

You know that when you were pagans, you were enticed and led astray to idols that could not speak. 3 Therefore I want you to understand that no one speaking by the Spirit of God ever says "Let Jesus be cursed!" and no one can say "Jesus is Lord" except by the Holy Spirit. 4 Now there are varieties of gifts, but the same Spirit; 5 and there are varieties of services, but the same Lord; 6 and there are varieties of activities, but it is the same God who activates all of them in everyone.

Eph 3:8–9

Although I am the very least of all the saints, this grace was given to me to bring to the Gentiles the news of the boundless riches of Christ, 9 and to make everyone see[a] what is the plan of the mystery hidden for ages in God who created all things

Eph 4:4–6

There is one body and one Spirit, just as you were called to the one hope of your calling, 5 one Lord, one faith, one baptism, 6 one God and Father of all, who is above all and through all and in all.

Col 1:15–17

Who[b] is the image of the invisible God, the firstborn of all creation; 16 for in him all things in heaven and on earth were created, things visible and invisible, whether thrones or dominions or rulers or powers—all things have been created through him and for him. 17 He himself is before all things, and in him all things hold together.

1 Thess 1:9–10

For the people of those regions report about us what kind of welcome we had among you, and how you turned to God from idols, to serve a living and true God, 10 and to wait for his Son from heaven, whom he raised from the dead—Jesus, who rescues us from the wrath that is coming.

1 Tim 1:17

To the King of the ages, immortal, invisible, the only God, be honor and glory forever and ever. Amen.

1 Tim 6:13–16

In the presence of God, who gives life to all things, and of Christ Jesus, who in his testimony before Pontius Pilate made the good confession, I charge you 14 to keep the commandment without spot or blame until the manifestation of our Lord Jesus Christ, 15 which he will bring about at the right time—he who is the blessed and only Sovereign, the King of kings and Lord of lords. 16 It is he alone who has immortality and dwells in unapproachable light, whom no one has ever seen or can see; to him be honor and eternal dominion. Amen.

Acts 14:14–17

When the apostles Barnabas and Paul heard of it, they tore their clothes and rushed out into the crowd, shouting, 15 "Friends, why are you doing this? We are mortals just like you, and we bring you good news, that you should turn from these worthless things to the living God, who made the heaven and the earth and the sea and all that is in them. 16 In past generations he allowed all the nations to follow their own ways; 17 yet he has not left himself without a witness in doing good—giving you rains from heaven and fruitful seasons, and filling you with food and your hearts with joy."

Acts 17:22–28

Then Paul stood in front of the Areopagus and said, "Athenians, I see how extremely religious you are in every way. 23 For as I went through the city and looked carefully at the objects of your worship, I found among them an altar with the inscription, 'To an unknown god.' What therefore you worship as unknown, this I proclaim to you. 24 The God who made the world and everything in it, he who is Lord of heaven and earth, does not live in shrines made by human hands, 25 nor is he served by human hands, as though he needed anything, since he himself gives to all mortals life and breath and all things. 26 From one ancestor[c] he made all nations to inhabit the whole earth, and he allotted the times of their existence and the boundaries of the places where they would live, 27 so that they would search for God[d] and perhaps grope for him and find him—though indeed he is not far from each one of us. 28 For 'In him we live and move and have our being'; as even some of your own poets have said, 'For we too are his offspring.'

Cf. Rom 3:29–30; 16:25–27; 1 Cor 10:14–22; 2 Cor 6:14–7:1; Gal 3:19–22; 1 Tim 2:5–7; 4:3–5; 4:8–10; Acts 19:23–27.

24. *Idolatry and Dehumanization*

Rom 1:18–32

For the wrath of God is revealed from heaven against all ungodliness and wickedness of those who by their wickedness suppress the truth. 19 For what can be known about God is plain

§ 23 [a] **Eph 3:9** *to make everyone see* Other ancient authorities read *to bring to light* [b] **Col 1:15** *Who* NRSV translates *He* [c] **Acts 17:26** *From one ancestor* Other ancient authorities read *From one blood* [d] **Acts 17:27** *God* Other ancient authorities read *the Lord*

γὰρ αὐτοῖς ἐφανέρωσεν. 20 τὰ γὰρ ἀόρατα αὐτοῦ ἀπὸ κτίσεως κόσμου τοῖς ποιήμασιν νοούμενα καθορᾶται, ἥ τε ἀΐδιος αὐτοῦ δύναμις καὶ θειότης, εἰς τὸ εἶναι αὐτοὺς ἀναπολογήτους, 21 διότι γνόντες τὸν θεὸν οὐχ ὡς θεὸν ἐδόξασαν ἢ ηὐχαρίστησαν, ἀλλ᾽ ἐματαιώθησαν ἐν τοῖς διαλογισμοῖς αὐτῶν καὶ ἐσκοτίσθη ἡ ἀσύνετος αὐτῶν καρδία. 22 φάσκοντες εἶναι σοφοὶ ἐμωράνθησαν 23 καὶ ἤλλαξαν τὴν δόξαν τοῦ ἀφθάρτου θεοῦ ἐν ὁμοιώματι εἰκόνος φθαρτοῦ ἀνθρώπου καὶ πετεινῶν καὶ τετραπόδων καὶ ἑρπετῶν. 24 Διὸ παρέδωκεν αὐτοὺς ὁ θεὸς ἐν ταῖς ἐπιθυμίαις τῶν καρδιῶν αὐτῶν εἰς ἀκαθαρσίαν τοῦ ἀτιμάζεσθαι τὰ σώματα αὐτῶν ἐν αὐτοῖς· 25 οἵτινες μετήλλαξαν τὴν ἀλήθειαν τοῦ θεοῦ ἐν τῷ ψεύδει καὶ ἐσεβάσθησαν καὶ ἐλάτρευσαν τῇ κτίσει παρὰ τὸν κτίσαντα, ὅς ἐστιν εὐλογητὸς εἰς τοὺς αἰῶνας, ἀμήν. 26 Διὰ τοῦτο παρέδωκεν αὐτοὺς ὁ θεὸς εἰς πάθη ἀτιμίας, αἵ τε γὰρ θήλειαι αὐτῶν μετήλλαξαν τὴν φυσικὴν χρῆσιν εἰς τὴν παρὰ φύσιν, 27 ὁμοίως τε καὶ οἱ ἄρσενες ἀφέντες τὴν φυσικὴν χρῆσιν τῆς θηλείας ἐξεκαύθησαν ἐν τῇ ὀρέξει αὐτῶν εἰς ἀλλήλους, ἄρσενες ἐν ἄρσεσιν τὴν ἀσχημοσύνην κατεργαζόμενοι καὶ τὴν ἀντιμισθίαν ἣν ἔδει τῆς πλάνης αὐτῶν ἐν ἑαυτοῖς ἀπολαμβάνοντες. 28 Καὶ καθὼς οὐκ ἐδοκίμασαν τὸν θεὸν ἔχειν ἐν ἐπιγνώσει, παρέδωκεν αὐτοὺς ὁ θεὸς εἰς ἀδόκιμον νοῦν, ποιεῖν τὰ μὴ καθήκοντα, 29 πεπληρωμένους πάσῃ ἀδικίᾳ πονηρίᾳ πλεονεξίᾳ κακίᾳ, μεστοὺς φθόνου φόνου ἔριδος δόλου κακοηθείας, ψιθυριστὰς 30 καταλάλους θεοστυγεῖς ὑβριστὰς ὑπερηφάνους ἀλαζόνας, ἐφευρετὰς κακῶν, γονεῦσιν ἀπειθεῖς, 31 ἀσυνέτους ἀσυνθέτους ἀστόργους ἀνελεήμονας· 32 οἵτινες τὸ δικαίωμα τοῦ θεοῦ ἐπιγνόντες ὅτι οἱ τὰ τοιαῦτα πράσσοντες ἄξιοι θανάτου εἰσίν, οὐ μόνον αὐτὰ ποιοῦσιν ἀλλὰ καὶ συνευδοκοῦσιν τοῖς πράσσουσιν.

Gal 4:8

Ἀλλὰ τότε μὲν οὐκ εἰδότες θεὸν ἐδουλεύσατε τοῖς φύσει μὴ οὖσιν θεοῖς

Eph 2:11–12

Διὸ μνημονεύετε ὅτι ποτὲ ὑμεῖς τὰ ἔθνη ἐν σαρκί, οἱ λεγόμενοι ἀκροβυστία ὑπὸ τῆς λεγομένης περιτομῆς ἐν σαρκὶ χειροποιήτου, 12 ὅτι ἦτε τῷ καιρῷ ἐκείνῳ χωρὶς Χριστοῦ, ἀπηλλοτριωμένοι τῆς πολιτείας τοῦ Ἰσραὴλ καὶ ξένοι τῶν διαθηκῶν τῆς ἐπαγγελίας, ἐλπίδα μὴ ἔχοντες καὶ ἄθεοι ἐν τῷ κόσμῳ.

Eph 4:17–19

Τοῦτο οὖν λέγω καὶ μαρτύρομαι ἐν κυρίῳ, μηκέτι ὑμᾶς περιπατεῖν, καθὼς καὶ τὰ ἔθνη περιπατεῖ ἐν ματαιότητι τοῦ νοὸς αὐτῶν, 18 ἐσκοτωμένοι τῇ διανοίᾳ ὄντες, ἀπηλλοτριωμένοι τῆς ζωῆς τοῦ θεοῦ διὰ τὴν ἄγνοιαν τὴν οὖσαν ἐν αὐτοῖς, διὰ τὴν πώρωσιν τῆς καρδίας αὐτῶν, 19 οἵτινες ἀπηλγηκότες ἑαυτοὺς παρέδωκαν τῇ ἀσελγείᾳ εἰς ἐργασίαν ἀκαθαρσίας πάσης ἐν πλεονεξίᾳ.

Eph 5:5–14

τοῦτο γὰρ ἴστε γινώσκοντες, ὅτι πᾶς πόρνος ἢ ἀκάθαρτος ἢ πλεονέκτης, ὅ ἐστιν εἰδωλολάτρης, οὐκ ἔχει κληρονομίαν ἐν τῇ βασιλείᾳ τοῦ Χριστοῦ καὶ θεοῦ. 6 Μηδεὶς ὑμᾶς ἀπατάτω κενοῖς λόγοις· διὰ ταῦτα γὰρ ἔρχεται ἡ ὀργὴ τοῦ θεοῦ ἐπὶ τοὺς υἱοὺς τῆς ἀπειθείας. 7 μὴ οὖν γίνεσθε συμμέτοχοι αὐτῶν· 8 ἦτε γάρ ποτε σκότος, νῦν δὲ φῶς ἐν κυρίῳ· ὡς τέκνα φωτὸς περιπατεῖτε 9 —ὁ γὰρ καρπὸς τοῦ φωτὸς ἐν πάσῃ ἀγαθωσύνῃ καὶ δικαιοσύνῃ καὶ ἀληθείᾳ— 10 δοκιμάζοντες τί ἐστιν εὐάρεστον τῷ κυρίῳ, 11 καὶ μὴ συγκοινωνεῖτε τοῖς ἔργοις τοῖς ἀκάρποις τοῦ σκότους, μᾶλλον δὲ καὶ ἐλέγχετε. 12 τὰ γὰρ κρυφῇ γινόμενα ὑπ᾽ αὐτῶν αἰσχρόν ἐστιν καὶ λέγειν, 13 τὰ δὲ πάντα ἐλεγχόμενα ὑπὸ τοῦ φωτὸς φανεροῦται, 14 πᾶν γὰρ τὸ φανερούμενον φῶς ἐστιν. διὸ λέγει· ἔγειρε, ὁ καθεύδων, καὶ ἀνάστα ἐκ τῶν νεκρῶν, καὶ ἐπιφαύσει σοι ὁ Χριστός.

Col 3:5–7

Νεκρώσατε οὖν τὰ μέλη τὰ ἐπὶ τῆς γῆς, πορνείαν ἀκαθαρσίαν πάθος ἐπιθυμίαν κακήν, καὶ τὴν πλεονεξίαν, ἥτις ἐστὶν εἰδωλολατρία, 6 δι᾽ ἃ ἔρχεται ἡ ὀργὴ τοῦ θεοῦ ⸂[ἐπὶ τοὺς υἱοὺς τῆς ἀπειθείας]⸃. 7 ἐν οἷς καὶ ὑμεῖς περιεπατήσατέ ποτε, ὅτε ἐζῆτε ἐν τούτοις

1 Thess 1:9–10

αὐτοὶ γὰρ περὶ ἡμῶν ἀπαγγέλλουσιν ὁποίαν εἴσοδον ἔσχομεν πρὸς ὑμᾶς, καὶ πῶς ἐπεστρέψατε πρὸς τὸν θεὸν ἀπὸ τῶν εἰδώλων δουλεύειν θεῷ ζῶντι καὶ ἀληθινῷ 10 καὶ ἀναμένειν τὸν υἱὸν αὐτοῦ ἐκ τῶν οὐρανῶν, ὃν ἤγειρεν ἐκ [τῶν] νεκρῶν, Ἰησοῦν τὸν ῥυόμενον ἡμᾶς ἐκ τῆς ὀργῆς τῆς ἐρχομένης.

1 Thess 4:5

μὴ ἐν πάθει ἐπιθυμίας καθάπερ καὶ τὰ ἔθνη τὰ μὴ εἰδότα τὸν θεόν

Titus 3:3

Ἦμεν γάρ ποτε καὶ ἡμεῖς ἀνόητοι, ἀπειθεῖς, πλανώμενοι, δουλεύοντες ἐπιθυμίαις καὶ ἡδοναῖς ποικίλαις, ἐν κακίᾳ καὶ φθόνῳ διάγοντες, στυγητοί, μισοῦντες ἀλλήλους.

Acts 14:14–18

Ἀκούσαντες δὲ οἱ ἀπόστολοι Βαρναβᾶς καὶ Παῦλος διαρρήξαντες τὰ ἱμάτια αὐτῶν ἐξεπήδησαν εἰς τὸν ὄχλον κράζοντες 15 καὶ λέγοντες· ἄνδρες, τί ταῦτα ποιεῖτε; καὶ ἡμεῖς ὁμοιοπαθεῖς ἐσμεν ὑμῖν ἄνθρωποι εὐαγγελιζόμενοι ὑμᾶς ἀπὸ τούτων τῶν ματαίων ἐπιστρέφειν ἐπὶ θεὸν ζῶντα, ὃς ἐποίησεν τὸν οὐρανὸν καὶ τὴν γῆν καὶ τὴν θάλασσαν καὶ πάντα τὰ ἐν αὐτοῖς· 16 ὃς ἐν ταῖς παρῳχημέναις γενεαῖς εἴασεν πάντα τὰ ἔθνη πορεύεσθαι ταῖς ὁδοῖς αὐτῶν· 17 καίτοι οὐκ ἀμάρτυρον αὐτὸν ἀφῆκεν ἀγαθουργῶν, οὐρανόθεν ὑμῖν ὑετοὺς διδοὺς καὶ καιροὺς καρποφόρους, ἐμπιπλῶν τροφῆς καὶ εὐφροσύνης τὰς καρδίας ὑμῶν. 18 καὶ ταῦτα λέγοντες μόλις κατέπαυσαν τοὺς ὄχλους τοῦ μὴ θύειν αὐτοῖς.

Acts 17:16

Ἐν δὲ ταῖς Ἀθήναις ἐκδεχομένου αὐτοὺς τοῦ Παύλου παρωξύνετο τὸ πνεῦμα αὐτοῦ ἐν αὐτῷ θεωροῦντος κατείδωλον οὖσαν τὴν πόλιν.

Acts 17:29–30

γένος οὖν ὑπάρχοντες τοῦ θεοῦ οὐκ ὀφείλομεν νομίζειν χρυσῷ ἢ ἀργύρῳ ἢ λίθῳ, χαράγματι τέχνης καὶ ἐνθυμήσεως ἀνθρώπου, τὸ θεῖον εἶναι ὅμοιον. 30 τοὺς μὲν οὖν χρόνους τῆς ἀγνοίας ὑπεριδὼν ὁ θεός, τὰ νῦν παραγγέλλει τοῖς ἀνθρώποις πάντας πανταχοῦ μετανοεῖν

Acts 19:18–19

Πολλοί τε τῶν πεπιστευκότων ἤρχοντο ἐξομολογούμενοι καὶ ἀναγγέλλοντες τὰς πράξεις αὐτῶν. 19 ἱκανοὶ δὲ τῶν τὰ περίεργα πραξάντων συνενέγκαντες τὰς

§ 24 Col 3:6 *επι τους υιους της απειθειας* ℵ A C D I 33. 1739. 1881 *Byz*] *om.* 𝔓[46] B

to them, because God has shown it to them. 20 Ever since the creation of the world his eternal power and divine nature, invisible though they are, have been understood and seen through the things he has made. So they are without excuse; 21 for though they knew God, they did not honor him as God or give thanks to him, but they became futile in their thinking, and their senseless minds were darkened. 22 Claiming to be wise, they became fools; 23 and they exchanged the glory of the immortal God for images resembling a mortal human being or birds or four-footed animals or reptiles. 24 Therefore God gave them up in the lusts of their hearts to impurity, to the degrading of their bodies among themselves, 25 because they exchanged the truth about God for a lie and worshiped and served the creature rather than the Creator, who is blessed forever! Amen. 26 For this reason God gave them up to degrading passions. Their women exchanged natural intercourse for unnatural, 27 and in the same way also the men, giving up natural intercourse with women, were consumed with passion for one another. Men committed shameless acts with men and received in their own persons the due penalty for their error. 28 And since they did not see fit to acknowledge God, God gave them up to a debased mind and to things that should not be done. 29 They were filled with every kind of wickedness, evil, covetousness, malice. Full of envy, murder, strife, deceit, craftiness, they are gossips, 30 slanderers, God-haters, insolent, haughty, boastful, inventors of evil, rebellious toward parents, 31 foolish, faithless, heartless, ruthless. 32 They know God's decree, that those who practice such things deserve to die—yet they not only do them but even applaud others who practice them.

Gal 4:8

Formerly, when you did not know God, you were enslaved to beings that by nature are not gods.

Eph 2:11–12

So then, remember that at one time you Gentiles by birth, called "the uncircumcision" by those who are called "the circumcision"—a physical circumcision made in the flesh by human hands— 12 remember that you were at that time without Christ, being aliens from the commonwealth of Israel, and strangers to the covenants of promise, having no hope and without God in the world.

Eph 4:17–19

Now this I affirm and insist on in the Lord: you must no longer live as the Gentiles live, in the futility of their minds. 18 They are darkened in their understanding, alienated from the life of God because of their ignorance and hardness of heart. 19 They have lost all sensitivity and have abandoned themselves to licentiousness, greedy to practice every kind of impurity.

Eph 5:5–14

Be sure of this, that no fornicator or impure person, or one who is greedy (that is, an idolater), has any inheritance in the kingdom of Christ and of God. 6 Let no one deceive you with empty words, for because of these things the wrath of God comes on those who are disobedient. 7 Therefore do not be associated with them. 8 For once you were darkness, but now in the Lord you are light. Live as children of light— 9 for the fruit of the light is found in all that is good and right and true. 10 Try to find out what is pleasing to the Lord. 11 Take no part in the unfruitful works of darkness, but instead expose them. 12 For it is shameful even to mention what such people do secretly; 13 but everything exposed by the light becomes visible, 14 for everything that becomes visible is light. Therefore it says, "Sleeper, awake! Rise from the dead, and Christ will shine on you."

Col 3:5–7

Put to death, therefore, whatever in you is earthly: fornication, impurity, passion, evil desire, and greed (which is idolatry). 6 On account of these the wrath of God is coming on those who are disobedient.[a] 7 These are the ways you also once followed, when you were living that life.

1 Thess 1:9–10

For the people of those regions report about us what kind of welcome we had among you, and how you turned to God from idols, to serve a living and true God, 10 and to wait for his Son from heaven, whom he raised from the dead—Jesus, who rescues us from the wrath that is coming.

1 Thess 4:5

not with lustful passion, like the Gentiles who do not know God

Titus 3:3

For we ourselves were once foolish, disobedient, led astray, slaves to various passions and pleasures, passing our days in malice and envy, despicable, hating one another.

Acts 14:14–18

When the apostles Barnabas and Paul heard of it, they tore their clothes and rushed out into the crowd, shouting, 15 "Friends, why are you doing this? We are mortals just like you, and we bring you good news, that you should turn from these worthless things to the living God, who made the heaven and the earth and the sea and all that is in them. 16 In past generations he allowed all the nations to follow their own ways; 17 yet he has not left himself without a witness in doing good—giving you rains from heaven and fruitful seasons, and filling you with food and your hearts with joy." 18 Even with these words, they scarcely restrained the crowds from offering sacrifice to them.

Acts 17:16

While Paul was waiting for them in Athens, he was deeply distressed to see that the city was full of idols.

Acts 17:29–30

Since we are God's offspring, we ought not to think that the deity is like gold, or silver, or stone, an image formed by the art and imagination of mortals. 30 While God has overlooked the times of human ignorance, now he commands all people everywhere to repent

Acts 19:18–19

Also many of those who became believers confessed and disclosed their practices. 19 A number of those who practiced magic collected their books

§ 24 [a] **Col 3:6** *on those who are disobedient* Other ancient authorities lack *on those who are disobedient*

βίβλους κατέκαιον ἐνώπιον πάντων,
καὶ συνεψήφισαν τὰς τιμὰς αὐτῶν καὶ
εὗρον ἀργυρίου μυριάδας πέντε.

Acts 19:26

καὶ θεωρεῖτε καὶ ἀκούετε ὅτι οὐ μόνον
Ἐφέσου ἀλλὰ σχεδὸν πάσης τῆς Ἀσίας ὁ
Παῦλος οὗτος πείσας μετέστησεν ἱκανὸν
ὄχλον λέγων ὅτι οὐκ εἰσὶν θεοὶ οἱ διὰ
χειρῶν γινόμενοι.

Cf. 1 Cor 10:14–22; 12:1–3; and the conjunction of idolatry and associated deeds in several of the lists in § 16 Vice List.

See the corresponding theme § 49 The New Humanity in Christ.

25. The Wrath of God

Rom 1:18–23

Ἀποκαλύπτεται γὰρ ὀργὴ θεοῦ ἀπ᾽ οὐρα-
νοῦ ἐπὶ πᾶσαν ἀσέβειαν καὶ ἀδικίαν
ἀνθρώπων τῶν τὴν ἀλήθειαν ἐν ἀδικίᾳ
κατεχόντων, 19 διότι τὸ γνωστὸν τοῦ
θεοῦ φανερόν ἐστιν ἐν αὐτοῖς· ὁ θεὸς
γὰρ αὐτοῖς ἐφανέρωσεν. 20 τὰ γὰρ ἀό-
ρατα αὐτοῦ ἀπὸ κτίσεως κόσμου τοῖς
ποιήμασιν νοούμενα καθορᾶται, ἥ τε
ἀΐδιος αὐτοῦ δύναμις καὶ θειότης, εἰς
τὸ εἶναι αὐτοὺς ἀναπολογήτους, 21 διότι
γνόντες τὸν θεὸν οὐχ ὡς θεὸν ἐδόξασαν
ἢ ηὐχαρίστησαν, ἀλλ᾽ ἐματαιώθησαν ἐν
τοῖς διαλογισμοῖς αὐτῶν καὶ ἐσκοτίσθη
ἡ ἀσύνετος αὐτῶν καρδία. 22 φάσκον-
τες εἶναι σοφοὶ ἐμωράνθησαν 23 καὶ
ἤλλαξαν τὴν δόξαν τοῦ ἀφθάρτου θεοῦ
ἐν ὁμοιώματι εἰκόνος φθαρτοῦ ἀνθρώ-
που καὶ πετεινῶν καὶ τετραπόδων καὶ
ἑρπετῶν.

Rom 2:1–11

Διὸ ἀναπολόγητος εἶ, ὦ ἄνθρωπε πᾶς ὁ
κρίνων· ἐν ᾧ γὰρ κρίνεις τὸν ἕτερον, σε-
αυτὸν κατακρίνεις, τὰ γὰρ αὐτὰ πράσσεις
ὁ κρίνων. 2 οἴδαμεν δὲ ὅτι τὸ κρίμα τοῦ
θεοῦ ἐστιν κατὰ ἀλήθειαν ἐπὶ τοὺς τὰ
τοιαῦτα πράσσοντας. 3 λογίζῃ δὲ τοῦτο, ὦ
ἄνθρωπε ὁ κρίνων τοὺς τὰ τοιαῦτα πράσ-
σοντας καὶ ποιῶν αὐτά, ὅτι σὺ ἐκφεύξῃ
τὸ κρίμα τοῦ θεοῦ; 4 ἢ τοῦ πλούτου τῆς
χρηστότητος αὐτοῦ καὶ τῆς ἀνοχῆς καὶ
τῆς μακροθυμίας καταφρονεῖς, ἀγνοῶν
ὅτι τὸ χρηστὸν τοῦ θεοῦ εἰς μετάνοιάν
σε ἄγει; 5 κατὰ δὲ τὴν σκληρότητά σου
καὶ ἀμετανόητον καρδίαν θησαυρίζεις
σεαυτῷ ὀργὴν ἐν ἡμέρᾳ ὀργῆς καὶ ἀπο-
καλύψεως δικαιοκρισίας τοῦ θεοῦ 6 ὃς
ἀποδώσει ἑκάστῳ κατὰ τὰ ἔργα αὐτοῦ·
7 τοῖς μὲν καθ᾽ ὑπομονὴν ἔργου ἀγαθοῦ
δόξαν καὶ τιμὴν καὶ ἀφθαρσίαν ζητοῦσιν
ζωὴν αἰώνιον, 8 τοῖς δὲ ἐξ ἐριθείας καὶ
ἀπειθοῦσι τῇ ἀληθείᾳ πειθομένοις δὲ
τῇ ἀδικίᾳ ὀργὴ καὶ θυμός. 9 θλῖψις καὶ
στενοχωρία ἐπὶ πᾶσαν ψυχὴν ἀνθρώπου
τοῦ κατεργαζομένου τὸ κακόν, Ἰουδαίου
τε πρῶτον καὶ Ἕλληνος· 10 δόξα δὲ καὶ
τιμὴ καὶ εἰρήνη παντὶ τῷ ἐργαζομένῳ τὸ
ἀγαθόν, Ἰουδαίῳ τε πρῶτον καὶ Ἕλληνι·
11 οὐ γάρ ἐστιν προσωπολημψία παρὰ
τῷ θεῷ.

Rom 3:5–6

εἰ δὲ ἡ ἀδικία ἡμῶν θεοῦ δικαιοσύνην
συνίστησιν, τί ἐροῦμεν; μὴ ἄδικος ὁ θεὸς
ὁ ἐπιφέρων τὴν ὀργήν; κατὰ ἄνθρωπον
λέγω. 6 μὴ γένοιτο· ἐπεὶ πῶς κρινεῖ ὁ
θεὸς τὸν κόσμον;

Rom 5:8–10

συνίστησιν δὲ τὴν ἑαυτοῦ ἀγάπην εἰς ἡμᾶς
ὁ θεός, ὅτι ἔτι ἁμαρτωλῶν ὄντων ἡμῶν
Χριστὸς ὑπὲρ ἡμῶν ἀπέθανεν. 9 πολλῷ οὖν
μᾶλλον δικαιωθέντες νῦν ἐν τῷ αἵματι
αὐτοῦ σωθησόμεθα δι᾽ αὐτοῦ ἀπὸ τῆς
ὀργῆς. 10 εἰ γὰρ ἐχθροὶ ὄντες κατηλλά-
γημεν τῷ θεῷ διὰ τοῦ θανάτου τοῦ υἱοῦ
αὐτοῦ, πολλῷ μᾶλλον καταλλαγέντες
σωθησόμεθα ἐν τῇ ζωῇ αὐτοῦ

Rom 9:22–24

εἰ δὲ θέλων ὁ θεὸς ἐνδείξασθαι τὴν ὀργὴν
καὶ γνωρίσαι τὸ δυνατὸν αὐτοῦ ἤνεγκεν
ἐν πολλῇ μακροθυμίᾳ σκεύη ὀργῆς κα-
τηρτισμένα εἰς ἀπώλειαν, 23 καὶ ἵνα
γνωρίσῃ τὸν πλοῦτον τῆς δόξης αὐτοῦ
ἐπὶ σκεύη ἐλέους ἃ προητοίμασεν εἰς δό-
ξαν; 24 Οὓς καὶ ἐκάλεσεν ἡμᾶς οὐ μόνον
ἐξ Ἰουδαίων ἀλλὰ καὶ ἐξ ἐθνῶν

Eph 2:3

ἐν οἷς καὶ ἡμεῖς πάντες ἀνεστράφημέν
ποτε ἐν ταῖς ἐπιθυμίαις τῆς σαρκὸς ἡμῶν
ποιοῦντες τὰ θελήματα τῆς σαρκὸς καὶ
τῶν διανοιῶν, καὶ ἤμεθα τέκνα φύσει
ὀργῆς ὡς καὶ οἱ λοιποί

Eph 5:5–7

τοῦτο γὰρ ἴστε γινώσκοντες, ὅτι πᾶς πόρ-
νος ἢ ἀκάθαρτος ἢ πλεονέκτης, ὅ ἐστιν
εἰδωλολάτρης, οὐκ ἔχει κληρονομίαν
ἐν τῇ βασιλείᾳ τοῦ Χριστοῦ καὶ θεοῦ.
6 Μηδεὶς ὑμᾶς ἀπατάτω κενοῖς λόγοις·
διὰ ταῦτα γὰρ ἔρχεται ἡ ὀργὴ τοῦ θεοῦ
ἐπὶ τοὺς υἱοὺς τῆς ἀπειθείας. 7 μὴ οὖν
γίνεσθε συμμέτοχοι αὐτῶν

Col 3:5–7

Νεκρώσατε οὖν τὰ μέλη τὰ ἐπὶ τῆς γῆς,
πορνείαν ἀκαθαρσίαν πάθος ἐπιθυμίαν
κακήν, καὶ τὴν πλεονεξίαν, ἥτις ἐστὶν
εἰδωλολατρία, 6 δι᾽ ἃ ἔρχεται ἡ ὀργὴ τοῦ
θεοῦ ⸢[ἐπὶ τοὺς υἱοὺς τῆς ἀπειθείας]⸣.
7 ἐν οἷς καὶ ὑμεῖς περιεπατήσατέ ποτε,
ὅτε ἐζῆτε ἐν τούτοις

1 Thess 1:9–10

αὐτοὶ γὰρ περὶ ἡμῶν ἀπαγγέλλουσιν
ὁποίαν εἴσοδον ἔσχομεν πρὸς ὑμᾶς, καὶ
πῶς ἐπεστρέψατε πρὸς τὸν θεὸν ἀπὸ τῶν
εἰδώλων δουλεύειν θεῷ ζῶντι καὶ ἀλη-
θινῷ 10 καὶ ἀναμένειν τὸν υἱὸν αὐτοῦ
ἐκ τῶν οὐρανῶν, ὃν ἤγειρεν ἐκ [τῶν]
νεκρῶν, Ἰησοῦν τὸν ῥυόμενον ἡμᾶς ἐκ
τῆς ὀργῆς τῆς ἐρχομένης.

1 Thess 5:9–10

ὅτι οὐκ ἔθετο ἡμᾶς ὁ θεὸς εἰς ὀργὴν ἀλλὰ
εἰς περιποίησιν σωτηρίας διὰ τοῦ κυρίου
ἡμῶν Ἰησοῦ Χριστοῦ 10 τοῦ ἀποθανόντος
ὑπὲρ ἡμῶν, ἵνα εἴτε γρηγορῶμεν εἴτε
καθεύδωμεν ἅμα σὺν αὐτῷ ζήσωμεν.

§ 25 Col 3:6 *επι τους υιους της απειθειας* ℵ A C D I 33. 1739. 1881 *Byz*] *om.* 𝔓^{46} B

and burned them publicly; when the value of these books was calculated, it was found to come to fifty thousand silver coins.

Acts 19:26

You also see and hear that not only in Ephesus but in almost the whole of Asia this Paul has persuaded and drawn away a considerable number of people by saying that gods made with hands are not gods.

Cf. 1 Cor 10:14–22; 12:1–3; and the conjunction of idolatry and associated deeds in several of the lists in § 16 Vice List.

See the corresponding theme § 49 The New Humanity in Christ.

25. The Wrath of God

Rom 1:18–23

For the wrath of God is revealed from heaven against all ungodliness and wickedness of those who by their wickedness suppress the truth. **19** For what can be known about God is plain to them, because God has shown it to them. **20** Ever since the creation of the world his eternal power and divine nature, invisible though they are, have been understood and seen through the things he has made. So they are without excuse; **21** for though they knew God, they did not honor him as God or give thanks to him, but they became futile in their thinking, and their senseless minds were darkened. **22** Claiming to be wise, they became fools; **23** and they exchanged the glory of the immortal God for images resembling a mortal human being or birds or four-footed animals or reptiles.

Rom 2:1–11

Therefore you have no excuse, whoever you are, when you judge others; for in passing judgment on another you condemn yourself, because you, the judge, are doing the very same things. **2** You say, "We know that God's judgment on those who do such things is in accordance with truth." **3** Do you imagine, whoever you are, that when you judge those who do such things and yet do them yourself, you will escape the judgment of God? **4** Or do you despise the riches of his kindness and forbearance and patience? Do you not realize that God's kindness is meant to lead you to repentance? **5** But by your hard and impenitent heart you are storing up wrath for yourself on the day of wrath, when God's righteous judgment will be revealed. **6** For he will repay according to each one's deeds: **7** to those who by patiently doing good seek for glory and honor and immortality, he will give eternal life; **8** while for those who are self-seeking and who obey not the truth but wickedness, there will be wrath and fury. **9** There will be anguish and distress for everyone who does evil, the Jew first and also the Greek, **10** but glory and honor and peace for everyone who does good, the Jew first and also the Greek. **11** For God shows no partiality.

Rom 3:5–6

But if our injustice serves to confirm the justice of God, what should we say? That God is unjust to inflict wrath on us? (I speak in a human way.) **6** By no means! For then how could God judge the world?

Rom 5:8–10

But God proves his love for us in that while we still were sinners Christ died for us. **9** Much more surely then, now that we have been justified by his blood, will we be saved through him from the wrath of God. **10** For if while we were enemies, we were reconciled to God through the death of his Son, much more surely, having been reconciled, will we be saved by his life.

Rom 9:22–24

What if God, desiring to show his wrath and to make known his power, has endured with much patience the objects of wrath that are made for destruction; **23** and what if he has done so in order to make known the riches of his glory for the objects of mercy, which he has prepared beforehand for glory— **24** including us whom he has called, not from the Jews only but also from the Gentiles?

Eph 2:3

All of us once lived among them in the passions of our flesh, following the desires of flesh and senses, and we were by nature children of wrath, like everyone else.

Eph 5:5–7

Be sure of this, that no fornicator or impure person, or one who is greedy (that is, an idolater), has any inheritance in the kingdom of Christ and of God. **6** Let no one deceive you with empty words, for because of these things the wrath of God comes on those who are disobedient. **7** Therefore do not be associated with them.

Col 3:5–7

Put to death, therefore, whatever in you is earthly: fornication, impurity, passion, evil desire, and greed (which is idolatry). **6** On account of these the wrath of God is coming on those who are disobedient.[a] **7** These are the ways you also once followed, when you were living that life.

1 Thess 1:9–10

For the people of those regions report about us what kind of welcome we had among you, and how you turned to God from idols, to serve a living and true God, **10** and to wait for his Son from heaven, whom he raised from the dead—Jesus, who rescues us from the wrath that is coming.

1 Thess 5:9–10

For God has destined us not for wrath but for obtaining salvation through our Lord Jesus Christ, **10** who died for us, so that whether we are awake or asleep we may live with him.

§ 25 [a] **Col 3:6** ***on those who are disobedient*** Other ancient authorities lack *on those who are disobedient*

2 Thess 1:5–10

ἔνδειγμα τῆς δικαίας κρίσεως τοῦ θεοῦ εἰς τὸ καταξιωθῆναι ὑμᾶς τῆς βασιλείας τοῦ θεοῦ, ὑπὲρ ἧς καὶ πάσχετε, 6 εἴπερ δίκαιον παρὰ θεῷ ἀνταποδοῦναι τοῖς θλίβουσιν ὑμᾶς θλῖψιν 7 καὶ ὑμῖν τοῖς θλιβομένοις ἄνεσιν μεθ' ἡμῶν, ἐν τῇ ἀποκαλύψει τοῦ κυρίου Ἰησοῦ ἀπ' οὐρανοῦ μετ' ἀγγέλων δυνάμεως αὐτοῦ 8 ἐν πυρὶ φλογός, διδόντος ἐκδίκησιν τοῖς μὴ εἰδόσιν θεὸν καὶ τοῖς μὴ ὑπακούουσιν τῷ εὐαγγελίῳ τοῦ κυρίου ἡμῶν Ἰησοῦ, 9 οἵτινες δίκην τίσουσιν ὄλεθρον αἰώνιον ἀπὸ προσώπου τοῦ κυρίου καὶ ἀπὸ τῆς δόξης τῆς ἰσχύος αὐτοῦ, 10 ὅταν ἔλθῃ ἐνδοξασθῆναι ἐν τοῖς ἁγίοις αὐτοῦ καὶ θαυμασθῆναι ἐν πᾶσιν τοῖς πιστεύσασιν, ὅτι ἐπιστεύθη τὸ μαρτύριον ἡμῶν ἐφ' ὑμᾶς, ἐν τῇ ἡμέρᾳ ἐκείνῃ.

Cf. 1 Cor 5:3–5; 2 Cor 11:12–15; Phil 1:27–30; 3:17–4:1; 2 Tim 4:14.

See also § 96 The Righteous Judgment of God.

26. *The Advantages of the Jewish People*

Rom 3:1–4

Τί οὖν τὸ περισσὸν τοῦ Ἰουδαίου ἢ τίς ἡ ὠφέλεια τῆς περιτομῆς; 2 πολὺ κατὰ πάντα τρόπον. πρῶτον μὲν [γὰρ] ὅτι ἐπιστεύθησαν τὰ λόγια τοῦ θεοῦ. 3 τί γάρ; εἰ ἠπίστησάν τινες, μὴ ἡ ἀπιστία αὐτῶν τὴν πίστιν τοῦ θεοῦ καταργήσει; 4 μὴ γένοιτο· γινέσθω δὲ ὁ θεὸς ἀληθής, πᾶς δὲ ἄνθρωπος ψεύστης, καθὼς γέγραπται· ὅπως ἂν δικαιωθῇς ἐν τοῖς λόγοις σου καὶ νικήσεις ἐν τῷ κρίνεσθαί σε.

Rom 9:4–5

οἵτινές εἰσιν Ἰσραηλῖται, ὧν ἡ υἱοθεσία καὶ ἡ δόξα καὶ ⸀αἱ διαθῆκαι⸁ καὶ ἡ νομοθεσία καὶ ἡ λατρεία καὶ αἱ ἐπαγγελίαι, 5 ὧν οἱ πατέρες καὶ ἐξ ὧν ὁ Χριστὸς τὸ κατὰ σάρκα, ὁ ὢν ἐπὶ πάντων θεὸς εὐλογητὸς εἰς τοὺς αἰῶνας, ἀμήν.

Rom 15:7–9

Διὸ προσλαμβάνεσθε ἀλλήλους, καθὼς καὶ ὁ Χριστὸς προσελάβετο ὑμᾶς εἰς δόξαν τοῦ θεοῦ. 8 λέγω γὰρ Χριστὸν διάκονον γεγενῆσθαι περιτομῆς ὑπὲρ ἀληθείας θεοῦ, εἰς τὸ βεβαιῶσαι τὰς ἐπαγγελίας τῶν πατέρων, 9 τὰ δὲ ἔθνη ὑπὲρ ἐλέους δοξάσαι τὸν θεόν, καθὼς γέγραπται· διὰ τοῦτο ἐξομολογήσομαί σοι ἐν ἔθνεσιν καὶ τῷ ὀνόματί σου ψαλῶ.

Gal 2:15

Ἡμεῖς φύσει Ἰουδαῖοι καὶ οὐκ ἐξ ἐθνῶν ἁμαρτωλοί

Eph 2:11–12

Διὸ μνημονεύετε ὅτι ποτὲ ὑμεῖς τὰ ἔθνη ἐν σαρκί, οἱ λεγόμενοι ἀκροβυστία ὑπὸ τῆς λεγομένης περιτομῆς ἐν σαρκὶ χειροποιήτου, 12 ὅτι ἦτε τῷ καιρῷ ἐκείνῳ χωρὶς Χριστοῦ, ἀπηλλοτριωμένοι τῆς πολιτείας τοῦ Ἰσραὴλ καὶ ξένοι τῶν διαθηκῶν τῆς ἐπαγγελίας, ἐλπίδα μὴ ἔχοντες καὶ ἄθεοι ἐν τῷ κόσμῳ.

Phil 3:4–6

καίπερ ἐγὼ ἔχων πεποίθησιν καὶ ἐν σαρκί. Εἴ τις δοκεῖ ἄλλος πεποιθέναι ἐν σαρκί, ἐγὼ μᾶλλον· 5 περιτομῇ ὀκταήμερος, ἐκ γένους Ἰσραήλ, φυλῆς Βενιαμίν, Ἑβραῖος ἐξ Ἑβραίων, κατὰ νόμον Φαρισαῖος, 6 κατὰ ζῆλος διώκων τὴν ἐκκλησίαν, κατὰ δικαιοσύνην τὴν ἐν νόμῳ γενόμενος ἄμεμπτος.

2 Tim 3:14–17

Σὺ δὲ μένε ἐν οἷς ἔμαθες καὶ ἐπιστώθης, εἰδὼς παρὰ ⸀τίνων ἔμαθες, 15 καὶ ὅτι ἀπὸ βρέφους [τὰ] ἱερὰ γράμματα οἶδας, τὰ δυνάμενά σε σοφίσαι εἰς σωτηρίαν διὰ πίστεως τῆς ἐν Χριστῷ Ἰησοῦ. 16 πᾶσα γραφὴ θεόπνευστος καὶ ὠφέλιμος πρὸς διδασκαλίαν, πρὸς ἐλεγμόν, πρὸς ἐπανόρθωσιν, πρὸς παιδείαν τὴν ἐν δικαιοσύνῃ, 17 ἵνα ἄρτιος ᾖ ὁ τοῦ θεοῦ ἄνθρωπος, πρὸς πᾶν ἔργον ἀγαθὸν ἐξηρτισμένος.

Cf. Rom 11:11–24; 11:25–32; 15:25–27; 2 Cor 11:21b–22; 2 Tim 1:5; Acts 13:16–23; 13:26; 13:32–33.

27. *All Humanity under the Power of Sin and Death*

Rom 3:9–20

Τί οὖν; προεχόμεθα; οὐ πάντως· προῃτιασάμεθα γὰρ Ἰουδαίους τε καὶ Ἕλληνας πάντας ὑφ' ἁμαρτίαν εἶναι, 10 καθὼς γέγραπται ὅτι οὐκ ἔστιν δίκαιος οὐδὲ εἷς, 11 οὐκ ἔστιν ὁ συνίων, οὐκ ἔστιν ὁ ἐκζητῶν τὸν θεόν. 12 πάντες ἐξέκλιναν ἅμα ἠχρεώθησαν· οὐκ ἔστιν ὁ ποιῶν χρηστότητα, [οὐκ ἔστιν] ἕως ἑνός. 13 τάφος ἀνεῳγμένος ὁ λάρυγξ αὐτῶν, ταῖς γλώσσαις αὐτῶν ἐδολιοῦσαν, ἰὸς ἀσπίδων ὑπὸ τὰ χείλη αὐτῶν· 14 ὧν τὸ στόμα ἀρᾶς καὶ πικρίας γέμει, 15 ὀξεῖς οἱ πόδες αὐτῶν ἐκχέαι αἷμα, 16 σύντριμμα καὶ ταλαιπωρία ἐν ταῖς ὁδοῖς αὐτῶν, 17 καὶ ὁδὸν εἰρήνης οὐκ ἔγνωσαν. 18 οὐκ ἔστιν φόβος θεοῦ ἀπέναντι τῶν ὀφθαλμῶν αὐτῶν. 19 οἴδαμεν δὲ ὅτι ὅσα ὁ νόμος λέγει τοῖς ἐν τῷ νόμῳ λαλεῖ, ἵνα πᾶν στόμα φραγῇ καὶ ὑπόδικος γένηται πᾶς ὁ κόσμος τῷ θεῷ· 20 διότι ἐξ ἔργων νόμου οὐ δικαιωθήσεται πᾶσα σὰρξ ἐνώπιον αὐτοῦ, διὰ γὰρ νόμου ἐπίγνωσις ἁμαρτίας.

§ 26 **Rom 9:4** ***αι διαθηκαι*** ℵ C 33. 1739. 1881 *Byz*] η διαθηκη 𝔓[46] B D **2 Tim 3:14** ***τινων*** ℵ A C* 33. 1739. 1881] τινος C[3] D *Byz*

2 Thess 1:5–10

This is evidence of the righteous judgment of God, and is intended to make you worthy of the kingdom of God, for which you are also suffering. 6 For it is indeed just of God to repay with affliction those who afflict you, 7 and to give relief to the afflicted as well as to us, when the Lord Jesus is revealed from heaven with his mighty angels 8 in flaming fire, inflicting vengeance on those who do not know God and on those who do not obey the gospel of our Lord Jesus. 9 These will suffer the punishment of eternal destruction, separated from the presence of the Lord and from the glory of his might, 10 when he comes to be glorified by his saints and to be marveled at on that day among all who have believed, because our testimony to you was believed.

Cf. 1 Cor 5:3–5; 2 Cor 11:12–15; Phil 1:27–30; 3:17–4:1; 2 Tim 4:14.

See also § 96 The Righteous Judgment of God.

26. The Advantages of the Jewish People

Rom 3:1–4

Then what advantage has the Jew? Or what is the value of circumcision? 2 Much, in every way. For in the first place the Jews were entrusted with the oracles of God. 3 What if some were unfaithful? Will their faithlessness nullify the faithfulness of God? 4 By no means! Although everyone is a liar, let God be proved true, as it is written, "So that you may be justified in your words, and prevail in your judging."

Rom 9:4–5

They are Israelites, and to them belong the adoption, the glory, the covenants,[a] the giving of the law, the worship, and the promises; 5 to them belong the patriarchs, and from them, according to the flesh, comes the Messiah, who is over all, God blessed forever. Amen.

Rom 15:7–9

Welcome one another, therefore, just as Christ has welcomed you, for the glory of God. 8 For I tell you that Christ has become a servant of the circumcised on behalf of the truth of God in order that he might confirm the promises given to the patriarchs, 9 and in order that the Gentiles might glorify God for his mercy. As it is written, "Therefore I will confess you among the Gentiles, and sing praises to your name"

Gal 2:15

We ourselves are Jews by birth and not Gentile sinners

Eph 2:11–12

So then, remember that at one time you Gentiles by birth, called "the uncircumcision" by those who are called "the circumcision"—a physical circumcision made in the flesh by human hands— 12 remember that you were at that time without Christ, being aliens from the commonwealth of Israel, and strangers to the covenants of promise, having no hope and without God in the world.

Phil 3:4–6

even though I, too, have reason for confidence in the flesh. If anyone else has reason to be confident in the flesh, I have more: 5 circumcised on the eighth day, a member of the people of Israel, of the tribe of Benjamin, a Hebrew born of Hebrews; as to the law, a Pharisee; 6 as to zeal, a persecutor of the church; as to righteousness under the law, blameless.

2 Tim 3:14–17

But as for you, continue in what you have learned and firmly believed, knowing from whom[b] you learned it, 15 and how from childhood you have known the sacred writings that are able to instruct you for salvation through faith in Christ Jesus. 16 All scripture is inspired by God and is useful for teaching, for reproof, for correction, and for training in righteousness, 17 so that everyone who belongs to God may be proficient, equipped for every good work.

Cf. Rom 11:11–24; 11:25–32; 15:25–27; 2 Cor 11:21b–22; 2 Tim 1:5; Acts 13:16–23; 13:26; 13:32–33.

27. All Humanity under the Power of Sin and Death

Rom 3:9–20

What then? Are we any better off? No, not at all; for we have already charged that all, both Jews and Greeks, are under the power of sin, 10 as it is written: "There is no one who is righteous, not even one; 11 there is no one who has understanding, there is no one who seeks God. 12 All have turned aside, together they have become worthless; there is no one who shows kindness, there is not even one." 13 "Their throats are opened graves; they use their tongues to deceive." "The venom of vipers is under their lips." 14 "Their mouths are full of cursing and bitterness." 15 "Their feet are swift to shed blood; 16 ruin and misery are in their paths, 17 and the way of peace they have not known." 18 "There is no fear of God before their eyes." 19 Now we know that whatever the law says, it speaks to those who are under the law, so that every mouth may be silenced, and the whole world may be held accountable to God. 20 For "no human being will be justified in his sight" by deeds prescribed by the law, for through the law comes the knowledge of sin.

§ 26 [a] **Rom 9:4** *the covenants* Other ancient authorities read *the covenant* [b] **2 Tim 3:14** *whom* The Greek word for *whom* here is plural; in other ancient authorities it is singular.

Rom 3:22b–23

οὐ γάρ ἐστιν διαστολή, 23 πάντες γὰρ ἥμαρτον καὶ ὑστεροῦνται τῆς δόξης τοῦ θεοῦ

Rom 5:12–14

Διὰ τοῦτο ὥσπερ δι' ἑνὸς ἀνθρώπου ἡ ἁμαρτία εἰς τὸν κόσμον εἰσῆλθεν καὶ διὰ τῆς ἁμαρτίας ὁ θάνατος, καὶ οὕτως εἰς πάντας ἀνθρώπους ὁ θάνατος διῆλθεν, ἐφ' ᾧ πάντες ἥμαρτον· 13 ἄχρι γὰρ νόμου ἁμαρτία ἦν ἐν κόσμῳ, ἁμαρτία δὲ οὐκ ἐλλογεῖται μὴ ὄντος νόμου, 14 ἀλλὰ ἐβασίλευσεν ὁ θάνατος ἀπὸ Ἀδὰμ μέχρι Μωϋσέως καὶ ἐπὶ τοὺς μὴ ἁμαρτήσαντας ἐπὶ τῷ ὁμοιώματι τῆς παραβάσεως Ἀδὰμ ὅς ἐστιν τύπος τοῦ μέλλοντος.

Rom 6:20–21

ὅτε γὰρ δοῦλοι ἦτε τῆς ἁμαρτίας, ἐλεύθεροι ἦτε τῇ δικαιοσύνῃ. 21 τίνα οὖν καρπὸν εἴχετε τότε; ἐφ' οἷς νῦν ἐπαισχύνεσθε, τὸ γὰρ τέλος ἐκείνων θάνατος.

Rom 7:7–13

Τί οὖν ἐροῦμεν; ὁ νόμος ἁμαρτία; μὴ γένοιτο· ἀλλὰ τὴν ἁμαρτίαν οὐκ ἔγνων εἰ μὴ διὰ νόμου· τήν τε γὰρ ἐπιθυμίαν οὐκ ᾔδειν εἰ μὴ ὁ νόμος ἔλεγεν· οὐκ ἐπιθυμήσεις. 8 ἀφορμὴν δὲ λαβοῦσα ἡ ἁμαρτία διὰ τῆς ἐντολῆς κατειργάσατο ἐν ἐμοὶ πᾶσαν ἐπιθυμίαν· χωρὶς γὰρ νόμου ἁμαρτία νεκρά. 9 ἐγὼ δὲ ἔζων χωρὶς νόμου ποτέ, ἐλθούσης δὲ τῆς ἐντολῆς ἡ ἁμαρτία ἀνέζησεν, 10 ἐγὼ δὲ ἀπέθανον καὶ εὑρέθη μοι ἡ ἐντολὴ ἡ εἰς ζωήν, αὕτη εἰς θάνατον· 11 ἡ γὰρ ἁμαρτία ἀφορμὴν λαβοῦσα διὰ τῆς ἐντολῆς ἐξηπάτησέν με καὶ δι' αὐτῆς ἀπέκτεινεν. 12 ὥστε ὁ μὲν νόμος ἅγιος καὶ ἡ ἐντολὴ ἁγία καὶ δικαία καὶ ἀγαθή. 13 Τὸ οὖν ἀγαθὸν ἐμοὶ ἐγένετο θάνατος; μὴ γένοιτο· ἀλλὰ ἡ ἁμαρτία, ἵνα φανῇ ἁμαρτία, διὰ τοῦ ἀγαθοῦ μοι κατεργαζομένη θάνατον, ἵνα γένηται καθ' ὑπερβολὴν ἁμαρτωλὸς ἡ ἁμαρτία διὰ τῆς ἐντολῆς.

Rom 11:32

συνέκλεισεν γὰρ ὁ θεὸς τοὺς πάντας εἰς ἀπείθειαν, ἵνα τοὺς πάντας ἐλεήσῃ.

1 Cor 15:56

τὸ δὲ κέντρον τοῦ θανάτου ἡ ἁμαρτία, ἡ δὲ δύναμις τῆς ἁμαρτίας ὁ νόμος

Gal 2:16

εἰδότες [δὲ] ὅτι οὐ δικαιοῦται ἄνθρωπος ἐξ ἔργων νόμου ἐὰν μὴ διὰ πίστεως Ἰησοῦ Χριστοῦ, καὶ ἡμεῖς εἰς Χριστὸν Ἰησοῦν ἐπιστεύσαμεν, ἵνα δικαιωθῶμεν ἐκ πίστεως Χριστοῦ καὶ οὐκ ἐξ ἔργων νόμου, ὅτι ἐξ ἔργων νόμου οὐ δικαιωθήσεται πᾶσα σάρξ.

Gal 3:10–12

Ὅσοι γὰρ ἐξ ἔργων νόμου εἰσίν, ὑπὸ κατάραν εἰσίν· γέγραπται γὰρ ὅτι ἐπικατάρατος πᾶς ὃς οὐκ ἐμμένει πᾶσιν τοῖς γεγραμμένοις ἐν τῷ βιβλίῳ τοῦ νόμου τοῦ ποιῆσαι αὐτά. 11 ὅτι δὲ ἐν νόμῳ οὐδεὶς δικαιοῦται παρὰ τῷ θεῷ δῆλον, ὅτι ὁ δίκαιος ἐκ πίστεως ζήσεται· 12 ὁ δὲ νόμος οὐκ ἔστιν ἐκ πίστεως, ἀλλ' ὁ ποιήσας αὐτὰ ζήσεται ἐν αὐτοῖς.

Gal 3:21–22

ὁ οὖν νόμος κατὰ τῶν ἐπαγγελιῶν [τοῦ θεοῦ]; μὴ γένοιτο. εἰ γὰρ ἐδόθη νόμος ὁ δυνάμενος ζῳοποιῆσαι, ὄντως ἐκ νόμου ἂν ἦν ἡ δικαιοσύνη· 22 ἀλλὰ συνέκλεισεν ἡ γραφὴ τὰ πάντα ὑπὸ ἁμαρτίαν, ἵνα ἡ ἐπαγγελία ἐκ πίστεως Ἰησοῦ Χριστοῦ δοθῇ τοῖς πιστεύουσιν.

Acts 13:38–39

γνωστὸν οὖν ἔστω ὑμῖν, ἄνδρες ἀδελφοί, ὅτι διὰ τούτου ὑμῖν ἄφεσις ἁμαρτιῶν καταγγέλλεται, [καὶ] ἀπὸ πάντων ὧν οὐκ ἠδυνήθητε ἐν νόμῳ Μωϋσέως δικαιωθῆναι, 39 ἐν τούτῳ πᾶς ὁ πιστεύων δικαιοῦται.

Cf. Rom 1:18–32; 2:12–13; 2:17–24; 5:15–21; 6:16–19; 6:22–23; 7:5; 8:5–8; 1 Cor 15:21–22; Eph 2:1–3.

See the corresponding themes § 28 The Revelation of God's Righteousness; § 42 Liberation from Slavery; § 48 Life through Christ Jesus; and § 89 The Resurrection of the Body

28. The Revelation of God's Righteousness

Rom 1:16–17

Οὐ γὰρ ἐπαισχύνομαι τὸ εὐαγγέλιον, δύναμις γὰρ θεοῦ ἐστιν εἰς σωτηρίαν παντὶ τῷ πιστεύοντι, Ἰουδαίῳ τε πρῶτον καὶ Ἕλληνι. 17 δικαιοσύνη γὰρ θεοῦ ἐν αὐτῷ ἀποκαλύπτεται ἐκ πίστεως εἰς πίστιν, καθὼς γέγραπται· ὁ δὲ δίκαιος ἐκ πίστεως ζήσεται.

Rom 3:21–31

Νυνὶ δὲ χωρὶς νόμου δικαιοσύνη θεοῦ πεφανέρωται μαρτυρουμένη ὑπὸ τοῦ νόμου καὶ τῶν προφητῶν, 22 δικαιοσύνη δὲ θεοῦ διὰ πίστεως Ἰησοῦ Χριστοῦ εἰς πάντας τοὺς πιστεύοντας. οὐ γάρ ἐστιν διαστολή, 23 πάντες γὰρ ἥμαρτον καὶ ὑστεροῦνται τῆς δόξης τοῦ θεοῦ 24 δικαιούμενοι δωρεὰν τῇ αὐτοῦ χάριτι διὰ τῆς ἀπολυτρώσεως τῆς ἐν Χριστῷ Ἰησοῦ· 25 ὃν προέθετο ὁ θεὸς ἱλαστήριον διὰ [τῆς] πίστεως ἐν τῷ αὐτοῦ αἵματι εἰς ἔνδειξιν τῆς δικαιοσύνης αὐτοῦ διὰ τὴν πάρεσιν τῶν προγεγονότων ἁμαρτημάτων 26 ἐν τῇ ἀνοχῇ τοῦ θεοῦ, πρὸς τὴν ἔνδειξιν τῆς δικαιοσύνης αὐτοῦ ἐν τῷ νῦν καιρῷ, εἰς τὸ εἶναι αὐτὸν δίκαιον καὶ δικαιοῦντα τὸν ἐκ πίστεως Ἰησοῦ. 27 Ποῦ οὖν ἡ καύχησις; ἐξεκλείσθη. διὰ ποίου νόμου; τῶν ἔργων; οὐχί, ἀλλὰ διὰ νόμου πίστεως. 28 λογιζόμεθα γὰρ δικαιοῦσθαι πίστει ἄνθρωπον χωρὶς ἔργων νόμου. 29 ἢ Ἰουδαίων ὁ θεὸς μόνον; οὐχὶ καὶ ἐθνῶν; ναὶ καὶ ἐθνῶν, 30 εἴπερ εἷς ὁ θεὸς ὃς δικαιώσει περιτομὴν ἐκ πίστεως καὶ ἀκροβυστίαν διὰ τῆς πίστεως. 31 νόμον οὖν καταργοῦμεν διὰ τῆς πίστεως; μὴ γένοιτο· ἀλλὰ νόμον ἱστάνομεν.

Rom 9:30–10:13

Τί οὖν ἐροῦμεν; ὅτι ἔθνη τὰ μὴ διώκοντα δικαιοσύνην κατέλαβεν δικαιοσύνην, δικαιοσύνην δὲ τὴν ἐκ πίστεως, 31 Ἰσραὴλ δὲ διώκων νόμον δικαιοσύνης εἰς νόμον οὐκ ἔφθασεν. 32 διὰ τί; ὅτι οὐκ ἐκ πίστεως ἀλλ' ὡς ἐξ ἔργων· προσέκοψαν τῷ λίθῳ τοῦ προσκόμματος, 33 καθὼς

Rom 3:22b–23
For there is no distinction, 23 since all have sinned and fall short of the glory of God

Rom 5:12–14
Therefore, just as sin came into the world through one man, and death came through sin, and so death spread to all because all have sinned— 13 sin was indeed in the world before the law, but sin is not reckoned when there is no law. 14 Yet death exercised dominion from Adam to Moses, even over those whose sins were not like the transgression of Adam, who is a type of the one who was to come.

Rom 6:20–21
When you were slaves of sin, you were free in regard to righteousness. 21 So what fruit did you have then? Because of these things you are now ashamed, because the end of those things is death.

Rom 7:7–13
What then should we say? That the law is sin? By no means! Yet, if it had not been for the law, I would not have known sin. I would not have known what it is to covet if the law had not said, "You shall not covet." 8 But sin, seizing an opportunity in the commandment, produced in me all kinds of covetousness. Apart from the law sin lies dead. 9 I was once alive apart from the law, but when the commandment came, sin revived 10 and I died, and the very commandment that promised life proved to be death to me. 11 For sin, seizing an opportunity in the commandment, deceived me and through it killed me. 12 So the law is holy, and the commandment is holy and just and good. 13 Did what is good, then, bring death to me? By no means! It was sin, working death in me through what is good, in order that sin might be shown to be sin, and through the commandment might become sinful beyond measure.

Rom 11:32
For God has imprisoned all in disobedience so that he may be merciful to all.

1 Cor 15:56
The sting of death is sin, and the power of sin is the law.

Gal 2:16
yet we know that a person is justified not by the works of the law but through faith in Jesus Christ. And we have come to believe in Christ Jesus, so that we might be justified by faith in Christ, and not by doing the works of the law, because no one will be justified by the works of the law.

Gal 3:10–12
For all who rely on the works of the law are under a curse; for it is written, "Cursed is everyone who does not observe and obey all the things written in the book of the law." 11 Now it is evident that no one is justified before God by the law; for "The one who is righteous will live by faith." 12 But the law does not rest on faith; on the contrary, "Whoever does the works of the law will live by them."

Gal 3:21–22
Is the law then opposed to the promises of God? Certainly not! For if a law had been given that could make alive, then righteousness would indeed come through the law. 22 But the scripture has imprisoned all things under the power of sin, so that what was promised through faith in Jesus Christ might be given to those who believe.

Acts 13:38–39
Let it be known to you therefore, my brothers, that through this man forgiveness of sins is proclaimed to you; 39 by this Jesus everyone who believes is set free from all those sins from which you could not be freed by the law of Moses.

Cf. Rom 1:18–32; 2:12–13; 2:17–24; 5:15–21; 6:16–19; 6:22–23; 7:5; 8:5–8; 1 Cor 15:21–22; Eph 2:1–3.

See the corresponding themes § 28 The Revelation of God's Righteousness; § 42 Liberation from Slavery; § 48 Life through Christ Jesus; and § 89 The Resurrection of the Body

28. The Revelation of God's Righteousness

Rom 1:16–17
For I am not ashamed of the gospel; it is the power of God for salvation to everyone who has faith, to the Jew first and also to the Greek. 17 For in it the righteousness of God is revealed through faith for faith; as it is written, "The one who is righteous will live by faith."

Rom 3:21–31
But now, apart from law, the righteousness of God has been disclosed, and is attested by the law and the prophets, 22 the righteousness of God through faith in Jesus Christ for all who believe. For there is no distinction, 23 since all have sinned and fall short of the glory of God; 24 they are now justified by his grace as a gift, through the redemption that is in Christ Jesus, 25 whom God put forward as a sacrifice of atonement by his blood, effective through faith. He did this to show his righteousness, because in his divine forbearance he had passed over the sins previously committed; 26 it was to prove at the present time that he himself is righteous and that he justifies the one who has faith in Jesus. 27 Then what becomes of boasting? It is excluded. By what law? By that of works? No, but by the law of faith. 28 For we hold that a person is justified by faith apart from works prescribed by the law. 29 Or is God the God of Jews only? Is he not the God of Gentiles also? Yes, of Gentiles also, 30 since God is one; and he will justify the circumcised on the ground of faith and the uncircumcised through that same faith. 31 Do we then overthrow the law by this faith? By no means! On the contrary, we uphold the law.

Rom 9:30–10:13
What then are we to say? Gentiles, who did not strive for righteousness, have attained it, that is, righteousness through faith; 31 but Israel, who did strive for the righteousness that is based on the law, did not succeed in fulfilling that law. 32 Why not? Because they did not strive for it on the basis of faith, but as if it were based on works. They have stumbled over the stumbling stone, 33 as

γέγραπται· ἰδοὺ τίθημι ἐν Σιὼν λίθον προσκόμματος καὶ πέτραν σκανδάλου, καὶ ὁ πιστεύων ἐπ᾽ αὐτῷ οὐ καταισχυνθήσεται. **10** Ἀδελφοί, ἡ μὲν εὐδοκία τῆς ἐμῆς καρδίας καὶ ἡ δέησις πρὸς τὸν θεὸν ὑπὲρ αὐτῶν εἰς σωτηρίαν. **2** μαρτυρῶ γὰρ αὐτοῖς ὅτι ζῆλον θεοῦ ἔχουσιν ἀλλ᾽ οὐ κατ᾽ ἐπίγνωσιν· **3** ἀγνοοῦντες γὰρ τὴν τοῦ θεοῦ δικαιοσύνην καὶ τὴν ἰδίαν [δικαιοσύνην] ζητοῦντες στῆσαι, τῇ δικαιοσύνῃ τοῦ θεοῦ οὐχ ὑπετάγησαν. **4** τέλος γὰρ νόμου Χριστὸς εἰς δικαιοσύνην παντὶ τῷ πιστεύοντι. **5** Μωϋσῆς γὰρ γράφει τὴν δικαιοσύνην τὴν ἐκ [τοῦ] νόμου ὅτι ὁ ποιήσας αὐτὰ ἄνθρωπος ζήσεται ἐν ⸀αὐτοῖς. **6** ἡ δὲ ἐκ πίστεως δικαιοσύνη οὕτως λέγει· μὴ εἴπῃς ἐν τῇ καρδίᾳ σου· τίς ἀναβήσεται εἰς τὸν οὐρανόν; τοῦτ᾽ ἔστιν Χριστὸν καταγαγεῖν· **7** ἤ· τίς καταβήσεται εἰς τὴν ἄβυσσον; τοῦτ᾽ ἔστιν Χριστὸν ἐκ νεκρῶν ἀναγαγεῖν. **8** ἀλλὰ τί λέγει; ἐγγύς σου τὸ ῥῆμά ἐστιν ἐν τῷ στόματί σου καὶ ἐν τῇ καρδίᾳ σου, τοῦτ᾽ ἔστιν τὸ ῥῆμα τῆς πίστεως ὃ κηρύσσομεν. **9** ὅτι ἐὰν ὁμολογήσῃς ἐν τῷ στόματί σου κύριον Ἰησοῦν καὶ πιστεύσῃς ἐν τῇ καρδίᾳ σου ὅτι ὁ θεὸς αὐτὸν ἤγειρεν ἐκ νεκρῶν, σωθήσῃ· **10** καρδίᾳ γὰρ πιστεύεται εἰς δικαιοσύνην, στόματι δὲ ὁμολογεῖται εἰς σωτηρίαν. **11** λέγει γὰρ ἡ γραφή· πᾶς ὁ πιστεύων ἐπ᾽ αὐτῷ οὐ καταισχυνθήσεται. **12** οὐ γάρ ἐστιν διαστολὴ Ἰουδαίου τε καὶ Ἕλληνος, ὁ γὰρ αὐτὸς κύριος πάντων, πλουτῶν εἰς πάντας τοὺς ἐπικαλουμένους αὐτόν· **13** πᾶς γὰρ ὃς ἂν ἐπικαλέσηται τὸ ὄνομα κυρίου σωθήσεται.

1 Cor 1:29–31

ὅπως μὴ καυχήσηται πᾶσα σὰρξ ἐνώπιον τοῦ θεοῦ. **30** ἐξ αὐτοῦ δὲ ὑμεῖς ἐστε ἐν Χριστῷ Ἰησοῦ, ὃς ἐγενήθη σοφία ἡμῖν ἀπὸ θεοῦ, δικαιοσύνη τε καὶ ἁγιασμὸς καὶ ἀπολύτρωσις, **31** ἵνα καθὼς γέγραπται· ὁ καυχώμενος ἐν κυρίῳ καυχάσθω.

2 Cor 5:21

τὸν μὴ γνόντα ἁμαρτίαν ὑπὲρ ἡμῶν ἁμαρτίαν ἐποίησεν, ἵνα ἡμεῖς γενώμεθα δικαιοσύνη θεοῦ ἐν αὐτῷ.

Gal 2:15–21

Ἡμεῖς φύσει Ἰουδαῖοι καὶ οὐκ ἐξ ἐθνῶν ἁμαρτωλοί· **16** εἰδότες [δὲ] ὅτι οὐ δικαιοῦται ἄνθρωπος ἐξ ἔργων νόμου ἐὰν μὴ διὰ πίστεως Ἰησοῦ Χριστοῦ, καὶ ἡμεῖς εἰς Χριστὸν Ἰησοῦν ἐπιστεύσαμεν, ἵνα δικαιωθῶμεν ἐκ πίστεως Χριστοῦ καὶ οὐκ ἐξ ἔργων νόμου, ὅτι ἐξ ἔργων νόμου οὐ δικαιωθήσεται πᾶσα σάρξ. **17** εἰ δὲ ζητοῦντες δικαιωθῆναι ἐν Χριστῷ εὑρέθημεν καὶ αὐτοὶ ἁμαρτωλοί, ἆρα Χριστὸς ἁμαρτίας διάκονος; μὴ γένοιτο. **18** εἰ γὰρ ἃ κατέλυσα ταῦτα πάλιν οἰκοδομῶ, παραβάτην ἐμαυτὸν συνιστάνω. **19** ἐγὼ γὰρ διὰ νόμου νόμῳ ἀπέθανον, ἵνα θεῷ ζήσω. Χριστῷ συνεσταύρωμαι· **20** ζῶ δὲ οὐκέτι ἐγώ, ζῇ δὲ ἐν ἐμοὶ Χριστός· ὃ δὲ νῦν ζῶ ἐν σαρκί, ἐν πίστει ζῶ τῇ τοῦ υἱοῦ τοῦ θεοῦ τοῦ ἀγαπήσαντός με καὶ παραδόντος ἑαυτὸν ὑπὲρ ἐμοῦ. **21** Οὐκ ἀθετῶ τὴν χάριν τοῦ θεοῦ· εἰ γὰρ διὰ νόμου δικαιοσύνη, ἄρα Χριστὸς δωρεὰν ἀπέθανεν.

Gal 3:8

προϊδοῦσα δὲ ἡ γραφὴ ὅτι ἐκ πίστεως δικαιοῖ τὰ ἔθνη ὁ θεός, προευηγγελίσατο τῷ Ἀβραὰμ ὅτι ἐνευλογηθήσονται ἐν σοὶ πάντα τὰ ἔθνη

Gal 3:21–24

ὁ οὖν νόμος κατὰ τῶν ἐπαγγελιῶν [τοῦ θεοῦ]; μὴ γένοιτο. εἰ γὰρ ἐδόθη νόμος ὁ δυνάμενος ζῳοποιῆσαι, ὄντως ἐκ νόμου ἂν ἦν ἡ δικαιοσύνη· **22** ἀλλὰ συνέκλεισεν ἡ γραφὴ τὰ πάντα ὑπὸ ἁμαρτίαν, ἵνα ἡ ἐπαγγελία ἐκ πίστεως Ἰησοῦ Χριστοῦ δοθῇ τοῖς πιστεύουσιν. **23** Πρὸ τοῦ δὲ ἐλθεῖν τὴν πίστιν ὑπὸ νόμον ἐφρουρούμεθα συγκλειόμενοι εἰς τὴν μέλλουσαν πίστιν ἀποκαλυφθῆναι, **24** ὥστε ὁ νόμος παιδαγωγὸς ἡμῶν γέγονεν εἰς Χριστόν, ἵνα ἐκ πίστεως δικαιωθῶμεν

Eph 2:8–10

Τῇ γὰρ χάριτί ἐστε σεσῳσμένοι διὰ πίστεως· καὶ τοῦτο οὐκ ἐξ ὑμῶν, θεοῦ τὸ δῶρον· **9** οὐκ ἐξ ἔργων, ἵνα μή τις καυχήσηται. **10** αὐτοῦ γάρ ἐσμεν ποίημα, κτισθέντες ἐν Χριστῷ Ἰησοῦ ἐπὶ ἔργοις ἀγαθοῖς οἷς προητοίμασεν ὁ θεός, ἵνα ἐν αὐτοῖς περιπατήσωμεν.

Phil 3:9

καὶ εὑρεθῶ ἐν αὐτῷ, μὴ ἔχων ἐμὴν δικαιοσύνην τὴν ἐκ νόμου ἀλλὰ τὴν διὰ πίστεως Χριστοῦ, τὴν ἐκ θεοῦ δικαιοσύνην ἐπὶ τῇ πίστει

Titus 3:4–7

ὅτε δὲ ἡ χρηστότης καὶ ἡ φιλανθρωπία ἐπεφάνη τοῦ σωτῆρος ἡμῶν θεοῦ, **5** οὐκ ἐξ ἔργων τῶν ἐν δικαιοσύνῃ ἃ ἐποιήσαμεν ἡμεῖς ἀλλὰ κατὰ τὸ αὐτοῦ ἔλεος ἔσωσεν ἡμᾶς διὰ λουτροῦ παλιγγενεσίας καὶ ἀνακαινώσεως πνεύματος ἁγίου, **6** οὗ ἐξέχεεν ἐφ᾽ ἡμᾶς πλουσίως διὰ Ἰησοῦ Χριστοῦ τοῦ σωτῆρος ἡμῶν, **7** ἵνα δικαιωθέντες τῇ ἐκείνου χάριτι κληρονόμοι γενηθῶμεν κατ᾽ ἐλπίδα ζωῆς αἰωνίου.

Acts 13:38–39

γνωστὸν οὖν ἔστω ὑμῖν, ἄνδρες ἀδελφοί, ὅτι διὰ τούτου ὑμῖν ἄφεσις ἁμαρτιῶν καταγγέλλεται, [καὶ] ἀπὸ πάντων ὧν οὐκ ἠδυνήθητε ἐν νόμῳ Μωϋσέως δικαιωθῆναι, **39** ἐν τούτῳ πᾶς ὁ πιστεύων δικαιοῦται.

Cf. Rom 2:1–11; 2:12–13; 3:1–8; 4:1–25; 5:1; 5:6–11; 5:15–21; 6:12–23; 8:1–11; 8:31–39; 14:17–18.

29. The Son of God Made Flesh

Rom 1:3–4

περὶ τοῦ υἱοῦ αὐτοῦ τοῦ γενομένου ἐκ σπέρματος Δαυὶδ κατὰ σάρκα, **4** τοῦ ὁρισθέντος υἱοῦ θεοῦ ἐν δυνάμει κατὰ πνεῦμα ἁγιωσύνης ἐξ ἀναστάσεως νεκρῶν, Ἰησοῦ Χριστοῦ τοῦ κυρίου ἡμῶν

§ 28 Rom 10:5 *αυτοις* 𝔓46 ℵ2 D *Byz*] αυτη ℵ* A B 33. 1739. 1881

it is written, "See, I am laying in Zion a stone that will make people stumble, a rock that will make them fall, and whoever believes in him will not be put to shame." **10** Brothers and sisters, my heart's desire and prayer to God for them is that they may be saved. **2** I can testify that they have a zeal for God, but it is not enlightened. **3** For, being ignorant of the righteousness that comes from God, and seeking to establish their own, they have not submitted to God's righteousness. **4** For Christ is the goal[a] of the law so that there may be righteousness for everyone who believes. **5** Moses writes concerning the righteousness that comes from the law, that "the person who does these things will live by them."[b] **6** But the righteousness that comes from faith says, "Do not say in your heart, 'Who will ascend into heaven?'" (that is, to bring Christ down) **7** "or 'Who will descend into the abyss?'" (that is, to bring Christ up from the dead). **8** But what does it say? "The word is near you, on your lips and in your heart" (that is, the word of faith that we proclaim); **9** because if you confess with your lips that Jesus is Lord and believe in your heart that God raised him from the dead, you will be saved. **10** For one believes with the heart and so is justified, and one confesses with the mouth and so is saved. **11** The scripture says, "No one who believes in him will be put to shame." **12** For there is no distinction between Jew and Greek; the same Lord is Lord of all and is generous to all who call on him. **13** For, "Everyone who calls on the name of the Lord shall be saved."

1 Cor 1:29–31

so that no one might boast in the presence of God. **30** He is the source of your life in Christ Jesus, who became for us wisdom from God, and righteousness and sanctification and redemption, **31** in order that, as it is written, "Let the one who boasts, boast in the Lord."

2 Cor 5:21

For our sake he made him to be sin who knew no sin, so that in him we might become the righteousness of God.

Gal 2:15–21

We ourselves are Jews by birth and not Gentile sinners; **16** yet we know that a person is justified not by the works of the law but through faith in Jesus Christ. And we have come to believe in Christ Jesus, so that we might be justified by faith in Christ, and not by doing the works of the law, because no one will be justified by the works of the law. **17** But if, in our effort to be justified in Christ, we ourselves have been found to be sinners, is Christ then a servant of sin? Certainly not! **18** But if I build up again the very things that I once tore down, then I demonstrate that I am a transgressor. **19** For through the law I died to the law, so that I might live to God. I have been crucified with Christ; **20** and it is no longer I who live, but it is Christ who lives in me. And the life I now live in the flesh I live by faith in the Son of God, who loved me and gave himself for me. **21** I do not nullify the grace of God; for if justification comes through the law, then Christ died for nothing.

Gal 3:8

And the scripture, foreseeing that God would justify the Gentiles by faith, declared the gospel beforehand to Abraham, saying, "All the Gentiles shall be blessed in you."

Gal 3:21–24

Is the law then opposed to the promises of God? Certainly not! For if a law had been given that could make alive, then righteousness would indeed come through the law. **22** But the scripture has imprisoned all things under the power of sin, so that what was promised through faith in Jesus Christ might be given to those who believe. **23** Now before faith came, we were imprisoned and guarded under the law until faith would be revealed. **24** Therefore the law was our disciplinarian until Christ came, so that we might be justified by faith.

Eph 2:8–10

For by grace you have been saved through faith, and this is not your own doing; it is the gift of God— **9** not the result of works, so that no one may boast. **10** For we are what he has made us, created in Christ Jesus for good works, which God prepared beforehand to be our way of life.

Phil 3:9

and be found in him, not having a righteousness of my own that comes from the law, but one that comes through faith in Christ, the righteousness from God based on faith.

Titus 3:4–7

But when the goodness and loving kindness of God our Savior appeared, **5** he saved us, not because of any works of righteousness that we had done, but according to his mercy, through the water of rebirth and renewal by the Holy Spirit. **6** This Spirit he poured out on us richly through Jesus Christ our Savior, **7** so that, having been justified by his grace, we might become heirs according to the hope of eternal life.

Acts 13:38–39

Let it be known to you therefore, my brothers, that through this man forgiveness of sins is proclaimed to you; **39** by this Jesus everyone who believes is set free from all those sins from which you could not be freed by the law of Moses.

Cf. Rom 2:1–11; 2:12–13; 3:1–8; 4:1–25; 5:1; 5:6–11; 5:15–21; 6:12–23; 8:1–11; 8:31–39; 14:17–18.

29. The Son of God Made Flesh

Rom 1:3–4

the gospel concerning his Son, who was descended from David according to the flesh **4** and was declared to be Son of God with power according to the Spirit[a] of holiness by resurrection from the dead, Jesus Christ our Lord

§ 28 [a] **Rom 10:4** *goal* Or *end* (so NRSV) [b] **Rom 10:5** *them* Other ancient authorities read *it*, i.e., the righteousness that comes from the law **§ 29** [a] **Rom 1:4** *Spirit* NRSV alternate translation

Rom 8:3–4

Τὸ γὰρ ἀδύνατον τοῦ νόμου ἐν ᾧ ἠσθένει διὰ τῆς σαρκός, ὁ θεὸς τὸν ἑαυτοῦ υἱὸν πέμψας ἐν ὁμοιώματι σαρκὸς ἁμαρτίας καὶ περὶ ἁμαρτίας κατέκρινεν τὴν ἁμαρτίαν ἐν τῇ σαρκί, **4** ἵνα τὸ δικαίωμα τοῦ νόμου πληρωθῇ ἐν ἡμῖν τοῖς μὴ κατὰ σάρκα περιπατοῦσιν ἀλλὰ κατὰ πνεῦμα.

Rom 9:5

ὧν οἱ πατέρες καὶ ἐξ ὧν ὁ Χριστὸς τὸ κατὰ σάρκα, ὁ ὢν ἐπὶ πάντων θεὸς εὐλογητὸς εἰς τοὺς αἰῶνας, ἀμήν.

Rom 10:6–13

ἡ δὲ ἐκ πίστεως δικαιοσύνη οὕτως λέγει· μὴ εἴπῃς ἐν τῇ καρδίᾳ σου· τίς ἀναβήσεται εἰς τὸν οὐρανόν; τοῦτ᾽ ἔστιν Χριστὸν καταγαγεῖν· **7** ἤ· τίς καταβήσεται εἰς τὴν ἄβυσσον; τοῦτ᾽ ἔστιν Χριστὸν ἐκ νεκρῶν ἀναγαγεῖν. **8** ἀλλὰ τί λέγει; ἐγγύς σου τὸ ῥῆμά ἐστιν ἐν τῷ στόματί σου καὶ ἐν τῇ καρδίᾳ σου, τοῦτ᾽ ἔστιν τὸ ῥῆμα τῆς πίστεως ὃ κηρύσσομεν. **9** ὅτι ἐὰν ὁμολογήσῃς ἐν τῷ στόματί σου κύριον Ἰησοῦν καὶ πιστεύσῃς ἐν τῇ καρδίᾳ σου ὅτι ὁ θεὸς αὐτὸν ἤγειρεν ἐκ νεκρῶν, σωθήσῃ· **10** καρδίᾳ γὰρ πιστεύεται εἰς δικαιοσύνην, στόματι δὲ ὁμολογεῖται εἰς σωτηρίαν. **11** λέγει γὰρ ἡ γραφή· πᾶς ὁ πιστεύων ἐπ᾽ αὐτῷ οὐ καταισχυνθήσεται. **12** οὐ γάρ ἐστιν διαστολὴ Ἰουδαίου τε καὶ Ἕλληνος, ὁ γὰρ αὐτὸς κύριος πάντων, πλουτῶν εἰς πάντας τοὺς ἐπικαλουμένους αὐτόν· **13** πᾶς γὰρ ὃς ἂν ἐπικαλέσηται τὸ ὄνομα κυρίου σωθήσεται.

1 Cor 8:6

ἀλλ᾽ ἡμῖν εἷς θεὸς ὁ πατὴρ ἐξ οὗ τὰ πάντα καὶ ἡμεῖς εἰς αὐτόν, καὶ εἷς κύριος Ἰησοῦς Χριστὸς δι᾽ οὗ τὰ πάντα καὶ ἡμεῖς δι᾽ αὐτοῦ.

Gal 4:4–6

ὅτε δὲ ἦλθεν τὸ πλήρωμα τοῦ χρόνου, ἐξαπέστειλεν ὁ θεὸς τὸν υἱὸν αὐτοῦ, γενόμενον ἐκ γυναικός, γενόμενον ὑπὸ νόμον, **5** ἵνα τοὺς ὑπὸ νόμον ἐξαγοράσῃ, ἵνα τὴν υἱοθεσίαν ἀπολάβωμεν. **6** Ὅτι δέ ἐστε υἱοί, ἐξαπέστειλεν ὁ θεὸς τὸ πνεῦμα τοῦ υἱοῦ αὐτοῦ εἰς τὰς καρδίας ⸀ἡμῶν κρᾶζον· αββα ὁ πατήρ.

Phil 2:5–11

Τοῦτο φρονεῖτε ἐν ὑμῖν ὃ καὶ ἐν Χριστῷ Ἰησοῦ, **6** ὃς ἐν μορφῇ θεοῦ ὑπάρχων οὐχ ἁρπαγμὸν ἡγήσατο τὸ εἶναι ἴσα θεῷ, **7** ἀλλὰ ἑαυτὸν ἐκένωσεν μορφὴν δούλου λαβών, ἐν ὁμοιώματι ἀνθρώπων γενόμενος· καὶ σχήματι εὑρεθεὶς ὡς ἄνθρωπος **8** ἐταπείνωσεν ἑαυτὸν γενόμενος ὑπήκοος μέχρι θανάτου, θανάτου δὲ σταυροῦ. **9** διὸ καὶ ὁ θεὸς αὐτὸν ὑπερύψωσεν καὶ ἐχαρίσατο αὐτῷ τὸ ὄνομα τὸ ὑπὲρ πᾶν ὄνομα, **10** ἵνα ἐν τῷ ὀνόματι Ἰησοῦ πᾶν γόνυ κάμψῃ ἐπουρανίων καὶ ἐπιγείων καὶ καταχθονίων **11** καὶ πᾶσα γλῶσσα ἐξομολογήσηται ὅτι κύριος Ἰησοῦς Χριστὸς εἰς δόξαν θεοῦ πατρός.

Col 1:13–20

ὃς ἐρρύσατο ἡμᾶς ἐκ τῆς ἐξουσίας τοῦ σκότους καὶ μετέστησεν εἰς τὴν βασιλείαν τοῦ υἱοῦ τῆς ἀγάπης αὐτοῦ, **14** ἐν ᾧ ἔχομεν τὴν ⸀ἀπολύτρωσιν, τὴν ἄφεσιν τῶν ἁμαρτιῶν· **15** ὅς ἐστιν εἰκὼν τοῦ θεοῦ τοῦ ἀοράτου, πρωτότοκος πάσης κτίσεως, **16** ὅτι ἐν αὐτῷ ἐκτίσθη τὰ πάντα ἐν τοῖς οὐρανοῖς καὶ ἐπὶ τῆς γῆς, τὰ ὁρατὰ καὶ τὰ ἀόρατα, εἴτε θρόνοι εἴτε κυριότητες εἴτε ἀρχαὶ εἴτε ἐξουσίαι· τὰ πάντα δι᾽ αὐτοῦ καὶ εἰς αὐτὸν ἔκτισται· **17** καὶ αὐτός ἐστιν πρὸ πάντων καὶ τὰ πάντα ἐν αὐτῷ συνέστηκεν, **18** καὶ αὐτός ἐστιν ἡ κεφαλὴ τοῦ σώματος τῆς ἐκκλησίας· ὅς ἐστιν ἀρχή, πρωτότοκος ἐκ τῶν νεκρῶν, ἵνα γένηται ἐν πᾶσιν αὐτὸς πρωτεύων, **19** ὅτι ἐν αὐτῷ εὐδόκησεν πᾶν τὸ πλήρωμα κατοικῆσαι **20** καὶ δι᾽ αὐτοῦ ἀποκαταλλάξαι τὰ πάντα εἰς αὐτόν, εἰρηνοποιήσας διὰ τοῦ αἵματος τοῦ σταυροῦ αὐτοῦ, [δι᾽ αὐτοῦ] εἴτε τὰ ἐπὶ τῆς γῆς εἴτε τὰ ἐν τοῖς οὐρανοῖς.

Col 2:9

ὅτι ἐν αὐτῷ κατοικεῖ πᾶν τὸ πλήρωμα τῆς θεότητος σωματικῶς

1 Tim 3:16

καὶ ὁμολογουμένως μέγα ἐστὶν τὸ τῆς εὐσεβείας μυστήριον· ⸀ὃς ἐφανερώθη ἐν σαρκί, ἐδικαιώθη ἐν πνεύματι, ὤφθη ἀγγέλοις, ἐκηρύχθη ἐν ἔθνεσιν, ἐπιστεύθη ἐν κόσμῳ, ἀνελήμφθη ἐν δόξῃ.

Cf. 2 Cor 5:18–21; 8:9; 1 Tim 1:15; 2:5–6; Titus 2:11–14.

30. The Son of God's Redemptive Sharing in the Human Plight

Rom 8:3–4

Τὸ γὰρ ἀδύνατον τοῦ νόμου ἐν ᾧ ἠσθένει διὰ τῆς σαρκός, ὁ θεὸς τὸν ἑαυτοῦ υἱὸν πέμψας ἐν ὁμοιώματι σαρκὸς ἁμαρτίας καὶ περὶ ἁμαρτίας κατέκρινεν τὴν ἁμαρτίαν ἐν τῇ σαρκί, **4** ἵνα τὸ δικαίωμα τοῦ νόμου πληρωθῇ ἐν ἡμῖν τοῖς μὴ κατὰ σάρκα περιπατοῦσιν ἀλλὰ κατὰ πνεῦμα.

2 Cor 5:14–21

ἡ γὰρ ἀγάπη τοῦ Χριστοῦ συνέχει ἡμᾶς, κρίναντας τοῦτο, ὅτι εἷς ὑπὲρ πάντων ἀπέθανεν, ἄρα οἱ πάντες ἀπέθανον· **15** καὶ ὑπὲρ πάντων ἀπέθανεν, ἵνα οἱ ζῶντες μηκέτι ἑαυτοῖς ζῶσιν ἀλλὰ τῷ ὑπὲρ αὐτῶν ἀποθανόντι καὶ ἐγερθέντι. **16** Ὥστε ἡμεῖς ἀπὸ τοῦ νῦν οὐδένα οἴδαμεν κατὰ σάρκα· εἰ καὶ ἐγνώκαμεν κατὰ σάρκα Χριστόν, ἀλλὰ νῦν οὐκέτι γινώσκομεν. **17** ὥστε εἴ τις ἐν Χριστῷ, καινὴ κτίσις· τὰ ἀρχαῖα παρῆλθεν, ἰδοὺ γέγονεν καινά. **18** τὰ δὲ πάντα ἐκ τοῦ θεοῦ τοῦ καταλλάξαντος ἡμᾶς ἑαυτῷ διὰ Χριστοῦ καὶ δόντος ἡμῖν τὴν διακονίαν τῆς καταλλαγῆς, **19** ὡς ὅτι θεὸς ἦν ἐν Χριστῷ κόσμον καταλλάσσων ἑαυτῷ, μὴ λογιζόμενος αὐτοῖς

§ 29 **Gal 4:6** ***ημων*** 𝔓[46] ℵ A B C D* 1739. 1881] υμων D² 33 *Byz* **Col 1:14** ***απολυτρωσιν*** ℵ A B C D 33. 1739. 1881 *Byz*] *add.* δια του αιματος αυτου *pc* **1 Tim 3:16** ***ος*** ℵ* A* C* 33] ὃ D* ¦ θεος ℵᶜ Aᶜ C² D² 1739. 1881 *Byz*

Rom 8:3–4

For God has done what the law, weak-
ened by the flesh, could not do: by
sending his own Son in the likeness of
sinful flesh, and to deal with sin, he
condemned sin in the flesh, 4 so that
the just requirement of the law might
be fulfilled in us, who walk not accord-
ing to the flesh but according to the
Spirit.

Rom 9:5

to them belong the patriarchs, and from them, according to the flesh, comes the Messiah, who is over all, God blessed forever. Amen.

Rom 10:6–13

But the righteousness that comes from
faith says, "Do not say in your heart,
'Who will ascend into heaven?'" (that
is, to bring Christ down) 7 "or 'Who
will descend into the abyss?'" (that is,
to bring Christ up from the dead). 8 But
what does it say? "The word is near
you, on your lips and in your heart"
(that is, the word of faith that we pro-
claim); 9 because if you confess with
your lips that Jesus is Lord and believe
in your heart that God raised him from
the dead, you will be saved. 10 For one
believes with the heart and so is justi-
fied, and one confesses with the mouth
and so is saved. 11 The scripture says,
"No one who believes in him will be
put to shame." 12 For there is no distinc-
tion between Jew and Greek; the same
Lord is Lord of all and is generous to
all who call on him. 13 For, "Everyone
who calls on the name of the Lord shall
be saved."

1 Cor 8:6

yet for us there is one God, the Father, from whom are all things and for whom we exist, and one Lord, Jesus Christ, through whom are all things and through whom we exist.

Gal 4:4–6

But when the fullness of time had come,
God sent his Son, born of a woman,
born under the law, 5 in order to redeem
those who were under the law, so that
we might receive adoption as children.
6 And because you are children, God
has sent the Spirit of his Son into our[b]
hearts, crying, "Abba! Father!"

Phil 2:5–11

Let the same mind be in you that was
in Christ Jesus, 6 who, though he was
in the form of God, did not regard
equality with God as something to be
exploited, 7 but emptied himself, tak-
ing the form of a slave, being born in
human likeness. And being found in
human form, 8 he humbled himself
and became obedient to the point of
death— even death on a cross. 9 There-
fore God also highly exalted him and
gave him the name that is above every
name, 10 so that at the name of Jesus
every knee should bend, in heaven and
on earth and under the earth, 11 and
every tongue should confess that Jesus
Christ is Lord, to the glory of God the
Father.

Col 1:13–20

He has rescued us from the power of
darkness and transferred us into the
kingdom of his beloved Son, 14 in whom
we have redemption,[c] the forgiveness of
sins. 15 Who[d] is the image of the invis-
ible God, the firstborn of all creation;
16 for in him all things in heaven and on
earth were created, things visible and
invisible, whether thrones or dominions
or rulers or powers—all things have
been created through him and for him.
17 He himself is before all things, and
in him all things hold together. 18 He
is the head of the body, the church; he
is the beginning, the firstborn from the
dead, so that he might come to have first
place in everything. 19 For in him all the
fullness of God was pleased to dwell,
20 and through him God was pleased to
reconcile to himself all things, whether
on earth or in heaven, by making peace
through the blood of his cross.

Col 2:9

For in him the whole fullness of deity dwells bodily

1 Tim 3:16

Without any doubt, the mystery of our religion is great: Who[e] was revealed in flesh, vindicated by the Spirit,[f] seen by angels, proclaimed among Gentiles, believed in throughout the world, taken up in glory.

Cf. 2 Cor 5:18–21; 8:9; 1 Tim 1:15; 2:5–6; Titus 2:11–14.

30. The Son of God's Redemptive Sharing in the Human Plight

Rom 8:3–4

For God has done what the law, weak-
ened by the flesh, could not do: by
sending his own Son in the likeness of
sinful flesh, and to deal with sin, he con-
demned sin in the flesh, 4 so that the just
requirement of the law might be fulfilled
in us, who walk not according to the
flesh but according to the Spirit.

2 Cor 5:14–21

For the love of Christ urges us on, be-
cause we are convinced that one has
died for all; therefore all have died.
15 And he died for all, so that those who
live might live no longer for themselves,
but for him who died and was raised
for them. 16 From now on, therefore,
we regard no one from a human point
of view; even though we once knew
Christ from a human point of view, we
know him no longer in that way. 17 So if
anyone is in Christ, there is a new cre-
ation: everything old has passed away;
see, everything has become new! 18 All
this is from God, who reconciled us to
himself through Christ, and has given
us the ministry of reconciliation; 19 that
is, God was in Christ, reconciling[a] the
world to himself, not counting their

[b] **Gal 4:6** *our* Other ancient authorities read *your* [c] **Col 1:14** *redemption* Other ancient authorities add *through his blood* [d] **Col 1:15** *Who* NRSV translates *He* [e] **1 Tim 3:16** *Who* Other ancient authorities read *God*; others, *Which*. NRSV translates Gk *Who* as *He* [f] **1 Tim 3:16** *by the Spirit* NRSV alternate translation **§ 30** [a] **2 Cor 5:19** *God was in Christ, reconciling* Or possibly *in Christ God was reconciling* (so NRSV)

τὰ παραπτώματα αὐτῶν καὶ θέμενος ἐν ἡμῖν τὸν λόγον τῆς καταλλαγῆς. **20** Ὑπὲρ Χριστοῦ οὖν πρεσβεύομεν ὡς τοῦ θεοῦ παρακαλοῦντος δι᾽ ἡμῶν· δεόμεθα ὑπὲρ Χριστοῦ, καταλλάγητε τῷ θεῷ. **21** τὸν μὴ γνόντα ἁμαρτίαν ὑπὲρ ἡμῶν ἁμαρτίαν ἐποίησεν, ἵνα ἡμεῖς γενώμεθα δικαιοσύνη θεοῦ ἐν αὐτῷ.

2 Cor 8:8–9

Οὐ κατ᾽ ἐπιταγὴν λέγω ἀλλὰ διὰ τῆς ἑτέρων σπουδῆς καὶ τὸ τῆς ὑμετέρας ἀγάπης γνήσιον δοκιμάζων· **9** γινώσκετε γὰρ τὴν χάριν τοῦ κυρίου ἡμῶν Ἰησοῦ Χριστοῦ, ὅτι δι᾽ ὑμᾶς ἐπτώχευσεν πλούσιος ὤν, ἵνα ὑμεῖς τῇ ἐκείνου πτωχείᾳ πλουτήσητε.

Gal 2:19–21

ἐγὼ γὰρ διὰ νόμου νόμῳ ἀπέθανον, ἵνα θεῷ ζήσω. Χριστῷ συνεσταύρωμαι· **20** ζῶ δὲ οὐκέτι ἐγώ, ζῇ δὲ ἐν ἐμοὶ Χριστός· ὃ δὲ νῦν ζῶ ἐν σαρκί, ἐν πίστει ζῶ τῇ τοῦ υἱοῦ τοῦ θεοῦ τοῦ ἀγαπήσαντός με καὶ παραδόντος ἑαυτὸν ὑπὲρ ἐμοῦ. **21** Οὐκ ἀθετῶ τὴν χάριν τοῦ θεοῦ· εἰ γὰρ διὰ νόμου δικαιοσύνη, ἄρα Χριστὸς δωρεὰν ἀπέθανεν.

Gal 4:4–7

ὅτε δὲ ἦλθεν τὸ πλήρωμα τοῦ χρόνου, ἐξαπέστειλεν ὁ θεὸς τὸν υἱὸν αὐτοῦ, γενόμενον ἐκ γυναικός, γενόμενον ὑπὸ νόμον, **5** ἵνα τοὺς ὑπὸ νόμον ἐξαγοράσῃ, ἵνα τὴν υἱοθεσίαν ἀπολάβωμεν. **6** Ὅτι δέ ἐστε υἱοί, ἐξαπέστειλεν ὁ θεὸς τὸ πνεῦμα τοῦ υἱοῦ αὐτοῦ εἰς τὰς καρδίας ⸀ἡμῶν κρᾶζον· αββα ὁ πατήρ. **7** ὥστε οὐκέτι εἶ δοῦλος ἀλλὰ υἱός· εἰ δὲ υἱός, καὶ κληρονόμος ⸂διὰ θεοῦ⸃.

Eph 5:1–2

Γίνεσθε οὖν μιμηταὶ τοῦ θεοῦ ὡς τέκνα ἀγαπητὰ **2** καὶ περιπατεῖτε ἐν ἀγάπῃ, καθὼς καὶ ὁ Χριστὸς ἠγάπησεν ⸀ἡμᾶς καὶ παρέδωκεν ἑαυτὸν ὑπὲρ ἡμῶν προσφορὰν καὶ θυσίαν τῷ θεῷ εἰς ὀσμὴν εὐωδίας.

Phil 2:5–11

Τοῦτο φρονεῖτε ἐν ὑμῖν ὃ καὶ ἐν Χριστῷ Ἰησοῦ, **6** ὃς ἐν μορφῇ θεοῦ ὑπάρχων οὐχ ἁρπαγμὸν ἡγήσατο τὸ εἶναι ἴσα θεῷ, **7** ἀλλὰ ἑαυτὸν ἐκένωσεν μορφὴν δούλου λαβών, ἐν ὁμοιώματι ἀνθρώπων γενόμενος· καὶ σχήματι εὑρεθεὶς ὡς ἄνθρωπος **8** ἐταπείνωσεν ἑαυτὸν γενόμενος ὑπήκοος μέχρι θανάτου, θανάτου δὲ σταυροῦ. **9** διὸ καὶ ὁ θεὸς αὐτὸν ὑπερύψωσεν καὶ ἐχαρίσατο αὐτῷ τὸ ὄνομα τὸ ὑπὲρ πᾶν ὄνομα, **10** ἵνα ἐν τῷ ὀνόματι Ἰησοῦ πᾶν γόνυ κάμψῃ ἐπουρανίων καὶ ἐπιγείων καὶ καταχθονίων **11** καὶ πᾶσα γλῶσσα ἐξομολογήσηται ὅτι κύριος Ἰησοῦς Χριστὸς εἰς δόξαν θεοῦ πατρός.

1 Tim 1:15

πιστὸς ὁ λόγος καὶ πάσης ἀποδοχῆς ἄξιος, ὅτι Χριστὸς Ἰησοῦς ἦλθεν εἰς τὸν κόσμον ἁμαρτωλοὺς σῶσαι, ὧν πρῶτός εἰμι ἐγώ.

Titus 2:11–14

Ἐπεφάνη γὰρ ἡ χάρις τοῦ θεοῦ σωτήριος πᾶσιν ἀνθρώποις **12** παιδεύουσα ἡμᾶς, ἵνα ἀρνησάμενοι τὴν ἀσέβειαν καὶ τὰς κοσμικὰς ἐπιθυμίας σωφρόνως καὶ δικαίως καὶ εὐσεβῶς ζήσωμεν ἐν τῷ νῦν αἰῶνι, **13** προσδεχόμενοι τὴν μακαρίαν ἐλπίδα καὶ ἐπιφάνειαν τῆς δόξης τοῦ μεγάλου θεοῦ καὶ σωτῆρος ἡμῶν Ἰησοῦ Χριστοῦ, **14** ὃς ἔδωκεν ἑαυτὸν ὑπὲρ ἡμῶν, ἵνα λυτρώσηται ἡμᾶς ἀπὸ πάσης ἀνομίας καὶ καθαρίσῃ ἑαυτῷ λαὸν περιούσιον, ζηλωτὴν καλῶν ἔργων.

Cf. Rom 8:32; 10:6–13; 2 Cor 13:3–4; Gal 1:3–4; Eph 5:25–33; Col 1:13–20; 1 Tim 2:5–6; Titus 3:4–7.

See also § 32 The Love of God in Christ.

31. The Second Adam

Rom 5:12–21

Διὰ τοῦτο ὥσπερ δι᾽ ἑνὸς ἀνθρώπου ἡ ἁμαρτία εἰς τὸν κόσμον εἰσῆλθεν καὶ διὰ τῆς ἁμαρτίας ὁ θάνατος, καὶ οὕτως εἰς πάντας ἀνθρώπους ὁ θάνατος διῆλθεν, ἐφ᾽ ᾧ πάντες ἥμαρτον· **13** ἄχρι γὰρ νόμου ἁμαρτία ἦν ἐν κόσμῳ, ἁμαρτία δὲ οὐκ ἐλλογεῖται μὴ ὄντος νόμου, **14** ἀλλὰ ἐβασίλευσεν ὁ θάνατος ἀπὸ Ἀδὰμ μέχρι Μωϋσέως καὶ ἐπὶ τοὺς μὴ ἁμαρτήσαντας ἐπὶ τῷ ὁμοιώματι τῆς παραβάσεως Ἀδὰμ ὅς ἐστιν τύπος τοῦ μέλλοντος. **15** Ἀλλ᾽ οὐχ ὡς τὸ παράπτωμα, οὕτως καὶ τὸ χάρισμα· εἰ γὰρ τῷ τοῦ ἑνὸς παραπτώματι οἱ πολλοὶ ἀπέθανον, πολλῷ μᾶλλον ἡ χάρις τοῦ θεοῦ καὶ ἡ δωρεὰ ἐν χάριτι τῇ τοῦ ἑνὸς ἀνθρώπου Ἰησοῦ Χριστοῦ εἰς τοὺς πολλοὺς ἐπερίσσευσεν. **16** καὶ οὐχ ὡς δι᾽ ἑνὸς ἁμαρτήσαντος τὸ δώρημα· τὸ μὲν γὰρ κρίμα ἐξ ἑνὸς εἰς κατάκριμα, τὸ δὲ χάρισμα ἐκ πολλῶν παραπτωμάτων εἰς δικαίωμα. **17** εἰ γὰρ τῷ τοῦ ἑνὸς παραπτώματι ὁ θάνατος ἐβασίλευσεν διὰ τοῦ ἑνός, πολλῷ μᾶλλον οἱ τὴν περισσείαν τῆς χάριτος καὶ τῆς δωρεᾶς τῆς δικαιοσύνης λαμβάνοντες ἐν ζωῇ βασιλεύσουσιν διὰ τοῦ ἑνὸς Ἰησοῦ Χριστοῦ. **18** Ἄρα οὖν ὡς δι᾽ ἑνὸς παραπτώματος εἰς πάντας ἀνθρώπους εἰς κατάκριμα, οὕτως καὶ δι᾽ ἑνὸς δικαιώματος εἰς πάντας ἀνθρώπους εἰς δικαίωσιν ζωῆς· **19** ὥσπερ γὰρ διὰ τῆς παρακοῆς τοῦ ἑνὸς ἀνθρώπου ἁμαρτωλοὶ κατεστάθησαν οἱ πολλοί, οὕτως καὶ διὰ τῆς ὑπακοῆς τοῦ ἑνὸς δίκαιοι κατασταθήσονται οἱ πολλοί. **20** νόμος δὲ παρεισῆλθεν, ἵνα πλεονάσῃ τὸ παράπτωμα· οὗ δὲ ἐπλεόνασεν ἡ ἁμαρτία, ὑπερεπερίσσευσεν ἡ χάρις, **21** ἵνα ὥσπερ ἐβασίλευσεν ἡ ἁμαρτία ἐν τῷ θανάτῳ, οὕτως καὶ ἡ χάρις βασιλεύσῃ διὰ δικαιοσύνης εἰς ζωὴν αἰώνιον διὰ Ἰησοῦ Χριστοῦ τοῦ κυρίου ἡμῶν.

1 Cor 15:21–28

ἐπειδὴ γὰρ δι᾽ ἀνθρώπου θάνατος, καὶ δι᾽ ἀνθρώπου ἀνάστασις νεκρῶν. **22** ὥσπερ γὰρ ἐν τῷ Ἀδὰμ πάντες ἀποθνῄσκουσιν, οὕτως καὶ ἐν τῷ Χριστῷ πάντες ζῳοποιηθήσονται. **23** Ἕκαστος δὲ ἐν τῷ ἰδίῳ τάγματι· ἀπαρχὴ Χριστός, ἔπειτα οἱ τοῦ Χριστοῦ ἐν τῇ παρουσίᾳ αὐτοῦ, **24** εἶτα τὸ τέλος, ὅταν παραδιδῷ τὴν βασιλείαν τῷ θεῷ καὶ πατρί, ὅταν καταργήσῃ πᾶσαν ἀρχὴν καὶ πᾶσαν ἐξουσίαν καὶ δύναμιν. **25** δεῖ γὰρ αὐτὸν βασιλεύειν ἄχρι οὗ θῇ πάντας τοὺς ἐχθροὺς ὑπὸ τοὺς πόδας αὐτοῦ. **26** ἔσχατος ἐχθρὸς καταργεῖται ὁ θάνατος· **27** πάντα γὰρ ὑπέταξεν ὑπὸ τοὺς πόδας αὐτοῦ. ὅταν δὲ εἴπῃ ὅτι πάντα

§ 30 **Gal 4:6** ***ημων*** 𝔓^{46} ℵ A B C D* 1739. 1881] υμων D^{2} 33 *Byz* **Gal 4:7** ***δια θεου*** 𝔓^{46} ℵ* A B C* 33. 1739^{*vid}] θεου δια Χριστου ℵ^{2} C^{3} D *Byz* ¦ δια θεον 1881 ¦ δια Ιησου Χριστου 1739^{c} **Eph 5:2** ***ημας*** 𝔓^{46} ℵ^{2} D 33. 1739. 1881 *Byz*] υμας ℵ* A B

trespasses against them, and entrust-
ing the message of reconciliation to us.
20 So we are ambassadors for Christ,
since God is making his appeal through
us; we entreat you on behalf of Christ,
be reconciled to God. **21** For our sake
he made him to be sin who knew no
sin, so that in him we might become
the righteousness of God.

2 Cor 8:8–9

I do not say this as a command, but I
am testing the genuineness of your love
against the earnestness of others. **9** For
you know the grace[b] of our Lord Jesus
Christ, that though he was rich, yet for
your sakes he became poor, so that by
his poverty you might become rich.

Gal 2:19–21

For through the law I died to the law, so
that I might live to God. I have been cru-
cified with Christ; **20** and it is no longer
I who live, but it is Christ who lives in
me. And the life I now live in the flesh
I live by faith in the Son of God, who
loved me and gave himself for me. **21** I
do not nullify the grace of God; for
if justification comes through the law,
then Christ died for nothing.

Gal 4:4–7

But when the fullness of time had come,
God sent his Son, born of a woman,
born under the law, **5** in order to redeem
those who were under the law, so that
we might receive adoption as children.
6 And because you are children, God
has sent the Spirit of his Son into our[c]
hearts, crying, "Abba! Father!" **7** So you
are no longer a slave but a child, and if a
child then also an heir, through God.[d]

Eph 5:1–2

Therefore be imitators of God, as
beloved children, **2** and live in love, as
Christ loved us[e] and gave himself up
for us, a fragrant offering and sacrifice
to God.

Phil 2:5–11

Let the same mind be in you that was
in Christ Jesus, **6** who, though he was
in the form of God, did not regard
equality with God as something to be
exploited, **7** but emptied himself, tak-
ing the form of a slave, being born in
human likeness. And being found in
human form, **8** he humbled himself
and became obedient to the point of
death— even death on a cross. **9** There-
fore God also highly exalted him and
gave him the name that is above every
name, **10** so that at the name of Jesus
every knee should bend, in heaven and
on earth and under the earth, **11** and
every tongue should confess that Jesus
Christ is Lord, to the glory of God the
Father.

1 Tim 1:15

The saying is sure and worthy of full acceptance, that Christ Jesus came into the world to save sinners—of whom I am the foremost.

Titus 2:11–14

For the grace of God has appeared,
bringing salvation to all, **12** training
us to renounce impiety and worldly
passions, and in the present age to live
lives that are self-controlled, upright,
and godly, **13** while we wait for the
blessed hope and the manifestation of
the glory of our great God and Sav-
ior, Jesus Christ. **14** He it is who gave
himself for us that he might redeem us
from all iniquity and purify for himself
a people of his own who are zealous for
good deeds.

Cf. Rom 8:32; 10:6–13; 2 Cor 13:3–4; Gal 1:3–4; Eph 5:25–33; Col 1:13–20; 1 Tim 2:5–6; Titus 3:4–7.

See also § 32 The Love of God in Christ.

31. The Second Adam

Rom 5:12–21

Therefore, just as sin came into the
world through one man, and death
came through sin, and so death spread
to all because all have sinned— **13** sin
was indeed in the world before the law,
but sin is not reckoned when there is no
law. **14** Yet death exercised dominion
from Adam to Moses, even over those
whose sins were not like the transgres-
sion of Adam, who is a type of the one
who was to come. **15** But the free gift is
not like the trespass. For if the many
died through the one man's trespass,
much more surely have the grace of God
and the free gift in the grace of the one
man, Jesus Christ, abounded for the
many. **16** And the free gift is not like the
effect of the one man's sin. For the judg-
ment following one trespass brought
condemnation, but the free gift follow-
ing many trespasses brings justification.
17 If, because of the one man's trespass,
death exercised dominion through that
one, much more surely will those who
receive the abundance of grace and
the free gift of righteousness exercise
dominion in life through the one man,
Jesus Christ. **18** Therefore just as one
man's trespass led to condemnation for
all, so one man's act of righteousness
leads to justification and life for all.
19 For just as by the one man's disobe-
dience the many were made sinners, so
by the one man's obedience the many
will be made righteous. **20** But law came
in, with the result that the trespass mul-
tiplied; but where sin increased, grace
abounded all the more, **21** so that, just
as sin exercised dominion in death, so
grace might also exercise dominion
through justification leading to eternal
life through Jesus Christ our Lord.

1 Cor 15:21–28

For since death came through a human
being, the resurrection of the dead has
also come through a human being;
22 for as all die in Adam, so all will
be made alive in Christ. **23** But each in
his own order: Christ the first fruits,
then at his coming those who belong
to Christ. **24** Then comes the end, when
he hands over the kingdom to God the
Father, after he has destroyed every
ruler and every authority and power.
25 For he must reign until he has put all
his enemies under his feet. **26** The last
enemy to be destroyed is death. **27** For
"God has put all things in subjection

[b] **2 Cor 8:9** ***grace*** NRSV translates *generous act* [c] **Gal 4:6** ***our*** Other ancient authorities read *your* [d] **Gal 4:7** ***an heir, through God*** Other ancient authorities read *an heir of God through Christ* [e] **Eph 5:2** ***us*** Other ancient authorities read *you*

ὑποτέτακται, δῆλον ὅτι ἐκτὸς τοῦ ὑπο-
τάξαντος αὐτῷ τὰ πάντα. 28 ὅταν δὲ
ὑποταγῇ αὐτῷ τὰ πάντα, τότε [καὶ] αὐτὸς
ὁ υἱὸς ὑποταγήσεται τῷ ὑποτάξαντι
αὐτῷ τὰ πάντα, ἵνα ᾖ ὁ θεὸς [τὰ] πάν-
τα ἐν πᾶσιν.

1 Cor 15:42–49

Οὕτως καὶ ἡ ἀνάστασις τῶν νεκρῶν.
σπείρεται ἐν φθορᾷ, ἐγείρεται ἐν ἀφθαρ-
σίᾳ· 43 σπείρεται ἐν ἀτιμίᾳ, ἐγείρεται ἐν
δόξῃ· σπείρεται ἐν ἀσθενείᾳ, ἐγείρεται
ἐν δυνάμει· 44 σπείρεται σῶμα ψυχικόν,
ἐγείρεται σῶμα πνευματικόν. Εἰ ἔστιν
σῶμα ψυχικόν, ἔστιν καὶ πνευματικόν.
45 οὕτως καὶ γέγραπται· ἐγένετο ὁ πρῶ-
τος ἄνθρωπος Ἀδὰμ εἰς ψυχὴν ζῶσαν,
ὁ ἔσχατος Ἀδὰμ εἰς πνεῦμα ζῳοποιοῦν.
46 ἀλλ' οὐ πρῶτον τὸ πνευματικὸν ἀλλὰ
τὸ ψυχικόν, ἔπειτα τὸ πνευματικόν. 47 ὁ
πρῶτος ἄνθρωπος ἐκ γῆς χοϊκός, ὁ δεύ-
τερος ⸀ἄνθρωπος ἐξ οὐρανοῦ. 48 οἷος ὁ
χοϊκός, τοιοῦτοι καὶ οἱ χοϊκοί, καὶ οἷος ὁ
ἐπουράνιος, τοιοῦτοι καὶ οἱ ἐπουράνιοι·
49 καὶ καθὼς ἐφορέσαμεν τὴν εἰκόνα τοῦ
χοϊκοῦ, ⸀φορέσομεν καὶ τὴν εἰκόνα τοῦ
ἐπουρανίου.

Cf. Rom 8:29; 2 Cor 3:18; 4:4–6; Eph 1:22–23; Phil 3:20–21; Col 1:15; 1 Tim 2:5–6.

See also § 49 The New Humanity in Christ.

32. *The Love of God in Christ*

Rom 5:5–8

ἡ δὲ ἐλπὶς οὐ καταισχύνει, ὅτι ἡ ἀγάπη
τοῦ θεοῦ ἐκκέχυται ἐν ταῖς καρδίαις
ἡμῶν διὰ πνεύματος ἁγίου τοῦ δοθέν-
τος ἡμῖν. 6 Ἔτι γὰρ Χριστὸς ὄντων ἡμῶν
ἀσθενῶν ἔτι κατὰ καιρὸν ὑπὲρ ἀσεβῶν
ἀπέθανεν. 7 μόλις γὰρ ὑπὲρ δικαίου τις
ἀποθανεῖται· ὑπὲρ γὰρ τοῦ ἀγαθοῦ τάχα
τις καὶ τολμᾷ ἀποθανεῖν· 8 συνίστησιν
δὲ τὴν ἑαυτοῦ ἀγάπην εἰς ἡμᾶς ὁ θεός,
ὅτι ἔτι ἁμαρτωλῶν ὄντων ἡμῶν Χριστὸς
ὑπὲρ ἡμῶν ἀπέθανεν.

Rom 8:35–39

τίς ἡμᾶς χωρίσει ἀπὸ τῆς ἀγάπης τοῦ
Χριστοῦ; θλῖψις ἢ στενοχωρία ἢ διω-
γμὸς ἢ λιμὸς ἢ γυμνότης ἢ κίνδυνος ἢ
μάχαιρα; 36 καθὼς γέγραπται ὅτι ἕνεκεν
σοῦ θανατούμεθα ὅλην τὴν ἡμέραν,
ἐλογίσθημεν ὡς πρόβατα σφαγῆς. 37 ἀλλ'
ἐν τούτοις πᾶσιν ὑπερνικῶμεν διὰ τοῦ
ἀγαπήσαντος ἡμᾶς. 38 πέπεισμαι γὰρ ὅτι
οὔτε θάνατος οὔτε ζωὴ οὔτε ἄγγελοι οὔτε
ἀρχαὶ οὔτε ἐνεστῶτα οὔτε μέλλοντα οὔτε
δυνάμεις 39 οὔτε ὕψωμα οὔτε βάθος οὔτε
τις κτίσις ἑτέρα δυνήσεται ἡμᾶς χωρίσαι
ἀπὸ τῆς ἀγάπης τοῦ θεοῦ τῆς ἐν Χριστῷ
Ἰησοῦ τῷ κυρίῳ ἡμῶν.

2 Cor 5:14–21

ἡ γὰρ ἀγάπη τοῦ Χριστοῦ συνέχει ἡμᾶς,
κρίναντας τοῦτο, ὅτι εἷς ὑπὲρ πάντων
ἀπέθανεν, ἄρα οἱ πάντες ἀπέθανον· 15 καὶ
ὑπὲρ πάντων ἀπέθανεν, ἵνα οἱ ζῶντες
μηκέτι ἑαυτοῖς ζῶσιν ἀλλὰ τῷ ὑπὲρ αὐτῶν
ἀποθανόντι καὶ ἐγερθέντι. 16 Ὥστε ἡμεῖς
ἀπὸ τοῦ νῦν οὐδένα οἴδαμεν κατὰ σάρκα·
εἰ καὶ ἐγνώκαμεν κατὰ σάρκα Χριστόν,
ἀλλὰ νῦν οὐκέτι γινώσκομεν. 17 ὥστε εἴ
τις ἐν Χριστῷ, καινὴ κτίσις· τὰ ἀρχαῖα
παρῆλθεν, ἰδοὺ γέγονεν καινά. 18 τὰ δὲ
πάντα ἐκ τοῦ θεοῦ τοῦ καταλλάξαντος
ἡμᾶς ἑαυτῷ διὰ Χριστοῦ καὶ δόντος ἡμῖν
τὴν διακονίαν τῆς καταλλαγῆς, 19 ὡς
ὅτι θεὸς ἦν ἐν Χριστῷ κόσμον καταλ-
λάσσων ἑαυτῷ, μὴ λογιζόμενος αὐτοῖς
τὰ παραπτώματα αὐτῶν καὶ θέμενος ἐν
ἡμῖν τὸν λόγον τῆς καταλλαγῆς. 20 Ὑπὲρ
Χριστοῦ οὖν πρεσβεύομεν ὡς τοῦ θεοῦ
παρακαλοῦντος δι' ἡμῶν· δεόμεθα ὑπὲρ
Χριστοῦ, καταλλάγητε τῷ θεῷ. 21 τὸν μὴ
γνόντα ἁμαρτίαν ὑπὲρ ἡμῶν ἁμαρτίαν
ἐποίησεν, ἵνα ἡμεῖς γενώμεθα δικαιο-
σύνη θεοῦ ἐν αὐτῷ.

Gal 2:20

ζῶ δὲ οὐκέτι ἐγώ, ζῇ δὲ ἐν ἐμοὶ Χριστός·
ὃ δὲ νῦν ζῶ ἐν σαρκί, ἐν πίστει ζῶ τῇ τοῦ
υἱοῦ τοῦ θεοῦ τοῦ ἀγαπήσαντός με καὶ
παραδόντος ἑαυτὸν ὑπὲρ ἐμοῦ.

Eph 2:4–7

ὁ δὲ θεὸς πλούσιος ὢν ἐν ἐλέει, διὰ τὴν
πολλὴν ἀγάπην αὐτοῦ ἣν ἠγάπησεν
ἡμᾶς, 5 καὶ ὄντας ἡμᾶς νεκροὺς τοῖς
παραπτώμασιν συνεζωοποίησεν ⸂τῷ
Χριστῷ⸃, —χάριτί ἐστε σεσῳσμένοι—
6 καὶ συνήγειρεν καὶ συνεκάθισεν ἐν
τοῖς ἐπουρανίοις ἐν Χριστῷ Ἰησοῦ, 7 ἵνα
ἐνδείξηται ἐν τοῖς αἰῶσιν τοῖς ἐπερ-
χομένοις τὸ ὑπερβάλλον πλοῦτος τῆς
χάριτος αὐτοῦ ἐν χρηστότητι ἐφ' ἡμᾶς
ἐν Χριστῷ Ἰησοῦ.

Eph 3:14–19

Τούτου χάριν κάμπτω τὰ γόνατά μου
πρὸς τὸν ⸀πατέρα, 15 ἐξ οὗ πᾶσα πα-
τριὰ ἐν οὐρανοῖς καὶ ἐπὶ γῆς ὀνομάζε-
ται, 16 ἵνα δῷ ὑμῖν κατὰ τὸ πλοῦτος τῆς
δόξης αὐτοῦ δυνάμει κραταιωθῆναι
διὰ τοῦ πνεύματος αὐτοῦ εἰς τὸν ἔσω
ἄνθρωπον, 17 κατοικῆσαι τὸν Χριστὸν
διὰ τῆς πίστεως ἐν ταῖς καρδίαις ὑμῶν,
ἐν ἀγάπῃ ἐρριζωμένοι καὶ τεθεμελιω-
μένοι, 18 ἵνα ἐξισχύσητε καταλαβέσθαι
σὺν πᾶσιν τοῖς ἁγίοις τί τὸ πλάτος καὶ
μῆκος καὶ ὕψος καὶ βάθος, 19 γνῶναί
τε τὴν ὑπερβάλλουσαν τῆς γνώσεως
ἀγάπην τοῦ Χριστοῦ, ἵνα πληρωθῆτε
εἰς πᾶν τὸ πλήρωμα τοῦ θεοῦ.

Eph 5:1–2

Γίνεσθε οὖν μιμηταὶ τοῦ θεοῦ ὡς τέκνα
ἀγαπητὰ 2 καὶ περιπατεῖτε ἐν ἀγάπῃ, καθὼς

§ 31 **1 Cor 15:47** ***ανθρωπος*** א* B C D* 33. 1739*] *add.* ο κυριος א² A D¹ 1739^mg. 1881 *Byz* ¦ *add.* πνευματικος 𝔓⁴⁶ **1 Cor 15:49** ***φορεσομεν*** B I 1881] φορεσωμεν (+ δη 𝔓⁴⁶) 𝔓⁴⁶ א A C D 33. 1739 *Byz* **§ 32** **Eph 2:5** ***τω Χριστω*** א A D 1739. 1881 *Byz*] εν τω Χριστω 𝔓⁴⁶ B 33 **Eph 3:14** ***πατερα*** 𝔓⁴⁶ א* A B C 33. 1739] *add.* του κυριου ημων Ιησου Χριστου א² D 1881 *Byz*

under his feet." But when it says, "All things are put in subjection," it is plain that this does not include the one who put all things in subjection under him. **28** When all things are subjected to him, then the Son himself will also be subjected to the one who put all things in subjection under him, so that God may be all in all.

1 Cor 15:42–49

So it is with the resurrection of the dead. The body is sown in decay, it is raised in freedom from decay.[a] **43** It is sown in dishonor, it is raised in glory. It is sown in weakness, it is raised in power. **44** It is sown a body given life by the soul, it is raised a body given life by the Spirit. If there is a body given life by the soul, there is also a body given life by the Spirit. **45** Thus it is written, "The first man, Adam, became a living soul"; the last Adam became a life-giving Spirit. **46** But it is not the body given life by the Spirit that is first, but the body given life by the soul, and then the body given life by the Spirit.[b] **47** The first man was from the earth, a man of dust; the second man is[c] from heaven. **48** As was the man of dust, so are those who are of the dust; and as is the man of heaven, so are those who are of heaven. **49** Just as we have borne the image of the man of dust, we will[d] also bear the image of the man of heaven.

Cf. Rom 8:29; 2 Cor 3:18; 4:4–6; Eph 1:22–23; Phil 3:20–21; Col 1:15; 1 Tim 2:5–6.

See also § 49 The New Humanity in Christ.

32. The Love of God in Christ

Rom 5:5–8

and hope does not disappoint us, because God's love has been poured into our hearts through the Holy Spirit that has been given to us. **6** For while we were still weak, at the right time Christ died for the ungodly. **7** Indeed, rarely will anyone die for a righteous person—though perhaps for a good person someone might actually dare to die. **8** But God proves his love for us in that while we still were sinners Christ died for us.

Rom 8:35–39

Who will separate us from the love of Christ? Will hardship, or distress, or persecution, or famine, or nakedness, or peril, or sword? **36** As it is written, "For your sake we are being killed all day long; we are accounted as sheep to be slaughtered." **37** No, in all these things we are more than conquerors through him who loved us. **38** For I am convinced that neither death, nor life, nor angels, nor rulers, nor things present, nor things to come, nor powers, **39** nor height, nor depth, nor anything else in all creation, will be able to separate us from the love of God in Christ Jesus our Lord.

2 Cor 5:14–21

For the love of Christ urges us on, because we are convinced that one has died for all; therefore all have died. **15** And he died for all, so that those who live might live no longer for themselves, but for him who died and was raised for them. **16** From now on, therefore, we regard no one from a human point of view; even though we once knew Christ from a human point of view, we know him no longer in that way. **17** So if anyone is in Christ, there is a new creation: everything old has passed away; see, everything has become new! **18** All this is from God, who reconciled us to himself through Christ, and has given us the ministry of reconciliation; **19** that is, God was in Christ, reconciling[a] the world to himself, not counting their trespasses against them, and entrusting the message of reconciliation to us. **20** So we are ambassadors for Christ, since God is making his appeal through us; we entreat you on behalf of Christ, be reconciled to God. **21** For our sake he made him to be sin who knew no sin, so that in him we might become the righteousness of God.

Gal 2:20

and it is no longer I who live, but it is Christ who lives in me. And the life I now live in the flesh I live by faith in the Son of God, who loved me and gave himself for me.

Eph 2:4–7

But God, who is rich in mercy, out of the great love with which he loved us **5** even when we were dead through our trespasses, made us alive together with Christ[b]—by grace you have been saved— **6** and raised us up with him and seated us with him in the heavenly places in Christ Jesus, **7** so that in the ages to come he might show the immeasurable riches of his grace in kindness toward us in Christ Jesus.

Eph 3:14–19

For this reason I bow my knees before the Father,[c] **15** from whom the whole family[d] in heaven and on earth takes its name. **16** I pray that, according to the riches of his glory, he may grant that you may be strengthened in your inner being with power through his Spirit, **17** and that Christ may dwell in your hearts through faith, as you are being rooted and grounded in love. **18** I pray that you may have the power to comprehend, with all the saints, what is the breadth and length and height and depth, **19** and to know the love of Christ that surpasses knowledge, so that you may be filled with all the fullness of God.

Eph 5:1–2

Therefore be imitators of God, as beloved children, **2** and live in love, as

§ 31 [a] **1 Cor 15:42** Translation differs from NRSV [b] **1 Cor 15:44–46** Translation differs from NRSV [c] **1 Cor 15:47** ***is*** Other ancient authorities add *the Lord* [d] **1 Cor 15:49** ***we will*** Other ancient authorities read *let us* **§ 32** [a] **2 Cor 5:19** ***God was in Christ, reconciling*** Or possibly *in Christ God was reconciling* (so NRSV) [b] **Eph 2:5** ***together with Christ*** Other ancient authorities read *in Christ* [c] **Eph 3:14** ***the Father*** Other ancient authorities add *of our Lord Jesus Christ* [d] **Eph 3:15** ***the whole family*** Or *every family* (so NRSV)

καὶ ὁ Χριστὸς ἠγάπησεν ⸀ἡμᾶς καὶ παρέδωκεν ἑαυτὸν ὑπὲρ ἡμῶν προσφορὰν καὶ θυσίαν τῷ θεῷ εἰς ὀσμὴν εὐωδίας.

Eph 5:25–32

Οἱ ἄνδρες, ἀγαπᾶτε τὰς γυναῖκας, καθὼς καὶ ὁ Χριστὸς ἠγάπησεν τὴν ἐκκλησίαν καὶ ἑαυτὸν παρέδωκεν ὑπὲρ αὐτῆς, 26 ἵνα αὐτὴν ἁγιάσῃ καθαρίσας τῷ λουτρῷ τοῦ ὕδατος ἐν ῥήματι, 27 ἵνα παραστήσῃ αὐτὸς ἑαυτῷ ἔνδοξον τὴν ἐκκλησίαν, μὴ ἔχουσαν σπίλον ἢ ῥυτίδα ἤ τι τῶν τοιούτων, ἀλλ᾽ ἵνα ᾖ ἁγία καὶ ἄμωμος. 28 οὕτως ὀφείλουσιν [καὶ] οἱ ἄνδρες ἀγαπᾶν τὰς ἑαυτῶν γυναῖκας ὡς τὰ ἑαυτῶν σώματα. ὁ ἀγαπῶν τὴν ἑαυτοῦ γυναῖκα ἑαυτὸν ἀγαπᾷ. 29 Οὐδεὶς γάρ ποτε τὴν ἑαυτοῦ σάρκα ἐμίσησεν ἀλλὰ ἐκτρέφει καὶ θάλπει αὐτήν, καθὼς καὶ ὁ Χριστὸς τὴν ἐκκλησίαν, 30 ὅτι μέλη ἐσμὲν τοῦ σώματος ⸀αὐτοῦ. 31 ἀντὶ τούτου καταλείψει ἄνθρωπος [τὸν] πατέρα καὶ [τὴν] μητέρα καὶ προσκολληθήσεται πρὸς τὴν γυναῖκα αὐτοῦ, καὶ ἔσονται οἱ δύο εἰς σάρκα μίαν. 32 τὸ μυστήριον τοῦτο μέγα ἐστίν· ἐγὼ δὲ λέγω εἰς Χριστὸν καὶ εἰς τὴν ἐκκλησίαν.

2 Thess 2:16–17

Αὐτὸς δὲ ὁ κύριος ἡμῶν Ἰησοῦς Χριστὸς καὶ [ὁ] θεὸς ὁ πατὴρ ἡμῶν ὁ ἀγαπήσας ἡμᾶς καὶ δοὺς παράκλησιν αἰωνίαν καὶ ἐλπίδα ἀγαθὴν ἐν χάριτι, 17 παρακαλέσαι ὑμῶν τὰς καρδίας καὶ στηρίξαι ἐν παντὶ ἔργῳ καὶ λόγῳ ἀγαθῷ.

Cf. Rom 1:7; 15:30; 2 Cor 13:11; 13:13 [E 14]; Phil 2:1–2; Col 3:12–13; 1 Thess 1:4–5; 2 Thess 2:13–14; 3:5.

See also § 30 The Son of God's Redemptive Sharing in the Human Plight.

33. The Atoning Death of Christ

Rom 3:21–26

Νυνὶ δὲ χωρὶς νόμου δικαιοσύνη θεοῦ πεφανέρωται μαρτυρουμένη ὑπὸ τοῦ νόμου καὶ τῶν προφητῶν, 22 δικαιοσύνη δὲ θεοῦ διὰ πίστεως Ἰησοῦ Χριστοῦ εἰς πάντας τοὺς πιστεύοντας. οὐ γάρ ἐστιν διαστολή, 23 πάντες γὰρ ἥμαρτον καὶ ὑστεροῦνται τῆς δόξης τοῦ θεοῦ 24 δικαιούμενοι δωρεὰν τῇ αὐτοῦ χάριτι διὰ τῆς ἀπολυτρώσεως τῆς ἐν Χριστῷ Ἰησοῦ· 25 ὃν προέθετο ὁ θεὸς ἱλαστήριον διὰ [τῆς] πίστεως ἐν τῷ αὐτοῦ αἵματι εἰς ἔνδειξιν τῆς δικαιοσύνης αὐτοῦ διὰ τὴν πάρεσιν τῶν προγεγονότων ἁμαρτημάτων 26 ἐν τῇ ἀνοχῇ τοῦ θεοῦ, πρὸς τὴν ἔνδειξιν τῆς δικαιοσύνης αὐτοῦ ἐν τῷ νῦν καιρῷ, εἰς τὸ εἶναι αὐτὸν δίκαιον καὶ δικαιοῦντα τὸν ἐκ πίστεως Ἰησοῦ.

Rom 4:24–25

ἀλλὰ καὶ δι᾽ ἡμᾶς, οἷς μέλλει λογίζεσθαι, τοῖς πιστεύουσιν ἐπὶ τὸν ἐγείραντα Ἰησοῦν τὸν κύριον ἡμῶν ἐκ νεκρῶν, 25 ὃς παρεδόθη διὰ τὰ παραπτώματα ἡμῶν καὶ ἠγέρθη διὰ τὴν δικαίωσιν ἡμῶν.

Rom 5:6–11

Ἔτι γὰρ Χριστὸς ὄντων ἡμῶν ἀσθενῶν ἔτι κατὰ καιρὸν ὑπὲρ ἀσεβῶν ἀπέθανεν. 7 μόλις γὰρ ὑπὲρ δικαίου τις ἀποθανεῖται· ὑπὲρ γὰρ τοῦ ἀγαθοῦ τάχα τις καὶ τολμᾷ ἀποθανεῖν· 8 συνίστησιν δὲ τὴν ἑαυτοῦ ἀγάπην εἰς ἡμᾶς ὁ θεός, ὅτι ἔτι ἁμαρτωλῶν ὄντων ἡμῶν Χριστὸς ὑπὲρ ἡμῶν ἀπέθανεν. 9 πολλῷ οὖν μᾶλλον δικαιωθέντες νῦν ἐν τῷ αἵματι αὐτοῦ σωθησόμεθα δι᾽ αὐτοῦ ἀπὸ τῆς ὀργῆς. 10 εἰ γὰρ ἐχθροὶ ὄντες κατηλλάγημεν τῷ θεῷ διὰ τοῦ θανάτου τοῦ υἱοῦ αὐτοῦ, πολλῷ μᾶλλον καταλλαγέντες σωθησόμεθα ἐν τῇ ζωῇ αὐτοῦ· 11 οὐ μόνον δέ, ἀλλὰ καὶ καυχώμενοι ἐν τῷ θεῷ διὰ τοῦ κυρίου ἡμῶν Ἰησοῦ Χριστοῦ δι᾽ οὗ νῦν τὴν καταλλαγὴν ἐλάβομεν.

Rom 8:3–4

Τὸ γὰρ ἀδύνατον τοῦ νόμου ἐν ᾧ ἠσθένει διὰ τῆς σαρκός, ὁ θεὸς τὸν ἑαυτοῦ υἱὸν πέμψας ἐν ὁμοιώματι σαρκὸς ἁμαρτίας καὶ περὶ ἁμαρτίας κατέκρινεν τὴν ἁμαρτίαν ἐν τῇ σαρκί, 4 ἵνα τὸ δικαίωμα τοῦ νόμου πληρωθῇ ἐν ἡμῖν τοῖς μὴ κατὰ σάρκα περιπατοῦσιν ἀλλὰ κατὰ πνεῦμα.

Rom 8:32

ὅς γε τοῦ ἰδίου υἱοῦ οὐκ ἐφείσατο ἀλλὰ ὑπὲρ ἡμῶν πάντων παρέδωκεν αὐτόν, πῶς οὐχὶ καὶ σὺν αὐτῷ τὰ πάντα ἡμῖν χαρίσεται;

Rom 14:15

εἰ γὰρ διὰ βρῶμα ὁ ἀδελφός σου λυπεῖται, οὐκέτι κατὰ ἀγάπην περιπατεῖς· μὴ τῷ βρώματί σου ἐκεῖνον ἀπόλλυε ὑπὲρ οὗ Χριστὸς ἀπέθανεν.

1 Cor 5:7–8

ἐκκαθάρατε τὴν παλαιὰν ζύμην, ἵνα ἦτε νέον φύραμα, καθώς ἐστε ἄζυμοι· καὶ γὰρ τὸ πάσχα ἡμῶν ἐτύθη Χριστός. 8 ὥστε ἑορτάζωμεν μὴ ἐν ζύμῃ παλαιᾷ μηδὲ ἐν ζύμῃ κακίας καὶ πονηρίας ἀλλ᾽ ἐν ἀζύμοις εἰλικρινείας καὶ ἀληθείας.

1 Cor 6:20

ἠγοράσθητε γὰρ τιμῆς· δοξάσατε δὴ τὸν θεὸν ἐν τῷ σώματι ὑμῶν.

1 Cor 7:23

τιμῆς ἠγοράσθητε· μὴ γίνεσθε δοῦλοι ἀνθρώπων.

1 Cor 8:11

ἀπόλλυται γὰρ ὁ ἀσθενῶν ἐν τῇ σῇ γνώσει, ὁ ἀδελφὸς δι᾽ ὃν Χριστὸς ἀπέθανεν.

1 Cor 11:23–25

Ἐγὼ γὰρ παρέλαβον ἀπὸ τοῦ κυρίου, ὃ καὶ παρέδωκα ὑμῖν, ὅτι ὁ κύριος Ἰησοῦς ἐν τῇ νυκτὶ ᾗ παρεδίδετο ἔλαβεν ἄρτον 24 καὶ εὐχαριστήσας ἔκλασεν καὶ εἶπεν· τοῦτό μού ἐστιν τὸ σῶμα τὸ ὑπὲρ ⸀ὑμῶν· τοῦτο ποιεῖτε εἰς τὴν ἐμὴν ἀνάμνησιν. 25 ὡσαύτως καὶ τὸ ποτήριον μετὰ τὸ δειπνῆσαι λέγων· τοῦτο τὸ ποτήριον ἡ καινὴ διαθήκη ἐστὶν ἐν τῷ ἐμῷ αἵματι· τοῦτο ποιεῖτε, ὁσάκις ἐὰν πίνητε, εἰς τὴν ἐμὴν ἀνάμνησιν.

Eph 5:2 ***ημας*** 𝔓[46] ℵ[2] D 33. 1739. 1881 *Byz*] υμας ℵ* A B **Eph 5:30** ***αυτου*** 𝔓[46] ℵ* A B 048. 33. 1739*. 1881] *add.* εκ της σαρκος αυτου και εκ των οστεων αυτου ℵ[2] D 1739[mg] *Byz* **§ 33 1 Cor 11:24** ***υμων*** 𝔓[46] ℵ* A B C* 33. 1739*] *add.* κλωμενον ℵ[2] C[3] D[2] 1739[mg]. 1881 *Byz* ¦ *add.* θρυπτομενον D*

Christ loved us[e] and gave himself up for us, a fragrant offering and sacrifice to God.

Eph 5:25–32

Husbands, love your wives, just as Christ loved the church and gave himself up for her, **26** in order to make her holy by cleansing her with the washing of water by the word, **27** so as to present the church to himself in splendor, without a spot or wrinkle or anything of the kind—yes, so that she may be holy and without blemish. **28** In the same way, husbands should love their wives as they do their own bodies. He who loves his wife loves himself. **29** For no one ever hates his own body, but he nourishes and tenderly cares for it, just as Christ does for the church, **30** because we are members of his body.[f] **31** "For this reason a man will leave his father and mother and be joined to his wife, and the two will become one flesh." **32** This is a great mystery, and I am applying it to Christ and the church.

2 Thess 2:16–17

Now may our Lord Jesus Christ himself and God our Father, who loved us and through grace gave us eternal comfort and good hope, **17** comfort your hearts and strengthen them in every good work and word.

Cf. Rom 1:7; 15:30; 2 Cor 13:11; 13:13 [E 14]; Phil 2:1–2; Col 3:12–13; 1 Thess 1:4–5; 2 Thess 2:13–14; 3:5.

See also § 30 The Son of God's Redemptive Sharing in the Human Plight.

33. The Atoning Death of Christ

Rom 3:21–26

But now, apart from law, the righteousness of God has been disclosed, and is attested by the law and the prophets, **22** the righteousness of God through faith in Jesus Christ for all who believe. For there is no distinction, **23** since all have sinned and fall short of the glory of God; **24** they are now justified by his grace as a gift, through the redemption that is in Christ Jesus, **25** whom God put forward as a sacrifice of atonement by his blood, effective through faith. He did this to show his righteousness, because in his divine forbearance he had passed over the sins previously committed; **26** it was to prove at the present time that he himself is righteous and that he justifies the one who has faith in Jesus.

Rom 4:24–25

but for ours also. It will be reckoned to us who believe in him who raised Jesus our Lord from the dead, **25** who was handed over to death for our trespasses and was raised for our justification.

Rom 5:6–11

For while we were still weak, at the right time Christ died for the ungodly. **7** Indeed, rarely will anyone die for a righteous person—though perhaps for a good person someone might actually dare to die. **8** But God proves his love for us in that while we still were sinners Christ died for us. **9** Much more surely then, now that we have been justified by his blood, will we be saved through him from the wrath of God. **10** For if while we were enemies, we were reconciled to God through the death of his Son, much more surely, having been reconciled, will we be saved by his life. **11** But more than that, we even boast in God through our Lord Jesus Christ, through whom we have now received reconciliation.

Rom 8:3–4

For God has done what the law, weakened by the flesh, could not do: by sending his own Son in the likeness of sinful flesh, and to deal with sin, he condemned sin in the flesh, **4** so that the just requirement of the law might be fulfilled in us, who walk not according to the flesh but according to the Spirit.

Rom 8:32

He who did not withhold his own Son, but gave him up for all of us, will he not with him also give us everything else?

Rom 14:15

If your brother or sister is being injured by what you eat, you are no longer walking in love. Do not let what you eat cause the ruin of one for whom Christ died.

1 Cor 5:7–8

Clean out the old yeast so that you may be a new batch, as you really are unleavened. For our paschal lamb, Christ, has been sacrificed. **8** Therefore, let us celebrate the festival, not with the old yeast, the yeast of malice and evil, but with the unleavened bread of sincerity and truth.

1 Cor 6:20

For you were bought with a price; therefore glorify God in your body.

1 Cor 7:23

You were bought with a price; do not become slaves of human masters.

1 Cor 8:11

So by your knowledge those weak believers for whom Christ died are destroyed.

1 Cor 11:23–25

For I received from the Lord what I also handed on to you, that the Lord Jesus on the night when he was betrayed took a loaf of bread, **24** and when he had given thanks, he broke it and said, "This is my body that is for[a] you. Do this in remembrance of me." **25** In the same way he took the cup also, after supper, saying, "This cup is the new covenant in my blood. Do this, as often as you drink it, in remembrance of me."

[e] **Eph 5:2** ***us*** Other ancient authorities read *you* [f] **Eph 5:30** ***of his body*** Other ancient authorities add *of his flesh and of his bones* **§ 33** [a] **1 Cor 11:24** ***is for*** Other ancient authorities read *is broken for*

1 Cor 15:3–4

παρέδωκα γὰρ ὑμῖν ἐν πρώτοις, ὃ καὶ παρέλαβον, ὅτι Χριστὸς ἀπέθανεν ὑπὲρ τῶν ἁμαρτιῶν ἡμῶν κατὰ τὰς γραφὰς **4** καὶ ὅτι ἐτάφη καὶ ὅτι ἐγήγερται τῇ ἡμέρᾳ τῇ τρίτῃ κατὰ τὰς γραφὰς

2 Cor 5:14–21

ἡ γὰρ ἀγάπη τοῦ Χριστοῦ συνέχει ἡμᾶς, κρίναντας τοῦτο, ὅτι εἷς ὑπὲρ πάντων ἀπέθανεν, ἄρα οἱ πάντες ἀπέθανον· **15** καὶ ὑπὲρ πάντων ἀπέθανεν, ἵνα οἱ ζῶντες μηκέτι ἑαυτοῖς ζῶσιν ἀλλὰ τῷ ὑπὲρ αὐτῶν ἀποθανόντι καὶ ἐγερθέντι. **16** Ὥστε ἡμεῖς ἀπὸ τοῦ νῦν οὐδένα οἴδαμεν κατὰ σάρκα· εἰ καὶ ἐγνώκαμεν κατὰ σάρκα Χριστόν, ἀλλὰ νῦν οὐκέτι γινώσκομεν. **17** ὥστε εἴ τις ἐν Χριστῷ, καινὴ κτίσις· τὰ ἀρχαῖα παρῆλθεν, ἰδοὺ γέγονεν καινά. **18** τὰ δὲ πάντα ἐκ τοῦ θεοῦ τοῦ καταλλάξαντος ἡμᾶς ἑαυτῷ διὰ Χριστοῦ καὶ δόντος ἡμῖν τὴν διακονίαν τῆς καταλλαγῆς, **19** ὡς ὅτι θεὸς ἦν ἐν Χριστῷ κόσμον καταλλάσσων ἑαυτῷ, μὴ λογιζόμενος αὐτοῖς τὰ παραπτώματα αὐτῶν καὶ θέμενος ἐν ἡμῖν τὸν λόγον τῆς καταλλαγῆς. **20** Ὑπὲρ Χριστοῦ οὖν πρεσβεύομεν ὡς τοῦ θεοῦ παρακαλοῦντος δι' ἡμῶν· δεόμεθα ὑπὲρ Χριστοῦ, καταλλάγητε τῷ θεῷ. **21** τὸν μὴ γνόντα ἁμαρτίαν ὑπὲρ ἡμῶν ἁμαρτίαν ἐποίησεν, ἵνα ἡμεῖς γενώμεθα δικαιοσύνη θεοῦ ἐν αὐτῷ.

Gal 1:3–4

χάρις ὑμῖν καὶ εἰρήνη ἀπὸ θεοῦ πατρὸς ἡμῶν καὶ κυρίου Ἰησοῦ Χριστοῦ **4** τοῦ δόντος ἑαυτὸν ὑπὲρ τῶν ἁμαρτιῶν ἡμῶν, ὅπως ἐξέληται ἡμᾶς ἐκ τοῦ αἰῶνος τοῦ ἐνεστῶτος πονηροῦ κατὰ τὸ θέλημα τοῦ θεοῦ καὶ πατρὸς ἡμῶν

Gal 2:19–20

ἐγὼ γὰρ διὰ νόμου νόμῳ ἀπέθανον, ἵνα θεῷ ζήσω. Χριστῷ συνεσταύρωμαι· **20** ζῶ δὲ οὐκέτι ἐγώ, ζῇ δὲ ἐν ἐμοὶ Χριστός· ὃ δὲ νῦν ζῶ ἐν σαρκί, ἐν πίστει ζῶ τῇ τοῦ υἱοῦ τοῦ θεοῦ τοῦ ἀγαπήσαντός με καὶ παραδόντος ἑαυτὸν ὑπὲρ ἐμοῦ.

Gal 3:13–14

Χριστὸς ἡμᾶς ἐξηγόρασεν ἐκ τῆς κατάρας τοῦ νόμου γενόμενος ὑπὲρ ἡμῶν κατάρα, ὅτι γέγραπται· ἐπικατάρατος πᾶς ὁ κρεμάμενος ἐπὶ ξύλου, **14** ἵνα εἰς τὰ ἔθνη ἡ εὐλογία τοῦ Ἀβραὰμ γένηται ἐν Χριστῷ Ἰησοῦ, ἵνα τὴν ἐπαγγελίαν τοῦ πνεύματος λάβωμεν διὰ τῆς πίστεως.

Eph 1:7

Ἐν ᾧ ἔχομεν τὴν ἀπολύτρωσιν διὰ τοῦ αἵματος αὐτοῦ, τὴν ἄφεσιν τῶν παραπτωμάτων, κατὰ τὸ πλοῦτος τῆς χάριτος αὐτοῦ

Eph 2:11–18

Διὸ μνημονεύετε ὅτι ποτὲ ὑμεῖς τὰ ἔθνη ἐν σαρκί, οἱ λεγόμενοι ἀκροβυστία ὑπὸ τῆς λεγομένης περιτομῆς ἐν σαρκὶ χειροποιήτου, **12** ὅτι ἦτε τῷ καιρῷ ἐκείνῳ χωρὶς Χριστοῦ, ἀπηλλοτριωμένοι τῆς πολιτείας τοῦ Ἰσραὴλ καὶ ξένοι τῶν διαθηκῶν τῆς ἐπαγγελίας, ἐλπίδα μὴ ἔχοντες καὶ ἄθεοι ἐν τῷ κόσμῳ. **13** νυνὶ δὲ ἐν Χριστῷ Ἰησοῦ ὑμεῖς οἵ ποτε ὄντες μακρὰν ἐγενήθητε ἐγγὺς ἐν τῷ αἵματι τοῦ Χριστοῦ. **14** Αὐτὸς γάρ ἐστιν ἡ εἰρήνη ἡμῶν, ὁ ποιήσας τὰ ἀμφότερα ἓν καὶ τὸ μεσότοιχον τοῦ φραγμοῦ λύσας, τὴν ἔχθραν ἐν τῇ σαρκὶ αὐτοῦ, **15** τὸν νόμον τῶν ἐντολῶν ἐν δόγμασιν καταργήσας, ἵνα τοὺς δύο κτίσῃ ἐν αὐτῷ εἰς ἕνα καινὸν ἄνθρωπον ποιῶν εἰρήνην **16** καὶ ἀποκαταλλάξῃ τοὺς ἀμφοτέρους ἐν ἑνὶ σώματι τῷ θεῷ διὰ τοῦ σταυροῦ, ἀποκτείνας τὴν ἔχθραν ἐν αὐτῷ. **17** καὶ ἐλθὼν εὐηγγελίσατο εἰρήνην ὑμῖν τοῖς μακρὰν καὶ εἰρήνην τοῖς ἐγγύς· **18** ὅτι δι' αὐτοῦ ἔχομεν τὴν προσαγωγὴν οἱ ἀμφότεροι ἐν ἑνὶ πνεύματι πρὸς τὸν πατέρα.

Eph 5:1–2

Γίνεσθε οὖν μιμηταὶ τοῦ θεοῦ ὡς τέκνα ἀγαπητὰ **2** καὶ περιπατεῖτε ἐν ἀγάπῃ, καθὼς καὶ ὁ Χριστὸς ἠγάπησεν ⸀ἡμᾶς καὶ παρέδωκεν ἑαυτὸν ὑπὲρ ἡμῶν προσφορὰν καὶ θυσίαν τῷ θεῷ εἰς ὀσμὴν εὐωδίας.

Eph 5:25–27

Οἱ ἄνδρες, ἀγαπᾶτε τὰς γυναῖκας, καθὼς καὶ ὁ Χριστὸς ἠγάπησεν τὴν ἐκκλησίαν καὶ ἑαυτὸν παρέδωκεν ὑπὲρ αὐτῆς, **26** ἵνα αὐτὴν ἁγιάσῃ καθαρίσας τῷ λουτρῷ τοῦ ὕδατος ἐν ῥήματι, **27** ἵνα παραστήσῃ αὐτὸς ἑαυτῷ ἔνδοξον τὴν ἐκκλησίαν, μὴ ἔχουσαν σπίλον ἢ ῥυτίδα ἤ τι τῶν τοιούτων, ἀλλ' ἵνα ᾖ ἁγία καὶ ἄμωμος.

Col 1:19–22

ὅτι ἐν αὐτῷ εὐδόκησεν πᾶν τὸ πλήρωμα κατοικῆσαι **20** καὶ δι' αὐτοῦ ἀποκαταλλάξαι τὰ πάντα εἰς αὐτόν, εἰρηνοποιήσας διὰ τοῦ αἵματος τοῦ σταυροῦ αὐτοῦ, [δι' αὐτοῦ] εἴτε τὰ ἐπὶ τῆς γῆς εἴτε τὰ ἐν τοῖς οὐρανοῖς. **21** Καὶ ὑμᾶς ποτε ὄντας ἀπηλλοτριωμένους καὶ ἐχθροὺς τῇ διανοίᾳ ἐν τοῖς ἔργοις τοῖς πονηροῖς, **22** νυνὶ δὲ ⸀ἀποκατήλλαξεν ἐν τῷ σώματι τῆς σαρκὸς αὐτοῦ διὰ τοῦ θανάτου παραστῆσαι ὑμᾶς ἁγίους καὶ ἀμώμους καὶ ἀνεγκλήτους κατενώπιον αὐτοῦ

Col 2:13–15

καὶ ὑμᾶς νεκροὺς ὄντας [ἐν] τοῖς παραπτώμασιν καὶ τῇ ἀκροβυστίᾳ τῆς σαρκὸς ὑμῶν, συνεζωοποίησεν ⸀ὑμᾶς σὺν αὐτῷ, χαρισάμενος ἡμῖν πάντα τὰ παραπτώματα. **14** ἐξαλείψας τὸ καθ' ἡμῶν χειρόγραφον τοῖς δόγμασιν ὃ ἦν ὑπεναντίον ἡμῖν, καὶ αὐτὸ ἦρκεν ἐκ τοῦ μέσου προσηλώσας αὐτὸ τῷ σταυρῷ· **15** ἀπεκδυσάμενος τὰς ἀρχὰς καὶ τὰς ἐξουσίας ἐδειγμάτισεν ἐν παρρησίᾳ, θριαμβεύσας αὐτοὺς ἐν αὐτῷ.

1 Thess 5:9–10

ὅτι οὐκ ἔθετο ἡμᾶς ὁ θεὸς εἰς ὀργὴν ἀλλὰ εἰς περιποίησιν σωτηρίας διὰ τοῦ κυρίου ἡμῶν Ἰησοῦ Χριστοῦ **10** τοῦ ἀποθανόντος ὑπὲρ ἡμῶν, ἵνα εἴτε γρηγορῶμεν εἴτε καθεύδωμεν ἅμα σὺν αὐτῷ ζήσωμεν.

1 Tim 2:5–6

Εἷς γὰρ θεός, εἷς καὶ μεσίτης θεοῦ καὶ ἀνθρώπων, ἄνθρωπος Χριστὸς Ἰησοῦς, **6** ὁ δοὺς ἑαυτὸν ἀντίλυτρον ὑπὲρ πάντων, τὸ μαρτύριον καιροῖς ἰδίοις.

Titus 2:13–14

προσδεχόμενοι τὴν μακαρίαν ἐλπίδα καὶ ἐπιφάνειαν τῆς δόξης τοῦ μεγάλου θεοῦ καὶ σωτῆρος ἡμῶν Ἰησοῦ Χριστοῦ, **14** ὃς ἔδωκεν ἑαυτὸν ὑπὲρ ἡμῶν, ἵνα λυτρώσηται ἡμᾶς ἀπὸ πάσης ἀνομίας καὶ καθαρίσῃ ἑαυτῷ λαὸν περιούσιον, ζηλωτὴν καλῶν ἔργων.

Eph 5:2 ***ημας*** 𝔓46 ℵ2 D 33. 1739. 1881 *Byz*] υμας ℵ* A B **Col 1:22** ***αποκατηλλαξεν*** ℵ A C D2 048. 1739. 1881 *Byz*] αποκατηλλαγητε (𝔓46) B ¦ αποκαταλλαγεντες D* ¦ αποκατηλλακται 33 **Col 2:13** ***υμας*** ℵ* A C 1739. 1881] ημας 𝔓46 B 33 ¦ *om.* ℵ2 D *Byz*

1 Cor 15:3–4

For I handed on to you as of first importance what I in turn had received: that Christ died for our sins in accordance with the scriptures, **4** and that he was buried, and that he was raised on the third day in accordance with the scriptures

2 Cor 5:14–21

For the love of Christ urges us on, because we are convinced that one has died for all; therefore all have died. **15** And he died for all, so that those who live might live no longer for themselves, but for him who died and was raised for them. **16** From now on, therefore, we regard no one from a human point of view; even though we once knew Christ from a human point of view, we know him no longer in that way. **17** So if anyone is in Christ, there is a new creation: everything old has passed away; see, everything has become new! **18** All this is from God, who reconciled us to himself through Christ, and has given us the ministry of reconciliation; **19** that is, God was in Christ, reconciling[b] the world to himself, not counting their trespasses against them, and entrusting the message of reconciliation to us. **20** So we are ambassadors for Christ, since God is making his appeal through us; we entreat you on behalf of Christ, be reconciled to God. **21** For our sake he made him to be sin who knew no sin, so that in him we might become the righteousness of God.

Gal 1:3–4

Grace to you and peace from God our Father and the Lord Jesus Christ, **4** who gave himself for our sins to set us free from the present evil age, according to the will of our God and Father

Gal 2:19–20

For through the law I died to the law, so that I might live to God. I have been crucified with Christ; **20** and it is no longer I who live, but it is Christ who lives in me. And the life I now live in the flesh I live by faith in the Son of God, who loved me and gave himself for me.

Gal 3:13–14

Christ redeemed us from the curse of the law by becoming a curse for us—for it is written, "Cursed is everyone who hangs on a tree"— **14** in order that in Christ Jesus the blessing of Abraham might come to the Gentiles, so that we might receive the promise of the Spirit through faith.

Eph 1:7

In him we have redemption through his blood, the forgiveness of our trespasses, according to the riches of his grace

Eph 2:11–18

So then, remember that at one time you Gentiles by birth, called "the uncircumcision" by those who are called "the circumcision"—a physical circumcision made in the flesh by human hands— **12** remember that you were at that time without Christ, being aliens from the commonwealth of Israel, and strangers to the covenants of promise, having no hope and without God in the world. **13** But now in Christ Jesus you who once were far off have been brought near by the blood of Christ. **14** For he is our peace; in his flesh he has made both groups into one and has broken down the dividing wall, that is, the hostility between us. **15** He has abolished the law with its commandments and ordinances, that he might create in himself one new humanity in place of the two, thus making peace, **16** and might reconcile both groups to God in one body through the cross, thus putting to death that hostility through it. **17** So he came and proclaimed peace to you who were far off and peace to those who were near; **18** for through him both of us have access in one Spirit to the Father.

Eph 5:1–2

Therefore be imitators of God, as beloved children, **2** and live in love, as Christ loved us[c] and gave himself up for us, a fragrant offering and sacrifice to God.

Eph 5:25–27

Husbands, love your wives, just as Christ loved the church and gave himself up for her, **26** in order to make her holy by cleansing her with the washing of water by the word, **27** so as to present the church to himself in splendor, without a spot or wrinkle or anything of the kind—yes, so that she may be holy and without blemish.

Col 1:19–22

For in him all the fullness of God was pleased to dwell, **20** and through him God was pleased to reconcile to himself all things, whether on earth or in heaven, by making peace through the blood of his cross. **21** And you who were once estranged and hostile in mind, doing evil deeds, **22** he has now reconciled[d] in his fleshly body through death, so as to present you holy and blameless and irreproachable before him

Col 2:13–15

And when you were dead in trespasses and the uncircumcision of your flesh, God made you[e] alive together with him, when he forgave us all our trespasses, **14** erasing the record that stood against us with its legal demands. He set this aside, nailing it to the cross. **15** He disarmed the rulers and authorities and made a public example of them, triumphing over them in it.

1 Thess 5:9–10

For God has destined us not for wrath but for obtaining salvation through our Lord Jesus Christ, **10** who died for us, so that whether we are awake or asleep we may live with him.

1 Tim 2:5–6

For there is one God; there is also one mediator between God and humankind, Christ Jesus, himself human, **6** who gave himself a ransom for all —this was attested at the right time.

Titus 2:13–14

while we wait for the blessed hope and the manifestation of the glory of our great God and Savior, Jesus Christ. **14** He it is who gave himself for us that he might redeem us from all iniquity and purify for himself a people of his own who are zealous for good deeds.

[b] **2 Cor 5:19** ***God was in Christ, reconciling*** Or possibly *in Christ God was reconciling* (so NRSV) [c] **Eph 5:2** ***us*** Other ancient authorities read *you* [d] **Col 1:22** ***he has now reconciled*** Other ancient authorities read *you have now been reconciled* [e] **Col 2:13** ***made you*** Other ancient authorities read *made us*; others, *made*

Acts 20:28

προσέχετε ἑαυτοῖς καὶ παντὶ τῷ ποιμνίῳ, ἐν ᾧ ὑμᾶς τὸ πνεῦμα τὸ ἅγιον ἔθετο ἐπισκόπους ποιμαίνειν τὴν ἐκκλησίαν τοῦ ⸀θεοῦ, ἣν περιεποιήσατο διὰ τοῦ αἵματος τοῦ ἰδίου.

Cf. Rom 6:9–10; 8:34; 14:9; 1 Cor 1:13; 1:18–25; 2:1–5; 2:6–9; 2 Cor 13:4; Gal 3:1; 4:4–7; 6:11–16; Phil 2:8; 1 Thess 4:14.

See also § 40 Participation in Christ Crucified and Risen.

34. The Resurrection of Jesus

Rom 1:3–4

περὶ τοῦ υἱοῦ αὐτοῦ τοῦ γενομένου ἐκ σπέρματος Δαυὶδ κατὰ σάρκα, **4** τοῦ ὁρισθέντος υἱοῦ θεοῦ ἐν δυνάμει κατὰ πνεῦμα ἁγιωσύνης ἐξ ἀναστάσεως νεκρῶν, Ἰησοῦ Χριστοῦ τοῦ κυρίου ἡμῶν

Rom 4:24–25

ἀλλὰ καὶ δι᾽ ἡμᾶς, οἷς μέλλει λογίζεσθαι, τοῖς πιστεύουσιν ἐπὶ τὸν ἐγείραντα Ἰησοῦν τὸν κύριον ἡμῶν ἐκ νεκρῶν, **25** ὃς παρεδόθη διὰ τὰ παραπτώματα ἡμῶν καὶ ἠγέρθη διὰ τὴν δικαίωσιν ἡμῶν.

Rom 6:4

συνετάφημεν οὖν αὐτῷ διὰ τοῦ βαπτίσματος εἰς τὸν θάνατον, ἵνα ὥσπερ ἠγέρθη Χριστὸς ἐκ νεκρῶν διὰ τῆς δόξης τοῦ πατρός, οὕτως καὶ ἡμεῖς ἐν καινότητι ζωῆς περιπατήσωμεν.

Rom 6:9–10

εἰδότες ὅτι Χριστὸς ἐγερθεὶς ἐκ νεκρῶν οὐκέτι ἀποθνῄσκει, θάνατος αὐτοῦ οὐκέτι κυριεύει. **10** ὃ γὰρ ἀπέθανεν, τῇ ἁμαρτίᾳ ἀπέθανεν ἐφάπαξ· ὃ δὲ ζῇ, ζῇ τῷ θεῷ.

Rom 8:11

εἰ δὲ τὸ πνεῦμα τοῦ ἐγείραντος τὸν Ἰησοῦν ἐκ νεκρῶν οἰκεῖ ἐν ὑμῖν, ὁ ἐγείρας ⸂Χριστὸν ἐκ νεκρῶν⸃ ζῳοποιήσει καὶ τὰ θνητὰ σώματα ὑμῶν διὰ ⸂τοῦ ἐνοικοῦντος αὐτοῦ πνεύματος⸃ ἐν ὑμῖν.

Rom 8:34

τίς ὁ κατακρινῶν; Χριστὸς [Ἰησοῦς] ὁ ἀποθανών, μᾶλλον δὲ ⸀ἐγερθείς, ὃς καί ἐστιν ἐν δεξιᾷ τοῦ θεοῦ, ὃς καὶ ἐντυγχάνει ὑπὲρ ἡμῶν.

Rom 10:8–10

ἀλλὰ τί λέγει; ἐγγύς σου τὸ ῥῆμά ἐστιν ἐν τῷ στόματί σου καὶ ἐν τῇ καρδίᾳ σου, τοῦτ᾽ ἔστιν τὸ ῥῆμα τῆς πίστεως ὃ κηρύσσομεν. **9** ὅτι ἐὰν ὁμολογήσῃς ἐν τῷ στόματί σου κύριον Ἰησοῦν καὶ πιστεύσῃς ἐν τῇ καρδίᾳ σου ὅτι ὁ θεὸς αὐτὸν ἤγειρεν ἐκ νεκρῶν, σωθήσῃ· **10** καρδίᾳ γὰρ πιστεύεται εἰς δικαιοσύνην, στόματι δὲ ὁμολογεῖται εἰς σωτηρίαν.

Rom 14:9

εἰς τοῦτο γὰρ Χριστὸς ἀπέθανεν καὶ ἔζησεν, ἵνα καὶ νεκρῶν καὶ ζώντων κυριεύσῃ.

1 Cor 6:14

ὁ δὲ θεὸς καὶ τὸν κύριον ἤγειρεν καὶ ἡμᾶς ἐξεγερεῖ διὰ τῆς δυνάμεως αὐτοῦ.

1 Cor 15:3–8

παρέδωκα γὰρ ὑμῖν ἐν πρώτοις, ὃ καὶ παρέλαβον, ὅτι Χριστὸς ἀπέθανεν ὑπὲρ τῶν ἁμαρτιῶν ἡμῶν κατὰ τὰς γραφὰς **4** καὶ ὅτι ἐτάφη καὶ ὅτι ἐγήγερται τῇ ἡμέρᾳ τῇ τρίτῃ κατὰ τὰς γραφὰς **5** καὶ ὅτι ὤφθη Κηφᾷ εἶτα τοῖς δώδεκα· **6** ἔπειτα ὤφθη ἐπάνω πεντακοσίοις ἀδελφοῖς ἐφάπαξ, ἐξ ὧν οἱ πλείονες μένουσιν ἕως ἄρτι, τινὲς δὲ ἐκοιμήθησαν· **7** ἔπειτα ὤφθη Ἰακώβῳ εἶτα τοῖς ἀποστόλοις πᾶσιν· **8** ἔσχατον δὲ πάντων ὡσπερεὶ τῷ ἐκτρώματι ὤφθη κἀμοί.

1 Cor 15:12–19

Εἰ δὲ Χριστὸς κηρύσσεται ὅτι ἐκ νεκρῶν ἐγήγερται, πῶς λέγουσιν ἐν ὑμῖν τινες ὅτι ἀνάστασις νεκρῶν οὐκ ἔστιν; **13** εἰ δὲ ἀνάστασις νεκρῶν οὐκ ἔστιν, οὐδὲ Χριστὸς ἐγήγερται· **14** εἰ δὲ Χριστὸς οὐκ ἐγήγερται, κενὸν ἄρα [καὶ] τὸ κήρυγμα ἡμῶν, κενὴ καὶ ἡ πίστις ὑμῶν· **15** εὑρισκόμεθα δὲ καὶ ψευδομάρτυρες τοῦ θεοῦ, ὅτι ἐμαρτυρήσαμεν κατὰ τοῦ θεοῦ ὅτι ἤγειρεν τὸν Χριστόν, ὃν οὐκ ἤγειρεν εἴπερ ἄρα νεκροὶ οὐκ ἐγείρονται. **16** εἰ γὰρ νεκροὶ οὐκ ἐγείρονται, οὐδὲ Χριστὸς ἐγήγερται· **17** εἰ δὲ Χριστὸς οὐκ ἐγήγερται, ματαία ἡ πίστις ὑμῶν, ἔτι ἐστὲ ἐν ταῖς ἁμαρτίαις ὑμῶν, **18** ἄρα καὶ οἱ κοιμηθέντες ἐν Χριστῷ ἀπώλοντο. **19** εἰ ἐν τῇ ζωῇ ταύτῃ ἐν Χριστῷ ἠλπικότες ἐσμὲν μόνον, ἐλεεινότεροι πάντων ἀνθρώπων ἐσμέν.

1 Cor 15:20–23

Νυνὶ δὲ Χριστὸς ἐγήγερται ἐκ νεκρῶν ἀπαρχὴ τῶν κεκοιμημένων. **21** ἐπειδὴ γὰρ δι᾽ ἀνθρώπου θάνατος, καὶ δι᾽ ἀνθρώπου ἀνάστασις νεκρῶν. **22** ὥσπερ γὰρ ἐν τῷ Ἀδὰμ πάντες ἀποθνῄσκουσιν, οὕτως καὶ ἐν τῷ Χριστῷ πάντες ζῳοποιηθήσονται. **23** Ἕκαστος δὲ ἐν τῷ ἰδίῳ τάγματι· ἀπαρχὴ Χριστός, ἔπειτα οἱ τοῦ Χριστοῦ ἐν τῇ παρουσίᾳ αὐτοῦ

2 Cor 4:14

εἰδότες ὅτι ὁ ἐγείρας τὸν ⸀κύριον Ἰησοῦν καὶ ἡμᾶς σὺν Ἰησοῦ ἐγερεῖ καὶ παραστήσει σὺν ὑμῖν.

2 Cor 13:4

καὶ γὰρ ἐσταυρώθη ἐξ ἀσθενείας, ἀλλὰ ζῇ ἐκ δυνάμεως θεοῦ. καὶ γὰρ ἡμεῖς ἀσθενοῦμεν ⸀ἐν αὐτῷ, ἀλλὰ ζήσομεν σὺν αὐτῷ ἐκ δυνάμεως θεοῦ εἰς ὑμᾶς.

Gal 1:1

Παῦλος ἀπόστολος οὐκ ἀπ᾽ ἀνθρώπων οὐδὲ δι᾽ ἀνθρώπου ἀλλὰ διὰ Ἰησοῦ Χριστοῦ καὶ θεοῦ πατρὸς τοῦ ἐγείραντος αὐτὸν ἐκ νεκρῶν

Acts 20:28 ***θεου*** **א** B] κυριου 𝔓[74] A C* D E 33. 1739 ¦ κυριου και θεου *Byz* **§ 34** **Rom 8:11** ***Χριστον εκ νεκρων*** B D[2]] τον Χ. εκ ν. א[2] 33 *Byz* ¦ Χ. Ιησουν εκ ν. D* ¦ εκ ν. Χ. Ιησουν א* A (C Ι. Χ.) 1739. 1881 • ***του ενοικουντος αυτου πνευματος*** א A C[(*)]] το ενοικουν αυτου πνευμα B D 33. 1739. 1881 *Byz* **Rom 8:34** ***εγερθεις*** 𝔓[27vid] 𝔓[46] א[2] B D 1739. 1881 *Byz*] *add.* εκ νεκρων א* A C 33 **2 Cor 4:14** ***κυριον*** א C D 1881 *Byz*] *om.* 𝔓[46] B (33) (1739) **2 Cor 13:4** ***εν*** B D 33. 1739. 1881 *Byz*] συν א A

Acts 20:28
Keep watch over yourselves and over all the flock, of which the Holy Spirit has made you overseers, to shepherd the church of God[f] that he obtained with the blood of his own Son.

Cf. Rom 6:9–10; 8:34; 14:9; 1 Cor 1:13; 1:18–25; 2:1–5; 2:6–9; 2 Cor 13:4; Gal 3:1; 4:4–7; 6:11–16; Phil 2:8; 1 Thess 4:14.

See also § 40 Participation in Christ Crucified and Risen.

34. The Resurrection of Jesus

Rom 1:3–4
the gospel concerning his Son, who was descended from David according to the flesh **4** and was declared to be Son of God with power according to the Spirit[a] of holiness by resurrection from the dead, Jesus Christ our Lord

Rom 4:24–25
but for ours also. It will be reckoned to us who believe in him who raised Jesus our Lord from the dead, **25** who was handed over to death for our trespasses and was raised for our justification.

Rom 6:4
Therefore we have been buried with him by baptism into death, so that, just as Christ was raised from the dead by the glory of the Father, so we too might walk in newness of life.

Rom 6:9–10
We know that Christ, being raised from the dead, will never die again; death no longer has dominion over him. **10** The death he died, he died to sin, once for all; but the life he lives, he lives to God.

Rom 8:11
If the Spirit of him who raised Jesus from the dead dwells in you, he who raised Christ[b] from the dead will give life to your mortal bodies also through[c] his Spirit that dwells in you.

Rom 8:34
Who is to condemn? It is Christ Jesus, who died, yes, who was raised,[d] who is at the right hand of God, who indeed intercedes for us.

Rom 10:8–10
But what does it say? "The word is near you, on your lips and in your heart" (that is, the word of faith that we proclaim); **9** because if you confess with your lips that Jesus is Lord and believe in your heart that God raised him from the dead, you will be saved. **10** For one believes with the heart and so is justified, and one confesses with the mouth and so is saved.

Rom 14:9
For to this end Christ died and lived again, so that he might be Lord of both the dead and the living.

1 Cor 6:14
And God raised the Lord and will also raise us by his power.

1 Cor 15:3–8
For I handed on to you as of first importance what I in turn had received: that Christ died for our sins in accordance with the scriptures, **4** and that he was buried, and that he was raised on the third day in accordance with the scriptures, **5** and that he appeared to Cephas, then to the twelve. **6** Then he appeared to more than five hundred brothers and sisters at one time, most of whom are still alive, though some have died. **7** Then he appeared to James, then to all the apostles. **8** Last of all, as to one untimely born, he appeared also to me.

1 Cor 15:12–19
Now if Christ is proclaimed as raised from the dead, how can some of you say there is no resurrection of the dead? **13** If there is no resurrection of the dead, then Christ has not been raised; **14** and if Christ has not been raised, then our proclamation has been in vain and your faith has been in vain. **15** We are even found to be misrepresenting God, because we testified of God that he raised Christ—whom he did not raise if it is true that the dead are not raised. **16** For if the dead are not raised, then Christ has not been raised. **17** If Christ has not been raised, your faith is futile and you are still in your sins. **18** Then those also who have died in Christ have perished. **19** If for this life only we have hoped in Christ, we are of all people most to be pitied.

1 Cor 15:20–23
But in fact Christ has been raised from the dead, the first fruits of those who have died. **21** For since death came through a human being, the resurrection of the dead has also come through a human being; **22** for as all die in Adam, so all will be made alive in Christ. **23** But each in his own order: Christ the first fruits, then at his coming those who belong to Christ.

2 Cor 4:14
because we know that the one who raised the Lord[e] Jesus will raise us also with Jesus, and will bring us with you into his presence.

2 Cor 13:4
For he was crucified in weakness, but lives by the power of God. For we are weak in him,[f] but in dealing with you we will live with him by the power of God.

Gal 1:1
Paul an apostle—sent neither by human commission nor from human authorities, but through Jesus Christ and God the Father, who raised him from the dead

[f] **Acts 20:28** *of God* Other ancient authorities read *of the Lord* **§ 34** [a] **Rom 1:4** *Spirit* NRSV alternate translation [b] **Rom 8:11** *Christ* Other ancient authorities read *the Christ* or *Christ Jesus* or *Jesus Christ* [c] **Rom 8:11** *through* Other ancient authorities read *on account of* [d] **Rom 8:34** *raised* Other ancient authorities add *from the dead* [e] **2 Cor 4:14** *the Lord* Other ancient authorities lack *the Lord* [f] **2 Cor 13:4** *in him* Other ancient authorities read *with him*

Eph 1:19–20

καὶ τί τὸ ὑπερβάλλον μέγεθος τῆς δυνάμεως αὐτοῦ εἰς ἡμᾶς τοὺς πιστεύοντας κατὰ τὴν ἐνέργειαν τοῦ κράτους τῆς ἰσχύος αὐτοῦ. 20 Ἣν ⸀ἐνήργησεν ἐν τῷ Χριστῷ ἐγείρας αὐτὸν ἐκ νεκρῶν καὶ καθίσας ἐν δεξιᾷ αὐτοῦ ἐν τοῖς ἐπουρανίοις

Phil 3:10–11

τοῦ γνῶναι αὐτὸν καὶ τὴν δύναμιν τῆς ἀναστάσεως αὐτοῦ καὶ [τὴν] κοινωνίαν [τῶν] παθημάτων αὐτοῦ, συμμορφιζόμενος τῷ θανάτῳ αὐτοῦ, 11 εἴ πως καταντήσω εἰς τὴν ἐξανάστασιν τὴν ἐκ νεκρῶν.

Phil 3:20–21

ἡμῶν γὰρ τὸ πολίτευμα ἐν οὐρανοῖς ὑπάρχει, ἐξ οὗ καὶ σωτῆρα ἀπεκδεχόμεθα κύριον Ἰησοῦν Χριστόν, 21 ὃς μετασχηματίσει τὸ σῶμα τῆς ταπεινώσεως ἡμῶν σύμμορφον τῷ σώματι τῆς δόξης αὐτοῦ κατὰ τὴν ἐνέργειαν τοῦ δύνασθαι αὐτὸν καὶ ὑποτάξαι αὐτῷ τὰ πάντα.

Col 1:18

καὶ αὐτός ἐστιν ἡ κεφαλὴ τοῦ σώματος τῆς ἐκκλησίας· ὅς ἐστιν ἀρχή, πρωτότοκος ἐκ τῶν νεκρῶν, ἵνα γένηται ἐν πᾶσιν αὐτὸς πρωτεύων

Col 2:12

συνταφέντες αὐτῷ ἐν τῷ βαπτισμῷ, ἐν ᾧ καὶ συνηγέρθητε διὰ τῆς πίστεως τῆς ἐνεργείας τοῦ θεοῦ τοῦ ἐγείραντος αὐτὸν ἐκ νεκρῶν

1 Thess 1:9–10

αὐτοὶ γὰρ περὶ ἡμῶν ἀπαγγέλλουσιν ὁποίαν εἴσοδον ἔσχομεν πρὸς ὑμᾶς, καὶ πῶς ἐπεστρέψατε πρὸς τὸν θεὸν ἀπὸ τῶν εἰδώλων δουλεύειν θεῷ ζῶντι καὶ ἀληθινῷ 10 καὶ ἀναμένειν τὸν υἱὸν αὐτοῦ ἐκ τῶν οὐρανῶν, ὃν ἤγειρεν ἐκ [τῶν] νεκρῶν, Ἰησοῦν τὸν ῥυόμενον ἡμᾶς ἐκ τῆς ὀργῆς τῆς ἐρχομένης.

1 Thess 4:14

εἰ γὰρ πιστεύομεν ὅτι Ἰησοῦς ἀπέθανεν καὶ ἀνέστη, οὕτως καὶ ὁ θεὸς τοὺς κοιμηθέντας διὰ τοῦ Ἰησοῦ ἄξει σὺν αὐτῷ.

1 Tim 3:16

καὶ ὁμολογουμένως μέγα ἐστὶν τὸ τῆς εὐσεβείας μυστήριον· ⸀ὃς ἐφανερώθη ἐν σαρκί, ἐδικαιώθη ἐν πνεύματι, ὤφθη ἀγγέλοις, ἐκηρύχθη ἐν ἔθνεσιν, ἐπιστεύθη ἐν κόσμῳ, ἀνελήμφθη ἐν δόξῃ.

2 Tim 2:8

Μνημόνευε Ἰησοῦν Χριστὸν ἐγηγερμένον ἐκ νεκρῶν, ἐκ σπέρματος Δαυίδ, κατὰ τὸ εὐαγγέλιόν μου

Acts 13:30–37

ὁ δὲ θεὸς ἤγειρεν αὐτὸν ἐκ νεκρῶν, 31 ὃς ὤφθη ἐπὶ ἡμέρας πλείους τοῖς συναναβᾶσιν αὐτῷ ἀπὸ τῆς Γαλιλαίας εἰς Ἰερουσαλήμ, οἵτινες [νῦν] εἰσιν μάρτυρες αὐτοῦ πρὸς τὸν λαόν. 32 Καὶ ἡμεῖς ὑμᾶς εὐαγγελιζόμεθα τὴν πρὸς τοὺς πατέρας ἐπαγγελίαν γενομένην, 33 ὅτι ταύτην ὁ θεὸς ἐκπεπλήρωκεν τοῖς τέκνοις [αὐτῶν] ἡμῖν ἀναστήσας Ἰησοῦν ὡς καὶ ἐν τῷ ψαλμῷ γέγραπται τῷ δευτέρῳ· υἱός μου εἶ σύ, ἐγὼ σήμερον γεγέννηκά σε. 34 ὅτι δὲ ἀνέστησεν αὐτὸν ἐκ νεκρῶν μηκέτι μέλλοντα ὑποστρέφειν εἰς διαφθοράν, οὕτως εἴρηκεν ὅτι δώσω ὑμῖν τὰ ὅσια Δαυὶδ τὰ πιστά. 35 διότι καὶ ἐν ἑτέρῳ λέγει· οὐ δώσεις τὸν ὅσιόν σου ἰδεῖν διαφθοράν. 36 Δαυὶδ μὲν γὰρ ἰδίᾳ γενεᾷ ὑπηρετήσας τῇ τοῦ θεοῦ βουλῇ ἐκοιμήθη καὶ προσετέθη πρὸς τοὺς πατέρας αὐτοῦ καὶ εἶδεν διαφθοράν· 37 ὃν δὲ ὁ θεὸς ἤγειρεν, οὐκ εἶδεν διαφθοράν.

Acts 17:2–3

κατὰ δὲ τὸ εἰωθὸς τῷ Παύλῳ εἰσῆλθεν πρὸς αὐτοὺς καὶ ἐπὶ σάββατα τρία διελέξατο αὐτοῖς ἀπὸ τῶν γραφῶν, 3 διανοίγων καὶ παρατιθέμενος ὅτι τὸν χριστὸν ἔδει παθεῖν καὶ ἀναστῆναι ἐκ νεκρῶν καὶ ὅτι οὗτός ἐστιν ὁ χριστὸς [ὁ] Ἰησοῦς ὃν ἐγὼ καταγγέλλω ὑμῖν.

Acts 17:18

τινὲς δὲ καὶ τῶν Ἐπικουρείων καὶ Στοϊκῶν φιλοσόφων συνέβαλλον αὐτῷ, καί τινες ἔλεγον· τί ἂν θέλοι ὁ σπερμολόγος οὗτος λέγειν; οἱ δέ· ξένων δαιμονίων δοκεῖ καταγγελεὺς εἶναι, ὅτι τὸν Ἰησοῦν καὶ τὴν ἀνάστασιν εὐηγγελίζετο.

Acts 17:31–32

καθότι ἔστησεν ἡμέραν ἐν ᾗ μέλλει κρίνειν τὴν οἰκουμένην ἐν δικαιοσύνῃ, ἐν ἀνδρὶ ᾧ ὥρισεν, πίστιν παρασχὼν πᾶσιν ἀναστήσας αὐτὸν ἐκ νεκρῶν. 32 Ἀκούσαντες δὲ ἀνάστασιν νεκρῶν οἱ μὲν ἐχλεύαζον, οἱ δὲ εἶπαν· ἀκουσόμεθά σου περὶ τούτου καὶ πάλιν.

Acts 23:6

Γνοὺς δὲ ὁ Παῦλος ὅτι τὸ ἓν μέρος ἐστὶν Σαδδουκαίων τὸ δὲ ἕτερον Φαρισαίων ἔκραζεν ἐν τῷ συνεδρίῳ· ἄνδρες ἀδελφοί, ἐγὼ Φαρισαῖός εἰμι, υἱὸς Φαρισαίων, περὶ ἐλπίδος καὶ ἀναστάσεως νεκρῶν [ἐγὼ] κρίνομαι.

Acts 24:20–21

ἢ αὐτοὶ οὗτοι εἰπάτωσαν τί εὗρον ἀδίκημα στάντος μου ἐπὶ τοῦ συνεδρίου, 21 ἢ περὶ μιᾶς ταύτης φωνῆς ἧς ἐκέκραξα ἐν αὐτοῖς ἑστὼς ὅτι περὶ ἀναστάσεως νεκρῶν ἐγὼ κρίνομαι σήμερον ἐφ᾽ ὑμῶν.

Acts 25:18–19

περὶ οὗ σταθέντες οἱ κατήγοροι οὐδεμίαν αἰτίαν ἔφερον ὧν ἐγὼ ὑπενόουν ⸀πονηρῶν, 19 ζητήματα δέ τινα περὶ τῆς ἰδίας δεισιδαιμονίας εἶχον πρὸς αὐτὸν καὶ περί τινος Ἰησοῦ τεθνηκότος ὃν ἔφασκεν ὁ Παῦλος ζῆν.

Acts 26:6–8

καὶ νῦν ἐπ᾽ ἐλπίδι τῆς εἰς τοὺς πατέρας ἡμῶν ἐπαγγελίας γενομένης ὑπὸ τοῦ θεοῦ ἕστηκα κρινόμενος, 7 εἰς ἣν τὸ δωδεκάφυλον ἡμῶν ἐν ἐκτενείᾳ νύκτα καὶ ἡμέραν λατρεῦον ἐλπίζει καταντῆσαι, περὶ ἧς ἐλπίδος ἐγκαλοῦμαι ὑπὸ Ἰουδαίων, βασιλεῦ. 8 τί ἄπιστον κρίνεται παρ᾽ ὑμῖν εἰ ὁ θεὸς νεκροὺς ἐγείρει;

Acts 26:22–23

ἐπικουρίας οὖν τυχὼν τῆς ἀπὸ τοῦ θεοῦ ἄχρι τῆς ἡμέρας ταύτης ἕστηκα μαρτυρόμενος μικρῷ τε καὶ μεγάλῳ οὐδὲν ἐκτὸς λέγων ὧν τε οἱ προφῆται ἐλάλησαν μελλόντων γίνεσθαι καὶ Μωϋσῆς, 23 εἰ παθητὸς ὁ χριστός, εἰ πρῶτος ἐξ ἀναστάσεως νεκρῶν φῶς μέλλει καταγγέλλειν τῷ τε λαῷ καὶ τοῖς ἔθνεσιν.

Eph 1:20 ***ενηργησεν*** ℵ D 33. 1739. 1881 *Byz*] ενηργηκεν A B **1 Tim 3:16** ***ος*** ℵ* A* C* 33] ὃ D* ¦ θεος ℵ^c A^c C^2 D^2 1739. 1881 *Byz* **Acts 25:18** ***πονηρων*** ℵ^2 B E] πονηραν 𝔓^{74} A C* 33^{vid}. 1739 ¦ πονηρα ℵ* C^2 ¦ *om*. *Byz*

Eph 1:19–20
and what is the immeasurable greatness of his power for us who believe, according to the working of his great power. **20** God put this power to work[g] in Christ when he raised him from the dead and seated him at his right hand in the heavenly places

Phil 3:10–11
I want to know Christ and the power of his resurrection and the sharing of his sufferings by becoming like him in his death, **11** if somehow I may attain the resurrection from the dead.

Phil 3:20–21
But our citizenship is in heaven, and it is from there that we are expecting a Savior, the Lord Jesus Christ. **21** He will transform the body of our humiliation that it may be conformed to the body of his glory, by the power that also enables him to make all things subject to himself.

Col 1:18
He is the head of the body, the church; he is the beginning, the firstborn from the dead, so that he might come to have first place in everything.

Col 2:12
when you were buried with him in baptism, you were also raised with him through faith in the power of God, who raised him from the dead.

1 Thess 1:9–10
For the people of those regions report about us what kind of welcome we had among you, and how you turned to God from idols, to serve a living and true God, **10** and to wait for his Son from heaven, whom he raised from the dead—Jesus, who rescues us from the wrath that is coming.

1 Thess 4:14
For since we believe that Jesus died and rose again, even so, through Jesus, God will bring with him those who have died.

1 Tim 3:16
Without any doubt, the mystery of our religion is great: Who[h] was revealed in flesh, vindicated by the Spirit,[i] seen by angels, proclaimed among Gentiles, believed in throughout the world, taken up in glory.

2 Tim 2:8
Remember Jesus Christ, raised from the dead, a descendant of David—that is my gospel

Acts 13:30–37
But God raised him from the dead; **31** and for many days he appeared to those who came up with him from Galilee to Jerusalem, and they are now his witnesses to the people. **32** And we bring you the good news that what God promised to our ancestors **33** he has fulfilled for us, their children, by raising Jesus; as also it is written in the second psalm, 'You are my Son; today I have begotten you.' **34** As to his raising him from the dead, no more to return to corruption, he has spoken in this way, 'I will give you the holy promises made to David.' **35** Therefore he has also said in another psalm, 'You will not let your Holy One experience corruption.' **36** For David, after he had served the purpose of God in his own generation, died, was laid beside his ancestors, and experienced corruption; **37** but he whom God raised up experienced no corruption.

Acts 17:2–3
And Paul went in, as was his custom, and on three sabbath days argued with them from the scriptures, **3** explaining and proving that it was necessary for the Messiah to suffer and to rise from the dead, and saying, "This is the Messiah, Jesus whom I am proclaiming to you."

Acts 17:18
Also some Epicurean and Stoic philosophers debated with him. Some said, "What does this babbler want to say?" Others said, "He seems to be a proclaimer of foreign divinities." (This was because he was telling the good news about Jesus and the resurrection.)

Acts 17:31–32
because he has fixed a day on which he will have the world judged in righteousness by a man whom he has appointed, and of this he has given assurance to all by raising him from the dead." **32** When they heard of the resurrection of the dead, some scoffed; but others said, "We will hear you again about this."

Acts 23:6
When Paul noticed that some were Sadducees and others were Pharisees, he called out in the council, "Brothers, I am a Pharisee, a son of Pharisees. I am on trial concerning the hope of the resurrection of the dead."

Acts 24:20–21
Or let these men here tell what crime they had found when I stood before the council, **21** unless it was this one sentence that I called out while standing before them, 'It is about the resurrection of the dead that I am on trial before you today.'"

Acts 25:18–19
When the accusers stood up, they did not charge him with any of the crimes[j] that I was expecting. **19** Instead they had certain points of disagreement with him about their own religion and about a certain Jesus, who had died, but whom Paul asserted to be alive.

Acts 26:6–8
And now I stand here on trial on account of my hope in the promise made by God to our ancestors, **7** a promise that our twelve tribes hope to attain, as they earnestly worship day and night. It is for this hope, your Excellency, that I am accused by Jews! **8** Why is it thought incredible by any of you that God raises the dead?

Acts 26:22–23
To this day I have had help from God, and so I stand here, testifying to both small and great, saying nothing but what the prophets and Moses said would take place: **23** that the Messiah must suffer, and that, by being the first to rise from the dead, he would proclaim light both to our people and to the Gentiles.

[g] **Eph 1:20** ***put this power to work*** Other ancient authorities read *has put this power to work* [h] **1 Tim 3:16** ***Who*** Other ancient authorities read *God*; others, *Which*. NRSV translates Gk *Who* as *He* [i] **1 Tim 3:16** ***by the Spirit*** NRSV alternate translation [j] **Acts 25:18** ***with any of the crimes*** Other ancient authorities read *with anything*

Acts 28:20

διὰ ταύτην οὖν τὴν αἰτίαν παρεκάλεσα ὑμᾶς ἰδεῖν καὶ προσλαλῆσαι, ἕνεκεν γὰρ τῆς ἐλπίδος τοῦ Ἰσραὴλ τὴν ἅλυσιν ταύτην περίκειμαι.

See also § 40 Participation in Christ Crucified and Risen.

35. The Ascension of the Lord

Rom 8:34

τίς ὁ κατακρινῶν; Χριστὸς [Ἰησοῦς] ὁ ἀποθανών, μᾶλλον δὲ ⸀ἐγερθείς, ὃς καί ἐστιν ἐν δεξιᾷ τοῦ θεοῦ, ὃς καὶ ἐντυγχάνει ὑπὲρ ἡμῶν.

Eph 1:20–23

Ἣν ⸀ἐνήργησεν ἐν τῷ Χριστῷ ἐγείρας
αὐτὸν ἐκ νεκρῶν καὶ καθίσας ἐν δεξιᾷ
αὐτοῦ ἐν τοῖς ἐπουρανίοις **21** ὑπεράνω
πάσης ἀρχῆς καὶ ἐξουσίας καὶ δυνάμεως
καὶ κυριότητος καὶ παντὸς ὀνόματος
ὀνομαζομένου, οὐ μόνον ἐν τῷ αἰῶνι
τούτῳ ἀλλὰ καὶ ἐν τῷ μέλλοντι· **22** καὶ
πάντα ὑπέταξεν ὑπὸ τοὺς πόδας αὐτοῦ
καὶ αὐτὸν ἔδωκεν κεφαλὴν ὑπὲρ πάν-
τα τῇ ἐκκλησίᾳ, **23** ἥτις ἐστὶν τὸ σῶμα
αὐτοῦ, τὸ πλήρωμα τοῦ τὰ πάντα ἐν
πᾶσιν πληρουμένου.

Eph 4:8–10

διὸ λέγει· ἀναβὰς εἰς ὕψος ᾐχμαλώτευ-
σεν αἰχμαλωσίαν, ἔδωκεν δόματα τοῖς
ἀνθρώποις. **9** τὸ δὲ ἀνέβη τί ἐστιν, εἰ μὴ
ὅτι καὶ ⸀κατέβη εἰς τὰ κατώτερα [μέρη]
τῆς γῆς; **10** ὁ καταβὰς αὐτός ἐστιν καὶ ὁ
ἀναβὰς ὑπεράνω πάντων τῶν οὐρανῶν,
ἵνα πληρώσῃ τὰ πάντα.

Phil 2:9–11

διὸ καὶ ὁ θεὸς αὐτὸν ὑπερύψωσεν καὶ
ἐχαρίσατο αὐτῷ τὸ ὄνομα τὸ ὑπὲρ πᾶν
ὄνομα, **10** ἵνα ἐν τῷ ὀνόματι Ἰησοῦ πᾶν
γόνυ κάμψῃ ἐπουρανίων καὶ ἐπιγείων
καὶ καταχθονίων **11** καὶ πᾶσα γλῶσσα
ἐξομολογήσηται ὅτι κύριος Ἰησοῦς Χρι-
στὸς εἰς δόξαν θεοῦ πατρός.

Col 3:1

Εἰ οὖν συνηγέρθητε τῷ Χριστῷ, τὰ ἄνω ζητεῖτε, οὗ ὁ Χριστός ἐστιν ἐν δεξιᾷ τοῦ θεοῦ καθήμενος

1 Tim 3:16

καὶ ὁμολογουμένως μέγα ἐστὶν τὸ τῆς εὐσεβείας μυστήριον· ⸀ὃς ἐφανερώθη ἐν σαρκί, ἐδικαιώθη ἐν πνεύματι, ὤφθη ἀγγέλοις, ἐκηρύχθη ἐν ἔθνεσιν, ἐπιστεύθη ἐν κόσμῳ, ἀνελήμφθη ἐν δόξῃ.

36. The Mystery of God, Christ

Rom 16:25–27

⸂[Τῷ δὲ δυναμένῳ ὑμᾶς στηρίξαι κατὰ
τὸ εὐαγγέλιόν μου καὶ τὸ κήρυγμα Ἰη-
σοῦ Χριστοῦ, κατὰ ἀποκάλυψιν μυστη-
ρίου χρόνοις αἰωνίοις σεσιγημένου,
26 φανερωθέντος δὲ νῦν διά τε γραφῶν
προφητικῶν κατ' ἐπιταγὴν τοῦ αἰωνίου
θεοῦ εἰς ὑπακοὴν πίστεως εἰς πάντα τὰ
ἔθνη γνωρισθέντος, **27** μόνῳ σοφῷ θεῷ,
διὰ Ἰησοῦ Χριστοῦ, ⸀ᾧ ἡ δόξα εἰς τοὺς
⸀αἰῶνας, ἀμήν.]⸃

1 Cor 2:1–5

Κἀγὼ ἐλθὼν πρὸς ὑμᾶς, ἀδελφοί, ἦλθον
οὐ καθ' ὑπεροχὴν λόγου ἢ σοφίας καταγ-
γέλλων ὑμῖν τὸ ⸀μυστήριον τοῦ θεοῦ.
2 οὐ γὰρ ἔκρινά τι εἰδέναι ἐν ὑμῖν εἰ μὴ
Ἰησοῦν Χριστὸν καὶ τοῦτον ἐσταυρωμέ-
νον. **3** κἀγὼ ἐν ἀσθενείᾳ καὶ ἐν φόβῳ καὶ
ἐν τρόμῳ πολλῷ ἐγενόμην πρὸς ὑμᾶς,
4 καὶ ὁ λόγος μου καὶ τὸ κήρυγμά μου
οὐκ ἐν ⸂πειθοῖ[ς] σοφίας [λόγοις]⸃ ἀλλ'
ἐν ἀποδείξει πνεύματος καὶ δυνάμεως,
5 ἵνα ἡ πίστις ὑμῶν μὴ ᾖ ἐν σοφίᾳ ἀνθρώ-
πων ἀλλ' ἐν δυνάμει θεοῦ.

1 Cor 2:6–9

Σοφίαν δὲ λαλοῦμεν ἐν τοῖς τελείοις,
σοφίαν δὲ οὐ τοῦ αἰῶνος τούτου οὐδὲ
τῶν ἀρχόντων τοῦ αἰῶνος τούτου τῶν
καταργουμένων· **7** ἀλλὰ λαλοῦμεν θεοῦ
σοφίαν ἐν μυστηρίῳ τὴν ἀποκεκρυμ-
μένην, ἣν προώρισεν ὁ θεὸς πρὸ τῶν
αἰώνων εἰς δόξαν ἡμῶν, **8** ἣν οὐδεὶς τῶν
ἀρχόντων τοῦ αἰῶνος τούτου ἔγνωκεν·
εἰ γὰρ ἔγνωσαν, οὐκ ἂν τὸν κύριον τῆς
δόξης ἐσταύρωσαν. **9** ἀλλὰ καθὼς γέ-
γραπται· ἃ ὀφθαλμὸς οὐκ εἶδεν καὶ οὖς
οὐκ ἤκουσεν καὶ ἐπὶ καρδίαν ἀνθρώπου
οὐκ ἀνέβη, ἃ ἡτοίμασεν ὁ θεὸς τοῖς ἀγα-
πῶσιν αὐτόν.

Eph 3:1–13

Τούτου χάριν ἐγὼ Παῦλος ὁ δέσμιος τοῦ
Χριστοῦ [Ἰησοῦ] ὑπὲρ ὑμῶν τῶν ἐθνῶν
2 —εἴ γε ἠκούσατε τὴν οἰκονομίαν τῆς
χάριτος τοῦ θεοῦ τῆς δοθείσης μοι εἰς
ὑμᾶς, **3** [ὅτι] κατὰ ἀποκάλυψιν ἐγνωρίσθη
μοι τὸ μυστήριον, καθὼς προέγραψα ἐν
ὀλίγῳ, **4** πρὸς ὃ δύνασθε ἀναγινώσκοντες
νοῆσαι τὴν σύνεσίν μου ἐν τῷ μυστηρίῳ
τοῦ Χριστοῦ, **5** ὃ ἑτέραις γενεαῖς οὐκ
ἐγνωρίσθη τοῖς υἱοῖς τῶν ἀνθρώπων ὡς
νῦν ἀπεκαλύφθη τοῖς ἁγίοις ἀποστόλοις

§ 35 **Rom 8:34** ***εγερθεις*** 𝔓^{27vid} 𝔓^{46} א^{2} B D 1739. 1881 *Byz*] *add.* εκ νεκρων א* A C 33 **Eph 1:20** ***ενηργησεν*** א D 33. 1739. 1881 *Byz*] ενηργηκεν A B **Eph 4:9** ***κατεβη*** 𝔓^{46} א* A C* D I^{vid} 33. 1739. 1881] *add.* πρωτον א^{2} B C^{3} *Byz* **1 Tim 3:16** ***ος*** א* A* C* 33] ὃ D* ¦ θεος א^{c} A^{c} C^{2} D^{2} 1739. 1881 *Byz* **§ 36** **Rom 16:25–27** *pon. hic* 𝔓^{61} א B C D 1739] *pon. hic et p.* 14:23 A 33 ¦ *pon. p.* 14:23 *Byz* ¦ *pon. p.* 15:33 𝔓^{46} ¦ *om. pc* **Rom 16:27** ***ω*** 𝔓^{46} א A C D 33. 1739. 1881 *Byz*] *om.* B • ***αιωνας*** 𝔓^{46} B C 33. 1739. 1881 *Byz*] *add.* των αιωνων 𝔓^{61} א A D **1 Cor 2:1** ***μυστηριον*** 𝔓^{46vid} א* A C] μαρτυριον א^{2} B D 33. 1739. 1881 *Byz* **1 Cor 2:4** ***πειθοις σοφιας λογοις*** (א*) B D 33. 1739. 1881] πειθοις ανθρωπινης σοφιας λογοις א^{2} A C *Byz* ¦ πειθοις σοφιας 𝔓^{46} ¦ πειθοι σοφιας *cj*

Acts 28:20
For this reason therefore I have asked to see you and speak with you, since it is for the sake of the hope of Israel that I am bound with this chain.

See also § 40 Participation in Christ Crucified and Risen.

35. The Ascension of the Lord

Rom 8:34
Who is to condemn? It is Christ Jesus, who died, yes, who was raised,[a] who is at the right hand of God, who indeed intercedes for us.

Eph 1:20–23
God put this power to work[b] in Christ when he raised him from the dead and seated him at his right hand in the heavenly places, **21** far above all rule and authority and power and dominion, and above every name that is named, not only in this age but also in the age to come. **22** And he has put all things under his feet and has made him the head over all things for the church, **23** which is his body, the fullness of him who fills all in all.

Eph 4:8–10
Therefore it is said, "When he ascended on high he made captivity itself a captive; he gave gifts to his people." **9** (When it says, "He ascended," what does it mean but that he had also descended[c] into the lower parts of the earth? **10** He who descended is the same one who ascended far above all the heavens, so that he might fill all things.)

Phil 2:9–11
Therefore God also highly exalted him and gave him the name that is above every name, **10** so that at the name of Jesus every knee should bend, in heaven and on earth and under the earth, **11** and every tongue should confess that Jesus Christ is Lord, to the glory of God the Father.

Col 3:1
So if you have been raised with Christ, seek the things that are above, where Christ is, seated at the right hand of God.

1 Tim 3:16
Without any doubt, the mystery of our religion is great: Who[d] was revealed in flesh, vindicated by the Spirit,[e] seen by angels, proclaimed among Gentiles, believed in throughout the world, taken up in glory.

36. The Mystery of God, Christ

Rom 16:25–27
Now to God who is able to strengthen you according to my gospel and the proclamation of Jesus Christ, according to the revelation of the mystery that was kept secret for long ages **26** but is now disclosed, and through the prophetic writings is made known to all the Gentiles, according to the command of the eternal God, to bring about the obedience of faith— **27** to the only wise God, through Jesus Christ, to whom[a] be the glory forever![b] Amen.[c]

1 Cor 2:1–5
When I came to you, brothers and sisters, I did not come proclaiming the mystery[d] of God to you in lofty words or wisdom. **2** For I decided to know nothing among you except Jesus Christ, and him crucified. **3** And I came to you in weakness and in fear and in much trembling. **4** My speech and my proclamation were not with plausible words of wisdom,[e] but with a demonstration of the Spirit and of power, **5** so that your faith might rest not on human wisdom but on the power of God.

1 Cor 2:6–9
Yet among the mature we do speak wisdom, though it is not a wisdom of this age or of the rulers of this age, who are doomed to perish. **7** But we speak God's wisdom, secret and hidden, which God decreed before the ages for our glory. **8** None of the rulers of this age understood this; for if they had, they would not have crucified the Lord of glory. **9** But, as it is written, "What no eye has seen, nor ear heard, nor the human heart conceived, what God has prepared for those who love him"

Eph 3:1–13
This is the reason that I Paul am a prisoner for Christ Jesus for the sake of you Gentiles— **2** for surely you have already heard of the commission of God's grace that was given me for you, **3** and how the mystery was made known to me by revelation, as I wrote above in a few words, **4** a reading of which will enable you to perceive my understanding of the mystery of Christ. **5** In former generations this mystery was not made known to humankind, as it has now been revealed

§ 35 [a] **Rom 8:34** ***raised*** Other ancient authorities add *from the dead* [b] **Eph 1:20** ***put this power to work*** Other ancient authorities read *has put this power to work* [c] **Eph 4:9** ***descended*** Other ancient authorities add *first* [d] **1 Tim 3:16** ***Who*** Other ancient authorities read *God*; others, *Which*. NRSV translates Gk *Who* as *He* [e] **1 Tim 3:16** ***by the Spirit*** NRSV alternate translation **§ 36** [a] **Rom 16:27** ***to whom*** A few ancient authorities lack *to whom*. The verse then reads, *to the only wise God be the glory through Jesus Christ forever. Amen.* [b] **Rom 16:27** ***forever*** Other ancient authorities read *forever and ever* [c] **Rom 16:27** ***Amen*** Other ancient authorities include 16:25–27 after 14:23 or 15:33; a few lack these verses altogether [d] **1 Cor 2:1** ***mystery*** Other ancient authorities read *testimony* [e] **1 Cor 2:4** ***plausible words of wisdom*** Other ancient authorities provide evidence for the reading *the persuasiveness of wisdom*; others read *plausible words of human wisdom*

αὐτοῦ καὶ προφήταις ἐν πνεύματι, 6 εἶναι
τὰ ἔθνη συγκληρονόμα καὶ σύσσωμα
καὶ συμμέτοχα τῆς ἐπαγγελίας ἐν Χρι-
στῷ Ἰησοῦ διὰ τοῦ εὐαγγελίου, 7 οὗ
ἐγενήθην διάκονος κατὰ τὴν δωρεὰν
τῆς χάριτος τοῦ θεοῦ τῆς δοθείσης μοι
κατὰ τὴν ἐνέργειαν τῆς δυνάμεως αὐτοῦ.
8 Ἐμοὶ τῷ ἐλαχιστοτέρῳ πάντων ἁγίων
ἐδόθη ἡ χάρις αὕτη, τοῖς ἔθνεσιν εὐαγ-
γελίσασθαι τὸ ἀνεξιχνίαστον πλοῦτος
τοῦ Χριστοῦ 9 καὶ φωτίσαι ⸀[πάντας] τίς
ἡ οἰκονομία τοῦ μυστηρίου τοῦ ἀποκε-
κρυμμένου ἀπὸ τῶν αἰώνων ἐν τῷ θεῷ
τῷ τὰ πάντα κτίσαντι, 10 ἵνα γνωρισθῇ
νῦν ταῖς ἀρχαῖς καὶ ταῖς ἐξουσίαις ἐν
τοῖς ἐπουρανίοις διὰ τῆς ἐκκλησίας ἡ
πολυποίκιλος σοφία τοῦ θεοῦ, 11 κατὰ
πρόθεσιν τῶν αἰώνων ἣν ἐποίησεν ἐν
τῷ Χριστῷ Ἰησοῦ τῷ κυρίῳ ἡμῶν, 12 ἐν
ᾧ ἔχομεν τὴν παρρησίαν καὶ προσα-
γωγὴν ἐν πεποιθήσει διὰ τῆς πίστεως
αὐτοῦ. 13 διὸ αἰτοῦμαι μὴ ἐγκακεῖν ἐν
ταῖς θλίψεσίν μου ὑπὲρ ὑμῶν, ἥτις ἐστὶν
δόξα ὑμῶν.

Eph 6:19–20

καὶ ὑπὲρ ἐμοῦ, ἵνα μοι δοθῇ λόγος ἐν
ἀνοίξει τοῦ στόματός μου, ἐν παρρησίᾳ
γνωρίσαι τὸ μυστήριον ⸂τοῦ εὐαγγε-
λίου⸃, 20 ὑπὲρ οὗ πρεσβεύω ἐν ἁλύσει,
ἵνα ἐν αὐτῷ παρρησιάσωμαι ὡς δεῖ με
λαλῆσαι.

Col 1:24–29

Νῦν χαίρω ἐν τοῖς παθήμασιν ὑπὲρ ὑμῶν
καὶ ἀνταναπληρῶ τὰ ὑστερήματα τῶν
θλίψεων τοῦ Χριστοῦ ἐν τῇ σαρκί μου ὑπὲρ
τοῦ σώματος αὐτοῦ, ὅ ἐστιν ἡ ἐκκλησία,
25 ἧς ἐγενόμην ἐγὼ διάκονος κατὰ τὴν
οἰκονομίαν τοῦ θεοῦ τὴν δοθεῖσάν μοι
εἰς ὑμᾶς πληρῶσαι τὸν λόγον τοῦ θεοῦ,
26 τὸ μυστήριον τὸ ἀποκεκρυμμένον ἀπὸ
τῶν αἰώνων καὶ ἀπὸ τῶν γενεῶν—νῦν
δὲ ἐφανερώθη τοῖς ἁγίοις αὐτοῦ, 27 οἷς
ἠθέλησεν ὁ θεὸς γνωρίσαι τί τὸ πλοῦ-
τος τῆς δόξης τοῦ μυστηρίου τούτου ἐν
τοῖς ἔθνεσιν, ὅ ἐστιν Χριστὸς ἐν ὑμῖν, ἡ
ἐλπὶς τῆς δόξης· 28 ὃν ἡμεῖς καταγγέλ-
λομεν νουθετοῦντες πάντα ἄνθρωπον
καὶ διδάσκοντες πάντα ἄνθρωπον ἐν
πάσῃ σοφίᾳ, ἵνα παραστήσωμεν πάν-
τα ἄνθρωπον τέλειον ἐν Χριστῷ· 29 εἰς
ὃ καὶ κοπιῶ ἀγωνιζόμενος κατὰ τὴν
ἐνέργειαν αὐτοῦ τὴν ἐνεργουμένην ἐν
ἐμοὶ ἐν δυνάμει.

Col 2:1–3

Θέλω γὰρ ὑμᾶς εἰδέναι ἡλίκον ἀγῶνα
ἔχω ὑπὲρ ὑμῶν καὶ τῶν ἐν Λαοδικείᾳ
καὶ ὅσοι οὐχ ἑόρακαν τὸ πρόσωπόν μου
ἐν σαρκί, 2 ἵνα παρακληθῶσιν αἱ καρδίαι
αὐτῶν συμβιβασθέντες ἐν ἀγάπῃ καὶ
εἰς πᾶν πλοῦτος τῆς πληροφορίας τῆς
συνέσεως, εἰς ἐπίγνωσιν τοῦ μυστηρίου
⸂τοῦ θεοῦ, Χριστοῦ⸃, 3 ἐν ᾧ εἰσιν πάντες
οἱ θησαυροὶ τῆς σοφίας καὶ γνώσεως
ἀπόκρυφοι.

Col 4:3

προσευχόμενοι ἅμα καὶ περὶ ἡμῶν, ἵνα
ὁ θεὸς ἀνοίξῃ ἡμῖν θύραν τοῦ λόγου
λαλῆσαι τὸ μυστήριον τοῦ Χριστοῦ, δι'
ὃ καὶ δέδεμαι

1 Tim 3:16

καὶ ὁμολογουμένως μέγα ἐστὶν τὸ τῆς
εὐσεβείας μυστήριον· ⸀ὃς ἐφανερώθη
ἐν σαρκί, ἐδικαιώθη ἐν πνεύματι, ὤφθη
ἀγγέλοις, ἐκηρύχθη ἐν ἔθνεσιν, ἐπιστεύθη
ἐν κόσμῳ, ἀνελήμφθη ἐν δόξῃ.

See also § 37 Christ the Wisdom and Power of God; § 64 The Mystery of Gentile Inclusion in Israel.

37. Christ the Wisdom and Power of God

1 Cor 1:18–25

Ὁ λόγος γὰρ ὁ τοῦ σταυροῦ τοῖς μὲν ἀπολ-
λυμένοις μωρία ἐστίν, τοῖς δὲ σῳζομένοις
ἡμῖν δύναμις θεοῦ ἐστιν. 19 γέγραπται γάρ·
ἀπολῶ τὴν σοφίαν τῶν σοφῶν καὶ τὴν
σύνεσιν τῶν συνετῶν ἀθετήσω. 20 ποῦ
σοφός; ποῦ γραμματεύς; ποῦ συζητητὴς
τοῦ αἰῶνος τούτου; οὐχὶ ἐμώρανεν ὁ θεὸς
τὴν σοφίαν τοῦ κόσμου; 21 ἐπειδὴ γὰρ ἐν
τῇ σοφίᾳ τοῦ θεοῦ οὐκ ἔγνω ὁ κόσμος
διὰ τῆς σοφίας τὸν θεόν, εὐδόκησεν ὁ
θεὸς διὰ τῆς μωρίας τοῦ κηρύγματος
σῶσαι τοὺς πιστεύοντας· 22 ἐπειδὴ καὶ
Ἰουδαῖοι σημεῖα αἰτοῦσιν καὶ Ἕλληνες
σοφίαν ζητοῦσιν, 23 ἡμεῖς δὲ κηρύσσο-
μεν Χριστὸν ἐσταυρωμένον, Ἰουδαίοις
μὲν σκάνδαλον, ἔθνεσιν δὲ μωρίαν,
24 αὐτοῖς δὲ τοῖς κλητοῖς, Ἰουδαίοις τε
καὶ Ἕλλησιν, Χριστὸν θεοῦ δύναμιν
καὶ θεοῦ σοφίαν· 25 ὅτι τὸ μωρὸν τοῦ
θεοῦ σοφώτερον τῶν ἀνθρώπων ἐστὶν
καὶ τὸ ἀσθενὲς τοῦ θεοῦ ἰσχυρότερον
τῶν ἀνθρώπων.

1 Cor 1:26–31

Βλέπετε γὰρ τὴν κλῆσιν ὑμῶν, ἀδελ-
φοί, ὅτι οὐ πολλοὶ σοφοὶ κατὰ σάρκα,
οὐ πολλοὶ δυνατοί, οὐ πολλοὶ εὐγενεῖς·
27 ἀλλὰ τὰ μωρὰ τοῦ κόσμου ἐξελέξατο
ὁ θεός, ἵνα καταισχύνῃ τοὺς σοφούς, καὶ
τὰ ἀσθενῆ τοῦ κόσμου ἐξελέξατο ὁ θε-
ός, ἵνα καταισχύνῃ τὰ ἰσχυρά, 28 καὶ τὰ
ἀγενῆ τοῦ κόσμου καὶ τὰ ἐξουθενημένα
ἐξελέξατο ὁ θεός, τὰ μὴ ὄντα, ἵνα τὰ
ὄντα καταργήσῃ, 29 ὅπως μὴ καυχήση-
ται πᾶσα σὰρξ ἐνώπιον τοῦ θεοῦ. 30 ἐξ
αὐτοῦ δὲ ὑμεῖς ἐστε ἐν Χριστῷ Ἰησοῦ,
ὃς ἐγενήθη σοφία ἡμῖν ἀπὸ θεοῦ, δικαι-
οσύνη τε καὶ ἁγιασμὸς καὶ ἀπολύτρωσις,
31 ἵνα καθὼς γέγραπται· ὁ καυχώμενος
ἐν κυρίῳ καυχάσθω.

1 Cor 2:1–5

Κἀγὼ ἐλθὼν πρὸς ὑμᾶς, ἀδελφοί, ἦλθον
οὐ καθ' ὑπεροχὴν λόγου ἢ σοφίας καταγ-
γέλλων ὑμῖν τὸ ⸀μυστήριον τοῦ θεοῦ.
2 οὐ γὰρ ἔκρινά τι εἰδέναι ἐν ὑμῖν εἰ μὴ
Ἰησοῦν Χριστὸν καὶ τοῦτον ἐσταυρωμέ-
νον. 3 κἀγὼ ἐν ἀσθενείᾳ καὶ ἐν φόβῳ καὶ
ἐν τρόμῳ πολλῷ ἐγενόμην πρὸς ὑμᾶς,

Eph 3:9 ***παντας*** 𝔓[46] א[2] B C D 33 *Byz*] *om.* א* A 1739. 1881 **Eph 6:19** ***του ευαγγελιου*** א A D I 33. 1739. 1881 *Byz*] *om.* B **Col 2:2** ***του θεου, Χριστου*** 𝔓[46] B] του θεου πατρος (+ του A C) Χριστου א* A C 048[vid] ¦ του θεου και πατρος του Χριστου א[2] ¦ του θεου και πατρος και του Χριστου D[2] *Byz* ¦ του θεου ὅ εστιν Χριστος D* ¦ του θεου του εν Χριστω 33 ¦ του θεου D[1] 1881 ¦ του Χριστου (1739) **1 Tim 3:16** ***ος*** א* A* C* 33] ὃ D* ¦ θεος א[c] A[c] C[2] D[2] 1739. 1881 *Byz* **§ 37** **1 Cor 2:1** ***μυστηριον*** 𝔓[46vid] א* A C] μαρτυριον א[2] B D 33. 1739. 1881 *Byz*

to his holy apostles and prophets by the Spirit: **6** that is, the Gentiles have become fellow heirs, members of the same body, and sharers in the promise in Christ Jesus through the gospel. **7** Of this gospel I have become a servant according to the gift of God's grace that was given me by the working of his power. **8** Although I am the very least of all the saints, this grace was given to me to bring to the Gentiles the news of the boundless riches of Christ, **9** and to make everyone see[f] what is the plan of the mystery hidden for ages in God who created all things; **10** so that through the church the wisdom of God in its rich variety might now be made known to the rulers and authorities in the heavenly places. **11** This was in accordance with the eternal purpose that he has carried out in Christ Jesus our Lord, **12** in whom we have access to God in boldness and confidence through faith in him. **13** I pray therefore that you may not lose heart over my sufferings for you; they are your glory.

Eph 6:19–20

Pray also for me, so that when I speak, a message may be given to me to make known with boldness the mystery of the gospel,[g] **20** for which I am an ambassador in chains. Pray that I may declare it boldly, as I must speak.

Col 1:24–29

I am now rejoicing in my sufferings for your sake, and in my flesh I am completing what is lacking in Christ's afflictions for the sake of his body, that is, the church. **25** I became its servant according to God's commission that was given to me for you, to make the word of God fully known, **26** the mystery that has been hidden throughout the ages and generations but has now been revealed to his saints. **27** To them God chose to make known how great among the Gentiles are the riches of the glory of this mystery, which is Christ in you, the hope of glory. **28** It is he whom we proclaim, warning everyone and teaching everyone in all wisdom, so that we may present everyone mature in Christ. **29** For this I toil and struggle with all the energy that he powerfully inspires within me.

Col 2:1–3

For I want you to know how much I am struggling for you, and for those in Laodicea, and for all who have not seen me face to face. **2** I want their hearts to be encouraged and united in love, so that they may have all the riches of assured understanding and have the knowledge of God's mystery, that is, Christ himself,[h] **3** in whom are hidden all the treasures of wisdom and knowledge.

Col 4:3

At the same time pray for us as well that God will open to us a door for the word, that we may declare the mystery of Christ, for which I am in prison

1 Tim 3:16

Without any doubt, the mystery of our religion is great: Who[i] was revealed in flesh, vindicated by the Spirit,[j] seen by angels, proclaimed among Gentiles, believed in throughout the world, taken up in glory.

See also § 37 Christ the Wisdom and Power of God; § 64 The Mystery of Gentile Inclusion in Israel.

37. Christ the Wisdom and Power of God

1 Cor 1:18–25

For the message about the cross is foolishness to those who are perishing, but to us who are being saved it is the power of God. **19** For it is written, "I wll destroy the wisdom of the wise, and the discernment of the discerning I will thwart." **20** Where is the one who is wise? Where is the scribe? Where is the debater of this age? Has not God made foolish the wisdom of the world? **21** For since, in the wisdom of God, the world did not know God through wisdom, God decided, through the foolishness of our proclamation, to save those who believe. **22** For Jews demand signs and Greeks desire wisdom, **23** but we proclaim Christ crucified, a stumbling block to Jews and foolishness to Gentiles, **24** but to those who are the called, both Jews and Greeks, Christ the power of God and the wisdom of God. **25** For God's foolishness is wiser than human wisdom, and God's weakness is stronger than human strength.

1 Cor 1:26–31

Consider your own call, brothers and sisters: not many of you were wise by human standards, not many were powerful, not many were of noble birth. **27** But God chose what is foolish in the world to shame the wise; God chose what is weak in the world to shame the strong; **28** God chose what is low and despised in the world, things that are not, to reduce to nothing things that are, **29** so that no one might boast in the presence of God. **30** He is the source of your life in Christ Jesus, who became for us wisdom from God, and righteousness and sanctification and redemption, **31** in order that, as it is written, "Let the one who boasts, boast in the Lord."

1 Cor 2:1–5

When I came to you, brothers and sisters, I did not come proclaiming the mystery[a] of God to you in lofty words or wisdom. **2** For I decided to know nothing among you except Jesus Christ, and him crucified. **3** And I came to you in weakness and in fear and in much

[f] **Eph 3:9** ***to make everyone see*** Other ancient authorities read *to bring to light* [g] **Eph 6:19** ***of the gospel*** Other ancient authorities lack *of the gospel* [h] **Col 2:2** ***of God's mystery, that is, Christ himself*** Other ancient authorities read *of the mystery of God, the Father of Christ* or *of the mystery of God, both of the Father and of Christ* [i] **1 Tim 3:16** ***Who*** Other ancient authorities read *God*; others, *Which*. NRSV translates Gk *Who* as *He* [j] **1 Tim 3:16** ***by the Spirit*** NRSV alternate translation **§ 37** [a] **1 Cor 2:1** ***mystery*** Other ancient authorities read *testimony*

4 καὶ ὁ λόγος μου καὶ τὸ κήρυγμά μου
οὐκ ἐν ⸂πειθοῖ[ς] σοφίας [λόγοις]⸃ ἀλλ᾿
ἐν ἀποδείξει πνεύματος καὶ δυνάμεως,
5 ἵνα ἡ πίστις ὑμῶν μὴ ᾖ ἐν σοφίᾳ ἀνθρώ-
πων ἀλλ᾿ ἐν δυνάμει θεοῦ.

1 Cor 2:6–9

Σοφίαν δὲ λαλοῦμεν ἐν τοῖς τελείοις,
σοφίαν δὲ οὐ τοῦ αἰῶνος τούτου οὐδὲ
τῶν ἀρχόντων τοῦ αἰῶνος τούτου τῶν
καταργουμένων· 7 ἀλλὰ λαλοῦμεν θεοῦ
σοφίαν ἐν μυστηρίῳ τὴν ἀποκεκρυμ-
μένην, ἣν προώρισεν ὁ θεὸς πρὸ τῶν
αἰώνων εἰς δόξαν ἡμῶν, 8 ἣν οὐδεὶς τῶν
ἀρχόντων τοῦ αἰῶνος τούτου ἔγνωκεν·
εἰ γὰρ ἔγνωσαν, οὐκ ἂν τὸν κύριον τῆς
δόξης ἐσταύρωσαν. 9 ἀλλὰ καθὼς γέ-
γραπται· ἃ ὀφθαλμὸς οὐκ εἶδεν καὶ οὖς
οὐκ ἤκουσεν καὶ ἐπὶ καρδίαν ἀνθρώπου
οὐκ ἀνέβη, ἃ ἡτοίμασεν ὁ θεὸς τοῖς ἀγα-
πῶσιν αὐτόν.

1 Cor 2:10–16

ἡμῖν δὲ ἀπεκάλυψεν ὁ θεὸς διὰ τοῦ πνεύ-
ματος· τὸ γὰρ πνεῦμα πάντα ἐραυνᾷ,
καὶ τὰ βάθη τοῦ θεοῦ. 11 τίς γὰρ οἶδεν
ἀνθρώπων τὰ τοῦ ἀνθρώπου εἰ μὴ τὸ
πνεῦμα τοῦ ἀνθρώπου τὸ ἐν αὐτῷ; οὕτως
καὶ τὰ τοῦ θεοῦ οὐδεὶς ἔγνωκεν εἰ μὴ τὸ
πνεῦμα τοῦ θεοῦ. 12 ἡμεῖς δὲ οὐ τὸ πνεῦμα
τοῦ κόσμου ἐλάβομεν ἀλλὰ τὸ πνεῦμα
τὸ ἐκ τοῦ θεοῦ, ἵνα εἰδῶμεν τὰ ὑπὸ τοῦ
θεοῦ χαρισθέντα ἡμῖν· 13 ἃ καὶ λαλοῦμεν
οὐκ ἐν διδακτοῖς ἀνθρωπίνης σοφίας
λόγοις ἀλλ᾿ ἐν διδακτοῖς πνεύματος,
πνευματικοῖς πνευματικὰ συγκρίνον-
τες. 14 ψυχικὸς δὲ ἄνθρωπος οὐ δέχεται
τὰ τοῦ πνεύματος τοῦ θεοῦ· μωρία γὰρ
αὐτῷ ἐστιν καὶ οὐ δύναται γνῶναι, ὅτι
πνευματικῶς ἀνακρίνεται. 15 ὁ δὲ πνευ-
ματικὸς ἀνακρίνει [τὰ] πάντα, αὐτὸς
δὲ ὑπ᾿ οὐδενὸς ἀνακρίνεται. 16 τίς γὰρ
ἔγνω νοῦν κυρίου, ὃς συμβιβάσει αὐτόν;
ἡμεῖς δὲ νοῦν Χριστοῦ ἔχομεν.

1 Cor 3:18–23

Μηδεὶς ἑαυτὸν ἐξαπατάτω· εἴ τις δοκεῖ
σοφὸς εἶναι ἐν ὑμῖν ἐν τῷ αἰῶνι τούτῳ,
μωρὸς γενέσθω, ἵνα γένηται σοφός. 19 ἡ γὰρ
σοφία τοῦ κόσμου τούτου μωρία παρὰ τῷ
θεῷ ἐστιν. γέγραπται γάρ· ὁ δρασσόμενος
τοὺς σοφοὺς ἐν τῇ πανουργίᾳ αὐτῶν·
20 καὶ πάλιν· κύριος γινώσκει τοὺς δια-
λογισμοὺς τῶν σοφῶν ὅτι εἰσὶν μάταιοι.
21 ὥστε μηδεὶς καυχάσθω ἐν ἀνθρώποις·
πάντα γὰρ ὑμῶν ἐστιν, 22 εἴτε Παῦλος
εἴτε Ἀπολλῶς εἴτε Κηφᾶς, εἴτε κόσμος
εἴτε ζωὴ εἴτε θάνατος, εἴτε ἐνεστῶτα
εἴτε μέλλοντα· πάντα ὑμῶν, 23 ὑμεῖς δὲ
Χριστοῦ, Χριστὸς δὲ θεοῦ.

Eph 1:15–21

Διὰ τοῦτο κἀγὼ ἀκούσας τὴν καθ᾿ ὑμᾶς
πίστιν ἐν τῷ κυρίῳ Ἰησοῦ καὶ ⸂τὴν ἀγά-
πην τὴν⸃ εἰς πάντας τοὺς ἁγίους 16 οὐ
παύομαι εὐχαριστῶν ὑπὲρ ὑμῶν μνείαν
ποιούμενος ἐπὶ τῶν προσευχῶν μου,
17 ἵνα ὁ θεὸς τοῦ κυρίου ἡμῶν Ἰησοῦ
Χριστοῦ, ὁ πατὴρ τῆς δόξης, δώῃ ὑμῖν
πνεῦμα σοφίας καὶ ἀποκαλύψεως ἐν
ἐπιγνώσει αὐτοῦ, 18 πεφωτισμένους
τοὺς ὀφθαλμοὺς τῆς καρδίας [ὑμῶν]
εἰς τὸ εἰδέναι ὑμᾶς τίς ἐστιν ἡ ἐλπὶς τῆς
κλήσεως αὐτοῦ, τίς ὁ πλοῦτος τῆς δόξης
τῆς κληρονομίας αὐτοῦ ἐν τοῖς ἁγίοις,
19 καὶ τί τὸ ὑπερβάλλον μέγεθος τῆς
δυνάμεως αὐτοῦ εἰς ἡμᾶς τοὺς πιστεύ-
οντας κατὰ τὴν ἐνέργειαν τοῦ κράτους
τῆς ἰσχύος αὐτοῦ. 20 Ἣν ⸀ἐνήργησεν ἐν
τῷ Χριστῷ ἐγείρας αὐτὸν ἐκ νεκρῶν καὶ
καθίσας ἐν δεξιᾷ αὐτοῦ ἐν τοῖς ἐπου-
ρανίοις 21 ὑπεράνω πάσης ἀρχῆς καὶ
ἐξουσίας καὶ δυνάμεως καὶ κυριότητος
καὶ παντὸς ὀνόματος ὀνομαζομένου, οὐ
μόνον ἐν τῷ αἰῶνι τούτῳ ἀλλὰ καὶ ἐν
τῷ μέλλοντι

Eph 3:7–12

οὗ ἐγενήθην διάκονος κατὰ τὴν δωρεὰν
τῆς χάριτος τοῦ θεοῦ τῆς δοθείσης μοι
κατὰ τὴν ἐνέργειαν τῆς δυνάμεως αὐτοῦ.
8 Ἐμοὶ τῷ ἐλαχιστοτέρῳ πάντων ἁγίων
ἐδόθη ἡ χάρις αὕτη, τοῖς ἔθνεσιν εὐαγ-
γελίσασθαι τὸ ἀνεξιχνίαστον πλοῦτος
τοῦ Χριστοῦ 9 καὶ φωτίσαι ⸀[πάντας] τίς
ἡ οἰκονομία τοῦ μυστηρίου τοῦ ἀποκε-
κρυμμένου ἀπὸ τῶν αἰώνων ἐν τῷ θεῷ
τῷ τὰ πάντα κτίσαντι, 10 ἵνα γνωρισθῇ
νῦν ταῖς ἀρχαῖς καὶ ταῖς ἐξουσίαις ἐν
τοῖς ἐπουρανίοις διὰ τῆς ἐκκλησίας ἡ
πολυποίκιλος σοφία τοῦ θεοῦ, 11 κατὰ
πρόθεσιν τῶν αἰώνων ἣν ἐποίησεν ἐν τῷ
Χριστῷ Ἰησοῦ τῷ κυρίῳ ἡμῶν, 12 ἐν ᾧ
ἔχομεν τὴν παρρησίαν καὶ προσαγωγὴν
ἐν πεποιθήσει διὰ τῆς πίστεως αὐτοῦ.

Col 2:1–3

Θέλω γὰρ ὑμᾶς εἰδέναι ἡλίκον ἀγῶνα
ἔχω ὑπὲρ ὑμῶν καὶ τῶν ἐν Λαοδικείᾳ
καὶ ὅσοι οὐχ ἑόρακαν τὸ πρόσωπόν μου
ἐν σαρκί, 2 ἵνα παρακληθῶσιν αἱ καρδίαι
αὐτῶν συμβιβασθέντες ἐν ἀγάπῃ καὶ
εἰς πᾶν πλοῦτος τῆς πληροφορίας τῆς
συνέσεως, εἰς ἐπίγνωσιν τοῦ μυστηρίου
⸂τοῦ θεοῦ, Χριστοῦ⸃, 3 ἐν ᾧ εἰσιν πάντες
οἱ θησαυροὶ τῆς σοφίας καὶ γνώσεως
ἀπόκρυφοι.

Cf. Rom 1:16–17; 11:33–36; 16:25–27; 1 Cor 4:18–21; 2 Cor 11:21b–12:10; 13:1–4; Phil 4:10–13; Col 1:24–29.

See also § 36 The Mystery of God, Christ; § 139 Human Weakness and God's Power.

38. *Faith and Hearing*

Rom 1:16–17

Οὐ γὰρ ἐπαισχύνομαι τὸ εὐαγγέλιον,
δύναμις γὰρ θεοῦ ἐστιν εἰς σωτηρίαν
παντὶ τῷ πιστεύοντι, Ἰουδαίῳ τε πρῶ-
τον καὶ Ἕλληνι. 17 δικαιοσύνη γὰρ θεοῦ
ἐν αὐτῷ ἀποκαλύπτεται ἐκ πίστεως εἰς
πίστιν, καθὼς γέγραπται· ὁ δὲ δίκαιος
ἐκ πίστεως ζήσεται.

1 Cor 2:4 ***πειθοις σοφιας λογοις*** (ℵ*) B D 33. 1739. 1881] πειθοις ανθρωπινης σοφιας λογοις ℵ^{2} A C *Byz* ¦ πειθοις σοφιας 𝔓^{46} ¦ πειθοι σοφιας *cj* **Eph 1:15** ***την αγαπην την*** ℵ^{2} D^{1} *Byz*] την 𝔓^{46} ℵ* A B 33. 1739. 1881 ¦ την αγαπην D* **Eph 1:20** ***ενηργησεν*** ℵ D 33. 1739. 1881 *Byz*] ενηργηκεν A B **Eph 3:9** ***παντας*** 𝔓^{46} ℵ^{2} B C D 33 *Byz*] *om.* ℵ* A 1739. 1881 **Col 2:2** ***του θεου, Χριστου*** 𝔓^{46} B] του θεου πατρος (+ του A C) Χριστου ℵ* A C 048^{vid} ¦ του θεου και πατρος του Χριστου ℵ^{2} ¦ του θεου και πατρος και του Χριστου D^{2} *Byz* ¦ του θεου ὅ εστιν Χριστος D* ¦ του θεου του εν Χριστω 33 ¦ του θεου D^{1} 1881 ¦ του Χριστου (1739)

trembling. 4 My speech and my proclamation were not with plausible words of wisdom,[b] but with a demonstration of the Spirit and of power, 5 so that your faith might rest not on human wisdom but on the power of God.

1 Cor 2:6–9

Yet among the mature we do speak wisdom, though it is not a wisdom of this age or of the rulers of this age, who are doomed to perish. 7 But we speak God's wisdom, secret and hidden, which God decreed before the ages for our glory. 8 None of the rulers of this age understood this; for if they had, they would not have crucified the Lord of glory. 9 But, as it is written, "What no eye has seen, nor ear heard, nor the human heart conceived, what God has prepared for those who love him"

1 Cor 2:10–16

these things God has revealed to us through the Spirit; for the Spirit searches everything, even the depths of God. 11 For what human being knows what is truly human except the human spirit that is within? So also no one comprehends what is truly God's except the Spirit of God. 12 Now we have received not the spirit of the world, but the Spirit that is from God, so that we may understand the gifts bestowed on us by God. 13 And we speak of these things in words not taught by human wisdom but taught by the Spirit, interpreting spiritual things to those who are spiritual. 14 Those who are unspiritual do not receive the gifts of God's Spirit, for they are foolishness to them, and they are unable to understand them because they are spiritually discerned. 15 Those who are spiritual discern all things, and they are themselves subject to no one else's scrutiny. 16 "For who has known the mind of the Lord so as to instruct him?" But we have the mind of Christ.

1 Cor 3:18–23

Do not deceive yourselves. If you think that you are wise in this age, you should become fools so that you may become wise. 19 For the wisdom of this world is foolishness with God. For it is written, "He catches the wise in their craftiness," 20 and again, "The Lord knows the thoughts of the wise, that they are futile." 21 So let no one boast about human leaders. For all things are yours, 22 whether Paul or Apollos or Cephas or the world or life or death or the present or the future—all belong to you, 23 and you belong to Christ, and Christ belongs to God.

Eph 1:15–21

I have heard of your faith in the Lord Jesus and your love[c] toward all the saints, and for this reason 16 I do not cease to give thanks for you as I remember you in my prayers. 17 I pray that the God of our Lord Jesus Christ, the Father of glory, may give you a spirit of wisdom and revelation as you come to know him, 18 so that, with the eyes of your heart enlightened, you may know what is the hope to which he has called you, what are the riches of his glorious inheritance among the saints, 19 and what is the immeasurable greatness of his power for us who believe, according to the working of his great power. 20 God put this power to work[d] in Christ when he raised him from the dead and seated him at his right hand in the heavenly places, 21 far above all rule and authority and power and dominion, and above every name that is named, not only in this age but also in the age to come.

Eph 3:7–12

Of this gospel I have become a servant according to the gift of God's grace that was given me by the working of his power. 8 Although I am the very least of all the saints, this grace was given to me to bring to the Gentiles the news of the boundless riches of Christ, 9 and to make everyone see[e] what is the plan of the mystery hidden for ages in God who created all things; 10 so that through the church the wisdom of God in its rich variety might now be made known to the rulers and authorities in the heavenly places. 11 This was in accordance with the eternal purpose that he has carried out in Christ Jesus our Lord, 12 in whom we have access to God in boldness and confidence through faith in him.

Col 2:1–3

For I want you to know how much I am struggling for you, and for those in Laodicea, and for all who have not seen me face to face. 2 I want their hearts to be encouraged and united in love, so that they may have all the riches of assured understanding and have the knowledge of God's mystery, that is, Christ himself,[f] 3 in whom are hidden all the treasures of wisdom and knowledge.

Cf. Rom 1:16–17; 11:33–36; 16:25–27; 1 Cor 4:18–21; 2 Cor 11:21b–12:10; 13:1–4; Phil 4:10–13; Col 1:24–29.

See also § 36 The Mystery of God, Christ; § 139 Human Weakness and God's Power.

38. Faith and Hearing

Rom 1:16–17

For I am not ashamed of the gospel; it is the power of God for salvation to everyone who has faith, to the Jew first and also to the Greek. 17 For in it the righteousness of God is revealed through faith for faith; as it is written, "The one who is righteous will live by faith."

[b] **1 Cor 2:4** ***plausible words of wisdom*** Other ancient authorities provide evidence for the reading *the persuasiveness of wisdom*; others read *plausible words of human wisdom* [c] **Eph 1:15** ***and your love*** Other ancient authorities lack *and your love* [d] **Eph 1:20** ***put this power to work*** Other ancient authorities read *has put this power to work* [e] **Eph 3:9** ***to make everyone see*** Other ancient authorities read *to bring to light* [f] **Col 2:2** ***of God's mystery, that is, Christ himself*** Other ancient authorities read *of the mystery of God, the Father of Christ* or *of the mystery of God, both of the Father and of Christ*

Rom 10:5–13

Μωϋσῆς γὰρ γράφει τὴν δικαιοσύνην
τὴν ἐκ [τοῦ] νόμου ὅτι ὁ ποιήσας αὐτὰ
ἄνθρωπος ζήσεται ἐν ⸀αὐτοῖς. 6 ἡ δὲ ἐκ
πίστεως δικαιοσύνη οὕτως λέγει· μὴ
εἴπῃς ἐν τῇ καρδίᾳ σου· τίς ἀναβήσεται
εἰς τὸν οὐρανόν; τοῦτ᾽ ἔστιν Χριστὸν
καταγαγεῖν· 7 ἤ· τίς καταβήσεται εἰς τὴν
ἄβυσσον; τοῦτ᾽ ἔστιν Χριστὸν ἐκ νεκρῶν
ἀναγαγεῖν. 8 ἀλλὰ τί λέγει; ἐγγύς σου
τὸ ῥῆμά ἐστιν ἐν τῷ στόματί σου καὶ
ἐν τῇ καρδίᾳ σου, τοῦτ᾽ ἔστιν τὸ ῥῆμα
τῆς πίστεως ὃ κηρύσσομεν. 9 ὅτι ἐὰν
ὁμολογήσῃς ἐν τῷ στόματί σου κύριον
Ἰησοῦν καὶ πιστεύσῃς ἐν τῇ καρδίᾳ σου
ὅτι ὁ θεὸς αὐτὸν ἤγειρεν ἐκ νεκρῶν,
σωθήσῃ· 10 καρδίᾳ γὰρ πιστεύεται εἰς
δικαιοσύνην, στόματι δὲ ὁμολογεῖται εἰς
σωτηρίαν. 11 λέγει γὰρ ἡ γραφή· πᾶς ὁ
πιστεύων ἐπ᾽ αὐτῷ οὐ καταισχυνθήσεται.
12 οὐ γάρ ἐστιν διαστολὴ Ἰουδαίου τε καὶ
Ἕλληνος, ὁ γὰρ αὐτὸς κύριος πάντων,
πλουτῶν εἰς πάντας τοὺς ἐπικαλουμένους
αὐτόν· 13 πᾶς γὰρ ὃς ἂν ἐπικαλέσηται τὸ
ὄνομα κυρίου σωθήσεται.

Rom 10:14–17

Πῶς οὖν ἐπικαλέσωνται εἰς ὃν οὐκ ἐπί-
στευσαν; πῶς δὲ πιστεύσωσιν οὗ οὐκ
ἤκουσαν; πῶς δὲ ἀκούσωσιν χωρὶς κη-
ρύσσοντος; 15 πῶς δὲ κηρύξωσιν ἐὰν
μὴ ἀποσταλῶσιν; καθὼς γέγραπται· ὡς
ὡραῖοι οἱ πόδες τῶν εὐαγγελιζομένων
[τὰ] ἀγαθά. 16 Ἀλλ᾽ οὐ πάντες ὑπήκου-
σαν τῷ εὐαγγελίῳ. Ἠσαΐας γὰρ λέγει·
κύριε, τίς ἐπίστευσεν τῇ ἀκοῇ ἡμῶν;
17 ἄρα ἡ πίστις ἐξ ἀκοῆς, ἡ δὲ ἀκοὴ διὰ
ῥήματος ⸀Χριστοῦ.

1 Cor 1:18–25

Ὁ λόγος γὰρ ὁ τοῦ σταυροῦ τοῖς μὲν ἀπολ-
λυμένοις μωρία ἐστίν, τοῖς δὲ σῳζομένοις
ἡμῖν δύναμις θεοῦ ἐστιν. 19 γέγραπται γάρ·
ἀπολῶ τὴν σοφίαν τῶν σοφῶν καὶ τὴν
σύνεσιν τῶν συνετῶν ἀθετήσω. 20 ποῦ
σοφός; ποῦ γραμματεύς; ποῦ συζητητὴς
τοῦ αἰῶνος τούτου; οὐχὶ ἐμώρανεν ὁ θεὸς
τὴν σοφίαν τοῦ κόσμου; 21 ἐπειδὴ γὰρ ἐν
τῇ σοφίᾳ τοῦ θεοῦ οὐκ ἔγνω ὁ κόσμος
διὰ τῆς σοφίας τὸν θεόν, εὐδόκησεν ὁ
θεὸς διὰ τῆς μωρίας τοῦ κηρύγματος
σῶσαι τοὺς πιστεύοντας· 22 ἐπειδὴ καὶ
Ἰουδαῖοι σημεῖα αἰτοῦσιν καὶ Ἕλληνες
σοφίαν ζητοῦσιν, 23 ἡμεῖς δὲ κηρύσσο-
μεν Χριστὸν ἐσταυρωμένον, Ἰουδαίοις
μὲν σκάνδαλον, ἔθνεσιν δὲ μωρίαν,
24 αὐτοῖς δὲ τοῖς κλητοῖς, Ἰουδαίοις τε
καὶ Ἕλλησιν, Χριστὸν θεοῦ δύναμιν
καὶ θεοῦ σοφίαν· 25 ὅτι τὸ μωρὸν τοῦ
θεοῦ σοφώτερον τῶν ἀνθρώπων ἐστὶν
καὶ τὸ ἀσθενὲς τοῦ θεοῦ ἰσχυρότερον
τῶν ἀνθρώπων.

1 Cor 2:1–5

Κἀγὼ ἐλθὼν πρὸς ὑμᾶς, ἀδελφοί, ἦλθον
οὐ καθ᾽ ὑπεροχὴν λόγου ἢ σοφίας καταγ-
γέλλων ὑμῖν τὸ ⸀μυστήριον τοῦ θεοῦ.
2 οὐ γὰρ ἔκρινά τι εἰδέναι ἐν ὑμῖν εἰ μὴ
Ἰησοῦν Χριστὸν καὶ τοῦτον ἐσταυρωμέ-
νον. 3 κἀγὼ ἐν ἀσθενείᾳ καὶ ἐν φόβῳ καὶ
ἐν τρόμῳ πολλῷ ἐγενόμην πρὸς ὑμᾶς,
4 καὶ ὁ λόγος μου καὶ τὸ κήρυγμά μου
οὐκ ἐν ⸂πειθοῖ[ς] σοφίας [λόγοις]⸃ ἀλλ᾽
ἐν ἀποδείξει πνεύματος καὶ δυνάμεως,
5 ἵνα ἡ πίστις ὑμῶν μὴ ᾖ ἐν σοφίᾳ ἀνθρώ-
πων ἀλλ᾽ ἐν δυνάμει θεοῦ.

1 Cor 15:1–2

Γνωρίζω δὲ ὑμῖν, ἀδελφοί, τὸ εὐαγγέλιον
ὃ εὐηγγελισάμην ὑμῖν, ὃ καὶ παρελάβετε,
ἐν ᾧ καὶ ἑστήκατε, 2 δι᾽ οὗ καὶ σῴζεσθε,
τίνι λόγῳ εὐηγγελισάμην ὑμῖν εἰ κατέχετε,
ἐκτὸς εἰ μὴ εἰκῇ ἐπιστεύσατε.

Gal 3:1–5

Ὦ ἀνόητοι Γαλάται, τίς ὑμᾶς ἐβάσκανεν,
οἷς κατ᾽ ὀφθαλμοὺς Ἰησοῦς Χριστὸς
προεγράφη ἐσταυρωμένος; 2 τοῦτο μό-
νον θέλω μαθεῖν ἀφ᾽ ὑμῶν· ἐξ ἔργων
νόμου τὸ πνεῦμα ἐλάβετε ἢ ἐξ ἀκοῆς
πίστεως; 3 οὕτως ἀνόητοί ἐστε, ἐναρξά-
μενοι πνεύματι νῦν σαρκὶ ἐπιτελεῖσθε;
4 τοσαῦτα ἐπάθετε εἰκῇ; εἴ γε καὶ εἰκῇ.
5 ὁ οὖν ἐπιχορηγῶν ὑμῖν τὸ πνεῦμα καὶ
ἐνεργῶν δυνάμεις ἐν ὑμῖν, ἐξ ἔργων
νόμου ἢ ἐξ ἀκοῆς πίστεως;

Eph 1:13–14

Ἐν ᾧ καὶ ὑμεῖς ἀκούσαντες τὸν λόγον
τῆς ἀληθείας, τὸ εὐαγγέλιον τῆς σω-
τηρίας ὑμῶν, ἐν ᾧ καὶ πιστεύσαντες
ἐσφραγίσθητε τῷ πνεύματι τῆς ἐπαγγε-
λίας τῷ ἁγίῳ, 14 ⸀ὅ ἐστιν ἀρραβὼν τῆς
κληρονομίας ἡμῶν, εἰς ἀπολύτρωσιν
τῆς περιποιήσεως, εἰς ἔπαινον τῆς δό-
ξης αὐτοῦ.

1 Thess 1:5–6

ὅτι τὸ εὐαγγέλιον ἡμῶν οὐκ ἐγενήθη
εἰς ὑμᾶς ἐν λόγῳ μόνον ἀλλὰ καὶ ἐν
δυνάμει καὶ ἐν πνεύματι ἁγίῳ καὶ [ἐν]
πληροφορίᾳ πολλῇ, καθὼς οἴδατε οἷοι
ἐγενήθημεν [ἐν] ὑμῖν δι᾽ ὑμᾶς. 6 Καὶ ὑμεῖς
μιμηταὶ ἡμῶν ἐγενήθητε καὶ τοῦ κυρίου,
δεξάμενοι τὸν λόγον ἐν θλίψει πολλῇ
μετὰ χαρᾶς πνεύματος ἁγίου

1 Tim 4:16

ἔπεχε σεαυτῷ καὶ τῇ διδασκαλίᾳ, ἐπίμενε
αὐτοῖς· τοῦτο γὰρ ποιῶν καὶ σεαυτὸν
σώσεις καὶ τοὺς ἀκούοντάς σου.

Titus 1:1–4

Παῦλος δοῦλος θεοῦ, ἀπόστολος δὲ
Ἰησοῦ Χριστοῦ κατὰ πίστιν ἐκλεκτῶν
θεοῦ καὶ ἐπίγνωσιν ἀληθείας τῆς κατ᾽
εὐσέβειαν 2 ἐπ᾽ ἐλπίδι ζωῆς αἰωνίου, ἣν
ἐπηγγείλατο ὁ ἀψευδὴς θεὸς πρὸ χρό-
νων αἰωνίων, 3 ἐφανέρωσεν δὲ καιροῖς
ἰδίοις τὸν λόγον αὐτοῦ ἐν κηρύγματι, ὃ
ἐπιστεύθην ἐγὼ κατ᾽ ἐπιταγὴν τοῦ σω-
τῆρος ἡμῶν θεοῦ, 4 Τίτῳ γνησίῳ τέκνῳ
κατὰ κοινὴν πίστιν, χάρις ⸀καὶ εἰρήνη
ἀπὸ θεοῦ πατρὸς καὶ Χριστοῦ Ἰησοῦ τοῦ
σωτῆρος ἡμῶν.

Acts 16:14

καί τις γυνὴ ὀνόματι Λυδία, πορφυ-
ρόπωλις πόλεως Θυατείρων σεβομένη
τὸν θεόν, ἤκουεν, ἧς ὁ κύριος διήνοιξεν
τὴν καρδίαν προσέχειν τοῖς λαλουμένοις
ὑπὸ τοῦ Παύλου.

§ 38 **Rom 10:5** ***αυτοις*** 𝔓^{46} ℵ^{2} D *Byz*] αυτη ℵ* A B 33. 1739. 1881 **Rom 10:17** ***Χριστου*** 𝔓^{46vid} ℵ* B C D* 1739] θεου ℵ^{1} A D^{1} 33. 1881 *Byz* **1 Cor 2:1** ***μυστηριον*** 𝔓^{46vid} ℵ* A C] μαρτυριον ℵ^{2} B D 33. 1739. 1881 *Byz* **1 Cor 2:4** ***πειθοις σοφιας λογοις*** (ℵ*) B D 33. 1739. 1881] πειθοις ανθρωπινης σοφιας λογοις ℵ^{2} A C *Byz* ¦ πειθοις σοφιας 𝔓^{46} ¦ πειθοι σοφιας *cj* **Eph 1:14** ***ὅ*** 𝔓^{46} A B 1739. 1881] ος ℵ D 33 *Byz* **Titus 1:4** ***και*** ℵ C* D 088] ελεος A C^{2} *Byz* ¦ *om*. 1739. 1881 ¦ υμιν και 33

Rom 10:5–13

Moses writes concerning the righteousness that comes from the law, that "the person who does these things will live by them."[a] 6 But the righteousness that comes from faith says, "Do not say in your heart, 'Who will ascend into heaven?'" (that is, to bring Christ down) 7 "or 'Who will descend into the abyss?'" (that is, to bring Christ up from the dead). 8 But what does it say? "The word is near you, on your lips and in your heart" (that is, the word of faith that we proclaim); 9 because if you confess with your lips that Jesus is Lord and believe in your heart that God raised him from the dead, you will be saved. 10 For one believes with the heart and so is justified, and one confesses with the mouth and so is saved. 11 The scripture says, "No one who believes in him will be put to shame." 12 For there is no distinction between Jew and Greek; the same Lord is Lord of all and is generous to all who call on him. 13 For, "Everyone who calls on the name of the Lord shall be saved."

Rom 10:14–17

But how are they to call on one in whom they have not believed? And how are they to believe in one of whom they have never heard? And how are they to hear without someone to proclaim him? 15 And how are they to proclaim him unless they are sent? As it is written, "How beautiful are the feet of those who bring good news!" 16 But not all have obeyed the good news; for Isaiah says, "Lord, who has believed our message?" 17 So faith comes from what is heard, and what is heard comes through the word of Christ.[b]

1 Cor 1:18–25

For the message about the cross is foolishness to those who are perishing, but to us who are being saved it is the power of God. 19 For it is written, "I will destroy the wisdom of the wise, and the discernment of the discerning I will thwart." 20 Where is the one who is wise? Where is the scribe? Where is the debater of this age? Has not God made foolish the wisdom of the world? 21 For since, in the wisdom of God, the world did not know God through wisdom, God decided, through the foolishness of our proclamation, to save those who believe. 22 For Jews demand signs and Greeks desire wisdom, 23 but we proclaim Christ crucified, a stumbling block to Jews and foolishness to Gentiles, 24 but to those who are the called, both Jews and Greeks, Christ the power of God and the wisdom of God. 25 For God's foolishness is wiser than human wisdom, and God's weakness is stronger than human strength.

1 Cor 2:1–5

When I came to you, brothers and sisters, I did not come proclaiming the mystery[c] of God to you in lofty words or wisdom. 2 For I decided to know nothing among you except Jesus Christ, and him crucified. 3 And I came to you in weakness and in fear and in much trembling. 4 My speech and my proclamation were not with plausible words of wisdom,[d] but with a demonstration of the Spirit and of power, 5 so that your faith might rest not on human wisdom but on the power of God.

1 Cor 15:1–2

Now I would remind you, brothers and sisters, of the good news that I proclaimed to you, which you in turn received, in which also you stand, 2 through which also you are being saved, if you hold firmly to the message that I proclaimed to you—unless you have come to believe in vain.

Gal 3:1–5

You foolish Galatians! Who has bewitched you? It was before your eyes that Jesus Christ was publicly exhibited as crucified! 2 The only thing I want to learn from you is this: Did you receive the Spirit by doing the works of the law or by believing what you heard? 3 Are you so foolish? Having started with the Spirit, are you now ending with the flesh? 4 Did you experience so much for nothing?—if it really was for nothing. 5 Well then, does God supply you with the Spirit and work miracles among you by your doing the works of the law, or by your believing what you heard?

Eph 1:13–14

In him you also, when you had heard the word of truth, the gospel of your salvation, and had believed in him, were marked with the seal of the promised Holy Spirit; 14 this[e] is the pledge of our inheritance toward redemption as God's own people, to the praise of his glory.

1 Thess 1:5–6

because our message of the gospel came to you not in word only, but also in power and in the Holy Spirit and with full conviction; just as you know what kind of persons we proved to be among you for your sake. 6 And you became imitators of us and of the Lord, for in spite of persecution you received the word with joy inspired by the Holy Spirit

1 Tim 4:16

Pay close attention to yourself and to your teaching; continue in these things, for in doing this you will save both yourself and your hearers.

Titus 1:1–4

Paul, a servant of God and an apostle of Jesus Christ, for the sake of the faith of God's elect and the knowledge of the truth that is in accordance with godliness, 2 in the hope of eternal life that God, who never lies, promised before the ages began— 3 in due time he revealed his word through the proclamation with which I have been entrusted by the command of God our Savior, 4 To Titus, my loyal child in the faith we share: Grace and[f] peace from God the Father and Christ Jesus our Savior.

Acts 16:14

A certain woman named Lydia, a worshiper of God, was listening to us; she was from the city of Thyatira and a dealer in purple cloth. The Lord opened her heart to listen eagerly to what was said by Paul.

§ 38 [a] **Rom 10:5** ***them*** Other ancient authorities read *it*, i.e., the righteousness that comes from the law [b] **Rom 10:17** ***of Christ*** Other ancient authorities read *of God* [c] **1 Cor 2:1** ***mystery*** Other ancient authorities read *testimony* [d] **1 Cor 2:4** ***plausible words of wisdom*** Other ancient authorities provide evidence for the reading *the persuasiveness of wisdom*; others read *plausible words of human wisdom* [e] **Eph 1:14** ***this*** Other ancient authorities read *who* [f] **Titus 1:4** ***Grace and*** Other ancient authorities read *Grace, mercy*

Acts 16:30–34

καὶ προαγαγὼν αὐτοὺς ἔξω ἔφη· κύ-
ριοι, τί με δεῖ ποιεῖν ἵνα σωθῶ; **31** οἱ δὲ
εἶπαν· πίστευσον ἐπὶ τὸν κύριον Ἰησοῦν
καὶ σωθήσῃ σὺ καὶ ὁ οἶκός σου. **32** καὶ
ἐλάλησαν αὐτῷ τὸν λόγον τοῦ ⸀κυρίου
σὺν πᾶσιν τοῖς ἐν τῇ οἰκίᾳ αὐτοῦ. **33** καὶ
παραλαβὼν αὐτοὺς ἐν ἐκείνῃ τῇ ὥρᾳ
τῆς νυκτὸς ἔλουσεν ἀπὸ τῶν πληγῶν,
καὶ ἐβαπτίσθη αὐτὸς καὶ οἱ αὐτοῦ πάν-
τες παραχρῆμα, **34** ἀναγαγών τε αὐτοὺς
εἰς τὸν οἶκον παρέθηκεν τράπεζαν καὶ
ἠγαλλιάσατο πανοικεὶ πεπιστευκὼς
τῷ θεῷ.

Cf. Rom 1:5; 3:21–31; 4:23–25; 15:18–19; 16:25–27; Gal 2:15–21; Eph 2:8–10; 1 Thess 2:13; Acts 13:38–39; 14:27; 20:20–21; 26:16–18.

39. Baptism into Christ

Rom 6:1–11

Τί οὖν ἐροῦμεν; ἐπιμένωμεν τῇ ἁμαρ-
τίᾳ, ἵνα ἡ χάρις πλεονάσῃ; **2** μὴ γένοιτο.
οἵτινες ἀπεθάνομεν τῇ ἁμαρτίᾳ, πῶς ἔτι
ζήσομεν ἐν αὐτῇ; **3** ἢ ἀγνοεῖτε ὅτι, ὅσοι
ἐβαπτίσθημεν εἰς Χριστὸν Ἰησοῦν, εἰς
τὸν θάνατον αὐτοῦ ἐβαπτίσθημεν; **4** συν-
ετάφημεν οὖν αὐτῷ διὰ τοῦ βαπτίσμα-
τος εἰς τὸν θάνατον, ἵνα ὥσπερ ἠγέρθη
Χριστὸς ἐκ νεκρῶν διὰ τῆς δόξης τοῦ
πατρός, οὕτως καὶ ἡμεῖς ἐν καινότητι
ζωῆς περιπατήσωμεν. **5** εἰ γὰρ σύμφυτοι
γεγόναμεν τῷ ὁμοιώματι τοῦ θανάτου
αὐτοῦ, ἀλλὰ καὶ τῆς ἀναστάσεως ἐσό-
μεθα· **6** τοῦτο γινώσκοντες ὅτι ὁ παλαιὸς
ἡμῶν ἄνθρωπος συνεσταυρώθη, ἵνα
καταργηθῇ τὸ σῶμα τῆς ἁμαρτίας, τοῦ
μηκέτι δουλεύειν ἡμᾶς τῇ ἁμαρτίᾳ· **7** ὁ
γὰρ ἀποθανὼν δεδικαίωται ἀπὸ τῆς
ἁμαρτίας. **8** εἰ δὲ ἀπεθάνομεν σὺν Χριστῷ,
πιστεύομεν ὅτι καὶ συζήσομεν αὐτῷ,
9 εἰδότες ὅτι Χριστὸς ἐγερθεὶς ἐκ νεκρῶν
οὐκέτι ἀποθνῄσκει, θάνατος αὐτοῦ οὐκέτι
κυριεύει. **10** ὃ γὰρ ἀπέθανεν, τῇ ἁμαρτίᾳ
ἀπέθανεν ἐφάπαξ· ὃ δὲ ζῇ, ζῇ τῷ θεῷ.
11 οὕτως καὶ ὑμεῖς λογίζεσθε ἑαυτοὺς
[εἶναι] νεκροὺς μὲν τῇ ἁμαρτίᾳ ζῶντας
δὲ τῷ θεῷ ἐν Χριστῷ Ἰησοῦ.

1 Cor 6:9–11

Ἢ οὐκ οἴδατε ὅτι ἄδικοι θεοῦ βασιλείαν
οὐ κληρονομήσουσιν; μὴ πλανᾶσθε· οὔτε
πόρνοι οὔτε εἰδωλολάτραι οὔτε μοιχοὶ
οὔτε μαλακοὶ οὔτε ἀρσενοκοῖται **10** οὔτε
κλέπται οὔτε πλεονέκται, οὐ μέθυσοι, οὐ
λοίδοροι, οὐχ ἅρπαγες βασιλείαν θεοῦ
κληρονομήσουσιν. **11** καὶ ταῦτά τινες
ἦτε· ἀλλὰ ἀπελούσασθε, ἀλλὰ ἡγιά-
σθητε, ἀλλὰ ἐδικαιώθητε ἐν τῷ ὀνόματι
τοῦ κυρίου ⸂Ἰησοῦ Χριστοῦ⸃ καὶ ἐν τῷ
πνεύματι τοῦ θεοῦ ἡμῶν.

1 Cor 10:1–4

Οὐ θέλω γὰρ ὑμᾶς ἀγνοεῖν, ἀδελφοί,
ὅτι οἱ πατέρες ἡμῶν πάντες ὑπὸ τὴν νε-
φέλην ἦσαν καὶ πάντες διὰ τῆς θαλάσσης
διῆλθον **2** καὶ πάντες εἰς τὸν Μωϋσῆν
ἐβαπτίσθησαν ἐν τῇ νεφέλῃ καὶ ἐν τῇ
θαλάσσῃ **3** καὶ πάντες τὸ αὐτὸ πνευματι-
κὸν βρῶμα ἔφαγον **4** καὶ πάντες τὸ αὐτὸ
πνευματικὸν ἔπιον πόμα· ἔπινον γὰρ ἐκ
πνευματικῆς ἀκολουθούσης πέτρας, ἡ
πέτρα δὲ ἦν ὁ Χριστός.

1 Cor 12:12–13

Καθάπερ γὰρ τὸ σῶμα ἕν ἐστιν καὶ μέλη
πολλὰ ἔχει, πάντα δὲ τὰ μέλη τοῦ σώ-
ματος πολλὰ ὄντα ἕν ἐστιν σῶμα, οὕτως
καὶ ὁ Χριστός· **13** καὶ γὰρ ἐν ἑνὶ πνεύματι
ἡμεῖς πάντες εἰς ἓν σῶμα ἐβαπτίσθημεν,
εἴτε Ἰουδαῖοι εἴτε Ἕλληνες εἴτε δοῦλοι
εἴτε ἐλεύθεροι, καὶ πάντες ἓν πνεῦμα
ἐποτίσθημεν.

Gal 3:26–29

Πάντες γὰρ υἱοὶ θεοῦ ἐστε διὰ τῆς πί-
στεως ἐν Χριστῷ Ἰησοῦ· **27** ὅσοι γὰρ εἰς
Χριστὸν ἐβαπτίσθητε, Χριστὸν ἐνεδύσα-
σθε. **28** οὐκ ἔνι Ἰουδαῖος οὐδὲ Ἕλλην,
οὐκ ἔνι δοῦλος οὐδὲ ἐλεύθερος, οὐκ
ἔνι ἄρσεν καὶ θῆλυ· πάντες γὰρ ὑμεῖς
εἷς ἐστε ἐν Χριστῷ Ἰησοῦ. **29** εἰ δὲ ὑμεῖς
Χριστοῦ, ἄρα τοῦ Ἀβραὰμ σπέρμα ἐστέ,
κατ᾽ ἐπαγγελίαν κληρονόμοι.

Eph 4:4–6

Ἓν σῶμα καὶ ἓν πνεῦμα, καθὼς καὶ ἐκλή-
θητε ἐν μιᾷ ἐλπίδι τῆς κλήσεως ὑμῶν·
5 εἷς κύριος, μία πίστις, ἓν βάπτισμα, **6** εἷς
θεὸς καὶ πατὴρ πάντων, ὁ ἐπὶ πάντων
καὶ διὰ πάντων καὶ ἐν πᾶσιν.

Eph 5:25–27

Οἱ ἄνδρες, ἀγαπᾶτε τὰς γυναῖκας, καθὼς
καὶ ὁ Χριστὸς ἠγάπησεν τὴν ἐκκλησίαν
καὶ ἑαυτὸν παρέδωκεν ὑπὲρ αὐτῆς, **26** ἵνα
αὐτὴν ἁγιάσῃ καθαρίσας τῷ λουτρῷ τοῦ
ὕδατος ἐν ῥήματι, **27** ἵνα παραστήσῃ αὐτὸς
ἑαυτῷ ἔνδοξον τὴν ἐκκλησίαν, μὴ ἔχου-
σαν σπίλον ἢ ῥυτίδα ἤ τι τῶν τοιούτων,
ἀλλ᾽ ἵνα ᾖ ἁγία καὶ ἄμωμος.

Col 2:11–12

Ἐν ᾧ καὶ περιετμήθητε περιτομῇ ἀχει-
ροποιήτῳ ἐν τῇ ἀπεκδύσει τοῦ σώματος
τῆς σαρκός, ἐν τῇ περιτομῇ τοῦ Χριστοῦ,
12 συνταφέντες αὐτῷ ἐν τῷ βαπτισμῷ,
ἐν ᾧ καὶ συνηγέρθητε διὰ τῆς πίστεως
τῆς ἐνεργείας τοῦ θεοῦ τοῦ ἐγείραντος
αὐτὸν ἐκ νεκρῶν

Titus 3:4–7

ὅτε δὲ ἡ χρηστότης καὶ ἡ φιλανθρω-
πία ἐπεφάνη τοῦ σωτῆρος ἡμῶν θεοῦ,
5 οὐκ ἐξ ἔργων τῶν ἐν δικαιοσύνῃ ἃ
ἐποιήσαμεν ἡμεῖς ἀλλὰ κατὰ τὸ αὐτοῦ
ἔλεος ἔσωσεν ἡμᾶς διὰ λουτροῦ παλιγ-
γενεσίας καὶ ἀνακαινώσεως πνεύματος
ἁγίου, **6** οὗ ἐξέχεεν ἐφ᾽ ἡμᾶς πλουσίως
διὰ Ἰησοῦ Χριστοῦ τοῦ σωτῆρος ἡμῶν,
7 ἵνα δικαιωθέντες τῇ ἐκείνου χάριτι
κληρονόμοι γενηθῶμεν κατ᾽ ἐλπίδα
ζωῆς αἰωνίου.

Acts 16:14–15

καί τις γυνὴ ὀνόματι Λυδία, πορφυ-
ρόπωλις πόλεως Θυατείρων σεβομένη
τὸν θεόν, ἤκουεν, ἧς ὁ κύριος διήνοιξεν
τὴν καρδίαν προσέχειν τοῖς λαλουμένοις
ὑπὸ τοῦ Παύλου. **15** ὡς δὲ ἐβαπτίσθη καὶ
ὁ οἶκος αὐτῆς, παρεκάλεσεν λέγουσα·
εἰ κεκρίκατέ με πιστὴν τῷ κυρίῳ εἶναι,
εἰσελθόντες εἰς τὸν οἶκόν μου μένετε·
καὶ παρεβιάσατο ἡμᾶς.

Acts 16:30–33

καὶ προαγαγὼν αὐτοὺς ἔξω ἔφη· κύ-
ριοι, τί με δεῖ ποιεῖν ἵνα σωθῶ; **31** οἱ δὲ
εἶπαν· πίστευσον ἐπὶ τὸν κύριον Ἰησοῦν

Acts 16:32 ***κυριου*** 𝔓[45] 𝔓[74] ℵ[2] A C (D) E 33. 1739 *Byz*] θεου ℵ* B

§ 39 **1 Cor 6:11** ***Ιησου Χριστου*** 𝔓[11vid] 𝔓[46] ℵ D*] Ιησου A D[2] *Byz* ¦ ημων Ιησου Χριστου B C[vid] 33. 1739. 1881

Acts 16:30–34

Then he brought them outside and said, "Sirs, what must I do to be saved?" 31 They answered, "Believe on the Lord Jesus, and you will be saved, you and your household." 32 They spoke the word of the Lord[g] to him and to all who were in his house. 33 At the same hour of the night he took them and washed their wounds; then he and his entire family were baptized without delay. 34 He brought them up into the house and set food before them; and he and his entire household rejoiced that he had become a believer in God.

Cf. Rom 1:5; 3:21–31; 4:23–25; 15:18–19; 16:25–27; Gal 2:15–21; Eph 2:8–10; 1 Thess 2:13; Acts 13:38–39; 14:27; 20:20–21; 26:16–18.

39. Baptism into Christ

Rom 6:1–11

What then are we to say? Should we continue in sin in order that grace may abound? 2 By no means! How can we who died to sin go on living in it? 3 Do you not know that all of us who have been baptized into Christ Jesus were baptized into his death? 4 Therefore we have been buried with him by baptism into death, so that, just as Christ was raised from the dead by the glory of the Father, so we too might walk in newness of life. 5 For if we have been united with him in a death like his, we will certainly be united with him in a resurrection like his. 6 We know that our old humanity[a] was crucified with him so that the body of sin might be destroyed, and we might no longer be enslaved to sin. 7 For whoever has died is freed from sin. 8 But if we have died with Christ, we believe that we will also live with him. 9 We know that Christ, being raised from the dead, will never die again; death no longer has dominion over him. 10 The death he died, he died to sin, once for all; but the life he lives, he lives to God. 11 So you also must consider yourselves dead to sin and alive to God in Christ Jesus.

1 Cor 6:9–11

Do you not know that wrongdoers will not inherit the kingdom of God? Do not be deceived! Fornicators, idolaters, adulterers, male prostitutes, sodomites, 10 thieves, the greedy, drunkards, revilers, robbers—none of these will inherit the kingdom of God. 11 And this is what some of you used to be. But you were washed, you were sanctified, you were justified in the name of the Lord Jesus Christ[b] and in the Spirit of our God.

1 Cor 10:1–4

I do not want you to be unaware, brothers and sisters, that our ancestors were all under the cloud, and all passed through the sea, 2 and all were baptized into Moses in the cloud and in the sea, 3 and all ate the same spiritual food, 4 and all drank the same spiritual drink. For they drank from the spiritual rock that followed them, and the rock was Christ.

1 Cor 12:12–13

For just as the body is one and has many members, and all the members of the body, though many, are one body, so it is with Christ. 13 For in the one Spirit we were all baptized into one body—Jews or Greeks, slaves or free—and we were all made to drink of one Spirit.

Gal 3:26–29

for in Christ Jesus you are all children of God through faith. 27 As many of you as were baptized into Christ have clothed yourselves with Christ. 28 There is no longer Jew or Greek, there is no longer slave or free, there is no longer male and female; for all of you are one in Christ Jesus. 29 And if you belong to Christ, then you are Abraham's offspring, heirs according to the promise.

Eph 4:4–6

There is one body and one Spirit, just as you were called to the one hope of your calling, 5 one Lord, one faith, one baptism, 6 one God and Father of all, who is above all and through all and in all.

Eph 5:25–27

Husbands, love your wives, just as Christ loved the church and gave himself up for her, 26 in order to make her holy by cleansing her with the washing of water by the word, 27 so as to present the church to himself in splendor, without a spot or wrinkle or anything of the kind—yes, so that she may be holy and without blemish.

Col 2:11–12

In him also you were circumcised with a spiritual circumcision, by putting off the body of the flesh in the circumcision of Christ; 12 when you were buried with him in baptism, you were also raised with him through faith in the power of God, who raised him from the dead.

Titus 3:4–7

But when the goodness and loving kindness of God our Savior appeared, 5 he saved us, not because of any works of righteousness that we had done, but according to his mercy, through the water of rebirth and renewal by the Holy Spirit. 6 This Spirit he poured out on us richly through Jesus Christ our Savior, 7 so that, having been justified by his grace, we might become heirs according to the hope of eternal life.

Acts 16:14–15

A certain woman named Lydia, a worshiper of God, was listening to us; she was from the city of Thyatira and a dealer in purple cloth. The Lord opened her heart to listen eagerly to what was said by Paul. 15 When she and her household were baptized, she urged us, saying, "If you have judged me to be faithful to the Lord, come and stay at my home." And she prevailed upon us.

Acts 16:30–33

Then he brought them outside and said, "Sirs, what must I do to be saved?" 31 They answered, "Believe on the Lord Jesus, and you will be saved, you and

[g] **Acts 16:32** *word of the Lord* Other ancient authorities read *word of God* **§ 39** [a] **Rom 6:6** ***humanity*** NRSV translates *self* [b] **1 Cor 6:11** *the Lord Jesus Christ* Other ancient authorities read *the Lord Jesus* or *our Lord Jesus Christ*

καὶ σωθήσῃ σὺ καὶ ὁ οἶκός σου. 32 καὶ ἐλάλησαν αὐτῷ τὸν λόγον τοῦ ⸀κυρίου σὺν πᾶσιν τοῖς ἐν τῇ οἰκίᾳ αὐτοῦ. 33 καὶ παραλαβὼν αὐτοὺς ἐν ἐκείνῃ τῇ ὥρᾳ τῆς νυκτὸς ἔλουσεν ἀπὸ τῶν πληγῶν, καὶ ἐβαπτίσθη αὐτὸς καὶ οἱ αὐτοῦ πάντες παραχρῆμα

Acts 18:8

Κρίσπος δὲ ὁ ἀρχισυνάγωγος ἐπίστευσεν τῷ κυρίῳ σὺν ὅλῳ τῷ οἴκῳ αὐτοῦ, καὶ πολλοὶ τῶν Κορινθίων ἀκούοντες ἐπίστευον καὶ ἐβαπτίζοντο.

Acts 19:1–6

Ἐγένετο δὲ ἐν τῷ τὸν Ἀπολλῶ εἶναι ἐν Κορίνθῳ Παῦλον διελθόντα τὰ ἀνωτερικὰ μέρη [κατ]ελθεῖν εἰς Ἔφεσον καὶ εὑρεῖν τινας μαθητὰς 2 εἶπέν τε πρὸς αὐτούς· εἰ πνεῦμα ἅγιον ἐλάβετε πιστεύσαντες; οἱ δὲ πρὸς αὐτόν· ἀλλ᾽ οὐδ᾽ εἰ πνεῦμα ἅγιον ἔστιν ἠκούσαμεν. 3 εἶπέν τε· εἰς τί οὖν ἐβαπτίσθητε; οἱ δὲ εἶπαν· εἰς τὸ Ἰωάννου βάπτισμα. 4 εἶπεν δὲ Παῦλος· Ἰωάννης ἐβάπτισεν βάπτισμα μετανοίας τῷ λαῷ λέγων εἰς τὸν ἐρχόμενον μετ᾽ αὐτὸν ἵνα πιστεύσωσιν, τοῦτ᾽ ἔστιν εἰς τὸν Ἰησοῦν. 5 ἀκούσαντες δὲ ἐβαπτίσθησαν εἰς τὸ ὄνομα τοῦ κυρίου Ἰησοῦ, 6 καὶ ἐπιθέντος αὐτοῖς τοῦ Παύλου [τὰς] χεῖρας ἦλθε τὸ πνεῦμα τὸ ἅγιον ἐπ᾽ αὐτούς, ἐλάλουν τε γλώσσαις καὶ ἐπροφήτευον.

Acts 22:16

καὶ νῦν τί μέλλεις; ἀναστὰς βάπτισαι καὶ ἀπόλουσαι τὰς ἁμαρτίας σου ἐπικαλεσάμενος τὸ ὄνομα αὐτοῦ.

Cf. 1 Cor 1:13–17; Eph 4:20–24; Col 3:9–11.

40. Participation in Christ Crucified and Risen

Rom 6:1–11

Τί οὖν ἐροῦμεν; ἐπιμένωμεν τῇ ἁμαρτίᾳ, ἵνα ἡ χάρις πλεονάσῃ; 2 μὴ γένοιτο. οἵτινες ἀπεθάνομεν τῇ ἁμαρτίᾳ, πῶς ἔτι ζήσομεν ἐν αὐτῇ; 3 ἢ ἀγνοεῖτε ὅτι, ὅσοι ἐβαπτίσθημεν εἰς Χριστὸν Ἰησοῦν, εἰς τὸν θάνατον αὐτοῦ ἐβαπτίσθημεν; 4 συνετάφημεν οὖν αὐτῷ διὰ τοῦ βαπτίσματος εἰς τὸν θάνατον, ἵνα ὥσπερ ἠγέρθη Χριστὸς ἐκ νεκρῶν διὰ τῆς δόξης τοῦ πατρός, οὕτως καὶ ἡμεῖς ἐν καινότητι ζωῆς περιπατήσωμεν. 5 εἰ γὰρ σύμφυτοι γεγόναμεν τῷ ὁμοιώματι τοῦ θανάτου αὐτοῦ, ἀλλὰ καὶ τῆς ἀναστάσεως ἐσόμεθα· 6 τοῦτο γινώσκοντες ὅτι ὁ παλαιὸς ἡμῶν ἄνθρωπος συνεσταυρώθη, ἵνα καταργηθῇ τὸ σῶμα τῆς ἁμαρτίας, τοῦ μηκέτι δουλεύειν ἡμᾶς τῇ ἁμαρτίᾳ· 7 ὁ γὰρ ἀποθανὼν δεδικαίωται ἀπὸ τῆς ἁμαρτίας. 8 εἰ δὲ ἀπεθάνομεν σὺν Χριστῷ, πιστεύομεν ὅτι καὶ συζήσομεν αὐτῷ, 9 εἰδότες ὅτι Χριστὸς ἐγερθεὶς ἐκ νεκρῶν οὐκέτι ἀποθνῄσκει, θάνατος αὐτοῦ οὐκέτι κυριεύει. 10 ὃ γὰρ ἀπέθανεν, τῇ ἁμαρτίᾳ ἀπέθανεν ἐφάπαξ· ὃ δὲ ζῇ, ζῇ τῷ θεῷ. 11 οὕτως καὶ ὑμεῖς λογίζεσθε ἑαυτοὺς [εἶναι] νεκροὺς μὲν τῇ ἁμαρτίᾳ ζῶντας δὲ τῷ θεῷ ἐν Χριστῷ Ἰησοῦ.

Rom 7:4–6

ὥστε, ἀδελφοί μου, καὶ ὑμεῖς ἐθανατώθητε τῷ νόμῳ διὰ τοῦ σώματος τοῦ Χριστοῦ, εἰς τὸ γενέσθαι ὑμᾶς ἑτέρῳ, τῷ ἐκ νεκρῶν ἐγερθέντι, ἵνα καρποφορήσωμεν τῷ θεῷ. 5 ὅτε γὰρ ἦμεν ἐν τῇ σαρκί, τὰ παθήματα τῶν ἁμαρτιῶν τὰ διὰ τοῦ νόμου ἐνηργεῖτο ἐν τοῖς μέλεσιν ἡμῶν, εἰς τὸ καρποφορῆσαι τῷ θανάτῳ· 6 νυνὶ δὲ κατηργήθημεν ἀπὸ τοῦ νόμου ἀποθανόντες ἐν ᾧ κατειχόμεθα, ὥστε δουλεύειν ἡμᾶς ἐν καινότητι πνεύματος καὶ οὐ παλαιότητι γράμματος.

2 Cor 5:14–21

ἡ γὰρ ἀγάπη τοῦ Χριστοῦ συνέχει ἡμᾶς, κρίναντας τοῦτο, ὅτι εἷς ὑπὲρ πάντων ἀπέθανεν, ἄρα οἱ πάντες ἀπέθανον· 15 καὶ ὑπὲρ πάντων ἀπέθανεν, ἵνα οἱ ζῶντες μηκέτι ἑαυτοῖς ζῶσιν ἀλλὰ τῷ ὑπὲρ αὐτῶν ἀποθανόντι καὶ ἐγερθέντι. 16 Ὥστε ἡμεῖς ἀπὸ τοῦ νῦν οὐδένα οἴδαμεν κατὰ σάρκα· εἰ καὶ ἐγνώκαμεν κατὰ σάρκα Χριστόν, ἀλλὰ νῦν οὐκέτι γινώσκομεν. 17 ὥστε εἴ τις ἐν Χριστῷ, καινὴ κτίσις· τὰ ἀρχαῖα παρῆλθεν, ἰδοὺ γέγονεν καινά. 18 τὰ δὲ πάντα ἐκ τοῦ θεοῦ τοῦ καταλλάξαντος ἡμᾶς ἑαυτῷ διὰ Χριστοῦ καὶ δόντος ἡμῖν τὴν διακονίαν τῆς καταλλαγῆς, 19 ὡς ὅτι θεὸς ἦν ἐν Χριστῷ κόσμον καταλλάσσων ἑαυτῷ, μὴ λογιζόμενος αὐτοῖς τὰ παραπτώματα αὐτῶν καὶ θέμενος ἐν ἡμῖν τὸν λόγον τῆς καταλλαγῆς. 20 Ὑπὲρ Χριστοῦ οὖν πρεσβεύομεν ὡς τοῦ θεοῦ παρακαλοῦντος δι᾽ ἡμῶν· δεόμεθα ὑπὲρ Χριστοῦ, καταλλάγητε τῷ θεῷ. 21 τὸν μὴ γνόντα ἁμαρτίαν ὑπὲρ ἡμῶν ἁμαρτίαν ἐποίησεν, ἵνα ἡμεῖς γενώμεθα δικαιοσύνη θεοῦ ἐν αὐτῷ.

Gal 2:19–20

ἐγὼ γὰρ διὰ νόμου νόμῳ ἀπέθανον, ἵνα θεῷ ζήσω. Χριστῷ συνεσταύρωμαι· 20 ζῶ δὲ οὐκέτι ἐγώ, ζῇ δὲ ἐν ἐμοὶ Χριστός· ὃ δὲ νῦν ζῶ ἐν σαρκί, ἐν πίστει ζῶ τῇ τοῦ υἱοῦ τοῦ θεοῦ τοῦ ἀγαπήσαντός με καὶ παραδόντος ἑαυτὸν ὑπὲρ ἐμοῦ.

Gal 5:24–25

οἱ δὲ τοῦ Χριστοῦ [Ἰησοῦ] τὴν σάρκα ἐσταύρωσαν σὺν τοῖς παθήμασιν καὶ ταῖς ἐπιθυμίαις. 25 Εἰ ζῶμεν πνεύματι, πνεύματι καὶ στοιχῶμεν.

Gal 6:14–16

Ἐμοὶ δὲ μὴ γένοιτο καυχᾶσθαι εἰ μὴ ἐν τῷ σταυρῷ τοῦ κυρίου ἡμῶν Ἰησοῦ Χριστοῦ, δι᾽ οὗ ἐμοὶ κόσμος ἐσταύρωται κἀγὼ κόσμῳ. 15 ⸂οὔτε γὰρ⸃ περιτομή τί ἐστιν οὔτε ἀκροβυστία ἀλλὰ καινὴ κτίσις. 16 καὶ ὅσοι τῷ κανόνι τούτῳ ⸀στοιχήσουσιν, εἰρήνη ἐπ᾽ αὐτοὺς καὶ ἔλεος καὶ ἐπὶ τὸν Ἰσραὴλ τοῦ θεοῦ.

Eph 2:1–7

Καὶ ὑμᾶς ὄντας νεκροὺς τοῖς παραπτώμασιν καὶ ταῖς ἁμαρτίαις ὑμῶν, 2 ἐν αἷς ποτε περιεπατήσατε κατὰ τὸν αἰῶνα τοῦ κόσμου τούτου, κατὰ τὸν ἄρχοντα τῆς ἐξουσίας τοῦ ἀέρος, τοῦ πνεύματος τοῦ νῦν ἐνεργοῦντος ἐν τοῖς υἱοῖς τῆς ἀπειθείας· 3 ἐν οἷς καὶ ἡμεῖς πάντες ἀνεστράφημέν ποτε ἐν ταῖς ἐπιθυμίαις τῆς σαρκὸς ἡμῶν ποιοῦντες τὰ θελήματα τῆς σαρκὸς καὶ τῶν διανοιῶν, καὶ ἤμεθα τέκνα

Acts 16:32 ***κυριου*** 𝔓^{45} 𝔓^{74} א^{2} A C (D) E 33. 1739 *Byz*] θεου א* B **§ 40** **Gal 6:15** ***ουτε γαρ*** 𝔓^{46} B 33. 1739*] εν γαρ Χριστω Ιησου ουτε א A C D (1739^{c}). 1881 *Byz* **Gal 6:16** ***στοιχησουσιν*** א B C^{2} 33 *Byz*] στοιχουσιν A C* D 1739. 1881 ¦ στοιχησωσιν 𝔓^{46}

your household." 32 They spoke the word of the Lord[c] to him and to all who were in his house. 33 At the same hour of the night he took them and washed their wounds; then he and his entire family were baptized without delay.

Acts 18:8

Crispus, the official of the synagogue, became a believer in the Lord, together with all his household; and many of the Corinthians who heard Paul became believers and were baptized.

Acts 19:1–6

While Apollos was in Corinth, Paul passed through the interior regions and came to Ephesus, where he found some disciples. 2 He said to them, "Did you receive the Holy Spirit when you became believers?" They replied, "No, we have not even heard that there is a Holy Spirit." 3 Then he said, "Into what then were you baptized?" They answered, "Into John's baptism." 4 Paul said, "John baptized with the baptism of repentance, telling the people to believe in the one who was to come after him, that is, in Jesus." 5 On hearing this, they were baptized in the name of the Lord Jesus. 6 When Paul had laid his hands on them, the Holy Spirit came upon them, and they spoke in tongues and prophesied

Acts 22:16

And now why do you delay? Get up, be baptized, and have your sins washed away, calling on his name.

Cf. 1 Cor 1:13–17; Eph 4:20–24; Col 3:9–11.

40. Participation in Christ Crucified and Risen

Rom 6:1–11

What then are we to say? Should we continue in sin in order that grace may abound? 2 By no means! How can we who died to sin go on living in it? 3 Do you not know that all of us who have been baptized into Christ Jesus were baptized into his death? 4 Therefore we have been buried with him by baptism into death, so that, just as Christ was raised from the dead by the glory of the Father, so we too might walk in newness of life. 5 For if we have been united with him in a death like his, we will certainly be united with him in a resurrection like his. 6 We know that our old humanity[a] was crucified with him so that the body of sin might be destroyed, and we might no longer be enslaved to sin. 7 For whoever has died is freed from sin. 8 But if we have died with Christ, we believe that we will also live with him. 9 We know that Christ, being raised from the dead, will never die again; death no longer has dominion over him. 10 The death he died, he died to sin, once for all; but the life he lives, he lives to God. 11 So you also must consider yourselves dead to sin and alive to God in Christ Jesus.

Rom 7:4–6

In the same way, my friends, you have died to the law through the body of Christ, so that you may belong to another, to him who has been raised from the dead in order that we may bear fruit for God. 5 While we were living in the flesh, our sinful passions, aroused by the law, were at work in our members to bear fruit for death. 6 But now we are discharged from the law, dead to that which held us captive, so that we are slaves not under the old written code but in the new life of the Spirit.

2 Cor 5:14–21

For the love of Christ urges us on, because we are convinced that one has died for all; therefore all have died. 15 And he died for all, so that those who live might live no longer for themselves, but for him who died and was raised for them. 16 From now on, therefore, we regard no one from a human point of view; even though we once knew Christ from a human point of view, we know him no longer in that way. 17 So if anyone is in Christ, there is a new creation: everything old has passed away; see, everything has become new! 18 All this is from God, who reconciled us to himself through Christ, and has given us the ministry of reconciliation; 19 that is, God was in Christ, reconciling[b] the world to himself, not counting their trespasses against them, and entrusting the message of reconciliation to us. 20 So we are ambassadors for Christ, since God is making his appeal through us; we entreat you on behalf of Christ, be reconciled to God. 21 For our sake he made him to be sin who knew no sin, so that in him we might become the righteousness of God.

Gal 2:19–20

For through the law I died to the law, so that I might live to God. I have been crucified with Christ; 20 and it is no longer I who live, but it is Christ who lives in me. And the life I now live in the flesh I live by faith in the Son of God, who loved me and gave himself for me.

Gal 5:24–25

And those who belong to Christ Jesus have crucified the flesh with its passions and desires. 25 If we live by the Spirit, let us also be guided by the Spirit.

Gal 6:14–16

May I never boast of anything except the cross of our Lord Jesus Christ, by which the world has been crucified to me, and I to the world. 15 For[c] neither circumcision nor uncircumcision is anything; but a new creation is everything! 16 As for those who will follow[d] this rule—peace be upon them, and mercy, and upon the Israel of God.

Eph 2:1–7

You were dead through the trespasses and sins 2 in which you once lived, following the course of this world, following the ruler of the power of the air, the spirit that is now at work among those who are disobedient. 3 All of us once lived among them in the passions of our flesh, following the desires of

[c] **Acts 16:32** *word of the Lord* Other ancient authorities read *word of God* **§ 40** [a] **Rom 6:6** ***humanity*** NRSV translates *self* [b] **2 Cor 5:19** ***God was in Christ, reconciling*** Or possibly *in Christ God was reconciling* (so NRSV) [c] **Gal 6:15** ***For*** Other ancient authorities add *in Christ Jesus* [d] **Gal 6:16** ***will follow*** Other ancient authorities read *follow*

φύσει ὀργῆς ὡς καὶ οἱ λοιποί· **4** ὁ δὲ θεὸς
πλούσιος ὢν ἐν ἐλέει, διὰ τὴν πολλὴν
ἀγάπην αὐτοῦ ἣν ἠγάπησεν ἡμᾶς, **5** καὶ
ὄντας ἡμᾶς νεκροὺς τοῖς παραπτώμασιν
συνεζωοποίησεν ⸂τῷ Χριστῷ⸃, —χάριτί
ἐστε σεσῳσμένοι— **6** καὶ συνήγειρεν καὶ
συνεκάθισεν ἐν τοῖς ἐπουρανίοις ἐν
Χριστῷ Ἰησοῦ, **7** ἵνα ἐνδείξηται ἐν τοῖς
αἰῶσιν τοῖς ἐπερχομένοις τὸ ὑπερβάλλον
πλοῦτος τῆς χάριτος αὐτοῦ ἐν χρηστότητι
ἐφ᾽ ἡμᾶς ἐν Χριστῷ Ἰησοῦ.

Phil 3:8–11

ἀλλὰ μενοῦνγε καὶ ἡγοῦμαι πάντα ζη-
μίαν εἶναι διὰ τὸ ὑπερέχον τῆς γνώσεως
Χριστοῦ Ἰησοῦ τοῦ κυρίου μου, δι᾽ ὃν τὰ
πάντα ἐζημιώθην, καὶ ἡγοῦμαι σκύβαλα,
ἵνα Χριστὸν κερδήσω **9** καὶ εὑρεθῶ ἐν
αὐτῷ, μὴ ἔχων ἐμὴν δικαιοσύνην τὴν ἐκ
νόμου ἀλλὰ τὴν διὰ πίστεως Χριστοῦ,
τὴν ἐκ θεοῦ δικαιοσύνην ἐπὶ τῇ πίστει,
10 τοῦ γνῶναι αὐτὸν καὶ τὴν δύναμιν
τῆς ἀναστάσεως αὐτοῦ καὶ [τὴν] κοι-
νωνίαν [τῶν] παθημάτων αὐτοῦ, συμ-
μορφιζόμενος τῷ θανάτῳ αὐτοῦ, **11** εἴ
πως καταντήσω εἰς τὴν ἐξανάστασιν
τὴν ἐκ νεκρῶν.

Col 2:12–13

συνταφέντες αὐτῷ ἐν τῷ βαπτισμῷ,
ἐν ᾧ καὶ συνηγέρθητε διὰ τῆς πίστεως
τῆς ἐνεργείας τοῦ θεοῦ τοῦ ἐγείραντος
αὐτὸν ἐκ νεκρῶν· **13** καὶ ὑμᾶς νεκροὺς
ὄντας [ἐν] τοῖς παραπτώμασιν καὶ τῇ
ἀκροβυστίᾳ τῆς σαρκὸς ὑμῶν, συνεζω-
οποίησεν ⸀ὑμᾶς σὺν αὐτῷ, χαρισάμενος
ἡμῖν πάντα τὰ παραπτώματα.

Col 3:1–4

Εἰ οὖν συνηγέρθητε τῷ Χριστῷ, τὰ ἄνω
ζητεῖτε, οὗ ὁ Χριστός ἐστιν ἐν δεξιᾷ τοῦ
θεοῦ καθήμενος· **2** τὰ ἄνω φρονεῖτε, μὴ
τὰ ἐπὶ τῆς γῆς. **3** ἀπεθάνετε γὰρ καὶ ἡ
ζωὴ ὑμῶν κέκρυπται σὺν τῷ Χριστῷ
ἐν τῷ θεῷ· **4** ὅταν ὁ Χριστὸς φανερωθῇ,
ἡ ζωὴ ⸀ὑμῶν, τότε καὶ ὑμεῖς σὺν αὐτῷ
φανερωθήσεσθε ἐν δόξῃ.

2 Tim 2:11–13

πιστὸς ὁ λόγος· εἰ γὰρ συναπεθάνομεν,
καὶ συζήσομεν· **12** εἰ ὑπομένομεν, καὶ
συμβασιλεύσομεν· εἰ ἀρνησόμεθα, κἀκεῖ-
νος ἀρνήσεται ἡμᾶς· **13** εἰ ἀπιστοῦμεν,
ἐκεῖνος πιστὸς μένει, ἀρνήσασθαι γὰρ
ἑαυτὸν οὐ δύναται.

Cf. 1 Cor 6:12–20; 2 Cor 3:15–18; 4:10–12; Eph 1:19–20; Col 2:20–23; and consult a concordance for Paul's participatory formulas **ἐν Χριστῷ**, **ἐν κυρίῳ**, **εἰς Χριστόν**, and **σὺν Χριστῷ**.

See also § 44 The Gift of the Spirit; § 70 Belonging to Christ; and § 80 The Body of Christ.

41. The New Exodus

Rom 6:17–23

χάρις δὲ τῷ θεῷ ὅτι ἦτε δοῦλοι τῆς ἁμαρ-
τίας ὑπηκούσατε δὲ ἐκ καρδίας εἰς ὃν
παρεδόθητε τύπον διδαχῆς, **18** ἐλευθερω-
θέντες δὲ ἀπὸ τῆς ἁμαρτίας ἐδουλώθητε
τῇ δικαιοσύνῃ. **19** Ἀνθρώπινον λέγω
διὰ τὴν ἀσθένειαν τῆς σαρκὸς ὑμῶν.
ὥσπερ γὰρ παρεστήσατε τὰ μέλη ὑμῶν
δοῦλα τῇ ἀκαθαρσίᾳ καὶ τῇ ἀνομίᾳ εἰς
τὴν ἀνομίαν, οὕτως νῦν παραστήσατε
τὰ μέλη ὑμῶν δοῦλα τῇ δικαιοσύνῃ
εἰς ἁγιασμόν. **20** ὅτε γὰρ δοῦλοι ἦτε τῆς
ἁμαρτίας, ἐλεύθεροι ἦτε τῇ δικαιοσύνῃ.
21 τίνα οὖν καρπὸν εἴχετε τότε; ἐφ᾽ οἷς
νῦν ἐπαισχύνεσθε, τὸ γὰρ τέλος ἐκείνων
θάνατος. **22** νυνὶ δὲ ἐλευθερωθέντες ἀπὸ
τῆς ἁμαρτίας δουλωθέντες δὲ τῷ θεῷ
ἔχετε τὸν καρπὸν ὑμῶν εἰς ἁγιασμόν, τὸ
δὲ τέλος ζωὴν αἰώνιον. **23** τὰ γὰρ ὀψώνια
τῆς ἁμαρτίας θάνατος, τὸ δὲ χάρισμα τοῦ
θεοῦ ζωὴ αἰώνιος ἐν Χριστῷ Ἰησοῦ τῷ
κυρίῳ ἡμῶν.

1 Cor 5:6–8

Οὐ καλὸν τὸ καύχημα ὑμῶν. οὐκ οἴδατε
ὅτι μικρὰ ζύμη ὅλον τὸ φύραμα ζυμοῖ;
7 ἐκκαθάρατε τὴν παλαιὰν ζύμην, ἵνα
ἦτε νέον φύραμα, καθώς ἐστε ἄζυμοι·
καὶ γὰρ τὸ πάσχα ἡμῶν ἐτύθη Χριστός.
8 ὥστε ἑορτάζωμεν μὴ ἐν ζύμῃ παλαιᾷ
μηδὲ ἐν ζύμῃ κακίας καὶ πονηρίας ἀλλ᾽ ἐν
ἀζύμοις εἰλικρινείας καὶ ἀληθείας.

1 Cor 10:1–13

Οὐ θέλω γὰρ ὑμᾶς ἀγνοεῖν, ἀδελφοί,
ὅτι οἱ πατέρες ἡμῶν πάντες ὑπὸ τὴν
νεφέλην ἦσαν καὶ πάντες διὰ τῆς θα-
λάσσης διῆλθον **2** καὶ πάντες εἰς τὸν
Μωϋσῆν ἐβαπτίσθησαν ἐν τῇ νεφέλῃ
καὶ ἐν τῇ θαλάσσῃ **3** καὶ πάντες τὸ αὐτὸ
πνευματικὸν βρῶμα ἔφαγον **4** καὶ πάντες
τὸ αὐτὸ πνευματικὸν ἔπιον πόμα· ἔπι-
νον γὰρ ἐκ πνευματικῆς ἀκολουθούσης
πέτρας, ἡ πέτρα δὲ ἦν ὁ Χριστός. **5** Ἀλλ᾽
οὐκ ἐν τοῖς πλείοσιν αὐτῶν εὐδόκησεν ὁ
θεός, κατεστρώθησαν γὰρ ἐν τῇ ἐρήμῳ.
6 Ταῦτα δὲ τύποι ἡμῶν ἐγενήθησαν, εἰς
τὸ μὴ εἶναι ἡμᾶς ἐπιθυμητὰς κακῶν, κα-
θὼς κἀκεῖνοι ἐπεθύμησαν. **7** μηδὲ εἰδω-
λολάτραι γίνεσθε καθώς τινες αὐτῶν,
ὥσπερ γέγραπται· ἐκάθισεν ὁ λαὸς φαγεῖν
καὶ πεῖν καὶ ἀνέστησαν παίζειν. **8** μηδὲ
πορνεύωμεν, καθώς τινες αὐτῶν ἐπόρ-
νευσαν καὶ ἔπεσαν μιᾷ ἡμέρᾳ εἴκοσι
τρεῖς χιλιάδες. **9** μηδὲ ἐκπειράζωμεν τὸν
⸀Χριστόν, καθώς τινες αὐτῶν ἐπείρασαν
καὶ ὑπὸ τῶν ὄφεων ἀπώλλυντο. **10** μηδὲ
γογγύζετε, καθάπερ τινὲς αὐτῶν ἐγόγγυ-
σαν καὶ ἀπώλοντο ὑπὸ τοῦ ὀλοθρευτοῦ.
11 ταῦτα δὲ τυπικῶς συνέβαινεν ἐκείνοις,
ἐγράφη δὲ πρὸς νουθεσίαν ἡμῶν, εἰς
οὓς τὰ τέλη τῶν αἰώνων κατήντηκεν.
12 Ὥστε ὁ δοκῶν ἑστάναι βλεπέτω μὴ
πέσῃ. **13** πειρασμὸς ὑμᾶς οὐκ εἴληφεν εἰ
μὴ ἀνθρώπινος· πιστὸς δὲ ὁ θεός, ὃς οὐκ
ἐάσει ὑμᾶς πειρασθῆναι ὑπὲρ ὃ δύνασθε
ἀλλὰ ποιήσει σὺν τῷ πειρασμῷ καὶ τὴν
ἔκβασιν τοῦ δύνασθαι ὑπενεγκεῖν.

2 Cor 6:14–7:1

Μὴ γίνεσθε ἑτεροζυγοῦντες ἀπίστοις·
τίς γὰρ μετοχὴ δικαιοσύνῃ καὶ ἀνομίᾳ,

Eph 2:5 ***τω Χριστω*** ℵ A D 1739. 1881 *Byz*] εν τω Χριστω 𝔓46 B 33 **Col 2:13** ***υμας*** ℵ* A C 1739. 1881] ημας 𝔓46 B 33 ¦ *om.* ℵ2 D *Byz* **Col 3:4** ***υμων*** 𝔓46 ℵ C D* 33. 1881] ημων B(*) D1 1739 *Byz* **§ 41** **1 Cor 10:9** ***Χριστον*** 𝔓46 D 1739. 1881 *Byz*] κυριον ℵ B C 33 ¦ θεον A

flesh and senses, and we were by nature children of wrath, like everyone else. 4 But God, who is rich in mercy, out of the great love with which he loved us 5 even when we were dead through our trespasses, made us alive together with Christ[e]—by grace you have been saved— 6 and raised us up with him and seated us with him in the heavenly places in Christ Jesus, 7 so that in the ages to come he might show the immeasurable riches of his grace in kindness toward us in Christ Jesus.

Phil 3:8–11

More than that, I regard everything as loss because of the surpassing value of knowing Christ Jesus my Lord. For his sake I have suffered the loss of all things, and I regard them as rubbish, in order that I may gain Christ 9 and be found in him, not having a righteousness of my own that comes from the law, but one that comes through faith in Christ, the righteousness from God based on faith. 10 I want to know Christ and the power of his resurrection and the sharing of his sufferings by becoming like him in his death, 11 if somehow I may attain the resurrection from the dead.

Col 2:12–13

when you were buried with him in baptism, you were also raised with him through faith in the power of God, who raised him from the dead. 13 And when you were dead in trespasses and the uncircumcision of your flesh, God made you[f] alive together with him, when he forgave us all our trespasses

Col 3:1–4

So if you have been raised with Christ, seek the things that are above, where Christ is, seated at the right hand of God. 2 Set your minds on things that are above, not on things that are on earth, 3 for you have died, and your life is hidden with Christ in God. 4 When Christ who is your[g] life is revealed, then you also will be revealed with him in glory.

2 Tim 2:11–13

The saying is sure: If we have died with him, we will also live with him; 12 if we endure, we will also reign with him; if we deny him, he will also deny us; 13 if we are faithless, he remains faithful—for he cannot deny himself.

Cf. 1 Cor 6:12–20; 2 Cor 3:15–18; 4:10–12; Eph 1:19–20; Col 2:20–23; and consult a concordance for Paul's participatory formulas "in Christ," "in the Lord," "into Christ" and "with Christ."

See also § 44 The Gift of the Spirit; § 70 Belonging to Christ; and § 80 The Body of Christ.

41. The New Exodus

Rom 6:17–23

But thanks be to God that you, having once been slaves of sin, have become obedient from the heart to the form of teaching to which you were entrusted, 18 and that you, having been set free from sin, have become slaves of righteousness. 19 I am speaking in human terms because of your natural limitations. For just as you once presented your members as slaves to impurity and to greater and greater iniquity, so now present your members as slaves to righteousness for sanctification. 20 When you were slaves of sin, you were free in regard to righteousness. 21 So what fruit did you have then? Because of these things you are now ashamed, because the end of those things is death. 22 But now that you have been freed from sin and enslaved to God, the fruit you get is sanctification, and the end is eternal life.[a] 23 For the wages of sin is death, but the free gift of God is eternal life in Christ Jesus our Lord.

1 Cor 5:6–8

Your boasting is not a good thing. Do you not know that a little yeast leavens the whole batch of dough? 7 Clean out the old yeast so that you may be a new batch, as you really are unleavened. For our paschal lamb, Christ, has been sacrificed. 8 Therefore, let us celebrate the festival, not with the old yeast, the yeast of malice and evil, but with the unleavened bread of sincerity and truth.

1 Cor 10:1–13

I do not want you to be unaware, brothers and sisters, that our ancestors were all under the cloud, and all passed through the sea, 2 and all were baptized into Moses in the cloud and in the sea, 3 and all ate the same spiritual food, 4 and all drank the same spiritual drink. For they drank from the spiritual rock that followed them, and the rock was Christ. 5 Nevertheless, God was not pleased with most of them, and they were struck down in the wilderness. 6 Now these things occurred as examples for us, so that we might not desire evil as they did. 7 Do not become idolaters as some of them did; as it is written, "The people sat down to eat and drink, and they rose up to play." 8 We must not indulge in sexual immorality as some of them did, and twenty-three thousand fell in a single day. 9 We must not put Christ[b] to the test, as some of them did, and were destroyed by serpents. 10 And do not complain as some of them did, and were destroyed by the destroyer. 11 These things happened to them to serve as an example, and they were written down to instruct us, on whom the ends of the ages have come. 12 So if you think you are standing, watch out that you do not fall. 13 No testing has overtaken you that is not common to everyone. God is faithful, and he will not let you be tested beyond your strength, but with the testing he will also provide the way out so that you may be able to endure it.

2 Cor 6:14–7:1

Do not be mismatched with unbelievers. For what partnership is there between

[e] **Eph 2:5** ***together with Christ*** Other ancient authorities read *in Christ* [f] **Col 2:13** ***made you*** Other ancient authorities read *made us*; others, *made* [g] **Col 3:4** ***your*** Other ancient authorities read *our* **§ 41** [a] **Rom 6:21–22** Translation differs from NRSV [b] **1 Cor 10:9** ***Christ*** Other ancient authorities read *the Lord*

ἢ τίς κοινωνία φωτὶ πρὸς σκότος; 15 τίς
δὲ συμφώνησις Χριστοῦ πρὸς Βελιάρ, ἢ
τίς μερὶς πιστῷ μετὰ ἀπίστου; 16 τίς δὲ
συγκατάθεσις ναῷ θεοῦ μετὰ εἰδώλων;
⸀ἡμεῖς γὰρ ναὸς θεοῦ ἐσμεν⸁ ζῶντος,
καθὼς εἶπεν ὁ θεὸς ὅτι ἐνοικήσω ἐν
αὐτοῖς καὶ ἐμπεριπατήσω καὶ ἔσομαι
αὐτῶν θεὸς καὶ αὐτοὶ ἔσονταί μου λα-
ός. 17 διὸ ἐξέλθατε ἐκ μέσου αὐτῶν καὶ
ἀφορίσθητε, λέγει κύριος, καὶ ἀκαθάρτου
μὴ ἅπτεσθε· κἀγὼ εἰσδέξομαι ὑμᾶς 18 καὶ
ἔσομαι ὑμῖν εἰς πατέρα καὶ ὑμεῖς ἔσεσθέ
μοι εἰς υἱοὺς καὶ θυγατέρας, λέγει κύριος
παντοκράτωρ. **7** Ταύτας οὖν ἔχοντες τὰς
ἐπαγγελίας, ἀγαπητοί, καθαρίσωμεν
ἑαυτοὺς ἀπὸ παντὸς μολυσμοῦ σαρκὸς
καὶ πνεύματος, ἐπιτελοῦντες ἁγιωσύνην
ἐν φόβῳ θεοῦ.

Cf. in light of their biblical allusions Rom 3:24; Gal 4:8–9; 4:21–27; Titus 2:11–14; Acts 13:6–12; 26:16–18; 26:22–23.

See also § 42 Liberation from Slavery; § 45 The Temple of God; § 92 The Inheritance of the Saints.

42. Liberation from Slavery

Rom 6:12–23

Μὴ οὖν βασιλευέτω ἡ ἁμαρτία ἐν τῷ
θνητῷ ὑμῶν σώματι εἰς τὸ ὑπακούειν
ταῖς ἐπιθυμίαις αὐτοῦ, 13 μηδὲ παρι-
στάνετε τὰ μέλη ὑμῶν ὅπλα ἀδικίας τῇ
ἁμαρτίᾳ, ἀλλὰ παραστήσατε ἑαυτοὺς
τῷ θεῷ ὡσεὶ ἐκ νεκρῶν ζῶντας καὶ τὰ
μέλη ὑμῶν ὅπλα δικαιοσύνης τῷ θεῷ.
14 ἁμαρτία γὰρ ὑμῶν οὐ κυριεύσει· οὐ
γάρ ἐστε ὑπὸ νόμον ἀλλὰ ὑπὸ χάριν.
15 Τί οὖν; ἁμαρτήσωμεν, ὅτι οὐκ ἐσμὲν
ὑπὸ νόμον ἀλλὰ ὑπὸ χάριν; μὴ γένοιτο.
16 οὐκ οἴδατε ὅτι ᾧ παριστάνετε ἑαυτοὺς
δούλους εἰς ὑπακοήν, δοῦλοί ἐστε ᾧ
ὑπακούετε, ἤτοι ἁμαρτίας εἰς θάνατον
ἢ ὑπακοῆς εἰς δικαιοσύνην; 17 χάρις δὲ
τῷ θεῷ ὅτι ἦτε δοῦλοι τῆς ἁμαρτίας
ὑπηκούσατε δὲ ἐκ καρδίας εἰς ὃν πα-
ρεδόθητε τύπον διδαχῆς, 18 ἐλευθερω-
θέντες δὲ ἀπὸ τῆς ἁμαρτίας ἐδουλώθητε
τῇ δικαιοσύνῃ. 19 Ἀνθρώπινον λέγω
διὰ τὴν ἀσθένειαν τῆς σαρκὸς ὑμῶν.
ὥσπερ γὰρ παρεστήσατε τὰ μέλη ὑμῶν
δοῦλα τῇ ἀκαθαρσίᾳ καὶ τῇ ἀνομίᾳ εἰς
τὴν ἀνομίαν, οὕτως νῦν παραστήσατε
τὰ μέλη ὑμῶν δοῦλα τῇ δικαιοσύνῃ
εἰς ἁγιασμόν. 20 ὅτε γὰρ δοῦλοι ἦτε τῆς
ἁμαρτίας, ἐλεύθεροι ἦτε τῇ δικαιοσύνῃ.
21 τίνα οὖν καρπὸν εἴχετε τότε; ἐφ᾽ οἷς
νῦν ἐπαισχύνεσθε, τὸ γὰρ τέλος ἐκείνων
θάνατος. 22 νυνὶ δὲ ἐλευθερωθέντες ἀπὸ
τῆς ἁμαρτίας δουλωθέντες δὲ τῷ θεῷ
ἔχετε τὸν καρπὸν ὑμῶν εἰς ἁγιασμόν, τὸ
δὲ τέλος ζωὴν αἰώνιον. 23 τὰ γὰρ ὀψώνια
τῆς ἁμαρτίας θάνατος, τὸ δὲ χάρισμα τοῦ
θεοῦ ζωὴ αἰώνιος ἐν Χριστῷ Ἰησοῦ τῷ
κυρίῳ ἡμῶν.

Rom 7:4–6

ὥστε, ἀδελφοί μου, καὶ ὑμεῖς ἐθανατώ-
θητε τῷ νόμῳ διὰ τοῦ σώματος τοῦ
Χριστοῦ, εἰς τὸ γενέσθαι ὑμᾶς ἑτέρῳ,
τῷ ἐκ νεκρῶν ἐγερθέντι, ἵνα καρπο-
φορήσωμεν τῷ θεῷ. 5 ὅτε γὰρ ἦμεν ἐν
τῇ σαρκί, τὰ παθήματα τῶν ἁμαρτιῶν
τὰ διὰ τοῦ νόμου ἐνηργεῖτο ἐν τοῖς
μέλεσιν ἡμῶν, εἰς τὸ καρποφορῆσαι
τῷ θανάτῳ· 6 νυνὶ δὲ κατηργήθημεν
ἀπὸ τοῦ νόμου ἀποθανόντες ἐν ᾧ κα-
τειχόμεθα, ὥστε δουλεύειν ἡμᾶς ἐν
καινότητι πνεύματος καὶ οὐ παλαιότητι
γράμματος.

Rom 7:22–8:2

συνήδομαι γὰρ τῷ νόμῳ τοῦ θεοῦ κατὰ τὸν
ἔσω ἄνθρωπον, 23 βλέπω δὲ ἕτερον νόμον
ἐν τοῖς μέλεσίν μου ἀντιστρατευόμενον
τῷ νόμῳ τοῦ νοός μου καὶ αἰχμαλωτί-
ζοντά με ἐν τῷ νόμῳ τῆς ἁμαρτίας τῷ
ὄντι ἐν τοῖς μέλεσίν μου. 24 Ταλαίπωρος
ἐγὼ ἄνθρωπος· τίς με ῥύσεται ἐκ τοῦ
σώματος τοῦ θανάτου τούτου; 25 χάρις
δὲ τῷ θεῷ διὰ Ἰησοῦ Χριστοῦ τοῦ κυρίου
ἡμῶν. Ἄρα οὖν αὐτὸς ἐγὼ τῷ μὲν νοῒ
δουλεύω νόμῳ θεοῦ τῇ δὲ σαρκὶ νόμῳ
ἁμαρτίας. **8** Οὐδὲν ἄρα νῦν κατάκριμα
τοῖς ἐν Χριστῷ Ἰησοῦ. 2 ὁ γὰρ νόμος τοῦ
πνεύματος τῆς ζωῆς ἐν Χριστῷ Ἰησοῦ
ἠλευθέρωσέν ⸀σε ἀπὸ τοῦ νόμου τῆς
ἁμαρτίας καὶ τοῦ θανάτου.

1 Cor 7:21–23

δοῦλος ἐκλήθης, μή σοι μελέτω· ἀλλ᾽ εἰ
καὶ δύνασαι ἐλεύθερος γενέσθαι, μᾶλλον
χρῆσαι. 22 ὁ γὰρ ἐν κυρίῳ κληθεὶς δοῦ-
λος ἀπελεύθερος κυρίου ἐστίν, ὁμοίως
ὁ ἐλεύθερος κληθεὶς δοῦλός ἐστιν Χρι-
στοῦ. 23 τιμῆς ἠγοράσθητε· μὴ γίνεσθε
δοῦλοι ἀνθρώπων.

Gal 4:1–11

Λέγω δέ, ἐφ᾽ ὅσον χρόνον ὁ κληρονόμος
νήπιός ἐστιν, οὐδὲν διαφέρει δούλου κύ-
ριος πάντων ὤν, 2 ἀλλὰ ὑπὸ ἐπιτρόπους
ἐστὶν καὶ οἰκονόμους ἄχρι τῆς προθε-
σμίας τοῦ πατρός. 3 οὕτως καὶ ἡμεῖς, ὅτε
ἦμεν νήπιοι, ὑπὸ τὰ στοιχεῖα τοῦ κόσμου
ἤμεθα δεδουλωμένοι· 4 ὅτε δὲ ἦλθεν τὸ
πλήρωμα τοῦ χρόνου, ἐξαπέστειλεν
ὁ θεὸς τὸν υἱὸν αὐτοῦ, γενόμενον ἐκ
γυναικός, γενόμενον ὑπὸ νόμον, 5 ἵνα
τοὺς ὑπὸ νόμον ἐξαγοράσῃ, ἵνα τὴν υἱο-
θεσίαν ἀπολάβωμεν. 6 Ὅτι δέ ἐστε υἱοί,
ἐξαπέστειλεν ὁ θεὸς τὸ πνεῦμα τοῦ υἱοῦ
αὐτοῦ εἰς τὰς καρδίας ⸀ἡμῶν κρᾶζον·
αββα ὁ πατήρ. 7 ὥστε οὐκέτι εἶ δοῦλος
ἀλλὰ υἱός· εἰ δὲ υἱός, καὶ κληρονόμος
⸂διὰ θεοῦ⸃. 8 Ἀλλὰ τότε μὲν οὐκ εἰδότες
θεὸν ἐδουλεύσατε τοῖς φύσει μὴ οὖσιν
θεοῖς· 9 νῦν δὲ γνόντες θεόν, μᾶλλον δὲ
γνωσθέντες ὑπὸ θεοῦ, πῶς ἐπιστρέφετε
πάλιν ἐπὶ τὰ ἀσθενῆ καὶ πτωχὰ στοιχεῖα
οἷς πάλιν ἄνωθεν δουλεύειν θέλετε;
10 ἡμέρας παρατηρεῖσθε καὶ μῆνας καὶ
καιροὺς καὶ ἐνιαυτούς, 11 φοβοῦμαι ὑμᾶς
μή πως εἰκῇ κεκοπίακα εἰς ὑμᾶς.

Gal 4:21–5:1

Λέγετέ μοι, οἱ ὑπὸ νόμον θέλοντες εἶναι,
τὸν νόμον οὐκ ἀκούετε; 22 γέγραπται

2 Cor 6:16 ***ημεις γαρ ναος θεου εσμεν*** B D* 33. 1881] υμεις γαρ ναος θεου εστε 𝔓^{46} (א^{2}) C D^{2} *Byz* ¦ ημεις γαρ ναοι θεου εσμεν א* 1739 **§ 42** **Rom 8:2** ***σε*** א B 1739*] με A D 1739^{c}. 1881 *Byz* **Gal 4:6** ***ημων*** 𝔓^{46} א A B C D* 1739. 1881] υμων D^{2} 33 *Byz* **Gal 4:7** ***δια θεου*** 𝔓^{46} א* A B C* 33. 1739^{*vid}] θεου δια Χριστου א^{2} C^{3} D *Byz* ¦ δια θεον 1881 ¦ δια Ιησου Χριστου 1739^{c}

righteousness and lawlessness? Or what fellowship is there between light and darkness? 15 What agreement does Christ have with Beliar? Or what does a believer share with an unbeliever? 16 What agreement has the temple of God with idols? For we[c] are the temple of the living God; as God said, "I will live in them and walk among them, and I will be their God, and they shall be my people. 17 Therefore come out from them, and be separate from them, says the Lord, and touch nothing unclean; then I will welcome you, 18 and I will be your father, and you shall be my sons and daughters, says the Lord Almighty." **7** Since we have these promises, beloved, let us cleanse ourselves from every defilement of body and of spirit, making holiness perfect in the fear of God.

Cf. in light of their biblical allusions Rom 3:24; Gal 4:8–9; 4:21–27; Titus 2:11–14; Acts 13:6–12; 26:16–18; 26:22–23.

See also § 42 Liberation from Slavery; § 45 The Temple of God; § 92 The Inheritance of the Saints.

42. Liberation from Slavery

Rom 6:12–23

Therefore, do not let sin exercise dominion in your mortal bodies, to make you obey their passions. 13 No longer present your members to sin as weapons[a] of wickedness, but present yourselves to God as those who have been brought from death to life, and present your members to God as weapons[a] of righteousness. 14 For sin will have no dominion over you, since you are not under law but under grace. 15 What then? Should we sin because we are not under law but under grace? By no means! 16 Do you not know that if you present yourselves to anyone as obedient slaves, you are slaves of the one whom you obey, either of sin, which leads to death, or of obedience, which leads to righteousness? 17 But thanks be to God that you, having once been slaves of sin, have become obedient from the heart to the form of teaching to which you were entrusted, 18 and that you, having been set free from sin, have become slaves of righteousness. 19 I am speaking in human terms because of your natural limitations. For just as you once presented your members as slaves to impurity and to greater and greater iniquity, so now present your members as slaves to righteousness for sanctification. 20 When you were slaves of sin, you were free in regard to righteousness. 21 So what fruit did you have then? Because of these things you are now ashamed, because the end of those things is death. 22 But now that you have been freed from sin and enslaved to God, the fruit you get is sanctification, and the end is eternal life.[b] 23 For the wages of sin is death, but the free gift of God is eternal life in Christ Jesus our Lord.

Rom 7:4–6

In the same way, my friends, you have died to the law through the body of Christ, so that you may belong to another, to him who has been raised from the dead in order that we may bear fruit for God. 5 While we were living in the flesh, our sinful passions, aroused by the law, were at work in our members to bear fruit for death. 6 But now we are discharged from the law, dead to that which held us captive, so that we are slaves not under the old written code but in the new life of the Spirit.

Rom 7:22–8:2

For I delight in the law of God in my inmost self, 23 but I see in my members another law at war with the law of my mind, making me captive to the law of sin that dwells in my members. 24 Wretched man that I am! Who will rescue me from this body of death? 25 Thanks be to God through Jesus Christ our Lord! So then, with my mind I am a slave to the law of God, but with my flesh I am a slave to the law of sin. **8** There is therefore now no condemnation for those who are in Christ Jesus. 2 For the law of the Spirit of life in Christ Jesus has set you[c] free from the law of sin and of death.

1 Cor 7:21–23

Were you a slave when called? Do not be concerned about it. Even if you can gain your freedom, make use of your present condition now more than ever. 22 For whoever was called in the Lord as a slave is a freed person belonging to the Lord, just as whoever was free when called is a slave of Christ. 23 You were bought with a price; do not become slaves of human masters.

Gal 4:1–11

My point is this: heirs, as long as they are minors, are no better than slaves, though they are the owners of all the property; 2 but they remain under guardians and trustees until the date set by the father. 3 So with us; while we were minors, we were enslaved to the elemental spirits of the world. 4 But when the fullness of time had come, God sent his Son, born of a woman, born under the law, 5 in order to redeem those who were under the law, so that we might receive adoption as children. 6 And because you are children, God has sent the Spirit of his Son into our[d] hearts, crying, "Abba! Father!" 7 So you are no longer a slave but a child, and if a child then also an heir, through God.[e] 8 Formerly, when you did not know God, you were enslaved to beings that by nature are not gods. 9 Now, however, that you have come to know God, or rather to be known by God, how can you turn back again to the weak and beggarly elemental spirits? How can you want to be enslaved to them again? 10 You are observing special days, and months, and seasons, and years. 11 I am afraid that my work for you may have been wasted.

Gal 4:21–5:1

Tell me, you who desire to be subject to the law, will you not listen to the law? 22 For it is written that Abraham had

[c] **2 Cor 6:16** *we* Other ancient authorities read *you* **§ 42** [a] **Rom 6:13** *weapons* Or possibly *instruments* (so NRSV) [b] **Rom 6:21–22** Translation differs from NRSV [c] **Rom 8:2** *you* Other ancient authorities read *me* [d] **Gal 4:6** *our* Other ancient authorities read *your* [e] **Gal 4:7** *an heir, through God* Other ancient authorities read *an heir of God through Christ*

γὰρ ὅτι Ἀβραὰμ δύο υἱοὺς ἔσχεν, ἕνα ἐκ
τῆς παιδίσκης καὶ ἕνα ἐκ τῆς ἐλευθέρας.
23 ἀλλ᾽ ὁ μὲν ἐκ τῆς παιδίσκης κατὰ σάρ-
κα γεγέννηται, ὁ δὲ ἐκ τῆς ἐλευθέρας δι᾽
ἐπαγγελίας. **24** ἅτινά ἐστιν ἀλληγορούμενα·
αὗται γάρ εἰσιν δύο διαθῆκαι, μία μὲν
ἀπὸ ὄρους Σινᾶ εἰς δουλείαν γεννῶσα,
ἥτις ἐστὶν Ἁγάρ. **25** τὸ ⸀δὲ Ἁγὰρ Σινᾶ⸁
ὄρος ἐστὶν ἐν τῇ Ἀραβίᾳ· συστοιχεῖ δὲ τῇ
νῦν Ἰερουσαλήμ, δουλεύει γὰρ μετὰ τῶν
τέκνων αὐτῆς. **26** ἡ δὲ ἄνω Ἰερουσαλὴμ
ἐλευθέρα ἐστίν, ἥτις ἐστὶν μήτηρ ἡμῶν·
27 γέγραπται γάρ· εὐφράνθητι, στεῖρα ἡ
οὐ τίκτουσα, ῥῆξον καὶ βόησον, ἡ οὐκ
ὠδίνουσα· ὅτι πολλὰ τὰ τέκνα τῆς ἐρή-
μου μᾶλλον ἢ τῆς ἐχούσης τὸν ἄνδρα.
28 ⸀Ὑμεῖς δέ, ἀδελφοί, κατὰ Ἰσαὰκ ἐπαγ-
γελίας τέκνα ⸀ἐστέ. **29** ἀλλ᾽ ὥσπερ τότε ὁ
κατὰ σάρκα γεννηθεὶς ἐδίωκεν τὸν κατὰ
πνεῦμα, οὕτως καὶ νῦν. **30** ἀλλὰ τί λέγει
ἡ γραφή; ἔκβαλε τὴν παιδίσκην καὶ τὸν
υἱὸν αὐτῆς· οὐ γὰρ μὴ κληρονομήσει ὁ
υἱὸς τῆς παιδίσκης μετὰ τοῦ υἱοῦ τῆς
ἐλευθέρας. **31** διό, ἀδελφοί, οὐκ ἐσμὲν
παιδίσκης τέκνα ἀλλὰ τῆς ἐλευθέρας.
5 Τῇ ἐλευθερίᾳ ἡμᾶς Χριστὸς ἠλευθέρω-
σεν· στήκετε οὖν καὶ μὴ πάλιν ζυγῷ
δουλείας ἐνέχεσθε.

Titus 2:14

ὃς ἔδωκεν ἑαυτὸν ὑπὲρ ἡμῶν, ἵνα λυ-
τρώσηται ἡμᾶς ἀπὸ πάσης ἀνομίας καὶ
καθαρίσῃ ἑαυτῷ λαὸν περιούσιον, ζη-
λωτὴν καλῶν ἔργων.

Cf. Rom 3:24; 8:18–25; 1 Cor 1:30–31; 6:20; Gal 5:13–14.

43. The New Covenant

Rom 2:25–29

Περιτομὴ μὲν γὰρ ὠφελεῖ ἐὰν νόμον
πράσσῃς· ἐὰν δὲ παραβάτης νόμου ᾖς,
ἡ περιτομή σου ἀκροβυστία γέγονεν.
26 ἐὰν οὖν ἡ ἀκροβυστία τὰ δικαιώματα
τοῦ νόμου φυλάσσῃ, οὐχ ἡ ἀκροβυστία
αὐτοῦ εἰς περιτομὴν λογισθήσεται; **27** καὶ
κρινεῖ ἡ ἐκ φύσεως ἀκροβυστία τὸν νό-
μον τελοῦσα σὲ τὸν διὰ γράμματος καὶ
περιτομῆς παραβάτην νόμου. **28** οὐ γὰρ ὁ
ἐν τῷ φανερῷ Ἰουδαῖός ἐστιν οὐδὲ ἡ ἐν
τῷ φανερῷ ἐν σαρκὶ περιτομή, **29** ἀλλ᾽ ὁ
ἐν τῷ κρυπτῷ Ἰουδαῖος, καὶ περιτομὴ
καρδίας ἐν πνεύματι οὐ γράμματι, οὗ
ὁ ἔπαινος οὐκ ἐξ ἀνθρώπων ἀλλ᾽ ἐκ
τοῦ θεοῦ.

Rom 7:5–6

ὅτε γὰρ ἦμεν ἐν τῇ σαρκί, τὰ παθήματα
τῶν ἁμαρτιῶν τὰ διὰ τοῦ νόμου ἐνηρ-
γεῖτο ἐν τοῖς μέλεσιν ἡμῶν, εἰς τὸ καρ-
ποφορῆσαι τῷ θανάτῳ· **6** νυνὶ δὲ κατηρ-
γήθημεν ἀπὸ τοῦ νόμου ἀποθανόντες ἐν
ᾧ κατειχόμεθα, ὥστε δουλεύειν ἡμᾶς ἐν
καινότητι πνεύματος καὶ οὐ παλαιότητι
γράμματος.

Rom 8:3–4

Τὸ γὰρ ἀδύνατον τοῦ νόμου ἐν ᾧ ἠσθένει
διὰ τῆς σαρκός, ὁ θεὸς τὸν ἑαυτοῦ υἱὸν
πέμψας ἐν ὁμοιώματι σαρκὸς ἁμαρτίας καὶ
περὶ ἁμαρτίας κατέκρινεν τὴν ἁμαρτίαν
ἐν τῇ σαρκί, **4** ἵνα τὸ δικαίωμα τοῦ νόμου
πληρωθῇ ἐν ἡμῖν τοῖς μὴ κατὰ σάρκα
περιπατοῦσιν ἀλλὰ κατὰ πνεῦμα.

1 Cor 11:23–25

Ἐγὼ γὰρ παρέλαβον ἀπὸ τοῦ κυρίου, ὃ
καὶ παρέδωκα ὑμῖν, ὅτι ὁ κύριος Ἰησοῦς
ἐν τῇ νυκτὶ ᾗ παρεδίδετο ἔλαβεν ἄρτον
24 καὶ εὐχαριστήσας ἔκλασεν καὶ εἶπεν·
τοῦτό μού ἐστιν τὸ σῶμα τὸ ὑπὲρ ⸀ὑμῶν·
τοῦτο ποιεῖτε εἰς τὴν ἐμὴν ἀνάμνησιν.
25 ὡσαύτως καὶ τὸ ποτήριον μετὰ τὸ
δειπνῆσαι λέγων· τοῦτο τὸ ποτήριον ἡ
καινὴ διαθήκη ἐστὶν ἐν τῷ ἐμῷ αἵματι·
τοῦτο ποιεῖτε, ὁσάκις ἐὰν πίνητε, εἰς
τὴν ἐμὴν ἀνάμνησιν.

2 Cor 3:1–6

Ἀρχόμεθα πάλιν ἑαυτοὺς συνιστάνειν; ἢ
μὴ χρῄζομεν ὥς τινες συστατικῶν ἐπιστο-
λῶν πρὸς ὑμᾶς ἢ ἐξ ὑμῶν; **2** ἡ ἐπιστολὴ
ἡμῶν ὑμεῖς ἐστε, ἐγγεγραμμένη ἐν ταῖς
καρδίαις ⸀ἡμῶν, γινωσκομένη καὶ ἀνα-
γινωσκομένη ὑπὸ πάντων ἀνθρώπων,
3 φανερούμενοι ὅτι ἐστὲ ἐπιστολὴ Χριστοῦ
διακονηθεῖσα ὑφ᾽ ἡμῶν, ἐγγεγραμμένη
οὐ μέλανι ἀλλὰ πνεύματι θεοῦ ζῶντος,
οὐκ ἐν πλαξὶν λιθίναις ἀλλ᾽ ἐν πλαξὶν
καρδίαις σαρκίναις. **4** Πεποίθησιν δὲ
τοιαύτην ἔχομεν διὰ τοῦ Χριστοῦ πρὸς
τὸν θεόν. **5** οὐχ ὅτι ἀφ᾽ ἑαυτῶν ἱκανοί
ἐσμεν λογίσασθαί τι ὡς ἐξ ἑαυτῶν, ἀλλ᾽
ἡ ἱκανότης ἡμῶν ἐκ τοῦ θεοῦ, **6** ὃς καὶ
ἱκάνωσεν ἡμᾶς διακόνους καινῆς δια-
θήκης, οὐ γράμματος ἀλλὰ πνεύματος·
τὸ γὰρ γράμμα ἀποκτέννει, τὸ δὲ πνεῦμα
ζῳοποιεῖ.

2 Cor 3:7–18

Εἰ δὲ ἡ διακονία τοῦ θανάτου ἐν γράμ-
μασιν ἐντετυπωμένη λίθοις ἐγενήθη ἐν
δόξῃ, ὥστε μὴ δύνασθαι ἀτενίσαι τοὺς
υἱοὺς Ἰσραὴλ εἰς τὸ πρόσωπον Μωϋσέως
διὰ τὴν δόξαν τοῦ προσώπου αὐτοῦ τὴν
καταργουμένην, **8** πῶς οὐχὶ μᾶλλον ἡ δια-
κονία τοῦ πνεύματος ἔσται ἐν δόξῃ; **9** εἰ
γὰρ τῇ διακονίᾳ τῆς κατακρίσεως δόξα,
πολλῷ μᾶλλον περισσεύει ἡ διακονία
τῆς δικαιοσύνης δόξῃ. **10** καὶ γὰρ οὐ
δεδόξασται τὸ δεδοξασμένον ἐν τούτῳ
τῷ μέρει εἵνεκεν τῆς ὑπερβαλλούσης
δόξης. **11** εἰ γὰρ τὸ καταργούμενον διὰ
δόξης, πολλῷ μᾶλλον τὸ μένον ἐν δόξῃ.
12 Ἔχοντες οὖν τοιαύτην ἐλπίδα πολλῇ
παρρησίᾳ χρώμεθα **13** καὶ οὐ καθάπερ
Μωϋσῆς ἐτίθει κάλυμμα ἐπὶ τὸ πρόσωπον
αὐτοῦ πρὸς τὸ μὴ ἀτενίσαι τοὺς υἱοὺς
Ἰσραὴλ εἰς τὸ τέλος τοῦ καταργουμένου.
14 ἀλλὰ ἐπωρώθη τὰ νοήματα αὐτῶν.
ἄχρι γὰρ τῆς σήμερον ἡμέρας τὸ αὐτὸ
κάλυμμα ἐπὶ τῇ ἀναγνώσει τῆς παλαιᾶς
διαθήκης μένει, μὴ ἀνακαλυπτόμενον
ὅτι ἐν Χριστῷ καταργεῖται· **15** ἀλλ᾽ ἕως
σήμερον ἡνίκα ἂν ἀναγινώσκηται Μω-
ϋσῆς, κάλυμμα ἐπὶ τὴν καρδίαν αὐτῶν

Gal 4:25 ***δε Αγαρ Σινα*** A B D] γαρ Αγαρ Σινα 33. 1881 *Byz* ¦ γαρ Σινα ℵ C 1739 ¦ δε Σινα 𝔓⁴⁶ **Gal 4:28** ***υμεις*** *et* εστε 𝔓⁴⁶ B D* 33. 1739. 1881] ημεις *et* εσμεν ℵ A C D² *Byz* **§ 43 1 Cor 11:24** ***υμων*** 𝔓⁴⁶ ℵ* A B C* 33. 1739*] *add.* κλωμενον ℵ² C³ D² 1739ᵐᵍ. 1881 *Byz* ¦ *add.* θρυπτομενον D* **2 Cor 3:2** ***ημων*** 𝔓⁴⁶ A B C D 1739 *Byz*] υμων ℵ 33. 1881

two sons, one by a slave woman and the other by a free woman. 23 One, the child of the slave, was born according to the flesh; the other, the child of the free woman, was born through the promise. 24 Now this is an allegory: these women are two covenants. One woman, in fact, is Hagar, from Mount Sinai, bearing children for slavery. 25 Now Hagar is Mount Sinai in Arabia[f] and corresponds to the present Jerusalem, for she is in slavery with her children. 26 But the other woman corresponds to the Jerusalem above; she is free, and she is our mother. 27 For it is written, "Rejoice, you childless one, you who bear no children, burst into song and shout, you who endure no birth pangs; for the children of the desolate woman are more numerous than the children of the one who is married." 28 Now you,[g] my friends, are children of the promise, like Isaac. 29 But just as at that time the child who was born according to the flesh persecuted the child who was born according to the Spirit, so it is now also. 30 But what does the scripture say? "Drive out the slave and her child; for the child of the slave will not share the inheritance with the child of the free woman." 31 So then, friends, we are children, not of the slave but of the free woman. **5** For freedom Christ has set us free. Stand firm, therefore, and do not submit again to a yoke of slavery.

Titus 2:14

He it is who gave himself for us that he might redeem us from all iniquity and purify for himself a people of his own who are zealous for good deeds.

Cf. Rom 3:24; 8:18–25; 1 Cor 1:30–31; 6:20; Gal 5:13–14.

43. The New Covenant

Rom 2:25–29

Circumcision indeed is of value if you obey the law; but if you break the law, your circumcision has become uncircumcision. 26 So, if those who are uncircumcised keep the requirements of the law, will not their uncircumcision be regarded as circumcision? 27 Then those who are physically uncircumcised but keep the law will condemn you that have the written code and circumcision but break the law. 28 For a person is not a Jew who is one outwardly, nor is true circumcision something external and physical. 29 Rather, a person is a Jew who is one inwardly, and real circumcision is a matter of the heart—it is by the Spirit and not by the written letter. Such a person receives praise not from others but from God.[a]

Rom 7:5–6

While we were living in the flesh, our sinful passions, aroused by the law, were at work in our members to bear fruit for death. 6 But now we are discharged from the law, dead to that which held us captive, so that we are slaves not under the old written code but in the new life of the Spirit.

Rom 8:3–4

For God has done what the law, weakened by the flesh, could not do: by sending his own Son in the likeness of sinful flesh, and to deal with sin, he condemned sin in the flesh, 4 so that the just requirement of the law might be fulfilled in us, who walk not according to the flesh but according to the Spirit.

1 Cor 11:23–25

For I received from the Lord what I also handed on to you, that the Lord Jesus on the night when he was betrayed took a loaf of bread, 24 and when he had given thanks, he broke it and said, "This is my body that is for[b] you. Do this in remembrance of me." 25 In the same way he took the cup also, after supper, saying, "This cup is the new covenant in my blood. Do this, as often as you drink it, in remembrance of me."

2 Cor 3:1–6

Are we beginning to commend ourselves again? Surely we do not need, as some do, letters of recommendation to you or from you, do we? 2 You yourselves are our letter, written on our[c] hearts, to be known and read by all; 3 and you show that you are a letter of Christ, prepared by us, written not with ink but with the Spirit of the living God, not on tablets of stone but on tablets of human hearts. 4 Such is the confidence that we have through Christ toward God. 5 Not that we are competent of ourselves to claim anything as coming from us; our competence is from God, 6 who has made us competent to be ministers of a new covenant, not of the letter but of the Spirit; for the letter kills, but the Spirit gives life.[d]

2 Cor 3:7–18

Now if the ministry of death, chiseled in letters on stone tablets, came in glory so that the people of Israel could not gaze at Moses' face because of the glory of his face, a glory now set aside, 8 how much more will the ministry of the Spirit come in glory? 9 For if there was glory in the ministry of condemnation, much more does the ministry of justification abound in glory! 10 Indeed, what once had glory has lost its glory because of the greater glory; 11 for if what was set aside came through glory, much more has the permanent come in glory! 12 Since, then, we have such a hope, we act with great boldness, 13 not like Moses, who put a veil over his face to keep the people of Israel from gazing at the end of the glory that was being set aside. 14 But their minds were hardened. Indeed, to this very day, when they hear the reading of the old covenant, that same veil is still there, since only in Christ is it set aside. 15 Indeed, to this very day whenever Moses is read, a veil

[f] **Gal 4:25** *Now Hagar is Mount Sinai in Arabia* Other ancient authorities read *For Sinai is a mountain in Arabia* [g] **Gal 4:28** *you* Other ancient authorities read *we* **§ 43** [a] **Rom 2:29** Translation differs from NRSV [b] **1 Cor 11:24** *is for* Other ancient authorities read *is broken for* [c] **2 Cor 3:2** *our* Other ancient authorities read *your* [d] **2 Cor 3:6** Translation differs from NRSV

κεῖται· **16** ἡνίκα δὲ ἐὰν ἐπιστρέψῃ πρὸς
κύριον, περιαιρεῖται τὸ κάλυμμα. **17** ὁ δὲ
κύριος τὸ πνεῦμά ἐστιν· οὗ δὲ τὸ πνεῦμα
κυρίου, ἐλευθερία. **18** ἡμεῖς δὲ πάντες
ἀνακεκαλυμμένῳ προσώπῳ τὴν δόξαν
κυρίου κατοπτριζόμενοι τὴν αὐτὴν εἰκόνα
μεταμορφούμεθα ἀπὸ δόξης εἰς δόξαν
καθάπερ ἀπὸ κυρίου πνεύματος.

Phil 3:3

ἡμεῖς γάρ ἐσμεν ἡ περιτομή, οἱ πνεύ-
ματι ⸀θεοῦ λατρεύοντες καὶ καυχώμε-
νοι ἐν Χριστῷ Ἰησοῦ καὶ οὐκ ἐν σαρκὶ
πεποιθότες

1 Thess 4:8

τοιγαροῦν ὁ ἀθετῶν οὐκ ἄνθρωπον ἀθε-
τεῖ ἀλλὰ τὸν θεὸν τὸν [καὶ] διδόντα τὸ
πνεῦμα αὐτοῦ τὸ ἅγιον εἰς ὑμᾶς.

Cf. Rom 2:14–16; 10:4–10; 11:26–27; Gal 4:21–31; Titus 2:11–14.

44. The Gift of the Spirit

Rom 5:5

ἡ δὲ ἐλπὶς οὐ καταισχύνει, ὅτι ἡ ἀγάπη τοῦ
θεοῦ ἐκκέχυται ἐν ταῖς καρδίαις ἡμῶν διὰ
πνεύματος ἁγίου τοῦ δοθέντος ἡμῖν.

Rom 8:9–11

Ὑμεῖς δὲ οὐκ ἐστὲ ἐν σαρκὶ ἀλλὰ ἐν πνεύ-
ματι, εἴπερ πνεῦμα θεοῦ οἰκεῖ ἐν ὑμῖν. εἰ
δέ τις πνεῦμα Χριστοῦ οὐκ ἔχει, οὗτος
οὐκ ἔστιν αὐτοῦ. **10** εἰ δὲ Χριστὸς ἐν ὑμῖν,
τὸ μὲν σῶμα νεκρὸν διὰ ἁμαρτίαν τὸ δὲ
πνεῦμα ζωὴ διὰ δικαιοσύνην. **11** εἰ δὲ τὸ
πνεῦμα τοῦ ἐγείραντος τὸν Ἰησοῦν ἐκ
νεκρῶν οἰκεῖ ἐν ὑμῖν, ὁ ἐγείρας ⸂Χριστὸν
ἐκ νεκρῶν⸃ ζῳοποιήσει καὶ τὰ θνητὰ
σώματα ὑμῶν διὰ ⸂τοῦ ἐνοικοῦντος
αὐτοῦ πνεύματος⸃ ἐν ὑμῖν.

Rom 8:12–17

Ἄρα οὖν, ἀδελφοί, ὀφειλέται ἐσμὲν
οὐ τῇ σαρκὶ τοῦ κατὰ σάρκα ζῆν, **13** εἰ
γὰρ κατὰ σάρκα ζῆτε, μέλλετε ἀποθνῄ-
σκειν· εἰ δὲ πνεύματι τὰς πράξεις τοῦ
σώματος θανατοῦτε, ζήσεσθε. **14** ὅσοι
γὰρ πνεύματι θεοῦ ἄγονται, οὗτοι υἱοὶ
θεοῦ εἰσιν. **15** οὐ γὰρ ἐλάβετε πνεῦμα
δουλείας πάλιν εἰς φόβον ἀλλὰ ἐλάβετε
πνεῦμα υἱοθεσίας ἐν ᾧ κράζομεν· αββα
ὁ πατήρ. **16** αὐτὸ τὸ πνεῦμα συμμαρτυ-
ρεῖ τῷ πνεύματι ἡμῶν ὅτι ἐσμὲν τέκνα
θεοῦ. **17** εἰ δὲ τέκνα, καὶ κληρονόμοι·
κληρονόμοι μὲν θεοῦ, συγκληρονόμοι
δὲ Χριστοῦ, εἴπερ συμπάσχομεν ἵνα καὶ
συνδοξασθῶμεν.

Rom 8:23

οὐ μόνον δέ, ἀλλὰ καὶ αὐτοὶ τὴν ἀπαρ-
χὴν τοῦ πνεύματος ἔχοντες, ἡμεῖς καὶ
αὐτοὶ ἐν ἑαυτοῖς στενάζομεν υἱοθεσίαν
ἀπεκδεχόμενοι, τὴν ἀπολύτρωσιν τοῦ
σώματος ἡμῶν.

1 Cor 2:10–16

ἡμῖν δὲ ἀπεκάλυψεν ὁ θεὸς διὰ τοῦ πνεύ-
ματος· τὸ γὰρ πνεῦμα πάντα ἐραυνᾷ,
καὶ τὰ βάθη τοῦ θεοῦ. **11** τίς γὰρ οἶδεν
ἀνθρώπων τὰ τοῦ ἀνθρώπου εἰ μὴ τὸ
πνεῦμα τοῦ ἀνθρώπου τὸ ἐν αὐτῷ; οὕτως
καὶ τὰ τοῦ θεοῦ οὐδεὶς ἔγνωκεν εἰ μὴ τὸ
πνεῦμα τοῦ θεοῦ. **12** ἡμεῖς δὲ οὐ τὸ πνεῦμα
τοῦ κόσμου ἐλάβομεν ἀλλὰ τὸ πνεῦμα
τὸ ἐκ τοῦ θεοῦ, ἵνα εἰδῶμεν τὰ ὑπὸ τοῦ
θεοῦ χαρισθέντα ἡμῖν· **13** ἃ καὶ λαλοῦμεν
οὐκ ἐν διδακτοῖς ἀνθρωπίνης σοφίας
λόγοις ἀλλ᾽ ἐν διδακτοῖς πνεύματος,
πνευματικοῖς πνευματικὰ συγκρίνον-
τες. **14** ψυχικὸς δὲ ἄνθρωπος οὐ δέχεται
τὰ τοῦ πνεύματος τοῦ θεοῦ· μωρία γὰρ
αὐτῷ ἐστιν καὶ οὐ δύναται γνῶναι, ὅτι
πνευματικῶς ἀνακρίνεται. **15** ὁ δὲ πνευ-
ματικὸς ἀνακρίνει [τὰ] πάντα, αὐτὸς δὲ
ὑπ᾽ οὐδενὸς ἀνακρίνεται. **16** τίς γὰρ ἔγνω
νοῦν κυρίου, ὃς συμβιβάσει αὐτόν; ἡμεῖς
δὲ νοῦν Χριστοῦ ἔχομεν.

1 Cor 3:16–17

Οὐκ οἴδατε ὅτι ναὸς θεοῦ ἐστε καὶ τὸ
πνεῦμα τοῦ θεοῦ οἰκεῖ ἐν ὑμῖν; **17** εἴ τις
τὸν ναὸν τοῦ θεοῦ φθείρει, φθερεῖ τοῦ-
τον ὁ θεός· ὁ γὰρ ναὸς τοῦ θεοῦ ἅγιός
ἐστιν, οἵτινές ἐστε ὑμεῖς.

1 Cor 6:19–20

ἢ οὐκ οἴδατε ὅτι τὸ σῶμα ὑμῶν ναὸς
τοῦ ἐν ὑμῖν ἁγίου πνεύματός ἐστιν οὗ
ἔχετε ἀπὸ θεοῦ, καὶ οὐκ ἐστὲ ἑαυτῶν;
20 ἠγοράσθητε γὰρ τιμῆς· δοξάσατε δὴ
τὸν θεὸν ἐν τῷ σώματι ὑμῶν.

1 Cor 12:12–13

Καθάπερ γὰρ τὸ σῶμα ἕν ἐστιν καὶ μέλη
πολλὰ ἔχει, πάντα δὲ τὰ μέλη τοῦ σώ-
ματος πολλὰ ὄντα ἕν ἐστιν σῶμα, οὕτως
καὶ ὁ Χριστός· **13** καὶ γὰρ ἐν ἑνὶ πνεύματι
ἡμεῖς πάντες εἰς ἓν σῶμα ἐβαπτίσθημεν,
εἴτε Ἰουδαῖοι εἴτε Ἕλληνες εἴτε δοῦλοι
εἴτε ἐλεύθεροι, καὶ πάντες ἓν πνεῦμα
ἐποτίσθημεν.

Gal 3:1–3

Ὦ ἀνόητοι Γαλάται, τίς ὑμᾶς ἐβάσκανεν,
οἷς κατ᾽ ὀφθαλμοὺς Ἰησοῦς Χριστὸς προ-
εγράφη ἐσταυρωμένος; **2** τοῦτο μόνον
θέλω μαθεῖν ἀφ᾽ ὑμῶν· ἐξ ἔργων νόμου
τὸ πνεῦμα ἐλάβετε ἢ ἐξ ἀκοῆς πίστεως;
3 οὕτως ἀνόητοί ἐστε, ἐναρξάμενοι πνεύ-
ματι νῦν σαρκὶ ἐπιτελεῖσθε;

Gal 3:13–14

Χριστὸς ἡμᾶς ἐξηγόρασεν ἐκ τῆς κατάρας
τοῦ νόμου γενόμενος ὑπὲρ ἡμῶν κατάρα,
ὅτι γέγραπται· ἐπικατάρατος πᾶς ὁ κρε-
μάμενος ἐπὶ ξύλου, **14** ἵνα εἰς τὰ ἔθνη ἡ
εὐλογία τοῦ Ἀβραὰμ γένηται ἐν Χριστῷ
Ἰησοῦ, ἵνα τὴν ἐπαγγελίαν τοῦ πνεύματος
λάβωμεν διὰ τῆς πίστεως.

Gal 4:6

Ὅτι δέ ἐστε υἱοί, ἐξαπέστειλεν ὁ θεὸς τὸ
πνεῦμα τοῦ υἱοῦ αὐτοῦ εἰς τὰς καρδίας
⸀ἡμῶν κρᾶζον· αββα ὁ πατήρ.

1 Thess 1:5–6

ὅτι τὸ εὐαγγέλιον ἡμῶν οὐκ ἐγενήθη
εἰς ὑμᾶς ἐν λόγῳ μόνον ἀλλὰ καὶ ἐν

Phil 3:3 ***θεου*** ℵ* A B C D^{2} 33. 1739. 1881 *Byz*] θεω ℵ^{2} D* ¦ *om.* 𝔓^{46} **§ 44** **Rom 8:11** ***Χριστον εκ νεκρων*** B D^{2}] τον Χ. εκ ν. ℵ^{2} 33 *Byz* ¦ Χ. Ιησουν εκ ν. D* ¦ εκ ν. Χ. Ιησουν ℵ* A (C I. X.) 1739. 1881 • ***του ενοικουντος αυτου πνευματος*** ℵ A C$^{(*)}$] το ενοικουν αυτου πνευμα B D 33. 1739. 1881 *Byz* **Gal 4:6** ***ημων*** 𝔓^{46} ℵ A B C D* 1739. 1881] υμων D^{2} 33 *Byz*

lies over their minds; [16] but when one turns to the Lord, the veil is removed. [17] Now the Lord is the Spirit, and where the Spirit of the Lord is, there is freedom. [18] And all of us, with unveiled faces, seeing the glory of the Lord as though reflected in a mirror, are being transformed into the same image from one degree of glory to another; for this comes from the Lord, the Spirit.

Phil 3:3

For it is we who are the circumcision, who worship in the Spirit of God[e] and boast in Christ Jesus and have no confidence in the flesh

1 Thess 4:8

Therefore whoever rejects this rejects not human authority but God, who also gives his Holy Spirit to you.

Cf. Rom 2:14–16; 10:4–10; 11:26–27; Gal 4:21–31; Titus 2:11–14.

44. The Gift of the Spirit

Rom 5:5

and hope does not disappoint us, because God's love has been poured into our hearts through the Holy Spirit that has been given to us.

Rom 8:9–11

But you are not in the flesh; you are in the Spirit, since the Spirit of God dwells in you. Anyone who does not have the Spirit of Christ does not belong to him. [10] But if Christ is in you, though the body is dead because of sin, the Spirit is life because of righteousness. [11] If the Spirit of him who raised Jesus from the dead dwells in you, he who raised Christ[a] from the dead will give life to your mortal bodies also through[b] his Spirit that dwells in you.

Rom 8:12–17

So then, brothers and sisters, we are debtors, not to the flesh, to live according to the flesh— [13] for if you live according to the flesh, you will die; but if by the Spirit you put to death the deeds of the body, you will live. [14] For all who are led by the Spirit of God are children of God. [15] For you did not receive a spirit of slavery to fall back into fear, but you have received a spirit of adoption. When we cry, "Abba! Father!" [16] it is that very Spirit bearing witness with our spirit that we are children of God, [17] and if children, then heirs, heirs of God and joint heirs with Christ—if, in fact, we suffer with him so that we may also be glorified with him.

Rom 8:23

and not only the creation, but we ourselves, who have the first fruits of the Spirit, groan inwardly while we wait for adoption, the redemption of our bodies.

1 Cor 2:10–16

these things God has revealed to us through the Spirit; for the Spirit searches everything, even the depths of God. [11] For what human being knows what is truly human except the human spirit that is within? So also no one comprehends what is truly God's except the Spirit of God. [12] Now we have received not the spirit of the world, but the Spirit that is from God, so that we may understand the gifts bestowed on us by God. [13] And we speak of these things in words not taught by human wisdom but taught by the Spirit, interpreting spiritual things to those who are spiritual. [14] Those who are unspiritual do not receive the gifts of God's Spirit, for they are foolishness to them, and they are unable to understand them because they are spiritually discerned. [15] Those who are spiritual discern all things, and they are themselves subject to no one else's scrutiny. [16] "For who has known the mind of the Lord so as to instruct him?" But we have the mind of Christ.

1 Cor 3:16–17

Do you not know that you are God's temple and that God's Spirit dwells in you? [17] If anyone destroys God's temple, God will destroy that person. For God's temple is holy, and you are that temple.

1 Cor 6:19–20

Or do you not know that your body is a temple of the Holy Spirit within you, which you have from God, and that you are not your own? [20] For you were bought with a price; therefore glorify God in your body.

1 Cor 12:12–13

For just as the body is one and has many members, and all the members of the body, though many, are one body, so it is with Christ. [13] For in the one Spirit we were all baptized into one body—Jews or Greeks, slaves or free—and we were all made to drink of one Spirit.

Gal 3:1–3

You foolish Galatians! Who has bewitched you? It was before your eyes that Jesus Christ was publicly exhibited as crucified! [2] The only thing I want to learn from you is this: Did you receive the Spirit by doing the works of the law or by believing what you heard? [3] Are you so foolish? Having started with the Spirit, are you now ending with the flesh?

Gal 3:13–14

Christ redeemed us from the curse of the law by becoming a curse for us—for it is written, "Cursed is everyone who hangs on a tree"— [14] in order that in Christ Jesus the blessing of Abraham might come to the Gentiles, so that we might receive the promise of the Spirit through faith.

Gal 4:6

And because you are children, God has sent the Spirit of his Son into our[c] hearts, crying, "Abba! Father!"

1 Thess 1:5–6

because our message of the gospel came to you not in word only, but also

[e] **Phil 3:3** ***worship in the Spirit of God*** Other ancient authorities read *worship God in the Spirit* **§ 44** [a] **Rom 8:11** ***Christ*** Other ancient authorities read *the Christ* or *Christ Jesus* or *Jesus Christ* [b] **Rom 8:11** ***through*** Other ancient authorities read *on account of* [c] **Gal 4:6** ***our*** Other ancient authorities read *your*

δυνάμει καὶ ἐν πνεύματι ἁγίῳ καὶ [ἐν] πληροφορίᾳ πολλῇ, καθὼς οἴδατε οἷοι ἐγενήθημεν [ἐν] ὑμῖν δι᾽ ὑμᾶς. 6 Καὶ ὑμεῖς μιμηταὶ ἡμῶν ἐγενήθητε καὶ τοῦ κυρίου, δεξάμενοι τὸν λόγον ἐν θλίψει πολλῇ μετὰ χαρᾶς πνεύματος ἁγίου

1 Thess 4:8

τοιγαροῦν ὁ ἀθετῶν οὐκ ἄνθρωπον ἀθετεῖ ἀλλὰ τὸν θεὸν τὸν [καὶ] διδόντα τὸ πνεῦμα αὐτοῦ τὸ ἅγιον εἰς ὑμᾶς.

2 Tim 1:7–8

οὐ γὰρ ἔδωκεν ἡμῖν ὁ θεὸς πνεῦμα δειλίας ἀλλὰ δυνάμεως καὶ ἀγάπης καὶ σωφρονισμοῦ. 8 μὴ οὖν ἐπαισχυνθῇς τὸ μαρτύριον τοῦ κυρίου ἡμῶν μηδὲ ἐμὲ τὸν δέσμιον αὐτοῦ, ἀλλὰ συγκακοπάθησον τῷ εὐαγγελίῳ κατὰ δύναμιν θεοῦ

2 Tim 1:14

τὴν καλὴν παραθήκην φύλαξον διὰ πνεύματος ἁγίου τοῦ ἐνοικοῦντος ἐν ἡμῖν.

Titus 3:4–7

ὅτε δὲ ἡ χρηστότης καὶ ἡ φιλανθρωπία ἐπεφάνη τοῦ σωτῆρος ἡμῶν θεοῦ,
5 οὐκ ἐξ ἔργων τῶν ἐν δικαιοσύνῃ ἃ ἐποιήσαμεν ἡμεῖς ἀλλὰ κατὰ τὸ αὐτοῦ ἔλεος ἔσωσεν ἡμᾶς διὰ λουτροῦ παλιγγενεσίας καὶ ἀνακαινώσεως πνεύματος ἁγίου, 6 οὗ ἐξέχεεν ἐφ᾽ ἡμᾶς πλουσίως διὰ Ἰησοῦ Χριστοῦ τοῦ σωτῆρος ἡμῶν,
7 ἵνα δικαιωθέντες τῇ ἐκείνου χάριτι κληρονόμοι γενηθῶμεν κατ᾽ ἐλπίδα ζωῆς αἰωνίου.

Acts 19:1–6

Ἐγένετο δὲ ἐν τῷ τὸν Ἀπολλῶ εἶναι ἐν Κορίνθῳ Παῦλον διελθόντα τὰ ἀνωτερικὰ μέρη [κατ]ελθεῖν εἰς Ἔφεσον καὶ εὑρεῖν τινας μαθητὰς 2 εἶπέν τε πρὸς αὐτούς· εἰ πνεῦμα ἅγιον ἐλάβετε πιστεύσαντες; οἱ δὲ πρὸς αὐτόν· ἀλλ᾽ οὐδ᾽ εἰ πνεῦμα ἅγιον ἔστιν ἠκούσαμεν. 3 εἶπέν τε· εἰς τί οὖν ἐβαπτίσθητε; οἱ δὲ εἶπαν· εἰς τὸ Ἰωάννου βάπτισμα. 4 εἶπεν δὲ Παῦλος· Ἰωάννης ἐβάπτισεν βάπτισμα μετανοίας τῷ λαῷ λέγων εἰς τὸν ἐρχόμενον μετ᾽ αὐτὸν ἵνα πιστεύσωσιν, τοῦτ᾽ ἔστιν εἰς τὸν Ἰησοῦν.
5 ἀκούσαντες δὲ ἐβαπτίσθησαν εἰς τὸ ὄνομα τοῦ κυρίου Ἰησοῦ, 6 καὶ ἐπιθέντος αὐτοῖς τοῦ Παύλου [τὰς] χεῖρας ἦλθε τὸ πνεῦμα τὸ ἅγιον ἐπ᾽ αὐτούς, ἐλάλουν τε γλώσσαις καὶ ἐπροφήτευον.

See also § 43 The New Covenant; § 45 The Temple of God; § 47 The Spirit the Guarantee of the Resurrection; § 48 Life through Christ Jesus; § 52 The Flesh and the Spirit; and § 76 The Supply of the Spirit.

45. *The Temple of God*

1 Cor 3:16–17

Οὐκ οἴδατε ὅτι ναὸς θεοῦ ἐστε καὶ τὸ πνεῦμα τοῦ θεοῦ οἰκεῖ ἐν ὑμῖν; 17 εἴ τις τὸν ναὸν τοῦ θεοῦ φθείρει, φθερεῖ τοῦτον ὁ θεός· ὁ γὰρ ναὸς τοῦ θεοῦ ἅγιός ἐστιν, οἵτινές ἐστε ὑμεῖς.

1 Cor 6:19–20

ἢ οὐκ οἴδατε ὅτι τὸ σῶμα ὑμῶν ναὸς τοῦ ἐν ὑμῖν ἁγίου πνεύματός ἐστιν οὗ ἔχετε ἀπὸ θεοῦ, καὶ οὐκ ἐστὲ ἑαυτῶν;
20 ἠγοράσθητε γὰρ τιμῆς· δοξάσατε δὴ τὸν θεὸν ἐν τῷ σώματι ὑμῶν.

2 Cor 6:14–7:1

Μὴ γίνεσθε ἑτεροζυγοῦντες ἀπίστοις· τίς γὰρ μετοχὴ δικαιοσύνῃ καὶ ἀνομίᾳ, ἢ τίς κοινωνία φωτὶ πρὸς σκότος; 15 τίς δὲ συμφώνησις Χριστοῦ πρὸς Βελιάρ, ἢ τίς μερὶς πιστῷ μετὰ ἀπίστου; 16 τίς δὲ συγκατάθεσις ναῷ θεοῦ μετὰ εἰδώλων; ⸂ἡμεῖς γὰρ ναὸς θεοῦ ἐσμεν⸃ ζῶντος, καθὼς εἶπεν ὁ θεὸς ὅτι ἐνοικήσω ἐν αὐτοῖς καὶ ἐμπεριπατήσω καὶ ἔσομαι αὐτῶν θεὸς καὶ αὐτοὶ ἔσονταί μου λαός. 17 διὸ ἐξέλθατε ἐκ μέσου αὐτῶν καὶ ἀφορίσθητε, λέγει κύριος, καὶ ἀκαθάρτου μὴ ἅπτεσθε· κἀγὼ εἰσδέξομαι ὑμᾶς 18 καὶ ἔσομαι ὑμῖν εἰς πατέρα καὶ ὑμεῖς ἔσεσθέ μοι εἰς υἱοὺς καὶ θυγατέρας, λέγει κύριος παντοκράτωρ. 7 Ταύτας οὖν ἔχοντες τὰς ἐπαγγελίας, ἀγαπητοί, καθαρίσωμεν ἑαυτοὺς ἀπὸ παντὸς μολυσμοῦ σαρκὸς καὶ πνεύματος, ἐπιτελοῦντες ἁγιωσύνην ἐν φόβῳ θεοῦ.

Eph 2:19–22

Ἄρα οὖν οὐκέτι ἐστὲ ξένοι καὶ πάροικοι ἀλλὰ ἐστὲ συμπολῖται τῶν ἁγίων καὶ οἰκεῖοι τοῦ θεοῦ, 20 ἐποικοδομηθέντες ἐπὶ τῷ θεμελίῳ τῶν ἀποστόλων καὶ προφητῶν, ὄντος ἀκρογωνιαίου αὐτοῦ Χριστοῦ Ἰησοῦ, 21 ἐν ᾧ πᾶσα οἰκοδομὴ συναρμολογουμένη αὔξει εἰς ναὸν ἅγιον ἐν κυρίῳ, 22 ἐν ᾧ καὶ ὑμεῖς συνοικοδομεῖσθε εἰς κατοικητήριον τοῦ θεοῦ ἐν πνεύματι.

1 Tim 3:14–15

Ταῦτά σοι γράφω ἐλπίζων ἐλθεῖν πρὸς σὲ ἐν τάχει· 15 ἐὰν δὲ βραδύνω, ἵνα εἰδῇς πῶς δεῖ ἐν οἴκῳ θεοῦ ἀναστρέφεσθαι, ἥτις ἐστὶν ἐκκλησία θεοῦ ζῶντος, στῦλος καὶ ἑδραίωμα τῆς ἀληθείας.

Cf. Rom 8:9–11; 2 Thess 2:3–4.

46. *Access to God's Presence*

Rom 5:1–2

Δικαιωθέντες οὖν ἐκ πίστεως εἰρήνην ⸀ἔχομεν πρὸς τὸν θεὸν διὰ τοῦ κυρίου ἡμῶν Ἰησοῦ Χριστοῦ 2 δι᾽ οὗ καὶ τὴν προσαγωγὴν ἐσχήκαμεν ⸂[τῇ πίστει]⸃ εἰς τὴν χάριν ταύτην ἐν ᾗ ἑστήκαμεν καὶ καυχώμεθα ἐπ᾽ ἐλπίδι τῆς δόξης τοῦ θεοῦ.

§ 45 **2 Cor 6:16** ***ημεις γαρ ναος θεου εσμεν*** B D* 33. 1881] υμεις γαρ ναος θεου εστε 𝔓[46] (א[2]) C D[2] *Byz* ¦ ημεις γαρ ναοι θεου εσμεν א* 1739 **§ 46** **Rom 5:1** ***εχομεν*** א[1] B[2] 0220[vid]. 1739[c]. 1881] εχωμεν א* A B* C D 33. 1739* **Rom 5:2** ***τη πιστει*** א[*.2] C 33. 1739. 1881 *Byz*] εν τη πιστει א[1] A ¦ *om*. B D 0220

in power and in the Holy Spirit and with full conviction; just as you know what kind of persons we proved to be among you for your sake. **6** And you became imitators of us and of the Lord, for in spite of persecution you received the word with joy inspired by the Holy Spirit

1 Thess 4:8

Therefore whoever rejects this rejects not human authority but God, who also gives his Holy Spirit to you.

2 Tim 1:7–8

for God did not give us a spirit of cowardice, but rather a spirit of power and of love and of self-discipline. **8** Do not be ashamed, then, of the testimony about our Lord or of me his prisoner, but join with me in suffering for the gospel, relying on the power of God

2 Tim 1:14

Guard the good treasure entrusted to you, with the help of the Holy Spirit living in us.

Titus 3:4–7

But when the goodness and loving kindness of God our Savior appeared, **5** he saved us, not because of any works of righteousness that we had done, but according to his mercy, through the water of rebirth and renewal by the Holy Spirit. **6** This Spirit he poured out on us richly through Jesus Christ our Savior, **7** so that, having been justified by his grace, we might become heirs according to the hope of eternal life.

Acts 19:1–6

While Apollos was in Corinth, Paul passed through the interior regions and came to Ephesus, where he found some disciples. **2** He said to them, "Did you receive the Holy Spirit when you became believers?" They replied, "No, we have not even heard that there is a Holy Spirit." **3** Then he said, "Into what then were you baptized?" They answered, "Into John's baptism." **4** Paul said, "John baptized with the baptism of repentance, telling the people to believe in the one who was to come after him, that is, in Jesus." **5** On hearing this, they were baptized in the name of the Lord Jesus. **6** When Paul had laid his hands on them, the Holy Spirit came upon them, and they spoke in tongues and prophesied

See also § 43 The New Covenant; § 45 The Temple of God; § 47 The Spirit and the Guarantee of the Resurrection; § 48 Life through Jesus Christ; § 52 The Flesh and the Spirit; and § 76 The Supply of the Spirit.

45. The Temple of God

1 Cor 3:16–17

Do you not know that you are God's temple and that God's Spirit dwells in you? **17** If anyone destroys God's temple, God will destroy that person. For God's temple is holy, and you are that temple.

1 Cor 6:19–20

Or do you not know that your body is a temple of the Holy Spirit within you, which you have from God, and that you are not your own? **20** For you were bought with a price; therefore glorify God in your body.

2 Cor 6:14–7:1

Do not be mismatched with unbelievers. For what partnership is there between righteousness and lawlessness? Or what fellowship is there between light and darkness? **15** What agreement does Christ have with Beliar? Or what does a believer share with an unbeliever? **16** What agreement has the temple of God with idols? For we[a] are the temple of the living God; as God said, "I will live in them and walk among them, and I will be their God, and they shall be my people. **17** Therefore come out from them, and be separate from them, says the Lord, and touch nothing unclean; then I will welcome you, **18** and I will be your father, and you shall be my sons and daughters, says the Lord Almighty." **7** Since we have these promises, beloved, let us cleanse ourselves from every defilement of body and of spirit, making holiness perfect in the fear of God.

Eph 2:19–22

So then you are no longer strangers and aliens, but you are citizens with the saints and also members of the household of God, **20** built upon the foundation of the apostles and prophets, with Christ Jesus himself as the cornerstone. **21** In him the whole structure is joined together and grows into a holy temple in the Lord; **22** in whom you also are built together spiritually into a dwelling place for God.

1 Tim 3:14–15

I hope to come to you soon, but I am writing these instructions to you so that, **15** if I am delayed, you may know how one ought to behave in the household of God, which is the church of the living God, the pillar and bulwark of the truth.

Cf. Rom 8:9–11; 2 Thess 2:3–4.

46. Access to God's Presence

Rom 5:1–2

Therefore, since we are justified by faith, we[a] have peace with God through our Lord Jesus Christ, **2** through whom we have obtained access[b] to this grace in which we stand; and we boast in our hope of sharing the glory of God.

§ 45 [a] **2 Cor 6:16** *we* Other ancient authorities read *you* **§ 46** [a] **Rom 5:1** *we* Other ancient authorities read *let us* [b] **Rom 5:2** *obtained access* Other ancient authorities add *by faith*

2 Cor 4:14

εἰδότες ὅτι ὁ ἐγείρας τὸν ⸀κύριον Ἰησοῦν καὶ ἡμᾶς σὺν Ἰησοῦ ἐγερεῖ καὶ παραστήσει σὺν ὑμῖν.

Eph 2:17–18

καὶ ἐλθὼν εὐηγγελίσατο εἰρήνην ὑμῖν τοῖς μακρὰν καὶ εἰρήνην τοῖς ἐγγύς· **18** ὅτι δι᾽ αὐτοῦ ἔχομεν τὴν προσαγωγὴν οἱ ἀμφότεροι ἐν ἑνὶ πνεύματι πρὸς τὸν πατέρα.

Eph 3:11–12

κατὰ πρόθεσιν τῶν αἰώνων ἣν ἐποίησεν ἐν τῷ Χριστῷ Ἰησοῦ τῷ κυρίῳ ἡμῶν, **12** ἐν ᾧ ἔχομεν τὴν παρρησίαν καὶ προσαγωγὴν ἐν πεποιθήσει διὰ τῆς πίστεως αὐτοῦ.

Col 1:22

νυνὶ δὲ ⸀ἀποκατήλλαξεν ἐν τῷ σώματι τῆς σαρκὸς αὐτοῦ διὰ τοῦ θανάτου παραστῆσαι ὑμᾶς ἁγίους καὶ ἀμώμους καὶ ἀνεγκλήτους κατενώπιον αὐτοῦ

Cf. Rom 14:10–12; 2 Cor 11:2; Eph 5:25–27; Col 1:28; 1 Thess 2:19–20; 3:13.

See also § 45 The Temple of God.

47. The Spirit the Guarantee of the Resurrection

Rom 8:9–11

Ὑμεῖς δὲ οὐκ ἐστὲ ἐν σαρκὶ ἀλλὰ ἐν πνεύματι, εἴπερ πνεῦμα θεοῦ οἰκεῖ ἐν ὑμῖν. εἰ δέ τις πνεῦμα Χριστοῦ οὐκ ἔχει, οὗτος οὐκ ἔστιν αὐτοῦ. **10** εἰ δὲ Χριστὸς ἐν ὑμῖν, τὸ μὲν σῶμα νεκρὸν διὰ ἁμαρτίαν τὸ δὲ πνεῦμα ζωὴ διὰ δικαιοσύνην. **11** εἰ δὲ τὸ πνεῦμα τοῦ ἐγείραντος τὸν Ἰησοῦν ἐκ νεκρῶν οἰκεῖ ἐν ὑμῖν, ὁ ἐγείρας ⸂Χριστὸν ἐκ νεκρῶν⸃ ζῳοποιήσει καὶ τὰ θνητὰ σώματα ὑμῶν διὰ ⸂τοῦ ἐνοικοῦντος αὐτοῦ πνεύματος⸃ ἐν ὑμῖν.

Rom 8:18–25

Λογίζομαι γὰρ ὅτι οὐκ ἄξια τὰ παθήματα τοῦ νῦν καιροῦ πρὸς τὴν μέλλουσαν δόξαν ἀποκαλυφθῆναι εἰς ἡμᾶς. **19** ἡ γὰρ ἀποκαραδοκία τῆς κτίσεως τὴν ἀποκάλυψιν τῶν υἱῶν τοῦ θεοῦ ἀπεκδέχεται. **20** τῇ γὰρ ματαιότητι ἡ κτίσις ὑπετάγη, οὐχ ἑκοῦσα ἀλλὰ διὰ τὸν ὑποτάξαντα, ἐφ᾽ ἑλπίδι **21** ὅτι καὶ αὐτὴ ἡ κτίσις ἐλευθερωθήσεται ἀπὸ τῆς δουλείας τῆς φθορᾶς εἰς τὴν ἐλευθερίαν τῆς δόξης τῶν τέκνων τοῦ θεοῦ. **22** οἴδαμεν γὰρ ὅτι πᾶσα ἡ κτίσις συστενάζει καὶ συνωδίνει ἄχρι τοῦ νῦν· **23** οὐ μόνον δέ, ἀλλὰ καὶ αὐτοὶ τὴν ἀπαρχὴν τοῦ πνεύματος ἔχοντες, ἡμεῖς καὶ αὐτοὶ ἐν ἑαυτοῖς στενάζομεν υἱοθεσίαν ἀπεκδεχόμενοι, τὴν ἀπολύτρωσιν τοῦ σώματος ἡμῶν. **24** τῇ γὰρ ἐλπίδι ἐσώθημεν· ἐλπὶς δὲ βλεπομένη οὐκ ἔστιν ἐλπίς· ὃ γὰρ βλέπει τίς ⸀ἐλπίζει; **25** εἰ δὲ ὃ οὐ βλέπομεν ἐλπίζομεν, δι᾽ ὑπομονῆς ἀπεκδεχόμεθα.

2 Cor 1:18–22

πιστὸς δὲ ὁ θεὸς ὅτι ὁ λόγος ἡμῶν ὁ πρὸς ὑμᾶς οὐκ ἔστιν ναὶ καὶ οὔ. **19** ὁ τοῦ θεοῦ γὰρ υἱὸς Ἰησοῦς Χριστὸς ὁ ἐν ὑμῖν δι᾽ ἡμῶν κηρυχθείς, δι᾽ ἐμοῦ καὶ Σιλουανοῦ καὶ Τιμοθέου, οὐκ ἐγένετο ναὶ καὶ οὒ ἀλλὰ ναὶ ἐν αὐτῷ γέγονεν. **20** ὅσαι γὰρ ἐπαγγελίαι θεοῦ, ἐν αὐτῷ τὸ ναί· διὸ καὶ δι᾽ αὐτοῦ τὸ ἀμὴν τῷ θεῷ πρὸς δόξαν δι᾽ ἡμῶν. **21** ὁ δὲ βεβαιῶν ἡμᾶς σὺν ὑμῖν εἰς Χριστὸν καὶ χρίσας ἡμᾶς θεός, **22** ὁ καὶ σφραγισάμενος ἡμᾶς καὶ δοὺς τὸν ἀρραβῶνα τοῦ πνεύματος ἐν ταῖς καρδίαις ἡμῶν.

2 Cor 5:1–5

Οἴδαμεν γὰρ ὅτι ἐὰν ἡ ἐπίγειος ἡμῶν οἰκία τοῦ σκήνους καταλυθῇ, οἰκοδομὴν ἐκ θεοῦ ἔχομεν, οἰκίαν ἀχειροποίητον αἰώνιον ἐν τοῖς οὐρανοῖς. **2** καὶ γὰρ ἐν τούτῳ στενάζομεν τὸ οἰκητήριον ἡμῶν τὸ ἐξ οὐρανοῦ ἐπενδύσασθαι ἐπιποθοῦντες, **3** εἴ γε καὶ ⸀ἐκδυσάμενοι οὐ γυμνοὶ εὑρεθησόμεθα. **4** καὶ γὰρ οἱ ὄντες ἐν τῷ σκήνει στενάζομεν βαρούμενοι, ἐφ᾽ ᾧ οὐ θέλομεν ἐκδύσασθαι ἀλλ᾽ ἐπενδύσασθαι, ἵνα καταποθῇ τὸ θνητὸν ὑπὸ τῆς ζωῆς. **5** ὁ δὲ κατεργασάμενος ἡμᾶς εἰς αὐτὸ τοῦτο θεός, ὁ δοὺς ἡμῖν τὸν ἀρραβῶνα τοῦ πνεύματος.

Gal 6:7–8

Μὴ πλανᾶσθε, θεὸς οὐ μυκτηρίζεται. ὃ γὰρ ἐὰν σπείρῃ ἄνθρωπος, τοῦτο καὶ θερίσει· **8** ὅτι ὁ σπείρων εἰς τὴν σάρκα ἑαυτοῦ ἐκ τῆς σαρκὸς θερίσει φθοράν, ὁ δὲ σπείρων εἰς τὸ πνεῦμα ἐκ τοῦ πνεύματος θερίσει ζωὴν αἰώνιον.

Eph 1:13–14

Ἐν ᾧ καὶ ὑμεῖς ἀκούσαντες τὸν λόγον τῆς ἀληθείας, τὸ εὐαγγέλιον τῆς σωτηρίας ὑμῶν, ἐν ᾧ καὶ πιστεύσαντες ἐσφραγίσθητε τῷ πνεύματι τῆς ἐπαγγελίας τῷ ἁγίῳ, **14** ⸀ὅ ἐστιν ἀρραβὼν τῆς κληρονομίας ἡμῶν, εἰς ἀπολύτρωσιν τῆς περιποιήσεως, εἰς ἔπαινον τῆς δόξης αὐτοῦ.

Eph 4:30

καὶ μὴ λυπεῖτε τὸ πνεῦμα τὸ ἅγιον τοῦ θεοῦ, ἐν ᾧ ἐσφραγίσθητε εἰς ἡμέραν ἀπολυτρώσεως.

Col 1:27

οἷς ἠθέλησεν ὁ θεὸς γνωρίσαι τί τὸ πλοῦτος τῆς δόξης τοῦ μυστηρίου τούτου ἐν τοῖς ἔθνεσιν, ὅ ἐστιν Χριστὸς ἐν ὑμῖν, ἡ ἐλπὶς τῆς δόξης

See also § 89 The Resurrection of the Body; § 91 The Renewal of Creation.

2 Cor 4:14 ***κυριον*** ℵ C D 1881 *Byz*] *om.* 𝔓46 B (33) (1739) **Col 1:22** ***αποκατηλλαξεν*** ℵ A C D² 048. 1739. 1881 *Byz*] αποκατηλλαγητε (𝔓46) B ¦ αποκαταλλαγεντες D* ¦ αποκατηλλακται 33 **§ 47 Rom 8:11** ***Χριστον εκ νεκρων*** B D²] τον Χ. εκ ν. ℵ² 33 *Byz* ¦ Χ. Ιησουν εκ ν. D* ¦ εκ ν. Χ. Ιησουν ℵ* A (C Ι. Χ.) 1739. 1881 • ***του ενοικουντος αυτου πνευματος*** ℵ A C(*)] το ενοικουν αυτου πνευμα B D 33. 1739. 1881 *Byz* **Rom 8:24** ***ελπιζει*** 𝔓46 ℵ² B C D 33. 1739*. 1881 *Byz*] υπομενει ℵ* A 1739mg **2 Cor 5:3** ***εκδυσαμενοι*** D*.c] ενδυσαμενοι 𝔓46 ℵ B C D² 33. 1739. 1881 *Byz* **Eph 1:14** ***ὅ*** 𝔓46 A B 1739. 1881] ος ℵ D 33 *Byz*

2 Cor 4:14
because we know that the one who raised the Lord[c] Jesus will raise us also with Jesus, and will bring us with you into his presence.

Eph 2:17–18
So he came and proclaimed peace to
you who were far off and peace to those
who were near; 18 for through him both
of us have access in one Spirit to the
Father.

Eph 3:11–12
This was in accordance with the eter-
nal purpose that he has carried out in
Christ Jesus our Lord, 12 in whom we
have access to God in boldness and
confidence through faith in him.

Col 1:22
he has now reconciled[d] in his fleshly body through death, so as to present you holy and blameless and irreproachable before him

Cf. Rom 14:10–12; 2 Cor 11:2; Eph 5:25–27; Col 1:28; 1 Thess 2:19–20; 3:13.

See also § 45 The Temple of God.

47. The Spirit the Guarantee of the Resurrection

Rom 8:9–11
But you are not in the flesh; you are
in the Spirit, since the Spirit of God
dwells in you. Anyone who does not
have the Spirit of Christ does not be-
long to him. 10 But if Christ is in you,
though the body is dead because of
sin, the Spirit is life because of righ-
teousness. 11 If the Spirit of him who
raised Jesus from the dead dwells in
you, he who raised Christ[a] from the
dead will give life to your mortal bod-
ies also through[b] his Spirit that dwells
in you.

Rom 8:18–25
I consider that the sufferings of this
present time are not worth comparing
with the glory about to be revealed
to us. 19 For the creation waits with
eager longing for the revealing of the
children of God; 20 for the creation
was subjected to futility, not of its
own will but by the will of the one
who subjected it, in hope 21 that the
creation itself will be set free from its
bondage to decay and will obtain the
freedom of the glory of the children
of God. 22 We know that the whole
creation has been groaning in labor
pains until now; 23 and not only the
creation, but we ourselves, who have
the first fruits of the Spirit, groan in-
wardly while we wait for adoption,
the redemption of our bodies. 24 For
in hope we were saved. Now hope that
is seen is not hope. For who hopes[c]
for what is seen? 25 But if we hope for
what we do not see, we wait for it with
patience.

2 Cor 1:18–22
As surely as God is faithful, our word
to you has not been "Yes and No."
19 For the Son of God, Jesus Christ,
whom we proclaimed among you,
Silvanus and Timothy and I, was
not "Yes and No"; but in him it is
always "Yes." 20 For in him every one
of God's promises is a "Yes." For this
reason it is through him that we say
the "Amen," to the glory of God.
21 But it is God who establishes us
with you in Christ and has anointed
us, 22 by putting his seal on us and
giving us his Spirit in our hearts as a
first installment.

2 Cor 5:1–5
For we know that if the earthly tent we
live in is destroyed, we have a build-
ing from God, a house not made
with hands, eternal in the heavens.
2 For in this tent we groan, longing
to be clothed with our dwelling from
heaven— 3 if indeed, when we have
put it on[d] we will not be found naked.[e]
4 For while we are still in this tent, we
groan under our burden, because we
wish not to be unclothed but to be
further clothed, so that what is mortal
may be swallowed up by life. 5 He who
has prepared us for this very thing is
God, who has given us the Spirit as
a guarantee.

Gal 6:7–8
Do not be deceived; God is not mocked,
for you reap whatever you sow. 8 If you
sow to your own flesh, you will reap
corruption from the flesh; but if you
sow to the Spirit, you will reap eternal
life from the Spirit.

Eph 1:13–14
In him you also, when you had heard
the word of truth, the gospel of your
salvation, and had believed in him, were
marked with the seal of the promised
Holy Spirit; 14 this[f] is the pledge of
our inheritance toward redemption as
God's own people, to the praise of his
glory.

Eph 4:30
And do not grieve the Holy Spirit of God, with which you were marked with a seal for the day of redemption.

Col 1:27
To them God chose to make known how great among the Gentiles are the riches of the glory of this mystery, which is Christ in you, the hope of glory.

See also § 89 The Resurrection of the Body; § 91 The Renewal of Creation.

[c] **2 Cor 4:14** ***the Lord*** Other ancient authorities lack *the Lord* [d] **Col 1:22** ***he has now reconciled*** Other ancient authorities read *you have now been reconciled* **§ 47** [a] **Rom 8:11** ***Christ*** Other ancient authorities read *the Christ* or *Christ Jesus* or *Jesus Christ* [b] **Rom 8:11** ***through*** Other ancient authorities read *on account of* [c] **Rom 8:24** ***hopes*** Other ancient authorities read *awaits* [d] **2 Cor 5:3** ***put it on*** A few ancient authorities read *taken it off* [e] **2 Cor 5:2–3** Translation differs from NRSV [f] **Eph 1:14** ***this*** Other ancient authorities read *who*

48. Life through Christ Jesus

Rom 5:17–21

εἰ γὰρ τῷ τοῦ ἑνὸς παραπτώματι ὁ θάνατος ἐβασίλευσεν διὰ τοῦ ἑνός, πολλῷ μᾶλλον οἱ τὴν περισσείαν τῆς χάριτος καὶ τῆς δωρεᾶς τῆς δικαιοσύνης λαμβάνοντες ἐν ζωῇ βασιλεύσουσιν διὰ τοῦ ἑνὸς Ἰησοῦ Χριστοῦ. **18** Ἄρα οὖν ὡς δι᾽ ἑνὸς παραπτώματος εἰς πάντας ἀνθρώπους εἰς κατάκριμα, οὕτως καὶ δι᾽ ἑνὸς δικαιώματος εἰς πάντας ἀνθρώπους εἰς δικαίωσιν ζωῆς· **19** ὥσπερ γὰρ διὰ τῆς παρακοῆς τοῦ ἑνὸς ἀνθρώπου ἁμαρτωλοὶ κατεστάθησαν οἱ πολλοί, οὕτως καὶ διὰ τῆς ὑπακοῆς τοῦ ἑνὸς δίκαιοι κατασταθήσονται οἱ πολλοί. **20** νόμος δὲ παρεισῆλθεν, ἵνα πλεονάσῃ τὸ παράπτωμα· οὗ δὲ ἐπλεόνασεν ἡ ἁμαρτία, ὑπερεπερίσσευσεν ἡ χάρις, **21** ἵνα ὥσπερ ἐβασίλευσεν ἡ ἁμαρτία ἐν τῷ θανάτῳ, οὕτως καὶ ἡ χάρις βασιλεύσῃ διὰ δικαιοσύνης εἰς ζωὴν αἰώνιον διὰ Ἰησοῦ Χριστοῦ τοῦ κυρίου ἡμῶν.

Rom 6:4

συνετάφημεν οὖν αὐτῷ διὰ τοῦ βαπτίσματος εἰς τὸν θάνατον, ἵνα ὥσπερ ἠγέρθη Χριστὸς ἐκ νεκρῶν διὰ τῆς δόξης τοῦ πατρός, οὕτως καὶ ἡμεῖς ἐν καινότητι ζωῆς περιπατήσωμεν.

Rom 6:8–13

εἰ δὲ ἀπεθάνομεν σὺν Χριστῷ, πιστεύομεν ὅτι καὶ συζήσομεν αὐτῷ, **9** εἰδότες ὅτι Χριστὸς ἐγερθεὶς ἐκ νεκρῶν οὐκέτι ἀποθνῄσκει, θάνατος αὐτοῦ οὐκέτι κυριεύει. **10** ὃ γὰρ ἀπέθανεν, τῇ ἁμαρτίᾳ ἀπέθανεν ἐφάπαξ· ὃ δὲ ζῇ, ζῇ τῷ θεῷ. **11** οὕτως καὶ ὑμεῖς λογίζεσθε ἑαυτοὺς [εἶναι] νεκροὺς μὲν τῇ ἁμαρτίᾳ ζῶντας δὲ τῷ θεῷ ἐν Χριστῷ Ἰησοῦ. **12** Μὴ οὖν βασιλευέτω ἡ ἁμαρτία ἐν τῷ θνητῷ ὑμῶν σώματι εἰς τὸ ὑπακούειν ταῖς ἐπιθυμίαις αὐτοῦ, **13** μηδὲ παριστάνετε τὰ μέλη ὑμῶν ὅπλα ἀδικίας τῇ ἁμαρτίᾳ, ἀλλὰ παραστήσατε ἑαυτοὺς τῷ θεῷ ὡσεὶ ἐκ νεκρῶν ζῶντας καὶ τὰ μέλη ὑμῶν ὅπλα δικαιοσύνης τῷ θεῷ.

Rom 6:22–23

νυνὶ δὲ ἐλευθερωθέντες ἀπὸ τῆς ἁμαρτίας δουλωθέντες δὲ τῷ θεῷ ἔχετε τὸν καρπὸν ὑμῶν εἰς ἁγιασμόν, τὸ δὲ τέλος ζωὴν αἰώνιον. **23** τὰ γὰρ ὀψώνια τῆς ἁμαρτίας θάνατος, τὸ δὲ χάρισμα τοῦ θεοῦ ζωὴ αἰώνιος ἐν Χριστῷ Ἰησοῦ τῷ κυρίῳ ἡμῶν.

Rom 8:1–11

Οὐδὲν ἄρα νῦν κατάκριμα τοῖς ἐν Χριστῷ Ἰησοῦ. **2** ὁ γὰρ νόμος τοῦ πνεύματος τῆς ζωῆς ἐν Χριστῷ Ἰησοῦ ἠλευθέρωσέν ⸀σε ἀπὸ τοῦ νόμου τῆς ἁμαρτίας καὶ τοῦ θανάτου. **3** Τὸ γὰρ ἀδύνατον τοῦ νόμου ἐν ᾧ ἠσθένει διὰ τῆς σαρκός, ὁ θεὸς τὸν ἑαυτοῦ υἱὸν πέμψας ἐν ὁμοιώματι σαρκὸς ἁμαρτίας καὶ περὶ ἁμαρτίας κατέκρινεν τὴν ἁμαρτίαν ἐν τῇ σαρκί, **4** ἵνα τὸ δικαίωμα τοῦ νόμου πληρωθῇ ἐν ἡμῖν τοῖς μὴ κατὰ σάρκα περιπατοῦσιν ἀλλὰ κατὰ πνεῦμα. **5** οἱ γὰρ κατὰ σάρκα ὄντες τὰ τῆς σαρκὸς φρονοῦσιν, οἱ δὲ κατὰ πνεῦμα τὰ τοῦ πνεύματος. **6** τὸ γὰρ φρόνημα τῆς σαρκὸς θάνατος, τὸ δὲ φρόνημα τοῦ πνεύματος ζωὴ καὶ εἰρήνη· **7** διότι τὸ φρόνημα τῆς σαρκὸς ἔχθρα εἰς θεόν, τῷ γὰρ νόμῳ τοῦ θεοῦ οὐχ ὑποτάσσεται, οὐδὲ γὰρ δύναται· **8** οἱ δὲ ἐν σαρκὶ ὄντες θεῷ ἀρέσαι οὐ δύνανται. **9** Ὑμεῖς δὲ οὐκ ἐστὲ ἐν σαρκὶ ἀλλὰ ἐν πνεύματι, εἴπερ πνεῦμα θεοῦ οἰκεῖ ἐν ὑμῖν. εἰ δέ τις πνεῦμα Χριστοῦ οὐκ ἔχει, οὗτος οὐκ ἔστιν αὐτοῦ. **10** εἰ δὲ Χριστὸς ἐν ὑμῖν, τὸ μὲν σῶμα νεκρὸν διὰ ἁμαρτίαν τὸ δὲ πνεῦμα ζωὴ διὰ δικαιοσύνην. **11** εἰ δὲ τὸ πνεῦμα τοῦ ἐγείραντος τὸν Ἰησοῦν ἐκ νεκρῶν οἰκεῖ ἐν ὑμῖν, ὁ ἐγείρας ⸂Χριστὸν ἐκ νεκρῶν⸃ ζῳοποιήσει καὶ τὰ θνητὰ σώματα ὑμῶν διὰ ⸂τοῦ ἐνοικοῦντος αὐτοῦ πνεύματος⸃ ἐν ὑμῖν.

Rom 8:12–13

Ἄρα οὖν, ἀδελφοί, ὀφειλέται ἐσμὲν οὐ τῇ σαρκὶ τοῦ κατὰ σάρκα ζῆν, **13** εἰ γὰρ κατὰ σάρκα ζῆτε, μέλλετε ἀποθνῄσκειν· εἰ δὲ πνεύματι τὰς πράξεις τοῦ σώματος θανατοῦτε, ζήσεσθε.

1 Cor 15:20–23

Νυνὶ δὲ Χριστὸς ἐγήγερται ἐκ νεκρῶν ἀπαρχὴ τῶν κεκοιμημένων. **21** ἐπειδὴ γὰρ δι᾽ ἀνθρώπου θάνατος, καὶ δι᾽ ἀνθρώπου ἀνάστασις νεκρῶν. **22** ὥσπερ γὰρ ἐν τῷ Ἀδὰμ πάντες ἀποθνῄσκουσιν, οὕτως καὶ ἐν τῷ Χριστῷ πάντες ζῳοποιηθήσονται. **23** Ἕκαστος δὲ ἐν τῷ ἰδίῳ τάγματι· ἀπαρχὴ Χριστός, ἔπειτα οἱ τοῦ Χριστοῦ ἐν τῇ παρουσίᾳ αὐτοῦ

2 Cor 3:7–8

Εἰ δὲ ἡ διακονία τοῦ θανάτου ἐν γράμμασιν ἐντετυπωμένη λίθοις ἐγενήθη ἐν δόξῃ, ὥστε μὴ δύνασθαι ἀτενίσαι τοὺς υἱοὺς Ἰσραὴλ εἰς τὸ πρόσωπον Μωϋσέως διὰ τὴν δόξαν τοῦ προσώπου αὐτοῦ τὴν καταργουμένην, **8** πῶς οὐχὶ μᾶλλον ἡ διακονία τοῦ πνεύματος ἔσται ἐν δόξῃ;

Gal 2:19–20

ἐγὼ γὰρ διὰ νόμου νόμῳ ἀπέθανον, ἵνα θεῷ ζήσω. Χριστῷ συνεσταύρωμαι· **20** ζῶ δὲ οὐκέτι ἐγώ, ζῇ δὲ ἐν ἐμοὶ Χριστός· ὃ δὲ νῦν ζῶ ἐν σαρκί, ἐν πίστει ζῶ τῇ τοῦ υἱοῦ τοῦ θεοῦ τοῦ ἀγαπήσαντός με καὶ παραδόντος ἑαυτὸν ὑπὲρ ἐμοῦ.

Gal 6:7–8

Μὴ πλανᾶσθε, θεὸς οὐ μυκτηρίζεται. ὃ γὰρ ἐὰν σπείρῃ ἄνθρωπος, τοῦτο καὶ θερίσει· **8** ὅτι ὁ σπείρων εἰς τὴν σάρκα ἑαυτοῦ ἐκ τῆς σαρκὸς θερίσει φθοράν, ὁ δὲ σπείρων εἰς τὸ πνεῦμα ἐκ τοῦ πνεύματος θερίσει ζωὴν αἰώνιον.

Eph 2:4–7

ὁ δὲ θεὸς πλούσιος ὢν ἐν ἐλέει, διὰ τὴν πολλὴν ἀγάπην αὐτοῦ ἣν ἠγάπησεν ἡμᾶς, **5** καὶ ὄντας ἡμᾶς νεκροὺς τοῖς παραπτώμασιν συνεζωοποίησεν ⸂τῷ Χριστῷ⸃, —χάριτί ἐστε σεσῳσμένοι—

§ 48 **Rom 8:2** ***σε*** ℵ B 1739*] με A D 1739ᶜ. 1881 *Byz* **Rom 8:11** ***Χριστον εκ νεκρων*** B D²] τον Χ. εκ ν. ℵ² 33 *Byz* ¦ Χ. Ιησουν εκ ν. D* ¦ εκ ν. Χ. Ιησουν ℵ* A (C Ι. Χ.) 1739. 1881 • ***του ενοικουντος αυτου πνευματος*** ℵ A C⁽*⁾] το ενοικουν αυτου πνευμα B D 33. 1739. 1881 *Byz* **Eph 2:5** ***τω Χριστω*** ℵ A D 1739. 1881 *Byz*] εν τω Χριστω 𝔓46 B 33

48. Life through Christ Jesus

Rom 5:17–21

If, because of the one man's trespass, death exercised dominion through that one, much more surely will those who receive the abundance of grace and the free gift of righteousness exercise dominion in life through the one man, Jesus Christ. **18** Therefore just as one man's trespass led to condemnation for all, so one man's act of righteousness leads to justification and life for all. **19** For just as by the one man's disobedience the many were made sinners, so by the one man's obedience the many will be made righteous. **20** But law came in, with the result that the trespass multiplied; but where sin increased, grace abounded all the more, **21** so that, just as sin exercised dominion in death, so grace might also exercise dominion through justification leading to eternal life through Jesus Christ our Lord.

Rom 6:4

Therefore we have been buried with him by baptism into death, so that, just as Christ was raised from the dead by the glory of the Father, so we too might walk in newness of life.

Rom 6:8–13

But if we have died with Christ, we believe that we will also live with him. **9** We know that Christ, being raised from the dead, will never die again; death no longer has dominion over him. **10** The death he died, he died to sin, once for all; but the life he lives, he lives to God. **11** So you also must consider yourselves dead to sin and alive to God in Christ Jesus. **12** Therefore, do not let sin exercise dominion in your mortal bodies, to make you obey their passions. **13** No longer present your members to sin as weapons[a] of wickedness, but present yourselves to God as those who have been brought from death to life, and present your members to God as weapons[a] of righteousness.

Rom 6:22–23

But now that you have been freed from sin and enslaved to God, the fruit you get is sanctification, and the end is eternal life.[b] **23** For the wages of sin is death, but the free gift of God is eternal life in Christ Jesus our Lord.

Rom 8:1–11

There is therefore now no condemnation for those who are in Christ Jesus. **2** For the law of the Spirit of life in Christ Jesus has set you[c] free from the law of sin and of death. **3** For God has done what the law, weakened by the flesh, could not do: by sending his own Son in the likeness of sinful flesh, and to deal with sin, he condemned sin in the flesh, **4** so that the just requirement of the law might be fulfilled in us, who walk not according to the flesh but according to the Spirit. **5** For those who live according to the flesh set their minds on the things of the flesh, but those who live according to the Spirit set their minds on the things of the Spirit. **6** To set the mind on the flesh is death, but to set the mind on the Spirit is life and peace. **7** For this reason the mind that is set on the flesh is hostile to God; it does not submit to God's law—indeed it cannot, **8** and those who are in the flesh cannot please God. **9** But you are not in the flesh; you are in the Spirit, since the Spirit of God dwells in you. Anyone who does not have the Spirit of Christ does not belong to him. **10** But if Christ is in you, though the body is dead because of sin, the Spirit is life because of righteousness. **11** If the Spirit of him who raised Jesus from the dead dwells in you, he who raised Christ[d] from the dead will give life to your mortal bodies also through[e] his Spirit that dwells in you.

Rom 8:12–13

So then, brothers and sisters, we are debtors, not to the flesh, to live according to the flesh— **13** for if you live according to the flesh, you will die; but if by the Spirit you put to death the deeds of the body, you will live.

1 Cor 15:20–23

But in fact Christ has been raised from the dead, the first fruits of those who have died. **21** For since death came through a human being, the resurrection of the dead has also come through a human being; **22** for as all die in Adam, so all will be made alive in Christ. **23** But each in his own order: Christ the first fruits, then at his coming those who belong to Christ.

2 Cor 3:7–8

Now if the ministry of death, chiseled in letters on stone tablets, came in glory so that the people of Israel could not gaze at Moses' face because of the glory of his face, a glory now set aside, **8** how much more will the ministry of the Spirit come in glory?

Gal 2:19–20

For through the law I died to the law, so that I might live to God. I have been crucified with Christ; **20** and it is no longer I who live, but it is Christ who lives in me. And the life I now live in the flesh I live by faith in the Son of God, who loved me and gave himself for me.

Gal 6:7–8

Do not be deceived; God is not mocked, for you reap whatever you sow. **8** If you sow to your own flesh, you will reap corruption from the flesh; but if you sow to the Spirit, you will reap eternal life from the Spirit.

Eph 2:4–7

But God, who is rich in mercy, out of the great love with which he loved us **5** even when we were dead through our trespasses, made us alive together with Christ[f] —by grace you have been

§ 48 [a] **Rom 6:13** ***weapons*** Or possibly *instruments* (so NRSV) [b] **Rom 6:22** Translation differs from NRSV [c] **Rom 8:2** ***you*** Other ancient authorities read *me* [d] **Rom 8:11** ***Christ*** Other ancient authorities read *the Christ* or *Christ Jesus* or *Jesus Christ* [e] **Rom 8:11** ***through*** Other ancient authorities read *on account of* [f] **Eph 2:5** ***together with Christ*** Other ancient authorities read *in Christ*

6 καὶ συνήγειρεν καὶ συνεκάθισεν ἐν τοῖς ἐπουρανίοις ἐν Χριστῷ Ἰησοῦ, **7** ἵνα ἐνδείξηται ἐν τοῖς αἰῶσιν τοῖς ἐπερχομένοις τὸ ὑπερβάλλον πλοῦτος τῆς χάριτος αὐτοῦ ἐν χρηστότητι ἐφ᾽ ἡμᾶς ἐν Χριστῷ Ἰησοῦ.

Col 2:12–13

συνταφέντες αὐτῷ ἐν τῷ βαπτισμῷ, ἐν ᾧ καὶ συνηγέρθητε διὰ τῆς πίστεως τῆς ἐνεργείας τοῦ θεοῦ τοῦ ἐγείραντος αὐτὸν ἐκ νεκρῶν· **13** καὶ ὑμᾶς νεκροὺς ὄντας [ἐν] τοῖς παραπτώμασιν καὶ τῇ ἀκροβυστίᾳ τῆς σαρκὸς ὑμῶν, συνεζωοποίησεν ⸀ὑμᾶς σὺν αὐτῷ, χαρισάμενος ἡμῖν πάντα τὰ παραπτώματα.

Col 3:1–4

Εἰ οὖν συνηγέρθητε τῷ Χριστῷ, τὰ ἄνω ζητεῖτε, οὗ ὁ Χριστός ἐστιν ἐν δεξιᾷ τοῦ θεοῦ καθήμενος· **2** τὰ ἄνω φρονεῖτε, μὴ τὰ ἐπὶ τῆς γῆς. **3** ἀπεθάνετε γὰρ καὶ ἡ ζωὴ ὑμῶν κέκρυπται σὺν τῷ Χριστῷ ἐν τῷ θεῷ· **4** ὅταν ὁ Χριστὸς φανερωθῇ, ἡ ζωὴ ⸀ὑμῶν, τότε καὶ ὑμεῖς σὺν αὐτῷ φανερωθήσεσθε ἐν δόξῃ.

1 Thess 5:9–10

ὅτι οὐκ ἔθετο ἡμᾶς ὁ θεὸς εἰς ὀργὴν ἀλλὰ εἰς περιποίησιν σωτηρίας διὰ τοῦ κυρίου ἡμῶν Ἰησοῦ Χριστοῦ **10** τοῦ ἀποθανόντος ὑπὲρ ἡμῶν, ἵνα εἴτε γρηγορῶμεν εἴτε καθεύδωμεν ἅμα σὺν αὐτῷ ζήσωμεν.

2 Tim 1:1

Παῦλος ἀπόστολος Χριστοῦ Ἰησοῦ διὰ θελήματος θεοῦ κατ᾽ ἐπαγγελίαν ζωῆς τῆς ἐν Χριστῷ Ἰησοῦ

2 Tim 1:9–10

τοῦ σώσαντος ἡμᾶς καὶ καλέσαντος κλήσει ἁγίᾳ, οὐ κατὰ τὰ ἔργα ἡμῶν ἀλλὰ κατὰ ἰδίαν πρόθεσιν καὶ χάριν, τὴν δοθεῖσαν ἡμῖν ἐν Χριστῷ Ἰησοῦ πρὸ χρόνων αἰωνίων, **10** φανερωθεῖσαν δὲ νῦν διὰ τῆς ἐπιφανείας τοῦ σωτῆρος ἡμῶν Χριστοῦ Ἰησοῦ, καταργήσαντος μὲν τὸν θάνατον φωτίσαντος δὲ ζωὴν καὶ ἀφθαρσίαν διὰ τοῦ εὐαγγελίου

Cf. Rom 1:16–17; 2:7; 1 Cor 15:45–49; 2 Cor 2:15–16; 4:10–12; 13:4; Gal 3:11; 3:21–22; 5:25; Phil 2:16; 1 Tim 1:16; 4:8–10; 6:12; 6:17–19; Titus 1:2–3; 3:4–7.

49. The New Humanity in Christ

Rom 6:1–7

Τί οὖν ἐροῦμεν; ἐπιμένωμεν τῇ ἁμαρτίᾳ, ἵνα ἡ χάρις πλεονάσῃ; **2** μὴ γένοιτο. οἵτινες ἀπεθάνομεν τῇ ἁμαρτίᾳ, πῶς ἔτι ζήσομεν ἐν αὐτῇ; **3** ἢ ἀγνοεῖτε ὅτι, ὅσοι ἐβαπτίσθημεν εἰς Χριστὸν Ἰησοῦν, εἰς τὸν θάνατον αὐτοῦ ἐβαπτίσθημεν; **4** συνετάφημεν οὖν αὐτῷ διὰ τοῦ βαπτίσματος εἰς τὸν θάνατον, ἵνα ὥσπερ ἠγέρθη Χριστὸς ἐκ νεκρῶν διὰ τῆς δόξης τοῦ πατρός, οὕτως καὶ ἡμεῖς ἐν καινότητι ζωῆς περιπατήσωμεν. **5** εἰ γὰρ σύμφυτοι γεγόναμεν τῷ ὁμοιώματι τοῦ θανάτου αὐτοῦ, ἀλλὰ καὶ τῆς ἀναστάσεως ἐσόμεθα· **6** τοῦτο γινώσκοντες ὅτι ὁ παλαιὸς ἡμῶν ἄνθρωπος συνεσταυρώθη, ἵνα καταργηθῇ τὸ σῶμα τῆς ἁμαρτίας, τοῦ μηκέτι δουλεύειν ἡμᾶς τῇ ἁμαρτίᾳ· **7** ὁ γὰρ ἀποθανὼν δεδικαίωται ἀπὸ τῆς ἁμαρτίας.

Rom 8:29

ὅτι οὓς προέγνω, καὶ προώρισεν συμμόρφους τῆς εἰκόνος τοῦ υἱοῦ αὐτοῦ, εἰς τὸ εἶναι αὐτὸν πρωτότοκον ἐν πολλοῖς ἀδελφοῖς

1 Cor 15:45–49

οὕτως καὶ γέγραπται· ἐγένετο ὁ πρῶτος ἄνθρωπος Ἀδὰμ εἰς ψυχὴν ζῶσαν, ὁ ἔσχατος Ἀδὰμ εἰς πνεῦμα ζῳοποιοῦν. **46** ἀλλ᾽ οὐ πρῶτον τὸ πνευματικὸν ἀλλὰ τὸ ψυχικόν, ἔπειτα τὸ πνευματικόν. **47** ὁ πρῶτος ἄνθρωπος ἐκ γῆς χοϊκός, ὁ δεύτερος ⸀ἄνθρωπος ἐξ οὐρανοῦ. **48** οἷος ὁ χοϊκός, τοιοῦτοι καὶ οἱ χοϊκοί, καὶ οἷος ὁ ἐπουράνιος, τοιοῦτοι καὶ οἱ ἐπουράνιοι· **49** καὶ καθὼς ἐφορέσαμεν τὴν εἰκόνα τοῦ χοϊκοῦ, ⸀φορέσομεν καὶ τὴν εἰκόνα τοῦ ἐπουρανίου.

2 Cor 3:17–18

ὁ δὲ κύριος τὸ πνεῦμά ἐστιν· οὗ δὲ τὸ πνεῦμα κυρίου, ἐλευθερία. **18** ἡμεῖς δὲ πάντες ἀνακεκαλυμμένῳ προσώπῳ τὴν δόξαν κυρίου κατοπτριζόμενοι τὴν αὐτὴν εἰκόνα μεταμορφούμεθα ἀπὸ δόξης εἰς δόξαν καθάπερ ἀπὸ κυρίου πνεύματος.

2 Cor 4:4–6

ἐν οἷς ὁ θεὸς τοῦ αἰῶνος τούτου ἐτύφλωσεν τὰ νοήματα τῶν ἀπίστων εἰς τὸ μὴ αὐγάσαι τὸν φωτισμὸν τοῦ εὐαγγελίου τῆς δόξης τοῦ Χριστοῦ, ὅς ἐστιν εἰκὼν τοῦ θεοῦ. **5** Οὐ γὰρ ἑαυτοὺς κηρύσσομεν ἀλλὰ Ἰησοῦν Χριστὸν κύριον, ἑαυτοὺς δὲ δούλους ὑμῶν διὰ Ἰησοῦν. **6** ὅτι ὁ θεὸς ὁ εἰπών· ἐκ σκότους φῶς λάμψει, ὃς ἔλαμψεν ἐν ταῖς καρδίαις ἡμῶν πρὸς φωτισμὸν τῆς γνώσεως τῆς δόξης τοῦ θεοῦ ἐν προσώπῳ [Ἰησοῦ] Χριστοῦ.

Eph 2:14–18

Αὐτὸς γάρ ἐστιν ἡ εἰρήνη ἡμῶν, ὁ ποιήσας τὰ ἀμφότερα ἓν καὶ τὸ μεσότοιχον τοῦ φραγμοῦ λύσας, τὴν ἔχθραν ἐν τῇ σαρκὶ αὐτοῦ, **15** τὸν νόμον τῶν ἐντολῶν ἐν δόγμασιν καταργήσας, ἵνα τοὺς δύο κτίσῃ ἐν αὐτῷ εἰς ἕνα καινὸν ἄνθρωπον ποιῶν εἰρήνην **16** καὶ ἀποκαταλλάξῃ τοὺς ἀμφοτέρους ἐν ἑνὶ σώματι τῷ θεῷ διὰ τοῦ σταυροῦ, ἀποκτείνας τὴν ἔχθραν ἐν αὐτῷ. **17** καὶ ἐλθὼν εὐηγγελίσατο εἰρήνην ὑμῖν τοῖς μακρὰν καὶ εἰρήνην τοῖς ἐγγύς· **18** ὅτι δι᾽ αὐτοῦ ἔχομεν τὴν προσαγωγὴν οἱ ἀμφότεροι ἐν ἑνὶ πνεύματι πρὸς τὸν πατέρα.

Eph 4:20–24

Ὑμεῖς δὲ οὐχ οὕτως ἐμάθετε τὸν Χριστόν, **21** εἴ γε αὐτὸν ἠκούσατε καὶ ἐν αὐτῷ ἐδιδάχθητε, καθώς ἐστιν ἀλήθεια ἐν τῷ Ἰησοῦ, **22** ἀποθέσθαι ὑμᾶς κατὰ τὴν προτέραν ἀναστροφὴν τὸν παλαιὸν

Col 2:13 ***υμας*** ℵ* A C 1739. 1881] ημας 𝔓^{46} B 33 ¦ *om.* ℵ^{2} D *Byz* **Col 3:4** ***υμων*** 𝔓^{46} ℵ C D* 33. 1881] ημων B$^{(*)}$ D^{1} 1739 *Byz* **§ 49** **1 Cor 15:47** ***ανθρωπος*** ℵ* B C D* 33. 1739*] *add.* ο κυριος ℵ^{2} A D^{1} 1739^{mg}. 1881 *Byz* ¦ *add.* πνευματικος 𝔓^{46} **1 Cor 15:49** ***φορεσομεν*** B I 1881] φορεσωμεν (+ δη 𝔓^{46}) 𝔓^{46} ℵ A C D 33. 1739 *Byz*

saved— 6 and raised us up with him and seated us with him in the heavenly places in Christ Jesus, 7 so that in the ages to come he might show the immeasurable riches of his grace in kindness toward us in Christ Jesus.

Col 2:12–13

when you were buried with him in baptism, you were also raised with him through faith in the power of God, who raised him from the dead. 13 And when you were dead in trespasses and the uncircumcision of your flesh, God made you[g] alive together with him, when he forgave us all our trespasses

Col 3:1–4

So if you have been raised with Christ, seek the things that are above, where Christ is, seated at the right hand of God. 2 Set your minds on things that are above, not on things that are on earth, 3 for you have died, and your life is hidden with Christ in God. 4 When Christ who is your[h] life is revealed, then you also will be revealed with him in glory.

1 Thess 5:9–10

For God has destined us not for wrath but for obtaining salvation through our Lord Jesus Christ, 10 who died for us, so that whether we are awake or asleep we may live with him.

2 Tim 1:1

Paul, an apostle of Christ Jesus by the will of God, for the sake of the promise of life that is in Christ Jesus

2 Tim 1:9–10

who saved us and called us with a holy calling, not according to our works but according to his own purpose and grace. This grace was given to us in Christ Jesus before the ages began, 10 but it has now been revealed through the appearing of our Savior Christ Jesus, who abolished death and brought life and immortality to light through the gospel.

Cf. Rom 1:16–17; 2:7; 1 Cor 15:45–49; 2 Cor 2:15–16; 4:10–12; 13:4; Gal 3:11; 3:21–22; 5:25; Phil 2:16; 1 Tim 1:16; 4:8–10; 6:12; 6:17–19; Titus 1:2–3; 3:4–7.

49. The New Humanity in Christ

Rom 6:1–7

What then are we to say? Should we continue in sin in order that grace may abound? 2 By no means! How can we who died to sin go on living in it? 3 Do you not know that all of us who have been baptized into Christ Jesus were baptized into his death? 4 Therefore we have been buried with him by baptism into death, so that, just as Christ was raised from the dead by the glory of the Father, so we too might walk in newness of life. 5 For if we have been united with him in a death like his, we will certainly be united with him in a resurrection like his. 6 We know that our old humanity[a] was crucified with him so that the body of sin might be destroyed, and we might no longer be enslaved to sin. 7 For whoever has died is freed from sin.

Rom 8:29

For those whom he foreknew he also predestined to be conformed to the image of his Son, in order that he might be the firstborn within a large family.

1 Cor 15:45–49

Thus it is written, "The first man, Adam, became a living soul"; the last Adam became a life-giving Spirit. 46 But it is not the body given life by the Spirit that is first, but the body given life by the soul, and then the body given life by the Spirit.[b] 47 The first man was from the earth, a man of dust; the second man is[c] from heaven. 48 As was the man of dust, so are those who are of the dust; and as is the man of heaven, so are those who are of heaven. 49 Just as we have borne the image of the man of dust, we will[d] also bear the image of the man of heaven.

2 Cor 3:17–18

Now the Lord is the Spirit, and where the Spirit of the Lord is, there is freedom. 18 And all of us, with unveiled faces, seeing the glory of the Lord as though reflected in a mirror, are being transformed into the same image from one degree of glory to another; for this comes from the Lord, the Spirit.

2 Cor 4:4–6

In their case the god of this world has blinded the minds of the unbelievers, to keep them from seeing the light of the gospel of the glory of Christ, who is the image of God. 5 For we do not proclaim ourselves; we proclaim Jesus Christ as Lord and ourselves as your slaves for Jesus' sake. 6 For it is the God who said, "Let light shine out of darkness," who has shone in our hearts to give the light of the knowledge of the glory of God in the face of Jesus Christ.

Eph 2:14–18

For he is our peace; in his flesh he has made both groups into one and has broken down the dividing wall, that is, the hostility between us. 15 He has abolished the law with its commandments and ordinances, that he might create in himself one new humanity in place of the two, thus making peace, 16 and might reconcile both groups to God in one body through the cross, thus putting to death that hostility through it. 17 So he came and proclaimed peace to you who were far off and peace to those who were near; 18 for through him both of us have access in one Spirit to the Father.

Eph 4:20–24

That is not the way you learned Christ! 21 For surely you have heard about him and were taught in him, as truth is in Jesus. 22 You were taught, in regard to your former way of life, to put off your

[g] **Col 2:13** ***made you*** Other ancient authorities read *made us*; others, *made* [h] **Col 3:4** ***your*** Other ancient authorities read *our* **§ 49** [a] **Rom 6:6** ***humanity*** NRSV translates *self* [b] **1 Cor 15:45–46** Translation differs from NRSV [c] **1 Cor 15:47** ***is*** Other ancient authorities add *the Lord* [d] **1 Cor 15:49** ***we will*** Other ancient authorities read *let us*

ἄνθρωπον τὸν φθειρόμενον κατὰ τὰς
ἐπιθυμίας τῆς ἀπάτης, 23 ἀνανεοῦσθαι
δὲ τῷ πνεύματι τοῦ νοὸς ὑμῶν 24 καὶ
ἐνδύσασθαι τὸν καινὸν ἄνθρωπον τὸν
κατὰ θεὸν κτισθέντα ἐν δικαιοσύνῃ καὶ
ὁσιότητι τῆς ἀληθείας.

Col 3:9–11

μὴ ψεύδεσθε εἰς ἀλλήλους, ἀπεκδυσάμε-
νοι τὸν παλαιὸν ἄνθρωπον σὺν ταῖς
πράξεσιν αὐτοῦ 10 καὶ ἐνδυσάμενοι τὸν
νέον τὸν ἀνακαινούμενον εἰς ἐπίγνω-
σιν κατ' εἰκόνα τοῦ κτίσαντος αὐτόν,
11 ὅπου οὐκ ἔνι Ἕλλην καὶ Ἰουδαῖος,
περιτομὴ καὶ ἀκροβυστία, βάρβαρος,
Σκύθης, δοῦλος, ἐλεύθερος, ἀλλὰ [τὰ]
πάντα καὶ ἐν πᾶσιν Χριστός.

Cf. Rom 4:13–25; 6:17–23; 12:1–2, which express this theme by literary contrast with Rom 1:18–32; cf. also Rom 5:12–21; 13:11–14; 1 Cor 2:10–16; 2 Cor 5:14–17; Gal 3:26–29; 6:14–16; Eph 2:8–10; Phil 3:21; Col 1:15.

See the corresponding themes § 24 Idolatry and Dehumanization and § 31 The Second Adam.

50. *Children of God*

Rom 8:12–17

Ἄρα οὖν, ἀδελφοί, ὀφειλέται ἐσμὲν
οὐ τῇ σαρκὶ τοῦ κατὰ σάρκα ζῆν, 13 εἰ
γὰρ κατὰ σάρκα ζῆτε, μέλλετε ἀποθνῄ-
σκειν· εἰ δὲ πνεύματι τὰς πράξεις τοῦ
σώματος θανατοῦτε, ζήσεσθε. 14 ὅσοι
γὰρ πνεύματι θεοῦ ἄγονται, οὗτοι υἱοὶ
θεοῦ εἰσιν. 15 οὐ γὰρ ἐλάβετε πνεῦμα
δουλείας πάλιν εἰς φόβον ἀλλὰ ἐλάβετε
πνεῦμα υἱοθεσίας ἐν ᾧ κράζομεν· αββα
ὁ πατήρ. 16 αὐτὸ τὸ πνεῦμα συμμαρτυ-
ρεῖ τῷ πνεύματι ἡμῶν ὅτι ἐσμὲν τέκνα
θεοῦ. 17 εἰ δὲ τέκνα, καὶ κληρονόμοι·
κληρονόμοι μὲν θεοῦ, συγκληρονόμοι
δὲ Χριστοῦ, εἴπερ συμπάσχομεν ἵνα καὶ
συνδοξασθῶμεν.

Rom 8:18–23

Λογίζομαι γὰρ ὅτι οὐκ ἄξια τὰ παθήματα
τοῦ νῦν καιροῦ πρὸς τὴν μέλλουσαν δόξαν
ἀποκαλυφθῆναι εἰς ἡμᾶς. 19 ἡ γὰρ ἀπο-
καραδοκία τῆς κτίσεως τὴν ἀποκάλυψιν
τῶν υἱῶν τοῦ θεοῦ ἀπεκδέχεται. 20 τῇ
γὰρ ματαιότητι ἡ κτίσις ὑπετάγη, οὐχ
ἑκοῦσα ἀλλὰ διὰ τὸν ὑποτάξαντα, ἐφ'
ἑλπίδι 21 ὅτι καὶ αὐτὴ ἡ κτίσις ἐλευθερω-
θήσεται ἀπὸ τῆς δουλείας τῆς φθορᾶς εἰς
τὴν ἐλευθερίαν τῆς δόξης τῶν τέκνων
τοῦ θεοῦ. 22 οἴδαμεν γὰρ ὅτι πᾶσα ἡ
κτίσις συστενάζει καὶ συνωδίνει ἄχρι
τοῦ νῦν· 23 οὐ μόνον δέ, ἀλλὰ καὶ αὐτοὶ
τὴν ἀπαρχὴν τοῦ πνεύματος ἔχοντες,
ἡμεῖς καὶ αὐτοὶ ἐν ἑαυτοῖς στενάζομεν
υἱοθεσίαν ἀπεκδεχόμενοι, τὴν ἀπολύ-
τρωσιν τοῦ σώματος ἡμῶν.

Rom 8:29

ὅτι οὓς προέγνω, καὶ προώρισεν συμ-
μόρφους τῆς εἰκόνος τοῦ υἱοῦ αὐτοῦ, εἰς
τὸ εἶναι αὐτὸν πρωτότοκον ἐν πολλοῖς
ἀδελφοῖς

2 Cor 6:16–18

τίς δὲ συγκατάθεσις ναῷ θεοῦ μετὰ εἰδώ-
λων; ⸂ἡμεῖς γὰρ ναὸς θεοῦ ἐσμεν⸃ ζῶν-
τος, καθὼς εἶπεν ὁ θεὸς ὅτι ἐνοικήσω
ἐν αὐτοῖς καὶ ἐμπεριπατήσω καὶ ἔσομαι
αὐτῶν θεὸς καὶ αὐτοὶ ἔσονταί μου λα-
ός. 17 διὸ ἐξέλθατε ἐκ μέσου αὐτῶν καὶ
ἀφορίσθητε, λέγει κύριος, καὶ ἀκαθάρ-
του μὴ ἅπτεσθε· κἀγὼ εἰσδέξομαι ὑμᾶς
18 καὶ ἔσομαι ὑμῖν εἰς πατέρα καὶ ὑμεῖς
ἔσεσθέ μοι εἰς υἱοὺς καὶ θυγατέρας, λέγει
κύριος παντοκράτωρ.

Gal 3:26–29

Πάντες γὰρ υἱοὶ θεοῦ ἐστε διὰ τῆς πί-
στεως ἐν Χριστῷ Ἰησοῦ· 27 ὅσοι γὰρ εἰς
Χριστὸν ἐβαπτίσθητε, Χριστὸν ἐνεδύσα-
σθε. 28 οὐκ ἔνι Ἰουδαῖος οὐδὲ Ἕλλην,
οὐκ ἔνι δοῦλος οὐδὲ ἐλεύθερος, οὐκ
ἔνι ἄρσεν καὶ θῆλυ· πάντες γὰρ ὑμεῖς
εἷς ἐστε ἐν Χριστῷ Ἰησοῦ. 29 εἰ δὲ ὑμεῖς
Χριστοῦ, ἄρα τοῦ Ἀβραὰμ σπέρμα ἐστέ,
κατ' ἐπαγγελίαν κληρονόμοι.

Gal 4:4–7

ὅτε δὲ ἦλθεν τὸ πλήρωμα τοῦ χρόνου,
ἐξαπέστειλεν ὁ θεὸς τὸν υἱὸν αὐτοῦ,
γενόμενον ἐκ γυναικός, γενόμενον ὑπὸ
νόμον, 5 ἵνα τοὺς ὑπὸ νόμον ἐξαγοράσῃ,
ἵνα τὴν υἱοθεσίαν ἀπολάβωμεν. 6 Ὅτι
δέ ἐστε υἱοί, ἐξαπέστειλεν ὁ θεὸς τὸ
πνεῦμα τοῦ υἱοῦ αὐτοῦ εἰς τὰς καρδίας
⸀ἡμῶν κρᾶζον· αββα ὁ πατήρ. 7 ὥστε
οὐκέτι εἶ δοῦλος ἀλλὰ υἱός· εἰ δὲ υἱός,
καὶ κληρονόμος ⸂διὰ θεοῦ⸃.

Eph 1:5

προορίσας ἡμᾶς εἰς υἱοθεσίαν διὰ Ἰησοῦ
Χριστοῦ εἰς αὐτόν, κατὰ τὴν εὐδοκίαν
τοῦ θελήματος αὐτοῦ

Eph 5:1–2

Γίνεσθε οὖν μιμηταὶ τοῦ θεοῦ ὡς τέκνα
ἀγαπητὰ 2 καὶ περιπατεῖτε ἐν ἀγάπῃ,
καθὼς καὶ ὁ Χριστὸς ἠγάπησεν ⸀ἡμᾶς
καὶ παρέδωκεν ἑαυτὸν ὑπὲρ ἡμῶν προσ-
φορὰν καὶ θυσίαν τῷ θεῷ εἰς ὀσμὴν
εὐωδίας.

Phil 2:14–16

Πάντα ποιεῖτε χωρὶς γογγυσμῶν καὶ
διαλογισμῶν, 15 ἵνα γένησθε ἄμεμπτοι
καὶ ἀκέραιοι, τέκνα θεοῦ ἄμωμα μέσον
γενεᾶς σκολιᾶς καὶ διεστραμμένης, ἐν οἷς
φαίνεσθε ὡς φωστῆρες ἐν κόσμῳ, 16 λό-
γον ζωῆς ἐπέχοντες, εἰς καύχημα ἐμοὶ
εἰς ἡμέραν Χριστοῦ, ὅτι οὐκ εἰς κενὸν
ἔδραμον οὐδὲ εἰς κενὸν ἐκοπίασα.

Cf. 1 Cor 4:14–15; 1 Tim 1:1–2; 1:18; 2 Tim 1:2; 2:1; Titus 1:4; Phlm 10–11.

See also § 51 The Family of God.

§ 50 **2 Cor 6:16** ***ημεις γαρ ναος θεου εσμεν*** B D* 33. 1881] υμεις γαρ ναος θεου εστε 𝔓[46] (ℵ[2]) C D[2] *Byz* ¦ ημεις γαρ ναοι θεου εσμεν ℵ* 1739 **Gal 4:6** ***ημων*** 𝔓[46] ℵ A B C D* 1739. 1881] υμων D[2] 33 *Byz* **Gal 4:7** ***δια θεου*** 𝔓[46] ℵ* A B C* 33. 1739[*vid]] θεου δια Χριστου ℵ[2] C[3] D *Byz* ¦ δια θεον 1881 ¦ δια Ιησου Χριστου 1739[c] **Eph 5:2** ***ημας*** 𝔓[46] ℵ[2] D 33. 1739. 1881 *Byz*] υμας ℵ* A B

old humanity, which is being corrupted in accordance with its deceptive desires, **23** and to be renewed in the spirit of your minds, **24** and to clothe yourselves with the new humanity, created in the image of God in true righteousness and holiness.[e]

Col 3:9–11

Do not lie to one another, seeing that you have stripped off the old humanity[f] with its practices **10** and have clothed yourselves with the new humanity,[f] which is being renewed in knowledge according to the image of its creator. **11** In that renewal there is no longer Greek and Jew, circumcised and uncircumcised, barbarian, Scythian, slave and free; but Christ is all and in all!

Cf. Rom 4:13–25; 6:17–23; 12:1–2, which express this theme by literary contrast with Rom 1:18–32; cf. also Rom 5:12–21; 13:11–14; 1 Cor 2:10–16; 2 Cor 5:14–17; Gal 3:26–29; 6:14–16; Eph 2:8–10; Phil 3:21; Col 1:15.

See the corresponding themes § 24 Idolatry and Dehumanization and § 31 The Second Adam.

50. Children of God

Rom 8:12–17

So then, brothers and sisters, we are debtors, not to the flesh, to live according to the flesh— **13** for if you live according to the flesh, you will die; but if by the Spirit you put to death the deeds of the body, you will live. **14** For all who are led by the Spirit of God are children of God. **15** For you did not receive a spirit of slavery to fall back into fear, but you have received a spirit of adoption. When we cry, "Abba! Father!" **16** it is that very Spirit bearing witness with our spirit that we are children of God, **17** and if children, then heirs, heirs of God and joint heirs with Christ—if, in fact, we suffer with him so that we may also be glorified with him.

Rom 8:18–23

I consider that the sufferings of this present time are not worth comparing with the glory about to be revealed to us. **19** For the creation waits with eager longing for the revealing of the children of God; **20** for the creation was subjected to futility, not of its own will but by the will of the one who subjected it, in hope **21** that the creation itself will be set free from its bondage to decay and will obtain the freedom of the glory of the children of God. **22** We know that the whole creation has been groaning in labor pains until now; **23** and not only the creation, but we ourselves, who have the first fruits of the Spirit, groan inwardly while we wait for adoption, the redemption of our bodies.

Rom 8:29

For those whom he foreknew he also predestined to be conformed to the image of his Son, in order that he might be the firstborn within a large family.

2 Cor 6:16–18

What agreement has the temple of God with idols? For we[a] are the temple of the living God; as God said, "I will live in them and walk among them, and I will be their God, and they shall be my people. **17** Therefore come out from them, and be separate from them, says the Lord, and touch nothing unclean; then I will welcome you, **18** and I will be your father, and you shall be my sons and daughters, says the Lord Almighty."

Gal 3:26–29

for in Christ Jesus you are all children of God through faith. **27** As many of you as were baptized into Christ have clothed yourselves with Christ. **28** There is no longer Jew or Greek, there is no longer slave or free, there is no longer male and female; for all of you are one in Christ Jesus. **29** And if you belong to Christ, then you are Abraham's offspring, heirs according to the promise.

Gal 4:4–7

But when the fullness of time had come, God sent his Son, born of a woman, born under the law, **5** in order to redeem those who were under the law, so that we might receive adoption as children. **6** And because you are children, God has sent the Spirit of his Son into our[b] hearts, crying, "Abba! Father!" **7** So you are no longer a slave but a child, and if a child then also an heir, through God.[c]

Eph 1:5

He destined us for adoption as his children through Jesus Christ, according to the good pleasure of his will

Eph 5:1–2

Therefore be imitators of God, as beloved children, **2** and live in love, as Christ loved us[d] and gave himself up for us, a fragrant offering and sacrifice to God.

Phil 2:14–16

Do all things without murmuring and arguing, **15** so that you may be blameless and innocent, children of God without blemish in the midst of a crooked and perverse generation, in which you shine like stars in the world. **16** It is by your holding forth[e] the word of life that I can boast on the day of Christ that I did not run in vain or labor in vain.

Cf. 1 Cor 4:14–15; 1 Tim 1:1–2; 1:18; 2 Tim 1:2; 2:1; Titus 1:4; Phlm 10–11.

See also § 51 The Family of God.

[e] **Eph 4:22–24** Translation differs from NRSV [f] **Col 3:9–10** ***humanity*** NRSV translates *self* **§ 50** [a] **2 Cor 6:16** ***we*** Other ancient authorities read *you* [b] **Gal 4:6** ***our*** Other ancient authorities read *your* [c] **Gal 4:7** ***an heir, through God*** Other ancient authorities read *an heir of God through Christ* [d] **Eph 5:2** ***us*** Other ancient authorities read *you* [e] **Phil 2:16** ***holding forth*** NRSV translates *holding fast to*

51. *The Family of God*

Gal 6:10

Ἄρα οὖν ὡς καιρὸν ἔχομεν, ἐργαζώμεθα τὸ ἀγαθὸν πρὸς πάντας, μάλιστα δὲ πρὸς τοὺς οἰκείους τῆς πίστεως.

Eph 2:19–22

Ἄρα οὖν οὐκέτι ἐστὲ ξένοι καὶ πάροικοι ἀλλὰ ἐστὲ συμπολῖται τῶν ἁγίων καὶ οἰκεῖοι τοῦ θεοῦ, **20** ἐποικοδομηθέντες ἐπὶ τῷ θεμελίῳ τῶν ἀποστόλων καὶ προφητῶν, ὄντος ἀκρογωνιαίου αὐτοῦ Χριστοῦ Ἰησοῦ, **21** ἐν ᾧ πᾶσα οἰκοδομὴ συναρμολογουμένη αὔξει εἰς ναὸν ἅγιον ἐν κυρίῳ, **22** ἐν ᾧ καὶ ὑμεῖς συνοικοδομεῖσθε εἰς κατοικητήριον τοῦ θεοῦ ἐν πνεύματι.

Eph 3:14–15

Τούτου χάριν κάμπτω τὰ γόνατά μου πρὸς τὸν ⸀πατέρα, **15** ἐξ οὗ πᾶσα πατριὰ ἐν οὐρανοῖς καὶ ἐπὶ γῆς ὀνομάζεται

1 Tim 3:14–15

Ταῦτά σοι γράφω ἐλπίζων ἐλθεῖν πρὸς σὲ ἐν τάχει· **15** ἐὰν δὲ βραδύνω, ἵνα εἰδῇς πῶς δεῖ ἐν οἴκῳ θεοῦ ἀναστρέφεσθαι, ἥτις ἐστὶν ἐκκλησία θεοῦ ζῶντος, στῦλος καὶ ἑδραίωμα τῆς ἀληθείας.

1 Tim 5:1–2

Πρεσβυτέρῳ μὴ ἐπιπλήξῃς ἀλλὰ παρακάλει ὡς πατέρα, νεωτέρους ὡς ἀδελφούς, **2** πρεσβυτέρας ὡς μητέρας, νεωτέρας ὡς ἀδελφὰς ἐν πάσῃ ἁγνείᾳ.

Consult a concordance for Paul's strikingly frequent description of believers as **ἀδελφοί**; see also § 50 Children of God.

52. *The Flesh and the Spirit*

Rom 2:28–29

οὐ γὰρ ὁ ἐν τῷ φανερῷ Ἰουδαῖός ἐστιν οὐδὲ ἡ ἐν τῷ φανερῷ ἐν σαρκὶ περιτομή, **29** ἀλλ᾽ ὁ ἐν τῷ κρυπτῷ Ἰουδαῖος, καὶ περιτομὴ καρδίας ἐν πνεύματι οὐ γράμματι, οὗ ὁ ἔπαινος οὐκ ἐξ ἀνθρώπων ἀλλ᾽ ἐκ τοῦ θεοῦ.

Rom 7:4–6

ὥστε, ἀδελφοί μου, καὶ ὑμεῖς ἐθανατώθητε τῷ νόμῳ διὰ τοῦ σώματος τοῦ Χριστοῦ, εἰς τὸ γενέσθαι ὑμᾶς ἑτέρῳ, τῷ ἐκ νεκρῶν ἐγερθέντι, ἵνα καρποφορήσωμεν τῷ θεῷ. **5** ὅτε γὰρ ἦμεν ἐν τῇ σαρκί, τὰ παθήματα τῶν ἁμαρτιῶν τὰ διὰ τοῦ νόμου ἐνηργεῖτο ἐν τοῖς μέλεσιν ἡμῶν, εἰς τὸ καρποφορῆσαι τῷ θανάτῳ· **6** νυνὶ δὲ κατηργήθημεν ἀπὸ τοῦ νόμου ἀποθανόντες ἐν ᾧ κατειχόμεθα, ὥστε δουλεύειν ἡμᾶς ἐν καινότητι πνεύματος καὶ οὐ παλαιότητι γράμματος.

Rom 8:3–11

Τὸ γὰρ ἀδύνατον τοῦ νόμου ἐν ᾧ ἠσθένει διὰ τῆς σαρκός, ὁ θεὸς τὸν ἑαυτοῦ υἱὸν πέμψας ἐν ὁμοιώματι σαρκὸς ἁμαρτίας καὶ περὶ ἁμαρτίας κατέκρινεν τὴν ἁμαρτίαν ἐν τῇ σαρκί, **4** ἵνα τὸ δικαίωμα τοῦ νόμου πληρωθῇ ἐν ἡμῖν τοῖς μὴ κατὰ σάρκα περιπατοῦσιν ἀλλὰ κατὰ πνεῦμα. **5** οἱ γὰρ κατὰ σάρκα ὄντες τὰ τῆς σαρκὸς φρονοῦσιν, οἱ δὲ κατὰ πνεῦμα τὰ τοῦ πνεύματος. **6** τὸ γὰρ φρόνημα τῆς σαρκὸς θάνατος, τὸ δὲ φρόνημα τοῦ πνεύματος ζωὴ καὶ εἰρήνη· **7** διότι τὸ φρόνημα τῆς σαρκὸς ἔχθρα εἰς θεόν, τῷ γὰρ νόμῳ τοῦ θεοῦ οὐχ ὑποτάσσεται, οὐδὲ γὰρ δύναται· **8** οἱ δὲ ἐν σαρκὶ ὄντες θεῷ ἀρέσαι οὐ δύνανται. **9** Ὑμεῖς δὲ οὐκ ἐστὲ ἐν σαρκὶ ἀλλὰ ἐν πνεύματι, εἴπερ πνεῦμα θεοῦ οἰκεῖ ἐν ὑμῖν. εἰ δέ τις πνεῦμα Χριστοῦ οὐκ ἔχει, οὗτος οὐκ ἔστιν αὐτοῦ. **10** εἰ δὲ Χριστὸς ἐν ὑμῖν, τὸ μὲν σῶμα νεκρὸν διὰ ἁμαρτίαν τὸ δὲ πνεῦμα ζωὴ διὰ δικαιοσύνην. **11** εἰ δὲ τὸ πνεῦμα τοῦ ἐγείραντος τὸν Ἰησοῦν ἐκ νεκρῶν οἰκεῖ ἐν ὑμῖν, ὁ ἐγείρας ⸀Χριστὸν ἐκ νεκρῶν⸀ ζῳοποιήσει καὶ τὰ θνητὰ σώματα ὑμῶν διὰ ⸀τοῦ ἐνοικοῦντος αὐτοῦ πνεύματος⸀ ἐν ὑμῖν.

Rom 8:12–14

Ἄρα οὖν, ἀδελφοί, ὀφειλέται ἐσμὲν οὐ τῇ σαρκὶ τοῦ κατὰ σάρκα ζῆν, **13** εἰ γὰρ κατὰ σάρκα ζῆτε, μέλλετε ἀποθνῄσκειν· εἰ δὲ πνεύματι τὰς πράξεις τοῦ σώματος θανατοῦτε, ζήσεσθε. **14** ὅσοι γὰρ πνεύματι θεοῦ ἄγονται, οὗτοι υἱοὶ θεοῦ εἰσιν.

1 Cor 3:1–4

Κἀγώ, ἀδελφοί, οὐκ ἠδυνήθην λαλῆσαι ὑμῖν ὡς πνευματικοῖς ἀλλ᾽ ὡς σαρκίνοις, ὡς νηπίοις ἐν Χριστῷ. **2** γάλα ὑμᾶς ἐπότισα, οὐ βρῶμα· οὔπω γὰρ ἐδύνασθε. ἀλλ᾽ οὐδὲ ἔτι νῦν δύνασθε, **3** ἔτι γὰρ σαρκικοί ἐστε. ὅπου γὰρ ἐν ὑμῖν ζῆλος καὶ ἔρις, οὐχὶ σαρκικοί ἐστε καὶ κατὰ ἄνθρωπον περιπατεῖτε; **4** ὅταν γὰρ λέγῃ τις· ἐγὼ μέν εἰμι Παύλου, ἕτερος δέ· ἐγὼ Ἀπολλῶ, οὐκ ἄνθρωποί ἐστε;

Gal 3:2–3

τοῦτο μόνον θέλω μαθεῖν ἀφ᾽ ὑμῶν· ἐξ ἔργων νόμου τὸ πνεῦμα ἐλάβετε ἢ ἐξ ἀκοῆς πίστεως; **3** οὕτως ἀνόητοί ἐστε, ἐναρξάμενοι πνεύματι νῦν σαρκὶ ἐπιτελεῖσθε;

Gal 5:16–25

Λέγω δέ, πνεύματι περιπατεῖτε καὶ ἐπιθυμίαν σαρκὸς οὐ μὴ τελέσητε. **17** ἡ γὰρ σὰρξ ἐπιθυμεῖ κατὰ τοῦ πνεύματος, τὸ

§ 51 **Eph 3:14** ***πατερα*** 𝔓[46] ℵ* A B C 33. 1739] *add.* του κυριου ημων Ιησου Χριστου ℵ[2] D 1881 *Byz* **§ 52** **Rom 8:11** ***Χριστον εκ νεκρων*** B D[2]] τον Χ. εκ ν. ℵ[2] 33 *Byz* ¦ Χ. Ιησουν εκ ν. D* ¦ εκ ν. Χ. Ιησουν ℵ* A (C I. X.) 1739. 1881 • ***του ενοικουντος αυτου πνευματος*** ℵ A C[(*)]] το ενοικουν αυτου πνευμα B D 33. 1739. 1881 *Byz*

51. *The Family of God*

Gal 6:10

So then, whenever we have an opportunity, let us work for the good of all, and especially for those of the family of faith.

Eph 2:19–22

So then you are no longer strangers and aliens, but you are citizens with the saints and also members of the household of God, **20** built upon the foundation of the apostles and prophets, with Christ Jesus himself as the cornerstone. **21** In him the whole structure is joined together and grows into a holy temple in the Lord; **22** in whom you also are built together spiritually into a dwelling place for God.

Eph 3:14–15

For this reason I bow my knees before the Father,[a] **15** from whom the whole family[b] in heaven and on earth takes its name.

1 Tim 3:14–15

I hope to come to you soon, but I am writing these instructions to you so that, **15** if I am delayed, you may know how one ought to behave in the household of God, which is the church of the living God, the pillar and bulwark of the truth.

1 Tim 5:1–2

Do not speak harshly to an older man, but speak to him as to a father, to younger men as brothers, **2** to older women as mothers, to younger women as sisters—with absolute purity.

Consult a concordance for Paul's strikingly frequent description of believers as "brothers and sisters"; regrettably, this is frequently obscured in the NRSV translation. See also § 50 Children of God.

52. *The Flesh and the Spirit*

Rom 2:28–29

For a person is not a Jew who is one outwardly, nor is true circumcision something external and physical. **29** Rather, a person is a Jew who is one inwardly, and real circumcision is a matter of the heart—it is by the Spirit and not by the written letter. Such a person receives praise not from others but from God.[a]

Rom 7:4–6

In the same way, my friends, you have died to the law through the body of Christ, so that you may belong to another, to him who has been raised from the dead in order that we may bear fruit for God. **5** While we were living in the flesh, our sinful passions, aroused by the law, were at work in our members to bear fruit for death. **6** But now we are discharged from the law, dead to that which held us captive, so that we are slaves not under the old written code but in the new life of the Spirit.

Rom 8:3–11

For God has done what the law, weakened by the flesh, could not do: by sending his own Son in the likeness of sinful flesh, and to deal with sin, he condemned sin in the flesh, **4** so that the just requirement of the law might be fulfilled in us, who walk not according to the flesh but according to the Spirit. **5** For those who live according to the flesh set their minds on the things of the flesh, but those who live according to the Spirit set their minds on the things of the Spirit. **6** To set the mind on the flesh is death, but to set the mind on the Spirit is life and peace. **7** For this reason the mind that is set on the flesh is hostile to God; it does not submit to God's law—indeed it cannot, **8** and those who are in the flesh cannot please God. **9** But you are not in the flesh; you are in the Spirit, since the Spirit of God dwells in you. Anyone who does not have the Spirit of Christ does not belong to him. **10** But if Christ is in you, though the body is dead because of sin, the Spirit is life because of righteousness. **11** If the Spirit of him who raised Jesus from the dead dwells in you, he who raised Christ[b] from the dead will give life to your mortal bodies also through[c] his Spirit that dwells in you.

Rom 8:12–14

So then, brothers and sisters, we are debtors, not to the flesh, to live according to the flesh— **13** for if you live according to the flesh, you will die; but if by the Spirit you put to death the deeds of the body, you will live. **14** For all who are led by the Spirit of God are children of God.

1 Cor 3:1–4

And so, brothers and sisters, I could not speak to you as spiritual people, but rather as people of the flesh, as infants in Christ. **2** I fed you with milk, not solid food, for you were not ready for solid food. Even now you are still not ready, **3** for you are still of the flesh. For as long as there is jealousy and quarreling among you, are you not of the flesh, and behaving according to human inclinations? **4** For when one says, "I belong to Paul," and another, "I belong to Apollos," are you not merely human?

Gal 3:2–3

The only thing I want to learn from you is this: Did you receive the Spirit by doing the works of the law or by believing what you heard? **3** Are you so foolish? Having started with the Spirit, are you now ending with the flesh?

Gal 5:16–25

Walk[d] by the Spirit, I say, and do not gratify the desires of the flesh. **17** For what the flesh desires is opposed to

§ 51 [a] **Eph 3:14** ***the Father*** Other ancient authorities add *of our Lord Jesus Christ* [b] **Eph 3:15** ***the whole family*** Or *every family* (so NRSV) **§ 52** [a] **Rom 2:29** Translation differs from NRSV [b] **Rom 8:11** ***Christ*** Other ancient authorities read *the Christ* or *Christ Jesus* or *Jesus Christ* [c] **Rom 8:11** ***through*** Other ancient authorities read *on account of* [d] **Gal 5:16** ***Walk*** NRSV translates *Live*

δὲ πνεῦμα κατὰ τῆς σαρκός, ταῦτα γὰρ ἀλλήλοις ἀντίκειται, ἵνα μὴ ἃ ἐὰν θέλητε ταῦτα ποιῆτε. 18 εἰ δὲ πνεύματι ἄγεσθε, οὐκ ἐστὲ ὑπὸ νόμον. 19 φανερὰ δέ ἐστιν τὰ ἔργα τῆς σαρκός, ἅτινά ἐστιν πορνεία, ἀκαθαρσία, ἀσέλγεια, 20 εἰδωλολατρία, φαρμακεία, ἔχθραι, ἔρις, ζῆλος, θυμοί, ἐριθεῖαι, διχοστασίαι, αἱρέσεις, 21 ⸀φθόνοι, μέθαι, κῶμοι καὶ τὰ ὅμοια τούτοις, ἃ προλέγω ὑμῖν, καθὼς προεῖπον ὅτι οἱ τὰ τοιαῦτα πράσσοντες βασιλείαν θεοῦ οὐ κληρονομήσουσιν. 22 ὁ δὲ καρπὸς τοῦ πνεύματός ἐστιν ἀγάπη χαρὰ εἰρήνη, μακροθυμία χρηστότης ἀγαθωσύνη, πίστις 23 πραΰτης ἐγκράτεια· κατὰ τῶν τοιούτων οὐκ ἔστιν νόμος. 24 οἱ δὲ τοῦ Χριστοῦ [Ἰησοῦ] τὴν σάρκα ἐσταύρωσαν σὺν τοῖς παθήμασιν καὶ ταῖς ἐπιθυμίαις. 25 Εἰ ζῶμεν πνεύματι, πνεύματι καὶ στοιχῶμεν.

Gal 6:7–8

Μὴ πλανᾶσθε, θεὸς οὐ μυκτηρίζεται. ὃ γὰρ ἐὰν σπείρῃ ἄνθρωπος, τοῦτο καὶ θερίσει· 8 ὅτι ὁ σπείρων εἰς τὴν σάρκα ἑαυτοῦ ἐκ τῆς σαρκὸς θερίσει φθοράν, ὁ δὲ σπείρων εἰς τὸ πνεῦμα ἐκ τοῦ πνεύματος θερίσει ζωὴν αἰώνιον.

Phil 3:3

ἡμεῖς γάρ ἐσμεν ἡ περιτομή, οἱ πνεύματι ⸀θεοῦ λατρεύοντες καὶ καυχώμενοι ἐν Χριστῷ Ἰησοῦ καὶ οὐκ ἐν σαρκὶ πεποιθότες

Cf. Rom 1:3–4; 7:7–25; 15:27; 1 Cor 9:11; Gal 4:21–31; Eph 2:11–22; 1 Tim 3:16.

53. Salvation by Grace

Rom 3:21–26

Νυνὶ δὲ χωρὶς νόμου δικαιοσύνη θεοῦ πεφανέρωται μαρτυρουμένη ὑπὸ τοῦ νόμου καὶ τῶν προφητῶν, 22 δικαιοσύνη δὲ θεοῦ διὰ πίστεως Ἰησοῦ Χριστοῦ εἰς πάντας τοὺς πιστεύοντας. οὐ γάρ ἐστιν διαστολή, 23 πάντες γὰρ ἥμαρτον καὶ ὑστεροῦνται τῆς δόξης τοῦ θεοῦ 24 δικαιούμενοι δωρεὰν τῇ αὐτοῦ χάριτι διὰ τῆς ἀπολυτρώσεως τῆς ἐν Χριστῷ Ἰησοῦ· 25 ὃν προέθετο ὁ θεὸς ἱλαστήριον διὰ [τῆς] πίστεως ἐν τῷ αὐτοῦ αἵματι εἰς ἔνδειξιν τῆς δικαιοσύνης αὐτοῦ διὰ τὴν πάρεσιν τῶν προγεγονότων ἁμαρτημάτων 26 ἐν τῇ ἀνοχῇ τοῦ θεοῦ, πρὸς τὴν ἔνδειξιν τῆς δικαιοσύνης αὐτοῦ ἐν τῷ νῦν καιρῷ, εἰς τὸ εἶναι αὐτὸν δίκαιον καὶ δικαιοῦντα τὸν ἐκ πίστεως Ἰησοῦ.

Rom 4:1–8

Τί οὖν ἐροῦμεν ⸀εὑρηκέναι Ἀβραὰμ τὸν προπάτορα ἡμῶν κατὰ σάρκα; 2 εἰ γὰρ Ἀβραὰμ ἐξ ἔργων ἐδικαιώθη, ἔχει καύχημα, ἀλλ᾽ οὐ πρὸς θεόν. 3 τί γὰρ ἡ γραφὴ λέγει; ἐπίστευσεν δὲ Ἀβραὰμ τῷ θεῷ καὶ ἐλογίσθη αὐτῷ εἰς δικαιοσύνην. 4 τῷ δὲ ἐργαζομένῳ ὁ μισθὸς οὐ λογίζεται κατὰ χάριν ἀλλὰ κατὰ ὀφείλημα, 5 τῷ δὲ μὴ ἐργαζομένῳ πιστεύοντι δὲ ἐπὶ τὸν δικαιοῦντα τὸν ἀσεβῆ λογίζεται ἡ πίστις αὐτοῦ εἰς δικαιοσύνην· 6 καθάπερ καὶ Δαυὶδ λέγει τὸν μακαρισμὸν τοῦ ἀνθρώπου ᾧ ὁ θεὸς λογίζεται δικαιοσύνην χωρὶς ἔργων· 7 μακάριοι ὧν ἀφέθησαν αἱ ἀνομίαι καὶ ὧν ἐπεκαλύφθησαν αἱ ἁμαρτίαι· 8 μακάριος ἀνὴρ οὗ οὐ μὴ λογίσηται κύριος ἁμαρτίαν.

Rom 4:13–17

Οὐ γὰρ διὰ νόμου ἡ ἐπαγγελία τῷ Ἀβραὰμ ἢ τῷ σπέρματι αὐτοῦ, τὸ κληρονόμον αὐτὸν εἶναι κόσμου, ἀλλὰ διὰ δικαιοσύνης πίστεως. 14 εἰ γὰρ οἱ ἐκ νόμου κληρονόμοι, κεκένωται ἡ πίστις καὶ κατήργηται ἡ ἐπαγγελία· 15 ὁ γὰρ νόμος ὀργὴν κατεργάζεται· οὗ δὲ οὐκ ἔστιν νόμος οὐδὲ παράβασις. 16 Διὰ τοῦτο ἐκ πίστεως, ἵνα κατὰ χάριν, εἰς τὸ εἶναι βεβαίαν τὴν ἐπαγγελίαν παντὶ τῷ σπέρματι, οὐ τῷ ἐκ τοῦ νόμου μόνον ἀλλὰ καὶ τῷ ἐκ πίστεως Ἀβραάμ, ὅς ἐστιν πατὴρ πάντων ἡμῶν, 17 καθὼς γέγραπται ὅτι πατέρα πολλῶν ἐθνῶν τέθεικά σε, κατέναντι οὗ ἐπίστευσεν θεοῦ τοῦ ζῳοποιοῦντος τοὺς νεκροὺς καὶ καλοῦντος τὰ μὴ ὄντα ὡς ὄντα.

Rom 5:1–2

Δικαιωθέντες οὖν ἐκ πίστεως εἰρήνην ⸀ἔχομεν πρὸς τὸν θεὸν διὰ τοῦ κυρίου ἡμῶν Ἰησοῦ Χριστοῦ 2 δι᾽ οὗ καὶ τὴν προσαγωγὴν ἐσχήκαμεν ⸂[τῇ πίστει]⸃ εἰς τὴν χάριν ταύτην ἐν ᾗ ἑστήκαμεν καὶ καυχώμεθα ἐπ᾽ ἐλπίδι τῆς δόξης τοῦ θεοῦ.

Rom 5:15–21

Ἀλλ᾽ οὐχ ὡς τὸ παράπτωμα, οὕτως καὶ τὸ χάρισμα· εἰ γὰρ τῷ τοῦ ἑνὸς παραπτώματι οἱ πολλοὶ ἀπέθανον, πολλῷ μᾶλλον ἡ χάρις τοῦ θεοῦ καὶ ἡ δωρεὰ ἐν χάριτι τῇ τοῦ ἑνὸς ἀνθρώπου Ἰησοῦ Χριστοῦ εἰς τοὺς πολλοὺς ἐπερίσσευσεν. 16 καὶ οὐχ ὡς δι᾽ ἑνὸς ἁμαρτήσαντος τὸ δώρημα· τὸ μὲν γὰρ κρίμα ἐξ ἑνὸς εἰς κατάκριμα, τὸ δὲ χάρισμα ἐκ πολλῶν παραπτωμάτων εἰς δικαίωμα. 17 εἰ γὰρ τῷ τοῦ ἑνὸς παραπτώματι ὁ θάνατος ἐβασίλευσεν διὰ τοῦ ἑνός, πολλῷ μᾶλλον οἱ τὴν περισσείαν τῆς χάριτος καὶ τῆς δωρεᾶς τῆς δικαιοσύνης λαμβάνοντες ἐν ζωῇ βασιλεύσουσιν διὰ τοῦ ἑνὸς Ἰησοῦ Χριστοῦ. 18 Ἄρα οὖν ὡς δι᾽ ἑνὸς παραπτώματος εἰς πάντας ἀνθρώπους εἰς κατάκριμα, οὕτως καὶ δι᾽ ἑνὸς δικαιώματος εἰς πάντας ἀνθρώπους εἰς δικαίωσιν ζωῆς· 19 ὥσπερ γὰρ διὰ τῆς παρακοῆς τοῦ ἑνὸς ἀνθρώπου ἁμαρτωλοὶ κατεστάθησαν οἱ πολλοί, οὕτως καὶ διὰ τῆς ὑπακοῆς τοῦ ἑνὸς δίκαιοι κατασταθήσονται οἱ πολλοί. 20 νόμος δὲ παρεισῆλθεν, ἵνα πλεονάσῃ τὸ παράπτωμα· οὗ δὲ ἐπλεόνασεν ἡ ἁμαρτία, ὑπερεπερίσσευσεν ἡ χάρις, 21 ἵνα ὥσπερ ἐβασίλευσεν ἡ ἁμαρτία ἐν τῷ θανάτῳ, οὕτως καὶ ἡ χάρις βασιλεύσῃ διὰ δικαιοσύνης εἰς ζωὴν αἰώνιον διὰ Ἰησοῦ Χριστοῦ τοῦ κυρίου ἡμῶν.

Gal 5:21 ***φθονοι*** 𝔓[46] ℵ B 33] *add.* φονοι A C D 1739. 1881 *Byz* **Phil 3:3** ***θεου*** ℵ* A B C D[2] 33. 1739. 1881 *Byz*] θεω ℵ[2] D* ¦ *om.* 𝔓[46] **§ 53** **Rom 4:1** ***ευρηκεναι*** ℵ A C D 33. 1881 *Byz*] *om.* B (1739) **Rom 5:1** ***εχομεν*** ℵ[1] B[2] 0220[vid]. 1739[c]. 1881] εχωμεν ℵ* A B* C D 33. 1739* **Rom 5:2** ***τη πιστει*** ℵ*.[2] C 33. 1739. 1881 *Byz*] εν τη πιστει ℵ[1] A ¦ *om.* B D 0220

the Spirit, and what the Spirit desires is opposed to the flesh; for these are opposed to each other, to prevent you from doing what you want. 18 But if you are led by the Spirit, you are not subject to the law. 19 Now the works of the flesh are obvious: fornication, impurity, licentiousness, 20 idolatry, sorcery, enmities, strife, jealousy, anger, quarrels, dissensions, factions, 21 envy,[e] drunkenness, carousing, and things like these. I am warning you, as I warned you before: those who do such things will not inherit the kingdom of God. 22 By contrast, the fruit of the Spirit is love, joy, peace, patience, kindness, generosity, faithfulness, 23 gentleness, and self-control. There is no law against such things. 24 And those who belong to Christ Jesus have crucified the flesh with its passions and desires. 25 If we live by the Spirit, let us also be guided by the Spirit.

Gal 6:7–8

Do not be deceived; God is not mocked, for you reap whatever you sow. 8 If you sow to your own flesh, you will reap corruption from the flesh; but if you sow to the Spirit, you will reap eternal life from the Spirit.

Phil 3:3

For it is we who are the circumcision, who worship in the Spirit of God[f] and boast in Christ Jesus and have no confidence in the flesh

Cf. Rom 1:3–4; 7:7–25; 15:27; 1 Cor 9:11; Gal 4:21–31; Eph 2:11–22; 1 Tim 3:16.

53. Salvation by Grace

Rom 3:21–26

But now, apart from law, the righteousness of God has been disclosed, and is attested by the law and the prophets, 22 the righteousness of God through faith in Jesus Christ for all who believe. For there is no distinction, 23 since all have sinned and fall short of the glory of God; 24 they are now justified by his grace as a gift, through the redemption that is in Christ Jesus, 25 whom God put forward as a sacrifice of atonement by his blood, effective through faith. He did this to show his righteousness, because in his divine forbearance he had passed over the sins previously committed; 26 it was to prove at the present time that he himself is righteous and that he justifies the one who has faith in Jesus.

Rom 4:1–8

What then are we to say was gained by[a] Abraham, our ancestor according to the flesh? 2 For if Abraham was justified by works, he has something to boast about, but not before God. 3 For what does the scripture say? "Abraham believed God, and it was reckoned to him as righteousness." 4 Now to one who works, wages are not reckoned as a gift but as something due. 5 But to one who without works trusts him who justifies the ungodly, such faith is reckoned as righteousness. 6 So also David speaks of the blessedness of those to whom God reckons righteousness apart from works: 7 "Blessed are those whose iniquities are forgiven, and whose sins are covered; 8 blessed is the one against whom the Lord will not reckon sin."

Rom 4:13–17

For the promise that he would inherit the world did not come to Abraham or to his descendants through the law but through the righteousness of faith. 14 If it is the adherents of the law who are to be the heirs, faith is null and the promise is void. 15 For the law brings wrath; but where there is no law, neither is there violation. 16 For this reason it depends on faith, in order that the promise may rest on grace and be guaranteed to all his descendants, not only to the adherents of the law but also to those who share the faith of Abraham (for he is the father of all of us, 17 as it is written, "I have made you the father of many nations")—in the presence of the God in whom he believed, who gives life to the dead and calls into existence the things that do not exist.

Rom 5:1–2

Therefore, since we are justified by faith, we[b] have peace with God through our Lord Jesus Christ, 2 through whom we have obtained access[c] to this grace in which we stand; and we boast in our hope of sharing the glory of God.

Rom 5:15–21

But the free gift is not like the trespass. For if the many died through the one man's trespass, much more surely have the grace of God and the free gift in the grace of the one man, Jesus Christ, abounded for the many. 16 And the free gift is not like the effect of the one man's sin. For the judgment following one trespass brought condemnation, but the free gift following many trespasses brings justification. 17 If, because of the one man's trespass, death exercised dominion through that one, much more surely will those who receive the abundance of grace and the free gift of righteousness exercise dominion in life through the one man, Jesus Christ. 18 Therefore just as one man's trespass led to condemnation for all, so one man's act of righteousness leads to justification and life for all. 19 For just as by the one man's disobedience the many were made sinners, so by the one man's obedience the many will be made righteous. 20 But law came in, with the result that the trespass multiplied; but where sin increased, grace abounded all the more, 21 so that, just as sin exercised dominion in death, so grace might also exercise dominion through justification leading to eternal life through Jesus Christ our Lord.

[e] **Gal 5:21** *envy,* Other ancient authorities add *murder* [f] **Phil 3:3** *worship in the Spirit of God* Other ancient authorities read *worship God in the Spirit* **§ 53** [a] **Rom 4:1** *say was gained by* A few ancient authorities read *say about* [b] **Rom 5:1** *we* Other ancient authorities read *let us* [c] **Rom 5:2** *obtained access* Other ancient authorities add *by faith*

Rom 6:14–18

ἁμαρτία γὰρ ὑμῶν οὐ κυριεύσει· οὐ γάρ
ἐστε ὑπὸ νόμον ἀλλὰ ὑπὸ χάριν. **15** Τί οὖν;
ἁμαρτήσωμεν, ὅτι οὐκ ἐσμὲν ὑπὸ νόμον
ἀλλὰ ὑπὸ χάριν; μὴ γένοιτο. **16** οὐκ οἴδατε
ὅτι ᾧ παριστάνετε ἑαυτοὺς δούλους εἰς
ὑπακοήν, δοῦλοί ἐστε ᾧ ὑπακούετε, ἤτοι
ἁμαρτίας εἰς θάνατον ἢ ὑπακοῆς εἰς δι-
καιοσύνην; **17** χάρις δὲ τῷ θεῷ ὅτι ἦτε
δοῦλοι τῆς ἁμαρτίας ὑπηκούσατε δὲ ἐκ
καρδίας εἰς ὃν παρεδόθητε τύπον διδαχῆς,
18 ἐλευθερωθέντες δὲ ἀπὸ τῆς ἁμαρτίας
ἐδουλώθητε τῇ δικαιοσύνῃ.

Rom 11:5–6

οὕτως οὖν καὶ ἐν τῷ νῦν καιρῷ λεῖμμα
κατ᾽ ἐκλογὴν χάριτος γέγονεν· **6** εἰ δὲ
χάριτι, οὐκέτι ἐξ ἔργων, ἐπεὶ ἡ χάρις
οὐκέτι γίνεται ⸀χάρις.

2 Cor 6:1–2

Συνεργοῦντες δὲ καὶ παρακαλοῦμεν μὴ
εἰς κενὸν τὴν χάριν τοῦ θεοῦ δέξασθαι
ὑμᾶς· **2** λέγει γάρ· καιρῷ δεκτῷ ἐπήκουσά
σου καὶ ἐν ἡμέρᾳ σωτηρίας ἐβοήθησά
σοι. ἰδοὺ νῦν καιρὸς εὐπρόσδεκτος, ἰδοὺ
νῦν ἡμέρα σωτηρίας.

2 Cor 8:9

γινώσκετε γὰρ τὴν χάριν τοῦ κυρίου ἡμῶν
Ἰησοῦ Χριστοῦ, ὅτι δι᾽ ὑμᾶς ἐπτώχευσεν
πλούσιος ὤν, ἵνα ὑμεῖς τῇ ἐκείνου πτω-
χείᾳ πλουτήσητε.

Gal 2:19–21

ἐγὼ γὰρ διὰ νόμου νόμῳ ἀπέθανον, ἵνα
θεῷ ζήσω. Χριστῷ συνεσταύρωμαι· **20** ζῶ
δὲ οὐκέτι ἐγώ, ζῇ δὲ ἐν ἐμοὶ Χριστός· ὃ
δὲ νῦν ζῶ ἐν σαρκί, ἐν πίστει ζῶ τῇ τοῦ
υἱοῦ τοῦ θεοῦ τοῦ ἀγαπήσαντός με καὶ
παραδόντος ἑαυτὸν ὑπὲρ ἐμοῦ. **21** Οὐκ
ἀθετῶ τὴν χάριν τοῦ θεοῦ· εἰ γὰρ διὰ
νόμου δικαιοσύνη, ἄρα Χριστὸς δωρεὰν
ἀπέθανεν.

Gal 5:2–6

Ἴδε ἐγὼ Παῦλος λέγω ὑμῖν ὅτι ἐὰν πε-
ριτέμνησθε, Χριστὸς ὑμᾶς οὐδὲν ὠφελήσει.
3 μαρτύρομαι δὲ πάλιν παντὶ ἀνθρώπῳ
περιτεμνομένῳ ὅτι ὀφειλέτης ἐστὶν ὅλον
τὸν νόμον ποιῆσαι. **4** κατηργήθητε ἀπὸ
Χριστοῦ, οἵτινες ἐν νόμῳ δικαιοῦσθε, τῆς
χάριτος ἐξεπέσατε. **5** ἡμεῖς γὰρ πνεύματι
ἐκ πίστεως ἐλπίδα δικαιοσύνης ἀπεκδε-
χόμεθα. **6** ἐν γὰρ Χριστῷ Ἰησοῦ οὔτε πε-
ριτομή τι ἰσχύει οὔτε ἀκροβυστία ἀλλὰ
πίστις δι᾽ ἀγάπης ἐνεργουμένη.

Eph 1:6–7

εἰς ἔπαινον δόξης τῆς χάριτος αὐτοῦ ἧς
ἐχαρίτωσεν ἡμᾶς ἐν τῷ ἠγαπημένῳ. **7** Ἐν ᾧ
ἔχομεν τὴν ἀπολύτρωσιν διὰ τοῦ αἵματος
αὐτοῦ, τὴν ἄφεσιν τῶν παραπτωμάτων,
κατὰ τὸ πλοῦτος τῆς χάριτος αὐτοῦ

Eph 2:4–10

ὁ δὲ θεὸς πλούσιος ὢν ἐν ἐλέει, διὰ τὴν
πολλὴν ἀγάπην αὐτοῦ ἣν ἠγάπησεν
ἡμᾶς, **5** καὶ ὄντας ἡμᾶς νεκροὺς τοῖς
παραπτώμασιν συνεζωοποίησεν ⸂τῷ
Χριστῷ⸃, —χάριτί ἐστε σεσῳσμένοι—
6 καὶ συνήγειρεν καὶ συνεκάθισεν ἐν
τοῖς ἐπουρανίοις ἐν Χριστῷ Ἰησοῦ, **7** ἵνα
ἐνδείξηται ἐν τοῖς αἰῶσιν τοῖς ἐπερ-
χομένοις τὸ ὑπερβάλλον πλοῦτος τῆς
χάριτος αὐτοῦ ἐν χρηστότητι ἐφ᾽ ἡμᾶς
ἐν Χριστῷ Ἰησοῦ. **8** Τῇ γὰρ χάριτί ἐστε
σεσῳσμένοι διὰ πίστεως· καὶ τοῦτο οὐκ
ἐξ ὑμῶν, θεοῦ τὸ δῶρον· **9** οὐκ ἐξ ἔργων,
ἵνα μή τις καυχήσηται. **10** αὐτοῦ γάρ ἐσμεν
ποίημα, κτισθέντες ἐν Χριστῷ Ἰησοῦ ἐπὶ
ἔργοις ἀγαθοῖς οἷς προητοίμασεν ὁ θεός,
ἵνα ἐν αὐτοῖς περιπατήσωμεν.

2 Thess 2:16–17

Αὐτὸς δὲ ὁ κύριος ἡμῶν Ἰησοῦς Χριστὸς
καὶ [ὁ] θεὸς ὁ πατὴρ ἡμῶν ὁ ἀγαπήσας
ἡμᾶς καὶ δοὺς παράκλησιν αἰωνίαν καὶ
ἐλπίδα ἀγαθὴν ἐν χάριτι, **17** παρακαλέσαι
ὑμῶν τὰς καρδίας καὶ στηρίξαι ἐν παντὶ
ἔργῳ καὶ λόγῳ ἀγαθῷ.

2 Tim 1:9–10

τοῦ σώσαντος ἡμᾶς καὶ καλέσαντος κλήσει
ἁγίᾳ, οὐ κατὰ τὰ ἔργα ἡμῶν ἀλλὰ κατὰ
ἰδίαν πρόθεσιν καὶ χάριν, τὴν δοθεῖσαν
ἡμῖν ἐν Χριστῷ Ἰησοῦ πρὸ χρόνων αἰω-
νίων, **10** φανερωθεῖσαν δὲ νῦν διὰ τῆς
ἐπιφανείας τοῦ σωτῆρος ἡμῶν Χριστοῦ
Ἰησοῦ, καταργήσαντος μὲν τὸν θάνατον
φωτίσαντος δὲ ζωὴν καὶ ἀφθαρσίαν διὰ
τοῦ εὐαγγελίου

Titus 2:11–14

Ἐπεφάνη γὰρ ἡ χάρις τοῦ θεοῦ σωτήριος
πᾶσιν ἀνθρώποις **12** παιδεύουσα ἡμᾶς,
ἵνα ἀρνησάμενοι τὴν ἀσέβειαν καὶ τὰς
κοσμικὰς ἐπιθυμίας σωφρόνως καὶ δι-
καίως καὶ εὐσεβῶς ζήσωμεν ἐν τῷ νῦν
αἰῶνι, **13** προσδεχόμενοι τὴν μακαρίαν
ἐλπίδα καὶ ἐπιφάνειαν τῆς δόξης τοῦ
μεγάλου θεοῦ καὶ σωτῆρος ἡμῶν Ἰησοῦ
Χριστοῦ, **14** ὃς ἔδωκεν ἑαυτὸν ὑπὲρ ἡμῶν,
ἵνα λυτρώσηται ἡμᾶς ἀπὸ πάσης ἀνομίας
καὶ καθαρίσῃ ἑαυτῷ λαὸν περιούσιον,
ζηλωτὴν καλῶν ἔργων.

Titus 3:4–7

ὅτε δὲ ἡ χρηστότης καὶ ἡ φιλανθρω-
πία ἐπεφάνη τοῦ σωτῆρος ἡμῶν θεοῦ,
5 οὐκ ἐξ ἔργων τῶν ἐν δικαιοσύνῃ ἃ
ἐποιήσαμεν ἡμεῖς ἀλλὰ κατὰ τὸ αὐτοῦ
ἔλεος ἔσωσεν ἡμᾶς διὰ λουτροῦ παλιγ-
γενεσίας καὶ ἀνακαινώσεως πνεύματος
ἁγίου, **6** οὗ ἐξέχεεν ἐφ᾽ ἡμᾶς πλουσίως
διὰ Ἰησοῦ Χριστοῦ τοῦ σωτῆρος ἡμῶν,
7 ἵνα δικαιωθέντες τῇ ἐκείνου χάριτι
κληρονόμοι γενηθῶμεν κατ᾽ ἐλπίδα
ζωῆς αἰωνίου.

Cf. Rom 6:1–4; 2 Cor 4:13–15; Gal 1:6–9; Col 1:5–6; 2 Thess 1:11–12; 1 Tim 1:14; 2 Tim 2:1; Acts 13:43; 14:3; 20:24; 20:32.

Rom 11:6 ***χαρις*** 𝔓^{46} א* A C D 1739. 1881] *add.* ει δε εξ εργων ουκετι εστι χαρις, επει το εργον ουκετι εστιν εργον א^{2} (B) 33^{vid} *Byz* **Eph 2:5** ***τω Χριστω*** א A D 1739. 1881 *Byz*] εν τω Χριστω 𝔓^{46} B 33

Rom 6:14–18

For sin will have no dominion over you, since you are not under law but under grace. **15** What then? Should we sin because we are not under law but under grace? By no means! **16** Do you not know that if you present yourselves to anyone as obedient slaves, you are slaves of the one whom you obey, either of sin, which leads to death, or of obedience, which leads to righteousness? **17** But thanks be to God that you, having once been slaves of sin, have become obedient from the heart to the form of teaching to which you were entrusted, **18** and that you, having been set free from sin, have become slaves of righteousness.

Rom 11:5–6

So too at the present time there is a remnant, chosen by grace. **6** But if it is by grace, it is no longer on the basis of works, otherwise grace would no longer be grace.[d]

2 Cor 6:1–2

As we work together with him, we urge you also not to accept the grace of God in vain. **2** For he says, "At an acceptable time I have listened to you, and on a day of salvation I have helped you." See, now is the acceptable time; see, now is the day of salvation!

2 Cor 8:9

For you know the grace[e] of our Lord Jesus Christ, that though he was rich, yet for your sakes he became poor, so that by his poverty you might become rich.

Gal 2:19–21

For through the law I died to the law, so that I might live to God. I have been crucified with Christ; **20** and it is no longer I who live, but it is Christ who lives in me. And the life I now live in the flesh I live by faith in the Son of God, who loved me and gave himself for me. **21** I do not nullify the grace of God; for if justification comes through the law, then Christ died for nothing.

Gal 5:2–6

Listen! I, Paul, am telling you that if you let yourselves be circumcised, Christ will be of no benefit to you. **3** Once again I testify to every man who lets himself be circumcised that he is obliged to obey the entire law. **4** You who want to be justified by the law have cut yourselves off from Christ; you have fallen away from grace. **5** For through the Spirit, by faith, we eagerly wait for the hope of righteousness. **6** For in Christ Jesus neither circumcision nor uncircumcision counts for anything; the only thing that counts is faith working through love.

Eph 1:6–7

to the praise of his glorious grace that he freely bestowed on us in the Beloved. **7** In him we have redemption through his blood, the forgiveness of our trespasses, according to the riches of his grace

Eph 2:4–10

But God, who is rich in mercy, out of the great love with which he loved us **5** even when we were dead through our trespasses, made us alive together with Christ[f]—by grace you have been saved— **6** and raised us up with him and seated us with him in the heavenly places in Christ Jesus, **7** so that in the ages to come he might show the immeasurable riches of his grace in kindness toward us in Christ Jesus. **8** For by grace you have been saved through faith, and this is not your own doing; it is the gift of God— **9** not the result of works, so that no one may boast. **10** For we are what he has made us, created in Christ Jesus for good works, which God prepared beforehand to be our way of life.

2 Thess 2:16–17

Now may our Lord Jesus Christ himself and God our Father, who loved us and through grace gave us eternal comfort and good hope, **17** comfort your hearts and strengthen them in every good work and word.

2 Tim 1:9–10

who saved us and called us with a holy calling, not according to our works but according to his own purpose and grace. This grace was given to us in Christ Jesus before the ages began, **10** but it has now been revealed through the appearing of our Savior Christ Jesus, who abolished death and brought life and immortality to light through the gospel.

Titus 2:11–14

For the grace of God has appeared, bringing salvation to all, **12** training us to renounce impiety and worldly passions, and in the present age to live lives that are self-controlled, upright, and godly, **13** while we wait for the blessed hope and the manifestation of the glory of our great God and Savior, Jesus Christ. **14** He it is who gave himself for us that he might redeem us from all iniquity and purify for himself a people of his own who are zealous for good deeds.

Titus 3:4–7

But when the goodness and loving kindness of God our Savior appeared, **5** he saved us, not because of any works of righteousness that we had done, but according to his mercy, through the water of rebirth and renewal by the Holy Spirit. **6** This Spirit he poured out on us richly through Jesus Christ our Savior, **7** so that, having been justified by his grace, we might become heirs according to the hope of eternal life.

Cf. Rom 6:1–4; 2 Cor 4:13–15; Gal 1:6–9; Col 1:5–6; 2 Thess 1:11–12; 1 Tim 1:14; 2 Tim 2:1; Acts 13:43; 14:3; 20:24; 20:32.

[d] **Rom 11:6** ***grace*** Other ancient authorities add *But if it is by works, it is no longer on the basis of grace, otherwise work would no longer be work* [e] **2 Cor 8:9** ***grace*** NRSV translates *generous act* [f] **Eph 2:5** ***together with Christ*** Other ancient authorities read *in Christ*

54. Boasting in God

Rom 5:1–11

Δικαιωθέντες οὖν ἐκ πίστεως εἰρήνην ⸀ἔχομεν πρὸς τὸν θεὸν διὰ τοῦ κυρίου ἡμῶν Ἰησοῦ Χριστοῦ **2** δι᾽ οὗ καὶ τὴν προσαγωγὴν ἐσχήκαμεν ⸂[τῇ πίστει]⸃ εἰς τὴν χάριν ταύτην ἐν ᾗ ἑστήκαμεν καὶ καυχώμεθα ἐπ᾽ ἐλπίδι τῆς δόξης τοῦ θεοῦ. **3** οὐ μόνον δέ, ἀλλὰ καὶ καυχώμεθα ἐν ταῖς θλίψεσιν, εἰδότες ὅτι ἡ θλῖψις ὑπομονὴν κατεργάζεται, **4** ἡ δὲ ὑπομονὴ δοκιμήν, ἡ δὲ δοκιμὴ ἐλπίδα. **5** ἡ δὲ ἐλπὶς οὐ καταισχύνει, ὅτι ἡ ἀγάπη τοῦ θεοῦ ἐκκέχυται ἐν ταῖς καρδίαις ἡμῶν διὰ πνεύματος ἁγίου τοῦ δοθέντος ἡμῖν. **6** Ἔτι γὰρ Χριστὸς ὄντων ἡμῶν ἀσθενῶν ἔτι κατὰ καιρὸν ὑπὲρ ἀσεβῶν ἀπέθανεν. **7** μόλις γὰρ ὑπὲρ δικαίου τις ἀποθανεῖται· ὑπὲρ γὰρ τοῦ ἀγαθοῦ τάχα τις καὶ τολμᾷ ἀποθανεῖν· **8** συνίστησιν δὲ τὴν ἑαυτοῦ ἀγάπην εἰς ἡμᾶς ὁ θεός, ὅτι ἔτι ἁμαρτωλῶν ὄντων ἡμῶν Χριστὸς ὑπὲρ ἡμῶν ἀπέθανεν. **9** πολλῷ οὖν μᾶλλον δικαιωθέντες νῦν ἐν τῷ αἵματι αὐτοῦ σωθησόμεθα δι᾽ αὐτοῦ ἀπὸ τῆς ὀργῆς. **10** εἰ γὰρ ἐχθροὶ ὄντες κατηλλάγημεν τῷ θεῷ διὰ τοῦ θανάτου τοῦ υἱοῦ αὐτοῦ, πολλῷ μᾶλλον καταλλαγέντες σωθησόμεθα ἐν τῇ ζωῇ αὐτοῦ· **11** οὐ μόνον δέ, ἀλλὰ καὶ καυχώμενοι ἐν τῷ θεῷ διὰ τοῦ κυρίου ἡμῶν Ἰησοῦ Χριστοῦ δι᾽ οὗ νῦν τὴν καταλλαγὴν ἐλάβομεν.

Rom 15:16–19

εἰς τὸ εἶναί με λειτουργὸν Χριστοῦ Ἰησοῦ εἰς τὰ ἔθνη, ἱερουργοῦντα τὸ εὐαγγέλιον τοῦ θεοῦ, ἵνα γένηται ἡ προσφορὰ τῶν ἐθνῶν εὐπρόσδεκτος, ἡγιασμένη ἐν πνεύματι ἁγίῳ. **17** ἔχω οὖν [τὴν] καύχησιν ἐν Χριστῷ Ἰησοῦ τὰ πρὸς τὸν θεόν· **18** οὐ γὰρ τολμήσω τι λαλεῖν ὧν οὐ κατειργάσατο Χριστὸς δι᾽ ἐμοῦ εἰς ὑπακοὴν ἐθνῶν, λόγῳ καὶ ἔργῳ, **19** ἐν δυνάμει σημείων καὶ τεράτων, ἐν δυνάμει πνεύματος ⸀[θεοῦ]· ὥστε με ἀπὸ Ἰερουσαλὴμ καὶ κύκλῳ μέχρι τοῦ Ἰλλυρικοῦ πεπληρωκέναι τὸ εὐαγγέλιον τοῦ Χριστοῦ

1 Cor 1:26–31

Βλέπετε γὰρ τὴν κλῆσιν ὑμῶν, ἀδελφοί, ὅτι οὐ πολλοὶ σοφοὶ κατὰ σάρκα, οὐ πολλοὶ δυνατοί, οὐ πολλοὶ εὐγενεῖς· **27** ἀλλὰ τὰ μωρὰ τοῦ κόσμου ἐξελέξατο ὁ θεός, ἵνα καταισχύνῃ τοὺς σοφούς, καὶ τὰ ἀσθενῆ τοῦ κόσμου ἐξελέξατο ὁ θεός, ἵνα καταισχύνῃ τὰ ἰσχυρά, **28** καὶ τὰ ἀγενῆ τοῦ κόσμου καὶ τὰ ἐξουθενημένα ἐξελέξατο ὁ θεός, τὰ μὴ ὄντα, ἵνα τὰ ὄντα καταργήσῃ, **29** ὅπως μὴ καυχήσηται πᾶσα σὰρξ ἐνώπιον τοῦ θεοῦ. **30** ἐξ αὐτοῦ δὲ ὑμεῖς ἐστε ἐν Χριστῷ Ἰησοῦ, ὃς ἐγενήθη σοφία ἡμῖν ἀπὸ θεοῦ, δικαιοσύνη τε καὶ ἁγιασμὸς καὶ ἀπολύτρωσις, **31** ἵνα καθὼς γέγραπται· ὁ καυχώμενος ἐν κυρίῳ καυχάσθω.

2 Cor 1:12–14

Ἡ γὰρ καύχησις ἡμῶν αὕτη ἐστίν, τὸ μαρτύριον τῆς συνειδήσεως ἡμῶν, ὅτι ἐν ⸀ἁπλότητι καὶ εἰλικρινείᾳ τοῦ θεοῦ, [καὶ] οὐκ ἐν σοφίᾳ σαρκικῇ ἀλλ᾽ ἐν χάριτι θεοῦ, ἀνεστράφημεν ἐν τῷ κόσμῳ, περισσοτέρως δὲ πρὸς ὑμᾶς. **13** οὐ γὰρ ἄλλα γράφομεν ὑμῖν ἀλλ᾽ ἢ ἃ ἀναγινώσκετε ἢ καὶ ἐπιγινώσκετε· ἐλπίζω δὲ ὅτι ἕως τέλους ἐπιγνώσεσθε, **14** καθὼς καὶ ἐπέγνωτε ἡμᾶς ἀπὸ μέρους, ὅτι καύχημα ὑμῶν ἐσμεν καθάπερ καὶ ὑμεῖς ἡμῶν ἐν τῇ ἡμέρᾳ τοῦ κυρίου [ἡμῶν] Ἰησοῦ.

2 Cor 10:12–18

Οὐ γὰρ τολμῶμεν ἐγκρῖναι ἢ συγκρῖναι ἑαυτούς τισιν τῶν ἑαυτοὺς συνιστανόντων, ἀλλὰ αὐτοὶ ἐν ἑαυτοῖς ἑαυτοὺς μετροῦντες καὶ συγκρίνοντες ἑαυτοὺς ἑαυτοῖς οὐ συνιᾶσιν. **13** ἡμεῖς δὲ οὐκ εἰς τὰ ἄμετρα καυχησόμεθα ἀλλὰ κατὰ τὸ μέτρον τοῦ κανόνος οὗ ἐμέρισεν ἡμῖν ὁ θεὸς μέτρου, ἐφικέσθαι ἄχρι καὶ ὑμῶν. **14** οὐ γὰρ ὡς μὴ ἐφικνούμενοι εἰς ὑμᾶς ὑπερεκτείνομεν ἑαυτούς, ἄχρι γὰρ καὶ ὑμῶν ἐφθάσαμεν ἐν τῷ εὐαγγελίῳ τοῦ Χριστοῦ, **15** οὐκ εἰς τὰ ἄμετρα καυχώμενοι ἐν ἀλλοτρίοις κόποις, ἐλπίδα δὲ ἔχοντες αὐξανομένης τῆς πίστεως ὑμῶν ἐν ὑμῖν μεγαλυνθῆναι κατὰ τὸν κανόνα ἡμῶν εἰς περισσείαν **16** εἰς τὰ ὑπερέκεινα ὑμῶν εὐαγγελίσασθαι, οὐκ ἐν ἀλλοτρίῳ κανόνι εἰς τὰ ἕτοιμα καυχήσασθαι. **17** Ὁ δὲ καυχώμενος ἐν κυρίῳ καυχάσθω· **18** οὐ γὰρ ὁ ἑαυτὸν συνιστάνων, ἐκεῖνός ἐστιν δόκιμος, ἀλλὰ ὃν ὁ κύριος συνίστησιν.

Gal 6:11–16

Ἴδετε πηλίκοις ὑμῖν γράμμασιν ἔγραψα τῇ ἐμῇ χειρί. **12** Ὅσοι θέλουσιν εὐπροσωπῆσαι ἐν σαρκί, οὗτοι ἀναγκάζουσιν ὑμᾶς περιτέμνεσθαι, μόνον ἵνα τῷ σταυρῷ τοῦ Χριστοῦ μὴ διώκωνται. **13** οὐδὲ γὰρ οἱ περιτεμνόμενοι αὐτοὶ νόμον φυλάσσουσιν ἀλλὰ θέλουσιν ὑμᾶς περιτέμνεσθαι, ἵνα ἐν τῇ ὑμετέρᾳ σαρκὶ καυχήσωνται. **14** Ἐμοὶ δὲ μὴ γένοιτο καυχᾶσθαι εἰ μὴ ἐν τῷ σταυρῷ τοῦ κυρίου ἡμῶν Ἰησοῦ Χριστοῦ, δι᾽ οὗ ἐμοὶ κόσμος ἐσταύρωται κἀγὼ κόσμῳ. **15** ⸂οὔτε γὰρ⸃ περιτομή τί ἐστιν οὔτε ἀκροβυστία ἀλλὰ καινὴ κτίσις. **16** καὶ ὅσοι τῷ κανόνι τούτῳ ⸀στοιχήσουσιν, εἰρήνη ἐπ᾽ αὐτοὺς καὶ ἔλεος καὶ ἐπὶ τὸν Ἰσραὴλ τοῦ θεοῦ.

Phil 3:3

ἡμεῖς γάρ ἐσμεν ἡ περιτομή, οἱ πνεύματι ⸀θεοῦ λατρεύοντες καὶ καυχώμενοι ἐν Χριστῷ Ἰησοῦ καὶ οὐκ ἐν σαρκὶ πεποιθότες

Cf. Rom 4:1–2; 1 Cor 3:18–23; 2 Cor 5:11–12; 11:21b–12:10; Eph 2:8–10; Phil 1:26; 2:16. For boasting in God in action, see Rom 8:31–39; 1 Cor 15:54–57.

§ 54 **Rom 5:1** ***εχομεν*** ℵ¹ B² 0220vid. 1739c. 1881] εχωμεν ℵ* A B* C D 33. 1739* **Rom 5:2** ***τη πιστει*** ℵ*.² C 33. 1739. 1881 *Byz*] εν τη πιστει ℵ¹ A ¦ *om*. B D 0220 **Rom 15:19** ***θεου*** 𝔓⁴⁶ ℵ D¹ *Byz*] *om*. B ¦ αγιου A D*.² 33. 1739. 1881 **2 Cor 1:12** ***απλοτητι*** ℵ² D *Byz*] αγιοτητι 𝔓⁴⁶ ℵ* A B C 33. 1739. 1881 **Gal 6:15** ***ουτε γαρ*** 𝔓⁴⁶ B 33. 1739*] εν γαρ Χριστω Ιησου ουτε ℵ A C D (1739c). 1881 *Byz* **Gal 6:16** ***στοιχησουσιν*** ℵ B C² 33 *Byz*] στοιχουσιν A C* D 1739. 1881 ¦ στοιχησωσιν 𝔓⁴⁶ **Phil 3:3** ***θεου*** ℵ* A B C D² 33. 1739. 1881 *Byz*] θεω ℵ² D* ¦ *om*. 𝔓⁴⁶

54. Boasting in God

Rom 5:1–11

Therefore, since we are justified by faith, we[a] have peace with God through our Lord Jesus Christ, 2 through whom we have obtained access[b] to this grace in which we stand; and we boast in our hope of sharing the glory of God. 3 And not only that, but we also boast in our sufferings, knowing that suffering produces endurance, 4 and endurance produces character, and character produces hope, 5 and hope does not disappoint us, because God's love has been poured into our hearts through the Holy Spirit that has been given to us. 6 For while we were still weak, at the right time Christ died for the ungodly. 7 Indeed, rarely will anyone die for a righteous person—though perhaps for a good person someone might actually dare to die. 8 But God proves his love for us in that while we still were sinners Christ died for us. 9 Much more surely then, now that we have been justified by his blood, will we be saved through him from the wrath of God. 10 For if while we were enemies, we were reconciled to God through the death of his Son, much more surely, having been reconciled, will we be saved by his life. 11 But more than that, we even boast in God through our Lord Jesus Christ, through whom we have now received reconciliation.

Rom 15:16–19

to be a minister of Christ Jesus to the Gentiles in the priestly service of the gospel of God, so that the offering of the Gentiles may be acceptable, sanctified by the Holy Spirit. 17 In Christ Jesus, then, I have reason to boast of my work for God. 18 For I will not venture to speak of anything except what Christ has accomplished through me to win obedience from the Gentiles, by word and deed, 19 by the power of signs and wonders, by the power of the Spirit of God,[c] so that from Jerusalem and as far around as Illyricum I have fully proclaimed the good news of Christ.

1 Cor 1:26–31

Consider your own call, brothers and sisters: not many of you were wise by human standards, not many were powerful, not many were of noble birth. 27 But God chose what is foolish in the world to shame the wise; God chose what is weak in the world to shame the strong; 28 God chose what is low and despised in the world, things that are not, to reduce to nothing things that are, 29 so that no one might boast in the presence of God. 30 He is the source of your life in Christ Jesus, who became for us wisdom from God, and righteousness and sanctification and redemption, 31 in order that, as it is written, "Let the one who boasts, boast in the Lord."

2 Cor 1:12–14

Indeed, this is our boast, the testimony of our conscience: we have behaved in the world with frankness[d] and godly sincerity, not by earthly wisdom but by the grace of God—and all the more toward you. 13 For we write you nothing other than what you can read and also understand; I hope you will understand until the end— 14 as you have already understood us in part—that on the day of the Lord Jesus we are your boast even as you are our boast.

2 Cor 10:12–18

We do not dare to classify or compare ourselves with some of those who commend themselves. But when they measure themselves by one another, and compare themselves with one another, they do not show good sense. 13 We, however, will not boast beyond limits, but will keep within the field that God has assigned to us, to reach out even as far as you. 14 For we were not overstepping our limits when we reached you; we were the first to come all the way to you with the good news of Christ. 15 We do not boast beyond limits, that is, in the labors of others; but our hope is that, as your faith increases, our sphere of action among you may be greatly enlarged, 16 so that we may proclaim the good news in lands beyond you, without boasting of work already done in someone else's sphere of action. 17 "Let the one who boasts, boast in the Lord." 18 For it is not those who commend themselves that are approved, but those whom the Lord commends.

Gal 6:11–16

See what large letters I make when I am writing in my own hand! 12 It is those who want to make a good showing in the flesh that try to compel you to be circumcised—only that they may not be persecuted for the cross of Christ. 13 Even the circumcised do not themselves obey the law, but they want you to be circumcised so that they may boast about your flesh. 14 May I never boast of anything except the cross of our Lord Jesus Christ, by which the world has been crucified to me, and I to the world. 15 For[e] neither circumcision nor uncircumcision is anything; but a new creation is everything! 16 As for those who will follow[f] this rule—peace be upon them, and mercy, and upon the Israel of God.

Phil 3:3

For it is we who are the circumcision, who worship in the Spirit of God[g] and boast in Christ Jesus and have no confidence in the flesh

Cf. Rom 4:1–2; 1 Cor 3:18–23; 2 Cor 5:11–12; 11:21b–12:10; Eph 2:8–10; Phil 1:26; 2:16. For boasting in God in action, see Rom 8:31–39; 1 Cor 15:54–57.

§ 54 [a] **Rom 5:1** ***we*** Other ancient authorities read *let us* [b] **Rom 5:2** ***obtained access*** Other ancient authorities add *by faith* [c] **Rom 15:19** ***of the Spirit of God*** Other ancient authorities read *of the Spirit* or *of the Holy Spirit* [d] **2 Cor 1:12** ***frankness*** Other ancient authorities read *holiness* [e] **Gal 6:15** ***For*** Other ancient authorities add *in Christ Jesus* [f] **Gal 6:16** ***will follow*** Other ancient authorities read *follow* [g] **Phil 3:3** ***worship in the Spirit of God*** Other ancient authorities read *worship God in the Spirit*

55. *The Inclusion of the Gentiles*

Rom 11:17–24

Εἰ δέ τινες τῶν κλάδων ἐξεκλάσθησαν, σὺ δὲ ἀγριέλαιος ὢν ἐνεκεντρίσθης ἐν αὐτοῖς καὶ συγκοινωνὸς ⸀τῆς ῥίζης⸌ τῆς πιότητος τῆς ἐλαίας ἐγένου, 18 μὴ κατακαυχῶ τῶν κλάδων· εἰ δὲ κατακαυχᾶσαι οὐ σὺ τὴν ῥίζαν βαστάζεις ἀλλὰ ἡ ῥίζα σέ. 19 ἐρεῖς οὖν· ἐξεκλάσθησαν κλάδοι ἵνα ἐγὼ ἐγκεντρισθῶ. 20 καλῶς· τῇ ἀπιστίᾳ ἐξεκλάσθησαν, σὺ δὲ τῇ πίστει ἕστηκας. μὴ ὑψηλὰ φρόνει ἀλλὰ φοβοῦ· 21 εἰ γὰρ ὁ θεὸς τῶν κατὰ φύσιν κλάδων οὐκ ἐφείσατο, ⸀[μή πως]⸌ οὐδὲ σοῦ φείσεται. 22 ἴδε οὖν χρηστότητα καὶ ἀποτομίαν θεοῦ· ἐπὶ μὲν τοὺς πεσόντας ἀποτομία, ἐπὶ δὲ σὲ χρηστότης θεοῦ, ἐὰν ἐπιμένῃς τῇ χρηστότητι, ἐπεὶ καὶ σὺ ἐκκοπήσῃ. 23 κἀκεῖνοι δέ, ἐὰν μὴ ἐπιμένωσιν τῇ ἀπιστίᾳ, ἐγκεντρισθήσονται· δυνατὸς γάρ ἐστιν ὁ θεὸς πάλιν ἐγκεντρίσαι αὐτούς. 24 εἰ γὰρ σὺ ἐκ τῆς κατὰ φύσιν ἐξεκόπης ἀγριελαίου καὶ παρὰ φύσιν ἐνεκεντρίσθης εἰς καλλιέλαιον, πόσῳ μᾶλλον οὗτοι οἱ κατὰ φύσιν ἐγκεντρισθήσονται τῇ ἰδίᾳ ἐλαίᾳ.

Rom 15:7–13

Διὸ προσλαμβάνεσθε ἀλλήλους, καθὼς καὶ ὁ Χριστὸς προσελάβετο ὑμᾶς εἰς δόξαν τοῦ θεοῦ. 8 λέγω γὰρ Χριστὸν διάκονον γεγενῆσθαι περιτομῆς ὑπὲρ ἀληθείας θεοῦ, εἰς τὸ βεβαιῶσαι τὰς ἐπαγγελίας τῶν πατέρων, 9 τὰ δὲ ἔθνη ὑπὲρ ἐλέους δοξάσαι τὸν θεόν, καθὼς γέγραπται· διὰ τοῦτο ἐξομολογήσομαί σοι ἐν ἔθνεσιν καὶ τῷ ὀνόματί σου ψαλῶ. 10 καὶ πάλιν λέγει· εὐφράνθητε, ἔθνη, μετὰ τοῦ λαοῦ αὐτοῦ. 11 καὶ πάλιν· αἰνεῖτε, πάντα τὰ ἔθνη, τὸν κύριον καὶ ἐπαινεσάτωσαν αὐτὸν πάντες οἱ λαοί. 12 καὶ πάλιν Ἠσαΐας λέγει· ἔσται ἡ ῥίζα τοῦ Ἰεσσαὶ καὶ ὁ ἀνιστάμενος ἄρχειν ἐθνῶν, ἐπ᾽ αὐτῷ ἔθνη ἐλπιοῦσιν. 13 Ὁ δὲ θεὸς τῆς ἐλπίδος πληρώσαι ὑμᾶς πάσης χαρᾶς καὶ εἰρήνης ἐν τῷ πιστεύειν, εἰς τὸ περισσεύειν ὑμᾶς ἐν τῇ ἐλπίδι ἐν δυνάμει πνεύματος ἁγίου.

Rom 15:27

εὐδόκησαν γὰρ καὶ ὀφειλέται εἰσὶν αὐτῶν· εἰ γὰρ τοῖς πνευματικοῖς αὐτῶν ἐκοινώνησαν τὰ ἔθνη, ὀφείλουσιν καὶ ἐν τοῖς σαρκικοῖς λειτουργῆσαι αὐτοῖς.

Eph 2:11–22

Διὸ μνημονεύετε ὅτι ποτὲ ὑμεῖς τὰ ἔθνη ἐν σαρκί, οἱ λεγόμενοι ἀκροβυστία ὑπὸ τῆς λεγομένης περιτομῆς ἐν σαρκὶ χειροποιήτου, 12 ὅτι ἦτε τῷ καιρῷ ἐκείνῳ χωρὶς Χριστοῦ, ἀπηλλοτριωμένοι τῆς πολιτείας τοῦ Ἰσραὴλ καὶ ξένοι τῶν διαθηκῶν τῆς ἐπαγγελίας, ἐλπίδα μὴ ἔχοντες καὶ ἄθεοι ἐν τῷ κόσμῳ. 13 νυνὶ δὲ ἐν Χριστῷ Ἰησοῦ ὑμεῖς οἵ ποτε ὄντες μακρὰν ἐγενήθητε ἐγγὺς ἐν τῷ αἵματι τοῦ Χριστοῦ. 14 Αὐτὸς γάρ ἐστιν ἡ εἰρήνη ἡμῶν, ὁ ποιήσας τὰ ἀμφότερα ἓν καὶ τὸ μεσότοιχον τοῦ φραγμοῦ λύσας, τὴν ἔχθραν ἐν τῇ σαρκὶ αὐτοῦ, 15 τὸν νόμον τῶν ἐντολῶν ἐν δόγμασιν καταργήσας, ἵνα τοὺς δύο κτίσῃ ἐν αὐτῷ εἰς ἕνα καινὸν ἄνθρωπον ποιῶν εἰρήνην 16 καὶ ἀποκαταλλάξῃ τοὺς ἀμφοτέρους ἐν ἑνὶ σώματι τῷ θεῷ διὰ τοῦ σταυροῦ, ἀποκτείνας τὴν ἔχθραν ἐν αὐτῷ. 17 καὶ ἐλθὼν εὐηγγελίσατο εἰρήνην ὑμῖν τοῖς μακρὰν καὶ εἰρήνην τοῖς ἐγγύς· 18 ὅτι δι᾽ αὐτοῦ ἔχομεν τὴν προσαγωγὴν οἱ ἀμφότεροι ἐν ἑνὶ πνεύματι πρὸς τὸν πατέρα. 19 Ἄρα οὖν οὐκέτι ἐστὲ ξένοι καὶ πάροικοι ἀλλὰ ἐστὲ συμπολῖται τῶν ἁγίων καὶ οἰκεῖοι τοῦ θεοῦ, 20 ἐποικοδομηθέντες ἐπὶ τῷ θεμελίῳ τῶν ἀποστόλων καὶ προφητῶν, ὄντος ἀκρογωνιαίου αὐτοῦ Χριστοῦ Ἰησοῦ, 21 ἐν ᾧ πᾶσα οἰκοδομὴ συναρμολογουμένη αὔξει εἰς ναὸν ἅγιον ἐν κυρίῳ, 22 ἐν ᾧ καὶ ὑμεῖς συνοικοδομεῖσθε εἰς κατοικητήριον τοῦ θεοῦ ἐν πνεύματι.

Acts 13:46–47

παρρησιασάμενοί τε ὁ Παῦλος καὶ ὁ Βαρναβᾶς εἶπαν· ὑμῖν ἦν ἀναγκαῖον πρῶτον λαληθῆναι τὸν λόγον τοῦ θεοῦ· ἐπειδὴ ἀπωθεῖσθε αὐτὸν καὶ οὐκ ἀξίους κρίνετε ἑαυτοὺς τῆς αἰωνίου ζωῆς, ἰδοὺ στρεφόμεθα εἰς τὰ ἔθνη. 47 οὕτως γὰρ ἐντέταλται ἡμῖν ὁ κύριος· τέθεικά σε εἰς φῶς ἐθνῶν τοῦ εἶναί σε εἰς σωτηρίαν ἕως ἐσχάτου τῆς γῆς.

Acts 26:22–23

ἐπικουρίας οὖν τυχὼν τῆς ἀπὸ τοῦ θεοῦ ἄχρι τῆς ἡμέρας ταύτης ἕστηκα μαρτυρόμενος μικρῷ τε καὶ μεγάλῳ οὐδὲν ἐκτὸς λέγων ὧν τε οἱ προφῆται ἐλάλησαν μελλόντων γίνεσθαι καὶ Μωϋσῆς, 23 εἰ παθητὸς ὁ χριστός, εἰ πρῶτος ἐξ ἀναστάσεως νεκρῶν φῶς μέλλει καταγγέλλειν τῷ τε λαῷ καὶ τοῖς ἔθνεσιν.

Cf. Rom 15:14–21; 16:25–27; Gal 3:6–14; Col 2:11–15; Acts 15:1–35; 18:5–6; 21:25; 28:28.

See also § 59 Abraham's Covenant Family; § 64 The Mystery of Gentile Inclusion in Israel.

56. *Human Divisions Abolished in Christ*

Rom 10:5–13

Μωϋσῆς γὰρ γράφει τὴν δικαιοσύνην τὴν ἐκ [τοῦ] νόμου ὅτι ὁ ποιήσας αὐτὰ ἄνθρωπος ζήσεται ἐν ⸀αὐτοῖς. 6 ἡ δὲ ἐκ πίστεως δικαιοσύνη οὕτως λέγει· μὴ εἴπῃς ἐν τῇ καρδίᾳ σου· τίς ἀναβήσεται εἰς τὸν οὐρανόν; τοῦτ᾽ ἔστιν Χριστὸν καταγαγεῖν· 7 ἤ· τίς καταβήσεται εἰς τὴν ἄβυσσον; τοῦτ᾽ ἔστιν Χριστὸν ἐκ νεκρῶν ἀναγαγεῖν. 8 ἀλλὰ τί λέγει; ἐγγύς σου τὸ ῥῆμά ἐστιν ἐν τῷ στόματί σου καὶ ἐν τῇ καρδίᾳ σου, τοῦτ᾽ ἔστιν τὸ ῥῆμα τῆς πίστεως ὃ κηρύσσομεν. 9 ὅτι ἐὰν ὁμολογήσῃς ἐν τῷ στόματί σου κύριον

§ 55 **Rom 11:17** ***της ριζης*** ℵ* B C] της ριζης και ℵ^{2} A D^{2} 33. 1739. 1881 *Byz* ¦ *om.* 𝔓^{46} D* **Rom 11:21** ***μη πως*** 𝔓^{46} D 33 *Byz*] *om.* ℵ A B C 1739. 1881 **§ 56** **Rom 10:5** ***αυτοις*** 𝔓^{46} ℵ^{2} D *Byz*] αυτη ℵ* A B 33. 1739. 1881

55. *The Inclusion of the Gentiles*

Rom 11:17–24

But if some of the branches were broken off, and you, a wild olive shoot, were grafted in their place to share the rich root[a] of the olive tree, **18** do not boast over the branches. If you do boast, remember that it is not you that support the root, but the root that supports you. **19** You will say, "Branches were broken off so that I might be grafted in." **20** That is true. They were broken off because of their unbelief, but you stand only through faith. So do not become proud, but stand in awe. **21** For if God did not spare the natural branches, perhaps he will not spare you.[b] **22** Note then the kindness and the severity of God: severity toward those who have fallen, but God's kindness toward you, provided you continue in his kindness; otherwise you also will be cut off. **23** And even those of Israel, if they do not persist in unbelief, will be grafted in, for God has the power to graft them in again. **24** For if you have been cut from what is by nature a wild olive tree and grafted, contrary to nature, into a cultivated olive tree, how much more will these natural branches be grafted back into their own olive tree.

Rom 15:7–13

Welcome one another, therefore, just as Christ has welcomed you, for the glory of God. **8** For I tell you that Christ has become a servant of the circumcised on behalf of the truth of God in order that he might confirm the promises given to the patriarchs, **9** and in order that the Gentiles might glorify God for his mercy. As it is written, "Therefore I will confess you among the Gentiles, and sing praises to your name"; **10** and again he says, "Rejoice, O Gentiles, with his people"; **11** and again, "Praise the Lord, all you Gentiles, and let all the peoples praise him"; **12** and again Isaiah says, "The root of Jesse shall come, the one who rises to rule the Gentiles; in him the Gentiles shall hope." **13** May the God of hope fill you with all joy and peace in believing, so that you may abound in hope by the power of the Holy Spirit.

Rom 15:27

They were pleased to do this, and indeed they owe it to them; for if the Gentiles have come to share in their spiritual blessings, they ought also to be of service to them in material things.

Eph 2:11–22

So then, remember that at one time you Gentiles by birth, called "the uncircumcision" by those who are called "the circumcision"—a physical circumcision made in the flesh by human hands— **12** remember that you were at that time without Christ, being aliens from the commonwealth of Israel, and strangers to the covenants of promise, having no hope and without God in the world. **13** But now in Christ Jesus you who once were far off have been brought near by the blood of Christ. **14** For he is our peace; in his flesh he has made both groups into one and has broken down the dividing wall, that is, the hostility between us. **15** He has abolished the law with its commandments and ordinances, that he might create in himself one new humanity in place of the two, thus making peace, **16** and might reconcile both groups to God in one body through the cross, thus putting to death that hostility through it. **17** So he came and proclaimed peace to you who were far off and peace to those who were near; **18** for through him both of us have access in one Spirit to the Father. **19** So then you are no longer strangers and aliens, but you are citizens with the saints and also members of the household of God, **20** built upon the foundation of the apostles and prophets, with Christ Jesus himself as the cornerstone. **21** In him the whole structure is joined together and grows into a holy temple in the Lord; **22** in whom you also are built together spiritually into a dwelling place for God.

Acts 13:46–47

Then both Paul and Barnabas spoke out boldly, saying, "It was necessary that the word of God should be spoken first to you. Since you reject it and judge yourselves to be unworthy of eternal life, we are now turning to the Gentiles. **47** For so the Lord has commanded us, saying, 'I have set you to be a light for the Gentiles, so that you may bring salvation to the ends of the earth.'"

Acts 26:22–23

To this day I have had help from God, and so I stand here, testifying to both small and great, saying nothing but what the prophets and Moses said would take place: **23** that the Messiah must suffer, and that, by being the first to rise from the dead, he would proclaim light both to our people and to the Gentiles.

Cf. Rom 15:14–21; 16:25–27; Gal 3:6–14; Col 2:11–15; Acts 15:1–35; 18:5–6; 21:25; 28:28.

See also § 59 Abraham's Covenant Family; § 64 The Mystery of Gentile Inclusion in Israel.

56. *Human Divisions Abolished in Christ*

Rom 10:5–13

Moses writes concerning the righteousness that comes from the law, that "the person who does these things will live by them."[a] **6** But the righteousness that comes from faith says, "Do not say in your heart, 'Who will ascend into heaven?'" (that is, to bring Christ down) **7** "or 'Who will descend into the abyss?'" (that is, to bring Christ up from the dead). **8** But what does it say? "The word is near you, on your lips and in your heart" (that is, the word of faith that we proclaim); **9** because if you confess with your lips that Jesus is

§ 55 [a] **Rom 11:17** *the rich root* Other ancient authorities read *the richness* [b] **Rom 11:21** *perhaps he will not spare you* Other ancient authorities read *neither will he spare you* **§ 56** [a] **Rom 10:5** *them* Other ancient authorities read *it*, i.e., the righteousness that comes from the law

Ἰησοῦν καὶ πιστεύσῃς ἐν τῇ καρδίᾳ σου
ὅτι ὁ θεὸς αὐτὸν ἤγειρεν ἐκ νεκρῶν,
σωθήσῃ· 10 καρδίᾳ γὰρ πιστεύεται εἰς
δικαιοσύνην, στόματι δὲ ὁμολογεῖται εἰς
σωτηρίαν. 11 λέγει γὰρ ἡ γραφή· πᾶς ὁ
πιστεύων ἐπ᾽ αὐτῷ οὐ καταισχυνθήσεται.
12 οὐ γάρ ἐστιν διαστολὴ Ἰουδαίου τε καὶ
Ἕλληνος, ὁ γὰρ αὐτὸς κύριος πάντων,
πλουτῶν εἰς πάντας τοὺς ἐπικαλουμένους
αὐτόν· 13 πᾶς γὰρ ὃς ἂν ἐπικαλέσηται τὸ
ὄνομα κυρίου σωθήσεται.

1 Cor 7:17–24

Εἰ μὴ ἑκάστῳ ὡς ἐμέρισεν ὁ κύριος,
ἕκαστον ὡς κέκληκεν ὁ θεός, οὕτως πε-
ριπατείτω. καὶ οὕτως ἐν ταῖς ἐκκλησίαις
πάσαις διατάσσομαι. 18 περιτετμημένος
τις ἐκλήθη, μὴ ἐπισπάσθω· ἐν ἀκροβυ-
στίᾳ κέκληταί τις, μὴ περιτεμνέσθω. 19 ἡ
περιτομὴ οὐδέν ἐστιν καὶ ἡ ἀκροβυστία
οὐδέν ἐστιν, ἀλλὰ τήρησις ἐντολῶν θε-
οῦ. 20 ἕκαστος ἐν τῇ κλήσει ᾗ ἐκλήθη,
ἐν ταύτῃ μενέτω. 21 δοῦλος ἐκλήθης, μή
σοι μελέτω· ἀλλ᾽ εἰ καὶ δύνασαι ἐλεύ-
θερος γενέσθαι, μᾶλλον χρῆσαι. 22 ὁ
γὰρ ἐν κυρίῳ κληθεὶς δοῦλος ἀπελεύ-
θερος κυρίου ἐστίν, ὁμοίως ὁ ἐλεύθερος
κληθεὶς δοῦλός ἐστιν Χριστοῦ. 23 τιμῆς
ἠγοράσθητε· μὴ γίνεσθε δοῦλοι ἀνθρώ-
πων. 24 ἕκαστος ἐν ᾧ ἐκλήθη, ἀδελφοί,
ἐν τούτῳ μενέτω παρὰ θεῷ.

1 Cor 12:12–13

Καθάπερ γὰρ τὸ σῶμα ἕν ἐστιν καὶ μέλη
πολλὰ ἔχει, πάντα δὲ τὰ μέλη τοῦ σώ-
ματος πολλὰ ὄντα ἕν ἐστιν σῶμα, οὕτως
καὶ ὁ Χριστός· 13 καὶ γὰρ ἐν ἑνὶ πνεύματι
ἡμεῖς πάντες εἰς ἓν σῶμα ἐβαπτίσθημεν,
εἴτε Ἰουδαῖοι εἴτε Ἕλληνες εἴτε δοῦλοι
εἴτε ἐλεύθεροι, καὶ πάντες ἓν πνεῦμα
ἐποτίσθημεν.

Gal 3:26–29

Πάντες γὰρ υἱοὶ θεοῦ ἐστε διὰ τῆς πί-
στεως ἐν Χριστῷ Ἰησοῦ· 27 ὅσοι γὰρ εἰς
Χριστὸν ἐβαπτίσθητε, Χριστὸν ἐνεδύσα-
σθε. 28 οὐκ ἔνι Ἰουδαῖος οὐδὲ Ἕλλην,
οὐκ ἔνι δοῦλος οὐδὲ ἐλεύθερος, οὐκ
ἔνι ἄρσεν καὶ θῆλυ· πάντες γὰρ ὑμεῖς
εἷς ἐστε ἐν Χριστῷ Ἰησοῦ. 29 εἰ δὲ ὑμεῖς
Χριστοῦ, ἄρα τοῦ Ἀβραὰμ σπέρμα ἐστέ,
κατ᾽ ἐπαγγελίαν κληρονόμοι.

Gal 5:5–6

ἡμεῖς γὰρ πνεύματι ἐκ πίστεως ἐλπίδα
δικαιοσύνης ἀπεκδεχόμεθα. 6 ἐν γὰρ
Χριστῷ Ἰησοῦ οὔτε περιτομή τι ἰσχύει
οὔτε ἀκροβυστία ἀλλὰ πίστις δι᾽ ἀγάπης
ἐνεργουμένη.

Gal 6:14–16

Ἐμοὶ δὲ μὴ γένοιτο καυχᾶσθαι εἰ μὴ
ἐν τῷ σταυρῷ τοῦ κυρίου ἡμῶν Ἰησοῦ
Χριστοῦ, δι᾽ οὗ ἐμοὶ κόσμος ἐσταύρωται
κἀγὼ κόσμῳ. 15 ⸂οὔτε γὰρ⸃ περιτομή τί
ἐστιν οὔτε ἀκροβυστία ἀλλὰ καινὴ κτίσις.
16 καὶ ὅσοι τῷ κανόνι τούτῳ ⸀στοιχήσου-
σιν, εἰρήνη ἐπ᾽ αὐτοὺς καὶ ἔλεος καὶ ἐπὶ
τὸν Ἰσραὴλ τοῦ θεοῦ.

Eph 2:11–18

Διὸ μνημονεύετε ὅτι ποτὲ ὑμεῖς τὰ ἔθνη
ἐν σαρκί, οἱ λεγόμενοι ἀκροβυστία ὑπὸ
τῆς λεγομένης περιτομῆς ἐν σαρκὶ χει-
ροποιήτου, 12 ὅτι ἦτε τῷ καιρῷ ἐκείνῳ
χωρὶς Χριστοῦ, ἀπηλλοτριωμένοι τῆς
πολιτείας τοῦ Ἰσραὴλ καὶ ξένοι τῶν
διαθηκῶν τῆς ἐπαγγελίας, ἐλπίδα μὴ
ἔχοντες καὶ ἄθεοι ἐν τῷ κόσμῳ. 13 νυνὶ
δὲ ἐν Χριστῷ Ἰησοῦ ὑμεῖς οἵ ποτε ὄντες
μακρὰν ἐγενήθητε ἐγγὺς ἐν τῷ αἵματι
τοῦ Χριστοῦ. 14 Αὐτὸς γάρ ἐστιν ἡ εἰρήνη
ἡμῶν, ὁ ποιήσας τὰ ἀμφότερα ἓν καὶ τὸ
μεσότοιχον τοῦ φραγμοῦ λύσας, τὴν
ἔχθραν ἐν τῇ σαρκὶ αὐτοῦ, 15 τὸν νόμον
τῶν ἐντολῶν ἐν δόγμασιν καταργήσας,
ἵνα τοὺς δύο κτίσῃ ἐν αὐτῷ εἰς ἕνα και-
νὸν ἄνθρωπον ποιῶν εἰρήνην 16 καὶ
ἀποκαταλλάξῃ τοὺς ἀμφοτέρους ἐν ἑνὶ
σώματι τῷ θεῷ διὰ τοῦ σταυροῦ, ἀποκτεί-
νας τὴν ἔχθραν ἐν αὐτῷ. 17 καὶ ἐλθὼν
εὐηγγελίσατο εἰρήνην ὑμῖν τοῖς μακρὰν
καὶ εἰρήνην τοῖς ἐγγύς· 18 ὅτι δι᾽ αὐτοῦ
ἔχομεν τὴν προσαγωγὴν οἱ ἀμφότεροι
ἐν ἑνὶ πνεύματι πρὸς τὸν πατέρα.

Col 3:9–11

μὴ ψεύδεσθε εἰς ἀλλήλους, ἀπεκδυσάμε-
νοι τὸν παλαιὸν ἄνθρωπον σὺν ταῖς
πράξεσιν αὐτοῦ 10 καὶ ἐνδυσάμενοι τὸν
νέον τὸν ἀνακαινούμενον εἰς ἐπίγνω-
σιν κατ᾽ εἰκόνα τοῦ κτίσαντος αὐτόν,
11 ὅπου οὐκ ἔνι Ἕλλην καὶ Ἰουδαῖος,
περιτομὴ καὶ ἀκροβυστία, βάρβαρος,
Σκύθης, δοῦλος, ἐλεύθερος, ἀλλὰ [τὰ]
πάντα καὶ ἐν πᾶσιν Χριστός.

Cf. Rom 2:28–29; 3:21–31; Col 2:11–15; Acts 13:1.

See also § 49 The New Humanity in Christ.

57. One God of Both Jews and Gentiles

Rom 3:29–30

ἢ Ἰουδαίων ὁ θεὸς μόνον; οὐχὶ καὶ ἐθνῶν;
ναὶ καὶ ἐθνῶν, 30 εἴπερ εἷς ὁ θεὸς ὃς
δικαιώσει περιτομὴν ἐκ πίστεως καὶ
ἀκροβυστίαν διὰ τῆς πίστεως.

Rom 10:12–13

οὐ γάρ ἐστιν διαστολὴ Ἰουδαίου τε καὶ
Ἕλληνος, ὁ γὰρ αὐτὸς κύριος πάντων,
πλουτῶν εἰς πάντας τοὺς ἐπικαλουμένους
αὐτόν· 13 πᾶς γὰρ ὃς ἂν ἐπικαλέσηται τὸ
ὄνομα κυρίου σωθήσεται.

1 Tim 2:3–7

τοῦτο καλὸν καὶ ἀπόδεκτον ἐνώπιον τοῦ
σωτῆρος ἡμῶν θεοῦ, 4 ὃς πάντας ἀνθρώ-
πους θέλει σωθῆναι καὶ εἰς ἐπίγνωσιν
ἀληθείας ἐλθεῖν. 5 Εἷς γὰρ θεός, εἷς καὶ
μεσίτης θεοῦ καὶ ἀνθρώπων, ἄνθρω-
πος Χριστὸς Ἰησοῦς, 6 ὁ δοὺς ἑαυτὸν
ἀντίλυτρον ὑπὲρ πάντων, τὸ μαρτύριον
καιροῖς ἰδίοις. 7 εἰς ὃ ἐτέθην ἐγὼ κῆ-
ρυξ καὶ ἀπόστολος, ἀλήθειαν ⸀λέγω οὐ
ψεύδομαι, διδάσκαλος ἐθνῶν ἐν πίστει
καὶ ἀληθείᾳ.

Gal 6:15 ***ουτε γαρ*** 𝔓^{46} B 33. 1739*] εν γαρ Χριστω Ιησου ουτε ℵ A C D (1739^{c}). 1881 *Byz* **Gal 6:16** ***στοιχησουσιν*** ℵ B C^{2} 33 *Byz*] στοιχουσιν A C* D 1739. 1881 ¦ στοιχησωσιν 𝔓^{46} **§ 57** **1 Tim 2:7** ***λεγω*** ℵ^{2} A D* 1739. 1881] *add.* εν Χριστω ℵ* D^{2} 33^{vid} *Byz*

Lord and believe in your heart that God raised him from the dead, you will be saved. **10** For one believes with the heart and so is justified, and one confesses with the mouth and so is saved. **11** The scripture says, "No one who believes in him will be put to shame." **12** For there is no distinction between Jew and Greek; the same Lord is Lord of all and is generous to all who call on him. **13** For, "Everyone who calls on the name of the Lord shall be saved."

1 Cor 7:17–24

However that may be, let each of you lead the life that the Lord has assigned, to which God called you. This is my rule in all the churches. **18** Was anyone at the time of his call already circumcised? Let him not seek to remove the marks of circumcision. Was anyone at the time of his call uncircumcised? Let him not seek circumcision. **19** Circumcision is nothing, and uncircumcision is nothing; but obeying the commandments of God is everything. **20** Let each of you remain in the condition in which you were called. **21** Were you a slave when called? Do not be concerned about it. Even if you can gain your freedom, make use of your present condition now more than ever. **22** For whoever was called in the Lord as a slave is a freed person belonging to the Lord, just as whoever was free when called is a slave of Christ. **23** You were bought with a price; do not become slaves of human masters. **24** In whatever condition you were called, brothers and sisters, there remain with God.

1 Cor 12:12–13

For just as the body is one and has many members, and all the members of the body, though many, are one body, so it is with Christ. **13** For in the one Spirit we were all baptized into one body—Jews or Greeks, slaves or free—and we were all made to drink of one Spirit.

Gal 3:26–29

for in Christ Jesus you are all children of God through faith. **27** As many of you as were baptized into Christ have clothed yourselves with Christ. **28** There is no longer Jew or Greek, there is no longer slave or free, there is no longer male and female; for all of you are one in Christ Jesus. **29** And if you belong to Christ, then you are Abraham's offspring, heirs according to the promise.

Gal 5:5–6

For through the Spirit, by faith, we eagerly wait for the hope of righteousness. **6** For in Christ Jesus neither circumcision nor uncircumcision counts for anything; the only thing that counts is faith working through love.

Gal 6:14–16

May I never boast of anything except the cross of our Lord Jesus Christ, by which the world has been crucified to me, and I to the world. **15** For[b] neither circumcision nor uncircumcision is anything; but a new creation is everything! **16** As for those who will follow[c] this rule—peace be upon them, and mercy, and upon the Israel of God.

Eph 2:11–18

So then, remember that at one time you Gentiles by birth, called "the uncircumcision" by those who are called "the circumcision"—a physical circumcision made in the flesh by human hands— **12** remember that you were at that time without Christ, being aliens from the commonwealth of Israel, and strangers to the covenants of promise, having no hope and without God in the world. **13** But now in Christ Jesus you who once were far off have been brought near by the blood of Christ. **14** For he is our peace; in his flesh he has made both groups into one and has broken down the dividing wall, that is, the hostility between us. **15** He has abolished the law with its commandments and ordinances, that he might create in himself one new humanity in place of the two, thus making peace, **16** and might reconcile both groups to God in one body through the cross, thus putting to death that hostility through it. **17** So he came and proclaimed peace to you who were far off and peace to those who were near; **18** for through him both of us have access in one Spirit to the Father.

Col 3:9–11

Do not lie to one another, seeing that you have stripped off the old humanity[d] with its practices **10** and have clothed yourselves with the new humanity,[d] which is being renewed in knowledge according to the image of its creator. **11** In that renewal there is no longer Greek and Jew, circumcised and uncircumcised, barbarian, Scythian, slave and free; but Christ is all and in all!

Cf. Rom 2:28–29; 3:21–31; Col 2:11–15; Acts 13:1.

See also § 49 The New Humanity in Christ.

57. One God of Both Jews and Gentiles

Rom 3:29–30

Or is God the God of Jews only? Is he not the God of Gentiles also? Yes, of Gentiles also, **30** since God is one; and he will justify the circumcised on the ground of faith and the uncircumcised through that same faith.

Rom 10:12–13

For there is no distinction between Jew and Greek; the same Lord is Lord of all and is generous to all who call on him. **13** For, "Everyone who calls on the name of the Lord shall be saved."

1 Tim 2:3–7

This is right and is acceptable in the sight of God our Savior, **4** who desires everyone to be saved and to come to the knowledge of the truth. **5** For there is one God; there is also one mediator between God and humankind, Christ Jesus, himself human, **6** who gave himself a ransom for all—this was attested at the right time. **7** For this I was appointed a herald and an apostle (I am telling the truth,[a] I am not lying), a teacher of the Gentiles in faith and truth.

[b] **Gal 6:15** *For* Other ancient authorities add *in Christ Jesus* [c] **Gal 6:16** *will follow* Other ancient authorities read *follow* [d] **Col 3:9–10** *humanity* NRSV translates *self* **§ 57** [a] **1 Tim 2:7** *telling the truth* Other ancient authorities add *in Christ*

58. Circumcision of the Spirit

Rom 2:25–29

Περιτομὴ μὲν γὰρ ὠφελεῖ ἐὰν νόμον πράσσῃς· ἐὰν δὲ παραβάτης νόμου ᾖς, ἡ περιτομή σου ἀκροβυστία γέγονεν. **26** ἐὰν οὖν ἡ ἀκροβυστία τὰ δικαιώματα τοῦ νόμου φυλάσσῃ, οὐχ ἡ ἀκροβυστία αὐτοῦ εἰς περιτομὴν λογισθήσεται; **27** καὶ κρινεῖ ἡ ἐκ φύσεως ἀκροβυστία τὸν νόμον τελοῦσα σὲ τὸν διὰ γράμματος καὶ περιτομῆς παραβάτην νόμου. **28** οὐ γὰρ ὁ ἐν τῷ φανερῷ Ἰουδαῖός ἐστιν οὐδὲ ἡ ἐν τῷ φανερῷ ἐν σαρκὶ περιτομή, **29** ἀλλ᾽ ὁ ἐν τῷ κρυπτῷ Ἰουδαῖος, καὶ περιτομὴ καρδίας ἐν πνεύματι οὐ γράμματι, οὗ ὁ ἔπαινος οὐκ ἐξ ἀνθρώπων ἀλλ᾽ ἐκ τοῦ θεοῦ.

Rom 7:5–6

ὅτε γὰρ ἦμεν ἐν τῇ σαρκί, τὰ παθήματα τῶν ἁμαρτιῶν τὰ διὰ τοῦ νόμου ἐνηργεῖτο ἐν τοῖς μέλεσιν ἡμῶν, εἰς τὸ καρποφορῆσαι τῷ θανάτῳ· **6** νυνὶ δὲ κατηργήθημεν ἀπὸ τοῦ νόμου ἀποθανόντες ἐν ᾧ κατειχόμεθα, ὥστε δουλεύειν ἡμᾶς ἐν καινότητι πνεύματος καὶ οὐ παλαιότητι γράμματος.

2 Cor 3:3–6

φανερούμενοι ὅτι ἐστὲ ἐπιστολὴ Χριστοῦ διακονηθεῖσα ὑφ᾽ ἡμῶν, ἐγγεγραμμένη οὐ μέλανι ἀλλὰ πνεύματι θεοῦ ζῶντος, οὐκ ἐν πλαξὶν λιθίναις ἀλλ᾽ ἐν πλαξὶν καρδίαις σαρκίναις. **4** Πεποίθησιν δὲ τοιαύτην ἔχομεν διὰ τοῦ Χριστοῦ πρὸς τὸν θεόν. **5** οὐχ ὅτι ἀφ᾽ ἑαυτῶν ἱκανοί ἐσμεν λογίσασθαί τι ὡς ἐξ ἑαυτῶν, ἀλλ᾽ ἡ ἱκανότης ἡμῶν ἐκ τοῦ θεοῦ, **6** ὃς καὶ ἱκάνωσεν ἡμᾶς διακόνους καινῆς διαθήκης, οὐ γράμματος ἀλλὰ πνεύματος· τὸ γὰρ γράμμα ἀποκτέννει, τὸ δὲ πνεῦμα ζῳοποιεῖ.

Phil 3:2–3

Βλέπετε τοὺς κύνας, βλέπετε τοὺς κακοὺς ἐργάτας, βλέπετε τὴν κατατομήν. **3** ἡμεῖς γάρ ἐσμεν ἡ περιτομή, οἱ πνεύματι ⸀θεοῦ λατρεύοντες καὶ καυχώμενοι ἐν Χριστῷ Ἰησοῦ καὶ οὐκ ἐν σαρκὶ πεποιθότες

Col 2:11–12

Ἐν ᾧ καὶ περιετμήθητε περιτομῇ ἀχειροποιήτῳ ἐν τῇ ἀπεκδύσει τοῦ σώματος τῆς σαρκός, ἐν τῇ περιτομῇ τοῦ Χριστοῦ, **12** συνταφέντες αὐτῷ ἐν τῷ βαπτισμῷ, ἐν ᾧ καὶ συνηγέρθητε διὰ τῆς πίστεως τῆς ἐνεργείας τοῦ θεοῦ τοῦ ἐγείραντος αὐτὸν ἐκ νεκρῶν

Cf. Eph 2:11–18; 1 Cor 7:19; Gal 5:6; 6:14–16.

See also § 43 The New Covenant.

59. Abraham's Covenant Family

Rom 4:1–25

Τί οὖν ἐροῦμεν ⸀εὑρηκέναι Ἀβραὰμ τὸν προπάτορα ἡμῶν κατὰ σάρκα; **2** εἰ γὰρ Ἀβραὰμ ἐξ ἔργων ἐδικαιώθη, ἔχει καύχημα, ἀλλ᾽ οὐ πρὸς θεόν. **3** τί γὰρ ἡ γραφὴ λέγει; ἐπίστευσεν δὲ Ἀβραὰμ τῷ θεῷ καὶ ἐλογίσθη αὐτῷ εἰς δικαιοσύνην. **4** τῷ δὲ ἐργαζομένῳ ὁ μισθὸς οὐ λογίζεται κατὰ χάριν ἀλλὰ κατὰ ὀφείλημα, **5** τῷ δὲ μὴ ἐργαζομένῳ πιστεύοντι δὲ ἐπὶ τὸν δικαιοῦντα τὸν ἀσεβῆ λογίζεται ἡ πίστις αὐτοῦ εἰς δικαιοσύνην· **6** καθάπερ καὶ Δαυὶδ λέγει τὸν μακαρισμὸν τοῦ ἀνθρώπου ᾧ ὁ θεὸς λογίζεται δικαιοσύνην χωρὶς ἔργων· **7** μακάριοι ὧν ἀφέθησαν αἱ ἀνομίαι καὶ ὧν ἐπεκαλύφθησαν αἱ ἁμαρτίαι· **8** μακάριος ἀνὴρ οὗ οὐ μὴ λογίσηται κύριος ἁμαρτίαν. **9** Ὁ μακαρισμὸς οὖν οὗτος ἐπὶ τὴν περιτομὴν ἢ καὶ ἐπὶ τὴν ἀκροβυστίαν; λέγομεν γάρ· ἐλογίσθη τῷ Ἀβραὰμ ἡ πίστις εἰς δικαιοσύνην. **10** πῶς οὖν ἐλογίσθη; ἐν περιτομῇ ὄντι ἢ ἐν ἀκροβυστίᾳ; οὐκ ἐν περιτομῇ ἀλλ᾽ ἐν ἀκροβυστίᾳ· **11** καὶ σημεῖον ἔλαβεν περιτομῆς σφραγῖδα τῆς δικαιοσύνης τῆς πίστεως τῆς ἐν τῇ ἀκροβυστίᾳ, εἰς τὸ εἶναι αὐτὸν πατέρα πάντων τῶν πιστευόντων δι᾽ ἀκροβυστίας, εἰς τὸ λογισθῆναι ⸀[καὶ] αὐτοῖς [τὴν] δικαιοσύνην, **12** καὶ πατέρα περιτομῆς τοῖς οὐκ ἐκ περιτομῆς μόνον ἀλλὰ καὶ τοῖς στοιχοῦσιν τοῖς ἴχνεσιν τῆς ἐν ἀκροβυστίᾳ πίστεως τοῦ πατρὸς ἡμῶν Ἀβραάμ. **13** Οὐ γὰρ διὰ νόμου ἡ ἐπαγγελία τῷ Ἀβραὰμ ἢ τῷ σπέρματι αὐτοῦ, τὸ κληρονόμον αὐτὸν εἶναι κόσμου, ἀλλὰ διὰ δικαιοσύνης πίστεως. **14** εἰ γὰρ οἱ ἐκ νόμου κληρονόμοι, κεκένωται ἡ πίστις καὶ κατήργηται ἡ ἐπαγγελία· **15** ὁ γὰρ νόμος ὀργὴν κατεργάζεται· οὗ δὲ οὐκ ἔστιν νόμος οὐδὲ παράβασις. **16** Διὰ τοῦτο ἐκ πίστεως, ἵνα κατὰ χάριν, εἰς τὸ εἶναι βεβαίαν τὴν ἐπαγγελίαν παντὶ τῷ σπέρματι, οὐ τῷ ἐκ τοῦ νόμου μόνον ἀλλὰ καὶ τῷ ἐκ πίστεως Ἀβραάμ, ὅς ἐστιν πατὴρ πάντων ἡμῶν, **17** καθὼς γέγραπται ὅτι πατέρα πολλῶν ἐθνῶν τέθεικά σε, κατέναντι οὗ ἐπίστευσεν θεοῦ τοῦ ζῳοποιοῦντος τοὺς νεκροὺς καὶ καλοῦντος τὰ μὴ ὄντα ὡς ὄντα. **18** Ὃς παρ᾽ ἐλπίδα ἐπ᾽ ἐλπίδι ἐπίστευσεν εἰς τὸ γενέσθαι αὐτὸν πατέρα πολλῶν ἐθνῶν κατὰ τὸ εἰρημένον· οὕτως ἔσται τὸ σπέρμα σου, **19** καὶ μὴ ἀσθενήσας τῇ πίστει κατενόησεν τὸ ἑαυτοῦ σῶμα ⸀[ἤδη] νενεκρωμένον, ἑκατονταετής που ὑπάρχων, καὶ τὴν νέκρωσιν τῆς μήτρας Σάρρας· **20** εἰς δὲ τὴν ἐπαγγελίαν τοῦ θεοῦ οὐ διεκρίθη τῇ ἀπιστίᾳ ἀλλ᾽ ἐνεδυναμώθη τῇ πίστει, δοὺς δόξαν τῷ θεῷ **21** καὶ πληροφορηθεὶς ὅτι ὃ ἐπήγγελται δυνατός ἐστιν καὶ ποιῆσαι. **22** διὸ [καὶ] ἐλογίσθη αὐτῷ εἰς δικαιοσύνην.

§ 58 **Phil 3:3** ***θεου*** א* A B C D² 33. 1739. 1881 *Byz*] θεω א² D* ¦ *om.* 𝔓⁴⁶ **§ 59** **Rom 4:1** ***ευρηκεναι*** א A C D 33. 1881 *Byz*] *om.* B (1739) **Rom 4:11** ***και*** א² C D *Byz*] *om.* א* A B 1739. 1881 **Rom 4:19** ***ηδη*** א A C D 33 *Byz*] *om.* B 1739. 1881

58. *Circumcision of the Spirit*

Rom 2:25–29

Circumcision indeed is of value if you obey the law; but if you break the law, your circumcision has become uncircumcision. 26 So, if those who are uncircumcised keep the requirements of the law, will not their uncircumcision be regarded as circumcision? 27 Then those who are physically uncircumcised but keep the law will condemn you that have the written code and circumcision but break the law. 28 For a person is not a Jew who is one outwardly, nor is true circumcision something external and physical. 29 Rather, a person is a Jew who is one inwardly, and real circumcision is a matter of the heart—it is by the Spirit and not by the written letter. Such a person receives praise not from others but from God.[a]

Rom 7:5–6

While we were living in the flesh, our sinful passions, aroused by the law, were at work in our members to bear fruit for death. 6 But now we are discharged from the law, dead to that which held us captive, so that we are slaves not under the old written code but in the new life of the Spirit.

2 Cor 3:3–6

and you show that you are a letter of Christ, prepared by us, written not with ink but with the Spirit of the living God, not on tablets of stone but on tablets of human hearts. 4 Such is the confidence that we have through Christ toward God. 5 Not that we are competent of ourselves to claim anything as coming from us; our competence is from God, 6 who has made us competent to be ministers of a new covenant, not of the letter but of the Spirit; for the letter kills, but the Spirit gives life.[b]

Phil 3:2–3

Beware of the dogs, beware of the evil workers, beware of those who mutilate the flesh! 3 For it is we who are the circumcision, who worship in the Spirit of God[c] and boast in Christ Jesus and have no confidence in the flesh

Col 2:11–12

In him also you were circumcised with a spiritual circumcision, by putting off the body of the flesh in the circumcision of Christ; 12 when you were buried with him in baptism, you were also raised with him through faith in the power of God, who raised him from the dead.

Cf. Eph 2:11–18; 1 Cor 7:19; Gal 5:6; 6:14–16.

See also § 43 The New Covenant.

59. *Abraham's Covenant Family*

Rom 4:1–25

What then are we to say was gained by[a] Abraham, our ancestor according to the flesh? 2 For if Abraham was justified by works, he has something to boast about, but not before God. 3 For what does the scripture say? "Abraham believed God, and it was reckoned to him as righteousness." 4 Now to one who works, wages are not reckoned as a gift but as something due. 5 But to one who without works trusts him who justifies the ungodly, such faith is reckoned as righteousness. 6 So also David speaks of the blessedness of those to whom God reckons righteousness apart from works: 7 "Blessed are those whose iniquities are forgiven, and whose sins are covered; 8 blessed is the one against whom the Lord will not reckon sin." 9 Is this blessedness, then, pronounced only on the circumcised, or also on the uncircumcised? We say, "Faith was reckoned to Abraham as righteousness." 10 How then was it reckoned to him? Was it before or after he had been circumcised? It was not after, but before he was circumcised. 11 He received the sign of circumcision as a seal of the righteousness that he had by faith while he was still uncircumcised. The purpose was to make him the ancestor of all who believe without being circumcised and who thus have righteousness reckoned to them,[b] 12 and likewise the ancestor of the circumcised who are not only circumcised but who also follow the example of the faith that our ancestor Abraham had before he was circumcised. 13 For the promise that he would inherit the world did not come to Abraham or to his descendants through the law but through the righteousness of faith. 14 If it is the adherents of the law who are to be the heirs, faith is null and the promise is void. 15 For the law brings wrath; but where there is no law, neither is there violation. 16 For this reason it depends on faith, in order that the promise may rest on grace and be guaranteed to all his descendants, not only to the adherents of the law but also to those who share the faith of Abraham (for he is the father of all of us, 17 as it is written, "I have made you the father of many nations")—in the presence of the God in whom he believed, who gives life to the dead and calls into existence the things that do not exist. 18 Hoping against hope, he believed that he would become "the father of many nations," according to what was said, "So numerous shall your descendants be." 19 He did not weaken in faith when he considered his own body, which was already[c] as good as dead (for he was about a hundred years old), or when he considered the barrenness of Sarah's womb. 20 No distrust made him waver concerning the promise of God, but he grew strong in his faith as he gave glory to God, 21 being fully convinced that God was able to do what he had promised. 22 Therefore his faith "was reckoned to him as righteousness."

§ 58 [a] **Rom 2:29** Translation differs from NRSV [b] **2 Cor 3:6** Translation differs from NRSV [c] **Phil 3:3** ***worship in the Spirit of God*** Other ancient authorities read *worship God in the Spirit* **§ 59** [a] **Rom 4:1** ***say was gained by*** A few ancient authorities read *say about* [b] **Rom 4:11** ***to them*** Other ancient authorities read *to them as well* [c] **Rom 4:19** ***already*** Other ancient authorities lack *already*

23 Οὐκ ἐγράφη δὲ δι᾽ αὐτὸν μόνον ὅτι
ἐλογίσθη αὐτῷ **24** ἀλλὰ καὶ δι᾽ ἡμᾶς,
οἷς μέλλει λογίζεσθαι, τοῖς πιστεύουσιν
ἐπὶ τὸν ἐγείραντα Ἰησοῦν τὸν κύριον
ἡμῶν ἐκ νεκρῶν, **25** ὃς παρεδόθη διὰ
τὰ παραπτώματα ἡμῶν καὶ ἠγέρθη διὰ
τὴν δικαίωσιν ἡμῶν.

Rom 9:6–9

Οὐχ οἷον δὲ ὅτι ἐκπέπτωκεν ὁ λόγος τοῦ
θεοῦ. οὐ γὰρ πάντες οἱ ἐξ Ἰσραὴλ οὗτοι
Ἰσραήλ· **7** οὐδ᾽ ὅτι εἰσὶν σπέρμα Ἀβραὰμ
πάντες τέκνα, ἀλλ᾽· ἐν Ἰσαὰκ κληθήσεταί
σοι σπέρμα. **8** τοῦτ᾽ ἔστιν, οὐ τὰ τέκνα
τῆς σαρκὸς ταῦτα τέκνα τοῦ θεοῦ ἀλλὰ
τὰ τέκνα τῆς ἐπαγγελίας λογίζεται εἰς
σπέρμα. **9** ἐπαγγελίας γὰρ ὁ λόγος οὗτος·
κατὰ τὸν καιρὸν τοῦτον ἐλεύσομαι καὶ
ἔσται τῇ Σάρρᾳ υἱός.

Gal 3:6–29

Καθὼς Ἀβραὰμ ἐπίστευσεν τῷ θεῷ, καὶ
ἐλογίσθη αὐτῷ εἰς δικαιοσύνην· **7** γι-
νώσκετε ἄρα ὅτι οἱ ἐκ πίστεως, οὗτοι
υἱοί εἰσιν Ἀβραάμ. **8** προϊδοῦσα δὲ ἡ
γραφὴ ὅτι ἐκ πίστεως δικαιοῖ τὰ ἔθνη
ὁ θεός, προευηγγελίσατο τῷ Ἀβραὰμ
ὅτι ἐνευλογηθήσονται ἐν σοὶ πάντα τὰ
ἔθνη· **9** ὥστε οἱ ἐκ πίστεως εὐλογοῦνται
σὺν τῷ πιστῷ Ἀβραάμ. **10** Ὅσοι γὰρ ἐξ
ἔργων νόμου εἰσίν, ὑπὸ κατάραν εἰσίν·
γέγραπται γὰρ ὅτι ἐπικατάρατος πᾶς ὃς
οὐκ ἐμμένει πᾶσιν τοῖς γεγραμμένοις ἐν
τῷ βιβλίῳ τοῦ νόμου τοῦ ποιῆσαι αὐτά.
11 ὅτι δὲ ἐν νόμῳ οὐδεὶς δικαιοῦται παρὰ
τῷ θεῷ δῆλον, ὅτι ὁ δίκαιος ἐκ πίστεως
ζήσεται· **12** ὁ δὲ νόμος οὐκ ἔστιν ἐκ πί-
στεως, ἀλλ᾽ ὁ ποιήσας αὐτὰ ζήσεται ἐν
αὐτοῖς. **13** Χριστὸς ἡμᾶς ἐξηγόρασεν
ἐκ τῆς κατάρας τοῦ νόμου γενόμενος
ὑπὲρ ἡμῶν κατάρα, ὅτι γέγραπται· ἐπι-
κατάρατος πᾶς ὁ κρεμάμενος ἐπὶ ξύλου,
14 ἵνα εἰς τὰ ἔθνη ἡ εὐλογία τοῦ Ἀβραὰμ
γένηται ἐν Χριστῷ Ἰησοῦ, ἵνα τὴν ἐπαγ-
γελίαν τοῦ πνεύματος λάβωμεν διὰ τῆς
πίστεως. **15** Ἀδελφοί, κατὰ ἄνθρωπον
λέγω· ὅμως ἀνθρώπου κεκυρωμένην
διαθήκην οὐδεὶς ἀθετεῖ ἢ ἐπιδιατάσσεται.
16 τῷ δὲ Ἀβραὰμ ἐρρέθησαν αἱ ἐπαγγε-
λίαι καὶ τῷ σπέρματι αὐτοῦ. οὐ λέγει· καὶ
τοῖς σπέρμασιν, ὡς ἐπὶ πολλῶν ἀλλ᾽ ὡς
ἐφ᾽ ἑνός· καὶ τῷ σπέρματί σου, ὅς ἐστιν
Χριστός. **17** τοῦτο δὲ λέγω· διαθήκην
προκεκυρωμένην ὑπὸ τοῦ θεοῦ ὁ μετὰ
τετρακόσια καὶ τριάκοντα ἔτη γεγονὼς
νόμος οὐκ ἀκυροῖ εἰς τὸ καταργῆσαι
τὴν ἐπαγγελίαν. **18** εἰ γὰρ ἐκ νόμου ἡ
κληρονομία, οὐκέτι ἐξ ἐπαγγελίας· τῷ
δὲ Ἀβραὰμ δι᾽ ἐπαγγελίας κεχάρισται ὁ
θεός. **19** Τί οὖν ὁ νόμος; τῶν παραβά-
σεων χάριν προσετέθη, ἄχρις οὗ ἔλθῃ
τὸ σπέρμα ᾧ ἐπήγγελται, διαταγεὶς δι᾽
ἀγγέλων ἐν χειρὶ μεσίτου. **20** ὁ δὲ μεσίτης
ἑνὸς οὐκ ἔστιν, ὁ δὲ θεὸς εἷς ἐστιν. **21** ὁ
οὖν νόμος κατὰ τῶν ἐπαγγελιῶν [τοῦ
θεοῦ]; μὴ γένοιτο. εἰ γὰρ ἐδόθη νόμος ὁ
δυνάμενος ζῳοποιῆσαι, ὄντως ἐκ νόμου
ἂν ἦν ἡ δικαιοσύνη· **22** ἀλλὰ συνέκλεισεν
ἡ γραφὴ τὰ πάντα ὑπὸ ἁμαρτίαν, ἵνα ἡ
ἐπαγγελία ἐκ πίστεως Ἰησοῦ Χριστοῦ
δοθῇ τοῖς πιστεύουσιν. **23** Πρὸ τοῦ δὲ
ἐλθεῖν τὴν πίστιν ὑπὸ νόμον ἐφρουρού-
μεθα συγκλειόμενοι εἰς τὴν μέλλουσαν
πίστιν ἀποκαλυφθῆναι, **24** ὥστε ὁ νόμος
παιδαγωγὸς ἡμῶν γέγονεν εἰς Χριστόν,
ἵνα ἐκ πίστεως δικαιωθῶμεν· **25** ἐλθούσης
δὲ τῆς πίστεως οὐκέτι ὑπὸ παιδαγωγόν
ἐσμεν. **26** Πάντες γὰρ υἱοὶ θεοῦ ἐστε διὰ
τῆς πίστεως ἐν Χριστῷ Ἰησοῦ· **27** ὅσοι
γὰρ εἰς Χριστὸν ἐβαπτίσθητε, Χριστὸν
ἐνεδύσασθε. **28** οὐκ ἔνι Ἰουδαῖος οὐδὲ
Ἕλλην, οὐκ ἔνι δοῦλος οὐδὲ ἐλεύθερος,
οὐκ ἔνι ἄρσεν καὶ θῆλυ· πάντες γὰρ ὑμεῖς
εἷς ἐστε ἐν Χριστῷ Ἰησοῦ. **29** εἰ δὲ ὑμεῖς
Χριστοῦ, ἄρα τοῦ Ἀβραὰμ σπέρμα ἐστέ,
κατ᾽ ἐπαγγελίαν κληρονόμοι.

Gal 4:21–31

Λέγετέ μοι, οἱ ὑπὸ νόμον θέλοντες εἶναι,
τὸν νόμον οὐκ ἀκούετε; **22** γέγραπται
γὰρ ὅτι Ἀβραὰμ δύο υἱοὺς ἔσχεν, ἕνα
ἐκ τῆς παιδίσκης καὶ ἕνα ἐκ τῆς ἐλευ-
θέρας. **23** ἀλλ᾽ ὁ μὲν ἐκ τῆς παιδίσκης
κατὰ σάρκα γεγέννηται, ὁ δὲ ἐκ τῆς
ἐλευθέρας δι᾽ ἐπαγγελίας. **24** ἅτινά ἐστιν
ἀλληγορούμενα· αὗται γάρ εἰσιν δύο
διαθῆκαι, μία μὲν ἀπὸ ὄρους Σινᾶ εἰς
δουλείαν γεννῶσα, ἥτις ἐστὶν Ἁγάρ.
25 τὸ ⸂δὲ Ἁγὰρ Σινᾶ⸃ ὄρος ἐστὶν ἐν τῇ
Ἀραβίᾳ· συστοιχεῖ δὲ τῇ νῦν Ἰερουσαλήμ,
δουλεύει γὰρ μετὰ τῶν τέκνων αὐτῆς.
26 ἡ δὲ ἄνω Ἰερουσαλὴμ ἐλευθέρα ἐστίν,
ἥτις ἐστὶν μήτηρ ἡμῶν· **27** γέγραπται
γάρ· εὐφράνθητι, στεῖρα ἡ οὐ τίκτουσα,
ῥῆξον καὶ βόησον, ἡ οὐκ ὠδίνουσα· ὅτι
πολλὰ τὰ τέκνα τῆς ἐρήμου μᾶλλον ἢ
τῆς ἐχούσης τὸν ἄνδρα. **28** ⸀Ὑμεῖς δέ,
ἀδελφοί, κατὰ Ἰσαὰκ ἐπαγγελίας τέκνα
⸀ἐστέ. **29** ἀλλ᾽ ὥσπερ τότε ὁ κατὰ σάρκα
γεννηθεὶς ἐδίωκεν τὸν κατὰ πνεῦμα,
οὕτως καὶ νῦν. **30** ἀλλὰ τί λέγει ἡ γρα-
φή; ἔκβαλε τὴν παιδίσκην καὶ τὸν υἱὸν
αὐτῆς· οὐ γὰρ μὴ κληρονομήσει ὁ υἱὸς τῆς
παιδίσκης μετὰ τοῦ υἱοῦ τῆς ἐλευθέρας.
31 διό, ἀδελφοί, οὐκ ἐσμὲν παιδίσκης
τέκνα ἀλλὰ τῆς ἐλευθέρας.

See also § 61 The Israel of God.

60. Children of the Promise

Rom 4:13–25

Οὐ γὰρ διὰ νόμου ἡ ἐπαγγελία τῷ Ἀβραὰμ
ἢ τῷ σπέρματι αὐτοῦ, τὸ κληρονόμον
αὐτὸν εἶναι κόσμου, ἀλλὰ διὰ δικαι-
οσύνης πίστεως. **14** εἰ γὰρ οἱ ἐκ νόμου
κληρονόμοι, κεκένωται ἡ πίστις καὶ
κατήργηται ἡ ἐπαγγελία· **15** ὁ γὰρ νόμος
ὀργὴν κατεργάζεται· οὗ δὲ οὐκ ἔστιν νόμος
οὐδὲ παράβασις. **16** Διὰ τοῦτο ἐκ πίστεως,
ἵνα κατὰ χάριν, εἰς τὸ εἶναι βεβαίαν τὴν
ἐπαγγελίαν παντὶ τῷ σπέρματι, οὐ τῷ

Gal 4:25 ***δε Αγαρ Σινα*** A B D] γαρ Αγαρ Σινα 33. 1881 *Byz* ¦ γαρ Σινα ℵ C 1739 ¦ δε Σινα 𝔓46 **Gal 4:28** ***υμεις*** *et* εστε 𝔓46 B D* 33. 1739. 1881] ημεις *et* εσμεν ℵ A C D2 *Byz*

23 Now the words, "it was reckoned to him," were written not for his sake alone, 24 but for ours also. It will be reckoned to us who believe in him who raised Jesus our Lord from the dead, 25 who was handed over to death for our trespasses and was raised for our justification.

Rom 9:6–9

It is not as though the word of God had failed. For not all Israelites truly belong to Israel, 7 and not all of Abraham's children are his true descendants; but "It is through Isaac that descendants shall be named for you." 8 This means that it is not the children of the flesh who are the children of God, but the children of the promise are counted as descendants. 9 For this is what the promise said, "About this time I will return and Sarah shall have a son."

Gal 3:6–29

Just as Abraham "believed God, and it was reckoned to him as righteousness," 7 so, you see, those who believe are the descendants of Abraham. 8 And the scripture, foreseeing that God would justify the Gentiles by faith, declared the gospel beforehand to Abraham, saying, "All the Gentiles shall be blessed in you." 9 For this reason, those who believe are blessed with Abraham who believed. 10 For all who rely on the works of the law are under a curse; for it is written, "Cursed is everyone who does not observe and obey all the things written in the book of the law." 11 Now it is evident that no one is justified before God by the law; for "The one who is righteous will live by faith." 12 But the law does not rest on faith; on the contrary, "Whoever does the works of the law will live by them." 13 Christ redeemed us from the curse of the law by becoming a curse for us—for it is written, "Cursed is everyone who hangs on a tree"— 14 in order that in Christ Jesus the blessing of Abraham might come to the Gentiles, so that we might receive the promise of the Spirit through faith. 15 Brothers and sisters, I give an example from daily life: once a person's will has been ratified, no one adds to it or annuls it. 16 Now the promises were made to Abraham and to his offspring; it does not say, "And to offsprings," as of many; but it says, "And to your offspring," that is, to one person, who is Christ. 17 My point is this: the law, which came four hundred thirty years later, does not annul a covenant previously ratified by God, so as to nullify the promise. 18 For if the inheritance comes from the law, it no longer comes from the promise; but God granted it to Abraham through the promise. 19 Why then the law? It was added because of transgressions, until the offspring would come to whom the promise had been made; and it was ordained through angels by a mediator. 20 Now a mediator involves more than one party; but God is one. 21 Is the law then opposed to the promises of God? Certainly not! For if a law had been given that could make alive, then righteousness would indeed come through the law. 22 But the scripture has imprisoned all things under the power of sin, so that what was promised through faith in Jesus Christ might be given to those who believe. 23 Now before faith came, we were imprisoned and guarded under the law until faith would be revealed. 24 Therefore the law was our disciplinarian until Christ came, so that we might be justified by faith. 25 But now that faith has come, we are no longer subject to a disciplinarian, 26 for in Christ Jesus you are all children of God through faith. 27 As many of you as were baptized into Christ have clothed yourselves with Christ. 28 There is no longer Jew or Greek, there is no longer slave or free, there is no longer male and female; for all of you are one in Christ Jesus. 29 And if you belong to Christ, then you are Abraham's offspring, heirs according to the promise.

Gal 4:21–31

Tell me, you who desire to be subject to the law, will you not listen to the law? 22 For it is written that Abraham had two sons, one by a slave woman and the other by a free woman. 23 One, the child of the slave, was born according to the flesh; the other, the child of the free woman, was born through the promise. 24 Now this is an allegory: these women are two covenants. One woman, in fact, is Hagar, from Mount Sinai, bearing children for slavery. 25 Now Hagar is Mount Sinai in Arabia[d] and corresponds to the present Jerusalem, for she is in slavery with her children. 26 But the other woman corresponds to the Jerusalem above; she is free, and she is our mother. 27 For it is written, "Rejoice, you childless one, you who bear no children, burst into song and shout, you who endure no birth pangs; for the children of the desolate woman are more numerous than the children of the one who is married." 28 Now you,[e] my friends, are children of the promise, like Isaac. 29 But just as at that time the child who was born according to the flesh persecuted the child who was born according to the Spirit, so it is now also. 30 But what does the scripture say? "Drive out the slave and her child; for the child of the slave will not share the inheritance with the child of the free woman." 31 So then, friends, we are children, not of the slave but of the free woman.

See also § 61 The Israel of God.

60. Children of the Promise

Rom 4:13–25

For the promise that he would inherit the world did not come to Abraham or to his descendants through the law but through the righteousness of faith. 14 If it is the adherents of the law who are to be the heirs, faith is null and the promise is void. 15 For the law brings wrath; but where there is no law, neither is there violation. 16 For this reason it depends on faith, in order that the promise may rest on grace and be guar-

[d] **Gal 4:25** *Now Hagar is Mount Sinai in Arabia* Other ancient authorities read *For Sinai is a mountain in Arabia* [e] **Gal 4:28** *you* Other ancient authorities read *we*

ἐκ τοῦ νόμου μόνον ἀλλὰ καὶ τῷ ἐκ πίστεως Ἀβραάμ, ὅς ἐστιν πατὴρ πάντων ἡμῶν, 17 καθὼς γέγραπται ὅτι πατέρα πολλῶν ἐθνῶν τέθεικά σε, κατέναντι οὗ ἐπίστευσεν θεοῦ τοῦ ζῳοποιοῦντος τοὺς νεκροὺς καὶ καλοῦντος τὰ μὴ ὄντα ὡς ὄντα. 18 Ὃς παρ' ἐλπίδα ἐπ' ἐλπίδι ἐπίστευσεν εἰς τὸ γενέσθαι αὐτὸν πατέρα πολλῶν ἐθνῶν κατὰ τὸ εἰρημένον· οὕτως ἔσται τὸ σπέρμα σου, 19 καὶ μὴ ἀσθενήσας τῇ πίστει κατενόησεν τὸ ἑαυτοῦ σῶμα ⸀[ἤδη] νενεκρωμένον, ἑκατονταετής που ὑπάρχων, καὶ τὴν νέκρωσιν τῆς μήτρας Σάρρας· 20 εἰς δὲ τὴν ἐπαγγελίαν τοῦ θεοῦ οὐ διεκρίθη τῇ ἀπιστίᾳ ἀλλ' ἐνεδυναμώθη τῇ πίστει, δοὺς δόξαν τῷ θεῷ 21 καὶ πληροφορηθεὶς ὅτι ὃ ἐπήγγελται δυνατός ἐστιν καὶ ποιῆσαι. 22 διὸ [καὶ] ἐλογίσθη αὐτῷ εἰς δικαιοσύνην. 23 Οὐκ ἐγράφη δὲ δι' αὐτὸν μόνον ὅτι ἐλογίσθη αὐτῷ 24 ἀλλὰ καὶ δι' ἡμᾶς, οἷς μέλλει λογίζεσθαι, τοῖς πιστεύουσιν ἐπὶ τὸν ἐγείραντα Ἰησοῦν τὸν κύριον ἡμῶν ἐκ νεκρῶν, 25 ὃς παρεδόθη διὰ τὰ παραπτώματα ἡμῶν καὶ ἠγέρθη διὰ τὴν δικαίωσιν ἡμῶν.

Rom 9:6–9

Οὐχ οἷον δὲ ὅτι ἐκπέπτωκεν ὁ λόγος τοῦ θεοῦ. οὐ γὰρ πάντες οἱ ἐξ Ἰσραὴλ οὗτοι Ἰσραήλ· 7 οὐδ' ὅτι εἰσὶν σπέρμα Ἀβραὰμ πάντες τέκνα, ἀλλ'· ἐν Ἰσαὰκ κληθήσεταί σοι σπέρμα. 8 τοῦτ' ἔστιν, οὐ τὰ τέκνα τῆς σαρκὸς ταῦτα τέκνα τοῦ θεοῦ ἀλλὰ τὰ τέκνα τῆς ἐπαγγελίας λογίζεται εἰς σπέρμα. 9 ἐπαγγελίας γὰρ ὁ λόγος οὗτος· κατὰ τὸν καιρὸν τοῦτον ἐλεύσομαι καὶ ἔσται τῇ Σάρρᾳ υἱός.

Gal 3:15–22

Ἀδελφοί, κατὰ ἄνθρωπον λέγω· ὅμως ἀνθρώπου κεκυρωμένην διαθήκην οὐδεὶς ἀθετεῖ ἢ ἐπιδιατάσσεται. 16 τῷ δὲ Ἀβραὰμ ἐρρέθησαν αἱ ἐπαγγελίαι καὶ τῷ σπέρματι αὐτοῦ. οὐ λέγει· καὶ τοῖς σπέρμασιν, ὡς ἐπὶ πολλῶν ἀλλ' ὡς ἐφ' ἑνός· καὶ τῷ σπέρματί σου, ὅς ἐστιν Χριστός. 17 τοῦτο δὲ λέγω· διαθήκην προκεκυρωμένην ὑπὸ τοῦ θεοῦ ὁ μετὰ τετρακόσια καὶ τριάκοντα ἔτη γεγονὼς νόμος οὐκ ἀκυροῖ εἰς τὸ καταργῆσαι τὴν ἐπαγγελίαν. 18 εἰ γὰρ ἐκ νόμου ἡ κληρονομία, οὐκέτι ἐξ ἐπαγγελίας· τῷ δὲ Ἀβραὰμ δι' ἐπαγγελίας κεχάρισται ὁ θεός. 19 Τί οὖν ὁ νόμος; τῶν παραβάσεων χάριν προσετέθη, ἄχρις οὗ ἔλθῃ τὸ σπέρμα ᾧ ἐπήγγελται, διαταγεὶς δι' ἀγγέλων ἐν χειρὶ μεσίτου. 20 ὁ δὲ μεσίτης ἑνὸς οὐκ ἔστιν, ὁ δὲ θεὸς εἷς ἐστιν. 21 ὁ οὖν νόμος κατὰ τῶν ἐπαγγελιῶν [τοῦ θεοῦ]; μὴ γένοιτο. εἰ γὰρ ἐδόθη νόμος ὁ δυνάμενος ζῳοποιῆσαι, ὄντως ἐκ νόμου ἂν ἦν ἡ δικαιοσύνη· 22 ἀλλὰ συνέκλεισεν ἡ γραφὴ τὰ πάντα ὑπὸ ἁμαρτίαν, ἵνα ἡ ἐπαγγελία ἐκ πίστεως Ἰησοῦ Χριστοῦ δοθῇ τοῖς πιστεύουσιν.

Gal 3:26–29

Πάντες γὰρ υἱοὶ θεοῦ ἐστε διὰ τῆς πίστεως ἐν Χριστῷ Ἰησοῦ· 27 ὅσοι γὰρ εἰς Χριστὸν ἐβαπτίσθητε, Χριστὸν ἐνεδύσασθε. 28 οὐκ ἔνι Ἰουδαῖος οὐδὲ Ἕλλην, οὐκ ἔνι δοῦλος οὐδὲ ἐλεύθερος, οὐκ ἔνι ἄρσεν καὶ θῆλυ· πάντες γὰρ ὑμεῖς εἷς ἐστε ἐν Χριστῷ Ἰησοῦ. 29 εἰ δὲ ὑμεῖς Χριστοῦ, ἄρα τοῦ Ἀβραὰμ σπέρμα ἐστέ, κατ' ἐπαγγελίαν κληρονόμοι.

Gal 4:21–31

Λέγετέ μοι, οἱ ὑπὸ νόμον θέλοντες εἶναι, τὸν νόμον οὐκ ἀκούετε; 22 γέγραπται γὰρ ὅτι Ἀβραὰμ δύο υἱοὺς ἔσχεν, ἕνα ἐκ τῆς παιδίσκης καὶ ἕνα ἐκ τῆς ἐλευθέρας. 23 ἀλλ' ὁ μὲν ἐκ τῆς παιδίσκης κατὰ σάρκα γεγέννηται, ὁ δὲ ἐκ τῆς ἐλευθέρας δι' ἐπαγγελίας. 24 ἅτινά ἐστιν ἀλληγορούμενα· αὗται γάρ εἰσιν δύο διαθῆκαι, μία μὲν ἀπὸ ὄρους Σινᾶ εἰς δουλείαν γεννῶσα, ἥτις ἐστὶν Ἁγάρ. 25 τὸ ⸂δὲ Ἁγὰρ Σινᾶ⸃ ὄρος ἐστὶν ἐν τῇ Ἀραβίᾳ· συστοιχεῖ δὲ τῇ νῦν Ἰερουσαλήμ, δουλεύει γὰρ μετὰ τῶν τέκνων αὐτῆς. 26 ἡ δὲ ἄνω Ἰερουσαλὴμ ἐλευθέρα ἐστίν, ἥτις ἐστὶν μήτηρ ἡμῶν· 27 γέγραπται γάρ· εὐφράνθητι, στεῖρα ἡ οὐ τίκτουσα, ῥῆξον καὶ βόησον, ἡ οὐκ ὠδίνουσα· ὅτι πολλὰ τὰ τέκνα τῆς ἐρήμου μᾶλλον ἢ τῆς ἐχούσης τὸν ἄνδρα. 28 ⸂⸀Ὑμεῖς δέ, ἀδελφοί, κατὰ Ἰσαὰκ ἐπαγγελίας τέκνα ⸀ἐστέ. 29 ἀλλ' ὥσπερ τότε ὁ κατὰ σάρκα γεννηθεὶς ἐδίωκεν τὸν κατὰ πνεῦμα, οὕτως καὶ νῦν. 30 ἀλλὰ τί λέγει ἡ γραφή; ἔκβαλε τὴν παιδίσκην καὶ τὸν υἱὸν αὐτῆς· οὐ γὰρ μὴ κληρονομήσει ὁ υἱὸς τῆς παιδίσκης μετὰ τοῦ υἱοῦ τῆς ἐλευθέρας. 31 διό, ἀδελφοί, οὐκ ἐσμὲν παιδίσκης τέκνα ἀλλὰ τῆς ἐλευθέρας.

2 Tim 1:1

Παῦλος ἀπόστολος Χριστοῦ Ἰησοῦ διὰ θελήματος θεοῦ κατ' ἐπαγγελίαν ζωῆς τῆς ἐν Χριστῷ Ἰησοῦ

Titus 1:1–3

Παῦλος δοῦλος θεοῦ, ἀπόστολος δὲ Ἰησοῦ Χριστοῦ κατὰ πίστιν ἐκλεκτῶν θεοῦ καὶ ἐπίγνωσιν ἀληθείας τῆς κατ' εὐσέβειαν 2 ἐπ' ἐλπίδι ζωῆς αἰωνίου, ἣν ἐπηγγείλατο ὁ ἀψευδὴς θεὸς πρὸ χρόνων αἰωνίων, 3 ἐφανέρωσεν δὲ καιροῖς ἰδίοις τὸν λόγον αὐτοῦ ἐν κηρύγματι, ὃ ἐπιστεύθην ἐγὼ κατ' ἐπιταγὴν τοῦ σωτῆρος ἡμῶν θεοῦ

61. *The Israel of God*

Rom 2:25–29

Περιτομὴ μὲν γὰρ ὠφελεῖ ἐὰν νόμον πράσσῃς· ἐὰν δὲ παραβάτης νόμου ᾖς, ἡ περιτομή σου ἀκροβυστία γέγονεν. 26 ἐὰν οὖν ἡ ἀκροβυστία τὰ δικαιώματα τοῦ νόμου φυλάσσῃ, οὐχ ἡ ἀκροβυστία αὐτοῦ εἰς περιτομὴν λογισθήσεται; 27 καὶ κρινεῖ ἡ ἐκ φύσεως ἀκροβυστία τὸν

§ 60 **Rom 4:19** ***ηδη*** ℵ A C D 33 *Byz*] *om.* B 1739. 1881 **Gal 4:25** ***δε Αγαρ Σινα*** A B D] γαρ Αγαρ Σινα 33. 1881 *Byz* ¦ γαρ Σινα ℵ C 1739 ¦ δε Σινα 𝔓46 **Gal 4:28** ***υμεις*** *et* εστε 𝔓46 B D* 33. 1739. 1881] ημεις *et* εσμεν ℵ A C D2 *Byz*

anteed to all his descendants, not only to the adherents of the law but also to those who share the faith of Abraham (for he is the father of all of us, 17 as it is written, "I have made you the father of many nations")—in the presence of the God in whom he believed, who gives life to the dead and calls into existence the things that do not exist. 18 Hoping against hope, he believed that he would become "the father of many nations," according to what was said, "So numerous shall your descendants be." 19 He did not weaken in faith when he considered his own body, which was already[a] as good as dead (for he was about a hundred years old), or when he considered the barrenness of Sarah's womb. 20 No distrust made him waver concerning the promise of God, but he grew strong in his faith as he gave glory to God, 21 being fully convinced that God was able to do what he had promised. 22 Therefore his faith "was reckoned to him as righteousness." 23 Now the words, "it was reckoned to him," were written not for his sake alone, 24 but for ours also. It will be reckoned to us who believe in him who raised Jesus our Lord from the dead, 25 who was handed over to death for our trespasses and was raised for our justification.

Rom 9:6–9

It is not as though the word of God had failed. For not all Israelites truly belong to Israel, 7 and not all of Abraham's children are his true descendants; but "It is through Isaac that descendants shall be named for you." 8 This means that it is not the children of the flesh who are the children of God, but the children of the promise are counted as descendants. 9 For this is what the promise said, "About this time I will return and Sarah shall have a son."

Gal 3:15–22

Brothers and sisters, I give an example from daily life: once a person's will has been ratified, no one adds to it or annuls it. 16 Now the promises were made to Abraham and to his offspring; it does not say, "And to offsprings," as of many; but it says, "And to your offspring," that is, to one person, who is Christ. 17 My point is this: the law, which came four hundred thirty years later, does not annul a covenant previously ratified by God, so as to nullify the promise. 18 For if the inheritance comes from the law, it no longer comes from the promise; but God granted it to Abraham through the promise. 19 Why then the law? It was added because of transgressions, until the offspring would come to whom the promise had been made; and it was ordained through angels by a mediator. 20 Now a mediator involves more than one party; but God is one. 21 Is the law then opposed to the promises of God? Certainly not! For if a law had been given that could make alive, then righteousness would indeed come through the law. 22 But the scripture has imprisoned all things under the power of sin, so that what was promised through faith in Jesus Christ might be given to those who believe.

Gal 3:26–29

for in Christ Jesus you are all children of God through faith. 27 As many of you as were baptized into Christ have clothed yourselves with Christ. 28 There is no longer Jew or Greek, there is no longer slave or free, there is no longer male and female; for all of you are one in Christ Jesus. 29 And if you belong to Christ, then you are Abraham's offspring, heirs according to the promise.

Gal 4:21–31

Tell me, you who desire to be subject to the law, will you not listen to the law? 22 For it is written that Abraham had two sons, one by a slave woman and the other by a free woman. 23 One, the child of the slave, was born according to the flesh; the other, the child of the free woman, was born through the promise. 24 Now this is an allegory: these women are two covenants. One woman, in fact, is Hagar, from Mount Sinai, bearing children for slavery. 25 Now Hagar is Mount Sinai in Arabia[b] and corresponds to the present Jerusalem, for she is in slavery with her children. 26 But the other woman corresponds to the Jerusalem above; she is free, and she is our mother. 27 For it is written, "Rejoice, you childless one, you who bear no children, burst into song and shout, you who endure no birth pangs; for the children of the desolate woman are more numerous than the children of the one who is married." 28 Now you,[c] my friends, are children of the promise, like Isaac. 29 But just as at that time the child who was born according to the flesh persecuted the child who was born according to the Spirit, so it is now also. 30 But what does the scripture say? "Drive out the slave and her child; for the child of the slave will not share the inheritance with the child of the free woman." 31 So then, friends, we are children, not of the slave but of the free woman.

2 Tim 1:1

Paul, an apostle of Christ Jesus by the will of God, for the sake of the promise of life that is in Christ Jesus

Titus 1:1–3

Paul, a servant of God and an apostle of Jesus Christ, for the sake of the faith of God's elect and the knowledge of the truth that is in accordance with godliness, 2 in the hope of eternal life that God, who never lies, promised before the ages began— 3 in due time he revealed his word through the proclamation with which I have been entrusted by the command of God our Savior

61. The Israel of God

Rom 2:25–29

Circumcision indeed is of value if you obey the law; but if you break the law, your circumcision has become uncircumcision. 26 So, if those who are uncircumcised keep the requirements of the law, will not their uncircumcision be regarded as circumcision? 27 Then those who are physically uncircumcised

§ 60 [a] **Rom 4:19** *already* Other ancient authorities lack *already* [b] **Gal 4:25** *Now Hagar is Mount Sinai in Arabia* Other ancient authorities read *For Sinai is a mountain in Arabia* [c] **Gal 4:28** *you* Other ancient authorities read *we*

νόμον τελοῦσα σὲ τὸν διὰ γράμματος καὶ περιτομῆς παραβάτην νόμου. 28 οὐ γὰρ ὁ ἐν τῷ φανερῷ Ἰουδαῖός ἐστιν οὐδὲ ἡ ἐν τῷ φανερῷ ἐν σαρκὶ περιτομή, 29 ἀλλ᾽ ὁ ἐν τῷ κρυπτῷ Ἰουδαῖος, καὶ περιτομὴ καρδίας ἐν πνεύματι οὐ γράμματι, οὗ ὁ ἔπαινος οὐκ ἐξ ἀνθρώπων ἀλλ᾽ ἐκ τοῦ θεοῦ.

Rom 9:6–9

Οὐχ οἷον δὲ ὅτι ἐκπέπτωκεν ὁ λόγος τοῦ θεοῦ. οὐ γὰρ πάντες οἱ ἐξ Ἰσραὴλ οὗτοι Ἰσραήλ· 7 οὐδ᾽ ὅτι εἰσὶν σπέρμα Ἀβραὰμ πάντες τέκνα, ἀλλ᾽· ἐν Ἰσαὰκ κληθήσεταί σοι σπέρμα. 8 τοῦτ᾽ ἔστιν, οὐ τὰ τέκνα τῆς σαρκὸς ταῦτα τέκνα τοῦ θεοῦ ἀλλὰ τὰ τέκνα τῆς ἐπαγγελίας λογίζεται εἰς σπέρμα. 9 ἐπαγγελίας γὰρ ὁ λόγος οὗτος· κατὰ τὸν καιρὸν τοῦτον ἐλεύσομαι καὶ ἔσται τῇ Σάρρᾳ υἱός.

Rom 11:1–6

Λέγω οὖν, μὴ ἀπώσατο ὁ θεὸς τὸν λαὸν αὐτοῦ; μὴ γένοιτο· καὶ γὰρ ἐγὼ Ἰσραηλίτης εἰμί, ἐκ σπέρματος Ἀβραάμ, φυλῆς Βενιαμίν. 2 οὐκ ἀπώσατο ὁ θεὸς τὸν λαὸν αὐτοῦ ὃν προέγνω. ἢ οὐκ οἴδατε ἐν Ἠλίᾳ τί λέγει ἡ γραφή, ὡς ἐντυγχάνει τῷ θεῷ κατὰ τοῦ Ἰσραήλ; 3 κύριε, τοὺς προφήτας σου ἀπέκτειναν, τὰ θυσιαστήριά σου κατέσκαψαν, κἀγὼ ὑπελείφθην μόνος καὶ ζητοῦσιν τὴν ψυχήν μου. 4 ἀλλὰ τί λέγει αὐτῷ ὁ χρηματισμός; κατέλιπον ἐμαυτῷ ἑπτακισχιλίους ἄνδρας, οἵτινες οὐκ ἔκαμψαν γόνυ τῇ Βάαλ. 5 οὕτως οὖν καὶ ἐν τῷ νῦν καιρῷ λεῖμμα κατ᾽ ἐκλογὴν χάριτος γέγονεν· 6 εἰ δὲ χάριτι, οὐκέτι ἐξ ἔργων, ἐπεὶ ἡ χάρις οὐκέτι γίνεται ⸀χάρις.

1 Cor 10:1–4

Οὐ θέλω γὰρ ὑμᾶς ἀγνοεῖν, ἀδελφοί, ὅτι οἱ πατέρες ἡμῶν πάντες ὑπὸ τὴν νεφέλην ἦσαν καὶ πάντες διὰ τῆς θαλάσσης διῆλθον 2 καὶ πάντες εἰς τὸν Μωϋσῆν ἐβαπτίσθησαν ἐν τῇ νεφέλῃ καὶ ἐν τῇ θαλάσσῃ 3 καὶ πάντες τὸ αὐτὸ πνευματικὸν βρῶμα ἔφαγον 4 καὶ πάντες τὸ αὐτὸ πνευματικὸν ἔπιον πόμα· ἔπινον γὰρ ἐκ πνευματικῆς ἀκολουθούσης πέτρας, ἡ πέτρα δὲ ἦν ὁ Χριστός.

Gal 6:14–16

Ἐμοὶ δὲ μὴ γένοιτο καυχᾶσθαι εἰ μὴ ἐν τῷ σταυρῷ τοῦ κυρίου ἡμῶν Ἰησοῦ Χριστοῦ, δι᾽ οὗ ἐμοὶ κόσμος ἐσταύρωται κἀγὼ κόσμῳ. 15 ⸂οὔτε γὰρ⸃ περιτομή τί ἐστιν οὔτε ἀκροβυστία ἀλλὰ καινὴ κτίσις. 16 καὶ ὅσοι τῷ κανόνι τούτῳ ⸀στοιχήσουσιν, εἰρήνη ἐπ᾽ αὐτοὺς καὶ ἔλεος καὶ ἐπὶ τὸν Ἰσραὴλ τοῦ θεοῦ.

Phil 3:3

ἡμεῖς γάρ ἐσμεν ἡ περιτομή, οἱ πνεύματι ⸀θεοῦ λατρεύοντες καὶ καυχώμενοι ἐν Χριστῷ Ἰησοῦ καὶ οὐκ ἐν σαρκὶ πεποιθότες

Cf. Rom 4:1–25; 9:24–29; 11:17–24; Gal 3:6–29; 4:21–31; Eph 2:11–22; Phil 1:27; 2:15; 3:20–21; Col 2:11–15.

See also § 59 Abraham's Covenant Family.

62. Circumcision in the Flesh

Rom 2:25–29

Περιτομὴ μὲν γὰρ ὠφελεῖ ἐὰν νόμον πράσσῃς· ἐὰν δὲ παραβάτης νόμου ἧς, ἡ περιτομή σου ἀκροβυστία γέγονεν. 26 ἐὰν οὖν ἡ ἀκροβυστία τὰ δικαιώματα τοῦ νόμου φυλάσσῃ, οὐχ ἡ ἀκροβυστία αὐτοῦ εἰς περιτομὴν λογισθήσεται; 27 καὶ κρινεῖ ἡ ἐκ φύσεως ἀκροβυστία τὸν νόμον τελοῦσα σὲ τὸν διὰ γράμματος καὶ περιτομῆς παραβάτην νόμου. 28 οὐ γὰρ ὁ ἐν τῷ φανερῷ Ἰουδαῖός ἐστιν οὐδὲ ἡ ἐν τῷ φανερῷ ἐν σαρκὶ περιτομή, 29 ἀλλ᾽ ὁ ἐν τῷ κρυπτῷ Ἰουδαῖος, καὶ περιτομὴ καρδίας ἐν πνεύματι οὐ γράμματι, οὗ ὁ ἔπαινος οὐκ ἐξ ἀνθρώπων ἀλλ᾽ ἐκ τοῦ θεοῦ.

Rom 3:1–4

Τί οὖν τὸ περισσὸν τοῦ Ἰουδαίου ἢ τίς ἡ ὠφέλεια τῆς περιτομῆς; 2 πολὺ κατὰ πάντα τρόπον. πρῶτον μὲν [γὰρ] ὅτι ἐπιστεύθησαν τὰ λόγια τοῦ θεοῦ. 3 τί γάρ; εἰ ἠπίστησάν τινες, μὴ ἡ ἀπιστία αὐτῶν τὴν πίστιν τοῦ θεοῦ καταργήσει; 4 μὴ γένοιτο· γινέσθω δὲ ὁ θεὸς ἀληθής, πᾶς δὲ ἄνθρωπος ψεύστης, καθὼς γέγραπται· ὅπως ἂν δικαιωθῇς ἐν τοῖς λόγοις σου καὶ νικήσεις ἐν τῷ κρίνεσθαί σε.

Rom 3:29–31

ἢ Ἰουδαίων ὁ θεὸς μόνον; οὐχὶ καὶ ἐθνῶν; ναὶ καὶ ἐθνῶν, 30 εἴπερ εἷς ὁ θεὸς ὃς δικαιώσει περιτομὴν ἐκ πίστεως καὶ ἀκροβυστίαν διὰ τῆς πίστεως. 31 νόμον οὖν καταργοῦμεν διὰ τῆς πίστεως; μὴ γένοιτο· ἀλλὰ νόμον ἱστάνομεν.

Rom 4:9–12

Ὁ μακαρισμὸς οὖν οὗτος ἐπὶ τὴν περιτομὴν ἢ καὶ ἐπὶ τὴν ἀκροβυστίαν; λέγομεν γάρ· ἐλογίσθη τῷ Ἀβραὰμ ἡ πίστις εἰς δικαιοσύνην. 10 πῶς οὖν ἐλογίσθη; ἐν περιτομῇ ὄντι ἢ ἐν ἀκροβυστίᾳ; οὐκ ἐν περιτομῇ ἀλλ᾽ ἐν ἀκροβυστίᾳ· 11 καὶ σημεῖον ἔλαβεν περιτομῆς σφραγῖδα τῆς δικαιοσύνης τῆς πίστεως τῆς ἐν τῇ ἀκροβυστίᾳ, εἰς τὸ εἶναι αὐτὸν πατέρα πάντων τῶν πιστευόντων δι᾽ ἀκροβυστίας, εἰς τὸ λογισθῆναι ⸀[καὶ] αὐτοῖς [τὴν] δικαιοσύνην, 12 καὶ πατέρα περιτομῆς τοῖς οὐκ ἐκ περιτομῆς μόνον ἀλλὰ καὶ τοῖς στοιχοῦσιν τοῖς ἴχνεσιν τῆς ἐν ἀκροβυστίᾳ πίστεως τοῦ πατρὸς ἡμῶν Ἀβραάμ.

§ 61 **Rom 11:6** ***χαρις*** 𝔓^{46} ℵ* A C D 1739. 1881] *add.* ει δε εξ εργων ουκετι εστι χαρις, επει το εργον ουκετι εστιν εργον ℵ^{2} (B) 33^{vid} *Byz* **Gal 6:15** ***ουτε γαρ*** 𝔓^{46} B 33. 1739*] εν γαρ Χριστω Ιησου ουτε ℵ A C D (1739^{c}). 1881 *Byz* **Gal 6:16** ***στοιχησουσιν*** ℵ B C^{2} 33 *Byz*] στοιχουσιν A C* D 1739. 1881 ¦ στοιχησωσιν 𝔓^{46} **Phil 3:3** ***θεου*** ℵ* A B C D^{2} 33. 1739. 1881 *Byz*] θεω ℵ^{2} D* ¦ *om.* 𝔓^{46} **§ 62** **Rom 4:11** ***και*** ℵ^{2} C D *Byz*] *om.* ℵ* A B 1739. 1881

but keep the law will condemn you that have the written code and circumcision but break the law. **28** For a person is not a Jew who is one outwardly, nor is true circumcision something external and physical. **29** Rather, a person is a Jew who is one inwardly, and real circumcision is a matter of the heart—it is by the Spirit and not by the written letter. Such a person receives praise not from others but from God.[a]

Rom 9:6–9

It is not as though the word of God had failed. For not all Israelites truly belong to Israel, **7** and not all of Abraham's children are his true descendants; but "It is through Isaac that descendants shall be named for you." **8** This means that it is not the children of the flesh who are the children of God, but the children of the promise are counted as descendants. **9** For this is what the promise said, "About this time I will return and Sarah shall have a son."

Rom 11:1–6

I ask, then, has God rejected his people? By no means! I myself am an Israelite, a descendant of Abraham, a member of the tribe of Benjamin. **2** God has not rejected his people whom he foreknew. Do you not know what the scripture says of Elijah, how he pleads with God against Israel? **3** "Lord, they have killed your prophets, they have demolished your altars; I alone am left, and they are seeking my life." **4** But what is the divine reply to him? "I have kept for myself seven thousand who have not bowed the knee to Baal." **5** So too at the present time there is a remnant, chosen by grace. **6** But if it is by grace, it is no longer on the basis of works, otherwise grace would no longer be grace.[b]

1 Cor 10:1–4

I do not want you to be unaware, brothers and sisters, that our ancestors were all under the cloud, and all passed through the sea, **2** and all were baptized into Moses in the cloud and in the sea, **3** and all ate the same spiritual food, **4** and all drank the same spiritual drink. For they drank from the spiritual rock that followed them, and the rock was Christ.

Gal 6:14–16

May I never boast of anything except the cross of our Lord Jesus Christ, by which the world has been crucified to me, and I to the world. **15** For[c] neither circumcision nor uncircumcision is anything; but a new creation is everything! **16** As for those who will follow[d] this rule—peace be upon them, and mercy, and upon the Israel of God.

Phil 3:3

For it is we who are the circumcision, who worship in the Spirit of God[e] and boast in Christ Jesus and have no confidence in the flesh

Cf. Rom 4:1–25; 9:24–29; 11:17–24; Gal 3:6–29; 4:21–31; Eph 2:11–22; Phil 1:27; 2:15; 3:20–21; Col 2:11–15.

See also § 59 Abraham's Covenant Family.

62. *Circumcision in the Flesh*

Rom 2:25–29

Circumcision indeed is of value if you obey the law; but if you break the law, your circumcision has become uncircumcision. **26** So, if those who are uncircumcised keep the requirements of the law, will not their uncircumcision be regarded as circumcision? **27** Then those who are physically uncircumcised but keep the law will condemn you that have the written code and circumcision but break the law. **28** For a person is not a Jew who is one outwardly, nor is true circumcision something external and physical. **29** Rather, a person is a Jew who is one inwardly, and real circumcision is a matter of the heart—it is by the Spirit and not by the written letter. Such a person receives praise not from others but from God.[a]

Rom 3:1–4

Then what advantage has the Jew? Or what is the value of circumcision? **2** Much, in every way. For in the first place the Jews were entrusted with the oracles of God. **3** What if some were unfaithful? Will their faithlessness nullify the faithfulness of God? **4** By no means! Although everyone is a liar, let God be proved true, as it is written, "So that you may be justified in your words, and prevail in your judging."

Rom 3:29–31

Or is God the God of Jews only? Is he not the God of Gentiles also? Yes, of Gentiles also, **30** since God is one; and he will justify the circumcised on the ground of faith and the uncircumcised through that same faith. **31** Do we then overthrow the law by this faith? By no means! On the contrary, we uphold the law.

Rom 4:9–12

Is this blessedness, then, pronounced only on the circumcised, or also on the uncircumcised? We say, "Faith was reckoned to Abraham as righteousness." **10** How then was it reckoned to him? Was it before or after he had been circumcised? It was not after, but before he was circumcised. **11** He received the sign of circumcision as a seal of the righteousness that he had by faith while he was still uncircumcised. The purpose was to make him the ancestor of all who believe without being circumcised and who thus have righteousness reckoned to them,[b] **12** and likewise the ancestor of the circumcised who are not only circumcised but who also follow the example of the faith that our ancestor Abraham had before he was circumcised.

§ 61 [a] **Rom 2:29** Translation differs from NRSV [b] **Rom 11:6** *grace* Other ancient authorities add *But if it is by works, it is no longer on the basis of grace, otherwise work would no longer be work* [c] **Gal 6:15** *For* Other ancient authorities add *in Christ Jesus* [d] **Gal 6:16** *will follow* Other ancient authorities read *follow* [e] **Phil 3:3** *worship in the Spirit of God* Other ancient authorities read *worship God in the Spirit* **§ 62** [a] **Rom 2:29** Translation differs from NRSV [b] **Rom 4:11** *to them* Other ancient authorities read *to them as well*

1 Cor 7:17–19

Εἰ μὴ ἑκάστῳ ὡς ἐμέρισεν ὁ κύριος, ἕκαστον ὡς κέκληκεν ὁ θεός, οὕτως περιπατείτω. καὶ οὕτως ἐν ταῖς ἐκκλησίαις πάσαις διατάσσομαι. **18** περιτετμημένος τις ἐκλήθη, μὴ ἐπισπάσθω· ἐν ἀκροβυστίᾳ κέκληταί τις, μὴ περιτεμνέσθω. **19** ἡ περιτομὴ οὐδέν ἐστιν καὶ ἡ ἀκροβυστία οὐδέν ἐστιν, ἀλλὰ τήρησις ἐντολῶν θεοῦ.

Gal 2:1–5

Ἔπειτα διὰ δεκατεσσάρων ἐτῶν πάλιν ἀνέβην εἰς Ἱεροσόλυμα μετὰ Βαρναβᾶ συμπαραλαβὼν καὶ Τίτον· **2** ἀνέβην δὲ κατὰ ἀποκάλυψιν· καὶ ἀνεθέμην αὐτοῖς τὸ εὐαγγέλιον ὃ κηρύσσω ἐν τοῖς ἔθνεσιν, κατ᾽ ἰδίαν δὲ τοῖς δοκοῦσιν, μή πως εἰς κενὸν τρέχω ἢ ἔδραμον. **3** ἀλλ᾽ οὐδὲ Τίτος ὁ σὺν ἐμοί, Ἕλλην ὤν, ἠναγκάσθη περιτμηθῆναι· **4** διὰ δὲ τοὺς παρεισάκτους ψευδαδέλφους, οἵτινες παρεισῆλθον κατασκοπῆσαι τὴν ἐλευθερίαν ἡμῶν ἣν ἔχομεν ἐν Χριστῷ Ἰησοῦ, ἵνα ἡμᾶς καταδουλώσουσιν, **5** οἷς οὐδὲ πρὸς ὥραν εἴξαμεν τῇ ὑποταγῇ, ἵνα ἡ ἀλήθεια τοῦ εὐαγγελίου διαμείνῃ πρὸς ὑμᾶς.

Gal 5:1–12

Τῇ ἐλευθερίᾳ ἡμᾶς Χριστὸς ἠλευθέρωσεν· στήκετε οὖν καὶ μὴ πάλιν ζυγῷ δουλείας ἐνέχεσθε. **2** Ἴδε ἐγὼ Παῦλος λέγω ὑμῖν ὅτι ἐὰν περιτέμνησθε, Χριστὸς ὑμᾶς οὐδὲν ὠφελήσει. **3** μαρτύρομαι δὲ πάλιν παντὶ ἀνθρώπῳ περιτεμνομένῳ ὅτι ὀφειλέτης ἐστὶν ὅλον τὸν νόμον ποιῆσαι. **4** κατηργήθητε ἀπὸ Χριστοῦ, οἵτινες ἐν νόμῳ δικαιοῦσθε, τῆς χάριτος ἐξεπέσατε. **5** ἡμεῖς γὰρ πνεύματι ἐκ πίστεως ἐλπίδα δικαιοσύνης ἀπεκδεχόμεθα. **6** ἐν γὰρ Χριστῷ Ἰησοῦ οὔτε περιτομή τι ἰσχύει οὔτε ἀκροβυστία ἀλλὰ πίστις δι᾽ ἀγάπης ἐνεργουμένη. **7** Ἐτρέχετε καλῶς· τίς ὑμᾶς ἐνέκοψεν [τῇ] ἀληθείᾳ μὴ πείθεσθαι; **8** ἡ πεισμονὴ οὐκ ἐκ τοῦ καλοῦντος ὑμᾶς. **9** μικρὰ ζύμη ὅλον τὸ φύραμα ζυμοῖ. **10** ἐγὼ πέποιθα εἰς ὑμᾶς ἐν κυρίῳ ὅτι οὐδὲν ἄλλο φρονήσετε· ὁ δὲ ταράσσων ὑμᾶς βαστάσει τὸ κρίμα, ὅστις ἐὰν ᾖ. **11** Ἐγὼ δέ, ἀδελφοί, εἰ περιτομὴν ἔτι κηρύσσω, τί ἔτι διώκομαι; ἄρα κατήργηται τὸ σκάνδαλον τοῦ σταυροῦ. **12** Ὄφελον καὶ ἀποκόψονται οἱ ἀναστατοῦντες ὑμᾶς.

Gal 6:11–16

Ἴδετε πηλίκοις ὑμῖν γράμμασιν ἔγραψα τῇ ἐμῇ χειρί. **12** Ὅσοι θέλουσιν εὐπροσωπῆσαι ἐν σαρκί, οὗτοι ἀναγκάζουσιν ὑμᾶς περιτέμνεσθαι, μόνον ἵνα τῷ σταυρῷ τοῦ Χριστοῦ μὴ διώκωνται. **13** οὐδὲ γὰρ οἱ περιτεμνόμενοι αὐτοὶ νόμον φυλάσσουσιν ἀλλὰ θέλουσιν ὑμᾶς περιτέμνεσθαι, ἵνα ἐν τῇ ὑμετέρᾳ σαρκὶ καυχήσωνται. **14** Ἐμοὶ δὲ μὴ γένοιτο καυχᾶσθαι εἰ μὴ ἐν τῷ σταυρῷ τοῦ κυρίου ἡμῶν Ἰησοῦ Χριστοῦ, δι᾽ οὗ ἐμοὶ κόσμος ἐσταύρωται κἀγὼ κόσμῳ. **15** ⸀οὔτε γὰρ⸀ περιτομή τί ἐστιν οὔτε ἀκροβυστία ἀλλὰ καινὴ κτίσις. **16** καὶ ὅσοι τῷ κανόνι τούτῳ ⸀στοιχήσουσιν, εἰρήνη ἐπ᾽ αὐτοὺς καὶ ἔλεος καὶ ἐπὶ τὸν Ἰσραὴλ τοῦ θεοῦ.

Cf. Eph 2:11–13; Acts 15:1–35; 16:1–3; 21:20–26.

See also § 58 Circumcision of the Spirit.

63. *The Disobedience of Israel according to the Flesh*

Rom 9:1–5

Ἀλήθειαν λέγω ἐν Χριστῷ, οὐ ψεύδομαι, συμμαρτυρούσης μοι τῆς συνειδήσεώς μου ἐν πνεύματι ἁγίῳ, **2** ὅτι λύπη μοί ἐστιν μεγάλη καὶ ἀδιάλειπτος ὀδύνη τῇ καρδίᾳ μου. **3** ηὐχόμην γὰρ ἀνάθεμα εἶναι αὐτὸς ἐγὼ ἀπὸ τοῦ Χριστοῦ ὑπὲρ τῶν ἀδελφῶν μου τῶν συγγενῶν μου κατὰ σάρκα, **4** οἵτινές εἰσιν Ἰσραηλῖται, ὧν ἡ υἱοθεσία καὶ ἡ δόξα καὶ ⸀αἱ διαθῆκαι⸀ καὶ ἡ νομοθεσία καὶ ἡ λατρεία καὶ αἱ ἐπαγγελίαι, **5** ὧν οἱ πατέρες καὶ ἐξ ὧν ὁ Χριστὸς τὸ κατὰ σάρκα, ὁ ὢν ἐπὶ πάντων θεὸς εὐλογητὸς εἰς τοὺς αἰῶνας, ἀμήν.

Rom 9:30–10:4

Τί οὖν ἐροῦμεν; ὅτι ἔθνη τὰ μὴ διώκοντα δικαιοσύνην κατέλαβεν δικαιοσύνην, δικαιοσύνην δὲ τὴν ἐκ πίστεως, **31** Ἰσραὴλ δὲ διώκων νόμον δικαιοσύνης εἰς νόμον οὐκ ἔφθασεν. **32** διὰ τί; ὅτι οὐκ ἐκ πίστεως ἀλλ᾽ ὡς ἐξ ἔργων· προσέκοψαν τῷ λίθῳ τοῦ προσκόμματος, **33** καθὼς γέγραπται· ἰδοὺ τίθημι ἐν Σιὼν λίθον προσκόμματος καὶ πέτραν σκανδάλου, καὶ ὁ πιστεύων ἐπ᾽ αὐτῷ οὐ καταισχυνθήσεται. **10** Ἀδελφοί, ἡ μὲν εὐδοκία τῆς ἐμῆς καρδίας καὶ ἡ δέησις πρὸς τὸν θεὸν ὑπὲρ αὐτῶν εἰς σωτηρίαν. **2** μαρτυρῶ γὰρ αὐτοῖς ὅτι ζῆλον θεοῦ ἔχουσιν ἀλλ᾽ οὐ κατ᾽ ἐπίγνωσιν· **3** ἀγνοοῦντες γὰρ τὴν τοῦ θεοῦ δικαιοσύνην καὶ τὴν ἰδίαν [δικαιοσύνην] ζητοῦντες στῆσαι, τῇ δικαιοσύνῃ τοῦ θεοῦ οὐχ ὑπετάγησαν. **4** τέλος γὰρ νόμου Χριστὸς εἰς δικαιοσύνην παντὶ τῷ πιστεύοντι.

Rom 10:19–21

ἀλλὰ λέγω, μὴ Ἰσραὴλ οὐκ ἔγνω; πρῶτος Μωϋσῆς λέγει· ἐγὼ παραζηλώσω ὑμᾶς ἐπ᾽ οὐκ ἔθνει, ἐπ᾽ ἔθνει ἀσυνέτῳ παροργιῶ ὑμᾶς. **20** Ἠσαΐας δὲ ἀποτολμᾷ καὶ λέγει· εὑρέθην [ἐν] τοῖς ἐμὲ μὴ ζητοῦσιν, ἐμφανὴς ἐγενόμην τοῖς ἐμὲ μὴ ἐπερωτῶσιν. **21** πρὸς δὲ τὸν Ἰσραὴλ λέγει· ὅλην τὴν ἡμέραν ἐξεπέτασα τὰς χεῖράς μου πρὸς λαὸν ἀπειθοῦντα καὶ ἀντιλέγοντα.

Rom 11:7–10

Τί οὖν; ὃ ἐπιζητεῖ Ἰσραήλ, τοῦτο οὐκ ἐπέτυχεν, ἡ δὲ ἐκλογὴ ἐπέτυχεν· οἱ δὲ λοιποὶ ἐπωρώθησαν, **8** καθὼς γέγραπται· ἔδωκεν αὐτοῖς ὁ θεὸς πνεῦμα κατανύξεως,

Gal 6:15 ***ουτε γαρ*** 𝔓[46] B 33. 1739*] εν γαρ Χριστω Ιησου ουτε א A C D (1739[c]). 1881 *Byz* **Gal 6:16** ***στοιχησουσιν*** א B C[2] 33 *Byz*] στοιχουσιν A C* D 1739. 1881 ¦ στοιχησωσιν 𝔓[46] **§ 63** **Rom 9:4** ***αι διαθηκαι*** א C 33. 1739. 1881 *Byz*] η διαθηκη 𝔓[46] B D

1 Cor 7:17–19

However that may be, let each of you lead the life that the Lord has assigned, to which God called you. This is my rule in all the churches. 18 Was anyone at the time of his call already circumcised? Let him not seek to remove the marks of circumcision. Was anyone at the time of his call uncircumcised? Let him not seek circumcision. 19 Circumcision is nothing, and uncircumcision is nothing; but obeying the commandments of God is everything.

Gal 2:1–5

Then after fourteen years I went up again to Jerusalem with Barnabas, taking Titus along with me. 2 I went up in response to a revelation. Then I laid before them (though only in a private meeting with the acknowledged leaders) the gospel that I proclaim among the Gentiles, in order to make sure that I was not running, or had not run, in vain. 3 But even Titus, who was with me, was not compelled to be circumcised, though he was a Greek. 4 But because of false believers secretly brought in, who slipped in to spy on the freedom we have in Christ Jesus, so that they might enslave us— 5 we did not submit to them even for a moment, so that the truth of the gospel might always remain with you.

Gal 5:1–12

For freedom Christ has set us free. Stand firm, therefore, and do not submit again to a yoke of slavery. 2 Listen! I, Paul, am telling you that if you let yourselves be circumcised, Christ will be of no benefit to you. 3 Once again I testify to every man who lets himself be circumcised that he is obliged to obey the entire law. 4 You who want to be justified by the law have cut yourselves off from Christ; you have fallen away from grace. 5 For through the Spirit, by faith, we eagerly wait for the hope of righteousness. 6 For in Christ Jesus neither circumcision nor uncircumcision counts for anything; the only thing that counts is faith working through love. 7 You were running well; who prevented you from obeying the truth? 8 Such persuasion does not come from the one who calls you. 9 A little yeast leavens the whole batch of dough. 10 I am confident about you in the Lord that you will not think otherwise. But whoever it is that is confusing you will pay the penalty. 11 But my friends, why am I still being persecuted if I am still preaching circumcision? In that case the offense of the cross has been removed. 12 I wish those who unsettle you would castrate themselves!

Gal 6:11–16

See what large letters I make when I am writing in my own hand! 12 It is those who want to make a good showing in the flesh that try to compel you to be circumcised—only that they may not be persecuted for the cross of Christ. 13 Even the circumcised do not themselves obey the law, but they want you to be circumcised so that they may boast about your flesh. 14 May I never boast of anything except the cross of our Lord Jesus Christ, by which the world has been crucified to me, and I to the world. 15 For[c] neither circumcision nor uncircumcision is anything; but a new creation is everything! 16 As for those who will follow[d] this rule—peace be upon them, and mercy, and upon the Israel of God.

Cf. Eph 2:11–13; Acts 15:1–35; 16:1–3; 21:20–26.

See also § 58 Circumcision of the Spirit.

63. *The Disobedience of Israel according to the Flesh*

Rom 9:1–5

I am speaking the truth in Christ—I am not lying; my conscience confirms it by the Holy Spirit— 2 I have great sorrow and unceasing anguish in my heart. 3 For I could wish that I myself were accursed and cut off from Christ for the sake of my own people, my kindred according to the flesh. 4 They are Israelites, and to them belong the adoption, the glory, the covenants,[a] the giving of the law, the worship, and the promises; 5 to them belong the patriarchs, and from them, according to the flesh, comes the Messiah, who is over all, God blessed forever. Amen.

Rom 9:30–10:4

What then are we to say? Gentiles, who did not strive for righteousness, have attained it, that is, righteousness through faith; 31 but Israel, who did strive for the righteousness that is based on the law, did not succeed in fulfilling that law. 32 Why not? Because they did not strive for it on the basis of faith, but as if it were based on works. They have stumbled over the stumbling stone, 33 as it is written, "See, I am laying in Zion a stone that will make people stumble, a rock that will make them fall, and whoever believes in him will not be put to shame." **10** Brothers and sisters, my heart's desire and prayer to God for them is that they may be saved. 2 I can testify that they have a zeal for God, but it is not enlightened. 3 For, being ignorant of the righteousness that comes from God, and seeking to establish their own, they have not submitted to God's righteousness. 4 For Christ is the goal[b] of the law so that there may be righteousness for everyone who believes.

Rom 10:19–21

Again I ask, did Israel not understand? First Moses says, "I will make you jealous of those who are not a nation; with a foolish nation I will make you angry." 20 Then Isaiah is so bold as to say, "I have been found by those who did not seek me; I have shown myself to those who did not ask for me." 21 But of Israel he says, "All day long I have held out my hands to a disobedient and contrary people."

Rom 11:7–10

What then? Israel failed to obtain what it was seeking. The elect obtained it, but the rest were hardened, 8 as it is written, "God gave them a sluggish spirit, eyes

[c] **Gal 6:15** *For* Other ancient authorities add *in Christ Jesus* [d] **Gal 6:16** *will follow* Other ancient authorities read *follow* **§ 63** [a] **Rom 9:4** *the covenants* Other ancient authorities read *the covenant* [b] **Rom 10:4** *goal* Or *end* (so NRSV)

ὀφθαλμοὺς τοῦ μὴ βλέπειν καὶ ὦτα τοῦ μὴ ἀκούειν, ἕως τῆς σήμερον ἡμέρας. **9** καὶ Δαυὶδ λέγει· γενηθήτω ἡ τράπεζα αὐτῶν εἰς παγίδα καὶ εἰς θήραν καὶ εἰς σκάνδαλον καὶ εἰς ἀνταπόδομα αὐτοῖς, **10** σκοτισθήτωσαν οἱ ὀφθαλμοὶ αὐτῶν τοῦ μὴ βλέπειν καὶ τὸν νῶτον αὐτῶν διὰ παντὸς σύγκαμψον.

Rom 11:11–24

Λέγω οὖν, μὴ ἔπταισαν ἵνα πέσωσιν; μὴ γένοιτο· ἀλλὰ τῷ αὐτῶν παραπτώματι ἡ σωτηρία τοῖς ἔθνεσιν εἰς τὸ παραζηλῶσαι αὐτούς. **12** εἰ δὲ τὸ παράπτωμα αὐτῶν πλοῦτος κόσμου καὶ τὸ ἥττημα αὐτῶν πλοῦτος ἐθνῶν, πόσῳ μᾶλλον τὸ πλήρωμα αὐτῶν. **13** Ὑμῖν δὲ λέγω τοῖς ἔθνεσιν· ἐφ' ὅσον μὲν οὖν εἰμι ἐγὼ ἐθνῶν ἀπόστολος, τὴν διακονίαν μου δοξάζω, **14** εἴ πως παραζηλώσω μου τὴν σάρκα καὶ σώσω τινὰς ἐξ αὐτῶν. **15** εἰ γὰρ ἡ ἀποβολὴ αὐτῶν καταλλαγὴ κόσμου, τίς ἡ πρόσλημψις εἰ μὴ ζωὴ ἐκ νεκρῶν; **16** εἰ δὲ ἡ ἀπαρχὴ ἁγία, καὶ τὸ φύραμα· καὶ εἰ ἡ ῥίζα ἁγία, καὶ οἱ κλάδοι. **17** Εἰ δέ τινες τῶν κλάδων ἐξεκλάσθησαν, σὺ δὲ ἀγριέλαιος ὢν ἐνεκεντρίσθης ἐν αὐτοῖς καὶ συγκοινωνὸς ⸂τῆς ῥίζης⸃ τῆς πιότητος τῆς ἐλαίας ἐγένου, **18** μὴ κατακαυχῶ τῶν κλάδων· εἰ δὲ κατακαυχᾶσαι οὐ σὺ τὴν ῥίζαν βαστάζεις ἀλλὰ ἡ ῥίζα σέ. **19** ἐρεῖς οὖν· ἐξεκλάσθησαν κλάδοι ἵνα ἐγὼ ἐγκεντρισθῶ. **20** καλῶς· τῇ ἀπιστίᾳ ἐξεκλάσθησαν, σὺ δὲ τῇ πίστει ἕστηκας. μὴ ὑψηλὰ φρόνει ἀλλὰ φοβοῦ· **21** εἰ γὰρ ὁ θεὸς τῶν κατὰ φύσιν κλάδων οὐκ ἐφείσατο, ⸂[μή πως]⸃ οὐδὲ σοῦ φείσεται. **22** ἴδε οὖν χρηστότητα καὶ ἀποτομίαν θεοῦ· ἐπὶ μὲν τοὺς πεσόντας ἀποτομία, ἐπὶ δὲ σὲ χρηστότης θεοῦ, ἐὰν ἐπιμένῃς τῇ χρηστότητι, ἐπεὶ καὶ σὺ ἐκκοπήσῃ. **23** κἀκεῖνοι δέ, ἐὰν μὴ ἐπιμένωσιν τῇ ἀπιστίᾳ, ἐγκεντρισθήσονται· δυνατὸς γάρ ἐστιν ὁ θεὸς πάλιν ἐγκεντρίσαι αὐτούς. **24** εἰ γὰρ σὺ ἐκ τῆς κατὰ φύσιν ἐξεκόπης ἀγριελαίου καὶ παρὰ φύσιν ἐνεκεντρίσθης εἰς καλλιέλαιον, πόσῳ μᾶλλον οὗτοι οἱ κατὰ φύσιν ἐγκεντρισθήσονται τῇ ἰδίᾳ ἐλαίᾳ.

Rom 11:25–32

Οὐ γὰρ θέλω ὑμᾶς ἀγνοεῖν, ἀδελφοί, τὸ μυστήριον τοῦτο, ἵνα μὴ ἦτε [παρ'] ἑαυτοῖς φρόνιμοι, ὅτι πώρωσις ἀπὸ μέρους τῷ Ἰσραὴλ γέγονεν ἄχρι οὗ τὸ πλήρωμα τῶν ἐθνῶν εἰσέλθῃ **26** καὶ οὕτως πᾶς Ἰσραὴλ σωθήσεται, καθὼς γέγραπται· ἥξει ἐκ Σιὼν ὁ ῥυόμενος, ἀποστρέψει ἀσεβείας ἀπὸ Ἰακώβ. **27** καὶ αὕτη αὐτοῖς ἡ παρ' ἐμοῦ διαθήκη, ὅταν ἀφέλωμαι τὰς ἁμαρτίας αὐτῶν. **28** κατὰ μὲν τὸ εὐαγγέλιον ἐχθροὶ δι' ὑμᾶς, κατὰ δὲ τὴν ἐκλογὴν ἀγαπητοὶ διὰ τοὺς πατέρας· **29** ἀμεταμέλητα γὰρ τὰ χαρίσματα καὶ ἡ κλῆσις τοῦ θεοῦ. **30** ὥσπερ γὰρ ὑμεῖς ποτε ἠπειθήσατε τῷ θεῷ, νῦν δὲ ἠλεήθητε τῇ τούτων ἀπειθείᾳ, **31** οὕτως καὶ οὗτοι νῦν ἠπείθησαν τῷ ὑμετέρῳ ἐλέει, ἵνα καὶ αὐτοὶ ⸀[νῦν] ἐλεηθῶσιν. **32** συνέκλεισεν γὰρ ὁ θεὸς τοὺς πάντας εἰς ἀπείθειαν, ἵνα τοὺς πάντας ἐλεήσῃ.

1 Cor 1:23–24

ἡμεῖς δὲ κηρύσσομεν Χριστὸν ἐσταυρωμένον, Ἰουδαίοις μὲν σκάνδαλον, ἔθνεσιν δὲ μωρίαν, **24** αὐτοῖς δὲ τοῖς κλητοῖς, Ἰουδαίοις τε καὶ Ἕλλησιν, Χριστὸν θεοῦ δύναμιν καὶ θεοῦ σοφίαν

1 Thess 2:14–16

Ὑμεῖς γὰρ μιμηταὶ ἐγενήθητε, ἀδελφοί, τῶν ἐκκλησιῶν τοῦ θεοῦ τῶν οὐσῶν ἐν τῇ Ἰουδαίᾳ ἐν Χριστῷ Ἰησοῦ, ὅτι τὰ αὐτὰ ἐπάθετε καὶ ὑμεῖς ὑπὸ τῶν ἰδίων συμφυλετῶν καθὼς καὶ αὐτοὶ ὑπὸ τῶν Ἰουδαίων, **15** τῶν καὶ τὸν κύριον ἀποκτεινάντων Ἰησοῦν καὶ ⸀τοὺς προφήτας καὶ ἡμᾶς ἐκδιωξάντων καὶ θεῷ μὴ ἀρεσκόντων καὶ πᾶσιν ἀνθρώποις ἐναντίων, **16** κωλυόντων ἡμᾶς τοῖς ἔθνεσιν λαλῆσαι ἵνα σωθῶσιν, εἰς τὸ ἀναπληρῶσαι αὐτῶν τὰς ἁμαρτίας πάντοτε. ἔφθασεν δὲ ἐπ' αὐτοὺς ἡ ὀργὴ εἰς τέλος.

Acts 13:26–27

Ἄνδρες ἀδελφοί, υἱοὶ γένους Ἀβραὰμ καὶ οἱ ἐν ὑμῖν φοβούμενοι τὸν θεόν, ⸀ἡμῖν ὁ λόγος τῆς σωτηρίας ταύτης ἐξαπεστάλη. **27** οἱ γὰρ κατοικοῦντες ἐν Ἰερουσαλὴμ καὶ οἱ ἄρχοντες αὐτῶν τοῦτον ἀγνοήσαντες καὶ τὰς φωνὰς τῶν προφητῶν τὰς κατὰ πᾶν σάββατον ἀναγινωσκομένας κρίναντες ἐπλήρωσαν

Acts 13:45–46

ἰδόντες δὲ οἱ Ἰουδαῖοι τοὺς ὄχλους ἐπλήσθησαν ζήλου καὶ ἀντέλεγον τοῖς ὑπὸ Παύλου λαλουμένοις βλασφημοῦντες. **46** παρρησιασάμενοί τε ὁ Παῦλος καὶ ὁ Βαρναβᾶς εἶπαν· ὑμῖν ἦν ἀναγκαῖον πρῶτον λαληθῆναι τὸν λόγον τοῦ θεοῦ· ἐπειδὴ ἀπωθεῖσθε αὐτὸν καὶ οὐκ ἀξίους κρίνετε ἑαυτοὺς τῆς αἰωνίου ζωῆς, ἰδοὺ στρεφόμεθα εἰς τὰ ἔθνη.

Acts 18:5–6

Ὡς δὲ κατῆλθον ἀπὸ τῆς Μακεδονίας ὅ τε Σιλᾶς καὶ ὁ Τιμόθεος, συνείχετο τῷ λόγῳ ὁ Παῦλος διαμαρτυρόμενος τοῖς Ἰουδαίοις εἶναι τὸν χριστὸν Ἰησοῦν. **6** ἀντιτασσομένων δὲ αὐτῶν καὶ βλασφημούντων ἐκτιναξάμενος τὰ ἱμάτια εἶπεν πρὸς αὐτούς· τὸ αἷμα ὑμῶν ἐπὶ τὴν κεφαλὴν ὑμῶν· καθαρὸς ἐγὼ ἀπὸ τοῦ νῦν εἰς τὰ ἔθνη πορεύσομαι.

Acts 19:9

ὡς δέ τινες ἐσκληρύνοντο καὶ ἠπείθουν κακολογοῦντες τὴν ὁδὸν ἐνώπιον τοῦ πλήθους, ἀποστὰς ἀπ' αὐτῶν ἀφώρισεν τοὺς μαθητὰς καθ' ἡμέραν διαλεγόμενος ἐν τῇ σχολῇ ⸀Τυράννου.

Acts 22:17–21

Ἐγένετο δέ μοι ὑποστρέψαντι εἰς Ἰερουσαλὴμ καὶ προσευχομένου μου ἐν τῷ ἱερῷ γενέσθαι με ἐν ἐκστάσει **18** καὶ ἰδεῖν αὐτὸν λέγοντά μοι· σπεῦσον καὶ ἔξελθε ἐν τάχει ἐξ Ἰερουσαλήμ, διότι οὐ παραδέξονταί σου μαρτυρίαν περὶ ἐμοῦ. **19** κἀγὼ εἶπον· κύριε, αὐτοὶ ἐπίστανται ὅτι ἐγὼ ἤμην φυλακίζων καὶ δέρων κατὰ τὰς συναγωγὰς τοὺς πιστεύοντας ἐπὶ σέ, **20** καὶ ὅτε ἐξεχύννετο τὸ αἷμα Στεφάνου

Rom 11:17 ***της ριζης*** ℵ* B C] της ριζης και ℵ^{2} A D^{2} 33. 1739. 1881 *Byz* ¦ *om.* 𝔓^{46} D* **Rom 11:21** ***μη πως*** 𝔓^{46} D 33 *Byz*] *om.* ℵ A B C 1739. 1881 **Rom 11:31** ***νυν*** ℵ B D^{*,c}] *om.* 𝔓^{46} A D^{2} 1739. 1881 *Byz* ¦ υστερον 33 **1 Thess 2:15** ***τους*** ℵ A B D* I 33. 1739. 1881] *add.* ιδιους D^{1} *Byz* **Acts 13:26** ***ημιν*** 𝔓^{74} ℵ A B D 33] υμιν 𝔓^{45} C E 1739 *Byz* **Acts 19:9** ***Τυραννου*** 𝔓^{74} ℵ A B 1739] *add.* τινος E *Byz* ¦ *add.* τινος απο ωρας ε εως δεκατης D

that would not see and ears that would
not hear, down to this very day." 9 And
David says, "Let their table become a
snare and a trap, a stumbling block and
a retribution for them; 10 let their eyes
be darkened so that they cannot see,
and keep their backs forever bent."

Rom 11:11–24

So I ask, have they stumbled so as to
fall? By no means! But through their
stumbling salvation has come to the
Gentiles, so as to make Israel jeal-
ous. 12 Now if their stumbling means
riches for the world, and if their defeat
means riches for Gentiles, how much
more will their full inclusion mean!
13 Now I am speaking to you Gentiles.
Inasmuch then as I am an apostle to
the Gentiles, I glorify my ministry 14 in
order to make my own people jealous,
and thus save some of them. 15 For
if their rejection is the reconciliation
of the world, what will their accep-
tance be but life from the dead! 16 If
the part of the dough offered as first
fruits is holy, then the whole batch is
holy; and if the root is holy, then the
branches also are holy. 17 But if some
of the branches were broken off, and
you, a wild olive shoot, were grafted
in their place to share the rich root[c] of
the olive tree, 18 do not boast over the
branches. If you do boast, remember
that it is not you that support the root,
but the root that supports you. 19 You
will say, "Branches were broken off so
that I might be grafted in." 20 That is
true. They were broken off because
of their unbelief, but you stand only
through faith. So do not become proud,
but stand in awe. 21 For if God did not
spare the natural branches, perhaps he
will not spare you.[d] 22 Note then the
kindness and the severity of God: sever-
ity toward those who have fallen, but
God's kindness toward you, provided
you continue in his kindness; otherwise
you also will be cut off. 23 And even
those of Israel, if they do not persist
in unbelief, will be grafted in, for God
has the power to graft them in again.
24 For if you have been cut from what is
by nature a wild olive tree and grafted,
contrary to nature, into a cultivated
olive tree, how much more will these
natural branches be grafted back into
their own olive tree.

Rom 11:25–32

So that you may not claim to be wiser
than you are, brothers and sisters, I
want you to understand this mystery: a
hardening has come upon part of Israel,
until the full number of the Gentiles
has come in. 26 And so all Israel will
be saved; as it is written, "Out of Zion
will come the Deliverer; he will ban-
ish ungodliness from Jacob." 27 "And
this is my covenant with them, when
I take away their sins." 28 As regards
the gospel they are enemies of God
for your sake; but as regards election
they are beloved, for the sake of their
ancestors; 29 for the gifts and the calling
of God are irrevocable. 30 Just as you
were once disobedient to God but have
now received mercy because of their
disobedience, 31 so they have now been
disobedient in order that, by the mercy
shown to you, they too may now[e] re-
ceive mercy. 32 For God has imprisoned
all in disobedience so that he may be
merciful to all.

1 Cor 1:23–24

but we proclaim Christ crucified, a
stumbling block to Jews and foolish-
ness to Gentiles, 24 but to those who
are the called, both Jews and Greeks,
Christ the power of God and the wis-
dom of God.

1 Thess 2:14–16

For you, brothers and sisters, became
imitators of the churches of God in
Christ Jesus that are in Judea, for you
suffered the same things from your own
compatriots as they did from the Jews,
15 who killed both the Lord Jesus and
the prophets,[f] and drove us out; they
displease God and oppose everyone
16 by hindering us from speaking to
the Gentiles so that they may be saved.
Thus they have constantly been filling
up the measure of their sins; but God's
wrath has overtaken them at last.

Acts 13:26–27

"My brothers, you descendants of
Abraham's family, and others who
fear God, to us[g] the message of this
salvation has been sent. 27 Because the
residents of Jerusalem and their leaders
did not recognize him or understand
the words of the prophets that are
read every sabbath, they fulfilled those
words by condemning him.

Acts 13:45–46

But when the Jews saw the crowds, they
were filled with jealousy; and blasphem-
ing, they contradicted what was spoken
by Paul. 46 Then both Paul and Barna-
bas spoke out boldly, saying, "It was
necessary that the word of God should
be spoken first to you. Since you reject
it and judge yourselves to be unworthy
of eternal life, we are now turning to
the Gentiles.

Acts 18:5–6

When Silas and Timothy arrived from
Macedonia, Paul was occupied with
proclaiming the word, testifying to the
Jews that the Messiah was Jesus. 6 When
they opposed and reviled him, in pro-
test he shook the dust from his clothes
and said to them, "Your blood be on
your own heads! I am innocent. From
now on I will go to the Gentiles."

Acts 19:9

When some stubbornly refused to be-
lieve and spoke evil of the Way before
the congregation, he left them, taking
the disciples with him, and argued daily
in the lecture hall of Tyrannus.[h]

Acts 22:17–21

"After I had returned to Jerusalem and
while I was praying in the temple, I fell
into a trance 18 and saw Jesus saying to
me, 'Hurry and get out of Jerusalem
quickly, because they will not accept
your testimony about me.' 19 And I said,
'Lord, they themselves know that in every
synagogue I imprisoned and beat those
who believed in you. 20 And while the

[c] **Rom 11:17** ***the rich root*** Other ancient authorities read *the richness* [d] **Rom 11:21** ***perhaps he will not spare you*** Other ancient authorities read *neither will he spare you* [e] **Rom 11:31** ***now*** Other ancient authorities lack *now* [f] **1 Thess 2:15** ***the prophets*** Other ancient authorities read *their own prophets* [g] **Acts 13:26** ***us*** Other ancient authorities read *you* [h] **Acts 19:9** ***of Tyrannus*** A few ancient authorities read *of a certain Tyrannus, from eleven o'clock in the morning to four in the afternoon*

τοῦ μάρτυρός σου, καὶ αὐτὸς ἤμην ἐφε-
στὼς καὶ συνευδοκῶν καὶ φυλάσσων τὰ
ἱμάτια τῶν ἀναιρούντων αὐτόν. 21 καὶ
εἶπεν πρός με· πορεύου, ὅτι ἐγὼ εἰς ἔθνη
μακρὰν ἐξαποστελῶ σε.

Acts 28:17–28

Ἐγένετο δὲ μετὰ ἡμέρας τρεῖς συγκαλέσα-
σθαι αὐτὸν τοὺς ὄντας τῶν Ἰουδαίων
πρώτους· συνελθόντων δὲ αὐτῶν ἔλεγεν
πρὸς αὐτούς· ἐγώ, ἄνδρες ἀδελφοί, οὐδὲν
ἐναντίον ποιήσας τῷ λαῷ ἢ τοῖς ἔθεσι
τοῖς πατρῴοις δέσμιος ἐξ Ἱεροσολύμων
παρεδόθην εἰς τὰς χεῖρας τῶν Ῥωμαίων,
18 οἵτινες ἀνακρίναντές με ἐβούλοντο
ἀπολῦσαι διὰ τὸ μηδεμίαν αἰτίαν θανάτου
ὑπάρχειν ἐν ἐμοί. 19 ἀντιλεγόντων δὲ
τῶν Ἰουδαίων ἠναγκάσθην ἐπικαλέ-
σασθαι Καίσαρα οὐχ ὡς τοῦ ἔθνους μου
ἔχων τι κατηγορεῖν. 20 διὰ ταύτην οὖν
τὴν αἰτίαν παρεκάλεσα ὑμᾶς ἰδεῖν καὶ
προσλαλῆσαι, ἕνεκεν γὰρ τῆς ἐλπίδος
τοῦ Ἰσραὴλ τὴν ἅλυσιν ταύτην περίκει-
μαι. 21 οἱ δὲ πρὸς αὐτὸν εἶπαν· ἡμεῖς οὔτε
γράμματα περὶ σοῦ ἐδεξάμεθα ἀπὸ τῆς
Ἰουδαίας οὔτε παραγενόμενός τις τῶν
ἀδελφῶν ἀπήγγειλεν ἢ ἐλάλησέν τι
περὶ σοῦ πονηρόν. 22 ἀξιοῦμεν δὲ παρὰ
σοῦ ἀκοῦσαι ἃ φρονεῖς, περὶ μὲν γὰρ τῆς
αἱρέσεως ταύτης γνωστὸν ἡμῖν ἐστιν
ὅτι πανταχοῦ ἀντιλέγεται. 23 Ταξάμενοι
δὲ αὐτῷ ἡμέραν ἦλθον πρὸς αὐτὸν εἰς
τὴν ξενίαν πλείονες οἷς ἐξετίθετο δια-
μαρτυρόμενος τὴν βασιλείαν τοῦ θεοῦ,
πείθων τε αὐτοὺς περὶ τοῦ Ἰησοῦ ἀπό τε
τοῦ νόμου Μωϋσέως καὶ τῶν προφητῶν,
ἀπὸ πρωῒ ἕως ἑσπέρας. 24 καὶ οἱ μὲν ἐπεί-
θοντο τοῖς λεγομένοις, οἱ δὲ ἠπίστουν·
25 ἀσύμφωνοι δὲ ὄντες πρὸς ἀλλήλους
ἀπελύοντο εἰπόντος τοῦ Παύλου ῥῆμα
ἕν, ὅτι καλῶς τὸ πνεῦμα τὸ ἅγιον ἐλά-
λησεν διὰ Ἠσαΐου τοῦ προφήτου πρὸς
τοὺς πατέρας ὑμῶν 26 λέγων· πορεύθητι
πρὸς τὸν λαὸν τοῦτον καὶ εἰπόν· ἀκοῇ
ἀκούσετε καὶ οὐ μὴ συνῆτε καὶ βλέποντες
βλέψετε καὶ οὐ μὴ ἴδητε· 27 ἐπαχύνθη γὰρ
ἡ καρδία τοῦ λαοῦ τούτου καὶ τοῖς ὠσὶν
βαρέως ἤκουσαν καὶ τοὺς ὀφθαλμοὺς
αὐτῶν ἐκάμμυσαν· μήποτε ἴδωσιν τοῖς
ὀφθαλμοῖς καὶ τοῖς ὠσὶν ἀκούσωσιν καὶ
τῇ καρδίᾳ συνῶσιν καὶ ἐπιστρέψωσιν,
καὶ ἰάσομαι αὐτούς. 28 γνωστὸν οὖν
ἔστω ὑμῖν ὅτι τοῖς ἔθνεσιν ἀπεστάλη
τοῦτο τὸ σωτήριον τοῦ θεοῦ· αὐτοὶ καὶ
⸀ἀκούσονται.

Cf. the accounts of persecution of Paul and his co-workers by Jewish leaders in Acts 17:5–7; 17:13–15; 18:12–17; and the extended narrative in the latter chapters of Acts of Paul's arrest in Jerusalem and resulting imprisonment.

64. The Mystery of Gentile Inclusion in Israel

Rom 11:25–32

Οὐ γὰρ θέλω ὑμᾶς ἀγνοεῖν, ἀδελφοί, τὸ
μυστήριον τοῦτο, ἵνα μὴ ἦτε [παρ'] ἑαυτοῖς
φρόνιμοι, ὅτι πώρωσις ἀπὸ μέρους τῷ
Ἰσραὴλ γέγονεν ἄχρι οὗ τὸ πλήρωμα τῶν
ἐθνῶν εἰσέλθῃ 26 καὶ οὕτως πᾶς Ἰσραὴλ
σωθήσεται, καθὼς γέγραπται· ἥξει ἐκ Σιὼν
ὁ ῥυόμενος, ἀποστρέψει ἀσεβείας ἀπὸ
Ἰακώβ. 27 καὶ αὕτη αὐτοῖς ἡ παρ' ἐμοῦ
διαθήκη, ὅταν ἀφέλωμαι τὰς ἁμαρτίας
αὐτῶν. 28 κατὰ μὲν τὸ εὐαγγέλιον ἐχθροὶ
δι' ὑμᾶς, κατὰ δὲ τὴν ἐκλογὴν ἀγαπητοὶ
διὰ τοὺς πατέρας· 29 ἀμεταμέλητα γὰρ
τὰ χαρίσματα καὶ ἡ κλῆσις τοῦ θεοῦ.
30 ὥσπερ γὰρ ὑμεῖς ποτε ἠπειθήσατε
τῷ θεῷ, νῦν δὲ ἠλεήθητε τῇ τούτων
ἀπειθείᾳ, 31 οὕτως καὶ οὗτοι νῦν ἠπεί-
θησαν τῷ ὑμετέρῳ ἐλέει, ἵνα καὶ αὐτοὶ
⸀[νῦν] ἐλεηθῶσιν. 32 συνέκλεισεν γὰρ
ὁ θεὸς τοὺς πάντας εἰς ἀπείθειαν, ἵνα
τοὺς πάντας ἐλεήσῃ.

Rom 16:25–27

⸂[Τῷ δὲ δυναμένῳ ὑμᾶς στηρίξαι κατὰ
τὸ εὐαγγέλιόν μου καὶ τὸ κήρυγμα Ἰη-
σοῦ Χριστοῦ, κατὰ ἀποκάλυψιν μυστη-
ρίου χρόνοις αἰωνίοις σεσιγημένου,
26 φανερωθέντος δὲ νῦν διά τε γραφῶν
προφητικῶν κατ' ἐπιταγὴν τοῦ αἰωνίου
θεοῦ εἰς ὑπακοὴν πίστεως εἰς πάντα τὰ
ἔθνη γνωρισθέντος, 27 μόνῳ σοφῷ θεῷ,
διὰ Ἰησοῦ Χριστοῦ, ⸀ᾧ ἡ δόξα εἰς τοὺς
⸀αἰῶνας, ἀμήν.]⸃

Eph 3:1–13

Τούτου χάριν ἐγὼ Παῦλος ὁ δέσμιος τοῦ
Χριστοῦ [Ἰησοῦ] ὑπὲρ ὑμῶν τῶν ἐθνῶν
2 —εἴ γε ἠκούσατε τὴν οἰκονομίαν τῆς
χάριτος τοῦ θεοῦ τῆς δοθείσης μοι εἰς
ὑμᾶς, 3 [ὅτι] κατὰ ἀποκάλυψιν ἐγνωρίσθη
μοι τὸ μυστήριον, καθὼς προέγραψα ἐν
ὀλίγῳ, 4 πρὸς ὃ δύνασθε ἀναγινώσκοντες
νοῆσαι τὴν σύνεσίν μου ἐν τῷ μυστηρίῳ
τοῦ Χριστοῦ, 5 ὃ ἑτέραις γενεαῖς οὐκ
ἐγνωρίσθη τοῖς υἱοῖς τῶν ἀνθρώπων
ὡς νῦν ἀπεκαλύφθη τοῖς ἁγίοις ἀποστό-
λοις αὐτοῦ καὶ προφήταις ἐν πνεύματι,
6 εἶναι τὰ ἔθνη συγκληρονόμα καὶ σύσ-
σωμα καὶ συμμέτοχα τῆς ἐπαγγελίας ἐν
Χριστῷ Ἰησοῦ διὰ τοῦ εὐαγγελίου, 7 οὗ
ἐγενήθην διάκονος κατὰ τὴν δωρεὰν
τῆς χάριτος τοῦ θεοῦ τῆς δοθείσης μοι
κατὰ τὴν ἐνέργειαν τῆς δυνάμεως αὐτοῦ.
8 Ἐμοὶ τῷ ἐλαχιστοτέρῳ πάντων ἁγίων
ἐδόθη ἡ χάρις αὕτη, τοῖς ἔθνεσιν εὐαγ-
γελίσασθαι τὸ ἀνεξιχνίαστον πλοῦτος
τοῦ Χριστοῦ 9 καὶ φωτίσαι ⸀[πάντας] τίς
ἡ οἰκονομία τοῦ μυστηρίου τοῦ ἀποκε-
κρυμμένου ἀπὸ τῶν αἰώνων ἐν τῷ θεῷ
τῷ τὰ πάντα κτίσαντι, 10 ἵνα γνωρισθῇ
νῦν ταῖς ἀρχαῖς καὶ ταῖς ἐξουσίαις ἐν
τοῖς ἐπουρανίοις διὰ τῆς ἐκκλησίας ἡ
πολυποίκιλος σοφία τοῦ θεοῦ, 11 κατὰ
πρόθεσιν τῶν αἰώνων ἣν ἐποίησεν ἐν τῷ
Χριστῷ Ἰησοῦ τῷ κυρίῳ ἡμῶν, 12 ἐν ᾧ
ἔχομεν τὴν παρρησίαν καὶ προσαγωγὴν

Acts 28:28 ***ακουσονται*** 𝔓[74vid] **א** A B E 048. 33. 1739] *add.* [v. 29] και ταυτα αυτου ειποντος απηλθον οι Ιουδαιοι πολλην εχοντες εν εαυτοις συζητησιν *Byz* **§ 64** **Rom 11:31** ***νυν*** **א** B D[*.c] *om.* 𝔓[46] A D[2] 1739. 1881 *Byz* ¦ υστερον 33 **Rom 16:25–27** *pon. hic* 𝔓[61] **א** B C D 1739] *pon. hic et p.* 14:23 A 33 ¦ *pon. p.* 14:23 *Byz* ¦ *pon. p.* 15:33 𝔓[46] ¦ *om. pc* **Rom 16:27** ***ω*** 𝔓[46] **א** A C D 33. 1739. 1881 *Byz*] *om.* B • ***αιωνας*** 𝔓[46] B C 33. 1739. 1881 *Byz*] *add.* των αιωνων 𝔓[61] **א** A D **Eph 3:9** ***παντας*** 𝔓[46] **א**[2] B C D 33 *Byz*] *om.* **א*** A 1739. 1881

blood of your witness Stephen was shed, I myself was standing by, approving and keeping the coats of those who killed him.' **21** Then he said to me, 'Go, for I will send you far away to the Gentiles.'"

Acts 28:17–28

Three days later he called together the local leaders of the Jews. When they had assembled, he said to them, "Brothers, though I had done nothing against our people or the customs of our ancestors, yet I was arrested in Jerusalem and handed over to the Romans. **18** When they had examined me, the Romans wanted to release me, because there was no reason for the death penalty in my case. **19** But when the Jews objected, I was compelled to appeal to the emperor—even though I had no charge to bring against my nation. **20** For this reason therefore I have asked to see you and speak with you, since it is for the sake of the hope of Israel that I am bound with this chain." **21** They replied, "We have received no letters from Judea about you, and none of the brothers coming here has reported or spoken anything evil about you. **22** But we would like to hear from you what you think, for with regard to this sect we know that everywhere it is spoken against." **23** After they had set a day to meet with him, they came to him at his lodgings in great numbers. From morning until evening he explained the matter to them, testifying to the kingdom of God and trying to convince them about Jesus both from the law of Moses and from the prophets. **24** Some were convinced by what he had said, while others refused to believe. **25** So they disagreed with each other; and as they were leaving, Paul made one further statement: "The Holy Spirit was right in saying to your ancestors through the prophet Isaiah, **26** 'Go to this people and say, You will indeed listen, but never understand, and you will indeed look, but never perceive. **27** For this people's heart has grown dull, and their ears are hard of hearing, and they have shut their eyes; so that they might not look with their eyes, and listen with their ears, and understand with their heart and turn— and I would heal them.' **28** Let it be known to you then that this salvation of God has been sent to the Gentiles; they will listen."[i]

Cf. the accounts of persecution of Paul and his co-workers by Jewish leaders in Acts 17:5–7; 17:13–15; 18:12–17; and the extended narrative in the latter chapters of Acts of Paul's arrest in Jerusalem and resulting imprisonment.

64. The Mystery of Gentile Inclusion in Israel

Rom 11:25–32

So that you may not claim to be wiser than you are, brothers and sisters, I want you to understand this mystery: a hardening has come upon part of Israel, until the full number of the Gentiles has come in. **26** And so all Israel will be saved; as it is written, "Out of Zion will come the Deliverer; he will banish ungodliness from Jacob." **27** "And this is my covenant with them, when I take away their sins." **28** As regards the gospel they are enemies of God for your sake; but as regards election they are beloved, for the sake of their ancestors; **29** for the gifts and the calling of God are irrevocable. **30** Just as you were once disobedient to God but have now received mercy because of their disobedience, **31** so they have now been disobedient in order that, by the mercy shown to you, they too may now[a] receive mercy. **32** For God has imprisoned all in disobedience so that he may be merciful to all.

Rom 16:25–27

Now to God who is able to strengthen you according to my gospel and the proclamation of Jesus Christ, according to the revelation of the mystery that was kept secret for long ages **26** but is now disclosed, and through the prophetic writings is made known to all the Gentiles, according to the command of the eternal God, to bring about the obedience of faith— **27** to the only wise God, through Jesus Christ, to whom[b] be the glory forever![c] Amen.[d]

Eph 3:1–13

This is the reason that I Paul am a prisoner for Christ Jesus for the sake of you Gentiles— **2** for surely you have already heard of the commission of God's grace that was given me for you, **3** and how the mystery was made known to me by revelation, as I wrote above in a few words, **4** a reading of which will enable you to perceive my understanding of the mystery of Christ. **5** In former generations this mystery was not made known to humankind, as it has now been revealed to his holy apostles and prophets by the Spirit: **6** that is, the Gentiles have become fellow heirs, members of the same body, and sharers in the promise in Christ Jesus through the gospel. **7** Of this gospel I have become a servant according to the gift of God's grace that was given me by the working of his power. **8** Although I am the very least of all the saints, this grace was given to me to bring to the Gentiles the news of the boundless riches of Christ, **9** and to make everyone see[e] what is the plan of the mystery hidden for ages in God who created all things; **10** so that through the church the wisdom of God in its rich variety might now be made known to the rulers and authorities in the heavenly places. **11** This was in accordance with the eternal purpose that he has carried out in Christ Jesus our Lord, **12** in whom we have access to God in boldness and confidence through

[i] **Acts 28:28** ***listen."*** Other ancient authorities add verse 29, *And when he had said these words, the Jews departed, arguing vigorously among themselves* **§ 64** [a] **Rom 11:31** ***now*** Other ancient authorities lack *now* [b] **Rom 16:27** ***to whom*** A few ancient authorities lack *to whom*. The verse then reads, *to the only wise God be the glory through Jesus Christ forever. Amen.* [c] **Rom 16:27** ***forever*** Other ancient authorities read *forever and ever* [d] **Rom 16:27** ***Amen*** Other ancient authorities include 16:25–27 after 14:23 or 15:33; a few lack these verses altogether [e] **Eph 3:9** ***to make everyone see*** Other ancient authorities read *to bring to light*

ἐν πεποιθήσει διὰ τῆς πίστεως αὐτοῦ.
13 διὸ αἰτοῦμαι μὴ ἐγκακεῖν ἐν ταῖς
θλίψεσίν μου ὑπὲρ ὑμῶν, ἥτις ἐστὶν
δόξα ὑμῶν.

Col 1:24–29

Νῦν χαίρω ἐν τοῖς παθήμασιν ὑπὲρ ὑμῶν
καὶ ἀνταναπληρῶ τὰ ὑστερήματα τῶν
θλίψεων τοῦ Χριστοῦ ἐν τῇ σαρκί μου ὑπὲρ
τοῦ σώματος αὐτοῦ, ὅ ἐστιν ἡ ἐκκλησία,
25 ἧς ἐγενόμην ἐγὼ διάκονος κατὰ τὴν
οἰκονομίαν τοῦ θεοῦ τὴν δοθεῖσάν μοι
εἰς ὑμᾶς πληρῶσαι τὸν λόγον τοῦ θεοῦ,
26 τὸ μυστήριον τὸ ἀποκεκρυμμένον ἀπὸ
τῶν αἰώνων καὶ ἀπὸ τῶν γενεῶν—νῦν
δὲ ἐφανερώθη τοῖς ἁγίοις αὐτοῦ, 27 οἷς
ἠθέλησεν ὁ θεὸς γνωρίσαι τί τὸ πλοῦ-
τος τῆς δόξης τοῦ μυστηρίου τούτου ἐν
τοῖς ἔθνεσιν, ὅ ἐστιν Χριστὸς ἐν ὑμῖν, ἡ
ἐλπὶς τῆς δόξης· 28 ὃν ἡμεῖς καταγγέλ-
λομεν νουθετοῦντες πάντα ἄνθρωπον
καὶ διδάσκοντες πάντα ἄνθρωπον ἐν
πάσῃ σοφίᾳ, ἵνα παραστήσωμεν πάν-
τα ἄνθρωπον τέλειον ἐν Χριστῷ· 29 εἰς
ὃ καὶ κοπιῶ ἀγωνιζόμενος κατὰ τὴν
ἐνέργειαν αὐτοῦ τὴν ἐνεργουμένην ἐν
ἐμοὶ ἐν δυνάμει.

1 Tim 3:16

καὶ ὁμολογουμένως μέγα ἐστὶν τὸ τῆς
εὐσεβείας μυστήριον· ⸀ὃς ἐφανερώθη
ἐν σαρκί, ἐδικαιώθη ἐν πνεύματι, ὤφθη
ἀγγέλοις, ἐκηρύχθη ἐν ἔθνεσιν, ἐπιστεύθη
ἐν κόσμῳ, ἀνελήμφθη ἐν δόξῃ.

See also § 55 The Inclusion of the Gentiles; § 36 The Mystery of God, Christ.

65. *Christ the Goal of the Law*

Rom 7:1–6

Ἢ ἀγνοεῖτε, ἀδελφοί, γινώσκουσιν γὰρ
νόμον λαλῶ, ὅτι ὁ νόμος κυριεύει τοῦ
ἀνθρώπου ἐφ᾽ ὅσον χρόνον ζῇ; 2 ἡ γὰρ
ὕπανδρος γυνὴ τῷ ζῶντι ἀνδρὶ δέδεται
νόμῳ· ἐὰν δὲ ἀποθάνῃ ὁ ἀνήρ, κατήργη-
ται ἀπὸ τοῦ νόμου τοῦ ἀνδρός. 3 ἄρα οὖν
ζῶντος τοῦ ἀνδρὸς μοιχαλὶς χρηματίσει
ἐὰν γένηται ἀνδρὶ ἑτέρῳ· ἐὰν δὲ ἀποθάνῃ
ὁ ἀνήρ, ἐλευθέρα ἐστὶν ἀπὸ τοῦ νόμου,
τοῦ μὴ εἶναι αὐτὴν μοιχαλίδα γενομένην
ἀνδρὶ ἑτέρῳ. 4 ὥστε, ἀδελφοί μου, καὶ
ὑμεῖς ἐθανατώθητε τῷ νόμῳ διὰ τοῦ
σώματος τοῦ Χριστοῦ, εἰς τὸ γενέσθαι
ὑμᾶς ἑτέρῳ, τῷ ἐκ νεκρῶν ἐγερθέντι, ἵνα
καρποφορήσωμεν τῷ θεῷ. 5 ὅτε γὰρ ἦμεν
ἐν τῇ σαρκί, τὰ παθήματα τῶν ἁμαρτιῶν
τὰ διὰ τοῦ νόμου ἐνηργεῖτο ἐν τοῖς μέλεσιν
ἡμῶν, εἰς τὸ καρποφορῆσαι τῷ θανάτῳ·
6 νυνὶ δὲ κατηργήθημεν ἀπὸ τοῦ νόμου
ἀποθανόντες ἐν ᾧ κατειχόμεθα, ὥστε
δουλεύειν ἡμᾶς ἐν καινότητι πνεύματος
καὶ οὐ παλαιότητι γράμματος.

Rom 10:1–13

Ἀδελφοί, ἡ μὲν εὐδοκία τῆς ἐμῆς καρδίας
καὶ ἡ δέησις πρὸς τὸν θεὸν ὑπὲρ αὐτῶν
εἰς σωτηρίαν. 2 μαρτυρῶ γὰρ αὐτοῖς
ὅτι ζῆλον θεοῦ ἔχουσιν ἀλλ᾽ οὐ κατ᾽
ἐπίγνωσιν· 3 ἀγνοοῦντες γὰρ τὴν τοῦ
θεοῦ δικαιοσύνην καὶ τὴν ἰδίαν [δικαιο-
σύνην] ζητοῦντες στῆσαι, τῇ δικαιοσύνῃ
τοῦ θεοῦ οὐχ ὑπετάγησαν. 4 τέλος γὰρ
νόμου Χριστὸς εἰς δικαιοσύνην παντὶ
τῷ πιστεύοντι. 5 Μωϋσῆς γὰρ γράφει
τὴν δικαιοσύνην τὴν ἐκ [τοῦ] νόμου
ὅτι ὁ ποιήσας αὐτὰ ἄνθρωπος ζήσεται
ἐν ⸀αὐτοῖς. 6 ἡ δὲ ἐκ πίστεως δικαιοσύνη
οὕτως λέγει· μὴ εἴπῃς ἐν τῇ καρδίᾳ σου·
τίς ἀναβήσεται εἰς τὸν οὐρανόν; τοῦτ᾽
ἔστιν Χριστὸν καταγαγεῖν· 7 ἤ· τίς κα-
ταβήσεται εἰς τὴν ἄβυσσον; τοῦτ᾽ ἔστιν
Χριστὸν ἐκ νεκρῶν ἀναγαγεῖν. 8 ἀλλὰ
τί λέγει; ἐγγύς σου τὸ ῥῆμά ἐστιν ἐν
τῷ στόματί σου καὶ ἐν τῇ καρδίᾳ σου,
τοῦτ᾽ ἔστιν τὸ ῥῆμα τῆς πίστεως ὃ κη-
ρύσσομεν. 9 ὅτι ἐὰν ὁμολογήσῃς ἐν τῷ
στόματί σου κύριον Ἰησοῦν καὶ πιστεύ-
σῃς ἐν τῇ καρδίᾳ σου ὅτι ὁ θεὸς αὐτὸν
ἤγειρεν ἐκ νεκρῶν, σωθήσῃ· 10 καρδίᾳ
γὰρ πιστεύεται εἰς δικαιοσύνην, στόματι
δὲ ὁμολογεῖται εἰς σωτηρίαν. 11 λέγει
γὰρ ἡ γραφή· πᾶς ὁ πιστεύων ἐπ᾽ αὐτῷ
οὐ καταισχυνθήσεται. 12 οὐ γάρ ἐστιν
διαστολὴ Ἰουδαίου τε καὶ Ἕλληνος,
ὁ γὰρ αὐτὸς κύριος πάντων, πλουτῶν
εἰς πάντας τοὺς ἐπικαλουμένους αὐτόν·
13 πᾶς γὰρ ὃς ἂν ἐπικαλέσηται τὸ ὄνομα
κυρίου σωθήσεται.

2 Cor 3:12–18

Ἔχοντες οὖν τοιαύτην ἐλπίδα πολλῇ
παρρησίᾳ χρώμεθα 13 καὶ οὐ καθάπερ
Μωϋσῆς ἐτίθει κάλυμμα ἐπὶ τὸ πρόσωπον
αὐτοῦ πρὸς τὸ μὴ ἀτενίσαι τοὺς υἱοὺς
Ἰσραὴλ εἰς τὸ τέλος τοῦ καταργουμένου.
14 ἀλλὰ ἐπωρώθη τὰ νοήματα αὐτῶν.
ἄχρι γὰρ τῆς σήμερον ἡμέρας τὸ αὐτὸ
κάλυμμα ἐπὶ τῇ ἀναγνώσει τῆς παλαιᾶς
διαθήκης μένει, μὴ ἀνακαλυπτόμενον
ὅτι ἐν Χριστῷ καταργεῖται· 15 ἀλλ᾽ ἕως
σήμερον ἡνίκα ἂν ἀναγινώσκηται Μω-
ϋσῆς, κάλυμμα ἐπὶ τὴν καρδίαν αὐτῶν
κεῖται· 16 ἡνίκα δὲ ἐὰν ἐπιστρέψῃ πρὸς
κύριον, περιαιρεῖται τὸ κάλυμμα. 17 ὁ δὲ
κύριος τὸ πνεῦμά ἐστιν· οὗ δὲ τὸ πνεῦμα
κυρίου, ἐλευθερία. 18 ἡμεῖς δὲ πάντες
ἀνακεκαλυμμένῳ προσώπῳ τὴν δόξαν
κυρίου κατοπτριζόμενοι τὴν αὐτὴν εἰκόνα
μεταμορφούμεθα ἀπὸ δόξης εἰς δόξαν
καθάπερ ἀπὸ κυρίου πνεύματος.

Gal 3:15–18

Ἀδελφοί, κατὰ ἄνθρωπον λέγω· ὅμως
ἀνθρώπου κεκυρωμένην διαθήκην οὐδεὶς
ἀθετεῖ ἢ ἐπιδιατάσσεται. 16 τῷ δὲ Ἀβραὰμ
ἐρρέθησαν αἱ ἐπαγγελίαι καὶ τῷ σπέρ-
ματι αὐτοῦ. οὐ λέγει· καὶ τοῖς σπέρμασιν,
ὡς ἐπὶ πολλῶν ἀλλ᾽ ὡς ἐφ᾽ ἑνός· καὶ τῷ
σπέρματί σου, ὅς ἐστιν Χριστός. 17 τοῦτο
δὲ λέγω· διαθήκην προκεκυρωμένην
ὑπὸ τοῦ θεοῦ ὁ μετὰ τετρακόσια καὶ τρι-
άκοντα ἔτη γεγονὼς νόμος οὐκ ἀκυροῖ
εἰς τὸ καταργῆσαι τὴν ἐπαγγελίαν. 18 εἰ
γὰρ ἐκ νόμου ἡ κληρονομία, οὐκέτι ἐξ
ἐπαγγελίας· τῷ δὲ Ἀβραὰμ δι᾽ ἐπαγγελίας
κεχάρισται ὁ θεός.

Gal 3:21–29

ὁ οὖν νόμος κατὰ τῶν ἐπαγγελιῶν [τοῦ
θεοῦ]; μὴ γένοιτο. εἰ γὰρ ἐδόθη νόμος ὁ
δυνάμενος ζῳοποιῆσαι, ὄντως ἐκ νόμου

1 Tim 3:16 *ος* א* A* C* 33] ὃ D* ¦ θεος א^{c} A^{c} C^{2} D^{2} 1739. 1881 *Byz*

§ 65 Rom 10:5 ***αυτοις*** 𝔓^{46} א^{2} D *Byz*] αυτη א* A B 33. 1739. 1881

faith in him. **13** I pray therefore that you may not lose heart over my sufferings for you; they are your glory.

Col 1:24–29

I am now rejoicing in my sufferings for your sake, and in my flesh I am completing what is lacking in Christ's afflictions for the sake of his body, that is, the church. **25** I became its servant according to God's commission that was given to me for you, to make the word of God fully known, **26** the mystery that has been hidden throughout the ages and generations but has now been revealed to his saints. **27** To them God chose to make known how great among the Gentiles are the riches of the glory of this mystery, which is Christ in you, the hope of glory. **28** It is he whom we proclaim, warning everyone and teaching everyone in all wisdom, so that we may present everyone mature in Christ. **29** For this I toil and struggle with all the energy that he powerfully inspires within me.

1 Tim 3:16

Without any doubt, the mystery of our religion is great: Who[f] was revealed in flesh, vindicated by the Spirit,[g] seen by angels, proclaimed among Gentiles, believed in throughout the world, taken up in glory.

See also § 55 The Inclusion of the Gentiles; § 36 The Mystery of God, Christ.

65. *Christ the Goal of the Law*

Rom 7:1–6

Do you not know, brothers and sisters—for I am speaking to those who know the law—that the law is binding on a person only during that person's lifetime? **2** Thus a married woman is bound by the law to her husband as long as he lives; but if her husband dies, she is discharged from the law concerning the husband. **3** Accordingly, she will be called an adulteress if she lives with another man while her husband is alive. But if her husband dies, she is free from that law, and if she marries another man, she is not an adulteress. **4** In the same way, my friends, you have died to the law through the body of Christ, so that you may belong to another, to him who has been raised from the dead in order that we may bear fruit for God. **5** While we were living in the flesh, our sinful passions, aroused by the law, were at work in our members to bear fruit for death. **6** But now we are discharged from the law, dead to that which held us captive, so that we are slaves not under the old written code but in the new life of the Spirit.

Rom 10:1–13

Brothers and sisters, my heart's desire and prayer to God for them is that they may be saved. **2** I can testify that they have a zeal for God, but it is not enlightened. **3** For, being ignorant of the righteousness that comes from God, and seeking to establish their own, they have not submitted to God's righteousness. **4** For Christ is the goal[a] of the law so that there may be righteousness for everyone who believes. **5** Moses writes concerning the righteousness that comes from the law, that "the person who does these things will live by them."[b] **6** But the righteousness that comes from faith says, "Do not say in your heart, 'Who will ascend into heaven?'" (that is, to bring Christ down) **7** "or 'Who will descend into the abyss?'" (that is, to bring Christ up from the dead). **8** But what does it say? "The word is near you, on your lips and in your heart" (that is, the word of faith that we proclaim); **9** because if you confess with your lips that Jesus is Lord and believe in your heart that God raised him from the dead, you will be saved. **10** For one believes with the heart and so is justified, and one confesses with the mouth and so is saved. **11** The scripture says, "No one who believes in him will be put to shame." **12** For there is no distinction between Jew and Greek; the same Lord is Lord of all and is generous to all who call on him. **13** For, "Everyone who calls on the name of the Lord shall be saved."

2 Cor 3:12–18

Since, then, we have such a hope, we act with great boldness, **13** not like Moses, who put a veil over his face to keep the people of Israel from gazing at the end of the glory that was being set aside. **14** But their minds were hardened. Indeed, to this very day, when they hear the reading of the old covenant, that same veil is still there, since only in Christ is it set aside. **15** Indeed, to this very day whenever Moses is read, a veil lies over their minds; **16** but when one turns to the Lord, the veil is removed. **17** Now the Lord is the Spirit, and where the Spirit of the Lord is, there is freedom. **18** And all of us, with unveiled faces, seeing the glory of the Lord as though reflected in a mirror, are being transformed into the same image from one degree of glory to another; for this comes from the Lord, the Spirit.

Gal 3:15–18

Brothers and sisters, I give an example from daily life: once a person's will has been ratified, no one adds to it or annuls it. **16** Now the promises were made to Abraham and to his offspring; it does not say, "And to offsprings," as of many; but it says, "And to your offspring," that is, to one person, who is Christ. **17** My point is this: the law, which came four hundred thirty years later, does not annul a covenant previously ratified by God, so as to nullify the promise. **18** For if the inheritance comes from the law, it no longer comes from the promise; but God granted it to Abraham through the promise.

Gal 3:21–29

Is the law then opposed to the promises of God? Certainly not! For if a law had been given that could make alive, then righteousness would indeed come

[f] **1 Tim 3:16** *Who* Other ancient authorities read *God*; others, *Which*. NRSV translates Gk *Who* as *He* [g] **1 Tim 3:16** *by the Spirit* NRSV alternate translation **§ 65** [a] **Rom 10:4** *goal* Or *end* (so NRSV) [b] **Rom 10:5** *them* Other ancient authorities read *it*, i.e., the righteousness that comes from the law

ἂν ἦν ἡ δικαιοσύνη· 22 ἀλλὰ συνέκλεισεν ἡ γραφὴ τὰ πάντα ὑπὸ ἁμαρτίαν, ἵνα ἡ ἐπαγγελία ἐκ πίστεως Ἰησοῦ Χριστοῦ δοθῇ τοῖς πιστεύουσιν. 23 Πρὸ τοῦ δὲ ἐλθεῖν τὴν πίστιν ὑπὸ νόμον ἐφρουρούμεθα συγκλειόμενοι εἰς τὴν μέλλουσαν πίστιν ἀποκαλυφθῆναι, 24 ὥστε ὁ νόμος παιδαγωγὸς ἡμῶν γέγονεν εἰς Χριστόν, ἵνα ἐκ πίστεως δικαιωθῶμεν· 25 ἐλθούσης δὲ τῆς πίστεως οὐκέτι ὑπὸ παιδαγωγόν ἐσμεν. 26 Πάντες γὰρ υἱοὶ θεοῦ ἐστε διὰ τῆς πίστεως ἐν Χριστῷ Ἰησοῦ· 27 ὅσοι γὰρ εἰς Χριστὸν ἐβαπτίσθητε, Χριστὸν ἐνεδύσασθε. 28 οὐκ ἔνι Ἰουδαῖος οὐδὲ Ἕλλην, οὐκ ἔνι δοῦλος οὐδὲ ἐλεύθερος, οὐκ ἔνι ἄρσεν καὶ θῆλυ· πάντες γὰρ ὑμεῖς εἷς ἐστε ἐν Χριστῷ Ἰησοῦ. 29 εἰ δὲ ὑμεῖς Χριστοῦ, ἄρα τοῦ Ἀβραὰμ σπέρμα ἐστέ, κατ᾽ ἐπαγγελίαν κληρονόμοι.

Acts 13:38–39

γνωστὸν οὖν ἔστω ὑμῖν, ἄνδρες ἀδελφοί, ὅτι διὰ τούτου ὑμῖν ἄφεσις ἁμαρτιῶν καταγγέλλεται, [καὶ] ἀπὸ πάντων ὧν οὐκ ἠδυνήθητε ἐν νόμῳ Μωϋσέως δικαιωθῆναι, 39 ἐν τούτῳ πᾶς ὁ πιστεύων δικαιοῦται.

Cf. Rom 15:8–12; Gal 2:19–20; Eph 2:11–22.

See also § 28 The Revelation of God's Righteousness.

66. The Function of the Law

Rom 3:19–20

οἴδαμεν δὲ ὅτι ὅσα ὁ νόμος λέγει τοῖς ἐν τῷ νόμῳ λαλεῖ, ἵνα πᾶν στόμα φραγῇ καὶ ὑπόδικος γένηται πᾶς ὁ κόσμος τῷ θεῷ· 20 διότι ἐξ ἔργων νόμου οὐ δικαιωθήσεται πᾶσα σὰρξ ἐνώπιον αὐτοῦ, διὰ γὰρ νόμου ἐπίγνωσις ἁμαρτίας.

Rom 4:15

ὁ γὰρ νόμος ὀργὴν κατεργάζεται· οὗ δὲ οὐκ ἔστιν νόμος οὐδὲ παράβασις.

Rom 5:20

νόμος δὲ παρεισῆλθεν, ἵνα πλεονάσῃ τὸ παράπτωμα· οὗ δὲ ἐπλεόνασεν ἡ ἁμαρτία, ὑπερεπερίσσευσεν ἡ χάρις,

Rom 7:5

ὅτε γὰρ ἦμεν ἐν τῇ σαρκί, τὰ παθήματα τῶν ἁμαρτιῶν τὰ διὰ τοῦ νόμου ἐνηργεῖτο ἐν τοῖς μέλεσιν ἡμῶν, εἰς τὸ καρποφορῆσαι τῷ θανάτῳ

Rom 7:7–25

Τί οὖν ἐροῦμεν; ὁ νόμος ἁμαρτία; μὴ γένοιτο· ἀλλὰ τὴν ἁμαρτίαν οὐκ ἔγνων εἰ μὴ διὰ νόμου· τήν τε γὰρ ἐπιθυμίαν οὐκ ᾔδειν εἰ μὴ ὁ νόμος ἔλεγεν· οὐκ ἐπιθυμήσεις. 8 ἀφορμὴν δὲ λαβοῦσα ἡ ἁμαρτία διὰ τῆς ἐντολῆς κατειργάσατο ἐν ἐμοὶ πᾶσαν ἐπιθυμίαν· χωρὶς γὰρ νόμου ἁμαρτία νεκρά. 9 ἐγὼ δὲ ἔζων χωρὶς νόμου ποτέ, ἐλθούσης δὲ τῆς ἐντολῆς ἡ ἁμαρτία ἀνέζησεν, 10 ἐγὼ δὲ ἀπέθανον καὶ εὑρέθη μοι ἡ ἐντολὴ ἡ εἰς ζωήν, αὕτη εἰς θάνατον· 11 ἡ γὰρ ἁμαρτία ἀφορμὴν λαβοῦσα διὰ τῆς ἐντολῆς ἐξηπάτησέν με καὶ δι᾽ αὐτῆς ἀπέκτεινεν. 12 ὥστε ὁ μὲν νόμος ἅγιος καὶ ἡ ἐντολὴ ἁγία καὶ δικαία καὶ ἀγαθή. 13 Τὸ οὖν ἀγαθὸν ἐμοὶ ἐγένετο θάνατος; μὴ γένοιτο· ἀλλὰ ἡ ἁμαρτία, ἵνα φανῇ ἁμαρτία, διὰ τοῦ ἀγαθοῦ μοι κατεργαζομένη θάνατον, ἵνα γένηται καθ᾽ ὑπερβολὴν ἁμαρτωλὸς ἡ ἁμαρτία διὰ τῆς ἐντολῆς. 14 Οἴδαμεν γὰρ ὅτι ὁ νόμος πνευματικός ἐστιν, ἐγὼ δὲ σάρκινός εἰμι πεπραμένος ὑπὸ τὴν ἁμαρτίαν. 15 ὃ γὰρ κατεργάζομαι οὐ γινώσκω· οὐ γὰρ ὃ θέλω τοῦτο πράσσω, ἀλλ᾽ ὃ μισῶ τοῦτο ποιῶ. 16 εἰ δὲ ὃ οὐ θέλω τοῦτο ποιῶ, σύμφημι τῷ νόμῳ ὅτι καλός. 17 νυνὶ δὲ οὐκέτι ἐγὼ κατεργάζομαι αὐτὸ ἀλλὰ ἡ οἰκοῦσα ἐν ἐμοὶ ἁμαρτία. 18 Οἶδα γὰρ ὅτι οὐκ οἰκεῖ ἐν ἐμοί, τοῦτ᾽ ἔστιν ἐν τῇ σαρκί μου, ἀγαθόν· τὸ γὰρ θέλειν παράκειταί μοι, τὸ δὲ κατεργάζεσθαι τὸ καλὸν οὔ· 19 οὐ γὰρ ὃ θέλω ποιῶ ἀγαθόν, ἀλλὰ ὃ οὐ θέλω κακὸν τοῦτο πράσσω. 20 εἰ δὲ ὃ οὐ θέλω [ἐγὼ] τοῦτο ποιῶ, οὐκέτι ἐγὼ κατεργάζομαι αὐτὸ ἀλλὰ ἡ οἰκοῦσα ἐν ἐμοὶ ἁμαρτία. 21 εὑρίσκω ἄρα τὸν νόμον, τῷ θέλοντι ἐμοὶ ποιεῖν τὸ καλόν, ὅτι ἐμοὶ τὸ κακὸν παράκειται· 22 συνήδομαι γὰρ τῷ νόμῳ τοῦ θεοῦ κατὰ τὸν ἔσω ἄνθρωπον, 23 βλέπω δὲ ἕτερον νόμον ἐν τοῖς μέλεσίν μου ἀντιστρατευόμενον τῷ νόμῳ τοῦ νοός μου καὶ αἰχμαλωτίζοντά με ἐν τῷ νόμῳ τῆς ἁμαρτίας τῷ ὄντι ἐν τοῖς μέλεσίν μου. 24 Ταλαίπωρος ἐγὼ ἄνθρωπος· τίς με ῥύσεται ἐκ τοῦ σώματος τοῦ θανάτου τούτου; 25 χάρις δὲ τῷ θεῷ διὰ Ἰησοῦ Χριστοῦ τοῦ κυρίου ἡμῶν. Ἄρα οὖν αὐτὸς ἐγὼ τῷ μὲν νοῒ δουλεύω νόμῳ θεοῦ τῇ δὲ σαρκὶ νόμῳ ἁμαρτίας.

1 Cor 15:56–57

τὸ δὲ κέντρον τοῦ θανάτου ἡ ἁμαρτία, ἡ δὲ δύναμις τῆς ἁμαρτίας ὁ νόμος· 57 τῷ δὲ θεῷ χάρις τῷ διδόντι ἡμῖν τὸ νῖκος διὰ τοῦ κυρίου ἡμῶν Ἰησοῦ Χριστοῦ.

2 Cor 3:7–9

Εἰ δὲ ἡ διακονία τοῦ θανάτου ἐν γράμμασιν ἐντετυπωμένη λίθοις ἐγενήθη ἐν δόξῃ, ὥστε μὴ δύνασθαι ἀτενίσαι τοὺς υἱοὺς Ἰσραὴλ εἰς τὸ πρόσωπον Μωϋσέως διὰ τὴν δόξαν τοῦ προσώπου αὐτοῦ τὴν καταργουμένην, 8 πῶς οὐχὶ μᾶλλον ἡ διακονία τοῦ πνεύματος ἔσται ἐν δόξῃ; 9 εἰ γὰρ τῇ διακονίᾳ τῆς κατακρίσεως δόξα, πολλῷ μᾶλλον περισσεύει ἡ διακονία τῆς δικαιοσύνης δόξῃ.

Gal 2:17–19

εἰ δὲ ζητοῦντες δικαιωθῆναι ἐν Χριστῷ εὑρέθημεν καὶ αὐτοὶ ἁμαρτωλοί, ἆρα Χριστὸς ἁμαρτίας διάκονος; μὴ γένοιτο. 18 εἰ γὰρ ἃ κατέλυσα ταῦτα πάλιν οἰκοδομῶ, παραβάτην ἐμαυτὸν συνιστάνω. 19 ἐγὼ γὰρ διὰ νόμου νόμῳ ἀπέθανον, ἵνα θεῷ ζήσω. Χριστῷ συνεσταύρωμαι

Gal 3:19–25

Τί οὖν ὁ νόμος; τῶν παραβάσεων χάριν προσετέθη, ἄχρις οὗ ἔλθῃ τὸ σπέρμα ᾧ ἐπήγγελται, διαταγεὶς δι᾽ ἀγγέλων ἐν χειρὶ μεσίτου. 20 ὁ δὲ μεσίτης ἑνὸς οὐκ ἔστιν, ὁ δὲ θεὸς εἷς ἐστιν. 21 ὁ οὖν νόμος κατὰ τῶν ἐπαγγελιῶν [τοῦ θεοῦ]; μὴ γένοιτο. εἰ γὰρ ἐδόθη νόμος ὁ δυνάμενος ζῳοποιῆσαι, ὄντως ἐκ νόμου ἂν ἦν ἡ δικαιοσύνη· 22 ἀλλὰ συνέκλεισεν ἡ γραφὴ τὰ πάντα ὑπὸ ἁμαρτίαν, ἵνα ἡ ἐπαγγελία ἐκ πίστεως Ἰησοῦ Χριστοῦ δοθῇ τοῖς πιστεύουσιν. 23 Πρὸ τοῦ δὲ

through the law. **22** But the scripture has
imprisoned all things under the power of
sin, so that what was promised through
faith in Jesus Christ might be given to
those who believe. **23** Now before faith
came, we were imprisoned and guarded
under the law until faith would be re-
vealed. **24** Therefore the law was our dis-
ciplinarian until Christ came, so that
we might be justified by faith. **25** But
now that faith has come, we are no
longer subject to a disciplinarian, **26** for
in Christ Jesus you are all children of
God through faith. **27** As many of you as
were baptized into Christ have clothed
yourselves with Christ. **28** There is no
longer Jew or Greek, there is no longer
slave or free, there is no longer male and
female; for all of you are one in Christ
Jesus. **29** And if you belong to Christ,
then you are Abraham's offspring, heirs
according to the promise.

Acts 13:38–39

Let it be known to you therefore, my
brothers, that through this man for-
giveness of sins is proclaimed to you;
39 by this Jesus everyone who believes is
set free from all those sins from which
you could not be freed by the law of
Moses.

Cf. Rom 15:8–12; Gal 2:19–20; Eph 2:11–22.

See also § 28 The Revelation of God's Righteousness.

66. The Function of the Law

Rom 3:19–20

Now we know that whatever the law
says, it speaks to those who are under
the law, so that every mouth may be
silenced, and the whole world may be
held accountable to God. **20** For "no
human being will be justified in his
sight" by deeds prescribed by the law,
for through the law comes the knowl-
edge of sin.

Rom 4:15

For the law brings wrath; but where there is no law, neither is there violation.

Rom 5:20

But law came in, with the result that the trespass multiplied; but where sin increased, grace abounded all the more

Rom 7:5

While we were living in the flesh, our sinful passions, aroused by the law, were at work in our members to bear fruit for death.

Rom 7:7–25

What then should we say? That the
law is sin? By no means! Yet, if it had
not been for the law, I would not have
known sin. I would not have known
what it is to covet if the law had not
said, "You shall not covet." **8** But sin,
seizing an opportunity in the com-
mandment, produced in me all kinds
of covetousness. Apart from the law sin
lies dead. **9** I was once alive apart from
the law, but when the commandment
came, sin revived **10** and I died, and the
very commandment that promised life
proved to be death to me. **11** For sin,
seizing an opportunity in the com-
mandment, deceived me and through
it killed me. **12** So the law is holy, and
the commandment is holy and just
and good. **13** Did what is good, then,
bring death to me? By no means! It
was sin, working death in me through
what is good, in order that sin might
be shown to be sin, and through the
commandment might become sinful
beyond measure. **14** For we know that
the law is spiritual; but I am of the flesh,
sold into slavery under sin. **15** I do not
understand my own actions. For I do
not do what I want, but I do the very
thing I hate. **16** Now if I do what I do
not want, I agree that the law is good.
17 But in fact it is no longer I that do it,
but sin that dwells within me. **18** For I
know that nothing good dwells within
me, that is, in my flesh. I can will what
is right, but I cannot do it. **19** For I do
not do the good I want, but the evil I
do not want is what I do. **20** Now if I
do what I do not want, it is no longer
I that do it, but sin that dwells within
me. **21** So I find it to be a law that when
I want to do what is good, evil lies close
at hand. **22** For I delight in the law of
God in my inmost self, **23** but I see in
my members another law at war with
the law of my mind, making me cap-
tive to the law of sin that dwells in my
members. **24** Wretched man that I am!
Who will rescue me from this body of
death? **25** Thanks be to God through
Jesus Christ our Lord! So then, with my
mind I am a slave to the law of God,
but with my flesh I am a slave to the
law of sin.

1 Cor 15:56–57

The sting of death is sin, and the power
of sin is the law. **57** But thanks be to
God, who gives us the victory through
our Lord Jesus Christ.

2 Cor 3:7–9

Now if the ministry of death, chiseled
in letters on stone tablets, came in glory
so that the people of Israel could not
gaze at Moses' face because of the
glory of his face, a glory now set aside,
8 how much more will the ministry of
the Spirit come in glory? **9** For if there
was glory in the ministry of condemna-
tion, much more does the ministry of
justification abound in glory!

Gal 2:17–19

But if, in our effort to be justified in
Christ, we ourselves have been found
to be sinners, is Christ then a servant
of sin? Certainly not! **18** But if I build
up again the very things that I once tore
down, then I demonstrate that I am a
transgressor. **19** For through the law I
died to the law, so that I might live to
God. I have been crucified with Christ

Gal 3:19–25

Why then the law? It was added because
of transgressions, until the offspring
would come to whom the promise had
been made; and it was ordained through
angels by a mediator. **20** Now a media-
tor involves more than one party; but
God is one. **21** Is the law then opposed
to the promises of God? Certainly
not! For if a law had been given that
could make alive, then righteousness
would indeed come through the law.
22 But the scripture has imprisoned all
things under the power of sin, so that
what was promised through faith in
Jesus Christ might be given to those
who believe. **23** Now before faith came,

ἐλθεῖν τὴν πίστιν ὑπὸ νόμον ἐφρουρούμεθα συγκλειόμενοι εἰς τὴν μέλλουσαν πίστιν ἀποκαλυφθῆναι, 24 ὥστε ὁ νόμος παιδαγωγὸς ἡμῶν γέγονεν εἰς Χριστόν, ἵνα ἐκ πίστεως δικαιωθῶμεν· 25 ἐλθούσης δὲ τῆς πίστεως οὐκέτι ὑπὸ παιδαγωγόν ἐσμεν.

1 Tim 1:8–11

Οἴδαμεν δὲ ὅτι καλὸς ὁ νόμος, ἐάν τις αὐτῷ νομίμως χρῆται, 9 εἰδὼς τοῦτο, ὅτι δικαίῳ νόμος οὐ κεῖται, ἀνόμοις δὲ καὶ ἀνυποτάκτοις, ἀσεβέσι καὶ ἁμαρτωλοῖς, ἀνοσίοις καὶ βεβήλοις, πατρολῴαις καὶ μητρολῴαις, ἀνδροφόνοις 10 πόρνοις ἀρσενοκοίταις ἀνδραποδισταῖς ψεύσταις ἐπιόρκοις, καὶ εἴ τι ἕτερον τῇ ὑγιαινούσῃ διδασκαλίᾳ ἀντίκειται 11 κατὰ τὸ εὐαγγέλιον τῆς δόξης τοῦ μακαρίου θεοῦ, ὃ ἐπιστεύθην ἐγώ.

67. *The Fulfillment of the Law through Faith and Love*

Rom 2:26–29

ἐὰν οὖν ἡ ἀκροβυστία τὰ δικαιώματα τοῦ νόμου φυλάσσῃ, οὐχ ἡ ἀκροβυστία αὐτοῦ εἰς περιτομὴν λογισθήσεται; 27 καὶ κρινεῖ ἡ ἐκ φύσεως ἀκροβυστία τὸν νόμον τελοῦσα σὲ τὸν διὰ γράμματος καὶ περιτομῆς παραβάτην νόμου. 28 οὐ γὰρ ὁ ἐν τῷ φανερῷ Ἰουδαῖός ἐστιν οὐδὲ ἡ ἐν τῷ φανερῷ ἐν σαρκὶ περιτομή, 29 ἀλλ᾽ ὁ ἐν τῷ κρυπτῷ Ἰουδαῖος, καὶ περιτομὴ καρδίας ἐν πνεύματι οὐ γράμματι, οὗ ὁ ἔπαινος οὐκ ἐξ ἀνθρώπων ἀλλ᾽ ἐκ τοῦ θεοῦ.

Rom 3:31

31 νόμον οὖν καταργοῦμεν διὰ τῆς πίστεως; μὴ γένοιτο· ἀλλὰ νόμον ἱστάνομεν.

Rom 8:3–4

Τὸ γὰρ ἀδύνατον τοῦ νόμου ἐν ᾧ ἠσθένει διὰ τῆς σαρκός, ὁ θεὸς τὸν ἑαυτοῦ υἱὸν πέμψας ἐν ὁμοιώματι σαρκὸς ἁμαρτίας καὶ περὶ ἁμαρτίας κατέκρινεν τὴν ἁμαρτίαν ἐν τῇ σαρκί, 4 ἵνα τὸ δικαίωμα τοῦ νόμου πληρωθῇ ἐν ἡμῖν τοῖς μὴ κατὰ σάρκα περιπατοῦσιν ἀλλὰ κατὰ πνεῦμα.

Rom 13:8–10

Μηδενὶ μηδὲν ὀφείλετε εἰ μὴ τὸ ἀλλήλους ἀγαπᾶν· ὁ γὰρ ἀγαπῶν τὸν ἕτερον νόμον πεπλήρωκεν. 9 τὸ γὰρ οὐ μοιχεύσεις, οὐ φονεύσεις, οὐ κλέψεις, οὐκ ἐπιθυμήσεις, καὶ εἴ τις ἑτέρα ἐντολή, ἐν τῷ λόγῳ τούτῳ ἀνακεφαλαιοῦται [ἐν τῷ]· ἀγαπήσεις τὸν πλησίον σου ὡς σεαυτόν. 10 ἡ ἀγάπη τῷ πλησίον κακὸν οὐκ ἐργάζεται· πλήρωμα οὖν νόμου ἡ ἀγάπη.

1 Cor 7:19

ἡ περιτομὴ οὐδέν ἐστιν καὶ ἡ ἀκροβυστία οὐδέν ἐστιν, ἀλλὰ τήρησις ἐντολῶν θεοῦ.

Gal 5:13–14

Ὑμεῖς γὰρ ἐπ᾽ ἐλευθερίᾳ ἐκλήθητε, ἀδελφοί· μόνον μὴ τὴν ἐλευθερίαν εἰς ἀφορμὴν τῇ σαρκί, ἀλλὰ διὰ τῆς ἀγάπης δουλεύετε ἀλλήλοις. 14 ὁ γὰρ πᾶς νόμος ἐν ἑνὶ λόγῳ πεπλήρωται, ἐν τῷ· ἀγαπήσεις τὸν πλησίον σου ὡς σεαυτόν.

Gal 5:22–24

ὁ δὲ καρπὸς τοῦ πνεύματός ἐστιν ἀγάπη χαρὰ εἰρήνη, μακροθυμία χρηστότης ἀγαθωσύνη, πίστις 23 πραΰτης ἐγκράτεια· κατὰ τῶν τοιούτων οὐκ ἔστιν νόμος. 24 οἱ δὲ τοῦ Χριστοῦ ['Ιησοῦ] τὴν σάρκα ἐσταύρωσαν σὺν τοῖς παθήμασιν καὶ ταῖς ἐπιθυμίαις.

1 Tim 1:5–7

τὸ δὲ τέλος τῆς παραγγελίας ἐστὶν ἀγάπη ἐκ καθαρᾶς καρδίας καὶ συνειδήσεως ἀγαθῆς καὶ πίστεως ἀνυποκρίτου, 6 ὧν τινες ἀστοχήσαντες ἐξετράπησαν εἰς ματαιολογίαν 7 θέλοντες εἶναι νομοδιδάσκαλοι, μὴ νοοῦντες μήτε ἃ λέγουσιν μήτε περὶ τίνων διαβεβαιοῦνται.

Cf. Rom 9:30–10:13.

See also § 65 Christ the Goal of the Law.

68. *Reconciliation with God*

Rom 5:6–10

Ἔτι γὰρ Χριστὸς ὄντων ἡμῶν ἀσθενῶν ἔτι κατὰ καιρὸν ὑπὲρ ἀσεβῶν ἀπέθανεν. 7 μόλις γὰρ ὑπὲρ δικαίου τις ἀποθανεῖται· ὑπὲρ γὰρ τοῦ ἀγαθοῦ τάχα τις καὶ τολμᾷ ἀποθανεῖν· 8 συνίστησιν δὲ τὴν ἑαυτοῦ ἀγάπην εἰς ἡμᾶς ὁ θεός, ὅτι ἔτι ἁμαρτωλῶν ὄντων ἡμῶν Χριστὸς ὑπὲρ ἡμῶν ἀπέθανεν. 9 πολλῷ οὖν μᾶλλον δικαιωθέντες νῦν ἐν τῷ αἵματι αὐτοῦ σωθησόμεθα δι᾽ αὐτοῦ ἀπὸ τῆς ὀργῆς. 10 εἰ γὰρ ἐχθροὶ ὄντες κατηλλάγημεν τῷ θεῷ διὰ τοῦ θανάτου τοῦ υἱοῦ αὐτοῦ, πολλῷ μᾶλλον καταλλαγέντες σωθησόμεθα ἐν τῇ ζωῇ αὐτοῦ

2 Cor 5:18–21

τὰ δὲ πάντα ἐκ τοῦ θεοῦ τοῦ καταλλάξαντος ἡμᾶς ἑαυτῷ διὰ Χριστοῦ καὶ δόντος ἡμῖν τὴν διακονίαν τῆς καταλλαγῆς, 19 ὡς ὅτι θεὸς ἦν ἐν Χριστῷ κόσμον καταλλάσσων ἑαυτῷ, μὴ λογιζόμενος αὐτοῖς τὰ παραπτώματα αὐτῶν καὶ θέμενος ἐν ἡμῖν τὸν λόγον τῆς καταλλαγῆς. 20 Ὑπὲρ Χριστοῦ οὖν πρεσβεύομεν ὡς τοῦ θεοῦ παρακαλοῦντος δι᾽ ἡμῶν· δεόμεθα ὑπὲρ Χριστοῦ, καταλλάγητε τῷ θεῷ. 21 τὸν μὴ γνόντα ἁμαρτίαν ὑπὲρ ἡμῶν ἁμαρτίαν ἐποίησεν, ἵνα ἡμεῖς γενώμεθα δικαιοσύνη θεοῦ ἐν αὐτῷ.

Eph 2:14–18

Αὐτὸς γάρ ἐστιν ἡ εἰρήνη ἡμῶν, ὁ ποιήσας τὰ ἀμφότερα ἓν καὶ τὸ μεσότοιχον τοῦ φραγμοῦ λύσας, τὴν ἔχθραν ἐν τῇ σαρκὶ αὐτοῦ, 15 τὸν νόμον τῶν ἐντολῶν

we were imprisoned and guarded under the law until faith would be revealed. [24] Therefore the law was our disciplinarian until Christ came, so that we might be justified by faith. [25] But now that faith has come, we are no longer subject to a disciplinarian

1 Tim 1:8–11

Now we know that the law is good, if one uses it legitimately. [9] This means understanding that the law is laid down not for the innocent but for the lawless and disobedient, for the godless and sinful, for the unholy and profane, for those who kill their father or mother, for murderers, [10] fornicators, sodomites, slave traders, liars, perjurers, and whatever else is contrary to the sound teaching [11] that conforms to the glorious gospel of the blessed God, which he entrusted to me.

67. The Fulfillment of the Law through Faith and Love

Rom 2:26–29

So, if those who are uncircumcised keep the requirements of the law, will not their uncircumcision be regarded as circumcision? [27] Then those who are physically uncircumcised but keep the law will condemn you that have the written code and circumcision but break the law. [28] For a person is not a Jew who is one outwardly, nor is true circumcision something external and physical. [29] Rather, a person is a Jew who is one inwardly, and real circumcision is a matter of the heart—it is by the Spirit and not by the written letter. Such a person receives praise not from others but from God.[a]

Rom 3:31

Do we then overthrow the law by this faith? By no means! On the contrary, we uphold the law.

Rom 8:3–4

For God has done what the law, weakened by the flesh, could not do: by sending his own Son in the likeness of sinful flesh, and to deal with sin, he condemned sin in the flesh, [4] so that the just requirement of the law might be fulfilled in us, who walk not according to the flesh but according to the Spirit.

Rom 13:8–10

Owe no one anything, except to love one another; for the one who loves another has fulfilled the law. [9] The commandments, "You shall not commit adultery; You shall not murder; You shall not steal; You shall not covet"; and any other commandment, are summed up in this word, "Love your neighbor as yourself." [10] Love does no wrong to a neighbor; therefore, love is the fulfilling of the law.

1 Cor 7:19

Circumcision is nothing, and uncircumcision is nothing; but obeying the commandments of God is everything.

Gal 5:13–14

For you were called to freedom, brothers and sisters; only do not use your freedom as an opportunity for self-indulgence, but through love become slaves to one another. [14] For the whole law is summed up in a single commandment, "You shall love your neighbor as yourself."

Gal 5:22–24

By contrast, the fruit of the Spirit is love, joy, peace, patience, kindness, generosity, faithfulness, [23] gentleness, and self-control. There is no law against such things. [24] And those who belong to Christ Jesus have crucified the flesh with its passions and desires.

1 Tim 1:5–7

But the aim of such instruction is love that comes from a pure heart, a good conscience, and sincere faith. [6] Some people have deviated from these and turned to meaningless talk, [7] desiring to be teachers of the law, without understanding either what they are saying or the things about which they make assertions.

Cf. Rom 9:30–10:13.

See also § 65 Christ the Goal of the Law.

68. Reconciliation with God

Rom 5:6–10

For while we were still weak, at the right time Christ died for the ungodly. [7] Indeed, rarely will anyone die for a righteous person—though perhaps for a good person someone might actually dare to die. [8] But God proves his love for us in that while we still were sinners Christ died for us. [9] Much more surely then, now that we have been justified by his blood, will we be saved through him from the wrath of God. [10] For if while we were enemies, we were reconciled to God through the death of his Son, much more surely, having been reconciled, will we be saved by his life.

2 Cor 5:18–21

All this is from God, who reconciled us to himself through Christ, and has given us the ministry of reconciliation; [19] that is, God was in Christ, reconciling[a] the world to himself, not counting their trespasses against them, and entrusting the message of reconciliation to us. [20] So we are ambassadors for Christ, since God is making his appeal through us; we entreat you on behalf of Christ, be reconciled to God. [21] For our sake he made him to be sin who knew no sin, so that in him we might become the righteousness of God.

Eph 2:14–18

For he is our peace; in his flesh he has made both groups into one and has broken down the dividing wall, that is, the hostility between us. [15] He has

§ 67 [a] **Rom 2:29** Translation differs from NRSV **§ 68** [a] **2 Cor 5:19** *God was in Christ, reconciling* Or possibly *in Christ God was reconciling* (so NRSV)

ἐν δόγμασιν καταργήσας, ἵνα τοὺς δύο κτίσῃ ἐν αὐτῷ εἰς ἕνα καινὸν ἄνθρωπον ποιῶν εἰρήνην [16] καὶ ἀποκαταλλάξῃ τοὺς ἀμφοτέρους ἐν ἑνὶ σώματι τῷ θεῷ διὰ τοῦ σταυροῦ, ἀποκτείνας τὴν ἔχθραν ἐν αὐτῷ. [17] καὶ ἐλθὼν εὐηγγελίσατο εἰρήνην ὑμῖν τοῖς μακρὰν καὶ εἰρήνην τοῖς ἐγγύς· [18] ὅτι δι᾽ αὐτοῦ ἔχομεν τὴν προσαγωγὴν οἱ ἀμφότεροι ἐν ἑνὶ πνεύματι πρὸς τὸν πατέρα.

Col 1:19–22

ὅτι ἐν αὐτῷ εὐδόκησεν πᾶν τὸ πλήρωμα κατοικῆσαι [20] καὶ δι᾽ αὐτοῦ ἀποκαταλλάξαι τὰ πάντα εἰς αὐτόν, εἰρηνοποιήσας διὰ τοῦ αἵματος τοῦ σταυροῦ αὐτοῦ, [δι᾽ αὐτοῦ] εἴτε τὰ ἐπὶ τῆς γῆς εἴτε τὰ ἐν τοῖς οὐρανοῖς. [21] Καὶ ὑμᾶς ποτε ὄντας ἀπηλλοτριωμένους καὶ ἐχθροὺς τῇ διανοίᾳ ἐν τοῖς ἔργοις τοῖς πονηροῖς, [22] νυνὶ δὲ ⸀ἀποκατήλλαξεν ἐν τῷ σώματι τῆς σαρκὸς αὐτοῦ διὰ τοῦ θανάτου παραστῆσαι ὑμᾶς ἁγίους καὶ ἀμώμους καὶ ἀνεγκλήτους κατενώπιον αὐτοῦ

Cf. Rom 5:1; 11:13–16; 1 Tim 2:5–7.

69. The Chosen People of God

Rom 8:28–30

Οἴδαμεν δὲ ὅτι τοῖς ἀγαπῶσιν τὸν θεὸν πάντα ⸀συνεργεῖ εἰς ἀγαθόν, τοῖς κατὰ πρόθεσιν κλητοῖς οὖσιν. [29] ὅτι οὓς προέγνω, καὶ προώρισεν συμμόρφους τῆς εἰκόνος τοῦ υἱοῦ αὐτοῦ, εἰς τὸ εἶναι αὐτὸν πρωτότοκον ἐν πολλοῖς ἀδελφοῖς· [30] οὓς δὲ προώρισεν, τούτους καὶ ἐκάλεσεν· καὶ οὓς ἐκάλεσεν, τούτους καὶ ἐδικαίωσεν· οὓς δὲ ἐδικαίωσεν, τούτους καὶ ἐδόξασεν.

Rom 8:33

τίς ἐγκαλέσει κατὰ ἐκλεκτῶν θεοῦ; θεὸς ὁ δικαιῶν

Eph 1:3–12

Εὐλογητὸς ὁ θεὸς καὶ πατὴρ τοῦ κυρίου ἡμῶν Ἰησοῦ Χριστοῦ, ὁ εὐλογήσας ἡμᾶς ἐν πάσῃ εὐλογίᾳ πνευματικῇ ἐν τοῖς ἐπουρανίοις ἐν Χριστῷ, [4] καθὼς ἐξελέξατο ἡμᾶς ἐν αὐτῷ πρὸ καταβολῆς κόσμου εἶναι ἡμᾶς ἁγίους καὶ ἀμώμους κατενώπιον αὐτοῦ ἐν ἀγάπῃ, [5] προορίσας ἡμᾶς εἰς υἱοθεσίαν διὰ Ἰησοῦ Χριστοῦ εἰς αὐτόν, κατὰ τὴν εὐδοκίαν τοῦ θελήματος αὐτοῦ, [6] εἰς ἔπαινον δόξης τῆς χάριτος αὐτοῦ ἧς ἐχαρίτωσεν ἡμᾶς ἐν τῷ ἠγαπημένῳ. [7] Ἐν ᾧ ἔχομεν τὴν ἀπολύτρωσιν διὰ τοῦ αἵματος αὐτοῦ, τὴν ἄφεσιν τῶν παραπτωμάτων, κατὰ τὸ πλοῦτος τῆς χάριτος αὐτοῦ [8] ἧς ἐπερίσσευσεν εἰς ἡμᾶς, ἐν πάσῃ σοφίᾳ καὶ φρονήσει, [9] γνωρίσας ἡμῖν τὸ μυστήριον τοῦ θελήματος αὐτοῦ, κατὰ τὴν εὐδοκίαν αὐτοῦ ἣν προέθετο ἐν αὐτῷ [10] εἰς οἰκονομίαν τοῦ πληρώματος τῶν καιρῶν, ἀνακεφαλαιώσασθαι τὰ πάντα ἐν τῷ Χριστῷ, τὰ ἐπὶ τοῖς οὐρανοῖς καὶ τὰ ἐπὶ τῆς γῆς ἐν αὐτῷ. [11] Ἐν ᾧ καὶ ἐκληρώθημεν προορισθέντες κατὰ πρόθεσιν τοῦ τὰ πάντα ἐνεργοῦντος κατὰ τὴν βουλὴν τοῦ θελήματος αὐτοῦ [12] εἰς τὸ εἶναι ἡμᾶς εἰς ἔπαινον δόξης αὐτοῦ τοὺς προηλπικότας ἐν τῷ Χριστῷ.

Col 3:12

Ἐνδύσασθε οὖν, ὡς ἐκλεκτοὶ τοῦ θεοῦ ἅγιοι καὶ ἠγαπημένοι, σπλάγχνα οἰκτιρμοῦ χρηστότητα ταπεινοφροσύνην πραΰτητα μακροθυμίαν

1 Thess 1:2–5

Εὐχαριστοῦμεν τῷ θεῷ πάντοτε περὶ πάντων ὑμῶν μνείαν ποιούμενοι ἐπὶ τῶν προσευχῶν ἡμῶν, ἀδιαλείπτως [3] μνημονεύοντες ὑμῶν τοῦ ἔργου τῆς πίστεως καὶ τοῦ κόπου τῆς ἀγάπης καὶ τῆς ὑπομονῆς τῆς ἐλπίδος τοῦ κυρίου ἡμῶν Ἰησοῦ Χριστοῦ ἔμπροσθεν τοῦ θεοῦ καὶ πατρὸς ἡμῶν, [4] εἰδότες, ἀδελφοὶ ἠγαπημένοι ὑπὸ [τοῦ] θεοῦ, τὴν ἐκλογὴν ὑμῶν, [5] ὅτι τὸ εὐαγγέλιον ἡμῶν οὐκ ἐγενήθη εἰς ὑμᾶς ἐν λόγῳ μόνον ἀλλὰ καὶ ἐν δυνάμει καὶ ἐν πνεύματι ἁγίῳ καὶ [ἐν] πληροφορίᾳ πολλῇ, καθὼς οἴδατε οἷοι ἐγενήθημεν [ἐν] ὑμῖν δι᾽ ὑμᾶς.

1 Thess 5:9–10

ὅτι οὐκ ἔθετο ἡμᾶς ὁ θεὸς εἰς ὀργὴν ἀλλὰ εἰς περιποίησιν σωτηρίας διὰ τοῦ κυρίου ἡμῶν Ἰησοῦ Χριστοῦ [10] τοῦ ἀποθανόντος ὑπὲρ ἡμῶν, ἵνα εἴτε γρηγορῶμεν εἴτε καθεύδωμεν ἅμα σὺν αὐτῷ ζήσωμεν.

2 Thess 2:13–15

Ἡμεῖς δὲ ὀφείλομεν εὐχαριστεῖν τῷ θεῷ πάντοτε περὶ ὑμῶν, ἀδελφοὶ ἠγαπημένοι ὑπὸ κυρίου, ὅτι εἵλατο ὑμᾶς ὁ θεὸς ⸀ἀπαρχὴν εἰς σωτηρίαν ἐν ἁγιασμῷ πνεύματος καὶ πίστει ἀληθείας, [14] εἰς ὃ [καὶ] ἐκάλεσεν ὑμᾶς διὰ τοῦ εὐαγγελίου ἡμῶν εἰς περιποίησιν δόξης τοῦ κυρίου ἡμῶν Ἰησοῦ Χριστοῦ. [15] Ἄρα οὖν, ἀδελφοί, στήκετε καὶ κρατεῖτε τὰς παραδόσεις ἃς ἐδιδάχθητε εἴτε διὰ λόγου εἴτε δι᾽ ἐπιστολῆς ἡμῶν.

Acts 13:48

Ἀκούοντα δὲ τὰ ἔθνη ἔχαιρον καὶ ἐδόξαζον τὸν λόγον τοῦ κυρίου καὶ ἐπίστευσαν ὅσοι ἦσαν τεταγμένοι εἰς ζωὴν αἰώνιον

Cf. Rom 9:6–29; 11:1–6; 11:7–10; 16:13; 1 Cor 1:18–25; 1:26–31; 2 Tim 1:9–10; 2:10; 2:19–21; Titus 1:1; 2:14.

70. Belonging to Christ

Rom 8:9

Ὑμεῖς δὲ οὐκ ἐστὲ ἐν σαρκὶ ἀλλὰ ἐν πνεύματι, εἴπερ πνεῦμα θεοῦ οἰκεῖ ἐν ὑμῖν. εἰ δέ τις πνεῦμα Χριστοῦ οὐκ ἔχει, οὗτος οὐκ ἔστιν αὐτοῦ.

Rom 14:7–9

οὐδεὶς γὰρ ἡμῶν ἑαυτῷ ζῇ καὶ οὐδεὶς ἑαυτῷ ἀποθνῄσκει· [8] ἐάν τε γὰρ ζῶμεν,

§ 68 **Col 1:22** ***αποκατηλλαξεν*** ℵ A C D^2 048. 1739. 1881 *Byz*] αποκατηλλαγητε ($\mathfrak{P}^{46}$) B ¦ αποκαταλλαγεντες D* ¦ αποκατηλλακται 33 **§ 69** **Rom 8:28** ***συνεργει*** ℵ C D 33. 1739. 1881 *Byz*] *add.* ο θεος $\mathfrak{P}^{46}$ A B **2 Thess 2:13** ***απαρχην*** B 33. 1739. 1881] απ αρχης ℵ D *Byz*

abolished the law with its commandments and ordinances, that he might create in himself one new humanity in place of the two, thus making peace,
16 and might reconcile both groups to God in one body through the cross, thus putting to death that hostility through
it. 17 So he came and proclaimed peace to you who were far off and peace to those who were near; 18 for through him both of us have access in one Spirit to the Father.

Col 1:19–22

For in him all the fullness of God was
pleased to dwell, 20 and through him God was pleased to reconcile to himself all things, whether on earth or in heaven, by making peace through the
blood of his cross. 21 And you who were once estranged and hostile in mind,
doing evil deeds, 22 he has now reconciled[b] in his fleshly body through death, so as to present you holy and blameless and irreproachable before him

Cf. Rom 5:1; 11:13–16; 1 Tim 2:5–7.

69. The Chosen People of God

Rom 8:28–30

We know that all things work together for good[a] for those who love God, who are called according to his purpose.
29 For those whom he foreknew he also predestined to be conformed to the image of his Son, in order that he might be the firstborn within a large family.
30 And those whom he predestined he also called; and those whom he called he also justified; and those whom he justified he also glorified.

Rom 8:33

Who will bring any charge against God's elect? It is God who justifies.

Eph 1:3–12

Blessed be the God and Father of our Lord Jesus Christ, who has blessed us in Christ with every spiritual blessing
in the heavenly places, 4 just as he chose us in Christ before the foundation of the world to be holy and blameless be-
fore him in love. 5 He destined us for adoption as his children through Jesus Christ, according to the good pleasure
of his will, 6 to the praise of his glorious grace that he freely bestowed on us in
the Beloved. 7 In him we have redemption through his blood, the forgiveness of our trespasses, according to the
riches of his grace 8 that he lavished on
us. With all wisdom and insight 9 he has made known to us the mystery of his will, according to his good pleasure
that he set forth in Christ, 10 as a plan for the fullness of time, to gather up all things in him, things in heaven and
things on earth. 11 In Christ we have also obtained an inheritance, having been destined according to the purpose of him who accomplishes all things ac-
cording to his counsel and will, 12 so that we, who were the first to set our hope on Christ, might live for the praise of his glory.

Col 3:12

As God's chosen ones, holy and beloved, clothe yourselves with compassion, kindness, humility, meekness, and patience.

1 Thess 1:2–5

We always give thanks to God for all of you and mention you in our prayers,
constantly 3 remembering before our God and Father your work of faith and labor of love and steadfastness of hope
in our Lord Jesus Christ. 4 For we know, brothers and sisters beloved by God,
that he has chosen you, 5 because our message of the gospel came to you not in word only, but also in power and in the Holy Spirit and with full conviction; just as you know what kind of persons we proved to be among you for your sake.

1 Thess 5:9–10

For God has destined us not for wrath but for obtaining salvation through our
Lord Jesus Christ, 10 who died for us, so that whether we are awake or asleep we may live with him.

2 Thess 2:13–15

But we must always give thanks to God for you, brothers and sisters beloved by the Lord, because God chose you as the first fruits[b] for salvation through sanctification by the Spirit and through
belief in the truth. 14 For this purpose he called you through our proclamation of the good news, so that you may obtain
the glory of our Lord Jesus Christ. 15 So then, brothers and sisters, stand firm and hold fast to the traditions that you were taught by us, either by word of mouth or by our letter.

Acts 13:48

When the Gentiles heard this, they were glad and praised the word of the Lord; and as many as had been destined for eternal life became believers.

Cf. Rom 9:6–29; 11:1–6; 11:7–10; 16:13; 1 Cor 1:18–25; 1:26–31; 2 Tim 1:9–10; 2:10; 2:19–21; Titus 1:1; 2:14.

70. Belonging to Christ

Rom 8:9

But you are not in the flesh; you are in the Spirit, since the Spirit of God dwells in you. Anyone who does not have the Spirit of Christ does not belong to him.

Rom 14:7–9

We do not live to ourselves, and we do
not die to ourselves. 8 If we live, we live

[b] **Col 1:22** ***he has now reconciled*** Other ancient authorities read *you have now been reconciled* **§ 69** [a] **Rom 8:28** ***all things work together for good*** Other ancient authorities read *God makes all things work together for good*, or *in all things God works for good* [b] **2 Thess 2:13** ***as the first fruits*** Other ancient authorities read *from the beginning*

τῷ κυρίῳ ζῶμεν, ἐάν τε ἀποθνῄσκω-
μεν, τῷ κυρίῳ ἀποθνῄσκομεν. ἐάν τε
οὖν ζῶμεν ἐάν τε ἀποθνῄσκωμεν, τοῦ
κυρίου ἐσμέν. 9 εἰς τοῦτο γὰρ Χριστὸς
ἀπέθανεν καὶ ἔζησεν, ἵνα καὶ νεκρῶν
καὶ ζώντων κυριεύσῃ.

1 Cor 3:21–23

ὥστε μηδεὶς καυχάσθω ἐν ἀνθρώποις·
πάντα γὰρ ὑμῶν ἐστιν, 22 εἴτε Παῦλος
εἴτε Ἀπολλῶς εἴτε Κηφᾶς, εἴτε κόσμος
εἴτε ζωὴ εἴτε θάνατος, εἴτε ἐνεστῶτα
εἴτε μέλλοντα· πάντα ὑμῶν, 23 ὑμεῖς δὲ
Χριστοῦ, Χριστὸς δὲ θεοῦ.

1 Cor 6:19–20

ἢ οὐκ οἴδατε ὅτι τὸ σῶμα ὑμῶν ναὸς
τοῦ ἐν ὑμῖν ἁγίου πνεύματός ἐστιν οὗ
ἔχετε ἀπὸ θεοῦ, καὶ οὐκ ἐστὲ ἑαυτῶν;
20 ἠγοράσθητε γὰρ τιμῆς· δοξάσατε δὴ
τὸν θεὸν ἐν τῷ σώματι ὑμῶν.

Cf. 1 Cor 1:12; 7:23; 15:23; 2 Cor 10:7; Gal 3:29; 5:24–25; 2 Tim 2:16–19; Acts 20:28.

71. The Church's Betrothal to Christ

2 Cor 11:1–4

Ὄφελον ἀνείχεσθέ μου μικρόν τι ἀφρο-
σύνης· ἀλλὰ καὶ ἀνέχεσθέ μου. 2 ζηλῶ γὰρ
ὑμᾶς θεοῦ ζήλῳ, ἡρμοσάμην γὰρ ὑμᾶς
ἑνὶ ἀνδρὶ παρθένον ἁγνὴν παραστῆσαι
τῷ Χριστῷ· 3 φοβοῦμαι δὲ μή πως, ὡς ὁ
ὄφις ἐξηπάτησεν Εὕαν ἐν τῇ πανουργίᾳ
αὐτοῦ, φθαρῇ τὰ νοήματα ὑμῶν ἀπὸ τῆς
ἁπλότητος ⸀[καὶ τῆς ἁγνότητος]⸀ τῆς εἰς
τὸν Χριστόν. 4 εἰ μὲν γὰρ ὁ ἐρχόμενος
ἄλλον Ἰησοῦν κηρύσσει ὃν οὐκ ἐκη-
ρύξαμεν, ἢ πνεῦμα ἕτερον λαμβάνετε
ὃ οὐκ ἐλάβετε, ἢ εὐαγγέλιον ἕτερον ὃ
οὐκ ἐδέξασθε, καλῶς ἀνέχεσθε.

Eph 5:25–33

Οἱ ἄνδρες, ἀγαπᾶτε τὰς γυναῖκας, καθὼς
καὶ ὁ Χριστὸς ἠγάπησεν τὴν ἐκκλησίαν
καὶ ἑαυτὸν παρέδωκεν ὑπὲρ αὐτῆς, 26 ἵνα
αὐτὴν ἁγιάσῃ καθαρίσας τῷ λουτρῷ
τοῦ ὕδατος ἐν ῥήματι, 27 ἵνα παραστήσῃ
αὐτὸς ἑαυτῷ ἔνδοξον τὴν ἐκκλησίαν,
μὴ ἔχουσαν σπίλον ἢ ῥυτίδα ἤ τι τῶν
τοιούτων, ἀλλ' ἵνα ᾖ ἁγία καὶ ἄμωμος.
28 οὕτως ὀφείλουσιν [καὶ] οἱ ἄνδρες
ἀγαπᾶν τὰς ἑαυτῶν γυναῖκας ὡς τὰ
ἑαυτῶν σώματα. ὁ ἀγαπῶν τὴν ἑαυτοῦ
γυναῖκα ἑαυτὸν ἀγαπᾷ. 29 Οὐδεὶς γάρ
ποτε τὴν ἑαυτοῦ σάρκα ἐμίσησεν ἀλλὰ
ἐκτρέφει καὶ θάλπει αὐτήν, καθὼς καὶ
ὁ Χριστὸς τὴν ἐκκλησίαν, 30 ὅτι μέλη
ἐσμὲν τοῦ σώματος ⸀αὐτοῦ. 31 ἀντὶ τού-
του καταλείψει ἄνθρωπος [τὸν] πατέρα
καὶ [τὴν] μητέρα καὶ προσκολληθήσεται
πρὸς τὴν γυναῖκα αὐτοῦ, καὶ ἔσονται οἱ
δύο εἰς σάρκα μίαν. 32 τὸ μυστήριον τοῦτο
μέγα ἐστίν· ἐγὼ δὲ λέγω εἰς Χριστὸν καὶ
εἰς τὴν ἐκκλησίαν. 33 πλὴν καὶ ὑμεῖς οἱ
καθ' ἕνα, ἕκαστος τὴν ἑαυτοῦ γυναῖκα
οὕτως ἀγαπάτω ὡς ἑαυτόν, ἡ δὲ γυνὴ
ἵνα φοβῆται τὸν ἄνδρα.

Cf. Rom 7:1–6; 1 Cor 6:16–17.

72. Then and Now

Rom 6:17–23

χάρις δὲ τῷ θεῷ ὅτι ἦτε δοῦλοι τῆς ἁμαρ-
τίας ὑπηκούσατε δὲ ἐκ καρδίας εἰς ὃν
παρεδόθητε τύπον διδαχῆς, 18 ἐλευθερω-
θέντες δὲ ἀπὸ τῆς ἁμαρτίας ἐδουλώθητε
τῇ δικαιοσύνῃ. 19 Ἀνθρώπινον λέγω
διὰ τὴν ἀσθένειαν τῆς σαρκὸς ὑμῶν.
ὥσπερ γὰρ παρεστήσατε τὰ μέλη ὑμῶν
δοῦλα τῇ ἀκαθαρσίᾳ καὶ τῇ ἀνομίᾳ εἰς
τὴν ἀνομίαν, οὕτως νῦν παραστήσατε
τὰ μέλη ὑμῶν δοῦλα τῇ δικαιοσύνῃ
εἰς ἁγιασμόν. 20 ὅτε γὰρ δοῦλοι ἦτε τῆς
ἁμαρτίας, ἐλεύθεροι ἦτε τῇ δικαιοσύνῃ.
21 τίνα οὖν καρπὸν εἴχετε τότε; ἐφ' οἷς
νῦν ἐπαισχύνεσθε, τὸ γὰρ τέλος ἐκείνων
θάνατος. 22 νυνὶ δὲ ἐλευθερωθέντες ἀπὸ
τῆς ἁμαρτίας δουλωθέντες δὲ τῷ θεῷ
ἔχετε τὸν καρπὸν ὑμῶν εἰς ἁγιασμόν, τὸ
δὲ τέλος ζωὴν αἰώνιον. 23 τὰ γὰρ ὀψώνια
τῆς ἁμαρτίας θάνατος, τὸ δὲ χάρισμα τοῦ
θεοῦ ζωὴ αἰώνιος ἐν Χριστῷ Ἰησοῦ τῷ
κυρίῳ ἡμῶν.

2 Cor 5:14–17

ἡ γὰρ ἀγάπη τοῦ Χριστοῦ συνέχει ἡμᾶς,
κρίναντας τοῦτο, ὅτι εἷς ὑπὲρ πάντων
ἀπέθανεν, ἄρα οἱ πάντες ἀπέθανον· 15 καὶ
ὑπὲρ πάντων ἀπέθανεν, ἵνα οἱ ζῶντες
μηκέτι ἑαυτοῖς ζῶσιν ἀλλὰ τῷ ὑπὲρ αὐτῶν
ἀποθανόντι καὶ ἐγερθέντι. 16 Ὥστε ἡμεῖς
ἀπὸ τοῦ νῦν οὐδένα οἴδαμεν κατὰ σάρκα·
εἰ καὶ ἐγνώκαμεν κατὰ σάρκα Χριστόν,
ἀλλὰ νῦν οὐκέτι γινώσκομεν. 17 ὥστε εἴ
τις ἐν Χριστῷ, καινὴ κτίσις· τὰ ἀρχαῖα
παρῆλθεν, ἰδοὺ γέγονεν καινά.

Gal 1:23–24

μόνον δὲ ἀκούοντες ἦσαν ὅτι ὁ διώκων
ἡμᾶς ποτε νῦν εὐαγγελίζεται τὴν πίστιν
ἥν ποτε ἐπόρθει, 24 καὶ ἐδόξαζον ἐν
ἐμοὶ τὸν θεόν.

Gal 4:8–9

Ἀλλὰ τότε μὲν οὐκ εἰδότες θεὸν ἐδου-
λεύσατε τοῖς φύσει μὴ οὖσιν θεοῖς· 9 νῦν
δὲ γνόντες θεόν, μᾶλλον δὲ γνωσθέντες
ὑπὸ θεοῦ, πῶς ἐπιστρέφετε πάλιν ἐπὶ τὰ
ἀσθενῆ καὶ πτωχὰ στοιχεῖα οἷς πάλιν
ἄνωθεν δουλεύειν θέλετε;

Eph 2:1–7

Καὶ ὑμᾶς ὄντας νεκροὺς τοῖς παραπτώ-
μασιν καὶ ταῖς ἁμαρτίαις ὑμῶν, 2 ἐν αἷς
ποτε περιεπατήσατε κατὰ τὸν αἰῶνα
τοῦ κόσμου τούτου, κατὰ τὸν ἄρχοντα
τῆς ἐξουσίας τοῦ ἀέρος, τοῦ πνεύματος
τοῦ νῦν ἐνεργοῦντος ἐν τοῖς υἱοῖς τῆς
ἀπειθείας· 3 ἐν οἷς καὶ ἡμεῖς πάντες ἀνε-
στράφημέν ποτε ἐν ταῖς ἐπιθυμίαις τῆς
σαρκὸς ἡμῶν ποιοῦντες τὰ θελήματα τῆς

§ 71 **2 Cor 11:3** ***και της αγνοτητος*** 𝔓46 א* B (D*) 33] *om.* א2 D(2) 1739. 1881 *Byz* **Eph 5:30** ***αυτου*** 𝔓46 א* A B 048. 33. 1739*. 1881] *add.* εκ της σαρκος αυτου και εκ των οστεων αυτου א2 D 1739mg *Byz*

to the Lord, and if we die, we die to the Lord; so then, whether we live or whether we die, we are the Lord's. **9** For to this end Christ died and lived again, so that he might be Lord of both the dead and the living.

1 Cor 3:21–23

So let no one boast about human leaders. For all things are yours, **22** whether Paul or Apollos or Cephas or the world or life or death or the present or the future—all belong to you, **23** and you belong to Christ, and Christ belongs to God.

1 Cor 6:19–20

Or do you not know that your body is a temple of the Holy Spirit within you, which you have from God, and that you are not your own? **20** For you were bought with a price; therefore glorify God in your body.

Cf. 1 Cor 1:12; 7:23; 15:23; 2 Cor 10:7; Gal 3:29; 5:24–25; 2 Tim 2:16–19; Acts 20:28.

71. The Church's Betrothal to Christ

2 Cor 11:1–4

I wish you would bear with me in a little foolishness. Do bear with me! **2** I feel a divine jealousy for you, for I promised you in marriage to one husband, to present you as a chaste virgin to Christ. **3** But I am afraid that as the serpent deceived Eve by its cunning, your thoughts will be led astray from a sincere and pure[a] devotion to Christ. **4** For if someone comes and proclaims another Jesus than the one we proclaimed, or if you receive a different spirit from the one you received, or a different gospel from the one you accepted, you submit to it readily enough.

Eph 5:25–33

Husbands, love your wives, just as Christ loved the church and gave himself up for her, **26** in order to make her holy by cleansing her with the washing of water by the word, **27** so as to present the church to himself in splendor, without a spot or wrinkle or anything of the kind—yes, so that she may be holy and without blemish. **28** In the same way, husbands should love their wives as they do their own bodies. He who loves his wife loves himself. **29** For no one ever hates his own body, but he nourishes and tenderly cares for it, just as Christ does for the church, **30** because we are members of his body.[b] **31** "For this reason a man will leave his father and mother and be joined to his wife, and the two will become one flesh." **32** This is a great mystery, and I am applying it to Christ and the church. **33** Each of you, however, should love his wife as himself, and a wife should respect her husband.

Cf. Rom 7:1–6; 1 Cor 6:16–17.

72. Then and Now

Rom 6:17–23

But thanks be to God that you, having once been slaves of sin, have become obedient from the heart to the form of teaching to which you were entrusted, **18** and that you, having been set free from sin, have become slaves of righteousness. **19** I am speaking in human terms because of your natural limitations. For just as you once presented your members as slaves to impurity and to greater and greater iniquity, so now present your members as slaves to righteousness for sanctification. **20** When you were slaves of sin, you were free in regard to righteousness. **21** So what fruit did you have then? Because of these things you are now ashamed, because the end of those things is death. **22** But now that you have been freed from sin and enslaved to God, the fruit you get is sanctification, and the end is eternal life.[a] **23** For the wages of sin is death, but the free gift of God is eternal life in Christ Jesus our Lord.

2 Cor 5:14–17

For the love of Christ urges us on, because we are convinced that one has died for all; therefore all have died. **15** And he died for all, so that those who live might live no longer for themselves, but for him who died and was raised for them. **16** From now on, therefore, we regard no one from a human point of view; even though we once knew Christ from a human point of view, we know him no longer in that way. **17** So if anyone is in Christ, there is a new creation: everything old has passed away; see, everything has become new!

Gal 1:23–24

they only heard it said, "The one who formerly was persecuting us is now proclaiming the faith he once tried to destroy." **24** And they glorified God because of me.

Gal 4:8–9

Formerly, when you did not know God, you were enslaved to beings that by nature are not gods. **9** Now, however, that you have come to know God, or rather to be known by God, how can you turn back again to the weak and beggarly elemental spirits? How can you want to be enslaved to them again?

Eph 2:1–7

You were dead through the trespasses and sins **2** in which you once lived, following the course of this world, following the ruler of the power of the air, the spirit that is now at work among those who are disobedient. **3** All of us once lived among them in the passions of our flesh, following the desires of

§ 71 [a] **2 Cor 11:3** *and pure* Other ancient authorities lack *and pure* [b] **Eph 5:30** *of his body* Other ancient authorities add *of his flesh and of his bones* **§ 72** [a] **Rom 6:21–22** Translation differs from NRSV

σαρκὸς καὶ τῶν διανοιῶν, καὶ ἤμεθα τέκνα
φύσει ὀργῆς ὡς καὶ οἱ λοιποί· 4 ὁ δὲ θεὸς
πλούσιος ὢν ἐν ἐλέει, διὰ τὴν πολλὴν
ἀγάπην αὐτοῦ ἣν ἠγάπησεν ἡμᾶς, 5 καὶ
ὄντας ἡμᾶς νεκροὺς τοῖς παραπτώμασιν
συνεζωοποίησεν ⸂τῷ Χριστῷ⸃, —χάριτί
ἐστε σεσῳσμένοι— 6 καὶ συνήγειρεν καὶ
συνεκάθισεν ἐν τοῖς ἐπουρανίοις ἐν
Χριστῷ Ἰησοῦ, 7 ἵνα ἐνδείξηται ἐν τοῖς
αἰῶσιν τοῖς ἐπερχομένοις τὸ ὑπερβάλλον
πλοῦτος τῆς χάριτος αὐτοῦ ἐν χρηστότητι
ἐφ᾽ ἡμᾶς ἐν Χριστῷ Ἰησοῦ.

Eph 2:11–13

Διὸ μνημονεύετε ὅτι ποτὲ ὑμεῖς τὰ ἔθνη
ἐν σαρκί, οἱ λεγόμενοι ἀκροβυστία ὑπὸ
τῆς λεγομένης περιτομῆς ἐν σαρκὶ χει-
ροποιήτου, 12 ὅτι ἦτε τῷ καιρῷ ἐκείνῳ
χωρὶς Χριστοῦ, ἀπηλλοτριωμένοι τῆς
πολιτείας τοῦ Ἰσραὴλ καὶ ξένοι τῶν
διαθηκῶν τῆς ἐπαγγελίας, ἐλπίδα μὴ
ἔχοντες καὶ ἄθεοι ἐν τῷ κόσμῳ. 13 νυνὶ
δὲ ἐν Χριστῷ Ἰησοῦ ὑμεῖς οἵ ποτε ὄντες
μακρὰν ἐγενήθητε ἐγγὺς ἐν τῷ αἵματι
τοῦ Χριστοῦ.

Eph 2:19–20

Ἄρα οὖν οὐκέτι ἐστὲ ξένοι καὶ πάροικοι
ἀλλὰ ἐστὲ συμπολῖται τῶν ἁγίων καὶ
οἰκεῖοι τοῦ θεοῦ, 20 ἐποικοδομηθέντες
ἐπὶ τῷ θεμελίῳ τῶν ἀποστόλων καὶ
προφητῶν, ὄντος ἀκρογωνιαίου αὐτοῦ
Χριστοῦ Ἰησοῦ

Eph 5:8

ἦτε γάρ ποτε σκότος, νῦν δὲ φῶς ἐν κυ-
ρίῳ· ὡς τέκνα φωτὸς περιπατεῖτε

Col 1:21–23

Καὶ ὑμᾶς ποτε ὄντας ἀπηλλοτριωμένους
καὶ ἐχθροὺς τῇ διανοίᾳ ἐν τοῖς ἔργοις τοῖς
πονηροῖς, 22 νυνὶ δὲ ⸀ἀποκατήλλαξεν
ἐν τῷ σώματι τῆς σαρκὸς αὐτοῦ διὰ τοῦ
θανάτου παραστῆσαι ὑμᾶς ἁγίους καὶ
ἀμώμους καὶ ἀνεγκλήτους κατενώπιον
αὐτοῦ, 23 εἴ γε ἐπιμένετε τῇ πίστει τεθεμε-
λιωμένοι καὶ ἑδραῖοι καὶ μὴ μετακινού-
μενοι ἀπὸ τῆς ἐλπίδος τοῦ εὐαγγελίου
οὗ ἠκούσατε, τοῦ κηρυχθέντος ἐν πάσῃ
κτίσει τῇ ὑπὸ τὸν οὐρανόν, οὗ ἐγενόμην
ἐγὼ Παῦλος διάκονος.

Col 2:12–13

συνταφέντες αὐτῷ ἐν τῷ βαπτισμῷ,
ἐν ᾧ καὶ συνηγέρθητε διὰ τῆς πίστεως
τῆς ἐνεργείας τοῦ θεοῦ τοῦ ἐγείραντος
αὐτὸν ἐκ νεκρῶν· 13 καὶ ὑμᾶς νεκροὺς
ὄντας [ἐν] τοῖς παραπτώμασιν καὶ τῇ
ἀκροβυστίᾳ τῆς σαρκὸς ὑμῶν, συνεζω-
οποίησεν ⸀ὑμᾶς σὺν αὐτῷ, χαρισάμενος
ἡμῖν πάντα τὰ παραπτώματα.

Col 3:5–11

Νεκρώσατε οὖν τὰ μέλη τὰ ἐπὶ τῆς γῆς,
πορνείαν ἀκαθαρσίαν πάθος ἐπιθυμίαν
κακήν, καὶ τὴν πλεονεξίαν, ἥτις ἐστὶν
εἰδωλολατρία, 6 δι᾽ ἃ ἔρχεται ἡ ὀργὴ τοῦ
θεοῦ ⸂[ἐπὶ τοὺς υἱοὺς τῆς ἀπειθείας]⸃.
7 ἐν οἷς καὶ ὑμεῖς περιεπατήσατέ ποτε,
ὅτε ἐζῆτε ἐν τούτοις· 8 νυνὶ δὲ ἀπόθε-
σθε καὶ ὑμεῖς τὰ πάντα, ὀργήν, θυμόν,
κακίαν, βλασφημίαν, αἰσχρολογίαν ἐκ
τοῦ στόματος ὑμῶν· 9 μὴ ψεύδεσθε εἰς
ἀλλήλους, ἀπεκδυσάμενοι τὸν παλαιὸν
ἄνθρωπον σὺν ταῖς πράξεσιν αὐτοῦ 10 καὶ
ἐνδυσάμενοι τὸν νέον τὸν ἀνακαινού-
μενον εἰς ἐπίγνωσιν κατ᾽ εἰκόνα τοῦ
κτίσαντος αὐτόν, 11 ὅπου οὐκ ἔνι Ἕλλην
καὶ Ἰουδαῖος, περιτομὴ καὶ ἀκροβυστία,
βάρβαρος, Σκύθης, δοῦλος, ἐλεύθερος,
ἀλλὰ [τὰ] πάντα καὶ ἐν πᾶσιν Χριστός.

1 Tim 1:12–16

Χάριν ἔχω τῷ ἐνδυναμώσαντί με Χρι-
στῷ Ἰησοῦ τῷ κυρίῳ ἡμῶν, ὅτι πιστόν
με ἡγήσατο θέμενος εἰς διακονίαν 13 τὸ
πρότερον ὄντα βλάσφημον καὶ διώκτην
καὶ ὑβριστήν, ἀλλὰ ἠλεήθην, ὅτι ἀγνοῶν
ἐποίησα ἐν ἀπιστίᾳ· 14 ὑπερεπλεόνασεν
δὲ ἡ χάρις τοῦ κυρίου ἡμῶν μετὰ πί-
στεως καὶ ἀγάπης τῆς ἐν Χριστῷ Ἰησοῦ.
15 πιστὸς ὁ λόγος καὶ πάσης ἀποδοχῆς
ἄξιος, ὅτι Χριστὸς Ἰησοῦς ἦλθεν εἰς τὸν
κόσμον ἁμαρτωλοὺς σῶσαι, ὧν πρῶτός
εἰμι ἐγώ. 16 ἀλλὰ διὰ τοῦτο ἠλεήθην,
ἵνα ἐν ἐμοὶ πρώτῳ ἐνδείξηται Χριστὸς
Ἰησοῦς τὴν ἅπασαν μακροθυμίαν πρὸς
ὑποτύπωσιν τῶν μελλόντων πιστεύειν
ἐπ᾽ αὐτῷ εἰς ζωὴν αἰώνιον.

Titus 3:3–7

Ἦμεν γάρ ποτε καὶ ἡμεῖς ἀνόητοι, ἀπει-
θεῖς, πλανώμενοι, δουλεύοντες ἐπιθυμί-
αις καὶ ἡδοναῖς ποικίλαις, ἐν κακίᾳ καὶ
φθόνῳ διάγοντες, στυγητοί, μισοῦντες
ἀλλήλους. 4 ὅτε δὲ ἡ χρηστότης καὶ ἡ φι-
λανθρωπία ἐπεφάνη τοῦ σωτῆρος ἡμῶν
θεοῦ, 5 οὐκ ἐξ ἔργων τῶν ἐν δικαιοσύνῃ
ἃ ἐποιήσαμεν ἡμεῖς ἀλλὰ κατὰ τὸ αὐτοῦ
ἔλεος ἔσωσεν ἡμᾶς διὰ λουτροῦ παλιγ-
γενεσίας καὶ ἀνακαινώσεως πνεύματος
ἁγίου, 6 οὗ ἐξέχεεν ἐφ᾽ ἡμᾶς πλουσίως
διὰ Ἰησοῦ Χριστοῦ τοῦ σωτῆρος ἡμῶν,
7 ἵνα δικαιωθέντες τῇ ἐκείνου χάριτι
κληρονόμοι γενηθῶμεν κατ᾽ ἐλπίδα
ζωῆς αἰωνίου.

Phlm 10–11

παρακαλῶ σε περὶ τοῦ ἐμοῦ τέκνου, ὃν
ἐγέννησα ἐν τοῖς δεσμοῖς, Ὀνήσιμον,
11 τόν ποτέ σοι ἄχρηστον νυνὶ δὲ [καὶ]
σοὶ καὶ ἐμοὶ εὔχρηστον

Cf. Rom 5:6–11; 6:1–4; 7:4–6; 1 Cor 7:17–24; Gal 2:19–20; Acts 9:1–22; 19:18–19; 22:1–16; 26:9–23.

73. Joy in the Lord

Rom 12:12

τῇ ἐλπίδι χαίροντες, τῇ θλίψει ὑπομένον-
τες, τῇ προσευχῇ προσκαρτεροῦντες

Rom 14:17

οὐ γάρ ἐστιν ἡ βασιλεία τοῦ θεοῦ βρῶσις
καὶ πόσις ἀλλὰ δικαιοσύνη καὶ εἰρήνη
καὶ χαρὰ ἐν πνεύματι ἁγίῳ

Rom 15:8–13

λέγω γὰρ Χριστὸν διάκονον γεγενῆσθαι
περιτομῆς ὑπὲρ ἀληθείας θεοῦ, εἰς τὸ βε

§ 72 **Eph 2:5** ***τω Χριστω*** ℵ A D 1739. 1881 *Byz*] εν τω Χριστω 𝔓^{46} B 33 **Col 1:22** ***αποκατηλλαξεν*** ℵ A C D^{2} 048. 1739. 1881 *Byz*] αποκατηλλαγητε (𝔓^{46}) B ¦ αποκαταλλαγεντες D* ¦ αποκατηλλακται 33 **Col 2:13** ***υμας*** ℵ* A C 1739. 1881] ημας 𝔓^{46} B 33 ¦ *om.* ℵ^{2} D *Byz* **Col 3:6** ***επι τους υιους της απειθειας*** ℵ A C D I 33. 1739. 1881 *Byz*] *om.* 𝔓^{46} B

flesh and senses, and we were by nature children of wrath, like everyone else. 4 But God, who is rich in mercy, out of the great love with which he loved us 5 even when we were dead through our trespasses, made us alive together with Christ[b]—by grace you have been saved— 6 and raised us up with him and seated us with him in the heavenly places in Christ Jesus, 7 so that in the ages to come he might show the immeasurable riches of his grace in kindness toward us in Christ Jesus.

Eph 2:11–13

So then, remember that at one time you Gentiles by birth, called "the uncircumcision" by those who are called "the circumcision"—a physical circumcision made in the flesh by human hands— 12 remember that you were at that time without Christ, being aliens from the commonwealth of Israel, and strangers to the covenants of promise, having no hope and without God in the world. 13 But now in Christ Jesus you who once were far off have been brought near by the blood of Christ.

Eph 2:19–20

So then you are no longer strangers and aliens, but you are citizens with the saints and also members of the household of God, 20 built upon the foundation of the apostles and prophets, with Christ Jesus himself as the cornerstone.

Eph 5:8

For once you were darkness, but now in the Lord you are light. Live as children of light

Col 1:21–23

And you who were once estranged and hostile in mind, doing evil deeds, 22 he has now reconciled[c] in his fleshly body through death, so as to present you holy and blameless and irreproachable before him— 23 provided that you continue securely established and steadfast in the faith, without shifting from the hope promised by the gospel that you heard, which has been proclaimed to every creature under heaven. I, Paul, became a servant of this gospel.

Col 2:12–13

when you were buried with him in baptism, you were also raised with him through faith in the power of God, who raised him from the dead. 13 And when you were dead in trespasses and the uncircumcision of your flesh, God made you[d] alive together with him, when he forgave us all our trespasses

Col 3:5–11

Put to death, therefore, whatever in you is earthly: fornication, impurity, passion, evil desire, and greed (which is idolatry). 6 On account of these the wrath of God is coming on those who are disobedient.[e] 7 These are the ways you also once followed, when you were living that life. 8 But now you must get rid of all such things—anger, wrath, malice, slander, and abusive language from your mouth. 9 Do not lie to one another, seeing that you have stripped off the old humanity[f] with its practices 10 and have clothed yourselves with the new humanity,[f] which is being renewed in knowledge according to the image of its creator. 11 In that renewal there is no longer Greek and Jew, circumcised and uncircumcised, barbarian, Scythian, slave and free; but Christ is all and in all!

1 Tim 1:12–16

I am grateful to Christ Jesus our Lord, who has strengthened me, because he judged me faithful and appointed me to his service, 13 even though I was formerly a blasphemer, a persecutor, and a man of violence. But I received mercy because I had acted ignorantly in unbelief, 14 and the grace of our Lord overflowed for me with the faith and love that are in Christ Jesus. 15 The saying is sure and worthy of full acceptance, that Christ Jesus came into the world to save sinners—of whom I am the foremost. 16 But for that very reason I received mercy, so that in me, as the foremost, Jesus Christ might display the utmost patience, making me an example to those who would come to believe in him for eternal life.

Titus 3:3–7

For we ourselves were once foolish, disobedient, led astray, slaves to various passions and pleasures, passing our days in malice and envy, despicable, hating one another. 4 But when the goodness and loving kindness of God our Savior appeared, 5 he saved us, not because of any works of righteousness that we had done, but according to his mercy, through the water of rebirth and renewal by the Holy Spirit. 6 This Spirit he poured out on us richly through Jesus Christ our Savior, 7 so that, having been justified by his grace, we might become heirs according to the hope of eternal life.

Phlm 10–11

I am appealing to you for my child, Onesimus, whose father I have become during my imprisonment. 11 Formerly he was useless to you, but now he is indeed useful both to you and to me.

Cf. Rom 5:6–11; 6:1–4; 7:4–6; 1 Cor 7:17–24; Gal 2:19–20; Acts 9:1–22; 19:18–19; 22:1–16; 26:9–23.

73. Joy in the Lord

Rom 12:12

Rejoice in hope, be patient in suffering, persevere in prayer.

Rom 14:17

For the kingdom of God is not food and drink but righteousness and peace and joy in the Holy Spirit.

Rom 15:8–13

For I tell you that Christ has become a servant of the circumcised on behalf of the truth of God in order that he might

[b] **Eph 2:5** ***together with Christ*** Other ancient authorities read *in Christ* [c] **Col 1:22** ***he has now reconciled*** Other ancient authorities read *you have now been reconciled* [d] **Col 2:13** ***made you*** Other ancient authorities read *made us*; others, *made* [e] **Col 3:6** ***on those who are disobedient*** Other ancient authorities lack *on those who are disobedient* [f] **Col 3:9–10** ***humanity*** NRSV translates *self*

βαιῶσαι τὰς ἐπαγγελίας τῶν πατέρων, 9 τὰ
δὲ ἔθνη ὑπὲρ ἐλέους δοξάσαι τὸν θεόν,
καθὼς γέγραπται· διὰ τοῦτο ἐξομολογήσο-
μαί σοι ἐν ἔθνεσιν καὶ τῷ ὀνόματί σου
ψαλῶ. 10 καὶ πάλιν λέγει· εὐφράνθητε,
ἔθνη, μετὰ τοῦ λαοῦ αὐτοῦ. 11 καὶ πάλιν·
αἰνεῖτε, πάντα τὰ ἔθνη, τὸν κύριον καὶ
ἐπαινεσάτωσαν αὐτὸν πάντες οἱ λαοί.
12 καὶ πάλιν Ἠσαΐας λέγει· ἔσται ἡ ῥίζα
τοῦ Ἰεσσαὶ καὶ ὁ ἀνιστάμενος ἄρχειν
ἐθνῶν, ἐπ' αὐτῷ ἔθνη ἐλπιοῦσιν. 13 Ὁ
δὲ θεὸς τῆς ἐλπίδος πληρώσαι ὑμᾶς πά-
σης χαρᾶς καὶ εἰρήνης ἐν τῷ πιστεύειν,
εἰς τὸ περισσεύειν ὑμᾶς ἐν τῇ ἐλπίδι ἐν
δυνάμει πνεύματος ἁγίου.

2 Cor 1:24

οὐχ ὅτι κυριεύομεν ὑμῶν τῆς πίστεως ἀλλὰ συνεργοί ἐσμεν τῆς χαρᾶς ὑμῶν· τῇ γὰρ πίστει ἑστήκατε.

2 Cor 6:10

ὡς λυπούμενοι ἀεὶ δὲ χαίροντες, ὡς πτωχοὶ πολλοὺς δὲ πλουτίζοντες, ὡς μηδὲν ἔχοντες καὶ πάντα κατέχοντες.

2 Cor 8:2

ὅτι ἐν πολλῇ δοκιμῇ θλίψεως ἡ περισσεία τῆς χαρᾶς αὐτῶν καὶ ἡ κατὰ βάθους πτωχεία αὐτῶν ἐπερίσσευσεν εἰς τὸ πλοῦτος τῆς ἁπλότητος αὐτῶν

Gal 5:22–23

ὁ δὲ καρπὸς τοῦ πνεύματός ἐστιν ἀγάπη
χαρὰ εἰρήνη, μακροθυμία χρηστότης
ἀγαθωσύνη, πίστις 23 πραΰτης ἐγκράτεια·
κατὰ τῶν τοιούτων οὐκ ἔστιν νόμος.

Eph 5:18–20

καὶ μὴ μεθύσκεσθε οἴνῳ, ἐν ᾧ ἐστιν
ἀσωτία, ἀλλὰ πληροῦσθε ἐν πνεύματι,
19 λαλοῦντες ἑαυτοῖς [ἐν] ψαλμοῖς καὶ
ὕμνοις καὶ ᾠδαῖς πνευματικαῖς, ᾄδον-
τες καὶ ψάλλοντες τῇ καρδίᾳ ὑμῶν τῷ
κυρίῳ, 20 εὐχαριστοῦντες πάντοτε ὑπὲρ
πάντων ἐν ὀνόματι τοῦ κυρίου ἡμῶν
Ἰησοῦ Χριστοῦ τῷ θεῷ καὶ πατρί.

Phil 1:18a

Τί γάρ; πλὴν ὅτι παντὶ τρόπῳ, εἴτε προφάσει εἴτε ἀληθείᾳ, Χριστὸς καταγγέλλεται, καὶ ἐν τούτῳ χαίρω.

Phil 1:25

καὶ τοῦτο πεποιθὼς οἶδα ὅτι μενῶ καὶ παραμενῶ πᾶσιν ὑμῖν εἰς τὴν ὑμῶν προκοπὴν καὶ χαρὰν τῆς πίστεως

Phil 2:17–18

Ἀλλὰ εἰ καὶ σπένδομαι ἐπὶ τῇ θυσίᾳ καὶ
λειτουργίᾳ τῆς πίστεως ὑμῶν, χαίρω καὶ
συγχαίρω πᾶσιν ὑμῖν· 18 τὸ δὲ αὐτὸ καὶ
ὑμεῖς χαίρετε καὶ συγχαίρετέ μοι.

Phil 3:1a

Τὸ λοιπόν, ἀδελφοί μου, χαίρετε ἐν κυρίῳ.

Phil 4:1

Ὥστε, ἀδελφοί μου ἀγαπητοὶ καὶ ἐπιπόθητοι, χαρὰ καὶ στέφανός μου, οὕτως στήκετε ἐν κυρίῳ, ἀγαπητοί.

Phil 4:4–7

Χαίρετε ἐν κυρίῳ πάντοτε· πάλιν ἐρῶ,
χαίρετε. 5 τὸ ἐπιεικὲς ὑμῶν γνωσθήτω
πᾶσιν ἀνθρώποις. ὁ κύριος ἐγγύς. 6 μηδὲν
μεριμνᾶτε, ἀλλ' ἐν παντὶ τῇ προσευχῇ καὶ
τῇ δεήσει μετὰ εὐχαριστίας τὰ αἰτήματα
ὑμῶν γνωριζέσθω πρὸς τὸν θεόν. 7 καὶ
ἡ εἰρήνη τοῦ θεοῦ ἡ ὑπερέχουσα πάντα
νοῦν φρουρήσει τὰς καρδίας ὑμῶν καὶ τὰ
νοήματα ὑμῶν ἐν Χριστῷ Ἰησοῦ.

Col 1:11–12

ἐν πάσῃ δυνάμει δυναμούμενοι κατὰ
τὸ κράτος τῆς δόξης αὐτοῦ εἰς πᾶσαν
ὑπομονὴν καὶ μακροθυμίαν. Μετὰ
χαρᾶς 12 εὐχαριστοῦντες τῷ πατρὶ τῷ
⸀ἱκανώσαντι ⸀ὑμᾶς εἰς τὴν μερίδα τοῦ
κλήρου τῶν ἁγίων ἐν τῷ φωτί

Col 3:15–17

καὶ ἡ εἰρήνη τοῦ Χριστοῦ βραβευέτω ἐν
ταῖς καρδίαις ὑμῶν, εἰς ἣν καὶ ἐκλήθητε
ἐν ἑνὶ σώματι· καὶ εὐχάριστοι γίνεσθε.
16 Ὁ λόγος τοῦ ⸀Χριστοῦ ἐνοικείτω ἐν
ὑμῖν πλουσίως, ἐν πάσῃ σοφίᾳ διδά-
σκοντες καὶ νουθετοῦντες ἑαυτούς,
ψαλμοῖς ὕμνοις ᾠδαῖς πνευματικαῖς
ἐν [τῇ] χάριτι ᾄδοντες ἐν ταῖς καρδίαις
ὑμῶν τῷ ⸀θεῷ· 17 καὶ πᾶν ὅ τι ἐὰν ποιῆτε
ἐν λόγῳ ἢ ἐν ἔργῳ, πάντα ἐν ὀνόματι
κυρίου Ἰησοῦ, εὐχαριστοῦντες τῷ θεῷ
πατρὶ δι' αὐτοῦ.

1 Thess 1:6–7

Καὶ ὑμεῖς μιμηταὶ ἡμῶν ἐγενήθητε καὶ
τοῦ κυρίου, δεξάμενοι τὸν λόγον ἐν
θλίψει πολλῇ μετὰ χαρᾶς πνεύματος
ἁγίου, 7 ὥστε γενέσθαι ὑμᾶς τύπον πᾶ-
σιν τοῖς πιστεύουσιν ἐν τῇ Μακεδονίᾳ
καὶ ἐν τῇ Ἀχαΐᾳ.

1 Thess 2:19–20

τίς γὰρ ἡμῶν ἐλπὶς ἢ χαρὰ ἢ στέφανος
καυχήσεως—ἢ οὐχὶ καὶ ὑμεῖς—ἔμπροσ-
θεν τοῦ κυρίου ἡμῶν Ἰησοῦ ἐν τῇ αὐτοῦ
παρουσίᾳ; 20 ὑμεῖς γάρ ἐστε ἡ δόξα ἡμῶν
καὶ ἡ χαρά.

1 Thess 5:16–18

Πάντοτε χαίρετε, 17 ἀδιαλείπτως προσ-
εύχεσθε, 18 ἐν παντὶ εὐχαριστεῖτε· τοῦτο
γὰρ θέλημα θεοῦ ἐν Χριστῷ Ἰησοῦ εἰς
ὑμᾶς.

Acts 13:48–52

Ἀκούοντα δὲ τὰ ἔθνη ἔχαιρον καὶ ἐδόξαζον
τὸν λόγον τοῦ κυρίου καὶ ἐπίστευσαν
ὅσοι ἦσαν τεταγμένοι εἰς ζωὴν αἰώ-
νιον· 49 διεφέρετο δὲ ὁ λόγος τοῦ κυρίου
δι' ὅλης τῆς χώρας. 50 οἱ δὲ Ἰουδαῖοι
παρώτρυναν τὰς σεβομένας γυναῖκας
τὰς εὐσχήμονας καὶ τοὺς πρώτους τῆς
πόλεως καὶ ἐπήγειραν διωγμὸν ἐπὶ τὸν
Παῦλον καὶ Βαρναβᾶν καὶ ἐξέβαλον
αὐτοὺς ἀπὸ τῶν ὁρίων αὐτῶν. 51 οἱ δὲ
ἐκτιναξάμενοι τὸν κονιορτὸν τῶν ποδῶν
ἐπ' αὐτοὺς ἦλθον εἰς Ἰκόνιον, 52 οἵ τε
μαθηταὶ ἐπληροῦντο χαρᾶς καὶ πνεύ-
ματος ἁγίου.

Acts 16:34

ἀναγαγών τε αὐτοὺς εἰς τὸν οἶκον παρέθηκεν τράπεζαν καὶ ἠγαλλιάσατο πανοικεὶ πεπιστευκὼς τῷ θεῷ.

Cf. Rom 15:32; 2 Cor 7:2–4; 13:11; Phil 1:3–5; 2:2; 2:29–30; Col 1:24; 1 Thess 3:9.

See also the expressions of joy within the Pauline epistolary thanksgivings, in § 2 Thanksgiving.

§ 73 **Col 1:12** ***ικανωσαντι*** 𝔓^{46} 𝔓^{61vid} ℵ A C D^{2} I 1739. 1881 *Byz*] καλεσαντι D* 33 ¦ καλεσαντι και ικανωσαντι B • ***υμας*** ℵ B 1739. 1881] ημας A C D 33 *Byz* **Col 3:16** ***Χριστου*** 𝔓^{46} ℵ^{2} B C^{2} D 1739. 1881 *Byz*] κυριου ℵ* I ¦ θεου A C* 33 • ***θεω*** 𝔓^{46vid} ℵ A B C* D* 33. 1739. 1881] κυριω C^{2} D^{2} *Byz*

confirm the promises given to the patriarchs, **9** and in order that the Gentiles might glorify God for his mercy. As it is written, "Therefore I will confess you among the Gentiles, and sing praises to your name"; **10** and again he says, "Rejoice, O Gentiles, with his people"; **11** and again, "Praise the Lord, all you Gentiles, and let all the peoples praise him"; **12** and again Isaiah says, "The root of Jesse shall come, the one who rises to rule the Gentiles; in him the Gentiles shall hope." **13** May the God of hope fill you with all joy and peace in believing, so that you may abound in hope by the power of the Holy Spirit.

2 Cor 1:24

I do not mean to imply that we lord it over your faith; rather, we are workers with you for your joy, because you stand firm in the faith.

2 Cor 6:10

as sorrowful, yet always rejoicing; as poor, yet making many rich; as having nothing, and yet possessing everything.

2 Cor 8:2

for during a severe ordeal of affliction, their abundant joy and their extreme poverty have overflowed in a wealth of generosity on their part.

Gal 5:22–23

By contrast, the fruit of the Spirit is love, joy, peace, patience, kindness, generosity, faithfulness, **23** gentleness, and self-control. There is no law against such things.

Eph 5:18–20

Do not get drunk with wine, for that is debauchery; but be filled with the Spirit, **19** as you sing psalms and hymns and spiritual songs among yourselves, singing and making melody to the Lord in your hearts, **20** giving thanks to God the Father at all times and for everything in the name of our Lord Jesus Christ.

Phil 1:18a

What does it matter? Just this, that Christ is proclaimed in every way, whether out of false motives or true; and in that I rejoice.

Phil 1:25

Since I am convinced of this, I know that I will remain and continue with all of you for your progress and joy in faith

Phil 2:17–18

But even if I am being poured out as a libation over the sacrifice and the offering of your faith, I am glad and rejoice with all of you— **18** and in the same way you also must be glad and rejoice with me.

Phil 3:1a

Finally, my brothers and sisters, rejoice in the Lord.

Phil 4:1

Therefore, my brothers and sisters, whom I love and long for, my joy and crown, stand firm in the Lord in this way, my beloved.

Phil 4:4–7

Rejoice in the Lord always; again I will say, Rejoice. **5** Let your gentleness be known to everyone. The Lord is near. **6** Do not worry about anything, but in everything by prayer and supplication with thanksgiving let your requests be made known to God. **7** And the peace of God, which surpasses all understanding, will guard your hearts and your minds in Christ Jesus.

Col 1:11–12

May you be made strong with all the strength that comes from his glorious power, and may you be prepared to endure everything with patience, while joyfully **12** giving thanks to the Father, who has enabled[a] you[b] to share in the inheritance of the saints in the light.

Col 3:15–17

And let the peace of Christ rule in your hearts, to which indeed you were called in the one body. And be thankful. **16** Let the word of Christ[c] dwell in you richly; teach and admonish one another in all wisdom; and with gratitude in your hearts sing psalms, hymns, and spiritual songs to God.[d] **17** And whatever you do, in word or deed, do everything in the name of the Lord Jesus, giving thanks to God the Father through him.

1 Thess 1:6–7

And you became imitators of us and of the Lord, for in spite of persecution you received the word with joy inspired by the Holy Spirit, **7** so that you became an example to all the believers in Macedonia and in Achaia.

1 Thess 2:19–20

For what is our hope or joy or crown of boasting before our Lord Jesus at his coming? Is it not you? **20** Yes, you are our glory and joy!

1 Thess 5:16–18

Rejoice always, **17** pray without ceasing, **18** give thanks in all circumstances; for this is the will of God in Christ Jesus for you.

Acts 13:48–52

When the Gentiles heard this, they were glad and praised the word of the Lord; and as many as had been destined for eternal life became believers. **49** Thus the word of the Lord spread throughout the region. **50** But the Jews incited the devout women of high standing and the leading men of the city, and stirred up persecution against Paul and Barnabas, and drove them out of their region. **51** So they shook the dust off their feet in protest against them, and went to Iconium. **52** And the disciples were filled with joy and with the Holy Spirit.

Acts 16:34

He brought them up into the house and set food before them; and he and his entire household rejoiced that he had become a believer in God.

Cf. Rom 15:32; 2 Cor 7:2–4; 13:11; Phil 1:3–5; 2:2; 2:29–30; Col 1:24; 1 Thess 3:9.

See also the expressions of joy within the Pauline epistolary thanksgivings, in § 2 Thanksgiving.

§ 73 [a] **Col 1:12** *enabled* Other ancient authorities read *called* [b] **Col 1:12** *you* Other ancient authorities read *us* [c] **Col 3:16** *of Christ* Other ancient authorities read *of God,* or *of the Lord* [d] **Col 3:16** *to God* Other ancient authorities read *to the Lord*

74. The Peace of God

Rom 14:17

οὐ γάρ ἐστιν ἡ βασιλεία τοῦ θεοῦ βρῶσις καὶ πόσις ἀλλὰ δικαιοσύνη καὶ εἰρήνη καὶ χαρὰ ἐν πνεύματι ἁγίῳ

Rom 15:13

Ὁ δὲ θεὸς τῆς ἐλπίδος πληρώσαι ὑμᾶς πάσης χαρᾶς καὶ εἰρήνης ἐν τῷ πιστεύειν, εἰς τὸ περισσεύειν ὑμᾶς ἐν τῇ ἐλπίδι ἐν δυνάμει πνεύματος ἁγίου.

1 Cor 14:32–33a

καὶ πνεύματα προφητῶν προφήταις ὑποτάσσεται, **33** οὐ γάρ ἐστιν ἀκαταστασίας ὁ θεὸς ἀλλὰ εἰρήνης.

2 Cor 13:11

Λοιπόν, ἀδελφοί, χαίρετε, καταρτίζεσθε, παρακαλεῖσθε, τὸ αὐτὸ φρονεῖτε, εἰρηνεύετε, καὶ ὁ θεὸς τῆς ἀγάπης καὶ εἰρήνης ἔσται μεθ᾿ ὑμῶν.

Eph 2:14–18

Αὐτὸς γάρ ἐστιν ἡ εἰρήνη ἡμῶν, ὁ ποιήσας τὰ ἀμφότερα ἓν καὶ τὸ μεσότοιχον τοῦ φραγμοῦ λύσας, τὴν ἔχθραν ἐν τῇ σαρκὶ αὐτοῦ, **15** τὸν νόμον τῶν ἐντολῶν ἐν δόγμασιν καταργήσας, ἵνα τοὺς δύο κτίσῃ ἐν αὐτῷ εἰς ἕνα καινὸν ἄνθρωπον ποιῶν εἰρήνην **16** καὶ ἀποκαταλλάξῃ τοὺς ἀμφοτέρους ἐν ἑνὶ σώματι τῷ θεῷ διὰ τοῦ σταυροῦ, ἀποκτείνας τὴν ἔχθραν ἐν αὐτῷ. **17** καὶ ἐλθὼν εὐηγγελίσατο εἰρήνην ὑμῖν τοῖς μακρὰν καὶ εἰρήνην τοῖς ἐγγύς· **18** ὅτι δι᾿ αὐτοῦ ἔχομεν τὴν προσαγωγὴν οἱ ἀμφότεροι ἐν ἑνὶ πνεύματι πρὸς τὸν πατέρα.

Phil 4:4–9

Χαίρετε ἐν κυρίῳ πάντοτε· πάλιν ἐρῶ, χαίρετε. **5** τὸ ἐπιεικὲς ὑμῶν γνωσθήτω πᾶσιν ἀνθρώποις. ὁ κύριος ἐγγύς. **6** μηδὲν μεριμνᾶτε, ἀλλ᾿ ἐν παντὶ τῇ προσευχῇ καὶ τῇ δεήσει μετὰ εὐχαριστίας τὰ αἰτήματα ὑμῶν γνωριζέσθω πρὸς τὸν θεόν. **7** καὶ ἡ εἰρήνη τοῦ θεοῦ ἡ ὑπερέχουσα πάντα νοῦν φρουρήσει τὰς καρδίας ὑμῶν καὶ τὰ νοήματα ὑμῶν ἐν Χριστῷ Ἰησοῦ. **8** Τὸ λοιπόν, ἀδελφοί, ὅσα ἐστὶν ἀληθῆ, ὅσα σεμνά, ὅσα δίκαια, ὅσα ἁγνά, ὅσα προσφιλῆ, ὅσα εὔφημα, εἴ τις ἀρετὴ καὶ εἴ τις ἔπαινος, ταῦτα λογίζεσθε· **9** ἃ καὶ ἐμάθετε καὶ παρελάβετε καὶ ἠκούσατε καὶ εἴδετε ἐν ἐμοί, ταῦτα πράσσετε· καὶ ὁ θεὸς τῆς εἰρήνης ἔσται μεθ᾿ ὑμῶν.

Col 1:19–20

ὅτι ἐν αὐτῷ εὐδόκησεν πᾶν τὸ πλήρωμα κατοικῆσαι **20** καὶ δι᾿ αὐτοῦ ἀποκαταλλάξαι τὰ πάντα εἰς αὐτόν, εἰρηνοποιήσας διὰ τοῦ αἵματος τοῦ σταυροῦ αὐτοῦ, [δι᾿ αὐτοῦ] εἴτε τὰ ἐπὶ τῆς γῆς εἴτε τὰ ἐν τοῖς οὐρανοῖς.

Col 3:15

καὶ ἡ εἰρήνη τοῦ Χριστοῦ βραβευέτω ἐν ταῖς καρδίαις ὑμῶν, εἰς ἣν καὶ ἐκλήθητε ἐν ἑνὶ σώματι· καὶ εὐχάριστοι γίνεσθε.

2 Thess 3:16

Αὐτὸς δὲ ὁ κύριος τῆς εἰρήνης δῴη ὑμῖν τὴν εἰρήνην διὰ παντὸς ἐν παντὶ ⸀τρόπῳ. ὁ κύριος μετὰ πάντων ὑμῶν.

Cf. Rom 5:1; 15:33; 16:17–20; 1 Cor 7:15; Eph 4:1–3; 1 Thess 5:12–13; 5:23–24.

For the "peace wish" with which Paul regularly opens his letters, see also § 1 Salutation.

75. Sanctification

Rom 6:17–23

χάρις δὲ τῷ θεῷ ὅτι ἦτε δοῦλοι τῆς ἁμαρτίας ὑπηκούσατε δὲ ἐκ καρδίας εἰς ὃν παρεδόθητε τύπον διδαχῆς, **18** ἐλευθερωθέντες δὲ ἀπὸ τῆς ἁμαρτίας ἐδουλώθητε τῇ δικαιοσύνῃ. **19** Ἀνθρώπινον λέγω διὰ τὴν ἀσθένειαν τῆς σαρκὸς ὑμῶν. ὥσπερ γὰρ παρεστήσατε τὰ μέλη ὑμῶν δοῦλα τῇ ἀκαθαρσίᾳ καὶ τῇ ἀνομίᾳ εἰς τὴν ἀνομίαν, οὕτως νῦν παραστήσατε τὰ μέλη ὑμῶν δοῦλα τῇ δικαιοσύνῃ εἰς ἁγιασμόν. **20** ὅτε γὰρ δοῦλοι ἦτε τῆς ἁμαρτίας, ἐλεύθεροι ἦτε τῇ δικαιοσύνῃ. **21** τίνα οὖν καρπὸν εἴχετε τότε; ἐφ᾿ οἷς νῦν ἐπαισχύνεσθε, τὸ γὰρ τέλος ἐκείνων θάνατος. **22** νυνὶ δὲ ἐλευθερωθέντες ἀπὸ τῆς ἁμαρτίας δουλωθέντες δὲ τῷ θεῷ ἔχετε τὸν καρπὸν ὑμῶν εἰς ἁγιασμόν, τὸ δὲ τέλος ζωὴν αἰώνιον. **23** τὰ γὰρ ὀψώνια τῆς ἁμαρτίας θάνατος, τὸ δὲ χάρισμα τοῦ θεοῦ ζωὴ αἰώνιος ἐν Χριστῷ Ἰησοῦ τῷ κυρίῳ ἡμῶν.

1 Cor 1:2

τῇ ἐκκλησίᾳ τοῦ θεοῦ τῇ οὔσῃ ἐν Κορίνθῳ, ἡγιασμένοις ἐν Χριστῷ Ἰησοῦ, κλητοῖς ἁγίοις, σὺν πᾶσιν τοῖς ἐπικαλουμένοις τὸ ὄνομα τοῦ κυρίου ἡμῶν Ἰησοῦ Χριστοῦ ἐν παντὶ τόπῳ, αὐτῶν καὶ ἡμῶν

1 Cor 1:30–31

ἐξ αὐτοῦ δὲ ὑμεῖς ἐστε ἐν Χριστῷ Ἰησοῦ, ὃς ἐγενήθη σοφία ἡμῖν ἀπὸ θεοῦ, δικαιοσύνη τε καὶ ἁγιασμὸς καὶ ἀπολύτρωσις, **31** ἵνα καθὼς γέγραπται· ὁ καυχώμενος ἐν κυρίῳ καυχάσθω.

1 Cor 6:11

καὶ ταῦτά τινες ἦτε· ἀλλὰ ἀπελούσασθε, ἀλλὰ ἡγιάσθητε, ἀλλὰ ἐδικαιώθητε ἐν τῷ ὀνόματι τοῦ κυρίου ⸂Ἰησοῦ Χριστοῦ⸃ καὶ ἐν τῷ πνεύματι τοῦ θεοῦ ἡμῶν.

Eph 5:25–27

Οἱ ἄνδρες, ἀγαπᾶτε τὰς γυναῖκας, καθὼς καὶ ὁ Χριστὸς ἠγάπησεν τὴν ἐκκλησίαν καὶ ἑαυτὸν παρέδωκεν ὑπὲρ αὐτῆς, **26** ἵνα αὐτὴν ἁγιάσῃ καθαρίσας τῷ λουτρῷ τοῦ ὕδατος ἐν ῥήματι, **27** ἵνα παραστήσῃ αὐτὸς ἑαυτῷ ἔνδοξον τὴν ἐκκλησίαν, μὴ ἔχουσαν σπίλον ἢ ῥυτίδα ἤ τι τῶν τοιούτων, ἀλλ᾿ ἵνα ᾖ ἁγία καὶ ἄμωμος.

1 Thess 4:3–8

Τοῦτο γάρ ἐστιν θέλημα τοῦ θεοῦ, ὁ ἁγιασμὸς ὑμῶν, ἀπέχεσθαι ὑμᾶς ἀπὸ

§ 74 **2 Thess 3:16** ***τροπω*** ℵ A^c B D^2 1739. 1881 *Byz*] τοπω A* D* 33 **§ 75** **1 Cor 6:11** ***Ιησου Χριστου*** $\mathfrak{P}^{11vid}$ $\mathfrak{P}^{46}$ ℵ D*] Ιησου A D^2 *Byz* ¦ ημων Ιησου Χριστου B C^{vid} 33. 1739. 1881

74. The Peace of God

Rom 14:17

For the kingdom of God is not food and drink but righteousness and peace and joy in the Holy Spirit.

Rom 15:13

May the God of hope fill you with all joy and peace in believing, so that you may abound in hope by the power of the Holy Spirit.

1 Cor 14:32–33a

And the spirits of prophets are subject to the prophets, **33** for God is a God not of disorder but of peace.

2 Cor 13:11

Finally, brothers and sisters, farewell. Put things in order, listen to my appeal, agree with one another, live in peace; and the God of love and peace will be with you.

Eph 2:14–18

For he is our peace; in his flesh he has made both groups into one and has broken down the dividing wall, that is, the hostility between us. **15** He has abolished the law with its commandments and ordinances, that he might create in himself one new humanity in place of the two, thus making peace, **16** and might reconcile both groups to God in one body through the cross, thus putting to death that hostility through it. **17** So he came and proclaimed peace to you who were far off and peace to those who were near; **18** for through him both of us have access in one Spirit to the Father.

Phil 4:4–9

Rejoice in the Lord always; again I will say, Rejoice. **5** Let your gentleness be known to everyone. The Lord is near. **6** Do not worry about anything, but in everything by prayer and supplication with thanksgiving let your requests be made known to God. **7** And the peace of God, which surpasses all understanding, will guard your hearts and your minds in Christ Jesus. **8** Finally, beloved, whatever is true, whatever is honorable, whatever is just, whatever is pure, whatever is pleasing, whatever is commendable, if there is any excellence and if there is anything worthy of praise, think about these things. **9** Keep on doing the things that you have learned and received and heard and seen in me, and the God of peace will be with you.

Col 1:19–20

For in him all the fullness of God was pleased to dwell, **20** and through him God was pleased to reconcile to himself all things, whether on earth or in heaven, by making peace through the blood of his cross.

Col 3:15

And let the peace of Christ rule in your hearts, to which indeed you were called in the one body. And be thankful.

2 Thess 3:16

Now may the Lord of peace himself give you peace at all times in all ways.[a] The Lord be with all of you.

Cf. Rom 5:1; 15:33; 16:17–20; 1 Cor 7:15; Eph 4:1–3; 1 Thess 5:12–13; 5:23–24.

For the "peace wish" with which Paul regularly opens his letters, see also § 1 Salutation.

75. Sanctification

Rom 6:17–23

But thanks be to God that you, having once been slaves of sin, have become obedient from the heart to the form of teaching to which you were entrusted, **18** and that you, having been set free from sin, have become slaves of righteousness. **19** I am speaking in human terms because of your natural limitations. For just as you once presented your members as slaves to impurity and to greater and greater iniquity, so now present your members as slaves to righteousness for sanctification. **20** When you were slaves of sin, you were free in regard to righteousness. **21** So what fruit did you have then? Because of these things you are now ashamed, because the end of those things is death. **22** But now that you have been freed from sin and enslaved to God, the fruit you get is sanctification, and the end is eternal life.[a] **23** For the wages of sin is death, but the free gift of God is eternal life in Christ Jesus our Lord.

1 Cor 1:2

To the church of God that is in Corinth, to those who are sanctified in Christ Jesus, called to be saints, together with all those who in every place call on the name of our Lord Jesus Christ, both their Lord and ours

1 Cor 1:30–31

He is the source of your life in Christ Jesus, who became for us wisdom from God, and righteousness and sanctification and redemption, **31** in order that, as it is written, "Let the one who boasts, boast in the Lord."

1 Cor 6:11

And this is what some of you used to be. But you were washed, you were sanctified, you were justified in the name of the Lord Jesus Christ[b] and in the Spirit of our God.

Eph 5:25–27

Husbands, love your wives, just as Christ loved the church and gave himself up for her, **26** in order to make her holy by cleansing her with the washing of water by the word, **27** so as to present the church to himself in splendor, without a spot or wrinkle or anything of the kind—yes, so that she may be holy and without blemish.

1 Thess 4:3–8

For this is the will of God, your sanctification: that you abstain from fornica-

§ 74 [a] **2 Thess 3:16** *ways* Other ancient authorities read *places* **§ 75** [a] **Rom 6:21–22** Translation differs from NRSV [b] **1 Cor 6:11** *the Lord Jesus Christ* Other ancient authorities read *the Lord Jesus* or *our Lord Jesus Christ*

τῆς πορνείας, 4 εἰδέναι ἕκαστον ὑμῶν τὸ ἑαυτοῦ σκεῦος κτᾶσθαι ἐν ἁγιασμῷ καὶ τιμῇ, 5 μὴ ἐν πάθει ἐπιθυμίας καθάπερ καὶ τὰ ἔθνη τὰ μὴ εἰδότα τὸν θεόν, 6 τὸ μὴ ὑπερβαίνειν καὶ πλεονεκτεῖν ἐν τῷ πράγματι τὸν ἀδελφὸν αὐτοῦ, διότι ἔκδικος κύριος περὶ πάντων τούτων, καθὼς καὶ προείπαμεν ὑμῖν καὶ διεμαρτυράμεθα. 7 οὐ γὰρ ἐκάλεσεν ἡμᾶς ὁ θεὸς ἐπὶ ἀκαθαρσίᾳ ἀλλ᾽ ἐν ἁγιασμῷ. 8 τοιγαροῦν ὁ ἀθετῶν οὐκ ἄνθρωπον ἀθετεῖ ἀλλὰ τὸν θεὸν τὸν [καὶ] διδόντα τὸ πνεῦμα αὐτοῦ τὸ ἅγιον εἰς ὑμᾶς.

1 Thess 5:23–24

Αὐτὸς δὲ ὁ θεὸς τῆς εἰρήνης ἁγιάσαι ὑμᾶς ὁλοτελεῖς, καὶ ὁλόκληρον ὑμῶν τὸ πνεῦμα καὶ ἡ ψυχὴ καὶ τὸ σῶμα ἀμέμπτως ἐν τῇ παρουσίᾳ τοῦ κυρίου ἡμῶν Ἰησοῦ Χριστοῦ τηρηθείη. 24 πιστὸς ὁ καλῶν ὑμᾶς, ὃς καὶ ποιήσει.

2 Thess 2:13–14

Ἡμεῖς δὲ ὀφείλομεν εὐχαριστεῖν τῷ θεῷ πάντοτε περὶ ὑμῶν, ἀδελφοὶ ἠγαπημένοι ὑπὸ κυρίου, ὅτι εἵλατο ὑμᾶς ὁ θεὸς ⌜ἀπαρχὴν εἰς σωτηρίαν ἐν ἁγιασμῷ πνεύματος καὶ πίστει ἀληθείας, 14 εἰς ὃ [καὶ] ἐκάλεσεν ὑμᾶς διὰ τοῦ εὐαγγελίου ἡμῶν εἰς περιποίησιν δόξης τοῦ κυρίου ἡμῶν Ἰησοῦ Χριστοῦ.

1 Tim 2:15

σωθήσεται δὲ διὰ τῆς τεκνογονίας, ἐὰν μείνωσιν ἐν πίστει καὶ ἀγάπῃ καὶ ἁγιασμῷ μετὰ σωφροσύνης

Acts 20:32

Καὶ τὰ νῦν παρατίθεμαι ὑμᾶς τῷ θεῷ καὶ τῷ λόγῳ τῆς χάριτος αὐτοῦ, τῷ δυναμένῳ οἰκοδομῆσαι καὶ δοῦναι τὴν κληρονομίαν ἐν τοῖς ἡγιασμένοις πᾶσιν.

Acts 26:18

ἀνοῖξαι ὀφθαλμοὺς αὐτῶν, τοῦ ἐπιστρέψαι ἀπὸ σκότους εἰς φῶς καὶ τῆς ἐξουσίας τοῦ σατανᾶ ἐπὶ τὸν θεόν, τοῦ λαβεῖν αὐτοὺς ἄφεσιν ἁμαρτιῶν καὶ κλῆρον ἐν τοῖς ἡγιασμένοις πίστει τῇ εἰς ἐμέ.

Cf. Rom 15:15–16; 1 Cor 1:8–9; 7:14; Col 1:21–23; 1 Thess 3:11–13; 2 Thess 2:16–17; 3:3–5; 2 Tim 2:21.

76. The Supply of the Spirit

Gal 3:5

ὁ οὖν ἐπιχορηγῶν ὑμῖν τὸ πνεῦμα καὶ ἐνεργῶν δυνάμεις ἐν ὑμῖν, ἐξ ἔργων νόμου ἢ ἐξ ἀκοῆς πίστεως;

Eph 4:15–16

ἀληθεύοντες δὲ ἐν ἀγάπῃ αὐξήσωμεν εἰς αὐτὸν τὰ πάντα, ὅς ἐστιν ἡ κεφαλή, Χριστός, 16 ἐξ οὗ πᾶν τὸ σῶμα συναρμολογούμενον καὶ συμβιβαζόμενον διὰ πάσης ἁφῆς τῆς ἐπιχορηγίας κατ᾽ ἐνέργειαν ἐν μέτρῳ ἑνὸς ἑκάστου μέρους τὴν αὔξησιν τοῦ σώματος ποιεῖται εἰς οἰκοδομὴν ἑαυτοῦ ἐν ἀγάπῃ.

Phil 1:19–20

οἶδα γὰρ ὅτι τοῦτό μοι ἀποβήσεται εἰς σωτηρίαν διὰ τῆς ὑμῶν δεήσεως καὶ ἐπιχορηγίας τοῦ πνεύματος Ἰησοῦ Χριστοῦ 20 κατὰ τὴν ἀποκαραδοκίαν καὶ ἐλπίδα μου, ὅτι ἐν οὐδενὶ αἰσχυνθήσομαι ἀλλ᾽ ἐν πάσῃ παρρησίᾳ ὡς πάντοτε καὶ νῦν μεγαλυνθήσεται Χριστὸς ἐν τῷ σώματί μου, εἴτε διὰ ζωῆς εἴτε διὰ θανάτου.

Col 2:19

καὶ οὐ κρατῶν τὴν κεφαλήν, ἐξ οὗ πᾶν τὸ σῶμα διὰ τῶν ἁφῶν καὶ συνδέσμων ἐπιχορηγούμενον καὶ συμβιβαζόμενον αὔξει τὴν αὔξησιν τοῦ θεοῦ.

1 Thess 4:8

τοιγαροῦν ὁ ἀθετῶν οὐκ ἄνθρωπον ἀθετεῖ ἀλλὰ τὸν θεὸν τὸν [καὶ] διδόντα τὸ πνεῦμα αὐτοῦ τὸ ἅγιον εἰς ὑμᾶς.

77. Walking by the Spirit

Rom 8:1–11

Οὐδὲν ἄρα νῦν κατάκριμα τοῖς ἐν Χριστῷ Ἰησοῦ. 2 ὁ γὰρ νόμος τοῦ πνεύματος τῆς ζωῆς ἐν Χριστῷ Ἰησοῦ ἠλευθέρωσέν ⌜σε ἀπὸ τοῦ νόμου τῆς ἁμαρτίας καὶ τοῦ θανάτου. 3 Τὸ γὰρ ἀδύνατον τοῦ νόμου ἐν ᾧ ἠσθένει διὰ τῆς σαρκός, ὁ θεὸς τὸν ἑαυτοῦ υἱὸν πέμψας ἐν ὁμοιώματι σαρκὸς ἁμαρτίας καὶ περὶ ἁμαρτίας κατέκρινεν τὴν ἁμαρτίαν ἐν τῇ σαρκί, 4 ἵνα τὸ δικαίωμα τοῦ νόμου πληρωθῇ ἐν ἡμῖν τοῖς μὴ κατὰ σάρκα περιπατοῦσιν ἀλλὰ κατὰ πνεῦμα. 5 οἱ γὰρ κατὰ σάρκα ὄντες τὰ τῆς σαρκὸς φρονοῦσιν, οἱ δὲ κατὰ πνεῦμα τὰ τοῦ πνεύματος. 6 τὸ γὰρ φρόνημα τῆς σαρκὸς θάνατος, τὸ δὲ φρόνημα τοῦ πνεύματος ζωὴ καὶ εἰρήνη· 7 διότι τὸ φρόνημα τῆς σαρκὸς ἔχθρα εἰς θεόν, τῷ γὰρ νόμῳ τοῦ θεοῦ οὐχ ὑποτάσσεται, οὐδὲ γὰρ δύναται· 8 οἱ δὲ ἐν σαρκὶ ὄντες θεῷ ἀρέσαι οὐ δύνανται. 9 Ὑμεῖς δὲ οὐκ ἐστὲ ἐν σαρκὶ ἀλλὰ ἐν πνεύματι, εἴπερ πνεῦμα θεοῦ οἰκεῖ ἐν ὑμῖν. εἰ δέ τις πνεῦμα Χριστοῦ οὐκ ἔχει, οὗτος οὐκ ἔστιν αὐτοῦ. 10 εἰ δὲ Χριστὸς ἐν ὑμῖν, τὸ μὲν σῶμα νεκρὸν διὰ ἁμαρτίαν τὸ δὲ πνεῦμα ζωὴ διὰ δικαιοσύνην. 11 εἰ δὲ τὸ πνεῦμα τοῦ ἐγείραντος τὸν Ἰησοῦν ἐκ νεκρῶν οἰκεῖ ἐν ὑμῖν, ὁ ἐγείρας ⌜Χριστὸν ἐκ νεκρῶν⌝ ζῳοποιήσει καὶ τὰ θνητὰ σώματα ὑμῶν διὰ ⌜τοῦ ἐνοικοῦντος αὐτοῦ πνεύματος⌝ ἐν ὑμῖν.

2 Thess 2:13 ***απαρχην*** B 33. 1739. 1881] απ αρχης ℵ D *Byz* **§ 77 Rom 8:2** ***σε*** ℵ B 1739*] με A D 1739ᶜ. 1881 *Byz* **Rom 8:11** ***Χριστον εκ νεκρων*** B D²] τον Χ. εκ ν. ℵ² 33 *Byz* ¦ Χ. Ιησουν εκ ν. D* ¦ εκ ν. Χ. Ιησουν ℵ* A (C I. X.) 1739. 1881 • ***του ενοικουντος αυτου πνευματος*** ℵ A C⁽*⁾] το ενοικουν αυτου πνευμα B D 33. 1739. 1881 *Byz*

tion; [4] that each one of you know how to control your own body in holiness and honor, [5] not with lustful passion, like the Gentiles who do not know God; [6] that no one wrong or exploit a brother or sister in this matter, because the Lord is an avenger in all these things, just as we have already told you beforehand and solemnly warned you. [7] For God did not call us to impurity but in holiness. [8] Therefore whoever rejects this rejects not human authority but God, who also gives his Holy Spirit to you.

1 Thess 5:23–24

May the God of peace himself sanctify you entirely; and may your spirit and soul and body be kept sound and blameless at the coming of our Lord Jesus Christ. [24] The one who calls you is faithful, and he will do this.

2 Thess 2:13–14

But we must always give thanks to God for you, brothers and sisters beloved by the Lord, because God chose you as the first fruits[c] for salvation through sanctification by the Spirit and through belief in the truth. [14] For this purpose he called you through our proclamation of the good news, so that you may obtain the glory of our Lord Jesus Christ.

1 Tim 2:15

Yet she will be saved through childbearing, provided they continue in faith and love and holiness, with modesty.

Acts 20:32

And now I commend you to God and to the message of his grace, a message that is able to build you up and to give you the inheritance among all who are sanctified.

Acts 26:18

to open their eyes so that they may turn from darkness to light and from the power of Satan to God, so that they may receive forgiveness of sins and a place among those who are sanctified by faith in me.

Cf. Rom 15:15–16; 1 Cor 1:8–9; 7:14; Col 1:21–23; 1 Thess 3:11–13; 2 Thess 2:16–17; 3:3–5; 2 Tim 2:21.

76. The Supply of the Spirit

Gal 3:5

Well then, does God supply you with the Spirit and work miracles among you by your doing the works of the law, or by your believing what you heard?

Eph 4:15–16

But speaking the truth in love, we must grow up in every way into him who is the head, into Christ, [16] from whom the whole body, joined and knit together by every ligament by which it is supplied,[a] as each part is working properly, promotes the body's growth in building itself up in love.

Phil 1:19–20

for I know that through your prayers and the supply of the Spirit of Jesus Christ this will turn out for my deliverance.[b] [20] It is my eager expectation and hope that I will not be put to shame in any way, but that by my speaking with all boldness, Christ will be exalted now as always in my body, whether by life or by death.

Col 2:19

and not holding fast to the head, from whom the whole body, richly supplied[c] and held together by its ligaments and sinews, grows with a growth that is from God.

1 Thess 4:8

Therefore whoever rejects this rejects not human authority but God, who also gives his Holy Spirit to you.

77. Walking by the Spirit

Rom 8:1–11

There is therefore now no condemnation for those who are in Christ Jesus. [2] For the law of the Spirit of life in Christ Jesus has set you[a] free from the law of sin and of death. [3] For God has done what the law, weakened by the flesh, could not do: by sending his own Son in the likeness of sinful flesh, and to deal with sin, he condemned sin in the flesh, [4] so that the just requirement of the law might be fulfilled in us, who walk not according to the flesh but according to the Spirit. [5] For those who live according to the flesh set their minds on the things of the flesh, but those who live according to the Spirit set their minds on the things of the Spirit. [6] To set the mind on the flesh is death, but to set the mind on the Spirit is life and peace. [7] For this reason the mind that is set on the flesh is hostile to God; it does not submit to God's law—indeed it cannot, [8] and those who are in the flesh cannot please God. [9] But you are not in the flesh; you are in the Spirit, since the Spirit of God dwells in you. Anyone who does not have the Spirit of Christ does not belong to him. [10] But if Christ is in you, though the body is dead because of sin, the Spirit is life because of righteousness. [11] If the Spirit of him who raised Jesus from the dead dwells in you, he who raised Christ[b] from the dead will give life to your mortal bodies also through[c] his Spirit that dwells in you.

[c] **2 Thess 2:13** ***as the first fruits*** Other ancient authorities read *from the beginning* **§ 76** [a] **Eph 4:16** ***by which it is supplied*** NRSV translates *with which it is equipped* [b] **Phil 1:19** Translation differs from NRSV [c] **Col 2:19** ***richly supplied*** NRSV translates *nourished* **§ 77** [a] **Rom 8:2** ***you*** Other ancient authorities read *me* [b] **Rom 8:11** ***Christ*** Other ancient authorities read *the Christ* or *Christ Jesus* or *Jesus Christ* [c] **Rom 8:11** ***through*** Other ancient authorities read *on account of*

Rom 8:12–14

Ἄρα οὖν, ἀδελφοί, ὀφειλέται ἐσμὲν οὐ τῇ σαρκὶ τοῦ κατὰ σάρκα ζῆν, **13** εἰ γὰρ κατὰ σάρκα ζῆτε, μέλλετε ἀποθνῄσκειν· εἰ δὲ πνεύματι τὰς πράξεις τοῦ σώματος θανατοῦτε, ζήσεσθε. **14** ὅσοι γὰρ πνεύματι θεοῦ ἄγονται, οὗτοι υἱοὶ θεοῦ εἰσιν.

Rom 13:11–14

Καὶ τοῦτο εἰδότες τὸν καιρόν, ὅτι ὥρα ἤδη ὑμᾶς ἐξ ὕπνου ἐγερθῆναι, νῦν γὰρ ἐγγύτερον ἡμῶν ἡ σωτηρία ἢ ὅτε ἐπιστεύσαμεν. **12** ἡ νὺξ προέκοψεν, ἡ δὲ ἡμέρα ἤγγικεν. ἀποθώμεθα οὖν τὰ ἔργα τοῦ σκότους, ἐνδυσώμεθα [δὲ] τὰ ὅπλα τοῦ φωτός. **13** ὡς ἐν ἡμέρᾳ εὐσχημόνως περιπατήσωμεν, μὴ κώμοις καὶ μέθαις, μὴ κοίταις καὶ ἀσελγείαις, μὴ ἔριδι καὶ ζήλῳ, **14** ἀλλὰ ἐνδύσασθε τὸν κύριον Ἰησοῦν Χριστὸν καὶ τῆς σαρκὸς πρόνοιαν μὴ ποιεῖσθε εἰς ἐπιθυμίας.

Gal 5:4–6

κατηργήθητε ἀπὸ Χριστοῦ, οἵτινες ἐν νόμῳ δικαιοῦσθε, τῆς χάριτος ἐξεπέσατε. **5** ἡμεῖς γὰρ πνεύματι ἐκ πίστεως ἐλπίδα δικαιοσύνης ἀπεκδεχόμεθα. **6** ἐν γὰρ Χριστῷ Ἰησοῦ οὔτε περιτομή τι ἰσχύει οὔτε ἀκροβυστία ἀλλὰ πίστις δι᾽ ἀγάπης ἐνεργουμένη.

Gal 5:16–25

Λέγω δέ, πνεύματι περιπατεῖτε καὶ ἐπιθυμίαν σαρκὸς οὐ μὴ τελέσητε. **17** ἡ γὰρ σὰρξ ἐπιθυμεῖ κατὰ τοῦ πνεύματος, τὸ δὲ πνεῦμα κατὰ τῆς σαρκός, ταῦτα γὰρ ἀλλήλοις ἀντίκειται, ἵνα μὴ ἃ ἐὰν θέλητε ταῦτα ποιῆτε. **18** εἰ δὲ πνεύματι ἄγεσθε, οὐκ ἐστὲ ὑπὸ νόμον. **19** φανερὰ δέ ἐστιν τὰ ἔργα τῆς σαρκός, ἅτινά ἐστιν πορνεία, ἀκαθαρσία, ἀσέλγεια, **20** εἰδωλολατρία, φαρμακεία, ἔχθραι, ἔρις, ζῆλος, θυμοί, ἐριθεῖαι, διχοστασίαι, αἱρέσεις, **21** ⸀φθόνοι, μέθαι, κῶμοι καὶ τὰ ὅμοια τούτοις, ἃ προλέγω ὑμῖν, καθὼς προεῖπον ὅτι οἱ τὰ τοιαῦτα πράσσοντες βασιλείαν θεοῦ οὐ κληρονομήσουσιν. **22** ὁ δὲ καρπὸς τοῦ πνεύματός ἐστιν ἀγάπη χαρὰ εἰρήνη, μακροθυμία χρηστότης ἀγαθωσύνη, πίστις **23** πραΰτης ἐγκράτεια· κατὰ τῶν τοιούτων οὐκ ἔστιν νόμος. **24** οἱ δὲ τοῦ Χριστοῦ [Ἰησοῦ] τὴν σάρκα ἐσταύρωσαν σὺν τοῖς παθήμασιν καὶ ταῖς ἐπιθυμίαις. **25** Εἰ ζῶμεν πνεύματι, πνεύματι καὶ στοιχῶμεν.

Gal 6:7–10

Μὴ πλανᾶσθε, θεὸς οὐ μυκτηρίζεται. ὃ γὰρ ἐὰν σπείρῃ ἄνθρωπος, τοῦτο καὶ θερίσει· **8** ὅτι ὁ σπείρων εἰς τὴν σάρκα ἑαυτοῦ ἐκ τῆς σαρκὸς θερίσει φθοράν, ὁ δὲ σπείρων εἰς τὸ πνεῦμα ἐκ τοῦ πνεύματος θερίσει ζωὴν αἰώνιον. **9** τὸ δὲ καλὸν ποιοῦντες μὴ ἐγκακῶμεν, καιρῷ γὰρ ἰδίῳ θερίσομεν μὴ ἐκλυόμενοι. **10** Ἄρα οὖν ὡς καιρὸν ἔχομεν, ἐργαζώμεθα τὸ ἀγαθὸν πρὸς πάντας, μάλιστα δὲ πρὸς τοὺς οἰκείους τῆς πίστεως.

Cf. Rom 6:4; 7:14–25; Gal 2:19–20; Eph 4:20–24; 6:10–20; 1 Thess 5:8.

78. The Inner Person

Rom 7:18–25

Οἶδα γὰρ ὅτι οὐκ οἰκεῖ ἐν ἐμοί, τοῦτ᾽ ἔστιν ἐν τῇ σαρκί μου, ἀγαθόν· τὸ γὰρ θέλειν παράκειταί μοι, τὸ δὲ κατεργάζεσθαι τὸ καλὸν οὔ· **19** οὐ γὰρ ὃ θέλω ποιῶ ἀγαθόν, ἀλλὰ ὃ οὐ θέλω κακὸν τοῦτο πράσσω. **20** εἰ δὲ ὃ οὐ θέλω [ἐγὼ] τοῦτο ποιῶ, οὐκέτι ἐγὼ κατεργάζομαι αὐτὸ ἀλλὰ ἡ οἰκοῦσα ἐν ἐμοὶ ἁμαρτία. **21** εὑρίσκω ἄρα τὸν νόμον, τῷ θέλοντι ἐμοὶ ποιεῖν τὸ καλόν, ὅτι ἐμοὶ τὸ κακὸν παράκειται· **22** συνήδομαι γὰρ τῷ νόμῳ τοῦ θεοῦ κατὰ τὸν ἔσω ἄνθρωπον, **23** βλέπω δὲ ἕτερον νόμον ἐν τοῖς μέλεσίν μου ἀντιστρατευόμενον τῷ νόμῳ τοῦ νοός μου καὶ αἰχμαλωτίζοντά με ἐν τῷ νόμῳ τῆς ἁμαρτίας τῷ ὄντι ἐν τοῖς μέλεσίν μου. **24** Ταλαίπωρος ἐγὼ ἄνθρωπος· τίς με ῥύσεται ἐκ τοῦ σώματος τοῦ θανάτου τούτου; **25** χάρις δὲ τῷ θεῷ διὰ Ἰησοῦ Χριστοῦ τοῦ κυρίου ἡμῶν. Ἄρα οὖν αὐτὸς ἐγὼ τῷ μὲν νοῒ δουλεύω νόμῳ θεοῦ τῇ δὲ σαρκὶ νόμῳ ἁμαρτίας.

2 Cor 4:16–18

Διὸ οὐκ ἐγκακοῦμεν, ἀλλ᾽ εἰ καὶ ὁ ἔξω ἡμῶν ἄνθρωπος διαφθείρεται, ἀλλ᾽ ὁ ἔσω ἡμῶν ἀνακαινοῦται ἡμέρᾳ καὶ ἡμέρᾳ. **17** τὸ γὰρ παραυτίκα ἐλαφρὸν τῆς θλίψεως ἡμῶν καθ᾽ ὑπερβολὴν εἰς ὑπερβολὴν αἰώνιον βάρος δόξης κατεργάζεται ἡμῖν, **18** μὴ σκοπούντων ἡμῶν τὰ βλεπόμενα ἀλλὰ τὰ μὴ βλεπόμενα· τὰ γὰρ βλεπόμενα πρόσκαιρα, τὰ δὲ μὴ βλεπόμενα αἰώνια.

Eph 3:14–19

Τούτου χάριν κάμπτω τὰ γόνατά μου πρὸς τὸν ⸀πατέρα, **15** ἐξ οὗ πᾶσα πατριὰ ἐν οὐρανοῖς καὶ ἐπὶ γῆς ὀνομάζεται, **16** ἵνα δῷ ὑμῖν κατὰ τὸ πλοῦτος τῆς δόξης αὐτοῦ δυνάμει κραταιωθῆναι διὰ τοῦ πνεύματος αὐτοῦ εἰς τὸν ἔσω ἄνθρωπον, **17** κατοικῆσαι τὸν Χριστὸν διὰ τῆς πίστεως ἐν ταῖς καρδίαις ὑμῶν, ἐν ἀγάπῃ ἐρριζωμένοι καὶ τεθεμελιωμένοι, **18** ἵνα ἐξισχύσητε καταλαβέσθαι σὺν πᾶσιν τοῖς ἁγίοις τί τὸ πλάτος καὶ μῆκος καὶ ὕψος καὶ βάθος, **19** γνῶναί τε τὴν ὑπερβάλλουσαν τῆς γνώσεως ἀγάπην τοῦ Χριστοῦ, ἵνα πληρωθῆτε εἰς πᾶν τὸ πλήρωμα τοῦ θεοῦ.

See also § 49 The New Humanity in Christ.

Gal 5:21 ***φθονοι*** 𝔓[46] ℵ B 33] *add.* φονοι A C D 1739. 1881 *Byz* **§ 78** **Eph 3:14** ***πατερα*** 𝔓[46] ℵ* A B C 33. 1739] *add.* του κυριου ημων Ιησου Χριστου ℵ[2] D 1881 *Byz*

Rom 8:12–14

So then, brothers and sisters, we are debtors, not to the flesh, to live according to the flesh— **13** for if you live according to the flesh, you will die; but if by the Spirit you put to death the deeds of the body, you will live. **14** For all who are led by the Spirit of God are children of God.

Rom 13:11–14

Besides this, you know what time it is, how it is now the moment for you to wake from sleep. For salvation is nearer to us now than when we became believers; **12** the night is far gone, the day is near. Let us then lay aside the works of darkness and put on the armor of light; **13** let us walk[d] honorably as in the day, not in reveling and drunkenness, not in debauchery and licentiousness, not in quarreling and jealousy. **14** Instead, put on the Lord Jesus Christ, and make no provision for the flesh, to gratify its desires.

Gal 5:4–6

You who want to be justified by the law have cut yourselves off from Christ; you have fallen away from grace. **5** For through the Spirit, by faith, we eagerly wait for the hope of righteousness. **6** For in Christ Jesus neither circumcision nor uncircumcision counts for anything; the only thing that counts is faith working through love.

Gal 5:16–25

Walk[e] by the Spirit, I say, and do not gratify the desires of the flesh. **17** For what the flesh desires is opposed to the Spirit, and what the Spirit desires is opposed to the flesh; for these are opposed to each other, to prevent you from doing what you want. **18** But if you are led by the Spirit, you are not subject to the law. **19** Now the works of the flesh are obvious: fornication, impurity, licentiousness, **20** idolatry, sorcery, enmities, strife, jealousy, anger, quarrels, dissensions, factions, **21** envy,[f] drunkenness, carousing, and things like these. I am warning you, as I warned you before: those who do such things will not inherit the kingdom of God. **22** By contrast, the fruit of the Spirit is love, joy, peace, patience, kindness, generosity, faithfulness, **23** gentleness, and self-control. There is no law against such things. **24** And those who belong to Christ Jesus have crucified the flesh with its passions and desires. **25** If we live by the Spirit, let us also be guided by the Spirit.

Gal 6:7–10

Do not be deceived; God is not mocked, for you reap whatever you sow. **8** If you sow to your own flesh, you will reap corruption from the flesh; but if you sow to the Spirit, you will reap eternal life from the Spirit. **9** So let us not grow weary in doing what is right, for we will reap at harvest time, if we do not give up. **10** So then, whenever we have an opportunity, let us work for the good of all, and especially for those of the family of faith.

Cf. Rom 6:4; 7:14–25; Gal 2:19–20; Eph 4:20–24; 6:10–20; 1 Thess 5:8.

78. The Inner Person

Rom 7:18–25

For I know that nothing good dwells within me, that is, in my flesh. I can will what is right, but I cannot do it. **19** For I do not do the good I want, but the evil I do not want is what I do. **20** Now if I do what I do not want, it is no longer I that do it, but sin that dwells within me. **21** So I find it to be a law that when I want to do what is good, evil lies close at hand. **22** For I delight in the law of God in my inmost self, **23** but I see in my members another law at war with the law of my mind, making me captive to the law of sin that dwells in my members. **24** Wretched man that I am! Who will rescue me from this body of death? **25** Thanks be to God through Jesus Christ our Lord! So then, with my mind I am a slave to the law of God, but with my flesh I am a slave to the law of sin.

2 Cor 4:16–18

So we do not lose heart. Even though our outer nature is wasting away, our inner nature is being renewed day by day. **17** For this slight momentary affliction is preparing us for an eternal weight of glory beyond all measure, **18** because we look not at what is presently seen but at what is not presently seen; for what is presently seen is temporary, but what is not presently seen is eternal.[a]

Eph 3:14–19

For this reason I bow my knees before the Father,[b] **15** from whom the whole family[c] in heaven and on earth takes its name. **16** I pray that, according to the riches of his glory, he may grant that you may be strengthened in your inner being with power through his Spirit, **17** and that Christ may dwell in your hearts through faith, as you are being rooted and grounded in love. **18** I pray that you may have the power to comprehend, with all the saints, what is the breadth and length and height and depth, **19** and to know the love of Christ that surpasses knowledge, so that you may be filled with all the fullness of God.

See also § 49 The New Humanity in Christ.

[d] **Rom 13:13** ***walk*** NRSV translates *live* [e] **Gal 5:16** ***Walk*** NRSV translates *Live* [f] **Gal 5:21** ***envy*** Other ancient authorities add *murder* **§ 78** [a] **2 Cor 4:18** Translation differs from NRSV [b] **Eph 3:14** ***the Father*** Other ancient authorities add *of our Lord Jesus Christ* [c] **Eph 3:15** ***the whole family*** Or *every family* (so NRSV)

79. The Lord's Supper

1 Cor 10:1–4

Οὐ θέλω γὰρ ὑμᾶς ἀγνοεῖν, ἀδελφοί, ὅτι οἱ πατέρες ἡμῶν πάντες ὑπὸ τὴν νεφέλην ἦσαν καὶ πάντες διὰ τῆς θαλάσσης διῆλθον **2** καὶ πάντες εἰς τὸν Μωϋσῆν ἐβαπτίσθησαν ἐν τῇ νεφέλῃ καὶ ἐν τῇ θαλάσσῃ **3** καὶ πάντες τὸ αὐτὸ πνευματικὸν βρῶμα ἔφαγον **4** καὶ πάντες τὸ αὐτὸ πνευματικὸν ἔπιον πόμα· ἔπινον γὰρ ἐκ πνευματικῆς ἀκολουθούσης πέτρας, ἡ πέτρα δὲ ἦν ὁ Χριστός.

1 Cor 10:14–22

Διόπερ, ἀγαπητοί μου, φεύγετε ἀπὸ τῆς εἰδωλολατρίας. **15** ὡς φρονίμοις λέγω· κρίνατε ὑμεῖς ὅ φημι. **16** Τὸ ποτήριον τῆς εὐλογίας ὃ εὐλογοῦμεν, οὐχὶ κοινωνία ἐστὶν τοῦ αἵματος τοῦ Χριστοῦ; τὸν ἄρτον ὃν κλῶμεν, οὐχὶ κοινωνία τοῦ σώματος τοῦ Χριστοῦ ἐστιν; **17** ὅτι εἷς ἄρτος, ἓν σῶμα οἱ πολλοί ἐσμεν, οἱ γὰρ πάντες ἐκ τοῦ ἑνὸς ἄρτου μετέχομεν. **18** βλέπετε τὸν Ἰσραὴλ κατὰ σάρκα· οὐχ οἱ ἐσθίοντες τὰς θυσίας κοινωνοὶ τοῦ θυσιαστηρίου εἰσίν; **19** Τί οὖν φημι; ὅτι εἰδωλόθυτόν τί ἐστιν ἢ ὅτι εἴδωλόν τί ἐστιν; **20** ἀλλ' ὅτι ἃ θύουσιν, δαιμονίοις καὶ οὐ θεῷ ⸀[θύουσιν]· οὐ θέλω δὲ ὑμᾶς κοινωνοὺς τῶν δαιμονίων γίνεσθαι. **21** οὐ δύνασθε ποτήριον κυρίου πίνειν καὶ ποτήριον δαιμονίων, οὐ δύνασθε τραπέζης κυρίου μετέχειν καὶ τραπέζης δαιμονίων. **22** ἢ παραζηλοῦμεν τὸν κύριον; μὴ ἰσχυρότεροι αὐτοῦ ἐσμεν;

1 Cor 11:17–34

Τοῦτο δὲ παραγγέλλων οὐκ ἐπαινῶ ὅτι οὐκ εἰς τὸ κρεῖσσον ἀλλὰ εἰς τὸ ἧσσον συνέρχεσθε. **18** πρῶτον μὲν γὰρ συνερχομένων ὑμῶν ἐν ἐκκλησίᾳ ἀκούω σχίσματα ἐν ὑμῖν ὑπάρχειν καὶ μέρος τι πιστεύω. **19** δεῖ γὰρ καὶ αἱρέσεις ἐν ὑμῖν εἶναι, ἵνα [καὶ] οἱ δόκιμοι φανεροὶ γένωνται ἐν ὑμῖν. **20** Συνερχομένων οὖν ὑμῶν ἐπὶ τὸ αὐτὸ οὐκ ἔστιν κυριακὸν δεῖπνον φαγεῖν· **21** ἕκαστος γὰρ τὸ ἴδιον δεῖπνον προλαμβάνει ἐν τῷ φαγεῖν, καὶ ὃς μὲν πεινᾷ ὃς δὲ μεθύει. **22** μὴ γὰρ οἰκίας οὐκ ἔχετε εἰς τὸ ἐσθίειν καὶ πίνειν; ἢ τῆς ἐκκλησίας τοῦ θεοῦ καταφρονεῖτε, καὶ καταισχύνετε τοὺς μὴ ἔχοντας; τί εἴπω ὑμῖν; ἐπαινέσω ὑμᾶς; ἐν τούτῳ οὐκ ἐπαινῶ. **23** Ἐγὼ γὰρ παρέλαβον ἀπὸ τοῦ κυρίου, ὃ καὶ παρέδωκα ὑμῖν, ὅτι ὁ κύριος Ἰησοῦς ἐν τῇ νυκτὶ ᾗ παρεδίδετο ἔλαβεν ἄρτον **24** καὶ εὐχαριστήσας ἔκλασεν καὶ εἶπεν· τοῦτό μού ἐστιν τὸ σῶμα τὸ ὑπὲρ ⸀ὑμῶν· τοῦτο ποιεῖτε εἰς τὴν ἐμὴν ἀνάμνησιν. **25** ὡσαύτως καὶ τὸ ποτήριον μετὰ τὸ δειπνῆσαι λέγων· τοῦτο τὸ ποτήριον ἡ καινὴ διαθήκη ἐστὶν ἐν τῷ ἐμῷ αἵματι· τοῦτο ποιεῖτε, ὁσάκις ἐὰν πίνητε, εἰς τὴν ἐμὴν ἀνάμνησιν. **26** ὁσάκις γὰρ ἐὰν ἐσθίητε τὸν ἄρτον τοῦτον καὶ τὸ ποτήριον πίνητε, τὸν θάνατον τοῦ κυρίου καταγγέλλετε ἄχρι οὗ ἔλθῃ. **27** Ὥστε ὃς ἂν ἐσθίῃ τὸν ἄρτον ἢ πίνῃ τὸ ποτήριον τοῦ κυρίου ἀναξίως, ἔνοχος ἔσται τοῦ σώματος καὶ τοῦ αἵματος τοῦ κυρίου. **28** δοκιμαζέτω δὲ ἄνθρωπος ἑαυτὸν καὶ οὕτως ἐκ τοῦ ἄρτου ἐσθιέτω καὶ ἐκ τοῦ ποτηρίου πινέτω· **29** ὁ γὰρ ἐσθίων καὶ ⸀πίνων κρίμα ἑαυτῷ ἐσθίει καὶ πίνει μὴ διακρίνων τὸ ⸀σῶμα. **30** διὰ τοῦτο ἐν ὑμῖν πολλοὶ ἀσθενεῖς καὶ ἄρρωστοι καὶ κοιμῶνται ἱκανοί. **31** εἰ δὲ ἑαυτοὺς διεκρίνομεν, οὐκ ἂν ἐκρινόμεθα· **32** κρινόμενοι δὲ ὑπὸ [τοῦ] κυρίου παιδευόμεθα, ἵνα μὴ σὺν τῷ κόσμῳ κατακριθῶμεν. **33** Ὥστε, ἀδελφοί μου, συνερχόμενοι εἰς τὸ φαγεῖν ἀλλήλους ἐκδέχεσθε. **34** εἴ τις πεινᾷ, ἐν οἴκῳ ἐσθιέτω, ἵνα μὴ εἰς κρίμα συνέρχησθε. τὰ δὲ λοιπὰ ὡς ἂν ἔλθω διατάξομαι.

1 Cor 12:13

καὶ γὰρ ἐν ἑνὶ πνεύματι ἡμεῖς πάντες εἰς ἓν σῶμα ἐβαπτίσθημεν, εἴτε Ἰουδαῖοι εἴτε Ἕλληνες εἴτε δοῦλοι εἴτε ἐλεύθεροι, καὶ πάντες ἓν πνεῦμα ἐποτίσθημεν.

Acts 20:7–12

Ἐν δὲ τῇ μιᾷ τῶν σαββάτων συνηγμένων ἡμῶν κλάσαι ἄρτον, ὁ Παῦλος διελέγετο αὐτοῖς μέλλων ἐξιέναι τῇ ἐπαύριον, παρέτεινέν τε τὸν λόγον μέχρι μεσονυκτίου. **8** ἦσαν δὲ λαμπάδες ἱκαναὶ ἐν τῷ ὑπερῴῳ οὗ ἦμεν συνηγμένοι. **9** καθεζόμενος δέ τις νεανίας ὀνόματι Εὔτυχος ἐπὶ τῆς θυρίδος, καταφερόμενος ὕπνῳ βαθεῖ διαλεγομένου τοῦ Παύλου ἐπὶ πλεῖον, κατενεχθεὶς ἀπὸ τοῦ ὕπνου ἔπεσεν ἀπὸ τοῦ τριστέγου κάτω καὶ ἤρθη νεκρός. **10** καταβὰς δὲ ὁ Παῦλος ἐπέπεσεν αὐτῷ καὶ συμπεριλαβὼν εἶπεν· μὴ θορυβεῖσθε, ἡ γὰρ ψυχὴ αὐτοῦ ἐν αὐτῷ ἐστιν. **11** ἀναβὰς δὲ καὶ κλάσας τὸν ἄρτον καὶ γευσάμενος ἐφ' ἱκανόν τε ὁμιλήσας ἄχρι αὐγῆς, οὕτως ἐξῆλθεν. **12** ἤγαγον δὲ τὸν παῖδα ζῶντα καὶ παρεκλήθησαν οὐ μετρίως.

80. The Body of Christ

Rom 12:4–5

καθάπερ γὰρ ἐν ἑνὶ σώματι πολλὰ μέλη ἔχομεν, τὰ δὲ μέλη πάντα οὐ τὴν αὐτὴν ἔχει πρᾶξιν, **5** οὕτως οἱ πολλοὶ ἓν σῶμά ἐσμεν ἐν Χριστῷ, τὸ δὲ καθ' εἷς ἀλλήλων μέλη.

1 Cor 6:15–17

οὐκ οἴδατε ὅτι τὰ σώματα ὑμῶν μέλη Χριστοῦ ἐστιν; ἄρας οὖν τὰ μέλη τοῦ Χριστοῦ ποιήσω πόρνης μέλη; μὴ γένοιτο. **16** [ἢ] οὐκ οἴδατε ὅτι ὁ κολλώμενος τῇ πόρνῃ ἓν σῶμά ἐστιν; ἔσονται γάρ, φησίν, οἱ δύο εἰς σάρκα μίαν. **17** ὁ δὲ κολλώμενος τῷ κυρίῳ ἓν πνεῦμά ἐστιν.

§ 79 **1 Cor 10:20** ***θυουσιν*** B D] θυουσιν τα εθνη $\mathfrak{P}^{46vid}$ ℵ A C 33^{vid}. 1739 ¦ θυει τα εθνη 1881 *Byz* **1 Cor 11:24** ***υμων*** $\mathfrak{P}^{46}$ ℵ* A B C* 33. 1739*] *add.* κλωμενον $ℵ^{2}$ C^{3} D^{2} 1739^{mg}. 1881 *Byz* ¦ *add.* θρυπτομενον D* **1 Cor 11:29** ***πινων*** $\mathfrak{P}^{46}$ ℵ* A B C* 33. 1739] *add.* αναξιως $ℵ^{2}$ C^{3} D 1881 *Byz* • ***σωμα*** $\mathfrak{P}^{46}$ ℵ* A B C* 33. 1739. 1881*] *add.* του κυριου $ℵ^{2}$ C^{3} D 1881^{c} *Byz*

79. The Lord's Supper

1 Cor 10:1–4

I do not want you to be unaware, brothers and sisters, that our ancestors were all under the cloud, and all passed through the sea, **2** and all were baptized into Moses in the cloud and in the sea, **3** and all ate the same spiritual food, **4** and all drank the same spiritual drink. For they drank from the spiritual rock that followed them, and the rock was Christ.

1 Cor 10:14–22

Therefore, my dear friends, flee from the worship of idols. **15** I speak as to sensible people; judge for yourselves what I say. **16** The cup of blessing that we bless, is it not a sharing in the blood of Christ? The bread that we break, is it not a sharing in the body of Christ? **17** Because there is one bread, we who are many are one body, for we all partake of the one bread. **18** Consider the people of Israel; are not those who eat the sacrifices partners in the altar? **19** What do I imply then? That food sacrificed to idols is anything, or that an idol is anything? **20** No, I imply that what pagans sacrifice,[a] they sacrifice to demons and not to God. I do not want you to be partners with demons. **21** You cannot drink the cup of the Lord and the cup of demons. You cannot partake of the table of the Lord and the table of demons. **22** Or are we provoking the Lord to jealousy? Are we stronger than he?

1 Cor 11:17–34

Now in the following instructions I do not commend you, because when you come together it is not for the better but for the worse. **18** For, to begin with, when you come together as a church, I hear that there are divisions among you; and to some extent I believe it. **19** Indeed, there have to be factions among you, for only so will it become clear who among you are genuine. **20** When you come together, it is not really to eat the Lord's supper. **21** For when the time comes to eat, each of you goes ahead with your own supper, and one goes hungry and another becomes drunk. **22** What! Do you not have homes to eat and drink in? Or do you show contempt for the church of God and humiliate those who have nothing? What should I say to you? Should I commend you? In this matter I do not commend you! **23** For I received from the Lord what I also handed on to you, that the Lord Jesus on the night when he was betrayed took a loaf of bread, **24** and when he had given thanks, he broke it and said, "This is my body that is for[b] you. Do this in remembrance of me." **25** In the same way he took the cup also, after supper, saying, "This cup is the new covenant in my blood. Do this, as often as you drink it, in remembrance of me." **26** For as often as you eat this bread and drink the cup, you proclaim the Lord's death until he comes. **27** Whoever, therefore, eats the bread or drinks the cup of the Lord in an unworthy manner will be answerable for the body and blood of the Lord. **28** Examine yourselves, and only then eat of the bread and drink of the cup. **29** For all who eat and drink[c] without discerning the body,[d] eat and drink judgment against themselves. **30** For this reason many of you are weak and ill, and some have died. **31** But if we judged ourselves, we would not be judged. **32** But when we are judged by the Lord, we are disciplined so that we may not be condemned along with the world. **33** So then, my brothers and sisters, when you come together to eat, wait for one another. **34** If you are hungry, eat at home, so that when you come together, it will not be for your condemnation. About the other things I will give instructions when I come.

1 Cor 12:13

For in the one Spirit we were all baptized into one body—Jews or Greeks, slaves or free—and we were all made to drink of one Spirit.

Acts 20:7–12

On the first day of the week, when we met to break bread, Paul was holding a discussion with them; since he intended to leave the next day, he continued speaking until midnight. **8** There were many lamps in the room upstairs where we were meeting. **9** A young man named Eutychus, who was sitting in the window, began to sink off into a deep sleep while Paul talked still longer. Overcome by sleep, he fell to the ground three floors below and was picked up dead. **10** But Paul went down, and bending over him took him in his arms, and said, "Do not be alarmed, for his life is in him." **11** Then Paul went upstairs, and after he had broken bread and eaten, he continued to converse with them until dawn; then he left. **12** Meanwhile they had taken the boy away alive and were not a little comforted.

80. The Body of Christ

Rom 12:4–5

For as in one body we have many members, and not all the members have the same function, **5** so we, who are many, are one body in Christ, and individually we are members one of another.

1 Cor 6:15–17

Do you not know that your bodies are members of Christ? Should I therefore take the members of Christ and make them members of a prostitute? Never! **16** Do you not know that whoever is united to a prostitute becomes one body with her? For it is said, "The two shall be one flesh." **17** But anyone united to the Lord becomes one spirit with him.

§ 79 [a] **1 Cor 10:20** ***pagans sacrifice*** Other ancient authorities read *they sacrifice* [b] **1 Cor 11:24** ***is for*** Other ancient authorities read *is broken for* [c] **1 Cor 11:29** ***eat and drink*** Other ancient authorities add *in an unworthy manner* [d] **1 Cor 11:29** ***the body*** Other ancient authorities read *the Lord's body*

1 Cor 10:16–17

Τὸ ποτήριον τῆς εὐλογίας ὃ εὐλογοῦμεν,
οὐχὶ κοινωνία ἐστὶν τοῦ αἵματος τοῦ
Χριστοῦ; τὸν ἄρτον ὃν κλῶμεν, οὐχὶ
κοινωνία τοῦ σώματος τοῦ Χριστοῦ
ἐστιν; **17** ὅτι εἷς ἄρτος, ἓν σῶμα οἱ πολλοί
ἐσμεν, οἱ γὰρ πάντες ἐκ τοῦ ἑνὸς ἄρτου
μετέχομεν.

1 Cor 12:12–27

Καθάπερ γὰρ τὸ σῶμα ἕν ἐστιν καὶ μέλη
πολλὰ ἔχει, πάντα δὲ τὰ μέλη τοῦ σώ-
ματος πολλὰ ὄντα ἕν ἐστιν σῶμα, οὕτως
καὶ ὁ Χριστός· **13** καὶ γὰρ ἐν ἑνὶ πνεύματι
ἡμεῖς πάντες εἰς ἓν σῶμα ἐβαπτίσθημεν,
εἴτε Ἰουδαῖοι εἴτε Ἕλληνες εἴτε δοῦλοι
εἴτε ἐλεύθεροι, καὶ πάντες ἓν πνεῦμα
ἐποτίσθημεν. **14** Καὶ γὰρ τὸ σῶμα οὐκ
ἔστιν ἓν μέλος ἀλλὰ πολλά. **15** ἐὰν εἴπῃ
ὁ πούς· ὅτι οὐκ εἰμὶ χείρ, οὐκ εἰμὶ ἐκ
τοῦ σώματος, οὐ παρὰ τοῦτο οὐκ ἔστιν
ἐκ τοῦ σώματος; **16** καὶ ἐὰν εἴπῃ τὸ οὖς·
ὅτι οὐκ εἰμὶ ὀφθαλμός, οὐκ εἰμὶ ἐκ τοῦ
σώματος, οὐ παρὰ τοῦτο οὐκ ἔστιν ἐκ
τοῦ σώματος; **17** εἰ ὅλον τὸ σῶμα ὀφθαλ-
μός, ποῦ ἡ ἀκοή; εἰ ὅλον ἀκοή, ποῦ ἡ
ὄσφρησις; **18** νυνὶ δὲ ὁ θεὸς ἔθετο τὰ
μέλη, ἓν ἕκαστον αὐτῶν ἐν τῷ σώματι
καθὼς ἠθέλησεν. **19** εἰ δὲ ἦν τὰ πάντα
ἓν μέλος, ποῦ τὸ σῶμα; **20** νῦν δὲ πολλὰ
μὲν μέλη, ἓν δὲ σῶμα. **21** οὐ δύναται δὲ
ὁ ὀφθαλμὸς εἰπεῖν τῇ χειρί· χρείαν σου
οὐκ ἔχω, ἢ πάλιν ἡ κεφαλὴ τοῖς ποσίν·
χρείαν ὑμῶν οὐκ ἔχω· **22** ἀλλὰ πολλῷ
μᾶλλον τὰ δοκοῦντα μέλη τοῦ σώματος
ἀσθενέστερα ὑπάρχειν ἀναγκαῖά ἐστιν,
23 καὶ ἃ δοκοῦμεν ἀτιμότερα εἶναι τοῦ
σώματος τούτοις τιμὴν περισσοτέραν
περιτίθεμεν, καὶ τὰ ἀσχήμονα ἡμῶν
εὐσχημοσύνην περισσοτέραν ἔχει, **24** τὰ
δὲ εὐσχήμονα ἡμῶν οὐ χρείαν ἔχει.
ἀλλὰ ὁ θεὸς συνεκέρασεν τὸ σῶμα τῷ
ὑστερουμένῳ περισσοτέραν δοὺς τιμήν,
25 ἵνα μὴ ᾖ σχίσμα ἐν τῷ σώματι ἀλλὰ
τὸ αὐτὸ ὑπὲρ ἀλλήλων μεριμνῶσιν τὰ
μέλη. **26** καὶ εἴτε πάσχει ἓν μέλος, συμ-
πάσχει πάντα τὰ μέλη· εἴτε δοξάζεται
[ἓν] μέλος, συγχαίρει πάντα τὰ μέλη.
27 Ὑμεῖς δέ ἐστε σῶμα Χριστοῦ καὶ μέλη
ἐκ μέρους.

Eph 1:22–23

καὶ πάντα ὑπέταξεν ὑπὸ τοὺς πόδας
αὐτοῦ καὶ αὐτὸν ἔδωκεν κεφαλὴν ὑπὲρ
πάντα τῇ ἐκκλησίᾳ, **23** ἥτις ἐστὶν τὸ σῶμα
αὐτοῦ, τὸ πλήρωμα τοῦ τὰ πάντα ἐν
πᾶσιν πληρουμένου.

Eph 4:4–16

Ἓν σῶμα καὶ ἓν πνεῦμα, καθὼς καὶ
ἐκλήθητε ἐν μιᾷ ἐλπίδι τῆς κλήσεως
ὑμῶν· **5** εἷς κύριος, μία πίστις, ἓν βάπτι-
σμα, **6** εἷς θεὸς καὶ πατὴρ πάντων, ὁ ἐπὶ
πάντων καὶ διὰ πάντων καὶ ἐν πᾶσιν.
7 Ἑνὶ δὲ ἑκάστῳ ἡμῶν ἐδόθη ἡ χάρις
κατὰ τὸ μέτρον τῆς δωρεᾶς τοῦ Χριστοῦ.
8 διὸ λέγει· ἀναβὰς εἰς ὕψος ᾐχμαλώτευ-
σεν αἰχμαλωσίαν, ἔδωκεν δόματα τοῖς
ἀνθρώποις. **9** τὸ δὲ ἀνέβη τί ἐστιν, εἰ μὴ
ὅτι καὶ ⸀κατέβη εἰς τὰ κατώτερα [μέρη]
τῆς γῆς; **10** ὁ καταβὰς αὐτός ἐστιν καὶ ὁ
ἀναβὰς ὑπεράνω πάντων τῶν οὐρανῶν,
ἵνα πληρώσῃ τὰ πάντα. **11** Καὶ αὐτὸς
ἔδωκεν τοὺς μὲν ἀποστόλους, τοὺς δὲ
προφήτας, τοὺς δὲ εὐαγγελιστάς, τοὺς
δὲ ποιμένας καὶ διδασκάλους, **12** πρὸς
τὸν καταρτισμὸν τῶν ἁγίων εἰς ἔργον
διακονίας, εἰς οἰκοδομὴν τοῦ σώματος
τοῦ Χριστοῦ, **13** μέχρι καταντήσωμεν
οἱ πάντες εἰς τὴν ἑνότητα τῆς πίστεως
καὶ τῆς ἐπιγνώσεως τοῦ υἱοῦ τοῦ θεοῦ,
εἰς ἄνδρα τέλειον, εἰς μέτρον ἡλικίας
τοῦ πληρώματος τοῦ Χριστοῦ, **14** ἵνα
μηκέτι ὦμεν νήπιοι, κλυδωνιζόμενοι
καὶ περιφερόμενοι παντὶ ἀνέμῳ τῆς
διδασκαλίας ἐν τῇ κυβείᾳ τῶν ἀνθρώ-
πων, ἐν πανουργίᾳ πρὸς τὴν μεθοδείαν
τῆς πλάνης, **15** ἀληθεύοντες δὲ ἐν ἀγάπῃ
αὐξήσωμεν εἰς αὐτὸν τὰ πάντα, ὅς ἐστιν
ἡ κεφαλή, Χριστός, **16** ἐξ οὗ πᾶν τὸ σῶμα
συναρμολογούμενον καὶ συμβιβαζόμενον
διὰ πάσης ἁφῆς τῆς ἐπιχορηγίας κατ'
ἐνέργειαν ἐν μέτρῳ ἑνὸς ἑκάστου μέρους
τὴν αὔξησιν τοῦ σώματος ποιεῖται εἰς
οἰκοδομὴν ἑαυτοῦ ἐν ἀγάπῃ.

Eph 4:25

Διὸ ἀποθέμενοι τὸ ψεῦδος λαλεῖτε ἀλή-
θειαν ἕκαστος μετὰ τοῦ πλησίον αὐτοῦ,
ὅτι ἐσμὲν ἀλλήλων μέλη.

Eph 5:22–32

αἱ γυναῖκες τοῖς ἰδίοις ⸀ἀνδράσιν ὡς
τῷ κυρίῳ, **23** ὅτι ἀνήρ ἐστιν κεφαλὴ τῆς
γυναικὸς ὡς καὶ ὁ Χριστὸς κεφαλὴ τῆς
ἐκκλησίας, αὐτὸς σωτὴρ τοῦ σώματος·
24 ἀλλὰ ὡς ἡ ἐκκλησία ὑποτάσσεται τῷ
Χριστῷ, οὕτως καὶ αἱ γυναῖκες τοῖς ἀνδρά-
σιν ἐν παντί. **25** Οἱ ἄνδρες, ἀγαπᾶτε τὰς
γυναῖκας, καθὼς καὶ ὁ Χριστὸς ἠγάπησεν
τὴν ἐκκλησίαν καὶ ἑαυτὸν παρέδωκεν
ὑπὲρ αὐτῆς, **26** ἵνα αὐτὴν ἁγιάσῃ καθαρίσας
τῷ λουτρῷ τοῦ ὕδατος ἐν ῥήματι, **27** ἵνα
παραστήσῃ αὐτὸς ἑαυτῷ ἔνδοξον τὴν
ἐκκλησίαν, μὴ ἔχουσαν σπίλον ἢ ῥυτίδα
ἤ τι τῶν τοιούτων, ἀλλ' ἵνα ᾖ ἁγία καὶ
ἄμωμος. **28** οὕτως ὀφείλουσιν [καὶ] οἱ
ἄνδρες ἀγαπᾶν τὰς ἑαυτῶν γυναῖκας ὡς
τὰ ἑαυτῶν σώματα. ὁ ἀγαπῶν τὴν ἑαυτοῦ
γυναῖκα ἑαυτὸν ἀγαπᾷ. **29** Οὐδεὶς γάρ
ποτε τὴν ἑαυτοῦ σάρκα ἐμίσησεν ἀλλὰ
ἐκτρέφει καὶ θάλπει αὐτήν, καθὼς καὶ
ὁ Χριστὸς τὴν ἐκκλησίαν, **30** ὅτι μέλη
ἐσμὲν τοῦ σώματος ⸀αὐτοῦ. **31** ἀντὶ τού-
του καταλείψει ἄνθρωπος [τὸν] πατέρα
καὶ [τὴν] μητέρα καὶ προσκολληθήσεται
πρὸς τὴν γυναῖκα αὐτοῦ, καὶ ἔσονται
οἱ δύο εἰς σάρκα μίαν. **32** τὸ μυστήριον
τοῦτο μέγα ἐστίν· ἐγὼ δὲ λέγω εἰς Χρι-
στὸν καὶ εἰς τὴν ἐκκλησίαν.

Col 1:18

καὶ αὐτός ἐστιν ἡ κεφαλὴ τοῦ σώματος
τῆς ἐκκλησίας· ὅς ἐστιν ἀρχή, πρωτότο-
κος ἐκ τῶν νεκρῶν, ἵνα γένηται ἐν πᾶσιν
αὐτὸς πρωτεύων

Col 1:24

Νῦν χαίρω ἐν τοῖς παθήμασιν ὑπὲρ ὑμῶν
καὶ ἀνταναπληρῶ τὰ ὑστερήματα τῶν
θλίψεων τοῦ Χριστοῦ ἐν τῇ σαρκί μου
ὑπὲρ τοῦ σώματος αὐτοῦ, ὅ ἐστιν ἡ
ἐκκλησία

Col 2:16–19

Μὴ οὖν τις ὑμᾶς κρινέτω ἐν βρώσει καὶ
ἐν πόσει ἢ ἐν μέρει ἑορτῆς ἢ νεομηνίας
ἢ σαββάτων· **17** ἅ ἐστιν σκιὰ τῶν μελλόν-
των, τὸ δὲ σῶμα τοῦ Χριστοῦ. **18** μηδεὶς
ὑμᾶς καταβραβευέτω θέλων ἐν ταπεινο-
φροσύνῃ καὶ θρησκείᾳ τῶν ἀγγέλων, ⸀ἃ
ἑόρακεν ἐμβατεύων, εἰκῇ φυσιούμενος

§ 80 **Eph 4:9** ***κατεβη*** 𝔓[46] ℵ* A C* D I[vid] 33. 1739. 1881] *add.* πρωτον ℵ[2] B C[3] *Byz* **Eph 5:22** ***ανδρασιν*** 𝔓[46] B] *add.* υποτασσεσθωσαν ℵ A I 33. 1739. 1881 ¦ *add.* υποτασσεσθε (D) *Byz* **Eph 5:30** ***αυτου*** 𝔓[46] ℵ* A B 048. 33. 1739*. 1881] *add.* εκ της σαρκος αυτου και εκ των οστεων αυτου ℵ[2] D 1739[mg] *Byz* **Col 2:18** ***ἃ*** 𝔓[46] ℵ* A B D* I 33. 1739] ἃ μη ℵ[2] C D[1] 1881 *Byz*

1 Cor 10:16–17

The cup of blessing that we bless, is it not a sharing in the blood of Christ? The bread that we break, is it not a sharing in the body of Christ? **17** Because there is one bread, we who are many are one body, for we all partake of the one bread.

1 Cor 12:12–27

For just as the body is one and has many members, and all the members of the body, though many, are one body, so it is with Christ. **13** For in the one Spirit we were all baptized into one body—Jews or Greeks, slaves or free—and we were all made to drink of one Spirit. **14** Indeed, the body does not consist of one member but of many. **15** If the foot would say, "Because I am not a hand, I do not belong to the body," that would not make it any less a part of the body. **16** And if the ear would say, "Because I am not an eye, I do not belong to the body," that would not make it any less a part of the body. **17** If the whole body were an eye, where would the hearing be? If the whole body were hearing, where would the sense of smell be? **18** But as it is, God arranged the members in the body, each one of them, as he chose. **19** If all were a single member, where would the body be? **20** As it is, there are many members, yet one body. **21** The eye cannot say to the hand, "I have no need of you," nor again the head to the feet, "I have no need of you." **22** On the contrary, the members of the body that seem to be weaker are indispensable, **23** and those members of the body that we think less honorable we clothe with greater honor, and our less respectable members are treated with greater respect; **24** whereas our more respectable members do not need this. But God has so arranged the body, giving the greater honor to the inferior member, **25** that there may be no dissension within the body, but the members may have the same care for one another. **26** If one member suffers, all suffer together with it; if one member is honored, all rejoice together with it. **27** Now you are the body of Christ and individually members of it.

Eph 1:22–23

And he has put all things under his feet and has made him the head over all things for the church, **23** which is his body, the fullness of him who fills all in all.

Eph 4:4–16

There is one body and one Spirit, just as you were called to the one hope of your calling, **5** one Lord, one faith, one baptism, **6** one God and Father of all, who is above all and through all and in all. **7** But each of us was given grace according to the measure of Christ's gift. **8** Therefore it is said, "When he ascended on high he made captivity itself a captive; he gave gifts to his people." **9** (When it says, "He ascended," what does it mean but that he had also descended[a] into the lower parts of the earth? **10** He who descended is the same one who ascended far above all the heavens, so that he might fill all things.) **11** The gifts he gave were that some would be apostles, some prophets, some evangelists, some pastors and teachers, **12** to equip the saints for the work of ministry, for building up the body of Christ, **13** until all of us come to the unity of the faith and of the knowledge of the Son of God, to maturity, to the measure of the full stature of Christ. **14** We must no longer be children, tossed to and fro and blown about by every wind of doctrine, by people's trickery, by their craftiness in deceitful scheming. **15** But speaking the truth in love, we must grow up in every way into him who is the head, into Christ, **16** from whom the whole body, joined and knit together by every ligament by which it is supplied,[b] as each part is working properly, promotes the body's growth in building itself up in love.

Eph 4:25

So then, putting away falsehood, let all of us speak the truth to our neighbors, for we are members of one another.

Eph 5:22–32

Wives, be subject[c] to your husbands as you are to the Lord. **23** For the husband is the head of the wife just as Christ is the head of the church, the body of which he is the Savior. **24** Just as the church is subject to Christ, so also wives ought to be, in everything, to their husbands. **25** Husbands, love your wives, just as Christ loved the church and gave himself up for her, **26** in order to make her holy by cleansing her with the washing of water by the word, **27** so as to present the church to himself in splendor, without a spot or wrinkle or anything of the kind—yes, so that she may be holy and without blemish. **28** In the same way, husbands should love their wives as they do their own bodies. He who loves his wife loves himself. **29** For no one ever hates his own body, but he nourishes and tenderly cares for it, just as Christ does for the church, **30** because we are members of his body.[d] **31** "For this reason a man will leave his father and mother and be joined to his wife, and the two will become one flesh." **32** This is a great mystery, and I am applying it to Christ and the church.

Col 1:18

He is the head of the body, the church; he is the beginning, the firstborn from the dead, so that he might come to have first place in everything.

Col 1:24

I am now rejoicing in my sufferings for your sake, and in my flesh I am completing what is lacking in Christ's afflictions for the sake of his body, that is, the church.

Col 2:16–19

Therefore do not let anyone condemn you in matters of food and drink or of observing festivals, new moons, or sabbaths. **17** These are only a shadow of what is to come, but the substance belongs to Christ. **18** Do not let anyone disqualify you, insisting on self-abasement and worship of angels, dwelling on visions,[e] puffed up without cause by

§ 80 [a] **Eph 4:9** *descended* Other ancient authorities add *first* [b] **Eph 4:16** ***by which it is supplied*** NRSV translates *with which it is equipped* [c] **Eph 5:22** ***Wives, be subject*** Other ancient authorities read *Wives should be subject* [d] **Eph 5:30** ***of his body*** Other ancient authorities add *of his flesh and of his bones* [e] **Col 2:18** ***visions*** lit. *things which he has seen* Other ancient authorities read *false visions* lit. *things which he has not seen*

ὑπὸ τοῦ νοὸς τῆς σαρκὸς αὐτοῦ, **19** καὶ οὐ κρατῶν τὴν κεφαλήν, ἐξ οὗ πᾶν τὸ σῶμα διὰ τῶν ἁφῶν καὶ συνδέσμων ἐπιχορηγούμενον καὶ συμβιβαζόμενον αὔξει τὴν αὔξησιν τοῦ θεοῦ.

Col 3:15

καὶ ἡ εἰρήνη τοῦ Χριστοῦ βραβευέτω ἐν ταῖς καρδίαις ὑμῶν, εἰς ἣν καὶ ἐκλήθητε ἐν ἑνὶ σώματι· καὶ εὐχάριστοι γίνεσθε.

81. Christ the Head of the Church

Eph 1:22–23

καὶ πάντα ὑπέταξεν ὑπὸ τοὺς πόδας αὐτοῦ καὶ αὐτὸν ἔδωκεν κεφαλὴν ὑπὲρ πάντα τῇ ἐκκλησίᾳ, **23** ἥτις ἐστὶν τὸ σῶμα αὐτοῦ, τὸ πλήρωμα τοῦ τὰ πάντα ἐν πᾶσιν πληρουμένου.

Eph 4:11–16

Καὶ αὐτὸς ἔδωκεν τοὺς μὲν ἀποστόλους, τοὺς δὲ προφήτας, τοὺς δὲ εὐαγγελιστάς, τοὺς δὲ ποιμένας καὶ διδασκάλους, **12** πρὸς τὸν καταρτισμὸν τῶν ἁγίων εἰς ἔργον διακονίας, εἰς οἰκοδομὴν τοῦ σώματος τοῦ Χριστοῦ, **13** μέχρι καταντήσωμεν οἱ πάντες εἰς τὴν ἑνότητα τῆς πίστεως καὶ τῆς ἐπιγνώσεως τοῦ υἱοῦ τοῦ θεοῦ, εἰς ἄνδρα τέλειον, εἰς μέτρον ἡλικίας τοῦ πληρώματος τοῦ Χριστοῦ, **14** ἵνα μηκέτι ὦμεν νήπιοι, κλυδωνιζόμενοι καὶ περιφερόμενοι παντὶ ἀνέμῳ τῆς διδασκαλίας ἐν τῇ κυβείᾳ τῶν ἀνθρώπων, ἐν πανουργίᾳ πρὸς τὴν μεθοδείαν τῆς πλάνης, **15** ἀληθεύοντες δὲ ἐν ἀγάπῃ αὐξήσωμεν εἰς αὐτὸν τὰ πάντα, ὅς ἐστιν ἡ κεφαλή, Χριστός, **16** ἐξ οὗ πᾶν τὸ σῶμα συναρμολογούμενον καὶ συμβιβαζόμενον διὰ πάσης ἁφῆς τῆς ἐπιχορηγίας κατ᾽ ἐνέργειαν ἐν μέτρῳ ἑνὸς ἑκάστου μέρους τὴν αὔξησιν τοῦ σώματος ποιεῖται εἰς οἰκοδομὴν ἑαυτοῦ ἐν ἀγάπῃ.

Eph 5:22–32

αἱ γυναῖκες τοῖς ἰδίοις ⸀ἀνδράσιν ὡς τῷ κυρίῳ, **23** ὅτι ἀνήρ ἐστιν κεφαλὴ τῆς γυναικὸς ὡς καὶ ὁ Χριστὸς κεφαλὴ τῆς ἐκκλησίας, αὐτὸς σωτὴρ τοῦ σώματος· **24** ἀλλὰ ὡς ἡ ἐκκλησία ὑποτάσσεται τῷ Χριστῷ, οὕτως καὶ αἱ γυναῖκες τοῖς ἀνδράσιν ἐν παντί. **25** Οἱ ἄνδρες, ἀγαπᾶτε τὰς γυναῖκας, καθὼς καὶ ὁ Χριστὸς ἠγάπησεν τὴν ἐκκλησίαν καὶ ἑαυτὸν παρέδωκεν ὑπὲρ αὐτῆς, **26** ἵνα αὐτὴν ἁγιάσῃ καθαρίσας τῷ λουτρῷ τοῦ ὕδατος ἐν ῥήματι, **27** ἵνα παραστήσῃ αὐτὸς ἑαυτῷ ἔνδοξον τὴν ἐκκλησίαν, μὴ ἔχουσαν σπίλον ἢ ῥυτίδα ἤ τι τῶν τοιούτων, ἀλλ᾽ ἵνα ᾖ ἁγία καὶ ἄμωμος. **28** οὕτως ὀφείλουσιν [καὶ] οἱ ἄνδρες ἀγαπᾶν τὰς ἑαυτῶν γυναῖκας ὡς τὰ ἑαυτῶν σώματα. ὁ ἀγαπῶν τὴν ἑαυτοῦ γυναῖκα ἑαυτὸν ἀγαπᾷ. **29** Οὐδεὶς γάρ ποτε τὴν ἑαυτοῦ σάρκα ἐμίσησεν ἀλλὰ ἐκτρέφει καὶ θάλπει αὐτήν, καθὼς καὶ ὁ Χριστὸς τὴν ἐκκλησίαν, **30** ὅτι μέλη ἐσμὲν τοῦ σώματος ⸀αὐτοῦ. **31** ἀντὶ τούτου καταλείψει ἄνθρωπος [τὸν] πατέρα καὶ [τὴν] μητέρα καὶ προσκολληθήσεται πρὸς τὴν γυναῖκα αὐτοῦ, καὶ ἔσονται οἱ δύο εἰς σάρκα μίαν. **32** τὸ μυστήριον τοῦτο μέγα ἐστίν· ἐγὼ δὲ λέγω εἰς Χριστὸν καὶ εἰς τὴν ἐκκλησίαν.

Col 1:18

καὶ αὐτός ἐστιν ἡ κεφαλὴ τοῦ σώματος τῆς ἐκκλησίας· ὅς ἐστιν ἀρχή, πρωτότοκος ἐκ τῶν νεκρῶν, ἵνα γένηται ἐν πᾶσιν αὐτὸς πρωτεύων

Col 2:16–19

Μὴ οὖν τις ὑμᾶς κρινέτω ἐν βρώσει καὶ ἐν πόσει ἢ ἐν μέρει ἑορτῆς ἢ νεομηνίας ἢ σαββάτων· **17** ἅ ἐστιν σκιὰ τῶν μελλόντων, τὸ δὲ σῶμα τοῦ Χριστοῦ. **18** μηδεὶς ὑμᾶς καταβραβευέτω θέλων ἐν ταπεινοφροσύνῃ καὶ θρησκείᾳ τῶν ἀγγέλων, ⸀ἃ ἑόρακεν ἐμβατεύων, εἰκῇ φυσιούμενος ὑπὸ τοῦ νοὸς τῆς σαρκὸς αὐτοῦ, **19** καὶ οὐ κρατῶν τὴν κεφαλήν, ἐξ οὗ πᾶν τὸ σῶμα διὰ τῶν ἁφῶν καὶ συνδέσμων ἐπιχορηγούμενον καὶ συμβιβαζόμενον αὔξει τὴν αὔξησιν τοῦ θεοῦ.

Cf. 1 Cor 11:2–16.

See also § 80 The Body of Christ.

82. Authorities and Powers

Rom 8:38–39

πέπεισμαι γὰρ ὅτι οὔτε θάνατος οὔτε ζωὴ οὔτε ἄγγελοι οὔτε ἀρχαὶ οὔτε ἐνεστῶτα οὔτε μέλλοντα οὔτε δυνάμεις **39** οὔτε ὕψωμα οὔτε βάθος οὔτε τις κτίσις ἑτέρα δυνήσεται ἡμᾶς χωρίσαι ἀπὸ τῆς ἀγάπης τοῦ θεοῦ τῆς ἐν Χριστῷ Ἰησοῦ τῷ κυρίῳ ἡμῶν.

1 Cor 2:6–8

Σοφίαν δὲ λαλοῦμεν ἐν τοῖς τελείοις, σοφίαν δὲ οὐ τοῦ αἰῶνος τούτου οὐδὲ τῶν ἀρχόντων τοῦ αἰῶνος τούτου τῶν καταργουμένων· **7** ἀλλὰ λαλοῦμεν θεοῦ σοφίαν ἐν μυστηρίῳ τὴν ἀποκεκρυμμένην, ἣν προώρισεν ὁ θεὸς πρὸ τῶν αἰώνων εἰς δόξαν ἡμῶν, **8** ἣν οὐδεὶς τῶν ἀρχόντων τοῦ αἰῶνος τούτου ἔγνωκεν· εἰ γὰρ ἔγνωσαν, οὐκ ἂν τὸν κύριον τῆς δόξης ἐσταύρωσαν.

1 Cor 15:23–28

Ἕκαστος δὲ ἐν τῷ ἰδίῳ τάγματι· ἀπαρχὴ Χριστός, ἔπειτα οἱ τοῦ Χριστοῦ ἐν τῇ παρουσίᾳ αὐτοῦ, **24** εἶτα τὸ τέλος, ὅταν παραδιδῷ τὴν βασιλείαν τῷ θεῷ καὶ πατρί, ὅταν καταργήσῃ πᾶσαν ἀρχὴν καὶ πᾶσαν ἐξουσίαν καὶ δύναμιν. **25** δεῖ γὰρ αὐτὸν βασιλεύειν ἄχρι οὗ θῇ πάντας τοὺς ἐχθροὺς ὑπὸ τοὺς πόδας αὐτοῦ. **26** ἔσχατος

§ 81 **Eph 5:22** ***ανδρασιν*** 𝔓46 B] *add.* υποτασσεσθωσαν ℵ A I 33. 1739. 1881 ¦ *add.* υποτασσεσθε (D) *Byz* **Eph 5:30** ***αυτου*** 𝔓46 ℵ* A B 048. 33. 1739*. 1881] *add.* εκ της σαρκος αυτου και εκ των οστεων αυτου ℵ2 D 1739mg *Byz* **Col 2:18** ***ἃ*** 𝔓46 ℵ* A B D* I 33. 1739] ἃ μη ℵ2 C D1 1881 *Byz*

a human way of thinking, 19 and not holding fast to the head, from whom the whole body, richly supplied[f] and held together by its ligaments and sinews, grows with a growth that is from God.

Col 3:15

And let the peace of Christ rule in your hearts, to which indeed you were called in the one body. And be thankful.

81. Christ the Head of the Church

Eph 1:22–23

And he has put all things under his feet and has made him the head over all things for the church, 23 which is his body, the fullness of him who fills all in all.

Eph 4:11–16

The gifts he gave were that some would be apostles, some prophets, some evangelists, some pastors and teachers, 12 to equip the saints for the work of ministry, for building up the body of Christ, 13 until all of us come to the unity of the faith and of the knowledge of the Son of God, to maturity, to the measure of the full stature of Christ. 14 We must no longer be children, tossed to and fro and blown about by every wind of doctrine, by people's trickery, by their craftiness in deceitful scheming. 15 But speaking the truth in love, we must grow up in every way into him who is the head, into Christ, 16 from whom the whole body, joined and knit together by every ligament by which it is supplied,[a] as each part is working properly, promotes the body's growth in building itself up in love.

Eph 5:22–32

Wives, be subject[b] to your husbands as you are to the Lord. 23 For the husband is the head of the wife just as Christ is the head of the church, the body of which he is the Savior. 24 Just as the church is subject to Christ, so also wives ought to be, in everything, to their husbands. 25 Husbands, love your wives, just as Christ loved the church and gave himself up for her, 26 in order to make her holy by cleansing her with the washing of water by the word, 27 so as to present the church to himself in splendor, without a spot or wrinkle or anything of the kind—yes, so that she may be holy and without blemish. 28 In the same way, husbands should love their wives as they do their own bodies. He who loves his wife loves himself. 29 For no one ever hates his own body, but he nourishes and tenderly cares for it, just as Christ does for the church, 30 because we are members of his body.[c] 31 "For this reason a man will leave his father and mother and be joined to his wife, and the two will become one flesh." 32 This is a great mystery, and I am applying it to Christ and the church.

Col 1:18

He is the head of the body, the church; he is the beginning, the firstborn from the dead, so that he might come to have first place in everything.

Col 2:16–19

Therefore do not let anyone condemn you in matters of food and drink or of observing festivals, new moons, or sabbaths. 17 These are only a shadow of what is to come, but the substance belongs to Christ. 18 Do not let anyone disqualify you, insisting on self-abasement and worship of angels, dwelling on visions,[d] puffed up without cause by a human way of thinking, 19 and not holding fast to the head, from whom the whole body, richly supplied[e] and held together by its ligaments and sinews, grows with a growth that is from God.

Cf. 1 Cor 11:2–16.

See also § 80 The Body of Christ.

82. Authorities and Powers

Rom 8:38–39

For I am convinced that neither death, nor life, nor angels, nor rulers, nor things present, nor things to come, nor powers, 39 nor height, nor depth, nor anything else in all creation, will be able to separate us from the love of God in Christ Jesus our Lord.

1 Cor 2:6–8

Yet among the mature we do speak wisdom, though it is not a wisdom of this age or of the rulers of this age, who are doomed to perish. 7 But we speak God's wisdom, secret and hidden, which God decreed before the ages for our glory. 8 None of the rulers of this age understood this; for if they had, they would not have crucified the Lord of glory.

1 Cor 15:23–28

But each in his own order: Christ the first fruits, then at his coming those who belong to Christ. 24 Then comes the end, when he hands over the kingdom to God the Father, after he has destroyed every ruler and every authority and power. 25 For he must reign until he has put all his enemies under his feet. 26 The last enemy to be destroyed is

[f] Col 2:19 ***richly supplied*** NRSV translates *nourished*

§ 81 [a] Eph 4:16 ***by which it is supplied*** NRSV translates *with which it is equipped* [b] Eph 5:22 ***Wives, be subject*** Other ancient authorities read *Wives should be subject* [c] Eph 5:30 ***of his body*** Other ancient authorities add *of his flesh and of his bones* [d] Col 2:18 ***visions*** lit. *things which he has seen* Other ancient authorities read *false visions* lit. *things which he has not seen* [e] Col 2:19 ***richly supplied*** NRSV translates *nourished*

ἐχθρὸς καταργεῖται ὁ θάνατος· **27** πάντα
γὰρ ὑπέταξεν ὑπὸ τοὺς πόδας αὐτοῦ.
ὅταν δὲ εἴπῃ ὅτι πάντα ὑποτέτακται,
δῆλον ὅτι ἐκτὸς τοῦ ὑποτάξαντος αὐτῷ
τὰ πάντα. **28** ὅταν δὲ ὑποταγῇ αὐτῷ τὰ
πάντα, τότε [καὶ] αὐτὸς ὁ υἱὸς ὑποταγή-
σεται τῷ ὑποτάξαντι αὐτῷ τὰ πάντα, ἵνα
ᾖ ὁ θεὸς [τὰ] πάντα ἐν πᾶσιν.

Eph 1:20–23

Ἣν ⸀ἐνήργησεν ἐν τῷ Χριστῷ ἐγείρας
αὐτὸν ἐκ νεκρῶν καὶ καθίσας ἐν δεξιᾷ
αὐτοῦ ἐν τοῖς ἐπουρανίοις **21** ὑπεράνω
πάσης ἀρχῆς καὶ ἐξουσίας καὶ δυνάμεως
καὶ κυριότητος καὶ παντὸς ὀνόματος
ὀνομαζομένου, οὐ μόνον ἐν τῷ αἰῶνι
τούτῳ ἀλλὰ καὶ ἐν τῷ μέλλοντι· **22** καὶ
πάντα ὑπέταξεν ὑπὸ τοὺς πόδας αὐτοῦ
καὶ αὐτὸν ἔδωκεν κεφαλὴν ὑπὲρ πάν-
τα τῇ ἐκκλησίᾳ, **23** ἥτις ἐστὶν τὸ σῶμα
αὐτοῦ, τὸ πλήρωμα τοῦ τὰ πάντα ἐν
πᾶσιν πληρουμένου.

Eph 2:2

ἐν αἷς ποτε περιεπατήσατε κατὰ τὸν
αἰῶνα τοῦ κόσμου τούτου, κατὰ τὸν
ἄρχοντα τῆς ἐξουσίας τοῦ ἀέρος, τοῦ
πνεύματος τοῦ νῦν ἐνεργοῦντος ἐν τοῖς
υἱοῖς τῆς ἀπειθείας

Eph 3:8–11

Ἐμοὶ τῷ ἐλαχιστοτέρῳ πάντων ἁγίων
ἐδόθη ἡ χάρις αὕτη, τοῖς ἔθνεσιν εὐαγ-
γελίσασθαι τὸ ἀνεξιχνίαστον πλοῦτος
τοῦ Χριστοῦ **9** καὶ φωτίσαι ⸀[πάντας] τίς
ἡ οἰκονομία τοῦ μυστηρίου τοῦ ἀποκε-
κρυμμένου ἀπὸ τῶν αἰώνων ἐν τῷ θεῷ
τῷ τὰ πάντα κτίσαντι, **10** ἵνα γνωρισθῇ
νῦν ταῖς ἀρχαῖς καὶ ταῖς ἐξουσίαις ἐν
τοῖς ἐπουρανίοις διὰ τῆς ἐκκλησίας ἡ
πολυποίκιλος σοφία τοῦ θεοῦ, **11** κατὰ
πρόθεσιν τῶν αἰώνων ἣν ἐποίησεν ἐν
τῷ Χριστῷ Ἰησοῦ τῷ κυρίῳ ἡμῶν

Eph 6:11–12

ἐνδύσασθε τὴν πανοπλίαν τοῦ θεοῦ
πρὸς τὸ δύνασθαι ὑμᾶς στῆναι πρὸς τὰς
μεθοδείας τοῦ διαβόλου· **12** ὅτι οὐκ ἔστιν
⸀ἡμῖν ἡ πάλη πρὸς αἷμα καὶ σάρκα ἀλλὰ
πρὸς τὰς ἀρχάς, πρὸς τὰς ἐξουσίας, πρὸς
τοὺς κοσμοκράτορας τοῦ σκότους τού-
του, πρὸς τὰ πνευματικὰ τῆς πονηρίας
ἐν τοῖς ἐπουρανίοις.

Phil 2:9–11

διὸ καὶ ὁ θεὸς αὐτὸν ὑπερύψωσεν καὶ
ἐχαρίσατο αὐτῷ τὸ ὄνομα τὸ ὑπὲρ πᾶν
ὄνομα, **10** ἵνα ἐν τῷ ὀνόματι Ἰησοῦ πᾶν
γόνυ κάμψῃ ἐπουρανίων καὶ ἐπιγείων
καὶ καταχθονίων **11** καὶ πᾶσα γλῶσσα
ἐξομολογήσηται ὅτι κύριος Ἰησοῦς Χρι-
στὸς εἰς δόξαν θεοῦ πατρός.

Col 1:13

ὃς ἐρρύσατο ἡμᾶς ἐκ τῆς ἐξουσίας τοῦ
σκότους καὶ μετέστησεν εἰς τὴν βασιλείαν
τοῦ υἱοῦ τῆς ἀγάπης αὐτοῦ

Col 1:16

ὅτι ἐν αὐτῷ ἐκτίσθη τὰ πάντα ἐν τοῖς
οὐρανοῖς καὶ ἐπὶ τῆς γῆς, τὰ ὁρατὰ καὶ
τὰ ἀόρατα, εἴτε θρόνοι εἴτε κυριότητες
εἴτε ἀρχαὶ εἴτε ἐξουσίαι· τὰ πάντα δι'
αὐτοῦ καὶ εἰς αὐτὸν ἔκτισται

Col 2:8–10

Βλέπετε μή τις ὑμᾶς ἔσται ὁ συλαγωγῶν
διὰ τῆς φιλοσοφίας καὶ κενῆς ἀπάτης κατὰ
τὴν παράδοσιν τῶν ἀνθρώπων, κατὰ τὰ
στοιχεῖα τοῦ κόσμου καὶ οὐ κατὰ Χριστόν·
9 ὅτι ἐν αὐτῷ κατοικεῖ πᾶν τὸ πλήρωμα
τῆς θεότητος σωματικῶς, **10** καὶ ἐστὲ ἐν
αὐτῷ πεπληρωμένοι, ὅς ἐστιν ἡ κεφαλὴ
πάσης ἀρχῆς καὶ ἐξουσίας.

Col 2:13–15

καὶ ὑμᾶς νεκροὺς ὄντας [ἐν] τοῖς παρα-
πτώμασιν καὶ τῇ ἀκροβυστίᾳ τῆς σαρκὸς
ὑμῶν, συνεζωοποίησεν ⸀ὑμᾶς σὺν αὐτῷ,
χαρισάμενος ἡμῖν πάντα τὰ παραπτώματα.
14 ἐξαλείψας τὸ καθ' ἡμῶν χειρόγραφον
τοῖς δόγμασιν ὃ ἦν ὑπεναντίον ἡμῖν, καὶ
αὐτὸ ἦρκεν ἐκ τοῦ μέσου προσηλώσας αὐτὸ
τῷ σταυρῷ· **15** ἀπεκδυσάμενος τὰς ἀρχὰς
καὶ τὰς ἐξουσίας ἐδειγμάτισεν ἐν παρρη-
σίᾳ, θριαμβεύσας αὐτοὺς ἐν αὐτῷ.

On the activity of Satan see further Rom 16:17–20; 1 Cor 5:3–5; 7:5; 2 Cor 2:5–11; 4:4–6; 11:2–3; 11:12–15; 12:7–10; Eph 4:26–27; 6:16; 1 Thess 2:17–18; 3:5; 2 Thess 2:8–12; 3:3; 1 Tim 1:19–20; 3:6–7; 5:14–15; 2 Tim 2:25–26; Acts 13:6–12; 19:13–20; 26:16–18.

See also § 83 The Elemental Powers/Principles of the Universe; and § 121 Governing Authorities.

83. The Elemental Powers/Principles of the Universe

Gal 4:1–3

Λέγω δέ, ἐφ' ὅσον χρόνον ὁ κληρονόμος
νήπιός ἐστιν, οὐδὲν διαφέρει δούλου
κύριος πάντων ὤν, **2** ἀλλὰ ὑπὸ ἐπιτρό-
πους ἐστὶν καὶ οἰκονόμους ἄχρι τῆς
προθεσμίας τοῦ πατρός. **3** οὕτως καὶ
ἡμεῖς, ὅτε ἦμεν νήπιοι, ὑπὸ τὰ στοιχεῖα
τοῦ κόσμου ἤμεθα δεδουλωμένοι

Gal 4:8–11

Ἀλλὰ τότε μὲν οὐκ εἰδότες θεὸν ἐδου-
λεύσατε τοῖς φύσει μὴ οὖσιν θεοῖς· **9** νῦν
δὲ γνόντες θεόν, μᾶλλον δὲ γνωσθέντες
ὑπὸ θεοῦ, πῶς ἐπιστρέφετε πάλιν ἐπὶ τὰ
ἀσθενῆ καὶ πτωχὰ στοιχεῖα οἷς πάλιν
ἄνωθεν δουλεύειν θέλετε; **10** ἡμέρας
παρατηρεῖσθε καὶ μῆνας καὶ καιροὺς
καὶ ἐνιαυτούς, **11** φοβοῦμαι ὑμᾶς μή πως
εἰκῇ κεκοπίακα εἰς ὑμᾶς.

Col 2:8–10

Βλέπετε μή τις ὑμᾶς ἔσται ὁ συλαγωγῶν
διὰ τῆς φιλοσοφίας καὶ κενῆς ἀπάτης κατὰ
τὴν παράδοσιν τῶν ἀνθρώπων, κατὰ τὰ
στοιχεῖα τοῦ κόσμου καὶ οὐ κατὰ Χριστόν·
9 ὅτι ἐν αὐτῷ κατοικεῖ πᾶν τὸ πλήρωμα
τῆς θεότητος σωματικῶς, **10** καὶ ἐστὲ ἐν
αὐτῷ πεπληρωμένοι, ὅς ἐστιν ἡ κεφαλὴ
πάσης ἀρχῆς καὶ ἐξουσίας.

Col 2:20–23

Εἰ ἀπεθάνετε σὺν Χριστῷ ἀπὸ τῶν στοι-
χείων τοῦ κόσμου, τί ὡς ζῶντες ἐν κόσμῳ
δογματίζεσθε; **21** μὴ ἅψῃ μηδὲ γεύσῃ
μηδὲ θίγῃς, **22** ἅ ἐστιν πάντα εἰς φθορὰν

§ 82 **Eph 1:20** ***ενηργησεν*** ℵ D 33. 1739. 1881 *Byz*] ενηργηκεν A B **Eph 3:9** ***παντας*** 𝔓46 ℵ2 B C D 33 *Byz*] *om.* ℵ* A 1739. 1881 **Eph 6:12** ***ημιν*** ℵ A D2 I 33. 1739. 1881 *Byz*] υμιν 𝔓46 B D* **Col 2:13** ***υμας*** ℵ* A C 1739. 1881] ημας 𝔓46 B 33 ¦ *om.* ℵ2 D *Byz*

death. 27 For "God has put all things in subjection under his feet." But when it says, "All things are put in subjection," it is plain that this does not include the one who put all things in subjection under him. 28 When all things are subjected to him, then the Son himself will also be subjected to the one who put all things in subjection under him, so that God may be all in all.

Eph 1:20–23

God put this power to work[a] in Christ when he raised him from the dead and seated him at his right hand in the heavenly places, 21 far above all rule and authority and power and dominion, and above every name that is named, not only in this age but also in the age to come. 22 And he has put all things under his feet and has made him the head over all things for the church, 23 which is his body, the fullness of him who fills all in all.

Eph 2:2

in which you once lived, following the course of this world, following the ruler of the power of the air, the spirit that is now at work among those who are disobedient.

Eph 3:8–11

Although I am the very least of all the saints, this grace was given to me to bring to the Gentiles the news of the boundless riches of Christ, 9 and to make everyone see[b] what is the plan of the mystery hidden for ages in God who created all things; 10 so that through the church the wisdom of God in its rich variety might now be made known to the rulers and authorities in the heavenly places. 11 This was in accordance with the eternal purpose that he has carried out in Christ Jesus our Lord

Eph 6:11–12

Put on the whole armor of God, so that you may be able to stand against the wiles of the devil. 12 For our[c] struggle is not against enemies of blood and flesh, but against the rulers, against the authorities, against the cosmic powers of this present darkness, against the spiritual forces of evil in the heavenly places.

Phil 2:9–11

Therefore God also highly exalted him and gave him the name that is above every name, 10 so that at the name of Jesus every knee should bend, in heaven and on earth and under the earth, 11 and every tongue should confess that Jesus Christ is Lord, to the glory of God the Father.

Col 1:13

He has rescued us from the power of darkness and transferred us into the kingdom of his beloved Son

Col 1:16

for in him all things in heaven and on earth were created, things visible and invisible, whether thrones or dominions or rulers or powers—all things have been created through him and for him.

Col 2:8–10

See to it that no one takes you captive through philosophy and empty deceit, according to human tradition, according to the elemental spirits of the universe, and not according to Christ. 9 For in him the whole fullness of deity dwells bodily, 10 and you have come to fullness in him, who is the head of every ruler and authority.

Col 2:13–15

And when you were dead in trespasses and the uncircumcision of your flesh, God made you[d] alive together with him, when he forgave us all our trespasses, 14 erasing the record that stood against us with its legal demands. He set this aside, nailing it to the cross. 15 He disarmed the rulers and authorities and made a public example of them, triumphing over them in it.

On the activity of Satan see further Rom 16:17–20; 1 Cor 5:3–5; 7:5; 2 Cor 2:5–11; 4:4–6; 11:2–3; 11:12–15; 12:7–10; Eph 4:26–27; 6:16; 1 Thess 2:17–18; 3:5; 2 Thess 2:8–12; 3:3; 1 Tim 1:19–20; 3:6–7; 5:14–15; 2 Tim 2:25–26; Acts 13:6–12; 19:13–20; 26:16–18.

See also § 83 The Elemental Powers/Principles of the Universe and § 121 Governing Authorities.

83. The Elemental Powers/Principles of the Universe

Gal 4:1–3

My point is this: heirs, as long as they are minors, are no better than slaves, though they are the owners of all the property; 2 but they remain under guardians and trustees until the date set by the father. 3 So with us; while we were minors, we were enslaved to the elemental spirits of the world.

Gal 4:8–11

Formerly, when you did not know God, you were enslaved to beings that by nature are not gods. 9 Now, however, that you have come to know God, or rather to be known by God, how can you turn back again to the weak and beggarly elemental spirits? How can you want to be enslaved to them again? 10 You are observing special days, and months, and seasons, and years. 11 I am afraid that my work for you may have been wasted.

Col 2:8–10

See to it that no one takes you captive through philosophy and empty deceit, according to human tradition, according to the elemental spirits of the universe, and not according to Christ. 9 For in him the whole fullness of deity dwells bodily, 10 and you have come to fullness in him, who is the head of every ruler and authority.

Col 2:20–23

If with Christ you died to the elemental spirits of the universe, why do you live as if you still belonged to the world? Why do you submit to regulations, 21 "Do not handle, Do not taste, Do not touch"? 22 All these

§ 82 [a] **Eph 1:20** ***put this power to work*** Other ancient authorities read *has put this power to work* [b] **Eph 3:9** ***to make everyone see*** Other ancient authorities read *to bring to light* [c] **Eph 6:12** ***our*** Other ancient authorities read *your* [d] **Col 2:13** ***made you*** Other ancient authorities read *made us*; others, *made*

τῇ ἀποχρήσει, κατὰ τὰ ἐντάλματα καὶ διδασκαλίας τῶν ἀνθρώπων, **23** ἅτινά ἐστιν λόγον μὲν ἔχοντα σοφίας ἐν ἐθελοθρησκίᾳ καὶ ταπεινοφροσύνῃ [καὶ] ἀφειδίᾳ σώματος, οὐκ ἐν τιμῇ τινι πρὸς πλησμονὴν τῆς σαρκός.

84. Spiritual Warfare

Rom 6:13

μηδὲ παριστάνετε τὰ μέλη ὑμῶν ὅπλα ἀδικίας τῇ ἁμαρτίᾳ, ἀλλὰ παραστήσατε ἑαυτοὺς τῷ θεῷ ὡσεὶ ἐκ νεκρῶν ζῶντας καὶ τὰ μέλη ὑμῶν ὅπλα δικαιοσύνης τῷ θεῷ.

Rom 13:11–14

Καὶ τοῦτο εἰδότες τὸν καιρόν, ὅτι ὥρα ἤδη ὑμᾶς ἐξ ὕπνου ἐγερθῆναι, νῦν γὰρ ἐγγύτερον ἡμῶν ἡ σωτηρία ἢ ὅτε ἐπιστεύσαμεν. **12** ἡ νὺξ προέκοψεν, ἡ δὲ ἡμέρα ἤγγικεν. ἀποθώμεθα οὖν τὰ ἔργα τοῦ σκότους, ἐνδυσώμεθα [δὲ] τὰ ὅπλα τοῦ φωτός. **13** ὡς ἐν ἡμέρᾳ εὐσχημόνως περιπατήσωμεν, μὴ κώμοις καὶ μέθαις, μὴ κοίταις καὶ ἀσελγείαις, μὴ ἔριδι καὶ ζήλῳ, **14** ἀλλὰ ἐνδύσασθε τὸν κύριον Ἰησοῦν Χριστὸν καὶ τῆς σαρκὸς πρόνοιαν μὴ ποιεῖσθε εἰς ἐπιθυμίας.

2 Cor 6:7

ἐν λόγῳ ἀληθείας, ἐν δυνάμει θεοῦ· διὰ τῶν ὅπλων τῆς δικαιοσύνης τῶν δεξιῶν καὶ ἀριστερῶν

2 Cor 10:1–6

Αὐτὸς δὲ ἐγὼ Παῦλος παρακαλῶ ὑμᾶς διὰ τῆς πραΰτητος καὶ ἐπιεικείας τοῦ Χριστοῦ, ὃς κατὰ πρόσωπον μὲν ταπεινὸς ἐν ὑμῖν, ἀπὼν δὲ θαρρῶ εἰς ὑμᾶς· **2** δέομαι δὲ τὸ μὴ παρὼν θαρρῆσαι τῇ πεποιθήσει ᾗ λογίζομαι τολμῆσαι ἐπί τινας τοὺς λογιζομένους ἡμᾶς ὡς κατὰ σάρκα περιπατοῦντας. **3** Ἐν σαρκὶ γὰρ περιπατοῦντες οὐ κατὰ σάρκα στρατευόμεθα, **4** τὰ γὰρ ὅπλα τῆς στρατείας ἡμῶν οὐ σαρκικὰ ἀλλὰ δυνατὰ τῷ θεῷ πρὸς καθαίρεσιν ὀχυρωμάτων, λογισμοὺς καθαιροῦντες **5** καὶ πᾶν ὕψωμα ἐπαιρόμενον κατὰ τῆς γνώσεως τοῦ θεοῦ, καὶ αἰχμαλωτίζοντες πᾶν νόημα εἰς τὴν ὑπακοὴν τοῦ Χριστοῦ, **6** καὶ ἐν ἑτοίμῳ ἔχοντες ἐκδικῆσαι πᾶσαν παρακοήν, ὅταν πληρωθῇ ὑμῶν ἡ ὑπακοή.

Eph 6:10–20

Τοῦ λοιποῦ, ἐνδυναμοῦσθε ἐν κυρίῳ καὶ ἐν τῷ κράτει τῆς ἰσχύος αὐτοῦ. **11** ἐνδύσασθε τὴν πανοπλίαν τοῦ θεοῦ πρὸς τὸ δύνασθαι ὑμᾶς στῆναι πρὸς τὰς μεθοδείας τοῦ διαβόλου· **12** ὅτι οὐκ ἔστιν ⸀ἡμῖν ἡ πάλη πρὸς αἷμα καὶ σάρκα ἀλλὰ πρὸς τὰς ἀρχάς, πρὸς τὰς ἐξουσίας, πρὸς τοὺς κοσμοκράτορας τοῦ σκότους τούτου, πρὸς τὰ πνευματικὰ τῆς πονηρίας ἐν τοῖς ἐπουρανίοις. **13** διὰ τοῦτο ἀναλάβετε τὴν πανοπλίαν τοῦ θεοῦ, ἵνα δυνηθῆτε ἀντιστῆναι ἐν τῇ ἡμέρᾳ τῇ πονηρᾷ καὶ ἅπαντα κατεργασάμενοι στῆναι. **14** στῆτε οὖν περιζωσάμενοι τὴν ὀσφὺν ὑμῶν ἐν ἀληθείᾳ καὶ ἐνδυσάμενοι τὸν θώρακα τῆς δικαιοσύνης **15** καὶ ὑποδησάμενοι τοὺς πόδας ἐν ἑτοιμασίᾳ τοῦ εὐαγγελίου τῆς εἰρήνης, **16** ἐν πᾶσιν ἀναλαβόντες τὸν θυρεὸν τῆς πίστεως, ἐν ᾧ δυνήσεσθε πάντα τὰ βέλη τοῦ πονηροῦ [τὰ] πεπυρωμένα σβέσαι· **17** καὶ τὴν περικεφαλαίαν τοῦ σωτηρίου δέξασθε καὶ τὴν μάχαιραν τοῦ πνεύματος, ὅ ἐστιν ῥῆμα θεοῦ. **18** Διὰ πάσης προσευχῆς καὶ δεήσεως προσευχόμενοι ἐν παντὶ καιρῷ ἐν πνεύματι, καὶ εἰς αὐτὸ ἀγρυπνοῦντες ἐν πάσῃ προσκαρτερήσει καὶ δεήσει περὶ πάντων τῶν ἁγίων **19** καὶ ὑπὲρ ἐμοῦ, ἵνα μοι δοθῇ λόγος ἐν ἀνοίξει τοῦ στόματός μου, ἐν παρρησίᾳ γνωρίσαι τὸ μυστήριον ⸂τοῦ εὐαγγελίου⸃, **20** ὑπὲρ οὗ πρεσβεύω ἐν ἁλύσει, ἵνα ἐν αὐτῷ παρρησιάσωμαι ὡς δεῖ με λαλῆσαι.

Phil 2:25

Ἀναγκαῖον δὲ ἡγησάμην Ἐπαφρόδιτον τὸν ἀδελφὸν καὶ συνεργὸν καὶ συστρατιώτην μου, ὑμῶν δὲ ἀπόστολον καὶ λειτουργὸν τῆς χρείας μου, πέμψαι πρὸς ὑμᾶς

1 Thess 5:8

ἡμεῖς δὲ ἡμέρας ὄντες νήφωμεν ἐνδυσάμενοι θώρακα πίστεως καὶ ἀγάπης καὶ περικεφαλαίαν ἐλπίδα σωτηρίας

1 Tim 1:18–20

Ταύτην τὴν παραγγελίαν παρατίθεμαί σοι, τέκνον Τιμόθεε, κατὰ τὰς προαγούσας ἐπὶ σὲ προφητείας, ἵνα στρατεύῃ ἐν αὐταῖς τὴν καλὴν στρατείαν **19** ἔχων πίστιν καὶ ἀγαθὴν συνείδησιν, ἥν τινες ἀπωσάμενοι περὶ τὴν πίστιν ἐναυάγησαν, **20** ὧν ἐστιν Ὑμέναιος καὶ Ἀλέξανδρος, οὓς παρέδωκα τῷ σατανᾷ, ἵνα παιδευθῶσιν μὴ βλασφημεῖν.

2 Tim 2:1–7

Σὺ οὖν, τέκνον μου, ἐνδυναμοῦ ἐν τῇ χάριτι τῇ ἐν Χριστῷ Ἰησοῦ, **2** καὶ ἃ ἤκουσας παρ' ἐμοῦ διὰ πολλῶν μαρτύρων, ταῦτα παράθου πιστοῖς ἀνθρώποις, οἵτινες ἱκανοὶ ἔσονται καὶ ἑτέρους διδάξαι. **3** Συγκακοπάθησον ὡς καλὸς στρατιώτης Χριστοῦ Ἰησοῦ. **4** οὐδεὶς στρατευόμενος ἐμπλέκεται ταῖς τοῦ βίου πραγματείαις, ἵνα τῷ στρατολογήσαντι ἀρέσῃ. **5** ἐὰν δὲ καὶ ἀθλῇ τις, οὐ στεφανοῦται ἐὰν μὴ νομίμως ἀθλήσῃ. **6** τὸν κοπιῶντα γεωργὸν δεῖ πρῶτον τῶν καρπῶν μεταλαμβάνειν. **7** νόει ὃ λέγω· δώσει γάρ σοι ὁ κύριος σύνεσιν ἐν πᾶσιν.

Phlm 2

καὶ Ἀπφίᾳ τῇ ἀδελφῇ καὶ Ἀρχίππῳ τῷ συστρατιώτῃ ἡμῶν καὶ τῇ κατ' οἶκόν σου ἐκκλησίᾳ

Cf. Rom 7:22–23; 1 Cor 9:7; Phil 1:27–30; 4:7.

§ 84 **Eph 6:12** ***ημιν*** ℵ A D^{2} I 33. 1739. 1881 *Byz*] υμιν $\mathfrak{P}^{46}$ B D* **Eph 6:19** ***του ευαγγελιου*** ℵ A D I 33. 1739. 1881 *Byz*] *om.* B

regulations refer to things that perish with use; they are simply human commands and teachings. **23** These have indeed an appearance of wisdom in promoting self-imposed piety, humility, and severe treatment of the body, but they are of no value in checking self-indulgence.

Note: The phrase "elemental spirits" in the passages above translates the Greek word στοιχεῖα. There is no consensus among scholars as to the meaning(s) of this term within the Pauline corpus. Some interpreters understand the term to refer to personal spiritual beings, angelic or demonic, while others understand it to refer to particular philosophical or religious teachings. The NRSV translation adopts the first view; interpreters who adopt the second view translate the term as "rudimentary principles" and the like.

84. Spiritual Warfare

Rom 6:13

No longer present your members to sin as weapons[a] of wickedness, but present yourselves to God as those who have been brought from death to life, and present your members to God as weapons[a] of righteousness.

Rom 13:11–14

Besides this, you know what time it is, how it is now the moment for you to wake from sleep. For salvation is nearer to us now than when we became believers; **12** the night is far gone, the day is near. Let us then lay aside the works of darkness and put on the armor of light; **13** let us walk[b] honorably as in the day, not in reveling and drunkenness, not in debauchery and licentiousness, not in quarreling and jealousy. **14** Instead, put on the Lord Jesus Christ, and make no provision for the flesh, to gratify its desires.

2 Cor 6:7

truthful speech, and the power of God; with the weapons of righteousness for the right hand and for the left

2 Cor 10:1–6

I myself, Paul, appeal to you by the meekness and gentleness of Christ—I who am humble when face to face with you, but bold toward you when I am away!— **2** I ask that when I am present I need not show boldness by daring to oppose those who think we are acting according to human standards. **3** Indeed, we live as human beings, but we do not wage war according to human standards; **4** for the weapons of our warfare are not merely human, but they have divine power to destroy strongholds. We destroy arguments **5** and every proud obstacle raised up against the knowledge of God, and we take every thought captive to obey Christ. **6** We are ready to punish every disobedience when your obedience is complete.

Eph 6:10–20

Finally, be strong in the Lord and in the strength of his power. **11** Put on the whole armor of God, so that you may be able to stand against the wiles of the devil. **12** For our[c] struggle is not against enemies of blood and flesh, but against the rulers, against the authorities, against the cosmic powers of this present darkness, against the spiritual forces of evil in the heavenly places. **13** Therefore take up the whole armor of God, so that you may be able to withstand on that evil day, and having done everything, to stand firm. **14** Stand therefore, and fasten the belt of truth around your waist, and put on the breastplate of righteousness. **15** As shoes for your feet put on whatever will make you ready to proclaim the gospel of peace. **16** With all of these, take the shield of faith, with which you will be able to quench all the flaming arrows of the evil one. **17** Take the helmet of salvation, and the sword of the Spirit, which is the word of God. **18** Pray in the Spirit at all times in every prayer and supplication. To that end keep alert and always persevere in supplication for all the saints. **19** Pray also for me, so that when I speak, a message may be given to me to make known with boldness the mystery of the gospel,[d] **20** for which I am an ambassador in chains. Pray that I may declare it boldly, as I must speak.

Phil 2:25

Still, I think it necessary to send to you Epaphroditus—my brother and co-worker and fellow soldier, your messenger and minister to my need

1 Thess 5:8

But since we belong to the day, let us be sober, and put on the breastplate of faith and love, and for a helmet the hope of salvation.

1 Tim 1:18–20

I am giving you these instructions, Timothy, my child, in accordance with the prophecies made earlier about you, so that by following them you may fight the good fight, **19** having faith and a good conscience. By rejecting conscience, certain persons have suffered shipwreck in the faith; **20** among them are Hymenaeus and Alexander, whom I have turned over to Satan, so that they may learn not to blaspheme.

2 Tim 2:1–7

You then, my child, be strong in the grace that is in Christ Jesus; **2** and what you have heard from me through many witnesses entrust to faithful people who will be able to teach others as well. **3** Share in suffering like a good soldier of Christ Jesus. **4** No one serving in the army gets entangled in everyday affairs; the soldier's aim is to please the enlisting officer. **5** And in the case of an athlete, no one is crowned without competing according to the rules. **6** It is the farmer who does the work who ought to have the first share of the crops. **7** Think over what I say, for the Lord will give you understanding in all things.

Phlm 2

to Apphia our sister, to Archippus our fellow soldier, and to the church in your house

Cf. Rom 7:22–23; 1 Cor 9:7; Phil 1:27–30; 4:7.

§ 84 [a] **Rom 6:13** *weapons* Or possibly instruments (so NRSV) [b] **Rom 13:13** *walk* NRSV translates *live* [c] **Eph 6:12** *our* Other ancient authorities read *your* [d] **Eph 6:19** *of the gospel* Other ancient authorities lack *of the gospel*

85. Standing Firm in the Faith

Rom 11:17–22

Εἰ δέ τινες τῶν κλάδων ἐξεκλάσθησαν, σὺ δὲ ἀγριέλαιος ὢν ἐνεκεντρίσθης ἐν αὐτοῖς καὶ συγκοινωνὸς ⸂τῆς ῥίζης⸃ τῆς πιότητος τῆς ἐλαίας ἐγένου, 18 μὴ κατακαυχῶ τῶν κλάδων· εἰ δὲ κατακαυχᾶσαι οὐ σὺ τὴν ῥίζαν βαστάζεις ἀλλὰ ἡ ῥίζα σέ. 19 ἐρεῖς οὖν· ἐξεκλάσθησαν κλάδοι ἵνα ἐγὼ ἐγκεντρισθῶ. 20 καλῶς· τῇ ἀπιστίᾳ ἐξεκλάσθησαν, σὺ δὲ τῇ πίστει ἕστηκας. μὴ ὑψηλὰ φρόνει ἀλλὰ φοβοῦ· 21 εἰ γὰρ ὁ θεὸς τῶν κατὰ φύσιν κλάδων οὐκ ἐφείσατο, ⸂[μή πως]⸃ οὐδὲ σοῦ φείσεται. 22 ἴδε οὖν χρηστότητα καὶ ἀποτομίαν θεοῦ· ἐπὶ μὲν τοὺς πεσόντας ἀποτομία, ἐπὶ δὲ σὲ χρηστότης θεοῦ, ἐὰν ἐπιμένῃς τῇ χρηστότητι, ἐπεὶ καὶ σὺ ἐκκοπήσῃ.

1 Cor 1:8–9

ὃς καὶ βεβαιώσει ὑμᾶς ἕως τέλους ἀνεγκλήτους ἐν τῇ ἡμέρᾳ τοῦ κυρίου ἡμῶν Ἰησοῦ [Χριστοῦ]. 9 πιστὸς ὁ θεός, δι᾿ οὗ ἐκλήθητε εἰς κοινωνίαν τοῦ υἱοῦ αὐτοῦ Ἰησοῦ Χριστοῦ τοῦ κυρίου ἡμῶν.

1 Cor 10:11–13

ταῦτα δὲ τυπικῶς συνέβαινεν ἐκείνοις, ἐγράφη δὲ πρὸς νουθεσίαν ἡμῶν, εἰς οὓς τὰ τέλη τῶν αἰώνων κατήντηκεν. 12 Ὥστε ὁ δοκῶν ἑστάναι βλεπέτω μὴ πέσῃ. 13 πειρασμὸς ὑμᾶς οὐκ εἴληφεν εἰ μὴ ἀνθρώπινος· πιστὸς δὲ ὁ θεός, ὃς οὐκ ἐάσει ὑμᾶς πειρασθῆναι ὑπὲρ ὃ δύνασθε ἀλλὰ ποιήσει σὺν τῷ πειρασμῷ καὶ τὴν ἔκβασιν τοῦ δύνασθαι ὑπενεγκεῖν.

1 Cor 15:1–2

Γνωρίζω δὲ ὑμῖν, ἀδελφοί, τὸ εὐαγγέλιον ὃ εὐηγγελισάμην ὑμῖν, ὃ καὶ παρελάβετε, ἐν ᾧ καὶ ἑστήκατε, 2 δι᾿ οὗ καὶ σῴζεσθε, τίνι λόγῳ εὐηγγελισάμην ὑμῖν εἰ κατέχετε, ἐκτὸς εἰ μὴ εἰκῇ ἐπιστεύσατε.

1 Cor 15:56–58

τὸ δὲ κέντρον τοῦ θανάτου ἡ ἁμαρτία, ἡ δὲ δύναμις τῆς ἁμαρτίας ὁ νόμος· 57 τῷ δὲ θεῷ χάρις τῷ διδόντι ἡμῖν τὸ νῖκος διὰ τοῦ κυρίου ἡμῶν Ἰησοῦ Χριστοῦ. 58 Ὥστε, ἀδελφοί μου ἀγαπητοί, ἑδραῖοι γίνεσθε, ἀμετακίνητοι, περισσεύοντες ἐν τῷ ἔργῳ τοῦ κυρίου πάντοτε, εἰδότες ὅτι ὁ κόπος ὑμῶν οὐκ ἔστιν κενὸς ἐν κυρίῳ.

1 Cor 16:13–14

Γρηγορεῖτε, στήκετε ἐν τῇ πίστει, ἀνδρίζεσθε, κραταιοῦσθε. 14 πάντα ὑμῶν ἐν ἀγάπῃ γινέσθω.

2 Cor 1:18–24

πιστὸς δὲ ὁ θεὸς ὅτι ὁ λόγος ἡμῶν ὁ πρὸς ὑμᾶς οὐκ ἔστιν ναὶ καὶ οὔ. 19 ὁ τοῦ θεοῦ γὰρ υἱὸς Ἰησοῦς Χριστὸς ὁ ἐν ὑμῖν δι᾿ ἡμῶν κηρυχθείς, δι᾿ ἐμοῦ καὶ Σιλουανοῦ καὶ Τιμοθέου, οὐκ ἐγένετο ναὶ καὶ οὒ ἀλλὰ ναὶ ἐν αὐτῷ γέγονεν. 20 ὅσαι γὰρ ἐπαγγελίαι θεοῦ, ἐν αὐτῷ τὸ ναί· διὸ καὶ δι᾿ αὐτοῦ τὸ ἀμὴν τῷ θεῷ πρὸς δόξαν δι᾿ ἡμῶν. 21 ὁ δὲ βεβαιῶν ἡμᾶς σὺν ὑμῖν εἰς Χριστὸν καὶ χρίσας ἡμᾶς θεός, 22 ὁ καὶ σφραγισάμενος ἡμᾶς καὶ δοὺς τὸν ἀρραβῶνα τοῦ πνεύματος ἐν ταῖς καρδίαις ἡμῶν. 23 Ἐγὼ δὲ μάρτυρα τὸν θεὸν ἐπικαλοῦμαι ἐπὶ τὴν ἐμὴν ψυχήν, ὅτι φειδόμενος ὑμῶν οὐκέτι ἦλθον εἰς Κόρινθον. 24 οὐχ ὅτι κυριεύομεν ὑμῶν τῆς πίστεως ἀλλὰ συνεργοί ἐσμεν τῆς χαρᾶς ὑμῶν· τῇ γὰρ πίστει ἑστήκατε.

Gal 5:1–2

Τῇ ἐλευθερίᾳ ἡμᾶς Χριστὸς ἠλευθέρωσεν· στήκετε οὖν καὶ μὴ πάλιν ζυγῷ δουλείας ἐνέχεσθε. 2 Ἴδε ἐγὼ Παῦλος λέγω ὑμῖν ὅτι ἐὰν περιτέμνησθε, Χριστὸς ὑμᾶς οὐδὲν ὠφελήσει.

Eph 6:10–20

Τοῦ λοιποῦ, ἐνδυναμοῦσθε ἐν κυρίῳ καὶ ἐν τῷ κράτει τῆς ἰσχύος αὐτοῦ. 11 ἐνδύσασθε τὴν πανοπλίαν τοῦ θεοῦ πρὸς τὸ δύνασθαι ὑμᾶς στῆναι πρὸς τὰς μεθοδείας τοῦ διαβόλου· 12 ὅτι οὐκ ἔστιν ⸀ἡμῖν ἡ πάλη πρὸς αἷμα καὶ σάρκα ἀλλὰ πρὸς τὰς ἀρχάς, πρὸς τὰς ἐξουσίας, πρὸς τοὺς κοσμοκράτορας τοῦ σκότους τούτου, πρὸς τὰ πνευματικὰ τῆς πονηρίας ἐν τοῖς ἐπουρανίοις. 13 διὰ τοῦτο ἀναλάβετε τὴν πανοπλίαν τοῦ θεοῦ, ἵνα δυνηθῆτε ἀντιστῆναι ἐν τῇ ἡμέρᾳ τῇ πονηρᾷ καὶ ἅπαντα κατεργασάμενοι στῆναι. 14 στῆτε οὖν περιζωσάμενοι τὴν ὀσφὺν ὑμῶν ἐν ἀληθείᾳ καὶ ἐνδυσάμενοι τὸν θώρακα τῆς δικαιοσύνης 15 καὶ ὑποδησάμενοι τοὺς πόδας ἐν ἑτοιμασίᾳ τοῦ εὐαγγελίου τῆς εἰρήνης, 16 ἐν πᾶσιν ἀναλαβόντες τὸν θυρεὸν τῆς πίστεως, ἐν ᾧ δυνήσεσθε πάντα τὰ βέλη τοῦ πονηροῦ [τὰ] πεπυρωμένα σβέσαι· 17 καὶ τὴν περικεφαλαίαν τοῦ σωτηρίου δέξασθε καὶ τὴν μάχαιραν τοῦ πνεύματος, ὅ ἐστιν ῥῆμα θεοῦ. 18 Διὰ πάσης προσευχῆς καὶ δεήσεως προσευχόμενοι ἐν παντὶ καιρῷ ἐν πνεύματι, καὶ εἰς αὐτὸ ἀγρυπνοῦντες ἐν πάσῃ προσκαρτερήσει καὶ δεήσει περὶ πάντων τῶν ἁγίων 19 καὶ ὑπὲρ ἐμοῦ, ἵνα μοι δοθῇ λόγος ἐν ἀνοίξει τοῦ στόματός μου, ἐν παρρησίᾳ γνωρίσαι τὸ μυστήριον ⸂τοῦ εὐαγγελίου⸃, 20 ὑπὲρ οὗ πρεσβεύω ἐν ἁλύσει, ἵνα ἐν αὐτῷ παρρησιάσωμαι ὡς δεῖ με λαλῆσαι.

Phil 1:27–28

Μόνον ἀξίως τοῦ εὐαγγελίου τοῦ Χριστοῦ πολιτεύεσθε, ἵνα εἴτε ἐλθὼν καὶ ἰδὼν ὑμᾶς εἴτε ἀπὼν ἀκούω τὰ περὶ ὑμῶν, ὅτι στήκετε ἐν ἑνὶ πνεύματι, μιᾷ ψυχῇ συναθλοῦντες τῇ πίστει τοῦ εὐαγγελίου 28 καὶ μὴ πτυρόμενοι ἐν μηδενὶ ὑπὸ τῶν ἀντικειμένων, ἥτις ἐστὶν αὐτοῖς ἔνδειξις ἀπωλείας, ὑμῶν δὲ σωτηρίας, καὶ τοῦτο ἀπὸ θεοῦ

Phil 3:17–4:1

Συμμιμηταί μου γίνεσθε, ἀδελφοί, καὶ σκοπεῖτε τοὺς οὕτω περιπατοῦντας καθὼς ἔχετε τύπον ἡμᾶς. 18 πολλοὶ γὰρ περιπατοῦσιν οὓς πολλάκις ἔλεγον ὑμῖν, νῦν δὲ καὶ κλαίων λέγω, τοὺς ἐχθροὺς τοῦ σταυροῦ τοῦ Χριστοῦ, 19 ὧν τὸ τέλος ἀπώλεια, ὧν ὁ θεὸς ἡ κοιλία καὶ ἡ δόξα ἐν τῇ αἰσχύνῃ αὐτῶν, οἱ τὰ ἐπίγεια

---

§ 85 **Rom 11:17** ***της ριζης*** א* B C] της ριζης και א² A D² 33. 1739. 1881 *Byz* ¦ *om.* 𝔓⁴⁶ D* **Rom 11:21** ***μη πως*** 𝔓⁴⁶ D 33 *Byz*] *om.* א A B C 1739. 1881 **Eph 6:12** ***ημιν*** א A D² I 33. 1739. 1881 *Byz*] υμιν 𝔓⁴⁶ B D* **Eph 6:19** ***του ευαγγελιου*** א A D I 33. 1739. 1881 *Byz*] *om.* B

85. Standing Firm in the Faith

Rom 11:17–22

But if some of the branches were broken off, and you, a wild olive shoot, were grafted in their place to share the rich root[a] of the olive tree, **18** do not boast over the branches. If you do boast, remember that it is not you that support the root, but the root that supports you. **19** You will say, "Branches were broken off so that I might be grafted in." **20** That is true. They were broken off because of their unbelief, but you stand only through faith. So do not become proud, but stand in awe. **21** For if God did not spare the natural branches, perhaps he will not spare you.[b] **22** Note then the kindness and the severity of God: severity toward those who have fallen, but God's kindness toward you, provided you continue in his kindness; otherwise you also will be cut off.

1 Cor 1:8–9

He will also strengthen you to the end, so that you may be blameless on the day of our Lord Jesus Christ. **9** God is faithful; by him you were called into the fellowship of his Son, Jesus Christ our Lord.

1 Cor 10:11–13

These things happened to them to serve as an example, and they were written down to instruct us, on whom the ends of the ages have come. **12** So if you think you are standing, watch out that you do not fall. **13** No testing has overtaken you that is not common to everyone. God is faithful, and he will not let you be tested beyond your strength, but with the testing he will also provide the way out so that you may be able to endure it.

1 Cor 15:1–2

Now I would remind you, brothers and sisters, of the good news that I proclaimed to you, which you in turn received, in which also you stand, **2** through which also you are being saved, if you hold firmly to the message that I proclaimed to you—unless you have come to believe in vain.

1 Cor 15:56–58

The sting of death is sin, and the power of sin is the law. **57** But thanks be to God, who gives us the victory through our Lord Jesus Christ. **58** Therefore, my beloved, be steadfast, immovable, always excelling in the work of the Lord, because you know that in the Lord your labor is not in vain.

1 Cor 16:13–14

Keep alert, stand firm in your faith, be courageous, be strong. **14** Let all that you do be done in love.

2 Cor 1:18–24

As surely as God is faithful, our word to you has not been "Yes and No." **19** For the Son of God, Jesus Christ, whom we proclaimed among you, Silvanus and Timothy and I, was not "Yes and No"; but in him it is always "Yes." **20** For in him every one of God's promises is a "Yes." For this reason it is through him that we say the "Amen," to the glory of God. **21** But it is God who establishes us with you in Christ and has anointed us, **22** by putting his seal on us and giving us his Spirit in our hearts as a first installment. **23** But I call on God as witness against me: it was to spare you that I did not come again to Corinth. **24** I do not mean to imply that we lord it over your faith; rather, we are workers with you for your joy, because you stand firm in the faith.

Gal 5:1–2

For freedom Christ has set us free. Stand firm, therefore, and do not submit again to a yoke of slavery. **2** Listen! I, Paul, am telling you that if you let yourselves be circumcised, Christ will be of no benefit to you.

Eph 6:10–20

Finally, be strong in the Lord and in the strength of his power. **11** Put on the whole armor of God, so that you may be able to stand against the wiles of the devil. **12** For our[c] struggle is not against enemies of blood and flesh, but against the rulers, against the authorities, against the cosmic powers of this present darkness, against the spiritual forces of evil in the heavenly places. **13** Therefore take up the whole armor of God, so that you may be able to withstand on that evil day, and having done everything, to stand firm. **14** Stand therefore, and fasten the belt of truth around your waist, and put on the breastplate of righteousness. **15** As shoes for your feet put on whatever will make you ready to proclaim the gospel of peace. **16** With all of these, take the shield of faith, with which you will be able to quench all the flaming arrows of the evil one. **17** Take the helmet of salvation, and the sword of the Spirit, which is the word of God. **18** Pray in the Spirit at all times in every prayer and supplication. To that end keep alert and always persevere in supplication for all the saints. **19** Pray also for me, so that when I speak, a message may be given to me to make known with boldness the mystery of the gospel,[d] **20** for which I am an ambassador in chains. Pray that I may declare it boldly, as I must speak.

Phil 1:27–28

Only, live your life in a manner worthy of the gospel of Christ, so that, whether I come and see you or am absent and hear about you, I will know that you are standing firm in one spirit, striving side by side with one mind for the faith of the gospel, **28** and are in no way intimidated by your opponents. For them this is evidence of their destruction, but of your salvation. And this is God's doing.

Phil 3:17–4:1

Brothers and sisters, join in imitating me, and observe those who live according to the example you have in us. **18** For many live as enemies of the cross of Christ; I have often told you of them, and now I tell you even with tears. **19** Their end is destruction; their god is the belly; and their glory is in their shame; their minds are set

§ 85 [a] **Rom 11:17** *the rich root* Other ancient authorities read *the richness* [b] **Rom 11:21** *perhaps he will not spare you* Other ancient authorities read *neither will he spare you* [c] **Eph 6:12** *our* Other ancient authorities read *your* [d] **Eph 6:19** *of the gospel* Other ancient authorities lack *of the gospel*

φρονοῦντες. 20 ἡμῶν γὰρ τὸ πολίτευμα
ἐν οὐρανοῖς ὑπάρχει, ἐξ οὗ καὶ σωτῆρα
ἀπεκδεχόμεθα κύριον Ἰησοῦν Χριστόν,
21 ὃς μετασχηματίσει τὸ σῶμα τῆς ταπει-
νώσεως ἡμῶν σύμμορφον τῷ σώματι
τῆς δόξης αὐτοῦ κατὰ τὴν ἐνέργειαν τοῦ
δύνασθαι αὐτὸν καὶ ὑποτάξαι αὐτῷ τὰ
πάντα. **4** Ὥστε, ἀδελφοί μου ἀγαπητοὶ
καὶ ἐπιπόθητοι, χαρὰ καὶ στέφανός μου,
οὕτως στήκετε ἐν κυρίῳ, ἀγαπητοί.

Col 1:22–23

νυνὶ δὲ ⸀ἀποκατήλλαξεν ἐν τῷ σώματι
τῆς σαρκὸς αὐτοῦ διὰ τοῦ θανάτου πα-
ραστῆσαι ὑμᾶς ἁγίους καὶ ἀμώμους καὶ
ἀνεγκλήτους κατενώπιον αὐτοῦ, 23 εἴ γε
ἐπιμένετε τῇ πίστει τεθεμελιωμένοι καὶ
ἑδραῖοι καὶ μὴ μετακινούμενοι ἀπὸ τῆς
ἐλπίδος τοῦ εὐαγγελίου οὗ ἠκούσατε,
τοῦ κηρυχθέντος ἐν πάσῃ κτίσει τῇ ὑπὸ
τὸν οὐρανόν, οὗ ἐγενόμην ἐγὼ Παῦλος
διάκονος.

Col 2:6–7

Ὡς οὖν παρελάβετε τὸν Χριστὸν Ἰη-
σοῦν τὸν κύριον, ἐν αὐτῷ περιπατεῖτε,
7 ἐρριζωμένοι καὶ ἐποικοδομούμενοι
ἐν αὐτῷ καὶ βεβαιούμενοι τῇ πίστει
καθὼς ἐδιδάχθητε, περισσεύοντες ἐν
εὐχαριστίᾳ.

1 Thess 3:1–13

Διὸ μηκέτι στέγοντες εὐδοκήσαμεν κα-
ταλειφθῆναι ἐν Ἀθήναις μόνοι 2 καὶ
ἐπέμψαμεν Τιμόθεον, τὸν ἀδελφὸν
ἡμῶν καὶ ⸂συνεργὸν τοῦ θεοῦ⸃ ἐν τῷ
εὐαγγελίῳ τοῦ Χριστοῦ, εἰς τὸ στηρίξαι
ὑμᾶς καὶ παρακαλέσαι ὑπὲρ τῆς πίστεως
ὑμῶν 3 τὸ μηδένα σαίνεσθαι ἐν ταῖς
θλίψεσιν ταύταις. αὐτοὶ γὰρ οἴδατε ὅτι
εἰς τοῦτο κείμεθα· 4 καὶ γὰρ ὅτε πρὸς
ὑμᾶς ἦμεν, προελέγομεν ὑμῖν ὅτι μέλ-
λομεν θλίβεσθαι, καθὼς καὶ ἐγένετο καὶ
οἴδατε. 5 διὰ τοῦτο κἀγὼ μηκέτι στέγων
ἔπεμψα εἰς τὸ γνῶναι τὴν πίστιν ὑμῶν,
μή πως ἐπείρασεν ὑμᾶς ὁ πειράζων καὶ
εἰς κενὸν γένηται ὁ κόπος ἡμῶν. 6 Ἄρτι
δὲ ἐλθόντος Τιμοθέου πρὸς ἡμᾶς ἀφ'
ὑμῶν καὶ εὐαγγελισαμένου ἡμῖν τὴν
πίστιν καὶ τὴν ἀγάπην ὑμῶν καὶ ὅτι
ἔχετε μνείαν ἡμῶν ἀγαθὴν πάντοτε,
ἐπιποθοῦντες ἡμᾶς ἰδεῖν καθάπερ καὶ
ἡμεῖς ὑμᾶς, 7 διὰ τοῦτο παρεκλήθημεν,
ἀδελφοί, ἐφ' ὑμῖν ἐπὶ πάσῃ τῇ ἀνάγκῃ καὶ
θλίψει ἡμῶν διὰ τῆς ὑμῶν πίστεως, 8 ὅτι
νῦν ζῶμεν ἐὰν ὑμεῖς στήκετε ἐν κυρίῳ.
9 τίνα γὰρ εὐχαριστίαν δυνάμεθα τῷ
θεῷ ἀνταποδοῦναι περὶ ὑμῶν ἐπὶ πάσῃ
τῇ χαρᾷ ᾗ χαίρομεν δι' ὑμᾶς ἔμπροσθεν
τοῦ θεοῦ ἡμῶν, 10 νυκτὸς καὶ ἡμέρας
ὑπερεκπερισσοῦ δεόμενοι εἰς τὸ ἰδεῖν
ὑμῶν τὸ πρόσωπον καὶ καταρτίσαι τὰ
ὑστερήματα τῆς πίστεως ὑμῶν; 11 Αὐτὸς
δὲ ὁ θεὸς καὶ πατὴρ ἡμῶν καὶ ὁ κύριος
ἡμῶν Ἰησοῦς κατευθύναι τὴν ὁδὸν ἡμῶν
πρὸς ὑμᾶς· 12 ὑμᾶς δὲ ὁ κύριος πλεονάσαι
καὶ περισσεύσαι τῇ ἀγάπῃ εἰς ἀλλήλους
καὶ εἰς πάντας καθάπερ καὶ ἡμεῖς εἰς
ὑμᾶς, 13 εἰς τὸ στηρίξαι ὑμῶν τὰς καρδίας
ἀμέμπτους ἐν ἁγιωσύνῃ ἔμπροσθεν τοῦ
θεοῦ καὶ πατρὸς ἡμῶν ἐν τῇ παρουσίᾳ
τοῦ κυρίου ἡμῶν Ἰησοῦ μετὰ πάντων
τῶν ἁγίων αὐτοῦ, [ἀμήν].

1 Thess 5:23–24

Αὐτὸς δὲ ὁ θεὸς τῆς εἰρήνης ἁγιάσαι
ὑμᾶς ὁλοτελεῖς, καὶ ὁλόκληρον ὑμῶν τὸ
πνεῦμα καὶ ἡ ψυχὴ καὶ τὸ σῶμα ἀμέμ-
πτως ἐν τῇ παρουσίᾳ τοῦ κυρίου ἡμῶν
Ἰησοῦ Χριστοῦ τηρηθείη. 24 πιστὸς ὁ
καλῶν ὑμᾶς, ὃς καὶ ποιήσει.

2 Thess 1:11–12

Εἰς ὃ καὶ προσευχόμεθα πάντοτε περὶ
ὑμῶν, ἵνα ὑμᾶς ἀξιώσῃ τῆς κλήσεως ὁ
θεὸς ἡμῶν καὶ πληρώσῃ πᾶσαν εὐδοκίαν
ἀγαθωσύνης καὶ ἔργον πίστεως ἐν δυ-
νάμει, 12 ὅπως ἐνδοξασθῇ τὸ ὄνομα τοῦ
κυρίου ἡμῶν Ἰησοῦ ἐν ὑμῖν, καὶ ὑμεῖς
ἐν αὐτῷ, κατὰ τὴν χάριν τοῦ θεοῦ ἡμῶν
καὶ κυρίου Ἰησοῦ Χριστοῦ.

2 Thess 2:13–17

Ἡμεῖς δὲ ὀφείλομεν εὐχαριστεῖν τῷ θεῷ
πάντοτε περὶ ὑμῶν, ἀδελφοὶ ἠγαπημέ-
νοι ὑπὸ κυρίου, ὅτι εἵλατο ὑμᾶς ὁ θεὸς
⸀ἀπαρχὴν εἰς σωτηρίαν ἐν ἁγιασμῷ
πνεύματος καὶ πίστει ἀληθείας, 14 εἰς
ὃ [καὶ] ἐκάλεσεν ὑμᾶς διὰ τοῦ εὐαγγε-
λίου ἡμῶν εἰς περιποίησιν δόξης τοῦ
κυρίου ἡμῶν Ἰησοῦ Χριστοῦ. 15 Ἄρα
οὖν, ἀδελφοί, στήκετε καὶ κρατεῖτε τὰς
παραδόσεις ἃς ἐδιδάχθητε εἴτε διὰ λόγου
εἴτε δι' ἐπιστολῆς ἡμῶν. 16 Αὐτὸς δὲ ὁ
κύριος ἡμῶν Ἰησοῦς Χριστὸς καὶ [ὁ]
θεὸς ὁ πατὴρ ἡμῶν ὁ ἀγαπήσας ἡμᾶς καὶ
δοὺς παράκλησιν αἰωνίαν καὶ ἐλπίδα
ἀγαθὴν ἐν χάριτι, 17 παρακαλέσαι ὑμῶν
τὰς καρδίας καὶ στηρίξαι ἐν παντὶ ἔργῳ
καὶ λόγῳ ἀγαθῷ.

2 Thess 3:3–5

Πιστὸς δέ ἐστιν ὁ κύριος, ὃς στηρίξει
ὑμᾶς καὶ φυλάξει ἀπὸ τοῦ πονηροῦ.
4 πεποίθαμεν δὲ ἐν κυρίῳ ἐφ' ὑμᾶς, ὅτι
ἃ παραγγέλλομεν [καὶ] ποιεῖτε καὶ ποι-
ήσετε. 5 Ὁ δὲ κύριος κατευθύναι ὑμῶν
τὰς καρδίας εἰς τὴν ἀγάπην τοῦ θεοῦ καὶ
εἰς τὴν ὑπομονὴν τοῦ Χριστοῦ.

Cf. Rom 1:11–12; 2:7–8; 14:2–4; 16:25–27; Phil 1:5–6; 2:12–13; Col 1:11; 1 Thess 1:3; 2 Thess 1:4–5; 2 Tim 2:11–13; Acts 13:43; 14:21–22; 20:32.

86. Faith and Sight

Rom 8:18–25

Λογίζομαι γὰρ ὅτι οὐκ ἄξια τὰ παθήματα
τοῦ νῦν καιροῦ πρὸς τὴν μέλλουσαν δόξαν
ἀποκαλυφθῆναι εἰς ἡμᾶς. 19 ἡ γὰρ ἀπο-
καραδοκία τῆς κτίσεως τὴν ἀποκάλυψιν
τῶν υἱῶν τοῦ θεοῦ ἀπεκδέχεται. 20 τῇ
γὰρ ματαιότητι ἡ κτίσις ὑπετάγη, οὐχ
ἑκοῦσα ἀλλὰ διὰ τὸν ὑποτάξαντα, ἐφ'
ἑλπίδι 21 ὅτι καὶ αὐτὴ ἡ κτίσις ἐλευθερω-
θήσεται ἀπὸ τῆς δουλείας τῆς φθορᾶς εἰς
τὴν ἐλευθερίαν τῆς δόξης τῶν τέκνων
τοῦ θεοῦ. 22 οἴδαμεν γὰρ ὅτι πᾶσα ἡ
κτίσις συστενάζει καὶ συνωδίνει ἄχρι
τοῦ νῦν· 23 οὐ μόνον δέ, ἀλλὰ καὶ αὐτοὶ
τὴν ἀπαρχὴν τοῦ πνεύματος ἔχοντες,
ἡμεῖς καὶ αὐτοὶ ἐν ἑαυτοῖς στενάζομεν
υἱοθεσίαν ἀπεκδεχόμενοι, τὴν ἀπολύτρω-
σιν τοῦ σώματος ἡμῶν. 24 τῇ γὰρ ἐλπίδι
ἐσώθημεν· ἐλπὶς δὲ βλεπομένη οὐκ ἔστιν

Col 1:22 ***αποκατηλλαξεν*** ℵ A C D² 048. 1739. 1881 *Byz*] αποκατηλλαγητε (𝔓⁴⁶) B ¦ αποκαταλλαγεντες D* ¦ αποκατηλλακται 33 **1 Thess 3:2** ***συνεργον του θεου*** D* 33] συνεργον B ¦ διακονον του θεου ℵ A 1739. 1881 ¦ διακονον του θεου και συνεργον ημων D² *Byz* **2 Thess 2:13** ***απαρχην*** B 33. 1739. 1881] απ αρχης ℵ D *Byz*

on earthly things. 20 But our citizenship is in heaven, and it is from there that we are expecting a Savior, the Lord Jesus Christ. 21 He will transform the body of our humiliation that it may be conformed to the body of his glory, by the power that also enables him to make all things subject to himself. **4** Therefore, my brothers and sisters, whom I love and long for, my joy and crown, stand firm in the Lord in this way, my beloved.

Col 1:22–23

he has now reconciled[e] in his fleshly body through death, so as to present you holy and blameless and irreproachable before him— 23 provided that you continue securely established and steadfast in the faith, without shifting from the hope promised by the gospel that you heard, which has been proclaimed to every creature under heaven. I, Paul, became a servant of this gospel.

Col 2:6–7

As you therefore have received Christ Jesus the Lord, continue to live your lives in him, 7 rooted and built up in him and established in the faith, just as you were taught, abounding in thanksgiving.

1 Thess 3:1–13

Therefore when we could bear it no longer, we decided to be left alone in Athens; 2 and we sent Timothy, our brother and co-worker for God[f] in proclaiming the gospel of Christ, to strengthen and encourage you for the sake of your faith, 3 so that no one would be shaken by these persecutions. Indeed, you yourselves know that this is what we are destined for. 4 In fact, when we were with you, we told you beforehand that we were to suffer persecution; so it turned out, as you know. 5 For this reason, when I could bear it no longer, I sent to find out about your faith; I was afraid that somehow the tempter had tempted you and that our labor had been in vain. 6 But Timothy has just now come to us from you, and has brought us the good news of your faith and love. He has told us also that you always remember us kindly and long to see us—just as we long to see you. 7 For this reason, brothers and sisters, during all our distress and persecution we have been encouraged about you through your faith. 8 For we now live, if you continue to stand firm in the Lord. 9 How can we thank God enough for you in return for all the joy that we feel before our God because of you? 10 Night and day we pray most earnestly that we may see you face to face and restore whatever is lacking in your faith. 11 Now may our God and Father himself and our Lord Jesus direct our way to you. 12 And may the Lord make you increase and abound in love for one another and for all, just as we abound in love for you. 13 And may he so strengthen your hearts in holiness that you may be blameless before our God and Father at the coming of our Lord Jesus with all his saints.

1 Thess 5:23–24

May the God of peace himself sanctify you entirely; and may your spirit and soul and body be kept sound and blameless at the coming of our Lord Jesus Christ. 24 The one who calls you is faithful, and he will do this.

2 Thess 1:11–12

To this end we always pray for you, asking that our God will make you worthy of his call and will fulfill by his power every good resolve and work of faith, 12 so that the name of our Lord Jesus may be glorified in you, and you in him, according to the grace of our God and the Lord Jesus Christ.

2 Thess 2:13–17

But we must always give thanks to God for you, brothers and sisters beloved by the Lord, because God chose you as the first fruits[g] for salvation through sanctification by the Spirit and through belief in the truth. 14 For this purpose he called you through our proclamation of the good news, so that you may obtain the glory of our Lord Jesus Christ. 15 So then, brothers and sisters, stand firm and hold fast to the traditions that you were taught by us, either by word of mouth or by our letter. 16 Now may our Lord Jesus Christ himself and God our Father, who loved us and through grace gave us eternal comfort and good hope, 17 comfort your hearts and strengthen them in every good work and word.

2 Thess 3:3–5

But the Lord is faithful; he will strengthen you and guard you from the evil one. 4 And we have confidence in the Lord concerning you, that you are doing and will go on doing the things that we command. 5 May the Lord direct your hearts to the love of God and to the steadfastness of Christ.

Cf. Rom 1:11–12; 2:7–8; 14:2–4; 16:25–27; Phil 1:5–6; 2:12–13; Col 1:11; 1 Thess 1:3; 2 Thess 1:4–5; 2 Tim 2:11–13; Acts 13:43; 14:21–22; 20:32.

86. Faith and Sight

Rom 8:18–25

I consider that the sufferings of this present time are not worth comparing with the glory about to be revealed to us. 19 For the creation waits with eager longing for the revealing of the children of God; 20 for the creation was subjected to futility, not of its own will but by the will of the one who subjected it, in hope 21 that the creation itself will be set free from its bondage to decay and will obtain the freedom of the glory of the children of God. 22 We know that the whole creation has been groaning in labor pains until now; 23 and not only the creation, but we ourselves, who have the first fruits of the Spirit, groan inwardly while we wait for adoption, the redemption of our bodies. 24 For in hope we were saved. Now hope that is seen is not

[e] **Col 1:22** ***he has now reconciled*** Other ancient authorities read *you have now been reconciled* [f] **1 Thess 3:2** ***co-worker for God*** lit. *God's co-worker* Other ancient authorities read *God's minister* or *God's minister and our co-worker* [g] **2 Thess 2:13** ***as the first fruits*** Other ancient authorities read *from the beginning*

ἐλπίς· ὃ γὰρ βλέπει τίς ⸀ἐλπίζει; 25 εἰ δὲ ὃ οὐ βλέπομεν ἐλπίζομεν, δι᾽ ὑπομονῆς ἀπεκδεχόμεθα.

2 Cor 4:16–5:10

Διὸ οὐκ ἐγκακοῦμεν, ἀλλ᾽ εἰ καὶ ὁ ἔξω ἡμῶν ἄνθρωπος διαφθείρεται, ἀλλ᾽ ὁ ἔσω ἡμῶν ἀνακαινοῦται ἡμέρᾳ καὶ ἡμέρᾳ. 17 τὸ γὰρ παραυτίκα ἐλαφρὸν τῆς θλίψεως ἡμῶν καθ᾽ ὑπερβολὴν εἰς ὑπερβολὴν αἰώνιον βάρος δόξης κατεργάζεται ἡμῖν, 18 μὴ σκοπούντων ἡμῶν τὰ βλεπόμενα ἀλλὰ τὰ μὴ βλεπόμενα· τὰ γὰρ βλεπόμενα πρόσκαιρα, τὰ δὲ μὴ βλεπόμενα αἰώνια.

5 Οἴδαμεν γὰρ ὅτι ἐὰν ἡ ἐπίγειος ἡμῶν οἰκία τοῦ σκήνους καταλυθῇ, οἰκοδομὴν ἐκ θεοῦ ἔχομεν, οἰκίαν ἀχειροποίητον αἰώνιον ἐν τοῖς οὐρανοῖς. 2 καὶ γὰρ ἐν τούτῳ στενάζομεν τὸ οἰκητήριον ἡμῶν τὸ ἐξ οὐρανοῦ ἐπενδύσασθαι ἐπιποθοῦντες, 3 εἴ γε καὶ ⸀ἐκδυσάμενοι οὐ γυμνοὶ εὑρεθησόμεθα. 4 καὶ γὰρ οἱ ὄντες ἐν τῷ σκήνει στενάζομεν βαρούμενοι, ἐφ᾽ ᾧ οὐ θέλομεν ἐκδύσασθαι ἀλλ᾽ ἐπενδύσασθαι, ἵνα καταποθῇ τὸ θνητὸν ὑπὸ τῆς ζωῆς. 5 ὁ δὲ κατεργασάμενος ἡμᾶς εἰς αὐτὸ τοῦτο θεός, ὁ δοὺς ἡμῖν τὸν ἀρραβῶνα τοῦ πνεύματος. 6 Θαρροῦντες οὖν πάντοτε καὶ εἰδότες ὅτι ἐνδημοῦντες ἐν τῷ σώματι ἐκδημοῦμεν ἀπὸ τοῦ κυρίου· 7 διὰ πίστεως γὰρ περιπατοῦμεν, οὐ διὰ εἴδους· 8 θαρροῦμεν δὲ καὶ εὐδοκοῦμεν μᾶλλον ἐκδημῆσαι ἐκ τοῦ σώματος καὶ ἐνδημῆσαι πρὸς τὸν κύριον. 9 διὸ καὶ φιλοτιμούμεθα, εἴτε ἐνδημοῦντες εἴτε ἐκδημοῦντες, εὐάρεστοι αὐτῷ εἶναι. 10 τοὺς γὰρ πάντας ἡμᾶς φανερωθῆναι δεῖ ἔμπροσθεν τοῦ βήματος τοῦ Χριστοῦ, ἵνα κομίσηται ἕκαστος τὰ διὰ τοῦ σώματος πρὸς ἃ ἔπραξεν, εἴτε ἀγαθὸν εἴτε φαῦλον.

Cf. 1 Cor 13:12; Gal 5:5.

87. The Intermediate State

2 Cor 5:6–10

Θαρροῦντες οὖν πάντοτε καὶ εἰδότες ὅτι ἐνδημοῦντες ἐν τῷ σώματι ἐκδημοῦμεν ἀπὸ τοῦ κυρίου· 7 διὰ πίστεως γὰρ περιπατοῦμεν, οὐ διὰ εἴδους· 8 θαρροῦμεν δὲ καὶ εὐδοκοῦμεν μᾶλλον ἐκδημῆσαι ἐκ τοῦ σώματος καὶ ἐνδημῆσαι πρὸς τὸν κύριον. 9 διὸ καὶ φιλοτιμούμεθα, εἴτε ἐνδημοῦντες εἴτε ἐκδημοῦντες, εὐάρεστοι αὐτῷ εἶναι. 10 τοὺς γὰρ πάντας ἡμᾶς φανερωθῆναι δεῖ ἔμπροσθεν τοῦ βήματος τοῦ Χριστοῦ, ἵνα κομίσηται ἕκαστος τὰ διὰ τοῦ σώματος πρὸς ἃ ἔπραξεν, εἴτε ἀγαθὸν εἴτε φαῦλον.

Phil 1:21–26

Ἐμοὶ γὰρ τὸ ζῆν Χριστὸς καὶ τὸ ἀποθανεῖν κέρδος. 22 εἰ δὲ τὸ ζῆν ἐν σαρκί, τοῦτό μοι καρπὸς ἔργου, καὶ τί αἱρήσομαι οὐ γνωρίζω. 23 συνέχομαι δὲ ἐκ τῶν δύο, τὴν ἐπιθυμίαν ἔχων εἰς τὸ ἀναλῦσαι καὶ σὺν Χριστῷ εἶναι, πολλῷ [γὰρ] μᾶλλον κρεῖσσον· 24 τὸ δὲ ἐπιμένειν [ἐν] τῇ σαρκὶ ἀναγκαιότερον δι᾽ ὑμᾶς. 25 καὶ τοῦτο πεποιθὼς οἶδα ὅτι μενῶ καὶ παραμενῶ πᾶσιν ὑμῖν εἰς τὴν ὑμῶν προκοπὴν καὶ χαρὰν τῆς πίστεως, 26 ἵνα τὸ καύχημα ὑμῶν περισσεύῃ ἐν Χριστῷ Ἰησοῦ ἐν ἐμοὶ διὰ τῆς ἐμῆς παρουσίας πάλιν πρὸς ὑμᾶς.

88. The Second Coming of Christ

1 Cor 1:7–8

ὥστε ὑμᾶς μὴ ὑστερεῖσθαι ἐν μηδενὶ χαρίσματι ἀπεκδεχομένους τὴν ἀποκάλυψιν τοῦ κυρίου ἡμῶν Ἰησοῦ Χριστοῦ· 8 ὃς καὶ βεβαιώσει ὑμᾶς ἕως τέλους ἀνεγκλήτους ἐν τῇ ἡμέρᾳ τοῦ κυρίου ἡμῶν Ἰησοῦ [Χριστοῦ].

1 Cor 4:5

ὥστε μὴ πρὸ καιροῦ τι κρίνετε ἕως ἂν ἔλθῃ ὁ κύριος, ὃς καὶ φωτίσει τὰ κρυπτὰ τοῦ σκότους καὶ φανερώσει τὰς βουλὰς τῶν καρδιῶν· καὶ τότε ὁ ἔπαινος γενήσεται ἑκάστῳ ἀπὸ τοῦ θεοῦ.

1 Cor 15:20–28

Νυνὶ δὲ Χριστὸς ἐγήγερται ἐκ νεκρῶν ἀπαρχὴ τῶν κεκοιμημένων. 21 ἐπειδὴ γὰρ δι᾽ ἀνθρώπου θάνατος, καὶ δι᾽ ἀνθρώπου ἀνάστασις νεκρῶν. 22 ὥσπερ γὰρ ἐν τῷ Ἀδὰμ πάντες ἀποθνῄσκουσιν, οὕτως καὶ ἐν τῷ Χριστῷ πάντες ζῳοποιηθήσονται. 23 Ἕκαστος δὲ ἐν τῷ ἰδίῳ τάγματι· ἀπαρχὴ Χριστός, ἔπειτα οἱ τοῦ Χριστοῦ ἐν τῇ παρουσίᾳ αὐτοῦ, 24 εἶτα τὸ τέλος, ὅταν παραδιδῷ τὴν βασιλείαν τῷ θεῷ καὶ πατρί, ὅταν καταργήσῃ πᾶσαν ἀρχὴν καὶ πᾶσαν ἐξουσίαν καὶ δύναμιν. 25 δεῖ γὰρ αὐτὸν βασιλεύειν ἄχρι οὗ θῇ πάντας τοὺς ἐχθροὺς ὑπὸ τοὺς πόδας αὐτοῦ. 26 ἔσχατος ἐχθρὸς καταργεῖται ὁ θάνατος· 27 πάντα γὰρ ὑπέταξεν ὑπὸ τοὺς πόδας αὐτοῦ. ὅταν δὲ εἴπῃ ὅτι πάντα ὑποτέτακται, δῆλον ὅτι ἐκτὸς τοῦ ὑποτάξαντος αὐτῷ τὰ πάντα. 28 ὅταν δὲ ὑποταγῇ αὐτῷ τὰ πάντα, τότε [καὶ] αὐτὸς ὁ υἱὸς ὑποταγήσεται τῷ ὑποτάξαντι αὐτῷ τὰ πάντα, ἵνα ᾖ ὁ θεὸς [τὰ] πάντα ἐν πᾶσιν.

Phil 3:20–21

ἡμῶν γὰρ τὸ πολίτευμα ἐν οὐρανοῖς ὑπάρχει, ἐξ οὗ καὶ σωτῆρα ἀπεκδεχόμεθα κύριον Ἰησοῦν Χριστόν, 21 ὃς μετασχηματίσει τὸ σῶμα τῆς ταπεινώσεως ἡμῶν σύμμορφον τῷ σώματι τῆς δόξης αὐτοῦ κατὰ τὴν ἐνέργειαν τοῦ δύνασθαι αὐτὸν καὶ ὑποτάξαι αὐτῷ τὰ πάντα.

Col 3:3–4

ἀπεθάνετε γὰρ καὶ ἡ ζωὴ ὑμῶν κέκρυπται σὺν τῷ Χριστῷ ἐν τῷ θεῷ· 4 ὅταν ὁ Χριστὸς φανερωθῇ, ἡ ζωὴ ⸀ὑμῶν, τότε καὶ ὑμεῖς σὺν αὐτῷ φανερωθήσεσθε ἐν δόξῃ.

§ 86 **Rom 8:24** ***ελπιζει*** 𝔓^{46} ℵ^{2} B C D 33. 1739*. 1881 *Byz*] υπομενει ℵ* A 1739^{mg} **2 Cor 5:3** ***εκδυσαμενοι*** D^{*,c}] ενδυσαμενοι 𝔓^{46} ℵ B C D^{2} 33. 1739. 1881 *Byz* **§ 88** **Col 3:4** ***υμων*** 𝔓^{46} ℵ C D* 33. 1881] ημων B$^{(*)}$ D^{1} 1739 *Byz*

hope. For who hopes[a] for what is seen? **25** But if we hope for what we do not see, we wait for it with patience.

2 Cor 4:16–5:10

So we do not lose heart. Even though our outer nature is wasting away, our inner nature is being renewed day by day. **17** For this slight momentary affliction is preparing us for an eternal weight of glory beyond all measure, **18** because we look not at what is presently seen but at what is not presently seen; for what is presently seen is temporary, but what is not presently seen is eternal.[b] **5** For we know that if the earthly tent we live in is destroyed, we have a building from God, a house not made with hands, eternal in the heavens. **2** For in this tent we groan, longing to be clothed with our dwelling from heaven— **3** if indeed, when we have put it on[c] we will not be found naked.[d] **4** For while we are still in this tent, we groan under our burden, because we wish not to be unclothed but to be further clothed, so that what is mortal may be swallowed up by life. **5** He who has prepared us for this very thing is God, who has given us the Spirit as a guarantee. **6** So we are always confident; even though we know that while we are at home in the body we are away from the Lord— **7** for we walk by faith, not by sight. **8** Yes, we do have confidence, and we would rather be away from the body and at home with the Lord. **9** So whether we are at home or away, we make it our aim to please him. **10** For all of us must appear before the judgment seat of Christ, so that each may receive recompense for what has been done in the body, whether good or evil.

Cf. 1 Cor 13:12; Gal 5:5.

87. The Intermediate State

2 Cor 5:6–10

So we are always confident; even though we know that while we are at home in the body we are away from the Lord— **7** for we walk by faith, not by sight. **8** Yes, we do have confidence, and we would rather be away from the body and at home with the Lord. **9** So whether we are at home or away, we make it our aim to please him. **10** For all of us must appear before the judgment seat of Christ, so that each may receive recompense for what has been done in the body, whether good or evil.

Phil 1:21–26

For to me, living is Christ and dying is gain. **22** If I am to live in the flesh, that means fruitful labor for me; and I do not know which I prefer. **23** I am hard pressed between the two: my desire is to depart and be with Christ, for that is far better; **24** but to remain in the flesh is more necessary for you. **25** Since I am convinced of this, I know that I will remain and continue with all of you for your progress and joy in faith, **26** so that I may share abundantly in your boasting in Christ Jesus when I come to you again.

88. The Second Coming of Christ

1 Cor 1:7–8

so that you are not lacking in any spiritual gift as you wait for the revealing of our Lord Jesus Christ. **8** He will also strengthen you to the end, so that you may be blameless on the day of our Lord Jesus Christ.

1 Cor 4:5

Therefore do not pronounce judgment before the time, before the Lord comes, who will bring to light the things now hidden in darkness and will disclose the purposes of the heart. Then each one will receive commendation from God.

1 Cor 15:20–28

But in fact Christ has been raised from the dead, the first fruits of those who have died. **21** For since death came through a human being, the resurrection of the dead has also come through a human being; **22** for as all die in Adam, so all will be made alive in Christ. **23** But each in his own order: Christ the first fruits, then at his coming those who belong to Christ. **24** Then comes the end, when he hands over the kingdom to God the Father, after he has destroyed every ruler and every authority and power. **25** For he must reign until he has put all his enemies under his feet. **26** The last enemy to be destroyed is death. **27** For "God has put all things in subjection under his feet." But when it says, "All things are put in subjection," it is plain that this does not include the one who put all things in subjection under him. **28** When all things are subjected to him, then the Son himself will also be subjected to the one who put all things in subjection under him, so that God may be all in all.

Phil 3:20–21

But our citizenship is in heaven, and it is from there that we are expecting a Savior, the Lord Jesus Christ. **21** He will transform the body of our humiliation that it may be conformed to the body of his glory, by the power that also enables him to make all things subject to himself.

Col 3:3–4

for you have died, and your life is hidden with Christ in God. **4** When Christ who is your[a] life is revealed, then you also will be revealed with him in glory.

§ 86 [a] **Rom 8:24** *hopes* Other ancient authorities read *awaits* [b] **2 Cor 4:18** Translation differs from NRSV [c] **2 Cor 5:3** *put it on* A few ancient authorities read *taken it off* [d] **2 Cor 5:2–3** Translation differs from NRSV **§ 88** [a] **Col 3:4** *your* Other ancient authorities read *our*

1 Thess 1:9–10

αὐτοὶ γὰρ περὶ ἡμῶν ἀπαγγέλλουσιν ὁποίαν εἴσοδον ἔσχομεν πρὸς ὑμᾶς, καὶ πῶς ἐπεστρέψατε πρὸς τὸν θεὸν ἀπὸ τῶν εἰδώλων δουλεύειν θεῷ ζῶντι καὶ ἀληθινῷ **10** καὶ ἀναμένειν τὸν υἱὸν αὐτοῦ ἐκ τῶν οὐρανῶν, ὃν ἤγειρεν ἐκ [τῶν] νεκρῶν, Ἰησοῦν τὸν ῥυόμενον ἡμᾶς ἐκ τῆς ὀργῆς τῆς ἐρχομένης.

1 Thess 2:19

τίς γὰρ ἡμῶν ἐλπὶς ἢ χαρὰ ἢ στέφανος καυχήσεως—ἢ οὐχὶ καὶ ὑμεῖς—ἔμπροσθεν τοῦ κυρίου ἡμῶν Ἰησοῦ ἐν τῇ αὐτοῦ παρουσίᾳ;

1 Thess 3:13

εἰς τὸ στηρίξαι ὑμῶν τὰς καρδίας ἀμέμπτους ἐν ἁγιωσύνῃ ἔμπροσθεν τοῦ θεοῦ καὶ πατρὸς ἡμῶν ἐν τῇ παρουσίᾳ τοῦ κυρίου ἡμῶν Ἰησοῦ μετὰ πάντων τῶν ἁγίων αὐτοῦ, [ἀμήν].

1 Thess 4:13–18

Οὐ θέλομεν δὲ ὑμᾶς ἀγνοεῖν, ἀδελφοί, περὶ τῶν κοιμωμένων, ἵνα μὴ λυπῆσθε καθὼς καὶ οἱ λοιποὶ οἱ μὴ ἔχοντες ἐλπίδα. **14** εἰ γὰρ πιστεύομεν ὅτι Ἰησοῦς ἀπέθανεν καὶ ἀνέστη, οὕτως καὶ ὁ θεὸς τοὺς κοιμηθέντας διὰ τοῦ Ἰησοῦ ἄξει σὺν αὐτῷ. **15** Τοῦτο γὰρ ὑμῖν λέγομεν ἐν λόγῳ κυρίου, ὅτι ἡμεῖς οἱ ζῶντες οἱ περιλειπόμενοι εἰς τὴν παρουσίαν τοῦ κυρίου οὐ μὴ φθάσωμεν τοὺς κοιμηθέντας· **16** ὅτι αὐτὸς ὁ κύριος ἐν κελεύσματι, ἐν φωνῇ ἀρχαγγέλου καὶ ἐν σάλπιγγι θεοῦ, καταβήσεται ἀπ' οὐρανοῦ καὶ οἱ νεκροὶ ἐν Χριστῷ ἀναστήσονται πρῶτον, **17** ἔπειτα ἡμεῖς οἱ ζῶντες οἱ περιλειπόμενοι ἅμα σὺν αὐτοῖς ἁρπαγησόμεθα ἐν νεφέλαις εἰς ἀπάντησιν τοῦ κυρίου εἰς ἀέρα· καὶ οὕτως πάντοτε σὺν κυρίῳ ἐσόμεθα. **18** Ὥστε παρακαλεῖτε ἀλλήλους ἐν τοῖς λόγοις τούτοις.

1 Thess 5:1–11

Περὶ δὲ τῶν χρόνων καὶ τῶν καιρῶν, ἀδελφοί, οὐ χρείαν ἔχετε ὑμῖν γράφεσθαι, **2** αὐτοὶ γὰρ ἀκριβῶς οἴδατε ὅτι ἡμέρα κυρίου ὡς κλέπτης ἐν νυκτὶ οὕτως ἔρχεται. **3** ὅταν λέγωσιν· εἰρήνη καὶ ἀσφάλεια, τότε αἰφνίδιος αὐτοῖς ἐφίσταται ὄλεθρος ὥσπερ ἡ ὠδὶν τῇ ἐν γαστρὶ ἐχούσῃ, καὶ οὐ μὴ ἐκφύγωσιν. **4** ὑμεῖς δέ, ἀδελφοί, οὐκ ἐστὲ ἐν σκότει, ἵνα ἡ ἡμέρα ὑμᾶς ὡς κλέπτης καταλάβῃ· **5** πάντες γὰρ ὑμεῖς υἱοὶ φωτός ἐστε καὶ υἱοὶ ἡμέρας. Οὐκ ἐσμὲν νυκτὸς οὐδὲ σκότους· **6** ἄρα οὖν μὴ καθεύδωμεν ὡς οἱ λοιποὶ ἀλλὰ γρηγορῶμεν καὶ νήφωμεν. **7** Οἱ γὰρ καθεύδοντες νυκτὸς καθεύδουσιν καὶ οἱ μεθυσκόμενοι νυκτὸς μεθύουσιν· **8** ἡμεῖς δὲ ἡμέρας ὄντες νήφωμεν ἐνδυσάμενοι θώρακα πίστεως καὶ ἀγάπης καὶ περικεφαλαίαν ἐλπίδα σωτηρίας· **9** ὅτι οὐκ ἔθετο ἡμᾶς ὁ θεὸς εἰς ὀργὴν ἀλλὰ εἰς περιποίησιν σωτηρίας διὰ τοῦ κυρίου ἡμῶν Ἰησοῦ Χριστοῦ **10** τοῦ ἀποθανόντος ὑπὲρ ἡμῶν, ἵνα εἴτε γρηγορῶμεν εἴτε καθεύδωμεν ἅμα σὺν αὐτῷ ζήσωμεν. **11** Διὸ παρακαλεῖτε ἀλλήλους καὶ οἰκοδομεῖτε εἷς τὸν ἕνα, καθὼς καὶ ποιεῖτε.

1 Thess 5:23

Αὐτὸς δὲ ὁ θεὸς τῆς εἰρήνης ἁγιάσαι ὑμᾶς ὁλοτελεῖς, καὶ ὁλόκληρον ὑμῶν τὸ πνεῦμα καὶ ἡ ψυχὴ καὶ τὸ σῶμα ἀμέμπτως ἐν τῇ παρουσίᾳ τοῦ κυρίου ἡμῶν Ἰησοῦ Χριστοῦ τηρηθείη.

2 Thess 1:5–10

ἔνδειγμα τῆς δικαίας κρίσεως τοῦ θεοῦ εἰς τὸ καταξιωθῆναι ὑμᾶς τῆς βασιλείας τοῦ θεοῦ, ὑπὲρ ἧς καὶ πάσχετε, **6** εἴπερ δίκαιον παρὰ θεῷ ἀνταποδοῦναι τοῖς θλίβουσιν ὑμᾶς θλῖψιν **7** καὶ ὑμῖν τοῖς θλιβομένοις ἄνεσιν μεθ' ἡμῶν, ἐν τῇ ἀποκαλύψει τοῦ κυρίου Ἰησοῦ ἀπ' οὐρανοῦ μετ' ἀγγέλων δυνάμεως αὐτοῦ **8** ἐν πυρὶ φλογός, διδόντος ἐκδίκησιν τοῖς μὴ εἰδόσιν θεὸν καὶ τοῖς μὴ ὑπακούουσιν τῷ εὐαγγελίῳ τοῦ κυρίου ἡμῶν Ἰησοῦ, **9** οἵτινες δίκην τίσουσιν ὄλεθρον αἰώνιον ἀπὸ προσώπου τοῦ κυρίου καὶ ἀπὸ τῆς δόξης τῆς ἰσχύος αὐτοῦ, **10** ὅταν ἔλθῃ ἐνδοξασθῆναι ἐν τοῖς ἁγίοις αὐτοῦ καὶ θαυμασθῆναι ἐν πᾶσιν τοῖς πιστεύσασιν, ὅτι ἐπιστεύθη τὸ μαρτύριον ἡμῶν ἐφ' ὑμᾶς, ἐν τῇ ἡμέρᾳ ἐκείνῃ.

2 Thess 2:1–2

Ἐρωτῶμεν δὲ ὑμᾶς, ἀδελφοί, ὑπὲρ τῆς παρουσίας τοῦ κυρίου ἡμῶν Ἰησοῦ Χριστοῦ καὶ ἡμῶν ἐπισυναγωγῆς ἐπ' αὐτὸν **2** εἰς τὸ μὴ ταχέως σαλευθῆναι ὑμᾶς ἀπὸ τοῦ νοὸς μηδὲ θροεῖσθαι, μήτε διὰ πνεύματος μήτε διὰ λόγου μήτε δι' ἐπιστολῆς ὡς δι' ἡμῶν, ὡς ὅτι ἐνέστηκεν ἡ ἡμέρα τοῦ κυρίου

2 Thess 2:8

καὶ τότε ἀποκαλυφθήσεται ὁ ἄνομος, ὃν ὁ κύριος ⸀[Ἰησοῦς] ⸀ἀνελεῖ τῷ πνεύματι τοῦ στόματος αὐτοῦ καὶ καταργήσει τῇ ἐπιφανείᾳ τῆς παρουσίας αὐτοῦ

1 Tim 6:13–16

παραγγέλλω [σοι] ἐνώπιον τοῦ θεοῦ τοῦ ζῳογονοῦντος τὰ πάντα καὶ Χριστοῦ Ἰησοῦ τοῦ μαρτυρήσαντος ἐπὶ Ποντίου Πιλάτου τὴν καλὴν ὁμολογίαν, **14** τηρῆσαί σε τὴν ἐντολὴν ἄσπιλον ἀνεπίλημπτον μέχρι τῆς ἐπιφανείας τοῦ κυρίου ἡμῶν Ἰησοῦ Χριστοῦ, **15** ἣν καιροῖς ἰδίοις δείξει ὁ μακάριος καὶ μόνος δυνάστης, ὁ βασιλεὺς τῶν βασιλευόντων καὶ κύριος τῶν κυριευόντων, **16** ὁ μόνος ἔχων ἀθανασίαν, φῶς οἰκῶν ἀπρόσιτον, ὃν εἶδεν οὐδεὶς ἀνθρώπων οὐδὲ ἰδεῖν δύναται· ᾧ τιμὴ καὶ κράτος αἰώνιον, ἀμήν.

2 Tim 4:1

Διαμαρτύρομαι ἐνώπιον τοῦ θεοῦ καὶ Χριστοῦ Ἰησοῦ τοῦ μέλλοντος κρίνειν ζῶντας καὶ νεκρούς, καὶ τὴν ἐπιφάνειαν αὐτοῦ καὶ τὴν βασιλείαν αὐτοῦ

Titus 2:11–14

Ἐπεφάνη γὰρ ἡ χάρις τοῦ θεοῦ σωτήριος πᾶσιν ἀνθρώποις **12** παιδεύουσα ἡμᾶς, ἵνα ἀρνησάμενοι τὴν ἀσέβειαν καὶ τὰς κοσμικὰς ἐπιθυμίας σωφρόνως καὶ δικαίως καὶ εὐσεβῶς ζήσωμεν ἐν τῷ νῦν αἰῶνι, **13** προσδεχόμενοι τὴν μακαρίαν ἐλπίδα καὶ ἐπιφάνειαν τῆς δόξης τοῦ μεγάλου θεοῦ καὶ σωτῆρος ἡμῶν Ἰησοῦ Χριστοῦ, **14** ὃς ἔδωκεν ἑαυτὸν ὑπὲρ ἡμῶν, ἵνα λυτρώσηται ἡμᾶς ἀπὸ πάσης ἀνομίας καὶ καθαρίσῃ ἑαυτῷ λαὸν περιούσιον, ζηλωτὴν καλῶν ἔργων.

Cf. Rom 2:16; 1 Cor 5:5; 2 Cor 1:12–14; Phil 1:6; 1:9–11; 2:15–16; 2 Tim 1:16–18; 4:7–8; Acts 17:30–31.

2 Thess 2:8 ***Ιησους*** ℵ A D* 33] *om.* B D² 1739. 1881 *Byz* • ***ανελει*** A B] ανελοι (ℵ*) D*vid 33. 1739 ¦ αναλωσει D² 1881 *Byz*

1 Thess 1:9–10

For the people of those regions report about us what kind of welcome we had among you, and how you turned to God from idols, to serve a living and true God, **10** and to wait for his Son from heaven, whom he raised from the dead—Jesus, who rescues us from the wrath that is coming.

1 Thess 2:19

For what is our hope or joy or crown of boasting before our Lord Jesus at his coming? Is it not you?

1 Thess 3:13

And may he so strengthen your hearts in holiness that you may be blameless before our God and Father at the coming of our Lord Jesus with all his saints.

1 Thess 4:13–18

But we do not want you to be uninformed, brothers and sisters, about those who have died, so that you may not grieve as others do who have no hope. **14** For since we believe that Jesus died and rose again, even so, through Jesus, God will bring with him those who have died. **15** For this we declare to you by the word of the Lord, that we who are alive, who are left until the coming of the Lord, will by no means precede those who have died. **16** For the Lord himself, with a cry of command, with the archangel's call and with the sound of God's trumpet, will descend from heaven, and the dead in Christ will rise first. **17** Then we who are alive, who are left, will be caught up in the clouds together with them to meet the Lord in the air; and so we will be with the Lord forever. **18** Therefore encourage one another with these words.

1 Thess 5:1–11

Now concerning the times and the seasons, brothers and sisters, you do not need to have anything written to you. **2** For you yourselves know very well that the day of the Lord will come like a thief in the night. **3** When they say, "There is peace and security," then sudden destruction will come upon them, as labor pains come upon a pregnant woman, and there will be no escape! **4** But you, beloved, are not in darkness, for that day to surprise you like a thief; **5** for you are all children of light and children of the day; we are not of the night or of darkness. **6** So then let us not fall asleep as others do, but let us keep awake and be sober; **7** for those who sleep sleep at night, and those who are drunk get drunk at night. **8** But since we belong to the day, let us be sober, and put on the breastplate of faith and love, and for a helmet the hope of salvation. **9** For God has destined us not for wrath but for obtaining salvation through our Lord Jesus Christ, **10** who died for us, so that whether we are awake or asleep we may live with him. **11** Therefore encourage one another and build up each other, as indeed you are doing.

1 Thess 5:23

May the God of peace himself sanctify you entirely; and may your spirit and soul and body be kept sound and blameless at the coming of our Lord Jesus Christ.

2 Thess 1:5–10

This is evidence of the righteous judgment of God, and is intended to make you worthy of the kingdom of God, for which you are also suffering. **6** For it is indeed just of God to repay with affliction those who afflict you, **7** and to give relief to the afflicted as well as to us, when the Lord Jesus is revealed from heaven with his mighty angels **8** in flaming fire, inflicting vengeance on those who do not know God and on those who do not obey the gospel of our Lord Jesus. **9** These will suffer the punishment of eternal destruction, separated from the presence of the Lord and from the glory of his might, **10** when he comes to be glorified by his saints and to be marveled at on that day among all who have believed, because our testimony to you was believed.

2 Thess 2:1–2

As to the coming of our Lord Jesus Christ and our being gathered together to him, we beg you, brothers and sisters, **2** not to be quickly shaken in mind or alarmed, either by spirit or by word or by letter, as though from us, to the effect that the day of the Lord is already here.

2 Thess 2:8

And then the lawless one will be revealed, whom the Lord Jesus[b] will destroy[c] with the breath of his mouth, annihilating him by the manifestation of his coming.

1 Tim 6:13–16

In the presence of God, who gives life to all things, and of Christ Jesus, who in his testimony before Pontius Pilate made the good confession, I charge you **14** to keep the commandment without spot or blame until the manifestation of our Lord Jesus Christ, **15** which he will bring about at the right time—he who is the blessed and only Sovereign, the King of kings and Lord of lords. **16** It is he alone who has immortality and dwells in unapproachable light, whom no one has ever seen or can see; to him be honor and eternal dominion. Amen.

2 Tim 4:1

In the presence of God and of Christ Jesus, who is to judge the living and the dead, and in view of his appearing and his kingdom, I solemnly urge you

Titus 2:11–14

For the grace of God has appeared, bringing salvation to all, **12** training us to renounce impiety and worldly passions, and in the present age to live lives that are self-controlled, upright, and godly, **13** while we wait for the blessed hope and the manifestation of the glory of our great God and Savior, Jesus Christ. **14** He it is who gave himself for us that he might redeem us from all iniquity and purify for himself a people of his own who are zealous for good deeds.

Cf. Rom 2:16; 1 Cor 5:5; 2 Cor 1:12–14; Phil 1:6; 1:9–11; 2:15–16; 2 Tim 1:16–18; 4:7–8; Acts 17:30–31.

[b] **2 Thess 2:8** *Jesus* Other ancient authorities lack *Jesus* [c] **2 Thess 2:8** *destroy* Other ancient authorities read *consume*

89. The Resurrection of the Body

Rom 8:9–11

Ὑμεῖς δὲ οὐκ ἐστὲ ἐν σαρκὶ ἀλλὰ ἐν πνεύ-
ματι, εἴπερ πνεῦμα θεοῦ οἰκεῖ ἐν ὑμῖν. εἰ
δέ τις πνεῦμα Χριστοῦ οὐκ ἔχει, οὗτος
οὐκ ἔστιν αὐτοῦ. 10 εἰ δὲ Χριστὸς ἐν ὑμῖν,
τὸ μὲν σῶμα νεκρὸν διὰ ἁμαρτίαν τὸ δὲ
πνεῦμα ζωὴ διὰ δικαιοσύνην. 11 εἰ δὲ τὸ
πνεῦμα τοῦ ἐγείραντος τὸν Ἰησοῦν ἐκ
νεκρῶν οἰκεῖ ἐν ὑμῖν, ὁ ἐγείρας ⸂Χριστὸν
ἐκ νεκρῶν⸃ ζῳοποιήσει καὶ τὰ θνητὰ
σώματα ὑμῶν διὰ ⸂τοῦ ἐνοικοῦντος
αὐτοῦ πνεύματος⸃ ἐν ὑμῖν.

Rom 8:18–25

Λογίζομαι γὰρ ὅτι οὐκ ἄξια τὰ παθήματα
τοῦ νῦν καιροῦ πρὸς τὴν μέλλουσαν δόξαν
ἀποκαλυφθῆναι εἰς ἡμᾶς. 19 ἡ γὰρ ἀπο-
καραδοκία τῆς κτίσεως τὴν ἀποκάλυψιν
τῶν υἱῶν τοῦ θεοῦ ἀπεκδέχεται. 20 τῇ
γὰρ ματαιότητι ἡ κτίσις ὑπετάγη, οὐχ
ἑκοῦσα ἀλλὰ διὰ τὸν ὑποτάξαντα, ἐφ᾽
ἑλπίδι 21 ὅτι καὶ αὐτὴ ἡ κτίσις ἐλευθερω-
θήσεται ἀπὸ τῆς δουλείας τῆς φθορᾶς εἰς
τὴν ἐλευθερίαν τῆς δόξης τῶν τέκνων
τοῦ θεοῦ. 22 οἴδαμεν γὰρ ὅτι πᾶσα ἡ
κτίσις συστενάζει καὶ συνωδίνει ἄχρι
τοῦ νῦν· 23 οὐ μόνον δέ, ἀλλὰ καὶ αὐτοὶ
τὴν ἀπαρχὴν τοῦ πνεύματος ἔχοντες,
ἡμεῖς καὶ αὐτοὶ ἐν ἑαυτοῖς στενάζομεν
υἱοθεσίαν ἀπεκδεχόμενοι, τὴν ἀπολύ-
τρωσιν τοῦ σώματος ἡμῶν. 24 τῇ γὰρ
ἐλπίδι ἐσώθημεν· ἐλπὶς δὲ βλεπομένη
οὐκ ἔστιν ἐλπίς· ὃ γὰρ βλέπει τίς ⸀ἐλπί-
ζει; 25 εἰ δὲ ὃ οὐ βλέπομεν ἐλπίζομεν, δι᾽
ὑπομονῆς ἀπεκδεχόμεθα.

1 Cor 6:13–14

τὰ βρώματα τῇ κοιλίᾳ καὶ ἡ κοιλία τοῖς
βρώμασιν, ὁ δὲ θεὸς καὶ ταύτην καὶ
ταῦτα καταργήσει. τὸ δὲ σῶμα οὐ τῇ
πορνείᾳ ἀλλὰ τῷ κυρίῳ, καὶ ὁ κύριος
τῷ σώματι· 14 ὁ δὲ θεὸς καὶ τὸν κύριον
ἤγειρεν καὶ ἡμᾶς ἐξεγερεῖ διὰ τῆς δυ-
νάμεως αὐτοῦ.

1 Cor 15:20–28

Νυνὶ δὲ Χριστὸς ἐγήγερται ἐκ νεκρῶν
ἀπαρχὴ τῶν κεκοιμημένων. 21 ἐπειδὴ γὰρ
δι᾽ ἀνθρώπου θάνατος, καὶ δι᾽ ἀνθρώπου
ἀνάστασις νεκρῶν. 22 ὥσπερ γὰρ ἐν τῷ
Ἀδὰμ πάντες ἀποθνῄσκουσιν, οὕτως καὶ
ἐν τῷ Χριστῷ πάντες ζῳοποιηθήσον-
ται. 23 Ἕκαστος δὲ ἐν τῷ ἰδίῳ τάγματι·
ἀπαρχὴ Χριστός, ἔπειτα οἱ τοῦ Χριστοῦ
ἐν τῇ παρουσίᾳ αὐτοῦ, 24 εἶτα τὸ τέλος,
ὅταν παραδιδῷ τὴν βασιλείαν τῷ θεῷ καὶ
πατρί, ὅταν καταργήσῃ πᾶσαν ἀρχὴν καὶ
πᾶσαν ἐξουσίαν καὶ δύναμιν. 25 δεῖ γὰρ
αὐτὸν βασιλεύειν ἄχρι οὗ θῇ πάντας τοὺς
ἐχθροὺς ὑπὸ τοὺς πόδας αὐτοῦ. 26 ἔσχατος
ἐχθρὸς καταργεῖται ὁ θάνατος· 27 πάντα
γὰρ ὑπέταξεν ὑπὸ τοὺς πόδας αὐτοῦ.
ὅταν δὲ εἴπῃ ὅτι πάντα ὑποτέτακται,
δῆλον ὅτι ἐκτὸς τοῦ ὑποτάξαντος αὐτῷ
τὰ πάντα. 28 ὅταν δὲ ὑποταγῇ αὐτῷ τὰ
πάντα, τότε [καὶ] αὐτὸς ὁ υἱὸς ὑποταγή-
σεται τῷ ὑποτάξαντι αὐτῷ τὰ πάντα, ἵνα
ᾖ ὁ θεὸς [τὰ] πάντα ἐν πᾶσιν.

1 Cor 15:35–58

Ἀλλὰ ἐρεῖ τις· πῶς ἐγείρονται οἱ νεκροί;
ποίῳ δὲ σώματι ἔρχονται; 36 ἄφρων,
σὺ ὃ σπείρεις, οὐ ζῳοποιεῖται ἐὰν μὴ
ἀποθάνῃ· 37 καὶ ὃ σπείρεις, οὐ τὸ σῶμα
τὸ γενησόμενον σπείρεις ἀλλὰ γυμνὸν
κόκκον εἰ τύχοι σίτου ἤ τινος τῶν λοιπῶν·
38 ὁ δὲ θεὸς δίδωσιν αὐτῷ σῶμα καθὼς
ἠθέλησεν, καὶ ἑκάστῳ τῶν σπερμάτων
ἴδιον σῶμα. 39 Οὐ πᾶσα σὰρξ ἡ αὐτὴ σὰρξ
ἀλλὰ ἄλλη μὲν ἀνθρώπων, ἄλλη δὲ σὰρξ
κτηνῶν, ἄλλη δὲ σὰρξ πτηνῶν, ἄλλη
δὲ ἰχθύων. 40 καὶ σώματα ἐπουράνια,
καὶ σώματα ἐπίγεια· ἀλλὰ ἑτέρα μὲν ἡ
τῶν ἐπουρανίων δόξα, ἑτέρα δὲ ἡ τῶν
ἐπιγείων. 41 ἄλλη δόξα ἡλίου, καὶ ἄλλη
δόξα σελήνης, καὶ ἄλλη δόξα ἀστέρων·
ἀστὴρ γὰρ ἀστέρος διαφέρει ἐν δόξῃ.
42 Οὕτως καὶ ἡ ἀνάστασις τῶν νεκρῶν.
σπείρεται ἐν φθορᾷ, ἐγείρεται ἐν ἀφθαρ-
σίᾳ· 43 σπείρεται ἐν ἀτιμίᾳ, ἐγείρεται ἐν
δόξῃ· σπείρεται ἐν ἀσθενείᾳ, ἐγείρεται
ἐν δυνάμει· 44 σπείρεται σῶμα ψυχικόν,
ἐγείρεται σῶμα πνευματικόν. Εἰ ἔστιν
σῶμα ψυχικόν, ἔστιν καὶ πνευματικόν.
45 οὕτως καὶ γέγραπται· ἐγένετο ὁ πρῶ-
τος ἄνθρωπος Ἀδὰμ εἰς ψυχὴν ζῶσαν,
ὁ ἔσχατος Ἀδὰμ εἰς πνεῦμα ζῳοποιοῦν.
46 ἀλλ᾽ οὐ πρῶτον τὸ πνευματικὸν ἀλλὰ
τὸ ψυχικόν, ἔπειτα τὸ πνευματικόν. 47 ὁ
πρῶτος ἄνθρωπος ἐκ γῆς χοϊκός, ὁ δεύ-
τερος ⸀ἄνθρωπος ἐξ οὐρανοῦ. 48 οἷος ὁ
χοϊκός, τοιοῦτοι καὶ οἱ χοϊκοί, καὶ οἷος
ὁ ἐπουράνιος, τοιοῦτοι καὶ οἱ ἐπου-
ράνιοι· 49 καὶ καθὼς ἐφορέσαμεν τὴν
εἰκόνα τοῦ χοϊκοῦ, ⸀φορέσομεν καὶ τὴν
εἰκόνα τοῦ ἐπουρανίου. 50 Τοῦτο δέ φημι,
ἀδελφοί, ὅτι σὰρξ καὶ αἷμα βασιλείαν
θεοῦ κληρονομῆσαι οὐ δύναται οὐδὲ
ἡ φθορὰ τὴν ἀφθαρσίαν κληρονομεῖ.
51 ἰδοὺ μυστήριον ὑμῖν λέγω· πάντες οὐ
κοιμηθησόμεθα, πάντες δὲ ἀλλαγησό-
μεθα, 52 ἐν ἀτόμῳ, ἐν ῥιπῇ ὀφθαλμοῦ, ἐν
τῇ ἐσχάτῃ σάλπιγγι· σαλπίσει γὰρ καὶ οἱ
νεκροὶ ἐγερθήσονται ἄφθαρτοι καὶ ἡμεῖς
ἀλλαγησόμεθα. 53 Δεῖ γὰρ τὸ φθαρτὸν
τοῦτο ἐνδύσασθαι ἀφθαρσίαν καὶ τὸ
θνητὸν τοῦτο ἐνδύσασθαι ἀθανασίαν.
54 ὅταν δὲ τὸ φθαρτὸν τοῦτο ἐνδύσηται
ἀφθαρσίαν καὶ τὸ θνητὸν τοῦτο ἐνδύ-
σηται ἀθανασίαν, τότε γενήσεται ὁ λόγος
ὁ γεγραμμένος· κατεπόθη ὁ θάνατος εἰς
νῖκος. 55 ποῦ σου, θάνατε, τὸ νῖκος; ποῦ
σου, θάνατε, τὸ κέντρον; 56 τὸ δὲ κέντρον
τοῦ θανάτου ἡ ἁμαρτία, ἡ δὲ δύναμις
τῆς ἁμαρτίας ὁ νόμος· 57 τῷ δὲ θεῷ χά-
ρις τῷ διδόντι ἡμῖν τὸ νῖκος διὰ τοῦ
κυρίου ἡμῶν Ἰησοῦ Χριστοῦ. 58 Ὥστε,
ἀδελφοί μου ἀγαπητοί, ἑδραῖοι γίνεσθε,
ἀμετακίνητοι, περισσεύοντες ἐν τῷ ἔργῳ
τοῦ κυρίου πάντοτε, εἰδότες ὅτι ὁ κόπος
ὑμῶν οὐκ ἔστιν κενὸς ἐν κυρίῳ.

2 Cor 4:13–14

Ἔχοντες δὲ τὸ αὐτὸ πνεῦμα τῆς πίστεως
κατὰ τὸ γεγραμμένον· ἐπίστευσα, διὸ

§ 89 **Rom 8:11** ***Χριστον εκ νεκρων*** B D^{2}] τον Χ. εκ ν. ℵ^{2} 33 *Byz* ¦ Χ. Ιησουν εκ ν. D* ¦ εκ ν. Χ. Ιησουν ℵ* A (C I. X.) 1739. 1881 • ***του ενοικουντος αυτου πνευματος*** ℵ A C$^{(*)}$] το ενοικουν αυτου πνευμα B D 33. 1739. 1881 *Byz* **Rom 8:24** ***ελπιζει*** 𝔓^{46} ℵ^{2} B C D 33. 1739*. 1881 *Byz*] υπομενει ℵ* A 1739^{mg} **1 Cor 15:47** ***ανθρωπος*** ℵ* B C D* 33. 1739*] *add.* ο κυριος ℵ^{2} A D^{1} 1739^{mg}. 1881 *Byz* ¦ *add.* πνευματικος 𝔓^{46} **1 Cor 15:49** ***φορεσομεν*** B I 1881] φορεσωμεν (+ δη 𝔓^{46}) 𝔓^{46} ℵ A C D 33. 1739 *Byz*

89. The Resurrection of the Body

Rom 8:9–11

But you are not in the flesh; you are in the Spirit, since the Spirit of God dwells in you. Anyone who does not have the Spirit of Christ does not belong to him. **10** But if Christ is in you, though the body is dead because of sin, the Spirit is life because of righteousness. **11** If the Spirit of him who raised Jesus from the dead dwells in you, he who raised Christ[a] from the dead will give life to your mortal bodies also through[b] his Spirit that dwells in you.

Rom 8:18–25

I consider that the sufferings of this present time are not worth comparing with the glory about to be revealed to us. **19** For the creation waits with eager longing for the revealing of the children of God; **20** for the creation was subjected to futility, not of its own will but by the will of the one who subjected it, in hope **21** that the creation itself will be set free from its bondage to decay and will obtain the freedom of the glory of the children of God. **22** We know that the whole creation has been groaning in labor pains until now; **23** and not only the creation, but we ourselves, who have the first fruits of the Spirit, groan inwardly while we wait for adoption, the redemption of our bodies. **24** For in hope we were saved. Now hope that is seen is not hope. For who hopes[c] for what is seen? **25** But if we hope for what we do not see, we wait for it with patience.

1 Cor 6:13–14

"Food is meant for the stomach and the stomach for food," and God will destroy both one and the other. The body is meant not for fornication but for the Lord, and the Lord for the body. **14** And God raised the Lord and will also raise us by his power.

1 Cor 15:20–28

But in fact Christ has been raised from the dead, the first fruits of those who have died. **21** For since death came through a human being, the resurrection of the dead has also come through a human being; **22** for as all die in Adam, so all will be made alive in Christ. **23** But each in his own order: Christ the first fruits, then at his coming those who belong to Christ. **24** Then comes the end, when he hands over the kingdom to God the Father, after he has destroyed every ruler and every authority and power. **25** For he must reign until he has put all his enemies under his feet. **26** The last enemy to be destroyed is death. **27** For "God has put all things in subjection under his feet." But when it says, "All things are put in subjection," it is plain that this does not include the one who put all things in subjection under him. **28** When all things are subjected to him, then the Son himself will also be subjected to the one who put all things in subjection under him, so that God may be all in all.

1 Cor 15:35–58

But someone will ask, "How are the dead raised? With what kind of body do they come?" **36** Fool! What you sow does not come to life unless it dies. **37** And as for what you sow, you do not sow the body that is to be, but a bare seed, perhaps of wheat or of some other grain. **38** But God gives it a body as he has chosen, and to each kind of seed its own body. **39** Not all flesh is alike, but there is one flesh for human beings, another for animals, another for birds, and another for fish. **40** There are both heavenly bodies and earthly bodies, but the glory of the heavenly is one thing, and that of the earthly is another. **41** There is one glory of the sun, and another glory of the moon, and another glory of the stars; indeed, star differs from star in glory. **42** So it is with the resurrection of the dead. The body is sown in decay, it is raised in freedom from decay.[d] **43** It is sown in dishonor, it is raised in glory. It is sown in weakness, it is raised in power. **44** It is sown a body given life by the soul, it is raised a body given life by the Spirit. If there is a body given life by the soul, there is also a body given life by the Spirit. **45** Thus it is written, "The first man, Adam, became a living soul"; the last Adam became a life-giving Spirit. **46** But it is not the body given life by the Spirit that is first, but the body given life by the soul, and then the body given life by the Spirit.[e] **47** The first man was from the earth, a man of dust; the second man is[f] from heaven. **48** As was the man of dust, so are those who are of the dust; and as is the man of heaven, so are those who are of heaven. **49** Just as we have borne the image of the man of dust, we will[g] also bear the image of the man of heaven. **50** What I am saying, brothers and sisters, is this: flesh and blood cannot inherit the kingdom of God, nor does the perishable inherit the imperishable. **51** Listen, I will tell you a mystery! We will not all die, but we will all be changed, **52** in a moment, in the twinkling of an eye, at the last trumpet. For the trumpet will sound, and the dead will be raised imperishable, and we will be changed. **53** For this perishable body must put on imperishability, and this mortal body must put on immortality. **54** When this perishable body puts on imperishability, and this mortal body puts on immortality, then the saying that is written will be fulfilled: "Death has been swallowed up in victory." **55** "Where, O death, is your victory? Where, O death, is your sting?" **56** The sting of death is sin, and the power of sin is the law. **57** But thanks be to God, who gives us the victory through our Lord Jesus Christ. **58** Therefore, my beloved, be steadfast, immovable, always excelling in the work of the Lord, because you know that in the Lord your labor is not in vain.

2 Cor 4:13–14

But just as we have the same spirit of faith that is in accordance with

§ 89 [a] **Rom 8:11** ***Christ*** Other ancient authorities read *the Christ* or *Christ Jesus* or *Jesus Christ* [b] **Rom 8:11** ***through*** Other ancient authorities read *on account of* [c] **Rom 8:24** ***hopes*** Other ancient authorities read *awaits* [d] **1 Cor 15:42** Translation differs from NRSV [e] **1 Cor 15:44–46** Translation differs from NRSV [f] **1 Cor 15:47** ***is*** Other ancient authorities add *the Lord* [g] **1 Cor 15:49** ***we will*** Other ancient authorities read *let us*

ἐλάλησα, καὶ ἡμεῖς πιστεύομεν, διὸ καὶ λαλοῦμεν, **14** εἰδότες ὅτι ὁ ἐγείρας τὸν ⸀κύριον Ἰησοῦν καὶ ἡμᾶς σὺν Ἰησοῦ ἐγερεῖ καὶ παραστήσει σὺν ὑμῖν.

2 Cor 5:1–5

Οἴδαμεν γὰρ ὅτι ἐὰν ἡ ἐπίγειος ἡμῶν οἰκία τοῦ σκήνους καταλυθῇ, οἰκοδομὴν ἐκ θεοῦ ἔχομεν, οἰκίαν ἀχειροποίητον αἰώνιον ἐν τοῖς οὐρανοῖς. **2** καὶ γὰρ ἐν τούτῳ στενάζομεν τὸ οἰκητήριον ἡμῶν τὸ ἐξ οὐρανοῦ ἐπενδύσασθαι ἐπιποθοῦντες, **3** εἴ γε καὶ ⸀ἐκδυσάμενοι οὐ γυμνοὶ εὑρεθησόμεθα. **4** καὶ γὰρ οἱ ὄντες ἐν τῷ σκήνει στενάζομεν βαρούμενοι, ἐφ᾿ ᾧ οὐ θέλομεν ἐκδύσασθαι ἀλλ᾿ ἐπενδύσασθαι, ἵνα καταποθῇ τὸ θνητὸν ὑπὸ τῆς ζωῆς. **5** ὁ δὲ κατεργασάμενος ἡμᾶς εἰς αὐτὸ τοῦτο θεός, ὁ δοὺς ἡμῖν τὸν ἀρραβῶνα τοῦ πνεύματος.

Gal 6:7–8

Μὴ πλανᾶσθε, θεὸς οὐ μυκτηρίζεται. ὃ γὰρ ἐὰν σπείρῃ ἄνθρωπος, τοῦτο καὶ θερίσει· **8** ὅτι ὁ σπείρων εἰς τὴν σάρκα ἑαυτοῦ ἐκ τῆς σαρκὸς θερίσει φθοράν, ὁ δὲ σπείρων εἰς τὸ πνεῦμα ἐκ τοῦ πνεύματος θερίσει ζωὴν αἰώνιον.

Phil 3:10–11

τοῦ γνῶναι αὐτὸν καὶ τὴν δύναμιν τῆς ἀναστάσεως αὐτοῦ καὶ [τὴν] κοινωνίαν [τῶν] παθημάτων αὐτοῦ, συμμορφιζόμενος τῷ θανάτῳ αὐτοῦ, **11** εἴ πως καταντήσω εἰς τὴν ἐξανάστασιν τὴν ἐκ νεκρῶν.

Phil 3:20–21

ἡμῶν γὰρ τὸ πολίτευμα ἐν οὐρανοῖς ὑπάρχει, ἐξ οὗ καὶ σωτῆρα ἀπεκδεχόμεθα κύριον Ἰησοῦν Χριστόν, **21** ὃς μετασχηματίσει τὸ σῶμα τῆς ταπεινώσεως ἡμῶν σύμμορφον τῷ σώματι τῆς δόξης αὐτοῦ κατὰ τὴν ἐνέργειαν τοῦ δύνασθαι αὐτὸν καὶ ὑποτάξαι αὐτῷ τὰ πάντα.

Col 1:18

καὶ αὐτός ἐστιν ἡ κεφαλὴ τοῦ σώματος τῆς ἐκκλησίας· ὅς ἐστιν ἀρχή, πρωτότοκος ἐκ τῶν νεκρῶν, ἵνα γένηται ἐν πᾶσιν αὐτὸς πρωτεύων

1 Thess 4:13–18

Οὐ θέλομεν δὲ ὑμᾶς ἀγνοεῖν, ἀδελφοί, περὶ τῶν κοιμωμένων, ἵνα μὴ λυπῆσθε καθὼς καὶ οἱ λοιποὶ οἱ μὴ ἔχοντες ἐλπίδα. **14** εἰ γὰρ πιστεύομεν ὅτι Ἰησοῦς ἀπέθανεν καὶ ἀνέστη, οὕτως καὶ ὁ θεὸς τοὺς κοιμηθέντας διὰ τοῦ Ἰησοῦ ἄξει σὺν αὐτῷ. **15** Τοῦτο γὰρ ὑμῖν λέγομεν ἐν λόγῳ κυρίου, ὅτι ἡμεῖς οἱ ζῶντες οἱ περιλειπόμενοι εἰς τὴν παρουσίαν τοῦ κυρίου οὐ μὴ φθάσωμεν τοὺς κοιμηθέντας· **16** ὅτι αὐτὸς ὁ κύριος ἐν κελεύσματι, ἐν φωνῇ ἀρχαγγέλου καὶ ἐν σάλπιγγι θεοῦ, καταβήσεται ἀπ᾿ οὐρανοῦ καὶ οἱ νεκροὶ ἐν Χριστῷ ἀναστήσονται πρῶτον, **17** ἔπειτα ἡμεῖς οἱ ζῶντες οἱ περιλειπόμενοι ἅμα σὺν αὐτοῖς ἁρπαγησόμεθα ἐν νεφέλαις εἰς ἀπάντησιν τοῦ κυρίου εἰς ἀέρα· καὶ οὕτως πάντοτε σὺν κυρίῳ ἐσόμεθα. **18** Ὥστε παρακαλεῖτε ἀλλήλους ἐν τοῖς λόγοις τούτοις.

1 Thess 5:23

Αὐτὸς δὲ ὁ θεὸς τῆς εἰρήνης ἁγιάσαι ὑμᾶς ὁλοτελεῖς, καὶ ὁλόκληρον ὑμῶν τὸ πνεῦμα καὶ ἡ ψυχὴ καὶ τὸ σῶμα ἀμέμπτως ἐν τῇ παρουσίᾳ τοῦ κυρίου ἡμῶν Ἰησοῦ Χριστοῦ τηρηθείη.

2 Tim 1:9–10

τοῦ σώσαντος ἡμᾶς καὶ καλέσαντος κλήσει ἁγίᾳ, οὐ κατὰ τὰ ἔργα ἡμῶν ἀλλὰ κατὰ ἰδίαν πρόθεσιν καὶ χάριν, τὴν δοθεῖσαν ἡμῖν ἐν Χριστῷ Ἰησοῦ πρὸ χρόνων αἰωνίων, **10** φανερωθεῖσαν δὲ νῦν διὰ τῆς ἐπιφανείας τοῦ σωτῆρος ἡμῶν Χριστοῦ Ἰησοῦ, καταργήσαντος μὲν τὸν θάνατον φωτίσαντος δὲ ζωὴν καὶ ἀφθαρσίαν διὰ τοῦ εὐαγγελίου

Acts 24:14–15

ὁμολογῶ δὲ τοῦτό σοι ὅτι κατὰ τὴν ὁδὸν ἣν λέγουσιν αἵρεσιν, οὕτως λατρεύω τῷ πατρῴῳ θεῷ πιστεύων πᾶσι τοῖς κατὰ τὸν νόμον καὶ τοῖς ἐν τοῖς προφήταις γεγραμμένοις, **15** ἐλπίδα ἔχων εἰς τὸν θεὸν ἣν καὶ αὐτοὶ οὗτοι προσδέχονται, ἀνάστασιν μέλλειν ⸀ἔσεσθαι δικαίων τε καὶ ἀδίκων.

Cf. Rom 4:17; 2 Cor 13:3–4; Gal 5:5; Col 3:4; Acts 17:31–32; 23:6–9; 24:20–21; 26:6–8; 26:22–23; 28:20.

See also § 34 The Resurrection of Jesus; § 90 Warning against Those Who Deny the Bodily Resurrection; § 93 The Glory to Be Revealed.

90. Warning against Those Who Deny the Bodily Resurrection

1 Cor 15:12–19

Εἰ δὲ Χριστὸς κηρύσσεται ὅτι ἐκ νεκρῶν ἐγήγερται, πῶς λέγουσιν ἐν ὑμῖν τινες ὅτι ἀνάστασις νεκρῶν οὐκ ἔστιν; **13** εἰ δὲ ἀνάστασις νεκρῶν οὐκ ἔστιν, οὐδὲ Χριστὸς ἐγήγερται· **14** εἰ δὲ Χριστὸς οὐκ ἐγήγερται, κενὸν ἄρα [καὶ] τὸ κήρυγμα ἡμῶν, κενὴ καὶ ἡ πίστις ὑμῶν· **15** εὑρισκόμεθα δὲ καὶ ψευδομάρτυρες τοῦ θεοῦ, ὅτι ἐμαρτυρήσαμεν κατὰ τοῦ θεοῦ ὅτι ἤγειρεν τὸν Χριστόν, ὃν οὐκ ἤγειρεν εἴπερ ἄρα νεκροὶ οὐκ ἐγείρονται. **16** εἰ γὰρ νεκροὶ οὐκ ἐγείρονται, οὐδὲ Χριστὸς ἐγήγερται· **17** εἰ δὲ Χριστὸς οὐκ ἐγήγερται, ματαία ἡ πίστις ὑμῶν, ἔτι ἐστὲ ἐν ταῖς ἁμαρτίαις ὑμῶν, **18** ἄρα καὶ οἱ κοιμηθέντες ἐν Χριστῷ ἀπώλοντο. **19** εἰ ἐν τῇ ζωῇ ταύτῃ ἐν Χριστῷ ἠλπικότες ἐσμὲν μόνον, ἐλεεινότεροι πάντων ἀνθρώπων ἐσμέν.

1 Cor 15:29–34

Ἐπεὶ τί ποιήσουσιν οἱ βαπτιζόμενοι ὑπὲρ τῶν νεκρῶν; εἰ ὅλως νεκροὶ οὐκ ἐγείρονται, τί καὶ βαπτίζονται ὑπὲρ αὐτῶν; **30** Τί καὶ ἡμεῖς κινδυνεύομεν πᾶσαν ὥραν; **31** καθ᾿ ἡμέραν ἀποθνήσκω, νὴ τὴν ὑμετέραν καύχησιν, [ἀδελφοί], ἣν ἔχω ἐν Χριστῷ Ἰησοῦ τῷ κυρίῳ ἡμῶν. **32** εἰ κατὰ ἄνθρωπον ἐθηριομάχησα ἐν Ἐφέσῳ, τί μοι τὸ ὄφελος; εἰ νεκροὶ οὐκ ἐγείρονται, φάγωμεν καὶ πίωμεν, αὔριον γὰρ ἀποθνήσκομεν. **33** μὴ πλανᾶσθε·

2 Cor 4:14 ***κυριον*** א C D 1881 *Byz*] *om.* 𝔓46 B (33) (1739) **2 Cor 5:3** ***εκδυσαμενοι*** D*,c] ενδυσαμενοι 𝔓46 א B C D2 33. 1739. 1881 *Byz* **Acts 24:15** ***εσεσθαι*** 𝔓74 א A B C 33. 1739] *add.* νεκρων E *Byz*

scripture—"I believed, and so I spoke"—we also believe, and so we speak, 14 because we know that the one who raised the Lord[h] Jesus will raise us also with Jesus, and will bring us with you into his presence.

2 Cor 5:1–5

For we know that if the earthly tent we live in is destroyed, we have a building from God, a house not made with hands, eternal in the heavens. 2 For in this tent we groan, longing to be clothed with our dwelling from heaven— 3 if indeed, when we have put it on[i] we will not be found naked.[j] 4 For while we are still in this tent, we groan under our burden, because we wish not to be unclothed but to be further clothed, so that what is mortal may be swallowed up by life. 5 He who has prepared us for this very thing is God, who has given us the Spirit as a guarantee.

Gal 6:7–8

Do not be deceived; God is not mocked, for you reap whatever you sow. 8 If you sow to your own flesh, you will reap corruption from the flesh; but if you sow to the Spirit, you will reap eternal life from the Spirit.

Phil 3:10–11

I want to know Christ and the power of his resurrection and the sharing of his sufferings by becoming like him in his death, 11 if somehow I may attain the resurrection from the dead.

Phil 3:20–21

But our citizenship is in heaven, and it is from there that we are expecting a Savior, the Lord Jesus Christ. 21 He will transform the body of our humiliation that it may be conformed to the body of his glory, by the power that also enables him to make all things subject to himself.

Col 1:18

He is the head of the body, the church; he is the beginning, the firstborn from the dead, so that he might come to have first place in everything.

1 Thess 4:13–18

But we do not want you to be uninformed, brothers and sisters, about those who have died, so that you may not grieve as others do who have no hope. 14 For since we believe that Jesus died and rose again, even so, through Jesus, God will bring with him those who have died. 15 For this we declare to you by the word of the Lord, that we who are alive, who are left until the coming of the Lord, will by no means precede those who have died. 16 For the Lord himself, with a cry of command, with the archangel's call and with the sound of God's trumpet, will descend from heaven, and the dead in Christ will rise first. 17 Then we who are alive, who are left, will be caught up in the clouds together with them to meet the Lord in the air; and so we will be with the Lord forever. 18 Therefore encourage one another with these words.

1 Thess 5:23

May the God of peace himself sanctify you entirely; and may your spirit and soul and body be kept sound and blameless at the coming of our Lord Jesus Christ.

2 Tim 1:9–10

who saved us and called us with a holy calling, not according to our works but according to his own purpose and grace. This grace was given to us in Christ Jesus before the ages began, 10 but it has now been revealed through the appearing of our Savior Christ Jesus, who abolished death and brought life and immortality to light through the gospel.

Acts 24:14–15

But this I admit to you, that according to the Way, which they call a sect, I worship the God of our ancestors, believing everything laid down according to the law or written in the prophets. 15 I have a hope in God—a hope that they themselves also accept—that there will be a resurrection of both[k] the righteous and the unrighteous.

Cf. Rom 4:17; 2 Cor 13:3–4; Gal 5:5; Col 3:4; Acts 17:31–32; 23:6–9; 24:20–21; 26:6–8; 26:22–23; 28:20.

See also § 34 The Resurrection of Jesus; § 90 Warning against Those Who Deny the Bodily Resurrection; § 93 The Glory to Be Revealed.

90. Warning against Those Who Deny the Bodily Resurrection

1 Cor 15:12–19

Now if Christ is proclaimed as raised from the dead, how can some of you say there is no resurrection of the dead? 13 If there is no resurrection of the dead, then Christ has not been raised; 14 and if Christ has not been raised, then our proclamation has been in vain and your faith has been in vain. 15 We are even found to be misrepresenting God, because we testified of God that he raised Christ—whom he did not raise if it is true that the dead are not raised. 16 For if the dead are not raised, then Christ has not been raised. 17 If Christ has not been raised, your faith is futile and you are still in your sins. 18 Then those also who have died in Christ have perished. 19 If for this life only we have hoped in Christ, we are of all people most to be pitied.

1 Cor 15:29–34

Otherwise, what will those people do who receive baptism on behalf of the dead? If the dead are not raised at all, why are people baptized on their behalf? 30 And why are we putting ourselves in danger every hour? 31 I die every day! That is as certain, brothers and sisters, as my boasting of you—a boast that I make in Christ Jesus our Lord. 32 If with merely human hopes I fought with wild animals at Ephesus, what would I have gained by it? If the dead are not raised, "Let us eat and drink, for tomorrow we die." 33 Do not

[h] **2 Cor 4:14** *the Lord* Other ancient authorities lack *the Lord* [i] **2 Cor 5:3** *put it on* A few ancient authorities read *taken it off* [j] **2 Cor 5:2–3** Translation differs from NRSV [k] **Acts 24:15** *of both* Other ancient authorities read *of the dead, both of*

φθείρουσιν ἤθη χρηστὰ ὁμιλίαι κακαί. **34** ἐκνήψατε δικαίως καὶ μὴ ἁμαρτάνετε, ἀγνωσίαν γὰρ θεοῦ τινες ἔχουσιν, πρὸς ἐντροπὴν ὑμῖν λαλῶ.

2 Tim 2:14–21

Ταῦτα ὑπομίμνῃσκε διαμαρτυρόμενος ἐνώπιον τοῦ ⸀θεοῦ μὴ λογομαχεῖν, ἐπʼ οὐδὲν χρήσιμον, ἐπὶ καταστροφῇ τῶν ἀκουόντων. **15** σπούδασον σεαυτὸν δόκιμον παραστῆσαι τῷ θεῷ, ἐργάτην ἀνεπαίσχυντον, ὀρθοτομοῦντα τὸν λόγον τῆς ἀληθείας. **16** τὰς δὲ βεβήλους κενοφωνίας περιΐστασο· ἐπὶ πλεῖον γὰρ προκόψουσιν ἀσεβείας **17** καὶ ὁ λόγος αὐτῶν ὡς γάγγραινα νομὴν ἕξει. ὧν ἐστιν Ὑμέναιος καὶ Φίλητος, **18** οἵτινες περὶ τὴν ἀλήθειαν ἠστόχησαν, λέγοντες [τὴν] ἀνάστασιν ἤδη γεγονέναι, καὶ ἀνατρέπουσιν τήν τινων πίστιν. **19** ὁ μέντοι στερεὸς θεμέλιος τοῦ θεοῦ ἕστηκεν, ἔχων τὴν σφραγῖδα ταύτην· ἔγνω κύριος τοὺς ὄντας αὐτοῦ, καί· ἀποστήτω ἀπὸ ἀδικίας πᾶς ὁ ὀνομάζων τὸ ὄνομα κυρίου. **20** Ἐν μεγάλῃ δὲ οἰκίᾳ οὐκ ἔστιν μόνον σκεύη χρυσᾶ καὶ ἀργυρᾶ ἀλλὰ καὶ ξύλινα καὶ ὀστράκινα, καὶ ἃ μὲν εἰς τιμὴν ἃ δὲ εἰς ἀτιμίαν· **21** ἐὰν οὖν τις ἐκκαθάρῃ ἑαυτὸν ἀπὸ τούτων, ἔσται σκεῦος εἰς τιμήν, ἡγιασμένον, εὔχρηστον τῷ δεσπότῃ, εἰς πᾶν ἔργον ἀγαθὸν ἡτοιμασμένον.

Cf. Acts 23:6–9. With 2 Tim 2:14–21, cf. 1 Tim 1:18–20; 6:20–21.

91. The Renewal of Creation

Rom 8:18–25

Λογίζομαι γὰρ ὅτι οὐκ ἄξια τὰ παθήματα τοῦ νῦν καιροῦ πρὸς τὴν μέλλουσαν δόξαν ἀποκαλυφθῆναι εἰς ἡμᾶς. **19** ἡ γὰρ ἀποκαραδοκία τῆς κτίσεως τὴν ἀποκάλυψιν τῶν υἱῶν τοῦ θεοῦ ἀπεκδέχεται. **20** τῇ γὰρ ματαιότητι ἡ κτίσις ὑπετάγη, οὐχ ἑκοῦσα ἀλλὰ διὰ τὸν ὑποτάξαντα, ἐφʼ ἑλπίδι **21** ὅτι καὶ αὐτὴ ἡ κτίσις ἐλευθερωθήσεται ἀπὸ τῆς δουλείας τῆς φθορᾶς εἰς τὴν ἐλευθερίαν τῆς δόξης τῶν τέκνων τοῦ θεοῦ. **22** οἴδαμεν γὰρ ὅτι πᾶσα ἡ κτίσις συστενάζει καὶ συνωδίνει ἄχρι τοῦ νῦν· **23** οὐ μόνον δέ, ἀλλὰ καὶ αὐτοὶ τὴν ἀπαρχὴν τοῦ πνεύματος ἔχοντες, ἡμεῖς καὶ αὐτοὶ ἐν ἑαυτοῖς στενάζομεν υἱοθεσίαν ἀπεκδεχόμενοι, τὴν ἀπολύτρωσιν τοῦ σώματος ἡμῶν. **24** τῇ γὰρ ἐλπίδι ἐσώθημεν· ἐλπὶς δὲ βλεπομένη οὐκ ἔστιν ἐλπίς· ὃ γὰρ βλέπει τίς ⸀ἐλπίζει; **25** εἰ δὲ ὃ οὐ βλέπομεν ἐλπίζομεν, διʼ ὑπομονῆς ἀπεκδεχόμεθα.

2 Cor 4:17–18

τὸ γὰρ παραυτίκα ἐλαφρὸν τῆς θλίψεως ἡμῶν καθʼ ὑπερβολὴν εἰς ὑπερβολὴν αἰώνιον βάρος δόξης κατεργάζεται ἡμῖν, **18** μὴ σκοπούντων ἡμῶν τὰ βλεπόμενα ἀλλὰ τὰ μὴ βλεπόμενα· τὰ γὰρ βλεπόμενα πρόσκαιρα, τὰ δὲ μὴ βλεπόμενα αἰώνια.

Eph 1:9–12

γνωρίσας ἡμῖν τὸ μυστήριον τοῦ θελήματος αὐτοῦ, κατὰ τὴν εὐδοκίαν αὐτοῦ ἣν προέθετο ἐν αὐτῷ **10** εἰς οἰκονομίαν τοῦ πληρώματος τῶν καιρῶν, ἀνακεφαλαιώσασθαι τὰ πάντα ἐν τῷ Χριστῷ, τὰ ἐπὶ τοῖς οὐρανοῖς καὶ τὰ ἐπὶ τῆς γῆς ἐν αὐτῷ. **11** Ἐν ᾧ καὶ ἐκληρώθημεν προορισθέντες κατὰ πρόθεσιν τοῦ τὰ πάντα ἐνεργοῦντος κατὰ τὴν βουλὴν τοῦ θελήματος αὐτοῦ **12** εἰς τὸ εἶναι ἡμᾶς εἰς ἔπαινον δόξης αὐτοῦ τοὺς προηλπικότας ἐν τῷ Χριστῷ.

Phil 3:20–21

ἡμῶν γὰρ τὸ πολίτευμα ἐν οὐρανοῖς ὑπάρχει, ἐξ οὗ καὶ σωτῆρα ἀπεκδεχόμεθα κύριον Ἰησοῦν Χριστόν, **21** ὃς μετασχηματίσει τὸ σῶμα τῆς ταπεινώσεως ἡμῶν σύμμορφον τῷ σώματι τῆς δόξης αὐτοῦ κατὰ τὴν ἐνέργειαν τοῦ δύνασθαι αὐτὸν καὶ ὑποτάξαι αὐτῷ τὰ πάντα.

Col 1:15–20

ὅς ἐστιν εἰκὼν τοῦ θεοῦ τοῦ ἀοράτου, πρωτότοκος πάσης κτίσεως, **16** ὅτι ἐν αὐτῷ ἐκτίσθη τὰ πάντα ἐν τοῖς οὐρανοῖς καὶ ἐπὶ τῆς γῆς, τὰ ὁρατὰ καὶ τὰ ἀόρατα, εἴτε θρόνοι εἴτε κυριότητες εἴτε ἀρχαὶ εἴτε ἐξουσίαι· τὰ πάντα διʼ αὐτοῦ καὶ εἰς αὐτὸν ἔκτισται· **17** καὶ αὐτός ἐστιν πρὸ πάντων καὶ τὰ πάντα ἐν αὐτῷ συνέστηκεν, **18** καὶ αὐτός ἐστιν ἡ κεφαλὴ τοῦ σώματος τῆς ἐκκλησίας· ὅς ἐστιν ἀρχή, πρωτότοκος ἐκ τῶν νεκρῶν, ἵνα γένηται ἐν πᾶσιν αὐτὸς πρωτεύων, **19** ὅτι ἐν αὐτῷ εὐδόκησεν πᾶν τὸ πλήρωμα κατοικῆσαι **20** καὶ διʼ αὐτοῦ ἀποκαταλλάξαι τὰ πάντα εἰς αὐτόν, εἰρηνοποιήσας διὰ τοῦ αἵματος τοῦ σταυροῦ αὐτοῦ, [διʼ αὐτοῦ] εἴτε τὰ ἐπὶ τῆς γῆς εἴτε τὰ ἐν τοῖς οὐρανοῖς.

Cf. Rom 4:13; 1 Cor 15:23–28; 15:50–57; 2 Cor 5:17; Gal 5:5; 6:14–16; Phil 2:9–11.

See also § 92 The Inheritance of the Saints.

92. The Inheritance of the Saints

Rom 4:13–15

Οὐ γὰρ διὰ νόμου ἡ ἐπαγγελία τῷ Ἀβραὰμ ἢ τῷ σπέρματι αὐτοῦ, τὸ κληρονόμον αὐτὸν εἶναι κόσμου, ἀλλὰ διὰ δικαιοσύνης πίστεως. **14** εἰ γὰρ οἱ ἐκ νόμου κληρονόμοι, κεκένωται ἡ πίστις καὶ κατήργηται ἡ ἐπαγγελία· **15** ὁ γὰρ νόμος ὀργὴν κατεργάζεται· οὗ δὲ οὐκ ἔστιν νόμος οὐδὲ παράβασις.

Rom 8:15–21

οὐ γὰρ ἐλάβετε πνεῦμα δουλείας πάλιν εἰς φόβον ἀλλὰ ἐλάβετε πνεῦμα υἱοθεσίας ἐν ᾧ κράζομεν· αββα ὁ πατήρ. **16** αὐτὸ τὸ πνεῦμα συμμαρτυρεῖ τῷ πνεύματι

§ 90 2 Tim 2:14 *θεου* ℵ C I] κυριου A D 048. 1739. 1881 *Byz* **§ 91** Rom 8:24 *ελπιζει* 𝔓[46] ℵ[2] B C D 33. 1739*. 1881 *Byz*] υπομενει ℵ* A 1739[mg]

be deceived: "Bad company ruins good morals." **34** Come to a sober and right mind, and sin no more; for some people have no knowledge of God. I say this to your shame.

2 Tim 2:14–21

Remind them of this, and warn them before God[a] that they are to avoid wrangling over words, which does no good but only ruins those who are listening. **15** Do your best to present yourself to God as one approved by him, a worker who has no need to be ashamed, rightly explaining the word of truth. **16** Avoid profane chatter, for it will lead people into more and more impiety, **17** and their talk will spread like gangrene. Among them are Hymenaeus and Philetus, **18** who have swerved from the truth by claiming that the resurrection has already taken place. They are upsetting the faith of some. **19** But God's firm foundation stands, bearing this inscription: "The Lord knows those who are his," and, "Let everyone who calls on the name of the Lord turn away from wickedness." **20** In a large house there are utensils not only of gold and silver but also of wood and clay, some for special use, some for ordinary. **21** All who cleanse themselves of the things I have mentioned will become special utensils, dedicated and useful to the owner of the house, ready for every good work.

Cf. Acts 23:6–9. With 2 Tim 2:14–21, cf. 1 Tim 1:18–20; 6:20–21.

91. *The Renewal of Creation*

Rom 8:18–25

I consider that the sufferings of this present time are not worth comparing with the glory about to be revealed to us. **19** For the creation waits with eager longing for the revealing of the children of God; **20** for the creation was subjected to futility, not of its own will but by the will of the one who subjected it, in hope **21** that the creation itself will be set free from its bondage to decay and will obtain the freedom of the glory of the children of God. **22** We know that the whole creation has been groaning in labor pains until now; **23** and not only the creation, but we ourselves, who have the first fruits of the Spirit, groan inwardly while we wait for adoption, the redemption of our bodies. **24** For in hope we were saved. Now hope that is seen is not hope. For who hopes[a] for what is seen? **25** But if we hope for what we do not see, we wait for it with patience.

2 Cor 4:17–18

For this slight momentary affliction is preparing us for an eternal weight of glory beyond all measure, **18** because we look not at what is presently seen but at what is not presently seen; for what is presently seen is temporary, but what is not presently seen is eternal.[b]

Eph 1:9–12

he has made known to us the mystery of his will, according to his good pleasure that he set forth in Christ, **10** as a plan for the fullness of time, to gather up all things in him, things in heaven and things on earth. **11** In Christ we have also obtained an inheritance, having been destined according to the purpose of him who accomplishes all things according to his counsel and will, **12** so that we, who were the first to set our hope on Christ, might live for the praise of his glory.

Phil 3:20–21

But our citizenship is in heaven, and it is from there that we are expecting a Savior, the Lord Jesus Christ. **21** He will transform the body of our humiliation that it may be conformed to the body of his glory, by the power that also enables him to make all things subject to himself.

Col 1:15–20

Who[c] is the image of the invisible God, the firstborn of all creation; **16** for in him all things in heaven and on earth were created, things visible and invisible, whether thrones or dominions or rulers or powers—all things have been created through him and for him. **17** He himself is before all things, and in him all things hold together. **18** He is the head of the body, the church; he is the beginning, the firstborn from the dead, so that he might come to have first place in everything. **19** For in him all the fullness of God was pleased to dwell, **20** and through him God was pleased to reconcile to himself all things, whether on earth or in heaven, by making peace through the blood of his cross.

Cf. Rom 4:13; 1 Cor 15:23–28; 15:50–57; 2 Cor 5:17; Gal 5:5; 6:14–16; Phil 2:9–11.

See also § 92 The Inheritance of the Saints.

92. *The Inheritance of the Saints*

Rom 4:13–15

For the promise that he would inherit the world did not come to Abraham or to his descendants through the law but through the righteousness of faith. **14** If it is the adherents of the law who are to be the heirs, faith is null and the promise is void. **15** For the law brings wrath; but where there is no law, neither is there violation.

Rom 8:15–21

For you did not receive a spirit of slavery to fall back into fear, but you have received a spirit of adoption. When we cry, "Abba! Father!" **16** it is that very

§ 90 [a] **2 Tim 2:14** *God* Other ancient authorities read *the Lord* **§ 91** [a] **Rom 8:24** *hopes* Other ancient authorities read *awaits* [b] **2 Cor 4:18** Translation differs from NRSV [c] **Col 1:15** *Who* NRSV translates *He*

ἡμῶν ὅτι ἐσμὲν τέκνα θεοῦ. 17 εἰ δὲ τέκνα, καὶ κληρονόμοι· κληρονόμοι μὲν θεοῦ, συγκληρονόμοι δὲ Χριστοῦ, εἴπερ συμπάσχομεν ἵνα καὶ συνδοξασθῶμεν. 18 Λογίζομαι γὰρ ὅτι οὐκ ἄξια τὰ παθήματα τοῦ νῦν καιροῦ πρὸς τὴν μέλλουσαν δόξαν ἀποκαλυφθῆναι εἰς ἡμᾶς. 19 ἡ γὰρ ἀποκαραδοκία τῆς κτίσεως τὴν ἀποκάλυψιν τῶν υἱῶν τοῦ θεοῦ ἀπεκδέχεται. 20 τῇ γὰρ ματαιότητι ἡ κτίσις ὑπετάγη, οὐχ ἑκοῦσα ἀλλὰ διὰ τὸν ὑποτάξαντα, ἐφ' ἑλπίδι 21 ὅτι καὶ αὐτὴ ἡ κτίσις ἐλευθερωθήσεται ἀπὸ τῆς δουλείας τῆς φθορᾶς εἰς τὴν ἐλευθερίαν τῆς δόξης τῶν τέκνων τοῦ θεοῦ.

1 Cor 6:9–11

Ἢ οὐκ οἴδατε ὅτι ἄδικοι θεοῦ βασιλείαν οὐ κληρονομήσουσιν; μὴ πλανᾶσθε· οὔτε πόρνοι οὔτε εἰδωλολάτραι οὔτε μοιχοὶ οὔτε μαλακοὶ οὔτε ἀρσενοκοῖται 10 οὔτε κλέπται οὔτε πλεονέκται, οὐ μέθυσοι, οὐ λοίδοροι, οὐχ ἅρπαγες βασιλείαν θεοῦ κληρονομήσουσιν. 11 καὶ ταῦτά τινες ἦτε· ἀλλὰ ἀπελούσασθε, ἀλλὰ ἡγιάσθητε, ἀλλὰ ἐδικαιώθητε ἐν τῷ ὀνόματι τοῦ κυρίου ⸂Ἰησοῦ Χριστοῦ⸃ καὶ ἐν τῷ πνεύματι τοῦ θεοῦ ἡμῶν.

1 Cor 15:50–57

Τοῦτο δέ φημι, ἀδελφοί, ὅτι σὰρξ καὶ αἷμα βασιλείαν θεοῦ κληρονομῆσαι οὐ δύναται οὐδὲ ἡ φθορὰ τὴν ἀφθαρσίαν κληρονομεῖ. 51 ἰδοὺ μυστήριον ὑμῖν λέγω· πάντες οὐ κοιμηθησόμεθα, πάντες δὲ ἀλλαγησόμεθα, 52 ἐν ἀτόμῳ, ἐν ῥιπῇ ὀφθαλμοῦ, ἐν τῇ ἐσχάτῃ σάλπιγγι· σαλπίσει γὰρ καὶ οἱ νεκροὶ ἐγερθήσονται ἄφθαρτοι καὶ ἡμεῖς ἀλλαγησόμεθα. 53 Δεῖ γὰρ τὸ φθαρτὸν τοῦτο ἐνδύσασθαι ἀφθαρσίαν καὶ τὸ θνητὸν τοῦτο ἐνδύσασθαι ἀθανασίαν. 54 ὅταν δὲ τὸ φθαρτὸν τοῦτο ἐνδύσηται ἀφθαρσίαν καὶ τὸ θνητὸν τοῦτο ἐνδύσηται ἀθανασίαν, τότε γενήσεται ὁ λόγος ὁ γεγραμμένος· κατεπόθη ὁ θάνατος εἰς νῖκος. 55 ποῦ σου, θάνατε, τὸ νῖκος; ποῦ σου, θάνατε, τὸ κέντρον; 56 τὸ δὲ κέντρον τοῦ θανάτου ἡ ἁμαρτία, ἡ δὲ δύναμις τῆς ἁμαρτίας ὁ νόμος· 57 τῷ δὲ θεῷ χάρις τῷ διδόντι ἡμῖν τὸ νῖκος διὰ τοῦ κυρίου ἡμῶν Ἰησοῦ Χριστοῦ.

Gal 3:15–18

Ἀδελφοί, κατὰ ἄνθρωπον λέγω· ὅμως ἀνθρώπου κεκυρωμένην διαθήκην οὐδεὶς ἀθετεῖ ἢ ἐπιδιατάσσεται. 16 τῷ δὲ Ἀβραὰμ ἐρρέθησαν αἱ ἐπαγγελίαι καὶ τῷ σπέρματι αὐτοῦ. οὐ λέγει· καὶ τοῖς σπέρμασιν, ὡς ἐπὶ πολλῶν ἀλλ' ὡς ἐφ' ἑνός· καὶ τῷ σπέρματί σου, ὅς ἐστιν Χριστός. 17 τοῦτο δὲ λέγω· διαθήκην προκεκυρωμένην ὑπὸ τοῦ θεοῦ ὁ μετὰ τετρακόσια καὶ τριάκοντα ἔτη γεγονὼς νόμος οὐκ ἀκυροῖ εἰς τὸ καταργῆσαι τὴν ἐπαγγελίαν. 18 εἰ γὰρ ἐκ νόμου ἡ κληρονομία, οὐκέτι ἐξ ἐπαγγελίας· τῷ δὲ Ἀβραὰμ δι' ἐπαγγελίας κεχάρισται ὁ θεός.

Gal 3:26–29

Πάντες γὰρ υἱοὶ θεοῦ ἐστε διὰ τῆς πίστεως ἐν Χριστῷ Ἰησοῦ· 27 ὅσοι γὰρ εἰς Χριστὸν ἐβαπτίσθητε, Χριστὸν ἐνεδύσασθε. 28 οὐκ ἔνι Ἰουδαῖος οὐδὲ Ἕλλην, οὐκ ἔνι δοῦλος οὐδὲ ἐλεύθερος, οὐκ ἔνι ἄρσεν καὶ θῆλυ· πάντες γὰρ ὑμεῖς εἷς ἐστε ἐν Χριστῷ Ἰησοῦ. 29 εἰ δὲ ὑμεῖς Χριστοῦ, ἄρα τοῦ Ἀβραὰμ σπέρμα ἐστέ, κατ' ἐπαγγελίαν κληρονόμοι.

Gal 4:1–7

Λέγω δέ, ἐφ' ὅσον χρόνον ὁ κληρονόμος νήπιός ἐστιν, οὐδὲν διαφέρει δούλου κύριος πάντων ὤν, 2 ἀλλὰ ὑπὸ ἐπιτρόπους ἐστὶν καὶ οἰκονόμους ἄχρι τῆς προθεσμίας τοῦ πατρός. 3 οὕτως καὶ ἡμεῖς, ὅτε ἦμεν νήπιοι, ὑπὸ τὰ στοιχεῖα τοῦ κόσμου ἤμεθα δεδουλωμένοι· 4 ὅτε δὲ ἦλθεν τὸ πλήρωμα τοῦ χρόνου, ἐξαπέστειλεν ὁ θεὸς τὸν υἱὸν αὐτοῦ, γενόμενον ἐκ γυναικός, γενόμενον ὑπὸ νόμον, 5 ἵνα τοὺς ὑπὸ νόμον ἐξαγοράσῃ, ἵνα τὴν υἱοθεσίαν ἀπολάβωμεν. 6 Ὅτι δέ ἐστε υἱοί, ἐξαπέστειλεν ὁ θεὸς τὸ πνεῦμα τοῦ υἱοῦ αὐτοῦ εἰς τὰς καρδίας ⸀ἡμῶν κρᾶζον· αββα ὁ πατήρ. 7 ὥστε οὐκέτι εἶ δοῦλος ἀλλὰ υἱός· εἰ δὲ υἱός, καὶ κληρονόμος ⸂διὰ θεοῦ⸃.

Gal 4:28–31

⸀Ὑμεῖς δέ, ἀδελφοί, κατὰ Ἰσαὰκ ἐπαγγελίας τέκνα ⸀ἐστέ. 29 ἀλλ' ὥσπερ τότε ὁ κατὰ σάρκα γεννηθεὶς ἐδίωκεν τὸν κατὰ πνεῦμα, οὕτως καὶ νῦν. 30 ἀλλὰ τί λέγει ἡ γραφή; ἔκβαλε τὴν παιδίσκην καὶ τὸν υἱὸν αὐτῆς· οὐ γὰρ μὴ κληρονομήσει ὁ υἱὸς τῆς παιδίσκης μετὰ τοῦ υἱοῦ τῆς ἐλευθέρας. 31 διό, ἀδελφοί, οὐκ ἐσμὲν παιδίσκης τέκνα ἀλλὰ τῆς ἐλευθέρας.

Eph 1:13–21

Ἐν ᾧ καὶ ὑμεῖς ἀκούσαντες τὸν λόγον τῆς ἀληθείας, τὸ εὐαγγέλιον τῆς σωτηρίας ὑμῶν, ἐν ᾧ καὶ πιστεύσαντες ἐσφραγίσθητε τῷ πνεύματι τῆς ἐπαγγελίας τῷ ἁγίῳ, 14 ⸀ὅ ἐστιν ἀρραβὼν τῆς κληρονομίας ἡμῶν, εἰς ἀπολύτρωσιν τῆς περιποιήσεως, εἰς ἔπαινον τῆς δόξης αὐτοῦ. 15 Διὰ τοῦτο κἀγὼ ἀκούσας τὴν καθ' ὑμᾶς πίστιν ἐν τῷ κυρίῳ Ἰησοῦ καὶ ⸂τὴν ἀγάπην τὴν⸃ εἰς πάντας τοὺς ἁγίους 16 οὐ παύομαι εὐχαριστῶν ὑπὲρ ὑμῶν μνείαν ποιούμενος ἐπὶ τῶν προσευχῶν μου, 17 ἵνα ὁ θεὸς τοῦ κυρίου ἡμῶν Ἰησοῦ Χριστοῦ, ὁ πατὴρ τῆς δόξης, δώῃ ὑμῖν πνεῦμα σοφίας καὶ ἀποκαλύψεως ἐν ἐπιγνώσει αὐτοῦ, 18 πεφωτισμένους τοὺς ὀφθαλμοὺς τῆς καρδίας [ὑμῶν] εἰς τὸ εἰδέναι ὑμᾶς τίς ἐστιν ἡ ἐλπὶς τῆς κλήσεως αὐτοῦ, τίς ὁ πλοῦτος τῆς δόξης τῆς κληρονομίας αὐτοῦ ἐν τοῖς ἁγίοις, 19 καὶ τί τὸ ὑπερβάλλον μέγεθος τῆς δυνάμεως αὐτοῦ εἰς ἡμᾶς τοὺς πιστεύοντας κατὰ τὴν ἐνέργειαν τοῦ κράτους τῆς ἰσχύος αὐτοῦ. 20 Ἣν ⸀ἐνήργησεν ἐν τῷ Χριστῷ ἐγείρας αὐτὸν ἐκ νεκρῶν καὶ καθίσας ἐν δεξιᾷ αὐτοῦ ἐν τοῖς ἐπουρανίοις 21 ὑπεράνω πάσης ἀρχῆς καὶ ἐξουσίας καὶ δυνάμεως καὶ κυριότητος καὶ παντὸς ὀνόματος ὀνομαζομένου, οὐ μόνον ἐν τῷ αἰῶνι τούτῳ ἀλλὰ καὶ ἐν τῷ μέλλοντι

Eph 3:1–7

Τούτου χάριν ἐγὼ Παῦλος ὁ δέσμιος τοῦ Χριστοῦ [Ἰησοῦ] ὑπὲρ ὑμῶν τῶν ἐθνῶν 2 —εἴ γε ἠκούσατε τὴν οἰκονομίαν τῆς χάριτος τοῦ θεοῦ τῆς δοθείσης μοι εἰς ὑμᾶς, 3 [ὅτι] κατὰ ἀποκάλυψιν ἐγνωρίσθη

§ 92 **1 Cor 6:11** ***Ιησου Χριστου*** 𝔓^{11vid} 𝔓^{46} ℵ D*] Ιησου A D^{2} *Byz* ¦ ημων Ιησου Χριστου B C^{vid} 33. 1739. 1881 **Gal 4:6** ***ημων*** 𝔓^{46} ℵ A B C D* 1739. 1881] υμων D^{2} 33 *Byz* **Gal 4:7** ***δια θεου*** 𝔓^{46} ℵ* A B C* 33. 1739^{*vid}] θεου δια Χριστου ℵ^{2} C^{3} D *Byz* ¦ δια θεον 1881 ¦ δια Ιησου Χριστου 1739^{c} **Gal 4:28** ***υμεις*** *et* εστε 𝔓^{46} B D* 33. 1739. 1881] ημεις *et* εσμεν ℵ A C D^{2} *Byz* **Eph 1:14** ***ὅ*** 𝔓^{46} A B 1739. 1881] ος ℵ D 33 *Byz* **Eph 1:15** ***την αγαπην την*** ℵ^{2} D^{1} *Byz*] την 𝔓^{46} ℵ* A B 33. 1739. 1881 ¦ την αγαπην D* **Eph 1:20** ***ενηργησεν*** ℵ D 33. 1739. 1881 *Byz*] ενηργηκεν A B

Spirit bearing witness with our spirit that we are children of God, 17 and if children, then heirs, heirs of God and joint heirs with Christ—if, in fact, we suffer with him so that we may also be glorified with him. 18 I consider that the sufferings of this present time are not worth comparing with the glory about to be revealed to us. 19 For the creation waits with eager longing for the revealing of the children of God; 20 for the creation was subjected to futility, not of its own will but by the will of the one who subjected it, in hope 21 that the creation itself will be set free from its bondage to decay and will obtain the freedom of the glory of the children of God.

1 Cor 6:9–11

Do you not know that wrongdoers will not inherit the kingdom of God? Do not be deceived! Fornicators, idolaters, adulterers, male prostitutes, sodomites, 10 thieves, the greedy, drunkards, revilers, robbers—none of these will inherit the kingdom of God. 11 And this is what some of you used to be. But you were washed, you were sanctified, you were justified in the name of the Lord Jesus Christ[a] and in the Spirit of our God.

1 Cor 15:50–57

What I am saying, brothers and sisters, is this: flesh and blood cannot inherit the kingdom of God, nor does the perishable inherit the imperishable. 51 Listen, I will tell you a mystery! We will not all die, but we will all be changed, 52 in a moment, in the twinkling of an eye, at the last trumpet. For the trumpet will sound, and the dead will be raised imperishable, and we will be changed. 53 For this perishable body must put on imperishability, and this mortal body must put on immortality. 54 When this perishable body puts on imperishability, and this mortal body puts on immortality, then the saying that is written will be fulfilled: "Death has been swallowed up in victory." 55 "Where, O death, is your victory? Where, O death, is your sting?" 56 The sting of death is sin, and the power of sin is the law. 57 But thanks be to God, who gives us the victory through our Lord Jesus Christ.

Gal 3:15–18

Brothers and sisters, I give an example from daily life: once a person's will has been ratified, no one adds to it or annuls it. 16 Now the promises were made to Abraham and to his offspring; it does not say, "And to offsprings," as of many; but it says, "And to your offspring," that is, to one person, who is Christ. 17 My point is this: the law, which came four hundred thirty years later, does not annul a covenant previously ratified by God, so as to nullify the promise. 18 For if the inheritance comes from the law, it no longer comes from the promise; but God granted it to Abraham through the promise.

Gal 3:26–29

for in Christ Jesus you are all children of God through faith. 27 As many of you as were baptized into Christ have clothed yourselves with Christ. 28 There is no longer Jew or Greek, there is no longer slave or free, there is no longer male and female; for all of you are one in Christ Jesus. 29 And if you belong to Christ, then you are Abraham's offspring, heirs according to the promise.

Gal 4:1–7

My point is this: heirs, as long as they are minors, are no better than slaves, though they are the owners of all the property; 2 but they remain under guardians and trustees until the date set by the father. 3 So with us; while we were minors, we were enslaved to the elemental spirits of the world. 4 But when the fullness of time had come, God sent his Son, born of a woman, born under the law, 5 in order to redeem those who were under the law, so that we might receive adoption as children. 6 And because you are children, God has sent the Spirit of his Son into our[b] hearts, crying, "Abba! Father!" 7 So you are no longer a slave but a child, and if a child then also an heir, through God.[c]

Gal 4:28–31

Now you,[d] my friends, are children of the promise, like Isaac. 29 But just as at that time the child who was born according to the flesh persecuted the child who was born according to the Spirit, so it is now also. 30 But what does the scripture say? "Drive out the slave and her child; for the child of the slave will not share the inheritance with the child of the free woman." 31 So then, friends, we are children, not of the slave but of the free woman.

Eph 1:13–21

In him you also, when you had heard the word of truth, the gospel of your salvation, and had believed in him, were marked with the seal of the promised Holy Spirit; 14 this[e] is the pledge of our inheritance toward redemption as God's own people, to the praise of his glory. 15 I have heard of your faith in the Lord Jesus and your love[f] toward all the saints, and for this reason 16 I do not cease to give thanks for you as I remember you in my prayers. 17 I pray that the God of our Lord Jesus Christ, the Father of glory, may give you a spirit of wisdom and revelation as you come to know him, 18 so that, with the eyes of your heart enlightened, you may know what is the hope to which he has called you, what are the riches of his glorious inheritance among the saints, 19 and what is the immeasurable greatness of his power for us who believe, according to the working of his great power. 20 God put this power to work[g] in Christ when he raised him from the dead and seated him at his right hand in the heavenly places, 21 far above all rule and authority and power and dominion, and above every name that is named, not only in this age but also in the age to come.

Eph 3:1–7

This is the reason that I Paul am a prisoner for Christ Jesus for the sake of you Gentiles— 2 for surely you have already heard of the commission of God's grace that was given me for you, 3 and

§ 92 [a] **1 Cor 6:11** ***the Lord Jesus Christ*** Other ancient authorities read *the Lord Jesus* or *our Lord Jesus Christ* [b] **Gal 4:6** ***our*** Other ancient authorities read *your* [c] **Gal 4:7** ***an heir, through God*** Other ancient authorities read *an heir of God through Christ* [d] **Gal 4:28** ***you*** Other ancient authorities read *we* [e] **Eph 1:14** ***this*** Other ancient authorities read *who* [f] **Eph 1:15** ***and your love*** Other ancient authorities lack *and your love* [g] **Eph 1:20** ***put this power to work*** Other ancient authorities read *has put this power to work*

μοι τὸ μυστήριον, καθὼς προέγραψα ἐν ὀλίγῳ, **4** πρὸς ὃ δύνασθε ἀναγινώσκοντες νοῆσαι τὴν σύνεσίν μου ἐν τῷ μυστηρίῳ τοῦ Χριστοῦ, **5** ὃ ἑτέραις γενεαῖς οὐκ ἐγνωρίσθη τοῖς υἱοῖς τῶν ἀνθρώπων ὡς νῦν ἀπεκαλύφθη τοῖς ἁγίοις ἀποστόλοις αὐτοῦ καὶ προφήταις ἐν πνεύματι, **6** εἶναι τὰ ἔθνη συγκληρονόμα καὶ σύσσωμα καὶ συμμέτοχα τῆς ἐπαγγελίας ἐν Χριστῷ Ἰησοῦ διὰ τοῦ εὐαγγελίου, **7** οὗ ἐγενήθην διάκονος κατὰ τὴν δωρεὰν τῆς χάριτος τοῦ θεοῦ τῆς δοθείσης μοι κατὰ τὴν ἐνέργειαν τῆς δυνάμεως αὐτοῦ.

Eph 5:3–5

Πορνεία δὲ καὶ ἀκαθαρσία πᾶσα ἢ πλεονεξία μηδὲ ὀνομαζέσθω ἐν ὑμῖν, καθὼς πρέπει ἁγίοις, **4** καὶ αἰσχρότης καὶ μωρολογία ἢ εὐτραπελία, ἃ οὐκ ἀνῆκεν, ἀλλὰ μᾶλλον εὐχαριστία. **5** τοῦτο γὰρ ἴστε γινώσκοντες, ὅτι πᾶς πόρνος ἢ ἀκάθαρτος ἢ πλεονέκτης, ὅ ἐστιν εἰδωλολάτρης, οὐκ ἔχει κληρονομίαν ἐν τῇ βασιλείᾳ τοῦ Χριστοῦ καὶ θεοῦ.

Col 1:12

εὐχαριστοῦντες τῷ πατρὶ τῷ ⸀ἱκανώσαντι ⸀ὑμᾶς εἰς τὴν μερίδα τοῦ κλήρου τῶν ἁγίων ἐν τῷ φωτί

Col 3:22–25

Οἱ δοῦλοι, ὑπακούετε κατὰ πάντα τοῖς κατὰ σάρκα κυρίοις, μὴ ἐν ὀφθαλμοδουλίᾳ ὡς ἀνθρωπάρεσκοι, ἀλλ᾽ ἐν ἁπλότητι καρδίας φοβούμενοι τὸν κύριον. **23** ὃ ἐὰν ποιῆτε, ἐκ ψυχῆς ἐργάζεσθε ὡς τῷ κυρίῳ καὶ οὐκ ἀνθρώποις, **24** εἰδότες ὅτι ἀπὸ κυρίου ἀπολήμψεσθε τὴν ἀνταπόδοσιν τῆς κληρονομίας. τῷ κυρίῳ Χριστῷ δουλεύετε· **25** ὁ γὰρ ἀδικῶν κομίσεται ὃ ἠδίκησεν, καὶ οὐκ ἔστιν προσωπολημψία.

Titus 3:4–7

ὅτε δὲ ἡ χρηστότης καὶ ἡ φιλανθρωπία ἐπεφάνη τοῦ σωτῆρος ἡμῶν θεοῦ, **5** οὐκ ἐξ ἔργων τῶν ἐν δικαιοσύνῃ ἃ ἐποιήσαμεν ἡμεῖς ἀλλὰ κατὰ τὸ αὐτοῦ ἔλεος ἔσωσεν ἡμᾶς διὰ λουτροῦ παλιγγενεσίας καὶ ἀνακαινώσεως πνεύματος ἁγίου, **6** οὗ ἐξέχεεν ἐφ᾽ ἡμᾶς πλουσίως διὰ Ἰησοῦ Χριστοῦ τοῦ σωτῆρος ἡμῶν, **7** ἵνα δικαιωθέντες τῇ ἐκείνου χάριτι κληρονόμοι γενηθῶμεν κατ᾽ ἐλπίδα ζωῆς αἰωνίου.

Acts 20:32

Καὶ τὰ νῦν παρατίθεμαι ὑμᾶς τῷ θεῷ καὶ τῷ λόγῳ τῆς χάριτος αὐτοῦ, τῷ δυναμένῳ οἰκοδομῆσαι καὶ δοῦναι τὴν κληρονομίαν ἐν τοῖς ἡγιασμένοις πᾶσιν.

Acts 26:18

ἀνοῖξαι ὀφθαλμοὺς αὐτῶν, τοῦ ἐπιστρέψαι ἀπὸ σκότους εἰς φῶς καὶ τῆς ἐξουσίας τοῦ σατανᾶ ἐπὶ τὸν θεόν, τοῦ λαβεῖν αὐτοὺς ἄφεσιν ἁμαρτιῶν καὶ κλῆρον ἐν τοῖς ἡγιασμένοις πίστει τῇ εἰς ἐμέ.

Cf. 1 Cor 3:21–23; possibly Eph 1:11–12.

See also § 91 The Renewal of Creation.

93. The Glory to Be Revealed

Rom 5:1–2

Δικαιωθέντες οὖν ἐκ πίστεως εἰρήνην ⸀ἔχομεν πρὸς τὸν θεὸν διὰ τοῦ κυρίου ἡμῶν Ἰησοῦ Χριστοῦ **2** δι᾽ οὗ καὶ τὴν προσαγωγὴν ἐσχήκαμεν ⸂[τῇ πίστει]⸃ εἰς τὴν χάριν ταύτην ἐν ᾗ ἑστήκαμεν καὶ καυχώμεθα ἐπ᾽ ἐλπίδι τῆς δόξης τοῦ θεοῦ.

Rom 8:18–30

Λογίζομαι γὰρ ὅτι οὐκ ἄξια τὰ παθήματα τοῦ νῦν καιροῦ πρὸς τὴν μέλλουσαν δόξαν ἀποκαλυφθῆναι εἰς ἡμᾶς. **19** ἡ γὰρ ἀποκαραδοκία τῆς κτίσεως τὴν ἀποκάλυψιν τῶν υἱῶν τοῦ θεοῦ ἀπεκδέχεται. **20** τῇ γὰρ ματαιότητι ἡ κτίσις ὑπετάγη, οὐχ ἑκοῦσα ἀλλὰ διὰ τὸν ὑποτάξαντα, ἐφ᾽ ἑλπίδι **21** ὅτι καὶ αὐτὴ ἡ κτίσις ἐλευθερωθήσεται ἀπὸ τῆς δουλείας τῆς φθορᾶς εἰς τὴν ἐλευθερίαν τῆς δόξης τῶν τέκνων τοῦ θεοῦ. **22** οἴδαμεν γὰρ ὅτι πᾶσα ἡ κτίσις συστενάζει καὶ συνωδίνει ἄχρι τοῦ νῦν· **23** οὐ μόνον δέ, ἀλλὰ καὶ αὐτοὶ τὴν ἀπαρχὴν τοῦ πνεύματος ἔχοντες, ἡμεῖς καὶ αὐτοὶ ἐν ἑαυτοῖς στενάζομεν υἱοθεσίαν ἀπεκδεχόμενοι, τὴν ἀπολύτρωσιν τοῦ σώματος ἡμῶν. **24** τῇ γὰρ ἐλπίδι ἐσώθημεν· ἐλπὶς δὲ βλεπομένη οὐκ ἔστιν ἐλπίς· ὃ γὰρ βλέπει τίς ⸀ἐλπίζει; **25** εἰ δὲ ὃ οὐ βλέπομεν ἐλπίζομεν, δι᾽ ὑπομονῆς ἀπεκδεχόμεθα. **26** Ὡσαύτως δὲ καὶ τὸ πνεῦμα συναντιλαμβάνεται τῇ ἀσθενείᾳ ἡμῶν· τὸ γὰρ τί προσευξώμεθα καθὸ δεῖ οὐκ οἴδαμεν, ἀλλὰ αὐτὸ τὸ πνεῦμα ⸀ὑπερεντυγχάνει στεναγμοῖς ἀλαλήτοις· **27** ὁ δὲ ἐραυνῶν τὰς καρδίας οἶδεν τί τὸ φρόνημα τοῦ πνεύματος, ὅτι κατὰ θεὸν ἐντυγχάνει ὑπὲρ ἁγίων. **28** Οἴδαμεν δὲ ὅτι τοῖς ἀγαπῶσιν τὸν θεὸν πάντα ⸀συνεργεῖ εἰς ἀγαθόν, τοῖς κατὰ πρόθεσιν κλητοῖς οὖσιν. **29** ὅτι οὓς προέγνω, καὶ προώρισεν συμμόρφους τῆς εἰκόνος τοῦ υἱοῦ αὐτοῦ, εἰς τὸ εἶναι αὐτὸν πρωτότοκον ἐν πολλοῖς ἀδελφοῖς· **30** οὓς δὲ προώρισεν, τούτους καὶ ἐκάλεσεν· καὶ οὓς ἐκάλεσεν, τούτους καὶ ἐδικαίωσεν· οὓς δὲ ἐδικαίωσεν, τούτους καὶ ἐδόξασεν.

1 Cor 15:42–43

Οὕτως καὶ ἡ ἀνάστασις τῶν νεκρῶν. σπείρεται ἐν φθορᾷ, ἐγείρεται ἐν ἀφθαρσίᾳ· **43** σπείρεται ἐν ἀτιμίᾳ, ἐγείρεται ἐν δόξῃ· σπείρεται ἐν ἀσθενείᾳ, ἐγείρεται ἐν δυνάμει

2 Cor 4:17–5:5

τὸ γὰρ παραυτίκα ἐλαφρὸν τῆς θλίψεως ἡμῶν καθ᾽ ὑπερβολὴν εἰς ὑπερβολὴν αἰώνιον βάρος δόξης κατεργάζεται ἡμῖν, **18** μὴ σκοπούντων ἡμῶν τὰ βλεπόμενα ἀλλὰ τὰ μὴ βλεπόμενα· τὰ γὰρ βλεπόμενα

Col 1:12 ***ικανωσαντι*** 𝔓[46] 𝔓[61vid] ℵ A C D[2] I 1739. 1881 *Byz*] καλεσαντι D* 33 ¦ καλεσαντι και ικανωσαντι B • ***υμας*** ℵ B 1739. 1881] ημας A C D 33 *Byz* **§ 93** **Rom 5:1** ***εχομεν*** ℵ[1] B[2] 0220[vid]. 1739[c]. 1881] εχωμεν ℵ* A B* C D 33. 1739* **Rom 5:2** ***τη πιστει*** ℵ[*,2] C 33. 1739. 1881 *Byz*] εν τη πιστει ℵ[1] A ¦ *om.* B D 0220 **Rom 8:24** ***ελπιζει*** 𝔓[46] ℵ[2] B C D 33. 1739*. 1881 *Byz*] υπομενει ℵ* A 1739[mg] **Rom 8:26** ***υπερεντυγχανει*** ℵ* A B D 1739. 1881] *add.* υπερ ημων ℵ[2] C 33 *Byz* **Rom 8:28** ***συνεργει*** ℵ C D 33. 1739. 1881 *Byz*] *add.* ο θεος 𝔓[46] A B

how the mystery was made known to me by revelation, as I wrote above in a few words, **4** a reading of which will enable you to perceive my understanding of the mystery of Christ. **5** In former generations this mystery was not made known to humankind, as it has now been revealed to his holy apostles and prophets by the Spirit: **6** that is, the Gentiles have become fellow heirs, members of the same body, and sharers in the promise in Christ Jesus through the gospel. **7** Of this gospel I have become a servant according to the gift of God's grace that was given me by the working of his power.

Eph 5:3–5

But fornication and impurity of any kind, or greed, must not even be mentioned among you, as is proper among saints. **4** Entirely out of place is obscene, silly, and vulgar talk; but instead, let there be thanksgiving. **5** Be sure of this, that no fornicator or impure person, or one who is greedy (that is, an idolater), has any inheritance in the kingdom of Christ and of God.

Col 1:12

giving thanks to the Father, who has enabled[h] you[i] to share in the inheritance of the saints in the light.

Col 3:22–25

Slaves, obey your earthly masters in everything, not only while being watched and in order to please them, but wholeheartedly, fearing the Lord. **23** Whatever your task, put yourselves into it, as done for the Lord and not for your masters, **24** since you know that from the Lord you will receive the inheritance as your reward; you serve the Lord Christ. **25** For the wrongdoer will be paid back for whatever wrong has been done, and there is no partiality.

Titus 3:4–7

But when the goodness and loving kindness of God our Savior appeared, **5** he saved us, not because of any works of righteousness that we had done, but according to his mercy, through the water of rebirth and renewal by the Holy Spirit. **6** This Spirit he poured out on us richly through Jesus Christ our Savior, **7** so that, having been justified by his grace, we might become heirs according to the hope of eternal life.

Acts 20:32

And now I commend you to God and to the message of his grace, a message that is able to build you up and to give you the inheritance among all who are sanctified.

Acts 26:18

to open their eyes so that they may turn from darkness to light and from the power of Satan to God, so that they may receive forgiveness of sins and a place among those who are sanctified by faith in me.

Cf. 1 Cor 3:21–23; possibly Eph 1:11–12.

See also § 91 The Renewal of Creation.

93. The Glory to Be Revealed

Rom 5:1–2

Therefore, since we are justified by faith, we[a] have peace with God through our Lord Jesus Christ, **2** through whom we have obtained access[b] to this grace in which we stand; and we boast in our hope of sharing the glory of God.

Rom 8:18–30

I consider that the sufferings of this present time are not worth comparing with the glory about to be revealed to us. **19** For the creation waits with eager longing for the revealing of the children of God; **20** for the creation was subjected to futility, not of its own will but by the will of the one who subjected it, in hope **21** that the creation itself will be set free from its bondage to decay and will obtain the freedom of the glory of the children of God. **22** We know that the whole creation has been groaning in labor pains until now; **23** and not only the creation, but we ourselves, who have the first fruits of the Spirit, groan inwardly while we wait for adoption, the redemption of our bodies. **24** For in hope we were saved. Now hope that is seen is not hope. For who hopes[c] for what is seen? **25** But if we hope for what we do not see, we wait for it with patience. **26** Likewise the Spirit helps us in our weakness; for we do not know how to pray as we ought, but that very Spirit intercedes[d] with sighs too deep for words. **27** And God, who searches the heart, knows what is the mind of the Spirit, because the Spirit intercedes for the saints according to the will of God. **28** We know that all things work together for good[e] for those who love God, who are called according to his purpose. **29** For those whom he foreknew he also predestined to be conformed to the image of his Son, in order that he might be the firstborn within a large family. **30** And those whom he predestined he also called; and those whom he called he also justified; and those whom he justified he also glorified.

1 Cor 15:42–43

So it is with the resurrection of the dead. The body is sown in decay, it is raised in freedom from decay.[f] **43** It is sown in dishonor, it is raised in glory. It is sown in weakness, it is raised in power.

2 Cor 4:17–5:5

For this slight momentary affliction is preparing us for an eternal weight of glory beyond all measure, **18** because we look not at what is presently seen but at what is not presently seen; for what is

[h] **Col 1:12** ***enabled*** Other ancient authorities read *called* [i] **Col 1:12** ***you*** Other ancient authorities read *us* **§ 93** [a] **Rom 5:1** ***we*** Other ancient authorities read *let us* [b] **Rom 5:2** ***obtained access*** Other ancient authorities add *by faith* [c] **Rom 8:24** ***hopes*** Other ancient authorities read *awaits* [d] **Rom 8:26** ***intercedes*** Other ancient authorities add *for us* [e] **Rom 8:28** ***all things work together for good*** Other ancient authorities read *God makes all things work together for good*, or *in all things God works for good* [f] **1 Cor 15:42** Translation differs from NRSV

πρόσκαιρα, τὰ δὲ μὴ βλεπόμενα αἰώνια.
5 Οἴδαμεν γὰρ ὅτι ἐὰν ἡ ἐπίγειος ἡμῶν
οἰκία τοῦ σκήνους καταλυθῇ, οἰκοδομὴν
ἐκ θεοῦ ἔχομεν, οἰκίαν ἀχειροποίητον
αἰώνιον ἐν τοῖς οὐρανοῖς. **2** καὶ γὰρ ἐν
τούτῳ στενάζομεν τὸ οἰκητήριον ἡμῶν
τὸ ἐξ οὐρανοῦ ἐπενδύσασθαι ἐπιποθοῦν-
τες, **3** εἴ γε καὶ ⸀ἐκδυσάμενοι οὐ γυμνοὶ
εὑρεθησόμεθα. **4** καὶ γὰρ οἱ ὄντες ἐν τῷ
σκήνει στενάζομεν βαρούμενοι, ἐφ᾽ ᾧ οὐ
θέλομεν ἐκδύσασθαι ἀλλ᾽ ἐπενδύσασθαι,
ἵνα καταποθῇ τὸ θνητὸν ὑπὸ τῆς ζωῆς.
5 ὁ δὲ κατεργασάμενος ἡμᾶς εἰς αὐτὸ
τοῦτο θεός, ὁ δοὺς ἡμῖν τὸν ἀρραβῶνα
τοῦ πνεύματος.

Phil 3:20–21

ἡμῶν γὰρ τὸ πολίτευμα ἐν οὐρανοῖς
ὑπάρχει, ἐξ οὗ καὶ σωτῆρα ἀπεκδεχόμεθα
κύριον Ἰησοῦν Χριστόν, **21** ὃς μετασχη-
ματίσει τὸ σῶμα τῆς ταπεινώσεως ἡμῶν
σύμμορφον τῷ σώματι τῆς δόξης αὐτοῦ
κατὰ τὴν ἐνέργειαν τοῦ δύνασθαι αὐτὸν
καὶ ὑποτάξαι αὐτῷ τὰ πάντα.

Col 1:27

οἷς ἠθέλησεν ὁ θεὸς γνωρίσαι τί τὸ πλοῦ-
τος τῆς δόξης τοῦ μυστηρίου τούτου ἐν
τοῖς ἔθνεσιν, ὅ ἐστιν Χριστὸς ἐν ὑμῖν, ἡ
ἐλπὶς τῆς δόξης

Col 3:3–4

ἀπεθάνετε γὰρ καὶ ἡ ζωὴ ὑμῶν κέκρυ-
πται σὺν τῷ Χριστῷ ἐν τῷ θεῷ· **4** ὅταν
ὁ Χριστὸς φανερωθῇ, ἡ ζωὴ ⸀ὑμῶν,
τότε καὶ ὑμεῖς σὺν αὐτῷ φανερωθήσε-
σθε ἐν δόξῃ.

2 Thess 2:13–14

Ἡμεῖς δὲ ὀφείλομεν εὐχαριστεῖν τῷ θεῷ
πάντοτε περὶ ὑμῶν, ἀδελφοὶ ἠγαπημέ-
νοι ὑπὸ κυρίου, ὅτι εἵλατο ὑμᾶς ὁ θεὸς
⸀ἀπαρχὴν εἰς σωτηρίαν ἐν ἁγιασμῷ
πνεύματος καὶ πίστει ἀληθείας, **14** εἰς ὃ
[καὶ] ἐκάλεσεν ὑμᾶς διὰ τοῦ εὐαγγελίου
ἡμῶν εἰς περιποίησιν δόξης τοῦ κυρίου
ἡμῶν Ἰησοῦ Χριστοῦ.

2 Tim 2:10

διὰ τοῦτο πάντα ὑπομένω διὰ τοὺς ἐκλεκτούς, ἵνα καὶ αὐτοὶ σωτηρίας τύχωσιν τῆς ἐν Χριστῷ Ἰησοῦ μετὰ δόξης αἰωνίου.

Titus 2:13

προσδεχόμενοι τὴν μακαρίαν ἐλπίδα καὶ ἐπιφάνειαν τῆς δόξης τοῦ μεγάλου θεοῦ καὶ σωτῆρος ἡμῶν Ἰησοῦ Χριστοῦ

Cf. Rom 3:23; 9:22–24; 1 Cor 2:6–9; Eph 1:16–19; 2 Thess 1:11–12.

See also § 89 The Resurrection of the Body and § 91 The Renewal of Creation.

94. *The Judgment Seat of Christ*

Rom 2:16

ἐν ἡμέρᾳ ὅτε κρίνει ὁ θεὸς τὰ κρυπτὰ τῶν ἀνθρώπων κατὰ τὸ εὐαγγέλιόν μου διὰ ⸂Χριστοῦ Ἰησοῦ⸃.

Rom 14:10–12

Σὺ δὲ τί κρίνεις τὸν ἀδελφόν σου; ἢ καὶ
σὺ τί ἐξουθενεῖς τὸν ἀδελφόν σου; πάν-
τες γὰρ παραστησόμεθα τῷ βήματι τοῦ
⸀θεοῦ, **11** γέγραπται γάρ· ζῶ ἐγώ, λέγει
κύριος, ὅτι ἐμοὶ κάμψει πᾶν γόνυ καὶ
πᾶσα γλῶσσα ἐξομολογήσεται τῷ θεῷ.
12 ἄρα [οὖν] ἕκαστος ἡμῶν περὶ ἑαυτοῦ
λόγον δώσει [τῷ θεῷ].

1 Cor 4:3–5

ἐμοὶ δὲ εἰς ἐλάχιστόν ἐστιν, ἵνα ὑφ᾽ ὑμῶν
ἀνακριθῶ ἢ ὑπὸ ἀνθρωπίνης ἡμέρας·
ἀλλ᾽ οὐδὲ ἐμαυτὸν ἀνακρίνω. **4** οὐδὲν
γὰρ ἐμαυτῷ σύνοιδα, ἀλλ᾽ οὐκ ἐν τούτῳ
δεδικαίωμαι, ὁ δὲ ἀνακρίνων με κύριός
ἐστιν. **5** ὥστε μὴ πρὸ καιροῦ τι κρίνετε
ἕως ἂν ἔλθῃ ὁ κύριος, ὃς καὶ φωτίσει τὰ
κρυπτὰ τοῦ σκότους καὶ φανερώσει τὰς
βουλὰς τῶν καρδιῶν· καὶ τότε ὁ ἔπαινος
γενήσεται ἑκάστῳ ἀπὸ τοῦ θεοῦ.

2 Cor 5:6–10

Θαρροῦντες οὖν πάντοτε καὶ εἰδότες ὅτι
ἐνδημοῦντες ἐν τῷ σώματι ἐκδημοῦμεν
ἀπὸ τοῦ κυρίου· **7** διὰ πίστεως γὰρ πε-
ριπατοῦμεν, οὐ διὰ εἴδους· **8** θαρροῦμεν
δὲ καὶ εὐδοκοῦμεν μᾶλλον ἐκδημῆσαι
ἐκ τοῦ σώματος καὶ ἐνδημῆσαι πρὸς τὸν
κύριον. **9** διὸ καὶ φιλοτιμούμεθα, εἴτε
ἐνδημοῦντες εἴτε ἐκδημοῦντες, εὐάρεστοι
αὐτῷ εἶναι. **10** τοὺς γὰρ πάντας ἡμᾶς φα-
νερωθῆναι δεῖ ἔμπροσθεν τοῦ βήματος
τοῦ Χριστοῦ, ἵνα κομίσηται ἕκαστος τὰ
διὰ τοῦ σώματος πρὸς ἃ ἔπραξεν, εἴτε
ἀγαθὸν εἴτε φαῦλον.

Eph 6:8

εἰδότες ὅτι ἕκαστος ἐάν τι ποιήσῃ ἀγαθόν, τοῦτο κομίσεται παρὰ κυρίου εἴτε δοῦλος εἴτε ἐλεύθερος.

2 Tim 4:1–2

Διαμαρτύρομαι ἐνώπιον τοῦ θεοῦ καὶ
Χριστοῦ Ἰησοῦ τοῦ μέλλοντος κρίνειν
ζῶντας καὶ νεκρούς, καὶ τὴν ἐπιφάνειαν
αὐτοῦ καὶ τὴν βασιλείαν αὐτοῦ· **2** κήρυξον
τὸν λόγον, ἐπίστηθι εὐκαίρως ἀκαίρως,
ἔλεγξον, ἐπιτίμησον, παρακάλεσον, ἐν
πάσῃ μακροθυμίᾳ καὶ διδαχῇ.

2 Tim 4:8

λοιπὸν ἀπόκειταί μοι ὁ τῆς δικαιοσύνης στέφανος, ὃν ἀποδώσει μοι ὁ κύριος ἐν ἐκείνῃ τῇ ἡμέρᾳ, ὁ δίκαιος κριτής, οὐ μόνον δὲ ἐμοὶ ἀλλὰ καὶ πᾶσι τοῖς ἠγαπηκόσι τὴν ἐπιφάνειαν αὐτοῦ.

Acts 17:30–31

τοὺς μὲν οὖν χρόνους τῆς ἀγνοίας ὑπερ-
ιδὼν ὁ θεός, τὰ νῦν παραγγέλλει τοῖς
ἀνθρώποις πάντας πανταχοῦ μετανοεῖν,
31 καθότι ἔστησεν ἡμέραν ἐν ᾗ μέλλει
κρίνειν τὴν οἰκουμένην ἐν δικαιοσύνῃ, ἐν
ἀνδρὶ ᾧ ὥρισεν, πίστιν παρασχὼν πᾶσιν
ἀναστήσας αὐτὸν ἐκ νεκρῶν.

Cf. 1 Cor 3:10–17; Phil 2:10–11; Col 1:22–23.

See also § 88 The Second Coming of Christ; § 96 The Righteous Judgment of God.

2 Cor 5:3 ***εκδυσαμενοι*** D[*,c]] ενδυσαμενοι 𝔓[46] ℵ B C D[2] 33. 1739. 1881 *Byz* **Col 3:4** ***υμων*** 𝔓[46] ℵ C D* 33. 1881] ημων B[(*)] D[1] 1739 *Byz* **2 Thess 2:13** ***απαρχην*** B 33. 1739. 1881] απ αρχης ℵ D *Byz* **§ 94** **Rom 2:16** ***Χριστου Ιησου*** (ℵ[*vid]) B] Ιησου Χριστου ℵ[1] A D 33. 1739 *Byz* **Rom 14:10** ***θεου*** ℵ* A B C* D 1739] Χριστου ℵ[c] C[2] 048. 33. 1881 *Byz*

presently seen is temporary, but what is not presently seen is eternal.[g] **5** For we know that if the earthly tent we live in is destroyed, we have a building from God, a house not made with hands, eternal in the heavens. **2** For in this tent we groan, longing to be clothed with our dwelling from heaven— **3** if indeed, when we have put it on[h] we will not be found naked.[i] **4** For while we are still in this tent, we groan under our burden, because we wish not to be unclothed but to be further clothed, so that what is mortal may be swallowed up by life. **5** He who has prepared us for this very thing is God, who has given us the Spirit as a guarantee.

Phil 3:20–21

But our citizenship is in heaven, and it is from there that we are expecting a Savior, the Lord Jesus Christ. **21** He will transform the body of our humiliation that it may be conformed to the body of his glory, by the power that also enables him to make all things subject to himself.

Col 1:27

To them God chose to make known how great among the Gentiles are the riches of the glory of this mystery, which is Christ in you, the hope of glory.

Col 3:3–4

for you have died, and your life is hidden with Christ in God. **4** When Christ who is your[j] life is revealed, then you also will be revealed with him in glory.

2 Thess 2:13–14

But we must always give thanks to God for you, brothers and sisters beloved by the Lord, because God chose you as the first fruits[k] for salvation through sanctification by the Spirit and through belief in the truth. **14** For this purpose he called you through our proclamation of the good news, so that you may obtain the glory of our Lord Jesus Christ.

2 Tim 2:10

Therefore I endure everything for the sake of the elect, so that they may also obtain the salvation that is in Christ Jesus, with eternal glory.

Titus 2:13

while we wait for the blessed hope and the manifestation of the glory of our great God and Savior, Jesus Christ.

Cf. Rom 3:23; 9:22–24; 1 Cor 2:6–9; Eph 1:16–19; 2 Thess 1:11–12.

See also § 89 The Resurrection of the Body and § 91 The Renewal of Creation.

94. The Judgment Seat of Christ

Rom 2:16

on the day when, according to my gospel, God, through Jesus Christ,[a] will judge the secret thoughts of all.

Rom 14:10–12

Why do you pass judgment on your brother or sister? Or you, why do you despise your brother or sister? For we will all stand before the judgment seat of God.[b] **11** For it is written, "As I live, says the Lord, every knee shall bow to me, and every tongue shall give praise to God." **12** So then, each of us will be accountable to God.

1 Cor 4:3–5

But with me it is a very small thing that I should be judged by you or by any human court. I do not even judge myself. **4** I am not aware of anything against myself, but I am not thereby acquitted. It is the Lord who judges me. **5** Therefore do not pronounce judgment before the time, before the Lord comes, who will bring to light the things now hidden in darkness and will disclose the purposes of the heart. Then each one will receive commendation from God.

2 Cor 5:6–10

So we are always confident; even though we know that while we are at home in the body we are away from the Lord— **7** for we walk by faith, not by sight. **8** Yes, we do have confidence, and we would rather be away from the body and at home with the Lord. **9** So whether we are at home or away, we make it our aim to please him. **10** For all of us must appear before the judgment seat of Christ, so that each may receive recompense for what has been done in the body, whether good or evil.

Eph 6:8

knowing that whatever good we do, we will receive the same again from the Lord, whether we are slaves or free.

2 Tim 4:1–2

In the presence of God and of Christ Jesus, who is to judge the living and the dead, and in view of his appearing and his kingdom, I solemnly urge you: **2** proclaim the message; be persistent whether the time is favorable or unfavorable; convince, rebuke, and encourage, with the utmost patience in teaching.

2 Tim 4:8

From now on there is reserved for me the crown of righteousness, which the Lord, the righteous judge, will give me on that day, and not only to me but also to all who have longed for his appearing.

Acts 17:30–31

While God has overlooked the times of human ignorance, now he commands all people everywhere to repent, **31** because he has fixed a day on which he will have the world judged in righteousness by a man whom he has appointed, and of this he has given assurance to all by raising him from the dead.

Cf. 1 Cor 3:10–17; Phil 2:10–11; Col 1:22–23.

See also § 88 The Second Coming of Christ; § 96 The Righteous Judgment of God.

[g] **2 Cor 4:18** Translation differs from NRSV [h] **2 Cor 5:3** ***put it on*** A few ancient authorities read *taken it off* [i] **2 Cor 5:2–3** Translation differs from NRSV [j] **Col 3:4** ***your*** Other ancient authorities read *our* [k] **2 Thess 2:13** ***as the first fruits*** Other ancient authorities read *from the beginning* **§ 94** [a] **Rom 2:16** ***Jesus Christ*** Other ancient authorities read *Christ Jesus* [b] **Rom 14:10** ***of God*** Other ancient authorities read *of Christ*

95. *Judgment of the Secrets of the Heart*

Rom 2:16

ἐν ἡμέρᾳ ὅτε κρίνει ὁ θεὸς τὰ κρυπτὰ τῶν ἀνθρώπων κατὰ τὸ εὐαγγέλιόν μου διὰ ⸀Χριστοῦ Ἰησοῦ⸁.

Rom 2:28–29

οὐ γὰρ ὁ ἐν τῷ φανερῷ Ἰουδαῖός ἐστιν οὐδὲ ἡ ἐν τῷ φανερῷ ἐν σαρκὶ περιτομή, **29** ἀλλ' ὁ ἐν τῷ κρυπτῷ Ἰουδαῖος, καὶ περιτομὴ καρδίας ἐν πνεύματι οὐ γράμματι, οὗ ὁ ἔπαινος οὐκ ἐξ ἀνθρώπων ἀλλ' ἐκ τοῦ θεοῦ.

1 Cor 4:3–5

ἐμοὶ δὲ εἰς ἐλάχιστόν ἐστιν, ἵνα ὑφ' ὑμῶν ἀνακριθῶ ἢ ὑπὸ ἀνθρωπίνης ἡμέρας· ἀλλ' οὐδὲ ἐμαυτὸν ἀνακρίνω. **4** οὐδὲν γὰρ ἐμαυτῷ σύνοιδα, ἀλλ' οὐκ ἐν τούτῳ δεδικαίωμαι, ὁ δὲ ἀνακρίνων με κύριός ἐστιν. **5** ὥστε μὴ πρὸ καιροῦ τι κρίνετε ἕως ἂν ἔλθῃ ὁ κύριος, ὃς καὶ φωτίσει τὰ κρυπτὰ τοῦ σκότους καὶ φανερώσει τὰς βουλὰς τῶν καρδιῶν· καὶ τότε ὁ ἔπαινος γενήσεται ἑκάστῳ ἀπὸ τοῦ θεοῦ.

1 Thess 2:4

ἀλλὰ καθὼς δεδοκιμάσμεθα ὑπὸ τοῦ θεοῦ πιστευθῆναι τὸ εὐαγγέλιον, οὕτως λαλοῦμεν, οὐχ ὡς ἀνθρώποις ἀρέσκοντες ἀλλὰ θεῷ τῷ δοκιμάζοντι τὰς καρδίας ἡμῶν.

1 Tim 5:24–25

Τινῶν ἀνθρώπων αἱ ἁμαρτίαι πρόδηλοί εἰσιν προάγουσαι εἰς κρίσιν, τισὶν δὲ καὶ ἐπακολουθοῦσιν· **25** ὡσαύτως καὶ τὰ ἔργα τὰ καλὰ πρόδηλα, καὶ τὰ ἄλλως ἔχοντα κρυβῆναι οὐ δύνανται.

Cf. Rom 8:27; 1 Cor 14:24–25.

96. *The Righteous Judgment of God*

Rom 2:1–11

Διὸ ἀναπολόγητος εἶ, ὦ ἄνθρωπε πᾶς ὁ κρίνων· ἐν ᾧ γὰρ κρίνεις τὸν ἕτερον, σεαυτὸν κατακρίνεις, τὰ γὰρ αὐτὰ πράσσεις ὁ κρίνων. **2** οἴδαμεν δὲ ὅτι τὸ κρίμα τοῦ θεοῦ ἐστιν κατὰ ἀλήθειαν ἐπὶ τοὺς τὰ τοιαῦτα πράσσοντας. **3** λογίζῃ δὲ τοῦτο, ὦ ἄνθρωπε ὁ κρίνων τοὺς τὰ τοιαῦτα πράσσοντας καὶ ποιῶν αὐτά, ὅτι σὺ ἐκφεύξῃ τὸ κρίμα τοῦ θεοῦ; **4** ἢ τοῦ πλούτου τῆς χρηστότητος αὐτοῦ καὶ τῆς ἀνοχῆς καὶ τῆς μακροθυμίας καταφρονεῖς, ἀγνοῶν ὅτι τὸ χρηστὸν τοῦ θεοῦ εἰς μετάνοιάν σε ἄγει; **5** κατὰ δὲ τὴν σκληρότητά σου καὶ ἀμετανόητον καρδίαν θησαυρίζεις σεαυτῷ ὀργὴν ἐν ἡμέρᾳ ὀργῆς καὶ ἀποκαλύψεως δικαιοκρισίας τοῦ θεοῦ **6** ὃς ἀποδώσει ἑκάστῳ κατὰ τὰ ἔργα αὐτοῦ· **7** τοῖς μὲν καθ' ὑπομονὴν ἔργου ἀγαθοῦ δόξαν καὶ τιμὴν καὶ ἀφθαρσίαν ζητοῦσιν ζωὴν αἰώνιον, **8** τοῖς δὲ ἐξ ἐριθείας καὶ ἀπειθοῦσι τῇ ἀληθείᾳ πειθομένοις δὲ τῇ ἀδικίᾳ ὀργὴ καὶ θυμός. **9** θλῖψις καὶ στενοχωρία ἐπὶ πᾶσαν ψυχὴν ἀνθρώπου τοῦ κατεργαζομένου τὸ κακόν, Ἰουδαίου τε πρῶτον καὶ Ἕλληνος· **10** δόξα δὲ καὶ τιμὴ καὶ εἰρήνη παντὶ τῷ ἐργαζομένῳ τὸ ἀγαθόν, Ἰουδαίῳ τε πρῶτον καὶ Ἕλληνι· **11** οὐ γάρ ἐστιν προσωπολημψία παρὰ τῷ θεῷ.

2 Thess 1:5–10

ἔνδειγμα τῆς δικαίας κρίσεως τοῦ θεοῦ εἰς τὸ καταξιωθῆναι ὑμᾶς τῆς βασιλείας τοῦ θεοῦ, ὑπὲρ ἧς καὶ πάσχετε, **6** εἴπερ δίκαιον παρὰ θεῷ ἀνταποδοῦναι τοῖς θλίβουσιν ὑμᾶς θλῖψιν **7** καὶ ὑμῖν τοῖς θλιβομένοις ἄνεσιν μεθ' ἡμῶν, ἐν τῇ ἀποκαλύψει τοῦ κυρίου Ἰησοῦ ἀπ' οὐρανοῦ μετ' ἀγγέλων δυνάμεως αὐτοῦ **8** ἐν πυρὶ φλογός, διδόντος ἐκδίκησιν τοῖς μὴ εἰδόσιν θεὸν καὶ τοῖς μὴ ὑπακούουσιν τῷ εὐαγγελίῳ τοῦ κυρίου ἡμῶν Ἰησοῦ, **9** οἵτινες δίκην τίσουσιν ὄλεθρον αἰώνιον ἀπὸ προσώπου τοῦ κυρίου καὶ ἀπὸ τῆς δόξης τῆς ἰσχύος αὐτοῦ, **10** ὅταν ἔλθῃ ἐνδοξασθῆναι ἐν τοῖς ἁγίοις αὐτοῦ καὶ θαυμασθῆναι ἐν πᾶσιν τοῖς πιστεύσασιν, ὅτι ἐπιστεύθη τὸ μαρτύριον ἡμῶν ἐφ' ὑμᾶς, ἐν τῇ ἡμέρᾳ ἐκείνῃ.

2 Tim 4:8

λοιπὸν ἀπόκειταί μοι ὁ τῆς δικαιοσύνης στέφανος, ὃν ἀποδώσει μοι ὁ κύριος ἐν ἐκείνῃ τῇ ἡμέρᾳ, ὁ δίκαιος κριτής, οὐ μόνον δὲ ἐμοὶ ἀλλὰ καὶ πᾶσι τοῖς ἠγαπηκόσι τὴν ἐπιφάνειαν αὐτοῦ.

Acts 17:30–31

τοὺς μὲν οὖν χρόνους τῆς ἀγνοίας ὑπεριδὼν ὁ θεός, τὰ νῦν παραγγέλλει τοῖς ἀνθρώποις πάντας πανταχοῦ μετανοεῖν, **31** καθότι ἔστησεν ἡμέραν ἐν ᾗ μέλλει κρίνειν τὴν οἰκουμένην ἐν δικαιοσύνῃ, ἐν ἀνδρὶ ᾧ ὥρισεν, πίστιν παρασχὼν πᾶσιν ἀναστήσας αὐτὸν ἐκ νεκρῶν.

Acts 24:14–16

ὁμολογῶ δὲ τοῦτό σοι ὅτι κατὰ τὴν ὁδὸν ἣν λέγουσιν αἵρεσιν, οὕτως λατρεύω τῷ πατρῴῳ θεῷ πιστεύων πᾶσι τοῖς κατὰ τὸν νόμον καὶ τοῖς ἐν τοῖς προφήταις γεγραμμένοις, **15** ἐλπίδα ἔχων εἰς τὸν θεὸν ἣν καὶ αὐτοὶ οὗτοι προσδέχονται, ἀνάστασιν μέλλειν ⸀ἔσεσθαι δικαίων τε καὶ ἀδίκων. **16** ἐν τούτῳ καὶ αὐτὸς ἀσκῶ ἀπρόσκοπον συνείδησιν ἔχειν πρὸς τὸν θεὸν καὶ τοὺς ἀνθρώπους διὰ παντός.

Acts 24:24–25

Μετὰ δὲ ἡμέρας τινὰς παραγενόμενος ὁ Φῆλιξ σὺν Δρουσίλλῃ τῇ ἰδίᾳ γυναικὶ οὔσῃ Ἰουδαίᾳ μετεπέμψατο τὸν Παῦλον καὶ ἤκουσεν αὐτοῦ περὶ τῆς εἰς Χριστὸν Ἰησοῦν πίστεως. **25** διαλεγομένου δὲ αὐτοῦ περὶ δικαιοσύνης καὶ ἐγκρατείας καὶ τοῦ κρίματος τοῦ μέλλοντος, ἔμφοβος γενόμενος ὁ Φῆλιξ ἀπεκρίθη· τὸ νῦν ἔχον πορεύου, καιρὸν δὲ μεταλαβὼν μετακαλέσομαί σε,

Cf. Rom 1:24–32; 2:12–13; 2:16; 3:1–8; 1 Cor 3:10–17; 2 Cor 5:10; 11:15; Eph 6:8–9; Phil 3:17–4:1; Col 3:24–25; 1 Tim 5:24–25; 2 Tim 4:14.

See also § 94 The Judgment Seat of Christ.

§ 95 **Rom 2:16** ***Χριστου Ιησου*** (ℵ*vid) B] Ιησου Χριστου ℵ[1] A D 33. 1739 *Byz*

§ 96 **Acts 24:15** ***εσεσθαι*** 𝔓[74] ℵ A B C 33. 1739] *add*. νεκρων E *Byz*

95. Judgment of the Secrets of the Heart

Rom 2:16

on the day when, according to my gospel, God, through Jesus Christ,[a] will judge the secret thoughts of all.

Rom 2:28–29

For a person is not a Jew who is one outwardly, nor is true circumcision something external and physical. **29** Rather, a person is a Jew who is one inwardly, and real circumcision is a matter of the heart—it is by the Spirit and not by the written letter. Such a person receives praise not from others but from God.[b]

1 Cor 4:3–5

But with me it is a very small thing that I should be judged by you or by any human court. I do not even judge myself. **4** I am not aware of anything against myself, but I am not thereby acquitted. It is the Lord who judges me. **5** Therefore do not pronounce judgment before the time, before the Lord comes, who will bring to light the things now hidden in darkness and will disclose the purposes of the heart. Then each one will receive commendation from God.

1 Thess 2:4

but just as we have been approved by God to be entrusted with the message of the gospel, even so we speak, not to please mortals, but to please God who tests our hearts.

1 Tim 5:24–25

The sins of some people are conspicuous and precede them to judgment, while the sins of others follow them there. **25** So also good works are conspicuous; and even when they are not, they cannot remain hidden.

Cf. Rom 8:27; 1 Cor 14:24–25.

96. The Righteous Judgment of God

Rom 2:1–11

Therefore you have no excuse, whoever you are, when you judge others; for in passing judgment on another you condemn yourself, because you, the judge, are doing the very same things. **2** You say, "We know that God's judgment on those who do such things is in accordance with truth." **3** Do you imagine, whoever you are, that when you judge those who do such things and yet do them yourself, you will escape the judgment of God? **4** Or do you despise the riches of his kindness and forbearance and patience? Do you not realize that God's kindness is meant to lead you to repentance? **5** But by your hard and impenitent heart you are storing up wrath for yourself on the day of wrath, when God's righteous judgment will be revealed. **6** For he will repay according to each one's deeds: **7** to those who by patiently doing good seek for glory and honor and immortality, he will give eternal life; **8** while for those who are self-seeking and who obey not the truth but wickedness, there will be wrath and fury. **9** There will be anguish and distress for everyone who does evil, the Jew first and also the Greek, **10** but glory and honor and peace for everyone who does good, the Jew first and also the Greek. **11** For God shows no partiality.

2 Thess 1:5–10

This is evidence of the righteous judgment of God, and is intended to make you worthy of the kingdom of God, for which you are also suffering. **6** For it is indeed just of God to repay with affliction those who afflict you, **7** and to give relief to the afflicted as well as to us, when the Lord Jesus is revealed from heaven with his mighty angels **8** in flaming fire, inflicting vengeance on those who do not know God and on those who do not obey the gospel of our Lord Jesus. **9** These will suffer the punishment of eternal destruction, separated from the presence of the Lord and from the glory of his might, **10** when he comes to be glorified by his saints and to be marveled at on that day among all who have believed, because our testimony to you was believed.

2 Tim 4:8

From now on there is reserved for me the crown of righteousness, which the Lord, the righteous judge, will give me on that day, and not only to me but also to all who have longed for his appearing.

Acts 17:30–31

While God has overlooked the times of human ignorance, now he commands all people everywhere to repent, **31** because he has fixed a day on which he will have the world judged in righteousness by a man whom he has appointed, and of this he has given assurance to all by raising him from the dead.

Acts 24:14–16

But this I admit to you, that according to the Way, which they call a sect, I worship the God of our ancestors, believing everything laid down according to the law or written in the prophets. **15** I have a hope in God—a hope that they themselves also accept—that there will be a resurrection of both[a] the righteous and the unrighteous. **16** Therefore I do my best always to have a clear conscience toward God and all people.

Acts 24:24–25

Some days later when Felix came with his wife Drusilla, who was Jewish, he sent for Paul and heard him speak concerning faith in Christ Jesus. **25** And as he discussed justice, self-control, and the coming judgment, Felix became frightened and said, "Go away for the present; when I have an opportunity, I will send for you."

Cf. Rom 1:24–32; 2:12–13; 2:16; 3:1–8; 1 Cor 3:10–17; 2 Cor 5:10; 11:15; Eph 6:8–9; Phil 3:17–4:1; Col 3:24–25; 1 Tim 5:24–25; 2 Tim 4:14.

See also § 94 The Judgment Seat of Christ.

§ 95 [a] **Rom 2:16** *Jesus Christ* Other ancient authorities read *Christ Jesus* [b] **Rom 2:29** Translation differs from NRSV **§ 96** [a] **Acts 24:15** *of both* Other ancient authorities read *of the dead, both of*

97. *Fulfillment and Proclamation*

Rom 1:1–5

Παῦλος δοῦλος ⸀Χριστοῦ Ἰησοῦ⸃, κλητὸς
ἀπόστολος ἀφωρισμένος εἰς εὐαγγέ-
λιον θεοῦ, 2 ὃ προεπηγγείλατο διὰ τῶν
προφητῶν αὐτοῦ ἐν γραφαῖς ἁγίαις
3 περὶ τοῦ υἱοῦ αὐτοῦ τοῦ γενομένου
ἐκ σπέρματος Δαυὶδ κατὰ σάρκα, 4 τοῦ
ὁρισθέντος υἱοῦ θεοῦ ἐν δυνάμει κατὰ
πνεῦμα ἁγιωσύνης ἐξ ἀναστάσεως νε-
κρῶν, Ἰησοῦ Χριστοῦ τοῦ κυρίου ἡμῶν,
5 δι' οὗ ἐλάβομεν χάριν καὶ ἀποστολὴν εἰς
ὑπακοὴν πίστεως ἐν πᾶσιν τοῖς ἔθνεσιν
ὑπὲρ τοῦ ὀνόματος αὐτοῦ

Rom 3:21

Νυνὶ δὲ χωρὶς νόμου δικαιοσύνη θεοῦ πεφανέρωται μαρτυρουμένη ὑπὸ τοῦ νόμου καὶ τῶν προφητῶν

Rom 16:25–27

⸀[Τῷ δὲ δυναμένῳ ὑμᾶς στηρίξαι κατὰ
τὸ εὐαγγέλιόν μου καὶ τὸ κήρυγμα Ἰη-
σοῦ Χριστοῦ, κατὰ ἀποκάλυψιν μυστη-
ρίου χρόνοις αἰωνίοις σεσιγημένου,
26 φανερωθέντος δὲ νῦν διά τε γραφῶν
προφητικῶν κατ' ἐπιταγὴν τοῦ αἰωνίου
θεοῦ εἰς ὑπακοὴν πίστεως εἰς πάντα τὰ
ἔθνη γνωρισθέντος, 27 μόνῳ σοφῷ θεῷ,
διὰ Ἰησοῦ Χριστοῦ, ⸀ᾧ ἡ δόξα εἰς τοὺς
⸀αἰῶνας, ἀμήν.]⸃

1 Cor 15:1–4

Γνωρίζω δὲ ὑμῖν, ἀδελφοί, τὸ εὐαγγέλιον
ὃ εὐηγγελισάμην ὑμῖν, ὃ καὶ παρελάβετε,
ἐν ᾧ καὶ ἑστήκατε, 2 δι' οὗ καὶ σῴζεσθε,
τίνι λόγῳ εὐηγγελισάμην ὑμῖν εἰ κα-
τέχετε, ἐκτὸς εἰ μὴ εἰκῇ ἐπιστεύσατε.
3 παρέδωκα γὰρ ὑμῖν ἐν πρώτοις, ὃ καὶ
παρέλαβον, ὅτι Χριστὸς ἀπέθανεν ὑπὲρ
τῶν ἁμαρτιῶν ἡμῶν κατὰ τὰς γραφὰς
4 καὶ ὅτι ἐτάφη καὶ ὅτι ἐγήγερται τῇ
ἡμέρᾳ τῇ τρίτῃ κατὰ τὰς γραφὰς

1 Tim 2:5–7

Εἷς γὰρ θεός, εἷς καὶ μεσίτης θεοῦ καὶ
ἀνθρώπων, ἄνθρωπος Χριστὸς Ἰησοῦς,
6 ὁ δοὺς ἑαυτὸν ἀντίλυτρον ὑπὲρ πάν-
των, τὸ μαρτύριον καιροῖς ἰδίοις. 7 εἰς ὃ
ἐτέθην ἐγὼ κῆρυξ καὶ ἀπόστολος, ἀλή-
θειαν ⸀λέγω οὐ ψεύδομαι, διδάσκαλος
ἐθνῶν ἐν πίστει καὶ ἀληθείᾳ.

1 Tim 3:16

καὶ ὁμολογουμένως μέγα ἐστὶν τὸ τῆς εὐσεβείας μυστήριον· ⸀ὃς ἐφανερώθη ἐν σαρκί, ἐδικαιώθη ἐν πνεύματι, ὤφθη ἀγγέλοις, ἐκηρύχθη ἐν ἔθνεσιν, ἐπιστεύθη ἐν κόσμῳ, ἀνελήμφθη ἐν δόξῃ.

Titus 1:2–3

ἐπ' ἐλπίδι ζωῆς αἰωνίου, ἣν ἐπηγγείλατο
ὁ ἀψευδὴς θεὸς πρὸ χρόνων αἰωνίων,
3 ἐφανέρωσεν δὲ καιροῖς ἰδίοις τὸν λό-
γον αὐτοῦ ἐν κηρύγματι, ὃ ἐπιστεύθην
ἐγὼ κατ' ἐπιταγὴν τοῦ σωτῆρος ἡμῶν
θεοῦ

Acts 13:27–33

οἱ γὰρ κατοικοῦντες ἐν Ἰερουσαλὴμ καὶ
οἱ ἄρχοντες αὐτῶν τοῦτον ἀγνοήσαν-
τες καὶ τὰς φωνὰς τῶν προφητῶν τὰς
κατὰ πᾶν σάββατον ἀναγινωσκομένας
κρίναντες ἐπλήρωσαν, 28 καὶ μηδεμίαν
αἰτίαν θανάτου εὑρόντες ᾐτήσαντο Πι-
λᾶτον ἀναιρεθῆναι αὐτόν. 29 ὡς δὲ ἐτέ-
λεσαν πάντα τὰ περὶ αὐτοῦ γεγραμμένα,
καθελόντες ἀπὸ τοῦ ξύλου ἔθηκαν εἰς
μνημεῖον. 30 ὁ δὲ θεὸς ἤγειρεν αὐτὸν ἐκ
νεκρῶν, 31 ὃς ὤφθη ἐπὶ ἡμέρας πλείους
τοῖς συναναβᾶσιν αὐτῷ ἀπὸ τῆς Γα-
λιλαίας εἰς Ἰερουσαλήμ, οἵτινες [νῦν]
εἰσιν μάρτυρες αὐτοῦ πρὸς τὸν λαόν.
32 Καὶ ἡμεῖς ὑμᾶς εὐαγγελιζόμεθα τὴν
πρὸς τοὺς πατέρας ἐπαγγελίαν γενομέ-
νην, 33 ὅτι ταύτην ὁ θεὸς ἐκπεπλήρωκεν
τοῖς τέκνοις [αὐτῶν] ἡμῖν ἀναστήσας
Ἰησοῦν ὡς καὶ ἐν τῷ ψαλμῷ γέγραπται
τῷ δευτέρῳ· υἱός μου εἶ σύ, ἐγὼ σήμερον
γεγέννηκά σε.

Acts 17:2–3

κατὰ δὲ τὸ εἰωθὸς τῷ Παύλῳ εἰσῆλθεν πρὸς
αὐτοὺς καὶ ἐπὶ σάββατα τρία διελέξατο
αὐτοῖς ἀπὸ τῶν γραφῶν, 3 διανοίγων
καὶ παρατιθέμενος ὅτι τὸν χριστὸν ἔδει
παθεῖν καὶ ἀναστῆναι ἐκ νεκρῶν καὶ ὅτι
οὗτός ἐστιν ὁ χριστὸς [ὁ] Ἰησοῦς ὃν ἐγὼ
καταγγέλλω ὑμῖν.

Acts 26:22–23

ἐπικουρίας οὖν τυχὼν τῆς ἀπὸ τοῦ θεοῦ
ἄχρι τῆς ἡμέρας ταύτης ἕστηκα μαρτυ-
ρόμενος μικρῷ τε καὶ μεγάλῳ οὐδὲν
ἐκτὸς λέγων ὧν τε οἱ προφῆται ἐλάλησαν
μελλόντων γίνεσθαι καὶ Μωϋσῆς, 23 εἰ
παθητὸς ὁ χριστός, εἰ πρῶτος ἐξ ἀναστά-
σεως νεκρῶν φῶς μέλλει καταγγέλλειν
τῷ τε λαῷ καὶ τοῖς ἔθνεσιν.

Cf. Rom 15:8–12; 2 Tim 2:8; Acts 26:6–8.

See also § 98 The Role of Apostles and Missionary Proclaimers.

98. *The Role of Apostles and Missionary Proclaimers*

Rom 10:14–18

Πῶς οὖν ἐπικαλέσωνται εἰς ὃν οὐκ ἐπί-
στευσαν; πῶς δὲ πιστεύσωσιν οὗ οὐκ
ἤκουσαν; πῶς δὲ ἀκούσωσιν χωρὶς κη-
ρύσσοντος; 15 πῶς δὲ κηρύξωσιν ἐὰν
μὴ ἀποσταλῶσιν; καθὼς γέγραπται· ὡς

§ 97 **Rom 1:1** ***Χριστου Ιησου*** 𝔓^{10} B] Ιησου Χριστου 𝔓^{26} ℵ A 33. 1739. 1881 *Byz* **Rom 16:25–27** *pon. hic* 𝔓^{61} ℵ B C D 1739] *pon. hic et p.* 14:23 A 33 ¦ *pon. p.* 14:23 *Byz* ¦ *pon. p.* 15:33 𝔓^{46} ¦ *om. pc* **Rom 16:27** ***ω*** 𝔓^{46} ℵ A C D 33. 1739. 1881 *Byz*] *om.* B • ***αιωνας*** 𝔓^{46} B C 33. 1739. 1881 *Byz*] *add.* των αιωνων 𝔓^{61} ℵ A D **1 Tim 2:7** ***λεγω*** ℵ^{2} A D* 1739. 1881] *add.* εν Χριστω ℵ* D^{2} 33^{vid} *Byz* **1 Tim 3:16** ***ος*** ℵ* A* C* 33] ὃ D* ¦ θεος ℵ^{c} A^{c} C^{2} D^{2} 1739. 1881 *Byz*

97. Fulfillment and Proclamation

Rom 1:1–5

Paul, a servant of Jesus Christ,[a] called to be an apostle, set apart for the gospel of God, 2 which he promised beforehand through his prophets in the holy scriptures, 3 the gospel concerning his Son, who was descended from David according to the flesh 4 and was declared to be Son of God with power according to the Spirit[b] of holiness by resurrection from the dead, Jesus Christ our Lord, 5 through whom we have received grace and apostleship to bring about the obedience of faith among all the Gentiles for the sake of his name

Rom 3:21

But now, apart from law, the righteousness of God has been disclosed, and is attested by the law and the prophets

Rom 16:25–27

Now to God who is able to strengthen you according to my gospel and the proclamation of Jesus Christ, according to the revelation of the mystery that was kept secret for long ages 26 but is now disclosed, and through the prophetic writings is made known to all the Gentiles, according to the command of the eternal God, to bring about the obedience of faith— 27 to the only wise God, through Jesus Christ, to whom[c] be the glory forever![d] Amen.[e]

1 Cor 15:1–4

Now I would remind you, brothers and sisters, of the good news that I proclaimed to you, which you in turn received, in which also you stand, 2 through which also you are being saved, if you hold firmly to the message that I proclaimed to you—unless you have come to believe in vain. 3 For I handed on to you as of first importance what I in turn had received: that Christ died for our sins in accordance with the scriptures, 4 and that he was buried, and that he was raised on the third day in accordance with the scriptures

1 Tim 2:5–7

For there is one God; there is also one mediator between God and humankind, Christ Jesus, himself human, 6 who gave himself a ransom for all —this was attested at the right time. 7 For this I was appointed a herald and an apostle (I am telling the truth,[f] I am not lying), a teacher of the Gentiles in faith and truth.

1 Tim 3:16

Without any doubt, the mystery of our religion is great: Who[g] was revealed in flesh, vindicated by the Spirit,[h] seen by angels, proclaimed among Gentiles, believed in throughout the world, taken up in glory.

Titus 1:2–3

in the hope of eternal life that God, who never lies, promised before the ages began— 3 in due time he revealed his word through the proclamation with which I have been entrusted by the command of God our Savior

Acts 13:27–33

Because the residents of Jerusalem and their leaders did not recognize him or understand the words of the prophets that are read every sabbath, they fulfilled those words by condemning him. 28 Even though they found no cause for a sentence of death, they asked Pilate to have him killed. 29 When they had carried out everything that was written about him, they took him down from the tree and laid him in a tomb. 30 But God raised him from the dead; 31 and for many days he appeared to those who came up with him from Galilee to Jerusalem, and they are now his witnesses to the people. 32 And we bring you the good news that what God promised to our ancestors 33 he has fulfilled for us, their children, by raising Jesus; as also it is written in the second psalm, 'You are my Son; today I have begotten you.'

Acts 17:2–3

And Paul went in, as was his custom, and on three sabbath days argued with them from the scriptures, 3 explaining and proving that it was necessary for the Messiah to suffer and to rise from the dead, and saying, "This is the Messiah, Jesus whom I am proclaiming to you."

Acts 26:22–23

To this day I have had help from God, and so I stand here, testifying to both small and great, saying nothing but what the prophets and Moses said would take place: 23 that the Messiah must suffer, and that, by being the first to rise from the dead, he would proclaim light both to our people and to the Gentiles.

Cf. Rom 15:8–12; 2 Tim 2:8; Acts 26:6–8.

See also § 98 The Role of Apostles and Missionary Proclaimers.

98. The Role of Apostles and Missionary Proclaimers

Rom 10:14–18

But how are they to call on one in whom they have not believed? And how are they to believe in one of whom they have never heard? And how are they to hear without someone to proclaim him? 15 And how are they to proclaim him unless they are sent? As it is written, "How beautiful are the feet of those

§ 97 [a] **Rom 1:1** ***Jesus Christ*** Other ancient authorities read *Christ Jesus* [b] **Rom 1:4** ***Spirit*** NRSV alternate translation [c] **Rom 16:27** ***to whom*** A few ancient authorities lack *to whom*. The verse then reads, *to the only wise God be the glory through Jesus Christ forever. Amen.* [d] **Rom 16:27** ***forever*** Other ancient authorities read *forever and ever* [e] **Rom 16:27** ***Amen*** Other ancient authorities include 16:25–27 after 14:23 or 15:33; a few lack these verses altogether [f] **1 Tim 2:7** ***telling the truth*** Other ancient authorities add *in Christ* [g] **1 Tim 3:16** ***Who*** Other ancient authorities read *God*; others, *Which*. NRSV translates Gk *Who* as *He* [h] **1 Tim 3:16** ***by the Spirit*** NRSV alternate translation

ὡραῖοι οἱ πόδες τῶν εὐαγγελιζομένων [τὰ] ἀγαθά. **16** Ἀλλ᾽ οὐ πάντες ὑπήκουσαν τῷ εὐαγγελίῳ. Ἠσαΐας γὰρ λέγει· κύριε, τίς ἐπίστευσεν τῇ ἀκοῇ ἡμῶν; **17** ἄρα ἡ πίστις ἐξ ἀκοῆς, ἡ δὲ ἀκοὴ διὰ ῥήματος ⸀Χριστοῦ. **18** ἀλλὰ λέγω, μὴ οὐκ ἤκουσαν; μενοῦνγε· εἰς πᾶσαν τὴν γῆν ἐξῆλθεν ὁ φθόγγος αὐτῶν καὶ εἰς τὰ πέρατα τῆς οἰκουμένης τὰ ῥήματα αὐτῶν.

Rom 16:25–27

⸂[Τῷ δὲ δυναμένῳ ὑμᾶς στηρίξαι κατὰ τὸ εὐαγγέλιόν μου καὶ τὸ κήρυγμα Ἰησοῦ Χριστοῦ, κατὰ ἀποκάλυψιν μυστηρίου χρόνοις αἰωνίοις σεσιγημένου, **26** φανερωθέντος δὲ νῦν διά τε γραφῶν προφητικῶν κατ᾽ ἐπιταγὴν τοῦ αἰωνίου θεοῦ εἰς ὑπακοὴν πίστεως εἰς πάντα τὰ ἔθνη γνωρισθέντος, **27** μόνῳ σοφῷ θεῷ, διὰ Ἰησοῦ Χριστοῦ, ⸀ᾧ ἡ δόξα εἰς τοὺς ⸀αἰῶνας, ἀμήν.]⸃

1 Cor 3:5–15

Τί οὖν ἐστιν Ἀπολλῶς; τί δέ ἐστιν Παῦλος; διάκονοι δι᾽ ὧν ἐπιστεύσατε, καὶ ἑκάστῳ ὡς ὁ κύριος ἔδωκεν. **6** ἐγὼ ἐφύτευσα, Ἀπολλῶς ἐπότισεν, ἀλλὰ ὁ θεὸς ηὔξανεν· **7** ὥστε οὔτε ὁ φυτεύων ἐστίν τι οὔτε ὁ ποτίζων ἀλλ᾽ ὁ αὐξάνων θεός. **8** ὁ φυτεύων δὲ καὶ ὁ ποτίζων ἕν εἰσιν, ἕκαστος δὲ τὸν ἴδιον μισθὸν λήμψεται κατὰ τὸν ἴδιον κόπον· **9** θεοῦ γάρ ἐσμεν συνεργοί, θεοῦ γεώργιον, θεοῦ οἰκοδομή ἐστε. **10** Κατὰ τὴν χάριν τοῦ θεοῦ τὴν δοθεῖσάν μοι ὡς σοφὸς ἀρχιτέκτων θεμέλιον ἔθηκα, ἄλλος δὲ ἐποικοδομεῖ. ἕκαστος δὲ βλεπέτω πῶς ἐποικοδομεῖ. **11** θεμέλιον γὰρ ἄλλον οὐδεὶς δύναται θεῖναι παρὰ τὸν κείμενον, ὅς ἐστιν Ἰησοῦς Χριστός. **12** εἰ δέ τις ἐποικοδομεῖ ἐπὶ τὸν θεμέλιον χρυσόν, ἄργυρον, λίθους τιμίους, ξύλα, χόρτον, καλάμην, **13** ἑκάστου τὸ ἔργον φανερὸν γενήσεται, ἡ γὰρ ἡμέρα δηλώσει, ὅτι ἐν πυρὶ ἀποκαλύπτεται· καὶ ἑκάστου τὸ ἔργον ὁποῖόν ἐστιν τὸ πῦρ [αὐτὸ] δοκιμάσει. **14** εἴ τινος τὸ ἔργον μενεῖ ὃ ἐποικοδόμησεν, μισθὸν λήμψεται· **15** εἴ τινος τὸ ἔργον κατακαήσεται, ζημιωθήσεται, αὐτὸς δὲ σωθήσεται, οὕτως δὲ ὡς διὰ πυρός.

1 Cor 12:28–31

Καὶ οὓς μὲν ἔθετο ὁ θεὸς ἐν τῇ ἐκκλησίᾳ πρῶτον ἀποστόλους, δεύτερον προφήτας, τρίτον διδασκάλους, ἔπειτα δυνάμεις, ἔπειτα χαρίσματα ἰαμάτων, ἀντιλήμψεις, κυβερνήσεις, γένη γλωσσῶν. **29** μὴ πάντες ἀπόστολοι; μὴ πάντες προφῆται; μὴ πάντες διδάσκαλοι; μὴ πάντες δυνάμεις; **30** μὴ πάντες χαρίσματα ἔχουσιν ἰαμάτων; μὴ πάντες γλώσσαις λαλοῦσιν; μὴ πάντες διερμηνεύουσιν; **31** ζηλοῦτε δὲ τὰ χαρίσματα τὰ μείζονα. Καὶ ἔτι καθ᾽ ὑπερβολὴν ὁδὸν ὑμῖν δείκνυμι.

1 Cor 15:1–11

Γνωρίζω δὲ ὑμῖν, ἀδελφοί, τὸ εὐαγγέλιον ὃ εὐηγγελισάμην ὑμῖν, ὃ καὶ παρελάβετε, ἐν ᾧ καὶ ἑστήκατε, **2** δι᾽ οὗ καὶ σῴζεσθε, τίνι λόγῳ εὐηγγελισάμην ὑμῖν εἰ κατέχετε, ἐκτὸς εἰ μὴ εἰκῇ ἐπιστεύσατε. **3** παρέδωκα γὰρ ὑμῖν ἐν πρώτοις, ὃ καὶ παρέλαβον, ὅτι Χριστὸς ἀπέθανεν ὑπὲρ τῶν ἁμαρτιῶν ἡμῶν κατὰ τὰς γραφὰς **4** καὶ ὅτι ἐτάφη καὶ ὅτι ἐγήγερται τῇ ἡμέρᾳ τῇ τρίτῃ κατὰ τὰς γραφὰς **5** καὶ ὅτι ὤφθη Κηφᾷ εἶτα τοῖς δώδεκα· **6** ἔπειτα ὤφθη ἐπάνω πεντακοσίοις ἀδελφοῖς ἐφάπαξ, ἐξ ὧν οἱ πλείονες μένουσιν ἕως ἄρτι, τινὲς δὲ ἐκοιμήθησαν· **7** ἔπειτα ὤφθη Ἰακώβῳ εἶτα τοῖς ἀποστόλοις πᾶσιν· **8** ἔσχατον δὲ πάντων ὡσπερεὶ τῷ ἐκτρώματι ὤφθη κἀμοί. **9** Ἐγὼ γάρ εἰμι ὁ ἐλάχιστος τῶν ἀποστόλων ὃς οὐκ εἰμὶ ἱκανὸς καλεῖσθαι ἀπόστολος, διότι ἐδίωξα τὴν ἐκκλησίαν τοῦ θεοῦ· **10** χάριτι δὲ θεοῦ εἰμι ὅ εἰμι, καὶ ἡ χάρις αὐτοῦ ἡ εἰς ἐμὲ οὐ κενὴ ἐγενήθη, ἀλλὰ περισσότερον αὐτῶν πάντων ἐκοπίασα, οὐκ ἐγὼ δὲ ἀλλὰ ἡ χάρις τοῦ θεοῦ [ἡ] σὺν ἐμοί. **11** εἴτε οὖν ἐγὼ εἴτε ἐκεῖνοι, οὕτως κηρύσσομεν καὶ οὕτως ἐπιστεύσατε.

Gal 2:7–10

ἀλλὰ τοὐναντίον ἰδόντες ὅτι πεπίστευμαι τὸ εὐαγγέλιον τῆς ἀκροβυστίας καθὼς Πέτρος τῆς περιτομῆς, **8** ὁ γὰρ ἐνεργήσας Πέτρῳ εἰς ἀποστολὴν τῆς περιτομῆς ἐνήργησεν καὶ ἐμοὶ εἰς τὰ ἔθνη, **9** καὶ γνόντες τὴν χάριν τὴν δοθεῖσάν μοι, Ἰάκωβος καὶ Κηφᾶς καὶ Ἰωάννης, οἱ δοκοῦντες στῦλοι εἶναι, δεξιὰς ἔδωκαν ἐμοὶ καὶ Βαρναβᾷ κοινωνίας, ἵνα ἡμεῖς εἰς τὰ ἔθνη, αὐτοὶ δὲ εἰς τὴν περιτομήν· **10** μόνον τῶν πτωχῶν ἵνα μνημονεύωμεν, ὃ καὶ ἐσπούδασα αὐτὸ τοῦτο ποιῆσαι.

Eph 2:19–22

Ἄρα οὖν οὐκέτι ἐστὲ ξένοι καὶ πάροικοι ἀλλὰ ἐστὲ συμπολῖται τῶν ἁγίων καὶ οἰκεῖοι τοῦ θεοῦ, **20** ἐποικοδομηθέντες ἐπὶ τῷ θεμελίῳ τῶν ἀποστόλων καὶ προφητῶν, ὄντος ἀκρογωνιαίου αὐτοῦ Χριστοῦ Ἰησοῦ, **21** ἐν ᾧ πᾶσα οἰκοδομὴ συναρμολογουμένη αὔξει εἰς ναὸν ἅγιον ἐν κυρίῳ, **22** ἐν ᾧ καὶ ὑμεῖς συνοικοδομεῖσθε εἰς κατοικητήριον τοῦ θεοῦ ἐν πνεύματι.

Eph 4:11–16

Καὶ αὐτὸς ἔδωκεν τοὺς μὲν ἀποστόλους, τοὺς δὲ προφήτας, τοὺς δὲ εὐαγγελιστάς, τοὺς δὲ ποιμένας καὶ διδασκάλους, **12** πρὸς τὸν καταρτισμὸν τῶν ἁγίων εἰς ἔργον διακονίας, εἰς οἰκοδομὴν τοῦ σώματος τοῦ Χριστοῦ, **13** μέχρι καταντήσωμεν οἱ πάντες εἰς τὴν ἑνότητα τῆς πίστεως καὶ τῆς ἐπιγνώσεως τοῦ υἱοῦ τοῦ θεοῦ, εἰς ἄνδρα τέλειον, εἰς μέτρον ἡλικίας τοῦ πληρώματος τοῦ Χριστοῦ, **14** ἵνα μηκέτι ὦμεν νήπιοι, κλυδωνιζόμενοι καὶ περιφερόμενοι παντὶ ἀνέμῳ τῆς διδασκαλίας ἐν τῇ κυβείᾳ τῶν ἀνθρώπων, ἐν πανουργίᾳ πρὸς τὴν μεθοδείαν τῆς πλάνης, **15** ἀληθεύοντες δὲ ἐν ἀγάπῃ αὐξήσωμεν εἰς αὐτὸν τὰ πάντα, ὅς ἐστιν ἡ κεφαλή, Χριστός, **16** ἐξ οὗ πᾶν τὸ σῶμα συναρμολογούμενον καὶ συμβιβαζόμενον διὰ πάσης ἁφῆς τῆς ἐπιχορηγίας κατ᾽ ἐνέργειαν ἐν μέτρῳ ἑνὸς ἑκάστου μέρους

§ 98 **Rom 10:17** ***Χριστου*** 𝔓[46vid] ℵ* B C D* 1739] θεου ℵ[1] A D[1] 33. 1881 *Byz* **Rom 16:25–27** *pon. hic* 𝔓[61] ℵ B C D 1739] *pon. hic et p.* 14:23 A 33 ¦ *pon. p.* 14:23 *Byz* ¦ *pon. p.* 15:33 𝔓[46] ¦ *om. pc* **Rom 16:27** ***ω*** 𝔓[46] ℵ A C D 33. 1739. 1881 *Byz*] *om.* B • ***αιωνας*** 𝔓[46] B C 33. 1739. 1881 *Byz*] *add.* των αιωνων 𝔓[61] ℵ A D

who bring good news!" 16 But not all have obeyed the good news; for Isaiah says, "Lord, who has believed our message?" 17 So faith comes from what is heard, and what is heard comes through the word of Christ.[a] 18 But I ask, have they not heard? Indeed they have; for "Their voice has gone out to all the earth, and their words to the ends of the world."

Rom 16:25–27

Now to God who is able to strengthen you according to my gospel and the proclamation of Jesus Christ, according to the revelation of the mystery that was kept secret for long ages 26 but is now disclosed, and through the prophetic writings is made known to all the Gentiles, according to the command of the eternal God, to bring about the obedience of faith— 27 to the only wise God, through Jesus Christ, to whom[b] be the glory forever![c] Amen.[d]

1 Cor 3:5–15

What then is Apollos? What is Paul? Servants through whom you came to believe, as the Lord assigned to each. 6 I planted, Apollos watered, but God gave the growth. 7 So neither the one who plants nor the one who waters is anything, but only God who gives the growth. 8 The one who plants and the one who waters have a common purpose, and each will receive wages according to the labor of each. 9 For we are God's servants, working together; you are God's field, God's building. 10 According to the grace of God given to me, like a skilled master builder I laid a foundation, and someone else is building on it. Each builder must choose with care how to build on it. 11 For no one can lay any foundation other than the one that has been laid; that foundation is Jesus Christ. 12 Now if anyone builds on the foundation with gold, silver, precious stones, wood, hay, straw— 13 the work of each builder will become visible, for the Day will disclose it, because it will be revealed with fire, and the fire will test what sort of work each has done. 14 If what has been built on the foundation survives, the builder will receive a reward. 15 If the work is burned up, the builder will suffer loss; the builder will be saved, but only as through fire.

1 Cor 12:28–31

And God has appointed in the church first apostles, second prophets, third teachers; then deeds of power, then gifts of healing, forms of assistance, forms of leadership, various kinds of tongues. 29 Are all apostles? Are all prophets? Are all teachers? Do all work miracles? 30 Do all possess gifts of healing? Do all speak in tongues? Do all interpret? 31 But strive for the greater gifts. And I will show you a still more excellent way.

1 Cor 15:1–11

Now I would remind you, brothers and sisters, of the good news that I proclaimed to you, which you in turn received, in which also you stand, 2 through which also you are being saved, if you hold firmly to the message that I proclaimed to you—unless you have come to believe in vain. 3 For I handed on to you as of first importance what I in turn had received: that Christ died for our sins in accordance with the scriptures, 4 and that he was buried, and that he was raised on the third day in accordance with the scriptures, 5 and that he appeared to Cephas, then to the twelve. 6 Then he appeared to more than five hundred brothers and sisters at one time, most of whom are still alive, though some have died. 7 Then he appeared to James, then to all the apostles. 8 Last of all, as to one untimely born, he appeared also to me. 9 For I am the least of the apostles, unfit to be called an apostle, because I persecuted the church of God. 10 But by the grace of God I am what I am, and his grace toward me has not been in vain. On the contrary, I worked harder than any of them—though it was not I, but the grace of God that is with me. 11 Whether then it was I or they, so we proclaim and so you have come to believe.

Gal 2:7–10

On the contrary, when they saw that I had been entrusted with the gospel for the uncircumcised, just as Peter had been entrusted with the gospel for the circumcised 8 (for he who worked through Peter making him an apostle to the circumcised also worked through me in sending me to the Gentiles), 9 and when James and Cephas and John, who were acknowledged pillars, recognized the grace that had been given to me, they gave to Barnabas and me the right hand of fellowship, agreeing that we should go to the Gentiles and they to the circumcised. 10 They asked only one thing, that we remember the poor, which was actually what I was eager to do.

Eph 2:19–22

So then you are no longer strangers and aliens, but you are citizens with the saints and also members of the household of God, 20 built upon the foundation of the apostles and prophets, with Christ Jesus himself as the cornerstone. 21 In him the whole structure is joined together and grows into a holy temple in the Lord; 22 in whom you also are built together spiritually into a dwelling place for God.

Eph 4:11–16

The gifts he gave were that some would be apostles, some prophets, some evangelists, some pastors and teachers, 12 to equip the saints for the work of ministry, for building up the body of Christ, 13 until all of us come to the unity of the faith and of the knowledge of the Son of God, to maturity, to the measure of the full stature of Christ. 14 We must no longer be children, tossed to and fro and blown about by every wind of doctrine, by people's trickery, by their craftiness in deceitful scheming. 15 But speaking the truth in love, we must grow up in every way into him who is the head, into Christ, 16 from whom the whole body, joined and knit together by every ligament by which it is supplied,[e] as each part is working

§ 98 [a] **Rom 10:17** *of Christ* Other ancient authorities read *of God* [b] **Rom 16:27** *to whom* A few ancient authorities lack *to whom*. The verse then reads, *to the only wise God be the glory through Jesus Christ forever. Amen.* [c] **Rom 16:27** *forever* Other ancient authorities read *forever and ever* [d] **Rom 16:27** *Amen* Other ancient authorities include 16:25–27 after 14:23 or 15:33; a few lack these verses altogether [e] **Eph 4:16** *by which it is supplied* NRSV translates *with which it is equipped*

τὴν αὔξησιν τοῦ σώματος ποιεῖται εἰς
οἰκοδομὴν ἑαυτοῦ ἐν ἀγάπῃ.

Phil 1:12–18a

Γινώσκειν δὲ ὑμᾶς βούλομαι, ἀδελφοί,
ὅτι τὰ κατ' ἐμὲ μᾶλλον εἰς προκοπὴν τοῦ
εὐαγγελίου ἐλήλυθεν, **13** ὥστε τοὺς δε-
σμούς μου φανεροὺς ἐν Χριστῷ γενέσθαι
ἐν ὅλῳ τῷ πραιτωρίῳ καὶ τοῖς λοιποῖς
πᾶσιν, **14** καὶ τοὺς πλείονας τῶν ἀδελ-
φῶν ἐν κυρίῳ πεποιθότας τοῖς δεσμοῖς
μου περισσοτέρως τολμᾶν ἀφόβως τὸν
⸀λόγον λαλεῖν. **15** τινὲς μὲν καὶ διὰ φθό-
νον καὶ ἔριν, τινὲς δὲ καὶ δι' εὐδοκίαν
τὸν Χριστὸν κηρύσσουσιν· **16** οἱ μὲν ἐξ
ἀγάπης, εἰδότες ὅτι εἰς ἀπολογίαν τοῦ
εὐαγγελίου κεῖμαι, **17** οἱ δὲ ἐξ ἐριθείας
τὸν Χριστὸν καταγγέλλουσιν, οὐχ ἁγνῶς,
οἰόμενοι θλῖψιν ἐγείρειν τοῖς δεσμοῖς
μου. **18** Τί γάρ; πλὴν ὅτι παντὶ τρόπῳ,
εἴτε προφάσει εἴτε ἀληθείᾳ, Χριστὸς
καταγγέλλεται, καὶ ἐν τούτῳ χαίρω.

Col 1:3–8

Εὐχαριστοῦμεν τῷ θεῷ πατρὶ τοῦ κυρίου
ἡμῶν Ἰησοῦ Χριστοῦ πάντοτε περὶ ὑμῶν
προσευχόμενοι, **4** ἀκούσαντες τὴν πίστιν
ὑμῶν ἐν Χριστῷ Ἰησοῦ καὶ τὴν ἀγάπην
ἣν ἔχετε εἰς πάντας τοὺς ἁγίους **5** διὰ
τὴν ἐλπίδα τὴν ἀποκειμένην ὑμῖν ἐν
τοῖς οὐρανοῖς, ἣν προηκούσατε ἐν τῷ
λόγῳ τῆς ἀληθείας τοῦ εὐαγγελίου **6** τοῦ
παρόντος εἰς ὑμᾶς, καθὼς καὶ ἐν παντὶ
τῷ κόσμῳ ἐστὶν καρποφορούμενον καὶ
αὐξανόμενον καθὼς καὶ ἐν ὑμῖν, ἀφ' ἧς
ἡμέρας ἠκούσατε καὶ ἐπέγνωτε τὴν χάριν
τοῦ θεοῦ ἐν ἀληθείᾳ· **7** καθὼς ἐμάθετε
ἀπὸ Ἐπαφρᾶ τοῦ ἀγαπητοῦ συνδούλου
ἡμῶν, ὅς ἐστιν πιστὸς ὑπὲρ ⸀ὑμῶν διά-
κονος τοῦ Χριστοῦ, **8** ὁ καὶ δηλώσας ἡμῖν
τὴν ὑμῶν ἀγάπην ἐν πνεύματι.

Col 1:21–23

Καὶ ὑμᾶς ποτε ὄντας ἀπηλλοτριωμένους
καὶ ἐχθροὺς τῇ διανοίᾳ ἐν τοῖς ἔργοις τοῖς
πονηροῖς, **22** νυνὶ δὲ ⸀ἀποκατήλλαξεν
ἐν τῷ σώματι τῆς σαρκὸς αὐτοῦ διὰ τοῦ
θανάτου παραστῆσαι ὑμᾶς ἁγίους καὶ
ἀμώμους καὶ ἀνεγκλήτους κατενώπιον
αὐτοῦ, **23** εἴ γε ἐπιμένετε τῇ πίστει τεθεμε-
λιωμένοι καὶ ἑδραῖοι καὶ μὴ μετακινού-
μενοι ἀπὸ τῆς ἐλπίδος τοῦ εὐαγγελίου
οὗ ἠκούσατε, τοῦ κηρυχθέντος ἐν πάσῃ
κτίσει τῇ ὑπὸ τὸν οὐρανόν, οὗ ἐγενόμην
ἐγὼ Παῦλος διάκονος.

1 Tim 3:16

καὶ ὁμολογουμένως μέγα ἐστὶν τὸ τῆς
εὐσεβείας μυστήριον· ⸀ὃς ἐφανερώθη
ἐν σαρκί, ἐδικαιώθη ἐν πνεύματι, ὤφθη
ἀγγέλοις, ἐκηρύχθη ἐν ἔθνεσιν, ἐπιστεύθη
ἐν κόσμῳ, ἀνελήμφθη ἐν δόξῃ.

2 Tim 4:1–5

Διαμαρτύρομαι ἐνώπιον τοῦ θεοῦ καὶ
Χριστοῦ Ἰησοῦ τοῦ μέλλοντος κρίνειν
ζῶντας καὶ νεκρούς, καὶ τὴν ἐπιφάνειαν
αὐτοῦ καὶ τὴν βασιλείαν αὐτοῦ· **2** κή-
ρυξον τὸν λόγον, ἐπίστηθι εὐκαίρως
ἀκαίρως, ἔλεγξον, ἐπιτίμησον, παρακά-
λεσον, ἐν πάσῃ μακροθυμίᾳ καὶ διδαχῇ.
3 Ἔσται γὰρ καιρὸς ὅτε τῆς ὑγιαινούσης
διδασκαλίας οὐκ ἀνέξονται ἀλλὰ κατὰ
τὰς ἰδίας ἐπιθυμίας ἑαυτοῖς ἐπισωρεύ-
σουσιν διδασκάλους κνηθόμενοι τὴν
ἀκοὴν **4** καὶ ἀπὸ μὲν τῆς ἀληθείας τὴν
ἀκοὴν ἀποστρέψουσιν, ἐπὶ δὲ τοὺς μύ-
θους ἐκτραπήσονται. **5** Σὺ δὲ νῆφε ἐν
πᾶσιν, κακοπάθησον, ἔργον ποίησον
εὐαγγελιστοῦ, τὴν διακονίαν σου πλη-
ροφόρησον.

Cf. Rom 1:1–5; 15:14–21; 1 Cor 1:18–25; 4:9–13; 9:1–18; 2 Cor 2:14–17; 3:1–6; 3:7–18; 4:1–6; 5:18–6:2; Gal 3:1–5; Eph 3:1–13; Phil 4:2–3; Col 4:10–17; 1 Tim 2:5–7; 2 Tim 1:6–14; Titus 1:2–3; Acts 13:26–41; 13:46–47; 15:1–35; 16:4–5; 21:8–9; 22:14–15; 26:16–18; 28:28.

See also § 38 Faith and Hearing; § 99 Paul's Apostolic Commission; § 103 Stewards of God.

99. *Paul's Apostolic Commission*

Rom 1:1–5

Παῦλος δοῦλος ⸂Χριστοῦ Ἰησοῦ⸃, κλητὸς
ἀπόστολος ἀφωρισμένος εἰς εὐαγγέ-
λιον θεοῦ, **2** ὃ προεπηγγείλατο διὰ τῶν
προφητῶν αὐτοῦ ἐν γραφαῖς ἁγίαις
3 περὶ τοῦ υἱοῦ αὐτοῦ τοῦ γενομένου
ἐκ σπέρματος Δαυὶδ κατὰ σάρκα, **4** τοῦ
ὁρισθέντος υἱοῦ θεοῦ ἐν δυνάμει κατὰ
πνεῦμα ἁγιωσύνης ἐξ ἀναστάσεως νε-
κρῶν, Ἰησοῦ Χριστοῦ τοῦ κυρίου ἡμῶν,
5 δι' οὗ ἐλάβομεν χάριν καὶ ἀποστολὴν εἰς
ὑπακοὴν πίστεως ἐν πᾶσιν τοῖς ἔθνεσιν
ὑπὲρ τοῦ ὀνόματος αὐτοῦ

Rom 1:13–15

οὐ θέλω δὲ ὑμᾶς ἀγνοεῖν, ἀδελφοί, ὅτι
πολλάκις προεθέμην ἐλθεῖν πρὸς ὑμᾶς,
καὶ ἐκωλύθην ἄχρι τοῦ δεῦρο, ἵνα τινὰ
καρπὸν σχῶ καὶ ἐν ὑμῖν καθὼς καὶ ἐν τοῖς
λοιποῖς ἔθνεσιν. **14** Ἕλλησίν τε καὶ βαρ-
βάροις, σοφοῖς τε καὶ ἀνοήτοις ὀφειλέτης
εἰμί, **15** οὕτως τὸ κατ' ἐμὲ πρόθυμον καὶ
ὑμῖν τοῖς ἐν Ῥώμῃ εὐαγγελίσασθαι.

Rom 15:14–21

Πέπεισμαι δέ, ἀδελφοί μου, καὶ αὐτὸς
ἐγὼ περὶ ὑμῶν ὅτι καὶ αὐτοὶ μεστοί ἐστε
ἀγαθωσύνης, πεπληρωμένοι πάσης [τῆς]
γνώσεως, δυνάμενοι καὶ ἀλλήλους νου-
θετεῖν. **15** τολμηρότερον δὲ ἔγραψα ὑμῖν
ἀπὸ μέρους ὡς ἐπαναμιμνήσκων ὑμᾶς
διὰ τὴν χάριν τὴν δοθεῖσάν μοι ὑπὸ τοῦ
θεοῦ **16** εἰς τὸ εἶναί με λειτουργὸν Χρι-
στοῦ Ἰησοῦ εἰς τὰ ἔθνη, ἱερουργοῦντα
τὸ εὐαγγέλιον τοῦ θεοῦ, ἵνα γένηται ἡ
προσφορὰ τῶν ἐθνῶν εὐπρόσδεκτος,
ἡγιασμένη ἐν πνεύματι ἁγίῳ. **17** ἔχω
οὖν [τὴν] καύχησιν ἐν Χριστῷ Ἰησοῦ
τὰ πρὸς τὸν θεόν· **18** οὐ γὰρ τολμήσω τι
λαλεῖν ὧν οὐ κατειργάσατο Χριστὸς δι'
ἐμοῦ εἰς ὑπακοὴν ἐθνῶν, λόγῳ καὶ ἔργῳ,
19 ἐν δυνάμει σημείων καὶ τεράτων, ἐν

Phil 1:14 ***λογον*** 𝔓^{46} D^{2} 1739. 1881 *Byz*] *add.* του θεου ℵ A B (D*) 048^{vid}. 33 **Col 1:7** ***υμων*** ℵ^{2} C D^{1} 33. 1739. 1881 *Byz*] ημων 𝔓^{46} ℵ* A B D* **Col 1:22** ***αποκατηλλαξεν*** ℵ A C D^{2} 048. 1739. 1881 *Byz*] αποκατηλλαγητε (𝔓^{46}) B ¦ αποκαταλλαγεντες D* ¦ αποκατηλλακται 33 **1 Tim 3:16** ***ος*** ℵ* A* C* 33] ὃ D* ¦ θεος ℵ^{c} A^{c} C^{2} D^{2} 1739. 1881 *Byz* **§ 99** **Rom 1:1** ***Χριστου Ιησου*** 𝔓^{10} B] Ιησου Χριστου 𝔓^{26} ℵ A 33. 1739. 1881 *Byz*

properly, promotes the body's growth in building itself up in love.

Phil 1:12–18a

I want you to know, beloved, that what has happened to me has actually helped to spread the gospel, **13** so that it has become known throughout the whole imperial guard and to everyone else that my imprisonment is for Christ; **14** and most of the brothers and sisters, having been made confident in the Lord by my imprisonment, dare to speak the word[f] with greater boldness and without fear. **15** Some proclaim Christ from envy and rivalry, but others from goodwill. **16** These proclaim Christ out of love, knowing that I have been put here for the defense of the gospel; **17** the others proclaim Christ out of selfish ambition, not sincerely but intending to increase my suffering in my imprisonment. **18** What does it matter? Just this, that Christ is proclaimed in every way, whether out of false motives or true; and in that I rejoice.

Col 1:3–8

In our prayers for you we always thank God, the Father of our Lord Jesus Christ, **4** for we have heard of your faith in Christ Jesus and of the love that you have for all the saints, **5** because of the hope laid up for you in heaven. You have heard of this hope before in the word of the truth, the gospel **6** that has come to you. Just as it is bearing fruit and growing in the whole world, so it has been bearing fruit among yourselves from the day you heard it and truly comprehended the grace of God. **7** This you learned from Epaphras, our beloved fellow servant. He is a faithful minister of Christ on your[g] behalf, **8** and he has made known to us your love in the Spirit.

Col 1:21–23

And you who were once estranged and hostile in mind, doing evil deeds, **22** he has now reconciled[h] in his fleshly body through death, so as to present you holy and blameless and irreproachable before him— **23** provided that you continue securely established and steadfast in the faith, without shifting from the hope promised by the gospel that you heard, which has been proclaimed to every creature under heaven. I, Paul, became a servant of this gospel.

1 Tim 3:16

Without any doubt, the mystery of our religion is great: Who[i] was revealed in flesh, vindicated by the Spirit,[j] seen by angels, proclaimed among Gentiles, believed in throughout the world, taken up in glory.

2 Tim 4:1–5

In the presence of God and of Christ Jesus, who is to judge the living and the dead, and in view of his appearing and his kingdom, I solemnly urge you: **2** proclaim the message; be persistent whether the time is favorable or unfavorable; convince, rebuke, and encourage, with the utmost patience in teaching. **3** For the time is coming when people will not put up with sound doctrine, but having itching ears, they will accumulate for themselves teachers to suit their own desires, **4** and will turn away from listening to the truth and wander away to myths. **5** As for you, always be sober, endure suffering, do the work of an evangelist, carry out your ministry fully.

Cf. Rom 1:1–5; 15:14–21; 1 Cor 1:18–25; 4:9–13; 9:1–18; 2 Cor 2:14–17; 3:1–6; 3:7–18; 4:1–6; 5:18–6:2; Gal 3:1–5; Eph 3:1–13; Phil 4:2–3; Col 4:10–17; 1 Tim 2:5–7; 2 Tim 1:6–14; Titus 1:2–3; Acts 13:26–41; 13:46–47; 15:1–35; 16:4–5; 21:8–9; 22:14–15; 26:16–18; 28:28.

See also § 38 Faith and Hearing; § 99 Paul's Apostolic Commission; § 103 Stewards of God.

99. *Paul's Apostolic Commission*

Rom 1:1–5

Paul, a servant of Jesus Christ,[a] called to be an apostle, set apart for the gospel of God, **2** which he promised beforehand through his prophets in the holy scriptures, **3** the gospel concerning his Son, who was descended from David according to the flesh **4** and was declared to be Son of God with power according to the Spirit[b] of holiness by resurrection from the dead, Jesus Christ our Lord, **5** through whom we have received grace and apostleship to bring about the obedience of faith among all the Gentiles for the sake of his name

Rom 1:13–15

I want you to know, brothers and sisters, that I have often intended to come to you (but thus far have been prevented), in order that I may reap some harvest among you as I have among the rest of the Gentiles. **14** I am a debtor both to Greeks and to barbarians, both to the wise and to the foolish **15**—hence my eagerness to proclaim the gospel to you also who are in Rome.

Rom 15:14–21

I myself feel confident about you, my brothers and sisters, that you yourselves are full of goodness, filled with all knowledge, and able to instruct one another. **15** Nevertheless on some points I have written to you rather boldly by way of reminder, because of the grace given me by God **16** to be a minister of Christ Jesus to the Gentiles in the priestly service of the gospel of God, so that the offering of the Gentiles may be acceptable, sanctified by the Holy Spirit. **17** In Christ Jesus, then, I have reason to boast of my work for God. **18** For I will not venture to speak of anything except what Christ has accomplished through me to win obedience from the Gentiles, by word and deed, **19** by the power of signs and wonders, by the power of

[f] **Phil 1:14** *word* Other ancient authorities read *word of God* [g] **Col 1:7** *your* Other ancient authorities read *our* [h] **Col 1:22** *he has now reconciled* Other ancient authorities read *you have now been reconciled* [i] **1 Tim 3:16** *Who* Other ancient authorities read *God*; others, *Which*. NRSV translates Gk *Who* as *He* [j] **1 Tim 3:16** *by the Spirit* NRSV alternate translation **§ 99** [a] **Rom 1:1** *Jesus Christ* Other ancient authorities read *Christ Jesus* [b] **Rom 1:4** *Spirit* NRSV alternate translation

δυνάμει πνεύματος ⸀[θεοῦ]· ὥστε με ἀπὸ Ἰερουσαλὴμ καὶ κύκλῳ μέχρι τοῦ Ἰλλυρικοῦ πεπληρωκέναι τὸ εὐαγγέλιον τοῦ Χριστοῦ, **20** οὕτως δὲ φιλοτιμούμενον εὐαγγελίζεσθαι οὐχ ὅπου ὠνομάσθη Χριστός, ἵνα μὴ ἐπ᾽ ἀλλότριον θεμέλιον οἰκοδομῶ, **21** ἀλλὰ καθὼς γέγραπται· οἷς οὐκ ἀνηγγέλη περὶ αὐτοῦ ὄψονται, καὶ οἳ οὐκ ἀκηκόασιν συνήσουσιν.

1 Cor 9:1–2

Οὐκ εἰμὶ ἐλεύθερος; οὐκ εἰμὶ ἀπόστολος; οὐχὶ Ἰησοῦν τὸν κύριον ἡμῶν ἑόρακα; οὐ τὸ ἔργον μου ὑμεῖς ἐστε ἐν κυρίῳ; **2** εἰ ἄλλοις οὐκ εἰμὶ ἀπόστολος, ἀλλά γε ὑμῖν εἰμι· ἡ γὰρ σφραγίς μου τῆς ἀποστολῆς ὑμεῖς ἐστε ἐν κυρίῳ.

1 Cor 9:16–18

ἐὰν γὰρ εὐαγγελίζωμαι, οὐκ ἔστιν μοι καύχημα· ἀνάγκη γάρ μοι ἐπίκειται· οὐαὶ γάρ μοί ἐστιν ἐὰν μὴ εὐαγγελίσωμαι. **17** εἰ γὰρ ἑκὼν τοῦτο πράσσω, μισθὸν ἔχω· εἰ δὲ ἄκων, οἰκονομίαν πεπίστευμαι· **18** τίς οὖν μού ἐστιν ὁ μισθός; ἵνα εὐαγγελιζόμενος ἀδάπανον θήσω τὸ εὐαγγέλιον εἰς τὸ μὴ καταχρήσασθαι τῇ ἐξουσίᾳ μου ἐν τῷ εὐαγγελίῳ.

1 Cor 15:3–11

παρέδωκα γὰρ ὑμῖν ἐν πρώτοις, ὃ καὶ παρέλαβον, ὅτι Χριστὸς ἀπέθανεν ὑπὲρ τῶν ἁμαρτιῶν ἡμῶν κατὰ τὰς γραφὰς **4** καὶ ὅτι ἐτάφη καὶ ὅτι ἐγήγερται τῇ ἡμέρᾳ τῇ τρίτῃ κατὰ τὰς γραφὰς **5** καὶ ὅτι ὤφθη Κηφᾷ εἶτα τοῖς δώδεκα· **6** ἔπειτα ὤφθη ἐπάνω πεντακοσίοις ἀδελφοῖς ἐφάπαξ, ἐξ ὧν οἱ πλείονες μένουσιν ἕως ἄρτι, τινὲς δὲ ἐκοιμήθησαν· **7** ἔπειτα ὤφθη Ἰακώβῳ εἶτα τοῖς ἀποστόλοις πᾶσιν· **8** ἔσχατον δὲ πάντων ὡσπερεὶ τῷ ἐκτρώματι ὤφθη κἀμοί. **9** Ἐγὼ γάρ εἰμι ὁ ἐλάχιστος τῶν ἀποστόλων ὃς οὐκ εἰμὶ ἱκανὸς καλεῖσθαι ἀπόστολος, διότι ἐδίωξα τὴν ἐκκλησίαν τοῦ θεοῦ· **10** χάριτι δὲ θεοῦ εἰμι ὅ εἰμι, καὶ ἡ χάρις αὐτοῦ ἡ εἰς ἐμὲ οὐ κενὴ ἐγενήθη, ἀλλὰ περισσότερον αὐτῶν πάντων ἐκοπίασα, οὐκ ἐγὼ δὲ ἀλλὰ ἡ χάρις τοῦ θεοῦ [ἡ] σὺν ἐμοί. **11** εἴτε οὖν ἐγὼ εἴτε ἐκεῖνοι, οὕτως κηρύσσομεν καὶ οὕτως ἐπιστεύσατε.

2 Cor 2:14–17

Τῷ δὲ θεῷ χάρις τῷ πάντοτε θριαμβεύοντι ἡμᾶς ἐν τῷ Χριστῷ καὶ τὴν ὀσμὴν τῆς γνώσεως αὐτοῦ φανεροῦντι δι᾽ ἡμῶν ἐν παντὶ τόπῳ· **15** ὅτι Χριστοῦ εὐωδία ἐσμὲν τῷ θεῷ ἐν τοῖς σῳζομένοις καὶ ἐν τοῖς ἀπολλυμένοις, **16** οἷς μὲν ὀσμὴ ἐκ θανάτου εἰς θάνατον, οἷς δὲ ὀσμὴ ἐκ ζωῆς εἰς ζωήν. καὶ πρὸς ταῦτα τίς ἱκανός; **17** οὐ γάρ ἐσμεν ὡς οἱ ⸀πολλοὶ καπηλεύοντες τὸν λόγον τοῦ θεοῦ, ἀλλ᾽ ὡς ἐξ εἰλικρινείας, ἀλλ᾽ ὡς ἐκ θεοῦ κατέναντι θεοῦ ἐν Χριστῷ λαλοῦμεν.

2 Cor 3:1–6

Ἀρχόμεθα πάλιν ἑαυτοὺς συνιστάνειν; ἢ μὴ χρῄζομεν ὥς τινες συστατικῶν ἐπιστολῶν πρὸς ὑμᾶς ἢ ἐξ ὑμῶν; **2** ἡ ἐπιστολὴ ἡμῶν ὑμεῖς ἐστε, ἐγγεγραμμένη ἐν ταῖς καρδίαις ⸀ἡμῶν, γινωσκομένη καὶ ἀναγινωσκομένη ὑπὸ πάντων ἀνθρώπων, **3** φανερούμενοι ὅτι ἐστὲ ἐπιστολὴ Χριστοῦ διακονηθεῖσα ὑφ᾽ ἡμῶν, ἐγγεγραμμένη οὐ μέλανι ἀλλὰ πνεύματι θεοῦ ζῶντος, οὐκ ἐν πλαξὶν λιθίναις ἀλλ᾽ ἐν πλαξὶν καρδίαις σαρκίναις. **4** Πεποίθησιν δὲ τοιαύτην ἔχομεν διὰ τοῦ Χριστοῦ πρὸς τὸν θεόν. **5** οὐχ ὅτι ἀφ᾽ ἑαυτῶν ἱκανοί ἐσμεν λογίσασθαί τι ὡς ἐξ ἑαυτῶν, ἀλλ᾽ ἡ ἱκανότης ἡμῶν ἐκ τοῦ θεοῦ, **6** ὃς καὶ ἱκάνωσεν ἡμᾶς διακόνους καινῆς διαθήκης, οὐ γράμματος ἀλλὰ πνεύματος· τὸ γὰρ γράμμα ἀποκτέννει, τὸ δὲ πνεῦμα ζῳοποιεῖ.

2 Cor 5:18–6:2

τὰ δὲ πάντα ἐκ τοῦ θεοῦ τοῦ καταλλάξαντος ἡμᾶς ἑαυτῷ διὰ Χριστοῦ καὶ δόντος ἡμῖν τὴν διακονίαν τῆς καταλλαγῆς, **19** ὡς ὅτι θεὸς ἦν ἐν Χριστῷ κόσμον καταλλάσσων ἑαυτῷ, μὴ λογιζόμενος αὐτοῖς τὰ παραπτώματα αὐτῶν καὶ θέμενος ἐν ἡμῖν τὸν λόγον τῆς καταλλαγῆς. **20** Ὑπὲρ Χριστοῦ οὖν πρεσβεύομεν ὡς τοῦ θεοῦ παρακαλοῦντος δι᾽ ἡμῶν· δεόμεθα ὑπὲρ Χριστοῦ, καταλλάγητε τῷ θεῷ. **21** τὸν μὴ γνόντα ἁμαρτίαν ὑπὲρ ἡμῶν ἁμαρτίαν ἐποίησεν, ἵνα ἡμεῖς γενώμεθα δικαιοσύνη θεοῦ ἐν αὐτῷ. **6** Συνεργοῦντες δὲ καὶ παρακαλοῦμεν μὴ εἰς κενὸν τὴν χάριν τοῦ θεοῦ δέξασθαι ὑμᾶς· **2** λέγει γάρ· καιρῷ δεκτῷ ἐπήκουσά σου καὶ ἐν ἡμέρᾳ σωτηρίας ἐβοήθησά σοι. ἰδοὺ νῦν καιρὸς εὐπρόσδεκτος, ἰδοὺ νῦν ἡμέρα σωτηρίας.

Gal 1:13–17

Ἠκούσατε γὰρ τὴν ἐμὴν ἀναστροφήν ποτε ἐν τῷ Ἰουδαϊσμῷ, ὅτι καθ᾽ ὑπερβολὴν ἐδίωκον τὴν ἐκκλησίαν τοῦ θεοῦ καὶ ἐπόρθουν αὐτήν, **14** καὶ προέκοπτον ἐν τῷ Ἰουδαϊσμῷ ὑπὲρ πολλοὺς συνηλικιώτας ἐν τῷ γένει μου, περισσοτέρως ζηλωτὴς ὑπάρχων τῶν πατρικῶν μου παραδόσεων. **15** Ὅτε δὲ εὐδόκησεν [ὁ θεὸς] ὁ ἀφορίσας με ἐκ κοιλίας μητρός μου καὶ καλέσας διὰ τῆς χάριτος αὐτοῦ **16** ἀποκαλύψαι τὸν υἱὸν αὐτοῦ ἐν ἐμοί, ἵνα εὐαγγελίζωμαι αὐτὸν ἐν τοῖς ἔθνεσιν, εὐθέως οὐ προσανεθέμην σαρκὶ καὶ αἵματι **17** οὐδὲ ἀνῆλθον εἰς Ἱεροσόλυμα πρὸς τοὺς πρὸ ἐμοῦ ἀποστόλους, ἀλλὰ ἀπῆλθον εἰς Ἀραβίαν καὶ πάλιν ὑπέστρεψα εἰς Δαμασκόν.

Eph 3:1–13

Τούτου χάριν ἐγὼ Παῦλος ὁ δέσμιος τοῦ Χριστοῦ [Ἰησοῦ] ὑπὲρ ὑμῶν τῶν ἐθνῶν **2** —εἴ γε ἠκούσατε τὴν οἰκονομίαν τῆς χάριτος τοῦ θεοῦ τῆς δοθείσης μοι εἰς ὑμᾶς, **3** [ὅτι] κατὰ ἀποκάλυψιν ἐγνωρίσθη μοι τὸ μυστήριον, καθὼς προέγραψα ἐν ὀλίγῳ, **4** πρὸς ὃ δύνασθε ἀναγινώσκοντες νοῆσαι τὴν σύνεσίν μου ἐν τῷ μυστηρίῳ τοῦ Χριστοῦ, **5** ὃ ἑτέραις γενεαῖς οὐκ ἐγνωρίσθη τοῖς υἱοῖς τῶν ἀνθρώπων ὡς νῦν ἀπεκαλύφθη τοῖς ἁγίοις ἀποστόλοις αὐτοῦ καὶ προφήταις ἐν πνεύματι, **6** εἶναι τὰ ἔθνη συγκληρονόμα καὶ σύσσωμα καὶ συμμέτοχα τῆς ἐπαγγελίας ἐν Χριστῷ Ἰησοῦ διὰ τοῦ εὐαγγελίου, **7** οὗ ἐγενήθην διάκονος κατὰ τὴν δωρεὰν τῆς χάριτος τοῦ θεοῦ τῆς δοθείσης μοι κατὰ τὴν ἐνέργειαν τῆς δυνάμεως αὐτοῦ. **8** Ἐμοὶ τῷ ἐλαχιστοτέρῳ πάντων ἁγίων

Rom 15:19 ***θεου*** 𝔓[46] ℵ D[1] *Byz*] *om.* B ¦ αγιου A D[*.2] 33. 1739. 1881 **2 Cor 2:17** ***πολλοι*** ℵ A B C 33. 1739. 1881 *Byz*] λοιποι 𝔓[46] D **2 Cor 3:2** ***ημων*** 𝔓[46] A B C D 1739 *Byz*] υμων ℵ 33. 1881

the Spirit of God,[c] so that from Jerusalem and as far around as Illyricum I have fully proclaimed the good news of Christ. **20** Thus I make it my ambition to proclaim the good news, not where Christ has already been named, so that I do not build on someone else's foundation, **21** but as it is written, "Those who have never been told of him shall see, and those who have never heard of him shall understand."

1 Cor 9:1–2

Am I not free? Am I not an apostle? Have I not seen Jesus our Lord? Are you not my work in the Lord? **2** If I am not an apostle to others, at least I am to you; for you are the seal of my apostleship in the Lord.

1 Cor 9:16–18

If I proclaim the gospel, this gives me no ground for boasting, for an obligation is laid on me, and woe to me if I do not proclaim the gospel! **17** For if I do this of my own will, I have a reward; but if not of my own will, I am entrusted with a commission. **18** What then is my reward? Just this: that in my proclamation I may make the gospel free of charge, so as not to make full use of my rights in the gospel.

1 Cor 15:3–11

For I handed on to you as of first importance what I in turn had received: that Christ died for our sins in accordance with the scriptures, **4** and that he was buried, and that he was raised on the third day in accordance with the scriptures, **5** and that he appeared to Cephas, then to the twelve. **6** Then he appeared to more than five hundred brothers and sisters at one time, most of whom are still alive, though some have died. **7** Then he appeared to James, then to all the apostles. **8** Last of all, as to one untimely born, he appeared also to me. **9** For I am the least of the apostles, unfit to be called an apostle, because I persecuted the church of God. **10** But by the grace of God I am what I am, and his grace toward me has not been in vain. On the contrary, I worked harder than any of them—though it was not I, but the grace of God that is with me. **11** Whether then it was I or they, so we proclaim and so you have come to believe.

2 Cor 2:14–17

But thanks be to God, who in Christ always leads us in triumphal procession, and through us spreads in every place the fragrance that comes from knowing him. **15** For we are the aroma of Christ to God among those who are being saved and among those who are perishing; **16** to the one a fragrance from death to death, to the other a fragrance from life to life. Who is sufficient for these things? **17** For we are not peddlers of God's word like so many;[d] but in Christ we speak as persons of sincerity, as persons sent from God and standing in his presence.

2 Cor 3:1–6

Are we beginning to commend ourselves again? Surely we do not need, as some do, letters of recommendation to you or from you, do we? **2** You yourselves are our letter, written on our[e] hearts, to be known and read by all; **3** and you show that you are a letter of Christ, prepared by us, written not with ink but with the Spirit of the living God, not on tablets of stone but on tablets of human hearts. **4** Such is the confidence that we have through Christ toward God. **5** Not that we are competent of ourselves to claim anything as coming from us; our competence is from God, **6** who has made us competent to be ministers of a new covenant, not of the letter but of the Spirit; for the letter kills, but the Spirit gives life.[f]

2 Cor 5:18–6:2

All this is from God, who reconciled us to himself through Christ, and has given us the ministry of reconciliation; **19** that is, God was in Christ, reconciling[g] the world to himself, not counting their trespasses against them, and entrusting the message of reconciliation to us. **20** So we are ambassadors for Christ, since God is making his appeal through us; we entreat you on behalf of Christ, be reconciled to God. **21** For our sake he made him to be sin who knew no sin, so that in him we might become the righteousness of God. **6** As we work together with him, we urge you also not to accept the grace of God in vain. **2** For he says, "At an acceptable time I have listened to you, and on a day of salvation I have helped you." See, now is the acceptable time; see, now is the day of salvation!

Gal 1:13–17

You have heard, no doubt, of my earlier life in Judaism. I was violently persecuting the church of God and was trying to destroy it. **14** I advanced in Judaism beyond many among my people of the same age, for I was far more zealous for the traditions of my ancestors. **15** But when God, who had set me apart before I was born and called me through his grace, was pleased **16** to reveal his Son to me, so that I might proclaim him among the Gentiles, I did not confer with any human being, **17** nor did I go up to Jerusalem to those who were already apostles before me, but I went away at once into Arabia, and afterwards I returned to Damascus.

Eph 3:1–13

This is the reason that I Paul am a prisoner for Christ Jesus for the sake of you Gentiles— **2** for surely you have already heard of the commission of God's grace that was given me for you, **3** and how the mystery was made known to me by revelation, as I wrote above in a few words, **4** a reading of which will enable you to perceive my understanding of the mystery of Christ. **5** In former generations this mystery was not made known to humankind, as it has now been revealed to his holy apostles and prophets by the Spirit: **6** that is, the Gentiles have become fellow heirs, members of the same body, and sharers in the promise in Christ Jesus through the gospel. **7** Of this gospel I have become a servant according to the gift of God's grace that was given me by the working of his power. **8** Although I am the very

[c] **Rom 15:19** ***of the Spirit of God*** Other ancient authorities read *of the Spirit* or *of the Holy Spirit* [d] **2 Cor 2:17** ***like so many*** Other ancient authorities read *like the others* [e] **2 Cor 3:2** ***our*** Other ancient authorities read *your* [f] **2 Cor 3:6** Translation differs from NRSV [g] **2 Cor 5:19** ***God was in Christ, reconciling*** Or possibly *in Christ God was reconciling* (so NRSV)

ἐδόθη ἡ χάρις αὕτη, τοῖς ἔθνεσιν εὐαγγελίσασθαι τὸ ἀνεξιχνίαστον πλοῦτος τοῦ Χριστοῦ **9** καὶ φωτίσαι ⸀[πάντας] τίς ἡ οἰκονομία τοῦ μυστηρίου τοῦ ἀποκεκρυμμένου ἀπὸ τῶν αἰώνων ἐν τῷ θεῷ τῷ τὰ πάντα κτίσαντι, **10** ἵνα γνωρισθῇ νῦν ταῖς ἀρχαῖς καὶ ταῖς ἐξουσίαις ἐν τοῖς ἐπουρανίοις διὰ τῆς ἐκκλησίας ἡ πολυποίκιλος σοφία τοῦ θεοῦ, **11** κατὰ πρόθεσιν τῶν αἰώνων ἣν ἐποίησεν ἐν τῷ Χριστῷ Ἰησοῦ τῷ κυρίῳ ἡμῶν, **12** ἐν ᾧ ἔχομεν τὴν παρρησίαν καὶ προσαγωγὴν ἐν πεποιθήσει διὰ τῆς πίστεως αὐτοῦ. **13** διὸ αἰτοῦμαι μὴ ἐγκακεῖν ἐν ταῖς θλίψεσίν μου ὑπὲρ ὑμῶν, ἥτις ἐστὶν δόξα ὑμῶν.

Col 1:24–29

Νῦν χαίρω ἐν τοῖς παθήμασιν ὑπὲρ ὑμῶν καὶ ἀνταναπληρῶ τὰ ὑστερήματα τῶν θλίψεων τοῦ Χριστοῦ ἐν τῇ σαρκί μου ὑπὲρ τοῦ σώματος αὐτοῦ, ὅ ἐστιν ἡ ἐκκλησία, **25** ἧς ἐγενόμην ἐγὼ διάκονος κατὰ τὴν οἰκονομίαν τοῦ θεοῦ τὴν δοθεῖσάν μοι εἰς ὑμᾶς πληρῶσαι τὸν λόγον τοῦ θεοῦ, **26** τὸ μυστήριον τὸ ἀποκεκρυμμένον ἀπὸ τῶν αἰώνων καὶ ἀπὸ τῶν γενεῶν—νῦν δὲ ἐφανερώθη τοῖς ἁγίοις αὐτοῦ, **27** οἷς ἠθέλησεν ὁ θεὸς γνωρίσαι τί τὸ πλοῦτος τῆς δόξης τοῦ μυστηρίου τούτου ἐν τοῖς ἔθνεσιν, ὅ ἐστιν Χριστὸς ἐν ὑμῖν, ἡ ἐλπὶς τῆς δόξης· **28** ὃν ἡμεῖς καταγγέλλομεν νουθετοῦντες πάντα ἄνθρωπον καὶ διδάσκοντες πάντα ἄνθρωπον ἐν πάσῃ σοφίᾳ, ἵνα παραστήσωμεν πάντα ἄνθρωπον τέλειον ἐν Χριστῷ· **29** εἰς ὃ καὶ κοπιῶ ἀγωνιζόμενος κατὰ τὴν ἐνέργειαν αὐτοῦ τὴν ἐνεργουμένην ἐν ἐμοὶ ἐν δυνάμει.

1 Thess 2:4

ἀλλὰ καθὼς δεδοκιμάσμεθα ὑπὸ τοῦ θεοῦ πιστευθῆναι τὸ εὐαγγέλιον, οὕτως λαλοῦμεν, οὐχ ὡς ἀνθρώποις ἀρέσκοντες ἀλλὰ θεῷ τῷ δοκιμάζοντι τὰς καρδίας ἡμῶν.

1 Tim 2:5–7

Εἷς γὰρ θεός, εἷς καὶ μεσίτης θεοῦ καὶ ἀνθρώπων, ἄνθρωπος Χριστὸς Ἰησοῦς, **6** ὁ δοὺς ἑαυτὸν ἀντίλυτρον ὑπὲρ πάντων, τὸ μαρτύριον καιροῖς ἰδίοις. **7** εἰς ὃ ἐτέθην ἐγὼ κῆρυξ καὶ ἀπόστολος, ἀλήθειαν ⸀λέγω οὐ ψεύδομαι, διδάσκαλος ἐθνῶν ἐν πίστει καὶ ἀληθείᾳ.

2 Tim 1:11

εἰς ὃ ἐτέθην ἐγὼ κῆρυξ καὶ ἀπόστολος καὶ ⸀διδάσκαλος

Titus 1:2–3

ἐπ᾽ ἐλπίδι ζωῆς αἰωνίου, ἣν ἐπηγγείλατο ὁ ἀψευδὴς θεὸς πρὸ χρόνων αἰωνίων, **3** ἐφανέρωσεν δὲ καιροῖς ἰδίοις τὸν λόγον αὐτοῦ ἐν κηρύγματι, ὃ ἐπιστεύθην ἐγὼ κατ᾽ ἐπιταγὴν τοῦ σωτῆρος ἡμῶν θεοῦ

Acts 9:15–16

εἶπεν δὲ πρὸς αὐτὸν ὁ κύριος· πορεύου, ὅτι σκεῦος ἐκλογῆς ἐστίν μοι οὗτος τοῦ βαστάσαι τὸ ὄνομά μου ἐνώπιον ἐθνῶν τε καὶ βασιλέων υἱῶν τε Ἰσραήλ· **16** ἐγὼ γὰρ ὑποδείξω αὐτῷ ὅσα δεῖ αὐτὸν ὑπὲρ τοῦ ὀνόματός μου παθεῖν.

Acts 20:24

ἀλλ᾽ οὐδενὸς λόγου ποιοῦμαι τὴν ψυχὴν τιμίαν ἐμαυτῷ ὡς τελειῶσαι τὸν δρόμον μου καὶ τὴν διακονίαν ἣν ἔλαβον παρὰ τοῦ κυρίου Ἰησοῦ, διαμαρτύρασθαι τὸ εὐαγγέλιον τῆς χάριτος τοῦ θεοῦ.

Acts 26:16–18

ἀλλὰ ἀνάστηθι καὶ στῆθι ἐπὶ τοὺς πόδας σου· εἰς τοῦτο γὰρ ὤφθην σοι, προχειρίσασθαί σε ὑπηρέτην καὶ μάρτυρα ὧν τε εἶδές ⸀[με] ὧν τε ὀφθήσομαί σοι, **17** ἐξαιρούμενός σε ἐκ τοῦ λαοῦ καὶ ἐκ τῶν ἐθνῶν εἰς οὓς ἐγὼ ἀποστέλλω σε **18** ἀνοῖξαι ὀφθαλμοὺς αὐτῶν, τοῦ ἐπιστρέψαι ἀπὸ σκότους εἰς φῶς καὶ τῆς ἐξουσίας τοῦ σατανᾶ ἐπὶ τὸν θεόν, τοῦ λαβεῖν αὐτοὺς ἄφεσιν ἁμαρτιῶν καὶ κλῆρον ἐν τοῖς ἡγιασμένοις πίστει τῇ εἰς ἐμέ.

Cf. 1 Cor 1:17; 2 Cor 12:11–12; Gal 2:6–9; Acts 13:1–3; 14:4; 14:14–15.

See also § 100 The Divine Origin and Authority of Paul's Teaching. For the accounts in Paul and Acts of the event of Paul's conversion and call, see § 163 Paul's Commissioning by the Risen Lord.

100. The Divine Origin and Authority of Paul's Teaching

2 Cor 10:1–6

Αὐτὸς δὲ ἐγὼ Παῦλος παρακαλῶ ὑμᾶς διὰ τῆς πραΰτητος καὶ ἐπιεικείας τοῦ Χριστοῦ, ὃς κατὰ πρόσωπον μὲν ταπεινὸς ἐν ὑμῖν, ἀπὼν δὲ θαρρῶ εἰς ὑμᾶς· **2** δέομαι δὲ τὸ μὴ παρὼν θαρρῆσαι τῇ πεποιθήσει ᾗ λογίζομαι τολμῆσαι ἐπί τινας τοὺς λογιζομένους ἡμᾶς ὡς κατὰ σάρκα περιπατοῦντας. **3** Ἐν σαρκὶ γὰρ περιπατοῦντες οὐ κατὰ σάρκα στρατευόμεθα, **4** τὰ γὰρ ὅπλα τῆς στρατείας ἡμῶν οὐ σαρκικὰ ἀλλὰ δυνατὰ τῷ θεῷ πρὸς καθαίρεσιν ὀχυρωμάτων, λογισμοὺς καθαιροῦντες **5** καὶ πᾶν ὕψωμα ἐπαιρόμενον κατὰ τῆς γνώσεως τοῦ θεοῦ, καὶ αἰχμαλωτίζοντες πᾶν νόημα εἰς τὴν ὑπακοὴν τοῦ Χριστοῦ, **6** καὶ ἐν ἑτοίμῳ ἔχοντες ἐκδικῆσαι πᾶσαν παρακοήν, ὅταν πληρωθῇ ὑμῶν ἡ ὑπακοή.

2 Cor 13:10

Διὰ τοῦτο ταῦτα ἀπὼν γράφω, ἵνα παρὼν μὴ ἀποτόμως χρήσωμαι κατὰ τὴν ἐξουσίαν ἣν ὁ κύριος ἔδωκέν μοι εἰς οἰκοδομὴν καὶ οὐκ εἰς καθαίρεσιν.

Gal 1:11–12

Γνωρίζω γὰρ ὑμῖν, ἀδελφοί, τὸ εὐαγγέλιον τὸ εὐαγγελισθὲν ὑπ᾽ ἐμοῦ ὅτι οὐκ ἔστιν κατὰ ἄνθρωπον· **12** οὐδὲ γὰρ ἐγὼ παρὰ ἀνθρώπου παρέλαβον αὐτὸ οὔτε ἐδιδάχθην ἀλλὰ δι᾽ ἀποκαλύψεως Ἰησοῦ Χριστοῦ.

Gal 2:6–9

Ἀπὸ δὲ τῶν δοκούντων εἶναί τι,—ὁποῖοί ποτε ἦσαν οὐδέν μοι διαφέρει· πρόσωπον [ὁ] θεὸς ἀνθρώπου οὐ λαμβάνει—ἐμοὶ γὰρ οἱ δοκοῦντες οὐδὲν προσανέθεντο, **7** ἀλλὰ τοὐναντίον ἰδόντες ὅτι πεπίστευμαι τὸ εὐαγγέλιον τῆς ἀκροβυ

Eph 3:9 ***παντας*** 𝔓^{46} ℵ^{2} B C D 33 *Byz*] *om.* ℵ* A 1739. 1881 **1 Tim 2:7** ***λεγω*** ℵ^{2} A D* 1739. 1881] *add.* εν Χριστω ℵ* D^{2} 33^{vid} *Byz* **2 Tim 1:11** ***διδασκαλος*** ℵ* A I] *add.* εθνων ℵ^{2} C D 1739. 1881 *Byz* ¦ διακονος 33 **Acts 26:16** ***με*** B C^{*vid} 1739] *om.* 𝔓^{74} ℵ A C^{2} E *Byz*

least of all the saints, this grace was given to me to bring to the Gentiles the news of the boundless riches of Christ, **9** and to make everyone see[h] what is the plan of the mystery hidden for ages in God who created all things; **10** so that through the church the wisdom of God in its rich variety might now be made known to the rulers and authorities in the heavenly places. **11** This was in accordance with the eternal purpose that he has carried out in Christ Jesus our Lord, **12** in whom we have access to God in boldness and confidence through faith in him. **13** I pray therefore that you may not lose heart over my sufferings for you; they are your glory.

Col 1:24–29

I am now rejoicing in my sufferings for your sake, and in my flesh I am completing what is lacking in Christ's afflictions for the sake of his body, that is, the church. **25** I became its servant according to God's commission that was given to me for you, to make the word of God fully known, **26** the mystery that has been hidden throughout the ages and generations but has now been revealed to his saints. **27** To them God chose to make known how great among the Gentiles are the riches of the glory of this mystery, which is Christ in you, the hope of glory. **28** It is he whom we proclaim, warning everyone and teaching everyone in all wisdom, so that we may present everyone mature in Christ. **29** For this I toil and struggle with all the energy that he powerfully inspires within me.

1 Thess 2:4

but just as we have been approved by God to be entrusted with the message of the gospel, even so we speak, not to please mortals, but to please God who tests our hearts.

1 Tim 2:5–7

For there is one God; there is also one mediator between God and humankind, Christ Jesus, himself human, **6** who gave himself a ransom for all —this was attested at the right time. **7** For this I was appointed a herald and an apostle (I am telling the truth,[i] I am not lying), a teacher of the Gentiles in faith and truth.

2 Tim 1:11

For this gospel I was appointed a herald and an apostle and a teacher[j]

Titus 1:2–3

in the hope of eternal life that God, who never lies, promised before the ages began— **3** in due time he revealed his word through the proclamation with which I have been entrusted by the command of God our Savior

Acts 9:15–16

But the Lord said to him, "Go, for he is an instrument whom I have chosen to bring my name before Gentiles and kings and before the people of Israel; **16** I myself will show him how much he must suffer for the sake of my name."

Acts 20:24

But I do not count my life of any value to myself, if only I may finish my course and the ministry that I received from the Lord Jesus, to testify to the good news of God's grace.

Acts 26:16–18

But get up and stand on your feet; for I have appeared to you for this purpose, to appoint you to serve and testify to the things in which you have seen me[k] and to those in which I will appear to you. **17** I will rescue you from your people and from the Gentiles—to whom I am sending you **18** to open their eyes so that they may turn from darkness to light and from the power of Satan to God, so that they may receive forgiveness of sins and a place among those who are sanctified by faith in me.

Cf. 1 Cor 1:17; 2 Cor 12:11–12; Gal 2:6–9; Acts 13:1–3; 14:4; 14:14–15.

See also § 100 The Divine Origin and Authority of Paul's Teaching. For the accounts in Paul and Acts of the event of Paul's conversion and call, see § 163 Paul's Commissioning by the Risen Lord.

100. The Divine Origin and Authority of Paul's Teaching

2 Cor 10:1–6

I myself, Paul, appeal to you by the meekness and gentleness of Christ—I who am humble when face to face with you, but bold toward you when I am away!— **2** I ask that when I am present I need not show boldness by daring to oppose those who think we are acting according to human standards. **3** Indeed, we live as human beings, but we do not wage war according to human standards; **4** for the weapons of our warfare are not merely human, but they have divine power to destroy strongholds. We destroy arguments **5** and every proud obstacle raised up against the knowledge of God, and we take every thought captive to obey Christ. **6** We are ready to punish every disobedience when your obedience is complete.

2 Cor 13:10

So I write these things while I am away from you, so that when I come, I may not have to be severe in using the authority that the Lord has given me for building up and not for tearing down.

Gal 1:11–12

For I want you to know, brothers and sisters, that the gospel that was proclaimed by me is not of human origin; **12** for I did not receive it from a human source, nor was I taught it, but I received it through a revelation of Jesus Christ.

Gal 2:6–9

And from those who were supposed to be acknowledged leaders (what they actually were makes no difference to me; God shows no partiality)—those leaders contributed nothing to me. **7** On the contrary, when they saw that I had been entrusted with the gospel for the uncircumcised, just as Peter had been

[h] **Eph 3:9** ***to make everyone see*** Other ancient authorities read *to bring to light* [i] **1 Tim 2:7** ***telling the truth*** Other ancient authorities add *in Christ* [j] **2 Tim 1:11** ***teacher*** Other ancient authorities add *of the Gentiles* [k] **Acts 26:16** ***the things in which you have seen me*** Other ancient authorities read *the things that you have seen*

στίας καθὼς Πέτρος τῆς περιτομῆς, 8 ὁ
γὰρ ἐνεργήσας Πέτρῳ εἰς ἀποστολὴν
τῆς περιτομῆς ἐνήργησεν καὶ ἐμοὶ εἰς
τὰ ἔθνη, 9 καὶ γνόντες τὴν χάριν τὴν
δοθεῖσάν μοι, Ἰάκωβος καὶ Κηφᾶς καὶ
Ἰωάννης, οἱ δοκοῦντες στῦλοι εἶναι,
δεξιὰς ἔδωκαν ἐμοὶ καὶ Βαρναβᾷ κοι-
νωνίας, ἵνα ἡμεῖς εἰς τὰ ἔθνη, αὐτοὶ δὲ
εἰς τὴν περιτομήν

1 Thess 2:13

Καὶ διὰ τοῦτο καὶ ἡμεῖς εὐχαριστοῦμεν
τῷ θεῷ ἀδιαλείπτως, ὅτι παραλαβόντες
λόγον ἀκοῆς παρ' ἡμῶν τοῦ θεοῦ ἐδέξασθε
οὐ λόγον ἀνθρώπων ἀλλὰ καθώς ἐστιν
ἀληθῶς λόγον θεοῦ, ὃς καὶ ἐνεργεῖται
ἐν ὑμῖν τοῖς πιστεύουσιν.

Cf. 2 Cor 10:7–8; 1 Thess 2:4; 1 Tim 1:11; 2:5–7; 2 Tim 1:11; Titus 1:1–3.

See also § 99 Paul's Apostolic Commission; § 163 Paul's Commissioning by the Risen Lord.

101. *The Miraculous Signs Accompanying Paul's Message*

Rom 15:18–19

οὐ γὰρ τολμήσω τι λαλεῖν ὧν οὐ κατειργά-
σατο Χριστὸς δι' ἐμοῦ εἰς ὑπακοὴν ἐθνῶν,
λόγῳ καὶ ἔργῳ, 19 ἐν δυνάμει σημείων καὶ
τεράτων, ἐν δυνάμει πνεύματος ⸀[θεοῦ]·
ὥστε με ἀπὸ Ἰερουσαλὴμ καὶ κύκλῳ
μέχρι τοῦ Ἰλλυρικοῦ πεπληρωκέναι τὸ
εὐαγγέλιον τοῦ Χριστοῦ

1 Cor 2:4–5

καὶ ὁ λόγος μου καὶ τὸ κήρυγμά μου οὐκ
ἐν ⸂πειθοῖ[ς] σοφίας [λόγοις]⸃ ἀλλ' ἐν
ἀποδείξει πνεύματος καὶ δυνάμεως, 5 ἵνα
ἡ πίστις ὑμῶν μὴ ᾖ ἐν σοφίᾳ ἀνθρώπων
ἀλλ' ἐν δυνάμει θεοῦ.

2 Cor 12:1–10

Καυχᾶσθαι δεῖ, οὐ συμφέρον μέν, ἐλεύ-
σομαι δὲ εἰς ὀπτασίας καὶ ἀποκαλύψεις
κυρίου. 2 οἶδα ἄνθρωπον ἐν Χριστῷ πρὸ
ἐτῶν δεκατεσσάρων, εἴτε ἐν σώματι οὐκ
οἶδα, εἴτε ἐκτὸς τοῦ σώματος οὐκ οἶδα,
ὁ θεὸς οἶδεν, ἁρπαγέντα τὸν τοιοῦτον
ἕως τρίτου οὐρανοῦ. 3 καὶ οἶδα τὸν τοι-
οῦτον ἄνθρωπον, εἴτε ἐν σώματι εἴτε
χωρὶς τοῦ σώματος οὐκ οἶδα, ὁ θεὸς
οἶδεν, 4 ὅτι ἡρπάγη εἰς τὸν παράδεισον
καὶ ἤκουσεν ἄρρητα ῥήματα ἃ οὐκ ἐξὸν
ἀνθρώπῳ λαλῆσαι. 5 ὑπὲρ τοῦ τοιού-
του καυχήσομαι, ὑπὲρ δὲ ἐμαυτοῦ οὐ
καυχήσομαι εἰ μὴ ἐν ταῖς ἀσθενείαις.
6 Ἐὰν γὰρ θελήσω καυχήσασθαι, οὐκ
ἔσομαι ἄφρων, ἀλήθειαν γὰρ ἐρῶ· φεί-
δομαι δέ, μή τις εἰς ἐμὲ λογίσηται ὑπὲρ
ὃ βλέπει με ἢ ἀκούει [τι] ἐξ ἐμοῦ 7 καὶ
τῇ ὑπερβολῇ τῶν ἀποκαλύψεων. ⸀διὸ
ἵνα μὴ ὑπεραίρωμαι, ἐδόθη μοι σκόλοψ
τῇ σαρκί, ἄγγελος σατανᾶ, ἵνα με κο-
λαφίζῃ, ⸂ἵνα μὴ ὑπεραίρωμαι⸃. 8 ὑπὲρ
τούτου τρὶς τὸν κύριον παρεκάλεσα
ἵνα ἀποστῇ ἀπ' ἐμοῦ. 9 καὶ εἴρηκέν μοι·
ἀρκεῖ σοι ἡ χάρις μου, ἡ γὰρ ⸀δύναμις
ἐν ἀσθενείᾳ τελεῖται. Ἥδιστα οὖν μᾶλ-
λον καυχήσομαι ἐν ταῖς ἀσθενείαις μου,
ἵνα ἐπισκηνώσῃ ἐπ' ἐμὲ ἡ δύναμις τοῦ
Χριστοῦ. 10 διὸ εὐδοκῶ ἐν ἀσθενείαις,
ἐν ὕβρεσιν, ἐν ἀνάγκαις, ἐν διωγμοῖς
καὶ στενοχωρίαις, ὑπὲρ Χριστοῦ· ὅταν
γὰρ ἀσθενῶ, τότε δυνατός εἰμι.

2 Cor 12:11–12

Γέγονα ἄφρων, ὑμεῖς με ἠναγκάσατε.
ἐγὼ γὰρ ὤφειλον ὑφ' ὑμῶν συνίστα-
σθαι· οὐδὲν γὰρ ὑστέρησα τῶν ὑπερλίαν
ἀποστόλων εἰ καὶ οὐδέν εἰμι. 12 τὰ μὲν
σημεῖα τοῦ ἀποστόλου κατειργάσθη ἐν
ὑμῖν ἐν πάσῃ ὑπομονῇ, σημείοις τε καὶ
τέρασιν καὶ δυνάμεσιν.

Acts 14:3

ἱκανὸν μὲν οὖν χρόνον διέτριψαν παρ-
ρησιαζόμενοι ἐπὶ τῷ κυρίῳ τῷ μαρτυ-
ροῦντι [ἐπὶ] τῷ λόγῳ τῆς χάριτος αὐτοῦ,
διδόντι σημεῖα καὶ τέρατα γίνεσθαι διὰ
τῶν χειρῶν αὐτῶν.

Acts 15:12

Ἐσίγησεν δὲ πᾶν τὸ πλῆθος καὶ ἤκουον
Βαρναβᾶ καὶ Παύλου ἐξηγουμένων ὅσα
ἐποίησεν ὁ θεὸς σημεῖα καὶ τέρατα ἐν
τοῖς ἔθνεσιν δι' αὐτῶν.

Acts 19:11–12

Δυνάμεις τε οὐ τὰς τυχούσας ὁ θεὸς
ἐποίει διὰ τῶν χειρῶν Παύλου, 12 ὥστε
καὶ ἐπὶ τοὺς ἀσθενοῦντας ἀποφέρεσθαι
ἀπὸ τοῦ χρωτὸς αὐτοῦ σουδάρια ἢ σι-
μικίνθια καὶ ἀπαλλάσσεσθαι ἀπ' αὐτῶν
τὰς νόσους, τά τε πνεύματα τὰ πονηρὰ
ἐκπορεύεσθαι.

Cf. Acts 13:6–12; 14:8–13; 16:16–18; 16:25–31; 19:5–7; 20:7–12; 27:21–26; 27:39–44; 28:3–10; see also 1 Cor 1:22–25.

102. *Paul and the Twelve*

1 Cor 9:5

μὴ οὐκ ἔχομεν ἐξουσίαν ἀδελφὴν γυναῖκα
περιάγειν ὡς καὶ οἱ λοιποὶ ἀπόστολοι καὶ
οἱ ἀδελφοὶ τοῦ κυρίου καὶ Κηφᾶς;

1 Cor 15:1–11

Γνωρίζω δὲ ὑμῖν, ἀδελφοί, τὸ εὐαγγέλιον
ὃ εὐηγγελισάμην ὑμῖν, ὃ καὶ παρελάβετε,

§ 101 **Rom 15:19** ***θεου*** 𝔓^{46} ℵ D^{1} *Byz*] *om.* B ¦ αγιου A D^{*,2} 33. 1739. 1881 **1 Cor 2:4** ***πειθοις σοφιας λογοις*** (ℵ*) B D 33. 1739. 1881] πειθοις ανθρωπινης σοφιας λογοις ℵ^{2} A C *Byz* ¦ πειθοις σοφιας 𝔓^{46} ¦ πειθοι σοφιας *cj* **2 Cor 12:7** ***διο*** ℵ A B 33. 1739] *om.* 𝔓^{46} D 1881 *Byz* • ***ινα μη υπεραιρωμαι*** 𝔓^{46} ℵ^{2} B I^{vid} 1739. (1881) *Byz*] *om.* ℵ* A D 33 **2 Cor 12:9** ***δυναμις*** 𝔓^{46vid} ℵ* A* B D*] *add.* μου ℵ^{2} A^{c} D^{1} 33. 1739. 1881 *Byz*

entrusted with the gospel for the circumcised [8] (for he who worked through Peter making him an apostle to the circumcised also worked through me in sending me to the Gentiles), [9] and when James and Cephas and John, who were acknowledged pillars, recognized the grace that had been given to me, they gave to Barnabas and me the right hand of fellowship, agreeing that we should go to the Gentiles and they to the circumcised.

1 Thess 2:13

We also constantly give thanks to God for this, that when you received the word of God that you heard from us, you accepted it not as a human word but as what it really is, God's word, which is also at work in you believers.

Cf. 2 Cor 10:7–8; 1 Thess 2:4; 1 Tim 1:11; 2:5–7; 2 Tim 1:11; Titus 1:1–3.

See also § 99 Paul's Apostolic Commission; § 163 Paul's Commissioning by the Risen Lord.

101. The Miraculous Signs Accompanying Paul's Message

Rom 15:18–19

For I will not venture to speak of anything except what Christ has accomplished through me to win obedience from the Gentiles, by word and deed, [19] by the power of signs and wonders, by the power of the Spirit of God,[a] so that from Jerusalem and as far around as Illyricum I have fully proclaimed the good news of Christ.

1 Cor 2:4–5

My speech and my proclamation were not with plausible words of wisdom,[b] but with a demonstration of the Spirit and of power, [5] so that your faith might rest not on human wisdom but on the power of God.

2 Cor 12:1–10

It is necessary to boast; nothing is to be gained by it, but I will go on to visions and revelations of the Lord. [2] I know a person in Christ who fourteen years ago was caught up to the third heaven—whether in the body or out of the body I do not know; God knows. [3] And I know that such a person—whether in the body or out of the body I do not know; God knows— [4] was caught up into Paradise and heard things that are not to be told, that no mortal is permitted to repeat. [5] On behalf of such a one I will boast, but on my own behalf I will not boast, except of my weaknesses. [6] But if I wish to boast, I will not be a fool, for I will be speaking the truth. But I refrain from it, so that no one may think better of me than what is seen in me or heard from me, [7] even considering the exceptional character of the revelations. Therefore, to keep[c] me from being too elated, a thorn was given me in the flesh, a messenger of Satan to torment me, to keep me from being too elated.[d] [8] Three times I appealed to the Lord about this, that it would leave me, [9] but he said to me, "My grace is sufficient for you, for power[e] is made perfect in weakness." So, I will boast all the more gladly of my weaknesses, so that the power of Christ may dwell in me. [10] Therefore I am content with weaknesses, insults, hardships, persecutions, and calamities for the sake of Christ; for whenever I am weak, then I am strong.

2 Cor 12:11–12

I have been a fool! You forced me to it. Indeed you should have been the ones commending me, for I am not at all inferior to these super-apostles, even though I am nothing. [12] The signs of a true apostle were performed among you with utmost patience, signs and wonders and mighty works.

Acts 14:3

So they remained for a long time, speaking boldly for the Lord, who testified to the word of his grace by granting signs and wonders to be done through them.

Acts 15:12

The whole assembly kept silence, and listened to Barnabas and Paul as they told of all the signs and wonders that God had done through them among the Gentiles.

Acts 19:11–12

God did extraordinary miracles through Paul, [12] so that when the handkerchiefs or aprons that had touched his skin were brought to the sick, their diseases left them, and the evil spirits came out of them.

Cf. Acts 13:6–12; 14:8–13; 16:16–18; 16:25–31; 19:5–7; 20:7–12; 27:21–26; 27:39–44; 28:3–10; see also 1 Cor 1:22–25.

102. Paul and the Twelve

1 Cor 9:5

Do we not have the right to be accompanied by a believing wife, as do the other apostles and the brothers of the Lord and Cephas?

1 Cor 15:1–11

Now I would remind you, brothers and sisters, of the good news that I proclaimed to you, which you in turn

§ 101 [a] **Rom 15:19** *of the Spirit of God* Other ancient authorities read *of the Spirit* or *of the Holy Spirit* [b] **1 Cor 2:4** ***plausible words of wisdom*** Other ancient authorities provide evidence for the reading *the persuasiveness of wisdom*; others read *plausible words of human wisdom* [c] **2 Cor 12:7** ***Therefore, to keep*** Other ancient authorities read *To keep* [d] **2 Cor 12:7** ***to keep me from being too elated*** Other ancient authorities lack *to keep me from being too elated* [e] **2 Cor 12:9** ***power*** Other ancient authorities read *my power*

ἐν ᾧ καὶ ἑστήκατε, 2 δι᾽ οὗ καὶ σῴζεσθε, τίνι λόγῳ εὐηγγελισάμην ὑμῖν εἰ κατέχετε, ἐκτὸς εἰ μὴ εἰκῇ ἐπιστεύσατε. 3 παρέδωκα γὰρ ὑμῖν ἐν πρώτοις, ὃ καὶ παρέλαβον, ὅτι Χριστὸς ἀπέθανεν ὑπὲρ τῶν ἁμαρτιῶν ἡμῶν κατὰ τὰς γραφὰς 4 καὶ ὅτι ἐτάφη καὶ ὅτι ἐγήγερται τῇ ἡμέρᾳ τῇ τρίτῃ κατὰ τὰς γραφὰς 5 καὶ ὅτι ὤφθη Κηφᾷ εἶτα τοῖς δώδεκα· 6 ἔπειτα ὤφθη ἐπάνω πεντακοσίοις ἀδελφοῖς ἐφάπαξ, ἐξ ὧν οἱ πλείονες μένουσιν ἕως ἄρτι, τινὲς δὲ ἐκοιμήθησαν· 7 ἔπειτα ὤφθη Ἰακώβῳ εἶτα τοῖς ἀποστόλοις πᾶσιν· 8 ἔσχατον δὲ πάντων ὡσπερεὶ τῷ ἐκτρώματι ὤφθη κἀμοί. 9 Ἐγὼ γάρ εἰμι ὁ ἐλάχιστος τῶν ἀποστόλων ὃς οὐκ εἰμὶ ἱκανὸς καλεῖσθαι ἀπόστολος, διότι ἐδίωξα τὴν ἐκκλησίαν τοῦ θεοῦ· 10 χάριτι δὲ θεοῦ εἰμι ὅ εἰμι, καὶ ἡ χάρις αὐτοῦ ἡ εἰς ἐμὲ οὐ κενὴ ἐγενήθη, ἀλλὰ περισσότερον αὐτῶν πάντων ἐκοπίασα, οὐκ ἐγὼ δὲ ἀλλὰ ἡ χάρις τοῦ θεοῦ [ἡ] σὺν ἐμοί. 11 εἴτε οὖν ἐγὼ εἴτε ἐκεῖνοι, οὕτως κηρύσσομεν καὶ οὕτως ἐπιστεύσατε.

Gal 1:15–24

Ὅτε δὲ εὐδόκησεν [ὁ θεὸς] ὁ ἀφορίσας με ἐκ κοιλίας μητρός μου καὶ καλέσας διὰ τῆς χάριτος αὐτοῦ 16 ἀποκαλύψαι τὸν υἱὸν αὐτοῦ ἐν ἐμοί, ἵνα εὐαγγελίζωμαι αὐτὸν ἐν τοῖς ἔθνεσιν, εὐθέως οὐ προσανεθέμην σαρκὶ καὶ αἵματι 17 οὐδὲ ἀνῆλθον εἰς Ἱεροσόλυμα πρὸς τοὺς πρὸ ἐμοῦ ἀποστόλους, ἀλλὰ ἀπῆλθον εἰς Ἀραβίαν καὶ πάλιν ὑπέστρεψα εἰς Δαμασκόν. 18 Ἔπειτα μετὰ ἔτη τρία ἀνῆλθον εἰς Ἱεροσόλυμα ἱστορῆσαι Κηφᾶν καὶ ἐπέμεινα πρὸς αὐτὸν ἡμέρας δεκαπέντε, 19 ἕτερον δὲ τῶν ἀποστόλων οὐκ εἶδον εἰ μὴ Ἰάκωβον τὸν ἀδελφὸν τοῦ κυρίου. 20 ἃ δὲ γράφω ὑμῖν, ἰδοὺ ἐνώπιον τοῦ θεοῦ ὅτι οὐ ψεύδομαι. 21 Ἔπειτα ἦλθον εἰς τὰ κλίματα τῆς Συρίας καὶ τῆς Κιλικίας· 22 ἤμην δὲ ἀγνοούμενος τῷ προσώπῳ ταῖς ἐκκλησίαις τῆς Ἰουδαίας ταῖς ἐν Χριστῷ. 23 μόνον δὲ ἀκούοντες ἦσαν ὅτι ὁ διώκων ἡμᾶς ποτε νῦν εὐαγγελίζεται τὴν πίστιν ἥν ποτε ἐπόρθει, 24 καὶ ἐδόξαζον ἐν ἐμοὶ τὸν θεόν.

Gal 2:1–10

Ἔπειτα διὰ δεκατεσσάρων ἐτῶν πάλιν ἀνέβην εἰς Ἱεροσόλυμα μετὰ Βαρναβᾶ συμπαραλαβὼν καὶ Τίτον· 2 ἀνέβην δὲ κατὰ ἀποκάλυψιν· καὶ ἀνεθέμην αὐτοῖς τὸ εὐαγγέλιον ὃ κηρύσσω ἐν τοῖς ἔθνεσιν, κατ᾽ ἰδίαν δὲ τοῖς δοκοῦσιν, μή πως εἰς κενὸν τρέχω ἢ ἔδραμον. 3 ἀλλ᾽ οὐδὲ Τίτος ὁ σὺν ἐμοί, Ἕλλην ὤν, ἠναγκάσθη περιτμηθῆναι· 4 διὰ δὲ τοὺς παρεισάκτους ψευδαδέλφους, οἵτινες παρεισῆλθον κατασκοπῆσαι τὴν ἐλευθερίαν ἡμῶν ἣν ἔχομεν ἐν Χριστῷ Ἰησοῦ, ἵνα ἡμᾶς καταδουλώσουσιν, 5 οἷς οὐδὲ πρὸς ὥραν εἴξαμεν τῇ ὑποταγῇ, ἵνα ἡ ἀλήθεια τοῦ εὐαγγελίου διαμείνῃ πρὸς ὑμᾶς. 6 Ἀπὸ δὲ τῶν δοκούντων εἶναί τι, —ὁποῖοί ποτε ἦσαν οὐδέν μοι διαφέρει· πρόσωπον [ὁ] θεὸς ἀνθρώπου οὐ λαμβάνει—ἐμοὶ γὰρ οἱ δοκοῦντες οὐδὲν προσανέθεντο, 7 ἀλλὰ τοὐναντίον ἰδόντες ὅτι πεπίστευμαι τὸ εὐαγγέλιον τῆς ἀκροβυστίας καθὼς Πέτρος τῆς περιτομῆς, 8 ὁ γὰρ ἐνεργήσας Πέτρῳ εἰς ἀποστολὴν τῆς περιτομῆς ἐνήργησεν καὶ ἐμοὶ εἰς τὰ ἔθνη, 9 καὶ γνόντες τὴν χάριν τὴν δοθεῖσάν μοι, Ἰάκωβος καὶ Κηφᾶς καὶ Ἰωάννης, οἱ δοκοῦντες στῦλοι εἶναι, δεξιὰς ἔδωκαν ἐμοὶ καὶ Βαρναβᾷ κοινωνίας, ἵνα ἡμεῖς εἰς τὰ ἔθνη, αὐτοὶ δὲ εἰς τὴν περιτομήν· 10 μόνον τῶν πτωχῶν ἵνα μνημονεύωμεν, ὃ καὶ ἐσπούδασα αὐτὸ τοῦτο ποιῆσαι.

Gal 2:11–14

Ὅτε δὲ ἦλθεν Κηφᾶς εἰς Ἀντιόχειαν, κατὰ πρόσωπον αὐτῷ ἀντέστην, ὅτι κατεγνωσμένος ἦν. 12 πρὸ τοῦ γὰρ ἐλθεῖν τινας ἀπὸ Ἰακώβου μετὰ τῶν ἐθνῶν συνήσθιεν· ὅτε δὲ ἦλθον, ὑπέστελλεν καὶ ἀφώριζεν ἑαυτὸν φοβούμενος τοὺς ἐκ περιτομῆς. 13 καὶ συνυπεκρίθησαν αὐτῷ [καὶ] οἱ λοιποὶ Ἰουδαῖοι, ὥστε καὶ Βαρναβᾶς συναπήχθη αὐτῶν τῇ ὑποκρίσει. 14 ἀλλ᾽ ὅτε εἶδον ὅτι οὐκ ὀρθοποδοῦσιν πρὸς τὴν ἀλήθειαν τοῦ εὐαγγελίου, εἶπον τῷ Κηφᾷ ἔμπροσθεν πάντων· εἰ σὺ Ἰουδαῖος ὑπάρχων ἐθνικῶς καὶ οὐχὶ Ἰουδαϊκῶς ζῇς, πῶς τὰ ἔθνη ἀναγκάζεις ἰουδαΐζειν;

Cf. Acts 9:26–30; 11:27–30; 12:25; 13:27–33; 15:1–35; 18:22; see also 1 Cor 1:10–17; 3:18–23; 4:9–13; 12:28–31; Eph 2:19–22; 3:1–7.

103. Stewards of God

1 Cor 4:1–5

Οὕτως ἡμᾶς λογιζέσθω ἄνθρωπος ὡς ὑπηρέτας Χριστοῦ καὶ οἰκονόμους μυστηρίων θεοῦ. 2 ὧδε λοιπὸν ⸀ζητεῖται ἐν τοῖς οἰκονόμοις, ἵνα πιστός τις εὑρεθῇ. 3 ἐμοὶ δὲ εἰς ἐλάχιστόν ἐστιν, ἵνα ὑφ᾽ ὑμῶν ἀνακριθῶ ἢ ὑπὸ ἀνθρωπίνης ἡμέρας· ἀλλ᾽ οὐδὲ ἐμαυτὸν ἀνακρίνω. 4 οὐδὲν γὰρ ἐμαυτῷ σύνοιδα, ἀλλ᾽ οὐκ ἐν τούτῳ δεδικαίωμαι, ὁ δὲ ἀνακρίνων με κύριός ἐστιν. 5 ὥστε μὴ πρὸ καιροῦ τι κρίνετε ἕως ἂν ἔλθῃ ὁ κύριος, ὃς καὶ φωτίσει τὰ κρυπτὰ τοῦ σκότους καὶ φανερώσει τὰς βουλὰς τῶν καρδιῶν· καὶ τότε ὁ ἔπαινος γενήσεται ἑκάστῳ ἀπὸ τοῦ θεοῦ.

1 Cor 9:16–18

ἐὰν γὰρ εὐαγγελίζωμαι, οὐκ ἔστιν μοι καύχημα· ἀνάγκη γάρ μοι ἐπίκειται· οὐαὶ γάρ μοί ἐστιν ἐὰν μὴ εὐαγγελίσωμαι. 17 εἰ γὰρ ἑκὼν τοῦτο πράσσω, μισθὸν ἔχω· εἰ δὲ ἄκων, οἰκονομίαν πεπίστευμαι· 18 τίς οὖν μού ἐστιν ὁ μισθός; ἵνα εὐαγγελιζόμενος ἀδάπανον θήσω τὸ εὐαγγέλιον εἰς τὸ μὴ καταχρήσασθαι τῇ ἐξουσίᾳ μου ἐν τῷ εὐαγγελίῳ.

Eph 3:1–13

Τούτου χάριν ἐγὼ Παῦλος ὁ δέσμιος τοῦ Χριστοῦ [Ἰησοῦ] ὑπὲρ ὑμῶν τῶν ἐθνῶν 2 —εἴ γε ἠκούσατε τὴν οἰκονομίαν τῆς

§ 103 1 Cor 4:2 *ζητειται* B *Byz*] ζητειτε 𝔓46 ℵ(*) A C D 33. 1739. 1881

received, in which also you stand, 2 through which also you are being saved, if you hold firmly to the message that I proclaimed to you—unless you have come to believe in vain. 3 For I handed on to you as of first importance what I in turn had received: that Christ died for our sins in accordance with the scriptures, 4 and that he was buried, and that he was raised on the third day in accordance with the scriptures, 5 and that he appeared to Cephas, then to the twelve. 6 Then he appeared to more than five hundred brothers and sisters at one time, most of whom are still alive, though some have died. 7 Then he appeared to James, then to all the apostles. 8 Last of all, as to one untimely born, he appeared also to me. 9 For I am the least of the apostles, unfit to be called an apostle, because I persecuted the church of God. 10 But by the grace of God I am what I am, and his grace toward me has not been in vain. On the contrary, I worked harder than any of them—though it was not I, but the grace of God that is with me. 11 Whether then it was I or they, so we proclaim and so you have come to believe.

Gal 1:15–24

But when God, who had set me apart before I was born and called me through his grace, was pleased 16 to reveal his Son to me, so that I might proclaim him among the Gentiles, I did not confer with any human being, 17 nor did I go up to Jerusalem to those who were already apostles before me, but I went away at once into Arabia, and afterwards I returned to Damascus. 18 Then after three years I did go up to Jerusalem to visit Cephas and stayed with him fifteen days; 19 but I did not see any other apostle except James the Lord's brother. 20 In what I am writing to you, before God, I do not lie! 21 Then I went into the regions of Syria and Cilicia, 22 and I was still unknown by sight to the churches of Judea that are in Christ; 23 they only heard it said, "The one who formerly was persecuting us is now proclaiming the faith he once tried to destroy." 24 And they glorified God because of me.

Gal 2:1–10

Then after fourteen years I went up again to Jerusalem with Barnabas, taking Titus along with me. 2 I went up in response to a revelation. Then I laid before them (though only in a private meeting with the acknowledged leaders) the gospel that I proclaim among the Gentiles, in order to make sure that I was not running, or had not run, in vain. 3 But even Titus, who was with me, was not compelled to be circumcised, though he was a Greek. 4 But because of false believers secretly brought in, who slipped in to spy on the freedom we have in Christ Jesus, so that they might enslave us— 5 we did not submit to them even for a moment, so that the truth of the gospel might always remain with you. 6 And from those who were supposed to be acknowledged leaders (what they actually were makes no difference to me; God shows no partiality)—those leaders contributed nothing to me. 7 On the contrary, when they saw that I had been entrusted with the gospel for the uncircumcised, just as Peter had been entrusted with the gospel for the circumcised 8 (for he who worked through Peter making him an apostle to the circumcised also worked through me in sending me to the Gentiles), 9 and when James and Cephas and John, who were acknowledged pillars, recognized the grace that had been given to me, they gave to Barnabas and me the right hand of fellowship, agreeing that we should go to the Gentiles and they to the circumcised. 10 They asked only one thing, that we remember the poor, which was actually what I was eager to do.

Gal 2:11–14

But when Cephas came to Antioch, I opposed him to his face, because he stood self-condemned; 12 for until certain people came from James, he used to eat with the Gentiles. But after they came, he drew back and kept himself separate for fear of the circumcision faction. 13 And the other Jews joined him in this hypocrisy, so that even Barnabas was led astray by their hypocrisy. 14 But when I saw that they were not acting consistently with the truth of the gospel, I said to Cephas before them all, "If you, though a Jew, live like a Gentile and not like a Jew, how can you compel the Gentiles to live like Jews?"

Cf. Acts 9:26–30; 11:27–30; 12:25; 13:27–33; 15:1–35; 18:22; see also 1 Cor 1:10–17; 3:18–23; 4:9–13; 12:28–31; Eph 2:19–22; 3:1–7.

103. Stewards of God

1 Cor 4:1–5

Think of us in this way, as servants of Christ and stewards of God's mysteries. 2 Moreover, it is required[a] of stewards that they be found trustworthy. 3 But with me it is a very small thing that I should be judged by you or by any human court. I do not even judge myself. 4 I am not aware of anything against myself, but I am not thereby acquitted. It is the Lord who judges me. 5 Therefore do not pronounce judgment before the time, before the Lord comes, who will bring to light the things now hidden in darkness and will disclose the purposes of the heart. Then each one will receive commendation from God.

1 Cor 9:16–18

If I proclaim the gospel, this gives me no ground for boasting, for an obligation is laid on me, and woe to me if I do not proclaim the gospel! 17 For if I do this of my own will, I have a reward; but if not of my own will, I am entrusted with a commission. 18 What then is my reward? Just this: that in my proclamation I may make the gospel free of charge, so as not to make full use of my rights in the gospel.

Eph 3:1–13

This is the reason that I Paul am a prisoner for Christ Jesus for the sake of you Gentiles— 2 for surely you have already

§ 103 [a] 1 Cor 4:2 *it is required* Other ancient authorities read *you require*

χάριτος τοῦ θεοῦ τῆς δοθείσης μοι εἰς
ὑμᾶς, 3 [ὅτι] κατὰ ἀποκάλυψιν ἐγνωρίσθη
μοι τὸ μυστήριον, καθὼς προέγραψα ἐν
ὀλίγῳ, 4 πρὸς ὃ δύνασθε ἀναγινώσκοντες
νοῆσαι τὴν σύνεσίν μου ἐν τῷ μυστηρίῳ
τοῦ Χριστοῦ, 5 ὃ ἑτέραις γενεαῖς οὐκ
ἐγνωρίσθη τοῖς υἱοῖς τῶν ἀνθρώπων
ὡς νῦν ἀπεκαλύφθη τοῖς ἁγίοις ἀποστό-
λοις αὐτοῦ καὶ προφήταις ἐν πνεύματι,
6 εἶναι τὰ ἔθνη συγκληρονόμα καὶ σύσ-
σωμα καὶ συμμέτοχα τῆς ἐπαγγελίας ἐν
Χριστῷ Ἰησοῦ διὰ τοῦ εὐαγγελίου, 7 οὗ
ἐγενήθην διάκονος κατὰ τὴν δωρεὰν
τῆς χάριτος τοῦ θεοῦ τῆς δοθείσης μοι
κατὰ τὴν ἐνέργειαν τῆς δυνάμεως αὐτοῦ.
8 Ἐμοὶ τῷ ἐλαχιστοτέρῳ πάντων ἁγίων
ἐδόθη ἡ χάρις αὕτη, τοῖς ἔθνεσιν εὐαγ-
γελίσασθαι τὸ ἀνεξιχνίαστον πλοῦτος
τοῦ Χριστοῦ 9 καὶ φωτίσαι ⸀[πάντας] τίς
ἡ οἰκονομία τοῦ μυστηρίου τοῦ ἀποκε-
κρυμμένου ἀπὸ τῶν αἰώνων ἐν τῷ θεῷ
τῷ τὰ πάντα κτίσαντι, 10 ἵνα γνωρισθῇ
νῦν ταῖς ἀρχαῖς καὶ ταῖς ἐξουσίαις ἐν
τοῖς ἐπουρανίοις διὰ τῆς ἐκκλησίας ἡ
πολυποίκιλος σοφία τοῦ θεοῦ, 11 κατὰ
πρόθεσιν τῶν αἰώνων ἣν ἐποίησεν ἐν
τῷ Χριστῷ Ἰησοῦ τῷ κυρίῳ ἡμῶν, 12 ἐν
ᾧ ἔχομεν τὴν παρρησίαν καὶ προσα-
γωγὴν ἐν πεποιθήσει διὰ τῆς πίστεως
αὐτοῦ. 13 διὸ αἰτοῦμαι μὴ ἐγκακεῖν ἐν
ταῖς θλίψεσίν μου ὑπὲρ ὑμῶν, ἥτις ἐστὶν
δόξα ὑμῶν.

Col 1:24–29

Νῦν χαίρω ἐν τοῖς παθήμασιν ὑπὲρ ὑμῶν
καὶ ἀνταναπληρῶ τὰ ὑστερήματα τῶν
θλίψεων τοῦ Χριστοῦ ἐν τῇ σαρκί μου ὑπὲρ
τοῦ σώματος αὐτοῦ, ὅ ἐστιν ἡ ἐκκλησία,
25 ἧς ἐγενόμην ἐγὼ διάκονος κατὰ τὴν
οἰκονομίαν τοῦ θεοῦ τὴν δοθεῖσάν μοι
εἰς ὑμᾶς πληρῶσαι τὸν λόγον τοῦ θεοῦ,
26 τὸ μυστήριον τὸ ἀποκεκρυμμένον ἀπὸ
τῶν αἰώνων καὶ ἀπὸ τῶν γενεῶν—νῦν
δὲ ἐφανερώθη τοῖς ἁγίοις αὐτοῦ, 27 οἷς
ἠθέλησεν ὁ θεὸς γνωρίσαι τί τὸ πλοῦ-
τος τῆς δόξης τοῦ μυστηρίου τούτου ἐν
τοῖς ἔθνεσιν, ὅ ἐστιν Χριστὸς ἐν ὑμῖν, ἡ
ἐλπὶς τῆς δόξης· 28 ὃν ἡμεῖς καταγγέλ-
λομεν νουθετοῦντες πάντα ἄνθρωπον
καὶ διδάσκοντες πάντα ἄνθρωπον ἐν
πάσῃ σοφίᾳ, ἵνα παραστήσωμεν πάν-
τα ἄνθρωπον τέλειον ἐν Χριστῷ· 29 εἰς
ὃ καὶ κοπιῶ ἀγωνιζόμενος κατὰ τὴν
ἐνέργειαν αὐτοῦ τὴν ἐνεργουμένην ἐν
ἐμοὶ ἐν δυνάμει.

Titus 1:7–9

δεῖ γὰρ τὸν ἐπίσκοπον ἀνέγκλητον εἶναι ὡς
θεοῦ οἰκονόμον, μὴ αὐθάδη, μὴ ὀργίλον,
μὴ πάροινον, μὴ πλήκτην, μὴ αἰσχρο-
κερδῆ, 8 ἀλλὰ φιλόξενον φιλάγαθον
σώφρονα δίκαιον ὅσιον ἐγκρατῆ, 9 ἀντε-
χόμενον τοῦ κατὰ τὴν διδαχὴν πιστοῦ
λόγου, ἵνα δυνατὸς ᾖ καὶ παρακαλεῖν ἐν
τῇ διδασκαλίᾳ τῇ ὑγιαινούσῃ καὶ τοὺς
ἀντιλέγοντας ἐλέγχειν.

Cf. Eph 1:9–10; 1 Tim 1:3–4.

104. Ambassadors of Christ

2 Cor 5:18–21

τὰ δὲ πάντα ἐκ τοῦ θεοῦ τοῦ καταλλάξαν-
τος ἡμᾶς ἑαυτῷ διὰ Χριστοῦ καὶ δόντος
ἡμῖν τὴν διακονίαν τῆς καταλλαγῆς, 19 ὡς
ὅτι θεὸς ἦν ἐν Χριστῷ κόσμον καταλ-
λάσσων ἑαυτῷ, μὴ λογιζόμενος αὐτοῖς
τὰ παραπτώματα αὐτῶν καὶ θέμενος ἐν
ἡμῖν τὸν λόγον τῆς καταλλαγῆς. 20 Ὑπὲρ
Χριστοῦ οὖν πρεσβεύομεν ὡς τοῦ θεοῦ
παρακαλοῦντος δι᾽ ἡμῶν· δεόμεθα ὑπὲρ
Χριστοῦ, καταλλάγητε τῷ θεῷ. 21 τὸν μὴ
γνόντα ἁμαρτίαν ὑπὲρ ἡμῶν ἁμαρτίαν
ἐποίησεν, ἵνα ἡμεῖς γενώμεθα δικαιο-
σύνη θεοῦ ἐν αὐτῷ.

Eph 6:19–20

καὶ ὑπὲρ ἐμοῦ, ἵνα μοι δοθῇ λόγος ἐν
ἀνοίξει τοῦ στόματός μου, ἐν παρρησίᾳ
γνωρίσαι τὸ μυστήριον ⸂τοῦ εὐαγγε-
λίου⸃, 20 ὑπὲρ οὗ πρεσβεύω ἐν ἁλύσει,
ἵνα ἐν αὐτῷ παρρησιάσωμαι ὡς δεῖ με
λαλῆσαι.

Phlm 8–9

Διὸ πολλὴν ἐν Χριστῷ παρρησίαν ἔχων
ἐπιτάσσειν σοι τὸ ἀνῆκον 9 διὰ τὴν ἀγά-
πην μᾶλλον παρακαλῶ, τοιοῦτος ὢν ὡς
Παῦλος ⸀πρεσβύτης νυνὶ δὲ καὶ δέσμιος
Χριστοῦ Ἰησοῦ

105. Paul's Apostolic Life and Ministry

1 Cor 9:19–23

Ἐλεύθερος γὰρ ὢν ἐκ πάντων πᾶσιν
ἐμαυτὸν ἐδούλωσα, ἵνα τοὺς πλείονας
κερδήσω· 20 καὶ ἐγενόμην τοῖς Ἰουδαίοις
ὡς Ἰουδαῖος, ἵνα Ἰουδαίους κερδήσω·
τοῖς ὑπὸ νόμον ὡς ὑπὸ νόμον, μὴ ὢν
αὐτὸς ὑπὸ νόμον, ἵνα τοὺς ὑπὸ νόμον
κερδήσω· 21 τοῖς ἀνόμοις ὡς ἄνομος, μὴ
ὢν ἄνομος θεοῦ ἀλλ᾽ ἔννομος Χριστοῦ,
ἵνα κερδάνω τοὺς ἀνόμους· 22 ἐγενόμην
τοῖς ἀσθενέσιν ἀσθενής, ἵνα τοὺς ἀσθενεῖς
κερδήσω· τοῖς πᾶσιν γέγονα πάντα, ἵνα
πάντως τινὰς σώσω. 23 πάντα δὲ ποιῶ
διὰ τὸ εὐαγγέλιον, ἵνα συγκοινωνὸς
αὐτοῦ γένωμαι.

Eph 3:9 ***παντας*** 𝔓46 ℵ2 B C D 33 *Byz*] *om.* ℵ* A 1739. 1881 **§ 104** **Eph 6:19** ***του ευαγγελιου*** ℵ A D I 33. 1739. 1881 *Byz*] *om.* B **Phlm 9** ***πρεσβυτης*** *omnes*] πρεσβευτης *cj*

heard of the commission of God's
grace that was given me for you, **3** and
how the mystery was made known to
me by revelation, as I wrote above in a
few words, **4** a reading of which will en-
able you to perceive my understanding
of the mystery of Christ. **5** In former
generations this mystery was not made
known to humankind, as it has now
been revealed to his holy apostles and
prophets by the Spirit: **6** that is, the Gen-
tiles have become fellow heirs, members
of the same body, and sharers in the
promise in Christ Jesus through the
gospel. **7** Of this gospel I have become
a servant according to the gift of God's
grace that was given me by the working
of his power. **8** Although I am the very
least of all the saints, this grace was
given to me to bring to the Gentiles the
news of the boundless riches of Christ,
9 and to make everyone see[b] what is the
plan of the mystery hidden for ages in
God who created all things; **10** so that
through the church the wisdom of God
in its rich variety might now be made
known to the rulers and authorities in
the heavenly places. **11** This was in ac-
cordance with the eternal purpose that
he has carried out in Christ Jesus our
Lord, **12** in whom we have access to God
in boldness and confidence through
faith in him. **13** I pray therefore that you
may not lose heart over my sufferings
for you; they are your glory.

Col 1:24–29

I am now rejoicing in my sufferings for
your sake, and in my flesh I am com-
pleting what is lacking in Christ's af-
flictions for the sake of his body, that
is, the church. **25** I became its servant
according to God's commission that
was given to me for you, to make the
word of God fully known, **26** the mys-
tery that has been hidden throughout
the ages and generations but has now
been revealed to his saints. **27** To them
God chose to make known how great
among the Gentiles are the riches of the
glory of this mystery, which is Christ
in you, the hope of glory. **28** It is he
whom we proclaim, warning everyone
and teaching everyone in all wisdom,
so that we may present everyone mature
in Christ. **29** For this I toil and struggle
with all the energy that he powerfully
inspires within me.

Titus 1:7–9

For a bishop, as God's steward, must
be blameless; he must not be arrogant
or quick-tempered or addicted to wine
or violent or greedy for gain; **8** but he
must be hospitable, a lover of good-
ness, prudent, upright, devout, and
self-controlled. **9** He must have a firm
grasp of the word that is trustworthy in
accordance with the teaching, so that he
may be able both to preach with sound
doctrine and to refute those who con-
tradict it.

Cf. Eph 1:9–10; 1 Tim 1:3–4.

Note: the word translated as "commission" in 1 Cor 9:17, Eph 3:2, and Col 1:25, and as "plan" in Eph 3:9, is οἰκονομία ("stewardship"), a word closely related to οἰκονόμος ("steward"), found in 1 Cor 4:1–2 and Titus 1:7.

104. Ambassadors of Christ

2 Cor 5:18–21

All this is from God, who reconciled
us to himself through Christ, and has
given us the ministry of reconciliation;
19 that is, God was in Christ, reconcil-
ing[a] the world to himself, not counting
their trespasses against them, and en-
trusting the message of reconciliation
to us. **20** So we are ambassadors for
Christ, since God is making his appeal
through us; we entreat you on behalf of
Christ, be reconciled to God. **21** For our
sake he made him to be sin who knew
no sin, so that in him we might become
the righteousness of God.

Eph 6:19–20

Pray also for me, so that when I speak,
a message may be given to me to make
known with boldness the mystery of
the gospel,[b] **20** for which I am an ambas-
sador in chains. Pray that I may declare
it boldly, as I must speak.

Phlm 8–9

For this reason, though I am bold
enough in Christ to command you to
do your duty, **9** yet I would rather appeal
to you on the basis of love—and I, Paul,
do this as an old man,[c] and now also as
a prisoner of Christ Jesus.

105. Paul's Apostolic Life and Ministry

1 Cor 9:19–23

For though I am free with respect to
all, I have made myself a slave to all, so
that I might win more of them. **20** To
the Jews I became as a Jew, in order
to win Jews. To those under the law I
became as one under the law (though
I myself am not under the law) so that
I might win those under the law. **21** To
those outside the law I became as one
outside the law (though I am not free
from God's law but am under Christ's
law) so that I might win those outside
the law. **22** To the weak I became weak,
so that I might win the weak. I have
become all things to all people, that I
might by all means save some. **23** I do
it all for the sake of the gospel, so that
I may share in its blessings.

[b] **Eph 3:9** ***to make everyone see*** Other ancient authorities read *to bring to light* **§ 104** [a] **2 Cor 5:19** ***God was in Christ, reconciling*** Or possibly *in Christ God was reconciling* (so NRSV) [b] **Eph 6:19** ***of the gospel*** Other ancient authorities lack *of the gospel* [c] **Phlm 9** ***old man*** Some scholars conjecture that the original text read *ambassador*, or that the reading in the manuscripts is a spelling variant for *ambassador*

2 Cor 4:1–15

Διὰ τοῦτο, ἔχοντες τὴν διακονίαν ταύτην καθὼς ἠλεήθημεν, οὐκ ἐγκακοῦμεν 2 ἀλλὰ ἀπειπάμεθα τὰ κρυπτὰ τῆς αἰσχύνης, μὴ περιπατοῦντες ἐν πανουργίᾳ μηδὲ δολοῦντες τὸν λόγον τοῦ θεοῦ ἀλλὰ τῇ φανερώσει τῆς ἀληθείας συνιστάνοντες ἑαυτοὺς πρὸς πᾶσαν συνείδησιν ἀνθρώπων ἐνώπιον τοῦ θεοῦ. 3 εἰ δὲ καὶ ἔστιν κεκαλυμμένον τὸ εὐαγγέλιον ἡμῶν, ἐν τοῖς ἀπολλυμένοις ἐστὶν κεκαλυμμένον, 4 ἐν οἷς ὁ θεὸς τοῦ αἰῶνος τούτου ἐτύφλωσεν τὰ νοήματα τῶν ἀπίστων εἰς τὸ μὴ αὐγάσαι τὸν φωτισμὸν τοῦ εὐαγγελίου τῆς δόξης τοῦ Χριστοῦ, ὅς ἐστιν εἰκὼν τοῦ θεοῦ. 5 Οὐ γὰρ ἑαυτοὺς κηρύσσομεν ἀλλὰ Ἰησοῦν Χριστὸν κύριον, ἑαυτοὺς δὲ δούλους ὑμῶν διὰ Ἰησοῦν. 6 ὅτι ὁ θεὸς ὁ εἰπών· ἐκ σκότους φῶς λάμψει, ὃς ἔλαμψεν ἐν ταῖς καρδίαις ἡμῶν πρὸς φωτισμὸν τῆς γνώσεως τῆς δόξης τοῦ θεοῦ ἐν προσώπῳ [Ἰησοῦ] Χριστοῦ. 7 Ἔχομεν δὲ τὸν θησαυρὸν τοῦτον ἐν ὀστρακίνοις σκεύεσιν, ἵνα ἡ ὑπερβολὴ τῆς δυνάμεως ᾖ τοῦ θεοῦ καὶ μὴ ἐξ ἡμῶν· 8 ἐν παντὶ θλιβόμενοι ἀλλ' οὐ στενοχωρούμενοι, ἀπορούμενοι ἀλλ' οὐκ ἐξαπορούμενοι, 9 διωκόμενοι ἀλλ' οὐκ ἐγκαταλειπόμενοι, καταβαλλόμενοι ἀλλ' οὐκ ἀπολλύμενοι, 10 πάντοτε τὴν νέκρωσιν τοῦ Ἰησοῦ ἐν τῷ σώματι περιφέροντες, ἵνα καὶ ἡ ζωὴ τοῦ Ἰησοῦ ἐν τῷ σώματι ἡμῶν φανερωθῇ. 11 ἀεὶ γὰρ ἡμεῖς οἱ ζῶντες εἰς θάνατον παραδιδόμεθα διὰ Ἰησοῦν, ἵνα καὶ ἡ ζωὴ τοῦ Ἰησοῦ φανερωθῇ ἐν τῇ θνητῇ σαρκὶ ἡμῶν. 12 ὥστε ὁ θάνατος ἐν ἡμῖν ἐνεργεῖται, ἡ δὲ ζωὴ ἐν ὑμῖν. 13 Ἔχοντες δὲ τὸ αὐτὸ πνεῦμα τῆς πίστεως κατὰ τὸ γεγραμμένον· ἐπίστευσα, διὸ ἐλάλησα, καὶ ἡμεῖς πιστεύομεν, διὸ καὶ λαλοῦμεν, 14 εἰδότες ὅτι ὁ ἐγείρας τὸν ⸀κύριον Ἰησοῦν καὶ ἡμᾶς σὺν Ἰησοῦ ἐγερεῖ καὶ παραστήσει σὺν ὑμῖν. 15 τὰ γὰρ πάντα δι' ὑμᾶς, ἵνα ἡ χάρις πλεονάσασα διὰ τῶν πλειόνων τὴν εὐχαριστίαν περισσεύσῃ εἰς τὴν δόξαν τοῦ θεοῦ.

2 Cor 6:3–10

Μηδεμίαν ἐν μηδενὶ διδόντες προσκοπήν, ἵνα μὴ μωμηθῇ ἡ διακονία, 4 ἀλλ' ἐν παντὶ συνιστάντες ἑαυτοὺς ὡς θεοῦ διάκονοι, ἐν ὑπομονῇ πολλῇ, ἐν θλίψεσιν, ἐν ἀνάγκαις, ἐν στενοχωρίαις, 5 ἐν πληγαῖς, ἐν φυλακαῖς, ἐν ἀκαταστασίαις, ἐν κόποις, ἐν ἀγρυπνίαις, ἐν νηστείαις, 6 ἐν ἁγνότητι, ἐν γνώσει, ἐν μακροθυμίᾳ, ἐν χρηστότητι, ἐν πνεύματι ἁγίῳ, ἐν ἀγάπῃ ἀνυποκρίτῳ, 7 ἐν λόγῳ ἀληθείας, ἐν δυνάμει θεοῦ· διὰ τῶν ὅπλων τῆς δικαιοσύνης τῶν δεξιῶν καὶ ἀριστερῶν, 8 διὰ δόξης καὶ ἀτιμίας, διὰ δυσφημίας καὶ εὐφημίας· ὡς πλάνοι καὶ ἀληθεῖς, 9 ὡς ἀγνοούμενοι καὶ ἐπιγινωσκόμενοι, ὡς ἀποθνῄσκοντες καὶ ἰδοὺ ζῶμεν, ὡς παιδευόμενοι καὶ μὴ θανατούμενοι, 10 ὡς λυπούμενοι ἀεὶ δὲ χαίροντες, ὡς πτωχοὶ πολλοὺς δὲ πλουτίζοντες, ὡς μηδὲν ἔχοντες καὶ πάντα κατέχοντες.

1 Thess 2:1–12

Αὐτοὶ γὰρ οἴδατε, ἀδελφοί, τὴν εἴσοδον ἡμῶν τὴν πρὸς ὑμᾶς ὅτι οὐ κενὴ γέγονεν, 2 ἀλλὰ προπαθόντες καὶ ὑβρισθέντες, καθὼς οἴδατε, ἐν Φιλίπποις ἐπαρρησιασάμεθα ἐν τῷ θεῷ ἡμῶν λαλῆσαι πρὸς ὑμᾶς τὸ εὐαγγέλιον τοῦ θεοῦ ἐν πολλῷ ἀγῶνι. 3 ἡ γὰρ παράκλησις ἡμῶν οὐκ ἐκ πλάνης οὐδὲ ἐξ ἀκαθαρσίας οὐδὲ ἐν δόλῳ, 4 ἀλλὰ καθὼς δεδοκιμάσμεθα ὑπὸ τοῦ θεοῦ πιστευθῆναι τὸ εὐαγγέλιον, οὕτως λαλοῦμεν, οὐχ ὡς ἀνθρώποις ἀρέσκοντες ἀλλὰ θεῷ τῷ δοκιμάζοντι τὰς καρδίας ἡμῶν. 5 Οὔτε γάρ ποτε ἐν λόγῳ κολακείας ἐγενήθημεν, καθὼς οἴδατε, οὔτε ἐν προφάσει πλεονεξίας, θεὸς μάρτυς, 6 οὔτε ζητοῦντες ἐξ ἀνθρώπων δόξαν οὔτε ἀφ' ὑμῶν οὔτε ἀπ' ἄλλων, 7 δυνάμενοι ἐν βάρει εἶναι ὡς Χριστοῦ ἀπόστολοι. ἀλλὰ ἐγενήθημεν ⸀νήπιοι ἐν μέσῳ ὑμῶν, ὡς ἐὰν τροφὸς θάλπῃ τὰ ἑαυτῆς τέκνα, 8 οὕτως ὁμειρόμενοι ὑμῶν εὐδοκοῦμεν μεταδοῦναι ὑμῖν οὐ μόνον τὸ εὐαγγέλιον τοῦ θεοῦ ἀλλὰ καὶ τὰς ἑαυτῶν ψυχάς, διότι ἀγαπητοὶ ἡμῖν ἐγενήθητε. 9 Μνημονεύετε γάρ, ἀδελφοί, τὸν κόπον ἡμῶν καὶ τὸν μόχθον· νυκτὸς καὶ ἡμέρας ἐργαζόμενοι πρὸς τὸ μὴ ἐπιβαρῆσαί τινα ὑμῶν ἐκηρύξαμεν εἰς ὑμᾶς τὸ εὐαγγέλιον τοῦ θεοῦ. 10 ὑμεῖς μάρτυρες καὶ ὁ θεός, ὡς ὁσίως καὶ δικαίως καὶ ἀμέμπτως ὑμῖν τοῖς πιστεύουσιν ἐγενήθημεν, 11 καθάπερ οἴδατε, ὡς ἕνα ἕκαστον ὑμῶν ὡς πατὴρ τέκνα ἑαυτοῦ 12 παρακαλοῦντες ὑμᾶς καὶ παραμυθούμενοι καὶ μαρτυρόμενοι εἰς τὸ περιπατεῖν ὑμᾶς ἀξίως τοῦ θεοῦ τοῦ ⸀καλοῦντος ὑμᾶς εἰς τὴν ἑαυτοῦ βασιλείαν καὶ δόξαν.

Cf. 1 Cor 4:9–13; 2 Cor 1:3–11; 10:1–18; 11:5–21a; 11:21b–12:10; 12:11–18; Phil 1:12–26; 3:2–11; 3:12–16; 4:10–20; Acts 20:17–35.

106. A Door for the Message

1 Cor 16:5–9

Ἐλεύσομαι δὲ πρὸς ὑμᾶς ὅταν Μακεδονίαν διέλθω· Μακεδονίαν γὰρ διέρχομαι, 6 πρὸς ὑμᾶς δὲ τυχὸν παραμενῶ ἢ καὶ παραχειμάσω, ἵνα ὑμεῖς με προπέμψητε οὗ ἐὰν πορεύωμαι. 7 οὐ θέλω γὰρ ὑμᾶς ἄρτι ἐν παρόδῳ ἰδεῖν, ἐλπίζω γὰρ χρόνον τινὰ ἐπιμεῖναι πρὸς ὑμᾶς ἐὰν ὁ κύριος ἐπιτρέψῃ. 8 ἐπιμενῶ δὲ ἐν Ἐφέσῳ ἕως τῆς πεντηκοστῆς· 9 θύρα γάρ μοι ἀνέῳγεν μεγάλη καὶ ἐνεργής, καὶ ἀντικείμενοι πολλοί.

2 Cor 2:12–13

Ἐλθὼν δὲ εἰς τὴν Τρῳάδα εἰς τὸ εὐαγγέλιον τοῦ Χριστοῦ καὶ θύρας μοι ἀνεῳγμένης ἐν κυρίῳ, 13 οὐκ ἔσχηκα ἄνεσιν τῷ πνεύματί μου τῷ μὴ εὑρεῖν με Τίτον τὸν ἀδελφόν μου, ἀλλὰ ἀποταξάμενος αὐτοῖς ἐξῆλθον εἰς Μακεδονίαν.

Col 4:2–4

Τῇ προσευχῇ προσκαρτερεῖτε, γρηγοροῦντες ἐν αὐτῇ ἐν εὐχαριστίᾳ, 3 προσευχόμενοι ἅμα καὶ περὶ ἡμῶν, ἵνα ὁ θεὸς ἀνοίξῃ ἡμῖν θύραν τοῦ λόγου λαλῆσαι τὸ μυστήριον τοῦ Χριστοῦ, δι' ὃ καὶ δέδεμαι, 4 ἵνα φανερώσω αὐτὸ ὡς δεῖ με λαλῆσαι.

Cf. 1 Thess 1:9–10; 2:1–2.

§ 105 **2 Cor 4:14** ***κυριον*** ℵ C D 1881 *Byz*] *om.* 𝔓[46] B (33) (1739) **1 Thess 2:7** ***νηπιοι*** 𝔓[65] ℵ* B C* D* I] ηπιοι ℵ[2] A C[2] D[2] 33. 1739. 1881 *Byz* **1 Thess 2:12** ***καλουντος*** B D 33. 1739. 1881 *Byz*] καλεσαντος ℵ A

2 Cor 4:1–15

Therefore, since it is by God's mercy that we are engaged in this ministry, we do not lose heart. **2** We have renounced the shameful things that one hides; we refuse to practice cunning or to falsify God's word; but by the open statement of the truth we commend ourselves to the conscience of everyone in the sight of God. **3** And even if our gospel is veiled, it is veiled to those who are perishing. **4** In their case the god of this world has blinded the minds of the unbelievers, to keep them from seeing the light of the gospel of the glory of Christ, who is the image of God. **5** For we do not proclaim ourselves; we proclaim Jesus Christ as Lord and ourselves as your slaves for Jesus' sake. **6** For it is the God who said, "Let light shine out of darkness," who has shone in our hearts to give the light of the knowledge of the glory of God in the face of Jesus Christ. **7** But we have this treasure in clay jars, so that it may be made clear that this extraordinary power belongs to God and does not come from us. **8** We are afflicted in every way, but not crushed; perplexed, but not driven to despair; **9** persecuted, but not forsaken; struck down, but not destroyed; **10** always carrying in the body the death of Jesus, so that the life of Jesus may also be made visible in our bodies. **11** For while we live, we are always being given up to death for Jesus' sake, so that the life of Jesus may be made visible in our mortal flesh. **12** So death is at work in us, but life in you. **13** But just as we have the same spirit of faith that is in accordance with scripture—"I believed, and so I spoke"—we also believe, and so we speak, **14** because we know that the one who raised the Lord[a] Jesus will raise us also with Jesus, and will bring us with you into his presence. **15** Yes, everything is for your sake, so that grace, as it extends to more and more people, may increase thanksgiving, to the glory of God.

2 Cor 6:3–10

We are putting no obstacle in anyone's way, so that no fault may be found with our ministry, **4** but as servants of God we have commended ourselves in every way: through great endurance, in afflictions, hardships, calamities, **5** beatings, imprisonments, riots, labors, sleepless nights, hunger; **6** by purity, knowledge, patience, kindness, holiness of spirit, genuine love, **7** truthful speech, and the power of God; with the weapons of righteousness for the right hand and for the left; **8** in honor and dishonor, in ill repute and good repute. We are treated as impostors, and yet are true; **9** as unknown, and yet are well known; as dying, and see—we are alive; as punished, and yet not killed; **10** as sorrowful, yet always rejoicing; as poor, yet making many rich; as having nothing, and yet possessing everything.

1 Thess 2:1–12

You yourselves know, brothers and sisters, that our coming to you was not in vain, **2** but though we had already suffered and been shamefully mistreated at Philippi, as you know, we had courage in our God to declare to you the gospel of God in spite of great opposition. **3** For our appeal does not spring from deceit or impure motives or trickery, **4** but just as we have been approved by God to be entrusted with the message of the gospel, even so we speak, not to please mortals, but to please God who tests our hearts. **5** As you know and as God is our witness, we never came with words of flattery or with a pretext for greed; **6** nor did we seek praise from mortals, whether from you or from others, **7** though we might have made demands as apostles of Christ. But we were gentle[b] among you, like a nurse tenderly caring for her own children. **8** So deeply do we care for you that we are determined to share with you not only the gospel of God but also our own selves, because you have become very dear to us. **9** You remember our labor and toil, brothers and sisters; we worked night and day, so that we might not burden any of you while we proclaimed to you the gospel of God. **10** You are witnesses, and God also, how pure, upright, and blameless our conduct was toward you believers. **11** As you know, we dealt with each one of you like a father with his children, **12** urging and encouraging you and pleading that you lead a life worthy of God, who calls[c] you into his own kingdom and glory.

Cf. 1 Cor 4:9–13; 2 Cor 1:3–11; 10:1–18; 11:5–21a; 11:21b–12:10; 12:11–18; Phil 1:12–26; 3:2–11; 3:12–16; 4:10–20; Acts 20:17–35.

106. A Door for the Message

1 Cor 16:5–9

I will visit you after passing through Macedonia—for I intend to pass through Macedonia— **6** and perhaps I will stay with you or even spend the winter, so that you may send me on my way, wherever I go. **7** I do not want to see you now just in passing, for I hope to spend some time with you, if the Lord permits. **8** But I will stay in Ephesus until Pentecost, **9** for a wide door for effective work has opened to me, and there are many adversaries.

2 Cor 2:12–13

When I came to Troas to proclaim the good news of Christ, a door was opened for me in the Lord; **13** but my mind could not rest because I did not find my brother Titus there. So I said farewell to them and went on to Macedonia.

Col 4:2–4

Devote yourselves to prayer, keeping alert in it with thanksgiving. **3** At the same time pray for us as well that God will open to us a door for the word, that we may declare the mystery of Christ, for which I am in prison, **4** so that I may reveal it clearly, as I should.

Cf. 1 Thess 1:9–10; 2:1–2.

§ 105 [a] **2 Cor 4:14** *the Lord* Other ancient authorities lack *the Lord* [b] **1 Thess 2:7** *gentle* Other ancient authorities read *infants* [c] **1 Thess 2:12** *calls* Other ancient authorities read *called*

107. Paul's Founding Preaching

1 Cor 2:1–5

Κἀγὼ ἐλθὼν πρὸς ὑμᾶς, ἀδελφοί, ἦλθον οὐ καθ' ὑπεροχὴν λόγου ἢ σοφίας καταγγέλλων ὑμῖν τὸ ⸀μυστήριον τοῦ θεοῦ. 2 οὐ γὰρ ἔκρινά τι εἰδέναι ἐν ὑμῖν εἰ μὴ Ἰησοῦν Χριστὸν καὶ τοῦτον ἐσταυρωμένον. 3 κἀγὼ ἐν ἀσθενείᾳ καὶ ἐν φόβῳ καὶ ἐν τρόμῳ πολλῷ ἐγενόμην πρὸς ὑμᾶς, 4 καὶ ὁ λόγος μου καὶ τὸ κήρυγμά μου οὐκ ἐν ⸂πειθοῖ[ς] σοφίας [λόγοις]⸃ ἀλλ' ἐν ἀποδείξει πνεύματος καὶ δυνάμεως, 5 ἵνα ἡ πίστις ὑμῶν μὴ ᾖ ἐν σοφίᾳ ἀνθρώπων ἀλλ' ἐν δυνάμει θεοῦ.

1 Cor 15:1–11

Γνωρίζω δὲ ὑμῖν, ἀδελφοί, τὸ εὐαγγέλιον ὃ εὐηγγελισάμην ὑμῖν, ὃ καὶ παρελάβετε, ἐν ᾧ καὶ ἑστήκατε, 2 δι' οὗ καὶ σῴζεσθε, τίνι λόγῳ εὐηγγελισάμην ὑμῖν εἰ κατέχετε, ἐκτὸς εἰ μὴ εἰκῇ ἐπιστεύσατε. 3 παρέδωκα γὰρ ὑμῖν ἐν πρώτοις, ὃ καὶ παρέλαβον, ὅτι Χριστὸς ἀπέθανεν ὑπὲρ τῶν ἁμαρτιῶν ἡμῶν κατὰ τὰς γραφὰς 4 καὶ ὅτι ἐτάφη καὶ ὅτι ἐγήγερται τῇ ἡμέρᾳ τῇ τρίτῃ κατὰ τὰς γραφὰς 5 καὶ ὅτι ὤφθη Κηφᾷ εἶτα τοῖς δώδεκα· 6 ἔπειτα ὤφθη ἐπάνω πεντακοσίοις ἀδελφοῖς ἐφάπαξ, ἐξ ὧν οἱ πλείονες μένουσιν ἕως ἄρτι, τινὲς δὲ ἐκοιμήθησαν· 7 ἔπειτα ὤφθη Ἰακώβῳ εἶτα τοῖς ἀποστόλοις πᾶσιν· 8 ἔσχατον δὲ πάντων ὡσπερεὶ τῷ ἐκτρώματι ὤφθη κἀμοί. 9 Ἐγὼ γάρ εἰμι ὁ ἐλάχιστος τῶν ἀποστόλων ὃς οὐκ εἰμὶ ἱκανὸς καλεῖσθαι ἀπόστολος, διότι ἐδίωξα τὴν ἐκκλησίαν τοῦ θεοῦ· 10 χάριτι δὲ θεοῦ εἰμι ὅ εἰμι, καὶ ἡ χάρις αὐτοῦ ἡ εἰς ἐμὲ οὐ κενὴ ἐγενήθη, ἀλλὰ περισσότερον αὐτῶν πάντων ἐκοπίασα, οὐκ ἐγὼ δὲ ἀλλὰ ἡ χάρις τοῦ θεοῦ [ἡ] σὺν ἐμοί. 11 εἴτε οὖν ἐγὼ εἴτε ἐκεῖνοι, οὕτως κηρύσσομεν καὶ οὕτως ἐπιστεύσατε.

2 Cor 1:18–22

πιστὸς δὲ ὁ θεὸς ὅτι ὁ λόγος ἡμῶν ὁ πρὸς ὑμᾶς οὐκ ἔστιν ναὶ καὶ οὔ. 19 ὁ τοῦ θεοῦ γὰρ υἱὸς Ἰησοῦς Χριστὸς ὁ ἐν ὑμῖν δι' ἡμῶν κηρυχθείς, δι' ἐμοῦ καὶ Σιλουανοῦ καὶ Τιμοθέου, οὐκ ἐγένετο ναὶ καὶ οὒ ἀλλὰ ναὶ ἐν αὐτῷ γέγονεν. 20 ὅσαι γὰρ ἐπαγγελίαι θεοῦ, ἐν αὐτῷ τὸ ναί· διὸ καὶ δι' αὐτοῦ τὸ ἀμὴν τῷ θεῷ πρὸς δόξαν δι' ἡμῶν. 21 ὁ δὲ βεβαιῶν ἡμᾶς σὺν ὑμῖν εἰς Χριστὸν καὶ χρίσας ἡμᾶς θεός, 22 ὁ καὶ σφραγισάμενος ἡμᾶς καὶ δοὺς τὸν ἀρραβῶνα τοῦ πνεύματος ἐν ταῖς καρδίαις ἡμῶν.

Gal 3:1–2

Ὦ ἀνόητοι Γαλάται, τίς ὑμᾶς ἐβάσκανεν, οἷς κατ' ὀφθαλμοὺς Ἰησοῦς Χριστὸς προεγράφη ἐσταυρωμένος; 2 τοῦτο μόνον θέλω μαθεῖν ἀφ' ὑμῶν· ἐξ ἔργων νόμου τὸ πνεῦμα ἐλάβετε ἢ ἐξ ἀκοῆς πίστεως;

Gal 4:12–15

Γίνεσθε ὡς ἐγώ, ὅτι κἀγὼ ὡς ὑμεῖς, ἀδελφοί, δέομαι ὑμῶν. οὐδέν με ἠδικήσατε· 13 οἴδατε δὲ ὅτι δι' ἀσθένειαν τῆς σαρκὸς εὐηγγελισάμην ὑμῖν τὸ πρότερον, 14 καὶ τὸν πειρασμὸν ὑμῶν ἐν τῇ σαρκί μου οὐκ ἐξουθενήσατε οὐδὲ ἐξεπτύσατε, ἀλλὰ ὡς ἄγγελον θεοῦ ἐδέξασθέ με, ὡς Χριστὸν Ἰησοῦν. 15 ποῦ οὖν ὁ μακαρισμὸς ὑμῶν; μαρτυρῶ γὰρ ὑμῖν ὅτι εἰ δυνατὸν τοὺς ὀφθαλμοὺς ὑμῶν ἐξορύξαντες ἐδώκατέ μοι.

1 Thess 1:4–10

εἰδότες, ἀδελφοὶ ἠγαπημένοι ὑπὸ [τοῦ] θεοῦ, τὴν ἐκλογὴν ὑμῶν, 5 ὅτι τὸ εὐαγγέλιον ἡμῶν οὐκ ἐγενήθη εἰς ὑμᾶς ἐν λόγῳ μόνον ἀλλὰ καὶ ἐν δυνάμει καὶ ἐν πνεύματι ἁγίῳ καὶ [ἐν] πληροφορίᾳ πολλῇ, καθὼς οἴδατε οἷοι ἐγενήθημεν [ἐν] ὑμῖν δι' ὑμᾶς. 6 Καὶ ὑμεῖς μιμηταὶ ἡμῶν ἐγενήθητε καὶ τοῦ κυρίου, δεξάμενοι τὸν λόγον ἐν θλίψει πολλῇ μετὰ χαρᾶς πνεύματος ἁγίου, 7 ὥστε γενέσθαι ὑμᾶς τύπον πᾶσιν τοῖς πιστεύουσιν ἐν τῇ Μακεδονίᾳ καὶ ἐν τῇ Ἀχαΐᾳ. 8 ἀφ' ὑμῶν γὰρ ἐξήχηται ὁ λόγος τοῦ κυρίου οὐ μόνον ἐν τῇ Μακεδονίᾳ καὶ [ἐν τῇ] Ἀχαΐᾳ, ἀλλ' ἐν παντὶ τόπῳ ἡ πίστις ὑμῶν ἡ πρὸς τὸν θεὸν ἐξελήλυθεν, ὥστε μὴ χρείαν ἔχειν ἡμᾶς λαλεῖν τι. 9 αὐτοὶ γὰρ περὶ ἡμῶν ἀπαγγέλλουσιν ὁποίαν εἴσοδον ἔσχομεν πρὸς ὑμᾶς, καὶ πῶς ἐπεστρέψατε πρὸς τὸν θεὸν ἀπὸ τῶν εἰδώλων δουλεύειν θεῷ ζῶντι καὶ ἀληθινῷ 10 καὶ ἀναμένειν τὸν υἱὸν αὐτοῦ ἐκ τῶν οὐρανῶν, ὃν ἤγειρεν ἐκ [τῶν] νεκρῶν, Ἰησοῦν τὸν ῥυόμενον ἡμᾶς ἐκ τῆς ὀργῆς τῆς ἐρχομένης.

1 Thess 2:1–12

Αὐτοὶ γὰρ οἴδατε, ἀδελφοί, τὴν εἴσοδον ἡμῶν τὴν πρὸς ὑμᾶς ὅτι οὐ κενὴ γέγονεν, 2 ἀλλὰ προπαθόντες καὶ ὑβρισθέντες, καθὼς οἴδατε, ἐν Φιλίπποις ἐπαρρησιασάμεθα ἐν τῷ θεῷ ἡμῶν λαλῆσαι πρὸς ὑμᾶς τὸ εὐαγγέλιον τοῦ θεοῦ ἐν πολλῷ ἀγῶνι. 3 ἡ γὰρ παράκλησις ἡμῶν οὐκ ἐκ πλάνης οὐδὲ ἐξ ἀκαθαρσίας οὐδὲ ἐν δόλῳ, 4 ἀλλὰ καθὼς δεδοκιμάσμεθα ὑπὸ τοῦ θεοῦ πιστευθῆναι τὸ εὐαγγέλιον, οὕτως λαλοῦμεν, οὐχ ὡς ἀνθρώποις ἀρέσκοντες ἀλλὰ θεῷ τῷ δοκιμάζοντι τὰς καρδίας ἡμῶν. 5 Οὔτε γάρ ποτε ἐν λόγῳ κολακείας ἐγενήθημεν, καθὼς οἴδατε, οὔτε ἐν προφάσει πλεονεξίας, θεὸς μάρτυς, 6 οὔτε ζητοῦντες ἐξ ἀνθρώπων δόξαν οὔτε ἀφ' ὑμῶν οὔτε ἀπ' ἄλλων, 7 δυνάμενοι ἐν βάρει εἶναι ὡς Χριστοῦ ἀπόστολοι. ἀλλὰ ἐγενήθημεν ⸀νήπιοι ἐν μέσῳ ὑμῶν, ὡς ἐὰν τροφὸς θάλπῃ τὰ ἑαυτῆς τέκνα, 8 οὕτως ὁμειρόμενοι ὑμῶν εὐδοκοῦμεν μεταδοῦναι ὑμῖν οὐ μόνον τὸ εὐαγγέλιον τοῦ θεοῦ ἀλλὰ καὶ τὰς ἑαυτῶν ψυχάς, διότι ἀγαπητοὶ ἡμῖν ἐγενήθητε. 9 Μνημονεύετε γάρ, ἀδελφοί, τὸν κόπον ἡμῶν καὶ τὸν μόχθον· νυκτὸς καὶ ἡμέρας ἐργαζόμενοι πρὸς τὸ μὴ ἐπιβαρῆσαί τινα ὑμῶν ἐκηρύξαμεν εἰς ὑμᾶς τὸ εὐαγγέλιον τοῦ θεοῦ. 10 ὑμεῖς μάρτυρες καὶ ὁ θεός, ὡς ὁσίως καὶ δικαίως καὶ ἀμέμπτως ὑμῖν τοῖς πιστεύουσιν ἐγενήθημεν, 11 καθάπερ οἴδατε, ὡς ἕνα ἕκαστον ὑμῶν ὡς πατὴρ τέκνα ἑαυτοῦ 12 παρακαλοῦντες ὑμᾶς καὶ παραμυθούμενοι καὶ μαρτυρόμενοι εἰς τὸ περιπατεῖν ὑμᾶς ἀξίως τοῦ θεοῦ τοῦ ⸀καλοῦντος ὑμᾶς εἰς τὴν ἑαυτοῦ βασιλείαν καὶ δόξαν.

Cf. Rom 15:14–21; 1 Cor 1:14–17; 2 Tim 3:10–11; Acts 13:16–41; 14:14–18; 17:2–3; 17:22–31; 19:26.

§ 107 1 Cor 2:1 ***μυστηριον*** 𝔓^{46vid} ℵ* A C] μαρτυριον ℵ^2 B D 33. 1739. 1881 *Byz* 1 Cor 2:4 ***πειθοις σοφιας λογοις*** (ℵ*) B D 33. 1739. 1881] πειθοις ανθρωπινης σοφιας λογοις ℵ^2 A C *Byz* ¦ πειθοις σοφιας 𝔓^{46} ¦ πειθοι σοφιας *cj* 1 Thess 2:7 ***νηπιοι*** 𝔓^{65} ℵ* B C* D* I] ηπιοι ℵ^2 A C^2 D^2 33. 1739. 1881 *Byz* 1 Thess 2:12 ***καλουντος*** B D 33. 1739. 1881 *Byz*] καλεσαντος ℵ A

107. *Paul's Founding Preaching*

1 Cor 2:1–5

When I came to you, brothers and sisters, I did not come proclaiming the mystery[a] of God to you in lofty words or wisdom. 2 For I decided to know nothing among you except Jesus Christ, and him crucified. 3 And I came to you in weakness and in fear and in much trembling. 4 My speech and my proclamation were not with plausible words of wisdom,[b] but with a demonstration of the Spirit and of power, 5 so that your faith might rest not on human wisdom but on the power of God.

1 Cor 15:1–11

Now I would remind you, brothers and sisters, of the good news that I proclaimed to you, which you in turn received, in which also you stand, 2 through which also you are being saved, if you hold firmly to the message that I proclaimed to you—unless you have come to believe in vain. 3 For I handed on to you as of first importance what I in turn had received: that Christ died for our sins in accordance with the scriptures, 4 and that he was buried, and that he was raised on the third day in accordance with the scriptures, 5 and that he appeared to Cephas, then to the twelve. 6 Then he appeared to more than five hundred brothers and sisters at one time, most of whom are still alive, though some have died. 7 Then he appeared to James, then to all the apostles. 8 Last of all, as to one untimely born, he appeared also to me. 9 For I am the least of the apostles, unfit to be called an apostle, because I persecuted the church of God. 10 But by the grace of God I am what I am, and his grace toward me has not been in vain. On the contrary, I worked harder than any of them—though it was not I, but the grace of God that is with me. 11 Whether then it was I or they, so we proclaim and so you have come to believe.

2 Cor 1:18–22

As surely as God is faithful, our word to you has not been "Yes and No." 19 For the Son of God, Jesus Christ, whom we proclaimed among you, Silvanus and Timothy and I, was not "Yes and No"; but in him it is always "Yes." 20 For in him every one of God's promises is a "Yes." For this reason it is through him that we say the "Amen," to the glory of God. 21 But it is God who establishes us with you in Christ and has anointed us, 22 by putting his seal on us and giving us his Spirit in our hearts as a first installment.

Gal 3:1–2

You foolish Galatians! Who has bewitched you? It was before your eyes that Jesus Christ was publicly exhibited as crucified! 2 The only thing I want to learn from you is this: Did you receive the Spirit by doing the works of the law or by believing what you heard?

Gal 4:12–15

Friends, I beg you, become as I am, for I also have become as you are. You have done me no wrong. 13 You know that it was because of a physical infirmity that I first announced the gospel to you; 14 though my condition put you to the test, you did not scorn or despise me, but welcomed me as an angel of God, as Christ Jesus. 15 What has become of the goodwill you felt? For I testify that, had it been possible, you would have torn out your eyes and given them to me.

1 Thess 1:4–10

For we know, brothers and sisters beloved by God, that he has chosen you, 5 because our message of the gospel came to you not in word only, but also in power and in the Holy Spirit and with full conviction; just as you know what kind of persons we proved to be among you for your sake. 6 And you became imitators of us and of the Lord, for in spite of persecution you received the word with joy inspired by the Holy Spirit, 7 so that you became an example to all the believers in Macedonia and in Achaia. 8 For the word of the Lord has sounded forth from you not only in Macedonia and Achaia, but in every place your faith in God has become known, so that we have no need to speak about it. 9 For the people of those regions report about us what kind of welcome we had among you, and how you turned to God from idols, to serve a living and true God, 10 and to wait for his Son from heaven, whom he raised from the dead—Jesus, who rescues us from the wrath that is coming.

1 Thess 2:1–12

You yourselves know, brothers and sisters, that our coming to you was not in vain, 2 but though we had already suffered and been shamefully mistreated at Philippi, as you know, we had courage in our God to declare to you the gospel of God in spite of great opposition. 3 For our appeal does not spring from deceit or impure motives or trickery, 4 but just as we have been approved by God to be entrusted with the message of the gospel, even so we speak, not to please mortals, but to please God who tests our hearts. 5 As you know and as God is our witness, we never came with words of flattery or with a pretext for greed; 6 nor did we seek praise from mortals, whether from you or from others, 7 though we might have made demands as apostles of Christ. But we were gentle[c] among you, like a nurse tenderly caring for her own children. 8 So deeply do we care for you that we are determined to share with you not only the gospel of God but also our own selves, because you have become very dear to us. 9 You remember our labor and toil, brothers and sisters; we worked night and day, so that we might not burden any of you while we proclaimed to you the gospel of God. 10 You are witnesses, and God also, how pure, upright, and blameless our conduct was toward you believers. 11 As you know, we dealt with each one of you like a father with his children, 12 urging and encouraging you and pleading that you lead a life worthy of God, who calls[d] you into his own kingdom and glory.

Cf. Rom 15:14–21; 1 Cor 1:14–17; 2 Tim 3:10–11; Acts 13:16–41; 14:14–18; 17:2–3; 17:22–31; 19:26.

§ 107 [a] 1 Cor 2:1 *mystery* Other ancient authorities read *testimony* [b] 1 Cor 2:4 *plausible words of wisdom* Other ancient authorities provide evidence for the reading *the persuasiveness of wisdom*; others read *plausible words of human wisdom* [c] 1 Thess 2:7 *gentle* Other ancient authorities read *infants* [d] 1 Thess 2:12 *calls* Other ancient authorities read *called*

108. The Pattern of Teaching

Rom 6:17–18

χάρις δὲ τῷ θεῷ ὅτι ἦτε δοῦλοι τῆς ἁμαρ-
τίας ὑπηκούσατε δὲ ἐκ καρδίας εἰς ὃν
παρεδόθητε τύπον διδαχῆς, **18** ἐλευθερω-
θέντες δὲ ἀπὸ τῆς ἁμαρτίας ἐδουλώθητε
τῇ δικαιοσύνῃ.

Rom 16:17–20

Παρακαλῶ δὲ ὑμᾶς, ἀδελφοί, σκοπεῖν
τοὺς τὰς διχοστασίας καὶ τὰ σκάνδαλα
παρὰ τὴν διδαχὴν ἣν ὑμεῖς ἐμάθετε ποι-
οῦντας, καὶ ἐκκλίνετε ἀπ᾽ αὐτῶν· **18** οἱ
γὰρ τοιοῦτοι τῷ κυρίῳ ἡμῶν Χριστῷ οὐ
δουλεύουσιν ἀλλὰ τῇ ἑαυτῶν κοιλίᾳ,
καὶ διὰ τῆς χρηστολογίας καὶ εὐλογίας
ἐξαπατῶσιν τὰς καρδίας τῶν ἀκάκων.
19 ἡ γὰρ ὑμῶν ὑπακοὴ εἰς πάντας ἀφί-
κετο· ἐφ᾽ ὑμῖν οὖν χαίρω, θέλω δὲ ὑμᾶς
σοφοὺς εἶναι εἰς τὸ ἀγαθόν, ἀκεραίους
δὲ εἰς τὸ κακόν. **20** ὁ δὲ θεὸς τῆς εἰρήνης
συντρίψει τὸν σατανᾶν ὑπὸ τοὺς πόδας
ὑμῶν ἐν τάχει. ⸀Ἡ χάρις τοῦ κυρίου
ἡμῶν Ἰησοῦ μεθ᾽ ὑμῶν.⸃

1 Cor 11:2

Ἐπαινῶ δὲ ὑμᾶς ὅτι πάντα μου μέμνησθε
καί, καθὼς παρέδωκα ὑμῖν, τὰς παραδό-
σεις κατέχετε.

1 Cor 11:23–25

Ἐγὼ γὰρ παρέλαβον ἀπὸ τοῦ κυρίου, ὃ
καὶ παρέδωκα ὑμῖν, ὅτι ὁ κύριος Ἰησοῦς
ἐν τῇ νυκτὶ ᾗ παρεδίδετο ἔλαβεν ἄρτον
24 καὶ εὐχαριστήσας ἔκλασεν καὶ εἶπεν·
τοῦτό μού ἐστιν τὸ σῶμα τὸ ὑπὲρ ⸀ὑμῶν·
τοῦτο ποιεῖτε εἰς τὴν ἐμὴν ἀνάμνησιν.
25 ὡσαύτως καὶ τὸ ποτήριον μετὰ τὸ
δειπνῆσαι λέγων· τοῦτο τὸ ποτήριον ἡ
καινὴ διαθήκη ἐστὶν ἐν τῷ ἐμῷ αἵματι·
τοῦτο ποιεῖτε, ὁσάκις ἐὰν πίνητε, εἰς
τὴν ἐμὴν ἀνάμνησιν.

1 Cor 15:1–8

Γνωρίζω δὲ ὑμῖν, ἀδελφοί, τὸ εὐαγγέλιον
ὃ εὐηγγελισάμην ὑμῖν, ὃ καὶ παρελάβετε,
ἐν ᾧ καὶ ἑστήκατε, **2** δι᾽ οὗ καὶ σῴζεσθε,
τίνι λόγῳ εὐηγγελισάμην ὑμῖν εἰ κα-
τέχετε, ἐκτὸς εἰ μὴ εἰκῇ ἐπιστεύσατε.
3 παρέδωκα γὰρ ὑμῖν ἐν πρώτοις, ὃ καὶ
παρέλαβον, ὅτι Χριστὸς ἀπέθανεν ὑπὲρ
τῶν ἁμαρτιῶν ἡμῶν κατὰ τὰς γραφὰς
4 καὶ ὅτι ἐτάφη καὶ ὅτι ἐγήγερται τῇ
ἡμέρᾳ τῇ τρίτῃ κατὰ τὰς γραφὰς **5** καὶ ὅτι
ὤφθη Κηφᾷ εἶτα τοῖς δώδεκα· **6** ἔπειτα
ὤφθη ἐπάνω πεντακοσίοις ἀδελφοῖς
ἐφάπαξ, ἐξ ὧν οἱ πλείονες μένουσιν
ἕως ἄρτι, τινὲς δὲ ἐκοιμήθησαν· **7** ἔπειτα
ὤφθη Ἰακώβῳ εἶτα τοῖς ἀποστόλοις
πᾶσιν· **8** ἔσχατον δὲ πάντων ὡσπερεὶ τῷ
ἐκτρώματι ὤφθη κἀμοί.

Phil 4:9

ἃ καὶ ἐμάθετε καὶ παρελάβετε καὶ ἠκούσατε
καὶ εἴδετε ἐν ἐμοί, ταῦτα πράσσετε· καὶ ὁ
θεὸς τῆς εἰρήνης ἔσται μεθ᾽ ὑμῶν.

Col 2:6–7

Ὡς οὖν παρελάβετε τὸν Χριστὸν Ἰη-
σοῦν τὸν κύριον, ἐν αὐτῷ περιπατεῖτε,
7 ἐρριζωμένοι καὶ ἐποικοδομούμενοι
ἐν αὐτῷ καὶ βεβαιούμενοι τῇ πίστει
καθὼς ἐδιδάχθητε, περισσεύοντες ἐν
εὐχαριστίᾳ.

2 Thess 2:15

Ἄρα οὖν, ἀδελφοί, στήκετε καὶ κρατεῖτε
τὰς παραδόσεις ἃς ἐδιδάχθητε εἴτε διὰ
λόγου εἴτε δι᾽ ἐπιστολῆς ἡμῶν.

2 Thess 3:6

Παραγγέλλομεν δὲ ὑμῖν, ἀδελφοί, ἐν ὀνό-
ματι τοῦ κυρίου [ἡμῶν] Ἰησοῦ Χριστοῦ
στέλλεσθαι ὑμᾶς ἀπὸ παντὸς ἀδελφοῦ
ἀτάκτως περιπατοῦντος καὶ μὴ κατὰ
τὴν παράδοσιν ἣν ⸀παρελάβοσαν παρ᾽
ἡμῶν.

1 Tim 6:20–21

Ὦ Τιμόθεε, τὴν παραθήκην φύλαξον
ἐκτρεπόμενος τὰς βεβήλους κενοφω-
νίας καὶ ἀντιθέσεις τῆς ψευδωνύμου
γνώσεως, **21** ἥν τινες ἐπαγγελλόμενοι
περὶ τὴν πίστιν ἠστόχησαν. Ἡ χάρις
⸀μεθ᾽ ὑμῶν⸃.

2 Tim 1:13–14

Ὑποτύπωσιν ἔχε ὑγιαινόντων λόγων ὧν
παρ᾽ ἐμοῦ ἤκουσας ἐν πίστει καὶ ἀγάπῃ
τῇ ἐν Χριστῷ Ἰησοῦ· **14** τὴν καλὴν πα-
ραθήκην φύλαξον διὰ πνεύματος ἁγίου
τοῦ ἐνοικοῦντος ἐν ἡμῖν.

2 Tim 2:1–2

Σὺ οὖν, τέκνον μου, ἐνδυναμοῦ ἐν τῇ χά-
ριτι τῇ ἐν Χριστῷ Ἰησοῦ, **2** καὶ ἃ ἤκουσας
παρ᾽ ἐμοῦ διὰ πολλῶν μαρτύρων, ταῦτα
παράθου πιστοῖς ἀνθρώποις, οἵτινες ἱκα-
νοὶ ἔσονται καὶ ἑτέρους διδάξαι.

Titus 1:9

ἀντεχόμενον τοῦ κατὰ τὴν διδαχὴν πιστοῦ
λόγου, ἵνα δυνατὸς ᾖ καὶ παρακαλεῖν ἐν
τῇ διδασκαλίᾳ τῇ ὑγιαινούσῃ καὶ τοὺς
ἀντιλέγοντας ἐλέγχειν.

Cf. 1 Tim 1:18–20; 4:6–7; 6:3; 6:12; 6:13–14; 2 Tim 3:10–17; 4:1–5.

See also § 20 Summaries of the Faith.

109. The Function of Scripture

Rom 15:1–6

Ὀφείλομεν δὲ ἡμεῖς οἱ δυνατοὶ τὰ ἀσθε-
νήματα τῶν ἀδυνάτων βαστάζειν καὶ
μὴ ἑαυτοῖς ἀρέσκειν. **2** ἕκαστος ἡμῶν
τῷ πλησίον ἀρεσκέτω εἰς τὸ ἀγαθὸν
πρὸς οἰκοδομήν· **3** καὶ γὰρ ὁ Χριστὸς οὐχ
ἑαυτῷ ἤρεσεν, ἀλλὰ καθὼς γέγραπται·
οἱ ὀνειδισμοὶ τῶν ὀνειδιζόντων σε ἐπέ-
πεσαν ἐπ᾽ ἐμέ. **4** ὅσα γὰρ προεγράφη, εἰς
τὴν ἡμετέραν διδασκαλίαν ἐγράφη, ἵνα
διὰ τῆς ὑπομονῆς καὶ διὰ τῆς παρακλή-
σεως τῶν γραφῶν τὴν ἐλπίδα ἔχωμεν.

§ 108 **Rom 16:20** ***η χαρις του κυριου ημων Ιησου μεθ υμων*** 𝔓[46] ℵ B C 1881] η χαρις του κυριου ημων Ιησου Χριστου μεθ υμων A C 33. 1739 *Byz* ¦ *om. hic et pon. p.* 16:23 D **1 Cor 11:24** ***υμων*** 𝔓[46] ℵ* A B C* 33. 1739*] add. κλωμενον ℵ[2] C[3] D[2] 1739[mg]. 1881 Byz ¦ add. θρυπτομενον D* **2 Thess 3:6** ***παρελαβοσαν*** ℵ* A (D*) 33] παρελαβον ℵ[2] D[2] 1739. 1881 Byz ¦ παρελαβετε B **1 Tim 6:21** ***μεθ υμων*** ℵ* A 33] μετα σου D* 048[vid]. 1739*. 1881 ¦ μεθ υμων, αμην ℵ[2] ¦ μετα σου, αμην D[1] 1739[c] Byz

108. The Pattern of Teaching

Rom 6:17–18

But thanks be to God that you, having once been slaves of sin, have become obedient from the heart to the form of teaching to which you were entrusted, **18** and that you, having been set free from sin, have become slaves of righteousness.

Rom 16:17–20

I urge you, brothers and sisters, to keep an eye on those who cause dissensions and offenses, in opposition to the teaching that you have learned; avoid them. **18** For such people do not serve our Lord Christ, but their own appetites, and by smooth talk and flattery they deceive the hearts of the simple-minded. **19** For while your obedience is known to all, so that I rejoice over you, I want you to be wise in what is good and guileless in what is evil. **20** The God of peace will shortly crush Satan under your feet. The grace of our Lord Jesus Christ be with you.[a]

1 Cor 11:2

I commend you because you remember me in everything and maintain the traditions just as I handed them on to you.

1 Cor 11:23–25

For I received from the Lord what I also handed on to you, that the Lord Jesus on the night when he was betrayed took a loaf of bread, **24** and when he had given thanks, he broke it and said, "This is my body that is for[b] you. Do this in remembrance of me." **25** In the same way he took the cup also, after supper, saying, "This cup is the new covenant in my blood. Do this, as often as you drink it, in remembrance of me."

1 Cor 15:1–8

Now I would remind you, brothers and sisters, of the good news that I proclaimed to you, which you in turn received, in which also you stand, **2** through which also you are being saved, if you hold firmly to the message that I proclaimed to you—unless you have come to believe in vain. **3** For I handed on to you as of first importance what I in turn had received: that Christ died for our sins in accordance with the scriptures, **4** and that he was buried, and that he was raised on the third day in accordance with the scriptures, **5** and that he appeared to Cephas, then to the twelve. **6** Then he appeared to more than five hundred brothers and sisters at one time, most of whom are still alive, though some have died. **7** Then he appeared to James, then to all the apostles. **8** Last of all, as to one untimely born, he appeared also to me.

Phil 4:9

Keep on doing the things that you have learned and received and heard and seen in me, and the God of peace will be with you.

Col 2:6–7

As you therefore have received Christ Jesus the Lord, continue to live your lives in him, **7** rooted and built up in him and established in the faith, just as you were taught, abounding in thanksgiving.

2 Thess 2:15

So then, brothers and sisters, stand firm and hold fast to the traditions that you were taught by us, either by word of mouth or by our letter.

2 Thess 3:6

Now we command you, beloved, in the name of our Lord Jesus Christ, to keep away from believers who are living in idleness and not according to the tradition that they[c] received from us.

1 Tim 6:20–21

Timothy, guard what has been entrusted to you. Avoid the profane chatter and contradictions of what is falsely called knowledge; **21** by professing it some have missed the mark as regards the faith. Grace be with you.[d]

2 Tim 1:13–14

Hold to the standard of sound teaching that you have heard from me, in the faith and love that are in Christ Jesus. **14** Guard the good treasure entrusted to you, with the help of the Holy Spirit living in us.

2 Tim 2:1–2

You then, my child, be strong in the grace that is in Christ Jesus; **2** and what you have heard from me through many witnesses entrust to faithful people who will be able to teach others as well.

Titus 1:9

He must have a firm grasp of the word that is trustworthy in accordance with the teaching, so that he may be able both to preach with sound doctrine and to refute those who contradict it.

Cf. 1 Tim 1:18–20; 4:6–7; 6:3; 6:12; 6:13–14; 2 Tim 3:10–17; 4:1–5.

See also § 20 Summaries of the Faith.

109. The Function of Scripture

Rom 15:1–6

We who are strong ought to put up with the failings of the weak, and not to please ourselves. **2** Each of us must please our neighbor for the good purpose of building up the neighbor. **3** For Christ did not please himself; but, as it is written, "The insults of those who insult you have fallen on me." **4** For whatever was written in former days was written for our instruction, so that by steadfastness and by the encourage-

§ 108 [a] **Rom 16:20** *you* A few ancient authorities omit this sentence here and place it after verse 23 [b] **1 Cor 11:24** *is for* Other ancient authorities read *is broken for* [c] **2 Thess 3:6** *they* Other ancient authorities read *you* [d] **1 Tim 6:21** *you* The Greek word for *you* here is plural; in other ancient authorities it is singular. Other ancient authorities add *Amen*

5 ὁ δὲ θεὸς τῆς ὑπομονῆς καὶ τῆς παρα-
κλήσεως δῴη ὑμῖν τὸ αὐτὸ φρονεῖν ἐν
ἀλλήλοις κατὰ Χριστὸν Ἰησοῦν, **6** ἵνα
ὁμοθυμαδὸν ἐν ἑνὶ στόματι δοξάζητε
τὸν θεὸν καὶ πατέρα τοῦ κυρίου ἡμῶν
Ἰησοῦ Χριστοῦ.

Rom 16:25–27

⸂[Τῷ δὲ δυναμένῳ ὑμᾶς στηρίξαι κατὰ
τὸ εὐαγγέλιόν μου καὶ τὸ κήρυγμα Ἰη-
σοῦ Χριστοῦ, κατὰ ἀποκάλυψιν μυστη-
ρίου χρόνοις αἰωνίοις σεσιγημένου,
26 φανερωθέντος δὲ νῦν διά τε γραφῶν
προφητικῶν κατ᾽ ἐπιταγὴν τοῦ αἰωνίου
θεοῦ εἰς ὑπακοὴν πίστεως εἰς πάντα τὰ
ἔθνη γνωρισθέντος, **27** μόνῳ σοφῷ θεῷ,
διὰ Ἰησοῦ Χριστοῦ, ⸀ᾧ ἡ δόξα εἰς τοὺς
⸀αἰῶνας, ἀμήν.]⸃

1 Cor 10:1–11

Οὐ θέλω γὰρ ὑμᾶς ἀγνοεῖν, ἀδελφοί,
ὅτι οἱ πατέρες ἡμῶν πάντες ὑπὸ τὴν νε-
φέλην ἦσαν καὶ πάντες διὰ τῆς θαλάσσης
διῆλθον **2** καὶ πάντες εἰς τὸν Μωϋσῆν
ἐβαπτίσθησαν ἐν τῇ νεφέλῃ καὶ ἐν τῇ
θαλάσσῃ **3** καὶ πάντες τὸ αὐτὸ πνευματι-
κὸν βρῶμα ἔφαγον **4** καὶ πάντες τὸ αὐτὸ
πνευματικὸν ἔπιον πόμα· ἔπινον γὰρ ἐκ
πνευματικῆς ἀκολουθούσης πέτρας, ἡ
πέτρα δὲ ἦν ὁ Χριστός. **5** Ἀλλ᾽ οὐκ ἐν τοῖς
πλείοσιν αὐτῶν εὐδόκησεν ὁ θεός, κατε-
στρώθησαν γὰρ ἐν τῇ ἐρήμῳ. **6** Ταῦτα δὲ
τύποι ἡμῶν ἐγενήθησαν, εἰς τὸ μὴ εἶναι
ἡμᾶς ἐπιθυμητὰς κακῶν, καθὼς κἀκεῖνοι
ἐπεθύμησαν. **7** μηδὲ εἰδωλολάτραι γίνεσθε
καθώς τινες αὐτῶν, ὥσπερ γέγραπται·
ἐκάθισεν ὁ λαὸς φαγεῖν καὶ πεῖν καὶ
ἀνέστησαν παίζειν. **8** μηδὲ πορνεύωμεν,
καθώς τινες αὐτῶν ἐπόρνευσαν καὶ
ἔπεσαν μιᾷ ἡμέρᾳ εἴκοσι τρεῖς χιλιάδες.
9 μηδὲ ἐκπειράζωμεν τὸν ⸀Χριστόν, κα-
θώς τινες αὐτῶν ἐπείρασαν καὶ ὑπὸ τῶν
ὄφεων ἀπώλλυντο. **10** μηδὲ γογγύζετε,
καθάπερ τινὲς αὐτῶν ἐγόγγυσαν καὶ
ἀπώλοντο ὑπὸ τοῦ ὀλοθρευτοῦ. **11** ταῦτα
δὲ τυπικῶς συνέβαινεν ἐκείνοις, ἐγράφη
δὲ πρὸς νουθεσίαν ἡμῶν, εἰς οὓς τὰ τέλη
τῶν αἰώνων κατήντηκεν.

2 Tim 3:14–17

Σὺ δὲ μένε ἐν οἷς ἔμαθες καὶ ἐπιστώθης,
εἰδὼς παρὰ ⸀τίνων ἔμαθες, **15** καὶ ὅτι ἀπὸ
βρέφους [τὰ] ἱερὰ γράμματα οἶδας, τὰ
δυνάμενά σε σοφίσαι εἰς σωτηρίαν διὰ
πίστεως τῆς ἐν Χριστῷ Ἰησοῦ. **16** πᾶσα
γραφὴ θεόπνευστος καὶ ὠφέλιμος πρὸς
διδασκαλίαν, πρὸς ἐλεγμόν, πρὸς ἐπανόρ-
θωσιν, πρὸς παιδείαν τὴν ἐν δικαιοσύνῃ,
17 ἵνα ἄρτιος ᾖ ὁ τοῦ θεοῦ ἄνθρωπος, πρὸς
πᾶν ἔργον ἀγαθὸν ἐξηρτισμένος.

Acts 17:2–3

κατὰ δὲ τὸ εἰωθὸς τῷ Παύλῳ εἰσῆλθεν πρὸς
αὐτοὺς καὶ ἐπὶ σάββατα τρία διελέξατο
αὐτοῖς ἀπὸ τῶν γραφῶν, **3** διανοίγων
καὶ παρατιθέμενος ὅτι τὸν χριστὸν ἔδει
παθεῖν καὶ ἀναστῆναι ἐκ νεκρῶν καὶ ὅτι
οὗτός ἐστιν ὁ χριστὸς [ὁ] Ἰησοῦς ὃν ἐγὼ
καταγγέλλω ὑμῖν.

Cf. Rom 3:1–2; 3:21; 4:23–25; 2 Cor 3:12–18; Acts 9:22; 17:10–12; 26:22–23; 26:26–29.

110. Visions and Revelations

1 Cor 14:6

Νῦν δέ, ἀδελφοί, ἐὰν ἔλθω πρὸς ὑμᾶς γλώσσαις λαλῶν, τί ὑμᾶς ὠφελήσω ἐὰν μὴ ὑμῖν λαλήσω ἢ ἐν ἀποκαλύψει ἢ ἐν γνώσει ἢ ἐν προφητείᾳ ἢ [ἐν] διδαχῇ;

1 Cor 14:26–33a

Τί οὖν ἐστιν, ἀδελφοί; ὅταν συνέρχησθε,
ἕκαστος ψαλμὸν ἔχει, διδαχὴν ἔχει, ἀπο-
κάλυψιν ἔχει, γλῶσσαν ἔχει, ἑρμηνείαν
ἔχει· πάντα πρὸς οἰκοδομὴν γινέσθω.
27 εἴτε γλώσσῃ τις λαλεῖ, κατὰ δύο ἢ τὸ
πλεῖστον τρεῖς καὶ ἀνὰ μέρος, καὶ εἷς δι-
ερμηνευέτω· **28** ἐὰν δὲ μὴ ᾖ διερμηνευτής,
σιγάτω ἐν ἐκκλησίᾳ, ἑαυτῷ δὲ λαλείτω
καὶ τῷ θεῷ. **29** προφῆται δὲ δύο ἢ τρεῖς
λαλείτωσαν καὶ οἱ ἄλλοι διακρινέτωσαν·
30 ἐὰν δὲ ἄλλῳ ἀποκαλυφθῇ καθημένῳ,
ὁ πρῶτος σιγάτω. **31** δύνασθε γὰρ καθ᾽
ἕνα πάντες προφητεύειν, ἵνα πάντες
μανθάνωσιν καὶ πάντες παρακαλῶνται.
32 καὶ πνεύματα προφητῶν προφήταις
ὑποτάσσεται, **33** οὐ γάρ ἐστιν ἀκαταστα-
σίας ὁ θεὸς ἀλλὰ εἰρήνης.

2 Cor 12:1–10

Καυχᾶσθαι δεῖ, οὐ συμφέρον μέν, ἐλεύ-
σομαι δὲ εἰς ὀπτασίας καὶ ἀποκαλύψεις
κυρίου. **2** οἶδα ἄνθρωπον ἐν Χριστῷ πρὸ
ἐτῶν δεκατεσσάρων, εἴτε ἐν σώματι οὐκ
οἶδα, εἴτε ἐκτὸς τοῦ σώματος οὐκ οἶδα,
ὁ θεὸς οἶδεν, ἁρπαγέντα τὸν τοιοῦτον
ἕως τρίτου οὐρανοῦ. **3** καὶ οἶδα τὸν τοι-
οῦτον ἄνθρωπον, εἴτε ἐν σώματι εἴτε
χωρὶς τοῦ σώματος οὐκ οἶδα, ὁ θεὸς
οἶδεν, **4** ὅτι ἡρπάγη εἰς τὸν παράδεισον
καὶ ἤκουσεν ἄρρητα ῥήματα ἃ οὐκ ἐξὸν
ἀνθρώπῳ λαλῆσαι. **5** ὑπὲρ τοῦ τοιού-
του καυχήσομαι, ὑπὲρ δὲ ἐμαυτοῦ οὐ
καυχήσομαι εἰ μὴ ἐν ταῖς ἀσθενείαις.
6 Ἐὰν γὰρ θελήσω καυχήσασθαι, οὐκ
ἔσομαι ἄφρων, ἀλήθειαν γὰρ ἐρῶ· φεί-
δομαι δέ, μή τις εἰς ἐμὲ λογίσηται ὑπὲρ
ὃ βλέπει με ἢ ἀκούει [τι] ἐξ ἐμοῦ **7** καὶ
τῇ ὑπερβολῇ τῶν ἀποκαλύψεων. ⸀διὸ
ἵνα μὴ ὑπεραίρωμαι, ἐδόθη μοι σκόλοψ
τῇ σαρκί, ἄγγελος σατανᾶ, ἵνα με κο-
λαφίζῃ, ⸂ἵνα μὴ ὑπεραίρωμαι⸃. **8** ὑπὲρ
τούτου τρὶς τὸν κύριον παρεκάλεσα
ἵνα ἀποστῇ ἀπ᾽ ἐμοῦ. **9** καὶ εἴρηκέν μοι·
ἀρκεῖ σοι ἡ χάρις μου, ἡ γὰρ ⸀δύναμις
ἐν ἀσθενείᾳ τελεῖται. Ἥδιστα οὖν μᾶλ-
λον καυχήσομαι ἐν ταῖς ἀσθενείαις μου,

§ 109 **Rom 16:25–27** *pon. hic* 𝔓61 ℵ B C D 1739] *pon. hic et p.* 14:23 A 33 ¦ *pon. p.* 14:23 *Byz* ¦ *pon. p.* 15:33 𝔓46 ¦ *om. pc* **Rom 16:27** ***ω*** 𝔓46 ℵ A C D 33. 1739. 1881 *Byz*] *om.* B • ***αιωνας*** 𝔓46 B C 33. 1739. 1881 *Byz*] *add.* των αιωνων 𝔓61 ℵ A D **1 Cor 10:9** ***Χριστον*** 𝔓46 D 1739. 1881 *Byz*] κυριον ℵ B C 33 ¦ θεον A **2 Tim 3:14** ***τινων*** ℵ A C* 33. 1739. 1881] τινος C3 D *Byz* **§ 110** **2 Cor 12:7** ***διο*** ℵ A B 33. 1739] *om.* 𝔓46 D 1881 *Byz* • ***ινα μη υπεραιρωμαι*** 𝔓46 ℵ2 B Ivid 1739. (1881) *Byz*] *om.* ℵ* A D 33 **2 Cor 12:9** ***δυναμις*** 𝔓46vid ℵ* A* B D*] *add.* μου ℵ2 Ac D1 33. 1739. 1881 *Byz*

ment of the scriptures we might have hope. [5] May the God of steadfastness and encouragement grant you to live in harmony with one another, in accordance with Christ Jesus, [6] so that together you may with one voice glorify the God and Father of our Lord Jesus Christ.

Rom 16:25–27

Now to God who is able to strengthen you according to my gospel and the proclamation of Jesus Christ, according to the revelation of the mystery that was kept secret for long ages [26] but is now disclosed, and through the prophetic writings is made known to all the Gentiles, according to the command of the eternal God, to bring about the obedience of faith— [27] to the only wise God, through Jesus Christ, to whom[a] be the glory forever![b] Amen.[c]

1 Cor 10:1–11

I do not want you to be unaware, brothers and sisters, that our ancestors were all under the cloud, and all passed through the sea, [2] and all were baptized into Moses in the cloud and in the sea, [3] and all ate the same spiritual food, [4] and all drank the same spiritual drink. For they drank from the spiritual rock that followed them, and the rock was Christ. [5] Nevertheless, God was not pleased with most of them, and they were struck down in the wilderness. [6] Now these things occurred as examples for us, so that we might not desire evil as they did. [7] Do not become idolaters as some of them did; as it is written, "The people sat down to eat and drink, and they rose up to play." [8] We must not indulge in sexual immorality as some of them did, and twenty-three thousand fell in a single day. [9] We must not put Christ[d] to the test, as some of them did, and were destroyed by serpents. [10] And do not complain as some of them did, and were destroyed by the destroyer. [11] These things happened to them to serve as an example, and they were written down to instruct us, on whom the ends of the ages have come.

2 Tim 3:14–17

But as for you, continue in what you have learned and firmly believed, knowing from whom[e] you learned it, [15] and how from childhood you have known the sacred writings that are able to instruct you for salvation through faith in Christ Jesus. [16] All scripture is inspired by God and is useful for teaching, for reproof, for correction, and for training in righteousness, [17] so that everyone who belongs to God may be proficient, equipped for every good work.

Acts 17:2–3

And Paul went in, as was his custom, and on three sabbath days argued with them from the scriptures, [3] explaining and proving that it was necessary for the Messiah to suffer and to rise from the dead, and saying, "This is the Messiah, Jesus whom I am proclaiming to you."

Cf. Rom 3:1–2; 3:21; 4:23–25; 2 Cor 3:12–18; Acts 9:22; 17:10–12; 26:22–23; 26:26–29.

110. Visions and Revelations

1 Cor 14:6

Now, brothers and sisters, if I come to you speaking in tongues, how will I benefit you unless I speak to you in some revelation or knowledge or prophecy or teaching?

1 Cor 14:26–33a

What should be done then, my friends? When you come together, each one has a hymn, a lesson, a revelation, a tongue, or an interpretation. Let all things be done for building up. [27] If anyone speaks in a tongue, let there be only two or at most three, and each in turn; and let one interpret. [28] But if there is no one to interpret, let them be silent in church and speak to themselves and to God. [29] Let two or three prophets speak, and let the others weigh what is said. [30] If a revelation is made to someone else sitting nearby, let the first person be silent. [31] For you can all prophesy one by one, so that all may learn and all be encouraged. [32] And the spirits of prophets are subject to the prophets, [33] for God is a God not of disorder but of peace.

2 Cor 12:1–10

It is necessary to boast; nothing is to be gained by it, but I will go on to visions and revelations of the Lord. [2] I know a person in Christ who fourteen years ago was caught up to the third heaven—whether in the body or out of the body I do not know; God knows. [3] And I know that such a person—whether in the body or out of the body I do not know; God knows— [4] was caught up into Paradise and heard things that are not to be told, that no mortal is permitted to repeat. [5] On behalf of such a one I will boast, but on my own behalf I will not boast, except of my weaknesses. [6] But if I wish to boast, I will not be a fool, for I will be speaking the truth. But I refrain from it, so that no one may think better of me than what is seen in me or heard from me, [7] even considering the exceptional character of the revelations. Therefore, to keep[a] me from being too elated, a thorn was given me in the flesh, a messenger of Satan to torment me, to keep me from being too elated.[b] [8] Three times I appealed to the Lord about this, that it would leave me, [9] but he said to me, "My grace is sufficient for you, for power[c] is made perfect in weakness." So, I will boast all the more gladly of

§ 109 [a] **Rom 16:27** ***to whom*** A few ancient authorities lack *to whom*. The verse then reads, *to the only wise God be the glory through Jesus Christ forever. Amen.* [b] **Rom 16:27** ***forever*** Other ancient authorities read *forever and ever* [c] **Rom 16:27** ***Amen*** Other ancient authorities include 16:25–27 after 14:23 or 15:33; a few lack these verses altogether [d] **1 Cor 10:9** ***Christ*** Other ancient authorities read *the Lord* [e] **2 Tim 3:14** ***whom*** The Greek word for *whom* here is plural; in other ancient authorities it is singular. **§ 110** [a] **2 Cor 12:7** ***Therefore, to keep*** Other ancient authorities read *To keep* [b] **2 Cor 12:7** ***to keep me from being too elated*** Other ancient authorities lack *to keep me from being too elated* [c] **2 Cor 12:9** ***power*** Other ancient authorities read *my power*

ἵνα ἐπισκηνώσῃ ἐπ᾽ ἐμὲ ἡ δύναμις τοῦ
Χριστοῦ. 10 διὸ εὐδοκῶ ἐν ἀσθενείαις,
ἐν ὕβρεσιν, ἐν ἀνάγκαις, ἐν διωγμοῖς
καὶ στενοχωρίαις, ὑπὲρ Χριστοῦ· ὅταν
γὰρ ἀσθενῶ, τότε δυνατός εἰμι.

Gal 2:1–2

Ἔπειτα διὰ δεκατεσσάρων ἐτῶν πάλιν
ἀνέβην εἰς Ἱεροσόλυμα μετὰ Βαρναβᾶ
συμπαραλαβὼν καὶ Τίτον· 2 ἀνέβην δὲ
κατὰ ἀποκάλυψιν· καὶ ἀνεθέμην αὐτοῖς
τὸ εὐαγγέλιον ὃ κηρύσσω ἐν τοῖς ἔθνε-
σιν, κατ᾽ ἰδίαν δὲ τοῖς δοκοῦσιν, μή πως
εἰς κενὸν τρέχω ἢ ἔδραμον.

Eph 3:1–6

Τούτου χάριν ἐγὼ Παῦλος ὁ δέσμιος τοῦ
Χριστοῦ [Ἰησοῦ] ὑπὲρ ὑμῶν τῶν ἐθνῶν
2 —εἴ γε ἠκούσατε τὴν οἰκονομίαν τῆς
χάριτος τοῦ θεοῦ τῆς δοθείσης μοι εἰς
ὑμᾶς, 3 [ὅτι] κατὰ ἀποκάλυψιν ἐγνωρίσθη
μοι τὸ μυστήριον, καθὼς προέγραψα ἐν
ὀλίγῳ, 4 πρὸς ὃ δύνασθε ἀναγινώσκοντες
νοῆσαι τὴν σύνεσίν μου ἐν τῷ μυστηρίῳ
τοῦ Χριστοῦ, 5 ὃ ἑτέραις γενεαῖς οὐκ
ἐγνωρίσθη τοῖς υἱοῖς τῶν ἀνθρώπων ὡς
νῦν ἀπεκαλύφθη τοῖς ἁγίοις ἀποστόλοις
αὐτοῦ καὶ προφήταις ἐν πνεύματι, 6 εἶναι
τὰ ἔθνη συγκληρονόμα καὶ σύσσωμα καὶ
συμμέτοχα τῆς ἐπαγγελίας ἐν Χριστῷ
Ἰησοῦ διὰ τοῦ εὐαγγελίου

Col 2:18–19

μηδεὶς ὑμᾶς καταβραβευέτω θέλων ἐν
ταπεινοφροσύνῃ καὶ θρησκείᾳ τῶν ἀγγέ-
λων, ⸀ἃ ἑόρακεν ἐμβατεύων, εἰκῇ φυσι-
ούμενος ὑπὸ τοῦ νοὸς τῆς σαρκὸς αὐτοῦ,
19 καὶ οὐ κρατῶν τὴν κεφαλήν, ἐξ οὗ πᾶν
τὸ σῶμα διὰ τῶν ἁφῶν καὶ συνδέσμων
ἐπιχορηγούμενον καὶ συμβιβαζόμενον
αὔξει τὴν αὔξησιν τοῦ θεοῦ.

Cf. the reports of visions and revelations given to Paul in Acts 16:9–10; 18:9–11; 22:17–21; 23:11; 27:21–26. Cf. also Eph 1:15–20; Phil 3:15; 2 Thess 2:1–2; 1 Tim 4:1–5.

For the unique revelatory event in which Paul saw the risen Jesus and was commissioned as an apostle, see § 163 Paul's Commissioning by the Risen Lord.

111. Co-laboring for the Gospel

Rom 16:3–12

Ἀσπάσασθε Πρίσκαν καὶ Ἀκύλαν τοὺς
συνεργούς μου ἐν Χριστῷ Ἰησοῦ, 4 οἵτι-
νες ὑπὲρ τῆς ψυχῆς μου τὸν ἑαυτῶν
τράχηλον ὑπέθηκαν, οἷς οὐκ ἐγὼ μόνος
εὐχαριστῶ ἀλλὰ καὶ πᾶσαι αἱ ἐκκλησίαι
τῶν ἐθνῶν, 5 καὶ τὴν κατ᾽ οἶκον αὐτῶν
ἐκκλησίαν. ἀσπάσασθε Ἐπαίνετον τὸν
ἀγαπητόν μου, ὅς ἐστιν ἀπαρχὴ τῆς Ἀσίας
εἰς Χριστόν. 6 ἀσπάσασθε Μαρίαν, ἥτις
πολλὰ ἐκοπίασεν εἰς ὑμᾶς. 7 ἀσπάσασθε
Ἀνδρόνικον καὶ ⸀Ἰουνίαν τοὺς συγγενεῖς
μου καὶ συναιχμαλώτους μου, οἵτινές
εἰσιν ἐπίσημοι ἐν τοῖς ἀποστόλοις, οἳ καὶ
πρὸ ἐμοῦ γέγοναν ἐν Χριστῷ. 8 ἀσπά-
σασθε Ἀμπλιᾶτον τὸν ἀγαπητόν μου
ἐν κυρίῳ. 9 ἀσπάσασθε Οὐρβανὸν τὸν
συνεργὸν ἡμῶν ἐν Χριστῷ καὶ Στάχυν
τὸν ἀγαπητόν μου. 10 ἀσπάσασθε Ἀπελ-
λῆν τὸν δόκιμον ἐν Χριστῷ. ἀσπάσασθε
τοὺς ἐκ τῶν Ἀριστοβούλου. 11 ἀσπά-
σασθε Ἡρῳδίωνα τὸν συγγενῆ μου.
ἀσπάσασθε τοὺς ἐκ τῶν Ναρκίσσου τοὺς
ὄντας ἐν κυρίῳ. 12 ἀσπάσασθε Τρύφαιναν
καὶ Τρυφῶσαν τὰς κοπιώσας ἐν κυρίῳ.
ἀσπάσασθε Περσίδα τὴν ἀγαπητήν, ἥτις
πολλὰ ἐκοπίασεν ἐν κυρίῳ.

Rom 16:21

Ἀσπάζεται ὑμᾶς Τιμόθεος ὁ συνεργός μου
καὶ Λούκιος καὶ Ἰάσων καὶ Σωσίπατρος
οἱ συγγενεῖς μου.

1 Cor 3:5–9

Τί οὖν ἐστιν Ἀπολλῶς; τί δέ ἐστιν Παῦλος;
διάκονοι δι᾽ ὧν ἐπιστεύσατε, καὶ ἑκάστῳ
ὡς ὁ κύριος ἔδωκεν. 6 ἐγὼ ἐφύτευσα,
Ἀπολλῶς ἐπότισεν, ἀλλὰ ὁ θεὸς ηὔξανεν·
7 ὥστε οὔτε ὁ φυτεύων ἐστίν τι οὔτε ὁ
ποτίζων ἀλλ᾽ ὁ αὐξάνων θεός. 8 ὁ φυτεύων
δὲ καὶ ὁ ποτίζων ἕν εἰσιν, ἕκαστος δὲ τὸν
ἴδιον μισθὸν λήμψεται κατὰ τὸν ἴδιον
κόπον· 9 θεοῦ γάρ ἐσμεν συνεργοί, θεοῦ
γεώργιον, θεοῦ οἰκοδομή ἐστε.

1 Cor 16:10–12

Ἐὰν δὲ ἔλθῃ Τιμόθεος, βλέπετε, ἵνα
ἀφόβως γένηται πρὸς ὑμᾶς· τὸ γὰρ ἔργον
κυρίου ἐργάζεται ὡς κἀγώ· 11 μή τις
οὖν αὐτὸν ἐξουθενήσῃ. προπέμψατε
δὲ αὐτὸν ἐν εἰρήνῃ, ἵνα ἔλθῃ πρός με·
ἐκδέχομαι γὰρ αὐτὸν μετὰ τῶν ἀδελφῶν.
12 Περὶ δὲ Ἀπολλῶ τοῦ ἀδελφοῦ, πολλὰ
παρεκάλεσα αὐτόν, ἵνα ἔλθῃ πρὸς ὑμᾶς
μετὰ τῶν ἀδελφῶν· καὶ πάντως οὐκ ἦν
θέλημα ἵνα νῦν ἔλθῃ· ἐλεύσεται δὲ ὅταν
εὐκαιρήσῃ.

1 Cor 16:15–18

Παρακαλῶ δὲ ὑμᾶς, ἀδελφοί· οἴδατε τὴν
οἰκίαν Στεφανᾶ, ὅτι ἐστὶν ἀπαρχὴ τῆς
Ἀχαΐας καὶ εἰς διακονίαν τοῖς ἁγίοις
ἔταξαν ἑαυτούς· 16 ἵνα καὶ ὑμεῖς ὑπο-
τάσσησθε τοῖς τοιούτοις καὶ παντὶ τῷ
συνεργοῦντι καὶ κοπιῶντι. 17 χαίρω δὲ ἐπὶ
τῇ παρουσίᾳ Στεφανᾶ καὶ Φορτουνάτου
καὶ Ἀχαϊκοῦ, ὅτι τὸ ὑμέτερον ὑστέρημα
οὗτοι ἀνεπλήρωσαν· 18 ἀνέπαυσαν γὰρ
τὸ ἐμὸν πνεῦμα καὶ τὸ ὑμῶν. ἐπιγινώ-
σκετε οὖν τοὺς τοιούτους.

2 Cor 8:16–24

Χάρις δὲ τῷ θεῷ τῷ ⸀δόντι τὴν αὐτὴν
σπουδὴν ὑπὲρ ὑμῶν ἐν τῇ καρδίᾳ Τί-
του, 17 ὅτι τὴν μὲν παράκλησιν ἐδέξατο,
σπουδαιότερος δὲ ὑπάρχων αὐθαίρετος
ἐξῆλθεν πρὸς ὑμᾶς. 18 συνεπέμψαμεν δὲ
μετ᾽ αὐτοῦ τὸν ἀδελφὸν οὗ ὁ ἔπαινος ἐν
τῷ εὐαγγελίῳ διὰ πασῶν τῶν ἐκκλησιῶν,
19 οὐ μόνον δέ, ἀλλὰ καὶ χειροτονηθεὶς
ὑπὸ τῶν ἐκκλησιῶν συνέκδημος ἡμῶν
σὺν τῇ χάριτι ταύτῃ τῇ διακονουμένῃ
ὑφ᾽ ἡμῶν πρὸς τὴν ⸀[αὐτοῦ] τοῦ κυρίου
δόξαν καὶ προθυμίαν ἡμῶν, 20 στελλό

Col 2:18 ***ἃ*** 𝔓[46] ℵ* A B D* I 33. 1739] ἃ μη ℵ[2] C D[1] 1881 *Byz* **§ 111** **Rom 16:7** ***Ιουνιαν*** ℵ A B C D 33. 1739. 1881 *Byz* (*acc.* Ἰουνίαν B[2] D[2] 33. 1739. 1881 *Byz*; *sine acc.* ℵ A B* C D*)] Ιουλιαν 𝔓[46] **2 Cor 8:16** ***δοντι*** 𝔓[46] ℵ[2] D] διδοντι ℵ* B C I[vid] (33). 1739. 1881 *Byz* **2 Cor 8:19** ***αυτου*** ℵ D[1] 1881* *Byz*] *om.* B C D* ¦ αυτην 1739. 1881[c]

my weaknesses, so that the power of Christ may dwell in me. **10** Therefore I am content with weaknesses, insults, hardships, persecutions, and calamities for the sake of Christ; for whenever I am weak, then I am strong.

Gal 2:1–2

Then after fourteen years I went up again to Jerusalem with Barnabas, taking Titus along with me. **2** I went up in response to a revelation. Then I laid before them (though only in a private meeting with the acknowledged leaders) the gospel that I proclaim among the Gentiles, in order to make sure that I was not running, or had not run, in vain.

Eph 3:1–6

This is the reason that I Paul am a prisoner for Christ Jesus for the sake of you Gentiles—**2** for surely you have already heard of the commission of God's grace that was given me for you, **3** and how the mystery was made known to me by revelation, as I wrote above in a few words, **4** a reading of which will enable you to perceive my understanding of the mystery of Christ. **5** In former generations this mystery was not made known to humankind, as it has now been revealed to his holy apostles and prophets by the Spirit: **6** that is, the Gentiles have become fellow heirs, members of the same body, and sharers in the promise in Christ Jesus through the gospel.

Col 2:18–19

Do not let anyone disqualify you, insisting on self-abasement and worship of angels, dwelling on visions,[d] puffed up without cause by a human way of thinking, **19** and not holding fast to the head, from whom the whole body, richly supplied[e] and held together by its ligaments and sinews, grows with a growth that is from God.

Cf. the reports of visions and revelations given to Paul in Acts 16:9–10; 18:9–11; 22:17–21; 23:11; 27:21–26. Cf. also Eph 1:15–20; Phil 3:15; 2 Thess 2:1–2; 1 Tim 4:1–5.

For the unique revelatory event in which Paul saw the risen Jesus and was commissioned as an apostle, see § 163 Paul's Commissioning by the Risen Lord.

111. Co-laboring for the Gospel

Rom 16:3–12

Greet Prisca and Aquila, who work with me in Christ Jesus, **4** and who risked their necks for my life, to whom not only I give thanks, but also all the churches of the Gentiles. **5** Greet also the church in their house. Greet my beloved Epaenetus, who was the first convert in Asia for Christ. **6** Greet Mary, who has worked very hard among you. **7** Greet Andronicus and Junia,[a] my relatives who were in prison with me; they are prominent among the apostles, and they were in Christ before I was. **8** Greet Ampliatus, my beloved in the Lord. **9** Greet Urbanus, our co-worker in Christ, and my beloved Stachys. **10** Greet Apelles, who is approved in Christ. Greet those who belong to the family of Aristobulus. **11** Greet my relative Herodion. Greet those in the Lord who belong to the family of Narcissus. **12** Greet those workers in the Lord, Tryphaena and Tryphosa. Greet the beloved Persis, who has worked hard in the Lord.

Rom 16:21

Timothy, my co-worker, greets you; so do Lucius and Jason and Sosipater, my relatives.

1 Cor 3:5–9

What then is Apollos? What is Paul? Servants through whom you came to believe, as the Lord assigned to each. **6** I planted, Apollos watered, but God gave the growth. **7** So neither the one who plants nor the one who waters is anything, but only God who gives the growth. **8** The one who plants and the one who waters have a common purpose, and each will receive wages according to the labor of each. **9** For we are God's servants, working together; you are God's field, God's building.

1 Cor 16:10–12

If Timothy comes, see that he has nothing to fear among you, for he is doing the work of the Lord just as I am; **11** therefore let no one despise him. Send him on his way in peace, so that he may come to me; for I am expecting him with the brothers. **12** Now concerning our brother Apollos, I strongly urged him to visit you with the other brothers, but he was not at all willing to come now. He will come when he has the opportunity.

1 Cor 16:15–18

Now, brothers and sisters, you know that members of the household of Stephanas were the first converts in Achaia, and they have devoted themselves to the service of the saints; **16** I urge you to put yourselves at the service of such people, and of everyone who works and toils with them. **17** I rejoice at the coming of Stephanas and Fortunatus and Achaicus, because they have made up for your absence; **18** for they refreshed my spirit as well as yours. So give recognition to such persons.

2 Cor 8:16–24

But thanks be to God who put[b] in the heart of Titus the same eagerness for you that I myself have. **17** For he not only accepted our appeal, but since he is more eager than ever, he is going to you of his own accord. **18** With him we are sending the brother who is famous among all the churches for his proclaiming the good news; **19** and not only that, but he has also been appointed by the churches to travel with us while we are administering this generous undertaking for the glory of the Lord himself[c] and to show our goodwill. **20** We intend

[d] **Col 2:18** ***visions*** lit. *things which he has seen* Other ancient authorities read *false visions* lit. *things which he has not seen* [e] **Col 2:19** ***richly supplied*** NRSV translates *nourished* **§ 111** [a] **Rom 16:7** ***Junia*** Or possibly *Junias*; a few ancient authorities read *Julia* [b] **2 Cor 8:16** ***put*** Other ancient authorities read *puts* [c] **2 Cor 8:19** ***himself*** Other ancient authorities lack *himself*

μενοι τοῦτο, μή τις ἡμᾶς μωμήσηται ἐν τῇ ἁδρότητι ταύτῃ τῇ διακονουμένῃ ὑφ᾽ ἡμῶν· **21** προνοοῦμεν γὰρ καλὰ οὐ μόνον ἐνώπιον κυρίου ἀλλὰ καὶ ἐνώπιον ἀνθρώπων. **22** συνεπέμψαμεν δὲ αὐτοῖς τὸν ἀδελφὸν ἡμῶν ὃν ἐδοκιμάσαμεν ἐν πολλοῖς πολλάκις σπουδαῖον ὄντα, νυνὶ δὲ πολὺ σπουδαιότερον πεποιθήσει πολλῇ τῇ εἰς ὑμᾶς. **23** εἴτε ὑπὲρ Τίτου, κοινωνὸς ἐμὸς καὶ εἰς ὑμᾶς συνεργός· εἴτε ἀδελφοὶ ἡμῶν, ἀπόστολοι ἐκκλησιῶν, δόξα Χριστοῦ. **24** τὴν οὖν ἔνδειξιν τῆς ἀγάπης ὑμῶν καὶ ἡμῶν καυχήσεως ὑπὲρ ὑμῶν εἰς αὐτοὺς ἐνδεικνύμενοι εἰς πρόσωπον τῶν ἐκκλησιῶν.

Phil 2:25–30

Ἀναγκαῖον δὲ ἡγησάμην Ἐπαφρόδιτον τὸν ἀδελφὸν καὶ συνεργὸν καὶ συστρατιώτην μου, ὑμῶν δὲ ἀπόστολον καὶ λειτουργὸν τῆς χρείας μου, πέμψαι πρὸς ὑμᾶς, **26** ἐπειδὴ ἐπιποθῶν ἦν ⸂πάντας ὑμᾶς⸃ καὶ ἀδημονῶν, διότι ἠκούσατε ὅτι ἠσθένησεν. **27** καὶ γὰρ ἠσθένησεν παραπλήσιον θανάτῳ· ἀλλὰ ὁ θεὸς ἠλέησεν αὐτόν, οὐκ αὐτὸν δὲ μόνον ἀλλὰ καὶ ἐμέ, ἵνα μὴ λύπην ἐπὶ λύπην σχῶ. **28** σπουδαιοτέρως οὖν ἔπεμψα αὐτόν, ἵνα ἰδόντες αὐτὸν πάλιν χαρῆτε κἀγὼ ἀλυπότερος ὦ. **29** προσδέχεσθε οὖν αὐτὸν ἐν κυρίῳ μετὰ πάσης χαρᾶς καὶ τοὺς τοιούτους ἐντίμους ἔχετε, **30** ὅτι διὰ τὸ ἔργον ⸀Χριστοῦ μέχρι θανάτου ἤγγισεν παραβολευσάμενος τῇ ψυχῇ, ἵνα ἀναπληρώσῃ τὸ ὑμῶν ὑστέρημα τῆς πρός με λειτουργίας.

Phil 4:2–3

Εὐοδίαν παρακαλῶ καὶ Συντύχην παρακαλῶ τὸ αὐτὸ φρονεῖν ἐν κυρίῳ. **3** ναὶ ἐρωτῶ καὶ σέ, γνήσιε σύζυγε, συλλαμβάνου αὐταῖς, αἵτινες ἐν τῷ εὐαγγελίῳ συνήθλησάν μοι μετὰ καὶ Κλήμεντος καὶ τῶν λοιπῶν συνεργῶν μου, ὧν τὰ ὀνόματα ἐν βίβλῳ ζωῆς.

Col 1:7

καθὼς ἐμάθετε ἀπὸ Ἐπαφρᾶ τοῦ ἀγαπητοῦ συνδούλου ἡμῶν, ὅς ἐστιν πιστὸς ὑπὲρ ⸀ὑμῶν διάκονος τοῦ Χριστοῦ

1 Thess 3:1–2

Διὸ μηκέτι στέγοντες εὐδοκήσαμεν καταλειφθῆναι ἐν Ἀθήναις μόνοι **2** καὶ ἐπέμψαμεν Τιμόθεον, τὸν ἀδελφὸν ἡμῶν καὶ ⸂συνεργὸν τοῦ θεοῦ⸃ ἐν τῷ εὐαγγελίῳ τοῦ Χριστοῦ, εἰς τὸ στηρίξαι ὑμᾶς καὶ παρακαλέσαι ὑπὲρ τῆς πίστεως ὑμῶν

1 Thess 5:12–13

Ἐρωτῶμεν δὲ ὑμᾶς, ἀδελφοί, εἰδέναι τοὺς κοπιῶντας ἐν ὑμῖν καὶ προϊσταμένους ὑμῶν ἐν κυρίῳ καὶ νουθετοῦντας ὑμᾶς **13** καὶ ἡγεῖσθαι αὐτοὺς ὑπερεκπερισσοῦ ἐν ἀγάπῃ διὰ τὸ ἔργον αὐτῶν. εἰρηνεύετε ἐν ἑαυτοῖς.

1 Tim 5:17–18

Οἱ καλῶς προεστῶτες πρεσβύτεροι διπλῆς τιμῆς ἀξιούσθωσαν, μάλιστα οἱ κοπιῶντες ἐν λόγῳ καὶ διδασκαλίᾳ. **18** λέγει γὰρ ἡ γραφή· βοῦν ἀλοῶντα οὐ φιμώσεις, καί· ἄξιος ὁ ἐργάτης τοῦ μισθοῦ αὐτοῦ.

Phlm 1–2

Παῦλος δέσμιος Χριστοῦ Ἰησοῦ καὶ Τιμόθεος ὁ ἀδελφὸς Φιλήμονι τῷ ἀγαπητῷ καὶ συνεργῷ ἡμῶν **2** καὶ Ἀπφίᾳ τῇ ἀδελφῇ καὶ Ἀρχίππῳ τῷ συστρατιώτῃ ἡμῶν καὶ τῇ κατ᾽ οἶκόν σου ἐκκλησίᾳ

Phlm 13

ὃν ἐγὼ ἐβουλόμην πρὸς ἐμαυτὸν κατέχειν, ἵνα ὑπὲρ σοῦ μοι διακονῇ ἐν τοῖς δεσμοῖς τοῦ εὐαγγελίου

Phlm 23–24

Ἀσπάζεταί σε Ἐπαφρᾶς ὁ συναιχμάλωτός μου ἐν Χριστῷ Ἰησοῦ, **24** Μᾶρκος, Ἀρίσταρχος, Δημᾶς, Λουκᾶς, οἱ συνεργοί μου.

See also § 98 The Role of Apostles and Missionary Proclaimers; § 103 Stewards of God; § 112 Bishops, Elders, and Deacons. For Paul's major co-workers individually, see §§ 167–177.

112. Bishops, Elders, and Deacons

Rom 12:6–8

ἔχοντες δὲ χαρίσματα κατὰ τὴν χάριν τὴν δοθεῖσαν ἡμῖν διάφορα, εἴτε προφητείαν κατὰ τὴν ἀναλογίαν τῆς πίστεως, **7** εἴτε διακονίαν ἐν τῇ διακονίᾳ, εἴτε ὁ διδάσκων ἐν τῇ διδασκαλίᾳ, **8** εἴτε ὁ παρακαλῶν ἐν τῇ παρακλήσει· ὁ μεταδιδοὺς ἐν ἁπλότητι, ὁ προϊστάμενος ἐν σπουδῇ, ὁ ἐλεῶν ἐν ἱλαρότητι.

Rom 16:1–2

Συνίστημι δὲ ὑμῖν Φοίβην τὴν ἀδελφὴν ἡμῶν, οὖσαν [καὶ] διάκονον τῆς ἐκκλησίας τῆς ἐν Κεγχρεαῖς, **2** ἵνα αὐτὴν προσδέξησθε ἐν κυρίῳ ἀξίως τῶν ἁγίων καὶ παραστῆτε αὐτῇ ἐν ᾧ ἂν ὑμῶν χρῄζῃ πράγματι· καὶ γὰρ αὐτὴ προστάτις πολλῶν ἐγενήθη καὶ ἐμοῦ αὐτοῦ.

Phil 1:1–2

Παῦλος καὶ Τιμόθεος δοῦλοι Χριστοῦ Ἰησοῦ πᾶσιν τοῖς ἁγίοις ἐν Χριστῷ Ἰησοῦ τοῖς οὖσιν ἐν Φιλίπποις σὺν ἐπισκόποις καὶ διακόνοις, **2** χάρις ὑμῖν καὶ εἰρήνη ἀπὸ θεοῦ πατρὸς ἡμῶν καὶ κυρίου Ἰησοῦ Χριστοῦ.

1 Thess 5:12–13

Ἐρωτῶμεν δὲ ὑμᾶς, ἀδελφοί, εἰδέναι τοὺς κοπιῶντας ἐν ὑμῖν καὶ προϊσταμένους ὑμῶν ἐν κυρίῳ καὶ νουθετοῦντας ὑμᾶς **13** καὶ ἡγεῖσθαι αὐτοὺς ὑπερεκπερισσοῦ ἐν ἀγάπῃ διὰ τὸ ἔργον αὐτῶν. εἰρηνεύετε ἐν ἑαυτοῖς.

1 Tim 3:1–13

⸀πιστὸς ὁ λόγος. Εἴ τις ἐπισκοπῆς ὀρέγεται, καλοῦ ἔργου ἐπιθυμεῖ. **2** δεῖ οὖν τὸν ἐπίσκοπον ἀνεπίλημπτον εἶναι, μιᾶς γυναικὸς ἄνδρα, νηφάλιον σώφρονα κόσμιον φιλόξενον διδακτικόν, **3** μὴ πάροινον μὴ πλήκτην, ἀλλὰ ἐπιεικῆ ἄμαχον ἀφιλάργυρον, **4** τοῦ ἰδίου οἴκου καλῶς προϊστάμενον, τέκνα ἔχοντα ἐν ὑποταγῇ, μετὰ πάσης σεμνότητος **5** (εἰ δέ

Phil 2:26 ***παντας υμας*** ℵ^{2} 1739. 1881 *Byz*] υμας παντας B ¦ παντας υμας ιδειν ℵ* A C D I^{vid} 33 ¦ πεμψαι προς υμας 𝔓^{46vid} **Phil 2:30** ***Χριστου*** 𝔓^{46} B 1739. 1881] κυριου ℵ A 33 ¦ του Χριστου D *Byz* ¦ *om.* C **Col 1:7** ***υμων*** ℵ^{2} C D^{1} 33. 1739. 1881 *Byz*] ημων 𝔓^{46} ℵ* A B D* **1 Thess 3:2** ***συνεργον του θεου*** D* 33] συνεργον B ¦ διακονον του θεου ℵ A 1739. 1881 ¦ διακονον του θεου και συνεργον ημων D^{2} *Byz* **§ 112** **1 Tim 3:1** ***πιστος*** ℵ A D^{2} 33. 1739. 1881 *Byz*] ανθρωπινος D*

that no one should blame us about this generous gift that we are administering, **21** for we intend to do what is right not only in the Lord's sight but also in the sight of others. **22** And with them we are sending our brother whom we have often tested and found eager in many matters, but who is now more eager than ever because of his great confidence in you. **23** As for Titus, he is my partner and co-worker in your service; as for our brothers, they are messengers of the churches, the glory of Christ. **24** Therefore openly before the churches, show them the proof of your love and of our reason for boasting about you.

Phil 2:25–30

Still, I think it necessary to send to you Epaphroditus—my brother and co-worker and fellow soldier, your messenger and minister to my need; **26** for he has been longing for[d] all of you, and has been distressed because you heard that he was ill. **27** He was indeed so ill that he nearly died. But God had mercy on him, and not only on him but on me also, so that I would not have one sorrow after another. **28** I am the more eager to send him, therefore, in order that you may rejoice at seeing him again, and that I may be less anxious. **29** Welcome him then in the Lord with all joy, and honor such people, **30** because he came close to death for the work of Christ,[e] risking his life to make up for those services that you could not give me.

Phil 4:2–3

I urge Euodia and I urge Syntyche to be of the same mind in the Lord. **3** Yes, and I ask you also, my loyal companion, help these women, for they have struggled beside me in the work of the gospel, together with Clement and the rest of my co-workers, whose names are in the book of life.

Col 1:7

This you learned from Epaphras, our beloved fellow servant. He is a faithful minister of Christ on your[f] behalf

1 Thess 3:1–2

Therefore when we could bear it no longer, we decided to be left alone in Athens; **2** and we sent Timothy, our brother and co-worker for God[g] in proclaiming the gospel of Christ, to strengthen and encourage you for the sake of your faith

1 Thess 5:12–13

But we appeal to you, brothers and sisters, to respect those who labor among you, and have charge of you in the Lord and admonish you; **13** esteem them very highly in love because of their work. Be at peace among yourselves.

1 Tim 5:17–18

Let the elders who rule well be considered worthy of double honor, especially those who labor in preaching and teaching; **18** for the scripture says, "You shall not muzzle an ox while it is treading out the grain," and, "The laborer deserves to be paid."

Phlm 1–2

Paul, a prisoner of Christ Jesus, and Timothy our brother, To Philemon our dear friend and co-worker, **2** to Apphia our sister, to Archippus our fellow soldier, and to the church in your house

Phlm 13

I wanted to keep him with me, so that he might be of service to me in your place during my imprisonment for the gospel

Phlm 23–24

Epaphras, my fellow prisoner in Christ Jesus, sends greetings to you, **24** and so do Mark, Aristarchus, Demas, and Luke, my fellow workers.

See also § 98 The Role of Apostles and Missionary Proclaimers; § 103 Stewards of God; § 112 Bishops, Elders, and Deacons. For Paul's major co-workers individually, see §§ 167–177.

112. Bishops, Elders, and Deacons

Rom 12:6–8

We have gifts that differ according to the grace given to us: prophecy, in proportion to faith; **7** ministry, in ministering; the teacher, in teaching; **8** the exhorter, in exhortation; the giver, in generosity; the leader, in diligence; the compassionate, in cheerfulness.

Rom 16:1–2

I commend to you our sister Phoebe, a deacon of the church at Cenchreae, **2** so that you may welcome her in the Lord as is fitting for the saints, and help her in whatever she may require from you, for she has been a benefactor of many and of myself as well.

Phil 1:1–2

Paul and Timothy, servants of Christ Jesus, To all the saints in Christ Jesus who are in Philippi, with the bishops and deacons: **2** Grace to you and peace from God our Father and the Lord Jesus Christ.

1 Thess 5:12–13

But we appeal to you, brothers and sisters, to respect those who labor among you, and have charge of you in the Lord and admonish you; **13** esteem them very highly in love because of their work. Be at peace among yourselves.

1 Tim 3:1–13

The saying is sure:[a] whoever aspires to the office of bishop desires a noble task. **2** Now a bishop must be above reproach, married only once, temperate, sensible, respectable, hospitable, an apt teacher, **3** not a drunkard, not violent but gentle, not quarrelsome, and not a lover of money. **4** He must manage his own household well, keeping his children submissive and respectful in every way— **5** for if someone does not know

[d] **Phil 2:26** ***longing for*** Other ancient authorities read *longing to see* [e] **Phil 2:30** ***of Christ*** Other ancient authorities read *of the Lord* [f] **Col 1:7** ***your*** Other ancient authorities read *our* [g] **1 Thess 3:2** ***co-worker for God*** lit. *God's co-worker* Other ancient authorities read *God's minister* or *God's minister and our co-worker* **§ 112** [a] **1 Tim 3:1** ***The saying is sure*** A few ancient authorities read *The saying is commonly accepted*

τις τοῦ ἰδίου οἴκου προστῆναι οὐκ οἶδεν, πῶς ἐκκλησίας θεοῦ ἐπιμελήσεται;), 6 μὴ νεόφυτον, ἵνα μὴ τυφωθεὶς εἰς κρίμα ἐμπέσῃ τοῦ διαβόλου. 7 δεῖ δὲ καὶ μαρτυρίαν καλὴν ἔχειν ἀπὸ τῶν ἔξωθεν, ἵνα μὴ εἰς ὀνειδισμὸν ἐμπέσῃ καὶ παγίδα τοῦ διαβόλου. 8 Διακόνους ὡσαύτως σεμνούς, μὴ διλόγους, μὴ οἴνῳ πολλῷ προσέχοντας, μὴ αἰσχροκερδεῖς, 9 ἔχοντας τὸ μυστήριον τῆς πίστεως ἐν καθαρᾷ συνειδήσει. 10 καὶ οὗτοι δὲ δοκιμαζέσθωσαν πρῶτον, εἶτα διακονείτωσαν ἀνέγκλητοι ὄντες. 11 Γυναῖκας ὡσαύτως σεμνάς, μὴ διαβόλους, νηφαλίους, πιστὰς ἐν πᾶσιν. 12 διάκονοι ἔστωσαν μιᾶς γυναικὸς ἄνδρες, τέκνων καλῶς προϊστάμενοι καὶ τῶν ἰδίων οἴκων. 13 οἱ γὰρ καλῶς διακονήσαντες βαθμὸν ἑαυτοῖς καλὸν περιποιοῦνται καὶ πολλὴν παρρησίαν ἐν πίστει τῇ ἐν Χριστῷ Ἰησοῦ.

1 Tim 4:14

μὴ ἀμέλει τοῦ ἐν σοὶ χαρίσματος, ὃ ἐδόθη σοι διὰ προφητείας μετὰ ἐπιθέσεως τῶν χειρῶν τοῦ πρεσβυτερίου.

1 Tim 5:17–25

Οἱ καλῶς προεστῶτες πρεσβύτεροι διπλῆς τιμῆς ἀξιούσθωσαν, μάλιστα οἱ κοπιῶντες ἐν λόγῳ καὶ διδασκαλίᾳ. 18 λέγει γὰρ ἡ γραφή· βοῦν ἀλοῶντα οὐ φιμώσεις, καί· ἄξιος ὁ ἐργάτης τοῦ μισθοῦ αὐτοῦ. 19 κατὰ πρεσβυτέρου κατηγορίαν μὴ παραδέχου, ἐκτὸς εἰ μὴ ἐπὶ δύο ἢ τριῶν μαρτύρων. 20 Τοὺς ἁμαρτάνοντας ἐνώπιον πάντων ἔλεγχε, ἵνα καὶ οἱ λοιποὶ φόβον ἔχωσιν. 21 Διαμαρτύρομαι ἐνώπιον τοῦ θεοῦ καὶ Χριστοῦ Ἰησοῦ καὶ τῶν ἐκλεκτῶν ἀγγέλων, ἵνα ταῦτα φυλάξῃς χωρὶς προκρίματος, μηδὲν ποιῶν κατὰ πρόσκλισιν. 22 χεῖρας ταχέως μηδενὶ ἐπιτίθει μηδὲ κοινώνει ἁμαρτίαις ἀλλοτρίαις· σεαυτὸν ἁγνὸν τήρει. 23 Μηκέτι ὑδροπότει, ἀλλὰ οἴνῳ ὀλίγῳ χρῶ διὰ τὸν στόμαχον καὶ τὰς πυκνάς σου ἀσθενείας. 24 Τινῶν ἀνθρώπων αἱ ἁμαρτίαι πρόδηλοί εἰσιν προάγουσαι εἰς κρίσιν, τισὶν δὲ καὶ ἐπακολουθοῦσιν· 25 ὡσαύτως καὶ τὰ ἔργα τὰ καλὰ πρόδηλα, καὶ τὰ ἄλλως ἔχοντα κρυβῆναι οὐ δύνανται.

Titus 1:5–9

Τούτου χάριν ἀπέλιπόν σε ἐν Κρήτῃ, ἵνα τὰ λείποντα ἐπιδιορθώσῃ καὶ καταστήσῃς κατὰ πόλιν πρεσβυτέρους, ὡς ἐγώ σοι διεταξάμην, 6 εἴ τίς ἐστιν ἀνέγκλητος, μιᾶς γυναικὸς ἀνήρ, τέκνα ἔχων πιστά, μὴ ἐν κατηγορίᾳ ἀσωτίας ἢ ἀνυπότακτα. 7 δεῖ γὰρ τὸν ἐπίσκοπον ἀνέγκλητον εἶναι ὡς θεοῦ οἰκονόμον, μὴ αὐθάδη, μὴ ὀργίλον, μὴ πάροινον, μὴ πλήκτην, μὴ αἰσχροκερδῆ, 8 ἀλλὰ φιλόξενον φιλάγαθον σώφρονα δίκαιον ὅσιον ἐγκρατῆ, 9 ἀντεχόμενον τοῦ κατὰ τὴν διδαχὴν πιστοῦ λόγου, ἵνα δυνατὸς ᾖ καὶ παρακαλεῖν ἐν τῇ διδασκαλίᾳ τῇ ὑγιαινούσῃ καὶ τοὺς ἀντιλέγοντας ἐλέγχειν.

Acts 14:23

χειροτονήσαντες δὲ αὐτοῖς κατ᾽ ἐκκλησίαν πρεσβυτέρους, προσευξάμενοι μετὰ νηστειῶν παρέθεντο αὐτοὺς τῷ κυρίῳ εἰς ὃν πεπιστεύκεισαν.

Acts 20:17

Ἀπὸ δὲ τῆς Μιλήτου πέμψας εἰς Ἔφεσον μετεκαλέσατο τοὺς πρεσβυτέρους τῆς ἐκκλησίας.

Acts 20:28–31

προσέχετε ἑαυτοῖς καὶ παντὶ τῷ ποιμνίῳ, ἐν ᾧ ὑμᾶς τὸ πνεῦμα τὸ ἅγιον ἔθετο ἐπισκόπους ποιμαίνειν τὴν ἐκκλησίαν τοῦ ⸀θεοῦ, ἣν περιεποιήσατο διὰ τοῦ αἵματος τοῦ ἰδίου. 29 ἐγὼ οἶδα ὅτι εἰσελεύσονται μετὰ τὴν ἄφιξίν μου λύκοι βαρεῖς εἰς ὑμᾶς μὴ φειδόμενοι τοῦ ποιμνίου, 30 καὶ ἐξ ὑμῶν αὐτῶν ἀναστήσονται ἄνδρες λαλοῦντες διεστραμμένα τοῦ ἀποσπᾶν τοὺς μαθητὰς ὀπίσω αὐτῶν. 31 διὸ γρηγορεῖτε μνημονεύοντες ὅτι τριετίαν νύκτα καὶ ἡμέραν οὐκ ἐπαυσάμην μετὰ δακρύων νουθετῶν ἕνα ἕκαστον.

113. Participation of Paul's Churches in Mission

1 Cor 10:31–11:1

Εἴτε οὖν ἐσθίετε εἴτε πίνετε εἴτε τι ποιεῖτε, πάντα εἰς δόξαν θεοῦ ποιεῖτε. 32 ἀπρόσκοποι καὶ Ἰουδαίοις γίνεσθε καὶ Ἕλλησιν καὶ τῇ ἐκκλησίᾳ τοῦ θεοῦ, 33 καθὼς κἀγὼ πάντα πᾶσιν ἀρέσκω μὴ ζητῶν τὸ ἐμαυτοῦ σύμφορον ἀλλὰ τὸ τῶν πολλῶν, ἵνα σωθῶσιν. **11** μιμηταί μου γίνεσθε καθὼς κἀγὼ Χριστοῦ.

1 Cor 14:20–25

Ἀδελφοί, μὴ παιδία γίνεσθε ταῖς φρεσὶν ἀλλὰ τῇ κακίᾳ νηπιάζετε, ταῖς δὲ φρεσὶν τέλειοι γίνεσθε. 21 ἐν τῷ νόμῳ γέγραπται ὅτι ἐν ἑτερογλώσσοις καὶ ἐν χείλεσιν ἑτέρων λαλήσω τῷ λαῷ τούτῳ καὶ οὐδ᾽ οὕτως εἰσακούσονταί μου, λέγει κύριος. 22 ὥστε αἱ γλῶσσαι εἰς σημεῖόν εἰσιν οὐ τοῖς πιστεύουσιν ἀλλὰ τοῖς ἀπίστοις, ἡ δὲ προφητεία οὐ τοῖς ἀπίστοις ἀλλὰ τοῖς πιστεύουσιν. 23 Ἐὰν οὖν συνέλθῃ ἡ ἐκκλησία ὅλη ἐπὶ τὸ αὐτὸ καὶ πάντες λαλῶσιν γλώσσαις, εἰσέλθωσιν δὲ ἰδιῶται ἢ ἄπιστοι, οὐκ ἐροῦσιν ὅτι μαίνεσθε; 24 ἐὰν δὲ πάντες προφητεύωσιν, εἰσέλθῃ δέ τις ἄπιστος ἢ ἰδιώτης, ἐλέγχεται ὑπὸ πάντων, ἀνακρίνεται ὑπὸ πάντων, 25 τὰ κρυπτὰ τῆς καρδίας αὐτοῦ φανερὰ γίνεται, καὶ οὕτως πεσὼν ἐπὶ πρόσωπον προσκυνήσει τῷ θεῷ ἀπαγγέλλων ὅτι ὄντως ὁ θεὸς ἐν ὑμῖν ἐστιν.

1 Cor 16:6

πρὸς ὑμᾶς δὲ τυχὸν παραμενῶ ἢ καὶ παραχειμάσω, ἵνα ὑμεῖς με προπέμψητε οὗ ἐὰν πορεύωμαι.

2 Cor 11:8–9

ἄλλας ἐκκλησίας ἐσύλησα λαβὼν ὀψώνιον πρὸς τὴν ὑμῶν διακονίαν, 9 καὶ παρὼν πρὸς ὑμᾶς καὶ ὑστερηθεὶς οὐ κατενάρκησα οὐθενός· τὸ γὰρ ὑστέρημά μου προσανεπλήρωσαν οἱ ἀδελφοὶ ἐλθόντες ἀπὸ Μακεδονίας, καὶ ἐν παντὶ ἀβαρῆ ἐμαυτὸν ὑμῖν ἐτήρησα καὶ τηρήσω.

Acts 20:28 ***θεου*** ℵ B] κυριου 𝔓74 A C* D E 33. 1739 ¦ κυριου και θεου *Byz*

how to manage his own household, how can he take care of God's church? 6 He must not be a recent convert, or he may be puffed up with conceit and fall into the condemnation of the devil. 7 Moreover, he must be well thought of by outsiders, so that he may not fall into disgrace and the snare of the devil. 8 Deacons likewise must be serious, not double-tongued, not indulging in much wine, not greedy for money; 9 they must hold fast to the mystery of the faith with a clear conscience. 10 And let them first be tested; then, if they prove themselves blameless, let them serve as deacons. 11 Women likewise must be serious, not slanderers, but temperate, faithful in all things. 12 Let deacons be married only once, and let them manage their children and their households well; 13 for those who serve well as deacons gain a good standing for themselves and great boldness in the faith that is in Christ Jesus.

1 Tim 4:14

Do not neglect the gift that is in you, which was given to you through prophecy with the laying on of hands by the council of elders.

1 Tim 5:17–25

Let the elders who rule well be considered worthy of double honor, especially those who labor in preaching and teaching; 18 for the scripture says, "You shall not muzzle an ox while it is treading out the grain," and, "The laborer deserves to be paid." 19 Never accept any accusation against an elder except on the evidence of two or three witnesses. 20 As for those who persist in sin, rebuke them in the presence of all, so that the rest also may stand in fear. 21 In the presence of God and of Christ Jesus and of the elect angels, I warn you to keep these instructions without prejudice, doing nothing on the basis of partiality. 22 Do not ordain anyone hastily, and do not participate in the sins of others; keep yourself pure. 23 No longer drink only water, but take a little wine for the sake of your stomach and your frequent ailments. 24 The sins of some people are conspicuous and precede them to judgment, while the sins of others follow them there. 25 So also good works are conspicuous; and even when they are not, they cannot remain hidden.

Titus 1:5–9

I left you behind in Crete for this reason, so that you should put in order what remained to be done, and should appoint elders in every town, as I directed you: 6 someone who is blameless, married only once, whose children are believers, not accused of debauchery and not rebellious. 7 For a bishop, as God's steward, must be blameless; he must not be arrogant or quick-tempered or addicted to wine or violent or greedy for gain; 8 but he must be hospitable, a lover of goodness, prudent, upright, devout, and self-controlled. 9 He must have a firm grasp of the word that is trustworthy in accordance with the teaching, so that he may be able both to preach with sound doctrine and to refute those who contradict it.

Acts 14:23

And after they had appointed elders for them in each church, with prayer and fasting they entrusted them to the Lord in whom they had come to believe.

Acts 20:17

From Miletus he sent a message to Ephesus, asking the elders of the church to meet him.

Acts 20:28–31

Keep watch over yourselves and over all the flock, of which the Holy Spirit has made you overseers, to shepherd the church of God[b] that he obtained with the blood of his own Son. 29 I know that after I have gone, savage wolves will come in among you, not sparing the flock. 30 Some even from your own group will come distorting the truth in order to entice the disciples to follow them. 31 Therefore be alert, remembering that for three years I did not cease night or day to warn everyone with tears.

113. Participation of Paul's Churches in Mission

1 Cor 10:31–11:1

So, whether you eat or drink, or whatever you do, do everything for the glory of God. 32 Give no offense to Jews or to Greeks or to the church of God, 33 just as I try to please everyone in everything I do, not seeking my own advantage, but that of many, so that they may be saved. **11** Be imitators of me, as I am of Christ.

1 Cor 14:20–25

Brothers and sisters, do not be children in your thinking; rather, be infants in evil, but in thinking be adults. 21 In the law it is written, "By people of strange tongues and by the lips of foreigners I will speak to this people; yet even then they will not listen to me," says the Lord. 22 Tongues, then, are a sign not for believers but for unbelievers, while prophecy is not for unbelievers but for believers. 23 If, therefore, the whole church comes together and all speak in tongues, and outsiders or unbelievers enter, will they not say that you are out of your mind? 24 But if all prophesy, an unbeliever or outsider who enters is reproved by all and called to account by all. 25 After the secrets of the unbeliever's heart are disclosed, that person will bow down before God and worship him, declaring, "God is really among you."

1 Cor 16:6

and perhaps I will stay with you or even spend the winter, so that you may send me on my way, wherever I go.

2 Cor 11:8–9

I robbed other churches by accepting support from them in order to serve you. 9 And when I was with you and was in need, I did not burden anyone, for my needs were supplied by the friends who came from Macedonia. So I refrained and will continue to refrain from burdening you in any way.

[b] **Acts 20:28** *of God* Other ancient authorities read *of the Lord*

2 Cor 12:13

τί γάρ ἐστιν ὃ ἡσσώθητε ὑπὲρ τὰς λοιπὰς ἐκκλησίας, εἰ μὴ ὅτι αὐτὸς ἐγὼ οὐ κατενάρκησα ὑμῶν; χαρίσασθέ μοι τὴν ἀδικίαν ταύτην.

Eph 6:14–15

στῆτε οὖν περιζωσάμενοι τὴν ὀσφὺν ὑμῶν ἐν ἀληθείᾳ καὶ ἐνδυσάμενοι τὸν θώρακα τῆς δικαιοσύνης **15** καὶ ὑποδησάμενοι τοὺς πόδας ἐν ἑτοιμασίᾳ τοῦ εὐαγγελίου τῆς εἰρήνης

Eph 6:19–20

καὶ ὑπὲρ ἐμοῦ, ἵνα μοι δοθῇ λόγος ἐν ἀνοίξει τοῦ στόματός μου, ἐν παρρησίᾳ γνωρίσαι τὸ μυστήριον ⸂τοῦ εὐαγγελίου⸃, **20** ὑπὲρ οὗ πρεσβεύω ἐν ἁλύσει, ἵνα ἐν αὐτῷ παρρησιάσωμαι ὡς δεῖ με λαλῆσαι.

Phil 1:3–5

Εὐχαριστῶ τῷ θεῷ μου ἐπὶ πάσῃ τῇ μνείᾳ ὑμῶν **4** πάντοτε ἐν πάσῃ δεήσει μου ὑπὲρ πάντων ὑμῶν, μετὰ χαρᾶς τὴν δέησιν ποιούμενος, **5** ἐπὶ τῇ κοινωνίᾳ ὑμῶν εἰς τὸ εὐαγγέλιον ἀπὸ τῆς πρώτης ἡμέρας ἄχρι τοῦ νῦν

Phil 1:12–14

Γινώσκειν δὲ ὑμᾶς βούλομαι, ἀδελφοί, ὅτι τὰ κατ' ἐμὲ μᾶλλον εἰς προκοπὴν τοῦ εὐαγγελίου ἐλήλυθεν, **13** ὥστε τοὺς δεσμούς μου φανεροὺς ἐν Χριστῷ γενέσθαι ἐν ὅλῳ τῷ πραιτωρίῳ καὶ τοῖς λοιποῖς πᾶσιν, **14** καὶ τοὺς πλείονας τῶν ἀδελφῶν ἐν κυρίῳ πεποιθότας τοῖς δεσμοῖς μου περισσοτέρως τολμᾶν ἀφόβως τὸν ⸀λόγον λαλεῖν.

Phil 1:19–20

οἶδα γὰρ ὅτι τοῦτό μοι ἀποβήσεται εἰς σωτηρίαν διὰ τῆς ὑμῶν δεήσεως καὶ ἐπιχορηγίας τοῦ πνεύματος Ἰησοῦ Χριστοῦ **20** κατὰ τὴν ἀποκαραδοκίαν καὶ ἐλπίδα μου, ὅτι ἐν οὐδενὶ αἰσχυνθήσομαι ἀλλ' ἐν πάσῃ παρρησίᾳ ὡς πάντοτε καὶ νῦν μεγαλυνθήσεται Χριστὸς ἐν τῷ σώματί μου, εἴτε διὰ ζωῆς εἴτε διὰ θανάτου.

Phil 1:27–30

Μόνον ἀξίως τοῦ εὐαγγελίου τοῦ Χριστοῦ πολιτεύεσθε, ἵνα εἴτε ἐλθὼν καὶ ἰδὼν ὑμᾶς εἴτε ἀπὼν ἀκούω τὰ περὶ ὑμῶν, ὅτι στήκετε ἐν ἑνὶ πνεύματι, μιᾷ ψυχῇ συναθλοῦντες τῇ πίστει τοῦ εὐαγγελίου **28** καὶ μὴ πτυρόμενοι ἐν μηδενὶ ὑπὸ τῶν ἀντικειμένων, ἥτις ἐστὶν αὐτοῖς ἔνδειξις ἀπωλείας, ὑμῶν δὲ σωτηρίας, καὶ τοῦτο ἀπὸ θεοῦ· **29** ὅτι ὑμῖν ἐχαρίσθη τὸ ὑπὲρ Χριστοῦ, οὐ μόνον τὸ εἰς αὐτὸν πιστεύειν ἀλλὰ καὶ τὸ ὑπὲρ αὐτοῦ πάσχειν, **30** τὸν αὐτὸν ἀγῶνα ἔχοντες, οἷον εἴδετε ἐν ἐμοὶ καὶ νῦν ἀκούετε ἐν ἐμοί.

Phil 2:12–18

Ὥστε, ἀγαπητοί μου, καθὼς πάντοτε ὑπηκούσατε, μὴ ὡς ἐν τῇ παρουσίᾳ μου μόνον ἀλλὰ νῦν πολλῷ μᾶλλον ἐν τῇ ἀπουσίᾳ μου, μετὰ φόβου καὶ τρόμου τὴν ἑαυτῶν σωτηρίαν κατεργάζεσθε· **13** θεὸς γάρ ἐστιν ὁ ἐνεργῶν ἐν ὑμῖν καὶ τὸ θέλειν καὶ τὸ ἐνεργεῖν ὑπὲρ τῆς εὐδοκίας. **14** Πάντα ποιεῖτε χωρὶς γογγυσμῶν καὶ διαλογισμῶν, **15** ἵνα γένησθε ἄμεμπτοι καὶ ἀκέραιοι, τέκνα θεοῦ ἄμωμα μέσον γενεᾶς σκολιᾶς καὶ διεστραμμένης, ἐν οἷς φαίνεσθε ὡς φωστῆρες ἐν κόσμῳ, **16** λόγον ζωῆς ἐπέχοντες, εἰς καύχημα ἐμοὶ εἰς ἡμέραν Χριστοῦ, ὅτι οὐκ εἰς κενὸν ἔδραμον οὐδὲ εἰς κενὸν ἐκοπίασα. **17** Ἀλλὰ εἰ καὶ σπένδομαι ἐπὶ τῇ θυσίᾳ καὶ λειτουργίᾳ τῆς πίστεως ὑμῶν, χαίρω καὶ συγχαίρω πᾶσιν ὑμῖν· **18** τὸ δὲ αὐτὸ καὶ ὑμεῖς χαίρετε καὶ συγχαίρετέ μοι.

Phil 2:25–30

Ἀναγκαῖον δὲ ἡγησάμην Ἐπαφρόδιτον τὸν ἀδελφὸν καὶ συνεργὸν καὶ συστρατιώτην μου, ὑμῶν δὲ ἀπόστολον καὶ λειτουργὸν τῆς χρείας μου, πέμψαι πρὸς ὑμᾶς, **26** ἐπειδὴ ἐπιποθῶν ἦν ⸂πάντας ὑμᾶς⸃ καὶ ἀδημονῶν, διότι ἠκούσατε ὅτι ἠσθένησεν. **27** καὶ γὰρ ἠσθένησεν παραπλήσιον θανάτῳ· ἀλλὰ ὁ θεὸς ἠλέησεν αὐτόν, οὐκ αὐτὸν δὲ μόνον ἀλλὰ καὶ ἐμέ, ἵνα μὴ λύπην ἐπὶ λύπην σχῶ. **28** σπουδαιοτέρως οὖν ἔπεμψα αὐτόν, ἵνα ἰδόντες αὐτὸν πάλιν χαρῆτε κἀγὼ ἀλυπότερος ὦ. **29** προσδέχεσθε οὖν αὐτὸν ἐν κυρίῳ μετὰ πάσης χαρᾶς καὶ τοὺς τοιούτους ἐντίμους ἔχετε, **30** ὅτι διὰ τὸ ἔργον ⸀Χριστοῦ μέχρι θανάτου ἤγγισεν παραβολευσάμενος τῇ ψυχῇ, ἵνα ἀναπληρώσῃ τὸ ὑμῶν ὑστέρημα τῆς πρός με λειτουργίας.

Phil 4:10–20

Ἐχάρην δὲ ἐν κυρίῳ μεγάλως ὅτι ἤδη ποτὲ ἀνεθάλετε τὸ ὑπὲρ ἐμοῦ φρονεῖν, ἐφ' ᾧ καὶ ἐφρονεῖτε, ἠκαιρεῖσθε δέ. **11** οὐχ ὅτι καθ' ὑστέρησιν λέγω, ἐγὼ γὰρ ἔμαθον ἐν οἷς εἰμι αὐτάρκης εἶναι. **12** οἶδα καὶ ταπεινοῦσθαι, οἶδα καὶ περισσεύειν· ἐν παντὶ καὶ ἐν πᾶσιν μεμύημαι, καὶ χορτάζεσθαι καὶ πεινᾶν καὶ περισσεύειν καὶ ὑστερεῖσθαι· **13** πάντα ἰσχύω ἐν τῷ ἐνδυναμοῦντί με. **14** πλὴν καλῶς ἐποιήσατε συγκοινωνήσαντές μου τῇ θλίψει. **15** οἴδατε δὲ καὶ ὑμεῖς, Φιλιππήσιοι, ὅτι ἐν ἀρχῇ τοῦ εὐαγγελίου, ὅτε ἐξῆλθον ἀπὸ Μακεδονίας, οὐδεμία μοι ἐκκλησία ἐκοινώνησεν εἰς λόγον δόσεως καὶ λήμψεως εἰ μὴ ὑμεῖς μόνοι, **16** ὅτι καὶ ἐν Θεσσαλονίκῃ καὶ ἅπαξ καὶ δὶς εἰς τὴν χρείαν μοι ἐπέμψατε. **17** οὐχ ὅτι ἐπιζητῶ τὸ δόμα, ἀλλὰ ἐπιζητῶ τὸν καρπὸν τὸν πλεονάζοντα εἰς λόγον ὑμῶν. **18** ἀπέχω δὲ πάντα καὶ περισσεύω· πεπλήρωμαι δεξάμενος παρὰ Ἐπαφροδίτου τὰ παρ' ὑμῶν, ὀσμὴν εὐωδίας, θυσίαν δεκτήν, εὐάρεστον τῷ θεῷ. **19** ὁ δὲ θεός μου πληρώσει πᾶσαν χρείαν ὑμῶν κατὰ τὸ πλοῦτος αὐτοῦ ἐν δόξῃ ἐν Χριστῷ Ἰησοῦ. **20** τῷ δὲ θεῷ καὶ πατρὶ ἡμῶν ἡ δόξα εἰς τοὺς αἰῶνας τῶν αἰώνων, ἀμήν.

Col 4:2–6

Τῇ προσευχῇ προσκαρτερεῖτε, γρηγοροῦντες ἐν αὐτῇ ἐν εὐχαριστίᾳ, **3** προσευχόμενοι ἅμα καὶ περὶ ἡμῶν, ἵνα ὁ θεὸς ἀνοίξῃ ἡμῖν θύραν τοῦ λόγου λαλῆσαι τὸ μυστήριον τοῦ Χριστοῦ, δι' ὃ καὶ δέδεμαι, **4** ἵνα φανερώσω αὐτὸ ὡς δεῖ με λαλῆσαι. **5** Ἐν σοφίᾳ περιπατεῖτε πρὸς τοὺς ἔξω τὸν καιρὸν ἐξαγοραζόμενοι.

§ 113 **Eph 6:19** ***του ευαγγελιου*** ℵ A D I 33. 1739. 1881 *Byz*] *om*. B **Phil 1:14** ***λογον*** 𝔓^{46} D^{2} 1739. 1881 *Byz*] *add*. του θεου ℵ A B (D*) 048^{vid}. 33 **Phil 2:26** ***παντας υμας*** ℵ^{2} 1739. 1881 *Byz*] υμας παντας B ¦ παντας υμας ιδειν ℵ* A C D I^{vid} 33 ¦ πεμψαι προς υμας 𝔓^{46vid} **Phil 2:30** ***Χριστου*** 𝔓^{46} B 1739. 1881] κυριου ℵ A 33 ¦ του Χριστου D *Byz* ¦ *om*. C

2 Cor 12:13

How have you been worse off than the other churches, except that I myself did not burden you? Forgive me this wrong!

Eph 6:14–15

Stand therefore, and fasten the belt of truth around your waist, and put on the breastplate of righteousness. **15** As shoes for your feet put on whatever will make you ready to proclaim the gospel of peace.

Eph 6:19–20

Pray also for me, so that when I speak, a message may be given to me to make known with boldness the mystery of the gospel,[a] **20** for which I am an ambassador in chains. Pray that I may declare it boldly, as I must speak.

Phil 1:3–5

I thank my God every time I remember you, **4** constantly praying with joy in every one of my prayers for all of you, **5** because of your sharing in the gospel proclamation[b] from the first day until now.

Phil 1:12–14

I want you to know, beloved, that what has happened to me has actually helped to spread the gospel, **13** so that it has become known throughout the whole imperial guard and to everyone else that my imprisonment is for Christ; **14** and most of the brothers and sisters, having been made confident in the Lord by my imprisonment, dare to speak the word[c] with greater boldness and without fear.

Phil 1:19–20

for I know that through your prayers and the supply of the Spirit of Jesus Christ this will turn out for my deliverance.[d] **20** It is my eager expectation and hope that I will not be put to shame in any way, but that by my speaking with all boldness, Christ will be exalted now as always in my body, whether by life or by death.

Phil 1:27–30

Only, live your life in a manner worthy of the gospel of Christ, so that, whether I come and see you or am absent and hear about you, I will know that you are standing firm in one spirit, striving side by side with one mind for the faith of the gospel, **28** and are in no way intimidated by your opponents. For them this is evidence of their destruction, but of your salvation. And this is God's doing. **29** For he has graciously granted you the privilege not only of believing in Christ, but of suffering for him as well— **30** since you are having the same struggle that you saw I had and now hear that I still have.

Phil 2:12–18

Therefore, my beloved, just as you have always obeyed me, not only in my presence, but much more now in my absence, work out your own salvation with fear and trembling; **13** for it is God who is at work in you, enabling you both to will and to work for his good pleasure. **14** Do all things without murmuring and arguing, **15** so that you may be blameless and innocent, children of God without blemish in the midst of a crooked and perverse generation, in which you shine like stars in the world. **16** It is by your holding forth[e] the word of life that I can boast on the day of Christ that I did not run in vain or labor in vain. **17** But even if I am being poured out as a libation over the sacrifice and the offering of your faith, I am glad and rejoice with all of you— **18** and in the same way you also must be glad and rejoice with me.

Phil 2:25–30

Still, I think it necessary to send to you Epaphroditus—my brother and co-worker and fellow soldier, your messenger and minister to my need; **26** for he has been longing for[f] all of you, and has been distressed because you heard that he was ill. **27** He was indeed so ill that he nearly died. But God had mercy on him, and not only on him but on me also, so that I would not have one sorrow after another. **28** I am the more eager to send him, therefore, in order that you may rejoice at seeing him again, and that I may be less anxious. **29** Welcome him then in the Lord with all joy, and honor such people, **30** because he came close to death for the work of Christ,[g] risking his life to make up for those services that you could not give me.

Phil 4:10–20

I rejoice in the Lord greatly that now at last you have revived your concern for me; indeed, you were concerned for me, but had no opportunity to show it. **11** Not that I am referring to being in need; for I have learned to be content with whatever I have. **12** I know what it is to have little, and I know what it is to have plenty. In any and all circumstances I have learned the secret of being well-fed and of going hungry, of having plenty and of being in need. **13** I can do all things through him who strengthens me. **14** In any case, it was kind of you to share my distress. **15** You Philippians indeed know that in the early days of the gospel, when I left Macedonia, no church shared with me in the matter of giving and receiving, except you alone. **16** For even when I was in Thessalonica, you sent me help for my needs more than once. **17** Not that I seek the gift, but I seek the profit that accumulates to your account. **18** I have been paid in full and have more than enough; I am fully satisfied, now that I have received from Epaphroditus the gifts you sent, a fragrant offering, a sacrifice acceptable and pleasing to God. **19** And my God will fully satisfy every need of yours according to his riches in glory in Christ Jesus. **20** To our God and Father be glory forever and ever. Amen.

Col 4:2–6

Devote yourselves to prayer, keeping alert in it with thanksgiving. **3** At the same time pray for us as well that God will open to us a door for the word, that we may declare the mystery of Christ, for which I am in prison, **4** so that I may reveal it clearly, as I should. **5** Conduct yourselves wisely toward outsiders,

§ 113 [a] **Eph 6:19** ***of the gospel*** Other ancient authorities lack *of the gospel* [b] **Phil 1:5** ***gospel proclamation*** NRSV translates *gospel* [c] **Phil 1:14** ***word*** Other ancient authorities read *word of God* [d] **Phil 1:19** Translation differs from NRSV [e] **Phil 2:16** ***holding forth*** NRSV translates *holding fast to* [f] **Phil 2:26** ***longing for*** Other ancient authorities read *longing to see* [g] **Phil 2:30** ***of Christ*** Other ancient authorities read *of the Lord*

6 ὁ λόγος ὑμῶν πάντοτε ἐν χάριτι, ἅλατι ἠρτυμένος, εἰδέναι πῶς δεῖ ὑμᾶς ἑνὶ ἑκάστῳ ἀποκρίνεσθαι.

1 Thess 1:5–8

ὅτι τὸ εὐαγγέλιον ἡμῶν οὐκ ἐγενήθη εἰς ὑμᾶς ἐν λόγῳ μόνον ἀλλὰ καὶ ἐν δυνάμει καὶ ἐν πνεύματι ἁγίῳ καὶ [ἐν] πληροφορίᾳ πολλῇ, καθὼς οἴδατε οἷοι ἐγενήθημεν [ἐν] ὑμῖν δι᾽ ὑμᾶς. **6** Καὶ ὑμεῖς μιμηταὶ ἡμῶν ἐγενήθητε καὶ τοῦ κυρίου, δεξάμενοι τὸν λόγον ἐν θλίψει πολλῇ μετὰ χαρᾶς πνεύματος ἁγίου, **7** ὥστε γενέσθαι ὑμᾶς τύπον πᾶσιν τοῖς πιστεύουσιν ἐν τῇ Μακεδονίᾳ καὶ ἐν τῇ Ἀχαΐᾳ. **8** ἀφ᾽ ὑμῶν γὰρ ἐξήχηται ὁ λόγος τοῦ κυρίου οὐ μόνον ἐν τῇ Μακεδονίᾳ καὶ [ἐν τῇ] Ἀχαΐᾳ, ἀλλ᾽ ἐν παντὶ τόπῳ ἡ πίστις ὑμῶν ἡ πρὸς τὸν θεὸν ἐξελήλυθεν, ὥστε μὴ χρείαν ἔχειν ἡμᾶς λαλεῖν τι.

2 Thess 3:1–2

Τὸ λοιπὸν προσεύχεσθε, ἀδελφοί, περὶ ἡμῶν, ἵνα ὁ λόγος τοῦ κυρίου τρέχῃ καὶ δοξάζηται καθὼς καὶ πρὸς ὑμᾶς, **2** καὶ ἵνα ῥυσθῶμεν ἀπὸ τῶν ἀτόπων καὶ πονηρῶν ἀνθρώπων· οὐ γὰρ πάντων ἡ πίστις.

1 Tim 2:1–4

Παρακαλῶ οὖν πρῶτον πάντων ποιεῖσθαι δεήσεις προσευχὰς ἐντεύξεις εὐχαριστίας ὑπὲρ πάντων ἀνθρώπων, **2** ὑπὲρ βασιλέων καὶ πάντων τῶν ἐν ὑπεροχῇ ὄντων, ἵνα ἤρεμον καὶ ἡσύχιον βίον διάγωμεν ἐν πάσῃ εὐσεβείᾳ καὶ σεμνότητι. **3** τοῦτο καλὸν καὶ ἀπόδεκτον ἐνώπιον τοῦ σωτῆρος ἡμῶν θεοῦ, **4** ὃς πάντας ἀνθρώπους θέλει σωθῆναι καὶ εἰς ἐπίγνωσιν ἀληθείας ἐλθεῖν.

1 Tim 6:1

Ὅσοι εἰσὶν ὑπὸ ζυγὸν δοῦλοι, τοὺς ἰδίους δεσπότας πάσης τιμῆς ἀξίους ἡγείσθωσαν, ἵνα μὴ τὸ ὄνομα τοῦ θεοῦ καὶ ἡ διδασκαλία βλασφημῆται.

Titus 2:4–5

ἵνα σωφρονίζωσιν τὰς νέας φιλάνδρους εἶναι, φιλοτέκνους **5** σώφρονας ἁγνὰς οἰκουργοὺς ἀγαθάς, ὑποτασσομένας τοῖς ἰδίοις ἀνδράσιν, ἵνα μὴ ὁ λόγος τοῦ θεοῦ βλασφημῆται.

Titus 2:9–10

Δούλους ἰδίοις δεσπόταις ὑποτάσσεσθαι ἐν πᾶσιν, εὐαρέστους εἶναι, μὴ ἀντιλέγοντας, **10** μὴ νοσφιζομένους, ἀλλὰ πᾶσαν πίστιν ἐνδεικνυμένους ἀγαθήν, ἵνα τὴν διδασκαλίαν τὴν τοῦ σωτῆρος ἡμῶν θεοῦ κοσμῶσιν ἐν πᾶσιν.

Cf. Acts 13:48–49; 19:8–10; and for the church of Rome (a congregation not founded by Paul) see Rom 1:8; 15:22–24; 15:30–32.

114. Exhortation to Verbal Mission and Proclamation

Eph 6:14–15

στῆτε οὖν περιζωσάμενοι τὴν ὀσφὺν ὑμῶν ἐν ἀληθείᾳ καὶ ἐνδυσάμενοι τὸν θώρακα τῆς δικαιοσύνης **15** καὶ ὑποδησάμενοι τοὺς πόδας ἐν ἑτοιμασίᾳ τοῦ εὐαγγελίου τῆς εἰρήνης

Phil 1:12–14

Γινώσκειν δὲ ὑμᾶς βούλομαι, ἀδελφοί, ὅτι τὰ κατ᾽ ἐμὲ μᾶλλον εἰς προκοπὴν τοῦ εὐαγγελίου ἐλήλυθεν, **13** ὥστε τοὺς δεσμούς μου φανεροὺς ἐν Χριστῷ γενέσθαι ἐν ὅλῳ τῷ πραιτωρίῳ καὶ τοῖς λοιποῖς πᾶσιν, **14** καὶ τοὺς πλείονας τῶν ἀδελφῶν ἐν κυρίῳ πεποιθότας τοῖς δεσμοῖς μου περισσοτέρως τολμᾶν ἀφόβως τὸν ⸀λόγον λαλεῖν.

Phil 2:12–16

Ὥστε, ἀγαπητοί μου, καθὼς πάντοτε ὑπηκούσατε, μὴ ὡς ἐν τῇ παρουσίᾳ μου μόνον ἀλλὰ νῦν πολλῷ μᾶλλον ἐν τῇ ἀπουσίᾳ μου, μετὰ φόβου καὶ τρόμου τὴν ἑαυτῶν σωτηρίαν κατεργάζεσθε· **13** θεὸς γάρ ἐστιν ὁ ἐνεργῶν ἐν ὑμῖν καὶ τὸ θέλειν καὶ τὸ ἐνεργεῖν ὑπὲρ τῆς εὐδοκίας. **14** Πάντα ποιεῖτε χωρὶς γογγυσμῶν καὶ διαλογισμῶν, **15** ἵνα γένησθε ἄμεμπτοι καὶ ἀκέραιοι, τέκνα θεοῦ ἄμωμα μέσον γενεᾶς σκολιᾶς καὶ διεστραμμένης, ἐν οἷς φαίνεσθε ὡς φωστῆρες ἐν κόσμῳ, **16** λόγον ζωῆς ἐπέχοντες, εἰς καύχημα ἐμοὶ εἰς ἡμέραν Χριστοῦ, ὅτι οὐκ εἰς κενὸν ἔδραμον οὐδὲ εἰς κενὸν ἐκοπίασα.

Col 4:5–6

Ἐν σοφίᾳ περιπατεῖτε πρὸς τοὺς ἔξω τὸν καιρὸν ἐξαγοραζόμενοι. **6** ὁ λόγος ὑμῶν πάντοτε ἐν χάριτι, ἅλατι ἠρτυμένος, εἰδέναι πῶς δεῖ ὑμᾶς ἑνὶ ἑκάστῳ ἀποκρίνεσθαι.

1 Thess 1:5–8

ὅτι τὸ εὐαγγέλιον ἡμῶν οὐκ ἐγενήθη εἰς ὑμᾶς ἐν λόγῳ μόνον ἀλλὰ καὶ ἐν δυνάμει καὶ ἐν πνεύματι ἁγίῳ καὶ [ἐν] πληροφορίᾳ πολλῇ, καθὼς οἴδατε οἷοι ἐγενήθημεν [ἐν] ὑμῖν δι᾽ ὑμᾶς. **6** Καὶ ὑμεῖς μιμηταὶ ἡμῶν ἐγενήθητε καὶ τοῦ κυρίου, δεξάμενοι τὸν λόγον ἐν θλίψει πολλῇ μετὰ χαρᾶς πνεύματος ἁγίου, **7** ὥστε γενέσθαι ὑμᾶς τύπον πᾶσιν τοῖς πιστεύουσιν ἐν τῇ Μακεδονίᾳ καὶ ἐν τῇ Ἀχαΐᾳ. **8** ἀφ᾽ ὑμῶν γὰρ ἐξήχηται ὁ λόγος τοῦ κυρίου οὐ μόνον ἐν τῇ Μακεδονίᾳ καὶ [ἐν τῇ] Ἀχαΐᾳ, ἀλλ᾽ ἐν παντὶ τόπῳ ἡ πίστις ὑμῶν ἡ πρὸς τὸν θεὸν ἐξελήλυθεν, ὥστε μὴ χρείαν ἔχειν ἡμᾶς λαλεῖν τι.

2 Tim 4:1–5

Διαμαρτύρομαι ἐνώπιον τοῦ θεοῦ καὶ Χριστοῦ Ἰησοῦ τοῦ μέλλοντος κρίνειν ζῶντας καὶ νεκρούς, καὶ τὴν ἐπιφάνειαν αὐτοῦ καὶ τὴν βασιλείαν αὐτοῦ· **2** κήρυξον τὸν λόγον, ἐπίστηθι εὐκαίρως ἀκαίρως, ἔλεγξον, ἐπιτίμησον, παρακάλεσον, ἐν πάσῃ μακροθυμίᾳ καὶ διδαχῇ. **3** Ἔσται γὰρ καιρὸς ὅτε τῆς ὑγιαινούσης διδασκαλίας οὐκ ἀνέξονται ἀλλὰ κατὰ τὰς ἰδίας ἐπιθυμίας ἑαυτοῖς ἐπισωρεύσουσιν διδασκάλους κνηθόμενοι τὴν ἀκοὴν **4** καὶ ἀπὸ μὲν τῆς ἀληθείας τὴν ἀκοὴν ἀποστρέψουσιν, ἐπὶ δὲ τοὺς μύθους ἐκτραπήσονται. **5** Σὺ δὲ νῆφε ἐν πᾶσιν, κακοπάθησον, ἔργον ποίησον εὐαγγελιστοῦ, τὴν διακονίαν σου πληροφόρησον.

Cf. Phil 1:3–5; 1:27–30; and the paradigmatic self-descriptions in Eph 6:18–20; Phil 1:18–20; and Col 4:3–4.

See also § 115 Paul's Example of Bold Speech.

§ 114 Phil 1:14 **λογον** 𝔓^{46} D^{2} 1739. 1881 *Byz*] *add*. του θεου א A B (D*) 048^{vid}. 33

making the most of the time. [6] Let your speech always be gracious, seasoned with salt, so that you may know how you ought to answer everyone.

1 Thess 1:5–8

because our message of the gospel came to you not in word only, but also in power and in the Holy Spirit and with full conviction; just as you know what kind of persons we proved to be among you for your sake. [6] And you became imitators of us and of the Lord, for in spite of persecution you received the word with joy inspired by the Holy Spirit, [7] so that you became an example to all the believers in Macedonia and in Achaia. [8] For the word of the Lord has sounded forth from you not only in Macedonia and Achaia, but in every place your faith in God has become known, so that we have no need to speak about it.

2 Thess 3:1–2

Finally, brothers and sisters, pray for us, so that the word of the Lord may spread rapidly and be glorified everywhere, just as it is among you, [2] and that we may be rescued from wicked and evil people; for not all have faith.

1 Tim 2:1–4

First of all, then, I urge that supplications, prayers, intercessions, and thanksgivings be made for everyone, [2] for kings and all who are in high positions, so that we may lead a quiet and peaceable life in all godliness and dignity. [3] This is right and is acceptable in the sight of God our Savior, [4] who desires everyone to be saved and to come to the knowledge of the truth.

1 Tim 6:1

Let all who are under the yoke of slavery regard their masters as worthy of all honor, so that the name of God and the teaching may not be blasphemed.

Titus 2:4–5

so that they may encourage the young women to love their husbands, to love their children, [5] to be self-controlled, chaste, good managers of the household, kind, being submissive to their husbands, so that the word of God may not be discredited.

Titus 2:9–10

Tell slaves to be submissive to their masters and to give satisfaction in every respect; they are not to talk back, [10] not to pilfer, but to show complete and perfect fidelity, so that in everything they may be an ornament to the doctrine of God our Savior.

Cf. Acts 13:48–49; 19:8–10; and for the church at Rome (a congregation not founded by Paul) see Rom 1:8; 15:22–24; 15:30–32.

114. Exhortation to Verbal Mission and Proclamation

Eph 6:14–15

Stand therefore, and fasten the belt of truth around your waist, and put on the breastplate of righteousness. [15] As shoes for your feet put on whatever will make you ready to proclaim the gospel of peace.

Phil 1:12–14

I want you to know, beloved, that what has happened to me has actually helped to spread the gospel, [13] so that it has become known throughout the whole imperial guard and to everyone else that my imprisonment is for Christ; [14] and most of the brothers and sisters, having been made confident in the Lord by my imprisonment, dare to speak the word[a] with greater boldness and without fear.

Phil 2:12–16

Therefore, my beloved, just as you have always obeyed me, not only in my presence, but much more now in my absence, work out your own salvation with fear and trembling; [13] for it is God who is at work in you, enabling you both to will and to work for his good pleasure. [14] Do all things without murmuring and arguing, [15] so that you may be blameless and innocent, children of God without blemish in the midst of a crooked and perverse generation, in which you shine like stars in the world. [16] It is by your holding forth[b] the word of life that I can boast on the day of Christ that I did not run in vain or labor in vain.

Col 4:5–6

Conduct yourselves wisely toward outsiders, making the most of the time. [6] Let your speech always be gracious, seasoned with salt, so that you may know how you ought to answer everyone.

1 Thess 1:5–8

because our message of the gospel came to you not in word only, but also in power and in the Holy Spirit and with full conviction; just as you know what kind of persons we proved to be among you for your sake. [6] And you became imitators of us and of the Lord, for in spite of persecution you received the word with joy inspired by the Holy Spirit, [7] so that you became an example to all the believers in Macedonia and in Achaia. [8] For the word of the Lord has sounded forth from you not only in Macedonia and Achaia, but in every place your faith in God has become known, so that we have no need to speak about it.

2 Tim 4:1–5

In the presence of God and of Christ Jesus, who is to judge the living and the dead, and in view of his appearing and his kingdom, I solemnly urge you: [2] proclaim the message; be persistent whether the time is favorable or unfavorable; convince, rebuke, and encourage, with the utmost patience in teaching. [3] For the time is coming when people will not put up with sound doctrine, but having itching ears, they will accumulate for themselves teachers to suit their own desires, [4] and will turn away from listening to the truth and wander away to myths. [5] As for you, always be sober, endure suffering, do the work of an evangelist, carry out your ministry fully.

Cf. Phil 1:3–5; 1:27–30; and the paradigmatic self-descriptions in Eph 6:18–20; Phil 1:18–20; and Col 4:3–4.

See also § 115 Paul's Example of Bold Speech.

§ 114 [a] **Phil 1:14** *word* Other ancient authorities read *word of God* [b] **Phil 2:16** *holding forth* NRSV translates *holding fast to*

115. Paul's Example of Bold Speech

Eph 6:18–20

Διὰ πάσης προσευχῆς καὶ δεήσεως προσευχόμενοι ἐν παντὶ καιρῷ ἐν πνεύματι, καὶ εἰς αὐτὸ ἀγρυπνοῦντες ἐν πάσῃ προσκαρτερήσει καὶ δεήσει περὶ πάντων τῶν ἁγίων **19** καὶ ὑπὲρ ἐμοῦ, ἵνα μοι δοθῇ λόγος ἐν ἀνοίξει τοῦ στόματός μου, ἐν παρρησίᾳ γνωρίσαι τὸ μυστήριον ⸂τοῦ εὐαγγελίου⸃, **20** ὑπὲρ οὗ πρεσβεύω ἐν ἁλύσει, ἵνα ἐν αὐτῷ παρρησιάσωμαι ὡς δεῖ με λαλῆσαι.

Phil 1:18–20

Τί γάρ; πλὴν ὅτι παντὶ τρόπῳ, εἴτε προφάσει εἴτε ἀληθείᾳ, Χριστὸς καταγγέλλεται, καὶ ἐν τούτῳ χαίρω. Ἀλλὰ καὶ χαρήσομαι, **19** οἶδα γὰρ ὅτι τοῦτό μοι ἀποβήσεται εἰς σωτηρίαν διὰ τῆς ὑμῶν δεήσεως καὶ ἐπιχορηγίας τοῦ πνεύματος Ἰησοῦ Χριστοῦ **20** κατὰ τὴν ἀποκαραδοκίαν καὶ ἐλπίδα μου, ὅτι ἐν οὐδενὶ αἰσχυνθήσομαι ἀλλ᾽ ἐν πάσῃ παρρησίᾳ ὡς πάντοτε καὶ νῦν μεγαλυνθήσεται Χριστὸς ἐν τῷ σώματί μου, εἴτε διὰ ζωῆς εἴτε διὰ θανάτου.

Col 4:3–4

προσευχόμενοι ἅμα καὶ περὶ ἡμῶν, ἵνα ὁ θεὸς ἀνοίξῃ ἡμῖν θύραν τοῦ λόγου λαλῆσαι τὸ μυστήριον τοῦ Χριστοῦ, δι᾽ ὃ καὶ δέδεμαι, **4** ἵνα φανερώσω αὐτὸ ὡς δεῖ με λαλῆσαι.

1 Thess 2:1–2

Αὐτοὶ γὰρ οἴδατε, ἀδελφοί, τὴν εἴσοδον ἡμῶν τὴν πρὸς ὑμᾶς ὅτι οὐ κενὴ γέγονεν, **2** ἀλλὰ προπαθόντες καὶ ὑβρισθέντες, καθὼς οἴδατε, ἐν Φιλίπποις ἐπαρρησιασάμεθα ἐν τῷ θεῷ ἡμῶν λαλῆσαι πρὸς ὑμᾶς τὸ εὐαγγέλιον τοῦ θεοῦ ἐν πολλῷ ἀγῶνι.

2 Tim 1:6–14

Δι᾽ ἣν αἰτίαν ἀναμιμνῄσκω σε ἀναζωπυρεῖν τὸ χάρισμα τοῦ θεοῦ, ὅ ἐστιν ἐν σοὶ διὰ τῆς ἐπιθέσεως τῶν χειρῶν μου. **7** οὐ γὰρ ἔδωκεν ἡμῖν ὁ θεὸς πνεῦμα δειλίας ἀλλὰ δυνάμεως καὶ ἀγάπης καὶ σωφρονισμοῦ. **8** μὴ οὖν ἐπαισχυνθῇς τὸ μαρτύριον τοῦ κυρίου ἡμῶν μηδὲ ἐμὲ τὸν δέσμιον αὐτοῦ, ἀλλὰ συγκακοπάθησον τῷ εὐαγγελίῳ κατὰ δύναμιν θεοῦ, **9** τοῦ σώσαντος ἡμᾶς καὶ καλέσαντος κλήσει ἁγίᾳ, οὐ κατὰ τὰ ἔργα ἡμῶν ἀλλὰ κατὰ ἰδίαν πρόθεσιν καὶ χάριν, τὴν δοθεῖσαν ἡμῖν ἐν Χριστῷ Ἰησοῦ πρὸ χρόνων αἰωνίων, **10** φανερωθεῖσαν δὲ νῦν διὰ τῆς ἐπιφανείας τοῦ σωτῆρος ἡμῶν Χριστοῦ Ἰησοῦ, καταργήσαντος μὲν τὸν θάνατον φωτίσαντος δὲ ζωὴν καὶ ἀφθαρσίαν διὰ τοῦ εὐαγγελίου **11** εἰς ὃ ἐτέθην ἐγὼ κῆρυξ καὶ ἀπόστολος καὶ ⸀διδάσκαλος, **12** δι᾽ ἣν αἰτίαν καὶ ταῦτα πάσχω· ἀλλ᾽ οὐκ ἐπαισχύνομαι, οἶδα γὰρ ᾧ πεπίστευκα καὶ πέπεισμαι ὅτι δυνατός ἐστιν τὴν παραθήκην μου φυλάξαι εἰς ἐκείνην τὴν ἡμέραν. **13** Ὑποτύπωσιν ἔχε ὑγιαινόντων λόγων ὧν παρ᾽ ἐμοῦ ἤκουσας ἐν πίστει καὶ ἀγάπῃ τῇ ἐν Χριστῷ Ἰησοῦ· **14** τὴν καλὴν παραθήκην φύλαξον διὰ πνεύματος ἁγίου τοῦ ἐνοικοῦντος ἐν ἡμῖν.

2 Tim 4:16–18

Ἐν τῇ πρώτῃ μου ἀπολογίᾳ οὐδείς μοι παρεγένετο, ἀλλὰ πάντες με ἐγκατέλιπον· μὴ αὐτοῖς λογισθείη· **17** ὁ δὲ κύριός μοι παρέστη καὶ ἐνεδυνάμωσέν με, ἵνα δι᾽ ἐμοῦ τὸ κήρυγμα πληροφορηθῇ καὶ ἀκούσωσιν πάντα τὰ ἔθνη, καὶ ἐρρύσθην ἐκ στόματος λέοντος. **18** ῥύσεταί με ὁ κύριος ἀπὸ παντὸς ἔργου πονηροῦ καὶ σώσει εἰς τὴν βασιλείαν αὐτοῦ τὴν ἐπουράνιον· ᾧ ἡ δόξα εἰς τοὺς αἰῶνας τῶν αἰώνων, ἀμήν.

Acts 9:27–28

Βαρναβᾶς δὲ ἐπιλαβόμενος αὐτὸν ἤγαγεν πρὸς τοὺς ἀποστόλους καὶ διηγήσατο αὐτοῖς πῶς ἐν τῇ ὁδῷ εἶδεν τὸν κύριον καὶ ὅτι ἐλάλησεν αὐτῷ καὶ πῶς ἐν Δαμασκῷ ἐπαρρησιάσατο ἐν τῷ ὀνόματι τοῦ Ἰησοῦ. **28** καὶ ἦν μετ᾽ αὐτῶν εἰσπορευόμενος καὶ ἐκπορευόμενος εἰς Ἰερουσαλήμ, παρρησιαζόμενος ἐν τῷ ὀνόματι τοῦ κυρίου

Acts 14:3

ἱκανὸν μὲν οὖν χρόνον διέτριψαν παρρησιαζόμενοι ἐπὶ τῷ κυρίῳ τῷ μαρτυροῦντι [ἐπὶ] τῷ λόγῳ τῆς χάριτος αὐτοῦ, διδόντι σημεῖα καὶ τέρατα γίνεσθαι διὰ τῶν χειρῶν αὐτῶν.

Acts 18:9–11

Εἶπεν δὲ ὁ κύριος ἐν νυκτὶ δι᾽ ὁράματος τῷ Παύλῳ· μὴ φοβοῦ, ἀλλὰ λάλει καὶ μὴ σιωπήσῃς, **10** διότι ἐγώ εἰμι μετὰ σοῦ καὶ οὐδεὶς ἐπιθήσεταί σοι τοῦ κακῶσαί σε, διότι λαός ἐστί μοι πολὺς ἐν τῇ πόλει ταύτῃ. **11** Ἐκάθισεν δὲ ἐνιαυτὸν καὶ μῆνας ἓξ διδάσκων ἐν αὐτοῖς τὸν λόγον τοῦ θεοῦ.

Acts 19:8

Εἰσελθὼν δὲ εἰς τὴν συναγωγὴν ἐπαρρησιάζετο ἐπὶ μῆνας τρεῖς διαλεγόμενος καὶ πείθων [τὰ] περὶ τῆς βασιλείας τοῦ θεοῦ.

Acts 26:24–29

Ταῦτα δὲ αὐτοῦ ἀπολογουμένου ὁ Φῆστος μεγάλῃ τῇ φωνῇ φησιν· μαίνῃ, Παῦλε· τὰ πολλά σε γράμματα εἰς μανίαν περιτρέπει. **25** ὁ δὲ Παῦλος· οὐ μαίνομαι, φησίν, κράτιστε Φῆστε, ἀλλὰ ἀληθείας καὶ σωφροσύνης ῥήματα ἀποφθέγγομαι. **26** ἐπίσταται γὰρ περὶ τούτων ὁ βασιλεὺς πρὸς ὃν καὶ παρρησιαζόμενος λαλῶ, λανθάνειν γὰρ αὐτόν [τι] τούτων οὐ πείθομαι οὐθέν· οὐ γάρ ἐστιν ἐν γωνίᾳ πεπραγμένον τοῦτο. **27** πιστεύεις, βασιλεῦ Ἀγρίππα, τοῖς προφήταις; οἶδα ὅτι πιστεύεις. **28** ὁ δὲ Ἀγρίππας πρὸς τὸν Παῦλον· ἐν ὀλίγῳ με πείθεις Χριστιανὸν ποιῆσαι. **29** ὁ δὲ Παῦλος· εὐξαίμην ἂν τῷ θεῷ καὶ ἐν ὀλίγῳ καὶ ἐν μεγάλῳ οὐ μόνον σὲ ἀλλὰ καὶ πάντας τοὺς ἀκούοντάς μου σήμερον γενέσθαι τοιούτους ὁποῖος καὶ ἐγώ εἰμι παρεκτὸς τῶν δεσμῶν τούτων.

Acts 28:30–31

Ἐνέμεινεν δὲ διετίαν ὅλην ἐν ἰδίῳ μισθώματι καὶ ἀπεδέχετο πάντας τοὺς εἰσπορευομένους πρὸς αὐτόν, **31** κηρύσσων τὴν βασιλείαν τοῦ θεοῦ καὶ διδάσκων τὰ περὶ τοῦ κυρίου Ἰησοῦ Χριστοῦ μετὰ πάσης παρρησίας ἀκωλύτως.

See also § 114 Exhortation to Verbal Mission and Proclamation.

§ 115 **Eph 6:19** ***του ευαγγελιου*** ℵ A D I 33. 1739. 1881 *Byz*] *om.* B **2 Tim 1:11** ***διδασκαλος*** ℵ* A I] *add.* εθνων ℵ² C D 1739. 1881 *Byz* ¦ διακονος 33

115. Paul's Example of Bold Speech

Eph 6:18–20

Pray in the Spirit at all times in every prayer and supplication. To that end keep alert and always persevere in supplication for all the saints. **19** Pray also for me, so that when I speak, a message may be given to me to make known with boldness the mystery of the gospel,[a] **20** for which I am an ambassador in chains. Pray that I may declare it boldly, as I must speak.

Phil 1:18–20

What does it matter? Just this, that Christ is proclaimed in every way, whether out of false motives or true; and in that I rejoice. Yes, and I will continue to rejoice, **19** for I know that through your prayers and the supply of the Spirit of Jesus Christ this will turn out for my deliverance.[b] **20** It is my eager expectation and hope that I will not be put to shame in any way, but that by my speaking with all boldness, Christ will be exalted now as always in my body, whether by life or by death.

Col 4:3–4

At the same time pray for us as well that God will open to us a door for the word, that we may declare the mystery of Christ, for which I am in prison, **4** so that I may reveal it clearly, as I should.

1 Thess 2:1–2

You yourselves know, brothers and sisters, that our coming to you was not in vain, **2** but though we had already suffered and been shamefully mistreated at Philippi, as you know, we had courage in our God to declare to you the gospel of God in spite of great opposition.

2 Tim 1:6–14

For this reason I remind you to rekindle the gift of God that is within you through the laying on of my hands; **7** for God did not give us a spirit of cowardice, but rather a spirit of power and of love and of self-discipline. **8** Do not be ashamed, then, of the testimony about our Lord or of me his prisoner, but join with me in suffering for the gospel, relying on the power of God, **9** who saved us and called us with a holy calling, not according to our works but according to his own purpose and grace. This grace was given to us in Christ Jesus before the ages began, **10** but it has now been revealed through the appearing of our Savior Christ Jesus, who abolished death and brought life and immortality to light through the gospel. **11** For this gospel I was appointed a herald and an apostle and a teacher,[c] **12** and for this reason I suffer as I do. But I am not ashamed, for I know the one in whom I have put my trust, and I am sure that he is able to guard until that day what I have entrusted to him. **13** Hold to the standard of sound teaching that you have heard from me, in the faith and love that are in Christ Jesus. **14** Guard the good treasure entrusted to you, with the help of the Holy Spirit living in us.

2 Tim 4:16–18

At my first defense no one came to my support, but all deserted me. May it not be counted against them! **17** But the Lord stood by me and gave me strength, so that through me the message might be fully proclaimed and all the Gentiles might hear it. So I was rescued from the lion's mouth. **18** The Lord will rescue me from every evil attack and save me for his heavenly kingdom. To him be the glory forever and ever. Amen.

Acts 9:27–28

But Barnabas took him, brought him to the apostles, and described for them how on the road he had seen the Lord, who had spoken to him, and how in Damascus he had spoken boldly in the name of Jesus. **28** So he went in and out among them in Jerusalem, speaking boldly in the name of the Lord.

Acts 14:3

So they remained for a long time, speaking boldly for the Lord, who testified to the word of his grace by granting signs and wonders to be done through them.

Acts 18:9–11

One night the Lord said to Paul in a vision, "Do not be afraid, but speak and do not be silent; **10** for I am with you, and no one will lay a hand on you to harm you, for there are many in this city who are my people." **11** He stayed there a year and six months, teaching the word of God among them.

Acts 19:8

He entered the synagogue and for three months spoke out boldly, and argued persuasively about the kingdom of God.

Acts 26:24–29

While he was making this defense, Festus exclaimed, "You are out of your mind, Paul! Too much learning is driving you insane!" **25** But Paul said, "I am not out of my mind, most excellent Festus, but I am speaking the sober truth. **26** Indeed the king knows about these things, and to him I speak freely; for I am certain that none of these things has escaped his notice, for this was not done in a corner. **27** King Agrippa, do you believe the prophets? I know that you believe." **28** Agrippa said to Paul, "Are you so quickly persuading me to become a Christian?" **29** Paul replied, "Whether quickly or not, I pray to God that not only you but also all who are listening to me today might become such as I am—except for these chains."

Acts 28:30–31

He lived there two whole years at his own expense and welcomed all who came to him, **31** proclaiming the kingdom of God and teaching about the Lord Jesus Christ with all boldness and without hindrance.

See also § 114 Exhortation to Verbal Mission and Proclamation.

§ 115 [a] **Eph 6:19** *of the gospel* Other ancient authorities lack *of the gospel* [b] **Phil 1:19** Translation differs from NRSV [c] **2 Tim 1:11** *teacher* Other ancient authorities add *of the Gentiles*

116. Exhortation to Unity

Rom 15:1–6

Ὀφείλομεν δὲ ἡμεῖς οἱ δυνατοὶ τὰ ἀσθενήματα τῶν ἀδυνάτων βαστάζειν καὶ μὴ ἑαυτοῖς ἀρέσκειν. 2 ἕκαστος ἡμῶν τῷ πλησίον ἀρεσκέτω εἰς τὸ ἀγαθὸν πρὸς οἰκοδομήν· 3 καὶ γὰρ ὁ Χριστὸς οὐχ ἑαυτῷ ἤρεσεν, ἀλλὰ καθὼς γέγραπται· οἱ ὀνειδισμοὶ τῶν ὀνειδιζόντων σε ἐπέπεσαν ἐπ᾽ ἐμέ. 4 ὅσα γὰρ προεγράφη, εἰς τὴν ἡμετέραν διδασκαλίαν ἐγράφη, ἵνα διὰ τῆς ὑπομονῆς καὶ διὰ τῆς παρακλήσεως τῶν γραφῶν τὴν ἐλπίδα ἔχωμεν. 5 ὁ δὲ θεὸς τῆς ὑπομονῆς καὶ τῆς παρακλήσεως δῴη ὑμῖν τὸ αὐτὸ φρονεῖν ἐν ἀλλήλοις κατὰ Χριστὸν Ἰησοῦν, 6 ἵνα ὁμοθυμαδὸν ἐν ἑνὶ στόματι δοξάζητε τὸν θεὸν καὶ πατέρα τοῦ κυρίου ἡμῶν Ἰησοῦ Χριστοῦ.

1 Cor 1:10–17

Παρακαλῶ δὲ ὑμᾶς, ἀδελφοί, διὰ τοῦ ὀνόματος τοῦ κυρίου ἡμῶν Ἰησοῦ Χριστοῦ, ἵνα τὸ αὐτὸ λέγητε πάντες καὶ μὴ ᾖ ἐν ὑμῖν σχίσματα, ἦτε δὲ κατηρτισμένοι ἐν τῷ αὐτῷ νοῒ καὶ ἐν τῇ αὐτῇ γνώμῃ. 11 ἐδηλώθη γάρ μοι περὶ ὑμῶν, ἀδελφοί μου, ὑπὸ τῶν Χλόης ὅτι ἔριδες ἐν ὑμῖν εἰσιν. 12 λέγω δὲ τοῦτο ὅτι ἕκαστος ὑμῶν λέγει· ἐγὼ μέν εἰμι Παύλου, ἐγὼ δὲ Ἀπολλῶ, ἐγὼ δὲ Κηφᾶ, ἐγὼ δὲ Χριστοῦ. 13 μεμέρισται ὁ Χριστός; μὴ Παῦλος ἐσταυρώθη ὑπὲρ ὑμῶν, ἢ εἰς τὸ ὄνομα Παύλου ἐβαπτίσθητε; 14 εὐχαριστῶ ⸂[τῷ θεῷ]⸃ ὅτι οὐδένα ὑμῶν ἐβάπτισα εἰ μὴ Κρίσπον καὶ Γάϊον, 15 ἵνα μή τις εἴπῃ ὅτι εἰς τὸ ἐμὸν ὄνομα ἐβαπτίσθητε. 16 ἐβάπτισα δὲ καὶ τὸν Στεφανᾶ οἶκον, λοιπὸν οὐκ οἶδα εἴ τινα ἄλλον ἐβάπτισα. 17 οὐ γὰρ ἀπέστειλέν με Χριστὸς βαπτίζειν ἀλλὰ εὐαγγελίζεσθαι, οὐκ ἐν σοφίᾳ λόγου, ἵνα μὴ κενωθῇ ὁ σταυρὸς τοῦ Χριστοῦ.

Eph 4:1–6

Παρακαλῶ οὖν ὑμᾶς ἐγὼ ὁ δέσμιος ἐν κυρίῳ ἀξίως περιπατῆσαι τῆς κλήσεως ἧς ἐκλήθητε, 2 μετὰ πάσης ταπεινοφροσύνης καὶ πραΰτητος, μετὰ μακροθυμίας, ἀνεχόμενοι ἀλλήλων ἐν ἀγάπῃ, 3 σπουδάζοντες τηρεῖν τὴν ἑνότητα τοῦ πνεύματος ἐν τῷ συνδέσμῳ τῆς εἰρήνης· 4 °Ἓν σῶμα καὶ ἓν πνεῦμα, καθὼς καὶ ἐκλήθητε ἐν μιᾷ ἐλπίδι τῆς κλήσεως ὑμῶν· 5 εἷς κύριος, μία πίστις, ἓν βάπτισμα, 6 εἷς θεὸς καὶ πατὴρ πάντων, ὁ ἐπὶ πάντων καὶ διὰ πάντων καὶ ἐν πᾶσιν.

Phil 2:1–4

Εἴ τις οὖν παράκλησις ἐν Χριστῷ, εἴ τι παραμύθιον ἀγάπης, εἴ τις κοινωνία πνεύματος, εἴ τις σπλάγχνα καὶ οἰκτιρμοί, 2 πληρώσατέ μου τὴν χαρὰν ἵνα τὸ αὐτὸ φρονῆτε, τὴν αὐτὴν ἀγάπην ἔχοντες, σύμψυχοι, τὸ ἓν φρονοῦντες, 3 μηδὲν κατ᾽ ἐριθείαν μηδὲ κατὰ κενοδοξίαν ἀλλὰ τῇ ταπεινοφροσύνῃ ἀλλήλους ἡγούμενοι ὑπερέχοντας ἑαυτῶν, 4 μὴ τὰ ἑαυτῶν ἕκαστος σκοποῦντες ἀλλὰ ⸀[καὶ] τὰ ἑτέρων ἕκαστοι.

Phil 4:2–3

Εὐοδίαν παρακαλῶ καὶ Συντύχην παρακαλῶ τὸ αὐτὸ φρονεῖν ἐν κυρίῳ. 3 ναὶ ἐρωτῶ καὶ σέ, γνήσιε σύζυγε, συλλαμβάνου αὐταῖς, αἵτινες ἐν τῷ εὐαγγελίῳ συνήθλησάν μοι μετὰ καὶ Κλήμεντος καὶ τῶν λοιπῶν συνεργῶν μου, ὧν τὰ ὀνόματα ἐν βίβλῳ ζωῆς.

Cf. Rom 12:16; 14:1–12; 14:13–23; 1 Cor 3:1–4; 8:7–13; 9:19–23; 10:23–11:1; 11:17–34; 2 Cor 11:29; 13:11; Phil 1:27–30; 1 Thess 5:14.

117. Warning against Deceivers and Charlatans

Rom 16:17–20

Παρακαλῶ δὲ ὑμᾶς, ἀδελφοί, σκοπεῖν τοὺς τὰς διχοστασίας καὶ τὰ σκάνδαλα παρὰ τὴν διδαχὴν ἣν ὑμεῖς ἐμάθετε ποιοῦντας, καὶ ἐκκλίνετε ἀπ᾽ αὐτῶν· 18 οἱ γὰρ τοιοῦτοι τῷ κυρίῳ ἡμῶν Χριστῷ οὐ δουλεύουσιν ἀλλὰ τῇ ἑαυτῶν κοιλίᾳ, καὶ διὰ τῆς χρηστολογίας καὶ εὐλογίας ἐξαπατῶσιν τὰς καρδίας τῶν ἀκάκων. 19 ἡ γὰρ ὑμῶν ὑπακοὴ εἰς πάντας ἀφίκετο· ἐφ᾽ ὑμῖν οὖν χαίρω, θέλω δὲ ὑμᾶς σοφοὺς εἶναι εἰς τὸ ἀγαθόν, ἀκεραίους δὲ εἰς τὸ κακόν. 20 ὁ δὲ θεὸς τῆς εἰρήνης συντρίψει τὸν σατανᾶν ὑπὸ τοὺς πόδας ὑμῶν ἐν τάχει. ⸂Ἡ χάρις τοῦ κυρίου ἡμῶν Ἰησοῦ μεθ᾽ ὑμῶν.⸃

2 Cor 11:1–4

Ὄφελον ἀνείχεσθέ μου μικρόν τι ἀφροσύνης· ἀλλὰ καὶ ἀνέχεσθέ μου. 2 ζηλῶ γὰρ ὑμᾶς θεοῦ ζήλῳ, ἡρμοσάμην γὰρ ὑμᾶς ἑνὶ ἀνδρὶ παρθένον ἁγνὴν παραστῆσαι τῷ Χριστῷ· 3 φοβοῦμαι δὲ μή πως, ὡς ὁ ὄφις ἐξηπάτησεν Εὕαν ἐν τῇ πανουργίᾳ αὐτοῦ, φθαρῇ τὰ νοήματα ὑμῶν ἀπὸ τῆς ἁπλότητος ⸂[καὶ τῆς ἁγνότητος]⸃ τῆς εἰς τὸν Χριστόν. 4 εἰ μὲν γὰρ ὁ ἐρχόμενος ἄλλον Ἰησοῦν κηρύσσει ὃν οὐκ ἐκηρύξαμεν, ἢ πνεῦμα ἕτερον λαμβάνετε ὃ οὐκ ἐλάβετε, ἢ εὐαγγέλιον ἕτερον ὃ οὐκ ἐδέξασθε, καλῶς ἀνέχεσθε.

2 Cor 11:12–15

°Ὃ δὲ ποιῶ, καὶ ποιήσω, ἵνα ἐκκόψω τὴν ἀφορμὴν τῶν θελόντων ἀφορμήν, ἵνα ἐν ᾧ καυχῶνται εὑρεθῶσιν καθὼς καὶ ἡμεῖς. 13 οἱ γὰρ τοιοῦτοι ψευδαπόστολοι, ἐργάται δόλιοι, μετασχηματιζόμενοι εἰς ἀποστόλους Χριστοῦ. 14 καὶ οὐ θαῦμα· αὐτὸς γὰρ ὁ σατανᾶς μετασχηματίζεται εἰς ἄγγελον φωτός. 15 οὐ μέγα οὖν εἰ καὶ οἱ διάκονοι αὐτοῦ μετασχηματίζονται ὡς διάκονοι δικαιοσύνης· ὧν τὸ τέλος ἔσται κατὰ τὰ ἔργα αὐτῶν.

Gal 1:6–9

Θαυμάζω ὅτι οὕτως ταχέως μετατίθεσθε ἀπὸ τοῦ καλέσαντος ὑμᾶς ἐν χάριτι [Χριστοῦ] εἰς ἕτερον εὐαγγέλιον, 7 ὃ οὐκ ἔστιν ἄλλο, εἰ μή τινές εἰσιν οἱ ταράσσοντες ὑμᾶς καὶ θέλοντες μεταστρέψαι τὸ εὐαγγέλιον τοῦ Χριστοῦ. 8 ἀλλὰ καὶ ἐὰν ἡμεῖς ἢ ἄγγελος ἐξ οὐρανοῦ εὐαγγελίζηται

§ 116 **1 Cor 1:14** ***τω θεω*** א² C D 1881 *Byz*] τω θεω μου A 33 ¦ *om.* א* B 1739 **Phil 2:4** ***και*** 𝔓⁴⁶ א A B C D² 33. 1739. 1881 *Byz*] *om.* D*.c **§ 117** **Rom 16:20** ***η χαρις του κυριου ημων Ιησου μεθ υμων*** 𝔓⁴⁶ א B 1881] η χαρις του κυριου ημων Ιησου Χριστου μεθ υμων A C 33. 1739 *Byz* ¦ *om. hic et pon. p.* 16:23 D **2 Cor 11:3** ***και της αγνοτητος*** 𝔓⁴⁶ א* B (D*) 33] *om.* א² D⁽²⁾ 1739. 1881 *Byz*

116. *Exhortation to Unity*

Rom 15:1–6

We who are strong ought to put up with the failings of the weak, and not to please ourselves. 2 Each of us must please our neighbor for the good purpose of building up the neighbor. 3 For Christ did not please himself; but, as it is written, "The insults of those who insult you have fallen on me." 4 For whatever was written in former days was written for our instruction, so that by steadfastness and by the encouragement of the scriptures we might have hope. 5 May the God of steadfastness and encouragement grant you to live in harmony with one another, in accordance with Christ Jesus, 6 so that together you may with one voice glorify the God and Father of our Lord Jesus Christ.

1 Cor 1:10–17

Now I appeal to you, brothers and sisters, by the name of our Lord Jesus Christ, that all of you be in agreement and that there be no divisions among you, but that you be united in the same mind and the same purpose. 11 For it has been reported to me by Chloe's people that there are quarrels among you, my brothers and sisters. 12 What I mean is that each of you says, "I belong to Paul," or "I belong to Apollos," or "I belong to Cephas," or "I belong to Christ." 13 Has Christ been divided? Was Paul crucified for you? Or were you baptized in the name of Paul? 14 I thank God[a] that I baptized none of you except Crispus and Gaius, 15 so that no one can say that you were baptized in my name. 16 (I did baptize also the household of Stephanas; beyond that, I do not know whether I baptized anyone else.) 17 For Christ did not send me to baptize but to proclaim the gospel, and not with eloquent wisdom, so that the cross of Christ might not be emptied of its power.

Eph 4:1–6

I therefore, the prisoner in the Lord, beg you to lead a life worthy of the calling to which you have been called, 2 with all humility and gentleness, with patience, bearing with one another in love, 3 making every effort to maintain the unity of the Spirit in the bond of peace. 4 There is one body and one Spirit, just as you were called to the one hope of your calling, 5 one Lord, one faith, one baptism, 6 one God and Father of all, who is above all and through all and in all.

Phil 2:1–4

If then there is any encouragement in Christ, any consolation from love, any sharing in the Spirit, any compassion and sympathy, 2 make my joy complete: be of the same mind, having the same love, being in full accord and of one mind. 3 Do nothing from selfish ambition or conceit, but in humility regard others as better than yourselves. 4 Let each of you look not to your own interests, but to the interests[b] of others.

Phil 4:2–3

I urge Euodia and I urge Syntyche to be of the same mind in the Lord. 3 Yes, and I ask you also, my loyal companion, help these women, for they have struggled beside me in the work of the gospel, together with Clement and the rest of my co-workers, whose names are in the book of life.

Cf. Rom 12:16; 14:1–12; 14:13–23; 1 Cor 3:1–4; 8:7–13; 9:19–23; 10:23–11:1; 11:17–34; 2 Cor 11:29; 13:11; Phil 1:27–30; 1 Thess 5:14.

117. *Warning against Deceivers and Charlatans*

Rom 16:17–20

I urge you, brothers and sisters, to keep an eye on those who cause dissensions and offenses, in opposition to the teaching that you have learned; avoid them. 18 For such people do not serve our Lord Christ, but their own appetites, and by smooth talk and flattery they deceive the hearts of the simple-minded. 19 For while your obedience is known to all, so that I rejoice over you, I want you to be wise in what is good and guileless in what is evil. 20 The God of peace will shortly crush Satan under your feet. The grace of our Lord Jesus Christ be with you.[a]

2 Cor 11:1–4

I wish you would bear with me in a little foolishness. Do bear with me! 2 I feel a divine jealousy for you, for I promised you in marriage to one husband, to present you as a chaste virgin to Christ. 3 But I am afraid that as the serpent deceived Eve by its cunning, your thoughts will be led astray from a sincere and pure[b] devotion to Christ. 4 For if someone comes and proclaims another Jesus than the one we proclaimed, or if you receive a different spirit from the one you received, or a different gospel from the one you accepted, you submit to it readily enough.

2 Cor 11:12–15

And what I do I will also continue to do, in order to deny an opportunity to those who want an opportunity to be recognized as our equals in what they boast about. 13 For such boasters are false apostles, deceitful workers, disguising themselves as apostles of Christ. 14 And no wonder! Even Satan disguises himself as an angel of light. 15 So it is not strange if his ministers also disguise themselves as ministers of righteousness. Their end will match their deeds.

Gal 1:6–9

I am astonished that you are so quickly deserting the one who called you in the grace of Christ and are turning to a different gospel— 7 not that there is another gospel, but there are some who are confusing you and want to pervert the gospel of Christ. 8 But even if we or an angel from heaven should proclaim

§ 116 [a] **1 Cor 1:14** ***I thank God*** Other ancient authorities read *I am thankful* or *I thank my God* [b] **Phil 2:4** ***to the interests*** Most ancient authorities read *also to the interests* **§ 117** [a] **Rom 16:20** ***you*** A few ancient authorities omit this sentence here and place it after verse 23 [b] **2 Cor 11:3** ***and pure*** Other ancient authorities lack *and pure*

[ὑμῖν] παρ' ὃ εὐηγγελισάμεθα ὑμῖν, ἀνάθεμα ἔστω. 9 ὡς προειρήκαμεν καὶ ἄρτι πάλιν λέγω· εἴ τις ὑμᾶς εὐαγγελίζεται παρ' ὃ παρελάβετε, ἀνάθεμα ἔστω.

Gal 2:3–5

ἀλλ' οὐδὲ Τίτος ὁ σὺν ἐμοί, Ἕλλην ὤν, ἠναγκάσθη περιτμηθῆναι· 4 διὰ δὲ τοὺς παρεισάκτους ψευδαδέλφους, οἵτινες παρεισῆλθον κατασκοπῆσαι τὴν ἐλευθερίαν ἡμῶν ἣν ἔχομεν ἐν Χριστῷ Ἰησοῦ, ἵνα ἡμᾶς καταδουλώσουσιν, 5 οἷς οὐδὲ πρὸς ὥραν εἴξαμεν τῇ ὑποταγῇ, ἵνα ἡ ἀλήθεια τοῦ εὐαγγελίου διαμείνῃ πρὸς ὑμᾶς.

Gal 5:7–12

Ἐτρέχετε καλῶς· τίς ὑμᾶς ἐνέκοψεν [τῇ] ἀληθείᾳ μὴ πείθεσθαι; 8 ἡ πεισμονὴ οὐκ ἐκ τοῦ καλοῦντος ὑμᾶς. 9 μικρὰ ζύμη ὅλον τὸ φύραμα ζυμοῖ. 10 ἐγὼ πέποιθα εἰς ὑμᾶς ἐν κυρίῳ ὅτι οὐδὲν ἄλλο φρονήσετε· ὁ δὲ ταράσσων ὑμᾶς βαστάσει τὸ κρίμα, ὅστις ἐὰν ᾖ. 11 Ἐγὼ δέ, ἀδελφοί, εἰ περιτομὴν ἔτι κηρύσσω, τί ἔτι διώκομαι; ἄρα κατήργηται τὸ σκάνδαλον τοῦ σταυροῦ. 12 Ὄφελον καὶ ἀποκόψονται οἱ ἀναστατοῦντες ὑμᾶς.

Gal 6:11–13

Ἴδετε πηλίκοις ὑμῖν γράμμασιν ἔγραψα τῇ ἐμῇ χειρί. 12 Ὅσοι θέλουσιν εὐπροσωπῆσαι ἐν σαρκί, οὗτοι ἀναγκάζουσιν ὑμᾶς περιτέμνεσθαι, μόνον ἵνα τῷ σταυρῷ τοῦ Χριστοῦ μὴ διώκωνται. 13 οὐδὲ γὰρ οἱ περιτεμνόμενοι αὐτοὶ νόμον φυλάσσουσιν ἀλλὰ θέλουσιν ὑμᾶς περιτέμνεσθαι, ἵνα ἐν τῇ ὑμετέρᾳ σαρκὶ καυχήσωνται.

Phil 3:2–11

Βλέπετε τοὺς κύνας, βλέπετε τοὺς κακοὺς ἐργάτας, βλέπετε τὴν κατατομήν. 3 ἡμεῖς γάρ ἐσμεν ἡ περιτομή, οἱ πνεύματι ⸀θεοῦ λατρεύοντες καὶ καυχώμενοι ἐν Χριστῷ Ἰησοῦ καὶ οὐκ ἐν σαρκὶ πεποιθότες, 4 καίπερ ἐγὼ ἔχων πεποίθησιν καὶ ἐν σαρκί. Εἴ τις δοκεῖ ἄλλος πεποιθέναι ἐν σαρκί, ἐγὼ μᾶλλον· 5 περιτομῇ ὀκταήμερος, ἐκ γένους Ἰσραήλ, φυλῆς Βενιαμίν, Ἑβραῖος ἐξ Ἑβραίων, κατὰ νόμον Φαρισαῖος, 6 κατὰ ζῆλος διώκων τὴν ἐκκλησίαν, κατὰ δικαιοσύνην τὴν ἐν νόμῳ γενόμενος ἄμεμπτος. 7 [Ἀλλὰ] ἅτινα ἦν μοι κέρδη, ταῦτα ἥγημαι διὰ τὸν Χριστὸν ζημίαν. 8 ἀλλὰ μενοῦνγε καὶ ἡγοῦμαι πάντα ζημίαν εἶναι διὰ τὸ ὑπερέχον τῆς γνώσεως Χριστοῦ Ἰησοῦ τοῦ κυρίου μου, δι' ὃν τὰ πάντα ἐζημιώθην, καὶ ἡγοῦμαι σκύβαλα, ἵνα Χριστὸν κερδήσω 9 καὶ εὑρεθῶ ἐν αὐτῷ, μὴ ἔχων ἐμὴν δικαιοσύνην τὴν ἐκ νόμου ἀλλὰ τὴν διὰ πίστεως Χριστοῦ, τὴν ἐκ θεοῦ δικαιοσύνην ἐπὶ τῇ πίστει, 10 τοῦ γνῶναι αὐτὸν καὶ τὴν δύναμιν τῆς ἀναστάσεως αὐτοῦ καὶ [τὴν] κοινωνίαν [τῶν] παθημάτων αὐτοῦ, συμμορφιζόμενος τῷ θανάτῳ αὐτοῦ, 11 εἴ πως καταντήσω εἰς τὴν ἐξανάστασιν τὴν ἐκ νεκρῶν.

Col 2:4–10

Τοῦτο λέγω, ἵνα μηδεὶς ὑμᾶς παραλογίζηται ἐν πιθανολογίᾳ. 5 εἰ γὰρ καὶ τῇ σαρκὶ ἄπειμι, ἀλλὰ τῷ πνεύματι σὺν ὑμῖν εἰμι, χαίρων καὶ βλέπων ὑμῶν τὴν τάξιν καὶ τὸ στερέωμα τῆς εἰς Χριστὸν πίστεως ὑμῶν. 6 Ὡς οὖν παρελάβετε τὸν Χριστὸν Ἰησοῦν τὸν κύριον, ἐν αὐτῷ περιπατεῖτε, 7 ἐρριζωμένοι καὶ ἐποικοδομούμενοι ἐν αὐτῷ καὶ βεβαιούμενοι τῇ πίστει καθὼς ἐδιδάχθητε, περισσεύοντες ἐν εὐχαριστίᾳ. 8 Βλέπετε μή τις ὑμᾶς ἔσται ὁ συλαγωγῶν διὰ τῆς φιλοσοφίας καὶ κενῆς ἀπάτης κατὰ τὴν παράδοσιν τῶν ἀνθρώπων, κατὰ τὰ στοιχεῖα τοῦ κόσμου καὶ οὐ κατὰ Χριστόν· 9 ὅτι ἐν αὐτῷ κατοικεῖ πᾶν τὸ πλήρωμα τῆς θεότητος σωματικῶς, 10 καὶ ἐστὲ ἐν αὐτῷ πεπληρωμένοι, ὅς ἐστιν ἡ κεφαλὴ πάσης ἀρχῆς καὶ ἐξουσίας.

Col 2:16–23

Μὴ οὖν τις ὑμᾶς κρινέτω ἐν βρώσει καὶ ἐν πόσει ἢ ἐν μέρει ἑορτῆς ἢ νεομηνίας ἢ σαββάτων· 17 ἅ ἐστιν σκιὰ τῶν μελλόντων, τὸ δὲ σῶμα τοῦ Χριστοῦ. 18 μηδεὶς ὑμᾶς καταβραβευέτω θέλων ἐν ταπεινοφροσύνῃ καὶ θρησκείᾳ τῶν ἀγγέλων, ⸀ἃ ἑόρακεν ἐμβατεύων, εἰκῇ φυσιούμενος ὑπὸ τοῦ νοὸς τῆς σαρκὸς αὐτοῦ, 19 καὶ οὐ κρατῶν τὴν κεφαλήν, ἐξ οὗ πᾶν τὸ σῶμα διὰ τῶν ἁφῶν καὶ συνδέσμων ἐπιχορηγούμενον καὶ συμβιβαζόμενον αὔξει τὴν αὔξησιν τοῦ θεοῦ. 20 Εἰ ἀπεθάνετε σὺν Χριστῷ ἀπὸ τῶν στοιχείων τοῦ κόσμου, τί ὡς ζῶντες ἐν κόσμῳ δογματίζεσθε; 21 μὴ ἅψῃ μηδὲ γεύσῃ μηδὲ θίγῃς, 22 ἅ ἐστιν πάντα εἰς φθορὰν τῇ ἀποχρήσει, κατὰ τὰ ἐντάλματα καὶ διδασκαλίας τῶν ἀνθρώπων, 23 ἅτινά ἐστιν λόγον μὲν ἔχοντα σοφίας ἐν ἐθελοθρησκίᾳ καὶ ταπεινοφροσύνῃ [καὶ] ἀφειδίᾳ σώματος, οὐκ ἐν τιμῇ τινι πρὸς πλησμονὴν τῆς σαρκός.

1 Tim 1:3–7

Καθὼς παρεκάλεσά σε προσμεῖναι ἐν Ἐφέσῳ πορευόμενος εἰς Μακεδονίαν, ἵνα παραγγείλῃς τισὶν μὴ ἑτεροδιδασκαλεῖν 4 μηδὲ προσέχειν μύθοις καὶ γενεαλογίαις ἀπεράντοις, αἵτινες ἐκζητήσεις παρέχουσιν μᾶλλον ἢ οἰκονομίαν θεοῦ τὴν ἐν πίστει. 5 τὸ δὲ τέλος τῆς παραγγελίας ἐστὶν ἀγάπη ἐκ καθαρᾶς καρδίας καὶ συνειδήσεως ἀγαθῆς καὶ πίστεως ἀνυποκρίτου, 6 ὧν τινες ἀστοχήσαντες ἐξετράπησαν εἰς ματαιολογίαν 7 θέλοντες εἶναι νομοδιδάσκαλοι, μὴ νοοῦντες μήτε ἃ λέγουσιν μήτε περὶ τίνων διαβεβαιοῦνται.

1 Tim 4:1–5

Τὸ δὲ πνεῦμα ῥητῶς λέγει ὅτι ἐν ὑστέροις καιροῖς ἀποστήσονταί τινες τῆς πίστεως προσέχοντες πνεύμασιν πλάνοις καὶ διδασκαλίαις δαιμονίων, 2 ἐν ὑποκρίσει ψευδολόγων, κεκαυστηριασμένων τὴν ἰδίαν συνείδησιν, 3 κωλυόντων γαμεῖν, ἀπέχεσθαι βρωμάτων, ἃ ὁ θεὸς ἔκτισεν εἰς μετάλημψιν μετὰ εὐχαριστίας τοῖς πιστοῖς καὶ ἐπεγνωκόσι τὴν ἀλήθειαν. 4 ὅτι πᾶν κτίσμα θεοῦ καλὸν καὶ οὐδὲν ἀπόβλητον μετὰ εὐχαριστίας λαμβανόμενον· 5 ἁγιάζεται γὰρ διὰ λόγου θεοῦ καὶ ἐντεύξεως.

Phil 3:3 *θεου* ℵ* A B C D^{2} 33. 1739. 1881 *Byz*] θεω ℵ^{2} D* ¦ *om.* 𝔓^{46} **Col 2:18** *ἃ* 𝔓^{46} ℵ* A B D* I 33. 1739] ἃ μη ℵ^{2} C D^{1} 1881 *Byz*

to you a gospel contrary to what we proclaimed to you, let that one be accursed! 9 As we have said before, so now I repeat, if anyone proclaims to you a gospel contrary to what you received, let that one be accursed!

Gal 2:3–5

But even Titus, who was with me, was not compelled to be circumcised, though he was a Greek. 4 But because of false believers secretly brought in, who slipped in to spy on the freedom we have in Christ Jesus, so that they might enslave us— 5 we did not submit to them even for a moment, so that the truth of the gospel might always remain with you.

Gal 5:7–12

You were running well; who prevented you from obeying the truth? 8 Such persuasion does not come from the one who calls you. 9 A little yeast leavens the whole batch of dough. 10 I am confident about you in the Lord that you will not think otherwise. But whoever it is that is confusing you will pay the penalty. 11 But my friends, why am I still being persecuted if I am still preaching circumcision? In that case the offense of the cross has been removed. 12 I wish those who unsettle you would castrate themselves!

Gal 6:11–13

See what large letters I make when I am writing in my own hand! 12 It is those who want to make a good showing in the flesh that try to compel you to be circumcised—only that they may not be persecuted for the cross of Christ. 13 Even the circumcised do not themselves obey the law, but they want you to be circumcised so that they may boast about your flesh.

Phil 3:2–11

Beware of the dogs, beware of the evil workers, beware of those who mutilate the flesh! 3 For it is we who are the circumcision, who worship in the Spirit of God[c] and boast in Christ Jesus and have no confidence in the flesh— 4 even though I, too, have reason for confidence in the flesh. If anyone else has reason to be confident in the flesh, I have more: 5 circumcised on the eighth day, a member of the people of Israel, of the tribe of Benjamin, a Hebrew born of Hebrews; as to the law, a Pharisee; 6 as to zeal, a persecutor of the church; as to righteousness under the law, blameless. 7 Yet whatever gains I had, these I have come to regard as loss because of Christ. 8 More than that, I regard everything as loss because of the surpassing value of knowing Christ Jesus my Lord. For his sake I have suffered the loss of all things, and I regard them as rubbish, in order that I may gain Christ 9 and be found in him, not having a righteousness of my own that comes from the law, but one that comes through faith in Christ, the righteousness from God based on faith. 10 I want to know Christ and the power of his resurrection and the sharing of his sufferings by becoming like him in his death, 11 if somehow I may attain the resurrection from the dead.

Col 2:4–10

I am saying this so that no one may deceive you with plausible arguments. 5 For though I am absent in body, yet I am with you in spirit, and I rejoice to see your morale and the firmness of your faith in Christ. 6 As you therefore have received Christ Jesus the Lord, continue to live your lives in him, 7 rooted and built up in him and established in the faith, just as you were taught, abounding in thanksgiving. 8 See to it that no one takes you captive through philosophy and empty deceit, according to human tradition, according to the elemental spirits of the universe, and not according to Christ. 9 For in him the whole fullness of deity dwells bodily, 10 and you have come to fullness in him, who is the head of every ruler and authority.

Col 2:16–23

Therefore do not let anyone condemn you in matters of food and drink or of observing festivals, new moons, or sabbaths. 17 These are only a shadow of what is to come, but the substance belongs to Christ. 18 Do not let anyone disqualify you, insisting on self-abasement and worship of angels, dwelling on visions,[d] puffed up without cause by a human way of thinking, 19 and not holding fast to the head, from whom the whole body, richly supplied[e] and held together by its ligaments and sinews, grows with a growth that is from God. 20 If with Christ you died to the elemental spirits of the universe, why do you live as if you still belonged to the world? Why do you submit to regulations, 21 "Do not handle, Do not taste, Do not touch"? 22 All these regulations refer to things that perish with use; they are simply human commands and teachings. 23 These have indeed an appearance of wisdom in promoting self-imposed piety, humility, and severe treatment of the body, but they are of no value in checking self-indulgence.

1 Tim 1:3–7

I urge you, as I did when I was on my way to Macedonia, to remain in Ephesus so that you may instruct certain people not to teach any different doctrine, 4 and not to occupy themselves with myths and endless genealogies that promote speculations rather than the divine training that is known by faith. 5 But the aim of such instruction is love that comes from a pure heart, a good conscience, and sincere faith. 6 Some people have deviated from these and turned to meaningless talk, 7 desiring to be teachers of the law, without understanding either what they are saying or the things about which they make assertions.

1 Tim 4:1–5

Now the Spirit expressly says that in later times some will renounce the faith by paying attention to deceitful spirits and teachings of demons, 2 through the hypocrisy of liars whose consciences are seared with a hot iron. 3 They forbid marriage and demand abstinence from foods, which God created to be received with thanksgiving by those who believe and know the truth. 4 For everything created by God is good, and nothing is to be rejected, provided it is received with thanksgiving; 5 for it is sanctified by God's word and by prayer.

[c] **Phil 3:3** ***worship in the Spirit of God*** Other ancient authorities read *worship God in the Spirit* [d] **Col 2:18** ***visions*** lit. *things which he has seen* Other ancient authorities read *false visions* lit. *things which he has not seen* [e] **Col 2:19** ***richly supplied*** NRSV translates *nourished*

1 Tim 6:3–5

εἴ τις ἑτεροδιδασκαλεῖ καὶ μὴ προσέρχεται ὑγιαίνουσιν λόγοις τοῖς τοῦ κυρίου ἡμῶν Ἰησοῦ Χριστοῦ καὶ τῇ κατ᾽ εὐσέβειαν διδασκαλίᾳ, **4** τετύφωται, μηδὲν ἐπιστάμενος, ἀλλὰ νοσῶν περὶ ζητήσεις καὶ λογομαχίας, ἐξ ὧν γίνεται φθόνος ἔρις βλασφημίαι, ὑπόνοιαι πονηραί, **5** διαπαρατριβαὶ διεφθαρμένων ἀνθρώπων τὸν νοῦν καὶ ἀπεστερημένων τῆς ἀληθείας, νομιζόντων πορισμὸν εἶναι τὴν ⸀εὐσέβειαν.

1 Tim 6:20–21

Ὦ Τιμόθεε, τὴν παραθήκην φύλαξον ἐκτρεπόμενος τὰς βεβήλους κενοφωνίας καὶ ἀντιθέσεις τῆς ψευδωνύμου γνώσεως, **21** ἥν τινες ἐπαγγελλόμενοι περὶ τὴν πίστιν ἠστόχησαν. Ἡ χάρις ⸂μεθ᾽ ὑμῶν⸃.

2 Tim 2:14–21

Ταῦτα ὑπομίμνῃσκε διαμαρτυρόμενος ἐνώπιον τοῦ ⸀θεοῦ μὴ λογομαχεῖν, ἐπ᾽ οὐδὲν χρήσιμον, ἐπὶ καταστροφῇ τῶν ἀκουόντων. **15** σπούδασον σεαυτὸν δόκιμον παραστῆσαι τῷ θεῷ, ἐργάτην ἀνεπαίσχυντον, ὀρθοτομοῦντα τὸν λόγον τῆς ἀληθείας. **16** τὰς δὲ βεβήλους κενοφωνίας περιΐστασο· ἐπὶ πλεῖον γὰρ προκόψουσιν ἀσεβείας **17** καὶ ὁ λόγος αὐτῶν ὡς γάγγραινα νομὴν ἕξει. ὧν ἐστιν Ὑμέναιος καὶ Φίλητος, **18** οἵτινες περὶ τὴν ἀλήθειαν ἠστόχησαν, λέγοντες [τὴν] ἀνάστασιν ἤδη γεγονέναι, καὶ ἀνατρέπουσιν τήν τινων πίστιν. **19** ὁ μέντοι στερεὸς θεμέλιος τοῦ θεοῦ ἕστηκεν, ἔχων τὴν σφραγῖδα ταύτην· ἔγνω κύριος τοὺς ὄντας αὐτοῦ, καί· ἀποστήτω ἀπὸ ἀδικίας πᾶς ὁ ὀνομάζων τὸ ὄνομα κυρίου. **20** Ἐν μεγάλῃ δὲ οἰκίᾳ οὐκ ἔστιν μόνον σκεύη χρυσᾶ καὶ ἀργυρᾶ ἀλλὰ καὶ ξύλινα καὶ ὀστράκινα, καὶ ἃ μὲν εἰς τιμὴν ἃ δὲ εἰς ἀτιμίαν· **21** ἐὰν οὖν τις ἐκκαθάρῃ ἑαυτὸν ἀπὸ τούτων, ἔσται σκεῦος εἰς τιμήν, ἡγιασμένον, εὔχρηστον τῷ δεσπότῃ, εἰς πᾶν ἔργον ἀγαθὸν ἡτοιμασμένον.

2 Tim 3:6–9

Ἐκ τούτων γάρ εἰσιν οἱ ἐνδύνοντες εἰς τὰς οἰκίας καὶ αἰχμαλωτίζοντες γυναικάρια σεσωρευμένα ἁμαρτίαις, ἀγόμενα ἐπιθυμίαις ποικίλαις, **7** πάντοτε μανθάνοντα καὶ μηδέποτε εἰς ἐπίγνωσιν ἀληθείας ἐλθεῖν δυνάμενα. **8** ὃν τρόπον δὲ Ἰάννης καὶ Ἰαμβρῆς ἀντέστησαν Μωϋσεῖ, οὕτως καὶ οὗτοι ἀνθίστανται τῇ ἀληθείᾳ, ἄνθρωποι κατεφθαρμένοι τὸν νοῦν, ἀδόκιμοι περὶ τὴν πίστιν. **9** ἀλλ᾽ οὐ προκόψουσιν ἐπὶ πλεῖον· ἡ γὰρ ἄνοια αὐτῶν ἔκδηλος ἔσται πᾶσιν, ὡς καὶ ἡ ἐκείνων ἐγένετο.

Titus 1:10–16

Εἰσὶν γὰρ πολλοὶ [καὶ] ἀνυπότακτοι, ματαιολόγοι καὶ φρεναπάται, μάλιστα οἱ ἐκ τῆς περιτομῆς, **11** οὓς δεῖ ἐπιστομίζειν, οἵτινες ὅλους οἴκους ἀνατρέπουσιν διδάσκοντες ἃ μὴ δεῖ αἰσχροῦ κέρδους χάριν. **12** εἶπέν τις ἐξ αὐτῶν ἴδιος αὐτῶν προφήτης· Κρῆτες ἀεὶ ψεῦσται, κακὰ θηρία, γαστέρες ἀργαί. **13** ἡ μαρτυρία αὕτη ἐστὶν ἀληθής. δι᾽ ἣν αἰτίαν ἔλεγχε αὐτοὺς ἀποτόμως, ἵνα ὑγιαίνωσιν ἐν τῇ πίστει, **14** μὴ προσέχοντες Ἰουδαϊκοῖς μύθοις καὶ ἐντολαῖς ἀνθρώπων ἀποστρεφομένων τὴν ἀλήθειαν. **15** πάντα καθαρὰ τοῖς καθαροῖς· τοῖς δὲ μεμιαμμένοις καὶ ἀπίστοις οὐδὲν καθαρόν, ἀλλὰ μεμίανται αὐτῶν καὶ ὁ νοῦς καὶ ἡ συνείδησις. **16** θεὸν ὁμολογοῦσιν εἰδέναι, τοῖς δὲ ἔργοις ἀρνοῦνται, βδελυκτοὶ ὄντες καὶ ἀπειθεῖς καὶ πρὸς πᾶν ἔργον ἀγαθὸν ἀδόκιμοι.

Titus 3:8–11

Πιστὸς ὁ λόγος· καὶ περὶ τούτων βούλομαί σε διαβεβαιοῦσθαι, ἵνα φροντίζωσιν καλῶν ἔργων προΐστασθαι οἱ πεπιστευκότες θεῷ· ταῦτά ἐστιν καλὰ καὶ ὠφέλιμα τοῖς ἀνθρώποις. **9** μωρὰς δὲ ζητήσεις καὶ γενεαλογίας καὶ ⸀ἔρεις καὶ μάχας νομικὰς περιΐστασο· εἰσὶν γὰρ ἀνωφελεῖς καὶ μάταιοι. **10** αἱρετικὸν ἄνθρωπον μετὰ μίαν καὶ δευτέραν νουθεσίαν παραιτοῦ, **11** εἰδὼς ὅτι ἐξέστραπται ὁ τοιοῦτος καὶ ἁμαρτάνει ὢν αὐτοκατάκριτος.

Acts 20:29–31

ἐγὼ οἶδα ὅτι εἰσελεύσονται μετὰ τὴν ἄφιξίν μου λύκοι βαρεῖς εἰς ὑμᾶς μὴ φειδόμενοι τοῦ ποιμνίου, **30** καὶ ἐξ ὑμῶν αὐτῶν ἀναστήσονται ἄνδρες λαλοῦντες διεστραμμένα τοῦ ἀποσπᾶν τοὺς μαθητὰς ὀπίσω αὐτῶν. **31** διὸ γρηγορεῖτε μνημονεύοντες ὅτι τριετίαν νύκτα καὶ ἡμέραν οὐκ ἐπαυσάμην μετὰ δακρύων νουθετῶν ἕνα ἕκαστον.

Cf. 1 Cor 11:17–19; 15:12–19; 15:29–34; 2 Cor 2:17; 10:1–18; 11:5–21a; 11:21b–12:10; 12:11–18; Gal 4:16–20; Phil 3:17–4:1; 2 Tim 1:15; 3:13; Acts 13:6–12; 15:1–35; 19:13–17.

See also § 116 Exhortation to Unity.

118. Spiritual Gifts

Rom 12:3–8

Λέγω γὰρ διὰ τῆς χάριτος τῆς δοθείσης μοι παντὶ τῷ ὄντι ἐν ὑμῖν μὴ ὑπερφρονεῖν παρ᾽ ὃ δεῖ φρονεῖν ἀλλὰ φρονεῖν εἰς τὸ σωφρονεῖν, ἑκάστῳ ὡς ὁ θεὸς ἐμέρισεν μέτρον πίστεως. **4** καθάπερ γὰρ ἐν ἑνὶ σώματι πολλὰ μέλη ἔχομεν, τὰ δὲ μέλη πάντα οὐ τὴν αὐτὴν ἔχει πρᾶξιν, **5** οὕτως οἱ πολλοὶ ἓν σῶμά ἐσμεν ἐν Χριστῷ, τὸ δὲ καθ᾽ εἷς ἀλλήλων μέλη. **6** ἔχοντες δὲ χαρίσματα κατὰ τὴν χάριν τὴν δοθεῖσαν ἡμῖν διάφορα, εἴτε προφητείαν κατὰ τὴν ἀναλογίαν τῆς πίστεως, **7** εἴτε διακονίαν ἐν τῇ διακονίᾳ, εἴτε ὁ διδάσκων ἐν τῇ διδασκαλίᾳ, **8** εἴτε ὁ παρακαλῶν ἐν τῇ παρακλήσει· ὁ μεταδιδοὺς ἐν ἁπλότητι, ὁ προϊστάμενος ἐν σπουδῇ, ὁ ἐλεῶν ἐν ἱλαρότητι.

1 Cor 12:1–31

Περὶ δὲ τῶν πνευματικῶν, ἀδελφοί, οὐ θέλω ὑμᾶς ἀγνοεῖν. **2** Οἴδατε ὅτι ὅτε ἔθνη ἦτε πρὸς τὰ εἴδωλα τὰ ἄφωνα ὡς ἂν ἤγεσθε

1 Tim 6:5 ***ευσεβειαν*** ℵ A D* 048. 33. 1739. 1881] *add.* αφιστασο απο των τοιουτων D^{2} *Byz* **1 Tim 6:21** ***μεθ υμων*** ℵ* A 33] μετα σου D* 048^{vid}. 1739*. 1881 ¦ μεθ υμων, αμην ℵ^{2} ¦ μετα σου, αμην D^{1} 1739^{c} *Byz* **2 Tim 2:14** ***θεου*** ℵ C I] κυριου A D 048. 1739. 1881 *Byz* **Titus 3:9** ***ερεις*** ℵ^{2} A C I 1739. 1881 *Byz*] εριν ℵ* D

1 Tim 6:3–5

Whoever teaches otherwise and does not agree with the sound words of our Lord Jesus Christ and the teaching that is in accordance with godliness, **4** is conceited, understanding nothing, and has a morbid craving for controversy and for disputes about words. From these come envy, dissension, slander, base suspicions, **5** and wrangling among those who are depraved in mind and bereft of the truth, imagining that godliness is a means of gain.[f]

1 Tim 6:20–21

Timothy, guard what has been entrusted to you. Avoid the profane chatter and contradictions of what is falsely called knowledge; **21** by professing it some have missed the mark as regards the faith. Grace be with you.[g]

2 Tim 2:14–21

Remind them of this, and warn them before God[h] that they are to avoid wrangling over words, which does no good but only ruins those who are listening. **15** Do your best to present yourself to God as one approved by him, a worker who has no need to be ashamed, rightly explaining the word of truth. **16** Avoid profane chatter, for it will lead people into more and more impiety, **17** and their talk will spread like gangrene. Among them are Hymenaeus and Philetus, **18** who have swerved from the truth by claiming that the resurrection has already taken place. They are upsetting the faith of some. **19** But God's firm foundation stands, bearing this inscription: "The Lord knows those who are his," and, "Let everyone who calls on the name of the Lord turn away from wickedness." **20** In a large house there are utensils not only of gold and silver but also of wood and clay, some for special use, some for ordinary. **21** All who cleanse themselves of the things I have mentioned will become special utensils, dedicated and useful to the owner of the house, ready for every good work.

2 Tim 3:6–9

For among them are those who make their way into households and captivate silly women, overwhelmed by their sins and swayed by all kinds of desires, **7** who are always being instructed and can never arrive at a knowledge of the truth. **8** As Jannes and Jambres opposed Moses, so these people, of corrupt mind and counterfeit faith, also oppose the truth. **9** But they will not make much progress, because, as in the case of those two men, their folly will become plain to everyone.

Titus 1:10–16

There are also many rebellious people, idle talkers and deceivers, especially those of the circumcision; **11** they must be silenced, since they are upsetting whole families by teaching for sordid gain what it is not right to teach. **12** It was one of them, their very own prophet, who said, "Cretans are always liars, vicious brutes, lazy gluttons." **13** That testimony is true. For this reason rebuke them sharply, so that they may become sound in the faith, **14** not paying attention to Jewish myths or to commandments of those who reject the truth. **15** To the pure all things are pure, but to the corrupt and unbelieving nothing is pure. Their very minds and consciences are corrupted. **16** They profess to know God, but they deny him by their actions. They are detestable, disobedient, unfit for any good work.

Titus 3:8–11

The saying is sure. I desire that you insist on these things, so that those who have come to believe in God may be careful to devote themselves to good works; these things are excellent and profitable to everyone. **9** But avoid stupid controversies, genealogies, dissensions,[i] and quarrels about the law, for they are unprofitable and worthless. **10** After a first and second admonition, have nothing more to do with anyone who causes divisions, **11** since you know that such a person is perverted and sinful, being self-condemned.

Acts 20:29–31

I know that after I have gone, savage wolves will come in among you, not sparing the flock. **30** Some even from your own group will come distorting the truth in order to entice the disciples to follow them. **31** Therefore be alert, remembering that for three years I did not cease night or day to warn everyone with tears.

Cf. 1 Cor 11:17–19; 15:12–19; 15:29–34; 2 Cor 2:17; 10:1–18; 11:5–21a; 11:21b–12:10; 12:11–18; Gal 4:16–20; Phil 3:17–4:1; 2 Tim 1:15; 3:13; Acts 13:6–12; 15:1–35; 19:13–17.

See also § 116 Exhortation to Unity.

118. Spiritual Gifts

Rom 12:3–8

For by the grace given to me I say to everyone among you not to think of yourself more highly than you ought to think, but to think with sober judgment, each according to the measure of faith that God has assigned. **4** For as in one body we have many members, and not all the members have the same function, **5** so we, who are many, are one body in Christ, and individually we are members one of another. **6** We have gifts that differ according to the grace given to us: prophecy, in proportion to faith; **7** ministry, in ministering; the teacher, in teaching; **8** the exhorter, in exhortation; the giver, in generosity; the leader, in diligence; the compassionate, in cheerfulness.

1 Cor 12:1–31

Now concerning spiritual gifts, brothers and sisters, I do not want you to be uninformed. **2** You know that when you were pagans, you were enticed and led astray to idols that could not speak.

[f] **1 Tim 6:5** ***gain*** Other ancient authorities add *Withdraw yourself from such people* [g] **1 Tim 6:21** ***you*** The Greek word for *you* here is plural; in other ancient authorities it is singular. Other ancient authorities add *Amen* [h] **2 Tim 2:14** ***God*** Other ancient authorities read *the Lord* [i] **Titus 3:9** ***dissensions*** Other ancient authorities read *dissension*

ἀπαγόμενοι. 3 διὸ γνωρίζω ὑμῖν ὅτι οὐδεὶς ἐν πνεύματι θεοῦ λαλῶν λέγει· Ἀνάθεμα Ἰησοῦς, καὶ οὐδεὶς δύναται εἰπεῖν· Κύριος Ἰησοῦς, εἰ μὴ ἐν πνεύματι ἁγίῳ. 4 Διαιρέσεις δὲ χαρισμάτων εἰσίν, τὸ δὲ αὐτὸ πνεῦμα· 5 καὶ διαιρέσεις διακονιῶν εἰσιν, καὶ ὁ αὐτὸς κύριος· 6 καὶ διαιρέσεις ἐνεργημάτων εἰσίν, ὁ δὲ αὐτὸς θεὸς ὁ ἐνεργῶν τὰ πάντα ἐν πᾶσιν. 7 ἑκάστῳ δὲ δίδοται ἡ φανέρωσις τοῦ πνεύματος πρὸς τὸ συμφέρον. 8 ᾧ μὲν γὰρ διὰ τοῦ πνεύματος δίδοται λόγος σοφίας, ἄλλῳ δὲ λόγος γνώσεως κατὰ τὸ αὐτὸ πνεῦμα, 9 ἑτέρῳ πίστις ἐν τῷ αὐτῷ πνεύματι, ἄλλῳ δὲ χαρίσματα ἰαμάτων ἐν τῷ ἑνὶ πνεύματι, 10 ἄλλῳ δὲ ἐνεργήματα δυνάμεων, ἄλλῳ [δὲ] προφητεία, ἄλλῳ [δὲ] διακρίσεις πνευμάτων, ἑτέρῳ γένη γλωσσῶν, ἄλλῳ δὲ ἑρμηνεία γλωσσῶν· 11 πάντα δὲ ταῦτα ἐνεργεῖ τὸ ἓν καὶ τὸ αὐτὸ πνεῦμα διαιροῦν ἰδίᾳ ἑκάστῳ καθὼς βούλεται. 12 Καθάπερ γὰρ τὸ σῶμα ἕν ἐστιν καὶ μέλη πολλὰ ἔχει, πάντα δὲ τὰ μέλη τοῦ σώματος πολλὰ ὄντα ἕν ἐστιν σῶμα, οὕτως καὶ ὁ Χριστός· 13 καὶ γὰρ ἐν ἑνὶ πνεύματι ἡμεῖς πάντες εἰς ἓν σῶμα ἐβαπτίσθημεν, εἴτε Ἰουδαῖοι εἴτε Ἕλληνες εἴτε δοῦλοι εἴτε ἐλεύθεροι, καὶ πάντες ἓν πνεῦμα ἐποτίσθημεν. 14 Καὶ γὰρ τὸ σῶμα οὐκ ἔστιν ἓν μέλος ἀλλὰ πολλά. 15 ἐὰν εἴπῃ ὁ πούς· ὅτι οὐκ εἰμὶ χείρ, οὐκ εἰμὶ ἐκ τοῦ σώματος, οὐ παρὰ τοῦτο οὐκ ἔστιν ἐκ τοῦ σώματος; 16 καὶ ἐὰν εἴπῃ τὸ οὖς· ὅτι οὐκ εἰμὶ ὀφθαλμός, οὐκ εἰμὶ ἐκ τοῦ σώματος, οὐ παρὰ τοῦτο οὐκ ἔστιν ἐκ τοῦ σώματος; 17 εἰ ὅλον τὸ σῶμα ὀφθαλμός, ποῦ ἡ ἀκοή; εἰ ὅλον ἀκοή, ποῦ ἡ ὄσφρησις; 18 νυνὶ δὲ ὁ θεὸς ἔθετο τὰ μέλη, ἓν ἕκαστον αὐτῶν ἐν τῷ σώματι καθὼς ἠθέλησεν. 19 εἰ δὲ ἦν τὰ πάντα ἓν μέλος, ποῦ τὸ σῶμα; 20 νῦν δὲ πολλὰ μὲν μέλη, ἓν δὲ σῶμα. 21 οὐ δύναται δὲ ὁ ὀφθαλμὸς εἰπεῖν τῇ χειρί· χρείαν σου οὐκ ἔχω, ἢ πάλιν ἡ κεφαλὴ τοῖς ποσίν· χρείαν ὑμῶν οὐκ ἔχω· 22 ἀλλὰ πολλῷ μᾶλλον τὰ δοκοῦντα μέλη τοῦ σώματος ἀσθενέστερα ὑπάρχειν ἀναγκαῖά ἐστιν, 23 καὶ ἃ δοκοῦμεν ἀτιμότερα εἶναι τοῦ σώματος τούτοις τιμὴν περισσοτέραν περιτίθεμεν, καὶ τὰ ἀσχήμονα ἡμῶν εὐσχημοσύνην περισσοτέραν ἔχει, 24 τὰ δὲ εὐσχήμονα ἡμῶν οὐ χρείαν ἔχει. ἀλλὰ ὁ θεὸς συνεκέρασεν τὸ σῶμα τῷ ὑστερουμένῳ περισσοτέραν δοὺς τιμήν, 25 ἵνα μὴ ᾖ σχίσμα ἐν τῷ σώματι ἀλλὰ τὸ αὐτὸ ὑπὲρ ἀλλήλων μεριμνῶσιν τὰ μέλη. 26 καὶ εἴτε πάσχει ἓν μέλος, συμπάσχει πάντα τὰ μέλη· εἴτε δοξάζεται [ἓν] μέλος, συγχαίρει πάντα τὰ μέλη. 27 Ὑμεῖς δέ ἐστε σῶμα Χριστοῦ καὶ μέλη ἐκ μέρους. 28 Καὶ οὓς μὲν ἔθετο ὁ θεὸς ἐν τῇ ἐκκλησίᾳ πρῶτον ἀποστόλους, δεύτερον προφήτας, τρίτον διδασκάλους, ἔπειτα δυνάμεις, ἔπειτα χαρίσματα ἰαμάτων, ἀντιλήμψεις, κυβερνήσεις, γένη γλωσσῶν. 29 μὴ πάντες ἀπόστολοι; μὴ πάντες προφῆται; μὴ πάντες διδάσκαλοι; μὴ πάντες δυνάμεις; 30 μὴ πάντες χαρίσματα ἔχουσιν ἰαμάτων; μὴ πάντες γλώσσαις λαλοῦσιν; μὴ πάντες διερμηνεύουσιν; 31 ζηλοῦτε δὲ τὰ χαρίσματα τὰ μείζονα. Καὶ ἔτι καθʼ ὑπερβολὴν ὁδὸν ὑμῖν δείκνυμι.

Eph 4:4–16

Ἓν σῶμα καὶ ἓν πνεῦμα, καθὼς καὶ ἐκλήθητε ἐν μιᾷ ἐλπίδι τῆς κλήσεως ὑμῶν· 5 εἷς κύριος, μία πίστις, ἓν βάπτισμα, 6 εἷς θεὸς καὶ πατὴρ πάντων, ὁ ἐπὶ πάντων καὶ διὰ πάντων καὶ ἐν πᾶσιν. 7 Ἑνὶ δὲ ἑκάστῳ ἡμῶν ἐδόθη ἡ χάρις κατὰ τὸ μέτρον τῆς δωρεᾶς τοῦ Χριστοῦ. 8 διὸ λέγει· ἀναβὰς εἰς ὕψος ᾐχμαλώτευσεν αἰχμαλωσίαν, ἔδωκεν δόματα τοῖς ἀνθρώποις. 9 τὸ δὲ ἀνέβη τί ἐστιν, εἰ μὴ ὅτι καὶ ⸀κατέβη εἰς τὰ κατώτερα [μέρη] τῆς γῆς; 10 ὁ καταβὰς αὐτός ἐστιν καὶ ὁ ἀναβὰς ὑπεράνω πάντων τῶν οὐρανῶν, ἵνα πληρώσῃ τὰ πάντα. 11 Καὶ αὐτὸς ἔδωκεν τοὺς μὲν ἀποστόλους, τοὺς δὲ προφήτας, τοὺς δὲ εὐαγγελιστάς, τοὺς δὲ ποιμένας καὶ διδασκάλους, 12 πρὸς τὸν καταρτισμὸν τῶν ἁγίων εἰς ἔργον διακονίας, εἰς οἰκοδομὴν τοῦ σώματος τοῦ Χριστοῦ, 13 μέχρι καταντήσωμεν οἱ πάντες εἰς τὴν ἑνότητα τῆς πίστεως καὶ τῆς ἐπιγνώσεως τοῦ υἱοῦ τοῦ θεοῦ, εἰς ἄνδρα τέλειον, εἰς μέτρον ἡλικίας τοῦ πληρώματος τοῦ Χριστοῦ, 14 ἵνα μηκέτι ὦμεν νήπιοι, κλυδωνιζόμενοι καὶ περιφερόμενοι παντὶ ἀνέμῳ τῆς διδασκαλίας ἐν τῇ κυβείᾳ τῶν ἀνθρώπων, ἐν πανουργίᾳ πρὸς τὴν μεθοδείαν τῆς πλάνης, 15 ἀληθεύοντες δὲ ἐν ἀγάπῃ αὐξήσωμεν εἰς αὐτὸν τὰ πάντα, ὅς ἐστιν ἡ κεφαλή, Χριστός, 16 ἐξ οὗ πᾶν τὸ σῶμα συναρμολογούμενον καὶ συμβιβαζόμενον διὰ πάσης ἁφῆς τῆς ἐπιχορηγίας κατʼ ἐνέργειαν ἐν μέτρῳ ἑνὸς ἑκάστου μέρους τὴν αὔξησιν τοῦ σώματος ποιεῖται εἰς οἰκοδομὴν ἑαυτοῦ ἐν ἀγάπῃ.

1 Tim 4:13–16

ἕως ἔρχομαι πρόσεχε τῇ ἀναγνώσει, τῇ παρακλήσει, τῇ διδασκαλίᾳ. 14 μὴ ἀμέλει τοῦ ἐν σοὶ χαρίσματος, ὃ ἐδόθη σοι διὰ προφητείας μετὰ ἐπιθέσεως τῶν χειρῶν τοῦ πρεσβυτερίου. 15 ταῦτα μελέτα, ἐν τούτοις ἴσθι, ἵνα σου ἡ προκοπὴ φανερὰ ᾖ πᾶσιν. 16 ἔπεχε σεαυτῷ καὶ τῇ διδασκαλίᾳ, ἐπίμενε αὐτοῖς· τοῦτο γὰρ ποιῶν καὶ σεαυτὸν σώσεις καὶ τοὺς ἀκούοντάς σου.

2 Tim 1:6–7

Διʼ ἣν αἰτίαν ἀναμιμνῄσκω σε ἀναζωπυρεῖν τὸ χάρισμα τοῦ θεοῦ, ὅ ἐστιν ἐν σοὶ διὰ τῆς ἐπιθέσεως τῶν χειρῶν μου. 7 οὐ γὰρ ἔδωκεν ἡμῖν ὁ θεὸς πνεῦμα δειλίας ἀλλὰ δυνάμεως καὶ ἀγάπης καὶ σωφρονισμοῦ.

Cf. Rom 1:11–12; 15:18–19; 1 Cor 1:7; 2:4–5; 7:7; 13:1–13; 14:1–40; 2 Cor 12:11–12; Gal 3:5; Acts 21:8–9.

See also § 119 Prophets and Prophecy.

119. Prophets and Prophecy

Rom 12:6–8

ἔχοντες δὲ χαρίσματα κατὰ τὴν χάριν τὴν δοθεῖσαν ἡμῖν διάφορα, εἴτε προφητείαν κατὰ τὴν ἀναλογίαν τῆς πίστεως, 7 εἴτε διακονίαν ἐν τῇ διακονίᾳ, εἴτε ὁ διδάσκων ἐν τῇ διδασκαλίᾳ, 8 εἴτε ὁ παρακαλῶν ἐν τῇ παρακλήσει· ὁ μεταδιδοὺς ἐν ἁπλότητι, ὁ προϊστάμενος ἐν σπουδῇ, ὁ ἐλεῶν ἐν ἱλαρότητι.

§ 118 Eph 4:9 *κατεβη* 𝔓[46] ℵ* A C* D I[vid] 33. 1739. 1881] *add.* πρωτον ℵ[2] B C[3] *Byz*

3 Therefore I want you to understand that no one speaking by the Spirit of God ever says "Let Jesus be cursed!" and no one can say "Jesus is Lord" except by the Holy Spirit. 4 Now there are varieties of gifts, but the same Spirit; 5 and there are varieties of services, but the same Lord; 6 and there are varieties of activities, but it is the same God who activates all of them in everyone. 7 To each is given the manifestation of the Spirit for the common good. 8 To one is given through the Spirit the utterance of wisdom, and to another the utterance of knowledge according to the same Spirit, 9 to another faith by the same Spirit, to another gifts of healing by the one Spirit, 10 to another the working of miracles, to another prophecy, to another the discernment of spirits, to another various kinds of tongues, to another the interpretation of tongues. 11 All these are activated by one and the same Spirit, who allots to each one individually just as the Spirit chooses. 12 For just as the body is one and has many members, and all the members of the body, though many, are one body, so it is with Christ. 13 For in the one Spirit we were all baptized into one body—Jews or Greeks, slaves or free—and we were all made to drink of one Spirit. 14 Indeed, the body does not consist of one member but of many. 15 If the foot would say, "Because I am not a hand, I do not belong to the body," that would not make it any less a part of the body. 16 And if the ear would say, "Because I am not an eye, I do not belong to the body," that would not make it any less a part of the body. 17 If the whole body were an eye, where would the hearing be? If the whole body were hearing, where would the sense of smell be? 18 But as it is, God arranged the members in the body, each one of them, as he chose. 19 If all were a single member, where would the body be? 20 As it is, there are many members, yet one body. 21 The eye cannot say to the hand, "I have no need of you," nor again the head to the feet, "I have no need of you." 22 On the contrary, the members of the body that seem to be weaker are indispensable, 23 and those members of the body that we think less honorable we clothe with greater honor, and our less respectable members are treated with greater respect; 24 whereas our more respectable members do not need this. But God has so arranged the body, giving the greater honor to the inferior member, 25 that there may be no dissension within the body, but the members may have the same care for one another. 26 If one member suffers, all suffer together with it; if one member is honored, all rejoice together with it. 27 Now you are the body of Christ and individually members of it. 28 And God has appointed in the church first apostles, second prophets, third teachers; then deeds of power, then gifts of healing, forms of assistance, forms of leadership, various kinds of tongues. 29 Are all apostles? Are all prophets? Are all teachers? Do all work miracles? 30 Do all possess gifts of healing? Do all speak in tongues? Do all interpret? 31 But strive for the greater gifts. And I will show you a still more excellent way.

Eph 4:4–16

There is one body and one Spirit, just as you were called to the one hope of your calling, 5 one Lord, one faith, one baptism, 6 one God and Father of all, who is above all and through all and in all. 7 But each of us was given grace according to the measure of Christ's gift. 8 Therefore it is said, "When he ascended on high he made captivity itself a captive; he gave gifts to his people." 9 (When it says, "He ascended," what does it mean but that he had also descended[a] into the lower parts of the earth? 10 He who descended is the same one who ascended far above all the heavens, so that he might fill all things.) 11 The gifts he gave were that some would be apostles, some prophets, some evangelists, some pastors and teachers, 12 to equip the saints for the work of ministry, for building up the body of Christ, 13 until all of us come to the unity of the faith and of the knowledge of the Son of God, to maturity, to the measure of the full stature of Christ. 14 We must no longer be children, tossed to and fro and blown about by every wind of doctrine, by people's trickery, by their craftiness in deceitful scheming. 15 But speaking the truth in love, we must grow up in every way into him who is the head, into Christ, 16 from whom the whole body, joined and knit together by every ligament by which it is supplied,[b] as each part is working properly, promotes the body's growth in building itself up in love.

1 Tim 4:13–16

Until I arrive, give attention to the public reading of scripture, to exhorting, to teaching. 14 Do not neglect the gift that is in you, which was given to you through prophecy with the laying on of hands by the council of elders. 15 Put these things into practice, devote yourself to them, so that all may see your progress. 16 Pay close attention to yourself and to your teaching; continue in these things, for in doing this you will save both yourself and your hearers.

2 Tim 1:6–7

For this reason I remind you to rekindle the gift of God that is within you through the laying on of my hands; 7 for God did not give us a spirit of cowardice, but rather a spirit of power and of love and of self-discipline.

Cf. Rom 1:11–12; 15:18–19; 1 Cor 1:7; 2:4–5; 7:7; 13:1–13; 14:1–40; 2 Cor 12:11–12; Gal 3:5; Acts 21:8–9.

See also § 119 Prophets and Prophecy.

119. Prophets and Prophecy

Rom 12:6–8

We have gifts that differ according to the grace given to us: prophecy, in proportion to faith; 7 ministry, in ministering; the teacher, in teaching; 8 the exhorter, in exhortation; the giver, in generosity; the leader, in diligence; the compassionate, in cheerfulness.

§ 118 [a] **Eph 4:9** *descended* Other ancient authorities add *first* [b] **Eph 4:16** *by which it is supplied* NRSV translates *with which it is equipped*

1 Cor 11:4–6

πᾶς ἀνὴρ προσευχόμενος ἢ προφητεύων κατὰ κεφαλῆς ἔχων καταισχύνει τὴν κεφαλὴν αὐτοῦ. 5 πᾶσα δὲ γυνὴ προσευχομένη ἢ προφητεύουσα ἀκατακαλύπτῳ τῇ κεφαλῇ καταισχύνει τὴν κεφαλὴν αὐτῆς· ἓν γάρ ἐστιν καὶ τὸ αὐτὸ τῇ ἐξυρημένῃ. 6 εἰ γὰρ οὐ κατακαλύπτεται γυνή, καὶ κειράσθω· εἰ δὲ αἰσχρὸν γυναικὶ τὸ κείρασθαι ἢ ξυρᾶσθαι, κατακαλυπτέσθω.

1 Cor 12:7–11

ἑκάστῳ δὲ δίδοται ἡ φανέρωσις τοῦ πνεύματος πρὸς τὸ συμφέρον. 8 ᾧ μὲν γὰρ διὰ τοῦ πνεύματος δίδοται λόγος σοφίας, ἄλλῳ δὲ λόγος γνώσεως κατὰ τὸ αὐτὸ πνεῦμα, 9 ἑτέρῳ πίστις ἐν τῷ αὐτῷ πνεύματι, ἄλλῳ δὲ χαρίσματα ἰαμάτων ἐν τῷ ἑνὶ πνεύματι, 10 ἄλλῳ δὲ ἐνεργήματα δυνάμεων, ἄλλῳ [δὲ] προφητεία, ἄλλῳ [δὲ] διακρίσεις πνευμάτων, ἑτέρῳ γένη γλωσσῶν, ἄλλῳ δὲ ἑρμηνεία γλωσσῶν· 11 πάντα δὲ ταῦτα ἐνεργεῖ τὸ ἓν καὶ τὸ αὐτὸ πνεῦμα διαιροῦν ἰδίᾳ ἑκάστῳ καθὼς βούλεται.

1 Cor 12:28–31a

Καὶ οὓς μὲν ἔθετο ὁ θεὸς ἐν τῇ ἐκκλησίᾳ πρῶτον ἀποστόλους, δεύτερον προφήτας, τρίτον διδασκάλους, ἔπειτα δυνάμεις, ἔπειτα χαρίσματα ἰαμάτων, ἀντιλήμψεις, κυβερνήσεις, γένη γλωσσῶν. 29 μὴ πάντες ἀπόστολοι; μὴ πάντες προφῆται; μὴ πάντες διδάσκαλοι; μὴ πάντες δυνάμεις; 30 μὴ πάντες χαρίσματα ἔχουσιν ἰαμάτων; μὴ πάντες γλώσσαις λαλοῦσιν; μὴ πάντες διερμηνεύουσιν; 31 ζηλοῦτε δὲ τὰ χαρίσματα τὰ μείζονα.

1 Cor 14:1–40

Διώκετε τὴν ἀγάπην, ζηλοῦτε δὲ τὰ πνευματικά, μᾶλλον δὲ ἵνα προφητεύητε. 2 ὁ γὰρ λαλῶν γλώσσῃ οὐκ ἀνθρώποις λαλεῖ ἀλλὰ θεῷ· οὐδεὶς γὰρ ἀκούει, πνεύματι δὲ λαλεῖ μυστήρια· 3 ὁ δὲ προφητεύων ἀνθρώποις λαλεῖ οἰκοδομὴν καὶ παράκλησιν καὶ παραμυθίαν. 4 ὁ λαλῶν γλώσσῃ ἑαυτὸν οἰκοδομεῖ· ὁ δὲ προφητεύων ἐκκλησίαν οἰκοδομεῖ. 5 θέλω δὲ πάντας ὑμᾶς λαλεῖν γλώσσαις, μᾶλλον δὲ ἵνα προφητεύητε· μείζων δὲ ὁ προφητεύων ἢ ὁ λαλῶν γλώσσαις ἐκτὸς εἰ μὴ διερμηνεύῃ, ἵνα ἡ ἐκκλησία οἰκοδομὴν λάβῃ. 6 Νῦν δέ, ἀδελφοί, ἐὰν ἔλθω πρὸς ὑμᾶς γλώσσαις λαλῶν, τί ὑμᾶς ὠφελήσω ἐὰν μὴ ὑμῖν λαλήσω ἢ ἐν ἀποκαλύψει ἢ ἐν γνώσει ἢ ἐν προφητείᾳ ἢ [ἐν] διδαχῇ; 7 ὅμως τὰ ἄψυχα φωνὴν διδόντα, εἴτε αὐλὸς εἴτε κιθάρα, ἐὰν διαστολὴν τοῖς φθόγγοις μὴ δῷ, πῶς γνωσθήσεται τὸ αὐλούμενον ἢ τὸ κιθαριζόμενον; 8 καὶ γὰρ ἐὰν ἄδηλον σάλπιγξ φωνὴν δῷ, τίς παρασκευάσεται εἰς πόλεμον; 9 οὕτως καὶ ὑμεῖς διὰ τῆς γλώσσης ἐὰν μὴ εὔσημον λόγον δῶτε, πῶς γνωσθήσεται τὸ λαλούμενον; ἔσεσθε γὰρ εἰς ἀέρα λαλοῦντες. 10 τοσαῦτα εἰ τύχοι γένη φωνῶν εἰσιν ἐν κόσμῳ καὶ οὐδὲν ἄφωνον· 11 ἐὰν οὖν μὴ εἰδῶ τὴν δύναμιν τῆς φωνῆς, ἔσομαι τῷ λαλοῦντι βάρβαρος καὶ ὁ λαλῶν ἐν ἐμοὶ βάρβαρος. 12 οὕτως καὶ ὑμεῖς, ἐπεὶ ζηλωταί ἐστε πνευμάτων, πρὸς τὴν οἰκοδομὴν τῆς ἐκκλησίας ζητεῖτε ἵνα περισσεύητε. 13 Διὸ ὁ λαλῶν γλώσσῃ προσευχέσθω ἵνα διερμηνεύῃ. 14 ἐὰν [γὰρ] προσεύχωμαι γλώσσῃ, τὸ πνεῦμά μου προσεύχεται, ὁ δὲ νοῦς μου ἄκαρπός ἐστιν. 15 τί οὖν ἐστιν; προσεύξομαι τῷ πνεύματι, προσεύξομαι δὲ καὶ τῷ νοΐ· ψαλῶ τῷ πνεύματι, ψαλῶ δὲ καὶ τῷ νοΐ. 16 ἐπεὶ ἐὰν εὐλογῇς [ἐν] πνεύματι, ὁ ἀναπληρῶν τὸν τόπον τοῦ ἰδιώτου πῶς ἐρεῖ τὸ ἀμὴν ἐπὶ τῇ σῇ εὐχαριστίᾳ; ἐπειδὴ τί λέγεις οὐκ οἶδεν· 17 σὺ μὲν γὰρ καλῶς εὐχαριστεῖς ἀλλ᾽ ὁ ἕτερος οὐκ οἰκοδομεῖται. 18 Εὐχαριστῶ τῷ θεῷ, πάντων ὑμῶν μᾶλλον γλώσσαις λαλῶ· 19 ἀλλὰ ἐν ἐκκλησίᾳ θέλω πέντε λόγους τῷ νοΐ μου λαλῆσαι, ἵνα καὶ ἄλλους κατηχήσω, ἢ μυρίους λόγους ἐν γλώσσῃ. 20 Ἀδελφοί, μὴ παιδία γίνεσθε ταῖς φρεσὶν ἀλλὰ τῇ κακίᾳ νηπιάζετε, ταῖς δὲ φρεσὶν τέλειοι γίνεσθε. 21 ἐν τῷ νόμῳ γέγραπται ὅτι ἐν ἑτερογλώσσοις καὶ ἐν χείλεσιν ἑτέρων λαλήσω τῷ λαῷ τούτῳ καὶ οὐδ᾽ οὕτως εἰσακούσονταί μου, λέγει κύριος. 22 ὥστε αἱ γλῶσσαι εἰς σημεῖόν εἰσιν οὐ τοῖς πιστεύουσιν ἀλλὰ τοῖς ἀπίστοις, ἡ δὲ προφητεία οὐ τοῖς ἀπίστοις ἀλλὰ τοῖς πιστεύουσιν. 23 Ἐὰν οὖν συνέλθῃ ἡ ἐκκλησία ὅλη ἐπὶ τὸ αὐτὸ καὶ πάντες λαλῶσιν γλώσσαις, εἰσέλθωσιν δὲ ἰδιῶται ἢ ἄπιστοι, οὐκ ἐροῦσιν ὅτι μαίνεσθε; 24 ἐὰν δὲ πάντες προφητεύωσιν, εἰσέλθῃ δέ τις ἄπιστος ἢ ἰδιώτης, ἐλέγχεται ὑπὸ πάντων, ἀνακρίνεται ὑπὸ πάντων, 25 τὰ κρυπτὰ τῆς καρδίας αὐτοῦ φανερὰ γίνεται, καὶ οὕτως πεσὼν ἐπὶ πρόσωπον προσκυνήσει τῷ θεῷ ἀπαγγέλλων ὅτι ὄντως ὁ θεὸς ἐν ὑμῖν ἐστιν. 26 Τί οὖν ἐστιν, ἀδελφοί; ὅταν συνέρχησθε, ἕκαστος ψαλμὸν ἔχει, διδαχὴν ἔχει, ἀποκάλυψιν ἔχει, γλῶσσαν ἔχει, ἑρμηνείαν ἔχει· πάντα πρὸς οἰκοδομὴν γινέσθω. 27 εἴτε γλώσσῃ τις λαλεῖ, κατὰ δύο ἢ τὸ πλεῖστον τρεῖς καὶ ἀνὰ μέρος, καὶ εἷς διερμηνευέτω· 28 ἐὰν δὲ μὴ ᾖ διερμηνευτής, σιγάτω ἐν ἐκκλησίᾳ, ἑαυτῷ δὲ λαλείτω καὶ τῷ θεῷ. 29 προφῆται δὲ δύο ἢ τρεῖς λαλείτωσαν καὶ οἱ ἄλλοι διακρινέτωσαν· 30 ἐὰν δὲ ἄλλῳ ἀποκαλυφθῇ καθημένῳ, ὁ πρῶτος σιγάτω. 31 δύνασθε γὰρ καθ᾽ ἕνα πάντες προφητεύειν, ἵνα πάντες μανθάνωσιν καὶ πάντες παρακαλῶνται. 32 καὶ πνεύματα προφητῶν προφήταις ὑποτάσσεται, 33 οὐ γάρ ἐστιν ἀκαταστασίας ὁ θεὸς ἀλλὰ εἰρήνης. Ὡς ἐν πάσαις ταῖς ἐκκλησίαις τῶν ἁγίων 34 ⸂αἱ γυναῖκες ἐν ταῖς ἐκκλησίαις σιγάτωσαν· οὐ γὰρ ἐπιτρέπεται αὐταῖς λαλεῖν, ἀλλὰ ὑποτασσέσθωσαν, καθὼς καὶ ὁ νόμος λέγει. 35 εἰ δέ τι μαθεῖν θέλουσιν, ἐν οἴκῳ τοὺς ἰδίους ἄνδρας ἐπερωτάτωσαν· αἰσχρὸν γάρ ἐστιν γυναικὶ λαλεῖν ἐν ἐκκλησίᾳ.⸃ 36 ἢ ἀφ᾽ ὑμῶν ὁ λόγος τοῦ θεοῦ ἐξῆλθεν, ἢ εἰς ὑμᾶς μόνους κατήντησεν; 37 Εἴ τις δοκεῖ προφήτης εἶναι ἢ πνευματικός, ἐπιγινωσκέτω ἃ γράφω ὑμῖν ὅτι κυρίου ἐστὶν ἐντολή· 38 εἰ δέ τις ἀγνοεῖ, ἀγνοεῖται. 39 Ὥστε, ἀδελφοί [μου], ζηλοῦτε τὸ προφητεύειν καὶ τὸ λαλεῖν μὴ κωλύετε γλώσσαις· 40 πάντα δὲ εὐσχημόνως καὶ κατὰ τάξιν γινέσθω.

Eph 2:19–22

Ἄρα οὖν οὐκέτι ἐστὲ ξένοι καὶ πάροικοι ἀλλὰ ἐστὲ συμπολῖται τῶν ἁγίων καὶ οἰκεῖοι τοῦ θεοῦ, 20 ἐποικοδομηθέντες ἐπὶ τῷ θεμελίῳ τῶν ἀποστόλων καὶ

§ 119 1 Cor 14:34–35 *pon. hic* 𝔓46 ℵ A B 33. 1739. 1881 *Byz*] *pon. p.* 14:40 D

1 Cor 11:4–6

Any man who prays or prophesies with something on his head disgraces his head, **5** but any woman who prays or prophesies with her head unveiled disgraces her head—it is one and the same thing as having her head shaved. **6** For if a woman will not veil herself, then she should cut off her hair; but if it is disgraceful for a woman to have her hair cut off or to be shaved, she should wear a veil.

1 Cor 12:7–11

To each is given the manifestation of the Spirit for the common good. **8** To one is given through the Spirit the utterance of wisdom, and to another the utterance of knowledge according to the same Spirit, **9** to another faith by the same Spirit, to another gifts of healing by the one Spirit, **10** to another the working of miracles, to another prophecy, to another the discernment of spirits, to another various kinds of tongues, to another the interpretation of tongues. **11** All these are activated by one and the same Spirit, who allots to each one individually just as the Spirit chooses.

1 Cor 12:28–31a

And God has appointed in the church first apostles, second prophets, third teachers; then deeds of power, then gifts of healing, forms of assistance, forms of leadership, various kinds of tongues. **29** Are all apostles? Are all prophets? Are all teachers? Do all work miracles? **30** Do all possess gifts of healing? Do all speak in tongues? Do all interpret? **31** But strive for the greater gifts.

1 Cor 14:1–40

Pursue love and strive for the spiritual gifts, and especially that you may prophesy. **2** For those who speak in a tongue do not speak to other people but to God; for nobody understands them, since they are speaking mysteries in the Spirit. **3** On the other hand, those who prophesy speak to other people for their upbuilding and encouragement and consolation. **4** Those who speak in a tongue build up themselves, but those who prophesy build up the church. **5** Now I would like all of you to speak in tongues, but even more to prophesy. One who prophesies is greater than one who speaks in tongues, unless someone interprets, so that the church may be built up. **6** Now, brothers and sisters, if I come to you speaking in tongues, how will I benefit you unless I speak to you in some revelation or knowledge or prophecy or teaching? **7** It is the same way with lifeless instruments that produce sound, such as the flute or the harp. If they do not give distinct notes, how will anyone know what is being played? **8** And if the bugle gives an indistinct sound, who will get ready for battle? **9** So with yourselves; if in a tongue you utter speech that is not intelligible, how will anyone know what is being said? For you will be speaking into the air. **10** There are doubtless many different kinds of sounds in the world, and nothing is without sound. **11** If then I do not know the meaning of a sound, I will be a foreigner to the speaker and the speaker a foreigner to me. **12** So with yourselves; since you are eager for spiritual gifts, strive to excel in them for building up the church. **13** Therefore, one who speaks in a tongue should pray for the power to interpret. **14** For if I pray in a tongue, my spirit prays but my mind is unproductive. **15** What should I do then? I will pray with the spirit, but I will pray with the mind also; I will sing praise with the spirit, but I will sing praise with the mind also. **16** Otherwise, if you say a blessing with the spirit, how can anyone in the position of an outsider say the "Amen" to your thanksgiving, since the outsider does not know what you are saying? **17** For you may give thanks well enough, but the other person is not built up. **18** I thank God that I speak in tongues more than all of you; **19** nevertheless, in church I would rather speak five words with my mind, in order to instruct others also, than ten thousand words in a tongue. **20** Brothers and sisters, do not be children in your thinking; rather, be infants in evil, but in thinking be adults. **21** In the law it is written, "By people of strange tongues and by the lips of foreigners I will speak to this people; yet even then they will not listen to me," says the Lord. **22** Tongues, then, are a sign not for believers but for unbelievers, while prophecy is not for unbelievers but for believers. **23** If, therefore, the whole church comes together and all speak in tongues, and outsiders or unbelievers enter, will they not say that you are out of your mind? **24** But if all prophesy, an unbeliever or outsider who enters is reproved by all and called to account by all. **25** After the secrets of the unbeliever's heart are disclosed, that person will bow down before God and worship him, declaring, "God is really among you." **26** What should be done then, my friends? When you come together, each one has a hymn, a lesson, a revelation, a tongue, or an interpretation. Let all things be done for building up. **27** If anyone speaks in a tongue, let there be only two or at most three, and each in turn; and let one interpret. **28** But if there is no one to interpret, let them be silent in church and speak to themselves and to God. **29** Let two or three prophets speak, and let the others weigh what is said. **30** If a revelation is made to someone else sitting nearby, let the first person be silent. **31** For you can all prophesy one by one, so that all may learn and all be encouraged. **32** And the spirits of prophets are subject to the prophets, **33** for God is a God not of disorder but of peace. (As in all the churches of the saints, **34** women should be silent in the churches. For they are not permitted to speak, but should be subordinate, as the law also says. **35** If there is anything they desire to know, let them ask their husbands at home. For it is shameful for a woman to speak in church.[a] **36** Or did the word of God originate with you? Or are you the only ones it has reached?) **37** Anyone who claims to be a prophet, or to have spiritual powers, must acknowledge that what I am writing to you is a command of the Lord. **38** Anyone who does not recognize this is not to be recognized. **39** So, my friends, be eager to prophesy, and do not forbid speaking in tongues; **40** but all things should be done decently and in order.

Eph 2:19–22

So then you are no longer strangers and aliens, but you are citizens with the saints and also members of the household of God, **20** built upon the foundation of the apostles and prophets, with

§ 119 [a] **1 Cor 14:35** *church* A few ancient authorities put verses 34–35 after verse 40

προφητῶν, ὄντος ἀκρογωνιαίου αὐτοῦ
Χριστοῦ Ἰησοῦ, 21 ἐν ᾧ πᾶσα οἰκοδομὴ
συναρμολογουμένη αὔξει εἰς ναὸν ἅγιον
ἐν κυρίῳ, 22 ἐν ᾧ καὶ ὑμεῖς συνοικοδο-
μεῖσθε εἰς κατοικητήριον τοῦ θεοῦ ἐν
πνεύματι.

Eph 3:1–7

Τούτου χάριν ἐγὼ Παῦλος ὁ δέσμιος τοῦ
Χριστοῦ [Ἰησοῦ] ὑπὲρ ὑμῶν τῶν ἐθνῶν
2 —εἴ γε ἠκούσατε τὴν οἰκονομίαν τῆς
χάριτος τοῦ θεοῦ τῆς δοθείσης μοι εἰς
ὑμᾶς, 3 [ὅτι] κατὰ ἀποκάλυψιν ἐγνωρίσθη
μοι τὸ μυστήριον, καθὼς προέγραψα ἐν
ὀλίγῳ, 4 πρὸς ὃ δύνασθε ἀναγινώσκοντες
νοῆσαι τὴν σύνεσίν μου ἐν τῷ μυστηρίῳ
τοῦ Χριστοῦ, 5 ὃ ἑτέραις γενεαῖς οὐκ
ἐγνωρίσθη τοῖς υἱοῖς τῶν ἀνθρώπων ὡς
νῦν ἀπεκαλύφθη τοῖς ἁγίοις ἀποστόλοις
αὐτοῦ καὶ προφήταις ἐν πνεύματι, 6 εἶναι
τὰ ἔθνη συγκληρονόμα καὶ σύσσωμα καὶ
συμμέτοχα τῆς ἐπαγγελίας ἐν Χριστῷ
Ἰησοῦ διὰ τοῦ εὐαγγελίου, 7 οὗ ἐγενήθην
διάκονος κατὰ τὴν δωρεὰν τῆς χάριτος
τοῦ θεοῦ τῆς δοθείσης μοι κατὰ τὴν
ἐνέργειαν τῆς δυνάμεως αὐτοῦ.

Eph 4:11–16

Καὶ αὐτὸς ἔδωκεν τοὺς μὲν ἀποστόλους,
τοὺς δὲ προφήτας, τοὺς δὲ εὐαγγελιστάς,
τοὺς δὲ ποιμένας καὶ διδασκάλους, 12 πρὸς
τὸν καταρτισμὸν τῶν ἁγίων εἰς ἔργον
διακονίας, εἰς οἰκοδομὴν τοῦ σώματος
τοῦ Χριστοῦ, 13 μέχρι καταντήσωμεν
οἱ πάντες εἰς τὴν ἑνότητα τῆς πίστεως
καὶ τῆς ἐπιγνώσεως τοῦ υἱοῦ τοῦ θεοῦ,
εἰς ἄνδρα τέλειον, εἰς μέτρον ἡλικίας
τοῦ πληρώματος τοῦ Χριστοῦ, 14 ἵνα
μηκέτι ὦμεν νήπιοι, κλυδωνιζόμενοι
καὶ περιφερόμενοι παντὶ ἀνέμῳ τῆς
διδασκαλίας ἐν τῇ κυβείᾳ τῶν ἀνθρώ-
πων, ἐν πανουργίᾳ πρὸς τὴν μεθοδείαν
τῆς πλάνης, 15 ἀληθεύοντες δὲ ἐν ἀγάπῃ
αὐξήσωμεν εἰς αὐτὸν τὰ πάντα, ὅς ἐστιν
ἡ κεφαλή, Χριστός, 16 ἐξ οὗ πᾶν τὸ σῶμα
συναρμολογούμενον καὶ συμβιβαζόμενον
διὰ πάσης ἁφῆς τῆς ἐπιχορηγίας κατ'
ἐνέργειαν ἐν μέτρῳ ἑνὸς ἑκάστου μέρους
τὴν αὔξησιν τοῦ σώματος ποιεῖται εἰς
οἰκοδομὴν ἑαυτοῦ ἐν ἀγάπῃ.

1 Thess 5:19–22

τὸ πνεῦμα μὴ σβέννυτε, 20 προφητείας
μὴ ἐξουθενεῖτε, 21 πάντα δὲ δοκιμάζετε,
τὸ καλὸν κατέχετε, 22 ἀπὸ παντὸς εἴδους
πονηροῦ ἀπέχεσθε.

Acts 11:27–30

Ἐν ταύταις δὲ ταῖς ἡμέραις κατῆλθον ἀπὸ
Ἱεροσολύμων προφῆται εἰς Ἀντιόχειαν.
28 ἀναστὰς δὲ εἷς ἐξ αὐτῶν ὀνόματι Ἅγα-
βος ἐσήμανεν διὰ τοῦ πνεύματος λιμὸν
μεγάλην μέλλειν ἔσεσθαι ἐφ' ὅλην τὴν
οἰκουμένην, ἥτις ἐγένετο ἐπὶ Κλαυδίου.
29 τῶν δὲ μαθητῶν, καθὼς εὐπορεῖτό τις,
ὥρισαν ἕκαστος αὐτῶν εἰς διακονίαν
πέμψαι τοῖς κατοικοῦσιν ἐν τῇ Ἰουδαίᾳ
ἀδελφοῖς· 30 ὃ καὶ ἐποίησαν ἀποστείλαν-
τες πρὸς τοὺς πρεσβυτέρους διὰ χειρὸς
Βαρναβᾶ καὶ Σαύλου.

Acts 13:1–3

Ἦσαν δὲ ἐν Ἀντιοχείᾳ κατὰ τὴν οὖσαν
ἐκκλησίαν προφῆται καὶ διδάσκαλοι ὅ
τε Βαρναβᾶς καὶ Συμεὼν ὁ καλούμενος
Νίγερ καὶ Λούκιος ὁ Κυρηναῖος, Μαναήν
τε Ἡρῴδου τοῦ τετραάρχου σύντροφος
καὶ Σαῦλος. 2 Λειτουργούντων δὲ αὐτῶν
τῷ κυρίῳ καὶ νηστευόντων εἶπεν τὸ
πνεῦμα τὸ ἅγιον· ἀφορίσατε δή μοι τὸν
Βαρναβᾶν καὶ Σαῦλον εἰς τὸ ἔργον ὃ
προσκέκλημαι αὐτούς. 3 τότε νηστεύ-
σαντες καὶ προσευξάμενοι καὶ ἐπιθέντες
τὰς χεῖρας αὐτοῖς ἀπέλυσαν.

Acts 15:30–35

Οἱ μὲν οὖν ἀπολυθέντες κατῆλθον εἰς
Ἀντιόχειαν, καὶ συναγαγόντες τὸ πλῆθος
ἐπέδωκαν τὴν ἐπιστολήν. 31 ἀναγνόντες
δὲ ἐχάρησαν ἐπὶ τῇ παρακλήσει. 32 Ἰούδας
τε καὶ Σιλᾶς καὶ αὐτοὶ προφῆται ὄντες
διὰ λόγου πολλοῦ παρεκάλεσαν τοὺς
ἀδελφοὺς καὶ ἐπεστήριξαν, 33 ποιήσαντες
δὲ χρόνον ἀπελύθησαν μετ' εἰρήνης ἀπὸ
τῶν ἀδελφῶν πρὸς τοὺς ἀποστείλαντας
⸀αὐτούς. 35 Παῦλος δὲ καὶ Βαρναβᾶς
διέτριβον ἐν Ἀντιοχείᾳ διδάσκοντες
καὶ εὐαγγελιζόμενοι μετὰ καὶ ἑτέρων
πολλῶν τὸν λόγον τοῦ κυρίου.

Acts 19:1–6

Ἐγένετο δὲ ἐν τῷ τὸν Ἀπολλῶ εἶναι ἐν
Κορίνθῳ Παῦλον διελθόντα τὰ ἀνωτερικὰ
μέρη [κατ]ελθεῖν εἰς Ἔφεσον καὶ εὑρεῖν
τινας μαθητὰς 2 εἶπέν τε πρὸς αὐτούς· εἰ
πνεῦμα ἅγιον ἐλάβετε πιστεύσαντες; οἱ
δὲ πρὸς αὐτόν· ἀλλ' οὐδ' εἰ πνεῦμα ἅγιον
ἔστιν ἠκούσαμεν. 3 εἶπέν τε· εἰς τί οὖν
ἐβαπτίσθητε; οἱ δὲ εἶπαν· εἰς τὸ Ἰωάννου
βάπτισμα. 4 εἶπεν δὲ Παῦλος· Ἰωάννης
ἐβάπτισεν βάπτισμα μετανοίας τῷ λαῷ
λέγων εἰς τὸν ἐρχόμενον μετ' αὐτὸν ἵνα
πιστεύσωσιν, τοῦτ' ἔστιν εἰς τὸν Ἰησοῦν.
5 ἀκούσαντες δὲ ἐβαπτίσθησαν εἰς τὸ
ὄνομα τοῦ κυρίου Ἰησοῦ, 6 καὶ ἐπιθέντος
αὐτοῖς τοῦ Παύλου [τὰς] χεῖρας ἦλθε τὸ
πνεῦμα τὸ ἅγιον ἐπ' αὐτούς, ἐλάλουν τε
γλώσσαις καὶ ἐπροφήτευον.

Acts 21:8–11

τῇ δὲ ἐπαύριον ἐξελθόντες ἤλθομεν εἰς
Καισάρειαν καὶ εἰσελθόντες εἰς τὸν οἶκον
Φιλίππου τοῦ εὐαγγελιστοῦ, ὄντος ἐκ
τῶν ἑπτά, ἐμείναμεν παρ' αὐτῷ. 9 τούτῳ
δὲ ἦσαν θυγατέρες τέσσαρες παρθένοι
προφητεύουσαι. 10 Ἐπιμενόντων δὲ
ἡμέρας πλείους κατῆλθέν τις ἀπὸ τῆς
Ἰουδαίας προφήτης ὀνόματι Ἅγαβος,
11 καὶ ἐλθὼν πρὸς ἡμᾶς καὶ ἄρας τὴν
ζώνην τοῦ Παύλου, δήσας ἑαυτοῦ τοὺς
πόδας καὶ τὰς χεῖρας εἶπεν· τάδε λέγει
τὸ πνεῦμα τὸ ἅγιον· τὸν ἄνδρα οὗ ἐστιν
ἡ ζώνη αὕτη, οὕτως δήσουσιν ἐν Ἰερου-
σαλὴμ οἱ Ἰουδαῖοι καὶ παραδώσουσιν
εἰς χεῖρας ἐθνῶν.

See also § 118 Spiritual Gifts.

120. Non-Vengeance

Rom 12:14–21

εὐλογεῖτε τοὺς διώκοντας [ὑμᾶς], εὐλο-
γεῖτε καὶ μὴ καταρᾶσθε. 15 χαίρειν μετὰ
χαιρόντων, κλαίειν μετὰ κλαιόντων.
16 τὸ αὐτὸ εἰς ἀλλήλους φρονοῦντες,
μὴ τὰ ὑψηλὰ φρονοῦντες ἀλλὰ τοῖς
ταπεινοῖς συναπαγόμενοι. μὴ γίνεσθε
φρόνιμοι παρ' ἑαυτοῖς. 17 μηδενὶ κα-
κὸν ἀντὶ κακοῦ ἀποδιδόντες, προνοού-
μενοι καλὰ ἐνώπιον πάντων ἀνθρώπων·
18 εἰ δυνατὸν τὸ ἐξ ὑμῶν, μετὰ πάντων
ἀνθρώπων εἰρηνεύοντες· 19 μὴ ἑαυτοὺς
ἐκδικοῦντες, ἀγαπητοί, ἀλλὰ δότε τόπον
τῇ ὀργῇ, γέγραπται γάρ· ἐμοὶ ἐκδίκησις,

Acts 15:33 *αυτους* 𝔓^{74} ℵ A B E *Byz*] *add.* [v. 34] εδοξε δε τω Σιλα επιμειναι αυτου (C) 33. 1739 ¦ *add.* εδοξε δε τω Σιλα επιμειναι προς αυτους, μονος δε Ιουδας επορευθη D

Christ Jesus himself as the cornerstone. [21] In him the whole structure is joined together and grows into a holy temple in the Lord; [22] in whom you also are built together spiritually into a dwelling place for God.

Eph 3:1–7

This is the reason that I Paul am a prisoner for Christ Jesus for the sake of you Gentiles— [2] for surely you have already heard of the commission of God's grace that was given me for you, [3] and how the mystery was made known to me by revelation, as I wrote above in a few words, [4] a reading of which will enable you to perceive my understanding of the mystery of Christ. [5] In former generations this mystery was not made known to humankind, as it has now been revealed to his holy apostles and prophets by the Spirit: [6] that is, the Gentiles have become fellow heirs, members of the same body, and sharers in the promise in Christ Jesus through the gospel. [7] Of this gospel I have become a servant according to the gift of God's grace that was given me by the working of his power.

Eph 4:11–16

The gifts he gave were that some would be apostles, some prophets, some evangelists, some pastors and teachers, [12] to equip the saints for the work of ministry, for building up the body of Christ, [13] until all of us come to the unity of the faith and of the knowledge of the Son of God, to maturity, to the measure of the full stature of Christ. [14] We must no longer be children, tossed to and fro and blown about by every wind of doctrine, by people's trickery, by their craftiness in deceitful scheming. [15] But speaking the truth in love, we must grow up in every way into him who is the head, into Christ, [16] from whom the whole body, joined and knit together by every ligament by which it is supplied,[b] as each part is working properly, promotes the body's growth in building itself up in love.

1 Thess 5:19–22

Do not quench the Spirit. [20] Do not despise the words of prophets, [21] but test everything; hold fast to what is good; [22] abstain from every form of evil.

Acts 11:27–30

At that time prophets came down from Jerusalem to Antioch. [28] One of them named Agabus stood up and predicted by the Spirit that there would be a severe famine over all the world; and this took place during the reign of Claudius. [29] The disciples determined that according to their ability, each would send relief to the believers living in Judea; [30] this they did, sending it to the elders by Barnabas and Saul.

Acts 13:1–3

Now in the church at Antioch there were prophets and teachers: Barnabas, Simeon who was called Niger, Lucius of Cyrene, Manaen a member of the court of Herod the ruler, and Saul. [2] While they were worshiping the Lord and fasting, the Holy Spirit said, "Set apart for me Barnabas and Saul for the work to which I have called them." [3] Then after fasting and praying they laid their hands on them and sent them off.

Acts 15:30–35

So they were sent off and went down to Antioch. When they gathered the congregation together, they delivered the letter. [31] When its members read it, they rejoiced at the exhortation. [32] Judas and Silas, who were themselves prophets, said much to encourage and strengthen the believers. [33] After they had been there for some time, they were sent off in peace by the believers to those who had sent them.[c] [35] But Paul and Barnabas remained in Antioch, and there, with many others, they taught and proclaimed the word of the Lord.

Acts 19:1–6

While Apollos was in Corinth, Paul passed through the interior regions and came to Ephesus, where he found some disciples. [2] He said to them, "Did you receive the Holy Spirit when you became believers?" They replied, "No, we have not even heard that there is a Holy Spirit." [3] Then he said, "Into what then were you baptized?" They answered, "Into John's baptism." [4] Paul said, "John baptized with the baptism of repentance, telling the people to believe in the one who was to come after him, that is, in Jesus." [5] On hearing this, they were baptized in the name of the Lord Jesus. [6] When Paul had laid his hands on them, the Holy Spirit came upon them, and they spoke in tongues and prophesied

Acts 21:8–11

The next day we left and came to Caesarea; and we went into the house of Philip the evangelist, one of the seven, and stayed with him. [9] He had four unmarried daughters who had the gift of prophecy. [10] While we were staying there for several days, a prophet named Agabus came down from Judea. [11] He came to us and took Paul's belt, bound his own feet and hands with it, and said, "Thus says the Holy Spirit, 'This is the way the Jews in Jerusalem will bind the man who owns this belt and will hand him over to the Gentiles.'"

See also § 118 Spiritual Gifts.

120. Non-Vengeance

Rom 12:14–21

Bless those who persecute you; bless and do not curse them. [15] Rejoice with those who rejoice, weep with those who weep. [16] Live in harmony with one another; do not be haughty, but associate with the lowly; do not claim to be wiser than you are. [17] Do not repay anyone evil for evil, but take thought for what is noble in the sight of all. [18] If it is possible, so far as it depends on you, live peaceably with all. [19] Beloved, never avenge yourselves, but leave room for the wrath of God; for it is written, "Vengeance is mine,

[b] **Eph 4:16** ***by which it is supplied*** NRSV translates *with which it is equipped* [c] **Acts 15:33** ***them*** Other ancient authorities add verse 34, *But it seemed good to Silas to remain there*

ἐγὼ ἀνταποδώσω, λέγει κύριος. **20** ἀλλὰ
ἐὰν πεινᾷ ὁ ἐχθρός σου, ψώμιζε αὐτόν·
ἐὰν διψᾷ, πότιζε αὐτόν· τοῦτο γὰρ ποιῶν
ἄνθρακας πυρὸς σωρεύσεις ἐπὶ τὴν κε-
φαλὴν αὐτοῦ. **21** μὴ νικῶ ὑπὸ τοῦ κακοῦ
ἀλλὰ νίκα ἐν τῷ ἀγαθῷ τὸ κακόν.

1 Cor 6:6–8

ἀλλὰ ἀδελφὸς μετὰ ἀδελφοῦ κρίνεται
καὶ τοῦτο ἐπὶ ἀπίστων; **7** Ἤδη μὲν [οὖν]
ὅλως ἥττημα ὑμῖν ἐστιν ὅτι κρίματα ἔχετε
μεθ᾽ ἑαυτῶν. διὰ τί οὐχὶ μᾶλλον ἀδικεῖ-
σθε; διὰ τί οὐχὶ μᾶλλον ἀποστερεῖσθε;
8 ἀλλὰ ὑμεῖς ἀδικεῖτε καὶ ἀποστερεῖτε,
καὶ τοῦτο ἀδελφούς.

1 Thess 5:15

ὁρᾶτε μή τις κακὸν ἀντὶ κακοῦ τινι ἀποδῷ,
ἀλλὰ πάντοτε τὸ ἀγαθὸν διώκετε [καὶ]
εἰς ἀλλήλους καὶ εἰς πάντας.

121. Governing Authorities

Rom 13:1–7

Πᾶσα ψυχὴ ἐξουσίαις ὑπερεχούσαις ὑπο-
τασσέσθω. οὐ γὰρ ἔστιν ἐξουσία εἰ μὴ ὑπὸ
θεοῦ, αἱ δὲ οὖσαι ὑπὸ θεοῦ τεταγμέναι
εἰσίν. **2** ὥστε ὁ ἀντιτασσόμενος τῇ ἐξουσίᾳ
τῇ τοῦ θεοῦ διαταγῇ ἀνθέστηκεν, οἱ δὲ
ἀνθεστηκότες ἑαυτοῖς κρίμα λήμψον-
ται. **3** οἱ γὰρ ἄρχοντες οὐκ εἰσὶν φόβος
τῷ ἀγαθῷ ἔργῳ ἀλλὰ τῷ κακῷ. θέλεις
δὲ μὴ φοβεῖσθαι τὴν ἐξουσίαν· τὸ ἀγα-
θὸν ποίει, καὶ ἕξεις ἔπαινον ἐξ αὐτῆς·
4 θεοῦ γὰρ διάκονός ἐστιν σοὶ εἰς τὸ
ἀγαθόν. ἐὰν δὲ τὸ κακὸν ποιῇς, φοβοῦ·
οὐ γὰρ εἰκῇ τὴν μάχαιραν φορεῖ· θεοῦ
γὰρ διάκονός ἐστιν ἔκδικος εἰς ὀργὴν
τῷ τὸ κακὸν πράσσοντι. **5** διὸ ἀνάγκη
ὑποτάσσεσθαι, οὐ μόνον διὰ τὴν ὀργὴν
ἀλλὰ καὶ διὰ τὴν συνείδησιν. **6** διὰ τοῦτο
γὰρ καὶ φόρους τελεῖτε· λειτουργοὶ γὰρ
θεοῦ εἰσιν εἰς αὐτὸ τοῦτο προσκαρτε-
ροῦντες. **7** ἀπόδοτε πᾶσιν τὰς ὀφειλάς,
τῷ τὸν φόρον τὸν φόρον, τῷ τὸ τέλος
τὸ τέλος, τῷ τὸν φόβον τὸν φόβον, τῷ
τὴν τιμὴν τὴν τιμήν.

1 Cor 2:6–8

Σοφίαν δὲ λαλοῦμεν ἐν τοῖς τελείοις,
σοφίαν δὲ οὐ τοῦ αἰῶνος τούτου οὐδὲ
τῶν ἀρχόντων τοῦ αἰῶνος τούτου τῶν
καταργουμένων· **7** ἀλλὰ λαλοῦμεν θεοῦ
σοφίαν ἐν μυστηρίῳ τὴν ἀποκεκρυμ-
μένην, ἣν προώρισεν ὁ θεὸς πρὸ τῶν
αἰώνων εἰς δόξαν ἡμῶν, **8** ἣν οὐδεὶς τῶν
ἀρχόντων τοῦ αἰῶνος τούτου ἔγνωκεν·
εἰ γὰρ ἔγνωσαν, οὐκ ἂν τὸν κύριον τῆς
δόξης ἐσταύρωσαν.

1 Cor 6:1–8

Τολμᾷ τις ὑμῶν πρᾶγμα ἔχων πρὸς τὸν
ἕτερον κρίνεσθαι ἐπὶ τῶν ἀδίκων καὶ
οὐχὶ ἐπὶ τῶν ἁγίων; **2** ἢ οὐκ οἴδατε ὅτι
οἱ ἅγιοι τὸν κόσμον κρινοῦσιν; καὶ εἰ
ἐν ὑμῖν κρίνεται ὁ κόσμος, ἀνάξιοί ἐστε
κριτηρίων ἐλαχίστων; **3** οὐκ οἴδατε ὅτι
ἀγγέλους κρινοῦμεν, μήτι γε βιωτικά;
4 βιωτικὰ μὲν οὖν κριτήρια ἐὰν ἔχητε,
τοὺς ἐξουθενημένους ἐν τῇ ἐκκλησίᾳ,
τούτους καθίζετε; **5** πρὸς ἐντροπὴν ὑμῖν
λέγω. οὕτως οὐκ ἔνι ἐν ὑμῖν οὐδεὶς σο-
φός, ὃς δυνήσεται διακρῖναι ἀνὰ μέσον
τοῦ ἀδελφοῦ αὐτοῦ; **6** ἀλλὰ ἀδελφὸς
μετὰ ἀδελφοῦ κρίνεται καὶ τοῦτο ἐπὶ
ἀπίστων; **7** Ἤδη μὲν [οὖν] ὅλως ἥττημα
ὑμῖν ἐστιν ὅτι κρίματα ἔχετε μεθ᾽ ἑαυ-
τῶν. διὰ τί οὐχὶ μᾶλλον ἀδικεῖσθε; διὰ
τί οὐχὶ μᾶλλον ἀποστερεῖσθε; **8** ἀλλὰ
ὑμεῖς ἀδικεῖτε καὶ ἀποστερεῖτε, καὶ τοῦ-
το ἀδελφούς.

1 Cor 15:23–25

Ἕκαστος δὲ ἐν τῷ ἰδίῳ τάγματι· ἀπαρχὴ
Χριστός, ἔπειτα οἱ τοῦ Χριστοῦ ἐν τῇ
παρουσίᾳ αὐτοῦ, **24** εἶτα τὸ τέλος, ὅταν
παραδιδῷ τὴν βασιλείαν τῷ θεῷ καὶ
πατρί, ὅταν καταργήσῃ πᾶσαν ἀρχὴν καὶ
πᾶσαν ἐξουσίαν καὶ δύναμιν. **25** δεῖ γὰρ
αὐτὸν βασιλεύειν ἄχρι οὗ θῇ πάντας τοὺς
ἐχθροὺς ὑπὸ τοὺς πόδας αὐτοῦ.

Eph 1:20–23

Ἣν ⸀ἐνήργησεν ἐν τῷ Χριστῷ ἐγείρας
αὐτὸν ἐκ νεκρῶν καὶ καθίσας ἐν δεξιᾷ
αὐτοῦ ἐν τοῖς ἐπουρανίοις **21** ὑπεράνω
πάσης ἀρχῆς καὶ ἐξουσίας καὶ δυνάμεως
καὶ κυριότητος καὶ παντὸς ὀνόματος
ὀνομαζομένου, οὐ μόνον ἐν τῷ αἰῶνι
τούτῳ ἀλλὰ καὶ ἐν τῷ μέλλοντι· **22** καὶ
πάντα ὑπέταξεν ὑπὸ τοὺς πόδας αὐτοῦ
καὶ αὐτὸν ἔδωκεν κεφαλὴν ὑπὲρ πάν-
τα τῇ ἐκκλησίᾳ, **23** ἥτις ἐστὶν τὸ σῶμα
αὐτοῦ, τὸ πλήρωμα τοῦ τὰ πάντα ἐν
πᾶσιν πληρουμένου.

Phil 1:12–14

Γινώσκειν δὲ ὑμᾶς βούλομαι, ἀδελφοί,
ὅτι τὰ κατ᾽ ἐμὲ μᾶλλον εἰς προκοπὴν τοῦ
εὐαγγελίου ἐλήλυθεν, **13** ὥστε τοὺς δε-
σμούς μου φανεροὺς ἐν Χριστῷ γενέσθαι
ἐν ὅλῳ τῷ πραιτωρίῳ καὶ τοῖς λοιποῖς
πᾶσιν, **14** καὶ τοὺς πλείονας τῶν ἀδελ-
φῶν ἐν κυρίῳ πεποιθότας τοῖς δεσμοῖς
μου περισσοτέρως τολμᾶν ἀφόβως τὸν
⸀λόγον λαλεῖν.

Phil 2:9–11

διὸ καὶ ὁ θεὸς αὐτὸν ὑπερύψωσεν καὶ
ἐχαρίσατο αὐτῷ τὸ ὄνομα τὸ ὑπὲρ πᾶν
ὄνομα, **10** ἵνα ἐν τῷ ὀνόματι Ἰησοῦ πᾶν
γόνυ κάμψῃ ἐπουρανίων καὶ ἐπιγείων
καὶ καταχθονίων **11** καὶ πᾶσα γλῶσσα
ἐξομολογήσηται ὅτι κύριος Ἰησοῦς Χρι-
στὸς εἰς δόξαν θεοῦ πατρός.

Phil 4:22

ἀσπάζονται ὑμᾶς πάντες οἱ ἅγιοι, μάλιστα
δὲ οἱ ἐκ τῆς Καίσαρος οἰκίας.

1 Tim 2:1–4

Παρακαλῶ οὖν πρῶτον πάντων ποι-
εῖσθαι δεήσεις προσευχὰς ἐντεύξεις
εὐχαριστίας ὑπὲρ πάντων ἀνθρώπων,
2 ὑπὲρ βασιλέων καὶ πάντων τῶν ἐν
ὑπεροχῇ ὄντων, ἵνα ἤρεμον καὶ ἡσύχιον
βίον διάγωμεν ἐν πάσῃ εὐσεβείᾳ καὶ σε-
μνότητι. **3** τοῦτο καλὸν καὶ ἀπόδεκτον
ἐνώπιον τοῦ σωτῆρος ἡμῶν θεοῦ, **4** ὃς
πάντας ἀνθρώπους θέλει σωθῆναι καὶ
εἰς ἐπίγνωσιν ἀληθείας ἐλθεῖν.

Titus 3:1

Ὑπομίμνῃσκε αὐτοὺς ἀρχαῖς ἐξουσίαις
ὑποτάσσεσθαι, πειθαρχεῖν, πρὸς πᾶν
ἔργον ἀγαθὸν ἑτοίμους εἶναι

§ 121 **Eph 1:20** *ενηργησεν* ℵ D 33. 1739. 1881 *Byz*] ενηργηκεν A B **Phil 1:14** *λογον* $\mathfrak{P}^{46}$ D^{2} 1739. 1881 *Byz*] *add.* του θεου ℵ A B (D*) 048^{vid}. 33

I will repay, says the Lord." 20 No, "if your enemies are hungry, feed them; if they are thirsty, give them something to drink; for by doing this you will heap burning coals on their heads." 21 Do not be overcome by evil, but overcome evil with good.

1 Cor 6:6–8

but a believer goes to court against a believer—and before unbelievers at that? 7 In fact, to have lawsuits at all with one another is already a defeat for you. Why not rather be wronged? Why not rather be defrauded? 8 But you yourselves wrong and defraud—and believers at that.

1 Thess 5:15

See that none of you repays evil for evil, but always seek to do good to one another and to all.

121. Governing Authorities

Rom 13:1–7

Let every person be subject to the governing authorities; for there is no authority except from God, and those authorities that exist have been instituted by God. 2 Therefore whoever resists authority resists what God has appointed, and those who resist will incur judgment. 3 For rulers are not a terror to good conduct, but to bad. Do you wish to have no fear of the authority? Then do what is good, and you will receive its approval; 4 for it is God's servant for your good. But if you do what is wrong, you should be afraid, for the authority does not bear the sword in vain! It is the servant of God to execute wrath on the wrongdoer. 5 Therefore one must be subject, not only because of wrath but also because of conscience. 6 For the same reason you also pay taxes, for the authorities are God's servants, busy with this very thing. 7 Pay to all what is due them—taxes to whom taxes are due, revenue to whom revenue is due, respect to whom respect is due, honor to whom honor is due.

1 Cor 2:6–8

Yet among the mature we do speak wisdom, though it is not a wisdom of this age or of the rulers of this age, who are doomed to perish. 7 But we speak God's wisdom, secret and hidden, which God decreed before the ages for our glory. 8 None of the rulers of this age understood this; for if they had, they would not have crucified the Lord of glory.

1 Cor 6:1–8

When any of you has a grievance against another, do you dare to take it to court before the unrighteous, instead of taking it before the saints? 2 Do you not know that the saints will judge the world? And if the world is to be judged by you, are you incompetent to try trivial cases? 3 Do you not know that we are to judge angels—to say nothing of ordinary matters? 4 If you have ordinary cases, then, do you appoint as judges those who have no standing in the church? 5 I say this to your shame. Can it be that there is no one among you wise enough to decide between one believer and another, 6 but a believer goes to court against a believer—and before unbelievers at that? 7 In fact, to have lawsuits at all with one another is already a defeat for you. Why not rather be wronged? Why not rather be defrauded? 8 But you yourselves wrong and defraud—and believers at that.

1 Cor 15:23–25

But each in his own order: Christ the first fruits, then at his coming those who belong to Christ. 24 Then comes the end, when he hands over the kingdom to God the Father, after he has destroyed every ruler and every authority and power. 25 For he must reign until he has put all his enemies under his feet.

Eph 1:20–23

God put this power to work[a] in Christ when he raised him from the dead and seated him at his right hand in the heavenly places, 21 far above all rule and authority and power and dominion, and above every name that is named, not only in this age but also in the age to come. 22 And he has put all things under his feet and has made him the head over all things for the church, 23 which is his body, the fullness of him who fills all in all.

Phil 1:12–14

I want you to know, beloved, that what has happened to me has actually helped to spread the gospel, 13 so that it has become known throughout the whole imperial guard and to everyone else that my imprisonment is for Christ; 14 and most of the brothers and sisters, having been made confident in the Lord by my imprisonment, dare to speak the word[b] with greater boldness and without fear.

Phil 2:9–11

Therefore God also highly exalted him and gave him the name that is above every name, 10 so that at the name of Jesus every knee should bend, in heaven and on earth and under the earth, 11 and every tongue should confess that Jesus Christ is Lord, to the glory of God the Father.

Phil 4:22

All the saints greet you, especially those of the emperor's household.

1 Tim 2:1–4

First of all, then, I urge that supplications, prayers, intercessions, and thanksgivings be made for everyone, 2 for kings and all who are in high positions, so that we may lead a quiet and peaceable life in all godliness and dignity. 3 This is right and is acceptable in the sight of God our Savior, 4 who desires everyone to be saved and to come to the knowledge of the truth.

Titus 3:1

Remind them to be subject to rulers and authorities, to be obedient, to be ready for every good work

§ 121 [a] **Eph 1:20** *put this power to work* Other ancient authorities read *has put this power to work* [b] **Phil 1:14** *word* Other ancient authorities read *word of God*

Acts 13:27
οἱ γὰρ κατοικοῦντες ἐν Ἰερουσαλὴμ καὶ
οἱ ἄρχοντες αὐτῶν τοῦτον ἀγνοήσαν-
τες καὶ τὰς φωνὰς τῶν προφητῶν τὰς
κατὰ πᾶν σάββατον ἀναγινωσκομένας
κρίναντες ἐπλήρωσαν

Acts 16:20–21
καὶ προσαγαγόντες αὐτοὺς τοῖς στρα-
τηγοῖς εἶπαν· οὗτοι οἱ ἄνθρωποι ἐκτα-
ράσσουσιν ἡμῶν τὴν πόλιν, Ἰουδαῖοι
ὑπάρχοντες, **21** καὶ καταγγέλλουσιν ἔθη
ἃ οὐκ ἔξεστιν ἡμῖν παραδέχεσθαι οὐδὲ
ποιεῖν Ῥωμαίοις οὖσιν.

Acts 17:6–7
μὴ εὑρόντες δὲ αὐτοὺς ἔσυρον Ἰάσονα
καί τινας ἀδελφοὺς ἐπὶ τοὺς πολιτάρχας
βοῶντες ὅτι οἱ τὴν οἰκουμένην ἀναστα-
τώσαντες οὗτοι καὶ ἐνθάδε πάρεισιν,
7 οὓς ὑποδέδεκται Ἰάσων· καὶ οὗτοι πάν-
τες ἀπέναντι τῶν δογμάτων Καίσαρος
πράσσουσιν βασιλέα ἕτερον λέγοντες
εἶναι Ἰησοῦν.

Cf. 2 Cor 11:32–33; Phil 1:18b–26; 1:27–30; 2 Tim 4:16–18; Acts 14:5–7; 18:12–17; and the extended narrative in the latter chapters of Acts of Paul's arrest in Jerusalem, imprisonment in Caesarea, and journey to Rome.

See also § 82 Authorities and Powers.

122. *The Love Command*

Rom 12:9–10
Ἡ ἀγάπη ἀνυπόκριτος. ἀποστυγοῦντες
τὸ πονηρόν, κολλώμενοι τῷ ἀγαθῷ, **10** τῇ
φιλαδελφίᾳ εἰς ἀλλήλους φιλόστοργοι,
τῇ τιμῇ ἀλλήλους προηγούμενοι

Rom 13:8–10
Μηδενὶ μηδὲν ὀφείλετε εἰ μὴ τὸ ἀλλήλους
ἀγαπᾶν· ὁ γὰρ ἀγαπῶν τὸν ἕτερον νόμον
πεπλήρωκεν. **9** τὸ γὰρ οὐ μοιχεύσεις, οὐ
φονεύσεις, οὐ κλέψεις, οὐκ ἐπιθυμήσεις,
καὶ εἴ τις ἑτέρα ἐντολή, ἐν τῷ λόγῳ τούτῳ
ἀνακεφαλαιοῦται [ἐν τῷ]· ἀγαπήσεις τὸν
πλησίον σου ὡς σεαυτόν. **10** ἡ ἀγάπη τῷ
πλησίον κακὸν οὐκ ἐργάζεται· πλήρωμα
οὖν νόμου ἡ ἀγάπη.

1 Cor 13:1–13
Ἐὰν ταῖς γλώσσαις τῶν ἀνθρώπων λαλῶ
καὶ τῶν ἀγγέλων, ἀγάπην δὲ μὴ ἔχω,
γέγονα χαλκὸς ἠχῶν ἢ κύμβαλον ἀλα-
λάζον. **2** καὶ ἐὰν ἔχω προφητείαν καὶ
εἰδῶ τὰ μυστήρια πάντα καὶ πᾶσαν τὴν
γνῶσιν καὶ ἐὰν ἔχω πᾶσαν τὴν πίστιν
ὥστε ὄρη μεθιστάναι, ἀγάπην δὲ μὴ
ἔχω, οὐθέν εἰμι. **3** κἂν ψωμίσω πάντα
τὰ ὑπάρχοντά μου καὶ ἐὰν παραδῶ τὸ
σῶμά μου ἵνα ⸀καυχήσωμαι, ἀγάπην δὲ
μὴ ἔχω, οὐδὲν ὠφελοῦμαι. **4** Ἡ ἀγάπη
μακροθυμεῖ, χρηστεύεται ἡ ἀγάπη, οὐ
ζηλοῖ, [ἡ ἀγάπη] οὐ περπερεύεται, οὐ
φυσιοῦται, **5** οὐκ ἀσχημονεῖ, οὐ ζητεῖ
τὰ ἑαυτῆς, οὐ παροξύνεται, οὐ λογίζε-
ται τὸ κακόν, **6** οὐ χαίρει ἐπὶ τῇ ἀδικίᾳ,
συγχαίρει δὲ τῇ ἀληθείᾳ· **7** πάντα στέγει,
πάντα πιστεύει, πάντα ἐλπίζει, πάντα
ὑπομένει. **8** Ἡ ἀγάπη οὐδέποτε πίπτει·
εἴτε δὲ προφητεῖαι, καταργηθήσονται·
εἴτε γλῶσσαι, παύσονται· εἴτε γνῶσις,
καταργηθήσεται. **9** ἐκ μέρους γὰρ γινώ-
σκομεν καὶ ἐκ μέρους προφητεύομεν·
10 ὅταν δὲ ἔλθῃ τὸ τέλειον, τὸ ἐκ μέρους
καταργηθήσεται. **11** ὅτε ἤμην νήπιος,
ἐλάλουν ὡς νήπιος, ἐφρόνουν ὡς νήπιος,
ἐλογιζόμην ὡς νήπιος· ὅτε γέγονα ἀνήρ,
κατήργηκα τὰ τοῦ νηπίου. **12** βλέπομεν
γὰρ ἄρτι δι᾽ ἐσόπτρου ἐν αἰνίγματι, τότε
δὲ πρόσωπον πρὸς πρόσωπον· ἄρτι γι-
νώσκω ἐκ μέρους, τότε δὲ ἐπιγνώσομαι
καθὼς καὶ ἐπεγνώσθην. **13** Νυνὶ δὲ μένει
πίστις, ἐλπίς, ἀγάπη, τὰ τρία ταῦτα· μεί-
ζων δὲ τούτων ἡ ἀγάπη.

1 Cor 16:13–14
Γρηγορεῖτε, στήκετε ἐν τῇ πίστει, ἀνδρί-
ζεσθε, κραταιοῦσθε. **14** πάντα ὑμῶν ἐν
ἀγάπῃ γινέσθω.

Gal 5:6
ἐν γὰρ Χριστῷ Ἰησοῦ οὔτε περιτομή τι
ἰσχύει οὔτε ἀκροβυστία ἀλλὰ πίστις δι᾽
ἀγάπης ἐνεργουμένη.

Gal 5:13–15
Ὑμεῖς γὰρ ἐπ᾽ ἐλευθερίᾳ ἐκλήθητε, ἀδελφοί·
μόνον μὴ τὴν ἐλευθερίαν εἰς ἀφορμὴν
τῇ σαρκί, ἀλλὰ διὰ τῆς ἀγάπης δουλεύ-
ετε ἀλλήλοις. **14** ὁ γὰρ πᾶς νόμος ἐν ἑνὶ
λόγῳ πεπλήρωται, ἐν τῷ· ἀγαπήσεις τὸν
πλησίον σου ὡς σεαυτόν. **15** εἰ δὲ ἀλλή-
λους δάκνετε καὶ κατεσθίετε, βλέπετε
μὴ ὑπ᾽ ἀλλήλων ἀναλωθῆτε.

Gal 5:22–24
ὁ δὲ καρπὸς τοῦ πνεύματός ἐστιν ἀγάπη
χαρὰ εἰρήνη, μακροθυμία χρηστότης
ἀγαθωσύνη, πίστις **23** πραΰτης ἐγκράτεια·
κατὰ τῶν τοιούτων οὐκ ἔστιν νόμος.
24 οἱ δὲ τοῦ Χριστοῦ [Ἰησοῦ] τὴν σάρκα
ἐσταύρωσαν σὺν τοῖς παθήμασιν καὶ
ταῖς ἐπιθυμίαις.

Eph 5:1–2
Γίνεσθε οὖν μιμηταὶ τοῦ θεοῦ ὡς τέκνα
ἀγαπητὰ **2** καὶ περιπατεῖτε ἐν ἀγάπῃ,
καθὼς καὶ ὁ Χριστὸς ἠγάπησεν ⸀ἡμᾶς
καὶ παρέδωκεν ἑαυτὸν ὑπὲρ ἡμῶν προσ-
φορὰν καὶ θυσίαν τῷ θεῷ εἰς ὀσμὴν
εὐωδίας.

Col 3:14
ἐπὶ πᾶσιν δὲ τούτοις τὴν ἀγάπην, ὅ ἐστιν
σύνδεσμος τῆς τελειότητος.

1 Thess 4:9–12
Περὶ δὲ τῆς φιλαδελφίας οὐ χρείαν ἔχε-
τε γράφειν ὑμῖν, αὐτοὶ γὰρ ὑμεῖς θεο-
δίδακτοί ἐστε εἰς τὸ ἀγαπᾶν ἀλλήλους,
10 καὶ γὰρ ποιεῖτε αὐτὸ εἰς πάντας τοὺς
ἀδελφοὺς [τοὺς] ἐν ὅλῃ τῇ Μακεδονίᾳ.
Παρακαλοῦμεν δὲ ὑμᾶς, ἀδελφοί, πε-
ρισσεύειν μᾶλλον **11** καὶ φιλοτιμεῖσθαι
ἡσυχάζειν καὶ πράσσειν τὰ ἴδια καὶ ἐργά-
ζεσθαι ταῖς [ἰδίαις] χερσὶν ὑμῶν, καθὼς
ὑμῖν παρηγγείλαμεν, **12** ἵνα περιπατῆτε
εὐσχημόνως πρὸς τοὺς ἔξω καὶ μηδενὸς
χρείαν ἔχητε.

1 Tim 1:5–7
τὸ δὲ τέλος τῆς παραγγελίας ἐστὶν ἀγάπη
ἐκ καθαρᾶς καρδίας καὶ συνειδήσεως
ἀγαθῆς καὶ πίστεως ἀνυποκρίτου, **6** ὧν

§ 122 **1 Cor 13:3** ***καυχησωμαι*** 𝔓46 ℵ A B 33. 1739*] καυθησομαι C D 1881* ¦ καυθησωμαι 1739c. 1881c *Byz* **Eph 5:2** ***ημας*** 𝔓46 ℵ2 D 33. 1739. 1881 *Byz*] υμας ℵ* A B

Acts 13:27

Because the residents of Jerusalem and their leaders did not recognize him or understand the words of the prophets that are read every sabbath, they fulfilled those words by condemning him.

Acts 16:20–21

When they had brought them before the magistrates, they said, "These men are disturbing our city; they are Jews
21 and are advocating customs that are not lawful for us as Romans to adopt or observe."

Acts 17:6–7

When they could not find them, they dragged Jason and some believers before the city authorities, shouting, "These people who have been turning the world upside down have come here also,
7 and Jason has entertained them as guests. They are all acting contrary to the decrees of the emperor, saying that there is another king named Jesus."

Cf. 2 Cor 11:32–33; Phil 1:18b–26; 1:27–30; 2 Tim 4:16–18; Acts 14:5–7; 18:12–17; and the extended narrative in the latter chapters of Acts of Paul's arrest in Jerusalem, imprisonment in Caesarea, and journey to Rome.

See also § 82 Authorities and Powers.

122. The Love Command

Rom 12:9–10

Let love be genuine; hate what is evil, hold fast to what is good;
10 love one another with mutual affection; outdo one another in showing honor.

Rom 13:8–10

Owe no one anything, except to love one another; for the one who loves another has fulfilled the law.
9 The commandments, "You shall not commit adultery; You shall not murder; You shall not steal; You shall not covet"; and any other commandment, are summed up in this word, "Love your neighbor as yourself."
10 Love does no wrong to a neighbor; therefore, love is the fulfilling of the law.

1 Cor 13:1–13

If I speak in the tongues of mortals and of angels, but do not have love, I am a noisy gong or a clanging cymbal.
2 And if I have prophetic powers, and understand all mysteries and all knowledge, and if I have all faith, so as to remove mountains, but do not have love, I am nothing.
3 If I give away all my possessions, and if I hand over my body so that I may boast,[a] but do not have love, I gain nothing.
4 Love is patient; love is kind; love is not envious or boastful or arrogant
5 or rude. It does not insist on its own way; it is not irritable or resentful;
6 it does not rejoice in wrongdoing, but rejoices in the truth.
7 It bears all things, believes all things, hopes all things, endures all things.
8 Love never ends. But as for prophecies, they will come to an end; as for tongues, they will cease; as for knowledge, it will come to an end.
9 For we know only in part, and we prophesy only in part;
10 but when the complete comes, the partial will come to an end.
11 When I was a child, I spoke like a child, I thought like a child, I reasoned like a child; when I became an adult, I put an end to childish ways.
12 For now we see in a mirror, dimly, but then we will see face to face. Now I know only in part; then I will know fully, even as I have been fully known.
13 And now faith, hope, and love abide, these three; and the greatest of these is love.

1 Cor 16:13–14

Keep alert, stand firm in your faith, be courageous, be strong.
14 Let all that you do be done in love.

Gal 5:6

For in Christ Jesus neither circumcision nor uncircumcision counts for anything; the only thing that counts is faith working through love.

Gal 5:13–15

For you were called to freedom, brothers and sisters; only do not use your freedom as an opportunity for self-indulgence, but through love become slaves to one another.
14 For the whole law is summed up in a single commandment, "You shall love your neighbor as yourself."
15 If, however, you bite and devour one another, take care that you are not consumed by one another.

Gal 5:22–24

By contrast, the fruit of the Spirit is love, joy, peace, patience, kindness, generosity, faithfulness,
23 gentleness, and self-control. There is no law against such things.
24 And those who belong to Christ Jesus have crucified the flesh with its passions and desires.

Eph 5:1–2

Therefore be imitators of God, as beloved children,
2 and live in love, as Christ loved us[b] and gave himself up for us, a fragrant offering and sacrifice to God.

Col 3:14

Above all, clothe yourselves with love, which binds everything together in perfect harmony.

1 Thess 4:9–12

Now concerning love of the brothers and sisters, you do not need to have anyone write to you, for you yourselves have been taught by God to love one another;
10 and indeed you do love all the brothers and sisters throughout Macedonia. But we urge you, beloved, to do so more and more,
11 to aspire to live quietly, to mind your own affairs, and to work with your hands, as we directed you,
12 so that you may behave properly toward outsiders and be dependent on no one.

1 Tim 1:5–7

But the aim of such instruction is love that comes from a pure heart, a good conscience, and sincere faith.
6 Some

§ 122 [a] **1 Cor 13:3** ***body so that I may boast*** Other ancient authorities read *body to be burned* [b] **Eph 5:2** ***us*** Other ancient authorities read *you*

τινες ἀστοχήσαντες ἐξετράπησαν εἰς ματαιολογίαν **7** θέλοντες εἶναι νομοδιδάσκαλοι, μὴ νοοῦντες μήτε ἃ λέγουσιν μήτε περὶ τίνων διαβεβαιοῦνται.

Cf. 1 Cor 8:1–3; Gal 6:1–2; Eph 4:15–16; Phil 2:1–4; 1 Thess 1:3; 3:12; 1 Tim 1:14; 2 Tim 1:13–14.

See also § 123 Faith, Hope, and Love.

123. Faith, Hope, and Love

1 Cor 13:7

πάντα στέγει, πάντα πιστεύει, πάντα ἐλπίζει, πάντα ὑπομένει.

1 Cor 13:13

Νυνὶ δὲ μένει πίστις, ἐλπίς, ἀγάπη, τὰ τρία ταῦτα· μείζων δὲ τούτων ἡ ἀγάπη.

Gal 5:5–6

ἡμεῖς γὰρ πνεύματι ἐκ πίστεως ἐλπίδα δικαιοσύνης ἀπεκδεχόμεθα. **6** ἐν γὰρ Χριστῷ Ἰησοῦ οὔτε περιτομή τι ἰσχύει οὔτε ἀκροβυστία ἀλλὰ πίστις δι᾽ ἀγάπης ἐνεργουμένη.

Eph 1:15–20

Διὰ τοῦτο κἀγὼ ἀκούσας τὴν καθ᾽ ὑμᾶς πίστιν ἐν τῷ κυρίῳ Ἰησοῦ καὶ ⸂τὴν ἀγάπην τὴν⸃ εἰς πάντας τοὺς ἁγίους **16** οὐ παύομαι εὐχαριστῶν ὑπὲρ ὑμῶν μνείαν ποιούμενος ἐπὶ τῶν προσευχῶν μου, **17** ἵνα ὁ θεὸς τοῦ κυρίου ἡμῶν Ἰησοῦ Χριστοῦ, ὁ πατὴρ τῆς δόξης, δώῃ ὑμῖν πνεῦμα σοφίας καὶ ἀποκαλύψεως ἐν ἐπιγνώσει αὐτοῦ, **18** πεφωτισμένους τοὺς ὀφθαλμοὺς τῆς καρδίας [ὑμῶν] εἰς τὸ εἰδέναι ὑμᾶς τίς ἐστιν ἡ ἐλπὶς τῆς κλήσεως αὐτοῦ, τίς ὁ πλοῦτος τῆς δόξης τῆς κληρονομίας αὐτοῦ ἐν τοῖς ἁγίοις, **19** καὶ τί τὸ ὑπερβάλλον μέγεθος τῆς δυνάμεως αὐτοῦ εἰς ἡμᾶς τοὺς πιστεύοντας κατὰ τὴν ἐνέργειαν τοῦ κράτους τῆς ἰσχύος αὐτοῦ. **20** Ἣν ⸀ἐνήργησεν ἐν τῷ Χριστῷ ἐγείρας αὐτὸν ἐκ νεκρῶν καὶ καθίσας ἐν δεξιᾷ αὐτοῦ ἐν τοῖς ἐπουρανίοις

Col 1:3–5

Εὐχαριστοῦμεν τῷ θεῷ πατρὶ τοῦ κυρίου ἡμῶν Ἰησοῦ Χριστοῦ πάντοτε περὶ ὑμῶν προσευχόμενοι, **4** ἀκούσαντες τὴν πίστιν ὑμῶν ἐν Χριστῷ Ἰησοῦ καὶ τὴν ἀγάπην ἣν ἔχετε εἰς πάντας τοὺς ἁγίους **5** διὰ τὴν ἐλπίδα τὴν ἀποκειμένην ὑμῖν ἐν τοῖς οὐρανοῖς, ἣν προηκούσατε ἐν τῷ λόγῳ τῆς ἀληθείας τοῦ εὐαγγελίου

1 Thess 1:3

μνημονεύοντες ὑμῶν τοῦ ἔργου τῆς πίστεως καὶ τοῦ κόπου τῆς ἀγάπης καὶ τῆς ὑπομονῆς τῆς ἐλπίδος τοῦ κυρίου ἡμῶν Ἰησοῦ Χριστοῦ ἔμπροσθεν τοῦ θεοῦ καὶ πατρὸς ἡμῶν

1 Thess 5:8

ἡμεῖς δὲ ἡμέρας ὄντες νήφωμεν ἐνδυσάμενοι θώρακα πίστεως καὶ ἀγάπης καὶ περικεφαλαίαν ἐλπίδα σωτηρίας

Cf. Rom 5:1–5; Eph 4:1–6. For the related triad of faith, love, and perseverance, see 2 Thess 1:3–4; 1 Tim 6:11; 2 Tim 3:10; Titus 2:2.

124. The Fruit of the Spirit

Rom 6:20–23

ὅτε γὰρ δοῦλοι ἦτε τῆς ἁμαρτίας, ἐλεύθεροι ἦτε τῇ δικαιοσύνῃ. **21** τίνα οὖν καρπὸν εἴχετε τότε; ἐφ᾽ οἷς νῦν ἐπαισχύνεσθε, τὸ γὰρ τέλος ἐκείνων θάνατος. **22** νυνὶ δὲ ἐλευθερωθέντες ἀπὸ τῆς ἁμαρτίας δουλωθέντες δὲ τῷ θεῷ ἔχετε τὸν καρπὸν ὑμῶν εἰς ἁγιασμόν, τὸ δὲ τέλος ζωὴν αἰώνιον. **23** τὰ γὰρ ὀψώνια τῆς ἁμαρτίας θάνατος, τὸ δὲ χάρισμα τοῦ θεοῦ ζωὴ αἰώνιος ἐν Χριστῷ Ἰησοῦ τῷ κυρίῳ ἡμῶν.

Rom 7:4–6

ὥστε, ἀδελφοί μου, καὶ ὑμεῖς ἐθανατώθητε τῷ νόμῳ διὰ τοῦ σώματος τοῦ Χριστοῦ, εἰς τὸ γενέσθαι ὑμᾶς ἑτέρῳ, τῷ ἐκ νεκρῶν ἐγερθέντι, ἵνα καρποφορήσωμεν τῷ θεῷ. **5** ὅτε γὰρ ἦμεν ἐν τῇ σαρκί, τὰ παθήματα τῶν ἁμαρτιῶν τὰ διὰ τοῦ νόμου ἐνηργεῖτο ἐν τοῖς μέλεσιν ἡμῶν, εἰς τὸ καρποφορῆσαι τῷ θανάτῳ· **6** νυνὶ δὲ κατηργήθημεν ἀπὸ τοῦ νόμου ἀποθανόντες ἐν ᾧ κατειχόμεθα, ὥστε δουλεύειν ἡμᾶς ἐν καινότητι πνεύματος καὶ οὐ παλαιότητι γράμματος.

Gal 5:22–24

ὁ δὲ καρπὸς τοῦ πνεύματός ἐστιν ἀγάπη χαρὰ εἰρήνη, μακροθυμία χρηστότης ἀγαθωσύνη, πίστις **23** πραΰτης ἐγκράτεια· κατὰ τῶν τοιούτων οὐκ ἔστιν νόμος. **24** οἱ δὲ τοῦ Χριστοῦ [Ἰησοῦ] τὴν σάρκα ἐσταύρωσαν σὺν τοῖς παθήμασιν καὶ ταῖς ἐπιθυμίαις.

Eph 5:8–14

ἦτε γάρ ποτε σκότος, νῦν δὲ φῶς ἐν κυρίῳ· ὡς τέκνα φωτὸς περιπατεῖτε **9** —ὁ γὰρ καρπὸς τοῦ φωτὸς ἐν πάσῃ ἀγαθωσύνῃ καὶ δικαιοσύνῃ καὶ ἀληθείᾳ— **10** δοκιμάζοντες τί ἐστιν εὐάρεστον τῷ κυρίῳ, **11** καὶ μὴ συγκοινωνεῖτε τοῖς ἔργοις τοῖς ἀκάρποις τοῦ σκότους, μᾶλλον δὲ καὶ ἐλέγχετε. **12** τὰ γὰρ κρυφῇ γινόμενα ὑπ᾽ αὐτῶν αἰσχρόν ἐστιν καὶ λέγειν, **13** τὰ δὲ πάντα ἐλεγχόμενα ὑπὸ τοῦ φωτὸς φανεροῦται, **14** πᾶν γὰρ τὸ φανερούμενον φῶς ἐστιν. διὸ λέγει· ἔγειρε, ὁ καθεύδων, καὶ ἀνάστα ἐκ τῶν νεκρῶν, καὶ ἐπιφαύσει σοι ὁ Χριστός.

Phil 1:9–11

Καὶ τοῦτο προσεύχομαι, ἵνα ἡ ἀγάπη ὑμῶν ἔτι μᾶλλον καὶ μᾶλλον περισσεύῃ ἐν ἐπιγνώσει καὶ πάσῃ αἰσθήσει **10** εἰς τὸ δοκιμάζειν ὑμᾶς τὰ διαφέροντα, ἵνα ἦτε εἰλικρινεῖς καὶ ἀπρόσκοποι εἰς ἡμέραν Χριστοῦ, **11** πεπληρωμένοι καρπὸν δικαιοσύνης τὸν διὰ Ἰησοῦ Χριστοῦ εἰς δόξαν καὶ ἔπαινον θεοῦ.

§ 123 **Eph 1:15** ***την αγαπην την*** ℵ^{2} D^{1} *Byz*] την 𝔓^{46} ℵ* A B 33. 1739. 1881 ¦ την αγαπην D* **Eph 1:20** ***ενηργησεν*** ℵ D 33. 1739. 1881 *Byz*] ενηργηκεν A B

people have deviated from these and turned to meaningless talk, 7 desiring to be teachers of the law, without understanding either what they are saying or the things about which they make assertions.

Cf. 1 Cor 8:1–3; Gal 6:1–2; Eph 4:15–16; Phil 2:1–4; 1 Thess 1:3; 3:12; 1 Tim 1:14; 2 Tim 1:13–14.

See also § 123 Faith, Hope, and Love.

123. Faith, Hope, and Love

1 Cor 13:7

It bears all things, believes all things, hopes all things, endures all things.

1 Cor 13:13

And now faith, hope, and love abide, these three; and the greatest of these is love.

Gal 5:5–6

For through the Spirit, by faith, we eagerly wait for the hope of righteousness.
6 For in Christ Jesus neither circumcision nor uncircumcision counts for anything; the only thing that counts is faith working through love.

Eph 1:15–20

I have heard of your faith in the Lord Jesus and your love[a] toward all the saints, and for this reason 16 I do not cease to give thanks for you as I remember you in my prayers. 17 I pray that the God of our Lord Jesus Christ, the Father of glory, may give you a spirit of wisdom and revelation as you come to know him, 18 so that, with the eyes of your heart enlightened, you may know what is the hope to which he has called you, what are the riches of his glorious inheritance among the saints,
19 and what is the immeasurable greatness of his power for us who believe, according to the working of his great power. 20 God put this power to work[b] in Christ when he raised him from the dead and seated him at his right hand in the heavenly places

Col 1:3–5

In our prayers for you we always thank God, the Father of our Lord Jesus Christ, 4 for we have heard of your faith in Christ Jesus and of the love that you have for all the saints, 5 because of the hope laid up for you in heaven. You have heard of this hope before in the word of the truth, the gospel

1 Thess 1:3

remembering before our God and Father your work of faith and labor of love and steadfastness of hope in our Lord Jesus Christ.

1 Thess 5:8

But since we belong to the day, let us be sober, and put on the breastplate of faith and love, and for a helmet the hope of salvation.

Cf. Rom 5:1–5; Eph 4:1–6. For the related triad of faith, love, and perseverance, see 2 Thess 1:3–4; 1 Tim 6:11; 2 Tim 3:10; Titus 2:2.

124. The Fruit of the Spirit

Rom 6:20–23

When you were slaves of sin, you were free in regard to righteousness. 21 So what fruit did you have then? Because of these things you are now ashamed, because the end of those things is death.
22 But now that you have been freed from sin and enslaved to God, the fruit you get is sanctification, and the end is eternal life.[a] 23 For the wages of sin is death, but the free gift of God is eternal life in Christ Jesus our Lord.

Rom 7:4–6

In the same way, my friends, you have died to the law through the body of Christ, so that you may belong to another, to him who has been raised from the dead in order that we may bear fruit for God. 5 While we were living in the flesh, our sinful passions, aroused by the law, were at work in our members to bear fruit for death. 6 But now we are discharged from the law, dead to that which held us captive, so that we are slaves not under the old written code but in the new life of the Spirit.

Gal 5:22–24

By contrast, the fruit of the Spirit is love, joy, peace, patience, kindness, generosity, faithfulness, 23 gentleness, and self-control. There is no law against such things. 24 And those who belong to Christ Jesus have crucified the flesh with its passions and desires.

Eph 5:8–14

For once you were darkness, but now in the Lord you are light. Live as children of light— 9 for the fruit of the light is found in all that is good and right and true. 10 Try to find out what is pleasing to the Lord. 11 Take no part in the unfruitful works of darkness, but instead expose them. 12 For it is shameful even to mention what such people do secretly; 13 but everything exposed by the light becomes visible, 14 for everything that becomes visible is light. Therefore it says, "Sleeper, awake! Rise from the dead, and Christ will shine on you."

Phil 1:9–11

And this is my prayer, that your love may overflow more and more with knowledge and full insight 10 to help you to determine what is best, so that in the day of Christ you may be pure and blameless, 11 having produced the harvest of righteousness that comes through Jesus Christ for the glory and praise of God.

§ 123 [a] **Eph 1:15** *and your love* Other ancient authorities lack *and your love* [b] **Eph 1:20** *put this power to work* Other ancient authorities read *has put this power to work* **§ 124** [a] **Rom 6:21–22** Translation differs from NRSV

Col 1:3–10

Εὐχαριστοῦμεν τῷ θεῷ πατρὶ τοῦ κυρίου ἡμῶν Ἰησοῦ Χριστοῦ πάντοτε περὶ ὑμῶν προσευχόμενοι, **4** ἀκούσαντες τὴν πίστιν ὑμῶν ἐν Χριστῷ Ἰησοῦ καὶ τὴν ἀγάπην ἣν ἔχετε εἰς πάντας τοὺς ἁγίους **5** διὰ τὴν ἐλπίδα τὴν ἀποκειμένην ὑμῖν ἐν τοῖς οὐρανοῖς, ἣν προηκούσατε ἐν τῷ λόγῳ τῆς ἀληθείας τοῦ εὐαγγελίου **6** τοῦ παρόντος εἰς ὑμᾶς, καθὼς καὶ ἐν παντὶ τῷ κόσμῳ ἐστὶν καρποφορούμενον καὶ αὐξανόμενον καθὼς καὶ ἐν ὑμῖν, ἀφ' ἧς ἡμέρας ἠκούσατε καὶ ἐπέγνωτε τὴν χάριν τοῦ θεοῦ ἐν ἀληθείᾳ· **7** καθὼς ἐμάθετε ἀπὸ Ἐπαφρᾶ τοῦ ἀγαπητοῦ συνδούλου ἡμῶν, ὅς ἐστιν πιστὸς ὑπὲρ ⸀ὑμῶν διάκονος τοῦ Χριστοῦ, **8** ὁ καὶ δηλώσας ἡμῖν τὴν ὑμῶν ἀγάπην ἐν πνεύματι. **9** Διὰ τοῦτο καὶ ἡμεῖς, ἀφ' ἧς ἡμέρας ἠκούσαμεν, οὐ παυόμεθα ὑπὲρ ὑμῶν προσευχόμενοι καὶ αἰτούμενοι, ἵνα πληρωθῆτε τὴν ἐπίγνωσιν τοῦ θελήματος αὐτοῦ ἐν πάσῃ σοφίᾳ καὶ συνέσει πνευματικῇ, **10** περιπατῆσαι ἀξίως τοῦ κυρίου εἰς πᾶσαν ἀρεσκείαν, ἐν παντὶ ἔργῳ ἀγαθῷ καρποφοροῦντες καὶ αὐξανόμενοι τῇ ἐπιγνώσει τοῦ θεοῦ

Cf. Rom 15:28; Gal 6:7–8; Phil 1:22; 4:17; Titus 3:14.

125. Humble Servanthood

Rom 12:3

Λέγω γὰρ διὰ τῆς χάριτος τῆς δοθείσης μοι παντὶ τῷ ὄντι ἐν ὑμῖν μὴ ὑπερφρονεῖν παρ' ὃ δεῖ φρονεῖν ἀλλὰ φρονεῖν εἰς τὸ σωφρονεῖν, ἑκάστῳ ὡς ὁ θεὸς ἐμέρισεν μέτρον πίστεως.

Rom 12:16

τὸ αὐτὸ εἰς ἀλλήλους φρονοῦντες, μὴ τὰ ὑψηλὰ φρονοῦντες ἀλλὰ τοῖς ταπεινοῖς συναπαγόμενοι. μὴ γίνεσθε φρόνιμοι παρ' ἑαυτοῖς.

1 Cor 13:4–5

Ἡ ἀγάπη μακροθυμεῖ, χρηστεύεται ἡ ἀγάπη, οὐ ζηλοῖ, [ἡ ἀγάπη] οὐ περπερεύεται, οὐ φυσιοῦται, **5** οὐκ ἀσχημονεῖ, οὐ ζητεῖ τὰ ἑαυτῆς, οὐ παροξύνεται, οὐ λογίζεται τὸ κακόν

Gal 5:13–15

Ὑμεῖς γὰρ ἐπ' ἐλευθερίᾳ ἐκλήθητε, ἀδελφοί· μόνον μὴ τὴν ἐλευθερίαν εἰς ἀφορμὴν τῇ σαρκί, ἀλλὰ διὰ τῆς ἀγάπης δουλεύετε ἀλλήλοις. **14** ὁ γὰρ πᾶς νόμος ἐν ἑνὶ λόγῳ πεπλήρωται, ἐν τῷ· ἀγαπήσεις τὸν πλησίον σου ὡς σεαυτόν. **15** εἰ δὲ ἀλλήλους δάκνετε καὶ κατεσθίετε, βλέπετε μὴ ὑπ' ἀλλήλων ἀναλωθῆτε.

Gal 5:25–6:5

Εἰ ζῶμεν πνεύματι, πνεύματι καὶ στοιχῶμεν. **26** μὴ γινώμεθα κενόδοξοι, ἀλλήλους προκαλούμενοι, ἀλλήλοις φθονοῦντες. **6** Ἀδελφοί, ἐὰν καὶ προλημφθῇ ἄνθρωπος ἔν τινι παραπτώματι, ὑμεῖς οἱ πνευματικοὶ καταρτίζετε τὸν τοιοῦτον ἐν πνεύματι πραΰτητος, σκοπῶν σεαυτὸν μὴ καὶ σὺ πειρασθῇς. **2** Ἀλλήλων τὰ βάρη βαστάζετε καὶ οὕτως ⸀ἀναπληρώσετε τὸν νόμον τοῦ Χριστοῦ. **3** εἰ γὰρ δοκεῖ τις εἶναί τι μηδὲν ὤν, φρεναπατᾷ ἑαυτόν. **4** τὸ δὲ ἔργον ἑαυτοῦ δοκιμαζέτω ἕκαστος, καὶ τότε εἰς ἑαυτὸν μόνον τὸ καύχημα ἕξει καὶ οὐκ εἰς τὸν ἕτερον· **5** ἕκαστος γὰρ τὸ ἴδιον φορτίον βαστάσει.

Eph 4:1–3

Παρακαλῶ οὖν ὑμᾶς ἐγὼ ὁ δέσμιος ἐν κυρίῳ ἀξίως περιπατῆσαι τῆς κλήσεως ἧς ἐκλήθητε, **2** μετὰ πάσης ταπεινοφροσύνης καὶ πραΰτητος, μετὰ μακροθυμίας, ἀνεχόμενοι ἀλλήλων ἐν ἀγάπῃ, **3** σπουδάζοντες τηρεῖν τὴν ἑνότητα τοῦ πνεύματος ἐν τῷ συνδέσμῳ τῆς εἰρήνης

Phil 2:1–4

Εἴ τις οὖν παράκλησις ἐν Χριστῷ, εἴ τι παραμύθιον ἀγάπης, εἴ τις κοινωνία πνεύματος, εἴ τις σπλάγχνα καὶ οἰκτιρμοί, **2** πληρώσατέ μου τὴν χαρὰν ἵνα τὸ αὐτὸ φρονῆτε, τὴν αὐτὴν ἀγάπην ἔχοντες, σύμψυχοι, τὸ ἓν φρονοῦντες, **3** μηδὲν κατ' ἐριθείαν μηδὲ κατὰ κενοδοξίαν ἀλλὰ τῇ ταπεινοφροσύνῃ ἀλλήλους ἡγούμενοι ὑπερέχοντας ἑαυτῶν, **4** μὴ τὰ ἑαυτῶν ἕκαστος σκοποῦντες ἀλλὰ ⸀[καὶ] τὰ ἑτέρων ἕκαστοι.

Col 3:12–13

Ἐνδύσασθε οὖν, ὡς ἐκλεκτοὶ τοῦ θεοῦ ἅγιοι καὶ ἠγαπημένοι, σπλάγχνα οἰκτιρμοῦ χρηστότητα ταπεινοφροσύνην πραΰτητα μακροθυμίαν, **13** ἀνεχόμενοι ἀλλήλων καὶ χαριζόμενοι ἑαυτοῖς ἐάν τις πρός τινα ἔχῃ μομφήν· καθὼς καὶ ὁ ⸀κύριος ἐχαρίσατο ὑμῖν, οὕτως καὶ ὑμεῖς

1 Tim 6:17–19

Τοῖς πλουσίοις ἐν τῷ νῦν αἰῶνι παράγγελλε μὴ ὑψηλοφρονεῖν μηδὲ ἠλπικέναι ἐπὶ πλούτου ἀδηλότητι ἀλλ' ἐπὶ θεῷ τῷ παρέχοντι ἡμῖν πάντα πλουσίως εἰς ἀπόλαυσιν, **18** ἀγαθοεργεῖν, πλουτεῖν ἐν ἔργοις καλοῖς, εὐμεταδότους εἶναι, κοινωνικούς, **19** ἀποθησαυρίζοντας ἑαυτοῖς θεμέλιον καλὸν εἰς τὸ μέλλον, ἵνα ἐπιλάβωνται τῆς ὄντως ζωῆς.

2 Tim 2:24–26

δοῦλον δὲ κυρίου οὐ δεῖ μάχεσθαι ἀλλὰ ἤπιον εἶναι πρὸς πάντας, διδακτικόν, ἀνεξίκακον, **25** ἐν πραΰτητι παιδεύοντα τοὺς ἀντιδιατιθεμένους, μήποτε δώῃ αὐτοῖς ὁ θεὸς μετάνοιαν εἰς ἐπίγνωσιν ἀληθείας **26** καὶ ἀνανήψωσιν ἐκ τῆς τοῦ διαβόλου παγίδος, ἐζωγρημένοι ὑπ' αὐτοῦ εἰς τὸ ἐκείνου θέλημα.

Titus 3:1–2

Ὑπομίμνῃσκε αὐτοὺς ἀρχαῖς ἐξουσίαις ὑποτάσσεσθαι, πειθαρχεῖν, πρὸς πᾶν ἔργον ἀγαθὸν ἑτοίμους εἶναι, **2** μηδένα βλασφημεῖν, ἀμάχους εἶναι, ἐπιεικεῖς, πᾶσαν ἐνδεικνυμένους πραΰτητα πρὸς πάντας ἀνθρώπους.

Cf. Rom 11:20–21; 12:10–11; 15:1–2; 1 Cor 9:19–23; 10:33–11:1; 2 Cor 4:5; 10:1–2; 11:7; Gal 5:22–23; Eph 5:21; Col 3:12; 1 Tim 6:11; Acts 20:18–19.

See also § 161 Gentleness toward All.

§ 124 **Col 1:7** ***υμων*** ℵ^{2} C D^{1} 33. 1739. 1881 *Byz*] ημων 𝔓^{46} ℵ* A B D* **§ 125** **Gal 6:2** ***αναπληρωσετε*** (𝔓^{46}) B] αναπληρωσατε ℵ A C D 33. 1739. 1881 *Byz* **Phil 2:4** ***και*** 𝔓^{46} ℵ A B C D^{2} 33. 1739. 1881 *Byz*] *om*. D$^{*.c}$ **Col 3:13** ***κυριος*** 𝔓^{46} A B D*] Χριστος ℵ^{2} C D^{1} 1739. 1881 *Byz* ¦ θεος ℵ* ¦ θεος εν Χριστω 33

Col 1:3–10

In our prayers for you we always thank God, the Father of our Lord Jesus Christ, 4 for we have heard of your faith in Christ Jesus and of the love that you have for all the saints, 5 because of the hope laid up for you in heaven. You have heard of this hope before in the word of the truth, the gospel 6 that has come to you. Just as it is bearing fruit and growing in the whole world, so it has been bearing fruit among yourselves from the day you heard it and truly comprehended the grace of God. 7 This you learned from Epaphras, our beloved fellow servant. He is a faithful minister of Christ on your[b] behalf, 8 and he has made known to us your love in the Spirit. 9 For this reason, since the day we heard it, we have not ceased praying for you and asking that you may be filled with the knowledge of God's will in all spiritual wisdom and understanding, 10 so that you may lead lives worthy of the Lord, fully pleasing to him, as you bear fruit in every good work and as you grow in the knowledge of God.

Cf. Rom 15:28; Gal 6:7–8; Phil 1:22; 4:17; Titus 3:14.

125. *Humble Servanthood*

Rom 12:3

For by the grace given to me I say to everyone among you not to think of yourself more highly than you ought to think, but to think with sober judgment, each according to the measure of faith that God has assigned.

Rom 12:16

Live in harmony with one another; do not be haughty, but associate with the lowly; do not claim to be wiser than you are.

1 Cor 13:4–5

Love is patient; love is kind; love is not envious or boastful or arrogant 5 or rude. It does not insist on its own way; it is not irritable or resentful

Gal 5:13–15

For you were called to freedom, brothers and sisters; only do not use your freedom as an opportunity for self-indulgence, but through love become slaves to one another. 14 For the whole law is summed up in a single commandment, "You shall love your neighbor as yourself." 15 If, however, you bite and devour one another, take care that you are not consumed by one another.

Gal 5:25–6:5

If we live by the Spirit, let us also be guided by the Spirit. 26 Let us not become conceited, competing against one another, envying one another. **6** My friends, if anyone is detected in a transgression, you who have received the Spirit should restore such a one in a spirit of gentleness. Take care that you yourselves are not tempted. 2 Bear one another's burdens, and in this way you will fulfill[a] the law of Christ. 3 For if those who are nothing think they are something, they deceive themselves. 4 All must test their own work; then that work, rather than their neighbor's work, will become a cause for pride. 5 For all must carry their own loads.

Eph 4:1–3

I therefore, the prisoner in the Lord, beg you to lead a life worthy of the calling to which you have been called, 2 with all humility and gentleness, with patience, bearing with one another in love, 3 making every effort to maintain the unity of the Spirit in the bond of peace.

Phil 2:1–4

If then there is any encouragement in Christ, any consolation from love, any sharing in the Spirit, any compassion and sympathy, 2 make my joy complete: be of the same mind, having the same love, being in full accord and of one mind. 3 Do nothing from selfish ambition or conceit, but in humility regard others as better than yourselves. 4 Let each of you look not to your own interests, but to the interests[b] of others.

Col 3:12–13

As God's chosen ones, holy and beloved, clothe yourselves with compassion, kindness, humility, meekness, and patience. 13 Bear with one another and, if anyone has a complaint against another, forgive each other; just as the Lord[c] has forgiven you, so you also must forgive.

1 Tim 6:17–19

As for those who in the present age are rich, command them not to be haughty, or to set their hopes on the uncertainty of riches, but rather on God who richly provides us with everything for our enjoyment. 18 They are to do good, to be rich in good works, generous, and ready to share, 19 thus storing up for themselves the treasure of a good foundation for the future, so that they may take hold of the life that really is life.

2 Tim 2:24–26

And the Lord's servant must not be quarrelsome but kindly to everyone, an apt teacher, patient, 25 correcting opponents with gentleness. God may perhaps grant that they will repent and come to know the truth, 26 and that they may escape from the snare of the devil, having been held captive by him to do his will.

Titus 3:1–2

Remind them to be subject to rulers and authorities, to be obedient, to be ready for every good work, 2 to speak evil of no one, to avoid quarreling, to be gentle, and to show every courtesy to everyone.

Cf. Rom 11:20–21; 12:10–11; 15:1–2; 1 Cor 9:19–23; 10:33–11:1; 2 Cor 4:5; 10:1–2; 11:7; Gal 5:22–23; Eph 5:21; Col 3:12; 1 Tim 6:11; Acts 20:18–19.

See also § 161 Gentleness toward All.

[b] **Col 1:7** ***your*** Other ancient authorities read *our* **§ 125** [a] **Gal 6:2** ***in this way you will fulfill*** Other ancient authorities read *in this way fulfill* [b] **Phil 2:4** ***to the interests*** Most ancient authorities read *also to the interests* [c] **Col 3:13** ***just as the Lord*** Other ancient authorities read *just as Christ*

126. Exhortation to Wakefulness

Rom 13:11–14

Καὶ τοῦτο εἰδότες τὸν καιρόν, ὅτι ὥρα ἤδη ὑμᾶς ἐξ ὕπνου ἐγερθῆναι, νῦν γὰρ ἐγγύτερον ἡμῶν ἡ σωτηρία ἢ ὅτε ἐπιστεύσαμεν. **12** ἡ νὺξ προέκοψεν, ἡ δὲ ἡμέρα ἤγγικεν. ἀποθώμεθα οὖν τὰ ἔργα τοῦ σκότους, ἐνδυσώμεθα [δὲ] τὰ ὅπλα τοῦ φωτός. **13** ὡς ἐν ἡμέρᾳ εὐσχημόνως περιπατήσωμεν, μὴ κώμοις καὶ μέθαις, μὴ κοίταις καὶ ἀσελγείαις, μὴ ἔριδι καὶ ζήλῳ, **14** ἀλλὰ ἐνδύσασθε τὸν κύριον Ἰησοῦν Χριστὸν καὶ τῆς σαρκὸς πρόνοιαν μὴ ποιεῖσθε εἰς ἐπιθυμίας.

Eph 5:8–14

ἦτε γάρ ποτε σκότος, νῦν δὲ φῶς ἐν κυρίῳ· ὡς τέκνα φωτὸς περιπατεῖτε **9**—ὁ γὰρ καρπὸς τοῦ φωτὸς ἐν πάσῃ ἀγαθωσύνῃ καὶ δικαιοσύνῃ καὶ ἀληθείᾳ— **10** δοκιμάζοντες τί ἐστιν εὐάρεστον τῷ κυρίῳ, **11** καὶ μὴ συγκοινωνεῖτε τοῖς ἔργοις τοῖς ἀκάρποις τοῦ σκότους, μᾶλλον δὲ καὶ ἐλέγχετε. **12** τὰ γὰρ κρυφῇ γινόμενα ὑπ᾽ αὐτῶν αἰσχρόν ἐστιν καὶ λέγειν, **13** τὰ δὲ πάντα ἐλεγχόμενα ὑπὸ τοῦ φωτὸς φανεροῦται, **14** πᾶν γὰρ τὸ φανερούμενον φῶς ἐστιν. διὸ λέγει· ἔγειρε, ὁ καθεύδων, καὶ ἀνάστα ἐκ τῶν νεκρῶν, καὶ ἐπιφαύσει σοι ὁ Χριστός.

1 Thess 5:1–11

Περὶ δὲ τῶν χρόνων καὶ τῶν καιρῶν, ἀδελφοί, οὐ χρείαν ἔχετε ὑμῖν γράφεσθαι, **2** αὐτοὶ γὰρ ἀκριβῶς οἴδατε ὅτι ἡμέρα κυρίου ὡς κλέπτης ἐν νυκτὶ οὕτως ἔρχεται. **3** ὅταν λέγωσιν· εἰρήνη καὶ ἀσφάλεια, τότε αἰφνίδιος αὐτοῖς ἐφίσταται ὄλεθρος ὥσπερ ἡ ὠδὶν τῇ ἐν γαστρὶ ἐχούσῃ, καὶ οὐ μὴ ἐκφύγωσιν. **4** ὑμεῖς δέ, ἀδελφοί, οὐκ ἐστὲ ἐν σκότει, ἵνα ἡ ἡμέρα ὑμᾶς ὡς κλέπτης καταλάβῃ· **5** πάντες γὰρ ὑμεῖς υἱοὶ φωτός ἐστε καὶ υἱοὶ ἡμέρας. Οὐκ ἐσμὲν νυκτὸς οὐδὲ σκότους· **6** ἄρα οὖν μὴ καθεύδωμεν ὡς οἱ λοιποὶ ἀλλὰ γρηγορῶμεν καὶ νήφωμεν. **7** Οἱ γὰρ καθεύδοντες νυκτὸς καθεύδουσιν καὶ οἱ μεθυσκόμενοι νυκτὸς μεθύουσιν· **8** ἡμεῖς δὲ ἡμέρας ὄντες νήφωμεν ἐνδυσάμενοι θώρακα πίστεως καὶ ἀγάπης καὶ περικεφαλαίαν ἐλπίδα σωτηρίας· **9** ὅτι οὐκ ἔθετο ἡμᾶς ὁ θεὸς εἰς ὀργὴν ἀλλὰ εἰς περιποίησιν σωτηρίας διὰ τοῦ κυρίου ἡμῶν Ἰησοῦ Χριστοῦ **10** τοῦ ἀποθανόντος ὑπὲρ ἡμῶν, ἵνα εἴτε γρηγορῶμεν εἴτε καθεύδωμεν ἅμα σὺν αὐτῷ ζήσωμεν. **11** Διὸ παρακαλεῖτε ἀλλήλους καὶ οἰκοδομεῖτε εἷς τὸν ἕνα, καθὼς καὶ ποιεῖτε.

Cf. 1 Cor 7:29–31; 16:13–14; Eph 6:10–20.

127. Sexual Immorality

Rom 1:24–27

Διὸ παρέδωκεν αὐτοὺς ὁ θεὸς ἐν ταῖς ἐπιθυμίαις τῶν καρδιῶν αὐτῶν εἰς ἀκαθαρσίαν τοῦ ἀτιμάζεσθαι τὰ σώματα αὐτῶν ἐν αὐτοῖς· **25** οἵτινες μετήλλαξαν τὴν ἀλήθειαν τοῦ θεοῦ ἐν τῷ ψεύδει καὶ ἐσεβάσθησαν καὶ ἐλάτρευσαν τῇ κτίσει παρὰ τὸν κτίσαντα, ὅς ἐστιν εὐλογητὸς εἰς τοὺς αἰῶνας, ἀμήν. **26** Διὰ τοῦτο παρέδωκεν αὐτοὺς ὁ θεὸς εἰς πάθη ἀτιμίας, αἵ τε γὰρ θήλειαι αὐτῶν μετήλλαξαν τὴν φυσικὴν χρῆσιν εἰς τὴν παρὰ φύσιν, **27** ὁμοίως τε καὶ οἱ ἄρσενες ἀφέντες τὴν φυσικὴν χρῆσιν τῆς θηλείας ἐξεκαύθησαν ἐν τῇ ὀρέξει αὐτῶν εἰς ἀλλήλους, ἄρσενες ἐν ἄρσεσιν τὴν ἀσχημοσύνην κατεργαζόμενοι καὶ τὴν ἀντιμισθίαν ἣν ἔδει τῆς πλάνης αὐτῶν ἐν ἑαυτοῖς ἀπολαμβάνοντες.

1 Cor 5:1–13

Ὅλως ἀκούεται ἐν ὑμῖν πορνεία, καὶ τοιαύτη πορνεία ἥτις οὐδὲ ἐν τοῖς ἔθνεσιν, ὥστε γυναῖκά τινα τοῦ πατρὸς ἔχειν. **2** καὶ ὑμεῖς πεφυσιωμένοι ἐστὲ καὶ οὐχὶ μᾶλλον ἐπενθήσατε, ἵνα ἀρθῇ ἐκ μέσου ὑμῶν ὁ τὸ ἔργον τοῦτο πράξας; **3** ἐγὼ μὲν γάρ, ἀπὼν τῷ σώματι παρὼν δὲ τῷ πνεύματι, ἤδη κέκρικα ὡς παρὼν τὸν οὕτως τοῦτο κατεργασάμενον· **4** ἐν τῷ ὀνόματι τοῦ κυρίου [ἡμῶν] Ἰησοῦ συναχθέντων ὑμῶν καὶ τοῦ ἐμοῦ πνεύματος σὺν τῇ δυνάμει τοῦ κυρίου ἡμῶν Ἰησοῦ, **5** παραδοῦναι τὸν τοιοῦτον τῷ σατανᾷ εἰς ὄλεθρον τῆς σαρκός, ἵνα τὸ πνεῦμα σωθῇ ἐν τῇ ἡμέρᾳ τοῦ ⸀κυρίου. **6** Οὐ καλὸν τὸ καύχημα ὑμῶν. οὐκ οἴδατε ὅτι μικρὰ ζύμη ὅλον τὸ φύραμα ζυμοῖ; **7** ἐκκαθάρατε τὴν παλαιὰν ζύμην, ἵνα ἦτε νέον φύραμα, καθώς ἐστε ἄζυμοι· καὶ γὰρ τὸ πάσχα ἡμῶν ἐτύθη Χριστός. **8** ὥστε ἑορτάζωμεν μὴ ἐν ζύμῃ παλαιᾷ μηδὲ ἐν ζύμῃ κακίας καὶ πονηρίας ἀλλ᾽ ἐν ἀζύμοις εἰλικρινείας καὶ ἀληθείας. **9** Ἔγραψα ὑμῖν ἐν τῇ ἐπιστολῇ μὴ συναναμίγνυσθαι πόρνοις, **10** οὐ πάντως τοῖς πόρνοις τοῦ κόσμου τούτου ἢ τοῖς πλεονέκταις καὶ ἅρπαξιν ἢ εἰδωλολάτραις, ἐπεὶ ὠφείλετε ἄρα ἐκ τοῦ κόσμου ἐξελθεῖν. **11** νῦν δὲ ἔγραψα ὑμῖν μὴ συναναμίγνυσθαι ἐάν τις ἀδελφὸς ὀνομαζόμενος ᾖ πόρνος ἢ πλεονέκτης ἢ εἰδωλολάτρης ἢ λοίδορος ἢ μέθυσος ἢ ἅρπαξ, τῷ τοιούτῳ μηδὲ συνεσθίειν. **12** τί γάρ μοι τοὺς ἔξω κρίνειν; οὐχὶ τοὺς ἔσω ὑμεῖς κρίνετε; **13** τοὺς δὲ ἔξω ὁ θεὸς κρινεῖ. ἐξάρατε τὸν πονηρὸν ἐξ ὑμῶν αὐτῶν.

1 Cor 6:12–20

Πάντα μοι ἔξεστιν ἀλλ᾽ οὐ πάντα συμφέρει· πάντα μοι ἔξεστιν ἀλλ᾽ οὐκ ἐγὼ ἐξουσιασθήσομαι ὑπό τινος. **13** τὰ βρώματα τῇ κοιλίᾳ καὶ ἡ κοιλία τοῖς βρώμασιν, ὁ δὲ θεὸς καὶ ταύτην καὶ ταῦτα καταργήσει. τὸ δὲ σῶμα οὐ τῇ πορνείᾳ ἀλλὰ τῷ κυρίῳ, καὶ ὁ κύριος τῷ σώματι· **14** ὁ δὲ θεὸς καὶ τὸν κύριον ἤγειρεν καὶ ἡμᾶς ἐξεγερεῖ διὰ τῆς δυνάμεως αὐτοῦ. **15** οὐκ οἴδατε ὅτι τὰ σώματα ὑμῶν μέλη Χριστοῦ ἐστιν; ἄρας οὖν τὰ μέλη τοῦ Χριστοῦ ποιήσω πόρνης μέλη; μὴ γένοιτο. **16** [ἢ] οὐκ οἴδατε ὅτι ὁ κολλώμενος τῇ πόρνῃ ἓν σῶμά ἐστιν; ἔσονται γάρ, φησίν, οἱ δύο εἰς σάρκα μίαν. **17** ὁ δὲ κολλώμενος τῷ

§ 127 1 Cor 5:5 ***κυριου*** 𝔓[46] B 1739] *add.* Ιησου 𝔓[61vid] ℵ *Byz* ¦ *add.* Ιησου Χριστου D ¦ *add.* ημων Ιησου Χριστου A 33. 1881

126. Exhortation to Wakefulness

Rom 13:11–14

Besides this, you know what time it is, how it is now the moment for you to wake from sleep. For salvation is nearer to us now than when we became believers; **12** the night is far gone, the day is near. Let us then lay aside the works of darkness and put on the armor of light; **13** let us walk[a] honorably as in the day, not in reveling and drunkenness, not in debauchery and licentiousness, not in quarreling and jealousy. **14** Instead, put on the Lord Jesus Christ, and make no provision for the flesh, to gratify its desires.

Eph 5:8–14

For once you were darkness, but now in the Lord you are light. Live as children of light— **9** for the fruit of the light is found in all that is good and right and true. **10** Try to find out what is pleasing to the Lord. **11** Take no part in the unfruitful works of darkness, but instead expose them. **12** For it is shameful even to mention what such people do secretly; **13** but everything exposed by the light becomes visible, **14** for everything that becomes visible is light. Therefore it says, "Sleeper, awake! Rise from the dead, and Christ will shine on you."

1 Thess 5:1–11

Now concerning the times and the seasons, brothers and sisters, you do not need to have anything written to you. **2** For you yourselves know very well that the day of the Lord will come like a thief in the night. **3** When they say, "There is peace and security," then sudden destruction will come upon them, as labor pains come upon a pregnant woman, and there will be no escape! **4** But you, beloved, are not in darkness, for that day to surprise you like a thief; **5** for you are all children of light and children of the day; we are not of the night or of darkness. **6** So then let us not fall asleep as others do, but let us keep awake and be sober; **7** for those who sleep sleep at night, and those who are drunk get drunk at night. **8** But since we belong to the day, let us be sober, and put on the breastplate of faith and love, and for a helmet the hope of salvation. **9** For God has destined us not for wrath but for obtaining salvation through our Lord Jesus Christ, **10** who died for us, so that whether we are awake or asleep we may live with him. **11** Therefore encourage one another and build up each other, as indeed you are doing.

Cf. 1 Cor 7:29–31; 16:13–14; Eph 6:10–20.

127. Sexual Immorality

Rom 1:24–27

Therefore God gave them up in the lusts of their hearts to impurity, to the degrading of their bodies among themselves, **25** because they exchanged the truth about God for a lie and worshiped and served the creature rather than the Creator, who is blessed forever! Amen. **26** For this reason God gave them up to degrading passions. Their women exchanged natural intercourse for unnatural, **27** and in the same way also the men, giving up natural intercourse with women, were consumed with passion for one another. Men committed shameless acts with men and received in their own persons the due penalty for their error.

1 Cor 5:1–13

It is actually reported that there is sexual immorality among you, and of a kind that is not found even among pagans; for a man is living with his father's wife. **2** And you are arrogant! Should you not rather have mourned, so that he who has done this would have been removed from among you? **3** For though absent in body, I am present in spirit; and as if present I have already pronounced judgment **4** in the name of the Lord Jesus on the man who has done such a thing. When you are assembled, and my spirit is present with the power of our Lord Jesus, **5** you are to hand this man over to Satan for the destruction of the flesh, so that his spirit may be saved in the day of the Lord.[a] **6** Your boasting is not a good thing. Do you not know that a little yeast leavens the whole batch of dough? **7** Clean out the old yeast so that you may be a new batch, as you really are unleavened. For our paschal lamb, Christ, has been sacrificed. **8** Therefore, let us celebrate the festival, not with the old yeast, the yeast of malice and evil, but with the unleavened bread of sincerity and truth. **9** I wrote to you in my letter not to associate with sexually immoral persons— **10** not at all meaning the immoral of this world, or the greedy and robbers, or idolaters, since you would then need to go out of the world. **11** But now I am writing to you not to associate with anyone who bears the name of brother or sister who is sexually immoral or greedy, or is an idolater, reviler, drunkard, or robber. Do not even eat with such a one. **12** For what have I to do with judging those outside? Is it not those who are inside that you are to judge? **13** God will judge those outside. "Drive out the wicked person from among you."

1 Cor 6:12–20

"All things are lawful for me," but not all things are beneficial. "All things are lawful for me," but I will not be dominated by anything. **13** "Food is meant for the stomach and the stomach for food," and God will destroy both one and the other. The body is meant not for fornication but for the Lord, and the Lord for the body. **14** And God raised the Lord and will also raise us by his power. **15** Do you not know that your bodies are members of Christ? Should I therefore take the members of Christ and make them members of a prostitute? Never! **16** Do you not know that whoever is united to a prostitute becomes one body with her? For it is said, "The two shall be one flesh." **17** But anyone

§ 126 [a] **Rom 13:13** *walk* NRSV translates *live* **§ 127** [a] **1 Cor 5:5** *the Lord* Other ancient authorities add *Jesus*

κυρίῳ ἓν πνεῦμά ἐστιν. **18** Φεύγετε τὴν πορνείαν. πᾶν ἁμάρτημα ὃ ἐὰν ποιήσῃ ἄνθρωπος ἐκτὸς τοῦ σώματός ἐστιν· ὁ δὲ πορνεύων εἰς τὸ ἴδιον σῶμα ἁμαρτάνει. **19** ἢ οὐκ οἴδατε ὅτι τὸ σῶμα ὑμῶν ναὸς τοῦ ἐν ὑμῖν ἁγίου πνεύματός ἐστιν οὗ ἔχετε ἀπὸ θεοῦ, καὶ οὐκ ἐστὲ ἑαυτῶν; **20** ἠγοράσθητε γὰρ τιμῆς· δοξάσατε δὴ τὸν θεὸν ἐν τῷ σώματι ὑμῶν.

Eph 5:3–7

Πορνεία δὲ καὶ ἀκαθαρσία πᾶσα ἢ πλεονεξία μηδὲ ὀνομαζέσθω ἐν ὑμῖν, καθὼς πρέπει ἁγίοις, **4** καὶ αἰσχρότης καὶ μωρολογία ἢ εὐτραπελία, ἃ οὐκ ἀνῆκεν, ἀλλὰ μᾶλλον εὐχαριστία. **5** τοῦτο γὰρ ἴστε γινώσκοντες, ὅτι πᾶς πόρνος ἢ ἀκάθαρτος ἢ πλεονέκτης, ὅ ἐστιν εἰδωλολάτρης, οὐκ ἔχει κληρονομίαν ἐν τῇ βασιλείᾳ τοῦ Χριστοῦ καὶ θεοῦ. **6** Μηδεὶς ὑμᾶς ἀπατάτω κενοῖς λόγοις· διὰ ταῦτα γὰρ ἔρχεται ἡ ὀργὴ τοῦ θεοῦ ἐπὶ τοὺς υἱοὺς τῆς ἀπειθείας. **7** μὴ οὖν γίνεσθε συμμέτοχοι αὐτῶν

Col 3:5–7

Νεκρώσατε οὖν τὰ μέλη τὰ ἐπὶ τῆς γῆς, πορνείαν ἀκαθαρσίαν πάθος ἐπιθυμίαν κακήν, καὶ τὴν πλεονεξίαν, ἥτις ἐστὶν εἰδωλολατρία, **6** δι᾽ ἃ ἔρχεται ἡ ὀργὴ τοῦ θεοῦ ⸀[ἐπὶ τοὺς υἱοὺς τῆς ἀπειθείας]⸃. **7** ἐν οἷς καὶ ὑμεῖς περιεπατήσατέ ποτε, ὅτε ἐζῆτε ἐν τούτοις

1 Thess 4:1–8

Λοιπὸν οὖν, ἀδελφοί, ἐρωτῶμεν ὑμᾶς καὶ παρακαλοῦμεν ἐν κυρίῳ Ἰησοῦ, ἵνα καθὼς παρελάβετε παρ᾽ ἡμῶν τὸ πῶς δεῖ ὑμᾶς περιπατεῖν καὶ ἀρέσκειν θεῷ, καθὼς καὶ περιπατεῖτε, ἵνα περισσεύητε μᾶλλον. **2** οἴδατε γὰρ τίνας παραγγελίας ἐδώκαμεν ὑμῖν διὰ τοῦ κυρίου Ἰησοῦ. **3** Τοῦτο γάρ ἐστιν θέλημα τοῦ θεοῦ, ὁ ἁγιασμὸς ὑμῶν, ἀπέχεσθαι ὑμᾶς ἀπὸ τῆς πορνείας, **4** εἰδέναι ἕκαστον ὑμῶν τὸ ἑαυτοῦ σκεῦος κτᾶσθαι ἐν ἁγιασμῷ καὶ τιμῇ, **5** μὴ ἐν πάθει ἐπιθυμίας καθάπερ καὶ τὰ ἔθνη τὰ μὴ εἰδότα τὸν θεόν, **6** τὸ μὴ ὑπερβαίνειν καὶ πλεονεκτεῖν ἐν τῷ πράγματι τὸν ἀδελφὸν αὐτοῦ, διότι ἔκδικος κύριος περὶ πάντων τούτων, καθὼς καὶ προείπαμεν ὑμῖν καὶ διεμαρτυράμεθα. **7** οὐ γὰρ ἐκάλεσεν ἡμᾶς ὁ θεὸς ἐπὶ ἀκαθαρσίᾳ ἀλλ᾽ ἐν ἁγιασμῷ. **8** τοιγαροῦν ὁ ἀθετῶν οὐκ ἄνθρωπον ἀθετεῖ ἀλλὰ τὸν θεὸν τὸν [καὶ] διδόντα τὸ πνεῦμα αὐτοῦ τὸ ἅγιον εἰς ὑμᾶς.

Cf. Rom 6:19; 13:11–14; 1 Cor 6:9–11; 7:2–5; 10:8; 2 Cor 12:20–21; Gal 5:19–21; Eph 4:17–19; 1 Thess 2:3–4; 1 Tim 1:8–11.

128. Wives and Husbands

1 Cor 7:2–5

διὰ δὲ τὰς πορνείας ἕκαστος τὴν ἑαυτοῦ γυναῖκα ἐχέτω καὶ ἑκάστη τὸν ἴδιον ἄνδρα ἐχέτω. **3** τῇ γυναικὶ ὁ ἀνὴρ τὴν ὀφειλὴν ἀποδιδότω, ὁμοίως δὲ καὶ ἡ γυνὴ τῷ ἀνδρί. **4** ἡ γυνὴ τοῦ ἰδίου σώματος οὐκ ἐξουσιάζει ἀλλὰ ὁ ἀνήρ, ὁμοίως δὲ καὶ ὁ ἀνὴρ τοῦ ἰδίου σώματος οὐκ ἐξουσιάζει ἀλλὰ ἡ γυνή. **5** μὴ ἀποστερεῖτε ἀλλήλους, εἰ μήτι ἂν ἐκ συμφώνου πρὸς καιρόν, ἵνα σχολάσητε τῇ προσευχῇ καὶ πάλιν ἐπὶ τὸ αὐτὸ ἦτε, ἵνα μὴ πειράζῃ ὑμᾶς ὁ σατανᾶς διὰ τὴν ἀκρασίαν ὑμῶν.

1 Cor 7:10–16

Τοῖς δὲ γεγαμηκόσιν παραγγέλλω, οὐκ ἐγὼ ἀλλὰ ὁ κύριος, γυναῖκα ἀπὸ ἀνδρὸς μὴ χωρισθῆναι, **11** —ἐὰν δὲ καὶ χωρισθῇ, μενέτω ἄγαμος ἢ τῷ ἀνδρὶ καταλλαγήτω, —καὶ ἄνδρα γυναῖκα μὴ ἀφιέναι. **12** Τοῖς δὲ λοιποῖς λέγω ἐγὼ οὐχ ὁ κύριος· εἴ τις ἀδελφὸς γυναῖκα ἔχει ἄπιστον καὶ αὕτη συνευδοκεῖ οἰκεῖν μετ᾽ αὐτοῦ, μὴ ἀφιέτω αὐτήν· **13** καὶ γυνὴ ⸀εἴ τις⸃ ἔχει ἄνδρα ἄπιστον καὶ οὗτος συνευδοκεῖ οἰκεῖν μετ᾽ αὐτῆς, μὴ ἀφιέτω τὸν ἄνδρα. **14** ἡγίασται γὰρ ὁ ἀνὴρ ὁ ἄπιστος ἐν τῇ γυναικὶ καὶ ἡγίασται ἡ γυνὴ ἡ ἄπιστος ἐν τῷ ἀδελφῷ· ἐπεὶ ἄρα τὰ τέκνα ὑμῶν ἀκάθαρτά ἐστιν, νῦν δὲ ἅγιά ἐστιν. **15** εἰ δὲ ὁ ἄπιστος χωρίζεται, χωριζέσθω· οὐ δεδούλωται ὁ ἀδελφὸς ἢ ἡ ἀδελφὴ ἐν τοῖς τοιούτοις· ἐν δὲ εἰρήνῃ κέκληκεν ⸀ὑμᾶς ὁ θεός. **16** τί γὰρ οἶδας, γύναι, εἰ τὸν ἄνδρα σώσεις; ἢ τί οἶδας, ἄνερ, εἰ τὴν γυναῖκα σώσεις;

1 Cor 7:39–40

Γυνὴ δέδεται ἐφ᾽ ὅσον χρόνον ζῇ ὁ ἀνὴρ αὐτῆς· ἐὰν δὲ κοιμηθῇ ὁ ἀνήρ, ἐλευθέρα ἐστὶν ᾧ θέλει γαμηθῆναι, μόνον ἐν κυρίῳ. **40** μακαριωτέρα δέ ἐστιν ἐὰν οὕτως μείνῃ, κατὰ τὴν ἐμὴν γνώμην· δοκῶ δὲ κἀγὼ πνεῦμα θεοῦ ἔχειν.

Eph 5:22–33

αἱ γυναῖκες τοῖς ἰδίοις ⸀ἀνδράσιν ὡς τῷ κυρίῳ, **23** ὅτι ἀνήρ ἐστιν κεφαλὴ τῆς γυναικὸς ὡς καὶ ὁ Χριστὸς κεφαλὴ τῆς ἐκκλησίας, αὐτὸς σωτὴρ τοῦ σώματος· **24** ἀλλὰ ὡς ἡ ἐκκλησία ὑποτάσσεται τῷ Χριστῷ, οὕτως καὶ αἱ γυναῖκες τοῖς ἀνδράσιν ἐν παντί. **25** Οἱ ἄνδρες, ἀγαπᾶτε τὰς γυναῖκας, καθὼς καὶ ὁ Χριστὸς ἠγάπησεν τὴν ἐκκλησίαν καὶ ἑαυτὸν παρέδωκεν ὑπὲρ αὐτῆς, **26** ἵνα αὐτὴν ἁγιάσῃ καθαρίσας τῷ λουτρῷ τοῦ ὕδατος ἐν ῥήματι, **27** ἵνα παραστήσῃ αὐτὸς ἑαυτῷ ἔνδοξον τὴν ἐκκλησίαν, μὴ ἔχουσαν σπίλον ἢ ῥυτίδα ἤ τι τῶν τοιούτων, ἀλλ᾽ ἵνα ᾖ ἁγία καὶ ἄμωμος. **28** οὕτως ὀφείλουσιν [καὶ] οἱ ἄνδρες ἀγαπᾶν τὰς ἑαυτῶν γυναῖκας ὡς τὰ ἑαυτῶν σώματα. ὁ ἀγαπῶν τὴν ἑαυτοῦ γυναῖκα ἑαυτὸν ἀγαπᾷ. **29** Οὐδεὶς γάρ ποτε τὴν ἑαυτοῦ σάρκα ἐμίσησεν ἀλλὰ ἐκτρέφει καὶ θάλπει αὐτήν, καθὼς καὶ ὁ Χριστὸς τὴν ἐκκλησίαν, **30** ὅτι μέλη ἐσμὲν τοῦ σώματος ⸀αὐτοῦ. **31** ἀντὶ τούτου καταλείψει ἄνθρωπος [τὸν] πατέρα καὶ [τὴν] μητέρα καὶ προσκολληθήσεται πρὸς τὴν γυναῖκα αὐτοῦ, καὶ ἔσονται οἱ δύο εἰς σάρκα μίαν. **32** τὸ μυστήριον τοῦτο μέγα ἐστίν· ἐγὼ δὲ λέγω εἰς Χριστὸν καὶ εἰς τὴν ἐκκλησίαν. **33** πλὴν καὶ ὑμεῖς οἱ

Col 3:6 ***επι τους υιους της απειθειας*** ℵ A C D I 33. 1739. 1881 *Byz*] *om.* 𝔓[46] B **§ 128** **1 Cor 7:13** ***ει τις*** 𝔓[46] ℵ D*] ητις A B D[2] 33. 1739. 1881 *Byz* **1 Cor 7:15** ***υμας*** ℵ* A C] ημας 𝔓[46] ℵ[2] B D 33. 1739. 1881 *Byz* **Eph 5:22** ***ανδρασιν*** 𝔓[46] B] *add.* υποτασσεσθωσαν ℵ A I 33. 1739. 1881 ¦ *add.* υποτασσεσθε (D) *Byz* **Eph 5:30** ***αυτου*** 𝔓[46] ℵ* A B 048. 33. 1739*. 1881] *add.* εκ της σαρκος αυτου και εκ των οστεων αυτου ℵ[2] D 1739[mg] *Byz*

united to the Lord becomes one spirit with him. **18** Shun fornication! Every sin that a person commits is outside the body; but the fornicator sins against the body itself. **19** Or do you not know that your body is a temple of the Holy Spirit within you, which you have from God, and that you are not your own? **20** For you were bought with a price; therefore glorify God in your body.

Eph 5:3–7

But fornication and impurity of any kind, or greed, must not even be mentioned among you, as is proper among saints. **4** Entirely out of place is obscene, silly, and vulgar talk; but instead, let there be thanksgiving. **5** Be sure of this, that no fornicator or impure person, or one who is greedy (that is, an idolater), has any inheritance in the kingdom of Christ and of God. **6** Let no one deceive you with empty words, for because of these things the wrath of God comes on those who are disobedient. **7** Therefore do not be associated with them.

Col 3:5–7

Put to death, therefore, whatever in you is earthly: fornication, impurity, passion, evil desire, and greed (which is idolatry). **6** On account of these the wrath of God is coming on those who are disobedient.[b] **7** These are the ways you also once followed, when you were living that life.

1 Thess 4:1–8

Finally, brothers and sisters, we ask and urge you in the Lord Jesus that, as you learned from us how you ought to live and to please God (as, in fact, you are doing), you should do so more and more. **2** For you know what instructions we gave you through the Lord Jesus. **3** For this is the will of God, your sanctification: that you abstain from fornication; **4** that each one of you know how to control your own body in holiness and honor, **5** not with lustful passion, like the Gentiles who do not know God; **6** that no one wrong or exploit a brother or sister in this matter, because the Lord is an avenger in all these things, just as we have already told you beforehand and solemnly warned you. **7** For God did not call us to impurity but in holiness. **8** Therefore whoever rejects this rejects not human authority but God, who also gives his Holy Spirit to you.

Cf. Rom 6:19; 13:11–14; 1 Cor 6:9–11; 7:2–5; 10:8; 2 Cor 12:20–21; Gal 5:19–21; Eph 4:17–19; 1 Thess 2:3–4; 1 Tim 1:8–11.

128. Wives and Husbands

1 Cor 7:2–5

But because of cases of sexual immorality, each man should have his own wife and each woman her own husband. **3** The husband should give to his wife her conjugal rights, and likewise the wife to her husband. **4** For the wife does not have authority over her own body, but the husband does; likewise the husband does not have authority over his own body, but the wife does. **5** Do not deprive one another except perhaps by agreement for a set time, to devote yourselves to prayer, and then come together again, so that Satan may not tempt you because of your lack of self-control.

1 Cor 7:10–16

To the married I give this command—not I but the Lord—that the wife should not separate from her husband **11** (but if she does separate, let her remain unmarried or else be reconciled to her husband), and that the husband should not divorce his wife. **12** To the rest I say—I and not the Lord—that if any believer has a wife who is an unbeliever, and she consents to live with him, he should not divorce her. **13** And if any woman[a] has a husband who is an unbeliever, and he consents to live with her, she should not divorce him. **14** For the unbelieving husband is made holy through his wife, and the unbelieving wife is made holy through her husband. Otherwise, your children would be unclean, but as it is, they are holy. **15** But if the unbelieving partner separates, let it be so; in such a case the brother or sister is not bound. It is to peace that God has called you.[b] **16** Wife, for all you know, you might save your husband. Husband, for all you know, you might save your wife.

1 Cor 7:39–40

A wife is bound as long as her husband lives. But if the husband dies, she is free to marry anyone she wishes, only in the Lord. **40** But in my judgment she is more blessed if she remains as she is. And I think that I too have the Spirit of God.

Eph 5:22–33

Wives, be subject[c] to your husbands as you are to the Lord. **23** For the husband is the head of the wife just as Christ is the head of the church, the body of which he is the Savior. **24** Just as the church is subject to Christ, so also wives ought to be, in everything, to their husbands. **25** Husbands, love your wives, just as Christ loved the church and gave himself up for her, **26** in order to make her holy by cleansing her with the washing of water by the word, **27** so as to present the church to himself in splendor, without a spot or wrinkle or anything of the kind—yes, so that she may be holy and without blemish. **28** In the same way, husbands should love their wives as they do their own bodies. He who loves his wife loves himself. **29** For no one ever hates his own body, but he nourishes and tenderly cares for it, just as Christ does for the church, **30** because we are members of his body.[d] **31** "For this reason a man will leave his father and mother and be joined to his wife, and the two will become one flesh." **32** This is a great mystery, and I am applying it to Christ and the church. **33** Each of you, however, should love

[b] **Col 3:6** *on those who are disobedient* Other ancient authorities lack *on those who are disobedient* **§ 128** [a] **1 Cor 7:13** *if any woman* Other ancient authorities read *a woman who* [b] **1 Cor 7:15** *you* Other ancient authorities read *us* [c] **Eph 5:22** *Wives, be subject* Other ancient authorities read *Wives should be subject* [d] **Eph 5:30** *of his body* Other ancient authorities add *of his flesh and of his bones*

καθ᾽ ἕνα, ἕκαστος τὴν ἑαυτοῦ γυναῖκα
οὕτως ἀγαπάτω ὡς ἑαυτόν, ἡ δὲ γυνὴ
ἵνα φοβῆται τὸν ἄνδρα.

Col 3:18–19

Αἱ γυναῖκες, ὑποτάσσεσθε τοῖς ἀνδράσιν
ὡς ἀνῆκεν ἐν κυρίῳ. 19 Οἱ ἄνδρες, ἀγα-
πᾶτε τὰς γυναῖκας καὶ μὴ πικραίνεσθε
πρὸς αὐτάς.

Titus 2:2–5

Πρεσβύτας νηφαλίους εἶναι, σεμνούς,
σώφρονας, ὑγιαίνοντας τῇ πίστει, τῇ
ἀγάπῃ, τῇ ὑπομονῇ· 3 πρεσβύτιδας ὡσαύ-
τως ἐν καταστήματι ἱεροπρεπεῖς, μὴ δι-
αβόλους μὴ οἴνῳ πολλῷ δεδουλωμένας,
καλοδιδασκάλους, 4 ἵνα σωφρονίζωσιν
τὰς νέας φιλάνδρους εἶναι, φιλοτέκνους
5 σώφρονας ἁγνὰς οἰκουργοὺς ἀγαθάς,
ὑποτασσομένας τοῖς ἰδίοις ἀνδράσιν, ἵνα
μὴ ὁ λόγος τοῦ θεοῦ βλασφημῆται.

Cf. Rom 7:1–3; 1 Cor 7:27; 14:35; 1 Tim 3:8–13; 5:14.

129. The Unmarried and Widows

1 Cor 7:1–9

Περὶ δὲ ὧν ἐγράψατε, καλὸν ἀνθρώπῳ
γυναικὸς μὴ ἅπτεσθαι· 2 διὰ δὲ τὰς πορ-
νείας ἕκαστος τὴν ἑαυτοῦ γυναῖκα ἐχέτω
καὶ ἑκάστη τὸν ἴδιον ἄνδρα ἐχέτω. 3 τῇ
γυναικὶ ὁ ἀνὴρ τὴν ὀφειλὴν ἀποδιδότω,
ὁμοίως δὲ καὶ ἡ γυνὴ τῷ ἀνδρί. 4 ἡ γυνὴ
τοῦ ἰδίου σώματος οὐκ ἐξουσιάζει ἀλλὰ
ὁ ἀνήρ, ὁμοίως δὲ καὶ ὁ ἀνὴρ τοῦ ἰδίου
σώματος οὐκ ἐξουσιάζει ἀλλὰ ἡ γυνή.
5 μὴ ἀποστερεῖτε ἀλλήλους, εἰ μήτι ἂν ἐκ
συμφώνου πρὸς καιρόν, ἵνα σχολάσητε
τῇ προσευχῇ καὶ πάλιν ἐπὶ τὸ αὐτὸ ἦτε,
ἵνα μὴ πειράζῃ ὑμᾶς ὁ σατανᾶς διὰ τὴν
ἀκρασίαν ὑμῶν. 6 τοῦτο δὲ λέγω κατὰ
συγγνώμην οὐ κατ᾽ ἐπιταγήν. 7 θέλω δὲ
πάντας ἀνθρώπους εἶναι ὡς καὶ ἐμαυ-
τόν· ἀλλὰ ἕκαστος ἴδιον ἔχει χάρισμα ἐκ
θεοῦ, ὁ μὲν οὕτως, ὁ δὲ οὕτως. 8 Λέγω
δὲ τοῖς ἀγάμοις καὶ ταῖς χήραις, καλὸν
αὐτοῖς ἐὰν μείνωσιν ὡς κἀγώ· 9 εἰ δὲ οὐκ
ἐγκρατεύονται, γαμησάτωσαν, κρεῖττον
γάρ ἐστιν γαμῆσαι ἢ πυροῦσθαι.

1 Cor 7:25–40

Περὶ δὲ τῶν παρθένων ἐπιταγὴν κυρίου
οὐκ ἔχω, γνώμην δὲ δίδωμι ὡς ἠλεημένος
ὑπὸ κυρίου πιστὸς εἶναι. 26 Νομίζω οὖν
τοῦτο καλὸν ὑπάρχειν διὰ τὴν ἐνεστῶσαν
ἀνάγκην, ὅτι καλὸν ἀνθρώπῳ τὸ οὕτως
εἶναι. 27 δέδεσαι γυναικί, μὴ ζήτει λύσιν·
λέλυσαι ἀπὸ γυναικός, μὴ ζήτει γυναῖκα.
28 ἐὰν δὲ καὶ γαμήσῃς, οὐχ ἥμαρτες, καὶ
ἐὰν γήμῃ ἡ παρθένος, οὐχ ἥμαρτεν·
θλῖψιν δὲ τῇ σαρκὶ ἕξουσιν οἱ τοιοῦτοι,
ἐγὼ δὲ ὑμῶν φείδομαι. 29 Τοῦτο δέ φημι,
ἀδελφοί, ὁ καιρὸς συνεσταλμένος ἐστίν·
τὸ λοιπόν, ἵνα καὶ οἱ ἔχοντες γυναῖκας
ὡς μὴ ἔχοντες ὦσιν 30 καὶ οἱ κλαίοντες
ὡς μὴ κλαίοντες καὶ οἱ χαίροντες ὡς
μὴ χαίροντες καὶ οἱ ἀγοράζοντες ὡς μὴ
κατέχοντες, 31 καὶ οἱ χρώμενοι τὸν κό-
σμον ὡς μὴ καταχρώμενοι· παράγει γὰρ
τὸ σχῆμα τοῦ κόσμου τούτου. 32 Θέλω
δὲ ὑμᾶς ἀμερίμνους εἶναι. ὁ ἄγαμος
μεριμνᾷ τὰ τοῦ κυρίου, πῶς ἀρέσῃ τῷ
κυρίῳ· 33 ὁ δὲ γαμήσας μεριμνᾷ τὰ τοῦ
κόσμου, πῶς ἀρέσῃ τῇ γυναικί, 34 καὶ
μεμέρισται. καὶ ἡ γυνὴ ἡ ἄγαμος καὶ ἡ
παρθένος μεριμνᾷ τὰ τοῦ κυρίου, ἵνα ᾖ
ἁγία καὶ τῷ σώματι καὶ τῷ πνεύματι· ἡ
δὲ γαμήσασα μεριμνᾷ τὰ τοῦ κόσμου,
πῶς ἀρέσῃ τῷ ἀνδρί. 35 τοῦτο δὲ πρὸς
τὸ ὑμῶν αὐτῶν σύμφορον λέγω, οὐχ
ἵνα βρόχον ὑμῖν ἐπιβάλω ἀλλὰ πρὸς
τὸ εὔσχημον καὶ εὐπάρεδρον τῷ κυρίῳ
ἀπερισπάστως. 36 Εἰ δέ τις ἀσχημονεῖν
ἐπὶ τὴν παρθένον αὐτοῦ νομίζει, ἐὰν ᾖ
ὑπέρακμος καὶ οὕτως ὀφείλει γίνεσθαι,
ὃ θέλει ποιείτω, οὐχ ἁμαρτάνει, γαμεί-
τωσαν. 37 ὃς δὲ ἕστηκεν ἐν τῇ καρδίᾳ
αὐτοῦ ἑδραῖος μὴ ἔχων ἀνάγκην, ἐξου-
σίαν δὲ ἔχει περὶ τοῦ ἰδίου θελήματος
καὶ τοῦτο κέκρικεν ἐν τῇ ἰδίᾳ καρδίᾳ,
τηρεῖν τὴν ἑαυτοῦ παρθένον, καλῶς ποι-
ήσει. 38 ὥστε καὶ ὁ γαμίζων τὴν ἑαυτοῦ
παρθένον καλῶς ποιεῖ καὶ ὁ μὴ γαμίζων
κρεῖσσον ποιήσει. 39 Γυνὴ δέδεται ἐφ᾽
ὅσον χρόνον ζῇ ὁ ἀνὴρ αὐτῆς· ἐὰν δὲ
κοιμηθῇ ὁ ἀνήρ, ἐλευθέρα ἐστὶν ᾧ θέλει
γαμηθῆναι, μόνον ἐν κυρίῳ. 40 μακαρι-
ωτέρα δέ ἐστιν ἐὰν οὕτως μείνῃ, κατὰ
τὴν ἐμὴν γνώμην· δοκῶ δὲ κἀγὼ πνεῦμα
θεοῦ ἔχειν.

1 Tim 4:1–5

Τὸ δὲ πνεῦμα ῥητῶς λέγει ὅτι ἐν ὑστέροις
καιροῖς ἀποστήσονταί τινες τῆς πίστεως
προσέχοντες πνεύμασιν πλάνοις καὶ
διδασκαλίαις δαιμονίων, 2 ἐν ὑποκρίσει
ψευδολόγων, κεκαυστηριασμένων τὴν
ἰδίαν συνείδησιν, 3 κωλυόντων γαμεῖν,
ἀπέχεσθαι βρωμάτων, ἃ ὁ θεὸς ἔκτισεν
εἰς μετάλημψιν μετὰ εὐχαριστίας τοῖς
πιστοῖς καὶ ἐπεγνωκόσι τὴν ἀλήθειαν.
4 ὅτι πᾶν κτίσμα θεοῦ καλὸν καὶ οὐδὲν
ἀπόβλητον μετὰ εὐχαριστίας λαμβα-
νόμενον· 5 ἁγιάζεται γὰρ διὰ λόγου θεοῦ
καὶ ἐντεύξεως.

1 Tim 5:3–16

Χήρας τίμα τὰς ὄντως χήρας. 4 εἰ δέ τις
χήρα τέκνα ἢ ἔκγονα ἔχει, μανθανέτω-
σαν πρῶτον τὸν ἴδιον οἶκον εὐσεβεῖν
καὶ ἀμοιβὰς ἀποδιδόναι τοῖς προγόνοις·
τοῦτο γάρ ἐστιν ἀπόδεκτον ἐνώπιον τοῦ
θεοῦ. 5 ἡ δὲ ὄντως χήρα καὶ μεμονωμένη
ἤλπικεν ἐπὶ ⸀θεὸν καὶ προσμένει ταῖς
δεήσεσιν καὶ ταῖς προσευχαῖς νυκτὸς
καὶ ἡμέρας, 6 ἡ δὲ σπαταλῶσα ζῶσα τέ-
θνηκεν. 7 καὶ ταῦτα παράγγελλε, ἵνα
ἀνεπίλημπτοι ὦσιν. 8 εἰ δέ τις τῶν ἰδίων
καὶ μάλιστα οἰκείων οὐ προνοεῖ, τὴν πί-
στιν ἤρνηται καὶ ἔστιν ἀπίστου χείρων.
9 Χήρα καταλεγέσθω μὴ ἔλαττον ἐτῶν
ἑξήκοντα γεγονυῖα, ἑνὸς ἀνδρὸς γυνή,
10 ἐν ἔργοις καλοῖς μαρτυρουμένη, εἰ ἐτε-
κνοτρόφησεν, εἰ ἐξενοδόχησεν, εἰ ἁγίων
πόδας ἔνιψεν, εἰ θλιβομένοις ἐπήρκεσεν,
εἰ παντὶ ἔργῳ ἀγαθῷ ἐπηκολούθησεν.
11 νεωτέρας δὲ χήρας παραιτοῦ· ὅταν

§ 129 1 Tim 5:5 *θεον* C 048] τον θεον ℵ^2 A D^2 1739. 1881 *Byz* ¦ κυριον ℵ* ¦ τον κυριον D*

his wife as himself, and a wife should respect her husband.

Col 3:18–19

Wives, be subject to your husbands, as is fitting in the Lord. 19 Husbands, love your wives and never treat them harshly.

Titus 2:2–5

Tell the older men to be temperate, serious, prudent, and sound in faith, in love, and in endurance. 3 Likewise, tell the older women to be reverent in behavior, not to be slanderers or slaves to drink; they are to teach what is good, 4 so that they may encourage the young women to love their husbands, to love their children, 5 to be self-controlled, chaste, good managers of the household, kind, being submissive to their husbands, so that the word of God may not be discredited.

Cf. Rom 7:1–3; 1 Cor 7:27; 14:35; 1 Tim 3:8–13; 5:14.

129. The Unmarried and Widows

1 Cor 7:1–9

Now concerning the matters about which you wrote: "It is well for a man not to touch a woman." 2 But because of cases of sexual immorality, each man should have his own wife and each woman her own husband. 3 The husband should give to his wife her conjugal rights, and likewise the wife to her husband. 4 For the wife does not have authority over her own body, but the husband does; likewise the husband does not have authority over his own body, but the wife does. 5 Do not deprive one another except perhaps by agreement for a set time, to devote yourselves to prayer, and then come together again, so that Satan may not tempt you because of your lack of self-control. 6 This I say by way of concession, not of command. 7 I wish that all were as I myself am. But each has a particular gift from God, one having one kind and another a different kind. 8 To the unmarried and the widows I say that it is well for them to remain unmarried as I am. 9 But if they are not practicing self-control, they should marry. For it is better to marry than to be aflame with passion.

1 Cor 7:25–40

Now concerning virgins, I have no command of the Lord, but I give my opinion as one who by the Lord's mercy is trustworthy. 26 I think that, in view of the impending crisis, it is well for you to remain as you are. 27 Are you bound to a wife? Do not seek to be free. Are you free from a wife? Do not seek a wife. 28 But if you marry, you do not sin, and if a virgin marries, she does not sin. Yet those who marry will experience distress in this life, and I would spare you that. 29 I mean, brothers and sisters, the appointed time has grown short; from now on, let even those who have wives be as though they had none, 30 and those who mourn as though they were not mourning, and those who rejoice as though they were not rejoicing, and those who buy as though they had no possessions, 31 and those who deal with the world as though they had no dealings with it. For the present form of this world is passing away. 32 I want you to be free from anxieties. The unmarried man is anxious about the affairs of the Lord, how to please the Lord; 33 but the married man is anxious about the affairs of the world, how to please his wife, 34 and his interests are divided. And the unmarried woman and the virgin are anxious about the affairs of the Lord, so that they may be holy in body and spirit; but the married woman is anxious about the affairs of the world, how to please her husband. 35 I say this for your own benefit, not to put any restraint upon you, but to promote good order and unhindered devotion to the Lord. 36 If anyone thinks that he is not behaving properly toward his fiancée, if his passions are strong, and so it has to be, let him marry as he wishes; it is no sin. Let them marry. 37 But if someone stands firm in his resolve, being under no necessity but having his own desire under control, and has determined in his own mind to keep her as his fiancée, he will do well. 38 So then, he who marries his fiancée does well; and he who refrains from marriage will do better. 39 A wife is bound as long as her husband lives. But if the husband dies, she is free to marry anyone she wishes, only in the Lord. 40 But in my judgment she is more blessed if she remains as she is. And I think that I too have the Spirit of God.

1 Tim 4:1–5

Now the Spirit expressly says that in later times some will renounce the faith by paying attention to deceitful spirits and teachings of demons, 2 through the hypocrisy of liars whose consciences are seared with a hot iron. 3 They forbid marriage and demand abstinence from foods, which God created to be received with thanksgiving by those who believe and know the truth. 4 For everything created by God is good, and nothing is to be rejected, provided it is received with thanksgiving; 5 for it is sanctified by God's word and by prayer.

1 Tim 5:3–16

Honor widows who are really widows. 4 If a widow has children or grandchildren, they should first learn their religious duty to their own family and make some repayment to their parents; for this is pleasing in God's sight. 5 The real widow, left alone, has set her hope on God[a] and continues in supplications and prayers night and day; 6 but the widow who lives for pleasure is dead even while she lives. 7 Give these commands as well, so that they may be above reproach. 8 And whoever does not provide for relatives, and especially for family members, has denied the faith and is worse than an unbeliever. 9 Let a widow be put on the list if she is not less than sixty years old and has been married only once; 10 she must be well attested for her good works, as one who has brought up children, shown hospitality, washed the saints' feet, helped the afflicted, and devoted herself to doing good in every way. 11 But refuse to put

§ 129 [a] **1 Tim 5:5** *God* Other ancient authorities read *the Lord*

γὰρ καταστρηνιάσωσιν τοῦ Χριστοῦ, γαμεῖν θέλουσιν **12** ἔχουσαι κρίμα ὅτι τὴν πρώτην πίστιν ἠθέτησαν· **13** ἅμα δὲ καὶ ἀργαὶ μανθάνουσιν περιερχόμεναι τὰς οἰκίας, οὐ μόνον δὲ ἀργαὶ ἀλλὰ καὶ φλύαροι καὶ περίεργοι, λαλοῦσαι τὰ μὴ δέοντα. **14** Βούλομαι οὖν νεωτέρας γαμεῖν, τεκνογονεῖν, οἰκοδεσποτεῖν, μηδεμίαν ἀφορμὴν διδόναι τῷ ἀντικειμένῳ λοιδορίας χάριν· **15** ἤδη γάρ τινες ἐξετράπησαν ὀπίσω τοῦ σατανᾶ. **16** εἴ τις ⸀πιστὴ ἔχει χήρας, ἐπαρκείτω αὐταῖς καὶ μὴ βαρείσθω ἡ ἐκκλησία, ἵνα ταῖς ὄντως χήραις ἐπαρκέσῃ.

Acts 21:8–9

τῇ δὲ ἐπαύριον ἐξελθόντες ἤλθομεν εἰς Καισάρειαν καὶ εἰσελθόντες εἰς τὸν οἶκον Φιλίππου τοῦ εὐαγγελιστοῦ, ὄντος ἐκ τῶν ἑπτά, ἐμείναμεν παρ' αὐτῷ. **9** τούτῳ δὲ ἦσαν θυγατέρες τέσσαρες παρθένοι προφητεύουσαι.

130. Children and Parents

Eph 6:1–4

Τὰ τέκνα, ὑπακούετε τοῖς γονεῦσιν ὑμῶν ⸀[ἐν κυρίῳ]⸁· τοῦτο γάρ ἐστιν δίκαιον. **2** τίμα τὸν πατέρα σου καὶ τὴν μητέρα, ἥτις ἐστὶν ἐντολὴ πρώτη ἐν ἐπαγγελίᾳ, **3** ἵνα εὖ σοι γένηται καὶ ἔσῃ μακροχρόνιος ἐπὶ τῆς γῆς. **4** Καὶ οἱ πατέρες, μὴ παροργίζετε τὰ τέκνα ὑμῶν ἀλλὰ ἐκτρέφετε αὐτὰ ἐν παιδείᾳ καὶ νουθεσίᾳ κυρίου.

Col 3:20–21

Τὰ τέκνα, ὑπακούετε τοῖς γονεῦσιν κατὰ πάντα, τοῦτο γὰρ εὐάρεστόν ἐστιν ἐν κυρίῳ. **21** Οἱ πατέρες, μὴ ἐρεθίζετε τὰ τέκνα ὑμῶν, ἵνα μὴ ἀθυμῶσιν.

Cf. 1 Cor 7:14; 1 Tim 3:2–5; 3:12; 5:14; 2 Tim 3:14–15; Titus 2:3–5.

131. Slaves and Masters

1 Cor 7:21–24

δοῦλος ἐκλήθης, μή σοι μελέτω· ἀλλ' εἰ καὶ δύνασαι ἐλεύθερος γενέσθαι, μᾶλλον χρῆσαι. **22** ὁ γὰρ ἐν κυρίῳ κληθεὶς δοῦλος ἀπελεύθερος κυρίου ἐστίν, ὁμοίως ὁ ἐλεύθερος κληθεὶς δοῦλός ἐστιν Χριστοῦ. **23** τιμῆς ἠγοράσθητε· μὴ γίνεσθε δοῦλοι ἀνθρώπων. **24** ἕκαστος ἐν ᾧ ἐκλήθη, ἀδελφοί, ἐν τούτῳ μενέτω παρὰ θεῷ.

1 Cor 12:13

καὶ γὰρ ἐν ἑνὶ πνεύματι ἡμεῖς πάντες εἰς ἓν σῶμα ἐβαπτίσθημεν, εἴτε Ἰουδαῖοι εἴτε Ἕλληνες εἴτε δοῦλοι εἴτε ἐλεύθεροι, καὶ πάντες ἓν πνεῦμα ἐποτίσθημεν.

Gal 3:26–29

Πάντες γὰρ υἱοὶ θεοῦ ἐστε διὰ τῆς πίστεως ἐν Χριστῷ Ἰησοῦ· **27** ὅσοι γὰρ εἰς Χριστὸν ἐβαπτίσθητε, Χριστὸν ἐνεδύσασθε. **28** οὐκ ἔνι Ἰουδαῖος οὐδὲ Ἕλλην, οὐκ ἔνι δοῦλος οὐδὲ ἐλεύθερος, οὐκ ἔνι ἄρσεν καὶ θῆλυ· πάντες γὰρ ὑμεῖς εἷς ἐστε ἐν Χριστῷ Ἰησοῦ. **29** εἰ δὲ ὑμεῖς Χριστοῦ, ἄρα τοῦ Ἀβραὰμ σπέρμα ἐστέ, κατ' ἐπαγγελίαν κληρονόμοι.

Eph 6:5–9

Οἱ δοῦλοι, ὑπακούετε τοῖς κατὰ σάρκα κυρίοις μετὰ φόβου καὶ τρόμου ἐν ἁπλότητι τῆς καρδίας ὑμῶν ὡς τῷ Χριστῷ, **6** μὴ κατ' ὀφθαλμοδουλίαν ὡς ἀνθρωπάρεσκοι ἀλλ' ὡς δοῦλοι Χριστοῦ ποιοῦντες τὸ θέλημα τοῦ θεοῦ ἐκ ψυχῆς, **7** μετ' εὐνοίας δουλεύοντες ὡς τῷ κυρίῳ καὶ οὐκ ἀνθρώποις, **8** εἰδότες ὅτι ἕκαστος ἐάν τι ποιήσῃ ἀγαθόν, τοῦτο κομίσεται παρὰ κυρίου εἴτε δοῦλος εἴτε ἐλεύθερος. **9** Καὶ οἱ κύριοι, τὰ αὐτὰ ποιεῖτε πρὸς αὐτούς, ἀνιέντες τὴν ἀπειλήν, εἰδότες ὅτι καὶ αὐτῶν καὶ ὑμῶν ὁ κύριός ἐστιν ἐν οὐρανοῖς καὶ προσωπολημψία οὐκ ἔστιν παρ' αὐτῷ.

Col 3:10–11

καὶ ἐνδυσάμενοι τὸν νέον τὸν ἀνακαινούμενον εἰς ἐπίγνωσιν κατ' εἰκόνα τοῦ κτίσαντος αὐτόν, **11** ὅπου οὐκ ἔνι Ἕλλην καὶ Ἰουδαῖος, περιτομὴ καὶ ἀκροβυστία, βάρβαρος, Σκύθης, δοῦλος, ἐλεύθερος, ἀλλὰ [τὰ] πάντα καὶ ἐν πᾶσιν Χριστός.

Col 3:22–4:1

Οἱ δοῦλοι, ὑπακούετε κατὰ πάντα τοῖς κατὰ σάρκα κυρίοις, μὴ ἐν ὀφθαλμοδουλίᾳ ὡς ἀνθρωπάρεσκοι, ἀλλ' ἐν ἁπλότητι καρδίας φοβούμενοι τὸν κύριον. **23** ὃ ἐὰν ποιῆτε, ἐκ ψυχῆς ἐργάζεσθε ὡς τῷ κυρίῳ καὶ οὐκ ἀνθρώποις, **24** εἰδότες ὅτι ἀπὸ κυρίου ἀπολήμψεσθε τὴν ἀνταπόδοσιν τῆς κληρονομίας. τῷ κυρίῳ Χριστῷ δουλεύετε· **25** ὁ γὰρ ἀδικῶν κομίσεται ὃ ἠδίκησεν, καὶ οὐκ ἔστιν προσωπολημψία. **4** Οἱ κύριοι, τὸ δίκαιον καὶ τὴν ἰσότητα τοῖς δούλοις παρέχεσθε, εἰδότες ὅτι καὶ ὑμεῖς ἔχετε κύριον ἐν οὐρανῷ.

1 Tim 1:8–11

Οἴδαμεν δὲ ὅτι καλὸς ὁ νόμος, ἐάν τις αὐτῷ νομίμως χρῆται, **9** εἰδὼς τοῦτο, ὅτι δικαίῳ νόμος οὐ κεῖται, ἀνόμοις δὲ καὶ ἀνυποτάκτοις, ἀσεβέσι καὶ ἁμαρτωλοῖς, ἀνοσίοις καὶ βεβήλοις, πατρολῴαις καὶ μητρολῴαις, ἀνδροφόνοις **10** πόρνοις ἀρσενοκοίταις ἀνδραποδισταῖς ψεύσταις ἐπιόρκοις, καὶ εἴ τι ἕτερον τῇ ὑγιαινούσῃ διδασκαλίᾳ ἀντίκειται **11** κατὰ τὸ εὐαγ

1 Tim 5:16 ***πιστη*** ℵ A C 048. 33. 1739. 1881] πιστος ἢ πιστη D *Byz* **§ 130** **Eph 6:1** ***εν κυριω*** $\mathfrak{P}^{46}$ ℵ A D¹ I^{vid} 33. 1739. 1881 *Byz*] *om.* B D*

younger widows on the list; for when their sensual desires alienate them from Christ, they want to marry, 12 and so they incur condemnation for having violated their first pledge. 13 Besides that, they learn to be idle, gadding about from house to house; and they are not merely idle, but also gossips and busybodies, saying what they should not say. 14 So I would have younger widows marry, bear children, and manage their households, so as to give the adversary no occasion to revile us. 15 For some have already turned away to follow Satan. 16 If any believing woman[b] has relatives who are really widows, let her assist them; let the church not be burdened, so that it can assist those who are real widows.

Acts 21:8–9

The next day we left and came to Caesarea; and we went into the house of Philip the evangelist, one of the seven, and stayed with him. 9 He had four unmarried daughters who had the gift of prophecy.

130. Children and Parents

Eph 6:1–4

Children, obey your parents in the Lord,[a] for this is right. 2 "Honor your father and mother"—this is the first commandment with a promise: 3 "so that it may be well with you and you may live long on the earth." 4 And, fathers, do not provoke your children to anger, but bring them up in the discipline and instruction of the Lord.

Col 3:20–21

Children, obey your parents in everything, for this is your acceptable duty in the Lord. 21 Fathers, do not provoke your children, or they may lose heart.

Cf. 1 Cor 7:14; 1 Tim 3:2–5; 3:12; 5:14; 2 Tim 3:14–15; Titus 2:3–5.

131. Slaves and Masters

1 Cor 7:21–24

Were you a slave when called? Do not be concerned about it. Even if you can gain your freedom, make use of your present condition now more than ever. 22 For whoever was called in the Lord as a slave is a freed person belonging to the Lord, just as whoever was free when called is a slave of Christ. 23 You were bought with a price; do not become slaves of human masters. 24 In whatever condition you were called, brothers and sisters, there remain with God.

1 Cor 12:13

For in the one Spirit we were all baptized into one body—Jews or Greeks, slaves or free—and we were all made to drink of one Spirit.

Gal 3:26–29

for in Christ Jesus you are all children of God through faith. 27 As many of you as were baptized into Christ have clothed yourselves with Christ. 28 There is no longer Jew or Greek, there is no longer slave or free, there is no longer male and female; for all of you are one in Christ Jesus. 29 And if you belong to Christ, then you are Abraham's offspring, heirs according to the promise.

Eph 6:5–9

Slaves, obey your earthly masters with fear and trembling, in singleness of heart, as you obey Christ; 6 not only while being watched, and in order to please them, but as slaves of Christ, doing the will of God from the heart. 7 Render service with enthusiasm, as to the Lord and not to men and women, 8 knowing that whatever good we do, we will receive the same again from the Lord, whether we are slaves or free. 9 And, masters, do the same to them. Stop threatening them, for you know that both of you have the same Master in heaven, and with him there is no partiality.

Col 3:10–11

and have clothed yourselves with the new humanity,[a] which is being renewed in knowledge according to the image of its creator. 11 In that renewal there is no longer Greek and Jew, circumcised and uncircumcised, barbarian, Scythian, slave and free; but Christ is all and in all!

Col 3:22–4:1

Slaves, obey your earthly masters in everything, not only while being watched and in order to please them, but wholeheartedly, fearing the Lord. 23 Whatever your task, put yourselves into it, as done for the Lord and not for your masters, 24 since you know that from the Lord you will receive the inheritance as your reward; you serve the Lord Christ. 25 For the wrongdoer will be paid back for whatever wrong has been done, and there is no partiality. **4** Masters, treat your slaves justly and fairly, for you know that you also have a Master in heaven.

1 Tim 1:8–11

Now we know that the law is good, if one uses it legitimately. 9 This means understanding that the law is laid down not for the innocent but for the lawless and disobedient, for the godless and sinful, for the unholy and profane, for those who kill their father or mother, for murderers, 10 fornicators, sodomites, slave traders, liars, perjurers, and whatever else is contrary to the sound teaching 11 that conforms to

[b] 1 Tim 5:16 *believing woman* Other ancient authorities read *believing man or woman* § 130 [a] Eph 6:1 *in the Lord* Other ancient authorities lack *in the Lord* § 131 [a] Col 3:10 *humanity* NRSV translates *self*

γέλιον τῆς δόξης τοῦ μακαρίου θεοῦ, ὃ ἐπιστεύθην ἐγώ.

1 Tim 6:1–2

Ὅσοι εἰσὶν ὑπὸ ζυγὸν δοῦλοι, τοὺς ἰδίους δεσπότας πάσης τιμῆς ἀξίους ἡγείσθωσαν, ἵνα μὴ τὸ ὄνομα τοῦ θεοῦ καὶ ἡ διδασκαλία βλασφημῆται. **2** οἱ δὲ πιστοὺς ἔχοντες δεσπότας μὴ καταφρονείτωσαν, ὅτι ἀδελφοί εἰσιν, ἀλλὰ μᾶλλον δουλευέτωσαν, ὅτι πιστοί εἰσιν καὶ ἀγαπητοὶ οἱ τῆς εὐεργεσίας ἀντιλαμβανόμενοι. Ταῦτα δίδασκε καὶ παρακάλει.

Titus 2:9–10

Δούλους ἰδίοις δεσπόταις ὑποτάσσεσθαι ἐν πᾶσιν, εὐαρέστους εἶναι, μὴ ἀντιλέγοντας, **10** μὴ νοσφιζομένους, ἀλλὰ πᾶσαν πίστιν ἐνδεικνυμένους ἀγαθήν, ἵνα τὴν διδασκαλίαν τὴν τοῦ σωτῆρος ἡμῶν θεοῦ κοσμῶσιν ἐν πᾶσιν.

Phlm 8–22

Διὸ πολλὴν ἐν Χριστῷ παρρησίαν ἔχων ἐπιτάσσειν σοι τὸ ἀνῆκον **9** διὰ τὴν ἀγάπην μᾶλλον παρακαλῶ, τοιοῦτος ὢν ὡς Παῦλος ⸀πρεσβύτης νυνὶ δὲ καὶ δέσμιος Χριστοῦ Ἰησοῦ· **10** παρακαλῶ σε περὶ τοῦ ἐμοῦ τέκνου, ὃν ἐγέννησα ἐν τοῖς δεσμοῖς, Ὀνήσιμον, **11** τόν ποτέ σοι ἄχρηστον νυνὶ δὲ [καὶ] σοὶ καὶ ἐμοὶ εὔχρηστον, **12** ὃν ἀνέπεμψά σοι, αὐτόν, τοῦτ᾽ ἔστιν τὰ ἐμὰ σπλάγχνα· **13** ὃν ἐγὼ ἐβουλόμην πρὸς ἐμαυτὸν κατέχειν, ἵνα ὑπὲρ σοῦ μοι διακονῇ ἐν τοῖς δεσμοῖς τοῦ εὐαγγελίου, **14** χωρὶς δὲ τῆς σῆς γνώμης οὐδὲν ἠθέλησα ποιῆσαι, ἵνα μὴ ὡς κατὰ ἀνάγκην τὸ ἀγαθόν σου ᾖ ἀλλὰ κατὰ ἑκούσιον. **15** Τάχα γὰρ διὰ τοῦτο ἐχωρίσθη πρὸς ὥραν, ἵνα αἰώνιον αὐτὸν ἀπέχῃς, **16** οὐκέτι ὡς δοῦλον ἀλλ᾽ ὑπὲρ δοῦλον, ἀδελφὸν ἀγαπητόν, μάλιστα ἐμοί, πόσῳ δὲ μᾶλλον σοὶ καὶ ἐν σαρκὶ καὶ ἐν κυρίῳ. **17** εἰ οὖν με ἔχεις κοινωνόν, προσλαβοῦ αὐτὸν ὡς ἐμέ. **18** εἰ δέ τι ἠδίκησέν σε ἢ ὀφείλει, τοῦτο ἐμοὶ ἐλλόγα. **19** ἐγὼ Παῦλος ἔγραψα τῇ ἐμῇ χειρί, ἐγὼ ἀποτίσω· ἵνα μὴ λέγω σοι ὅτι καὶ σεαυτόν μοι προσοφείλεις. **20** ναὶ ἀδελφέ, ἐγώ σου ὀναίμην ἐν κυρίῳ· ἀνάπαυσόν μου τὰ σπλάγχνα ἐν Χριστῷ. **21** Πεποιθὼς τῇ ὑπακοῇ σου ἔγραψά σοι, εἰδὼς ὅτι καὶ ὑπὲρ ἃ λέγω ποιήσεις. **22** ἅμα δὲ καὶ ἑτοίμαζέ μοι ξενίαν· ἐλπίζω γὰρ ὅτι διὰ τῶν προσευχῶν ὑμῶν χαρισθήσομαι ὑμῖν.

132. Purity Laws and Sabbath Keeping

Rom 14:1–12

Τὸν δὲ ἀσθενοῦντα τῇ πίστει προσλαμβάνεσθε, μὴ εἰς διακρίσεις διαλογισμῶν. **2** ὃς μὲν πιστεύει φαγεῖν πάντα, ὁ δὲ ἀσθενῶν λάχανα ἐσθίει. **3** ὁ ἐσθίων τὸν μὴ ἐσθίοντα μὴ ἐξουθενείτω, ὁ δὲ μὴ ἐσθίων τὸν ἐσθίοντα μὴ κρινέτω, ὁ θεὸς γὰρ αὐτὸν προσελάβετο. **4** σὺ τίς εἶ ὁ κρίνων ἀλλότριον οἰκέτην; τῷ ἰδίῳ κυρίῳ στήκει ἢ πίπτει· σταθήσεται δέ, δυνατεῖ γὰρ ὁ ⸀κύριος στῆσαι αὐτόν. **5** Ὃς μὲν [γὰρ] κρίνει ἡμέραν παρ᾽ ἡμέραν, ὃς δὲ κρίνει πᾶσαν ἡμέραν· ἕκαστος ἐν τῷ ἰδίῳ νοῒ πληροφορείσθω. **6** ὁ φρονῶν τὴν ἡμέραν κυρίῳ φρονεῖ· καὶ ὁ ἐσθίων κυρίῳ ἐσθίει, εὐχαριστεῖ γὰρ τῷ θεῷ· καὶ ὁ μὴ ἐσθίων κυρίῳ οὐκ ἐσθίει καὶ εὐχαριστεῖ τῷ θεῷ. **7** οὐδεὶς γὰρ ἡμῶν ἑαυτῷ ζῇ καὶ οὐδεὶς ἑαυτῷ ἀποθνῄσκει· **8** ἐάν τε γὰρ ζῶμεν, τῷ κυρίῳ ζῶμεν, ἐάν τε ἀποθνῄσκωμεν, τῷ κυρίῳ ἀποθνῄσκομεν. ἐάν τε οὖν ζῶμεν ἐάν τε ἀποθνῄσκωμεν, τοῦ κυρίου ἐσμέν. **9** εἰς τοῦτο γὰρ Χριστὸς ἀπέθανεν καὶ ἔζησεν, ἵνα καὶ νεκρῶν καὶ ζώντων κυριεύσῃ. **10** Σὺ δὲ τί κρίνεις τὸν ἀδελφόν σου; ἢ καὶ σὺ τί ἐξουθενεῖς τὸν ἀδελφόν σου; πάντες γὰρ παραστησόμεθα τῷ βήματι τοῦ ⸀θεοῦ, **11** γέγραπται γάρ· ζῶ ἐγώ, λέγει κύριος, ὅτι ἐμοὶ κάμψει πᾶν γόνυ καὶ πᾶσα γλῶσσα ἐξομολογήσεται τῷ θεῷ. **12** ἄρα [οὖν] ἕκαστος ἡμῶν περὶ ἑαυτοῦ λόγον δώσει [τῷ θεῷ].

Gal 2:11–14

Ὅτε δὲ ἦλθεν Κηφᾶς εἰς Ἀντιόχειαν, κατὰ πρόσωπον αὐτῷ ἀντέστην, ὅτι κατεγνωσμένος ἦν. **12** πρὸ τοῦ γὰρ ἐλθεῖν τινας ἀπὸ Ἰακώβου μετὰ τῶν ἐθνῶν συνήσθιεν· ὅτε δὲ ἦλθον, ὑπέστελλεν καὶ ἀφώριζεν ἑαυτὸν φοβούμενος τοὺς ἐκ περιτομῆς. **13** καὶ συνυπεκρίθησαν αὐτῷ [καὶ] οἱ λοιποὶ Ἰουδαῖοι, ὥστε καὶ Βαρναβᾶς συναπήχθη αὐτῶν τῇ ὑποκρίσει. **14** ἀλλ᾽ ὅτε εἶδον ὅτι οὐκ ὀρθοποδοῦσιν πρὸς τὴν ἀλήθειαν τοῦ εὐαγγελίου, εἶπον τῷ Κηφᾷ ἔμπροσθεν πάντων· εἰ σὺ Ἰουδαῖος ὑπάρχων ἐθνικῶς καὶ οὐχὶ Ἰουδαϊκῶς ζῇς, πῶς τὰ ἔθνη ἀναγκάζεις ἰουδαΐζειν;

Gal 4:8–11

Ἀλλὰ τότε μὲν οὐκ εἰδότες θεὸν ἐδουλεύσατε τοῖς φύσει μὴ οὖσιν θεοῖς· **9** νῦν δὲ γνόντες θεόν, μᾶλλον δὲ γνωσθέντες ὑπὸ θεοῦ, πῶς ἐπιστρέφετε πάλιν ἐπὶ τὰ ἀσθενῆ καὶ πτωχὰ στοιχεῖα οἷς πάλιν ἄνωθεν δουλεύειν θέλετε; **10** ἡμέρας παρατηρεῖσθε καὶ μῆνας καὶ καιροὺς καὶ ἐνιαυτούς, **11** φοβοῦμαι ὑμᾶς μή πως εἰκῇ κεκοπίακα εἰς ὑμᾶς.

Col 2:16–23

Μὴ οὖν τις ὑμᾶς κρινέτω ἐν βρώσει καὶ ἐν πόσει ἢ ἐν μέρει ἑορτῆς ἢ νεομηνίας ἢ σαββάτων· **17** ἅ ἐστιν σκιὰ τῶν μελλόντων, τὸ δὲ σῶμα τοῦ Χριστοῦ. **18** μηδεὶς ὑμᾶς καταβραβευέτω θέλων ἐν ταπεινοφροσύνῃ καὶ θρησκείᾳ τῶν ἀγγέλων, ⸀ἃ ἑόρακεν ἐμβατεύων, εἰκῇ φυσιούμενος ὑπὸ τοῦ νοὸς τῆς σαρκὸς

§ 131 **Phlm 9** ***πρεσβυτης*** *omnes*] πρεσβευτης *cj* **§ 132** **Rom 14:4** ***κυριος*** 𝔓46 ℵ A B C] θεος D 048. 33. 1739. 1881 *Byz* **Rom 14:10** ***θεου*** ℵ* A B C* D 1739] Χριστου ℵc C2 048. 33. 1881 *Byz* **Col 2:18** ***ἃ*** 𝔓46 ℵ* A B D* I 33. 1739] ἃ μη ℵ2 C D1 1881 *Byz*

the glorious gospel of the blessed God, which he entrusted to me.

1 Tim 6:1–2

Let all who are under the yoke of slavery regard their masters as worthy of all honor, so that the name of God and the teaching may not be blasphemed. **2** Those who have believing masters must not be disrespectful to them on the ground that they are members of the church; rather they must serve them all the more, since those who benefit by their service are believers and beloved. Teach and urge these duties.

Titus 2:9–10

Tell slaves to be submissive to their masters and to give satisfaction in every respect; they are not to talk back, **10** not to pilfer, but to show complete and perfect fidelity, so that in everything they may be an ornament to the doctrine of God our Savior.

Phlm 8–22

For this reason, though I am bold enough in Christ to command you to do your duty, **9** yet I would rather appeal to you on the basis of love—and I, Paul, do this as an old man,[b] and now also as a prisoner of Christ Jesus. **10** I am appealing to you for my child, Onesimus, whose father I have become during my imprisonment. **11** Formerly he was useless to you, but now he is indeed useful both to you and to me. **12** I am sending him, that is, my own heart, back to you. **13** I wanted to keep him with me, so that he might be of service to me in your place during my imprisonment for the gospel; **14** but I preferred to do nothing without your consent, in order that your good deed might be voluntary and not something forced. **15** Perhaps this is the reason he was separated from you for a while, so that you might have him back forever, **16** no longer as a slave but more than a slave, a beloved brother—especially to me but how much more to you, both in the flesh and in the Lord. **17** So if you consider me your partner, welcome him as you would welcome me. **18** If he has wronged you in any way, or owes you anything, charge that to my account. **19** I, Paul, am writing this with my own hand: I will repay it. I say nothing about your owing me even your own self. **20** Yes, brother, let me have this benefit from you in the Lord! Refresh my heart in Christ. **21** Confident of your obedience, I am writing to you, knowing that you will do even more than I say. **22** One thing more—prepare a guest room for me, for I am hoping through your prayers to be restored to you.

132. Purity Laws and Sabbath Keeping

Rom 14:1–12

Welcome those who are weak in faith, but not for the purpose of quarreling over opinions. **2** Some believe in eating anything, while the weak eat only vegetables. **3** Those who eat must not despise those who abstain, and those who abstain must not pass judgment on those who eat; for God has welcomed them. **4** Who are you to pass judgment on servants of another? It is before their own lord that they stand or fall. And they will be upheld, for the Lord[a] is able to make them stand. **5** Some judge one day to be better than another, while others judge all days to be alike. Let all be fully convinced in their own minds. **6** Those who observe the day, observe it in honor of the Lord. Also those who eat, eat in honor of the Lord, since they give thanks to God; while those who abstain, abstain in honor of the Lord and give thanks to God. **7** We do not live to ourselves, and we do not die to ourselves. **8** If we live, we live to the Lord, and if we die, we die to the Lord; so then, whether we live or whether we die, we are the Lord's. **9** For to this end Christ died and lived again, so that he might be Lord of both the dead and the living. **10** Why do you pass judgment on your brother or sister? Or you, why do you despise your brother or sister? For we will all stand before the judgment seat of God.[b] **11** For it is written, "As I live, says the Lord, every knee shall bow to me, and every tongue shall give praise to God." **12** So then, each of us will be accountable to God.

Gal 2:11–14

But when Cephas came to Antioch, I opposed him to his face, because he stood self-condemned; **12** for until certain people came from James, he used to eat with the Gentiles. But after they came, he drew back and kept himself separate for fear of the circumcision faction. **13** And the other Jews joined him in this hypocrisy, so that even Barnabas was led astray by their hypocrisy. **14** But when I saw that they were not acting consistently with the truth of the gospel, I said to Cephas before them all, "If you, though a Jew, live like a Gentile and not like a Jew, how can you compel the Gentiles to live like Jews?"

Gal 4:8–11

Formerly, when you did not know God, you were enslaved to beings that by nature are not gods. **9** Now, however, that you have come to know God, or rather to be known by God, how can you turn back again to the weak and beggarly elemental spirits? How can you want to be enslaved to them again? **10** You are observing special days, and months, and seasons, and years. **11** I am afraid that my work for you may have been wasted.

Col 2:16–23

Therefore do not let anyone condemn you in matters of food and drink or of observing festivals, new moons, or sabbaths. **17** These are only a shadow of what is to come, but the substance belongs to Christ. **18** Do not let anyone disqualify you, insisting on self-abasement and worship of angels, dwelling on visions,[c] puffed up without cause by

[b] **Phlm 9** *old man* Some scholars conjecture that the original text read *ambassador*, or that the reading in the manuscripts is a spelling variant for *ambassador* **§ 132** [a] **Rom 14:4** *for the Lord* Other ancient authorities read *for God* [b] **Rom 14:10** *of God* Other ancient authorities read *of Christ* [c] **Col 2:18** *visions* lit. *things which he has seen* Other ancient authorities read *false visions* lit. *things which he has not seen*

αὐτοῦ, 19 καὶ οὐ κρατῶν τὴν κεφαλήν, ἐξ οὗ πᾶν τὸ σῶμα διὰ τῶν ἁφῶν καὶ συνδέσμων ἐπιχορηγούμενον καὶ συμβιβαζόμενον αὔξει τὴν αὔξησιν τοῦ θεοῦ. 20 Εἰ ἀπεθάνετε σὺν Χριστῷ ἀπὸ τῶν στοιχείων τοῦ κόσμου, τί ὡς ζῶντες ἐν κόσμῳ δογματίζεσθε; 21 μὴ ἅψῃ μηδὲ γεύσῃ μηδὲ θίγῃς, 22 ἅ ἐστιν πάντα εἰς φθορὰν τῇ ἀποχρήσει, κατὰ τὰ ἐντάλματα καὶ διδασκαλίας τῶν ἀνθρώπων, 23 ἅτινά ἐστιν λόγον μὲν ἔχοντα σοφίας ἐν ἐθελοθρησκίᾳ καὶ ταπεινοφροσύνῃ [καὶ] ἀφειδίᾳ σώματος, οὐκ ἐν τιμῇ τινι πρὸς πλησμονὴν τῆς σαρκός.

1 Tim 4:1–5

Τὸ δὲ πνεῦμα ῥητῶς λέγει ὅτι ἐν ὑστέροις καιροῖς ἀποστήσονταί τινες τῆς πίστεως προσέχοντες πνεύμασιν πλάνοις καὶ διδασκαλίαις δαιμονίων, 2 ἐν ὑποκρίσει ψευδολόγων, κεκαυστηριασμένων τὴν ἰδίαν συνείδησιν, 3 κωλυόντων γαμεῖν, ἀπέχεσθαι βρωμάτων, ἃ ὁ θεὸς ἔκτισεν εἰς μετάλημψιν μετὰ εὐχαριστίας τοῖς πιστοῖς καὶ ἐπεγνωκόσι τὴν ἀλήθειαν. 4 ὅτι πᾶν κτίσμα θεοῦ καλὸν καὶ οὐδὲν ἀπόβλητον μετὰ εὐχαριστίας λαμβανόμενον· 5 ἁγιάζεται γὰρ διὰ λόγου θεοῦ καὶ ἐντεύξεως.

Titus 1:10–16

Εἰσὶν γὰρ πολλοὶ [καὶ] ἀνυπότακτοι, ματαιολόγοι καὶ φρεναπάται, μάλιστα οἱ ἐκ τῆς περιτομῆς, 11 οὓς δεῖ ἐπιστομίζειν, οἵτινες ὅλους οἴκους ἀνατρέπουσιν διδάσκοντες ἃ μὴ δεῖ αἰσχροῦ κέρδους χάριν. 12 εἶπέν τις ἐξ αὐτῶν ἴδιος αὐτῶν προφήτης· Κρῆτες ἀεὶ ψεῦσται, κακὰ θηρία, γαστέρες ἀργαί. 13 ἡ μαρτυρία αὕτη ἐστὶν ἀληθής. δι' ἣν αἰτίαν ἔλεγχε αὐτοὺς ἀποτόμως, ἵνα ὑγιαίνωσιν ἐν τῇ πίστει, 14 μὴ προσέχοντες Ἰουδαϊκοῖς μύθοις καὶ ἐντολαῖς ἀνθρώπων ἀποστρεφομένων τὴν ἀλήθειαν. 15 πάντα καθαρὰ τοῖς καθαροῖς· τοῖς δὲ μεμιαμμένοις καὶ ἀπίστοις οὐδὲν καθαρόν, ἀλλὰ μεμίανται αὐτῶν καὶ ὁ νοῦς καὶ ἡ συνείδησις. 16 θεὸν ὁμολογοῦσιν εἰδέναι, τοῖς δὲ ἔργοις ἀρνοῦνται, βδελυκτοὶ ὄντες καὶ ἀπειθεῖς καὶ πρὸς πᾶν ἔργον ἀγαθὸν ἀδόκιμοι.

Cf. Rom 14:13–23; 15:1–6; Acts 15:13–29; 21:25.

See also § 134 Weak and Strong; § 135 Purity and Impurity.

133. Food Offered to Idols

1 Cor 8:1–13

Περὶ δὲ τῶν εἰδωλοθύτων, οἴδαμεν ὅτι πάντες γνῶσιν ἔχομεν. ἡ γνῶσις φυσιοῖ, ἡ δὲ ἀγάπη οἰκοδομεῖ· 2 εἴ τις δοκεῖ ἐγνωκέναι τι, οὔπω ἔγνω καθὼς δεῖ γνῶναι· 3 εἰ δέ τις ἀγαπᾷ τὸν θεόν, οὗτος ἔγνωσται ὑπ' αὐτοῦ. 4 Περὶ τῆς βρώσεως οὖν τῶν εἰδωλοθύτων, οἴδαμεν ὅτι οὐδὲν εἴδωλον ἐν κόσμῳ καὶ ὅτι οὐδεὶς θεὸς εἰ μὴ εἷς. 5 καὶ γὰρ εἴπερ εἰσὶν λεγόμενοι θεοὶ εἴτε ἐν οὐρανῷ εἴτε ἐπὶ γῆς, ὥσπερ εἰσὶν θεοὶ πολλοὶ καὶ κύριοι πολλοί, 6 ἀλλ' ἡμῖν εἷς θεὸς ὁ πατὴρ ἐξ οὗ τὰ πάντα καὶ ἡμεῖς εἰς αὐτόν, καὶ εἷς κύριος Ἰησοῦς Χριστὸς δι' οὗ τὰ πάντα καὶ ἡμεῖς δι' αὐτοῦ. 7 Ἀλλ' οὐκ ἐν πᾶσιν ἡ γνῶσις· τινὲς δὲ τῇ συνηθείᾳ ἕως ἄρτι τοῦ εἰδώλου ὡς εἰδωλόθυτον ἐσθίουσιν, καὶ ἡ συνείδησις αὐτῶν ἀσθενὴς οὖσα μολύνεται. 8 βρῶμα δὲ ἡμᾶς οὐ παραστήσει τῷ θεῷ· οὔτε ἐὰν μὴ φάγωμεν ὑστερούμεθα, οὔτε ἐὰν φάγωμεν περισσεύομεν. 9 βλέπετε δὲ μή πως ἡ ἐξουσία ὑμῶν αὕτη πρόσκομμα γένηται τοῖς ἀσθενέσιν. 10 ἐὰν γάρ τις ἴδῃ σὲ τὸν ἔχοντα γνῶσιν ἐν εἰδωλείῳ κατακείμενον, οὐχὶ ἡ συνείδησις αὐτοῦ ἀσθενοῦς ὄντος οἰκοδομηθήσεται εἰς τὸ τὰ εἰδωλόθυτα ἐσθίειν; 11 ἀπόλλυται γὰρ ὁ ἀσθενῶν ἐν τῇ σῇ γνώσει, ὁ ἀδελφὸς δι' ὃν Χριστὸς ἀπέθανεν. 12 οὕτως δὲ ἁμαρτάνοντες εἰς τοὺς ἀδελφοὺς καὶ τύπτοντες αὐτῶν τὴν συνείδησιν ἀσθενοῦσαν εἰς Χριστὸν ἁμαρτάνετε. 13 διόπερ εἰ βρῶμα σκανδαλίζει τὸν ἀδελφόν μου, οὐ μὴ φάγω κρέα εἰς τὸν αἰῶνα, ἵνα μὴ τὸν ἀδελφόν μου σκανδαλίσω.

1 Cor 10:14–22

Διόπερ, ἀγαπητοί μου, φεύγετε ἀπὸ τῆς εἰδωλολατρίας. 15 ὡς φρονίμοις λέγω· κρίνατε ὑμεῖς ὅ φημι. 16 Τὸ ποτήριον τῆς εὐλογίας ὃ εὐλογοῦμεν, οὐχὶ κοινωνία ἐστὶν τοῦ αἵματος τοῦ Χριστοῦ; τὸν ἄρτον ὃν κλῶμεν, οὐχὶ κοινωνία τοῦ σώματος τοῦ Χριστοῦ ἐστιν; 17 ὅτι εἷς ἄρτος, ἓν σῶμα οἱ πολλοί ἐσμεν, οἱ γὰρ πάντες ἐκ τοῦ ἑνὸς ἄρτου μετέχομεν. 18 βλέπετε τὸν Ἰσραὴλ κατὰ σάρκα· οὐχ οἱ ἐσθίοντες τὰς θυσίας κοινωνοὶ τοῦ θυσιαστηρίου εἰσίν; 19 Τί οὖν φημι; ὅτι εἰδωλόθυτόν τί ἐστιν ἢ ὅτι εἴδωλόν τί ἐστιν; 20 ἀλλ' ὅτι ἃ θύουσιν, δαιμονίοις καὶ οὐ θεῷ ⸀[θύουσιν]· οὐ θέλω δὲ ὑμᾶς κοινωνοὺς τῶν δαιμονίων γίνεσθαι. 21 οὐ δύνασθε ποτήριον κυρίου πίνειν καὶ ποτήριον δαιμονίων, οὐ δύνασθε τραπέζης κυρίου μετέχειν καὶ τραπέζης δαιμονίων. 22 ἢ παραζηλοῦμεν τὸν κύριον; μὴ ἰσχυρότεροι αὐτοῦ ἐσμεν;

1 Cor 10:23–11:1

Πάντα ἔξεστιν ἀλλ' οὐ πάντα συμφέρει· πάντα ἔξεστιν ἀλλ' οὐ πάντα οἰκοδομεῖ. 24 μηδεὶς τὸ ἑαυτοῦ ζητείτω ἀλλὰ τὸ τοῦ ἑτέρου. 25 Πᾶν τὸ ἐν μακέλλῳ πωλούμενον ἐσθίετε μηδὲν ἀνακρίνοντες διὰ τὴν συνείδησιν· 26 τοῦ κυρίου γὰρ ἡ γῆ καὶ τὸ πλήρωμα αὐτῆς. 27 εἴ τις καλεῖ ὑμᾶς τῶν ἀπίστων καὶ θέλετε πορεύεσθαι, πᾶν τὸ παρατιθέμενον ὑμῖν ἐσθίετε μηδὲν ἀνακρίνοντες διὰ τὴν συνείδησιν. 28 ἐὰν δέ τις ὑμῖν εἴπῃ· τοῦτο ἱερόθυτόν ἐστιν, μὴ ἐσθίετε δι' ἐκεῖνον τὸν μηνύσαντα καὶ τὴν συνείδησιν· 29 συνείδησιν δὲ λέγω οὐχὶ τὴν ἑαυτοῦ ἀλλὰ

§ 133 1 Cor 10:20 *θυουσιν* B D] θυουσιν τα εθνη 𝔓[46vid] ℵ A C 33[vid]. 1739 ¦ θυει τα εθνη 1881 *Byz*

a human way of thinking, [19] and not holding fast to the head, from whom the whole body, richly supplied[d] and held together by its ligaments and sinews, grows with a growth that is from God. [20] If with Christ you died to the elemental spirits of the universe, why do you live as if you still belonged to the world? Why do you submit to regulations, [21] "Do not handle, Do not taste, Do not touch"? [22] All these regulations refer to things that perish with use; they are simply human commands and teachings. [23] These have indeed an appearance of wisdom in promoting self-imposed piety, humility, and severe treatment of the body, but they are of no value in checking self-indulgence.

1 Tim 4:1–5

Now the Spirit expressly says that in later times some will renounce the faith by paying attention to deceitful spirits and teachings of demons, [2] through the hypocrisy of liars whose consciences are seared with a hot iron. [3] They forbid marriage and demand abstinence from foods, which God created to be received with thanksgiving by those who believe and know the truth. [4] For everything created by God is good, and nothing is to be rejected, provided it is received with thanksgiving; [5] for it is sanctified by God's word and by prayer.

Titus 1:10–16

There are also many rebellious people, idle talkers and deceivers, especially those of the circumcision; [11] they must be silenced, since they are upsetting whole families by teaching for sordid gain what it is not right to teach. [12] It was one of them, their very own prophet, who said, "Cretans are always liars, vicious brutes, lazy gluttons." [13] That testimony is true. For this reason rebuke them sharply, so that they may become sound in the faith, [14] not paying attention to Jewish myths or to commandments of those who reject the truth. [15] To the pure all things are pure, but to the corrupt and unbelieving nothing is pure. Their very minds and consciences are corrupted. [16] They profess to know God, but they deny him by their actions. They are detestable, disobedient, unfit for any good work.

Cf. Rom 14:13–23; 15:1–6; Acts 15:13–29; 21:25.

See also § 134 Weak and Strong; § 135 Purity and Impurity.

133. Food Offered to Idols

1 Cor 8:1–13

Now concerning food sacrificed to idols: we know that "all of us possess knowledge." Knowledge puffs up, but love builds up. [2] Anyone who claims to know something does not yet have the necessary knowledge; [3] but anyone who loves God is known by him. [4] Hence, as to the eating of food offered to idols, we know that "no idol in the world really exists," and that "there is no God but one." [5] Indeed, even though there may be so-called gods in heaven or on earth—as in fact there are many gods and many lords— [6] yet for us there is one God, the Father, from whom are all things and for whom we exist, and one Lord, Jesus Christ, through whom are all things and through whom we exist. [7] It is not everyone, however, who has this knowledge. Since some have become so accustomed to idols until now, they still think of the food they eat as food offered to an idol; and their conscience, being weak, is defiled. [8] "Food will not bring us close to God." We are no worse off if we do not eat, and no better off if we do. [9] But take care that this liberty of yours does not somehow become a stumbling block to the weak. [10] For if others see you, who possess knowledge, eating in the temple of an idol, might they not, since their conscience is weak, be encouraged to the point of eating food sacrificed to idols? [11] So by your knowledge those weak believers for whom Christ died are destroyed. [12] But when you thus sin against members of your family, and wound their conscience when it is weak, you sin against Christ. [13] Therefore, if food is a cause of their falling, I will never eat meat, so that I may not cause one of them to fall.

1 Cor 10:14–22

Therefore, my dear friends, flee from the worship of idols. [15] I speak as to sensible people; judge for yourselves what I say. [16] The cup of blessing that we bless, is it not a sharing in the blood of Christ? The bread that we break, is it not a sharing in the body of Christ? [17] Because there is one bread, we who are many are one body, for we all partake of the one bread. [18] Consider the people of Israel; are not those who eat the sacrifices partners in the altar? [19] What do I imply then? That food sacrificed to idols is anything, or that an idol is anything? [20] No, I imply that what pagans sacrifice,[a] they sacrifice to demons and not to God. I do not want you to be partners with demons. [21] You cannot drink the cup of the Lord and the cup of demons. You cannot partake of the table of the Lord and the table of demons. [22] Or are we provoking the Lord to jealousy? Are we stronger than he?

1 Cor 10:23–11:1

"All things are lawful," but not all things are beneficial. "All things are lawful," but not all things build up. [24] Do not seek your own advantage, but that of the other. [25] Eat whatever is sold in the meat market without raising any question on the ground of conscience, [26] for "the earth and its fullness are the Lord's." [27] If an unbeliever invites you to a meal and you are disposed to go, eat whatever is set before you without raising any question on the ground of conscience. [28] But if someone says to you, "This has been offered in sacrifice," then do not eat it, out of consideration for the one who informed you, and for the sake of conscience— [29] I mean the other's conscience, not your own. For

[d] Col 2:19 *richly supplied* NRSV translates *nourished* **§ 133** [a] 1 Cor 10:20 *pagans sacrifice* Other ancient authorities read *they sacrifice*

τὴν τοῦ ἑτέρου. ἱνατί γὰρ ἡ ἐλευθερία μου κρίνεται ὑπὸ ἄλλης συνειδήσεως; **30** εἰ ἐγὼ χάριτι μετέχω, τί βλασφημοῦμαι ὑπὲρ οὗ ἐγὼ εὐχαριστῶ; **31** Εἴτε οὖν ἐσθίετε εἴτε πίνετε εἴτε τι ποιεῖτε, πάντα εἰς δόξαν θεοῦ ποιεῖτε. **32** ἀπρόσκοποι καὶ Ἰουδαίοις γίνεσθε καὶ Ἕλλησιν καὶ τῇ ἐκκλησίᾳ τοῦ θεοῦ, **33** καθὼς κἀγὼ πάντα πᾶσιν ἀρέσκω μὴ ζητῶν τὸ ἐμαυτοῦ σύμφορον ἀλλὰ τὸ τῶν πολλῶν, ἵνα σωθῶσιν. **11** μιμηταί μου γίνεσθε καθὼς κἀγὼ Χριστοῦ.

Acts 15:19–21

διὸ ἐγὼ κρίνω μὴ παρενοχλεῖν τοῖς ἀπὸ τῶν ἐθνῶν ἐπιστρέφουσιν ἐπὶ τὸν θεόν, **20** ἀλλὰ ἐπιστεῖλαι αὐτοῖς τοῦ ἀπέχεσθαι τῶν ἀλισγημάτων τῶν εἰδώλων καὶ τῆς πορνείας ⸂καὶ τοῦ πνικτοῦ⸃ καὶ τοῦ αἵματος. **21** Μωϋσῆς γὰρ ἐκ γενεῶν ἀρχαίων κατὰ πόλιν τοὺς κηρύσσοντας αὐτὸν ἔχει ἐν ταῖς συναγωγαῖς κατὰ πᾶν σάββατον ἀναγινωσκόμενος.

Acts 15:28–29

ἔδοξεν γὰρ τῷ πνεύματι τῷ ἁγίῳ καὶ ἡμῖν μηδὲν πλέον ἐπιτίθεσθαι ὑμῖν βάρος πλὴν τούτων τῶν ἐπάναγκες, **29** ἀπέχεσθαι εἰδωλοθύτων καὶ αἵματος ⸂καὶ πνικτῶν⸃ καὶ πορνείας, ἐξ ὧν διατηροῦντες ἑαυτοὺς εὖ πράξετε. Ἔρρωσθε.

Acts 21:25

περὶ δὲ τῶν πεπιστευκότων ἐθνῶν ἡμεῖς ἐπεστείλαμεν κρίναντες φυλάσσεσθαι αὐτοὺς τό τε εἰδωλόθυτον καὶ αἷμα ⸂καὶ πνικτὸν⸃ καὶ πορνείαν.

Cf. possibly Rom 14:1–12; 14:13–23; 15:1–6.

134. Weak and Strong

Rom 14:1–12

Τὸν δὲ ἀσθενοῦντα τῇ πίστει προσλαμβάνεσθε, μὴ εἰς διακρίσεις διαλογισμῶν. **2** ὃς μὲν πιστεύει φαγεῖν πάντα, ὁ δὲ ἀσθενῶν λάχανα ἐσθίει. **3** ὁ ἐσθίων τὸν μὴ ἐσθίοντα μὴ ἐξουθενείτω, ὁ δὲ μὴ ἐσθίων τὸν ἐσθίοντα μὴ κρινέτω, ὁ θεὸς γὰρ αὐτὸν προσελάβετο. **4** σὺ τίς εἶ ὁ κρίνων ἀλλότριον οἰκέτην; τῷ ἰδίῳ κυρίῳ στήκει ἢ πίπτει· σταθήσεται δέ, δυνατεῖ γὰρ ὁ ⸀κύριος στῆσαι αὐτόν. **5** Ὃς μὲν [γὰρ] κρίνει ἡμέραν παρ᾽ ἡμέραν, ὃς δὲ κρίνει πᾶσαν ἡμέραν· ἕκαστος ἐν τῷ ἰδίῳ νοῒ πληροφορείσθω. **6** ὁ φρονῶν τὴν ἡμέραν κυρίῳ φρονεῖ· καὶ ὁ ἐσθίων κυρίῳ ἐσθίει, εὐχαριστεῖ γὰρ τῷ θεῷ· καὶ ὁ μὴ ἐσθίων κυρίῳ οὐκ ἐσθίει καὶ εὐχαριστεῖ τῷ θεῷ. **7** οὐδεὶς γὰρ ἡμῶν ἑαυτῷ ζῇ καὶ οὐδεὶς ἑαυτῷ ἀποθνῄσκει· **8** ἐάν τε γὰρ ζῶμεν, τῷ κυρίῳ ζῶμεν, ἐάν τε ἀποθνῄσκωμεν, τῷ κυρίῳ ἀποθνῄσκομεν. ἐάν τε οὖν ζῶμεν ἐάν τε ἀποθνῄσκωμεν, τοῦ κυρίου ἐσμέν. **9** εἰς τοῦτο γὰρ Χριστὸς ἀπέθανεν καὶ ἔζησεν, ἵνα καὶ νεκρῶν καὶ ζώντων κυριεύσῃ. **10** Σὺ δὲ τί κρίνεις τὸν ἀδελφόν σου; ἢ καὶ σὺ τί ἐξουθενεῖς τὸν ἀδελφόν σου; πάντες γὰρ παραστησόμεθα τῷ βήματι τοῦ ⸀θεοῦ, **11** γέγραπται γάρ· ζῶ ἐγώ, λέγει κύριος, ὅτι ἐμοὶ κάμψει πᾶν γόνυ καὶ πᾶσα γλῶσσα ἐξομολογήσεται τῷ θεῷ. **12** ἄρα [οὖν] ἕκαστος ἡμῶν περὶ ἑαυτοῦ λόγον δώσει [τῷ θεῷ].

Rom 14:13–23

Μηκέτι οὖν ἀλλήλους κρίνωμεν· ἀλλὰ τοῦτο κρίνατε μᾶλλον, τὸ μὴ τιθέναι πρόσκομμα τῷ ἀδελφῷ ἢ σκάνδαλον. **14** οἶδα καὶ πέπεισμαι ἐν κυρίῳ Ἰησοῦ ὅτι οὐδὲν κοινὸν δι᾽ ἑαυτοῦ, εἰ μὴ τῷ λογιζομένῳ τι κοινὸν εἶναι, ἐκείνῳ κοινόν. **15** εἰ γὰρ διὰ βρῶμα ὁ ἀδελφός σου λυπεῖται, οὐκέτι κατὰ ἀγάπην περιπατεῖς· μὴ τῷ βρώματί σου ἐκεῖνον ἀπόλλυε ὑπὲρ οὗ Χριστὸς ἀπέθανεν. **16** μὴ βλασφημείσθω οὖν ὑμῶν τὸ ἀγαθόν. **17** οὐ γάρ ἐστιν ἡ βασιλεία τοῦ θεοῦ βρῶσις καὶ πόσις ἀλλὰ δικαιοσύνη καὶ εἰρήνη καὶ χαρὰ ἐν πνεύματι ἁγίῳ· **18** ὁ γὰρ ἐν τούτῳ δουλεύων τῷ Χριστῷ εὐάρεστος τῷ θεῷ καὶ δόκιμος τοῖς ἀνθρώποις. **19** Ἄρα οὖν τὰ τῆς εἰρήνης ⸀διώκωμεν καὶ τὰ τῆς οἰκοδομῆς τῆς εἰς ἀλλήλους. **20** μὴ ἕνεκεν βρώματος κατάλυε τὸ ἔργον τοῦ θεοῦ. πάντα μὲν καθαρά, ἀλλὰ κακὸν τῷ ἀνθρώπῳ τῷ διὰ προσκόμματος ἐσθίοντι. **21** καλὸν τὸ μὴ φαγεῖν κρέα μηδὲ πιεῖν οἶνον μηδὲ ἐν ᾧ ὁ ἀδελφός σου ⸀προσκόπτει. **22** σὺ πίστιν [ἣν] ἔχεις κατὰ σεαυτὸν ἔχε ἐνώπιον τοῦ θεοῦ. μακάριος ὁ μὴ κρίνων ἑαυτὸν ἐν ᾧ δοκιμάζει· **23** ὁ δὲ διακρινόμενος ἐὰν φάγῃ κατακέκριται, ὅτι οὐκ ἐκ πίστεως· πᾶν δὲ ὃ οὐκ ἐκ πίστεως ἁμαρτία ἐστίν.

Rom 15:1–6

Ὀφείλομεν δὲ ἡμεῖς οἱ δυνατοὶ τὰ ἀσθενήματα τῶν ἀδυνάτων βαστάζειν καὶ μὴ ἑαυτοῖς ἀρέσκειν. **2** ἕκαστος ἡμῶν τῷ πλησίον ἀρεσκέτω εἰς τὸ ἀγαθὸν πρὸς οἰκοδομήν· **3** καὶ γὰρ ὁ Χριστὸς οὐχ ἑαυτῷ ἤρεσεν, ἀλλὰ καθὼς γέγραπται· οἱ ὀνειδισμοὶ τῶν ὀνειδιζόντων σε ἐπέπεσαν ἐπ᾽ ἐμέ. **4** ὅσα γὰρ προεγράφη, εἰς τὴν ἡμετέραν διδασκαλίαν ἐγράφη, ἵνα διὰ τῆς ὑπομονῆς καὶ διὰ τῆς παρακλήσεως τῶν γραφῶν τὴν ἐλπίδα ἔχωμεν. **5** ὁ δὲ θεὸς τῆς ὑπομονῆς καὶ τῆς παρακλήσεως δῴη ὑμῖν τὸ αὐτὸ φρονεῖν ἐν ἀλλήλοις κατὰ Χριστὸν Ἰησοῦν, **6** ἵνα ὁμοθυμαδὸν ἐν ἑνὶ στόματι δοξάζητε τὸν θεὸν καὶ πατέρα τοῦ κυρίου ἡμῶν Ἰησοῦ Χριστοῦ.

Acts 15:20 ***και του πνικτου*** 𝔓^{45} ℵ C E 1739 *Byz*] και πνικτου 𝔓^{74} A B 33 ¦ *om.* D **Acts 15:29** ***και πνικτων*** ℵ* A* B C] και πνικτου 𝔓^{74} ℵ^{2} A^{c} E 33. 1739 *Byz* ¦ *om.* D **Acts 21:25** ***και πνικτον*** 𝔓^{74} ℵ A B C (E) 33. 1739] *om.* D **§ 134** **Rom 14:4** ***κυριος*** 𝔓^{46} ℵ A B C] θεος D 048. 33. 1739. 1881 *Byz* **Rom 14:10** ***θεου*** ℵ* A B C* D 1739] Χριστου ℵ^{c} C^{2} 048. 33. 1881 *Byz* **Rom 14:19** ***διωκωμεν*** C D 33. 1739. 1881 *Byz*] διωκομεν ℵ A B 048 **Rom 14:21** ***προσκοπτει*** ℵ* A C 048. 1739] *add.* η σκανδαλιζεται η ασθενει 𝔓^{46vid} ℵ^{2} B D 33. 1881 *Byz*

why should my liberty be subject to the judgment of someone else's conscience? 30 If I partake with thankfulness, why should I be denounced because of that for which I give thanks? 31 So, whether you eat or drink, or whatever you do, do everything for the glory of God. 32 Give no offense to Jews or to Greeks or to the church of God, 33 just as I try to please everyone in everything I do, not seeking my own advantage, but that of many, so that they may be saved. 11 Be imitators of me, as I am of Christ.

Acts 15:19–21

Therefore I have reached the decision that we should not trouble those Gentiles who are turning to God, 20 but we should write to them to abstain only from things polluted by idols and from fornication and from whatever has been strangled[b] and from blood. 21 For in every city, for generations past, Moses has had those who proclaim him, for he has been read aloud every sabbath in the synagogues.

Acts 15:28–29

For it has seemed good to the Holy Spirit and to us to impose on you no further burden than these essentials: 29 that you abstain from what has been sacrificed to idols and from blood and from what is strangled[c] and from fornication. If you keep yourselves from these, you will do well. Farewell.

Acts 21:25

But as for the Gentiles who have become believers, we have sent a letter with our judgment that they should abstain from what has been sacrificed to idols and from blood and from what is strangled[d] and from fornication.

Cf. possibly Rom 14:1–12; 14:13–23; 15:1–6.

134. Weak and Strong

Rom 14:1–12

Welcome those who are weak in faith, but not for the purpose of quarreling over opinions. 2 Some believe in eating anything, while the weak eat only vegetables. 3 Those who eat must not despise those who abstain, and those who abstain must not pass judgment on those who eat; for God has welcomed them. 4 Who are you to pass judgment on servants of another? It is before their own lord that they stand or fall. And they will be upheld, for the Lord[a] is able to make them stand. 5 Some judge one day to be better than another, while others judge all days to be alike. Let all be fully convinced in their own minds. 6 Those who observe the day, observe it in honor of the Lord. Also those who eat, eat in honor of the Lord, since they give thanks to God; while those who abstain, abstain in honor of the Lord and give thanks to God. 7 We do not live to ourselves, and we do not die to ourselves. 8 If we live, we live to the Lord, and if we die, we die to the Lord; so then, whether we live or whether we die, we are the Lord's. 9 For to this end Christ died and lived again, so that he might be Lord of both the dead and the living. 10 Why do you pass judgment on your brother or sister? Or you, why do you despise your brother or sister? For we will all stand before the judgment seat of God.[b] 11 For it is written, "As I live, says the Lord, every knee shall bow to me, and every tongue shall give praise to God." 12 So then, each of us will be accountable to God.

Rom 14:13–23

Let us therefore no longer pass judgment on one another, but resolve instead never to put a stumbling block or hindrance in the way of another. 14 I know and am persuaded in the Lord Jesus that nothing is unclean in itself; but it is unclean for anyone who thinks it unclean. 15 If your brother or sister is being injured by what you eat, you are no longer walking in love. Do not let what you eat cause the ruin of one for whom Christ died. 16 So do not let your good be spoken of as evil. 17 For the kingdom of God is not food and drink but righteousness and peace and joy in the Holy Spirit. 18 The one who thus serves Christ is acceptable to God and has human approval. 19 Let us then pursue[c] what makes for peace and for mutual upbuilding. 20 Do not, for the sake of food, destroy the work of God. Everything is indeed clean, but it is wrong for you to make others fall by what you eat; 21 it is good not to eat meat or drink wine or do anything that makes your brother or sister stumble.[d] 22 The faith that you have, have as your own conviction before God. Blessed are those who have no reason to condemn themselves because of what they approve. 23 But those who have doubts are condemned if they eat, because they do not act from faith; for whatever does not proceed from faith is sin.

Rom 15:1–6

We who are strong ought to put up with the failings of the weak, and not to please ourselves. 2 Each of us must please our neighbor for the good purpose of building up the neighbor. 3 For Christ did not please himself; but, as it is written, "The insults of those who insult you have fallen on me." 4 For whatever was written in former days was written for our instruction, so that by steadfastness and by the encouragement of the scriptures we might have hope. 5 May the God of steadfastness and encouragement grant you to live in harmony with one another, in accordance with Christ Jesus, 6 so that together you may with one voice glorify the God and Father of our Lord Jesus Christ.

[b] **Acts 15:20** ***and from whatever has been strangled*** A few ancient authorities lack *and from whatever has been strangled* [c] **Acts 15:29** ***and from what is strangled*** A few ancient authorities lack *and from what is strangled* [d] **Acts 21:25** ***and from what is strangled*** A few ancient authorities lack *and from what is strangled* **§ 134** [a] **Rom 14:4** ***for the Lord*** Other ancient authorities read *for God* [b] **Rom 14:10** ***of God*** Other ancient authorities read *of Christ* [c] **Rom 14:19** ***Let us then pursue*** Other ancient authorities read *We then pursue* [d] **Rom 14:21** ***stumble*** Other ancient authorities add *or be upset or be weakened*

1 Cor 8:7–13

Ἀλλʼ οὐκ ἐν πᾶσιν ἡ γνῶσις· τινὲς δὲ
τῇ συνηθείᾳ ἕως ἄρτι τοῦ εἰδώλου ὡς
εἰδωλόθυτον ἐσθίουσιν, καὶ ἡ συνείδησις
αὐτῶν ἀσθενὴς οὖσα μολύνεται. 8 βρῶ-
μα δὲ ἡμᾶς οὐ παραστήσει τῷ θεῷ· οὔτε
ἐὰν μὴ φάγωμεν ὑστερούμεθα, οὔτε ἐὰν
φάγωμεν περισσεύομεν. 9 βλέπετε δὲ μή
πως ἡ ἐξουσία ὑμῶν αὕτη πρόσκομμα
γένηται τοῖς ἀσθενέσιν. 10 ἐὰν γάρ τις
ἴδῃ σὲ τὸν ἔχοντα γνῶσιν ἐν εἰδωλείῳ
κατακείμενον, οὐχὶ ἡ συνείδησις αὐτοῦ
ἀσθενοῦς ὄντος οἰκοδομηθήσεται εἰς τὸ
τὰ εἰδωλόθυτα ἐσθίειν; 11 ἀπόλλυται γὰρ
ὁ ἀσθενῶν ἐν τῇ σῇ γνώσει, ὁ ἀδελφὸς
διʼ ὃν Χριστὸς ἀπέθανεν. 12 οὕτως δὲ
ἁμαρτάνοντες εἰς τοὺς ἀδελφοὺς καὶ
τύπτοντες αὐτῶν τὴν συνείδησιν ἀσθε-
νοῦσαν εἰς Χριστὸν ἁμαρτάνετε. 13 διόπερ
εἰ βρῶμα σκανδαλίζει τὸν ἀδελφόν μου,
οὐ μὴ φάγω κρέα εἰς τὸν αἰῶνα, ἵνα μὴ
τὸν ἀδελφόν μου σκανδαλίσω.

1 Cor 9:22

ἐγενόμην τοῖς ἀσθενέσιν ἀσθενής, ἵνα
τοὺς ἀσθενεῖς κερδήσω· τοῖς πᾶσιν γέγονα
πάντα, ἵνα πάντως τινὰς σώσω.

1 Cor 10:23–11:1

Πάντα ἔξεστιν ἀλλʼ οὐ πάντα συμφέρει·
πάντα ἔξεστιν ἀλλʼ οὐ πάντα οἰκοδομεῖ.
24 μηδεὶς τὸ ἑαυτοῦ ζητείτω ἀλλὰ τὸ τοῦ
ἑτέρου. 25 Πᾶν τὸ ἐν μακέλλῳ πωλού-
μενον ἐσθίετε μηδὲν ἀνακρίνοντες διὰ
τὴν συνείδησιν· 26 τοῦ κυρίου γὰρ ἡ γῆ
καὶ τὸ πλήρωμα αὐτῆς. 27 εἴ τις καλεῖ
ὑμᾶς τῶν ἀπίστων καὶ θέλετε πορεύε-
σθαι, πᾶν τὸ παρατιθέμενον ὑμῖν ἐσθίετε
μηδὲν ἀνακρίνοντες διὰ τὴν συνείδησιν.
28 ἐὰν δέ τις ὑμῖν εἴπῃ· τοῦτο ἱερόθυ-
τόν ἐστιν, μὴ ἐσθίετε διʼ ἐκεῖνον τὸν
μηνύσαντα καὶ τὴν συνείδησιν· 29 συν-
είδησιν δὲ λέγω οὐχὶ τὴν ἑαυτοῦ ἀλλὰ
τὴν τοῦ ἑτέρου. ἱνατί γὰρ ἡ ἐλευθερία
μου κρίνεται ὑπὸ ἄλλης συνειδήσεως;
30 εἰ ἐγὼ χάριτι μετέχω, τί βλασφημοῦ-
μαι ὑπὲρ οὗ ἐγὼ εὐχαριστῶ; 31 Εἴτε οὖν
ἐσθίετε εἴτε πίνετε εἴτε τι ποιεῖτε, πάντα
εἰς δόξαν θεοῦ ποιεῖτε. 32 ἀπρόσκοποι
καὶ Ἰουδαίοις γίνεσθε καὶ Ἕλλησιν καὶ
τῇ ἐκκλησίᾳ τοῦ θεοῦ, 33 καθὼς κἀγὼ
πάντα πᾶσιν ἀρέσκω μὴ ζητῶν τὸ ἐμαυ-
τοῦ σύμφορον ἀλλὰ τὸ τῶν πολλῶν,
ἵνα σωθῶσιν. **11** μιμηταί μου γίνεσθε
καθὼς κἀγὼ Χριστοῦ.

2 Cor 11:29

τίς ἀσθενεῖ καὶ οὐκ ἀσθενῶ; τίς σκανδα-
λίζεται καὶ οὐκ ἐγὼ πυροῦμαι;

1 Thess 5:14

Παρακαλοῦμεν δὲ ὑμᾶς, ἀδελφοί, νου-
θετεῖτε τοὺς ἀτάκτους, παραμυθεῖσθε τοὺς
ὀλιγοψύχους, ἀντέχεσθε τῶν ἀσθενῶν,
μακροθυμεῖτε πρὸς πάντας.

See also § 132 Purity Laws and Sabbath Keeping; § 133 Food Offered to Idols; § 135 Purity and Impurity.

135. Purity and Impurity

Rom 14:13–23

Μηκέτι οὖν ἀλλήλους κρίνωμεν· ἀλλὰ
τοῦτο κρίνατε μᾶλλον, τὸ μὴ τιθέναι
πρόσκομμα τῷ ἀδελφῷ ἢ σκάνδαλον.
14 οἶδα καὶ πέπεισμαι ἐν κυρίῳ Ἰησοῦ
ὅτι οὐδὲν κοινὸν διʼ ἑαυτοῦ, εἰ μὴ τῷ
λογιζομένῳ τι κοινὸν εἶναι, ἐκείνῳ κοι-
νόν. 15 εἰ γὰρ διὰ βρῶμα ὁ ἀδελφός σου
λυπεῖται, οὐκέτι κατὰ ἀγάπην περιπατεῖς·
μὴ τῷ βρώματί σου ἐκεῖνον ἀπόλλυε
ὑπὲρ οὗ Χριστὸς ἀπέθανεν. 16 μὴ βλα-
σφημείσθω οὖν ὑμῶν τὸ ἀγαθόν. 17 οὐ
γάρ ἐστιν ἡ βασιλεία τοῦ θεοῦ βρῶσις
καὶ πόσις ἀλλὰ δικαιοσύνη καὶ εἰρήνη
καὶ χαρὰ ἐν πνεύματι ἁγίῳ· 18 ὁ γὰρ ἐν
τούτῳ δουλεύων τῷ Χριστῷ εὐάρεστος
τῷ θεῷ καὶ δόκιμος τοῖς ἀνθρώποις.
19 Ἄρα οὖν τὰ τῆς εἰρήνης ⸀διώκωμεν
καὶ τὰ τῆς οἰκοδομῆς τῆς εἰς ἀλλήλους.
20 μὴ ἕνεκεν βρώματος κατάλυε τὸ ἔργον
τοῦ θεοῦ. πάντα μὲν καθαρά, ἀλλὰ κα-
κὸν τῷ ἀνθρώπῳ τῷ διὰ προσκόμματος
ἐσθίοντι. 21 καλὸν τὸ μὴ φαγεῖν κρέα
μηδὲ πιεῖν οἶνον μηδὲ ἐν ᾧ ὁ ἀδελφός
σου ⸀προσκόπτει. 22 σὺ πίστιν [ἣν] ἔχεις
κατὰ σεαυτὸν ἔχε ἐνώπιον τοῦ θεοῦ.
μακάριος ὁ μὴ κρίνων ἑαυτὸν ἐν ᾧ δο-
κιμάζει· 23 ὁ δὲ διακρινόμενος ἐὰν φάγῃ
κατακέκριται, ὅτι οὐκ ἐκ πίστεως· πᾶν δὲ
ὃ οὐκ ἐκ πίστεως ἁμαρτία ἐστίν.

1 Cor 8:7–13

Ἀλλʼ οὐκ ἐν πᾶσιν ἡ γνῶσις· τινὲς δὲ
τῇ συνηθείᾳ ἕως ἄρτι τοῦ εἰδώλου ὡς
εἰδωλόθυτον ἐσθίουσιν, καὶ ἡ συνείδησις
αὐτῶν ἀσθενὴς οὖσα μολύνεται. 8 βρῶ-
μα δὲ ἡμᾶς οὐ παραστήσει τῷ θεῷ· οὔτε
ἐὰν μὴ φάγωμεν ὑστερούμεθα, οὔτε ἐὰν
φάγωμεν περισσεύομεν. 9 βλέπετε δὲ μή
πως ἡ ἐξουσία ὑμῶν αὕτη πρόσκομμα
γένηται τοῖς ἀσθενέσιν. 10 ἐὰν γάρ τις
ἴδῃ σὲ τὸν ἔχοντα γνῶσιν ἐν εἰδωλείῳ
κατακείμενον, οὐχὶ ἡ συνείδησις αὐτοῦ
ἀσθενοῦς ὄντος οἰκοδομηθήσεται εἰς τὸ
τὰ εἰδωλόθυτα ἐσθίειν; 11 ἀπόλλυται γὰρ
ὁ ἀσθενῶν ἐν τῇ σῇ γνώσει, ὁ ἀδελφὸς
διʼ ὃν Χριστὸς ἀπέθανεν. 12 οὕτως δὲ
ἁμαρτάνοντες εἰς τοὺς ἀδελφοὺς καὶ
τύπτοντες αὐτῶν τὴν συνείδησιν ἀσθε-
νοῦσαν εἰς Χριστὸν ἁμαρτάνετε. 13 διόπερ
εἰ βρῶμα σκανδαλίζει τὸν ἀδελφόν μου,
οὐ μὴ φάγω κρέα εἰς τὸν αἰῶνα, ἵνα μὴ
τὸν ἀδελφόν μου σκανδαλίσω.

1 Tim 4:1–5

Τὸ δὲ πνεῦμα ῥητῶς λέγει ὅτι ἐν ὑστέροις
καιροῖς ἀποστήσονταί τινες τῆς πίστεως
προσέχοντες πνεύμασιν πλάνοις καὶ
διδασκαλίαις δαιμονίων, 2 ἐν ὑποκρίσει
ψευδολόγων, κεκαυστηριασμένων τὴν
ἰδίαν συνείδησιν, 3 κωλυόντων γαμεῖν,
ἀπέχεσθαι βρωμάτων, ἃ ὁ θεὸς ἔκτισεν
εἰς μετάλημψιν μετὰ εὐχαριστίας τοῖς
πιστοῖς καὶ ἐπεγνωκόσι τὴν ἀλήθειαν.
4 ὅτι πᾶν κτίσμα θεοῦ καλὸν καὶ οὐδὲν

§ 135 Rom 14:19 ***διωκωμεν*** C D 33. 1739. 1881 *Byz*] διωκομεν א A B 048 Rom 14:21 ***προσκοπτει*** א* A C 048. 1739] *add*. η σκανδαλιζεται η ασθενει 𝔓[46vid] א[2] B D 33. 1881 *Byz*

1 Cor 8:7–13

It is not everyone, however, who has this knowledge. Since some have become so accustomed to idols until now, they still think of the food they eat as food offered to an idol; and their conscience, being weak, is defiled. **8** "Food will not bring us close to God." We are no worse off if we do not eat, and no better off if we do. **9** But take care that this liberty of yours does not somehow become a stumbling block to the weak. **10** For if others see you, who possess knowledge, eating in the temple of an idol, might they not, since their conscience is weak, be encouraged to the point of eating food sacrificed to idols? **11** So by your knowledge those weak believers for whom Christ died are destroyed. **12** But when you thus sin against members of your family, and wound their conscience when it is weak, you sin against Christ. **13** Therefore, if food is a cause of their falling, I will never eat meat, so that I may not cause one of them to fall.

1 Cor 9:22

To the weak I became weak, so that I might win the weak. I have become all things to all people, that I might by all means save some.

1 Cor 10:23–11:1

"All things are lawful," but not all things are beneficial. "All things are lawful," but not all things build up. **24** Do not seek your own advantage, but that of the other. **25** Eat whatever is sold in the meat market without raising any question on the ground of conscience, **26** for "the earth and its fullness are the Lord's." **27** If an unbeliever invites you to a meal and you are disposed to go, eat whatever is set before you without raising any question on the ground of conscience. **28** But if someone says to you, "This has been offered in sacrifice," then do not eat it, out of consideration for the one who informed you, and for the sake of conscience— **29** I mean the other's conscience, not your own. For why should my liberty be subject to the judgment of someone else's conscience? **30** If I partake with thankfulness, why should I be denounced because of that for which I give thanks? **31** So, whether you eat or drink, or whatever you do, do everything for the glory of God. **32** Give no offense to Jews or to Greeks or to the church of God, **33** just as I try to please everyone in everything I do, not seeking my own advantage, but that of many, so that they may be saved. **11** Be imitators of me, as I am of Christ.

2 Cor 11:29

Who is weak, and I am not weak? Who is made to stumble, and I am not indignant?

1 Thess 5:14

And we urge you, beloved, to admonish the idlers, encourage the fainthearted, help the weak, be patient with all of them.

See also § 132 Purity Laws and Sabbath Keeping; § 133 Food Offered to Idols; § 135 Purity and Impurity.

135. Purity and Impurity

Rom 14:13–23

Let us therefore no longer pass judgment on one another, but resolve instead never to put a stumbling block or hindrance in the way of another. **14** I know and am persuaded in the Lord Jesus that nothing is unclean in itself; but it is unclean for anyone who thinks it unclean. **15** If your brother or sister is being injured by what you eat, you are no longer walking in love. Do not let what you eat cause the ruin of one for whom Christ died. **16** So do not let your good be spoken of as evil. **17** For the kingdom of God is not food and drink but righteousness and peace and joy in the Holy Spirit. **18** The one who thus serves Christ is acceptable to God and has human approval. **19** Let us then pursue[a] what makes for peace and for mutual upbuilding. **20** Do not, for the sake of food, destroy the work of God. Everything is indeed clean, but it is wrong for you to make others fall by what you eat; **21** it is good not to eat meat or drink wine or do anything that makes your brother or sister stumble.[b] **22** The faith that you have, have as your own conviction before God. Blessed are those who have no reason to condemn themselves because of what they approve. **23** But those who have doubts are condemned if they eat, because they do not act from faith; for whatever does not proceed from faith is sin.

1 Cor 8:7–13

It is not everyone, however, who has this knowledge. Since some have become so accustomed to idols until now, they still think of the food they eat as food offered to an idol; and their conscience, being weak, is defiled. **8** "Food will not bring us close to God." We are no worse off if we do not eat, and no better off if we do. **9** But take care that this liberty of yours does not somehow become a stumbling block to the weak. **10** For if others see you, who possess knowledge, eating in the temple of an idol, might they not, since their conscience is weak, be encouraged to the point of eating food sacrificed to idols? **11** So by your knowledge those weak believers for whom Christ died are destroyed. **12** But when you thus sin against members of your family, and wound their conscience when it is weak, you sin against Christ. **13** Therefore, if food is a cause of their falling, I will never eat meat, so that I may not cause one of them to fall.

1 Tim 4:1–5

Now the Spirit expressly says that in later times some will renounce the faith by paying attention to deceitful spirits and teachings of demons, **2** through the hypocrisy of liars whose consciences are seared with a hot iron. **3** They forbid marriage and demand abstinence from foods, which God created to be received with thanksgiving by those who believe and know the truth. **4** For everything created by God is good, and nothing

§ 135 [a] **Rom 14:19** *Let us then pursue* Other ancient authorities read *We then pursue* [b] **Rom 14:21** *stumble* Other ancient authorities add *or be upset or be weakened*

ἀπόβλητον μετὰ εὐχαριστίας λαμβα-
νόμενον· 5 ἁγιάζεται γὰρ διὰ λόγου θεοῦ
καὶ ἐντεύξεως.

Titus 1:10–16

Εἰσὶν γὰρ πολλοὶ [καὶ] ἀνυπότακτοι,
ματαιολόγοι καὶ φρεναπάται, μάλιστα
οἱ ἐκ τῆς περιτομῆς, 11 οὓς δεῖ ἐπιστο-
μίζειν, οἵτινες ὅλους οἴκους ἀνατρέπουσιν
διδάσκοντες ἃ μὴ δεῖ αἰσχροῦ κέρδους
χάριν. 12 εἶπέν τις ἐξ αὐτῶν ἴδιος αὐτῶν
προφήτης· Κρῆτες ἀεὶ ψεῦσται, κακὰ
θηρία, γαστέρες ἀργαί. 13 ἡ μαρτυρία
αὕτη ἐστὶν ἀληθής. δι' ἣν αἰτίαν ἔλεγχε
αὐτοὺς ἀποτόμως, ἵνα ὑγιαίνωσιν ἐν τῇ
πίστει, 14 μὴ προσέχοντες Ἰουδαϊκοῖς
μύθοις καὶ ἐντολαῖς ἀνθρώπων ἀπο-
στρεφομένων τὴν ἀλήθειαν. 15 πάντα
καθαρὰ τοῖς καθαροῖς· τοῖς δὲ μεμιαμ-
μένοις καὶ ἀπίστοις οὐδὲν καθαρόν,
ἀλλὰ μεμίανται αὐτῶν καὶ ὁ νοῦς καὶ
ἡ συνείδησις. 16 θεὸν ὁμολογοῦσιν εἰδέ-
ναι, τοῖς δὲ ἔργοις ἀρνοῦνται, βδελυκτοὶ
ὄντες καὶ ἀπειθεῖς καὶ πρὸς πᾶν ἔργον
ἀγαθὸν ἀδόκιμοι.

Cf. Rom 14:1–12; 15:1–6; 1 Cor 6:12–13; 7:12–14.

See also § 132 Purity Laws and Sabbath Keeping; § 133 Food Offered to Idols; § 134 Weak and Strong.

136. Table Fellowship

1 Cor 5:9–13

Ἔγραψα ὑμῖν ἐν τῇ ἐπιστολῇ μὴ συν-
αναμίγνυσθαι πόρνοις, 10 οὐ πάντως
τοῖς πόρνοις τοῦ κόσμου τούτου ἢ τοῖς
πλεονέκταις καὶ ἅρπαξιν ἢ εἰδωλολά-
τραις, ἐπεὶ ὠφείλετε ἄρα ἐκ τοῦ κό-
σμου ἐξελθεῖν. 11 νῦν δὲ ἔγραψα ὑμῖν
μὴ συναναμίγνυσθαι ἐάν τις ἀδελφὸς
ὀνομαζόμενος ᾖ πόρνος ἢ πλεονέκτης
ἢ εἰδωλολάτρης ἢ λοίδορος ἢ μέθυσος
ἢ ἅρπαξ, τῷ τοιούτῳ μηδὲ συνεσθίειν.
12 τί γάρ μοι τοὺς ἔξω κρίνειν; οὐχὶ τοὺς
ἔσω ὑμεῖς κρίνετε; 13 τοὺς δὲ ἔξω ὁ θεὸς
κρινεῖ. ἐξάρατε τὸν πονηρὸν ἐξ ὑμῶν
αὐτῶν.

1 Cor 10:25–11:1

Πᾶν τὸ ἐν μακέλλῳ πωλούμενον ἐσθίετε
μηδὲν ἀνακρίνοντες διὰ τὴν συνείδησιν·
26 τοῦ κυρίου γὰρ ἡ γῆ καὶ τὸ πλήρωμα
αὐτῆς. 27 εἴ τις καλεῖ ὑμᾶς τῶν ἀπίστων
καὶ θέλετε πορεύεσθαι, πᾶν τὸ παρατι-
θέμενον ὑμῖν ἐσθίετε μηδὲν ἀνακρίνοντες
διὰ τὴν συνείδησιν. 28 ἐὰν δέ τις ὑμῖν
εἴπῃ· τοῦτο ἱερόθυτόν ἐστιν, μὴ ἐσθί-
ετε δι' ἐκεῖνον τὸν μηνύσαντα καὶ τὴν
συνείδησιν· 29 συνείδησιν δὲ λέγω οὐχὶ
τὴν ἑαυτοῦ ἀλλὰ τὴν τοῦ ἑτέρου. ἱνατί
γὰρ ἡ ἐλευθερία μου κρίνεται ὑπὸ ἄλλης
συνειδήσεως; 30 εἰ ἐγὼ χάριτι μετέχω, τί
βλασφημοῦμαι ὑπὲρ οὗ ἐγὼ εὐχαριστῶ;
31 Εἴτε οὖν ἐσθίετε εἴτε πίνετε εἴτε τι
ποιεῖτε, πάντα εἰς δόξαν θεοῦ ποιεῖτε.
32 ἀπρόσκοποι καὶ Ἰουδαίοις γίνεσθε
καὶ Ἕλλησιν καὶ τῇ ἐκκλησίᾳ τοῦ θεοῦ,
33 καθὼς κἀγὼ πάντα πᾶσιν ἀρέσκω μὴ
ζητῶν τὸ ἐμαυτοῦ σύμφορον ἀλλὰ τὸ τῶν
πολλῶν, ἵνα σωθῶσιν. **11** μιμηταί μου
γίνεσθε καθὼς κἀγὼ Χριστοῦ.

Gal 2:11–14

Ὅτε δὲ ἦλθεν Κηφᾶς εἰς Ἀντιόχειαν,
κατὰ πρόσωπον αὐτῷ ἀντέστην, ὅτι κα-
τεγνωσμένος ἦν. 12 πρὸ τοῦ γὰρ ἐλθεῖν
τινας ἀπὸ Ἰακώβου μετὰ τῶν ἐθνῶν
συνήσθιεν· ὅτε δὲ ἦλθον, ὑπέστελλεν καὶ
ἀφώριζεν ἑαυτὸν φοβούμενος τοὺς ἐκ
περιτομῆς. 13 καὶ συνυπεκρίθησαν αὐτῷ
[καὶ] οἱ λοιποὶ Ἰουδαῖοι, ὥστε καὶ Βαρ-
ναβᾶς συναπήχθη αὐτῶν τῇ ὑποκρίσει.
14 ἀλλ' ὅτε εἶδον ὅτι οὐκ ὀρθοποδοῦσιν
πρὸς τὴν ἀλήθειαν τοῦ εὐαγγελίου,
εἶπον τῷ Κηφᾷ ἔμπροσθεν πάντων· εἰ
σὺ Ἰουδαῖος ὑπάρχων ἐθνικῶς καὶ οὐχὶ
Ἰουδαϊκῶς ζῇς, πῶς τὰ ἔθνη ἀναγκάζεις
ἰουδαΐζειν;

Acts 16:14–15

καί τις γυνὴ ὀνόματι Λυδία, πορφυ-
ρόπωλις πόλεως Θυατείρων σεβομένη
τὸν θεόν, ἤκουεν, ἧς ὁ κύριος διήνοιξεν
τὴν καρδίαν προσέχειν τοῖς λαλουμένοις
ὑπὸ τοῦ Παύλου. 15 ὡς δὲ ἐβαπτίσθη καὶ
ὁ οἶκος αὐτῆς, παρεκάλεσεν λέγουσα·
εἰ κεκρίκατέ με πιστὴν τῷ κυρίῳ εἶναι,
εἰσελθόντες εἰς τὸν οἶκόν μου μένετε·
καὶ παρεβιάσατο ἡμᾶς.

Acts 16:32–34

καὶ ἐλάλησαν αὐτῷ τὸν λόγον τοῦ ⸀κυ-
ρίου σὺν πᾶσιν τοῖς ἐν τῇ οἰκίᾳ αὐτοῦ.
33 καὶ παραλαβὼν αὐτοὺς ἐν ἐκείνῃ
τῇ ὥρᾳ τῆς νυκτὸς ἔλουσεν ἀπὸ τῶν
πληγῶν, καὶ ἐβαπτίσθη αὐτὸς καὶ οἱ
αὐτοῦ πάντες παραχρῆμα, 34 ἀναγαγών
τε αὐτοὺς εἰς τὸν οἶκον παρέθηκεν τρά-
πεζαν καὶ ἠγαλλιάσατο πανοικεὶ πεπι-
στευκὼς τῷ θεῷ.

Acts 20:7–12

Ἐν δὲ τῇ μιᾷ τῶν σαββάτων συνηγμένων
ἡμῶν κλάσαι ἄρτον, ὁ Παῦλος διελέγετο
αὐτοῖς μέλλων ἐξιέναι τῇ ἐπαύριον, πα-
ρέτεινέν τε τὸν λόγον μέχρι μεσονυκτίου.
8 ἦσαν δὲ λαμπάδες ἱκαναὶ ἐν τῷ ὑπερῴῳ
οὗ ἦμεν συνηγμένοι. 9 καθεζόμενος δέ
τις νεανίας ὀνόματι Εὔτυχος ἐπὶ τῆς
θυρίδος, καταφερόμενος ὕπνῳ βαθεῖ
διαλεγομένου τοῦ Παύλου ἐπὶ πλεῖον,
κατενεχθεὶς ἀπὸ τοῦ ὕπνου ἔπεσεν ἀπὸ
τοῦ τριστέγου κάτω καὶ ἤρθη νεκρός.
10 καταβὰς δὲ ὁ Παῦλος ἐπέπεσεν αὐτῷ
καὶ συμπεριλαβὼν εἶπεν· μὴ θορυβεῖ-
σθε, ἡ γὰρ ψυχὴ αὐτοῦ ἐν αὐτῷ ἐστιν.
11 ἀναβὰς δὲ καὶ κλάσας τὸν ἄρτον καὶ
γευσάμενος ἐφ' ἱκανόν τε ὁμιλήσας
ἄχρι αὐγῆς, οὕτως ἐξῆλθεν. 12 ἤγαγον
δὲ τὸν παῖδα ζῶντα καὶ παρεκλήθησαν
οὐ μετρίως.

Acts 27:33–38

Ἄχρι δὲ οὗ ἡμέρα ἤμελλεν γίνεσθαι, πα-
ρεκάλει ὁ Παῦλος ἅπαντας μεταλαβεῖν
τροφῆς λέγων· τεσσαρεσκαιδεκάτην
σήμερον ἡμέραν προσδοκῶντες ἄσιτοι
διατελεῖτε μηθὲν προσλαβόμενοι. 34 διὸ
παρακαλῶ ὑμᾶς μεταλαβεῖν τροφῆς·
τοῦτο γὰρ πρὸς τῆς ὑμετέρας σωτηρίας
ὑπάρχει, οὐδενὸς γὰρ ὑμῶν θρὶξ ἀπὸ τῆς
κεφαλῆς ἀπολεῖται. 35 εἴπας δὲ ταῦτα

§ 136 **Acts 16:32** ***κυριου*** 𝔓45 𝔓74 ℵ2 A C (D) E 33. 1739 *Byz*] θεου ℵ* B

is to be rejected, provided it is received with thanksgiving; **5** for it is sanctified by God's word and by prayer.

Titus 1:10–16

There are also many rebellious people, idle talkers and deceivers, especially those of the circumcision; **11** they must be silenced, since they are upsetting whole families by teaching for sordid gain what it is not right to teach. **12** It was one of them, their very own prophet, who said, "Cretans are always liars, vicious brutes, lazy gluttons." **13** That testimony is true. For this reason rebuke them sharply, so that they may become sound in the faith, **14** not paying attention to Jewish myths or to commandments of those who reject the truth. **15** To the pure all things are pure, but to the corrupt and unbelieving nothing is pure. Their very minds and consciences are corrupted. **16** They profess to know God, but they deny him by their actions. They are detestable, disobedient, unfit for any good work.

Cf. Rom 14:1–12; 15:1–6; 1 Cor 6:12–13; 7:12–14.

See also § 132 Purity Laws and Sabbath Keeping; § 133 Food Offered to Idols; § 134 Weak and Strong.

136. Table Fellowship

1 Cor 5:9–13

I wrote to you in my letter not to associate with sexually immoral persons— **10** not at all meaning the immoral of this world, or the greedy and robbers, or idolaters, since you would then need to go out of the world. **11** But now I am writing to you not to associate with anyone who bears the name of brother or sister who is sexually immoral or greedy, or is an idolater, reviler, drunkard, or robber. Do not even eat with such a one. **12** For what have I to do with judging those outside? Is it not those who are inside that you are to judge? **13** God will judge those outside. "Drive out the wicked person from among you."

1 Cor 10:25–11:1

Eat whatever is sold in the meat market without raising any question on the ground of conscience, **26** for "the earth and its fullness are the Lord's." **27** If an unbeliever invites you to a meal and you are disposed to go, eat whatever is set before you without raising any question on the ground of conscience. **28** But if someone says to you, "This has been offered in sacrifice," then do not eat it, out of consideration for the one who informed you, and for the sake of conscience— **29** I mean the other's conscience, not your own. For why should my liberty be subject to the judgment of someone else's conscience? **30** If I partake with thankfulness, why should I be denounced because of that for which I give thanks? **31** So, whether you eat or drink, or whatever you do, do everything for the glory of God. **32** Give no offense to Jews or to Greeks or to the church of God, **33** just as I try to please everyone in everything I do, not seeking my own advantage, but that of many, so that they may be saved. **11** Be imitators of me, as I am of Christ.

Gal 2:11–14

But when Cephas came to Antioch, I opposed him to his face, because he stood self-condemned; **12** for until certain people came from James, he used to eat with the Gentiles. But after they came, he drew back and kept himself separate for fear of the circumcision faction. **13** And the other Jews joined him in this hypocrisy, so that even Barnabas was led astray by their hypocrisy. **14** But when I saw that they were not acting consistently with the truth of the gospel, I said to Cephas before them all, "If you, though a Jew, live like a Gentile and not like a Jew, how can you compel the Gentiles to live like Jews?"

Acts 16:14–15

A certain woman named Lydia, a worshiper of God, was listening to us; she was from the city of Thyatira and a dealer in purple cloth. The Lord opened her heart to listen eagerly to what was said by Paul. **15** When she and her household were baptized, she urged us, saying, "If you have judged me to be faithful to the Lord, come and stay at my home." And she prevailed upon us.

Acts 16:32–34

They spoke the word of the Lord[a] to him and to all who were in his house. **33** At the same hour of the night he took them and washed their wounds; then he and his entire family were baptized without delay. **34** He brought them up into the house and set food before them; and he and his entire household rejoiced that he had become a believer in God.

Acts 20:7–12

On the first day of the week, when we met to break bread, Paul was holding a discussion with them; since he intended to leave the next day, he continued speaking until midnight. **8** There were many lamps in the room upstairs where we were meeting. **9** A young man named Eutychus, who was sitting in the window, began to sink off into a deep sleep while Paul talked still longer. Overcome by sleep, he fell to the ground three floors below and was picked up dead. **10** But Paul went down, and bending over him took him in his arms, and said, "Do not be alarmed, for his life is in him." **11** Then Paul went upstairs, and after he had broken bread and eaten, he continued to converse with them until dawn; then he left. **12** Meanwhile they had taken the boy away alive and were not a little comforted.

Acts 27:33–38

Just before daybreak, Paul urged all of them to take some food, saying, "Today is the fourteenth day that you have been in suspense and remaining without food, having eaten nothing. **34** Therefore I urge you to take some food, for it will help you survive; for none of you will lose a hair from your heads." **35** After he had said this, he took bread;

§ 136 [a] **Acts 16:32** *word of the Lord* Other ancient authorities read *word of God*

καὶ λαβὼν ἄρτον εὐχαρίστησεν τῷ θεῷ ἐνώπιον πάντων καὶ κλάσας ἤρξατο ἐσθίειν. **36** εὔθυμοι δὲ γενόμενοι πάντες καὶ αὐτοὶ προσελάβοντο τροφῆς. **37** ἤμεθα δὲ αἱ πᾶσαι ψυχαὶ ἐν τῷ πλοίῳ ⸂διακόσιαι ἑβδομήκοντα ἕξ⸃. **38** κορεσθέντες δὲ τροφῆς ἐκούφιζον τὸ πλοῖον ἐκβαλλόμενοι τὸν σῖτον εἰς τὴν θάλασσαν.

Cf. 1 Cor 10:14–22; 11:17–34.

137. Paul's Example of Social Flexibility

1 Cor 9:19–23

Ἐλεύθερος γὰρ ὢν ἐκ πάντων πᾶσιν ἐμαυτὸν ἐδούλωσα, ἵνα τοὺς πλείονας κερδήσω· **20** καὶ ἐγενόμην τοῖς Ἰουδαίοις ὡς Ἰουδαῖος, ἵνα Ἰουδαίους κερδήσω· τοῖς ὑπὸ νόμον ὡς ὑπὸ νόμον, μὴ ὢν αὐτὸς ὑπὸ νόμον, ἵνα τοὺς ὑπὸ νόμον κερδήσω· **21** τοῖς ἀνόμοις ὡς ἄνομος, μὴ ὢν ἄνομος θεοῦ ἀλλ' ἔννομος Χριστοῦ, ἵνα κερδάνω τοὺς ἀνόμους· **22** ἐγενόμην τοῖς ἀσθενέσιν ἀσθενής, ἵνα τοὺς ἀσθενεῖς κερδήσω· τοῖς πᾶσιν γέγονα πάντα, ἵνα πάντως τινὰς σώσω. **23** πάντα δὲ ποιῶ διὰ τὸ εὐαγγέλιον, ἵνα συγκοινωνὸς αὐτοῦ γένωμαι.

1 Cor 10:33–11:1

καθὼς κἀγὼ πάντα πᾶσιν ἀρέσκω μὴ ζητῶν τὸ ἐμαυτοῦ σύμφορον ἀλλὰ τὸ τῶν πολλῶν, ἵνα σωθῶσιν. **11** μιμηταί μου γίνεσθε καθὼς κἀγὼ Χριστοῦ.

2 Cor 11:29

τίς ἀσθενεῖ καὶ οὐκ ἀσθενῶ; τίς σκανδαλίζεται καὶ οὐκ ἐγὼ πυροῦμαι;

Acts 16:1–3

Κατήντησεν δὲ [καὶ] εἰς Δέρβην καὶ εἰς Λύστραν. καὶ ἰδοὺ μαθητής τις ἦν ἐκεῖ ὀνόματι Τιμόθεος, υἱὸς γυναικὸς Ἰουδαίας πιστῆς, πατρὸς δὲ Ἕλληνος, **2** ὃς ἐμαρτυρεῖτο ὑπὸ τῶν ἐν Λύστροις καὶ Ἰκονίῳ ἀδελφῶν. **3** τοῦτον ἠθέλησεν ὁ Παῦλος σὺν αὐτῷ ἐξελθεῖν, καὶ λαβὼν περιέτεμεν αὐτὸν διὰ τοὺς Ἰουδαίους τοὺς ὄντας ἐν τοῖς τόποις ἐκείνοις· ᾔδεισαν γὰρ ἅπαντες ὅτι Ἕλλην ὁ πατὴρ αὐτοῦ ὑπῆρχεν.

Acts 21:20–26

Οἱ δὲ ἀκούσαντες ἐδόξαζον τὸν θεὸν εἶπόν τε αὐτῷ· θεωρεῖς, ἀδελφέ, πόσαι μυριάδες εἰσὶν ἐν τοῖς Ἰουδαίοις τῶν πεπιστευκότων καὶ πάντες ζηλωταὶ τοῦ νόμου ὑπάρχουσιν· **21** κατηχήθησαν δὲ περὶ σοῦ ὅτι ἀποστασίαν διδάσκεις ἀπὸ Μωϋσέως τοὺς κατὰ τὰ ἔθνη πάντας Ἰουδαίους λέγων μὴ περιτέμνειν αὐτοὺς τὰ τέκνα μηδὲ τοῖς ἔθεσιν περιπατεῖν. **22** τί οὖν ἐστιν; πάντως ⸀ἀκούσονται ὅτι ἐλήλυθας. **23** τοῦτο οὖν ποίησον ὅ σοι λέγομεν· εἰσὶν ἡμῖν ἄνδρες τέσσαρες εὐχὴν ἔχοντες ἐφ' ἑαυτῶν. **24** τούτους παραλαβὼν ἁγνίσθητι σὺν αὐτοῖς καὶ δαπάνησον ἐπ' αὐτοῖς ἵνα ξυρήσονται τὴν κεφαλήν, καὶ γνώσονται πάντες ὅτι ὧν κατήχηνται περὶ σοῦ οὐδέν ἐστιν ἀλλὰ στοιχεῖς καὶ αὐτὸς φυλάσσων τὸν νόμον. **25** περὶ δὲ τῶν πεπιστευκότων ἐθνῶν ἡμεῖς ἐπεστείλαμεν κρίναντες φυλάσσεσθαι αὐτοὺς τό τε εἰδωλόθυτον καὶ αἷμα ⸂καὶ πνικτὸν⸃ καὶ πορνείαν. **26** Τότε ὁ Παῦλος παραλαβὼν τοὺς ἄνδρας τῇ ἐχομένῃ ἡμέρᾳ σὺν αὐτοῖς ἁγνισθείς, εἰσῄει εἰς τὸ ἱερὸν διαγγέλλων τὴν ἐκπλήρωσιν τῶν ἡμερῶν τοῦ ἁγνισμοῦ ἕως οὗ προσηνέχθη ὑπὲρ ἑνὸς ἑκάστου αὐτῶν ἡ προσφορά.

Cf. Acts 19:37; 28:11.

See also § 136 Table Fellowship.

138. The Apostle's Jewish Identity

Rom 11:1

Λέγω οὖν, μὴ ἀπώσατο ὁ θεὸς τὸν λαὸν αὐτοῦ; μὴ γένοιτο· καὶ γὰρ ἐγὼ Ἰσραηλίτης εἰμί, ἐκ σπέρματος Ἀβραάμ, φυλῆς Βενιαμίν.

1 Cor 7:17–19

Εἰ μὴ ἑκάστῳ ὡς ἐμέρισεν ὁ κύριος, ἕκαστον ὡς κέκληκεν ὁ θεός, οὕτως περιπατείτω. καὶ οὕτως ἐν ταῖς ἐκκλησίαις πάσαις διατάσσομαι. **18** περιτετμημένος τις ἐκλήθη, μὴ ἐπισπάσθω· ἐν ἀκροβυστίᾳ κέκληταί τις, μὴ περιτεμνέσθω. **19** ἡ περιτομὴ οὐδέν ἐστιν καὶ ἡ ἀκροβυστία οὐδέν ἐστιν, ἀλλὰ τήρησις ἐντολῶν θεοῦ.

2 Cor 11:22

Ἑβραῖοί εἰσιν; κἀγώ. Ἰσραηλῖταί εἰσιν; κἀγώ. σπέρμα Ἀβραάμ εἰσιν; κἀγώ.

Gal 1:13–14

Ἠκούσατε γὰρ τὴν ἐμὴν ἀναστροφήν ποτε ἐν τῷ Ἰουδαϊσμῷ, ὅτι καθ' ὑπερβολὴν ἐδίωκον τὴν ἐκκλησίαν τοῦ θεοῦ καὶ ἐπόρθουν αὐτήν, **14** καὶ προέκοπτον ἐν τῷ Ἰουδαϊσμῷ ὑπὲρ πολλοὺς συνηλικιώτας ἐν τῷ γένει μου, περισσοτέρως ζηλωτὴς ὑπάρχων τῶν πατρικῶν μου παραδόσεων.

Gal 2:15

Ἡμεῖς φύσει Ἰουδαῖοι καὶ οὐκ ἐξ ἐθνῶν ἁμαρτωλοί

Phil 3:4–6

καίπερ ἐγὼ ἔχων πεποίθησιν καὶ ἐν σαρκί. Εἴ τις δοκεῖ ἄλλος πεποιθέναι ἐν σαρκί, ἐγὼ μᾶλλον· **5** περιτομῇ ὀκταήμερος, ἐκ γένους Ἰσραήλ, φυλῆς Βενιαμίν, Ἑβραῖος ἐξ Ἑβραίων, κατὰ νόμον Φαρισαῖος, **6** κατὰ ζῆλος διώκων τὴν

Acts 27:37 ***διακοσιαι εβδομηκοντα εξ*** ℵ C 33. 1739 *Byz*] ως εβδομηκοντα εξ B ¦ διακοσιαι εβδομηκοντα πεντε A **§ 137 Acts 21:22** ***ακουσονται*** B C*vid 1739*] δει συνελθειν πληθος· ακουσονται γαρ 𝔓74 ℵ(*) A (C2) (D) E 33. 1739v.l. (*Byz*) **Acts 21:25** ***και πνικτον*** 𝔓74 ℵ A B C (E) 33. 1739] *om*. D

and giving thanks to God in the presence of all, he broke it and began to eat. 36 Then all of them were encouraged and took food for themselves. 37 (We were in all two hundred seventy-six[b] persons in the ship.) 38 After they had satisfied their hunger, they lightened the ship by throwing the wheat into the sea.

Cf. 1 Cor 10:14–22; 11:17–34.

137. *Paul's Example of Social Flexibility*

1 Cor 9:19–23

For though I am free with respect to all, I have made myself a slave to all, so that I might win more of them. 20 To the Jews I became as a Jew, in order to win Jews. To those under the law I became as one under the law (though I myself am not under the law) so that I might win those under the law. 21 To those outside the law I became as one outside the law (though I am not free from God's law but am under Christ's law) so that I might win those outside the law. 22 To the weak I became weak, so that I might win the weak. I have become all things to all people, that I might by all means save some. 23 I do it all for the sake of the gospel, so that I may share in its blessings.

1 Cor 10:33–11:1

just as I try to please everyone in everything I do, not seeking my own advantage, but that of many, so that they may be saved. **11** Be imitators of me, as I am of Christ.

2 Cor 11:29

Who is weak, and I am not weak? Who is made to stumble, and I am not indignant?

Acts 16:1–3

Paul went on also to Derbe and to Lystra, where there was a disciple named Timothy, the son of a Jewish woman who was a believer; but his father was a Greek. 2 He was well spoken of by the believers in Lystra and Iconium. 3 Paul wanted Timothy to accompany him; and he took him and had him circumcised because of the Jews who were in those places, for they all knew that his father was a Greek.

Acts 21:20–26

When they heard it, they praised God. Then they said to him, "You see, brother, how many thousands of believers there are among the Jews, and they are all zealous for the law. 21 They have been told about you that you teach all the Jews living among the Gentiles to forsake Moses, and that you tell them not to circumcise their children or observe the customs. 22 What then is to be done? They will certainly hear[a] that you have come. 23 So do what we tell you. We have four men who are under a vow. 24 Join these men, go through the rite of purification with them, and pay for the shaving of their heads. Thus all will know that there is nothing in what they have been told about you, but that you yourself observe and guard the law. 25 But as for the Gentiles who have become believers, we have sent a letter with our judgment that they should abstain from what has been sacrificed to idols and from blood and from what is strangled[b] and from fornication." 26 Then Paul took the men, and the next day, having purified himself, he entered the temple with them, making public the completion of the days of purification when the sacrifice would be made for each of them.

Cf. Acts 19:37; 28:11.

See also § 136 Table Fellowship.

138. *The Apostle's Jewish Identity*

Rom 11:1

I ask, then, has God rejected his people? By no means! I myself am an Israelite, a descendant of Abraham, a member of the tribe of Benjamin.

1 Cor 7:17–19

However that may be, let each of you lead the life that the Lord has assigned, to which God called you. This is my rule in all the churches. 18 Was anyone at the time of his call already circumcised? Let him not seek to remove the marks of circumcision. Was anyone at the time of his call uncircumcised? Let him not seek circumcision. 19 Circumcision is nothing, and uncircumcision is nothing; but obeying the commandments of God is everything.

2 Cor 11:22

Are they Hebrews? So am I. Are they Israelites? So am I. Are they descendants of Abraham? So am I.

Gal 1:13–14

You have heard, no doubt, of my earlier life in Judaism. I was violently persecuting the church of God and was trying to destroy it. 14 I advanced in Judaism beyond many among my people of the same age, for I was far more zealous for the traditions of my ancestors.

Gal 2:15

We ourselves are Jews by birth and not Gentile sinners

Phil 3:4–6

even though I, too, have reason for confidence in the flesh. If anyone else has reason to be confident in the flesh, I have more: 5 circumcised on the eighth day, a member of the people of Israel, of the tribe of Benjamin, a Hebrew born of Hebrews; as to the law, a Pharisee; 6 as to zeal, a persecutor of

[b] **Acts 27:37** *two hundred seventy-six* A few ancient authorities read *about seventy-six* **§ 137** [a] **Acts 21:22** *They will certainly hear* Other ancient authorities read *A multitude must certainly come together; for they will hear* [b] **Acts 21:25** *and from what is strangled* A few ancient authorities lack *and from what is strangled*

ἐκκλησίαν, κατὰ δικαιοσύνην τὴν ἐν νόμῳ γενόμενος ἄμεμπτος.

2 Tim 1:3

Χάριν ἔχω τῷ θεῷ, ᾧ λατρεύω ἀπὸ προγόνων ἐν καθαρᾷ συνειδήσει, ὡς ἀδιάλειπτον ἔχω τὴν περὶ σοῦ μνείαν ἐν ταῖς δεήσεσίν μου νυκτὸς καὶ ἡμέρας

Acts 16:1–3

Κατήντησεν δὲ [καὶ] εἰς Δέρβην καὶ εἰς Λύστραν. καὶ ἰδοὺ μαθητής τις ἦν ἐκεῖ ὀνόματι Τιμόθεος, υἱὸς γυναικὸς Ἰουδαίας πιστῆς, πατρὸς δὲ Ἕλληνος, **2** ὃς ἐμαρτυρεῖτο ὑπὸ τῶν ἐν Λύστροις καὶ Ἰκονίῳ ἀδελφῶν. **3** τοῦτον ἠθέλησεν ὁ Παῦλος σὺν αὐτῷ ἐξελθεῖν, καὶ λαβὼν περιέτεμεν αὐτὸν διὰ τοὺς Ἰουδαίους τοὺς ὄντας ἐν τοῖς τόποις ἐκείνοις· ᾔδεισαν γὰρ ἅπαντες ὅτι Ἕλλην ὁ πατὴρ αὐτοῦ ὑπῆρχεν.

Acts 16:20–21

καὶ προσαγαγόντες αὐτοὺς τοῖς στρατηγοῖς εἶπαν· οὗτοι οἱ ἄνθρωποι ἐκταράσσουσιν ἡμῶν τὴν πόλιν, Ἰουδαῖοι ὑπάρχοντες, **21** καὶ καταγγέλλουσιν ἔθη ἃ οὐκ ἔξεστιν ἡμῖν παραδέχεσθαι οὐδὲ ποιεῖν Ῥωμαίοις οὖσιν.

Acts 18:18

Ὁ δὲ Παῦλος ἔτι προσμείνας ἡμέρας ἱκανὰς τοῖς ἀδελφοῖς ἀποταξάμενος ἐξέπλει εἰς τὴν Συρίαν, καὶ σὺν αὐτῷ Πρίσκιλλα καὶ Ἀκύλας, κειράμενος ἐν Κεγχρεαῖς τὴν κεφαλήν, εἶχεν γὰρ εὐχήν.

Acts 20:16

κεκρίκει γὰρ ὁ Παῦλος παραπλεῦσαι τὴν Ἔφεσον, ὅπως μὴ γένηται αὐτῷ χρονοτριβῆσαι ἐν τῇ Ἀσίᾳ· ἔσπευδεν γὰρ εἰ δυνατὸν εἴη αὐτῷ τὴν ἡμέραν τῆς πεντηκοστῆς γενέσθαι εἰς Ἱεροσόλυμα.

Acts 21:20–26

Οἱ δὲ ἀκούσαντες ἐδόξαζον τὸν θεὸν εἶπόν τε αὐτῷ· θεωρεῖς, ἀδελφέ, πόσαι μυριάδες εἰσὶν ἐν τοῖς Ἰουδαίοις τῶν πεπιστευκότων καὶ πάντες ζηλωταὶ τοῦ νόμου ὑπάρχουσιν· **21** κατηχήθησαν δὲ περὶ σοῦ ὅτι ἀποστασίαν διδάσκεις ἀπὸ Μωϋσέως τοὺς κατὰ τὰ ἔθνη πάντας Ἰουδαίους λέγων μὴ περιτέμνειν αὐτοὺς τὰ τέκνα μηδὲ τοῖς ἔθεσιν περιπατεῖν. **22** τί οὖν ἐστιν; πάντως ⸀ἀκούσονται ὅτι ἐλήλυθας. **23** τοῦτο οὖν ποίησον ὅ σοι λέγομεν· εἰσὶν ἡμῖν ἄνδρες τέσσαρες εὐχὴν ἔχοντες ἐφ᾽ ἑαυτῶν. **24** τούτους παραλαβὼν ἁγνίσθητι σὺν αὐτοῖς καὶ δαπάνησον ἐπ᾽ αὐτοῖς ἵνα ξυρήσονται τὴν κεφαλήν, καὶ γνώσονται πάντες ὅτι ὧν κατήχηνται περὶ σοῦ οὐδέν ἐστιν ἀλλὰ στοιχεῖς καὶ αὐτὸς φυλάσσων τὸν νόμον. **25** περὶ δὲ τῶν πεπιστευκότων ἐθνῶν ἡμεῖς ἐπεστείλαμεν κρίναντες φυλάσσεσθαι αὐτοὺς τό τε εἰδωλόθυτον καὶ αἷμα ⸂καὶ πνικτὸν⸃ καὶ πορνείαν. **26** Τότε ὁ Παῦλος παραλαβὼν τοὺς ἄνδρας τῇ ἐχομένῃ ἡμέρᾳ σὺν αὐτοῖς ἁγνισθείς, εἰσῄει εἰς τὸ ἱερὸν διαγγέλλων τὴν ἐκπλήρωσιν τῶν ἡμερῶν τοῦ ἁγνισμοῦ ἕως οὗ προσηνέχθη ὑπὲρ ἑνὸς ἑκάστου αὐτῶν ἡ προσφορά.

Acts 21:39–22:5

εἶπεν δὲ ὁ Παῦλος· ἐγὼ ἄνθρωπος μέν εἰμι Ἰουδαῖος, Ταρσεὺς τῆς Κιλικίας, οὐκ ἀσήμου πόλεως πολίτης· δέομαι δέ σου, ἐπίτρεψόν μοι λαλῆσαι πρὸς τὸν λαόν. **40** ἐπιτρέψαντος δὲ αὐτοῦ ὁ Παῦλος ἑστὼς ἐπὶ τῶν ἀναβαθμῶν κατέσεισεν τῇ χειρὶ τῷ λαῷ. πολλῆς δὲ σιγῆς γενομένης προσεφώνησεν τῇ Ἑβραΐδι διαλέκτῳ λέγων· **22** Ἄνδρες ἀδελφοὶ καὶ πατέρες, ἀκούσατέ μου τῆς πρὸς ὑμᾶς νυνὶ ἀπολογίας. **2** ἀκούσαντες δὲ ὅτι τῇ Ἑβραΐδι διαλέκτῳ προσεφώνει αὐτοῖς, μᾶλλον παρέσχον ἡσυχίαν. καὶ φησίν· **3** ἐγώ εἰμι ἀνὴρ Ἰουδαῖος, γεγεννημένος ἐν Ταρσῷ τῆς Κιλικίας, ἀνατεθραμμένος δὲ ἐν τῇ πόλει ταύτῃ, παρὰ τοὺς πόδας Γαμαλιὴλ πεπαιδευμένος κατὰ ἀκρίβειαν τοῦ πατρῴου νόμου, ζηλωτὴς ὑπάρχων τοῦ θεοῦ καθὼς πάντες ὑμεῖς ἐστε σήμερον· **4** ὃς ταύτην τὴν ὁδὸν ἐδίωξα ἄχρι θανάτου δεσμεύων καὶ παραδιδοὺς εἰς φυλακὰς ἄνδρας τε καὶ γυναῖκας, **5** ὡς καὶ ὁ ἀρχιερεὺς μαρτυρεῖ μοι καὶ πᾶν τὸ πρεσβυτέριον, παρ᾽ ὧν καὶ ἐπιστολὰς δεξάμενος πρὸς τοὺς ἀδελφοὺς εἰς Δαμασκὸν ἐπορευόμην, ἄξων καὶ τοὺς ἐκεῖσε ὄντας δεδεμένους εἰς Ἰερουσαλὴμ ἵνα τιμωρηθῶσιν.

Acts 23:1

Ἀτενίσας δὲ ὁ Παῦλος τῷ συνεδρίῳ εἶπεν· ἄνδρες ἀδελφοί, ἐγὼ πάσῃ συνειδήσει ἀγαθῇ πεπολίτευμαι τῷ θεῷ ἄχρι ταύτης τῆς ἡμέρας.

Acts 23:6

Γνοὺς δὲ ὁ Παῦλος ὅτι τὸ ἓν μέρος ἐστὶν Σαδδουκαίων τὸ δὲ ἕτερον Φαρισαίων ἔκραζεν ἐν τῷ συνεδρίῳ· ἄνδρες ἀδελφοί, ἐγὼ Φαρισαῖός εἰμι, υἱὸς Φαρισαίων, περὶ ἐλπίδος καὶ ἀναστάσεως νεκρῶν [ἐγὼ] κρίνομαι.

Acts 24:14–21

ὁμολογῶ δὲ τοῦτό σοι ὅτι κατὰ τὴν ὁδὸν ἣν λέγουσιν αἵρεσιν, οὕτως λατρεύω τῷ πατρῴῳ θεῷ πιστεύων πᾶσι τοῖς κατὰ τὸν νόμον καὶ τοῖς ἐν τοῖς προφήταις γεγραμμένοις, **15** ἐλπίδα ἔχων εἰς τὸν θεὸν ἣν καὶ αὐτοὶ οὗτοι προσδέχονται, ἀνάστασιν μέλλειν ⸀ἔσεσθαι δικαίων τε καὶ ἀδίκων. **16** ἐν τούτῳ καὶ αὐτὸς ἀσκῶ ἀπρόσκοπον συνείδησιν ἔχειν πρὸς τὸν θεὸν καὶ τοὺς ἀνθρώπους διὰ παντός. **17** δι᾽ ἐτῶν δὲ πλειόνων ἐλεημοσύνας ποιήσων εἰς τὸ ἔθνος μου παρεγενόμην καὶ προσφοράς, **18** ἐν αἷς εὗρόν με ἡγνισμένον ἐν τῷ ἱερῷ οὐ μετὰ ὄχλου οὐδὲ μετὰ θορύβου, **19** τινὲς δὲ ἀπὸ τῆς Ἀσίας Ἰουδαῖοι, οὓς ἔδει ἐπὶ σοῦ παρεῖναι καὶ κατηγορεῖν εἴ τι ἔχοιεν πρὸς ἐμέ. **20** ἢ αὐτοὶ οὗτοι εἰπάτωσαν τί εὗρον ἀδίκημα στάντος μου ἐπὶ τοῦ συνεδρίου, **21** ἢ περὶ μιᾶς ταύτης φωνῆς ἧς ἐκέκραξα ἐν αὐτοῖς ἑστὼς ὅτι περὶ ἀναστάσεως νεκρῶν ἐγὼ κρίνομαι σήμερον ἐφ᾽ ὑμῶν.

Acts 26:2–8

Περὶ πάντων ὧν ἐγκαλοῦμαι ὑπὸ Ἰουδαίων, βασιλεῦ Ἀγρίππα, ἥγημαι ἐμαυτὸν μακάριον ἐπὶ σοῦ μέλλων σήμερον ἀπολογεῖσθαι **3** μάλιστα γνώστην ὄντα σε πάντων τῶν κατὰ Ἰουδαίους ἐθῶν τε καὶ ζητημάτων, διὸ δέομαι μακροθύμως ἀκοῦσαί μου. **4** Τὴν μὲν οὖν βίωσίν μου [τὴν] ἐκ νεότητος τὴν ἀπ᾽ ἀρχῆς γενομένην ἐν τῷ ἔθνει μου ἔν τε Ἱεροσολύμοις ἴσασι πάντες [οἱ] Ἰουδαῖοι **5** προγινώσκοντές με ἄνωθεν, ἐὰν θέλωσι μαρτυρεῖν, ὅτι κατὰ τὴν ἀκριβεστάτην αἵρεσιν τῆς ἡμετέρας θρησκείας ἔζησα Φαρισαῖος. **6** καὶ νῦν ἐπ᾽ ἐλπίδι τῆς εἰς τοὺς πατέρας ἡμῶν

§ 138 **Acts 21:22** ***ακουσονται*** B C*vid 1739*] δει συνελθειν πληθος· ακουσονται γαρ 𝔓74 ℵ(*) A (C²) (D) E 33. 1739v.l. (*Byz*) **Acts 21:25** ***και πνικτον*** 𝔓74 ℵ A B C (E) 33. 1739] *om.* D **Acts 24:15** ***εσεσθαι*** 𝔓74 ℵ A B C 33. 1739] *add.* νεκρων E *Byz*

the church; as to righteousness under the law, blameless.

2 Tim 1:3

I am grateful to God—whom I worship with a clear conscience, as my ancestors did—when I remember you constantly in my prayers night and day.

Acts 16:1–3

Paul went on also to Derbe and to Lystra, where there was a disciple named Timothy, the son of a Jewish woman who was a believer; but his father was a Greek. **2** He was well spoken of by the believers in Lystra and Iconium. **3** Paul wanted Timothy to accompany him; and he took him and had him circumcised because of the Jews who were in those places, for they all knew that his father was a Greek.

Acts 16:20–21

When they had brought them before the magistrates, they said, "These men are disturbing our city; they are Jews **21** and are advocating customs that are not lawful for us as Romans to adopt or observe."

Acts 18:18

After staying there for a considerable time, Paul said farewell to the believers and sailed for Syria, accompanied by Priscilla and Aquila. At Cenchreae he had his hair cut, for he was under a vow.

Acts 20:16

For Paul had decided to sail past Ephesus, so that he might not have to spend time in Asia; he was eager to be in Jerusalem, if possible, on the day of Pentecost.

Acts 21:20–26

When they heard it, they praised God. Then they said to him, "You see, brother, how many thousands of believers there are among the Jews, and they are all zealous for the law. **21** They have been told about you that you teach all the Jews living among the Gentiles to forsake Moses, and that you tell them not to circumcise their children or observe the customs. **22** What then is to be done? They will certainly hear[a] that you have come. **23** So do what we tell you. We have four men who are under a vow. **24** Join these men, go through the rite of purification with them, and pay for the shaving of their heads. Thus all will know that there is nothing in what they have been told about you, but that you yourself observe and guard the law. **25** But as for the Gentiles who have become believers, we have sent a letter with our judgment that they should abstain from what has been sacrificed to idols and from blood and from what is strangled[b] and from fornication." **26** Then Paul took the men, and the next day, having purified himself, he entered the temple with them, making public the completion of the days of purification when the sacrifice would be made for each of them.

Acts 21:39–22:5

Paul replied, "I am a Jew, from Tarsus in Cilicia, a citizen of an important city; I beg you, let me speak to the people." **40** When he had given him permission, Paul stood on the steps and motioned to the people for silence; and when there was a great hush, he addressed them in the Hebrew language, saying: **22** "Brothers and fathers, listen to the defense that I now make before you." **2** When they heard him addressing them in Hebrew, they became even more quiet. Then he said: **3** "I am a Jew, born in Tarsus in Cilicia, but brought up in this city at the feet of Gamaliel, educated strictly according to our ancestral law, being zealous for God, just as all of you are today. **4** I persecuted this Way up to the point of death by binding both men and women and putting them in prison, **5** as the high priest and the whole council of elders can testify about me. From them I also received letters to the brothers in Damascus, and I went there in order to bind those who were there and to bring them back to Jerusalem for punishment.

Acts 23:1

While Paul was looking intently at the council he said, "Brothers, up to this day I have lived my life with a clear conscience before God."

Acts 23:6

When Paul noticed that some were Sadducees and others were Pharisees, he called out in the council, "Brothers, I am a Pharisee, a son of Pharisees. I am on trial concerning the hope of the resurrection of the dead."

Acts 24:14–21

But this I admit to you, that according to the Way, which they call a sect, I worship the God of our ancestors, believing everything laid down according to the law or written in the prophets. **15** I have a hope in God—a hope that they themselves also accept—that there will be a resurrection of both[c] the righteous and the unrighteous. **16** Therefore I do my best always to have a clear conscience toward God and all people. **17** Now after some years I came to bring alms to my nation and to offer sacrifices. **18** While I was doing this, they found me in the temple, completing the rite of purification, without any crowd or disturbance. **19** But there were some Jews from Asia—they ought to be here before you to make an accusation, if they have anything against me. **20** Or let these men here tell what crime they had found when I stood before the council, **21** unless it was this one sentence that I called out while standing before them, 'It is about the resurrection of the dead that I am on trial before you today.'"

Acts 26:2–8

"I consider myself fortunate that it is before you, King Agrippa, I am to make my defense today against all the accusations of the Jews, **3** because you are especially familiar with all the customs and controversies of the Jews; therefore I beg of you to listen to me patiently. **4** "All the Jews know my way of life from my youth, a life spent from the beginning among my own people and in Jerusalem. **5** They have known for a long time, if they are willing to testify, that I have belonged to the strictest sect of our religion and lived as a Pharisee. **6** And now I stand here

§ 138 [a] **Acts 21:22** ***They will certainly hear*** Other ancient authorities read *A multitude must certainly come together; for they will hear* [b] **Acts 21:25** ***and from what is strangled*** A few ancient authorities lack *and from what is strangled* [c] **Acts 24:15** ***of both*** Other ancient authorities read *of the dead, both of*

ἐπαγγελίας γενομένης ὑπὸ τοῦ θεοῦ ἕστηκα κρινόμενος, 7 εἰς ἣν τὸ δωδεκάφυλον ἡμῶν ἐν ἐκτενείᾳ νύκτα καὶ ἡμέραν λατρεῦον ἐλπίζει καταντῆσαι, περὶ ἧς ἐλπίδος ἐγκαλοῦμαι ὑπὸ Ἰουδαίων, βασιλεῦ. 8 τί ἄπιστον κρίνεται παρ' ὑμῖν εἰ ὁ θεὸς νεκροὺς ἐγείρει;

Acts 28:17–20

Ἐγένετο δὲ μετὰ ἡμέρας τρεῖς συγκαλέσασθαι αὐτὸν τοὺς ὄντας τῶν Ἰουδαίων πρώτους· συνελθόντων δὲ αὐτῶν ἔλεγεν πρὸς αὐτούς· ἐγώ, ἄνδρες ἀδελφοί, οὐδὲν ἐναντίον ποιήσας τῷ λαῷ ἢ τοῖς ἔθεσι τοῖς πατρῴοις δέσμιος ἐξ Ἱεροσολύμων παρεδόθην εἰς τὰς χεῖρας τῶν Ῥωμαίων, 18 οἵτινες ἀνακρίναντές με ἐβούλοντο ἀπολῦσαι διὰ τὸ μηδεμίαν αἰτίαν θανάτου ὑπάρχειν ἐν ἐμοί. 19 ἀντιλεγόντων δὲ τῶν Ἰουδαίων ἠναγκάσθην ἐπικαλέσασθαι Καίσαρα οὐχ ὡς τοῦ ἔθνους μου ἔχων τι κατηγορεῖν. 20 διὰ ταύτην οὖν τὴν αἰτίαν παρεκάλεσα ὑμᾶς ἰδεῖν καὶ προσλαλῆσαι, ἕνεκεν γὰρ τῆς ἐλπίδος τοῦ Ἰσραὴλ τὴν ἅλυσιν ταύτην περίκειμαι.

Cf. Rom 9:3; 16:7; 16:11; 16:21; 2 Cor 11:24; Acts 18:21 (v.l.); 20:6; 27:9–10.

139. Human Weakness and God's Power

Rom 8:26–27

Ὡσαύτως δὲ καὶ τὸ πνεῦμα συναντιλαμβάνεται τῇ ἀσθενείᾳ ἡμῶν· τὸ γὰρ τί προσευξώμεθα καθὸ δεῖ οὐκ οἴδαμεν, ἀλλὰ αὐτὸ τὸ πνεῦμα ⸀ὑπερεντυγχάνει στεναγμοῖς ἀλαλήτοις· 27 ὁ δὲ ἐραυνῶν τὰς καρδίας οἶδεν τί τὸ φρόνημα τοῦ πνεύματος, ὅτι κατὰ θεὸν ἐντυγχάνει ὑπὲρ ἁγίων.

1 Cor 1:26–31

Βλέπετε γὰρ τὴν κλῆσιν ὑμῶν, ἀδελφοί, ὅτι οὐ πολλοὶ σοφοὶ κατὰ σάρκα, οὐ πολλοὶ δυνατοί, οὐ πολλοὶ εὐγενεῖς· 27 ἀλλὰ τὰ μωρὰ τοῦ κόσμου ἐξελέξατο ὁ θεός, ἵνα καταισχύνῃ τοὺς σοφούς, καὶ τὰ ἀσθενῆ τοῦ κόσμου ἐξελέξατο ὁ θεός, ἵνα καταισχύνῃ τὰ ἰσχυρά, 28 καὶ τὰ ἀγενῆ τοῦ κόσμου καὶ τὰ ἐξουθενημένα ἐξελέξατο ὁ θεός, τὰ μὴ ὄντα, ἵνα τὰ ὄντα καταργήσῃ, 29 ὅπως μὴ καυχήσηται πᾶσα σὰρξ ἐνώπιον τοῦ θεοῦ. 30 ἐξ αὐτοῦ δὲ ὑμεῖς ἐστε ἐν Χριστῷ Ἰησοῦ, ὃς ἐγενήθη σοφία ἡμῖν ἀπὸ θεοῦ, δικαιοσύνη τε καὶ ἁγιασμὸς καὶ ἀπολύτρωσις, 31 ἵνα καθὼς γέγραπται· ὁ καυχώμενος ἐν κυρίῳ καυχάσθω.

1 Cor 2:1–5

Κἀγὼ ἐλθὼν πρὸς ὑμᾶς, ἀδελφοί, ἦλθον οὐ καθ' ὑπεροχὴν λόγου ἢ σοφίας καταγγέλλων ὑμῖν τὸ ⸀μυστήριον τοῦ θεοῦ. 2 οὐ γὰρ ἔκρινά τι εἰδέναι ἐν ὑμῖν εἰ μὴ Ἰησοῦν Χριστὸν καὶ τοῦτον ἐσταυρωμένον. 3 κἀγὼ ἐν ἀσθενείᾳ καὶ ἐν φόβῳ καὶ ἐν τρόμῳ πολλῷ ἐγενόμην πρὸς ὑμᾶς, 4 καὶ ὁ λόγος μου καὶ τὸ κήρυγμά μου οὐκ ἐν ⸂πειθοῖ[ς] σοφίας [λόγοις]⸃ ἀλλ' ἐν ἀποδείξει πνεύματος καὶ δυνάμεως, 5 ἵνα ἡ πίστις ὑμῶν μὴ ᾖ ἐν σοφίᾳ ἀνθρώπων ἀλλ' ἐν δυνάμει θεοῦ.

1 Cor 4:9–13

δοκῶ γάρ, ὁ θεὸς ἡμᾶς τοὺς ἀποστόλους ἐσχάτους ἀπέδειξεν ὡς ἐπιθανατίους, ὅτι θέατρον ἐγενήθημεν τῷ κόσμῳ καὶ ἀγγέλοις καὶ ἀνθρώποις. 10 ἡμεῖς μωροὶ διὰ Χριστόν, ὑμεῖς δὲ φρόνιμοι ἐν Χριστῷ· ἡμεῖς ἀσθενεῖς, ὑμεῖς δὲ ἰσχυροί· ὑμεῖς ἔνδοξοι, ἡμεῖς δὲ ἄτιμοι. 11 ἄχρι τῆς ἄρτι ὥρας καὶ πεινῶμεν καὶ διψῶμεν καὶ γυμνιτεύομεν καὶ κολαφιζόμεθα καὶ ἀστατοῦμεν 12 καὶ κοπιῶμεν ἐργαζόμενοι ταῖς ἰδίαις χερσίν· λοιδορούμενοι εὐλογοῦμεν, διωκόμενοι ἀνεχόμεθα, 13 δυσφημούμενοι παρακαλοῦμεν· ὡς περικαθάρματα τοῦ κόσμου ἐγενήθημεν, πάντων περίψημα ἕως ἄρτι.

2 Cor 1:3–11

Εὐλογητὸς ὁ θεὸς καὶ πατὴρ τοῦ κυρίου ἡμῶν Ἰησοῦ Χριστοῦ, ὁ πατὴρ τῶν οἰκτιρμῶν καὶ θεὸς πάσης παρακλήσεως, 4 ὁ παρακαλῶν ἡμᾶς ἐπὶ πάσῃ τῇ θλίψει ἡμῶν εἰς τὸ δύνασθαι ἡμᾶς παρακαλεῖν τοὺς ἐν πάσῃ θλίψει διὰ τῆς παρακλήσεως ἧς παρακαλούμεθα αὐτοὶ ὑπὸ τοῦ θεοῦ. 5 ὅτι καθὼς περισσεύει τὰ παθήματα τοῦ Χριστοῦ εἰς ἡμᾶς, οὕτως διὰ τοῦ Χριστοῦ περισσεύει καὶ ἡ παράκλησις ἡμῶν. 6 εἴτε δὲ θλιβόμεθα, ὑπὲρ τῆς ὑμῶν παρακλήσεως καὶ σωτηρίας· εἴτε παρακαλούμεθα, ὑπὲρ τῆς ὑμῶν παρακλήσεως τῆς ἐνεργουμένης ἐν ὑπομονῇ τῶν αὐτῶν παθημάτων ὧν καὶ ἡμεῖς πάσχομεν. 7 καὶ ἡ ἐλπὶς ἡμῶν βεβαία ὑπὲρ ὑμῶν εἰδότες ὅτι ὡς κοινωνοί ἐστε τῶν παθημάτων, οὕτως καὶ τῆς παρακλήσεως. 8 Οὐ γὰρ θέλομεν ὑμᾶς ἀγνοεῖν, ἀδελφοί, ὑπὲρ τῆς θλίψεως ἡμῶν τῆς γενομένης ἐν τῇ Ἀσίᾳ, ὅτι καθ' ὑπερβολὴν ὑπὲρ δύναμιν ἐβαρήθημεν ὥστε ἐξαπορηθῆναι ἡμᾶς καὶ τοῦ ζῆν· 9 ἀλλὰ αὐτοὶ ἐν ἑαυτοῖς τὸ ἀπόκριμα τοῦ θανάτου ἐσχήκαμεν, ἵνα μὴ πεποιθότες ὦμεν ἐφ' ἑαυτοῖς ἀλλ' ἐπὶ τῷ θεῷ τῷ ἐγείροντι τοὺς νεκρούς· 10 ὃς ἐκ ⸂τηλικούτου θανάτου⸃ ἐρρύσατο ἡμᾶς καὶ ῥύσεται, εἰς ὃν ἠλπίκαμεν [ὅτι] καὶ ἔτι ῥύσεται, 11 συνυπουργούντων καὶ ὑμῶν ὑπὲρ ἡμῶν τῇ δεήσει, ἵνα ἐκ πολλῶν προσώπων τὸ εἰς ἡμᾶς χάρισμα διὰ πολλῶν εὐχαριστηθῇ ὑπὲρ ⸀ἡμῶν.

2 Cor 4:7–12

Ἔχομεν δὲ τὸν θησαυρὸν τοῦτον ἐν ὀστρακίνοις σκεύεσιν, ἵνα ἡ ὑπερβολὴ τῆς δυνάμεως ᾖ τοῦ θεοῦ καὶ μὴ ἐξ ἡμῶν· 8 ἐν παντὶ θλιβόμενοι ἀλλ' οὐ στενοχωρούμενοι, ἀπορούμενοι ἀλλ' οὐκ ἐξαπορούμενοι, 9 διωκόμενοι ἀλλ' οὐκ ἐγκαταλειπόμενοι, καταβαλλόμενοι ἀλλ' οὐκ ἀπολλύμενοι, 10 πάντοτε τὴν νέκρωσιν τοῦ Ἰησοῦ ἐν τῷ σώματι περιφέροντες, ἵνα καὶ ἡ ζωὴ τοῦ Ἰησοῦ ἐν τῷ σώματι ἡμῶν φανερωθῇ. 11 ἀεὶ γὰρ ἡμεῖς οἱ ζῶντες εἰς θάνατον παραδιδόμεθα διὰ Ἰησοῦν, ἵνα καὶ ἡ ζωὴ

§ 139 Rom 8:26 ***υπερεντυγχανει*** ℵ* A B D 1739. 1881] *add.* υπερ ημων ℵ^{2} C 33 *Byz* 1 Cor 2:1 ***μυστηριον*** 𝔓^{46vid} ℵ* A C] μαρτυριον ℵ^{2} B D 33. 1739. 1881 *Byz* 1 Cor 2:4 ***πειθοις σοφιας λογοις*** (ℵ*) B D 33. 1739. 1881] πειθοις ανθρωπινης σοφιας λογοις ℵ^{2} A C *Byz* ¦ πειθοις σοφιας 𝔓^{46} ¦ πειθοι σοφιας *cj* 2 Cor 1:10 ***τηλικουτου θανατου*** ℵ A B C D 33. 1739*. 1881 *Byz*] τηλικουτων θανατων 𝔓^{46} 1739^{mg} 2 Cor 1:11 ***ημων*** 𝔓^{46c} ℵ A C D* 33. 1739. 1881 *Byz*^{pt}] υμων 𝔓^{46*} B D^{2} *Byz*^{pt}

on trial on account of my hope in the promise made by God to our ancestors, **7** a promise that our twelve tribes hope to attain, as they earnestly worship day and night. It is for this hope, your Excellency, that I am accused by Jews! **8** Why is it thought incredible by any of you that God raises the dead?

Acts 28:17–20

Three days later he called together the local leaders of the Jews. When they had assembled, he said to them, "Brothers, though I had done nothing against our people or the customs of our ancestors, yet I was arrested in Jerusalem and handed over to the Romans. **18** When they had examined me, the Romans wanted to release me, because there was no reason for the death penalty in my case. **19** But when the Jews objected, I was compelled to appeal to the emperor—even though I had no charge to bring against my nation. **20** For this reason therefore I have asked to see you and speak with you, since it is for the sake of the hope of Israel that I am bound with this chain."

Cf. Rom 9:3; 16:7; 16:11; 16:21; 2 Cor 11:24; Acts 18:21 (v.l.); 20:6; 27:9–10.

139. Human Weakness and God's Power

Rom 8:26–27

Likewise the Spirit helps us in our weakness; for we do not know how to pray as we ought, but that very Spirit intercedes[a] with sighs too deep for words. **27** And God, who searches the heart, knows what is the mind of the Spirit, because the Spirit intercedes for the saints according to the will of God.

1 Cor 1:26–31

Consider your own call, brothers and sisters: not many of you were wise by human standards, not many were powerful, not many were of noble birth. **27** But God chose what is foolish in the world to shame the wise; God chose what is weak in the world to shame the strong; **28** God chose what is low and despised in the world, things that are not, to reduce to nothing things that are, **29** so that no one might boast in the presence of God. **30** He is the source of your life in Christ Jesus, who became for us wisdom from God, and righteousness and sanctification and redemption, **31** in order that, as it is written, "Let the one who boasts, boast in the Lord."

1 Cor 2:1–5

When I came to you, brothers and sisters, I did not come proclaiming the mystery[b] of God to you in lofty words or wisdom. **2** For I decided to know nothing among you except Jesus Christ, and him crucified. **3** And I came to you in weakness and in fear and in much trembling. **4** My speech and my proclamation were not with plausible words of wisdom,[c] but with a demonstration of the Spirit and of power, **5** so that your faith might rest not on human wisdom but on the power of God.

1 Cor 4:9–13

For I think that God has exhibited us apostles as last of all, as though sentenced to death, because we have become a spectacle to the world, to angels and to mortals. **10** We are fools for the sake of Christ, but you are wise in Christ. We are weak, but you are strong. You are held in honor, but we in disrepute. **11** To the present hour we are hungry and thirsty, we are poorly clothed and beaten and homeless, **12** and we grow weary from the work of our own hands. When reviled, we bless; when persecuted, we endure; **13** when slandered, we speak kindly. We have become like the rubbish of the world, the dregs of all things, to this very day.

2 Cor 1:3–11

Blessed be the God and Father of our Lord Jesus Christ, the Father of mercies and the God of all consolation, **4** who consoles us in all our affliction, so that we may be able to console those who are in any affliction with the consolation with which we ourselves are consoled by God. **5** For just as the sufferings of Christ are abundant for us, so also our consolation is abundant through Christ. **6** If we are being afflicted, it is for your consolation and salvation; if we are being consoled, it is for your consolation, which you experience when you patiently endure the same sufferings that we are also suffering. **7** Our hope for you is unshaken; for we know that as you share in our sufferings, so also you share in our consolation. **8** We do not want you to be unaware, brothers and sisters, of the affliction we experienced in Asia; for we were so utterly, unbearably crushed that we despaired of life itself. **9** Indeed, we felt that we had received the sentence of death so that we would rely not on ourselves but on God who raises the dead. **10** He who rescued us from so deadly a peril[d] will continue to rescue us; on him we have set our hope that he will rescue us again, **11** as you also join in helping us by your prayers, so that many will give thanks on our[e] behalf for the blessing granted us through the prayers of many.

2 Cor 4:7–12

But we have this treasure in clay jars, so that it may be made clear that this extraordinary power belongs to God and does not come from us. **8** We are afflicted in every way, but not crushed; perplexed, but not driven to despair; **9** persecuted, but not forsaken; struck down, but not destroyed; **10** always carrying in the body the death of Jesus, so that the life of Jesus may also be made visible in our bodies. **11** For while we live, we are always being given up to death for Jesus' sake, so that the life

§ 139 [a] **Rom 8:26** ***intercedes*** Other ancient authorities add *for us* [b] **1 Cor 2:1** ***mystery*** Other ancient authorities read *testimony* [c] **1 Cor 2:4** ***plausible words of wisdom*** Other ancient authorities provide evidence for the reading *the persuasiveness of wisdom*; others read *plausible words of human wisdom* [d] **2 Cor 1:10** ***so deadly a peril*** lit. *so great a death* Other ancient authorities read *perils so deadly* lit. *such great deaths* [e] **2 Cor 1:11** ***our*** Other ancient authorities read *your*

τοῦ Ἰησοῦ φανερωθῇ ἐν τῇ θνητῇ σαρκὶ
ἡμῶν. 12 ὥστε ὁ θάνατος ἐν ἡμῖν ἐνερ-
γεῖται, ἡ δὲ ζωὴ ἐν ὑμῖν.

2 Cor 11:21b–12:10

Ἐν ᾧ δ' ἄν τις τολμᾷ, ἐν ἀφροσύνῃ
λέγω, τολμῶ κἀγώ. 22 Ἑβραῖοί εἰσιν;
κἀγώ. Ἰσραηλῖταί εἰσιν; κἀγώ. σπέρμα
Ἀβραάμ εἰσιν; κἀγώ. 23 διάκονοι Χριστοῦ
εἰσιν; παραφρονῶν λαλῶ, ὑπὲρ ἐγώ·
ἐν κόποις περισσοτέρως, ἐν φυλακαῖς
περισσοτέρως, ἐν πληγαῖς ὑπερβαλ-
λόντως, ἐν θανάτοις πολλάκις. 24 Ὑπὸ
Ἰουδαίων πεντάκις τεσσεράκοντα παρὰ
μίαν ἔλαβον, 25 τρὶς ἐρραβδίσθην, ἅπαξ
ἐλιθάσθην, τρὶς ἐναυάγησα, νυχθήμερον
ἐν τῷ βυθῷ πεποίηκα· 26 ὁδοιπορίαις
πολλάκις, κινδύνοις ποταμῶν, κινδύνοις
λῃστῶν, κινδύνοις ἐκ γένους, κινδύνοις ἐξ
ἐθνῶν, κινδύνοις ἐν πόλει, κινδύνοις ἐν
ἐρημίᾳ, κινδύνοις ἐν θαλάσσῃ, κινδύνοις
ἐν ψευδαδέλφοις, 27 κόπῳ καὶ μόχθῳ,
ἐν ἀγρυπνίαις πολλάκις, ἐν λιμῷ καὶ
δίψει, ἐν νηστείαις πολλάκις, ἐν ψύχει
καὶ γυμνότητι· 28 χωρὶς τῶν παρεκτὸς ἡ
ἐπίστασίς μοι ἡ καθ' ἡμέραν, ἡ μέριμνα
πασῶν τῶν ἐκκλησιῶν. 29 τίς ἀσθενεῖ
καὶ οὐκ ἀσθενῶ; τίς σκανδαλίζεται καὶ
οὐκ ἐγὼ πυροῦμαι; 30 Εἰ καυχᾶσθαι δεῖ,
τὰ τῆς ἀσθενείας μου καυχήσομαι. 31 ὁ
θεὸς καὶ πατὴρ τοῦ κυρίου Ἰησοῦ οἶδεν,
ὁ ὢν εὐλογητὸς εἰς τοὺς αἰῶνας, ὅτι οὐ
ψεύδομαι. 32 ἐν Δαμασκῷ ὁ ἐθνάρχης
Ἀρέτα τοῦ βασιλέως ἐφρούρει τὴν πό-
λιν Δαμασκηνῶν πιάσαι ⸀με, 33 καὶ διὰ
θυρίδος ἐν σαργάνῃ ἐχαλάσθην διὰ τοῦ
τείχους καὶ ἐξέφυγον τὰς χεῖρας αὐτοῦ.
12 Καυχᾶσθαι δεῖ, οὐ συμφέρον μέν,
ἐλεύσομαι δὲ εἰς ὀπτασίας καὶ ἀποκαλύ-
ψεις κυρίου. 2 οἶδα ἄνθρωπον ἐν Χριστῷ
πρὸ ἐτῶν δεκατεσσάρων, εἴτε ἐν σώματι
οὐκ οἶδα, εἴτε ἐκτὸς τοῦ σώματος οὐκ
οἶδα, ὁ θεὸς οἶδεν, ἁρπαγέντα τὸν τοι-
οῦτον ἕως τρίτου οὐρανοῦ. 3 καὶ οἶδα
τὸν τοιοῦτον ἄνθρωπον, εἴτε ἐν σώματι
εἴτε χωρὶς τοῦ σώματος οὐκ οἶδα, ὁ θεὸς
οἶδεν, 4 ὅτι ἡρπάγη εἰς τὸν παράδεισον
καὶ ἤκουσεν ἄρρητα ῥήματα ἃ οὐκ ἐξὸν
ἀνθρώπῳ λαλῆσαι. 5 ὑπὲρ τοῦ τοιού-
του καυχήσομαι, ὑπὲρ δὲ ἐμαυτοῦ οὐ
καυχήσομαι εἰ μὴ ἐν ταῖς ἀσθενείαις.
6 Ἐὰν γὰρ θελήσω καυχήσασθαι, οὐκ
ἔσομαι ἄφρων, ἀλήθειαν γὰρ ἐρῶ· φεί-
δομαι δέ, μή τις εἰς ἐμὲ λογίσηται ὑπὲρ
ὃ βλέπει με ἢ ἀκούει [τι] ἐξ ἐμοῦ 7 καὶ
τῇ ὑπερβολῇ τῶν ἀποκαλύψεων. ⸀διὸ
ἵνα μὴ ὑπεραίρωμαι, ἐδόθη μοι σκόλοψ
τῇ σαρκί, ἄγγελος σατανᾶ, ἵνα με κο-
λαφίζῃ, ⸂ἵνα μὴ ὑπεραίρωμαι⸃. 8 ὑπὲρ
τούτου τρὶς τὸν κύριον παρεκάλεσα
ἵνα ἀποστῇ ἀπ' ἐμοῦ. 9 καὶ εἴρηκέν μοι·
ἀρκεῖ σοι ἡ χάρις μου, ἡ γὰρ ⸀δύναμις
ἐν ἀσθενείᾳ τελεῖται. Ἥδιστα οὖν μᾶλ-
λον καυχήσομαι ἐν ταῖς ἀσθενείαις μου,
ἵνα ἐπισκηνώσῃ ἐπ' ἐμὲ ἡ δύναμις τοῦ
Χριστοῦ. 10 διὸ εὐδοκῶ ἐν ἀσθενείαις,
ἐν ὕβρεσιν, ἐν ἀνάγκαις, ἐν διωγμοῖς
καὶ στενοχωρίαις, ὑπὲρ Χριστοῦ· ὅταν
γὰρ ἀσθενῶ, τότε δυνατός εἰμι.

2 Cor 13:3–4

ἐπεὶ δοκιμὴν ζητεῖτε τοῦ ἐν ἐμοὶ λαλοῦντος
Χριστοῦ, ὃς εἰς ὑμᾶς οὐκ ἀσθενεῖ ἀλλὰ
δυνατεῖ ἐν ὑμῖν. 4 καὶ γὰρ ἐσταυρώθη ἐξ
ἀσθενείας, ἀλλὰ ζῇ ἐκ δυνάμεως θεοῦ.
καὶ γὰρ ἡμεῖς ἀσθενοῦμεν ⸀ἐν αὐτῷ,
ἀλλὰ ζήσομεν σὺν αὐτῷ ἐκ δυνάμεως
θεοῦ εἰς ὑμᾶς.

Phil 4:10–13

Ἐχάρην δὲ ἐν κυρίῳ μεγάλως ὅτι ἤδη ποτὲ
ἀνεθάλετε τὸ ὑπὲρ ἐμοῦ φρονεῖν, ἐφ' ᾧ
καὶ ἐφρονεῖτε, ἠκαιρεῖσθε δέ. 11 οὐχ ὅτι
καθ' ὑστέρησιν λέγω, ἐγὼ γὰρ ἔμαθον
ἐν οἷς εἰμι αὐτάρκης εἶναι. 12 οἶδα καὶ
ταπεινοῦσθαι, οἶδα καὶ περισσεύειν· ἐν
παντὶ καὶ ἐν πᾶσιν μεμύημαι, καὶ χορ-
τάζεσθαι καὶ πεινᾶν καὶ περισσεύειν
καὶ ὑστερεῖσθαι· 13 πάντα ἰσχύω ἐν τῷ
ἐνδυναμοῦντί με.

See also § 37 Christ the Wisdom and Power of God.

140. Imprisonment for the Gospel

Eph 3:1

Τούτου χάριν ἐγὼ Παῦλος ὁ δέσμιος
τοῦ Χριστοῦ [Ἰησοῦ] ὑπὲρ ὑμῶν τῶν
ἐθνῶν

Eph 3:13

διὸ αἰτοῦμαι μὴ ἐγκακεῖν ἐν ταῖς θλίψεσίν
μου ὑπὲρ ὑμῶν, ἥτις ἐστὶν δόξα ὑμῶν.

Eph 4:1

Παρακαλῶ οὖν ὑμᾶς ἐγὼ ὁ δέσμιος ἐν
κυρίῳ ἀξίως περιπατῆσαι τῆς κλήσεως
ἧς ἐκλήθητε

Eph 6:18–20

Διὰ πάσης προσευχῆς καὶ δεήσεως προσ-
ευχόμενοι ἐν παντὶ καιρῷ ἐν πνεύματι,
καὶ εἰς αὐτὸ ἀγρυπνοῦντες ἐν πάσῃ προσ-
καρτερήσει καὶ δεήσει περὶ πάντων τῶν
ἁγίων 19 καὶ ὑπὲρ ἐμοῦ, ἵνα μοι δοθῇ
λόγος ἐν ἀνοίξει τοῦ στόματός μου, ἐν
παρρησίᾳ γνωρίσαι τὸ μυστήριον ⸂τοῦ
εὐαγγελίου⸃, 20 ὑπὲρ οὗ πρεσβεύω ἐν
ἁλύσει, ἵνα ἐν αὐτῷ παρρησιάσωμαι ὡς
δεῖ με λαλῆσαι.

Phil 1:7

Καθώς ἐστιν δίκαιον ἐμοὶ τοῦτο φρονεῖν
ὑπὲρ πάντων ὑμῶν διὰ τὸ ἔχειν με ἐν
τῇ καρδίᾳ ὑμᾶς, ἔν τε τοῖς δεσμοῖς μου
καὶ ἐν τῇ ἀπολογίᾳ καὶ βεβαιώσει τοῦ
εὐαγγελίου συγκοινωνούς μου τῆς χά-
ριτος πάντας ὑμᾶς ὄντας.

Phil 1:12–26

Γινώσκειν δὲ ὑμᾶς βούλομαι, ἀδελφοί,
ὅτι τὰ κατ' ἐμὲ μᾶλλον εἰς προκοπὴν τοῦ
εὐαγγελίου ἐλήλυθεν, 13 ὥστε τοὺς δε-
σμούς μου φανεροὺς ἐν Χριστῷ γενέσθαι

2 Cor 11:32 ***με*** B D*] *add.* θελων ℵ D^{2} 33. (1739). 1881 *Byz* **2 Cor 12:7** ***διο*** ℵ A B 33. 1739] *om.* 𝔓^{46} D 1881 *Byz* • ***ινα μη υπεραιρωμαι*** 𝔓^{46} ℵ^{2} B I^{vid} 1739. (1881) *Byz*] *om.* ℵ* A D 33 **2 Cor 12:9** ***δυναμις*** 𝔓^{46vid} ℵ* A* B D*] *add.* μου ℵ^{2} A^{c} D^{1} 33. 1739. 1881 *Byz* **2 Cor 13:4** ***εν*** B D 33. 1739. 1881 *Byz*] συν ℵ A **§ 140** **Eph 6:19** ***του ευαγγελιου*** ℵ A D I 33. 1739. 1881 *Byz*] *om.* B

of Jesus may be made visible in our mortal flesh. 12 So death is at work in us, but life in you.

2 Cor 11:21b–12:10

But whatever anyone dares to boast of—I am speaking as a fool—I also dare to boast of that. 22 Are they Hebrews? So am I. Are they Israelites? So am I. Are they descendants of Abraham? So am I. 23 Are they ministers of Christ? I am talking like a madman—I am a better one: with far greater labors, far more imprisonments, with countless floggings, and often near death. 24 Five times I have received from the Jews the forty lashes minus one. 25 Three times I was beaten with rods. Once I received a stoning. Three times I was shipwrecked; for a night and a day I was adrift at sea; 26 on frequent journeys, in danger from rivers, danger from bandits, danger from my own people, danger from Gentiles, danger in the city, danger in the wilderness, danger at sea, danger from false brothers and sisters; 27 in toil and hardship, through many a sleepless night, hungry and thirsty, often without food, cold and naked. 28 And, besides other things, I am under daily pressure because of my anxiety for all the churches. 29 Who is weak, and I am not weak? Who is made to stumble, and I am not indignant? 30 If I must boast, I will boast of the things that show my weakness. 31 The God and Father of the Lord Jesus (blessed be he forever!) knows that I do not lie. 32 In Damascus, the governor under King Aretas guarded the city of Damascus in order to[f] seize me, 33 but I was let down in a basket through a window in the wall, and escaped from his hands. **12** It is necessary to boast; nothing is to be gained by it, but I will go on to visions and revelations of the Lord. 2 I know a person in Christ who fourteen years ago was caught up to the third heaven—whether in the body or out of the body I do not know; God knows. 3 And I know that such a person—whether in the body or out of the body I do not know; God knows— 4 was caught up into Paradise and heard things that are not to be told, that no mortal is permitted to repeat. 5 On behalf of such a one I will boast, but on my own behalf I will not boast, except of my weaknesses. 6 But if I wish to boast, I will not be a fool, for I will be speaking the truth. But I refrain from it, so that no one may think better of me than what is seen in me or heard from me, 7 even considering the exceptional character of the revelations. Therefore, to keep[g] me from being too elated, a thorn was given me in the flesh, a messenger of Satan to torment me, to keep me from being too elated.[h] 8 Three times I appealed to the Lord about this, that it would leave me, 9 but he said to me, "My grace is sufficient for you, for power[i] is made perfect in weakness." So, I will boast all the more gladly of my weaknesses, so that the power of Christ may dwell in me. 10 Therefore I am content with weaknesses, insults, hardships, persecutions, and calamities for the sake of Christ; for whenever I am weak, then I am strong.

2 Cor 13:3–4

since you desire proof that Christ is speaking in me. He is not weak in dealing with you, but is powerful in you. 4 For he was crucified in weakness, but lives by the power of God. For we are weak in him,[j] but in dealing with you we will live with him by the power of God.

Phil 4:10–13

I rejoice in the Lord greatly that now at last you have revived your concern for me; indeed, you were concerned for me, but had no opportunity to show it. 11 Not that I am referring to being in need; for I have learned to be content with whatever I have. 12 I know what it is to have little, and I know what it is to have plenty. In any and all circumstances I have learned the secret of being well-fed and of going hungry, of having plenty and of being in need. 13 I can do all things through him who strengthens me.

See also § 37 Christ the Wisdom and Power of God.

140. Imprisonment for the Gospel

Eph 3:1

This is the reason that I Paul am a prisoner for Christ Jesus for the sake of you Gentiles

Eph 3:13

I pray therefore that you may not lose heart over my sufferings for you; they are your glory.

Eph 4:1

I therefore, the prisoner in the Lord, beg you to lead a life worthy of the calling to which you have been called

Eph 6:18–20

Pray in the Spirit at all times in every prayer and supplication. To that end keep alert and always persevere in supplication for all the saints. 19 Pray also for me, so that when I speak, a message may be given to me to make known with boldness the mystery of the gospel,[a] 20 for which I am an ambassador in chains. Pray that I may declare it boldly, as I must speak.

Phil 1:7

It is right for me to think this way about all of you, because you hold me in your heart, for all of you share in God's grace with me, both in my imprisonment and in the defense and confirmation of the gospel.

Phil 1:12–26

I want you to know, beloved, that what has happened to me has actually helped to spread the gospel, 13 so that it has become known throughout the whole

[f] **2 Cor 11:32** ***in order to*** Other ancient authorities read *and wanted to* [g] **2 Cor 12:7** ***Therefore, to keep*** Other ancient authorities read *To keep* [h] **2 Cor 12:7** ***to keep me from being too elated*** Other ancient authorities lack *to keep me from being too elated* [i] **2 Cor 12:9** ***power*** Other ancient authorities read *my power* [j] **2 Cor 13:4** ***in him*** Other ancient authorities read *with him* **§ 140** [a] **Eph 6:19** ***of the gospel*** Other ancient authorities lack *of the gospel*

ἐν ὅλῳ τῷ πραιτωρίῳ καὶ τοῖς λοιποῖς πᾶσιν, **14** καὶ τοὺς πλείονας τῶν ἀδελφῶν ἐν κυρίῳ πεποιθότας τοῖς δεσμοῖς μου περισσοτέρως τολμᾶν ἀφόβως τὸν ⸀λόγον λαλεῖν. **15** τινὲς μὲν καὶ διὰ φθόνον καὶ ἔριν, τινὲς δὲ καὶ δι' εὐδοκίαν τὸν Χριστὸν κηρύσσουσιν· **16** οἱ μὲν ἐξ ἀγάπης, εἰδότες ὅτι εἰς ἀπολογίαν τοῦ εὐαγγελίου κεῖμαι, **17** οἱ δὲ ἐξ ἐριθείας τὸν Χριστὸν καταγγέλλουσιν, οὐχ ἁγνῶς, οἰόμενοι θλῖψιν ἐγείρειν τοῖς δεσμοῖς μου. **18** Τί γάρ; πλὴν ὅτι παντὶ τρόπῳ, εἴτε προφάσει εἴτε ἀληθείᾳ, Χριστὸς καταγγέλλεται, καὶ ἐν τούτῳ χαίρω. Ἀλλὰ καὶ χαρήσομαι, **19** οἶδα γὰρ ὅτι τοῦτό μοι ἀποβήσεται εἰς σωτηρίαν διὰ τῆς ὑμῶν δεήσεως καὶ ἐπιχορηγίας τοῦ πνεύματος Ἰησοῦ Χριστοῦ **20** κατὰ τὴν ἀποκαραδοκίαν καὶ ἐλπίδα μου, ὅτι ἐν οὐδενὶ αἰσχυνθήσομαι ἀλλ' ἐν πάσῃ παρρησίᾳ ὡς πάντοτε καὶ νῦν μεγαλυνθήσεται Χριστὸς ἐν τῷ σώματί μου, εἴτε διὰ ζωῆς εἴτε διὰ θανάτου. **21** Ἐμοὶ γὰρ τὸ ζῆν Χριστὸς καὶ τὸ ἀποθανεῖν κέρδος. **22** εἰ δὲ τὸ ζῆν ἐν σαρκί, τοῦτό μοι καρπὸς ἔργου, καὶ τί αἱρήσομαι οὐ γνωρίζω. **23** συνέχομαι δὲ ἐκ τῶν δύο, τὴν ἐπιθυμίαν ἔχων εἰς τὸ ἀναλῦσαι καὶ σὺν Χριστῷ εἶναι, πολλῷ [γὰρ] μᾶλλον κρεῖσσον· **24** τὸ δὲ ἐπιμένειν [ἐν] τῇ σαρκὶ ἀναγκαιότερον δι' ὑμᾶς. **25** καὶ τοῦτο πεποιθὼς οἶδα ὅτι μενῶ καὶ παραμενῶ πᾶσιν ὑμῖν εἰς τὴν ὑμῶν προκοπὴν καὶ χαρὰν τῆς πίστεως, **26** ἵνα τὸ καύχημα ὑμῶν περισσεύῃ ἐν Χριστῷ Ἰησοῦ ἐν ἐμοὶ διὰ τῆς ἐμῆς παρουσίας πάλιν πρὸς ὑμᾶς.

Col 4:3–4

προσευχόμενοι ἅμα καὶ περὶ ἡμῶν, ἵνα ὁ θεὸς ἀνοίξῃ ἡμῖν θύραν τοῦ λόγου λαλῆσαι τὸ μυστήριον τοῦ Χριστοῦ, δι' ὃ καὶ δέδεμαι, **4** ἵνα φανερώσω αὐτὸ ὡς δεῖ με λαλῆσαι.

Col 4:18

Ὁ ἀσπασμὸς τῇ ἐμῇ χειρὶ Παύλου. μνημονεύετέ μου τῶν δεσμῶν. ἡ χάρις μεθ' ⸀ὑμῶν.

2 Tim 1:8

μὴ οὖν ἐπαισχυνθῇς τὸ μαρτύριον τοῦ κυρίου ἡμῶν μηδὲ ἐμὲ τὸν δέσμιον αὐτοῦ, ἀλλὰ συγκακοπάθησον τῷ εὐαγγελίῳ κατὰ δύναμιν θεοῦ

2 Tim 1:16–18

δῴη ἔλεος ὁ κύριος τῷ Ὀνησιφόρου οἴκῳ, ὅτι πολλάκις με ἀνέψυξεν καὶ τὴν ἅλυσίν μου οὐκ ἐπαισχύνθη, **17** ἀλλὰ γενόμενος ἐν Ῥώμῃ σπουδαίως ἐζήτησέν με καὶ εὗρεν· **18** δῴη αὐτῷ ὁ κύριος εὑρεῖν ἔλεος παρὰ κυρίου ἐν ἐκείνῃ τῇ ἡμέρᾳ. καὶ ὅσα ἐν Ἐφέσῳ διηκόνησεν, βέλτιον σὺ γινώσκεις.

2 Tim 2:8–10

Μνημόνευε Ἰησοῦν Χριστὸν ἐγηγερμένον ἐκ νεκρῶν, ἐκ σπέρματος Δαυίδ, κατὰ τὸ εὐαγγέλιόν μου, **9** ἐν ᾧ κακοπαθῶ μέχρι δεσμῶν ὡς κακοῦργος, ἀλλὰ ὁ λόγος τοῦ θεοῦ οὐ δέδεται· **10** διὰ τοῦτο πάντα ὑπομένω διὰ τοὺς ἐκλεκτούς, ἵνα καὶ αὐτοὶ σωτηρίας τύχωσιν τῆς ἐν Χριστῷ Ἰησοῦ μετὰ δόξης αἰωνίου.

2 Tim 4:16–18

Ἐν τῇ πρώτῃ μου ἀπολογίᾳ οὐδείς μοι παρεγένετο, ἀλλὰ πάντες με ἐγκατέλιπον· μὴ αὐτοῖς λογισθείη· **17** ὁ δὲ κύριός μοι παρέστη καὶ ἐνεδυνάμωσέν με, ἵνα δι' ἐμοῦ τὸ κήρυγμα πληροφορηθῇ καὶ ἀκούσωσιν πάντα τὰ ἔθνη, καὶ ἐρρύσθην ἐκ στόματος λέοντος. **18** ῥύσεταί με ὁ κύριος ἀπὸ παντὸς ἔργου πονηροῦ καὶ σώσει εἰς τὴν βασιλείαν αὐτοῦ τὴν ἐπουράνιον· ᾧ ἡ δόξα εἰς τοὺς αἰῶνας τῶν αἰώνων, ἀμήν.

Phlm 1

Παῦλος δέσμιος Χριστοῦ Ἰησοῦ καὶ Τιμόθεος ὁ ἀδελφὸς Φιλήμονι τῷ ἀγαπητῷ καὶ συνεργῷ ἡμῶν

Phlm 8–14

Διὸ πολλὴν ἐν Χριστῷ παρρησίαν ἔχων ἐπιτάσσειν σοι τὸ ἀνῆκον **9** διὰ τὴν ἀγάπην μᾶλλον παρακαλῶ, τοιοῦτος ὢν ὡς Παῦλος ⸀πρεσβύτης νυνὶ δὲ καὶ δέσμιος Χριστοῦ Ἰησοῦ· **10** παρακαλῶ σε περὶ τοῦ ἐμοῦ τέκνου, ὃν ἐγέννησα ἐν τοῖς δεσμοῖς, Ὀνήσιμον, **11** τόν ποτέ σοι ἄχρηστον νυνὶ δὲ [καὶ] σοὶ καὶ ἐμοὶ εὔχρηστον, **12** ὃν ἀνέπεμψά σοι, αὐτόν, τοῦτ' ἔστιν τὰ ἐμὰ σπλάγχνα· **13** ὃν ἐγὼ ἐβουλόμην πρὸς ἐμαυτὸν κατέχειν, ἵνα ὑπὲρ σοῦ μοι διακονῇ ἐν τοῖς δεσμοῖς τοῦ εὐαγγελίου, **14** χωρὶς δὲ τῆς σῆς γνώμης οὐδὲν ἠθέλησα ποιῆσαι, ἵνα μὴ ὡς κατὰ ἀνάγκην τὸ ἀγαθόν σου ᾖ ἀλλὰ κατὰ ἑκούσιον.

Cf. Rom 16:7; Phil 4:22; Col 4:10; Phlm 22; 23–24; Acts 16:16–40; 20:22–24; 21:10–14; and the narrative in the latter chapters of Acts of Paul's imprisonments in Jerusalem, Caesarea, and Rome.

See also § 142 Paul's Example of Suffering in behalf of Christ.

141. Suffering and Affliction in Christ

Rom 5:3–5

οὐ μόνον δέ, ἀλλὰ καὶ καυχώμεθα ἐν ταῖς θλίψεσιν, εἰδότες ὅτι ἡ θλῖψις ὑπομονὴν κατεργάζεται, **4** ἡ δὲ ὑπομονὴ δοκιμήν, ἡ δὲ δοκιμὴ ἐλπίδα. **5** ἡ δὲ ἐλπὶς οὐ καταισχύνει, ὅτι ἡ ἀγάπη τοῦ θεοῦ ἐκκέχυται ἐν ταῖς καρδίαις ἡμῶν διὰ πνεύματος ἁγίου τοῦ δοθέντος ἡμῖν.

Rom 8:18–39

Λογίζομαι γὰρ ὅτι οὐκ ἄξια τὰ παθήματα τοῦ νῦν καιροῦ πρὸς τὴν μέλλουσαν δόξαν ἀποκαλυφθῆναι εἰς ἡμᾶς. **19** ἡ γὰρ ἀποκαραδοκία τῆς κτίσεως τὴν ἀποκάλυψιν τῶν υἱῶν τοῦ θεοῦ ἀπεκδέχεται. **20** τῇ γὰρ ματαιότητι ἡ κτίσις ὑπετάγη, οὐχ ἑκοῦσα ἀλλὰ διὰ τὸν ὑποτάξαντα, ἐφ' ἐλπίδι

Phil 1:14 ***λογον*** 𝔓^{46} D^{2} 1739. 1881 *Byz*] *add.* του θεου ℵ A B (D*) 048^{vid}. 33 **Col 4:18** ***υμων*** ℵ* A B C 048. 33. 1739*. 1881] *add.* αμην ℵ^{2} D 1739^{c} *Byz* **Phlm 9** ***πρεσβυτης*** *omnes*] πρεσβευτης *cj*

imperial guard and to everyone else that
my imprisonment is for Christ; **14** and
most of the brothers and sisters, hav-
ing been made confident in the Lord
by my imprisonment, dare to speak
the word[b] with greater boldness and
without fear. **15** Some proclaim Christ
from envy and rivalry, but others from
goodwill. **16** These proclaim Christ out
of love, knowing that I have been put
here for the defense of the gospel; **17** the
others proclaim Christ out of selfish
ambition, not sincerely but intending
to increase my suffering in my impris-
onment. **18** What does it matter? Just
this, that Christ is proclaimed in every
way, whether out of false motives or
true; and in that I rejoice. Yes, and I will
continue to rejoice, **19** for I know that
through your prayers and the supply
of the Spirit of Jesus Christ this will
turn out for my deliverance.[c] **20** It is my
eager expectation and hope that I will
not be put to shame in any way, but
that by my speaking with all boldness,
Christ will be exalted now as always in
my body, whether by life or by death.
21 For to me, living is Christ and dying
is gain. **22** If I am to live in the flesh, that
means fruitful labor for me; and I do
not know which I prefer. **23** I am hard
pressed between the two: my desire is
to depart and be with Christ, for that is
far better; **24** but to remain in the flesh
is more necessary for you. **25** Since I am
convinced of this, I know that I will
remain and continue with all of you
for your progress and joy in faith, **26** so
that I may share abundantly in your
boasting in Christ Jesus when I come
to you again.

Col 4:3–4

At the same time pray for us as well
that God will open to us a door for
the word, that we may declare the
mystery of Christ, for which I am in
prison, **4** so that I may reveal it clearly,
as I should.

Col 4:18

I, Paul, write this greeting with my own hand. Remember my chains. Grace be with you.[d]

2 Tim 1:8

Do not be ashamed, then, of the testimony about our Lord or of me his prisoner, but join with me in suffering for the gospel, relying on the power of God

2 Tim 1:16–18

May the Lord grant mercy to the house-
hold of Onesiphorus, because he often
refreshed me and was not ashamed of
my chain; **17** when he arrived in Rome,
he eagerly searched for me and found
me **18**—may the Lord grant that he will
find mercy from the Lord on that day!
And you know very well how much ser-
vice he rendered in Ephesus.

2 Tim 2:8–10

Remember Jesus Christ, raised from the
dead, a descendant of David—that is
my gospel, **9** for which I suffer hardship,
even to the point of being chained like
a criminal. But the word of God is not
chained. **10** Therefore I endure every-
thing for the sake of the elect, so that
they may also obtain the salvation that
is in Christ Jesus, with eternal glory.

2 Tim 4:16–18

At my first defense no one came to my
support, but all deserted me. May it
not be counted against them! **17** But the
Lord stood by me and gave me strength,
so that through me the message might
be fully proclaimed and all the Gentiles
might hear it. So I was rescued from the
lion's mouth. **18** The Lord will rescue
me from every evil attack and save me
for his heavenly kingdom. To him be the
glory forever and ever. Amen.

Phlm 1

Paul, a prisoner of Christ Jesus, and Timothy our brother, To Philemon our dear friend and co-worker

Phlm 8–14

For this reason, though I am bold
enough in Christ to command you to
do your duty, **9** yet I would rather appeal
to you on the basis of love—and I, Paul,
do this as an old man,[e] and now also as
a prisoner of Christ Jesus. **10** I am ap-
pealing to you for my child, Onesimus,
whose father I have become during my
imprisonment. **11** Formerly he was use-
less to you, but now he is indeed useful
both to you and to me. **12** I am sending
him, that is, my own heart, back to you.
13 I wanted to keep him with me, so
that he might be of service to me in
your place during my imprisonment
for the gospel; **14** but I preferred to do
nothing without your consent, in order
that your good deed might be voluntary
and not something forced.

Cf. Rom 16:7; Phil 4:22; Col 4:10; Phlm 22; 23–24; Acts 16:16–40; 20:22–24; 21:10–14; and the narrative in the latter chapters of Acts of Paul's imprisonments in Jerusalem, Caesarea, and Rome.

See also § 142 Paul's Example of Suffering in behalf of Christ.

141. Suffering and Affliction in Christ

Rom 5:3–5

And not only that, but we also boast in
our sufferings, knowing that suffering
produces endurance, **4** and endurance
produces character, and character pro-
duces hope, **5** and hope does not disap-
point us, because God's love has been
poured into our hearts through the
Holy Spirit that has been given to us.

Rom 8:18–39

I consider that the sufferings of this
present time are not worth comparing
with the glory about to be revealed to
us. **19** For the creation waits with eager
longing for the revealing of the chil-
dren of God; **20** for the creation was
subjected to futility, not of its own will
but by the will of the one who subjected

[b] **Phil 1:14** ***word*** Other ancient authorities read *word of God* [c] **Phil 1:19** Translation differs from NRSV [d] **Col 4:18** ***you*** Other ancient authorities add *Amen* [e] **Phlm 9** ***old man*** Some scholars conjecture that the original text read *ambassador*, or that the reading in the manuscripts is a spelling variant for *ambassador*

21 ὅτι καὶ αὐτὴ ἡ κτίσις ἐλευθερωθήσε-
ται ἀπὸ τῆς δουλείας τῆς φθορᾶς εἰς τὴν
ἐλευθερίαν τῆς δόξης τῶν τέκνων τοῦ
θεοῦ. 22 οἴδαμεν γὰρ ὅτι πᾶσα ἡ κτίσις
συστενάζει καὶ συνωδίνει ἄχρι τοῦ νῦν·
23 οὐ μόνον δέ, ἀλλὰ καὶ αὐτοὶ τὴν ἀπαρ-
χὴν τοῦ πνεύματος ἔχοντες, ἡμεῖς καὶ
αὐτοὶ ἐν ἑαυτοῖς στενάζομεν υἱοθεσίαν
ἀπεκδεχόμενοι, τὴν ἀπολύτρωσιν τοῦ
σώματος ἡμῶν. 24 τῇ γὰρ ἐλπίδι ἐσώ-
θημεν· ἐλπὶς δὲ βλεπομένη οὐκ ἔστιν
ἐλπίς· ὃ γὰρ βλέπει τίς ⸀ἐλπίζει; 25 εἰ δὲ
ὃ οὐ βλέπομεν ἐλπίζομεν, δι᾽ ὑπομονῆς
ἀπεκδεχόμεθα. 26 Ὡσαύτως δὲ καὶ τὸ
πνεῦμα συναντιλαμβάνεται τῇ ἀσθενείᾳ
ἡμῶν· τὸ γὰρ τί προσευξώμεθα καθὸ
δεῖ οὐκ οἴδαμεν, ἀλλὰ αὐτὸ τὸ πνεῦμα
⸀ὑπερεντυγχάνει στεναγμοῖς ἀλαλήτοις·
27 ὁ δὲ ἐραυνῶν τὰς καρδίας οἶδεν τί τὸ
φρόνημα τοῦ πνεύματος, ὅτι κατὰ θεὸν
ἐντυγχάνει ὑπὲρ ἁγίων. 28 Οἴδαμεν δὲ
ὅτι τοῖς ἀγαπῶσιν τὸν θεὸν πάντα ⸀συν-
εργεῖ εἰς ἀγαθόν, τοῖς κατὰ πρόθεσιν
κλητοῖς οὖσιν. 29 ὅτι οὓς προέγνω, καὶ
προώρισεν συμμόρφους τῆς εἰκόνος
τοῦ υἱοῦ αὐτοῦ, εἰς τὸ εἶναι αὐτὸν πρω-
τότοκον ἐν πολλοῖς ἀδελφοῖς· 30 οὓς δὲ
προώρισεν, τούτους καὶ ἐκάλεσεν· καὶ
οὓς ἐκάλεσεν, τούτους καὶ ἐδικαίωσεν·
οὓς δὲ ἐδικαίωσεν, τούτους καὶ ἐδόξασεν.
31 Τί οὖν ἐροῦμεν πρὸς ταῦτα; εἰ ὁ θεὸς
ὑπὲρ ἡμῶν, τίς καθ᾽ ἡμῶν; 32 ὅς γε τοῦ
ἰδίου υἱοῦ οὐκ ἐφείσατο ἀλλὰ ὑπὲρ ἡμῶν
πάντων παρέδωκεν αὐτόν, πῶς οὐχὶ καὶ
σὺν αὐτῷ τὰ πάντα ἡμῖν χαρίσεται; 33 τίς
ἐγκαλέσει κατὰ ἐκλεκτῶν θεοῦ; θεὸς ὁ
δικαιῶν· 34 τίς ὁ κατακρινῶν; Χριστὸς
[Ἰησοῦς] ὁ ἀποθανών, μᾶλλον δὲ ⸀ἐγερ-
θείς, ὅς καί ἐστιν ἐν δεξιᾷ τοῦ θεοῦ, ὃς
καὶ ἐντυγχάνει ὑπὲρ ἡμῶν. 35 τίς ἡμᾶς
χωρίσει ἀπὸ τῆς ἀγάπης τοῦ Χριστοῦ;
θλῖψις ἢ στενοχωρία ἢ διωγμὸς ἢ λιμὸς
ἢ γυμνότης ἢ κίνδυνος ἢ μάχαιρα; 36 κα-
θὼς γέγραπται ὅτι ἕνεκεν σοῦ θανατού-
μεθα ὅλην τὴν ἡμέραν, ἐλογίσθημεν
ὡς πρόβατα σφαγῆς. 37 ἀλλ᾽ ἐν τούτοις
πᾶσιν ὑπερνικῶμεν διὰ τοῦ ἀγαπήσαντος
ἡμᾶς. 38 πέπεισμαι γὰρ ὅτι οὔτε θάνατος
οὔτε ζωὴ οὔτε ἄγγελοι οὔτε ἀρχαὶ οὔτε
ἐνεστῶτα οὔτε μέλλοντα οὔτε δυνάμεις
39 οὔτε ὕψωμα οὔτε βάθος οὔτε τις κτίσις
ἑτέρα δυνήσεται ἡμᾶς χωρίσαι ἀπὸ τῆς
ἀγάπης τοῦ θεοῦ τῆς ἐν Χριστῷ Ἰησοῦ
τῷ κυρίῳ ἡμῶν.

Phil 1:27–30

Μόνον ἀξίως τοῦ εὐαγγελίου τοῦ Χριστοῦ
πολιτεύεσθε, ἵνα εἴτε ἐλθὼν καὶ ἰδὼν
ὑμᾶς εἴτε ἀπὼν ἀκούω τὰ περὶ ὑμῶν,
ὅτι στήκετε ἐν ἑνὶ πνεύματι, μιᾷ ψυχῇ
συναθλοῦντες τῇ πίστει τοῦ εὐαγγελίου
28 καὶ μὴ πτυρόμενοι ἐν μηδενὶ ὑπὸ τῶν
ἀντικειμένων, ἥτις ἐστὶν αὐτοῖς ἔνδειξις
ἀπωλείας, ὑμῶν δὲ σωτηρίας, καὶ τοῦτο
ἀπὸ θεοῦ· 29 ὅτι ὑμῖν ἐχαρίσθη τὸ ὑπὲρ
Χριστοῦ, οὐ μόνον τὸ εἰς αὐτὸν πιστεύειν
ἀλλὰ καὶ τὸ ὑπὲρ αὐτοῦ πάσχειν, 30 τὸν
αὐτὸν ἀγῶνα ἔχοντες, οἷον εἴδετε ἐν
ἐμοὶ καὶ νῦν ἀκούετε ἐν ἐμοί.

1 Thess 1:6

Καὶ ὑμεῖς μιμηταὶ ἡμῶν ἐγενήθητε καὶ τοῦ
κυρίου, δεξάμενοι τὸν λόγον ἐν θλίψει
πολλῇ μετὰ χαρᾶς πνεύματος ἁγίου

1 Thess 2:13–14

Καὶ διὰ τοῦτο καὶ ἡμεῖς εὐχαριστοῦμεν
τῷ θεῷ ἀδιαλείπτως, ὅτι παραλαβόν-
τες λόγον ἀκοῆς παρ᾽ ἡμῶν τοῦ θεοῦ
ἐδέξασθε οὐ λόγον ἀνθρώπων ἀλλὰ
καθώς ἐστιν ἀληθῶς λόγον θεοῦ, ὃς
καὶ ἐνεργεῖται ἐν ὑμῖν τοῖς πιστεύου-
σιν. 14 Ὑμεῖς γὰρ μιμηταὶ ἐγενήθητε,
ἀδελφοί, τῶν ἐκκλησιῶν τοῦ θεοῦ τῶν
οὐσῶν ἐν τῇ Ἰουδαίᾳ ἐν Χριστῷ Ἰησοῦ,
ὅτι τὰ αὐτὰ ἐπάθετε καὶ ὑμεῖς ὑπὸ τῶν
ἰδίων συμφυλετῶν καθὼς καὶ αὐτοὶ ὑπὸ
τῶν Ἰουδαίων

1 Thess 3:1–5

Διὸ μηκέτι στέγοντες εὐδοκήσαμεν κα-
ταλειφθῆναι ἐν Ἀθήναις μόνοι 2 καὶ
ἐπέμψαμεν Τιμόθεον, τὸν ἀδελφὸν ἡμῶν
καὶ ⸂συνεργὸν τοῦ θεοῦ⸃ ἐν τῷ εὐαγγε-
λίῳ τοῦ Χριστοῦ, εἰς τὸ στηρίξαι ὑμᾶς
καὶ παρακαλέσαι ὑπὲρ τῆς πίστεως ὑμῶν
3 τὸ μηδένα σαίνεσθαι ἐν ταῖς θλίψεσιν
ταύταις. αὐτοὶ γὰρ οἴδατε ὅτι εἰς τοῦτο
κείμεθα· 4 καὶ γὰρ ὅτε πρὸς ὑμᾶς ἦμεν,
προελέγομεν ὑμῖν ὅτι μέλλομεν θλί-
βεσθαι, καθὼς καὶ ἐγένετο καὶ οἴδατε.
5 διὰ τοῦτο κἀγὼ μηκέτι στέγων ἔπεμψα
εἰς τὸ γνῶναι τὴν πίστιν ὑμῶν, μή πως
ἐπείρασεν ὑμᾶς ὁ πειράζων καὶ εἰς κενὸν
γένηται ὁ κόπος ἡμῶν.

2 Thess 1:4–8

ὥστε αὐτοὺς ἡμᾶς ἐν ὑμῖν ἐγκαυχᾶσθαι
ἐν ταῖς ἐκκλησίαις τοῦ θεοῦ ὑπὲρ τῆς
ὑπομονῆς ὑμῶν καὶ πίστεως ἐν πᾶσιν
τοῖς διωγμοῖς ὑμῶν καὶ ταῖς θλίψεσιν
αἷς ἀνέχεσθε, 5 ἔνδειγμα τῆς δικαίας
κρίσεως τοῦ θεοῦ εἰς τὸ καταξιωθῆναι
ὑμᾶς τῆς βασιλείας τοῦ θεοῦ, ὑπὲρ ἧς
καὶ πάσχετε, 6 εἴπερ δίκαιον παρὰ θεῷ
ἀνταποδοῦναι τοῖς θλίβουσιν ὑμᾶς θλῖ-
ψιν 7 καὶ ὑμῖν τοῖς θλιβομένοις ἄνεσιν
μεθ᾽ ἡμῶν, ἐν τῇ ἀποκαλύψει τοῦ κυ-
ρίου Ἰησοῦ ἀπ᾽ οὐρανοῦ μετ᾽ ἀγγέλων
δυνάμεως αὐτοῦ 8 ἐν πυρὶ φλογός, δι-
δόντος ἐκδίκησιν τοῖς μὴ εἰδόσιν θεὸν
καὶ τοῖς μὴ ὑπακούουσιν τῷ εὐαγγελίῳ
τοῦ κυρίου ἡμῶν Ἰησοῦ

2 Tim 1:6–14

Δι᾽ ἣν αἰτίαν ἀναμιμνῄσκω σε ἀναζωπυ-
ρεῖν τὸ χάρισμα τοῦ θεοῦ, ὅ ἐστιν ἐν
σοὶ διὰ τῆς ἐπιθέσεως τῶν χειρῶν μου.
7 οὐ γὰρ ἔδωκεν ἡμῖν ὁ θεὸς πνεῦμα
δειλίας ἀλλὰ δυνάμεως καὶ ἀγάπης καὶ
σωφρονισμοῦ. 8 μὴ οὖν ἐπαισχυνθῇς τὸ
μαρτύριον τοῦ κυρίου ἡμῶν μηδὲ ἐμὲ τὸν
δέσμιον αὐτοῦ, ἀλλὰ συγκακοπάθησον
τῷ εὐαγγελίῳ κατὰ δύναμιν θεοῦ, 9 τοῦ
σώσαντος ἡμᾶς καὶ καλέσαντος κλήσει
ἁγίᾳ, οὐ κατὰ τὰ ἔργα ἡμῶν ἀλλὰ κατὰ
ἰδίαν πρόθεσιν καὶ χάριν, τὴν δοθεῖσαν
ἡμῖν ἐν Χριστῷ Ἰησοῦ πρὸ χρόνων αἰω-
νίων, 10 φανερωθεῖσαν δὲ νῦν διὰ τῆς
ἐπιφανείας τοῦ σωτῆρος ἡμῶν Χριστοῦ
Ἰησοῦ, καταργήσαντος μὲν τὸν θάνατον
φωτίσαντος δὲ ζωὴν καὶ ἀφθαρσίαν διὰ
τοῦ εὐαγγελίου 11 εἰς ὃ ἐτέθην ἐγὼ κῆρυξ

§ 141 **Rom 8:24** ***ελπιζει*** 𝔓[46] א[2] B C D 33. 1739*. 1881 *Byz*] υπομενει א* A 1739[mg] **Rom 8:26** ***υπερεντυγχανει*** א* A B D 1739. 1881] *add.* υπερ ημων א[2] C 33 *Byz* **Rom 8:28** ***συνεργει*** א C D 33. 1739. 1881 *Byz*] *add.* ο θεος 𝔓[46] A B **Rom 8:34** ***εγερθεις*** 𝔓[27vid] 𝔓[46] א[2] B D 1739. 1881 *Byz*] *add.* εκ νεκρων א* A C 33 **1 Thess 3:2** ***συνεργον του θεου*** D* 33] συνεργον B ¦ διακονον του θεου א A 1739. 1881 ¦ διακονον του θεου και συνεργον ημων D[2] *Byz*

it, in hope **21** that the creation itself will be set free from its bondage to decay and will obtain the freedom of the glory of the children of God. **22** We know that the whole creation has been groaning in labor pains until now; **23** and not only the creation, but we ourselves, who have the first fruits of the Spirit, groan inwardly while we wait for adoption, the redemption of our bodies. **24** For in hope we were saved. Now hope that is seen is not hope. For who hopes[a] for what is seen? **25** But if we hope for what we do not see, we wait for it with patience. **26** Likewise the Spirit helps us in our weakness; for we do not know how to pray as we ought, but that very Spirit intercedes[b] with sighs too deep for words. **27** And God, who searches the heart, knows what is the mind of the Spirit, because the Spirit intercedes for the saints according to the will of God. **28** We know that all things work together for good[c] for those who love God, who are called according to his purpose. **29** For those whom he foreknew he also predestined to be conformed to the image of his Son, in order that he might be the firstborn within a large family. **30** And those whom he predestined he also called; and those whom he called he also justified; and those whom he justified he also glorified. **31** What then are we to say about these things? If God is for us, who is against us? **32** He who did not withhold his own Son, but gave him up for all of us, will he not with him also give us everything else? **33** Who will bring any charge against God's elect? It is God who justifies. **34** Who is to condemn? It is Christ Jesus, who died, yes, who was raised,[d] who is at the right hand of God, who indeed intercedes for us. **35** Who will separate us from the love of Christ? Will hardship, or distress, or persecution, or famine, or nakedness, or peril, or sword? **36** As it is written, "For your sake we are being killed all day long; we are accounted as sheep to be slaughtered." **37** No, in all these things we are more than conquerors through him who loved us. **38** For I am convinced that neither death, nor life, nor angels, nor rulers, nor things present, nor things to come, nor powers, **39** nor height, nor depth, nor anything else in all creation, will be able to separate us from the love of God in Christ Jesus our Lord.

Phil 1:27–30

Only, live your life in a manner worthy of the gospel of Christ, so that, whether I come and see you or am absent and hear about you, I will know that you are standing firm in one spirit, striving side by side with one mind for the faith of the gospel, **28** and are in no way intimidated by your opponents. For them this is evidence of their destruction, but of your salvation. And this is God's doing. **29** For he has graciously granted you the privilege not only of believing in Christ, but of suffering for him as well— **30** since you are having the same struggle that you saw I had and now hear that I still have.

1 Thess 1:6

And you became imitators of us and of the Lord, for in spite of persecution you received the word with joy inspired by the Holy Spirit

1 Thess 2:13–14

We also constantly give thanks to God for this, that when you received the word of God that you heard from us, you accepted it not as a human word but as what it really is, God's word, which is also at work in you believers. **14** For you, brothers and sisters, became imitators of the churches of God in Christ Jesus that are in Judea, for you suffered the same things from your own compatriots as they did from the Jews

1 Thess 3:1–5

Therefore when we could bear it no longer, we decided to be left alone in Athens; **2** and we sent Timothy, our brother and co-worker for God[e] in proclaiming the gospel of Christ, to strengthen and encourage you for the sake of your faith, **3** so that no one would be shaken by these persecutions. Indeed, you yourselves know that this is what we are destined for. **4** In fact, when we were with you, we told you beforehand that we were to suffer persecution; so it turned out, as you know. **5** For this reason, when I could bear it no longer, I sent to find out about your faith; I was afraid that somehow the tempter had tempted you and that our labor had been in vain.

2 Thess 1:4–8

Therefore we ourselves boast of you among the churches of God for your steadfastness and faith during all your persecutions and the afflictions that you are enduring. **5** This is evidence of the righteous judgment of God, and is intended to make you worthy of the kingdom of God, for which you are also suffering. **6** For it is indeed just of God to repay with affliction those who afflict you, **7** and to give relief to the afflicted as well as to us, when the Lord Jesus is revealed from heaven with his mighty angels **8** in flaming fire, inflicting vengeance on those who do not know God and on those who do not obey the gospel of our Lord Jesus.

2 Tim 1:6–14

For this reason I remind you to rekindle the gift of God that is within you through the laying on of my hands; **7** for God did not give us a spirit of cowardice, but rather a spirit of power and of love and of self-discipline. **8** Do not be ashamed, then, of the testimony about our Lord or of me his prisoner, but join with me in suffering for the gospel, relying on the power of God, **9** who saved us and called us with a holy calling, not according to our works but according to his own purpose and grace. This grace was given to us in Christ Jesus before the ages began, **10** but it has now been revealed through the appearing of our Savior Christ Jesus, who abolished death and brought life and immortality to light through the gospel. **11** For this

§ 141 [a] **Rom 8:24** ***hopes*** Other ancient authorities read *awaits* [b] **Rom 8:26** ***intercedes*** Other ancient authorities add *for us* [c] **Rom 8:28** ***all things work together for good*** Other ancient authorities read *God makes all things work together for good* or *in all things God works for good* [d] **Rom 8:34** ***raised*** Other ancient authorities add *from the dead* [e] **1 Thess 3:2** ***co-worker for God*** lit. *God's co-worker* Other ancient authorities read *God's minister* or *God's minister and our co-worker*

καὶ ἀπόστολος καὶ ⸀διδάσκαλος, 12 δι' ἣν αἰτίαν καὶ ταῦτα πάσχω· ἀλλ' οὐκ ἐπαισχύνομαι, οἶδα γὰρ ᾧ πεπίστευκα καὶ πέπεισμαι ὅτι δυνατός ἐστιν τὴν παραθήκην μου φυλάξαι εἰς ἐκείνην τὴν ἡμέραν. 13 Ὑποτύπωσιν ἔχε ὑγιαινόντων λόγων ὧν παρ' ἐμοῦ ἤκουσας ἐν πίστει καὶ ἀγάπῃ τῇ ἐν Χριστῷ Ἰησοῦ· 14 τὴν καλὴν παραθήκην φύλαξον διὰ πνεύματος ἁγίου τοῦ ἐνοικοῦντος ἐν ἡμῖν.

2 Tim 2:1–13

Σὺ οὖν, τέκνον μου, ἐνδυναμοῦ ἐν τῇ χάριτι τῇ ἐν Χριστῷ Ἰησοῦ, 2 καὶ ἃ ἤκουσας παρ' ἐμοῦ διὰ πολλῶν μαρτύρων, ταῦτα παράθου πιστοῖς ἀνθρώποις, οἵτινες ἱκανοὶ ἔσονται καὶ ἑτέρους διδάξαι. 3 Συγκακοπάθησον ὡς καλὸς στρατιώτης Χριστοῦ Ἰησοῦ. 4 οὐδεὶς στρατευόμενος ἐμπλέκεται ταῖς τοῦ βίου πραγματείαις, ἵνα τῷ στρατολογήσαντι ἀρέσῃ. 5 ἐὰν δὲ καὶ ἀθλῇ τις, οὐ στεφανοῦται ἐὰν μὴ νομίμως ἀθλήσῃ. 6 τὸν κοπιῶντα γεωργὸν δεῖ πρῶτον τῶν καρπῶν μεταλαμβάνειν. 7 νόει ὃ λέγω· δώσει γάρ σοι ὁ κύριος σύνεσιν ἐν πᾶσιν. 8 Μνημόνευε Ἰησοῦν Χριστὸν ἐγηγερμένον ἐκ νεκρῶν, ἐκ σπέρματος Δαυίδ, κατὰ τὸ εὐαγγέλιόν μου, 9 ἐν ᾧ κακοπαθῶ μέχρι δεσμῶν ὡς κακοῦργος, ἀλλὰ ὁ λόγος τοῦ θεοῦ οὐ δέδεται· 10 διὰ τοῦτο πάντα ὑπομένω διὰ τοὺς ἐκλεκτούς, ἵνα καὶ αὐτοὶ σωτηρίας τύχωσιν τῆς ἐν Χριστῷ Ἰησοῦ μετὰ δόξης αἰωνίου. 11 πιστὸς ὁ λόγος· εἰ γὰρ συναπεθάνομεν, καὶ συζήσομεν· 12 εἰ ὑπομένομεν, καὶ συμβασιλεύσομεν· εἰ ἀρνησόμεθα, κἀκεῖνος ἀρνήσεται ἡμᾶς· 13 εἰ ἀπιστοῦμεν, ἐκεῖνος πιστὸς μένει, ἀρνήσασθαι γὰρ ἑαυτὸν οὐ δύναται.

Acts 14:22

ἐπιστηρίζοντες τὰς ψυχὰς τῶν μαθητῶν, παρακαλοῦντες ἐμμένειν τῇ πίστει καὶ ὅτι διὰ πολλῶν θλίψεων δεῖ ἡμᾶς εἰσελθεῖν εἰς τὴν βασιλείαν τοῦ θεοῦ.

Cf. Rom 12:12; 12:14; 12:17–21.

See also § 142 Paul's Example of Suffering in behalf of Christ.

142. Paul's Example of Suffering in behalf of Christ

1 Cor 4:9–13

δοκῶ γάρ, ὁ θεὸς ἡμᾶς τοὺς ἀποστόλους ἐσχάτους ἀπέδειξεν ὡς ἐπιθανατίους, ὅτι θέατρον ἐγενήθημεν τῷ κόσμῳ καὶ ἀγγέλοις καὶ ἀνθρώποις. 10 ἡμεῖς μωροὶ διὰ Χριστόν, ὑμεῖς δὲ φρόνιμοι ἐν Χριστῷ· ἡμεῖς ἀσθενεῖς, ὑμεῖς δὲ ἰσχυροί· ὑμεῖς ἔνδοξοι, ἡμεῖς δὲ ἄτιμοι. 11 ἄχρι τῆς ἄρτι ὥρας καὶ πεινῶμεν καὶ διψῶμεν καὶ γυμνιτεύομεν καὶ κολαφιζόμεθα καὶ ἀστατοῦμεν 12 καὶ κοπιῶμεν ἐργαζόμενοι ταῖς ἰδίαις χερσίν· λοιδορούμενοι εὐλογοῦμεν, διωκόμενοι ἀνεχόμεθα, 13 δυσφημούμενοι παρακαλοῦμεν· ὡς περικαθάρματα τοῦ κόσμου ἐγενήθημεν, πάντων περίψημα ἕως ἄρτι.

2 Cor 1:3–11

Εὐλογητὸς ὁ θεὸς καὶ πατὴρ τοῦ κυρίου ἡμῶν Ἰησοῦ Χριστοῦ, ὁ πατὴρ τῶν οἰκτιρμῶν καὶ θεὸς πάσης παρακλήσεως, 4 ὁ παρακαλῶν ἡμᾶς ἐπὶ πάσῃ τῇ θλίψει ἡμῶν εἰς τὸ δύνασθαι ἡμᾶς παρακαλεῖν τοὺς ἐν πάσῃ θλίψει διὰ τῆς παρακλήσεως ἧς παρακαλούμεθα αὐτοὶ ὑπὸ τοῦ θεοῦ. 5 ὅτι καθὼς περισσεύει τὰ παθήματα τοῦ Χριστοῦ εἰς ἡμᾶς, οὕτως διὰ τοῦ Χριστοῦ περισσεύει καὶ ἡ παράκλησις ἡμῶν. 6 εἴτε δὲ θλιβόμεθα, ὑπὲρ τῆς ὑμῶν παρακλήσεως καὶ σωτηρίας· εἴτε παρακαλούμεθα, ὑπὲρ τῆς ὑμῶν παρακλήσεως τῆς ἐνεργουμένης ἐν ὑπομονῇ τῶν αὐτῶν παθημάτων ὧν καὶ ἡμεῖς πάσχομεν. 7 καὶ ἡ ἐλπὶς ἡμῶν βεβαία ὑπὲρ ὑμῶν εἰδότες ὅτι ὡς κοινωνοί ἐστε τῶν παθημάτων, οὕτως καὶ τῆς παρακλήσεως. 8 Οὐ γὰρ θέλομεν ὑμᾶς ἀγνοεῖν, ἀδελφοί, ὑπὲρ τῆς θλίψεως ἡμῶν τῆς γενομένης ἐν τῇ Ἀσίᾳ, ὅτι καθ' ὑπερβολὴν ὑπὲρ δύναμιν ἐβαρήθημεν ὥστε ἐξαπορηθῆναι ἡμᾶς καὶ τοῦ ζῆν· 9 ἀλλὰ αὐτοὶ ἐν ἑαυτοῖς τὸ ἀπόκριμα τοῦ θανάτου ἐσχήκαμεν, ἵνα μὴ πεποιθότες ὦμεν ἐφ' ἑαυτοῖς ἀλλ' ἐπὶ τῷ θεῷ τῷ ἐγείροντι τοὺς νεκρούς· 10 ὃς ἐκ ⸂τηλικούτου θανάτου⸃ ἐρρύσατο ἡμᾶς καὶ ῥύσεται, εἰς ὃν ἠλπίκαμεν [ὅτι] καὶ ἔτι ῥύσεται, 11 συνυπουργούντων καὶ ὑμῶν ὑπὲρ ἡμῶν τῇ δεήσει, ἵνα ἐκ πολλῶν προσώπων τὸ εἰς ἡμᾶς χάρισμα διὰ πολλῶν εὐχαριστηθῇ ὑπὲρ ⸀ἡμῶν.

2 Cor 4:7–12

Ἔχομεν δὲ τὸν θησαυρὸν τοῦτον ἐν ὀστρακίνοις σκεύεσιν, ἵνα ἡ ὑπερβολὴ τῆς δυνάμεως ᾖ τοῦ θεοῦ καὶ μὴ ἐξ ἡμῶν· 8 ἐν παντὶ θλιβόμενοι ἀλλ' οὐ στενοχωρούμενοι, ἀπορούμενοι ἀλλ' οὐκ ἐξαπορούμενοι, 9 διωκόμενοι ἀλλ' οὐκ ἐγκαταλειπόμενοι, καταβαλλόμενοι ἀλλ' οὐκ ἀπολλύμενοι, 10 πάντοτε τὴν νέκρωσιν τοῦ Ἰησοῦ ἐν τῷ σώματι περιφέροντες, ἵνα καὶ ἡ ζωὴ τοῦ Ἰησοῦ ἐν τῷ σώματι ἡμῶν φανερωθῇ. 11 ἀεὶ γὰρ ἡμεῖς οἱ ζῶντες εἰς θάνατον παραδιδόμεθα διὰ Ἰησοῦν, ἵνα καὶ ἡ ζωὴ τοῦ Ἰησοῦ φανερωθῇ ἐν τῇ θνητῇ σαρκὶ ἡμῶν. 12 ὥστε ὁ θάνατος ἐν ἡμῖν ἐνεργεῖται, ἡ δὲ ζωὴ ἐν ὑμῖν.

2 Cor 4:16–18

Διὸ οὐκ ἐγκακοῦμεν, ἀλλ' εἰ καὶ ὁ ἔξω ἡμῶν ἄνθρωπος διαφθείρεται, ἀλλ' ὁ ἔσω ἡμῶν ἀνακαινοῦται ἡμέρᾳ καὶ ἡμέρᾳ. 17 τὸ γὰρ παραυτίκα ἐλαφρὸν τῆς θλίψεως ἡμῶν καθ' ὑπερβολὴν εἰς ὑπερβολὴν αἰώνιον βάρος δόξης κατεργάζεται ἡμῖν, 18 μὴ σκοπούντων ἡμῶν τὰ βλεπόμενα ἀλλὰ τὰ μὴ βλεπόμενα· τὰ γὰρ βλεπόμενα πρόσκαιρα, τὰ δὲ μὴ βλεπόμενα αἰώνια.

2 Cor 6:3–10

Μηδεμίαν ἐν μηδενὶ διδόντες προσκοπήν, ἵνα μὴ μωμηθῇ ἡ διακονία, 4 ἀλλ'

2 Tim 1:11 ***διδασκαλος*** ℵ* A I] *add.* εθνων ℵ^{2} C D 1739. 1881 *Byz* ¦ διακονος 33 **§ 142** **2 Cor 1:10** ***τηλικουτου θανατου*** ℵ A B C D 33. 1739*. 1881 *Byz*] τηλικουτων θανατων $\mathfrak{P}^{46}$ 1739^{mg} **2 Cor 1:11** ***ημων*** $\mathfrak{P}^{46c}$ ℵ A C D* 33. 1739. 1881 *Byz*^{pt}] υμων $\mathfrak{P}^{46*}$ B D^{2} *Byz*^{pt}

gospel I was appointed a herald and an apostle and a teacher,[f] [12] and for this reason I suffer as I do. But I am not ashamed, for I know the one in whom I have put my trust, and I am sure that he is able to guard until that day what I have entrusted to him. [13] Hold to the standard of sound teaching that you have heard from me, in the faith and love that are in Christ Jesus. [14] Guard the good treasure entrusted to you, with the help of the Holy Spirit living in us.

2 Tim 2:1–13

You then, my child, be strong in the grace that is in Christ Jesus; [2] and what you have heard from me through many witnesses entrust to faithful people who will be able to teach others as well. [3] Share in suffering like a good soldier of Christ Jesus. [4] No one serving in the army gets entangled in everyday affairs; the soldier's aim is to please the enlisting officer. [5] And in the case of an athlete, no one is crowned without competing according to the rules. [6] It is the farmer who does the work who ought to have the first share of the crops. [7] Think over what I say, for the Lord will give you understanding in all things. [8] Remember Jesus Christ, raised from the dead, a descendant of David—that is my gospel, [9] for which I suffer hardship, even to the point of being chained like a criminal. But the word of God is not chained. [10] Therefore I endure everything for the sake of the elect, so that they may also obtain the salvation that is in Christ Jesus, with eternal glory. [11] The saying is sure: If we have died with him, we will also live with him; [12] if we endure, we will also reign with him; if we deny him, he will also deny us; [13] if we are faithless, he remains faithful— for he cannot deny himself.

Acts 14:22

There they strengthened the souls of the disciples and encouraged them to continue in the faith, saying, "It is through many persecutions that we must enter the kingdom of God."

Cf. Rom 12:12; 12:14; 12:17–21.

See also § 142 Paul's Example of Suffering in behalf of Christ.

142. Paul's Example of Suffering in behalf of Christ

1 Cor 4:9–13

For I think that God has exhibited us apostles as last of all, as though sentenced to death, because we have become a spectacle to the world, to angels and to mortals. [10] We are fools for the sake of Christ, but you are wise in Christ. We are weak, but you are strong. You are held in honor, but we in disrepute. [11] To the present hour we are hungry and thirsty, we are poorly clothed and beaten and homeless, [12] and we grow weary from the work of our own hands. When reviled, we bless; when persecuted, we endure; [13] when slandered, we speak kindly. We have become like the rubbish of the world, the dregs of all things, to this very day.

2 Cor 1:3–11

Blessed be the God and Father of our Lord Jesus Christ, the Father of mercies and the God of all consolation, [4] who consoles us in all our affliction, so that we may be able to console those who are in any affliction with the consolation with which we ourselves are consoled by God. [5] For just as the sufferings of Christ are abundant for us, so also our consolation is abundant through Christ. [6] If we are being afflicted, it is for your consolation and salvation; if we are being consoled, it is for your consolation, which you experience when you patiently endure the same sufferings that we are also suffering. [7] Our hope for you is unshaken; for we know that as you share in our sufferings, so also you share in our consolation. [8] We do not want you to be unaware, brothers and sisters, of the affliction we experienced in Asia; for we were so utterly, unbearably crushed that we despaired of life itself. [9] Indeed, we felt that we had received the sentence of death so that we would rely not on ourselves but on God who raises the dead. [10] He who rescued us from so deadly a peril[a] will continue to rescue us; on him we have set our hope that he will rescue us again, [11] as you also join in helping us by your prayers, so that many will give thanks on our[b] behalf for the blessing granted us through the prayers of many.

2 Cor 4:7–12

But we have this treasure in clay jars, so that it may be made clear that this extraordinary power belongs to God and does not come from us. [8] We are afflicted in every way, but not crushed; perplexed, but not driven to despair; [9] persecuted, but not forsaken; struck down, but not destroyed; [10] always carrying in the body the death of Jesus, so that the life of Jesus may also be made visible in our bodies. [11] For while we live, we are always being given up to death for Jesus' sake, so that the life of Jesus may be made visible in our mortal flesh. [12] So death is at work in us, but life in you.

2 Cor 4:16–18

So we do not lose heart. Even though our outer nature is wasting away, our inner nature is being renewed day by day. [17] For this slight momentary affliction is preparing us for an eternal weight of glory beyond all measure, [18] because we look not at what is presently seen but at what is not presently seen; for what is presently seen is temporary, but what is not presently seen is eternal.[c]

2 Cor 6:3–10

We are putting no obstacle in anyone's way, so that no fault may be found with our ministry, [4] but as servants of God

[f] **2 Tim 1:11** *teacher* Other ancient authorities add *of the Gentiles* **§ 142** [a] **2 Cor 1:10** *so deadly a peril* lit. *so great a death* Other ancient authorities read *perils so deadly* lit. *such great deaths* [b] **2 Cor 1:11** *our* Other ancient authorities read *your* [c] **2 Cor 4:18** Translation differs from NRSV

ἐν παντὶ συνιστάντες ἑαυτοὺς ὡς θεοῦ διάκονοι, ἐν ὑπομονῇ πολλῇ, ἐν θλίψεσιν, ἐν ἀνάγκαις, ἐν στενοχωρίαις, 5 ἐν πληγαῖς, ἐν φυλακαῖς, ἐν ἀκαταστασίαις, ἐν κόποις, ἐν ἀγρυπνίαις, ἐν νηστείαις, 6 ἐν ἁγνότητι, ἐν γνώσει, ἐν μακροθυμίᾳ, ἐν χρηστότητι, ἐν πνεύματι ἁγίῳ, ἐν ἀγάπῃ ἀνυποκρίτῳ, 7 ἐν λόγῳ ἀληθείας, ἐν δυνάμει θεοῦ· διὰ τῶν ὅπλων τῆς δικαιοσύνης τῶν δεξιῶν καὶ ἀριστερῶν, 8 διὰ δόξης καὶ ἀτιμίας, διὰ δυσφημίας καὶ εὐφημίας· ὡς πλάνοι καὶ ἀληθεῖς, 9 ὡς ἀγνοούμενοι καὶ ἐπιγινωσκόμενοι, ὡς ἀποθνῄσκοντες καὶ ἰδοὺ ζῶμεν, ὡς παιδευόμενοι καὶ μὴ θανατούμενοι, 10 ὡς λυπούμενοι ἀεὶ δὲ χαίροντες, ὡς πτωχοὶ πολλοὺς δὲ πλουτίζοντες, ὡς μηδὲν ἔχοντες καὶ πάντα κατέχοντες.

2 Cor 11:21b–33

Ἐν ᾧ δ' ἄν τις τολμᾷ, ἐν ἀφροσύνῃ λέγω, τολμῶ κἀγώ. 22 Ἑβραῖοί εἰσιν; κἀγώ. Ἰσραηλῖταί εἰσιν; κἀγώ. σπέρμα Ἀβραάμ εἰσιν; κἀγώ. 23 διάκονοι Χριστοῦ εἰσιν; παραφρονῶν λαλῶ, ὑπὲρ ἐγώ· ἐν κόποις περισσοτέρως, ἐν φυλακαῖς περισσοτέρως, ἐν πληγαῖς ὑπερβαλλόντως, ἐν θανάτοις πολλάκις. 24 Ὑπὸ Ἰουδαίων πεντάκις τεσσεράκοντα παρὰ μίαν ἔλαβον, 25 τρὶς ἐρραβδίσθην, ἅπαξ ἐλιθάσθην, τρὶς ἐναυάγησα, νυχθήμερον ἐν τῷ βυθῷ πεποίηκα· 26 ὁδοιπορίαις πολλάκις, κινδύνοις ποταμῶν, κινδύνοις λῃστῶν, κινδύνοις ἐκ γένους, κινδύνοις ἐξ ἐθνῶν, κινδύνοις ἐν πόλει, κινδύνοις ἐν ἐρημίᾳ, κινδύνοις ἐν θαλάσσῃ, κινδύνοις ἐν ψευδαδέλφοις, 27 κόπῳ καὶ μόχθῳ, ἐν ἀγρυπνίαις πολλάκις, ἐν λιμῷ καὶ δίψει, ἐν νηστείαις πολλάκις, ἐν ψύχει καὶ γυμνότητι· 28 χωρὶς τῶν παρεκτὸς ἡ ἐπίστασίς μοι ἡ καθ' ἡμέραν, ἡ μέριμνα πασῶν τῶν ἐκκλησιῶν. 29 τίς ἀσθενεῖ καὶ οὐκ ἀσθενῶ; τίς σκανδαλίζεται καὶ οὐκ ἐγὼ πυροῦμαι; 30 Εἰ καυχᾶσθαι δεῖ, τὰ τῆς ἀσθενείας μου καυχήσομαι. 31 ὁ θεὸς καὶ πατὴρ τοῦ κυρίου Ἰησοῦ οἶδεν, ὁ ὢν εὐλογητὸς εἰς τοὺς αἰῶνας, ὅτι οὐ ψεύδομαι. 32 ἐν Δαμασκῷ ὁ ἐθνάρχης Ἁρέτα τοῦ βασιλέως ἐφρούρει τὴν πόλιν Δαμασκηνῶν πιάσαι ⸀με, 33 καὶ διὰ θυρίδος ἐν σαργάνῃ ἐχαλάσθην διὰ τοῦ τείχους καὶ ἐξέφυγον τὰς χεῖρας αὐτοῦ.

2 Cor 12:1–10

Καυχᾶσθαι δεῖ, οὐ συμφέρον μέν, ἐλεύσομαι δὲ εἰς ὀπτασίας καὶ ἀποκαλύψεις κυρίου. 2 οἶδα ἄνθρωπον ἐν Χριστῷ πρὸ ἐτῶν δεκατεσσάρων, εἴτε ἐν σώματι οὐκ οἶδα, εἴτε ἐκτὸς τοῦ σώματος οὐκ οἶδα, ὁ θεὸς οἶδεν, ἁρπαγέντα τὸν τοιοῦτον ἕως τρίτου οὐρανοῦ. 3 καὶ οἶδα τὸν τοιοῦτον ἄνθρωπον, εἴτε ἐν σώματι εἴτε χωρὶς τοῦ σώματος οὐκ οἶδα, ὁ θεὸς οἶδεν, 4 ὅτι ἡρπάγη εἰς τὸν παράδεισον καὶ ἤκουσεν ἄρρητα ῥήματα ἃ οὐκ ἐξὸν ἀνθρώπῳ λαλῆσαι. 5 ὑπὲρ τοῦ τοιούτου καυχήσομαι, ὑπὲρ δὲ ἐμαυτοῦ οὐ καυχήσομαι εἰ μὴ ἐν ταῖς ἀσθενείαις. 6 Ἐὰν γὰρ θελήσω καυχήσασθαι, οὐκ ἔσομαι ἄφρων, ἀλήθειαν γὰρ ἐρῶ· φείδομαι δέ, μή τις εἰς ἐμὲ λογίσηται ὑπὲρ ὃ βλέπει με ἢ ἀκούει [τι] ἐξ ἐμοῦ 7 καὶ τῇ ὑπερβολῇ τῶν ἀποκαλύψεων. ⸀διὸ ἵνα μὴ ὑπεραίρωμαι, ἐδόθη μοι σκόλοψ τῇ σαρκί, ἄγγελος σατανᾶ, ἵνα με κολαφίζῃ, ⸂ἵνα μὴ ὑπεραίρωμαι⸃. 8 ὑπὲρ τούτου τρὶς τὸν κύριον παρεκάλεσα ἵνα ἀποστῇ ἀπ' ἐμοῦ. 9 καὶ εἴρηκέν μοι· ἀρκεῖ σοι ἡ χάρις μου, ἡ γὰρ ⸀δύναμις ἐν ἀσθενείᾳ τελεῖται. Ἥδιστα οὖν μᾶλλον καυχήσομαι ἐν ταῖς ἀσθενείαις μου, ἵνα ἐπισκηνώσῃ ἐπ' ἐμὲ ἡ δύναμις τοῦ Χριστοῦ. 10 διὸ εὐδοκῶ ἐν ἀσθενείαις, ἐν ὕβρεσιν, ἐν ἀνάγκαις, ἐν διωγμοῖς καὶ στενοχωρίαις, ὑπὲρ Χριστοῦ· ὅταν γὰρ ἀσθενῶ, τότε δυνατός εἰμι.

Eph 3:13

διὸ αἰτοῦμαι μὴ ἐγκακεῖν ἐν ταῖς θλίψεσίν μου ὑπὲρ ὑμῶν, ἥτις ἐστὶν δόξα ὑμῶν.

Phil 4:10–13

Ἐχάρην δὲ ἐν κυρίῳ μεγάλως ὅτι ἤδη ποτὲ ἀνεθάλετε τὸ ὑπὲρ ἐμοῦ φρονεῖν, ἐφ' ᾧ καὶ ἐφρονεῖτε, ἠκαιρεῖσθε δέ. 11 οὐχ ὅτι καθ' ὑστέρησιν λέγω, ἐγὼ γὰρ ἔμαθον ἐν οἷς εἰμι αὐτάρκης εἶναι. 12 οἶδα καὶ ταπεινοῦσθαι, οἶδα καὶ περισσεύειν· ἐν παντὶ καὶ ἐν πᾶσιν μεμύημαι, καὶ χορτάζεσθαι καὶ πεινᾶν καὶ περισσεύειν καὶ ὑστερεῖσθαι· 13 πάντα ἰσχύω ἐν τῷ ἐνδυναμοῦντί με.

Col 1:24

Νῦν χαίρω ἐν τοῖς παθήμασιν ὑπὲρ ὑμῶν καὶ ἀνταναπληρῶ τὰ ὑστερήματα τῶν θλίψεων τοῦ Χριστοῦ ἐν τῇ σαρκί μου ὑπὲρ τοῦ σώματος αὐτοῦ, ὅ ἐστιν ἡ ἐκκλησία

1 Thess 2:1–2

Αὐτοὶ γὰρ οἴδατε, ἀδελφοί, τὴν εἴσοδον ἡμῶν τὴν πρὸς ὑμᾶς ὅτι οὐ κενὴ γέγονεν, 2 ἀλλὰ προπαθόντες καὶ ὑβρισθέντες, καθὼς οἴδατε, ἐν Φιλίπποις ἐπαρρησιασάμεθα ἐν τῷ θεῷ ἡμῶν λαλῆσαι πρὸς ὑμᾶς τὸ εὐαγγέλιον τοῦ θεοῦ ἐν πολλῷ ἀγῶνι.

2 Tim 3:10–12

Σὺ δὲ παρηκολούθησάς μου τῇ διδασκαλίᾳ, τῇ ἀγωγῇ, τῇ προθέσει, τῇ πίστει, τῇ μακροθυμίᾳ, τῇ ἀγάπῃ, τῇ ὑπομονῇ, 11 τοῖς διωγμοῖς, τοῖς παθήμασιν, οἷά μοι ἐγένετο ἐν Ἀντιοχείᾳ, ἐν Ἰκονίῳ, ἐν Λύστροις, οἵους διωγμοὺς ὑπήνεγκα καὶ ἐκ πάντων με ἐρρύσατο ὁ κύριος. 12 καὶ πάντες δὲ οἱ θέλοντες εὐσεβῶς ζῆν ἐν Χριστῷ Ἰησοῦ διωχθήσονται.

Acts 9:16

ἐγὼ γὰρ ὑποδείξω αὐτῷ ὅσα δεῖ αὐτὸν ὑπὲρ τοῦ ὀνόματός μου παθεῖν.

Cf. the narrative of Paul's sufferings in Acts 13:48–52; 14:1–7; 14:19–20; 15:26; 16:22–25; 18:12–17; 19:23–40; 20:3; 20:18–19; 20:22–24; 21:10–14; 21:27–36; and the book's climactic narrative of Paul's arrest in Jerusalem and journey in chains to Rome. See also the paradigmatic self-descriptions in Phil 1:12–26; 3:2–11; 2 Tim 4:6–8; 4:16–18, and the function of Paul's example within the exhortations to suffering in Phil 1:27–30; 1 Thess 1:6–10; 2 Tim 1:6–14; and 2 Tim 2:1–13.

See also § 140 Imprisonment for the Gospel; § 141 Suffering and Affliction in Christ.

2 Cor 11:32 ***με*** B D*] *add.* θελων ℵ D² 33. (1739). 1881 *Byz* **2 Cor 12:7** ***διο*** ℵ A B 33. 1739] *om.* 𝔓⁴⁶ D 1881 *Byz* • ***ινα μη υπεραιρωμαι*** 𝔓⁴⁶ ℵ² B Iᵛⁱᵈ 1739. (1881) *Byz*] *om.* ℵ* A D 33 **2 Cor 12:9** ***δυναμις*** 𝔓⁴⁶ᵛⁱᵈ ℵ* A* B D*] *add.* μου ℵ² Aᶜ D¹ 33. 1739. 1881 *Byz*

we have commended ourselves in every way: through great endurance, in afflictions, hardships, calamities, **5** beatings, imprisonments, riots, labors, sleepless nights, hunger; **6** by purity, knowledge, patience, kindness, holiness of spirit, genuine love, **7** truthful speech, and the power of God; with the weapons of righteousness for the right hand and for the left; **8** in honor and dishonor, in ill repute and good repute. We are treated as impostors, and yet are true; **9** as unknown, and yet are well known; as dying, and see—we are alive; as punished, and yet not killed; **10** as sorrowful, yet always rejoicing; as poor, yet making many rich; as having nothing, and yet possessing everything.

2 Cor 11:21b–33

But whatever anyone dares to boast of—I am speaking as a fool—I also dare to boast of that. **22** Are they Hebrews? So am I. Are they Israelites? So am I. Are they descendants of Abraham? So am I. **23** Are they ministers of Christ? I am talking like a madman—I am a better one: with far greater labors, far more imprisonments, with countless floggings, and often near death. **24** Five times I have received from the Jews the forty lashes minus one. **25** Three times I was beaten with rods. Once I received a stoning. Three times I was shipwrecked; for a night and a day I was adrift at sea; **26** on frequent journeys, in danger from rivers, danger from bandits, danger from my own people, danger from Gentiles, danger in the city, danger in the wilderness, danger at sea, danger from false brothers and sisters; **27** in toil and hardship, through many a sleepless night, hungry and thirsty, often without food, cold and naked. **28** And, besides other things, I am under daily pressure because of my anxiety for all the churches. **29** Who is weak, and I am not weak? Who is made to stumble, and I am not indignant? **30** If I must boast, I will boast of the things that show my weakness. **31** The God and Father of the Lord Jesus (blessed be he forever!) knows that I do not lie. **32** In Damascus, the governor under King Aretas guarded the city of Damascus in order to[d] seize me, **33** but I was let down in a basket through a window in the wall, and escaped from his hands.

2 Cor 12:1–10

It is necessary to boast; nothing is to be gained by it, but I will go on to visions and revelations of the Lord. **2** I know a person in Christ who fourteen years ago was caught up to the third heaven—whether in the body or out of the body I do not know; God knows. **3** And I know that such a person—whether in the body or out of the body I do not know; God knows— **4** was caught up into Paradise and heard things that are not to be told, that no mortal is permitted to repeat. **5** On behalf of such a one I will boast, but on my own behalf I will not boast, except of my weaknesses. **6** But if I wish to boast, I will not be a fool, for I will be speaking the truth. But I refrain from it, so that no one may think better of me than what is seen in me or heard from me, **7** even considering the exceptional character of the revelations. Therefore, to keep[e] me from being too elated, a thorn was given me in the flesh, a messenger of Satan to torment me, to keep me from being too elated.[f] **8** Three times I appealed to the Lord about this, that it would leave me, **9** but he said to me, "My grace is sufficient for you, for power[g] is made perfect in weakness." So, I will boast all the more gladly of my weaknesses, so that the power of Christ may dwell in me. **10** Therefore I am content with weaknesses, insults, hardships, persecutions, and calamities for the sake of Christ; for whenever I am weak, then I am strong.

Eph 3:13

I pray therefore that you may not lose heart over my sufferings for you; they are your glory.

Phil 4:10–13

I rejoice in the Lord greatly that now at last you have revived your concern for me; indeed, you were concerned for me, but had no opportunity to show it. **11** Not that I am referring to being in need; for I have learned to be content with whatever I have. **12** I know what it is to have little, and I know what it is to have plenty. In any and all circumstances I have learned the secret of being well-fed and of going hungry, of having plenty and of being in need. **13** I can do all things through him who strengthens me.

Col 1:24

I am now rejoicing in my sufferings for your sake, and in my flesh I am completing what is lacking in Christ's afflictions for the sake of his body, that is, the church.

1 Thess 2:1–2

You yourselves know, brothers and sisters, that our coming to you was not in vain, **2** but though we had already suffered and been shamefully mistreated at Philippi, as you know, we had courage in our God to declare to you the gospel of God in spite of great opposition.

2 Tim 3:10–12

Now you have observed my teaching, my conduct, my aim in life, my faith, my patience, my love, my steadfastness, **11** my persecutions, and my suffering the things that happened to me in Antioch, Iconium, and Lystra. What persecutions I endured! Yet the Lord rescued me from all of them. **12** Indeed, all who want to live a godly life in Christ Jesus will be persecuted.

Acts 9:16

I myself will show him how much he must suffer for the sake of my name.

Cf. the narrative of Paul's sufferings in Acts 13:48–52; 14:1–7; 14:19–20; 15:26; 16:22–25; 18:12–17; 19:23–40; 20:3; 20:18–19; 20:22–24; 21:10–14; 21:27–36; and the book's climactic narrative of Paul's arrest in Jerusalem and journey in chains to Rome. See also the paradigmatic self-descriptions in Phil 1:12–26; 3:2–11; 2 Tim 4:6–8; 4:16–18, and the function of Paul's example within the exhortations to suffering in Phil 1:27–30; 1 Thess 1:6–10; 2 Tim 1:6–14; and 2 Tim 2:1–13.

See also § 140 Imprisonment for the Gospel; § 141 Suffering and Affliction in Christ.

[d] **2 Cor 11:32** ***in order to*** Other ancient authorities read *and wanted to* [e] **2 Cor 12:7** ***Therefore, to keep*** Other ancient authorities read *To keep* [f] **2 Cor 12:7** ***to keep me from being too elated*** Other ancient authorities lack *to keep me from being too elated* [g] **2 Cor 12:9** ***power*** Other ancient authorities read *my power*

143. The Athletic Metaphor

1 Cor 9:24–27

Οὐκ οἴδατε ὅτι οἱ ἐν σταδίῳ τρέχοντες πάντες μὲν τρέχουσιν, εἷς δὲ λαμβάνει τὸ βραβεῖον; οὕτως τρέχετε ἵνα καταλάβητε. 25 πᾶς δὲ ὁ ἀγωνιζόμενος πάντα ἐγκρατεύεται, ἐκεῖνοι μὲν οὖν ἵνα φθαρτὸν στέφανον λάβωσιν, ἡμεῖς δὲ ἄφθαρτον. 26 ἐγὼ τοίνυν οὕτως τρέχω ὡς οὐκ ἀδήλως, οὕτως πυκτεύω ὡς οὐκ ἀέρα δέρων· 27 ἀλλὰ ὑπωπιάζω μου τὸ σῶμα καὶ δουλαγωγῶ, μή πως ἄλλοις κηρύξας αὐτὸς ἀδόκιμος γένωμαι.

Gal 2:2

ἀνέβην δὲ κατὰ ἀποκάλυψιν· καὶ ἀνεθέμην αὐτοῖς τὸ εὐαγγέλιον ὃ κηρύσσω ἐν τοῖς ἔθνεσιν, κατ᾽ ἰδίαν δὲ τοῖς δοκοῦσιν, μή πως εἰς κενὸν τρέχω ἢ ἔδραμον.

Gal 5:7

Ἐτρέχετε καλῶς· τίς ὑμᾶς ἐνέκοψεν [τῇ] ἀληθείᾳ μὴ πείθεσθαι;

Phil 2:16

λόγον ζωῆς ἐπέχοντες, εἰς καύχημα ἐμοὶ εἰς ἡμέραν Χριστοῦ, ὅτι οὐκ εἰς κενὸν ἔδραμον οὐδὲ εἰς κενὸν ἐκοπίασα.

Phil 3:12–16

Οὐχ ὅτι ἤδη ἔλαβον ἢ ἤδη τετελείωμαι, διώκω δὲ εἰ καὶ καταλάβω, ἐφ᾽ ᾧ καὶ κατελήμφθην ὑπὸ Χριστοῦ [Ἰησοῦ]. 13 ἀδελφοί, ἐγὼ ἐμαυτὸν ⸀οὐ λογίζομαι κατειληφέναι· ἓν δέ, τὰ μὲν ὀπίσω ἐπιλανθανόμενος τοῖς δὲ ἔμπροσθεν ἐπεκτεινόμενος, 14 κατὰ σκοπὸν διώκω εἰς τὸ βραβεῖον τῆς ἄνω κλήσεως τοῦ θεοῦ ἐν Χριστῷ Ἰησοῦ. 15 Ὅσοι οὖν τέλειοι, τοῦτο φρονῶμεν· καὶ εἴ τι ἑτέρως φρονεῖτε, καὶ τοῦτο ὁ θεὸς ὑμῖν ἀποκαλύψει· 16 πλὴν εἰς ὃ ἐφθάσαμεν, τῷ αὐτῷ στοιχεῖν.

1 Thess 2:19–20

τίς γὰρ ἡμῶν ἐλπὶς ἢ χαρὰ ἢ στέφανος καυχήσεως—ἢ οὐχὶ καὶ ὑμεῖς—ἔμπροσθεν τοῦ κυρίου ἡμῶν Ἰησοῦ ἐν τῇ αὐτοῦ παρουσίᾳ; 20 ὑμεῖς γάρ ἐστε ἡ δόξα ἡμῶν καὶ ἡ χαρά.

1 Tim 4:6–10

Ταῦτα ὑποτιθέμενος τοῖς ἀδελφοῖς καλὸς ἔσῃ διάκονος Χριστοῦ Ἰησοῦ, ἐντρεφόμενος τοῖς λόγοις τῆς πίστεως καὶ τῆς καλῆς διδασκαλίας ᾗ παρηκολούθηκας· 7 τοὺς δὲ βεβήλους καὶ γραώδεις μύθους παραιτοῦ. Γύμναζε δὲ σεαυτὸν πρὸς εὐσέβειαν· 8 ἡ γὰρ σωματικὴ γυμνασία πρὸς ὀλίγον ἐστὶν ὠφέλιμος, ἡ δὲ εὐσέβεια πρὸς πάντα ὠφέλιμός ἐστιν ἐπαγγελίαν ἔχουσα ζωῆς τῆς νῦν καὶ τῆς μελλούσης. 9 πιστὸς ὁ λόγος καὶ πάσης ἀποδοχῆς ἄξιος· 10 εἰς τοῦτο γὰρ κοπιῶμεν καὶ ⸀ἀγωνιζόμεθα, ὅτι ἠλπίκαμεν ἐπὶ θεῷ ζῶντι, ὅς ἐστιν σωτὴρ πάντων ἀνθρώπων μάλιστα πιστῶν.

1 Tim 6:12

ἀγωνίζου τὸν καλὸν ἀγῶνα τῆς πίστεως, ἐπιλαβοῦ τῆς αἰωνίου ζωῆς, εἰς ἣν ἐκλήθης καὶ ὡμολόγησας τὴν καλὴν ὁμολογίαν ἐνώπιον πολλῶν μαρτύρων.

2 Tim 2:1–7

Σὺ οὖν, τέκνον μου, ἐνδυναμοῦ ἐν τῇ χάριτι τῇ ἐν Χριστῷ Ἰησοῦ, 2 καὶ ἃ ἤκουσας παρ᾽ ἐμοῦ διὰ πολλῶν μαρτύρων, ταῦτα παράθου πιστοῖς ἀνθρώποις, οἵτινες ἱκανοὶ ἔσονται καὶ ἑτέρους διδάξαι. 3 Συγκακοπάθησον ὡς καλὸς στρατιώτης Χριστοῦ Ἰησοῦ. 4 οὐδεὶς στρατευόμενος ἐμπλέκεται ταῖς τοῦ βίου πραγματείαις, ἵνα τῷ στρατολογήσαντι ἀρέσῃ. 5 ἐὰν δὲ καὶ ἀθλῇ τις, οὐ στεφανοῦται ἐὰν μὴ νομίμως ἀθλήσῃ. 6 τὸν κοπιῶντα γεωργὸν δεῖ πρῶτον τῶν καρπῶν μεταλαμβάνειν. 7 νόει ὃ λέγω· δώσει γάρ σοι ὁ κύριος σύνεσιν ἐν πᾶσιν.

2 Tim 4:6–8

Ἐγὼ γὰρ ἤδη σπένδομαι, καὶ ὁ καιρὸς τῆς ἀναλύσεώς μου ἐφέστηκεν. 7 τὸν καλὸν ἀγῶνα ἠγώνισμαι, τὸν δρόμον τετέλεκα, τὴν πίστιν τετήρηκα· 8 λοιπὸν ἀπόκειταί μοι ὁ τῆς δικαιοσύνης στέφανος, ὃν ἀποδώσει μοι ὁ κύριος ἐν ἐκείνῃ τῇ ἡμέρᾳ, ὁ δίκαιος κριτής, οὐ μόνον δὲ ἐμοὶ ἀλλὰ καὶ πᾶσι τοῖς ἠγαπηκόσι τὴν ἐπιφάνειαν αὐτοῦ.

Cf. Phil 1:27–30; 4:2–3; and possibly 1 Cor 4:9–13; 15:32; Col 2:16–19.

144. Spiritual Sacrifice

Rom 12:1

Παρακαλῶ οὖν ὑμᾶς, ἀδελφοί, διὰ τῶν οἰκτιρμῶν τοῦ θεοῦ παραστῆσαι τὰ σώματα ὑμῶν θυσίαν ζῶσαν ἁγίαν εὐάρεστον τῷ θεῷ, τὴν λογικὴν λατρείαν ὑμῶν

Rom 15:15–16

τολμηρότερον δὲ ἔγραψα ὑμῖν ἀπὸ μέρους ὡς ἐπαναμιμνήσκων ὑμᾶς διὰ τὴν χάριν τὴν δοθεῖσάν μοι ὑπὸ τοῦ θεοῦ 16 εἰς τὸ εἶναί με λειτουργὸν Χριστοῦ Ἰησοῦ εἰς τὰ ἔθνη, ἱερουργοῦντα τὸ εὐαγγέλιον τοῦ θεοῦ, ἵνα γένηται ἡ προσφορὰ τῶν ἐθνῶν εὐπρόσδεκτος, ἡγιασμένη ἐν πνεύματι ἁγίῳ.

Phil 2:17–18

Ἀλλὰ εἰ καὶ σπένδομαι ἐπὶ τῇ θυσίᾳ καὶ λειτουργίᾳ τῆς πίστεως ὑμῶν, χαίρω καὶ συγχαίρω πᾶσιν ὑμῖν· 18 τὸ δὲ αὐτὸ καὶ ὑμεῖς χαίρετε καὶ συγχαίρετέ μοι.

Phil 2:25–30

Ἀναγκαῖον δὲ ἡγησάμην Ἐπαφρόδιτον τὸν ἀδελφὸν καὶ συνεργὸν καὶ συστρατιώτην μου, ὑμῶν δὲ ἀπόστολον καὶ λειτουργὸν τῆς χρείας μου, πέμψαι πρὸς ὑμᾶς, 26 ἐπειδὴ ἐπιποθῶν ἦν

§ 143 Phil 3:13 *ου* $\mathfrak{P}^{46}$ B D^{2} 1739. 1881 *Byz*] ουπω ℵ A D* 33 1 Tim 4:10 *αγωνιζομεθα* ℵ* A C 33] ονειδιζομεθα $ℵ^{2}$ D 1739. 1881 *Byz*

143. *The Athletic Metaphor*

1 Cor 9:24–27

Do you not know that in a race the runners all compete, but only one receives the prize? Run in such a way that you may win it. **25** Athletes exercise self-control in all things; they do it to receive a perishable wreath, but we an imperishable one. **26** So I do not run aimlessly, nor do I box as though beating the air; **27** but I punish my body and enslave it, so that after proclaiming to others I myself should not be disqualified.

Gal 2:2

I went up in response to a revelation. Then I laid before them (though only in a private meeting with the acknowledged leaders) the gospel that I proclaim among the Gentiles, in order to make sure that I was not running, or had not run, in vain.

Gal 5:7

You were running well; who prevented you from obeying the truth?

Phil 2:16

It is by your holding forth[a] the word of life that I can boast on the day of Christ that I did not run in vain or labor in vain.

Phil 3:12–16

Not that I have already obtained this or have already reached the goal; but I press on to make it my own, because Christ Jesus has made me his own. **13** Beloved, I do not consider that I have made it my own;[b] but this one thing I do: forgetting what lies behind and straining forward to what lies ahead, **14** I press on toward the goal for the prize of the heavenly call of God in Christ Jesus. **15** Let those of us then who are mature be of the same mind; and if you think differently about anything, this too God will reveal to you. **16** Only let us hold fast to what we have attained.

1 Thess 2:19–20

For what is our hope or joy or crown of boasting before our Lord Jesus at his coming? Is it not you? **20** Yes, you are our glory and joy!

1 Tim 4:6–10

If you put these instructions before the brothers and sisters, you will be a good servant of Christ Jesus, nourished on the words of the faith and of the sound teaching that you have followed. **7** Have nothing to do with profane myths and old wives' tales. Train yourself in godliness, **8** for, while physical training is of some value, godliness is valuable in every way, holding promise for both the present life and the life to come. **9** The saying is sure and worthy of full acceptance. **10** For to this end we toil and struggle,[c] because we have our hope set on the living God, who is the Savior of all people, especially of those who believe.

1 Tim 6:12

Fight the good fight of the faith; take hold of the eternal life, to which you were called and for which you made the good confession in the presence of many witnesses.

2 Tim 2:1–7

You then, my child, be strong in the grace that is in Christ Jesus; **2** and what you have heard from me through many witnesses entrust to faithful people who will be able to teach others as well. **3** Share in suffering like a good soldier of Christ Jesus. **4** No one serving in the army gets entangled in everyday affairs; the soldier's aim is to please the enlisting officer. **5** And in the case of an athlete, no one is crowned without competing according to the rules. **6** It is the farmer who does the work who ought to have the first share of the crops. **7** Think over what I say, for the Lord will give you understanding in all things.

2 Tim 4:6–8

As for me, I am already being poured out as a libation, and the time of my departure has come. **7** I have fought the good fight, I have finished the race, I have kept the faith. **8** From now on there is reserved for me the crown of righteousness, which the Lord, the righteous judge, will give me on that day, and not only to me but also to all who have longed for his appearing.

Cf. Phil 1:27–30; 4:2–3; and possibly 1 Cor 4:9–13; 15:32; Col 2:16–19.

144. *Spiritual Sacrifice*

Rom 12:1

I appeal to you therefore, brothers and sisters, by the mercies of God, to present your bodies as a living sacrifice, holy and acceptable to God, which is your spiritual worship.

Rom 15:15–16

Nevertheless on some points I have written to you rather boldly by way of reminder, because of the grace given me by God **16** to be a minister of Christ Jesus to the Gentiles in the priestly service of the gospel of God, so that the offering of the Gentiles may be acceptable, sanctified by the Holy Spirit.

Phil 2:17–18

But even if I am being poured out as a libation over the sacrifice and the offering of your faith, I am glad and rejoice with all of you— **18** and in the same way you also must be glad and rejoice with me.

Phil 2:25–30

Still, I think it necessary to send to you Epaphroditus—my brother and co-worker and fellow soldier, your messenger and minister to my need; **26** for he

§ 143 [a] **Phil 2:16** ***holding forth*** NRSV translates *holding fast to* [b] **Phil 3:13** ***my own*** Other ancient authorities read *my own yet* [c] **1 Tim 4:10** ***struggle*** Other ancient authorities read *suffer reproach*

⸀πάντας ὑμᾶς⸀ καὶ ἀδημονῶν, διότι
ἠκούσατε ὅτι ἠσθένησεν. 27 καὶ γὰρ ἠσθέ-
νησεν παραπλήσιον θανάτῳ· ἀλλὰ ὁ θεὸς
ἠλέησεν αὐτόν, οὐκ αὐτὸν δὲ μόνον ἀλλὰ
καὶ ἐμέ, ἵνα μὴ λύπην ἐπὶ λύπην σχῶ.
28 σπουδαιοτέρως οὖν ἔπεμψα αὐτόν,
ἵνα ἰδόντες αὐτὸν πάλιν χαρῆτε κἀγὼ
ἀλυπότερος ὦ. 29 προσδέχεσθε οὖν αὐτὸν
ἐν κυρίῳ μετὰ πάσης χαρᾶς καὶ τοὺς
τοιούτους ἐντίμους ἔχετε, 30 ὅτι διὰ τὸ
ἔργον ⸀Χριστοῦ μέχρι θανάτου ἤγγισεν
παραβολευσάμενος τῇ ψυχῇ, ἵνα ἀνα-
πληρώσῃ τὸ ὑμῶν ὑστέρημα τῆς πρός
με λειτουργίας.

Phil 4:18

ἀπέχω δὲ πάντα καὶ περισσεύω· πεπλή-
ρωμαι δεξάμενος παρὰ Ἐπαφροδίτου
τὰ παρ' ὑμῶν, ὀσμὴν εὐωδίας, θυσίαν
δεκτήν, εὐάρεστον τῷ θεῷ.

2 Tim 4:6–8

Ἐγὼ γὰρ ἤδη σπένδομαι, καὶ ὁ καιρὸς
τῆς ἀναλύσεώς μου ἐφέστηκεν. 7 τὸν
καλὸν ἀγῶνα ἠγώνισμαι, τὸν δρόμον
τετέλεκα, τὴν πίστιν τετήρηκα· 8 λοι-
πὸν ἀπόκειταί μοι ὁ τῆς δικαιοσύνης
στέφανος, ὃν ἀποδώσει μοι ὁ κύριος
ἐν ἐκείνῃ τῇ ἡμέρᾳ, ὁ δίκαιος κριτής,
οὐ μόνον δὲ ἐμοὶ ἀλλὰ καὶ πᾶσι τοῖς
ἠγαπηκόσι τὴν ἐπιφάνειαν αὐτοῦ.

145. The Call to Imitation

1 Cor 4:14–21

Οὐκ ἐντρέπων ὑμᾶς γράφω ταῦτα ἀλλ'
ὡς τέκνα μου ἀγαπητὰ νουθετῶ[ν].
15 ἐὰν γὰρ μυρίους παιδαγωγοὺς ἔχητε
ἐν Χριστῷ ἀλλ' οὐ πολλοὺς πατέρας· ἐν
γὰρ Χριστῷ Ἰησοῦ διὰ τοῦ εὐαγγελίου
ἐγὼ ὑμᾶς ἐγέννησα. 16 Παρακαλῶ οὖν
ὑμᾶς, μιμηταί μου γίνεσθε. 17 Διὰ τοῦτο
ἔπεμψα ὑμῖν Τιμόθεον, ὅς ἐστίν μου
τέκνον ἀγαπητὸν καὶ πιστὸν ἐν κυρίῳ,
ὃς ὑμᾶς ἀναμνήσει τὰς ὁδούς μου τὰς
ἐν Χριστῷ [Ἰησοῦ], καθὼς πανταχοῦ ἐν
πάσῃ ἐκκλησίᾳ διδάσκω. 18 Ὡς μὴ ἐρχο-
μένου δέ μου πρὸς ὑμᾶς ἐφυσιώθησάν
τινες· 19 ἐλεύσομαι δὲ ταχέως πρὸς ὑμᾶς
ἐὰν ὁ κύριος θελήσῃ, καὶ γνώσομαι οὐ
τὸν λόγον τῶν πεφυσιωμένων ἀλλὰ τὴν
δύναμιν· 20 οὐ γὰρ ἐν λόγῳ ἡ βασιλεία
τοῦ θεοῦ ἀλλ' ἐν δυνάμει. 21 τί θέλετε;
ἐν ῥάβδῳ ἔλθω πρὸς ὑμᾶς ἢ ἐν ἀγάπῃ
πνεύματί τε πραΰτητος;

1 Cor 10:33–11:1

καθὼς κἀγὼ πάντα πᾶσιν ἀρέσκω μὴ
ζητῶν τὸ ἐμαυτοῦ σύμφορον ἀλλὰ τὸ
τῶν πολλῶν, ἵνα σωθῶσιν. **11** μιμηταί
μου γίνεσθε καθὼς κἀγὼ Χριστοῦ.

Eph 5:1–2

Γίνεσθε οὖν μιμηταὶ τοῦ θεοῦ ὡς τέκνα
ἀγαπητὰ 2 καὶ περιπατεῖτε ἐν ἀγάπῃ,
καθὼς καὶ ὁ Χριστὸς ἠγάπησεν ⸀ἡμᾶς
καὶ παρέδωκεν ἑαυτὸν ὑπὲρ ἡμῶν προσ-
φορὰν καὶ θυσίαν τῷ θεῷ εἰς ὀσμὴν
εὐωδίας.

Phil 2:5–11

Τοῦτο φρονεῖτε ἐν ὑμῖν ὃ καὶ ἐν Χριστῷ
Ἰησοῦ, 6 ὃς ἐν μορφῇ θεοῦ ὑπάρχων
οὐχ ἁρπαγμὸν ἡγήσατο τὸ εἶναι ἴσα
θεῷ, 7 ἀλλὰ ἑαυτὸν ἐκένωσεν μορφὴν
δούλου λαβών, ἐν ὁμοιώματι ἀνθρώ-
πων γενόμενος· καὶ σχήματι εὑρεθεὶς
ὡς ἄνθρωπος 8 ἐταπείνωσεν ἑαυτὸν
γενόμενος ὑπήκοος μέχρι θανάτου, θα-
νάτου δὲ σταυροῦ. 9 διὸ καὶ ὁ θεὸς αὐτὸν
ὑπερύψωσεν καὶ ἐχαρίσατο αὐτῷ τὸ
ὄνομα τὸ ὑπὲρ πᾶν ὄνομα, 10 ἵνα ἐν τῷ
ὀνόματι Ἰησοῦ πᾶν γόνυ κάμψῃ ἐπου-
ρανίων καὶ ἐπιγείων καὶ καταχθονίων
11 καὶ πᾶσα γλῶσσα ἐξομολογήσηται
ὅτι κύριος Ἰησοῦς Χριστὸς εἰς δόξαν
θεοῦ πατρός.

Phil 3:17–4:1

Συμμιμηταί μου γίνεσθε, ἀδελφοί, καὶ
σκοπεῖτε τοὺς οὕτω περιπατοῦντας κα-
θὼς ἔχετε τύπον ἡμᾶς. 18 πολλοὶ γὰρ
περιπατοῦσιν οὓς πολλάκις ἔλεγον ὑμῖν,
νῦν δὲ καὶ κλαίων λέγω, τοὺς ἐχθροὺς
τοῦ σταυροῦ τοῦ Χριστοῦ, 19 ὧν τὸ τέ-
λος ἀπώλεια, ὧν ὁ θεὸς ἡ κοιλία καὶ ἡ
δόξα ἐν τῇ αἰσχύνῃ αὐτῶν, οἱ τὰ ἐπίγεια
φρονοῦντες. 20 ἡμῶν γὰρ τὸ πολίτευμα
ἐν οὐρανοῖς ὑπάρχει, ἐξ οὗ καὶ σωτῆρα
ἀπεκδεχόμεθα κύριον Ἰησοῦν Χριστόν,
21 ὃς μετασχηματίσει τὸ σῶμα τῆς ταπει-
νώσεως ἡμῶν σύμμορφον τῷ σώματι
τῆς δόξης αὐτοῦ κατὰ τὴν ἐνέργειαν τοῦ
δύνασθαι αὐτὸν καὶ ὑποτάξαι αὐτῷ τὰ
πάντα. **4** Ὥστε, ἀδελφοί μου ἀγαπητοὶ
καὶ ἐπιπόθητοι, χαρὰ καὶ στέφανός μου,
οὕτως στήκετε ἐν κυρίῳ, ἀγαπητοί.

Phil 4:8–9

Τὸ λοιπόν, ἀδελφοί, ὅσα ἐστὶν ἀληθῆ,
ὅσα σεμνά, ὅσα δίκαια, ὅσα ἁγνά, ὅσα
προσφιλῆ, ὅσα εὔφημα, εἴ τις ἀρετὴ καὶ
εἴ τις ἔπαινος, ταῦτα λογίζεσθε· 9 ἃ καὶ
ἐμάθετε καὶ παρελάβετε καὶ ἠκούσατε
καὶ εἴδετε ἐν ἐμοί, ταῦτα πράσσετε· καὶ ὁ
θεὸς τῆς εἰρήνης ἔσται μεθ' ὑμῶν.

1 Thess 1:6–10

Καὶ ὑμεῖς μιμηταὶ ἡμῶν ἐγενήθητε καὶ
τοῦ κυρίου, δεξάμενοι τὸν λόγον ἐν θλί-
ψει πολλῇ μετὰ χαρᾶς πνεύματος ἁγίου,
7 ὥστε γενέσθαι ὑμᾶς τύπον πᾶσιν τοῖς
πιστεύουσιν ἐν τῇ Μακεδονίᾳ καὶ ἐν τῇ
Ἀχαΐᾳ. 8 ἀφ' ὑμῶν γὰρ ἐξήχηται ὁ λόγος
τοῦ κυρίου οὐ μόνον ἐν τῇ Μακεδονίᾳ
καὶ [ἐν τῇ] Ἀχαΐᾳ, ἀλλ' ἐν παντὶ τόπῳ ἡ
πίστις ὑμῶν ἡ πρὸς τὸν θεὸν ἐξελήλυθεν,
ὥστε μὴ χρείαν ἔχειν ἡμᾶς λαλεῖν τι.
9 αὐτοὶ γὰρ περὶ ἡμῶν ἀπαγγέλλουσιν
ὁποίαν εἴσοδον ἔσχομεν πρὸς ὑμᾶς, καὶ
πῶς ἐπεστρέψατε πρὸς τὸν θεὸν ἀπὸ τῶν
εἰδώλων δουλεύειν θεῷ ζῶντι καὶ ἀλη-
θινῷ 10 καὶ ἀναμένειν τὸν υἱὸν αὐτοῦ
ἐκ τῶν οὐρανῶν, ὃν ἤγειρεν ἐκ [τῶν]
νεκρῶν, Ἰησοῦν τὸν ῥυόμενον ἡμᾶς ἐκ
τῆς ὀργῆς τῆς ἐρχομένης.

1 Thess 2:14

Ὑμεῖς γὰρ μιμηταὶ ἐγενήθητε, ἀδελφοί,
τῶν ἐκκλησιῶν τοῦ θεοῦ τῶν οὐσῶν
ἐν τῇ Ἰουδαίᾳ ἐν Χριστῷ Ἰησοῦ, ὅτι τὰ

§ 144 **Phil 2:26** ***παντας υμας*** ℵ² 1739. 1881 *Byz*] υμας παντας B ¦ παντας υμας ιδειν ℵ* A C D I^vid 33 ¦ πεμψαι προς υμας 𝔓^46vid **Phil 2:30** ***Χριστου*** 𝔓^46 B 1739. 1881] κυριου ℵ A 33 ¦ του Χριστου D *Byz* ¦ *om.* C **§ 145** **Eph 5:2** ***ημας*** 𝔓^46 ℵ² D 33. 1739. 1881 *Byz*] υμας ℵ* A B

has been longing for[a] all of you, and has been distressed because you heard that he was ill. 27 He was indeed so ill that he nearly died. But God had mercy on him, and not only on him but on me also, so that I would not have one sorrow after another. 28 I am the more eager to send him, therefore, in order that you may rejoice at seeing him again, and that I may be less anxious. 29 Welcome him then in the Lord with all joy, and honor such people, 30 because he came close to death for the work of Christ,[b] risking his life to make up for those services that you could not give me.

Phil 4:18

I have been paid in full and have more than enough; I am fully satisfied, now that I have received from Epaphroditus the gifts you sent, a fragrant offering, a sacrifice acceptable and pleasing to God.

2 Tim 4:6–8

As for me, I am already being poured out as a libation, and the time of my departure has come. 7 I have fought the good fight, I have finished the race, I have kept the faith. 8 From now on there is reserved for me the crown of righteousness, which the Lord, the righteous judge, will give me on that day, and not only to me but also to all who have longed for his appearing.

145. The Call to Imitation

1 Cor 4:14–21

I am not writing this to make you ashamed, but to admonish you as my beloved children. 15 For though you might have ten thousand guardians in Christ, you do not have many fathers. Indeed, in Christ Jesus I became your father through the gospel. 16 I appeal to you, then, be imitators of me. 17 For this reason I sent you Timothy, who is my beloved and faithful child in the Lord, to remind you of my ways in Christ Jesus, as I teach them everywhere in every church. 18 But some of you, thinking that I am not coming to you, have become arrogant. 19 But I will come to you soon, if the Lord wills, and I will find out not the talk of these arrogant people but their power. 20 For the kingdom of God depends not on talk but on power. 21 What would you prefer? Am I to come to you with a stick, or with love in a spirit of gentleness?

1 Cor 10:33–11:1

just as I try to please everyone in everything I do, not seeking my own advantage, but that of many, so that they may be saved. **11** Be imitators of me, as I am of Christ.

Eph 5:1–2

Therefore be imitators of God, as beloved children, 2 and live in love, as Christ loved us[a] and gave himself up for us, a fragrant offering and sacrifice to God.

Phil 2:5–11

Let the same mind be in you that was in Christ Jesus, 6 who, though he was in the form of God, did not regard equality with God as something to be exploited, 7 but emptied himself, taking the form of a slave, being born in human likeness. And being found in human form, 8 he humbled himself and became obedient to the point of death— even death on a cross. 9 Therefore God also highly exalted him and gave him the name that is above every name, 10 so that at the name of Jesus every knee should bend, in heaven and on earth and under the earth, 11 and every tongue should confess that Jesus Christ is Lord, to the glory of God the Father.

Phil 3:17–4:1

Brothers and sisters, join in imitating me, and observe those who live according to the example you have in us. 18 For many live as enemies of the cross of Christ; I have often told you of them, and now I tell you even with tears. 19 Their end is destruction; their god is the belly; and their glory is in their shame; their minds are set on earthly things. 20 But our citizenship is in heaven, and it is from there that we are expecting a Savior, the Lord Jesus Christ. 21 He will transform the body of our humiliation that it may be conformed to the body of his glory, by the power that also enables him to make all things subject to himself. **4** Therefore, my brothers and sisters, whom I love and long for, my joy and crown, stand firm in the Lord in this way, my beloved.

Phil 4:8–9

Finally, beloved, whatever is true, whatever is honorable, whatever is just, whatever is pure, whatever is pleasing, whatever is commendable, if there is any excellence and if there is anything worthy of praise, think about these things. 9 Keep on doing the things that you have learned and received and heard and seen in me, and the God of peace will be with you.

1 Thess 1:6–10

And you became imitators of us and of the Lord, for in spite of persecution you received the word with joy inspired by the Holy Spirit, 7 so that you became an example to all the believers in Macedonia and in Achaia. 8 For the word of the Lord has sounded forth from you not only in Macedonia and Achaia, but in every place your faith in God has become known, so that we have no need to speak about it. 9 For the people of those regions report about us what kind of welcome we had among you, and how you turned to God from idols, to serve a living and true God, 10 and to wait for his Son from heaven, whom he raised from the dead—Jesus, who rescues us from the wrath that is coming.

1 Thess 2:14

For you, brothers and sisters, became imitators of the churches of God in Christ Jesus that are in Judea, for you

§ 144 [a] **Phil 2:26** *longing for* Other ancient authorities read *longing to see* [b] **Phil 2:30** *of Christ* Other ancient authorities read *of the Lord* **§ 145** [a] **Eph 5:2** *us* Other ancient authorities read *you*

αὐτὰ ἐπάθετε καὶ ὑμεῖς ὑπὸ τῶν ἰδίων
συμφυλετῶν καθὼς καὶ αὐτοὶ ὑπὸ τῶν
Ἰουδαίων

2 Thess 3:6–12

Παραγγέλλομεν δὲ ὑμῖν, ἀδελφοί, ἐν ὀνό-
ματι τοῦ κυρίου [ἡμῶν] Ἰησοῦ Χριστοῦ
στέλλεσθαι ὑμᾶς ἀπὸ παντὸς ἀδελφοῦ
ἀτάκτως περιπατοῦντος καὶ μὴ κατὰ
τὴν παράδοσιν ἣν ⸀παρελάβοσαν παρ'
ἡμῶν. 7 Αὐτοὶ γὰρ οἴδατε πῶς δεῖ μιμεῖ-
σθαι ἡμᾶς, ὅτι οὐκ ἠτακτήσαμεν ἐν ὑμῖν
8 οὐδὲ δωρεὰν ἄρτον ἐφάγομεν παρά
τινος, ἀλλ' ἐν κόπῳ καὶ μόχθῳ νυκτὸς
καὶ ἡμέρας ἐργαζόμενοι πρὸς τὸ μὴ ἐπι-
βαρῆσαί τινα ὑμῶν· 9 οὐχ ὅτι οὐκ ἔχομεν
ἐξουσίαν, ἀλλ' ἵνα ἑαυτοὺς τύπον δῶμεν
ὑμῖν εἰς τὸ μιμεῖσθαι ἡμᾶς. 10 καὶ γὰρ
ὅτε ἦμεν πρὸς ὑμᾶς, τοῦτο παρηγγέλλο-
μεν ὑμῖν, ὅτι εἴ τις οὐ θέλει ἐργάζεσθαι
μηδὲ ἐσθιέτω. 11 Ἀκούομεν γάρ τινας
περιπατοῦντας ἐν ὑμῖν ἀτάκτως μηδὲν
ἐργαζομένους ἀλλὰ περιεργαζομένους·
12 τοῖς δὲ τοιούτοις παραγγέλλομεν καὶ
παρακαλοῦμεν ἐν κυρίῳ Ἰησοῦ Χριστῷ,
ἵνα μετὰ ἡσυχίας ἐργαζόμενοι τὸν ἑαυ-
τῶν ἄρτον ἐσθίωσιν.

1 Tim 1:12–16

Χάριν ἔχω τῷ ἐνδυναμώσαντί με Χρι-
στῷ Ἰησοῦ τῷ κυρίῳ ἡμῶν, ὅτι πιστόν
με ἡγήσατο θέμενος εἰς διακονίαν 13 τὸ
πρότερον ὄντα βλάσφημον καὶ διώκτην
καὶ ὑβριστήν, ἀλλὰ ἠλεήθην, ὅτι ἀγνοῶν
ἐποίησα ἐν ἀπιστίᾳ· 14 ὑπερεπλεόνασεν
δὲ ἡ χάρις τοῦ κυρίου ἡμῶν μετὰ πί-
στεως καὶ ἀγάπης τῆς ἐν Χριστῷ Ἰησοῦ.
15 πιστὸς ὁ λόγος καὶ πάσης ἀποδοχῆς
ἄξιος, ὅτι Χριστὸς Ἰησοῦς ἦλθεν εἰς τὸν
κόσμον ἁμαρτωλοὺς σῶσαι, ὧν πρῶτός
εἰμι ἐγώ. 16 ἀλλὰ διὰ τοῦτο ἠλεήθην,
ἵνα ἐν ἐμοὶ πρώτῳ ἐνδείξηται Χριστὸς
Ἰησοῦς τὴν ἅπασαν μακροθυμίαν πρὸς
ὑποτύπωσιν τῶν μελλόντων πιστεύειν
ἐπ' αὐτῷ εἰς ζωὴν αἰώνιον.

Cf. Gal 4:12–20; Eph 5:25–33; and the apostle's paradigmatic self-descriptions in 1 Cor 4:9–13; 9:1–18; 9:19–23; 9:24–27; 2 Cor 1:3–11; 4:1–15; 4:16–5:10; 6:3–10; 11:21b–12:10; Eph 6:18–20; Phil 1:12–26; 3:2–11; 4:10–13; Col 4:3–4; 1 Thess 2:1–12; 2 Tim 1:12; 2:8–10; 3:10–17; 4:6–8; 4:16–18. See also the call to modeling and imitation in Phil 2:19–24; 2:25–30; 1 Tim 4:11–16; Titus 2:6–8.

See also § 115 Paul's Example of Bold Speech; § 137 Paul's Example of Social Flexibility; and § 142 Paul's Example of Suffering in behalf of Christ.

146. Forgiveness among the Saints

2 Cor 2:5–11

Εἰ δέ τις λελύπηκεν, οὐκ ἐμὲ λελύπη-
κεν, ἀλλὰ ἀπὸ μέρους, ἵνα μὴ ἐπιβαρῶ,
πάντας ὑμᾶς. 6 ἱκανὸν τῷ τοιούτῳ ἡ ἐπι-
τιμία αὕτη ἡ ὑπὸ τῶν πλειόνων, 7 ὥστε
τοὐναντίον μᾶλλον ὑμᾶς χαρίσασθαι καὶ
παρακαλέσαι, μή πως τῇ περισσοτέρᾳ
λύπῃ καταποθῇ ὁ τοιοῦτος. 8 διὸ πα-
ρακαλῶ ὑμᾶς κυρῶσαι εἰς αὐτὸν ἀγάπην·
9 εἰς τοῦτο γὰρ καὶ ἔγραψα, ἵνα γνῶ τὴν
δοκιμὴν ὑμῶν, εἰ εἰς πάντα ὑπήκοοί
ἐστε. 10 ᾧ δέ τι χαρίζεσθε, κἀγώ· καὶ
γὰρ ἐγὼ ὃ κεχάρισμαι, εἴ τι κεχάρισμαι,
δι' ὑμᾶς ἐν προσώπῳ Χριστοῦ, 11 ἵνα μὴ
πλεονεκτηθῶμεν ὑπὸ τοῦ σατανᾶ· οὐ γὰρ
αὐτοῦ τὰ νοήματα ἀγνοοῦμεν.

Eph 4:1–3

Παρακαλῶ οὖν ὑμᾶς ἐγὼ ὁ δέσμιος ἐν
κυρίῳ ἀξίως περιπατῆσαι τῆς κλήσεως
ἧς ἐκλήθητε, 2 μετὰ πάσης ταπεινοφρο-
σύνης καὶ πραΰτητος, μετὰ μακροθυμίας,
ἀνεχόμενοι ἀλλήλων ἐν ἀγάπῃ, 3 σπου-
δάζοντες τηρεῖν τὴν ἑνότητα τοῦ πνεύ-
ματος ἐν τῷ συνδέσμῳ τῆς εἰρήνης

Eph 4:31–32

πᾶσα πικρία καὶ θυμὸς καὶ ὀργὴ καὶ
κραυγὴ καὶ βλασφημία ἀρθήτω ἀφ'
ὑμῶν σὺν πάσῃ κακίᾳ. 32 γίνεσθε [δὲ]
εἰς ἀλλήλους χρηστοί, εὔσπλαγχνοι,
χαριζόμενοι ἑαυτοῖς, καθὼς καὶ ὁ θεὸς
ἐν Χριστῷ ἐχαρίσατο ⸀ὑμῖν.

Col 3:12–13

Ἐνδύσασθε οὖν, ὡς ἐκλεκτοὶ τοῦ θεοῦ
ἅγιοι καὶ ἠγαπημένοι, σπλάγχνα οἰκτιρμοῦ
χρηστότητα ταπεινοφροσύνην πραΰτητα
μακροθυμίαν, 13 ἀνεχόμενοι ἀλλήλων
καὶ χαριζόμενοι ἑαυτοῖς ἐάν τις πρός
τινα ἔχῃ μομφήν· καθὼς καὶ ὁ ⸀κύριος
ἐχαρίσατο ὑμῖν, οὕτως καὶ ὑμεῖς

147. Walking in Wisdom

Rom 12:2

καὶ μὴ συσχηματίζεσθε τῷ αἰῶνι τούτῳ,
ἀλλὰ μεταμορφοῦσθε τῇ ἀνακαινώσει
τοῦ νοὸς εἰς τὸ δοκιμάζειν ὑμᾶς τί τὸ
θέλημα τοῦ θεοῦ, τὸ ἀγαθὸν καὶ εὐά-
ρεστον καὶ τέλειον.

Eph 5:15–17

Βλέπετε οὖν ἀκριβῶς πῶς περιπατεῖτε
μὴ ὡς ἄσοφοι ἀλλ' ὡς σοφοί, 16 ἐξα-
γοραζόμενοι τὸν καιρόν, ὅτι αἱ ἡμέραι
πονηραί εἰσιν. 17 διὰ τοῦτο μὴ γίνεσθε
ἄφρονες, ἀλλὰ συνίετε τί τὸ θέλημα
τοῦ κυρίου.

Phil 1:9–11

Καὶ τοῦτο προσεύχομαι, ἵνα ἡ ἀγάπη
ὑμῶν ἔτι μᾶλλον καὶ μᾶλλον περισσεύῃ
ἐν ἐπιγνώσει καὶ πάσῃ αἰσθήσει 10 εἰς
τὸ δοκιμάζειν ὑμᾶς τὰ διαφέροντα, ἵνα
ἦτε εἰλικρινεῖς καὶ ἀπρόσκοποι εἰς ἡμέ-
ραν Χριστοῦ, 11 πεπληρωμένοι καρπὸν
δικαιοσύνης τὸν διὰ Ἰησοῦ Χριστοῦ εἰς
δόξαν καὶ ἔπαινον θεοῦ.

Col 1:9–10

Διὰ τοῦτο καὶ ἡμεῖς, ἀφ' ἧς ἡμέρας ἠκού-
σαμεν, οὐ παυόμεθα ὑπὲρ ὑμῶν προσευ-
χόμενοι καὶ αἰτούμενοι, ἵνα πληρωθῆτε
τὴν ἐπίγνωσιν τοῦ θελήματος αὐτοῦ ἐν

2 Thess 3:6 ***παρελαβοσαν*** א* A (D*) 33] παρελαβον א^{2} D^{2} 1739. 1881 *Byz* ¦ παρελαβετε B **§ 146** **Eph 4:32** ***υμιν*** 𝔓^{46} א A] ημιν 𝔓^{49} B D 33. 1739. 1881 *Byz* **Col 3:13** ***κυριος*** 𝔓^{46} A B D*] Χριστος א^{2} C D^{1} 1739. 1881 *Byz* ¦ θεος א* ¦ θεος εν Χριστω 33

suffered the same things from your own compatriots as they did from the Jews

2 Thess 3:6–12

Now we command you, beloved, in the name of our Lord Jesus Christ, to keep away from believers who are living in idleness and not according to the tradition that they[b] received from us. 7 For you yourselves know how you ought to imitate us; we were not idle when we were with you, 8 and we did not eat anyone's bread without paying for it; but with toil and labor we worked night and day, so that we might not burden any of you. 9 This was not because we do not have that right, but in order to give you an example to imitate. 10 For even when we were with you, we gave you this command: Anyone unwilling to work should not eat. 11 For we hear that some of you are living in idleness, mere busybodies, not doing any work. 12 Now such persons we command and exhort in the Lord Jesus Christ to do their work quietly and to earn their own living.

1 Tim 1:12–16

I am grateful to Christ Jesus our Lord, who has strengthened me, because he judged me faithful and appointed me to his service, 13 even though I was formerly a blasphemer, a persecutor, and a man of violence. But I received mercy because I had acted ignorantly in unbelief, 14 and the grace of our Lord overflowed for me with the faith and love that are in Christ Jesus. 15 The saying is sure and worthy of full acceptance, that Christ Jesus came into the world to save sinners—of whom I am the foremost. 16 But for that very reason I received mercy, so that in me, as the foremost, Jesus Christ might display the utmost patience, making me an example to those who would come to believe in him for eternal life.

Cf. Gal 4:12–20; Eph 5:25–33; and the apostle's paradigmatic self-descriptions in 1 Cor 4:9–13; 9:1–18; 9:19–23; 9:24–27; 2 Cor 1:3–11; 4:1–15; 4:16–5:10; 6:3–10; 11:21b–12:10; Eph 6:18–20; Phil 1:12–26; 3:2–11; 4:10–13; Col 4:3–4; 1 Thess 2:1–12; 2 Tim 1:12; 2:8–10; 3:10–17; 4:6–8; 4:16–18. See also the call to modeling and imitation in Phil 2:19–24; 2:25–30; 1 Tim 4:11–16; Titus 2:6–8.

See also § 115 Paul's Example of Bold Speech; § 137 Paul's Example of Social Flexibility; and § 142 Paul's Example of Suffering in behalf of Christ.

146. Forgiveness among the Saints

2 Cor 2:5–11

But if anyone has caused pain, he has caused it not to me, but to some extent—not to exaggerate it—to all of you. 6 This punishment by the majority is enough for such a person; 7 so now instead you should forgive and console him, so that he may not be overwhelmed by excessive sorrow. 8 So I urge you to reaffirm your love for him. 9 I wrote for this reason: to test you and to know whether you are obedient in everything. 10 Anyone whom you forgive, I also forgive. What I have forgiven, if I have forgiven anything, has been for your sake in the presence of Christ. 11 And we do this so that we may not be outwitted by Satan; for we are not ignorant of his designs.

Eph 4:1–3

I therefore, the prisoner in the Lord, beg you to lead a life worthy of the calling to which you have been called, 2 with all humility and gentleness, with patience, bearing with one another in love, 3 making every effort to maintain the unity of the Spirit in the bond of peace.

Eph 4:31–32

Put away from you all bitterness and wrath and anger and wrangling and slander, together with all malice, 32 and be kind to one another, tenderhearted, forgiving one another, as God in Christ has forgiven you.[a]

Col 3:12–13

As God's chosen ones, holy and beloved, clothe yourselves with compassion, kindness, humility, meekness, and patience. 13 Bear with one another and, if anyone has a complaint against another, forgive each other; just as the Lord[b] has forgiven you, so you also must forgive.

147. Walking in Wisdom

Rom 12:2

Do not be conformed to this world, but be transformed by the renewing of your minds, so that you may discern what is the will of God—what is good and acceptable and perfect.

Eph 5:15–17

Be careful then how you live, not as unwise people but as wise, 16 making the most of the time, because the days are evil. 17 So do not be foolish, but understand what the will of the Lord is.

Phil 1:9–11

And this is my prayer, that your love may overflow more and more with knowledge and full insight 10 to help you to determine what is best, so that in the day of Christ you may be pure and blameless, 11 having produced the harvest of righteousness that comes through Jesus Christ for the glory and praise of God.

Col 1:9–10

For this reason, since the day we heard it, we have not ceased praying for you and asking that you may be filled with the knowledge of God's will in all spiri-

[b] **2 Thess 3:6** *they* Other ancient authorities read *you* **§ 146** [a] **Eph 4:32** *you* Other ancient authorities read *us* [b] **Col 3:13** *just as the Lord* Other ancient authorities read *just as Christ*

πάσῃ σοφίᾳ καὶ συνέσει πνευματικῇ, 10 περιπατῆσαι ἀξίως τοῦ κυρίου εἰς πᾶσαν ἀρεσκείαν, ἐν παντὶ ἔργῳ ἀγαθῷ καρποφοροῦντες καὶ αὐξανόμενοι τῇ ἐπιγνώσει τοῦ θεοῦ

Col 4:5–6

Ἐν σοφίᾳ περιπατεῖτε πρὸς τοὺς ἔξω τὸν καιρὸν ἐξαγοραζόμενοι. 6 ὁ λόγος ὑμῶν πάντοτε ἐν χάριτι, ἅλατι ἠρτυμένος, εἰδέναι πῶς δεῖ ὑμᾶς ἑνὶ ἑκάστῳ ἀποκρίνεσθαι.

See also Paul's repeated use in Philippians of the verb *φρονέω* (1:7; 2:2 [twice]; 2:5; 3:15 [twice]; 3:19; 4:2–3; 4:10 [twice]), by which, it is argued, Paul calls the Philippians to a "practical wisdom" founded in Christ, a Christ-focused manner of thinking and living.

148. Thanksgiving to God

Rom 15:8–13

λέγω γὰρ Χριστὸν διάκονον γεγενῆσθαι περιτομῆς ὑπὲρ ἀληθείας θεοῦ, εἰς τὸ βεβαιῶσαι τὰς ἐπαγγελίας τῶν πατέρων, 9 τὰ δὲ ἔθνη ὑπὲρ ἐλέους δοξάσαι τὸν θεόν, καθὼς γέγραπται· διὰ τοῦτο ἐξομολογήσομαί σοι ἐν ἔθνεσιν καὶ τῷ ὀνόματί σου ψαλῶ. 10 καὶ πάλιν λέγει· εὐφράνθητε, ἔθνη, μετὰ τοῦ λαοῦ αὐτοῦ. 11 καὶ πάλιν· αἰνεῖτε, πάντα τὰ ἔθνη, τὸν κύριον καὶ ἐπαινεσάτωσαν αὐτὸν πάντες οἱ λαοί. 12 καὶ πάλιν Ἠσαΐας λέγει· ἔσται ἡ ῥίζα τοῦ Ἰεσσαὶ καὶ ὁ ἀνιστάμενος ἄρχειν ἐθνῶν, ἐπ᾽ αὐτῷ ἔθνη ἐλπιοῦσιν. 13 Ὁ δὲ θεὸς τῆς ἐλπίδος πληρώσαι ὑμᾶς πάσης χαρᾶς καὶ εἰρήνης ἐν τῷ πιστεύειν, εἰς τὸ περισσεύειν ὑμᾶς ἐν τῇ ἐλπίδι ἐν δυνάμει πνεύματος ἁγίου.

2 Cor 4:13–15

Ἔχοντες δὲ τὸ αὐτὸ πνεῦμα τῆς πίστεως κατὰ τὸ γεγραμμένον· ἐπίστευσα, διὸ ἐλάλησα, καὶ ἡμεῖς πιστεύομεν, διὸ καὶ λαλοῦμεν, 14 εἰδότες ὅτι ὁ ἐγείρας τὸν ⸀κύριον Ἰησοῦν καὶ ἡμᾶς σὺν Ἰησοῦ ἐγερεῖ καὶ παραστήσει σὺν ὑμῖν. 15 τὰ γὰρ πάντα δι᾽ ὑμᾶς, ἵνα ἡ χάρις πλεονάσασα διὰ τῶν πλειόνων τὴν εὐχαριστίαν περισσεύσῃ εἰς τὴν δόξαν τοῦ θεοῦ.

Eph 5:4

καὶ αἰσχρότης καὶ μωρολογία ἢ εὐτραπελία, ἃ οὐκ ἀνῆκεν, ἀλλὰ μᾶλλον εὐχαριστία.

Eph 5:18–20

καὶ μὴ μεθύσκεσθε οἴνῳ, ἐν ᾧ ἐστιν ἀσωτία, ἀλλὰ πληροῦσθε ἐν πνεύματι, 19 λαλοῦντες ἑαυτοῖς [ἐν] ψαλμοῖς καὶ ὕμνοις καὶ ᾠδαῖς πνευματικαῖς, ᾄδοντες καὶ ψάλλοντες τῇ καρδίᾳ ὑμῶν τῷ κυρίῳ, 20 εὐχαριστοῦντες πάντοτε ὑπὲρ πάντων ἐν ὀνόματι τοῦ κυρίου ἡμῶν Ἰησοῦ Χριστοῦ τῷ θεῷ καὶ πατρί.

Phil 4:6–7

μηδὲν μεριμνᾶτε, ἀλλ᾽ ἐν παντὶ τῇ προσευχῇ καὶ τῇ δεήσει μετὰ εὐχαριστίας τὰ αἰτήματα ὑμῶν γνωριζέσθω πρὸς τὸν θεόν. 7 καὶ ἡ εἰρήνη τοῦ θεοῦ ἡ ὑπερέχουσα πάντα νοῦν φρουρήσει τὰς καρδίας ὑμῶν καὶ τὰ νοήματα ὑμῶν ἐν Χριστῷ Ἰησοῦ.

Col 1:11–12

ἐν πάσῃ δυνάμει δυναμούμενοι κατὰ τὸ κράτος τῆς δόξης αὐτοῦ εἰς πᾶσαν ὑπομονὴν καὶ μακροθυμίαν. Μετὰ χαρᾶς 12 εὐχαριστοῦντες τῷ πατρὶ τῷ ⸀ἱκανώσαντι ⸀ὑμᾶς εἰς τὴν μερίδα τοῦ κλήρου τῶν ἁγίων ἐν τῷ φωτί

Col 2:6–7

Ὡς οὖν παρελάβετε τὸν Χριστὸν Ἰησοῦν τὸν κύριον, ἐν αὐτῷ περιπατεῖτε, 7 ἐρριζωμένοι καὶ ἐποικοδομούμενοι ἐν αὐτῷ καὶ βεβαιούμενοι τῇ πίστει καθὼς ἐδιδάχθητε, περισσεύοντες ἐν εὐχαριστίᾳ.

Col 3:15–17

καὶ ἡ εἰρήνη τοῦ Χριστοῦ βραβευέτω ἐν ταῖς καρδίαις ὑμῶν, εἰς ἣν καὶ ἐκλήθητε ἐν ἑνὶ σώματι· καὶ εὐχάριστοι γίνεσθε. 16 Ὁ λόγος τοῦ ⸀Χριστοῦ ἐνοικείτω ἐν ὑμῖν πλουσίως, ἐν πάσῃ σοφίᾳ διδάσκοντες καὶ νουθετοῦντες ἑαυτούς, ψαλμοῖς ὕμνοις ᾠδαῖς πνευματικαῖς ἐν [τῇ] χάριτι ᾄδοντες ἐν ταῖς καρδίαις ὑμῶν τῷ ⸀θεῷ· 17 καὶ πᾶν ὅ τι ἐὰν ποιῆτε ἐν λόγῳ ἢ ἐν ἔργῳ, πάντα ἐν ὀνόματι κυρίου Ἰησοῦ, εὐχαριστοῦντες τῷ θεῷ πατρὶ δι᾽ αὐτοῦ.

Col 4:2

Τῇ προσευχῇ προσκαρτερεῖτε, γρηγοροῦντες ἐν αὐτῇ ἐν εὐχαριστίᾳ

1 Thess 5:18

ἐν παντὶ εὐχαριστεῖτε· τοῦτο γὰρ θέλημα θεοῦ ἐν Χριστῷ Ἰησοῦ εἰς ὑμᾶς.

1 Tim 2:1–2

Παρακαλῶ οὖν πρῶτον πάντων ποιεῖσθαι δεήσεις προσευχὰς ἐντεύξεις εὐχαριστίας ὑπὲρ πάντων ἀνθρώπων, 2 ὑπὲρ βασιλέων καὶ πάντων τῶν ἐν ὑπεροχῇ ὄντων, ἵνα ἤρεμον καὶ ἡσύχιον βίον διάγωμεν ἐν πάσῃ εὐσεβείᾳ καὶ σεμνότητι.

Cf. Rom 1:21–23; 14:6; 1 Cor 10:29–30; 14:15–17; 2 Cor 9:10–15; 1 Thess 3:9–10; 1 Tim 4:3–5; Acts 27:35; 28:15.

See also § 73 Joy in the Lord. For the thanksgiving sections with which Paul begins his letters, see § 2 Thanksgiving.

149. Hymns and Psalms

1 Cor 14:26

Τί οὖν ἐστιν, ἀδελφοί; ὅταν συνέρχησθε, ἕκαστος ψαλμὸν ἔχει, διδαχὴν ἔχει, ἀποκάλυψιν ἔχει, γλῶσσαν ἔχει, ἑρμηνείαν ἔχει· πάντα πρὸς οἰκοδομὴν γινέσθω.

Eph 5:18–20

καὶ μὴ μεθύσκεσθε οἴνῳ, ἐν ᾧ ἐστιν ἀσωτία, ἀλλὰ πληροῦσθε ἐν πνεύματι,

§ 148 **2 Cor 4:14** ***κυριον*** ℵ C D 1881 *Byz*] *om.* 𝔓^{46} B (33) (1739) **Col 1:12** ***ικανωσαντι*** 𝔓^{46} 𝔓^{61vid} ℵ A C D^{2} I 1739. 1881 *Byz*] καλεσαντι D* 33 ¦ καλεσαντι και ικανωσαντι B • ***υμας*** ℵ B 1739. 1881] ημας A C D 33 *Byz* **Col 3:16** ***Χριστου*** 𝔓^{46} ℵ^{2} B C^{2} D 1739. 1881 *Byz*] κυριου ℵ* I ¦ θεου A C* 33 • ***θεω*** 𝔓^{46vid} ℵ A B C* D* 33. 1739. 1881] κυριω C^{2} D^{2} *Byz*

tual wisdom and understanding, [10] so that you may lead lives worthy of the Lord, fully pleasing to him, as you bear fruit in every good work and as you grow in the knowledge of God.

Col 4:5–6

Conduct yourselves wisely toward outsiders, making the most of the time. [6] Let your speech always be gracious, seasoned with salt, so that you may know how you ought to answer everyone.

See also Paul's repeated use in Philippians of the verb φρονέω (1:7; 2:2 [twice]; 2:5; 3:15 [twice]; 3:19; 4:2–3; 4:10 [twice]), by which, it is argued, Paul calls the Philippians to a "practical wisdom" founded in Christ, a Christ-focused manner of thinking and living.

148. Thanksgiving to God

Rom 15:8–13

For I tell you that Christ has become a servant of the circumcised on behalf of the truth of God in order that he might confirm the promises given to the patriarchs, [9] and in order that the Gentiles might glorify God for his mercy. As it is written, "Therefore I will confess you among the Gentiles, and sing praises to your name"; [10] and again he says, "Rejoice, O Gentiles, with his people"; [11] and again, "Praise the Lord, all you Gentiles, and let all the peoples praise him"; [12] and again Isaiah says, "The root of Jesse shall come, the one who rises to rule the Gentiles; in him the Gentiles shall hope." [13] May the God of hope fill you with all joy and peace in believing, so that you may abound in hope by the power of the Holy Spirit.

2 Cor 4:13–15

But just as we have the same spirit of faith that is in accordance with scripture—"I believed, and so I spoke"—we also believe, and so we speak, [14] because we know that the one who raised the Lord[a] Jesus will raise us also with Jesus, and will bring us with you into his presence. [15] Yes, everything is for your sake, so that grace, as it extends to more and more people, may increase thanksgiving, to the glory of God.

Eph 5:4

Entirely out of place is obscene, silly, and vulgar talk; but instead, let there be thanksgiving.

Eph 5:18–20

Do not get drunk with wine, for that is debauchery; but be filled with the Spirit, [19] as you sing psalms and hymns and spiritual songs among yourselves, singing and making melody to the Lord in your hearts, [20] giving thanks to God the Father at all times and for everything in the name of our Lord Jesus Christ.

Phil 4:6–7

Do not worry about anything, but in everything by prayer and supplication with thanksgiving let your requests be made known to God. [7] And the peace of God, which surpasses all understanding, will guard your hearts and your minds in Christ Jesus.

Col 1:11–12

May you be made strong with all the strength that comes from his glorious power, and may you be prepared to endure everything with patience, while joyfully [12] giving thanks to the Father, who has enabled[b] you[c] to share in the inheritance of the saints in the light.

Col 2:6–7

As you therefore have received Christ Jesus the Lord, continue to live your lives in him, [7] rooted and built up in him and established in the faith, just as you were taught, abounding in thanksgiving.

Col 3:15–17

And let the peace of Christ rule in your hearts, to which indeed you were called in the one body. And be thankful. [16] Let the word of Christ[d] dwell in you richly; teach and admonish one another in all wisdom; and with gratitude in your hearts sing psalms, hymns, and spiritual songs to God.[e] [17] And whatever you do, in word or deed, do everything in the name of the Lord Jesus, giving thanks to God the Father through him.

Col 4:2

Devote yourselves to prayer, keeping alert in it with thanksgiving.

1 Thess 5:18

give thanks in all circumstances; for this is the will of God in Christ Jesus for you.

1 Tim 2:1–2

First of all, then, I urge that supplications, prayers, intercessions, and thanksgivings be made for everyone, [2] for kings and all who are in high positions, so that we may lead a quiet and peaceable life in all godliness and dignity.

Cf. Rom 1:21–23; 14:6; 1 Cor 10:29–30; 14:15–17; 2 Cor 9:10–15; 1 Thess 3:9–10; 1 Tim 4:3–5; Acts 27:35; 28:15.

See also § 73 Joy in the Lord. For the thanksgiving sections with which Paul begins his letters, see § 2 Thanksgiving.

149. Hymns and Psalms

1 Cor 14:26

What should be done then, my friends? When you come together, each one has a hymn, a lesson, a revelation, a tongue, or an interpretation. Let all things be done for building up.

Eph 5:18–20

Do not get drunk with wine, for that is debauchery; but be filled with the

§ 148 [a] **2 Cor 4:14** *the Lord* Other ancient authorities lack *the Lord* [b] **Col 1:12** *enabled* Other ancient authorities read *called* [c] **Col 1:12** *you* Other ancient authorities read *us* [d] **Col 3:16** *of Christ* Other ancient authorities read *of God,* or *of the Lord* [e] **Col 3:16** *to God* Other ancient authorities read *to the Lord*

19 λαλοῦντες ἑαυτοῖς [ἐν] ψαλμοῖς καὶ ὕμνοις καὶ ᾠδαῖς πνευματικαῖς, ᾄδοντες καὶ ψάλλοντες τῇ καρδίᾳ ὑμῶν τῷ κυρίῳ, 20 εὐχαριστοῦντες πάντοτε ὑπὲρ πάντων ἐν ὀνόματι τοῦ κυρίου ἡμῶν Ἰησοῦ Χριστοῦ τῷ θεῷ καὶ πατρί.

Col 3:15–17

καὶ ἡ εἰρήνη τοῦ Χριστοῦ βραβευέτω ἐν ταῖς καρδίαις ὑμῶν, εἰς ἣν καὶ ἐκλήθητε ἐν ἑνὶ σώματι· καὶ εὐχάριστοι γίνεσθε. 16 Ὁ λόγος τοῦ ⸀Χριστοῦ ἐνοικείτω ἐν ὑμῖν πλουσίως, ἐν πάσῃ σοφίᾳ διδάσκοντες καὶ νουθετοῦντες ἑαυτούς, ψαλμοῖς ὕμνοις ᾠδαῖς πνευματικαῖς ἐν [τῇ] χάριτι ᾄδοντες ἐν ταῖς καρδίαις ὑμῶν τῷ ⸀θεῷ· 17 καὶ πᾶν ὅ τι ἐὰν ποιῆτε ἐν λόγῳ ἢ ἐν ἔργῳ, πάντα ἐν ὀνόματι κυρίου Ἰησοῦ, εὐχαριστοῦντες τῷ θεῷ πατρὶ δι᾿ αὐτοῦ.

Acts 16:25

Κατὰ δὲ τὸ μεσονύκτιον Παῦλος καὶ Σιλᾶς προσευχόμενοι ὕμνουν τὸν θεόν, ἐπηκροῶντο δὲ αὐτῶν οἱ δέσμιοι.

Cf. Rom 15:8–11; 1 Cor 14:15–17.

See also § 22 Proposed Hymn Fragments.

150. Instruction regarding Prayer

Rom 8:26–27

Ὡσαύτως δὲ καὶ τὸ πνεῦμα συναντιλαμβάνεται τῇ ἀσθενείᾳ ἡμῶν· τὸ γὰρ τί προσευξώμεθα καθὸ δεῖ οὐκ οἴδαμεν, ἀλλὰ αὐτὸ τὸ πνεῦμα ⸀ὑπερεντυγχάνει στεναγμοῖς ἀλαλήτοις· 27 ὁ δὲ ἐραυνῶν τὰς καρδίας οἶδεν τί τὸ φρόνημα τοῦ πνεύματος, ὅτι κατὰ θεὸν ἐντυγχάνει ὑπὲρ ἁγίων.

Rom 12:12

τῇ ἐλπίδι χαίροντες, τῇ θλίψει ὑπομένοντες, τῇ προσευχῇ προσκαρτεροῦντες

1 Cor 14:13–19

Διὸ ὁ λαλῶν γλώσσῃ προσευχέσθω ἵνα διερμηνεύῃ. 14 ἐὰν [γὰρ] προσεύχωμαι γλώσσῃ, τὸ πνεῦμά μου προσεύχεται, ὁ δὲ νοῦς μου ἄκαρπός ἐστιν. 15 τί οὖν ἐστιν; προσεύξομαι τῷ πνεύματι, προσεύξομαι δὲ καὶ τῷ νοΐ· ψαλῶ τῷ πνεύματι, ψαλῶ δὲ καὶ τῷ νοΐ. 16 ἐπεὶ ἐὰν εὐλογῇς [ἐν] πνεύματι, ὁ ἀναπληρῶν τὸν τόπον τοῦ ἰδιώτου πῶς ἐρεῖ τὸ ἀμὴν ἐπὶ τῇ σῇ εὐχαριστίᾳ; ἐπειδὴ τί λέγεις οὐκ οἶδεν· 17 σὺ μὲν γὰρ καλῶς εὐχαριστεῖς ἀλλ᾿ ὁ ἕτερος οὐκ οἰκοδομεῖται. 18 Εὐχαριστῶ τῷ θεῷ, πάντων ὑμῶν μᾶλλον γλώσσαις λαλῶ· 19 ἀλλὰ ἐν ἐκκλησίᾳ θέλω πέντε λόγους τῷ νοΐ μου λαλῆσαι, ἵνα καὶ ἄλλους κατηχήσω, ἢ μυρίους λόγους ἐν γλώσσῃ.

Eph 6:18–20

Διὰ πάσης προσευχῆς καὶ δεήσεως προσευχόμενοι ἐν παντὶ καιρῷ ἐν πνεύματι, καὶ εἰς αὐτὸ ἀγρυπνοῦντες ἐν πάσῃ προσκαρτερήσει καὶ δεήσει περὶ πάντων τῶν ἁγίων 19 καὶ ὑπὲρ ἐμοῦ, ἵνα μοι δοθῇ λόγος ἐν ἀνοίξει τοῦ στόματός μου, ἐν παρρησίᾳ γνωρίσαι τὸ μυστήριον ⸂τοῦ εὐαγγελίου⸃, 20 ὑπὲρ οὗ πρεσβεύω ἐν ἁλύσει, ἵνα ἐν αὐτῷ παρρησιάσωμαι ὡς δεῖ με λαλῆσαι.

Phil 4:6–7

μηδὲν μεριμνᾶτε, ἀλλ᾿ ἐν παντὶ τῇ προσευχῇ καὶ τῇ δεήσει μετὰ εὐχαριστίας τὰ αἰτήματα ὑμῶν γνωριζέσθω πρὸς τὸν θεόν. 7 καὶ ἡ εἰρήνη τοῦ θεοῦ ἡ ὑπερέχουσα πάντα νοῦν φρουρήσει τὰς καρδίας ὑμῶν καὶ τὰ νοήματα ὑμῶν ἐν Χριστῷ Ἰησοῦ.

Col 4:2–4

Τῇ προσευχῇ προσκαρτερεῖτε, γρηγοροῦντες ἐν αὐτῇ ἐν εὐχαριστίᾳ, 3 προσευχόμενοι ἅμα καὶ περὶ ἡμῶν, ἵνα ὁ θεὸς ἀνοίξῃ ἡμῖν θύραν τοῦ λόγου λαλῆσαι τὸ μυστήριον τοῦ Χριστοῦ, δι᾿ ὃ καὶ δέδεμαι, 4 ἵνα φανερώσω αὐτὸ ὡς δεῖ με λαλῆσαι.

1 Thess 5:17–18

ἀδιαλείπτως προσεύχεσθε, 18 ἐν παντὶ εὐχαριστεῖτε· τοῦτο γὰρ θέλημα θεοῦ ἐν Χριστῷ Ἰησοῦ εἰς ὑμᾶς.

1 Tim 2:1–4

Παρακαλῶ οὖν πρῶτον πάντων ποιεῖσθαι δεήσεις προσευχὰς ἐντεύξεις εὐχαριστίας ὑπὲρ πάντων ἀνθρώπων, 2 ὑπὲρ βασιλέων καὶ πάντων τῶν ἐν ὑπεροχῇ ὄντων, ἵνα ἤρεμον καὶ ἡσύχιον βίον διάγωμεν ἐν πάσῃ εὐσεβείᾳ καὶ σεμνότητι. 3 τοῦτο καλὸν καὶ ἀπόδεκτον ἐνώπιον τοῦ σωτῆρος ἡμῶν θεοῦ, 4 ὃς πάντας ἀνθρώπους θέλει σωθῆναι καὶ εἰς ἐπίγνωσιν ἀληθείας ἐλθεῖν.

1 Tim 2:8

Βούλομαι οὖν προσεύχεσθαι τοὺς ἄνδρας ἐν παντὶ τόπῳ ἐπαίροντας ὁσίους χεῖρας χωρὶς ὀργῆς καὶ διαλογισμοῦ.

Cf. Rom 8:15–17; Gal 4:6–7.

For prayers and requests for prayer in the Pauline letters, see § 12 Prayer and § 13 Request for Prayer.

151. Women, Men, Teaching, and Authority

Rom 16:1–2

Συνίστημι δὲ ὑμῖν Φοίβην τὴν ἀδελφὴν ἡμῶν, οὖσαν [καὶ] διάκονον τῆς ἐκκλησίας τῆς ἐν Κεγχρεαῖς, 2 ἵνα αὐτὴν προσδέξησθε ἐν κυρίῳ ἀξίως τῶν ἁγίων καὶ παραστῆτε αὐτῇ ἐν ᾧ ἂν ὑμῶν χρῄζῃ πράγματι· καὶ γὰρ αὐτὴ προστάτις πολλῶν ἐγενήθη καὶ ἐμοῦ αὐτοῦ.

Rom 16:3–16

Ἀσπάσασθε Πρίσκαν καὶ Ἀκύλαν τοὺς συνεργούς μου ἐν Χριστῷ Ἰησοῦ, 4 οἵτινες ὑπὲρ τῆς ψυχῆς μου τὸν ἑαυτῶν

§ 149 **Col 3:16** ***Χριστου*** 𝔓[46] ℵ[2] B C[2] D 1739. 1881 *Byz*] κυριου ℵ* I ¦ θεου A C* 33 • ***θεω*** 𝔓[46vid] ℵ A B C* D* 33. 1739. 1881] κυριω C[2] D[2] *Byz* **§ 150** **Rom 8:26** ***υπερεντυγχανει*** ℵ* A B D 1739. 1881] *add*. υπερ ημων ℵ[2] C 33 *Byz* **Eph 6:19** ***του ευαγγελιου*** ℵ A D I 33. 1739. 1881 *Byz*] *om*. B

Spirit, **19** as you sing psalms and hymns and spiritual songs among yourselves, singing and making melody to the Lord in your hearts, **20** giving thanks to God the Father at all times and for everything in the name of our Lord Jesus Christ.

Col 3:15–17

And let the peace of Christ rule in your hearts, to which indeed you were called in the one body. And be thankful. **16** Let the word of Christ[a] dwell in you richly; teach and admonish one another in all wisdom; and with gratitude in your hearts sing psalms, hymns, and spiritual songs to God.[b] **17** And whatever you do, in word or deed, do everything in the name of the Lord Jesus, giving thanks to God the Father through him.

Acts 16:25

About midnight Paul and Silas were praying and singing hymns to God, and the prisoners were listening to them.

Cf. Rom 15:8–11; 1 Cor 14:15–17.

See also § 22 Proposed Hymn Fragments.

150. Instruction regarding Prayer

Rom 8:26–27

Likewise the Spirit helps us in our weakness; for we do not know how to pray as we ought, but that very Spirit intercedes[a] with sighs too deep for words. **27** And God, who searches the heart, knows what is the mind of the Spirit, because the Spirit intercedes for the saints according to the will of God.

Rom 12:12

Rejoice in hope, be patient in suffering, persevere in prayer.

1 Cor 14:13–19

Therefore, one who speaks in a tongue should pray for the power to interpret. **14** For if I pray in a tongue, my spirit prays but my mind is unproductive. **15** What should I do then? I will pray with the spirit, but I will pray with the mind also; I will sing praise with the spirit, but I will sing praise with the mind also. **16** Otherwise, if you say a blessing with the spirit, how can anyone in the position of an outsider say the "Amen" to your thanksgiving, since the outsider does not know what you are saying? **17** For you may give thanks well enough, but the other person is not built up. **18** I thank God that I speak in tongues more than all of you; **19** nevertheless, in church I would rather speak five words with my mind, in order to instruct others also, than ten thousand words in a tongue.

Eph 6:18–20

Pray in the Spirit at all times in every prayer and supplication. To that end keep alert and always persevere in supplication for all the saints. **19** Pray also for me, so that when I speak, a message may be given to me to make known with boldness the mystery of the gospel,[b] **20** for which I am an ambassador in chains. Pray that I may declare it boldly, as I must speak.

Phil 4:6–7

Do not worry about anything, but in everything by prayer and supplication with thanksgiving let your requests be made known to God. **7** And the peace of God, which surpasses all understanding, will guard your hearts and your minds in Christ Jesus.

Col 4:2–4

Devote yourselves to prayer, keeping alert in it with thanksgiving. **3** At the same time pray for us as well that God will open to us a door for the word, that we may declare the mystery of Christ, for which I am in prison, **4** so that I may reveal it clearly, as I should.

1 Thess 5:17–18

pray without ceasing, **18** give thanks in all circumstances; for this is the will of God in Christ Jesus for you.

1 Tim 2:1–4

First of all, then, I urge that supplications, prayers, intercessions, and thanksgivings be made for everyone, **2** for kings and all who are in high positions, so that we may lead a quiet and peaceable life in all godliness and dignity. **3** This is right and is acceptable in the sight of God our Savior, **4** who desires everyone to be saved and to come to the knowledge of the truth.

1 Tim 2:8

I desire, then, that in every place the men should pray, lifting up holy hands without anger or argument

Cf. Rom 8:15–17; Gal 4:6–7.

For prayers and requests for prayer in the Pauline letters, see § 12 Prayer and § 13 Request for Prayer.

151. Women, Men, Teaching, and Authority

Rom 16:1–2

I commend to you our sister Phoebe, a deacon of the church at Cenchreae, **2** so that you may welcome her in the Lord as is fitting for the saints, and help her in whatever she may require from you, for she has been a benefactor of many and of myself as well.

Rom 16:3–16

Greet Prisca and Aquila, who work with me in Christ Jesus, **4** and who risked their necks for my life, to whom

§ 149 [a] **Col 3:16** *of Christ* Other ancient authorities read *of God,* or *of the Lord* [b] **Col 3:16** *to God* Other ancient authorities read *to the Lord* **§ 150** [a] **Rom 8:26** *intercedes* Other ancient authorities add *for us* [b] **Eph 6:19** *of the gospel* Other ancient authorities lack *of the gospel*

τράχηλον ὑπέθηκαν, οἷς οὐκ ἐγὼ μόνος εὐχαριστῶ ἀλλὰ καὶ πᾶσαι αἱ ἐκκλησίαι τῶν ἐθνῶν, 5 καὶ τὴν κατ᾽ οἶκον αὐτῶν ἐκκλησίαν. ἀσπάσασθε Ἐπαίνετον τὸν ἀγαπητόν μου, ὅς ἐστιν ἀπαρχὴ τῆς Ἀσίας εἰς Χριστόν. 6 ἀσπάσασθε Μαρίαν, ἥτις πολλὰ ἐκοπίασεν εἰς ὑμᾶς. 7 ἀσπάσασθε Ἀνδρόνικον καὶ ⸀Ἰουνίαν τοὺς συγγενεῖς μου καὶ συναιχμαλώτους μου, οἵτινές εἰσιν ἐπίσημοι ἐν τοῖς ἀποστόλοις, οἳ καὶ πρὸ ἐμοῦ γέγοναν ἐν Χριστῷ. 8 ἀσπάσασθε Ἀμπλιᾶτον τὸν ἀγαπητόν μου ἐν κυρίῳ. 9 ἀσπάσασθε Οὐρβανὸν τὸν συνεργὸν ἡμῶν ἐν Χριστῷ καὶ Στάχυν τὸν ἀγαπητόν μου. 10 ἀσπάσασθε Ἀπελλῆν τὸν δόκιμον ἐν Χριστῷ. ἀσπάσασθε τοὺς ἐκ τῶν Ἀριστοβούλου. 11 ἀσπάσασθε Ἡρῳδίωνα τὸν συγγενῆ μου. ἀσπάσασθε τοὺς ἐκ τῶν Ναρκίσσου τοὺς ὄντας ἐν κυρίῳ. 12 ἀσπάσασθε Τρύφαιναν καὶ Τρυφῶσαν τὰς κοπιώσας ἐν κυρίῳ. ἀσπάσασθε Περσίδα τὴν ἀγαπητήν, ἥτις πολλὰ ἐκοπίασεν ἐν κυρίῳ. 13 ἀσπάσασθε Ῥοῦφον τὸν ἐκλεκτὸν ἐν κυρίῳ καὶ τὴν μητέρα αὐτοῦ καὶ ἐμοῦ. 14 ἀσπάσασθε Ἀσύγκριτον, Φλέγοντα, Ἑρμῆν, Πατροβᾶν, Ἑρμᾶν καὶ τοὺς σὺν αὐτοῖς ἀδελφούς. 15 ἀσπάσασθε Φιλόλογον καὶ Ἰουλίαν, Νηρέα καὶ τὴν ἀδελφὴν αὐτοῦ, καὶ Ὀλυμπᾶν καὶ τοὺς σὺν αὐτοῖς πάντας ἁγίους. 16 ἀσπάσασθε ἀλλήλους ἐν φιλήματι ἁγίῳ. ἀσπάζονται ὑμᾶς αἱ ἐκκλησίαι πᾶσαι τοῦ Χριστοῦ.

1 Cor 11:2–16

Ἐπαινῶ δὲ ὑμᾶς ὅτι πάντα μου μέμνησθε καί, καθὼς παρέδωκα ὑμῖν, τὰς παραδόσεις κατέχετε. 3 Θέλω δὲ ὑμᾶς εἰδέναι ὅτι παντὸς ἀνδρὸς ἡ κεφαλὴ ὁ Χριστός ἐστιν, κεφαλὴ δὲ γυναικὸς ὁ ἀνήρ, κεφαλὴ δὲ τοῦ Χριστοῦ ὁ θεός. 4 πᾶς ἀνὴρ προσευχόμενος ἢ προφητεύων κατὰ κεφαλῆς ἔχων καταισχύνει τὴν κεφαλὴν αὐτοῦ. 5 πᾶσα δὲ γυνὴ προσευχομένη ἢ προφητεύουσα ἀκατακαλύπτῳ τῇ κεφαλῇ καταισχύνει τὴν κεφαλὴν αὐτῆς· ἓν γάρ ἐστιν καὶ τὸ αὐτὸ τῇ ἐξυρημένῃ. 6 εἰ γὰρ οὐ κατακαλύπτεται γυνή, καὶ κειράσθω· εἰ δὲ αἰσχρὸν γυναικὶ τὸ κείρασθαι ἢ ξυρᾶσθαι, κατακαλυπτέσθω. 7 Ἀνὴρ μὲν γὰρ οὐκ ὀφείλει κατακαλύπτεσθαι τὴν κεφαλὴν εἰκὼν καὶ δόξα θεοῦ ὑπάρχων· ἡ γυνὴ δὲ δόξα ἀνδρός ἐστιν. 8 οὐ γάρ ἐστιν ἀνὴρ ἐκ γυναικὸς ἀλλὰ γυνὴ ἐξ ἀνδρός· 9 καὶ γὰρ οὐκ ἐκτίσθη ἀνὴρ διὰ τὴν γυναῖκα ἀλλὰ γυνὴ διὰ τὸν ἄνδρα. 10 διὰ τοῦτο ὀφείλει ἡ γυνὴ ἐξουσίαν ἔχειν ἐπὶ τῆς κεφαλῆς διὰ τοὺς ἀγγέλους. 11 πλὴν οὔτε γυνὴ χωρὶς ἀνδρὸς οὔτε ἀνὴρ χωρὶς γυναικὸς ἐν κυρίῳ· 12 ὥσπερ γὰρ ἡ γυνὴ ἐκ τοῦ ἀνδρός, οὕτως καὶ ὁ ἀνὴρ διὰ τῆς γυναικός· τὰ δὲ πάντα ἐκ τοῦ θεοῦ. 13 Ἐν ὑμῖν αὐτοῖς κρίνατε· πρέπον ἐστὶν γυναῖκα ἀκατακάλυπτον τῷ θεῷ προσεύχεσθαι; 14 οὐδὲ ἡ φύσις αὐτὴ διδάσκει ὑμᾶς ὅτι ἀνὴρ μὲν ἐὰν κομᾷ ἀτιμία αὐτῷ ἐστιν, 15 γυνὴ δὲ ἐὰν κομᾷ δόξα αὐτῇ ἐστιν; ὅτι ἡ κόμη ἀντὶ περιβολαίου δέδοται [αὐτῇ]. 16 Εἰ δέ τις δοκεῖ φιλόνεικος εἶναι, ἡμεῖς τοιαύτην συνήθειαν οὐκ ἔχομεν οὐδὲ αἱ ἐκκλησίαι τοῦ θεοῦ.

1 Cor 14:26–36

Τί οὖν ἐστιν, ἀδελφοί; ὅταν συνέρχησθε, ἕκαστος ψαλμὸν ἔχει, διδαχὴν ἔχει, ἀποκάλυψιν ἔχει, γλῶσσαν ἔχει, ἑρμηνείαν ἔχει· πάντα πρὸς οἰκοδομὴν γινέσθω. 27 εἴτε γλώσσῃ τις λαλεῖ, κατὰ δύο ἢ τὸ πλεῖστον τρεῖς καὶ ἀνὰ μέρος, καὶ εἷς διερμηνευέτω· 28 ἐὰν δὲ μὴ ᾖ διερμηνευτής, σιγάτω ἐν ἐκκλησίᾳ, ἑαυτῷ δὲ λαλείτω καὶ τῷ θεῷ. 29 προφῆται δὲ δύο ἢ τρεῖς λαλείτωσαν καὶ οἱ ἄλλοι διακρινέτωσαν· 30 ἐὰν δὲ ἄλλῳ ἀποκαλυφθῇ καθημένῳ, ὁ πρῶτος σιγάτω. 31 δύνασθε γὰρ καθ᾽ ἕνα πάντες προφητεύειν, ἵνα πάντες μανθάνωσιν καὶ πάντες παρακαλῶνται. 32 καὶ πνεύματα προφητῶν προφήταις ὑποτάσσεται, 33 οὐ γάρ ἐστιν ἀκαταστασίας ὁ θεὸς ἀλλὰ εἰρήνης. Ὡς ἐν πάσαις ταῖς ἐκκλησίαις τῶν ἁγίων 34 ⸂αἱ γυναῖκες ἐν ταῖς ἐκκλησίαις σιγάτωσαν· οὐ γὰρ ἐπιτρέπεται αὐταῖς λαλεῖν, ἀλλὰ ὑποτασσέσθωσαν, καθὼς καὶ ὁ νόμος λέγει. 35 εἰ δέ τι μαθεῖν θέλουσιν, ἐν οἴκῳ τοὺς ἰδίους ἄνδρας ἐπερωτάτωσαν· αἰσχρὸν γάρ ἐστιν γυναικὶ λαλεῖν ἐν ἐκκλησίᾳ.⸃ 36 ἢ ἀφ᾽ ὑμῶν ὁ λόγος τοῦ θεοῦ ἐξῆλθεν, ἢ εἰς ὑμᾶς μόνους κατήντησεν;

Gal 3:26–29

Πάντες γὰρ υἱοὶ θεοῦ ἐστε διὰ τῆς πίστεως ἐν Χριστῷ Ἰησοῦ· 27 ὅσοι γὰρ εἰς Χριστὸν ἐβαπτίσθητε, Χριστὸν ἐνεδύσασθε. 28 οὐκ ἔνι Ἰουδαῖος οὐδὲ Ἕλλην, οὐκ ἔνι δοῦλος οὐδὲ ἐλεύθερος, οὐκ ἔνι ἄρσεν καὶ θῆλυ· πάντες γὰρ ὑμεῖς εἷς ἐστε ἐν Χριστῷ Ἰησοῦ. 29 εἰ δὲ ὑμεῖς Χριστοῦ, ἄρα τοῦ Ἀβραὰμ σπέρμα ἐστέ, κατ᾽ ἐπαγγελίαν κληρονόμοι.

Phil 4:2–3

Εὐοδίαν παρακαλῶ καὶ Συντύχην παρακαλῶ τὸ αὐτὸ φρονεῖν ἐν κυρίῳ. 3 ναὶ ἐρωτῶ καὶ σέ, γνήσιε σύζυγε, συλλαμβάνου αὐταῖς, αἵτινες ἐν τῷ εὐαγγελίῳ συνήθλησάν μοι μετὰ καὶ Κλήμεντος καὶ τῶν λοιπῶν συνεργῶν μου, ὧν τὰ ὀνόματα ἐν βίβλῳ ζωῆς.

Col 4:15

Ἀσπάσασθε τοὺς ἐν Λαοδικείᾳ ἀδελφοὺς καὶ Νύμφαν καὶ τὴν κατ᾽ οἶκον ⸀αὐτῆς ἐκκλησίαν.

1 Tim 2:8–15

Βούλομαι οὖν προσεύχεσθαι τοὺς ἄνδρας ἐν παντὶ τόπῳ ἐπαίροντας ὁσίους χεῖρας χωρὶς ὀργῆς καὶ διαλογισμοῦ. 9 Ὡσαύτως [καὶ] γυναῖκας ἐν καταστολῇ κοσμίῳ μετὰ αἰδοῦς καὶ σωφροσύνης κοσμεῖν ἑαυτάς, μὴ ἐν πλέγμασιν καὶ χρυσίῳ ἢ μαργαρίταις ἢ ἱματισμῷ πολυτελεῖ, 10 ἀλλ᾽ ὃ πρέπει γυναιξὶν ἐπαγγελλομέναις θεοσέβειαν, δι᾽ ἔργων ἀγαθῶν. 11 Γυνὴ ἐν ἡσυχίᾳ μανθανέτω ἐν πάσῃ ὑποταγῇ· 12 διδάσκειν δὲ γυναικὶ οὐκ ἐπιτρέπω οὐδὲ αὐθεντεῖν ἀνδρός, ἀλλ᾽ εἶναι ἐν ἡσυχίᾳ. 13 Ἀδὰμ γὰρ πρῶτος ἐπλάσθη, εἶτα Εὕα. 14 καὶ Ἀδὰμ οὐκ ἠπατήθη, ἡ δὲ γυνὴ ἐξαπατηθεῖσα ἐν παραβάσει γέγονεν· 15 σωθήσεται δὲ διὰ τῆς τεκνογονίας, ἐὰν μείνωσιν ἐν πίστει καὶ ἀγάπῃ καὶ ἁγιασμῷ μετὰ σωφροσύνης

2 Tim 1:3–5

Χάριν ἔχω τῷ θεῷ, ᾧ λατρεύω ἀπὸ προγόνων ἐν καθαρᾷ συνειδήσει, ὡς ἀδιάλειπτον ἔχω τὴν περὶ σοῦ μνείαν ἐν ταῖς δεήσεσίν μου νυκτὸς καὶ ἡμέρας, 4 ἐπιποθῶν σε ἰδεῖν, μεμνημένος σου τῶν δακρύων, ἵνα χαρᾶς πληρωθῶ, 5 ὑπόμνησιν λαβὼν τῆς ἐν σοὶ ἀνυποκρίτου πίστεως, ἥτις ἐνῴκησεν πρῶτον ἐν τῇ μάμμῃ σου Λωΐδι καὶ τῇ μητρί σου Εὐνίκῃ, πέπεισμαι δὲ ὅτι καὶ ἐν σοί.

§ 151 **Rom 16:7** ***Ιουνιαν*** ℵ A B C D 33. 1739. 1881 *Byz* (*acc.* Ἰουνίαν B^2 D^2 33. 1739. 1881 *Byz*; *sine acc.* ℵ A B* C D*)] Ιουλιαν 𝔓^{46} **1 Cor 14:34–35** *pon. hic* 𝔓^{46} ℵ A B 33. 1739. 1881 *Byz*] *pon. p.* 14:40 D **Col 4:15** ***αυτης*** B 1739$^{(*)}$. 1881] αυτου D *Byz* ¦ αυτων ℵ A C 33

not only I give thanks, but also all the churches of the Gentiles. 5 Greet also the church in their house. Greet my beloved Epaenetus, who was the first convert in Asia for Christ. 6 Greet Mary, who has worked very hard among you. 7 Greet Andronicus and Junia,[a] my relatives who were in prison with me; they are prominent among the apostles, and they were in Christ before I was. 8 Greet Ampliatus, my beloved in the Lord. 9 Greet Urbanus, our co-worker in Christ, and my beloved Stachys. 10 Greet Apelles, who is approved in Christ. Greet those who belong to the family of Aristobulus. 11 Greet my relative Herodion. Greet those in the Lord who belong to the family of Narcissus. 12 Greet those workers in the Lord, Tryphaena and Tryphosa. Greet the beloved Persis, who has worked hard in the Lord. 13 Greet Rufus, chosen in the Lord; and greet his mother—a mother to me also. 14 Greet Asyncritus, Phlegon, Hermes, Patrobas, Hermas, and the brothers and sisters who are with them. 15 Greet Philologus, Julia, Nereus and his sister, and Olympas, and all the saints who are with them. 16 Greet one another with a holy kiss. All the churches of Christ greet you.

1 Cor 11:2–16

I commend you because you remember me in everything and maintain the traditions just as I handed them on to you. 3 But I want you to understand that Christ is the head of every man, and the husband is the head of his wife, and God is the head of Christ. 4 Any man who prays or prophesies with something on his head disgraces his head, 5 but any woman who prays or prophesies with her head unveiled disgraces her head—it is one and the same thing as having her head shaved. 6 For if a woman will not veil herself, then she should cut off her hair; but if it is disgraceful for a woman to have her hair cut off or to be shaved, she should wear a veil. 7 For a man ought not to have his head veiled, since he is the image and reflection of God; but woman is the reflection of man. 8 Indeed, man was not made from woman, but woman from man. 9 Neither was man created for the sake of woman, but woman for the sake of man. 10 For this reason a woman ought to have a symbol of authority on her head, because of the angels. 11 Nevertheless, in the Lord woman is not independent of man or man independent of woman. 12 For just as woman came from man, so man comes through woman; but all things come from God. 13 Judge for yourselves: is it proper for a woman to pray to God with her head unveiled? 14 Does not nature itself teach you that if a man wears long hair, it is degrading to him, 15 but if a woman has long hair, it is her glory? For her hair is given to her for a covering. 16 But if anyone is disposed to be contentious—we have no such custom, nor do the churches of God.

1 Cor 14:26–36

What should be done then, my friends? When you come together, each one has a hymn, a lesson, a revelation, a tongue, or an interpretation. Let all things be done for building up. 27 If anyone speaks in a tongue, let there be only two or at most three, and each in turn; and let one interpret. 28 But if there is no one to interpret, let them be silent in church and speak to themselves and to God. 29 Let two or three prophets speak, and let the others weigh what is said. 30 If a revelation is made to someone else sitting nearby, let the first person be silent. 31 For you can all prophesy one by one, so that all may learn and all be encouraged. 32 And the spirits of prophets are subject to the prophets, 33 for God is a God not of disorder but of peace. (As in all the churches of the saints, 34 women should be silent in the churches. For they are not permitted to speak, but should be subordinate, as the law also says. 35 If there is anything they desire to know, let them ask their husbands at home. For it is shameful for a woman to speak in church.[b] 36 Or did the word of God originate with you? Or are you the only ones it has reached?)

Gal 3:26–29

for in Christ Jesus you are all children of God through faith. 27 As many of you as were baptized into Christ have clothed yourselves with Christ. 28 There is no longer Jew or Greek, there is no longer slave or free, there is no longer male and female; for all of you are one in Christ Jesus. 29 And if you belong to Christ, then you are Abraham's offspring, heirs according to the promise.

Phil 4:2–3

I urge Euodia and I urge Syntyche to be of the same mind in the Lord. 3 Yes, and I ask you also, my loyal companion, help these women, for they have struggled beside me in the work of the gospel, together with Clement and the rest of my co-workers, whose names are in the book of life.

Col 4:15

Give my greetings to the brothers and sisters in Laodicea, and to Nympha and the church in her[c] house.

1 Tim 2:8–15

I desire, then, that in every place the men should pray, lifting up holy hands without anger or argument; 9 also that the women should dress themselves modestly and decently in suitable clothing, not with their hair braided, or with gold, pearls, or expensive clothes, 10 but with good works, as is proper for women who profess reverence for God. 11 Let a woman learn in silence with full submission. 12 I permit no woman to teach or to have authority over a man; she is to keep silent. 13 For Adam was formed first, then Eve; 14 and Adam was not deceived, but the woman was deceived and became a transgressor. 15 Yet she will be saved through childbearing, provided they continue in faith and love and holiness, with modesty.

2 Tim 1:3–5

I am grateful to God—whom I worship with a clear conscience, as my ancestors did—when I remember you constantly in my prayers night and day. 4 Recalling your tears, I long to see you so that I may be filled with joy. 5 I am reminded of your sincere faith, a faith that lived first in your grandmother Lois and your mother Eunice and now, I am sure, lives in you.

§ 151 [a] **Rom 16:7** ***Junia*** Or possibly *Junias*; a few ancient authorities read *Julia* [b] **1 Cor 14:35** ***church*** A few ancient authorities put verses 34–35 after verse 40 [c] **Col 4:15** ***her*** Other ancient authorities read *his* (implying the masculine name *Nymphas*) or *their*

2 Tim 4:21

Σπούδασον πρὸ χειμῶνος ἐλθεῖν. Ἀσπάζεταί σε Εὔβουλος καὶ Πούδης καὶ Λίνος καὶ Κλαυδία καὶ οἱ ἀδελφοὶ πάντες.

Phlm 1–2

Παῦλος δέσμιος Χριστοῦ Ἰησοῦ καὶ Τιμόθεος ὁ ἀδελφὸς Φιλήμονι τῷ ἀγαπητῷ καὶ συνεργῷ ἡμῶν 2 καὶ Ἀπφίᾳ τῇ ἀδελφῇ καὶ Ἀρχίππῳ τῷ συστρατιώτῃ ἡμῶν καὶ τῇ κατ᾽ οἶκόν σου ἐκκλησίᾳ

Acts 18:24–26

Ἰουδαῖος δέ τις Ἀπολλῶς ὀνόματι, Ἀλεξανδρεὺς τῷ γένει, ἀνὴρ λόγιος, κατήντησεν εἰς Ἔφεσον, δυνατὸς ὢν ἐν ταῖς γραφαῖς. 25 οὗτος ἦν κατηχημένος τὴν ὁδὸν τοῦ κυρίου καὶ ζέων τῷ πνεύματι ἐλάλει καὶ ἐδίδασκεν ἀκριβῶς τὰ περὶ τοῦ Ἰησοῦ, ἐπιστάμενος μόνον τὸ βάπτισμα Ἰωάννου· 26 οὗτός τε ἤρξατο παρρησιάζεσθαι ἐν τῇ συναγωγῇ. ἀκούσαντες δὲ αὐτοῦ Πρίσκιλλα καὶ Ἀκύλας προσελάβοντο αὐτὸν καὶ ἀκριβέστερον αὐτῷ ἐξέθεντο τὴν ὁδὸν [τοῦ θεοῦ].

Acts 21:8–9

τῇ δὲ ἐπαύριον ἐξελθόντες ἤλθομεν εἰς Καισάρειαν καὶ εἰσελθόντες εἰς τὸν οἶκον Φιλίππου τοῦ εὐαγγελιστοῦ, ὄντος ἐκ τῶν ἑπτά, ἐμείναμεν παρ᾽ αὐτῷ. 9 τούτῳ δὲ ἦσαν θυγατέρες τέσσαρες παρθένοι προφητεύουσαι.

Cf. Acts 16:14–15; 16:40; 18:18–19. With 2 Tim 1:3–5, cf. 2 Tim 3:14–15.

152. Working for a Living

1 Cor 4:12

καὶ κοπιῶμεν ἐργαζόμενοι ταῖς ἰδίαις χερσίν· λοιδορούμενοι εὐλογοῦμεν, διωκόμενοι ἀνεχόμεθα

Eph 4:28

ὁ κλέπτων μηκέτι κλεπτέτω, μᾶλλον δὲ κοπιάτω ἐργαζόμενος ταῖς [ἰδίαις] χερσὶν τὸ ἀγαθόν, ἵνα ἔχῃ μεταδιδόναι τῷ χρείαν ἔχοντι.

1 Thess 2:9

Μνημονεύετε γάρ, ἀδελφοί, τὸν κόπον ἡμῶν καὶ τὸν μόχθον· νυκτὸς καὶ ἡμέρας ἐργαζόμενοι πρὸς τὸ μὴ ἐπιβαρῆσαί τινα ὑμῶν ἐκηρύξαμεν εἰς ὑμᾶς τὸ εὐαγγέλιον τοῦ θεοῦ.

1 Thess 4:10–12

καὶ γὰρ ποιεῖτε αὐτὸ εἰς πάντας τοὺς ἀδελφοὺς [τοὺς] ἐν ὅλῃ τῇ Μακεδονίᾳ. Παρακαλοῦμεν δὲ ὑμᾶς, ἀδελφοί, περισσεύειν μᾶλλον 11 καὶ φιλοτιμεῖσθαι ἡσυχάζειν καὶ πράσσειν τὰ ἴδια καὶ ἐργάζεσθαι ταῖς [ἰδίαις] χερσὶν ὑμῶν, καθὼς ὑμῖν παρηγγείλαμεν, 12 ἵνα περιπατῆτε εὐσχημόνως πρὸς τοὺς ἔξω καὶ μηδενὸς χρείαν ἔχητε.

1 Thess 5:14

Παρακαλοῦμεν δὲ ὑμᾶς, ἀδελφοί, νουθετεῖτε τοὺς ἀτάκτους, παραμυθεῖσθε τοὺς ὀλιγοψύχους, ἀντέχεσθε τῶν ἀσθενῶν, μακροθυμεῖτε πρὸς πάντας.

2 Thess 3:6–12

Παραγγέλλομεν δὲ ὑμῖν, ἀδελφοί, ἐν ὀνόματι τοῦ κυρίου [ἡμῶν] Ἰησοῦ Χριστοῦ στέλλεσθαι ὑμᾶς ἀπὸ παντὸς ἀδελφοῦ ἀτάκτως περιπατοῦντος καὶ μὴ κατὰ τὴν παράδοσιν ἣν ⸀παρελάβοσαν παρ᾽ ἡμῶν. 7 Αὐτοὶ γὰρ οἴδατε πῶς δεῖ μιμεῖσθαι ἡμᾶς, ὅτι οὐκ ἠτακτήσαμεν ἐν ὑμῖν 8 οὐδὲ δωρεὰν ἄρτον ἐφάγομεν παρά τινος, ἀλλ᾽ ἐν κόπῳ καὶ μόχθῳ νυκτὸς καὶ ἡμέρας ἐργαζόμενοι πρὸς τὸ μὴ ἐπιβαρῆσαί τινα ὑμῶν· 9 οὐχ ὅτι οὐκ ἔχομεν ἐξουσίαν, ἀλλ᾽ ἵνα ἑαυτοὺς τύπον δῶμεν ὑμῖν εἰς τὸ μιμεῖσθαι ἡμᾶς. 10 καὶ γὰρ ὅτε ἦμεν πρὸς ὑμᾶς, τοῦτο παρηγγέλλομεν ὑμῖν, ὅτι εἴ τις οὐ θέλει ἐργάζεσθαι μηδὲ ἐσθιέτω. 11 Ἀκούομεν γάρ τινας περιπατοῦντας ἐν ὑμῖν ἀτάκτως μηδὲν ἐργαζομένους ἀλλὰ περιεργαζομένους· 12 τοῖς δὲ τοιούτοις παραγγέλλομεν καὶ παρακαλοῦμεν ἐν κυρίῳ Ἰησοῦ Χριστῷ, ἵνα μετὰ ἡσυχίας ἐργαζόμενοι τὸν ἑαυτῶν ἄρτον ἐσθίωσιν.

1 Tim 5:13–14

ἅμα δὲ καὶ ἀργαὶ μανθάνουσιν περιερχόμεναι τὰς οἰκίας, οὐ μόνον δὲ ἀργαὶ ἀλλὰ καὶ φλύαροι καὶ περίεργοι, λαλοῦσαι τὰ μὴ δέοντα. 14 Βούλομαι οὖν νεωτέρας γαμεῖν, τεκνογονεῖν, οἰκοδεσποτεῖν, μηδεμίαν ἀφορμὴν διδόναι τῷ ἀντικειμένῳ λοιδορίας χάριν

Acts 18:1–3

Μετὰ ταῦτα χωρισθεὶς ἐκ τῶν Ἀθηνῶν ἦλθεν εἰς Κόρινθον. 2 καὶ εὑρών τινα Ἰουδαῖον ὀνόματι Ἀκύλαν, Ποντικὸν τῷ γένει προσφάτως ἐληλυθότα ἀπὸ τῆς Ἰταλίας καὶ Πρίσκιλλαν γυναῖκα αὐτοῦ, διὰ τὸ διατεταχέναι Κλαύδιον χωρίζεσθαι πάντας τοὺς Ἰουδαίους ἀπὸ τῆς Ῥώμης, προσῆλθεν αὐτοῖς 3 καὶ διὰ τὸ ὁμότεχνον εἶναι ἔμενεν παρ᾽ αὐτοῖς, καὶ ἠργάζετο· ἦσαν γὰρ σκηνοποιοὶ τῇ τέχνῃ.

Acts 20:33–35

ἀργυρίου ἢ χρυσίου ἢ ἱματισμοῦ οὐδενὸς ἐπεθύμησα· 34 αὐτοὶ γινώσκετε ὅτι ταῖς χρείαις μου καὶ τοῖς οὖσιν μετ᾽ ἐμοῦ ὑπηρέτησαν αἱ χεῖρες αὗται. 35 πάντα ὑπέδειξα ὑμῖν ὅτι οὕτως κοπιῶντας δεῖ ἀντιλαμβάνεσθαι τῶν ἀσθενούντων, μνημονεύειν τε τῶν λόγων τοῦ κυρίου Ἰησοῦ ὅτι αὐτὸς εἶπεν· μακάριόν ἐστιν μᾶλλον διδόναι ἢ λαμβάνειν.

153. Leading a Quiet Life

1 Thess 4:10–12

καὶ γὰρ ποιεῖτε αὐτὸ εἰς πάντας τοὺς ἀδελφοὺς [τοὺς] ἐν ὅλῃ τῇ Μακεδονίᾳ. Παρακαλοῦμεν δὲ ὑμᾶς, ἀδελφοί, περισσεύειν μᾶλλον 11 καὶ φιλοτιμεῖσθαι ἡσυχάζειν καὶ πράσσειν τὰ ἴδια καὶ ἐργάζεσθαι ταῖς [ἰδίαις] χερσὶν ὑμῶν, καθὼς ὑμῖν παρηγγείλαμεν, 12 ἵνα περιπατῆτε εὐσχημόνως πρὸς τοὺς ἔξω καὶ μηδενὸς χρείαν ἔχητε.

2 Thess 3:11–12

Ἀκούομεν γάρ τινας περιπατοῦντας ἐν ὑμῖν ἀτάκτως μηδὲν ἐργαζομένους ἀλλὰ περιεργαζομένους· 12 τοῖς δὲ τοιούτοις παραγγέλλομεν καὶ παρακαλοῦμεν ἐν

§ 152 **2 Thess 3:6** *παρελαβοσαν* ℵ* A (D*) 33] παρελαβον ℵ² D² 1739. 1881 *Byz* ¦ παρελαβετε B

2 Tim 4:21
Do your best to come before winter. Eubulus sends greetings to you, as do Pudens and Linus and Claudia and all the brothers and sisters.

Phlm 1–2
Paul, a prisoner of Christ Jesus, and Timothy our brother, To Philemon our dear friend and co-worker, **2** to Apphia our sister, to Archippus our fellow soldier, and to the church in your house

Acts 18:24–26
Now there came to Ephesus a Jew named Apollos, a native of Alexandria. He was an eloquent man, well-versed in the scriptures. **25** He had been instructed in the Way of the Lord; and he spoke with burning enthusiasm and taught accurately the things concerning Jesus, though he knew only the baptism of John. **26** He began to speak boldly in the synagogue; but when Priscilla and Aquila heard him, they took him aside and explained the Way of God to him more accurately.

Acts 21:8–9
The next day we left and came to Caesarea; and we went into the house of Philip the evangelist, one of the seven, and stayed with him. **9** He had four unmarried daughters who had the gift of prophecy.

Cf. Acts 16:14–15; 16:40; 18:18–19. With 2 Tim 1:3–5, cf. 2 Tim 3:14–15.

152. Working for a Living

1 Cor 4:12
and we grow weary from the work of our own hands. When reviled, we bless; when persecuted, we endure

Eph 4:28
Thieves must give up stealing; rather let them labor and work honestly with their own hands, so as to have something to share with the needy.

1 Thess 2:9
You remember our labor and toil, brothers and sisters; we worked night and day, so that we might not burden any of you while we proclaimed to you the gospel of God.

1 Thess 4:10–12
and indeed you do love all the brothers and sisters throughout Macedonia. But we urge you, beloved, to do so more and more, **11** to aspire to live quietly, to mind your own affairs, and to work with your hands, as we directed you, **12** so that you may behave properly toward outsiders and be dependent on no one.

1 Thess 5:14
And we urge you, beloved, to admonish the idlers, encourage the fainthearted, help the weak, be patient with all of them.

2 Thess 3:6–12
Now we command you, beloved, in the name of our Lord Jesus Christ, to keep away from believers who are living in idleness and not according to the tradition that they[a] received from us. **7** For you yourselves know how you ought to imitate us; we were not idle when we were with you, **8** and we did not eat anyone's bread without paying for it; but with toil and labor we worked night and day, so that we might not burden any of you. **9** This was not because we do not have that right, but in order to give you an example to imitate. **10** For even when we were with you, we gave you this command: Anyone unwilling to work should not eat. **11** For we hear that some of you are living in idleness, mere busybodies, not doing any work. **12** Now such persons we command and exhort in the Lord Jesus Christ to do their work quietly and to earn their own living.

1 Tim 5:13–14
Besides that, they learn to be idle, gadding about from house to house; and they are not merely idle, but also gossips and busybodies, saying what they should not say. **14** So I would have younger widows marry, bear children, and manage their households, so as to give the adversary no occasion to revile us.

Acts 18:1–3
After this Paul left Athens and went to Corinth. **2** There he found a Jew named Aquila, a native of Pontus, who had recently come from Italy with his wife Priscilla, because Claudius had ordered all Jews to leave Rome. Paul went to see them, **3** and, because he was of the same trade, he stayed with them, and they worked together—by trade they were tentmakers.

Acts 20:33–35
I coveted no one's silver or gold or clothing. **34** You know for yourselves that I worked with my own hands to support myself and my companions. **35** In all this I have given you an example that by such work we must support the weak, remembering the words of the Lord Jesus, for he himself said, 'It is more blessed to give than to receive.'

153. Leading a Quiet Life

1 Thess 4:10–12
and indeed you do love all the brothers and sisters throughout Macedonia. But we urge you, beloved, to do so more and more, **11** to aspire to live quietly, to mind your own affairs, and to work with your hands, as we directed you, **12** so that you may behave properly toward outsiders and be dependent on no one.

2 Thess 3:11–12
For we hear that some of you are living in idleness, mere busybodies, not doing any work. **12** Now such persons we command and exhort in the Lord

§ 152 [a] **2 Thess 3:6** *they* Other ancient authorities read *you*

κυρίῳ Ἰησοῦ Χριστῷ, ἵνα μετὰ ἡσυ-
χίας ἐργαζόμενοι τὸν ἑαυτῶν ἄρτον
ἐσθίωσιν.

1 Tim 2:1–7

Παρακαλῶ οὖν πρῶτον πάντων ποι-
εῖσθαι δεήσεις προσευχὰς ἐντεύξεις
εὐχαριστίας ὑπὲρ πάντων ἀνθρώπων,
2 ὑπὲρ βασιλέων καὶ πάντων τῶν ἐν
ὑπεροχῇ ὄντων, ἵνα ἤρεμον καὶ ἡσύχιον
βίον διάγωμεν ἐν πάσῃ εὐσεβείᾳ καὶ σε-
μνότητι. 3 τοῦτο καλὸν καὶ ἀπόδεκτον
ἐνώπιον τοῦ σωτῆρος ἡμῶν θεοῦ, 4 ὃς
πάντας ἀνθρώπους θέλει σωθῆναι καὶ
εἰς ἐπίγνωσιν ἀληθείας ἐλθεῖν. 5 Εἷς γὰρ
θεός, εἷς καὶ μεσίτης θεοῦ καὶ ἀνθρώ-
πων, ἄνθρωπος Χριστὸς Ἰησοῦς, 6 ὁ δοὺς
ἑαυτὸν ἀντίλυτρον ὑπὲρ πάντων, τὸ
μαρτύριον καιροῖς ἰδίοις. 7 εἰς ὃ ἐτέθην
ἐγὼ κῆρυξ καὶ ἀπόστολος, ἀλήθειαν
⸀λέγω οὐ ψεύδομαι, διδάσκαλος ἐθνῶν
ἐν πίστει καὶ ἀληθείᾳ.

Cf. 1 Tim 5:13–14.

154. *Contentment/Self-Sufficiency*

Phil 4:10–13

Ἐχάρην δὲ ἐν κυρίῳ μεγάλως ὅτι ἤδη ποτὲ
ἀνεθάλετε τὸ ὑπὲρ ἐμοῦ φρονεῖν, ἐφ' ᾧ
καὶ ἐφρονεῖτε, ἠκαιρεῖσθε δέ. 11 οὐχ ὅτι
καθ' ὑστέρησιν λέγω, ἐγὼ γὰρ ἔμαθον
ἐν οἷς εἰμι αὐτάρκης εἶναι. 12 οἶδα καὶ
ταπεινοῦσθαι, οἶδα καὶ περισσεύειν· ἐν
παντὶ καὶ ἐν πᾶσιν μεμύημαι, καὶ χορ-
τάζεσθαι καὶ πεινᾶν καὶ περισσεύειν
καὶ ὑστερεῖσθαι· 13 πάντα ἰσχύω ἐν τῷ
ἐνδυναμοῦντί με.

1 Tim 6:3–10

εἴ τις ἑτεροδιδασκαλεῖ καὶ μὴ προσέρχε-
ται ὑγιαίνουσιν λόγοις τοῖς τοῦ κυρίου
ἡμῶν Ἰησοῦ Χριστοῦ καὶ τῇ κατ' εὐσέ-
βειαν διδασκαλίᾳ, 4 τετύφωται, μηδὲν
ἐπιστάμενος, ἀλλὰ νοσῶν περὶ ζητήσεις
καὶ λογομαχίας, ἐξ ὧν γίνεται φθόνος
ἔρις βλασφημίαι, ὑπόνοιαι πονηραί,
5 διαπαρατριβαὶ διεφθαρμένων ἀνθρώ-
πων τὸν νοῦν καὶ ἀπεστερημένων τῆς
ἀληθείας, νομιζόντων πορισμὸν εἶναι
τὴν ⸀εὐσέβειαν. 6 Ἔστιν δὲ πορισμὸς μέ-
γας ἡ εὐσέβεια μετὰ αὐταρκείας· 7 οὐδὲν
γὰρ εἰσηνέγκαμεν εἰς τὸν κόσμον, ⸀ὅτι
οὐδὲ ἐξενεγκεῖν τι δυνάμεθα· 8 ἔχοντες
δὲ διατροφὰς καὶ σκεπάσματα, τούτοις
ἀρκεσθησόμεθα. 9 οἱ δὲ βουλόμενοι πλου-
τεῖν ἐμπίπτουσιν εἰς πειρασμὸν καὶ πα-
γίδα καὶ ἐπιθυμίας πολλὰς ἀνοήτους
καὶ βλαβεράς, αἵτινες βυθίζουσιν τοὺς
ἀνθρώπους εἰς ὄλεθρον καὶ ἀπώλειαν.
10 ῥίζα γὰρ πάντων τῶν κακῶν ἐστιν ἡ
φιλαργυρία, ἧς τινες ὀρεγόμενοι ἀπεπλα-
νήθησαν ἀπὸ τῆς πίστεως καὶ ἑαυτοὺς
περιέπειραν ὀδύναις πολλαῖς.

Cf. the warnings against greed and covetousness in several of the lists in § 16 Vice List.

155. *Support of the Gospel*

1 Cor 9:3–14

Ἡ ἐμὴ ἀπολογία τοῖς ἐμὲ ἀνακρίνουσίν
ἐστιν αὕτη. 4 μὴ οὐκ ἔχομεν ἐξουσίαν
φαγεῖν καὶ πεῖν; 5 μὴ οὐκ ἔχομεν ἐξου-
σίαν ἀδελφὴν γυναῖκα περιάγειν ὡς
καὶ οἱ λοιποὶ ἀπόστολοι καὶ οἱ ἀδελ-
φοὶ τοῦ κυρίου καὶ Κηφᾶς; 6 ἢ μόνος
ἐγὼ καὶ Βαρναβᾶς οὐκ ἔχομεν ἐξουσίαν
μὴ ἐργάζεσθαι; 7 Τίς στρατεύεται ἰδίοις
ὀψωνίοις ποτέ; τίς φυτεύει ἀμπελῶνα
καὶ τὸν καρπὸν αὐτοῦ οὐκ ἐσθίει; ἢ τίς
ποιμαίνει ποίμνην καὶ ἐκ τοῦ γάλακτος
τῆς ποίμνης οὐκ ἐσθίει; 8 Μὴ κατὰ ἄνθρω-
πον ταῦτα λαλῶ ἢ καὶ ὁ νόμος ταῦτα
οὐ λέγει; 9 ἐν γὰρ τῷ Μωϋσέως νόμῳ
γέγραπται· οὐ κημώσεις βοῦν ἀλοῶντα.
μὴ τῶν βοῶν μέλει τῷ θεῷ 10 ἢ δι' ἡμᾶς
πάντως λέγει; δι' ἡμᾶς γὰρ ἐγράφη ὅτι
ὀφείλει ἐπ' ἐλπίδι ὁ ἀροτριῶν ἀροτριᾶν
καὶ ὁ ἀλοῶν ἐπ' ἐλπίδι τοῦ μετέχειν.
11 εἰ ἡμεῖς ὑμῖν τὰ πνευματικὰ ἐσπεί-
ραμεν, μέγα εἰ ἡμεῖς ὑμῶν τὰ σαρκικὰ
θερίσομεν; 12 Εἰ ἄλλοι τῆς ὑμῶν ἐξουσίας
μετέχουσιν, οὐ μᾶλλον ἡμεῖς; ἀλλ' οὐκ
ἐχρησάμεθα τῇ ἐξουσίᾳ ταύτῃ, ἀλλὰ
πάντα στέγομεν, ἵνα μή τινα ἐγκοπὴν
δῶμεν τῷ εὐαγγελίῳ τοῦ Χριστοῦ. 13 Οὐκ
οἴδατε ὅτι οἱ τὰ ἱερὰ ἐργαζόμενοι [τὰ] ἐκ
τοῦ ἱεροῦ ἐσθίουσιν, οἱ τῷ θυσιαστηρίῳ
παρεδρεύοντες τῷ θυσιαστηρίῳ συμμε-
ρίζονται; 14 οὕτως καὶ ὁ κύριος διέταξεν
τοῖς τὸ εὐαγγέλιον καταγγέλλουσιν ἐκ
τοῦ εὐαγγελίου ζῆν.

Gal 6:6

Κοινωνείτω δὲ ὁ κατηχούμενος τὸν λόγον
τῷ κατηχοῦντι ἐν πᾶσιν ἀγαθοῖς.

1 Tim 5:17–18

Οἱ καλῶς προεστῶτες πρεσβύτεροι δι-
πλῆς τιμῆς ἀξιούσθωσαν, μάλιστα οἱ
κοπιῶντες ἐν λόγῳ καὶ διδασκαλίᾳ.
18 λέγει γὰρ ἡ γραφή· βοῦν ἀλοῶντα
οὐ φιμώσεις, καί· ἄξιος ὁ ἐργάτης τοῦ
μισθοῦ αὐτοῦ.

Cf. Rom 15:22–24; 16:23; Phil 1:3–5; 4:10–20; Titus 3:13; Acts 16:14–15; 16:40; 17:5–7; 18:7; 21:4–6; 21:7–8; 21:15–16; 24:22–23; 27:3; 28:13–14, and possibly 2 Tim 2:4–7.

See also § 156 Paul's Financial Practice.

§ 153 1 Tim 2:7 ***λεγω*** ℵ² A D* 1739. 1881] *add.* εν Χριστω ℵ* D² 33^vid *Byz* **§ 154** 1 Tim 6:5 ***ευσεβειαν*** ℵ A D* 048. 33. 1739. 1881] *add.* αφιστασο απο των τοιουτων D² *Byz* 1 Tim 6:7 ***οτι*** ℵ* A 048. 33. 1739. 1881] δηλον οτι ℵ² D² *Byz* ¦ αληθες οτι D*

Jesus Christ to do their work quietly and to earn their own living.

1 Tim 2:1–7

First of all, then, I urge that supplications, prayers, intercessions, and thanksgivings be made for everyone, **2** for kings and all who are in high positions, so that we may lead a quiet and peaceable life in all godliness and dignity. **3** This is right and is acceptable in the sight of God our Savior, **4** who desires everyone to be saved and to come to the knowledge of the truth. **5** For there is one God; there is also one mediator between God and humankind, Christ Jesus, himself human, **6** who gave himself a ransom for all —this was attested at the right time. **7** For this I was appointed a herald and an apostle (I am telling the truth,[a] I am not lying), a teacher of the Gentiles in faith and truth.

Cf. 1 Tim 5:13–14.

154. Contentment/Self-Sufficiency

Phil 4:10–13

I rejoice in the Lord greatly that now at last you have revived your concern for me; indeed, you were concerned for me, but had no opportunity to show it. **11** Not that I am referring to being in need; for I have learned to be content with whatever I have. **12** I know what it is to have little, and I know what it is to have plenty. In any and all circumstances I have learned the secret of being well-fed and of going hungry, of having plenty and of being in need. **13** I can do all things through him who strengthens me.

1 Tim 6:3–10

Whoever teaches otherwise and does not agree with the sound words of our Lord Jesus Christ and the teaching that is in accordance with godliness, **4** is conceited, understanding nothing, and has a morbid craving for controversy and for disputes about words. From these come envy, dissension, slander, base suspicions, **5** and wrangling among those who are depraved in mind and bereft of the truth, imagining that godliness is a means of gain.[a] **6** Of course, there is great gain in godliness combined with contentment; **7** for we brought nothing into the world, so that[b] we can take nothing out of it; **8** but if we have food and clothing, we will be content with these. **9** But those who want to be rich fall into temptation and are trapped by many senseless and harmful desires that plunge people into ruin and destruction. **10** For the love of money is a root of all kinds of evil, and in their eagerness to be rich some have wandered away from the faith and pierced themselves with many pains.

Cf. the warnings against greed and covetousness in several of the lists in § 16 Vice List.

155. Support of the Gospel

1 Cor 9:3–14

This is my defense to those who would examine me. **4** Do we not have the right to our food and drink? **5** Do we not have the right to be accompanied by a believing wife, as do the other apostles and the brothers of the Lord and Cephas? **6** Or is it only Barnabas and I who have no right to refrain from working for a living? **7** Who at any time pays the expenses for doing military service? Who plants a vineyard and does not eat any of its fruit? Or who tends a flock and does not get any of its milk? **8** Do I say this on human authority? Does not the law also say the same? **9** For it is written in the law of Moses, "You shall not muzzle an ox while it is treading out the grain." Is it for oxen that God is concerned? **10** Or does he not speak entirely for our sake? It was indeed written for our sake, for whoever plows should plow in hope and whoever threshes should thresh in hope of a share in the crop. **11** If we have sown spiritual good among you, is it too much if we reap your material benefits? **12** If others share this rightful claim on you, do not we still more? Nevertheless, we have not made use of this right, but we endure anything rather than put an obstacle in the way of the gospel of Christ. **13** Do you not know that those who are employed in the temple service get their food from the temple, and those who serve at the altar share in what is sacrificed on the altar? **14** In the same way, the Lord commanded that those who proclaim the gospel should get their living by the gospel.

Gal 6:6

Those who are taught the word must share in all good things with their teacher.

1 Tim 5:17–18

Let the elders who rule well be considered worthy of double honor, especially those who labor in preaching and teaching; **18** for the scripture says, "You shall not muzzle an ox while it is treading out the grain," and, "The laborer deserves to be paid."

Cf. Rom 15:22–24; 16:23; Phil 1:3–5; 4:10–20; Titus 3:13; Acts 16:14–15; 16:40; 17:5–7; 18:7; 21:4–6; 21:7–8; 21:15–16; 24:22–23; 27:3; 28:13–14; and possibly 2 Tim 2:4–7.

See also § 156 Paul's Financial Practice.

§ 153 [a] **1 Tim 2:7** ***telling the truth*** Other ancient authorities add *in Christ* **§ 154** [a] **1 Tim 6:5** ***gain*** Other ancient authorities add *Withdraw yourself from such people* [b] **1 Tim 6:7** ***world, so that*** Other ancient authorities read *world—it is certain that*

156. Paul's Financial Practice

1 Cor 9:1–18

Οὐκ εἰμὶ ἐλεύθερος; οὐκ εἰμὶ ἀπόστολος; οὐχὶ Ἰησοῦν τὸν κύριον ἡμῶν ἑόρακα; οὐ τὸ ἔργον μου ὑμεῖς ἐστε ἐν κυρίῳ; 2 εἰ ἄλλοις οὐκ εἰμὶ ἀπόστολος, ἀλλά γε ὑμῖν εἰμι· ἡ γὰρ σφραγίς μου τῆς ἀποστολῆς ὑμεῖς ἐστε ἐν κυρίῳ. 3 Ἡ ἐμὴ ἀπολογία τοῖς ἐμὲ ἀνακρίνουσίν ἐστιν αὕτη. 4 μὴ οὐκ ἔχομεν ἐξουσίαν φαγεῖν καὶ πεῖν; 5 μὴ οὐκ ἔχομεν ἐξουσίαν ἀδελφὴν γυναῖκα περιάγειν ὡς καὶ οἱ λοιποὶ ἀπόστολοι καὶ οἱ ἀδελφοὶ τοῦ κυρίου καὶ Κηφᾶς; 6 ἢ μόνος ἐγὼ καὶ Βαρναβᾶς οὐκ ἔχομεν ἐξουσίαν μὴ ἐργάζεσθαι; 7 Τίς στρατεύεται ἰδίοις ὀψωνίοις ποτέ; τίς φυτεύει ἀμπελῶνα καὶ τὸν καρπὸν αὐτοῦ οὐκ ἐσθίει; ἢ τίς ποιμαίνει ποίμνην καὶ ἐκ τοῦ γάλακτος τῆς ποίμνης οὐκ ἐσθίει; 8 Μὴ κατὰ ἄνθρωπον ταῦτα λαλῶ ἢ καὶ ὁ νόμος ταῦτα οὐ λέγει; 9 ἐν γὰρ τῷ Μωϋσέως νόμῳ γέγραπται· οὐ κημώσεις βοῦν ἀλοῶντα. μὴ τῶν βοῶν μέλει τῷ θεῷ 10 ἢ δι' ἡμᾶς πάντως λέγει; δι' ἡμᾶς γὰρ ἐγράφη ὅτι ὀφείλει ἐπ' ἐλπίδι ὁ ἀροτριῶν ἀροτριᾶν καὶ ὁ ἀλοῶν ἐπ' ἐλπίδι τοῦ μετέχειν. 11 εἰ ἡμεῖς ὑμῖν τὰ πνευματικὰ ἐσπείραμεν, μέγα εἰ ἡμεῖς ὑμῶν τὰ σαρκικὰ θερίσομεν; 12 Εἰ ἄλλοι τῆς ὑμῶν ἐξουσίας μετέχουσιν, οὐ μᾶλλον ἡμεῖς; ἀλλ' οὐκ ἐχρησάμεθα τῇ ἐξουσίᾳ ταύτῃ, ἀλλὰ πάντα στέγομεν, ἵνα μή τινα ἐγκοπὴν δῶμεν τῷ εὐαγγελίῳ τοῦ Χριστοῦ. 13 Οὐκ οἴδατε ὅτι οἱ τὰ ἱερὰ ἐργαζόμενοι [τὰ] ἐκ τοῦ ἱεροῦ ἐσθίουσιν, οἱ τῷ θυσιαστηρίῳ παρεδρεύοντες τῷ θυσιαστηρίῳ συμμερίζονται; 14 οὕτως καὶ ὁ κύριος διέταξεν τοῖς τὸ εὐαγγέλιον καταγγέλλουσιν ἐκ τοῦ εὐαγγελίου ζῆν. 15 Ἐγὼ δὲ οὐ κέχρημαι οὐδενὶ τούτων. Οὐκ ἔγραψα δὲ ταῦτα, ἵνα οὕτως γένηται ἐν ἐμοί· καλὸν γάρ μοι μᾶλλον ἀποθανεῖν ἤ—τὸ καύχημά μου οὐδεὶς κενώσει. 16 ἐὰν γὰρ εὐαγγελίζωμαι, οὐκ ἔστιν μοι καύχημα· ἀνάγκη γάρ μοι ἐπίκειται· οὐαὶ γάρ μοί ἐστιν ἐὰν μὴ εὐαγγελίσωμαι. 17 εἰ γὰρ ἑκὼν τοῦτο πράσσω, μισθὸν ἔχω· εἰ δὲ ἄκων, οἰκονομίαν πεπίστευμαι· 18 τίς οὖν μού ἐστιν ὁ μισθός; ἵνα εὐαγγελιζόμενος ἀδάπανον θήσω τὸ εὐαγγέλιον εἰς τὸ μὴ καταχρήσασθαι τῇ ἐξουσίᾳ μου ἐν τῷ εὐαγγελίῳ.

2 Cor 11:5–21a

Λογίζομαι γὰρ μηδὲν ὑστερηκέναι τῶν ὑπερλίαν ἀποστόλων. 6 εἰ δὲ καὶ ἰδιώτης τῷ λόγῳ, ἀλλ' οὐ τῇ γνώσει, ἀλλ' ἐν παντὶ φανερώσαντες ἐν πᾶσιν εἰς ὑμᾶς. 7 Ἢ ἁμαρτίαν ἐποίησα ἐμαυτὸν ταπεινῶν ἵνα ὑμεῖς ὑψωθῆτε, ὅτι δωρεὰν τὸ τοῦ θεοῦ εὐαγγέλιον εὐηγγελισάμην ὑμῖν; 8 ἄλλας ἐκκλησίας ἐσύλησα λαβὼν ὀψώνιον πρὸς τὴν ὑμῶν διακονίαν, 9 καὶ παρὼν πρὸς ὑμᾶς καὶ ὑστερηθεὶς οὐ κατενάρκησα οὐθενός· τὸ γὰρ ὑστέρημά μου προσανεπλήρωσαν οἱ ἀδελφοὶ ἐλθόντες ἀπὸ Μακεδονίας, καὶ ἐν παντὶ ἀβαρῆ ἐμαυτὸν ὑμῖν ἐτήρησα καὶ τηρήσω. 10 ἔστιν ἀλήθεια Χριστοῦ ἐν ἐμοὶ ὅτι ἡ καύχησις αὕτη οὐ φραγήσεται εἰς ἐμὲ ἐν τοῖς κλίμασιν τῆς Ἀχαΐας. 11 διὰ τί; ὅτι οὐκ ἀγαπῶ ὑμᾶς; ὁ θεὸς οἶδεν. 12 Ὃ δὲ ποιῶ, καὶ ποιήσω, ἵνα ἐκκόψω τὴν ἀφορμὴν τῶν θελόντων ἀφορμήν, ἵνα ἐν ᾧ καυχῶνται εὑρεθῶσιν καθὼς καὶ ἡμεῖς. 13 οἱ γὰρ τοιοῦτοι ψευδαπόστολοι, ἐργάται δόλιοι, μετασχηματιζόμενοι εἰς ἀποστόλους Χριστοῦ. 14 καὶ οὐ θαῦμα· αὐτὸς γὰρ ὁ σατανᾶς μετασχηματίζεται εἰς ἄγγελον φωτός. 15 οὐ μέγα οὖν εἰ καὶ οἱ διάκονοι αὐτοῦ μετασχηματίζονται ὡς διάκονοι δικαιοσύνης· ὧν τὸ τέλος ἔσται κατὰ τὰ ἔργα αὐτῶν. 16 Πάλιν λέγω, μή τίς με δόξῃ ἄφρονα εἶναι· εἰ δὲ μή γε, κἂν ὡς ἄφρονα δέξασθέ με, ἵνα κἀγὼ μικρόν τι καυχήσωμαι. 17 ὃ λαλῶ, οὐ κατὰ κύριον λαλῶ ἀλλ' ὡς ἐν ἀφροσύνῃ, ἐν ταύτῃ τῇ ὑποστάσει τῆς καυχήσεως. 18 ἐπεὶ πολλοὶ καυχῶνται κατὰ σάρκα, κἀγὼ ἀγὼ καυχήσομαι. 19 ἡδέως γὰρ ἀνέχεσθε τῶν ἀφρόνων φρόνιμοι ὄντες· 20 ἀνέχεσθε γὰρ εἴ τις ὑμᾶς καταδουλοῖ, εἴ τις κατεσθίει, εἴ τις λαμβάνει, εἴ τις ἐπαίρεται, εἴ τις εἰς πρόσωπον ὑμᾶς δέρει. 21 κατὰ ἀτιμίαν λέγω, ὡς ὅτι ἡμεῖς ἠσθενήκαμεν.

2 Cor 12:11–18

Γέγονα ἄφρων, ὑμεῖς με ἠναγκάσατε. ἐγὼ γὰρ ὤφειλον ὑφ' ὑμῶν συνίστασθαι· οὐδὲν γὰρ ὑστέρησα τῶν ὑπερλίαν ἀποστόλων εἰ καὶ οὐδέν εἰμι. 12 τὰ μὲν σημεῖα τοῦ ἀποστόλου κατειργάσθη ἐν ὑμῖν ἐν πάσῃ ὑπομονῇ, σημείοις τε καὶ τέρασιν καὶ δυνάμεσιν. 13 τί γάρ ἐστιν ὃ ἡσσώθητε ὑπὲρ τὰς λοιπὰς ἐκκλησίας, εἰ μὴ ὅτι αὐτὸς ἐγὼ οὐ κατενάρκησα ὑμῶν; χαρίσασθέ μοι τὴν ἀδικίαν ταύτην. 14 Ἰδοὺ τρίτον τοῦτο ἑτοίμως ἔχω ἐλθεῖν πρὸς ὑμᾶς, καὶ οὐ καταναρκήσω· οὐ γὰρ ζητῶ τὰ ὑμῶν ἀλλὰ ὑμᾶς. οὐ γὰρ ὀφείλει τὰ τέκνα τοῖς γονεῦσιν θησαυρίζειν ἀλλὰ οἱ γονεῖς τοῖς τέκνοις. 15 ἐγὼ δὲ ἥδιστα δαπανήσω καὶ ἐκδαπανηθήσομαι ὑπὲρ τῶν ψυχῶν ὑμῶν. εἰ περισσοτέρως ὑμᾶς ἀγαπῶ[ν], ἧσσον ἀγαπῶμαι; 16 Ἔστω δέ, ἐγὼ οὐ κατεβάρησα ὑμᾶς· ἀλλὰ ὑπάρχων πανοῦργος δόλῳ ὑμᾶς ἔλαβον. 17 μή τινα ὧν ἀπέσταλκα πρὸς ὑμᾶς, δι' αὐτοῦ ἐπλεονέκτησα ὑμᾶς; 18 παρεκάλεσα Τίτον καὶ συναπέστειλα τὸν ἀδελφόν· μήτι ἐπλεονέκτησεν ὑμᾶς Τίτος; οὐ τῷ αὐτῷ πνεύματι περιεπατήσαμεν; οὐ τοῖς αὐτοῖς ἴχνεσιν;

Phil 4:10–20

Ἐχάρην δὲ ἐν κυρίῳ μεγάλως ὅτι ἤδη ποτὲ ἀνεθάλετε τὸ ὑπὲρ ἐμοῦ φρονεῖν, ἐφ' ᾧ καὶ ἐφρονεῖτε, ἠκαιρεῖσθε δέ. 11 οὐχ ὅτι καθ' ὑστέρησιν λέγω, ἐγὼ γὰρ ἔμαθον ἐν οἷς εἰμι αὐτάρκης εἶναι. 12 οἶδα καὶ ταπεινοῦσθαι, οἶδα καὶ περισσεύειν· ἐν παντὶ καὶ ἐν πᾶσιν μεμύημαι, καὶ χορτάζεσθαι καὶ πεινᾶν καὶ περισσεύειν καὶ ὑστερεῖσθαι· 13 πάντα ἰσχύω ἐν τῷ ἐνδυναμοῦντί με. 14 πλὴν καλῶς ἐποιήσατε συγκοινωνήσαντές μου τῇ θλίψει. 15 οἴδατε δὲ καὶ ὑμεῖς, Φιλιππήσιοι, ὅτι ἐν ἀρχῇ τοῦ εὐαγγελίου, ὅτε ἐξῆλθον ἀπὸ Μακεδονίας, οὐδεμία μοι ἐκκλησία ἐκοινώνησεν εἰς λόγον δόσεως καὶ

156. Paul's Financial Practice

1 Cor 9:1–18

Am I not free? Am I not an apostle? Have I not seen Jesus our Lord? Are you not my work in the Lord? 2 If I am not an apostle to others, at least I am to you; for you are the seal of my apostleship in the Lord. 3 This is my defense to those who would examine me. 4 Do we not have the right to our food and drink? 5 Do we not have the right to be accompanied by a believing wife, as do the other apostles and the brothers of the Lord and Cephas? 6 Or is it only Barnabas and I who have no right to refrain from working for a living? 7 Who at any time pays the expenses for doing military service? Who plants a vineyard and does not eat any of its fruit? Or who tends a flock and does not get any of its milk? 8 Do I say this on human authority? Does not the law also say the same? 9 For it is written in the law of Moses, "You shall not muzzle an ox while it is treading out the grain." Is it for oxen that God is concerned? 10 Or does he not speak entirely for our sake? It was indeed written for our sake, for whoever plows should plow in hope and whoever threshes should thresh in hope of a share in the crop. 11 If we have sown spiritual good among you, is it too much if we reap your material benefits? 12 If others share this rightful claim on you, do not we still more? Nevertheless, we have not made use of this right, but we endure anything rather than put an obstacle in the way of the gospel of Christ. 13 Do you not know that those who are employed in the temple service get their food from the temple, and those who serve at the altar share in what is sacrificed on the altar? 14 In the same way, the Lord commanded that those who proclaim the gospel should get their living by the gospel. 15 But I have made no use of any of these rights, nor am I writing this so that they may be applied in my case. Indeed, I would rather die than that—no one will deprive me of my ground for boasting! 16 If I proclaim the gospel, this gives me no ground for boasting, for an obligation is laid on me, and woe to me if I do not proclaim the gospel! 17 For if I do this of my own will, I have a reward; but if not of my own will, I am entrusted with a commission. 18 What then is my reward? Just this: that in my proclamation I may make the gospel free of charge, so as not to make full use of my rights in the gospel.

2 Cor 11:5–21a

I think that I am not in the least inferior to these super-apostles. 6 I may be untrained in speech, but not in knowledge; certainly in every way and in all things we have made this evident to you. 7 Did I commit a sin by humbling myself so that you might be exalted, because I proclaimed God's good news to you free of charge? 8 I robbed other churches by accepting support from them in order to serve you. 9 And when I was with you and was in need, I did not burden anyone, for my needs were supplied by the friends who came from Macedonia. So I refrained and will continue to refrain from burdening you in any way. 10 As the truth of Christ is in me, this boast of mine will not be silenced in the regions of Achaia. 11 And why? Because I do not love you? God knows I do! 12 And what I do I will also continue to do, in order to deny an opportunity to those who want an opportunity to be recognized as our equals in what they boast about. 13 For such boasters are false apostles, deceitful workers, disguising themselves as apostles of Christ. 14 And no wonder! Even Satan disguises himself as an angel of light. 15 So it is not strange if his ministers also disguise themselves as ministers of righteousness. Their end will match their deeds. 16 I repeat, let no one think that I am a fool; but if you do, then accept me as a fool, so that I too may boast a little. 17 What I am saying in regard to this boastful confidence, I am saying not with the Lord's authority, but as a fool; 18 since many boast according to human standards, I will also boast. 19 For you gladly put up with fools, being wise yourselves! 20 For you put up with it when someone makes slaves of you, or preys upon you, or takes advantage of you, or puts on airs, or gives you a slap in the face. 21 To my shame, I must say, we were too weak for that!

2 Cor 12:11–18

I have been a fool! You forced me to it. Indeed you should have been the ones commending me, for I am not at all inferior to these super-apostles, even though I am nothing. 12 The signs of a true apostle were performed among you with utmost patience, signs and wonders and mighty works. 13 How have you been worse off than the other churches, except that I myself did not burden you? Forgive me this wrong! 14 Here I am, ready to come to you this third time. And I will not be a burden, because I do not want what is yours but you; for children ought not to lay up for their parents, but parents for their children. 15 I will most gladly spend and be spent for you. If I love you more, am I to be loved less? 16 Let it be assumed that I did not burden you. Nevertheless (you say) since I was crafty, I took you in by deceit. 17 Did I take advantage of you through any of those whom I sent to you? 18 I urged Titus to go, and sent the brother with him. Titus did not take advantage of you, did he? Did we not conduct ourselves with the same spirit? Did we not take the same steps?

Phil 4:10–20

I rejoice in the Lord greatly that now at last you have revived your concern for me; indeed, you were concerned for me, but had no opportunity to show it. 11 Not that I am referring to being in need; for I have learned to be content with whatever I have. 12 I know what it is to have little, and I know what it is to have plenty. In any and all circumstances I have learned the secret of being well-fed and of going hungry, of having plenty and of being in need. 13 I can do all things through him who strengthens me. 14 In any case, it was kind of you to share my distress. 15 You Philippians indeed know that in the early days of the gospel, when I left Macedonia, no church shared with me in the matter of giving and receiving,

λήμψεως εἰ μὴ ὑμεῖς μόνοι, **16** ὅτι καὶ ἐν Θεσσαλονίκῃ καὶ ἅπαξ καὶ δὶς εἰς τὴν χρείαν μοι ἐπέμψατε. **17** οὐχ ὅτι ἐπιζητῶ τὸ δόμα, ἀλλὰ ἐπιζητῶ τὸν καρπὸν τὸν πλεονάζοντα εἰς λόγον ὑμῶν. **18** ἀπέχω δὲ πάντα καὶ περισσεύω· πεπλήρωμαι δεξάμενος παρὰ Ἐπαφροδίτου τὰ παρ' ὑμῶν, ὀσμὴν εὐωδίας, θυσίαν δεκτήν, εὐάρεστον τῷ θεῷ. **19** ὁ δὲ θεός μου πληρώσει πᾶσαν χρείαν ὑμῶν κατὰ τὸ πλοῦτος αὐτοῦ ἐν δόξῃ ἐν Χριστῷ Ἰησοῦ. **20** τῷ δὲ θεῷ καὶ πατρὶ ἡμῶν ἡ δόξα εἰς τοὺς αἰῶνας τῶν αἰώνων, ἀμήν.

1 Thess 2:9–12

Μνημονεύετε γάρ, ἀδελφοί, τὸν κόπον ἡμῶν καὶ τὸν μόχθον· νυκτὸς καὶ ἡμέρας ἐργαζόμενοι πρὸς τὸ μὴ ἐπιβαρῆσαί τινα ὑμῶν ἐκηρύξαμεν εἰς ὑμᾶς τὸ εὐαγγέλιον τοῦ θεοῦ. **10** ὑμεῖς μάρτυρες καὶ ὁ θεός, ὡς ὁσίως καὶ δικαίως καὶ ἀμέμπτως ὑμῖν τοῖς πιστεύουσιν ἐγενήθημεν, **11** καθάπερ οἴδατε, ὡς ἕνα ἕκαστον ὑμῶν ὡς πατὴρ τέκνα ἑαυτοῦ **12** παρακαλοῦντες ὑμᾶς καὶ παραμυθούμενοι καὶ μαρτυρόμενοι εἰς τὸ περιπατεῖν ὑμᾶς ἀξίως τοῦ θεοῦ τοῦ ⸀καλοῦντος ὑμᾶς εἰς τὴν ἑαυτοῦ βασιλείαν καὶ δόξαν.

2 Thess 3:7–9

Αὐτοὶ γὰρ οἴδατε πῶς δεῖ μιμεῖσθαι ἡμᾶς, ὅτι οὐκ ἠτακτήσαμεν ἐν ὑμῖν **8** οὐδὲ δωρεὰν ἄρτον ἐφάγομεν παρά τινος, ἀλλ' ἐν κόπῳ καὶ μόχθῳ νυκτὸς καὶ ἡμέρας ἐργαζόμενοι πρὸς τὸ μὴ ἐπιβαρῆσαί τινα ὑμῶν· **9** οὐχ ὅτι οὐκ ἔχομεν ἐξουσίαν, ἀλλ' ἵνα ἑαυτοὺς τύπον δῶμεν ὑμῖν εἰς τὸ μιμεῖσθαι ἡμᾶς.

Acts 18:2–5

καὶ εὑρών τινα Ἰουδαῖον ὀνόματι Ἀκύλαν, Ποντικὸν τῷ γένει προσφάτως ἐληλυθότα ἀπὸ τῆς Ἰταλίας καὶ Πρίσκιλλαν γυναῖκα αὐτοῦ, διὰ τὸ διατεταχέναι Κλαύδιον χωρίζεσθαι πάντας τοὺς Ἰουδαίους ἀπὸ τῆς Ῥώμης, προσῆλθεν αὐτοῖς **3** καὶ διὰ τὸ ὁμότεχνον εἶναι ἔμενεν παρ' αὐτοῖς, καὶ ἠργάζετο· ἦσαν γὰρ σκηνοποιοὶ τῇ τέχνῃ. **4** διελέγετο δὲ ἐν τῇ συναγωγῇ κατὰ πᾶν σάββατον ἔπειθέν τε Ἰουδαίους καὶ Ἕλληνας. **5** Ὡς δὲ κατῆλθον ἀπὸ τῆς Μακεδονίας ὅ τε Σιλᾶς καὶ ὁ Τιμόθεος, συνείχετο τῷ λόγῳ ὁ Παῦλος διαμαρτυρόμενος τοῖς Ἰουδαίοις εἶναι τὸν χριστὸν Ἰησοῦν.

Acts 20:32–35

Καὶ τὰ νῦν παρατίθεμαι ὑμᾶς τῷ θεῷ καὶ τῷ λόγῳ τῆς χάριτος αὐτοῦ, τῷ δυναμένῳ οἰκοδομῆσαι καὶ δοῦναι τὴν κληρονομίαν ἐν τοῖς ἡγιασμένοις πᾶσιν. **33** ἀργυρίου ἢ χρυσίου ἢ ἱματισμοῦ οὐδενὸς ἐπεθύμησα· **34** αὐτοὶ γινώσκετε ὅτι ταῖς χρείαις μου καὶ τοῖς οὖσιν μετ' ἐμοῦ ὑπηρέτησαν αἱ χεῖρες αὗται. **35** πάντα ὑπέδειξα ὑμῖν ὅτι οὕτως κοπιῶντας δεῖ ἀντιλαμβάνεσθαι τῶν ἀσθενούντων, μνημονεύειν τε τῶν λόγων τοῦ κυρίου Ἰησοῦ ὅτι αὐτὸς εἶπεν· μακάριόν ἐστιν μᾶλλον διδόναι ἢ λαμβάνειν.

157. The Collection for the Saints

Rom 15:25–33

Νυνὶ δὲ πορεύομαι εἰς Ἰερουσαλὴμ διακονῶν τοῖς ἁγίοις. **26** εὐδόκησαν γὰρ Μακεδονία καὶ Ἀχαΐα κοινωνίαν τινὰ ποιήσασθαι εἰς τοὺς πτωχοὺς τῶν ἁγίων τῶν ἐν Ἰερουσαλήμ. **27** εὐδόκησαν γὰρ καὶ ὀφειλέται εἰσὶν αὐτῶν· εἰ γὰρ τοῖς πνευματικοῖς αὐτῶν ἐκοινώνησαν τὰ ἔθνη, ὀφείλουσιν καὶ ἐν τοῖς σαρκικοῖς λειτουργῆσαι αὐτοῖς. **28** τοῦτο οὖν ἐπιτελέσας καὶ σφραγισάμενος αὐτοῖς τὸν καρπὸν τοῦτον, ἀπελεύσομαι δι' ὑμῶν εἰς Σπανίαν· **29** οἶδα δὲ ὅτι ἐρχόμενος πρὸς ὑμᾶς ἐν πληρώματι ⸀εὐλογίας Χριστοῦ ἐλεύσομαι. **30** Παρακαλῶ δὲ ὑμᾶς[, ἀδελφοί,] διὰ τοῦ κυρίου ἡμῶν Ἰησοῦ Χριστοῦ καὶ διὰ τῆς ἀγάπης τοῦ πνεύματος συναγωνίσασθαί μοι ἐν ταῖς προσευχαῖς ὑπὲρ ἐμοῦ πρὸς τὸν θεόν, **31** ἵνα ῥυσθῶ ἀπὸ τῶν ἀπειθούντων ἐν τῇ Ἰουδαίᾳ καὶ ἡ ⸀διακονία μου ἡ εἰς Ἰερουσαλὴμ εὐπρόσδεκτος τοῖς ἁγίοις γένηται, **32** ἵνα ἐν χαρᾷ ἐλθὼν πρὸς ὑμᾶς διὰ θελήματος θεοῦ συναναπαύσωμαι ὑμῖν. **33** Ὁ δὲ θεὸς τῆς εἰρήνης μετὰ πάντων ὑμῶν, ἀμήν.

1 Cor 16:1–4

Περὶ δὲ τῆς λογείας τῆς εἰς τοὺς ἁγίους ὥσπερ διέταξα ταῖς ἐκκλησίαις τῆς Γαλατίας, οὕτως καὶ ὑμεῖς ποιήσατε. **2** κατὰ μίαν σαββάτου ἕκαστος ὑμῶν παρ' ἑαυτῷ τιθέτω θησαυρίζων ὅ τι ἐὰν εὐοδῶται, ἵνα μὴ ὅταν ἔλθω τότε λογεῖαι γίνωνται. **3** ὅταν δὲ παραγένωμαι, οὓς ἐὰν δοκιμάσητε, δι' ἐπιστολῶν τούτους πέμψω ἀπενεγκεῖν τὴν χάριν ὑμῶν εἰς Ἰερουσαλήμ· **4** ἐὰν δὲ ἄξιον ᾖ τοῦ κἀμὲ πορεύεσθαι, σὺν ἐμοὶ πορεύσονται.

Gal 2:9–10

καὶ γνόντες τὴν χάριν τὴν δοθεῖσάν μοι, Ἰάκωβος καὶ Κηφᾶς καὶ Ἰωάννης, οἱ δοκοῦντες στῦλοι εἶναι, δεξιὰς ἔδωκαν ἐμοὶ καὶ Βαρναβᾷ κοινωνίας, ἵνα ἡμεῖς εἰς τὰ ἔθνη, αὐτοὶ δὲ εἰς τὴν περιτομήν· **10** μόνον τῶν πτωχῶν ἵνα μνημονεύωμεν, ὃ καὶ ἐσπούδασα αὐτὸ τοῦτο ποιῆσαι.

Acts 11:27–30

Ἐν ταύταις δὲ ταῖς ἡμέραις κατῆλθον ἀπὸ Ἱεροσολύμων προφῆται εἰς Ἀντιόχειαν. **28** ἀναστὰς δὲ εἷς ἐξ αὐτῶν ὀνόματι Ἅγαβος ἐσήμανεν διὰ τοῦ πνεύματος λιμὸν μεγάλην μέλλειν ἔσεσθαι ἐφ' ὅλην τὴν οἰκουμένην, ἥτις ἐγένετο ἐπὶ Κλαυδίου. **29** τῶν δὲ μαθητῶν, καθὼς εὐπορεῖτό τις, ὥρισαν ἕκαστος αὐτῶν εἰς διακονίαν πέμψαι τοῖς κατοικοῦσιν ἐν τῇ Ἰουδαίᾳ ἀδελφοῖς· **30** ὃ καὶ ἐποίησαν ἀποστείλαντες πρὸς τοὺς πρεσβυτέρους διὰ χειρὸς Βαρναβᾶ καὶ Σαύλου.

Acts 12:25

Βαρναβᾶς δὲ καὶ Σαῦλος ὑπέστρεψαν ⸀εἰς Ἰερουσαλὴμ πληρώσαντες τὴν διακονίαν, συμπαραλαβόντες Ἰωάννην τὸν ἐπικληθέντα Μᾶρκον.

Acts 24:17–18

δι' ἐτῶν δὲ πλειόνων ἐλεημοσύνας ποιήσων εἰς τὸ ἔθνος μου παρεγενόμην

§ 156 **1 Thess 2:12** ***καλουντος*** B D 33. 1739. 1881 *Byz*] καλεσαντος ℵ A **§ 157** **Rom 15:29** ***ευλογιας*** 𝔓[46] ℵ* A B C D 1739. 1881] *add.* του ευαγγελιου του ℵ[2] 33 *Byz* **Rom 15:31** ***διακονια*** 𝔓[46] ℵ A C D[1] 33. 1739. 1881 *Byz*] δωροφορια B D* **Acts 12:25** ***εις*** ℵ B *Byz*] εξ 𝔓[74] A 33. 1739 ¦ απο D E

except you alone. 16 For even when I was in Thessalonica, you sent me help for my needs more than once. 17 Not that I seek the gift, but I seek the profit that accumulates to your account. 18 I have been paid in full and have more than enough; I am fully satisfied, now that I have received from Epaphroditus the gifts you sent, a fragrant offering, a sacrifice acceptable and pleasing to God. 19 And my God will fully satisfy every need of yours according to his riches in glory in Christ Jesus. 20 To our God and Father be glory forever and ever. Amen.

1 Thess 2:9–12

You remember our labor and toil, brothers and sisters; we worked night and day, so that we might not burden any of you while we proclaimed to you the gospel of God. 10 You are witnesses, and God also, how pure, upright, and blameless our conduct was toward you believers. 11 As you know, we dealt with each one of you like a father with his children, 12 urging and encouraging you and pleading that you lead a life worthy of God, who calls[a] you into his own kingdom and glory.

2 Thess 3:7–9

For you yourselves know how you ought to imitate us; we were not idle when we were with you, 8 and we did not eat anyone's bread without paying for it; but with toil and labor we worked night and day, so that we might not burden any of you. 9 This was not because we do not have that right, but in order to give you an example to imitate.

Acts 18:2–5

There he found a Jew named Aquila, a native of Pontus, who had recently come from Italy with his wife Priscilla, because Claudius had ordered all Jews to leave Rome. Paul went to see them, 3 and, because he was of the same trade, he stayed with them, and they worked together—by trade they were tentmakers. 4 Every sabbath he would argue in the synagogue and would try to convince Jews and Greeks. 5 When Silas and Timothy arrived from Macedonia, Paul was occupied with proclaiming the word, testifying to the Jews that the Messiah was Jesus.

Acts 20:32–35

And now I commend you to God and to the message of his grace, a message that is able to build you up and to give you the inheritance among all who are sanctified. 33 I coveted no one's silver or gold or clothing. 34 You know for yourselves that I worked with my own hands to support myself and my companions. 35 In all this I have given you an example that by such work we must support the weak, remembering the words of the Lord Jesus, for he himself said, 'It is more blessed to give than to receive.'"

157. The Collection for the Saints

Rom 15:25–33

At present, however, I am going to Jerusalem in a ministry to the saints; 26 for Macedonia and Achaia have been pleased to share their resources with the poor among the saints at Jerusalem. 27 They were pleased to do this, and indeed they owe it to them; for if the Gentiles have come to share in their spiritual blessings, they ought also to be of service to them in material things. 28 So, when I have completed this, and have delivered to them what has been collected, I will set out by way of you to Spain; 29 and I know that when I come to you, I will come in the fullness of the blessing[a] of Christ. 30 I appeal to you, brothers and sisters, by our Lord Jesus Christ and by the love of the Spirit, to join me in earnest prayer to God on my behalf, 31 that I may be rescued from the unbelievers in Judea, and that my ministry[b] to Jerusalem may be acceptable to the saints, 32 so that by God's will I may come to you with joy and be refreshed in your company. 33 The God of peace be with all of you. Amen.

1 Cor 16:1–4

Now concerning the collection for the saints: you should follow the directions I gave to the churches of Galatia. 2 On the first day of every week, each of you is to put aside and save whatever extra you earn, so that collections need not be taken when I come. 3 And when I arrive, I will send any whom you approve with letters to take your gift to Jerusalem. 4 If it seems advisable that I should go also, they will accompany me.

Gal 2:9–10

and when James and Cephas and John, who were acknowledged pillars, recognized the grace that had been given to me, they gave to Barnabas and me the right hand of fellowship, agreeing that we should go to the Gentiles and they to the circumcised. 10 They asked only one thing, that we remember the poor, which was actually what I was eager to do.

Acts 11:27–30

At that time prophets came down from Jerusalem to Antioch. 28 One of them named Agabus stood up and predicted by the Spirit that there would be a severe famine over all the world; and this took place during the reign of Claudius. 29 The disciples determined that according to their ability, each would send relief to the believers living in Judea; 30 this they did, sending it to the elders by Barnabas and Saul.

Acts 12:25

Then after completing their mission Barnabas and Saul returned to[c] Jerusalem and brought with them John, whose other name was Mark.

Acts 24:17–18

Now after some years I came to bring alms to my nation and to offer sacri-

§ 156 [a] **1 Thess 2:12** ***calls*** Other ancient authorities read *called* **§ 157** [a] **Rom 15:29** ***blessing*** Other ancient authorities add *of the gospel* [b] **Rom 15:31** ***my ministry*** Other ancient authorities read *my bringing of a gift* [c] **Acts 12:25** ***to*** Other ancient authorities read *from*

καὶ προσφοράς, 18 ἐν αἷς εὗρόν με ἡγνι-
σμένον ἐν τῷ ἱερῷ οὐ μετὰ ὄχλου οὐδὲ
μετὰ θορύβου

For Paul's fullest treatment of the collection, which space precludes providing in full here, see 2 Corinthians, chapters 8 and 9. On contributing to the needs of the saints more generally, see Rom 12:8; 12:13; Eph 4:28; 1 Tim 3:2; 5:9–10; 6:17–19; Titus 1:7–8; Acts 16:14–15; 20:33–35; 21:4; 21:8; 21:15–16; 24:22–23; 27:3.

158. Community Discipline

1 Cor 5:1–13

Ὅλως ἀκούεται ἐν ὑμῖν πορνεία, καὶ
τοιαύτη πορνεία ἥτις οὐδὲ ἐν τοῖς ἔθνε-
σιν, ὥστε γυναῖκά τινα τοῦ πατρὸς ἔχειν.
2 καὶ ὑμεῖς πεφυσιωμένοι ἐστὲ καὶ οὐχὶ
μᾶλλον ἐπενθήσατε, ἵνα ἀρθῇ ἐκ μέσου
ὑμῶν ὁ τὸ ἔργον τοῦτο πράξας; 3 ἐγὼ
μὲν γάρ, ἀπὼν τῷ σώματι παρὼν δὲ τῷ
πνεύματι, ἤδη κέκρικα ὡς παρὼν τὸν
οὕτως τοῦτο κατεργασάμενον· 4 ἐν τῷ
ὀνόματι τοῦ κυρίου [ἡμῶν] Ἰησοῦ συνα-
χθέντων ὑμῶν καὶ τοῦ ἐμοῦ πνεύματος
σὺν τῇ δυνάμει τοῦ κυρίου ἡμῶν Ἰησοῦ,
5 παραδοῦναι τὸν τοιοῦτον τῷ σατανᾷ
εἰς ὄλεθρον τῆς σαρκός, ἵνα τὸ πνεῦμα
σωθῇ ἐν τῇ ἡμέρᾳ τοῦ ⸀κυρίου. 6 Οὐ
καλὸν τὸ καύχημα ὑμῶν. οὐκ οἴδατε
ὅτι μικρὰ ζύμη ὅλον τὸ φύραμα ζυμοῖ;
7 ἐκκαθάρατε τὴν παλαιὰν ζύμην, ἵνα
ἦτε νέον φύραμα, καθώς ἐστε ἄζυμοι·
καὶ γὰρ τὸ πάσχα ἡμῶν ἐτύθη Χριστός.
8 ὥστε ἑορτάζωμεν μὴ ἐν ζύμῃ παλαιᾷ
μηδὲ ἐν ζύμῃ κακίας καὶ πονηρίας ἀλλ'
ἐν ἀζύμοις εἰλικρινείας καὶ ἀληθείας.
9 Ἔγραψα ὑμῖν ἐν τῇ ἐπιστολῇ μὴ συν-
αναμίγνυσθαι πόρνοις, 10 οὐ πάντως
τοῖς πόρνοις τοῦ κόσμου τούτου ἢ τοῖς
πλεονέκταις καὶ ἅρπαξιν ἢ εἰδωλολά-
τραις, ἐπεὶ ὠφείλετε ἄρα ἐκ τοῦ κό-
σμου ἐξελθεῖν. 11 νῦν δὲ ἔγραψα ὑμῖν
μὴ συναναμίγνυσθαι ἐάν τις ἀδελφὸς
ὀνομαζόμενος ᾖ πόρνος ἢ πλεονέκτης
ἢ εἰδωλολάτρης ἢ λοίδορος ἢ μέθυσος
ἢ ἅρπαξ, τῷ τοιούτῳ μηδὲ συνεσθίειν.
12 τί γάρ μοι τοὺς ἔξω κρίνειν; οὐχὶ τοὺς
ἔσω ὑμεῖς κρίνετε; 13 τοὺς δὲ ἔξω ὁ θεὸς
κρινεῖ. ἐξάρατε τὸν πονηρὸν ἐξ ὑμῶν
αὐτῶν.

2 Thess 3:6–15

Παραγγέλλομεν δὲ ὑμῖν, ἀδελφοί, ἐν ὀνό-
ματι τοῦ κυρίου [ἡμῶν] Ἰησοῦ Χριστοῦ
στέλλεσθαι ὑμᾶς ἀπὸ παντὸς ἀδελφοῦ
ἀτάκτως περιπατοῦντος καὶ μὴ κατὰ
τὴν παράδοσιν ἣν ⸀παρελάβοσαν παρ'
ἡμῶν. 7 Αὐτοὶ γὰρ οἴδατε πῶς δεῖ μιμεῖ-
σθαι ἡμᾶς, ὅτι οὐκ ἠτακτήσαμεν ἐν ὑμῖν
8 οὐδὲ δωρεὰν ἄρτον ἐφάγομεν παρά
τινος, ἀλλ' ἐν κόπῳ καὶ μόχθῳ νυκτὸς
καὶ ἡμέρας ἐργαζόμενοι πρὸς τὸ μὴ ἐπι-
βαρῆσαί τινα ὑμῶν· 9 οὐχ ὅτι οὐκ ἔχομεν
ἐξουσίαν, ἀλλ' ἵνα ἑαυτοὺς τύπον δῶμεν
ὑμῖν εἰς τὸ μιμεῖσθαι ἡμᾶς. 10 καὶ γὰρ
ὅτε ἦμεν πρὸς ὑμᾶς, τοῦτο παρηγγέλλο-
μεν ὑμῖν, ὅτι εἴ τις οὐ θέλει ἐργάζεσθαι
μηδὲ ἐσθιέτω. 11 Ἀκούομεν γάρ τινας
περιπατοῦντας ἐν ὑμῖν ἀτάκτως μηδὲν
ἐργαζομένους ἀλλὰ περιεργαζομένους·
12 τοῖς δὲ τοιούτοις παραγγέλλομεν καὶ
παρακαλοῦμεν ἐν κυρίῳ Ἰησοῦ Χριστῷ,
ἵνα μετὰ ἡσυχίας ἐργαζόμενοι τὸν ἑαυτῶν
ἄρτον ἐσθίωσιν. 13 Ὑμεῖς δέ, ἀδελφοί,
μὴ ἐγκακήσητε καλοποιοῦντες. 14 Εἰ
δέ τις οὐχ ὑπακούει τῷ λόγῳ ἡμῶν διὰ
τῆς ἐπιστολῆς, τοῦτον σημειοῦσθε μὴ
συναναμίγνυσθαι αὐτῷ, ἵνα ἐντραπῇ·
15 καὶ μὴ ὡς ἐχθρὸν ἡγεῖσθε, ἀλλὰ νου-
θετεῖτε ὡς ἀδελφόν.

1 Tim 1:18–20

Ταύτην τὴν παραγγελίαν παρατίθεμαί
σοι, τέκνον Τιμόθεε, κατὰ τὰς προαγού-
σας ἐπὶ σὲ προφητείας, ἵνα στρατεύῃ ἐν
αὐταῖς τὴν καλὴν στρατείαν 19 ἔχων
πίστιν καὶ ἀγαθὴν συνείδησιν, ἥν τινες
ἀπωσάμενοι περὶ τὴν πίστιν ἐναυάγησαν,
20 ὧν ἐστιν Ὑμέναιος καὶ Ἀλέξανδρος,
οὓς παρέδωκα τῷ σατανᾷ, ἵνα παιδευ-
θῶσιν μὴ βλασφημεῖν.

Cf. 2 Cor 10:1–6; 12:20–21; 13:1–4; 13:10; 1 Tim 5:19–22.

See also § 159 Restoration of a Fallen Brother or Sister.

159. Restoration of a Fallen Brother or Sister

2 Cor 2:5–11

Εἰ δέ τις λελύπηκεν, οὐκ ἐμὲ λελύπη-
κεν, ἀλλὰ ἀπὸ μέρους, ἵνα μὴ ἐπιβαρῶ,
πάντας ὑμᾶς. 6 ἱκανὸν τῷ τοιούτῳ ἡ
ἐπιτιμία αὕτη ἡ ὑπὸ τῶν πλειόνων,
7 ὥστε τοὐναντίον μᾶλλον ὑμᾶς χα-
ρίσασθαι καὶ παρακαλέσαι, μή πως τῇ
περισσοτέρᾳ λύπῃ καταποθῇ ὁ τοιοῦτος.
8 διὸ παρακαλῶ ὑμᾶς κυρῶσαι εἰς αὐτὸν
ἀγάπην· 9 εἰς τοῦτο γὰρ καὶ ἔγραψα, ἵνα
γνῶ τὴν δοκιμὴν ὑμῶν, εἰ εἰς πάντα ὑπή-
κοοί ἐστε. 10 ᾧ δέ τι χαρίζεσθε, κἀγώ· καὶ
γὰρ ἐγὼ ὃ κεχάρισμαι, εἴ τι κεχάρισμαι,
δι' ὑμᾶς ἐν προσώπῳ Χριστοῦ, 11 ἵνα μὴ
πλεονεκτηθῶμεν ὑπὸ τοῦ σατανᾶ· οὐ γὰρ
αὐτοῦ τὰ νοήματα ἀγνοοῦμεν.

2 Cor 7:8–13

Ὅτι εἰ καὶ ἐλύπησα ὑμᾶς ἐν τῇ ἐπιστολῇ,
οὐ μεταμέλομαι· εἰ καὶ μετεμελόμην,
βλέπω [γὰρ] ὅτι ἡ ἐπιστολὴ ἐκείνη εἰ καὶ
πρὸς ὥραν ἐλύπησεν ὑμᾶς, 9 νῦν χαίρω,
οὐχ ὅτι ἐλυπήθητε ἀλλ' ὅτι ἐλυπήθητε
εἰς μετάνοιαν· ἐλυπήθητε γὰρ κατὰ θεόν,
ἵνα ἐν μηδενὶ ζημιωθῆτε ἐξ ἡμῶν. 10 ἡ
γὰρ κατὰ θεὸν λύπη μετάνοιαν εἰς
σωτηρίαν ἀμεταμέλητον ἐργάζεται·
ἡ δὲ τοῦ κόσμου λύπη θάνατον κα-
τεργάζεται. 11 ἰδοὺ γὰρ αὐτὸ τοῦτο τὸ
κατὰ θεὸν λυπηθῆναι πόσην κατειργά-
σατο ὑμῖν σπουδήν, ἀλλὰ ἀπολογίαν,
ἀλλὰ ἀγανάκτησιν, ἀλλὰ φόβον, ἀλλὰ

§ 158 1 Cor 5:5 ***κυριου*** 𝔓46 B 1739] *add.* Ιησου 𝔓61vid ℵ *Byz* ¦ *add.* Ιησου Χριστου D ¦ *add.* ημων Ιησου Χριστου A 33. 1881 2 Thess 3:6 ***παρελαβοσαν*** ℵ* A (D*) 33] παρελαβον ℵ2 D2 1739. 1881 *Byz* ¦ παρελαβετε B

fices. **18** While I was doing this, they found me in the temple, completing the rite of purification, without any crowd or disturbance.

For Paul's fullest treatment of the collection, which space precludes providing in full here, see 2 Corinthians, chapters 8 and 9. On contributing to the needs of the saints more generally, see Rom 12:8; 12:13; Eph 4:28; 1 Tim 3:2; 5:9–10; 6:17–19; Titus 1:7–8; Acts 16:14–15; 20:33–35; 21:4; 21:8; 21:15–16; 24:22–23; 27:3.

158. Community Discipline

1 Cor 5:1–13

It is actually reported that there is sexual immorality among you, and of a kind that is not found even among pagans; for a man is living with his father's wife. **2** And you are arrogant! Should you not rather have mourned, so that he who has done this would have been removed from among you? **3** For though absent in body, I am present in spirit; and as if present I have already pronounced judgment **4** in the name of the Lord Jesus on the man who has done such a thing. When you are assembled, and my spirit is present with the power of our Lord Jesus, **5** you are to hand this man over to Satan for the destruction of the flesh, so that his spirit may be saved in the day of the Lord.[a] **6** Your boasting is not a good thing. Do you not know that a little yeast leavens the whole batch of dough? **7** Clean out the old yeast so that you may be a new batch, as you really are unleavened. For our paschal lamb, Christ, has been sacrificed. **8** Therefore, let us celebrate the festival, not with the old yeast, the yeast of malice and evil, but with the unleavened bread of sincerity and truth. **9** I wrote to you in my letter not to associate with sexually immoral persons— **10** not at all meaning the immoral of this world, or the greedy and robbers, or idolaters, since you would then need to go out of the world. **11** But now I am writing to you not to associate with anyone who bears the name of brother or sister who is sexually immoral or greedy, or is an idolater, reviler, drunkard, or robber. Do not even eat with such a one. **12** For what have I to do with judging those outside? Is it not those who are inside that you are to judge? **13** God will judge those outside. "Drive out the wicked person from among you."

2 Thess 3:6–15

Now we command you, beloved, in the name of our Lord Jesus Christ, to keep away from believers who are living in idleness and not according to the tradition that they[b] received from us. **7** For you yourselves know how you ought to imitate us; we were not idle when we were with you, **8** and we did not eat anyone's bread without paying for it; but with toil and labor we worked night and day, so that we might not burden any of you. **9** This was not because we do not have that right, but in order to give you an example to imitate. **10** For even when we were with you, we gave you this command: Anyone unwilling to work should not eat. **11** For we hear that some of you are living in idleness, mere busybodies, not doing any work. **12** Now such persons we command and exhort in the Lord Jesus Christ to do their work quietly and to earn their own living. **13** Brothers and sisters, do not be weary in doing what is right. **14** Take note of those who do not obey what we say in this letter; have nothing to do with them, so that they may be ashamed. **15** Do not regard them as enemies, but warn them as believers.

1 Tim 1:18–20

I am giving you these instructions, Timothy, my child, in accordance with the prophecies made earlier about you, so that by following them you may fight the good fight, **19** having faith and a good conscience. By rejecting conscience, certain persons have suffered shipwreck in the faith; **20** among them are Hymenaeus and Alexander, whom I have turned over to Satan, so that they may learn not to blaspheme.

Cf. 2 Cor 10:1–6; 12:20–21; 13:1–4; 13:10; 1 Tim 5:19–22.

See also § 159 Restoration of a Fallen Brother or Sister.

159. Restoration of a Fallen Brother or Sister

2 Cor 2:5–11

But if anyone has caused pain, he has caused it not to me, but to some extent—not to exaggerate it—to all of you. **6** This punishment by the majority is enough for such a person; **7** so now instead you should forgive and console him, so that he may not be overwhelmed by excessive sorrow. **8** So I urge you to reaffirm your love for him. **9** I wrote for this reason: to test you and to know whether you are obedient in everything. **10** Anyone whom you forgive, I also forgive. What I have forgiven, if I have forgiven anything, has been for your sake in the presence of Christ. **11** And we do this so that we may not be outwitted by Satan; for we are not ignorant of his designs.

2 Cor 7:8–13

For even if I made you sorry with my letter, I do not regret it (though I did regret it, for I see that I grieved you with that letter, though only briefly). **9** Now I rejoice, not because you were grieved, but because your grief led to repentance; for you felt a godly grief, so that you were not harmed in any way by us. **10** For godly grief produces a repentance that leads to salvation and brings no regret, but worldly grief produces death. **11** For see what earnestness this godly grief has produced in you, what eagerness to clear yourselves, what indignation, what alarm, what longing,

§ 158 [a] **1 Cor 5:5** *the Lord* Other ancient authorities add *Jesus* [b] **2 Thess 3:6** *they* Other ancient authorities read *you*

ἐπιπόθησιν, ἀλλὰ ζῆλον, ἀλλὰ ἐκδίκησιν. ἐν παντὶ συνεστήσατε ἑαυτοὺς ἁγνοὺς εἶναι τῷ πράγματι. 12 ἄρα εἰ καὶ ἔγραψα ὑμῖν, οὐχ ἕνεκεν τοῦ ἀδικήσαντος οὐδὲ ἕνεκεν τοῦ ἀδικηθέντος ἀλλ᾽ ἕνεκεν τοῦ φανερωθῆναι τὴν σπουδὴν ὑμῶν τὴν ὑπὲρ ἡμῶν πρὸς ὑμᾶς ἐνώπιον τοῦ θεοῦ. 13 διὰ τοῦτο παρακεκλήμεθα. Ἐπὶ δὲ τῇ παρακλήσει ἡμῶν περισσοτέρως μᾶλλον ἐχάρημεν ἐπὶ τῇ χαρᾷ Τίτου, ὅτι ἀναπέπαυται τὸ πνεῦμα αὐτοῦ ἀπὸ πάντων ὑμῶν

Gal 6:1–5

Ἀδελφοί, ἐὰν καὶ προλημφθῇ ἄνθρωπος ἔν τινι παραπτώματι, ὑμεῖς οἱ πνευματικοὶ καταρτίζετε τὸν τοιοῦτον ἐν πνεύματι πραΰτητος, σκοπῶν σεαυτὸν μὴ καὶ σὺ πειρασθῇς. 2 Ἀλλήλων τὰ βάρη βαστάζετε καὶ οὕτως ⸀ἀναπληρώσετε τὸν νόμον τοῦ Χριστοῦ. 3 εἰ γὰρ δοκεῖ τις εἶναί τι μηδὲν ὤν, φρεναπατᾷ ἑαυτόν. 4 τὸ δὲ ἔργον ἑαυτοῦ δοκιμαζέτω ἕκαστος, καὶ τότε εἰς ἑαυτὸν μόνον τὸ καύχημα ἕξει καὶ οὐκ εἰς τὸν ἕτερον· 5 ἕκαστος γὰρ τὸ ἴδιον φορτίον βαστάσει.

See also § 158 Community Discipline.

160. *Self-Examination*

1 Cor 11:27–32

Ὥστε ὃς ἂν ἐσθίῃ τὸν ἄρτον ἢ πίνῃ τὸ ποτήριον τοῦ κυρίου ἀναξίως, ἔνοχος ἔσται τοῦ σώματος καὶ τοῦ αἵματος τοῦ κυρίου. 28 δοκιμαζέτω δὲ ἄνθρωπος ἑαυτὸν καὶ οὕτως ἐκ τοῦ ἄρτου ἐσθιέτω καὶ ἐκ τοῦ ποτηρίου πινέτω· 29 ὁ γὰρ ἐσθίων καὶ ⸀πίνων κρίμα ἑαυτῷ ἐσθίει καὶ πίνει μὴ διακρίνων τὸ ⸀σῶμα. 30 διὰ τοῦτο ἐν ὑμῖν πολλοὶ ἀσθενεῖς καὶ ἄρρωστοι καὶ κοιμῶνται ἱκανοί. 31 εἰ δὲ ἑαυτοὺς διεκρίνομεν, οὐκ ἂν ἐκρινόμεθα· 32 κρινόμενοι δὲ ὑπὸ [τοῦ] κυρίου παιδευόμεθα, ἵνα μὴ σὺν τῷ κόσμῳ κατακριθῶμεν.

2 Cor 13:5–10

Ἑαυτοὺς πειράζετε εἰ ἐστὲ ἐν τῇ πίστει, ἑαυτοὺς δοκιμάζετε· ἢ οὐκ ἐπιγινώσκετε ἑαυτοὺς ὅτι Ἰησοῦς Χριστὸς ἐν ὑμῖν; εἰ μήτι ἀδόκιμοί ἐστε. 6 ἐλπίζω δὲ ὅτι γνώσεσθε ὅτι ἡμεῖς οὐκ ἐσμὲν ἀδόκιμοι. 7 εὐχόμεθα δὲ πρὸς τὸν θεὸν μὴ ποιῆσαι ὑμᾶς κακὸν μηδέν, οὐχ ἵνα ἡμεῖς δόκιμοι φανῶμεν, ἀλλ᾽ ἵνα ὑμεῖς τὸ καλὸν ποιῆτε, ἡμεῖς δὲ ὡς ἀδόκιμοι ὦμεν. 8 οὐ γὰρ δυνάμεθά τι κατὰ τῆς ἀληθείας ἀλλὰ ὑπὲρ τῆς ἀληθείας. 9 χαίρομεν γὰρ ὅταν ἡμεῖς ἀσθενῶμεν, ὑμεῖς δὲ δυνατοὶ ἦτε· τοῦτο καὶ εὐχόμεθα, τὴν ὑμῶν κατάρτισιν. 10 Διὰ τοῦτο ταῦτα ἀπὼν γράφω, ἵνα παρὼν μὴ ἀποτόμως χρήσωμαι κατὰ τὴν ἐξουσίαν ἣν ὁ κύριος ἔδωκέν μοι εἰς οἰκοδομὴν καὶ οὐκ εἰς καθαίρεσιν.

Gal 6:1–5

Ἀδελφοί, ἐὰν καὶ προλημφθῇ ἄνθρωπος ἔν τινι παραπτώματι, ὑμεῖς οἱ πνευματικοὶ καταρτίζετε τὸν τοιοῦτον ἐν πνεύματι πραΰτητος, σκοπῶν σεαυτὸν μὴ καὶ σὺ πειρασθῇς. 2 Ἀλλήλων τὰ βάρη βαστάζετε καὶ οὕτως ⸀ἀναπληρώσετε τὸν νόμον τοῦ Χριστοῦ. 3 εἰ γὰρ δοκεῖ τις εἶναί τι μηδὲν ὤν, φρεναπατᾷ ἑαυτόν. 4 τὸ δὲ ἔργον ἑαυτοῦ δοκιμαζέτω ἕκαστος, καὶ τότε εἰς ἑαυτὸν μόνον τὸ καύχημα ἕξει καὶ οὐκ εἰς τὸν ἕτερον· 5 ἕκαστος γὰρ τὸ ἴδιον φορτίον βαστάσει.

161. *Gentleness toward All*

Gal 6:1–5

Ἀδελφοί, ἐὰν καὶ προλημφθῇ ἄνθρωπος ἔν τινι παραπτώματι, ὑμεῖς οἱ πνευματικοὶ καταρτίζετε τὸν τοιοῦτον ἐν πνεύματι πραΰτητος, σκοπῶν σεαυτὸν μὴ καὶ σὺ πειρασθῇς. 2 Ἀλλήλων τὰ βάρη βαστάζετε καὶ οὕτως ⸀ἀναπληρώσετε τὸν νόμον τοῦ Χριστοῦ. 3 εἰ γὰρ δοκεῖ τις εἶναί τι μηδὲν ὤν, φρεναπατᾷ ἑαυτόν. 4 τὸ δὲ ἔργον ἑαυτοῦ δοκιμαζέτω ἕκαστος, καὶ τότε εἰς ἑαυτὸν μόνον τὸ καύχημα ἕξει καὶ οὐκ εἰς τὸν ἕτερον· 5 ἕκαστος γὰρ τὸ ἴδιον φορτίον βαστάσει.

Eph 4:1–3

Παρακαλῶ οὖν ὑμᾶς ἐγὼ ὁ δέσμιος ἐν κυρίῳ ἀξίως περιπατῆσαι τῆς κλήσεως ἧς ἐκλήθητε, 2 μετὰ πάσης ταπεινοφροσύνης καὶ πραΰτητος, μετὰ μακροθυμίας, ἀνεχόμενοι ἀλλήλων ἐν ἀγάπῃ, 3 σπουδάζοντες τηρεῖν τὴν ἑνότητα τοῦ πνεύματος ἐν τῷ συνδέσμῳ τῆς εἰρήνης

Eph 4:14–15

ἵνα μηκέτι ὦμεν νήπιοι, κλυδωνιζόμενοι καὶ περιφερόμενοι παντὶ ἀνέμῳ τῆς διδασκαλίας ἐν τῇ κυβείᾳ τῶν ἀνθρώπων, ἐν πανουργίᾳ πρὸς τὴν μεθοδείαν τῆς πλάνης, 15 ἀληθεύοντες δὲ ἐν ἀγάπῃ αὐξήσωμεν εἰς αὐτὸν τὰ πάντα, ὅς ἐστιν ἡ κεφαλή, Χριστός

Phil 4:4–5

Χαίρετε ἐν κυρίῳ πάντοτε· πάλιν ἐρῶ, χαίρετε. 5 τὸ ἐπιεικὲς ὑμῶν γνωσθήτω πᾶσιν ἀνθρώποις. ὁ κύριος ἐγγύς.

Col 3:12

Ἐνδύσασθε οὖν, ὡς ἐκλεκτοὶ τοῦ θεοῦ ἅγιοι καὶ ἠγαπημένοι, σπλάγχνα οἰκτιρμοῦ χρηστότητα ταπεινοφροσύνην πραΰτητα μακροθυμίαν

1 Thess 2:4–8

ἀλλὰ καθὼς δεδοκιμάσμεθα ὑπὸ τοῦ θεοῦ πιστευθῆναι τὸ εὐαγγέλιον, οὕτως λαλοῦμεν, οὐχ ὡς ἀνθρώποις ἀρέσκοντες ἀλλὰ θεῷ τῷ δοκιμάζοντι τὰς καρδίας ἡμῶν. 5 Οὔτε γάρ ποτε ἐν λόγῳ κολακείας

§ 159 Gal 6:2 ***αναπληρωσετε*** (𝔓46) B] αναπληρωσατε ℵ A C D 33. 1739. 1881 *Byz* **§ 160** 1 Cor 11:29 ***πινων*** 𝔓46 ℵ* A B C* 33. 1739] *add.* αναξιως ℵ2 C3 D 1881 *Byz* • ***σωμα*** 𝔓46 ℵ* A B C* 33. 1739. 1881*] *add.* του κυριου ℵ2 C3 D 1881c *Byz* Gal 6:2 ***αναπληρωσετε*** (𝔓46) B] αναπληρωσατε ℵ A C D 33. 1739. 1881 *Byz* **§ 161** Gal 6:2 ***αναπληρωσετε*** (𝔓46) B] αναπληρωσατε ℵ A C D 33. 1739. 1881 *Byz*

what zeal, what punishment! At every point you have proved yourselves guiltless in the matter. 12 So although I wrote to you, it was not on account of the one who did the wrong, nor on account of the one who was wronged, but in order that your zeal for us might be made known to you before God. 13 In this we find comfort. In addition to our own consolation, we rejoiced still more at the joy of Titus, because his mind has been set at rest by all of you.

Gal 6:1–5

My friends, if anyone is detected in a transgression, you who have received the Spirit should restore such a one in a spirit of gentleness. Take care that you yourselves are not tempted. 2 Bear one another's burdens, and in this way you will fulfill[a] the law of Christ. 3 For if those who are nothing think they are something, they deceive themselves. 4 All must test their own work; then that work, rather than their neighbor's work, will become a cause for pride. 5 For all must carry their own loads.

See also § 158 Community Discipline.

160. *Self-Examination*

1 Cor 11:27–32

Whoever, therefore, eats the bread or drinks the cup of the Lord in an unworthy manner will be answerable for the body and blood of the Lord. 28 Examine yourselves, and only then eat of the bread and drink of the cup. 29 For all who eat and drink [a] without discerning the body,[b] eat and drink judgment against themselves. 30 For this reason many of you are weak and ill, and some have died. 31 But if we judged ourselves, we would not be judged. 32 But when we are judged by the Lord, we are disciplined so that we may not be condemned along with the world.

2 Cor 13:5–10

Examine yourselves to see whether you are living in the faith. Test yourselves. Do you not realize that Jesus Christ is in you?—unless, indeed, you fail to meet the test! 6 I hope you will find out that we have not failed. 7 But we pray to God that you may not do anything wrong—not that we may appear to have met the test, but that you may do what is right, though we may seem to have failed. 8 For we cannot do anything against the truth, but only for the truth. 9 For we rejoice when we are weak and you are strong. This is what we pray for, that you may become perfect. 10 So I write these things while I am away from you, so that when I come, I may not have to be severe in using the authority that the Lord has given me for building up and not for tearing down.

Gal 6:1–5

My friends, if anyone is detected in a transgression, you who have received the Spirit should restore such a one in a spirit of gentleness. Take care that you yourselves are not tempted. 2 Bear one another's burdens, and in this way you will fulfill[c] the law of Christ. 3 For if those who are nothing think they are something, they deceive themselves. 4 All must test their own work; then that work, rather than their neighbor's work, will become a cause for pride. 5 For all must carry their own loads.

161. *Gentleness toward All*

Gal 6:1–5

My friends, if anyone is detected in a transgression, you who have received the Spirit should restore such a one in a spirit of gentleness. Take care that you yourselves are not tempted. 2 Bear one another's burdens, and in this way you will fulfill[a] the law of Christ. 3 For if those who are nothing think they are something, they deceive themselves. 4 All must test their own work; then that work, rather than their neighbor's work, will become a cause for pride. 5 For all must carry their own loads.

Eph 4:1–3

I therefore, the prisoner in the Lord, beg you to lead a life worthy of the calling to which you have been called, 2 with all humility and gentleness, with patience, bearing with one another in love, 3 making every effort to maintain the unity of the Spirit in the bond of peace.

Eph 4:14–15

We must no longer be children, tossed to and fro and blown about by every wind of doctrine, by people's trickery, by their craftiness in deceitful scheming. 15 But speaking the truth in love, we must grow up in every way into him who is the head, into Christ

Phil 4:4–5

Rejoice in the Lord always; again I will say, Rejoice. 5 Let your gentleness be known to everyone. The Lord is near.

Col 3:12

As God's chosen ones, holy and beloved, clothe yourselves with compassion, kindness, humility, meekness, and patience.

1 Thess 2:4–8

but just as we have been approved by God to be entrusted with the message of the gospel, even so we speak, not to please mortals, but to please God who tests our hearts. 5 As you know and as

§ 159 [a] **Gal 6:2** ***in this way you will fulfill*** Other ancient authorities read *in this way fulfill* **§ 160** [a] **1 Cor 11:29** ***eat and drink*** Other ancient authorities add *in an unworthy manner* [b] **1 Cor 11:29** ***the body*** Other ancient authorities read *the Lord's body* [c] **Gal 6:2** ***in this way you will fulfill*** Other ancient authorities read *in this way fulfill* **§ 161** [a] **Gal 6:2** ***in this way you will fulfill*** Other ancient authorities read *in this way fulfill*

ἐγενήθημεν, καθὼς οἴδατε, οὔτε ἐν προ-
φάσει πλεονεξίας, θεὸς μάρτυς, **6** οὔτε
ζητοῦντες ἐξ ἀνθρώπων δόξαν οὔτε ἀφ'
ὑμῶν οὔτε ἀπ' ἄλλων, **7** δυνάμενοι ἐν
βάρει εἶναι ὡς Χριστοῦ ἀπόστολοι. ἀλλὰ
ἐγενήθημεν ⸀νήπιοι ἐν μέσῳ ὑμῶν, ὡς
ἐὰν τροφὸς θάλπῃ τὰ ἑαυτῆς τέκνα,
8 οὕτως ὁμειρόμενοι ὑμῶν εὐδοκοῦμεν
μεταδοῦναι ὑμῖν οὐ μόνον τὸ εὐαγγέλιον
τοῦ θεοῦ ἀλλὰ καὶ τὰς ἑαυτῶν ψυχάς,
διότι ἀγαπητοὶ ἡμῖν ἐγενήθητε.

1 Thess 5:14

Παρακαλοῦμεν δὲ ὑμᾶς, ἀδελφοί, νου-
θετεῖτε τοὺς ἀτάκτους, παραμυθεῖσθε τοὺς
ὀλιγοψύχους, ἀντέχεσθε τῶν ἀσθενῶν,
μακροθυμεῖτε πρὸς πάντας.

1 Tim 3:2–3

δεῖ οὖν τὸν ἐπίσκοπον ἀνεπίλημπτον
εἶναι, μιᾶς γυναικὸς ἄνδρα, νηφάλιον
σώφρονα κόσμιον φιλόξενον διδακτι-
κόν, **3** μὴ πάροινον μὴ πλήκτην, ἀλλὰ
ἐπιεικῆ ἄμαχον ἀφιλάργυρον

2 Tim 2:22–26

Τὰς δὲ νεωτερικὰς ἐπιθυμίας φεῦγε,
δίωκε δὲ δικαιοσύνην πίστιν ἀγάπην
εἰρήνην μετὰ τῶν ἐπικαλουμένων τὸν
κύριον ἐκ καθαρᾶς καρδίας. **23** τὰς δὲ μω-
ρὰς καὶ ἀπαιδεύτους ζητήσεις παραιτοῦ,
εἰδὼς ὅτι γεννῶσιν μάχας· **24** δοῦλον δὲ
κυρίου οὐ δεῖ μάχεσθαι ἀλλὰ ἤπιον εἶναι
πρὸς πάντας, διδακτικόν, ἀνεξίκακον,
25 ἐν πραΰτητι παιδεύοντα τοὺς ἀντι-
διατιθεμένους, μήποτε δώῃ αὐτοῖς ὁ
θεὸς μετάνοιαν εἰς ἐπίγνωσιν ἀληθείας
26 καὶ ἀνανήψωσιν ἐκ τῆς τοῦ διαβόλου
παγίδος, ἐζωγρημένοι ὑπ' αὐτοῦ εἰς τὸ
ἐκείνου θέλημα.

Titus 3:1–2

Ὑπομίμνῃσκε αὐτοὺς ἀρχαῖς ἐξουσίαις
ὑποτάσσεσθαι, πειθαρχεῖν, πρὸς πᾶν
ἔργον ἀγαθὸν ἑτοίμους εἶναι, **2** μηδένα
βλασφημεῖν, ἀμάχους εἶναι, ἐπιεικεῖς,
πᾶσαν ἐνδεικνυμένους πραΰτητα πρὸς
πάντας ἀνθρώπους.

Cf. Gal 5:22–23; 1 Tim 6:11; 2 Tim 4:2.

See also § 125 Humble Servanthood.

162. Paul Prior to His Conversion and Call

1 Cor 15:9

Ἐγὼ γάρ εἰμι ὁ ἐλάχιστος τῶν ἀποστόλων
ὃς οὐκ εἰμὶ ἱκανὸς καλεῖσθαι ἀπόστολος,
διότι ἐδίωξα τὴν ἐκκλησίαν τοῦ θεοῦ

Gal 1:13–14

Ἠκούσατε γὰρ τὴν ἐμὴν ἀναστροφήν
ποτε ἐν τῷ Ἰουδαϊσμῷ, ὅτι καθ' ὑπερ-
βολὴν ἐδίωκον τὴν ἐκκλησίαν τοῦ θεοῦ
καὶ ἐπόρθουν αὐτήν, **14** καὶ προέκοπτον
ἐν τῷ Ἰουδαϊσμῷ ὑπὲρ πολλοὺς συνηλι-
κιώτας ἐν τῷ γένει μου, περισσοτέρως
ζηλωτὴς ὑπάρχων τῶν πατρικῶν μου
παραδόσεων.

Gal 1:22–23

ἤμην δὲ ἀγνοούμενος τῷ προσώπῳ ταῖς
ἐκκλησίαις τῆς Ἰουδαίας ταῖς ἐν Χριστῷ.
23 μόνον δὲ ἀκούοντες ἦσαν ὅτι ὁ διώ-
κων ἡμᾶς ποτε νῦν εὐαγγελίζεται τὴν
πίστιν ἥν ποτε ἐπόρθει

Phil 3:4–6

καίπερ ἐγὼ ἔχων πεποίθησιν καὶ ἐν
σαρκί. Εἴ τις δοκεῖ ἄλλος πεποιθέναι ἐν
σαρκί, ἐγὼ μᾶλλον· **5** περιτομῇ ὀκταή-
μερος, ἐκ γένους Ἰσραήλ, φυλῆς Βενι-
αμίν, Ἑβραῖος ἐξ Ἑβραίων, κατὰ νόμον
Φαρισαῖος, **6** κατὰ ζῆλος διώκων τὴν
ἐκκλησίαν, κατὰ δικαιοσύνην τὴν ἐν
νόμῳ γενόμενος ἄμεμπτος.

1 Tim 1:13–15

τὸ πρότερον ὄντα βλάσφημον καὶ διώ-
κτην καὶ ὑβριστήν, ἀλλὰ ἠλεήθην, ὅτι
ἀγνοῶν ἐποίησα ἐν ἀπιστίᾳ· **14** ὑπερε-
πλεόνασεν δὲ ἡ χάρις τοῦ κυρίου ἡμῶν
μετὰ πίστεως καὶ ἀγάπης τῆς ἐν Χριστῷ
Ἰησοῦ. **15** πιστὸς ὁ λόγος καὶ πάσης ἀπο-
δοχῆς ἄξιος, ὅτι Χριστὸς Ἰησοῦς ἦλθεν
εἰς τὸν κόσμον ἁμαρτωλοὺς σῶσαι, ὧν
πρῶτός εἰμι ἐγώ.

Acts 7:54–8:3

Ἀκούοντες δὲ ταῦτα διεπρίοντο ταῖς καρ-
δίαις αὐτῶν καὶ ἔβρυχον τοὺς ὀδόντας
ἐπ' αὐτόν. **55** ὑπάρχων δὲ πλήρης πνεύ-
ματος ἁγίου ἀτενίσας εἰς τὸν οὐρανὸν
εἶδεν δόξαν θεοῦ καὶ Ἰησοῦν ἑστῶτα ἐκ
δεξιῶν τοῦ θεοῦ **56** καὶ εἶπεν· ἰδοὺ θεωρῶ
τοὺς οὐρανοὺς διηνοιγμένους καὶ τὸν
υἱὸν τοῦ ἀνθρώπου ἐκ δεξιῶν ἑστῶτα
τοῦ θεοῦ. **57** κράξαντες δὲ φωνῇ μεγάλῃ
συνέσχον τὰ ὦτα αὐτῶν καὶ ὥρμησαν
ὁμοθυμαδὸν ἐπ' αὐτὸν **58** καὶ ἐκβαλόν-
τες ἔξω τῆς πόλεως ἐλιθοβόλουν. καὶ
οἱ μάρτυρες ἀπέθεντο τὰ ἱμάτια αὐτῶν
παρὰ τοὺς πόδας νεανίου καλουμένου
Σαύλου, **59** καὶ ἐλιθοβόλουν τὸν Στέ-
φανον ἐπικαλούμενον καὶ λέγοντα·
κύριε Ἰησοῦ, δέξαι τὸ πνεῦμά μου. **60** θεὶς
δὲ τὰ γόνατα ἔκραξεν φωνῇ μεγάλῃ·
κύριε, μὴ στήσῃς αὐτοῖς ταύτην τὴν
ἁμαρτίαν. καὶ τοῦτο εἰπὼν ἐκοιμήθη.
8 Σαῦλος δὲ ἦν συνευδοκῶν τῇ ἀναι-
ρέσει αὐτοῦ. Ἐγένετο δὲ ἐν ἐκείνῃ τῇ
ἡμέρᾳ διωγμὸς μέγας ἐπὶ τὴν ἐκκλησίαν
τὴν ἐν Ἱεροσολύμοις, πάντες δὲ διεσπά-
ρησαν κατὰ τὰς χώρας τῆς Ἰουδαίας
καὶ Σαμαρείας πλὴν τῶν ἀποστόλων.
2 συνεκόμισαν δὲ τὸν Στέφανον ἄνδρες
εὐλαβεῖς καὶ ἐποίησαν κοπετὸν μέγαν
ἐπ' αὐτῷ. **3** Σαῦλος δὲ ἐλυμαίνετο τὴν
ἐκκλησίαν κατὰ τοὺς οἴκους εἰσπορευ-
όμενος, σύρων τε ἄνδρας καὶ γυναῖκας
παρεδίδου εἰς φυλακήν.

Acts 9:1–2

Ὁ δὲ Σαῦλος ἔτι ἐμπνέων ἀπειλῆς καὶ
φόνου εἰς τοὺς μαθητὰς τοῦ κυρίου,
προσελθὼν τῷ ἀρχιερεῖ **2** ᾐτήσατο παρ'
αὐτοῦ ἐπιστολὰς εἰς Δαμασκὸν πρὸς τὰς
συναγωγάς, ὅπως ἐάν τινας εὕρῃ τῆς
ὁδοῦ ὄντας, ἄνδρας τε καὶ γυναῖκας,
δεδεμένους ἀγάγῃ εἰς Ἰερουσαλήμ.

Acts 9:13–14

ἀπεκρίθη δὲ Ἁνανίας· κύριε, ἤκουσα
ἀπὸ πολλῶν περὶ τοῦ ἀνδρὸς τούτου
ὅσα κακὰ τοῖς ἁγίοις σου ἐποίησεν ἐν
Ἰερουσαλήμ· **14** καὶ ὧδε ἔχει ἐξουσίαν
παρὰ τῶν ἀρχιερέων δῆσαι πάντας τοὺς
ἐπικαλουμένους τὸ ὄνομά σου.

Acts 9:21

ἐξίσταντο δὲ πάντες οἱ ἀκούοντες καὶ
ἔλεγον· οὐχ οὗτός ἐστιν ὁ πορθήσας εἰς
Ἰερουσαλὴμ τοὺς ἐπικαλουμένους τὸ

1 Thess 2:7 *νηπιοι* 𝔓65 ℵ* B C* D* I] ηπιοι ℵ2 A C2 D2 33. 1739. 1881 *Byz*

God is our witness, we never came with words of flattery or with a pretext for greed; [6] nor did we seek praise from mortals, whether from you or from others, [7] though we might have made demands as apostles of Christ. But we were gentle[b] among you, like a nurse tenderly caring for her own children. [8] So deeply do we care for you that we are determined to share with you not only the gospel of God but also our own selves, because you have become very dear to us.

1 Thess 5:14

And we urge you, beloved, to admonish the idlers, encourage the fainthearted, help the weak, be patient with all of them.

1 Tim 3:2–3

Now a bishop must be above reproach, married only once, temperate, sensible, respectable, hospitable, an apt teacher, [3] not a drunkard, not violent but gentle, not quarrelsome, and not a lover of money.

2 Tim 2:22–26

Shun youthful passions and pursue righteousness, faith, love, and peace, along with those who call on the Lord from a pure heart. [23] Have nothing to do with stupid and senseless controversies; you know that they breed quarrels. [24] And the Lord's servant must not be quarrelsome but kindly to everyone, an apt teacher, patient, [25] correcting opponents with gentleness. God may perhaps grant that they will repent and come to know the truth, [26] and that they may escape from the snare of the devil, having been held captive by him to do his will.

Titus 3:1–2

Remind them to be subject to rulers and authorities, to be obedient, to be ready for every good work, [2] to speak evil of no one, to avoid quarreling, to be gentle, and to show every courtesy to everyone.

Cf. Gal 5:22–23; 1 Tim 6:11; 2 Tim 4:2.

See also § 125 Humble Servanthood.

162. Paul Prior to His Conversion and Call

1 Cor 15:9

For I am the least of the apostles, unfit to be called an apostle, because I persecuted the church of God.

Gal 1:13–14

You have heard, no doubt, of my earlier life in Judaism. I was violently persecuting the church of God and was trying to destroy it. [14] I advanced in Judaism beyond many among my people of the same age, for I was far more zealous for the traditions of my ancestors.

Gal 1:22–23

and I was still unknown by sight to the churches of Judea that are in Christ; [23] they only heard it said, "The one who formerly was persecuting us is now proclaiming the faith he once tried to destroy."

Phil 3:4–6

even though I, too, have reason for confidence in the flesh. If anyone else has reason to be confident in the flesh, I have more: [5] circumcised on the eighth day, a member of the people of Israel, of the tribe of Benjamin, a Hebrew born of Hebrews; as to the law, a Pharisee; [6] as to zeal, a persecutor of the church; as to righteousness under the law, blameless.

1 Tim 1:13–15

even though I was formerly a blasphemer, a persecutor, and a man of violence. But I received mercy because I had acted ignorantly in unbelief, [14] and the grace of our Lord overflowed for me with the faith and love that are in Christ Jesus. [15] The saying is sure and worthy of full acceptance, that Christ Jesus came into the world to save sinners—of whom I am the foremost.

Acts 7:54–8:3

When they heard these things, they became enraged and ground their teeth at Stephen. [55] But filled with the Holy Spirit, he gazed into heaven and saw the glory of God and Jesus standing at the right hand of God. [56] "Look," he said, "I see the heavens opened and the Son of Man standing at the right hand of God!" [57] But they covered their ears, and with a loud shout all rushed together against him. [58] Then they dragged him out of the city and began to stone him; and the witnesses laid their coats at the feet of a young man named Saul. [59] While they were stoning Stephen, he prayed, "Lord Jesus, receive my spirit." [60] Then he knelt down and cried out in a loud voice, "Lord, do not hold this sin against them." When he had said this, he died. **8** And Saul approved of their killing him. That day a severe persecution began against the church in Jerusalem, and all except the apostles were scattered throughout the countryside of Judea and Samaria. [2] Devout men buried Stephen and made loud lamentation over him. [3] But Saul was ravaging the church by entering house after house; dragging off both men and women, he committed them to prison.

Acts 9:1–2

Meanwhile Saul, still breathing threats and murder against the disciples of the Lord, went to the high priest [2] and asked him for letters to the synagogues at Damascus, so that if he found any who belonged to the Way, men or women, he might bring them bound to Jerusalem.

Acts 9:13–14

But Ananias answered, "Lord, I have heard from many about this man, how much evil he has done to your saints in Jerusalem; [14] and here he has authority from the chief priests to bind all who invoke your name."

Acts 9:21

All who heard him were amazed and said, "Is not this the man who made havoc in Jerusalem among those who

[b] **1 Thess 2:7** *gentle* Other ancient authorities read *infants*

ὄνομα τοῦτο, καὶ ὧδε εἰς τοῦτο ἐληλύθει
ἵνα δεδεμένους αὐτοὺς ἀγάγῃ ἐπὶ τοὺς
ἀρχιερεῖς;

Acts 22:1–5

Ἄνδρες ἀδελφοὶ καὶ πατέρες, ἀκού-
σατέ μου τῆς πρὸς ὑμᾶς νυνὶ ἀπολογίας.
2 ἀκούσαντες δὲ ὅτι τῇ Ἑβραΐδι διαλέ-
κτῳ προσεφώνει αὐτοῖς, μᾶλλον πα-
ρέσχον ἡσυχίαν. καὶ φησίν· 3 ἐγώ εἰμι
ἀνὴρ Ἰουδαῖος, γεγεννημένος ἐν Ταρσῷ
τῆς Κιλικίας, ἀνατεθραμμένος δὲ ἐν τῇ
πόλει ταύτῃ, παρὰ τοὺς πόδας Γαμαλιὴλ
πεπαιδευμένος κατὰ ἀκρίβειαν τοῦ πα-
τρῴου νόμου, ζηλωτὴς ὑπάρχων τοῦ
θεοῦ καθὼς πάντες ὑμεῖς ἐστε σήμερον·
4 ὃς ταύτην τὴν ὁδὸν ἐδίωξα ἄχρι θα-
νάτου δεσμεύων καὶ παραδιδοὺς εἰς
φυλακὰς ἄνδρας τε καὶ γυναῖκας, 5 ὡς
καὶ ὁ ἀρχιερεὺς μαρτυρεῖ μοι καὶ πᾶν
τὸ πρεσβυτέριον, παρ' ὧν καὶ ἐπιστο-
λὰς δεξάμενος πρὸς τοὺς ἀδελφοὺς εἰς
Δαμασκὸν ἐπορευόμην, ἄξων καὶ τοὺς
ἐκεῖσε ὄντας δεδεμένους εἰς Ἰερουσαλὴμ
ἵνα τιμωρηθῶσιν.

Acts 22:19–20

κἀγὼ εἶπον· κύριε, αὐτοὶ ἐπίστανται ὅτι
ἐγὼ ἤμην φυλακίζων καὶ δέρων κατὰ
τὰς συναγωγὰς τοὺς πιστεύοντας ἐπὶ σέ,
20 καὶ ὅτε ἐξεχύννετο τὸ αἷμα Στεφάνου
τοῦ μάρτυρός σου, καὶ αὐτὸς ἤμην ἐφε-
στὼς καὶ συνευδοκῶν καὶ φυλάσσων τὰ
ἱμάτια τῶν ἀναιρούντων αὐτόν.

Acts 22:25–29

ὡς δὲ προέτειναν αὐτὸν τοῖς ἱμᾶσιν,
εἶπεν πρὸς τὸν ἑστῶτα ἑκατόνταρχον
ὁ Παῦλος· εἰ ἄνθρωπον Ῥωμαῖον καὶ
ἀκατάκριτον ἔξεστιν ὑμῖν μαστίζειν;
26 ἀκούσας δὲ ὁ ἑκατοντάρχης προσελ-
θὼν τῷ χιλιάρχῳ ἀπήγγειλεν λέγων· τί
μέλλεις ποιεῖν; ὁ γὰρ ἄνθρωπος οὗτος
Ῥωμαῖός ἐστιν. 27 προσελθὼν δὲ ὁ χι-
λίαρχος εἶπεν αὐτῷ· λέγε μοι, σὺ Ῥω-
μαῖος εἶ; ὁ δὲ ἔφη· ναί. 28 ἀπεκρίθη δὲ ὁ
χιλίαρχος· ἐγὼ πολλοῦ κεφαλαίου τὴν
πολιτείαν ταύτην ἐκτησάμην. ὁ δὲ Παῦλος
ἔφη· ἐγὼ δὲ καὶ γεγέννημαι. 29 εὐθέως
οὖν ἀπέστησαν ἀπ' αὐτοῦ οἱ μέλλοντες
αὐτὸν ἀνετάζειν, καὶ ὁ χιλίαρχος δὲ
ἐφοβήθη ἐπιγνοὺς ὅτι Ῥωμαῖός ἐστιν
καὶ ὅτι αὐτὸν ἦν δεδεκώς.

Acts 23:1

Ἀτενίσας δὲ ὁ Παῦλος τῷ συνεδρίῳ εἶπεν·
ἄνδρες ἀδελφοί, ἐγὼ πάσῃ συνειδήσει
ἀγαθῇ πεπολίτευμαι τῷ θεῷ ἄχρι ταύ-
της τῆς ἡμέρας.

Acts 23:6

Γνοὺς δὲ ὁ Παῦλος ὅτι τὸ ἓν μέρος ἐστὶν
Σαδδουκαίων τὸ δὲ ἕτερον Φαρισαίων
ἔκραζεν ἐν τῷ συνεδρίῳ· ἄνδρες ἀδελ-
φοί, ἐγὼ Φαρισαῖός εἰμι, υἱὸς Φαρισαίων,
περὶ ἐλπίδος καὶ ἀναστάσεως νεκρῶν
[ἐγὼ] κρίνομαι.

Acts 26:4–12

Τὴν μὲν οὖν βίωσίν μου [τὴν] ἐκ νεό-
τητος τὴν ἀπ' ἀρχῆς γενομένην ἐν τῷ
ἔθνει μου ἔν τε Ἱεροσολύμοις ἴσασι πάν-
τες [οἱ] Ἰουδαῖοι 5 προγινώσκοντές με
ἄνωθεν, ἐὰν θέλωσι μαρτυρεῖν, ὅτι κατὰ
τὴν ἀκριβεστάτην αἵρεσιν τῆς ἡμετέρας
θρησκείας ἔζησα Φαρισαῖος. 6 καὶ νῦν ἐπ'
ἐλπίδι τῆς εἰς τοὺς πατέρας ἡμῶν ἐπαγ-
γελίας γενομένης ὑπὸ τοῦ θεοῦ ἕστηκα
κρινόμενος, 7 εἰς ἣν τὸ δωδεκάφυλον
ἡμῶν ἐν ἐκτενείᾳ νύκτα καὶ ἡμέραν
λατρεῦον ἐλπίζει καταντῆσαι, περὶ ἧς
ἐλπίδος ἐγκαλοῦμαι ὑπὸ Ἰουδαίων, βα-
σιλεῦ. 8 τί ἄπιστον κρίνεται παρ' ὑμῖν εἰ
ὁ θεὸς νεκροὺς ἐγείρει; 9 Ἐγὼ μὲν οὖν
ἔδοξα ἐμαυτῷ πρὸς τὸ ὄνομα Ἰησοῦ τοῦ
Ναζωραίου δεῖν πολλὰ ἐναντία πρᾶξαι,
10 ὃ καὶ ἐποίησα ἐν Ἱεροσολύμοις, καὶ
πολλούς τε τῶν ἁγίων ἐγὼ ἐν φυλακαῖς
κατέκλεισα τὴν παρὰ τῶν ἀρχιερέων
ἐξουσίαν λαβὼν ἀναιρουμένων τε αὐτῶν
κατήνεγκα ψῆφον. 11 καὶ κατὰ πάσας τὰς
συναγωγὰς πολλάκις τιμωρῶν αὐτοὺς
ἠνάγκαζον βλασφημεῖν περισσῶς τε
ἐμμαινόμενος αὐτοῖς ἐδίωκον ἕως καὶ
εἰς τὰς ἔξω πόλεις. 12 Ἐν οἷς πορευό-
μενος εἰς τὴν Δαμασκὸν μετ' ἐξουσίας
καὶ ἐπιτροπῆς τῆς τῶν ἀρχιερέων

See also § 163 Paul's Commissioning by the Risen Lord.

163. Paul's Commissioning by the Risen Lord

1 Cor 9:1

Οὐκ εἰμὶ ἐλεύθερος; οὐκ εἰμὶ ἀπόστολος;
οὐχὶ Ἰησοῦν τὸν κύριον ἡμῶν ἑόρακα; οὐ
τὸ ἔργον μου ὑμεῖς ἐστε ἐν κυρίῳ;

1 Cor 15:3–11

παρέδωκα γὰρ ὑμῖν ἐν πρώτοις, ὃ καὶ
παρέλαβον, ὅτι Χριστὸς ἀπέθανεν ὑπὲρ
τῶν ἁμαρτιῶν ἡμῶν κατὰ τὰς γραφὰς
4 καὶ ὅτι ἐτάφη καὶ ὅτι ἐγήγερται τῇ ἡμέρᾳ
τῇ τρίτῃ κατὰ τὰς γραφὰς 5 καὶ ὅτι ὤφθη
Κηφᾷ εἶτα τοῖς δώδεκα· 6 ἔπειτα ὤφθη
ἐπάνω πεντακοσίοις ἀδελφοῖς ἐφάπαξ, ἐξ
ὧν οἱ πλείονες μένουσιν ἕως ἄρτι, τινὲς
δὲ ἐκοιμήθησαν· 7 ἔπειτα ὤφθη Ἰακώβῳ
εἶτα τοῖς ἀποστόλοις πᾶσιν· 8 ἔσχατον δὲ
πάντων ὡσπερεὶ τῷ ἐκτρώματι ὤφθη
κἀμοί. 9 Ἐγὼ γάρ εἰμι ὁ ἐλάχιστος τῶν
ἀποστόλων ὃς οὐκ εἰμὶ ἱκανὸς καλεῖσθαι
ἀπόστολος, διότι ἐδίωξα τὴν ἐκκλησίαν
τοῦ θεοῦ· 10 χάριτι δὲ θεοῦ εἰμι ὅ εἰμι,
καὶ ἡ χάρις αὐτοῦ ἡ εἰς ἐμὲ οὐ κενὴ
ἐγενήθη, ἀλλὰ περισσότερον αὐτῶν
πάντων ἐκοπίασα, οὐκ ἐγὼ δὲ ἀλλὰ ἡ
χάρις τοῦ θεοῦ [ἡ] σὺν ἐμοί. 11 εἴτε οὖν
ἐγὼ εἴτε ἐκεῖνοι, οὕτως κηρύσσομεν καὶ
οὕτως ἐπιστεύσατε.

Gal 1:13–24

Ἠκούσατε γὰρ τὴν ἐμὴν ἀναστροφήν
ποτε ἐν τῷ Ἰουδαϊσμῷ, ὅτι καθ' ὑπερ-
βολὴν ἐδίωκον τὴν ἐκκλησίαν τοῦ θεοῦ
καὶ ἐπόρθουν αὐτήν, 14 καὶ προέκοπτον
ἐν τῷ Ἰουδαϊσμῷ ὑπὲρ πολλοὺς συνηλι-
κιώτας ἐν τῷ γένει μου, περισσοτέρως
ζηλωτὴς ὑπάρχων τῶν πατρικῶν μου
παραδόσεων. 15 Ὅτε δὲ εὐδόκησεν [ὁ
θεὸς] ὁ ἀφορίσας με ἐκ κοιλίας μητρός
μου καὶ καλέσας διὰ τῆς χάριτος αὐτοῦ
16 ἀποκαλύψαι τὸν υἱὸν αὐτοῦ ἐν ἐμοί,
ἵνα εὐαγγελίζωμαι αὐτὸν ἐν τοῖς ἔθνε-
σιν, εὐθέως οὐ προσανεθέμην σαρκὶ καὶ
αἵματι 17 οὐδὲ ἀνῆλθον εἰς Ἱεροσόλυμα
πρὸς τοὺς πρὸ ἐμοῦ ἀποστόλους, ἀλλὰ
ἀπῆλθον εἰς Ἀραβίαν καὶ πάλιν ὑπέ-
στρεψα εἰς Δαμασκόν. 18 Ἔπειτα μετὰ
ἔτη τρία ἀνῆλθον εἰς Ἱεροσόλυμα ἱστο-
ρῆσαι Κηφᾶν καὶ ἐπέμεινα πρὸς αὐτὸν
ἡμέρας δεκαπέντε, 19 ἕτερον δὲ τῶν
ἀποστόλων οὐκ εἶδον εἰ μὴ Ἰάκωβον
τὸν ἀδελφὸν τοῦ κυρίου. 20 ἃ δὲ γρά-
φω ὑμῖν, ἰδοὺ ἐνώπιον τοῦ θεοῦ ὅτι
οὐ ψεύδομαι. 21 Ἔπειτα ἦλθον εἰς τὰ
κλίματα τῆς Συρίας καὶ τῆς Κιλικίας·
22 ἤμην δὲ ἀγνοούμενος τῷ προσώπῳ
ταῖς ἐκκλησίαις τῆς Ἰουδαίας ταῖς ἐν
Χριστῷ. 23 μόνον δὲ ἀκούοντες ἦσαν ὅτι

invoked this name? And has he not
come here for the purpose of bringing
them bound before the chief priests?"

Acts 22:1–5

"Brothers and fathers, listen to the
defense that I now make before you."
2 When they heard him addressing
them in Hebrew, they became even
more quiet. Then he said: 3 "I am a Jew,
born in Tarsus in Cilicia, but brought
up in this city at the feet of Gamaliel,
educated strictly according to our an-
cestral law, being zealous for God, just
as all of you are today. 4 I persecuted this
Way up to the point of death by bind-
ing both men and women and putting
them in prison, 5 as the high priest and
the whole council of elders can testify
about me. From them I also received
letters to the brothers in Damascus, and
I went there in order to bind those who
were there and to bring them back to
Jerusalem for punishment.

Acts 22:19–20

And I said, 'Lord, they themselves know
that in every synagogue I imprisoned
and beat those who believed in you.
20 And while the blood of your witness
Stephen was shed, I myself was stand-
ing by, approving and keeping the coats
of those who killed him.'

Acts 22:25–29

But when they had tied him up with
thongs, Paul said to the centurion who
was standing by, "Is it legal for you to
flog a Roman citizen who is uncon-
demned?" 26 When the centurion heard
that, he went to the tribune and said to
him, "What are you about to do? This
man is a Roman citizen." 27 The tribune
came and asked Paul, "Tell me, are you
a Roman citizen?" And he said, "Yes."
28 The tribune answered, "It cost me
a large sum of money to get my citi-
zenship." Paul said, "But I was born a
citizen." 29 Immediately those who were
about to examine him drew back from
him; and the tribune also was afraid,
for he realized that Paul was a Roman
citizen and that he had bound him.

Acts 23:1

While Paul was looking intently at the
council he said, "Brothers, up to this
day I have lived my life with a clear
conscience before God."

Acts 23:6

When Paul noticed that some were
Sadducees and others were Pharisees,
he called out in the council, "Brothers,
I am a Pharisee, a son of Pharisees. I
am on trial concerning the hope of the
resurrection of the dead."

Acts 26:4–12

"All the Jews know my way of life from
my youth, a life spent from the begin-
ning among my own people and in Je-
rusalem. 5 They have known for a long
time, if they are willing to testify, that I
have belonged to the strictest sect of our
religion and lived as a Pharisee. 6 And
now I stand here on trial on account
of my hope in the promise made by
God to our ancestors, 7 a promise that
our twelve tribes hope to attain, as they
earnestly worship day and night. It is
for this hope, your Excellency, that I am
accused by Jews! 8 Why is it thought
incredible by any of you that God raises
the dead? 9 "Indeed, I myself was con-
vinced that I ought to do many things
against the name of Jesus of Nazareth.
10 And that is what I did in Jerusalem;
with authority received from the chief
priests, I not only locked up many of
the saints in prison, but I also cast my
vote against them when they were being
condemned to death. 11 By punishing
them often in all the synagogues I tried
to force them to blaspheme; and since
I was so furiously enraged at them, I
pursued them even to foreign cities.
12 "With this in mind, I was traveling
to Damascus with the authority and
commission of the chief priests

See also § 163 Paul's Commissioning by the Risen Lord.

163. Paul's Commissioning by the Risen Lord

1 Cor 9:1

Am I not free? Am I not an apostle?
Have I not seen Jesus our Lord? Are
you not my work in the Lord?

1 Cor 15:3–11

For I handed on to you as of first im-
portance what I in turn had received:
that Christ died for our sins in accor-
dance with the scriptures, 4 and that he
was buried, and that he was raised on
the third day in accordance with the
scriptures, 5 and that he appeared to
Cephas, then to the twelve. 6 Then he
appeared to more than five hundred
brothers and sisters at one time, most
of whom are still alive, though some
have died. 7 Then he appeared to James,
then to all the apostles. 8 Last of all,
as to one untimely born, he appeared
also to me. 9 For I am the least of the
apostles, unfit to be called an apostle,
because I persecuted the church of God.
10 But by the grace of God I am what
I am, and his grace toward me has not
been in vain. On the contrary, I worked
harder than any of them—though it
was not I, but the grace of God that
is with me. 11 Whether then it was I or
they, so we proclaim and so you have
come to believe.

Gal 1:13–24

You have heard, no doubt, of my earlier
life in Judaism. I was violently persecut-
ing the church of God and was trying
to destroy it. 14 I advanced in Judaism
beyond many among my people of the
same age, for I was far more zealous for
the traditions of my ancestors. 15 But
when God, who had set me apart be-
fore I was born and called me through
his grace, was pleased 16 to reveal his
Son to me, so that I might proclaim
him among the Gentiles, I did not
confer with any human being, 17 nor
did I go up to Jerusalem to those who
were already apostles before me, but
I went away at once into Arabia, and
afterwards I returned to Damascus.
18 Then after three years I did go up to
Jerusalem to visit Cephas and stayed
with him fifteen days; 19 but I did not
see any other apostle except James the
Lord's brother. 20 In what I am writing
to you, before God, I do not lie! 21 Then
I went into the regions of Syria and
Cilicia, 22 and I was still unknown by
sight to the churches of Judea that are in
Christ; 23 they only heard it said, "The

ὁ διώκων ἡμᾶς ποτε νῦν εὐαγγελίζεται τὴν πίστιν ἥν ποτε ἐπόρθει, **24** καὶ ἐδόξαζον ἐν ἐμοὶ τὸν θεόν.

Phil 3:2–11

Βλέπετε τοὺς κύνας, βλέπετε τοὺς κακοὺς ἐργάτας, βλέπετε τὴν κατατομήν. **3** ἡμεῖς γάρ ἐσμεν ἡ περιτομή, οἱ πνεύματι ⸀θεοῦ λατρεύοντες καὶ καυχώμενοι ἐν Χριστῷ Ἰησοῦ καὶ οὐκ ἐν σαρκὶ πεποιθότες, **4** καίπερ ἐγὼ ἔχων πεποίθησιν καὶ ἐν σαρκί. Εἴ τις δοκεῖ ἄλλος πεποιθέναι ἐν σαρκί, ἐγὼ μᾶλλον· **5** περιτομῇ ὀκταήμερος, ἐκ γένους Ἰσραήλ, φυλῆς Βενιαμίν, Ἑβραῖος ἐξ Ἑβραίων, κατὰ νόμον Φαρισαῖος, **6** κατὰ ζῆλος διώκων τὴν ἐκκλησίαν, κατὰ δικαιοσύνην τὴν ἐν νόμῳ γενόμενος ἄμεμπτος. **7** [Ἀλλὰ] ἅτινα ἦν μοι κέρδη, ταῦτα ἥγημαι διὰ τὸν Χριστὸν ζημίαν. **8** ἀλλὰ μενοῦνγε καὶ ἡγοῦμαι πάντα ζημίαν εἶναι διὰ τὸ ὑπερέχον τῆς γνώσεως Χριστοῦ Ἰησοῦ τοῦ κυρίου μου, δι᾽ ὃν τὰ πάντα ἐζημιώθην, καὶ ἡγοῦμαι σκύβαλα, ἵνα Χριστὸν κερδήσω **9** καὶ εὑρεθῶ ἐν αὐτῷ, μὴ ἔχων ἐμὴν δικαιοσύνην τὴν ἐκ νόμου ἀλλὰ τὴν διὰ πίστεως Χριστοῦ, τὴν ἐκ θεοῦ δικαιοσύνην ἐπὶ τῇ πίστει, **10** τοῦ γνῶναι αὐτὸν καὶ τὴν δύναμιν τῆς ἀναστάσεως αὐτοῦ καὶ [τὴν] κοινωνίαν [τῶν] παθημάτων αὐτοῦ, συμμορφιζόμενος τῷ θανάτῳ αὐτοῦ, **11** εἴ πως καταντήσω εἰς τὴν ἐξανάστασιν τὴν ἐκ νεκρῶν.

1 Tim 1:12–17

Χάριν ἔχω τῷ ἐνδυναμώσαντί με Χριστῷ Ἰησοῦ τῷ κυρίῳ ἡμῶν, ὅτι πιστόν με ἡγήσατο θέμενος εἰς διακονίαν **13** τὸ πρότερον ὄντα βλάσφημον καὶ διώκτην καὶ ὑβριστήν, ἀλλὰ ἠλεήθην, ὅτι ἀγνοῶν ἐποίησα ἐν ἀπιστίᾳ· **14** ὑπερεπλεόνασεν δὲ ἡ χάρις τοῦ κυρίου ἡμῶν μετὰ πίστεως καὶ ἀγάπης τῆς ἐν Χριστῷ Ἰησοῦ. **15** πιστὸς ὁ λόγος καὶ πάσης ἀποδοχῆς ἄξιος, ὅτι Χριστὸς Ἰησοῦς ἦλθεν εἰς τὸν κόσμον ἁμαρτωλοὺς σῶσαι, ὧν πρῶτός εἰμι ἐγώ. **16** ἀλλὰ διὰ τοῦτο ἠλεήθην, ἵνα ἐν ἐμοὶ πρώτῳ ἐνδείξηται Χριστὸς Ἰησοῦς τὴν ἅπασαν μακροθυμίαν πρὸς ὑποτύπωσιν τῶν μελλόντων πιστεύειν ἐπ᾽ αὐτῷ εἰς ζωὴν αἰώνιον. **17** Τῷ δὲ βασιλεῖ τῶν αἰώνων, ἀφθάρτῳ ἀοράτῳ μόνῳ θεῷ, τιμὴ καὶ δόξα εἰς τοὺς αἰῶνας τῶν αἰώνων, ἀμήν.

Acts 9:1–22

Ὁ δὲ Σαῦλος ἔτι ἐμπνέων ἀπειλῆς καὶ φόνου εἰς τοὺς μαθητὰς τοῦ κυρίου, προσελθὼν τῷ ἀρχιερεῖ **2** ᾐτήσατο παρ᾽ αὐτοῦ ἐπιστολὰς εἰς Δαμασκὸν πρὸς τὰς συναγωγάς, ὅπως ἐάν τινας εὕρῃ τῆς ὁδοῦ ὄντας, ἄνδρας τε καὶ γυναῖκας, δεδεμένους ἀγάγῃ εἰς Ἰερουσαλήμ. **3** Ἐν δὲ τῷ πορεύεσθαι ἐγένετο αὐτὸν ἐγγίζειν τῇ Δαμασκῷ, ἐξαίφνης τε αὐτὸν περιήστραψεν φῶς ἐκ τοῦ οὐρανοῦ **4** καὶ πεσὼν ἐπὶ τὴν γῆν ἤκουσεν φωνὴν λέγουσαν αὐτῷ· Σαοὺλ Σαούλ, τί με διώκεις; **5** εἶπεν δέ· τίς εἶ, κύριε; ὁ δέ· ἐγώ εἰμι Ἰησοῦς ὃν σὺ διώκεις· **6** ἀλλὰ ἀνάστηθι καὶ εἴσελθε εἰς τὴν πόλιν καὶ λαληθήσεταί σοι ὅ τί σε δεῖ ποιεῖν. **7** οἱ δὲ ἄνδρες οἱ συνοδεύοντες αὐτῷ εἱστήκεισαν ἐνεοί, ἀκούοντες μὲν τῆς φωνῆς μηδένα δὲ θεωροῦντες. **8** ἠγέρθη δὲ Σαῦλος ἀπὸ τῆς γῆς, ἀνεῳγμένων δὲ τῶν ὀφθαλμῶν αὐτοῦ οὐδὲν ἔβλεπεν· χειραγωγοῦντες δὲ αὐτὸν εἰσήγαγον εἰς Δαμασκόν. **9** καὶ ἦν ἡμέρας τρεῖς μὴ βλέπων καὶ οὐκ ἔφαγεν οὐδὲ ἔπιεν. **10** Ἦν δέ τις μαθητὴς ἐν Δαμασκῷ ὀνόματι Ἁνανίας, καὶ εἶπεν πρὸς αὐτὸν ἐν ὁράματι ὁ κύριος· Ἁνανία. ὁ δὲ εἶπεν· ἰδοὺ ἐγώ, κύριε. **11** ὁ δὲ κύριος πρὸς αὐτόν· ἀναστὰς πορεύθητι ἐπὶ τὴν ῥύμην τὴν καλουμένην Εὐθεῖαν καὶ ζήτησον ἐν οἰκίᾳ Ἰούδα Σαῦλον ὀνόματι Ταρσέα· ἰδοὺ γὰρ προσεύχεται **12** καὶ εἶδεν ⸂ἄνδρα [ἐν ὁράματι]⸃ Ἁνανίαν ὀνόματι εἰσελθόντα καὶ ἐπιθέντα αὐτῷ [τὰς] χεῖρας ὅπως ἀναβλέψῃ. **13** ἀπεκρίθη δὲ Ἁνανίας· κύριε, ἤκουσα ἀπὸ πολλῶν περὶ τοῦ ἀνδρὸς τούτου ὅσα κακὰ τοῖς ἁγίοις σου ἐποίησεν ἐν Ἰερουσαλήμ· **14** καὶ ὧδε ἔχει ἐξουσίαν παρὰ τῶν ἀρχιερέων δῆσαι πάντας τοὺς ἐπικαλουμένους τὸ ὄνομά σου. **15** εἶπεν δὲ πρὸς αὐτὸν ὁ κύριος· πορεύου, ὅτι σκεῦος ἐκλογῆς ἐστίν μοι οὗτος τοῦ βαστάσαι τὸ ὄνομά μου ἐνώπιον ἐθνῶν τε καὶ βασιλέων υἱῶν τε Ἰσραήλ· **16** ἐγὼ γὰρ ὑποδείξω αὐτῷ ὅσα δεῖ αὐτὸν ὑπὲρ τοῦ ὀνόματός μου παθεῖν. **17** Ἀπῆλθεν δὲ Ἁνανίας καὶ εἰσῆλθεν εἰς τὴν οἰκίαν καὶ ἐπιθεὶς ἐπ᾽ αὐτὸν τὰς χεῖρας εἶπεν· Σαοὺλ ἀδελφέ, ὁ κύριος ἀπέσταλκέν με, Ἰησοῦς ὁ ὀφθείς σοι ἐν τῇ ὁδῷ ᾗ ἤρχου, ὅπως ἀναβλέψῃς καὶ πλησθῇς πνεύματος ἁγίου. **18** καὶ εὐθέως ἀπέπεσαν αὐτοῦ ἀπὸ τῶν ὀφθαλμῶν ὡς λεπίδες, ἀνέβλεψέν τε καὶ ἀναστὰς ἐβαπτίσθη **19** καὶ λαβὼν τροφὴν ἐνίσχυσεν. Ἐγένετο δὲ μετὰ τῶν ἐν Δαμασκῷ μαθητῶν ἡμέρας τινὰς **20** καὶ εὐθέως ἐν ταῖς συναγωγαῖς ἐκήρυσσεν τὸν Ἰησοῦν ὅτι οὗτός ἐστιν ὁ υἱὸς τοῦ θεοῦ. **21** ἐξίσταντο δὲ πάντες οἱ ἀκούοντες καὶ ἔλεγον· οὐχ οὗτός ἐστιν ὁ πορθήσας εἰς Ἰερουσαλὴμ τοὺς ἐπικαλουμένους τὸ ὄνομα τοῦτο, καὶ ὧδε εἰς τοῦτο ἐληλύθει ἵνα δεδεμένους αὐτοὺς ἀγάγῃ ἐπὶ τοὺς ἀρχιερεῖς; **22** Σαῦλος δὲ μᾶλλον ἐνεδυναμοῦτο καὶ συνέχυννεν [τοὺς] Ἰουδαίους τοὺς κατοικοῦντας ἐν Δαμασκῷ συμβιβάζων ὅτι οὗτός ἐστιν ὁ χριστός.

Acts 22:1–16

Ἄνδρες ἀδελφοὶ καὶ πατέρες, ἀκούσατέ μου τῆς πρὸς ὑμᾶς νυνὶ ἀπολογίας. **2** ἀκούσαντες δὲ ὅτι τῇ Ἑβραΐδι διαλέκτῳ προσεφώνει αὐτοῖς, μᾶλλον παρέσχον ἡσυχίαν. καὶ φησίν· **3** ἐγώ εἰμι ἀνὴρ Ἰουδαῖος, γεγεννημένος ἐν Ταρσῷ τῆς Κιλικίας, ἀνατεθραμμένος δὲ ἐν τῇ πόλει ταύτῃ, παρὰ τοὺς πόδας Γαμαλιὴλ πεπαιδευμένος κατὰ ἀκρίβειαν τοῦ πατρῴου νόμου, ζηλωτὴς ὑπάρχων τοῦ θεοῦ καθὼς πάντες ὑμεῖς ἐστε σήμερον· **4** ὃς ταύτην τὴν ὁδὸν ἐδίωξα ἄχρι θανάτου δεσμεύων καὶ παραδιδοὺς εἰς φυλακὰς ἄνδρας τε καὶ γυναῖκας, **5** ὡς καὶ ὁ ἀρχιερεὺς μαρτυρεῖ μοι καὶ πᾶν τὸ πρεσβυτέριον, παρ᾽ ὧν καὶ ἐπιστολὰς δεξάμενος πρὸς τοὺς ἀδελφοὺς εἰς Δαμασκὸν ἐπορευόμην, ἄξων καὶ τοὺς ἐκεῖσε ὄντας δεδεμένους εἰς Ἰερουσαλὴμ ἵνα τιμωρηθῶσιν. **6** Ἐγένετο δέ μοι πορευομένῳ καὶ ἐγγίζοντι τῇ Δαμασκῷ περὶ μεσημβρίαν ἐξαίφνης ἐκ τοῦ οὐρανοῦ περιαστράψαι φῶς ἱκανὸν περὶ ἐμέ, **7** ἔπεσά τε εἰς τὸ ἔδαφος καὶ ἤκουσα φωνῆς λεγούσης μοι· Σαοὺλ Σαούλ, τί με διώκεις; **8** ἐγὼ δὲ ἀπεκρίθην· τίς εἶ, κύριε; εἶπέν τε πρός με· ἐγώ εἰμι Ἰησοῦς

§ 163 **Phil 3:3** ***θεου*** ℵ* A B C D² 33. 1739. 1881 *Byz*] θεω ℵ² D* ¦ *om.* 𝔓⁴⁶ **Acts 9:12** ***ανδρα εν οραματι*** B C] ανδρα 𝔓⁷⁴ ℵ A ¦ εν οραματι ανδρα E 33. 1739 *Byz*

one who formerly was persecuting us is now proclaiming the faith he once tried to destroy." 24 And they glorified God because of me.

Phil 3:2–11

Beware of the dogs, beware of the evil workers, beware of those who mutilate the flesh! 3 For it is we who are the circumcision, who worship in the Spirit of God[a] and boast in Christ Jesus and have no confidence in the flesh— 4 even though I, too, have reason for confidence in the flesh. If anyone else has reason to be confident in the flesh, I have more: 5 circumcised on the eighth day, a member of the people of Israel, of the tribe of Benjamin, a Hebrew born of Hebrews; as to the law, a Pharisee; 6 as to zeal, a persecutor of the church; as to righteousness under the law, blameless. 7 Yet whatever gains I had, these I have come to regard as loss because of Christ. 8 More than that, I regard everything as loss because of the surpassing value of knowing Christ Jesus my Lord. For his sake I have suffered the loss of all things, and I regard them as rubbish, in order that I may gain Christ 9 and be found in him, not having a righteousness of my own that comes from the law, but one that comes through faith in Christ, the righteousness from God based on faith. 10 I want to know Christ and the power of his resurrection and the sharing of his sufferings by becoming like him in his death, 11 if somehow I may attain the resurrection from the dead.

1 Tim 1:12–17

I am grateful to Christ Jesus our Lord, who has strengthened me, because he judged me faithful and appointed me to his service, 13 even though I was formerly a blasphemer, a persecutor, and a man of violence. But I received mercy because I had acted ignorantly in unbelief, 14 and the grace of our Lord overflowed for me with the faith and love that are in Christ Jesus. 15 The saying is sure and worthy of full acceptance, that Christ Jesus came into the world to save sinners—of whom I am the foremost. 16 But for that very reason I received mercy, so that in me, as the foremost, Jesus Christ might display the utmost patience, making me an example to those who would come to believe in him for eternal life. 17 To the King of the ages, immortal, invisible, the only God, be honor and glory forever and ever. Amen.

Acts 9:1–22

Meanwhile Saul, still breathing threats and murder against the disciples of the Lord, went to the high priest 2 and asked him for letters to the synagogues at Damascus, so that if he found any who belonged to the Way, men or women, he might bring them bound to Jerusalem. 3 Now as he was going along and approaching Damascus, suddenly a light from heaven flashed around him. 4 He fell to the ground and heard a voice saying to him, "Saul, Saul, why do you persecute me?" 5 He asked, "Who are you, Lord?" The reply came, "I am Jesus, whom you are persecuting. 6 But get up and enter the city, and you will be told what you are to do." 7 The men who were traveling with him stood speechless because they heard the voice but saw no one. 8 Saul got up from the ground, and though his eyes were open, he could see nothing; so they led him by the hand and brought him into Damascus. 9 For three days he was without sight, and neither ate nor drank. 10 Now there was a disciple in Damascus named Ananias. The Lord said to him in a vision, "Ananias." He answered, "Here I am, Lord." 11 The Lord said to him, "Get up and go to the street called Straight, and at the house of Judas look for a man of Tarsus named Saul. At this moment he is praying, 12 and he has seen in a vision[b] a man named Ananias come in and lay his hands on him so that he might regain his sight." 13 But Ananias answered, "Lord, I have heard from many about this man, how much evil he has done to your saints in Jerusalem; 14 and here he has authority from the chief priests to bind all who invoke your name." 15 But the Lord said to him, "Go, for he is an instrument whom I have chosen to bring my name before Gentiles and kings and before the people of Israel; 16 I myself will show him how much he must suffer for the sake of my name." 17 So Ananias went and entered the house. He laid his hands on Saul and said, "Brother Saul, the Lord Jesus, who appeared to you on your way here, has sent me so that you may regain your sight and be filled with the Holy Spirit." 18 And immediately something like scales fell from his eyes, and his sight was restored. Then he got up and was baptized, 19 and after taking some food, he regained his strength. For several days he was with the disciples in Damascus, 20 and immediately he began to proclaim Jesus in the synagogues, saying, "He is the Son of God." 21 All who heard him were amazed and said, "Is not this the man who made havoc in Jerusalem among those who invoked this name? And has he not come here for the purpose of bringing them bound before the chief priests?" 22 Saul became increasingly more powerful and confounded the Jews who lived in Damascus by proving that Jesus was the Messiah.

Acts 22:1–16

"Brothers and fathers, listen to the defense that I now make before you." 2 When they heard him addressing them in Hebrew, they became even more quiet. Then he said: 3 "I am a Jew, born in Tarsus in Cilicia, but brought up in this city at the feet of Gamaliel, educated strictly according to our ancestral law, being zealous for God, just as all of you are today. 4 I persecuted this Way up to the point of death by binding both men and women and putting them in prison, 5 as the high priest and the whole council of elders can testify about me. From them I also received letters to the brothers in Damascus, and I went there in order to bind those who were there and to bring them back to Jerusalem for punishment. 6 "While I was on my way and approaching Damascus, about noon a great light from heaven suddenly shone about me. 7 I fell to the ground and heard a voice saying to me, 'Saul, Saul, why are you persecuting me?' 8 I answered, 'Who are you, Lord?' Then he said to me, 'I am Jesus of Nazareth whom you are

§ 163 [a] **Phil 3:3** *worship in the Spirit of God* Other ancient authorities read *worship God in the Spirit* [b] **Acts 9:12** *in a vision* Other ancient authorities lack *in a vision*

ὁ Ναζωραῖος, ὃν σὺ διώκεις. 9 οἱ δὲ σὺν
ἐμοὶ ὄντες τὸ μὲν φῶς ἐθεάσαντο τὴν
δὲ φωνὴν οὐκ ἤκουσαν τοῦ λαλοῦντός
μοι. 10 εἶπον δέ· τί ποιήσω, κύριε; ὁ δὲ
κύριος εἶπεν πρός με· ἀναστὰς πορεύου
εἰς Δαμασκὸν κἀκεῖ σοι λαληθήσεται
περὶ πάντων ὧν τέτακταί σοι ποιῆσαι.
11 ὡς δὲ οὐκ ἐνέβλεπον ἀπὸ τῆς δόξης
τοῦ φωτὸς ἐκείνου, χειραγωγούμενος
ὑπὸ τῶν συνόντων μοι ἦλθον εἰς Δαμα-
σκόν. 12 Ἁνανίας δέ τις, ἀνὴρ εὐλαβὴς
κατὰ τὸν νόμον, μαρτυρούμενος ὑπὸ
πάντων τῶν κατοικούντων Ἰουδαίων,
13 ἐλθὼν πρός με καὶ ἐπιστὰς εἶπέν μοι·
Σαοὺλ ἀδελφέ, ἀνάβλεψον. κἀγὼ αὐτῇ
τῇ ὥρᾳ ἀνέβλεψα εἰς αὐτόν. 14 ὁ δὲ εἶπεν·
ὁ θεὸς τῶν πατέρων ἡμῶν προεχειρίσατό
σε γνῶναι τὸ θέλημα αὐτοῦ καὶ ἰδεῖν
τὸν δίκαιον καὶ ἀκοῦσαι φωνὴν ἐκ τοῦ
στόματος αὐτοῦ, 15 ὅτι ἔσῃ μάρτυς αὐτῷ
πρὸς πάντας ἀνθρώπους ὧν ἑώρακας καὶ
ἤκουσας. 16 καὶ νῦν τί μέλλεις; ἀναστὰς
βάπτισαι καὶ ἀπόλουσαι τὰς ἁμαρτίας σου
ἐπικαλεσάμενος τὸ ὄνομα αὐτοῦ.

Acts 26:9–23

Ἐγὼ μὲν οὖν ἔδοξα ἐμαυτῷ πρὸς τὸ
ὄνομα Ἰησοῦ τοῦ Ναζωραίου δεῖν πολ-
λὰ ἐναντία πρᾶξαι, 10 ὃ καὶ ἐποίησα
ἐν Ἱεροσολύμοις, καὶ πολλούς τε τῶν
ἁγίων ἐγὼ ἐν φυλακαῖς κατέκλεισα τὴν
παρὰ τῶν ἀρχιερέων ἐξουσίαν λαβὼν
ἀναιρουμένων τε αὐτῶν κατήνεγκα ψῆ-
φον. 11 καὶ κατὰ πάσας τὰς συναγωγὰς
πολλάκις τιμωρῶν αὐτοὺς ἠνάγκαζον
βλασφημεῖν περισσῶς τε ἐμμαινόμε-
νος αὐτοῖς ἐδίωκον ἕως καὶ εἰς τὰς ἔξω
πόλεις. 12 Ἐν οἷς πορευόμενος εἰς τὴν
Δαμασκὸν μετ' ἐξουσίας καὶ ἐπιτροπῆς
τῆς τῶν ἀρχιερέων 13 ἡμέρας μέσης κατὰ
τὴν ὁδὸν εἶδον, βασιλεῦ, οὐρανόθεν ὑπὲρ
τὴν λαμπρότητα τοῦ ἡλίου περιλάμψαν
με φῶς καὶ τοὺς σὺν ἐμοὶ πορευομένους.
14 πάντων τε καταπεσόντων ἡμῶν εἰς
τὴν γῆν ἤκουσα φωνὴν λέγουσαν πρός
με τῇ Ἑβραΐδι διαλέκτῳ· Σαοὺλ Σαούλ,
τί με διώκεις; σκληρόν σοι πρὸς κέντρα
λακτίζειν. 15 ἐγὼ δὲ εἶπα· τίς εἶ, κύριε; ὁ
δὲ κύριος εἶπεν· ἐγώ εἰμι Ἰησοῦς ὃν σὺ
διώκεις. 16 ἀλλὰ ἀνάστηθι καὶ στῆθι ἐπὶ
τοὺς πόδας σου· εἰς τοῦτο γὰρ ὤφθην σοι,
προχειρίσασθαί σε ὑπηρέτην καὶ μάρτυρα
ὧν τε εἶδές ⸀[με] ὧν τε ὀφθήσομαί σοι,
17 ἐξαιρούμενός σε ἐκ τοῦ λαοῦ καὶ ἐκ
τῶν ἐθνῶν εἰς οὓς ἐγὼ ἀποστέλλω σε
18 ἀνοῖξαι ὀφθαλμοὺς αὐτῶν, τοῦ ἐπι-
στρέψαι ἀπὸ σκότους εἰς φῶς καὶ τῆς
ἐξουσίας τοῦ σατανᾶ ἐπὶ τὸν θεόν, τοῦ
λαβεῖν αὐτοὺς ἄφεσιν ἁμαρτιῶν καὶ
κλῆρον ἐν τοῖς ἡγιασμένοις πίστει τῇ
εἰς ἐμέ. 19 Ὅθεν, βασιλεῦ Ἀγρίππα, οὐκ
ἐγενόμην ἀπειθὴς τῇ οὐρανίῳ ὀπτασίᾳ
20 ἀλλὰ τοῖς ἐν Δαμασκῷ πρῶτόν τε καὶ
Ἱεροσολύμοις, πᾶσάν τε τὴν χώραν τῆς
Ἰουδαίας καὶ τοῖς ἔθνεσιν ἀπήγγελλον
μετανοεῖν καὶ ἐπιστρέφειν ἐπὶ τὸν θεόν,
ἄξια τῆς μετανοίας ἔργα πράσσοντας.
21 ἕνεκα τούτων με Ἰουδαῖοι συλλα-
βόμενοι [ὄντα] ἐν τῷ ἱερῷ ἐπειρῶντο
διαχειρίσασθαι. 22 ἐπικουρίας οὖν τυ-
χὼν τῆς ἀπὸ τοῦ θεοῦ ἄχρι τῆς ἡμέρας
ταύτης ἕστηκα μαρτυρόμενος μικρῷ
τε καὶ μεγάλῳ οὐδὲν ἐκτὸς λέγων ὧν
τε οἱ προφῆται ἐλάλησαν μελλόντων
γίνεσθαι καὶ Μωϋσῆς, 23 εἰ παθητὸς ὁ
χριστός, εἰ πρῶτος ἐξ ἀναστάσεως νε-
κρῶν φῶς μέλλει καταγγέλλειν τῷ τε
λαῷ καὶ τοῖς ἔθνεσιν.

Cf. 2 Cor 4:1–6.

See also § 99 Paul's Apostolic Commission.

164. Paul's Escape from Damascus

2 Cor 11:32–33

ἐν Δαμασκῷ ὁ ἐθνάρχης Ἁρέτα τοῦ βα-
σιλέως ἐφρούρει τὴν πόλιν Δαμασκηνῶν
πιάσαι ⸀με, 33 καὶ διὰ θυρίδος ἐν σαργάνῃ
ἐχαλάσθην διὰ τοῦ τείχους καὶ ἐξέφυγον
τὰς χεῖρας αὐτοῦ.

Acts 9:23–25

Ὡς δὲ ἐπληροῦντο ἡμέραι ἱκαναί, συν-
εβουλεύσαντο οἱ Ἰουδαῖοι ἀνελεῖν αὐτόν·
24 ἐγνώσθη δὲ τῷ Σαύλῳ ἡ ἐπιβουλὴ
αὐτῶν. παρετηροῦντο δὲ καὶ τὰς πύλας
ἡμέρας τε καὶ νυκτὸς ὅπως αὐτὸν ἀνέ-
λωσιν· 25 λαβόντες δὲ οἱ μαθηταὶ αὐτοῦ
νυκτὸς διὰ τοῦ τείχους καθῆκαν αὐτὸν
χαλάσαντες ἐν σπυρίδι.

165. Paul's Meeting with Apostles in Jerusalem

Gal 1:18–20

Ἔπειτα μετὰ ἔτη τρία ἀνῆλθον εἰς Ἱε-
ροσόλυμα ἱστορῆσαι Κηφᾶν καὶ ἐπέμεινα
πρὸς αὐτὸν ἡμέρας δεκαπέντε, 19 ἕτερον
δὲ τῶν ἀποστόλων οὐκ εἶδον εἰ μὴ Ἰά-
κωβον τὸν ἀδελφὸν τοῦ κυρίου. 20 ἃ δὲ
γράφω ὑμῖν, ἰδοὺ ἐνώπιον τοῦ θεοῦ ὅτι
οὐ ψεύδομαι.

Acts 9:26–30

Παραγενόμενος δὲ εἰς Ἰερουσαλὴμ ἐπεί-
ραζεν κολλᾶσθαι τοῖς μαθηταῖς, καὶ πάντες
ἐφοβοῦντο αὐτὸν μὴ πιστεύοντες ὅτι ἐστὶν
μαθητής. 27 Βαρναβᾶς δὲ ἐπιλαβόμενος
αὐτὸν ἤγαγεν πρὸς τοὺς ἀποστόλους καὶ
διηγήσατο αὐτοῖς πῶς ἐν τῇ ὁδῷ εἶδεν
τὸν κύριον καὶ ὅτι ἐλάλησεν αὐτῷ καὶ
πῶς ἐν Δαμασκῷ ἐπαρρησιάσατο ἐν τῷ
ὀνόματι τοῦ Ἰησοῦ. 28 καὶ ἦν μετ' αὐτῶν
εἰσπορευόμενος καὶ ἐκπορευόμενος εἰς
Ἰερουσαλήμ, παρρησιαζόμενος ἐν τῷ
ὀνόματι τοῦ κυρίου, 29 ἐλάλει τε καὶ
συνεζήτει πρὸς τοὺς Ἑλληνιστάς, οἱ δὲ
ἐπεχείρουν ἀνελεῖν αὐτόν. 30 ἐπιγνόν-
τες δὲ οἱ ἀδελφοὶ κατήγαγον αὐτὸν εἰς
Καισάρειαν καὶ ἐξαπέστειλαν αὐτὸν
εἰς Ταρσόν.

Cf. possibly Acts 22:17–21.

Acts 26:16 ***με*** B C*vid 1739] *om.* 𝔓74 ℵ A C2 E *Byz*   **§ 164** **2 Cor 11:32** ***με*** B D*] *add.* θελων ℵ D2 33. (1739). 1881 *Byz*

persecuting.' 9 Now those who were with me saw the light but did not hear the voice of the one who was speaking to me. 10 I asked, 'What am I to do, Lord?' The Lord said to me, 'Get up and go to Damascus; there you will be told everything that has been assigned to you to do.' 11 Since I could not see because of the brightness of that light, those who were with me took my hand and led me to Damascus. 12 "A certain Ananias, who was a devout man according to the law and well spoken of by all the Jews living there, 13 came to me; and standing beside me, he said, 'Brother Saul, regain your sight!' In that very hour I regained my sight and saw him. 14 Then he said, 'The God of our ancestors has chosen you to know his will, to see the Righteous One and to hear his own voice; 15 for you will be his witness to all the world of what you have seen and heard. 16 And now why do you delay? Get up, be baptized, and have your sins washed away, calling on his name.'

Acts 26:9–23

"Indeed, I myself was convinced that I ought to do many things against the name of Jesus of Nazareth. 10 And that is what I did in Jerusalem; with authority received from the chief priests, I not only locked up many of the saints in prison, but I also cast my vote against them when they were being condemned to death. 11 By punishing them often in all the synagogues I tried to force them to blaspheme; and since I was so furiously enraged at them, I pursued them even to foreign cities. 12 "With this in mind, I was traveling to Damascus with the authority and commission of the chief priests, 13 when at midday along the road, your Excellency, I saw a light from heaven, brighter than the sun, shining around me and my companions. 14 When we had all fallen to the ground, I heard a voice saying to me in the Hebrew language, 'Saul, Saul, why are you persecuting me? It hurts you to kick against the goads.' 15 I asked, 'Who are you, Lord?' The Lord answered, 'I am Jesus whom you are persecuting. 16 But get up and stand on your feet; for I have appeared to you for this purpose, to appoint you to serve and testify to the things in which you have seen me[c] and to those in which I will appear to you. 17 I will rescue you from your people and from the Gentiles—to whom I am sending you 18 to open their eyes so that they may turn from darkness to light and from the power of Satan to God, so that they may receive forgiveness of sins and a place among those who are sanctified by faith in me.' 19 "After that, King Agrippa, I was not disobedient to the heavenly vision, 20 but declared first to those in Damascus, then in Jerusalem and throughout the countryside of Judea, and also to the Gentiles, that they should repent and turn to God and do deeds consistent with repentance. 21 For this reason the Jews seized me in the temple and tried to kill me. 22 To this day I have had help from God, and so I stand here, testifying to both small and great, saying nothing but what the prophets and Moses said would take place: 23 that the Messiah must suffer, and that, by being the first to rise from the dead, he would proclaim light both to our people and to the Gentiles."

Cf. 2 Cor 4:1–6.

See also § 99 Paul's Apostolic Commission.

164. Paul's Escape from Damascus

2 Cor 11:32–33

In Damascus, the governor under King Aretas guarded the city of Damascus in order to[a] seize me, 33 but I was let down in a basket through a window in the wall, and escaped from his hands.

Acts 9:23–25

After some time had passed, the Jews plotted to kill him, 24 but their plot became known to Saul. They were watching the gates day and night so that they might kill him; 25 but his disciples took him by night and let him down through an opening in the wall, lowering him in a basket.

165. Paul's Meeting with Apostles in Jerusalem

Gal 1:18–20

Then after three years I did go up to Jerusalem to visit Cephas and stayed with him fifteen days; 19 but I did not see any other apostle except James the Lord's brother. 20 In what I am writing to you, before God, I do not lie!

Acts 9:26–30

When he had come to Jerusalem, he attempted to join the disciples; and they were all afraid of him, for they did not believe that he was a disciple. 27 But Barnabas took him, brought him to the apostles, and described for them how on the road he had seen the Lord, who had spoken to him, and how in Damascus he had spoken boldly in the name of Jesus. 28 So he went in and out among them in Jerusalem, speaking boldly in the name of the Lord. 29 He spoke and argued with the Hellenists; but they were attempting to kill him. 30 When the believers learned of it, they brought him down to Caesarea and sent him off to Tarsus.

Cf. possibly Acts 22:17–21.

[c] **Acts 26:16** *the things in which you have seen me* Other ancient authorities read *the things that you have seen* **§ 164** [a] **2 Cor 11:32** *in order to* Other ancient authorities read *and wanted to*

166. The Apostolic Council

Gal 2:1–10*

Ἔπειτα διὰ δεκατεσσάρων ἐτῶν πάλιν
ἀνέβην εἰς Ἱεροσόλυμα μετὰ Βαρναβᾶ
συμπαραλαβὼν καὶ Τίτον· **2** ἀνέβην δὲ
κατὰ ἀποκάλυψιν· καὶ ἀνεθέμην αὐτοῖς
τὸ εὐαγγέλιον ὃ κηρύσσω ἐν τοῖς ἔθνε-
σιν, κατʼ ἰδίαν δὲ τοῖς δοκοῦσιν, μή πως
εἰς κενὸν τρέχω ἢ ἔδραμον. **3** ἀλλʼ οὐδὲ
Τίτος ὁ σὺν ἐμοί, Ἕλλην ὤν, ἠναγκάσθη
περιτμηθῆναι· **4** διὰ δὲ τοὺς παρεισάκτους
ψευδαδέλφους, οἵτινες παρεισῆλθον
κατασκοπῆσαι τὴν ἐλευθερίαν ἡμῶν
ἣν ἔχομεν ἐν Χριστῷ Ἰησοῦ, ἵνα ἡμᾶς
καταδουλώσουσιν, **5** οἷς οὐδὲ πρὸς ὥραν
εἴξαμεν τῇ ὑποταγῇ, ἵνα ἡ ἀλήθεια τοῦ
εὐαγγελίου διαμείνῃ πρὸς ὑμᾶς. **6** Ἀπὸ δὲ
τῶν δοκούντων εἶναί τι, —ὁποῖοί ποτε
ἦσαν οὐδέν μοι διαφέρει· πρόσωπον [ὁ]
θεὸς ἀνθρώπου οὐ λαμβάνει—ἐμοὶ γὰρ οἱ
δοκοῦντες οὐδὲν προσανέθεντο, **7** ἀλλὰ
τοὐναντίον ἰδόντες ὅτι πεπίστευμαι τὸ
εὐαγγέλιον τῆς ἀκροβυστίας καθὼς Πέ-
τρος τῆς περιτομῆς, **8** ὁ γὰρ ἐνεργήσας
Πέτρῳ εἰς ἀποστολὴν τῆς περιτομῆς
ἐνήργησεν καὶ ἐμοὶ εἰς τὰ ἔθνη, **9** καὶ
γνόντες τὴν χάριν τὴν δοθεῖσάν μοι,
Ἰάκωβος καὶ Κηφᾶς καὶ Ἰωάννης, οἱ
δοκοῦντες στῦλοι εἶναι, δεξιὰς ἔδωκαν
ἐμοὶ καὶ Βαρναβᾷ κοινωνίας, ἵνα ἡμεῖς
εἰς τὰ ἔθνη, αὐτοὶ δὲ εἰς τὴν περιτομήν·
10 μόνον τῶν πτωχῶν ἵνα μνημονεύωμεν,
ὃ καὶ ἐσπούδασα αὐτὸ τοῦτο ποιῆσαι.

*Most interpreters identify the events of Galatians 2:1–10 with Paul's visit to Jerusalem recounted in Acts 15:1–35. Alternative views identify Galatians 2:1–10 with Paul's visit to Jerusalem in Acts 11:27–30 and 12:25, or with Paul's trip to Jerusalem in Acts 18:22, or with some combination of these Lucan accounts.

Acts 15:1–35

Καί τινες κατελθόντες ἀπὸ τῆς Ἰου-
δαίας ἐδίδασκον τοὺς ἀδελφοὺς ὅτι, ἐὰν
μὴ περιτμηθῆτε τῷ ἔθει τῷ Μωϋσέως,
οὐ δύνασθε σωθῆναι. **2** γενομένης δὲ
στάσεως καὶ ζητήσεως οὐκ ὀλίγης τῷ
Παύλῳ καὶ τῷ Βαρναβᾷ πρὸς αὐτούς,
ἔταξαν ἀναβαίνειν Παῦλον καὶ Βαρ-
ναβᾶν καί τινας ἄλλους ἐξ αὐτῶν πρὸς
τοὺς ἀποστόλους καὶ πρεσβυτέρους εἰς
Ἰερουσαλὴμ περὶ τοῦ ζητήματος τούτου.
3 Οἱ μὲν οὖν προπεμφθέντες ὑπὸ τῆς
ἐκκλησίας διήρχοντο τήν τε Φοινίκην καὶ
Σαμάρειαν ἐκδιηγούμενοι τὴν ἐπιστροφὴν
τῶν ἐθνῶν καὶ ἐποίουν χαρὰν μεγάλην
πᾶσιν τοῖς ἀδελφοῖς. **4** παραγενόμενοι
δὲ εἰς Ἰερουσαλὴμ παρεδέχθησαν ἀπὸ
τῆς ἐκκλησίας καὶ τῶν ἀποστόλων καὶ
τῶν πρεσβυτέρων, ἀνήγγειλάν τε ὅσα ὁ
θεὸς ἐποίησεν μετʼ αὐτῶν. **5** Ἐξανέστη-
σαν δέ τινες τῶν ἀπὸ τῆς αἱρέσεως τῶν
Φαρισαίων πεπιστευκότες λέγοντες ὅτι
δεῖ περιτέμνειν αὐτοὺς παραγγέλλειν τε
τηρεῖν τὸν νόμον Μωϋσέως. **6** Συνήχθη-
σάν τε οἱ ἀπόστολοι καὶ οἱ πρεσβύτεροι
ἰδεῖν περὶ τοῦ λόγου τούτου. **7** Πολλῆς
δὲ ζητήσεως γενομένης ἀναστὰς Πέτρος
εἶπεν πρὸς αὐτούς· ἄνδρες ἀδελφοί, ὑμεῖς
ἐπίστασθε ὅτι ἀφʼ ἡμερῶν ἀρχαίων ἐν
ὑμῖν ἐξελέξατο ὁ θεὸς διὰ τοῦ στόματός
μου ἀκοῦσαι τὰ ἔθνη τὸν λόγον τοῦ
εὐαγγελίου καὶ πιστεῦσαι. **8** καὶ ὁ καρ-
διογνώστης θεὸς ἐμαρτύρησεν αὐτοῖς
δοὺς τὸ πνεῦμα τὸ ἅγιον καθὼς καὶ ἡμῖν
9 καὶ οὐθὲν διέκρινεν μεταξὺ ἡμῶν τε καὶ
αὐτῶν τῇ πίστει καθαρίσας τὰς καρδίας
αὐτῶν. **10** νῦν οὖν τί πειράζετε τὸν θεὸν
ἐπιθεῖναι ζυγὸν ἐπὶ τὸν τράχηλον τῶν
μαθητῶν ὃν οὔτε οἱ πατέρες ἡμῶν οὔτε
ἡμεῖς ἰσχύσαμεν βαστάσαι; **11** ἀλλὰ διὰ
τῆς χάριτος τοῦ κυρίου Ἰησοῦ πιστεύο-
μεν σωθῆναι καθʼ ὃν τρόπον κἀκεῖνοι.
12 Ἐσίγησεν δὲ πᾶν τὸ πλῆθος καὶ ἤκουον
Βαρναβᾶ καὶ Παύλου ἐξηγουμένων ὅσα
ἐποίησεν ὁ θεὸς σημεῖα καὶ τέρατα ἐν
τοῖς ἔθνεσιν διʼ αὐτῶν. **13** Μετὰ δὲ τὸ
σιγῆσαι αὐτοὺς ἀπεκρίθη Ἰάκωβος λέ-
γων· ἄνδρες ἀδελφοί, ἀκούσατέ μου.
14 Συμεὼν ἐξηγήσατο καθὼς πρῶτον ὁ
θεὸς ἐπεσκέψατο λαβεῖν ἐξ ἐθνῶν λαὸν
τῷ ὀνόματι αὐτοῦ. **15** καὶ τούτῳ συμφω-
νοῦσιν οἱ λόγοι τῶν προφητῶν καθὼς
γέγραπται· **16** μετὰ ταῦτα ἀναστρέψω
καὶ ἀνοικοδομήσω τὴν σκηνὴν Δαυὶδ
τὴν πεπτωκυῖαν καὶ τὰ κατεσκαμμένα
αὐτῆς ἀνοικοδομήσω καὶ ἀνορθώσω
αὐτήν, **17** ὅπως ἂν ἐκζητήσωσιν οἱ κα-
τάλοιποι τῶν ἀνθρώπων τὸν κύριον
καὶ πάντα τὰ ἔθνη ἐφʼ οὓς ἐπικέκληται
τὸ ὄνομά μου ἐπʼ αὐτούς, λέγει κύριος
ποιῶν ⸀ταῦτα **18** γνωστὰ ἀπʼ αἰῶνος⸃.
19 διὸ ἐγὼ κρίνω μὴ παρενοχλεῖν τοῖς
ἀπὸ τῶν ἐθνῶν ἐπιστρέφουσιν ἐπὶ τὸν
θεόν, **20** ἀλλὰ ἐπιστεῖλαι αὐτοῖς τοῦ ἀπέ-
χεσθαι τῶν ἀλισγημάτων τῶν εἰδώλων
καὶ τῆς πορνείας ⸀καὶ τοῦ πνικτοῦ⸃ καὶ
τοῦ αἵματος. **21** Μωϋσῆς γὰρ ἐκ γενεῶν
ἀρχαίων κατὰ πόλιν τοὺς κηρύσσοντας
αὐτὸν ἔχει ἐν ταῖς συναγωγαῖς κατὰ πᾶν
σάββατον ἀναγινωσκόμενος. **22** Τότε ἔδοξε
τοῖς ἀποστόλοις καὶ τοῖς πρεσβυτέροις
σὺν ὅλῃ τῇ ἐκκλησίᾳ ἐκλεξαμένους
ἄνδρας ἐξ αὐτῶν πέμψαι εἰς Ἀντιόχειαν
σὺν τῷ Παύλῳ καὶ Βαρναβᾷ, Ἰούδαν
τὸν καλούμενον Βαρσαββᾶν καὶ Σιλᾶν,
ἄνδρας ἡγουμένους ἐν τοῖς ἀδελφοῖς,
23 γράψαντες διὰ χειρὸς αὐτῶν· Οἱ ἀπό-
στολοι καὶ οἱ πρεσβύτεροι ἀδελφοὶ τοῖς
κατὰ τὴν Ἀντιόχειαν καὶ Συρίαν καὶ
Κιλικίαν ἀδελφοῖς τοῖς ἐξ ἐθνῶν χαί-
ρειν. **24** Ἐπειδὴ ἠκούσαμεν ὅτι τινὲς ἐξ
ἡμῶν [ἐξελθόντες] ἐτάραξαν ὑμᾶς λόγοις
ἀνασκευάζοντες τὰς ψυχὰς ⸀ὑμῶν οἷς
οὐ διεστειλάμεθα, **25** ἔδοξεν ἡμῖν γενομέ-
νοις ὁμοθυμαδὸν ἐκλεξαμένοις ἄνδρας
πέμψαι πρὸς ὑμᾶς σὺν τοῖς ἀγαπητοῖς
ἡμῶν Βαρναβᾷ καὶ Παύλῳ, **26** ἀνθρώποις
παραδεδωκόσι τὰς ψυχὰς αὐτῶν ὑπὲρ
τοῦ ὀνόματος τοῦ κυρίου ἡμῶν Ἰησοῦ
Χριστοῦ. **27** ἀπεστάλκαμεν οὖν Ἰούδαν
καὶ Σιλᾶν καὶ αὐτοὺς διὰ λόγου ἀπαγ-
γέλλοντας τὰ αὐτά. **28** ἔδοξεν γὰρ τῷ
πνεύματι τῷ ἁγίῳ καὶ ἡμῖν μηδὲν πλέον
ἐπιτίθεσθαι ὑμῖν βάρος πλὴν τούτων
τῶν ἐπάναγκες, **29** ἀπέχεσθαι εἰδωλοθύ

§ 166 **Acts 15:17–18** ***ταυτα γνωστα απ αιωνος*** ℵ B C 33 (1739)] ταυτα· γνωστον απ αιωνος τω κυριω το εργον αυτου 𝔓^{74} A (D) ¦ ταυτα παντα· γνωστα απ αιωνος εστιν τω θεω παντα τα εργα αυτου (E) *Byz* **Acts 15:20** ***και του πνικτου*** 𝔓^{45} ℵ C E 1739 *Byz*] και πνικτου 𝔓^{74} A B 33 ¦ *om.* D **Acts 15:24** ***υμων*** 𝔓^{33} 𝔓^{45vid} 𝔓^{74} ℵ A B D 33] *add.* λεγοντες περιτεμνεσθαι (+ δει E) και τηρειν τον νομον C E 1739 *Byz*

166. The Apostolic Council

Gal 2:1–10*

Then after fourteen years I went up again to Jerusalem with Barnabas, taking Titus along with me. **2** I went up in response to a revelation. Then I laid before them (though only in a private meeting with the acknowledged leaders) the gospel that I proclaim among the Gentiles, in order to make sure that I was not running, or had not run, in vain. **3** But even Titus, who was with me, was not compelled to be circumcised, though he was a Greek. **4** But because of false believers secretly brought in, who slipped in to spy on the freedom we have in Christ Jesus, so that they might enslave us— **5** we did not submit to them even for a moment, so that the truth of the gospel might always remain with you. **6** And from those who were supposed to be acknowledged leaders (what they actually were makes no difference to me; God shows no partiality)—those leaders contributed nothing to me. **7** On the contrary, when they saw that I had been entrusted with the gospel for the uncircumcised, just as Peter had been entrusted with the gospel for the circumcised **8** (for he who worked through Peter making him an apostle to the circumcised also worked through me in sending me to the Gentiles), **9** and when James and Cephas and John, who were acknowledged pillars, recognized the grace that had been given to me, they gave to Barnabas and me the right hand of fellowship, agreeing that we should go to the Gentiles and they to the circumcised. **10** They asked only one thing, that we remember the poor, which was actually what I was eager to do.

* Most interpreters identify the events of Galatians 2:1–10 with Paul's visit to Jerusalem recounted in Acts 15:1–35. Alternative views identify Galatians 2:1–10 with Paul's visit to Jerusalem in Acts 11:27–30 and 12:25, or with Paul's trip to Jerusalem in Acts 18:22, or with some combination of these Lucan accounts.

Acts 15:1–35

Then certain individuals came down from Judea and were teaching the brothers, "Unless you are circumcised according to the custom of Moses, you cannot be saved." **2** And after Paul and Barnabas had no small dissension and debate with them, Paul and Barnabas and some of the others were appointed to go up to Jerusalem to discuss this question with the apostles and the elders. **3** So they were sent on their way by the church, and as they passed through both Phoenicia and Samaria, they reported the conversion of the Gentiles, and brought great joy to all the believers. **4** When they came to Jerusalem, they were welcomed by the church and the apostles and the elders, and they reported all that God had done with them. **5** But some believers who belonged to the sect of the Pharisees stood up and said, "It is necessary for them to be circumcised and ordered to keep the law of Moses." **6** The apostles and the elders met together to consider this matter. **7** After there had been much debate, Peter stood up and said to them, "My brothers, you know that in the early days God made a choice among you, that I should be the one through whom the Gentiles would hear the message of the good news and become believers. **8** And God, who knows the human heart, testified to them by giving them the Holy Spirit, just as he did to us; **9** and in cleansing their hearts by faith he has made no distinction between them and us. **10** Now therefore why are you putting God to the test by placing on the neck of the disciples a yoke that neither our ancestors nor we have been able to bear? **11** On the contrary, we believe that we will be saved through the grace of the Lord Jesus, just as they will." **12** The whole assembly kept silence, and listened to Barnabas and Paul as they told of all the signs and wonders that God had done through them among the Gentiles. **13** After they finished speaking, James replied, "My brothers, listen to me. **14** Simeon has related how God first looked favorably on the Gentiles, to take from among them a people for his name. **15** This agrees with the words of the prophets, as it is written, **16** 'After this I will return, and I will rebuild the dwelling of David, which has fallen; from its ruins I will rebuild it, and I will set it up, **17** so that all other peoples may seek the Lord— even all the Gentiles over whom my name has been called. Thus says the Lord, who has been making these things **18** known from long ago.'[a] **19** Therefore I have reached the decision that we should not trouble those Gentiles who are turning to God, **20** but we should write to them to abstain only from things polluted by idols and from fornication and from whatever has been strangled[b] and from blood. **21** For in every city, for generations past, Moses has had those who proclaim him, for he has been read aloud every sabbath in the synagogues." **22** Then the apostles and the elders, with the consent of the whole church, decided to choose men from among their members and to send them to Antioch with Paul and Barnabas. They sent Judas called Barsabbas, and Silas, leaders among the brothers, **23** with the following letter: "The brothers, both the apostles and the elders, to the believers of Gentile origin in Antioch and Syria and Cilicia, greetings. **24** Since we have heard that certain persons who have gone out from us, though with no instructions from us, have said things to disturb you and have unsettled your minds,[c] **25** we have decided unanimously to choose representatives and send them to you, along with our beloved Barnabas and Paul, **26** who have risked their lives for the sake of our Lord Jesus Christ. **27** We have therefore sent Judas and Silas, who themselves will tell you the same things by word of mouth. **28** For it has seemed good to the Holy Spirit and to us to impose on you no further burden than these essentials: **29** that you

§ 166 [a] **Acts 15:17–18** ***things known from long ago.*** Other ancient authorities read *things.* **18** *Known to the Lord from of old is his work.* [b] **Acts 15:20** ***and from whatever has been strangled*** A few ancient authorities lack *and from whatever has been strangled* [c] **Acts 15:24** ***minds*** Other ancient authorities add *saying, 'You must be circumcised and keep the law,'*

των καὶ αἵματος ⸀καὶ πνικτῶν⸁ καὶ πορνείας, ἐξ ὧν διατηροῦντες ἑαυτοὺς εὖ πράξετε. Ἔρρωσθε. 30 Οἱ μὲν οὖν ἀπολυθέντες κατῆλθον εἰς Ἀντιόχειαν, καὶ συναγαγόντες τὸ πλῆθος ἐπέδωκαν τὴν ἐπιστολήν. 31 ἀναγνόντες δὲ ἐχάρησαν ἐπὶ τῇ παρακλήσει. 32 Ἰούδας τε καὶ Σιλᾶς καὶ αὐτοὶ προφῆται ὄντες διὰ λόγου πολλοῦ παρεκάλεσαν τοὺς ἀδελφοὺς καὶ ἐπεστήριξαν, 33 ποιήσαντες δὲ χρόνον ἀπελύθησαν μετ' εἰρήνης ἀπὸ τῶν ἀδελφῶν πρὸς τοὺς ἀποστείλαντας ⸀αὐτούς. 35 Παῦλος δὲ καὶ Βαρναβᾶς διέτριβον ἐν Ἀντιοχείᾳ διδάσκοντες καὶ εὐαγγελιζόμενοι μετὰ καὶ ἑτέρων πολλῶν τὸν λόγον τοῦ κυρίου.

Acts 16:4–5

Ὡς δὲ διεπορεύοντο τὰς πόλεις, παρεδίδοσαν αὐτοῖς φυλάσσειν τὰ δόγματα τὰ κεκριμένα ὑπὸ τῶν ἀποστόλων καὶ πρεσβυτέρων τῶν ἐν Ἱεροσολύμοις. 5 Αἱ μὲν οὖν ἐκκλησίαι ἐστερεοῦντο τῇ πίστει καὶ ἐπερίσσευον τῷ ἀριθμῷ καθ' ἡμέραν.

Cf. Acts 11:27–30; 12:25; 18:22 (see note above).

167. Paul's Co-worker Timothy

Rom 16:21

Ἀσπάζεται ὑμᾶς Τιμόθεος ὁ συνεργός μου καὶ Λούκιος καὶ Ἰάσων καὶ Σωσίπατρος οἱ συγγενεῖς μου.

1 Cor 4:17

Διὰ τοῦτο ἔπεμψα ὑμῖν Τιμόθεον, ὅς ἐστίν μου τέκνον ἀγαπητὸν καὶ πιστὸν ἐν κυρίῳ, ὃς ὑμᾶς ἀναμνήσει τὰς ὁδούς μου τὰς ἐν Χριστῷ [Ἰησοῦ], καθὼς πανταχοῦ ἐν πάσῃ ἐκκλησίᾳ διδάσκω.

1 Cor 16:10–11

Ἐὰν δὲ ἔλθῃ Τιμόθεος, βλέπετε, ἵνα ἀφόβως γένηται πρὸς ὑμᾶς· τὸ γὰρ ἔργον κυρίου ἐργάζεται ὡς κἀγώ· 11 μή τις οὖν αὐτὸν ἐξουθενήσῃ. προπέμψατε δὲ αὐτὸν ἐν εἰρήνῃ, ἵνα ἔλθῃ πρός με· ἐκδέχομαι γὰρ αὐτὸν μετὰ τῶν ἀδελφῶν.

2 Cor 1:19–20

ὁ τοῦ θεοῦ γὰρ υἱὸς Ἰησοῦς Χριστὸς ὁ ἐν ὑμῖν δι' ἡμῶν κηρυχθείς, δι' ἐμοῦ καὶ Σιλουανοῦ καὶ Τιμοθέου, οὐκ ἐγένετο ναὶ καὶ οὒ ἀλλὰ ναὶ ἐν αὐτῷ γέγονεν. 20 ὅσαι γὰρ ἐπαγγελίαι θεοῦ, ἐν αὐτῷ τὸ ναί· διὸ καὶ δι' αὐτοῦ τὸ ἀμὴν τῷ θεῷ πρὸς δόξαν δι' ἡμῶν.

Phil 2:19–24

Ἐλπίζω δὲ ἐν κυρίῳ Ἰησοῦ Τιμόθεον ταχέως πέμψαι ὑμῖν, ἵνα κἀγὼ εὐψυχῶ γνοὺς τὰ περὶ ὑμῶν. 20 οὐδένα γὰρ ἔχω ἰσόψυχον, ὅστις γνησίως τὰ περὶ ὑμῶν μεριμνήσει· 21 οἱ πάντες γὰρ τὰ ἑαυτῶν ζητοῦσιν, οὐ τὰ Ἰησοῦ Χριστοῦ. 22 τὴν δὲ δοκιμὴν αὐτοῦ γινώσκετε, ὅτι ὡς πατρὶ τέκνον σὺν ἐμοὶ ἐδούλευσεν εἰς τὸ εὐαγγέλιον. 23 τοῦτον μὲν οὖν ἐλπίζω πέμψαι ὡς ἂν ἀφίδω τὰ περὶ ἐμὲ ἐξαυτῆς· 24 πέποιθα δὲ ἐν κυρίῳ ὅτι καὶ αὐτὸς ταχέως ἐλεύσομαι.

1 Thess 3:1–2

Διὸ μηκέτι στέγοντες εὐδοκήσαμεν καταλειφθῆναι ἐν Ἀθήναις μόνοι 2 καὶ ἐπέμψαμεν Τιμόθεον, τὸν ἀδελφὸν ἡμῶν καὶ ⸀συνεργὸν τοῦ θεοῦ⸁ ἐν τῷ εὐαγγελίῳ τοῦ Χριστοῦ, εἰς τὸ στηρίξαι ὑμᾶς καὶ παρακαλέσαι ὑπὲρ τῆς πίστεως ὑμῶν

1 Thess 3:6–7

Ἄρτι δὲ ἐλθόντος Τιμοθέου πρὸς ἡμᾶς ἀφ' ὑμῶν καὶ εὐαγγελισαμένου ἡμῖν τὴν πίστιν καὶ τὴν ἀγάπην ὑμῶν καὶ ὅτι ἔχετε μνείαν ἡμῶν ἀγαθὴν πάντοτε, ἐπιποθοῦντες ἡμᾶς ἰδεῖν καθάπερ καὶ ἡμεῖς ὑμᾶς, 7 διὰ τοῦτο παρεκλήθημεν, ἀδελφοί, ἐφ' ὑμῖν ἐπὶ πάσῃ τῇ ἀνάγκῃ καὶ θλίψει ἡμῶν διὰ τῆς ὑμῶν πίστεως

Acts 16:1–3

Κατήντησεν δὲ [καὶ] εἰς Δέρβην καὶ εἰς Λύστραν. καὶ ἰδοὺ μαθητής τις ἦν ἐκεῖ ὀνόματι Τιμόθεος, υἱὸς γυναικὸς Ἰουδαίας πιστῆς, πατρὸς δὲ Ἕλληνος, 2 ὃς ἐμαρτυρεῖτο ὑπὸ τῶν ἐν Λύστροις καὶ Ἰκονίῳ ἀδελφῶν. 3 τοῦτον ἠθέλησεν ὁ Παῦλος σὺν αὐτῷ ἐξελθεῖν, καὶ λαβὼν περιέτεμεν αὐτὸν διὰ τοὺς Ἰουδαίους τοὺς ὄντας ἐν τοῖς τόποις ἐκείνοις· ᾔδεισαν γὰρ ἅπαντες ὅτι Ἕλλην ὁ πατὴρ αὐτοῦ ὑπῆρχεν.

Acts 17:14–15

εὐθέως δὲ τότε τὸν Παῦλον ἐξαπέστειλαν οἱ ἀδελφοὶ πορεύεσθαι ἕως ἐπὶ τὴν θάλασσαν, ὑπέμεινάν τε ὅ τε Σιλᾶς καὶ ὁ Τιμόθεος ἐκεῖ. 15 οἱ δὲ καθιστάνοντες τὸν Παῦλον ἤγαγον ἕως Ἀθηνῶν, καὶ λαβόντες ἐντολὴν πρὸς τὸν Σιλᾶν καὶ τὸν Τιμόθεον ἵνα ὡς τάχιστα ἔλθωσιν πρὸς αὐτὸν ἐξῄεσαν.

Acts 18:5

Ὡς δὲ κατῆλθον ἀπὸ τῆς Μακεδονίας ὅ τε Σιλᾶς καὶ ὁ Τιμόθεος, συνείχετο τῷ λόγῳ ὁ Παῦλος διαμαρτυρόμενος τοῖς Ἰουδαίοις εἶναι τὸν χριστὸν Ἰησοῦν.

Acts 19:21–22

Ὡς δὲ ἐπληρώθη ταῦτα, ἔθετο ὁ Παῦλος ἐν τῷ πνεύματι διελθὼν τὴν Μακεδονίαν καὶ Ἀχαΐαν πορεύεσθαι εἰς Ἱεροσόλυμα εἰπὼν ὅτι μετὰ τὸ γενέσθαι με ἐκεῖ δεῖ με καὶ Ῥώμην ἰδεῖν. 22 ἀποστείλας δὲ εἰς τὴν Μακεδονίαν δύο τῶν διακονούντων αὐτῷ, Τιμόθεον καὶ Ἔραστον, αὐτὸς ἐπέσχεν χρόνον εἰς τὴν Ἀσίαν.

Acts 20:4

συνείπετο δὲ αὐτῷ Σώπατρος Πύρρου Βεροιαῖος, Θεσσαλονικέων δὲ Ἀρίσταρχος καὶ Σεκοῦνδος, καὶ Γάϊος Δερβαῖος καὶ Τιμόθεος, Ἀσιανοὶ δὲ Τύχικος καὶ Τρόφιμος.

Cf. 2 Cor 1:1–2; Phil 1:1–2; Col 1:1–2; 1 Thess 1:1; 2 Thess 1:1; Phlm 1; 1 Tim, passim; 2 Tim, passim.

Acts 15:29 ***και πνικτων*** א* A* B C] και πνικτου 𝔓74 א2 Ac E 33. 1739 *Byz* ¦ *om.* D **Acts 15:33** ***αυτους*** 𝔓74 א A B E *Byz*] *add.* [v. 34] εδοξε δε τω Σιλα επιμειναι αυτου (C) 33. 1739 ¦ *add.* εδοξε δε τω Σιλα επιμειναι προς αυτους, μονος δε Ιουδας επορευθη D **§ 167** **1 Thess 3:2** ***συνεργον του θεου*** D* 33] συνεργον B ¦ διακονον του θεου א A 1739. 1881 ¦ διακονον του θεου και συνεργον ημων D2 *Byz*

abstain from what has been sacrificed to idols and from blood and from what is strangled[d] and from fornication. If you keep yourselves from these, you will do well. Farewell." 30 So they were sent off and went down to Antioch. When they gathered the congregation together, they delivered the letter. 31 When its members read it, they rejoiced at the exhortation. 32 Judas and Silas, who were themselves prophets, said much to encourage and strengthen the believers. 33 After they had been there for some time, they were sent off in peace by the believers to those who had sent them.[e] 35 But Paul and Barnabas remained in Antioch, and there, with many others, they taught and proclaimed the word of the Lord.

Acts 16:4–5

As they went from town to town, they delivered to them for observance the decisions that had been reached by the apostles and elders who were in Jerusalem. 5 So the churches were strengthened in the faith and increased in numbers daily.

Cf. Acts 11:27–30; 12:25; 18:22 (see note above).

167. Paul's Co-worker Timothy

Rom 16:21

Timothy, my co-worker, greets you; so do Lucius and Jason and Sosipater, my relatives.

1 Cor 4:17

For this reason I sent you Timothy, who is my beloved and faithful child in the Lord, to remind you of my ways in Christ Jesus, as I teach them everywhere in every church.

1 Cor 16:10–11

If Timothy comes, see that he has nothing to fear among you, for he is doing the work of the Lord just as I am; 11 therefore let no one despise him. Send him on his way in peace, so that he may come to me; for I am expecting him with the brothers.

2 Cor 1:19–20

For the Son of God, Jesus Christ, whom we proclaimed among you, Silvanus and Timothy and I, was not "Yes and No"; but in him it is always "Yes." 20 For in him every one of God's promises is a "Yes." For this reason it is through him that we say the "Amen," to the glory of God.

Phil 2:19–24

I hope in the Lord Jesus to send Timothy to you soon, so that I may be cheered by news of you. 20 I have no one like him who will be genuinely concerned for your welfare. 21 All of them are seeking their own interests, not those of Jesus Christ. 22 But Timothy's worth you know, how like a son with a father he has served with me in the work of the gospel. 23 I hope therefore to send him as soon as I see how things go with me; 24 and I trust in the Lord that I will also come soon.

1 Thess 3:1–2

Therefore when we could bear it no longer, we decided to be left alone in Athens; 2 and we sent Timothy, our brother and co-worker for God[a] in proclaiming the gospel of Christ, to strengthen and encourage you for the sake of your faith

1 Thess 3:6–7

But Timothy has just now come to us from you, and has brought us the good news of your faith and love. He has told us also that you always remember us kindly and long to see us—just as we long to see you. 7 For this reason, brothers and sisters, during all our distress and persecution we have been encouraged about you through your faith.

Acts 16:1–3

Paul went on also to Derbe and to Lystra, where there was a disciple named Timothy, the son of a Jewish woman who was a believer; but his father was a Greek. 2 He was well spoken of by the believers in Lystra and Iconium. 3 Paul wanted Timothy to accompany him; and he took him and had him circumcised because of the Jews who were in those places, for they all knew that his father was a Greek.

Acts 17:14–15

Then the believers immediately sent Paul away to the coast, but Silas and Timothy remained behind. 15 Those who conducted Paul brought him as far as Athens; and after receiving instructions to have Silas and Timothy join him as soon as possible, they left him.

Acts 18:5

When Silas and Timothy arrived from Macedonia, Paul was occupied with proclaiming the word, testifying to the Jews that the Messiah was Jesus.

Acts 19:21–22

Now after these things had been accomplished, Paul resolved in the Spirit to go through Macedonia and Achaia, and then to go on to Jerusalem. He said, "After I have gone there, I must also see Rome." 22 So he sent two of his helpers, Timothy and Erastus, to Macedonia, while he himself stayed for some time longer in Asia.

Acts 20:4

He was accompanied by Sopater son of Pyrrhus from Beroea, by Aristarchus and Secundus from Thessalonica, by Gaius from Derbe, and by Timothy, as well as by Tychicus and Trophimus from Asia.

Cf. 2 Cor 1:1–2; Phil 1:1–2; Col 1:1–2; 1 Thess 1:1; 2 Thess 1:1; Phlm 1; 1 Tim, passim; 2 Tim, passim.

[d] **Acts 15:29** ***and from what is strangled*** A few ancient authorities lack *and from what is strangled* [e] **Acts 15:33** ***them*** Other ancient authorities add verse 34, *But it seemed good to Silas to remain there* **§ 167** [a] **1 Thess 3:2** ***co-worker for God*** lit. *God's co-worker* Other ancient authorities read *God's minister* or *God's minister and our co-worker*

168. Paul's Co-worker Barnabas

1 Cor 9:6–7

ἢ μόνος ἐγὼ καὶ Βαρναβᾶς οὐκ ἔχομεν
ἐξουσίαν μὴ ἐργάζεσθαι; 7 Τίς στρατεύ-
εται ἰδίοις ὀψωνίοις ποτέ; τίς φυτεύει
ἀμπελῶνα καὶ τὸν καρπὸν αὐτοῦ οὐκ
ἐσθίει; ἢ τίς ποιμαίνει ποίμνην καὶ ἐκ τοῦ
γάλακτος τῆς ποίμνης οὐκ ἐσθίει;

Gal 2:1–2

Ἔπειτα διὰ δεκατεσσάρων ἐτῶν πάλιν
ἀνέβην εἰς Ἱεροσόλυμα μετὰ Βαρναβᾶ
συμπαραλαβὼν καὶ Τίτον· 2 ἀνέβην δὲ
κατὰ ἀποκάλυψιν· καὶ ἀνεθέμην αὐτοῖς
τὸ εὐαγγέλιον ὃ κηρύσσω ἐν τοῖς ἔθνε-
σιν, κατ' ἰδίαν δὲ τοῖς δοκοῦσιν, μή πως
εἰς κενὸν τρέχω ἢ ἔδραμον.

Gal 2:9

καὶ γνόντες τὴν χάριν τὴν δοθεῖσάν μοι,
Ἰάκωβος καὶ Κηφᾶς καὶ Ἰωάννης, οἱ δο-
κοῦντες στῦλοι εἶναι, δεξιὰς ἔδωκαν ἐμοὶ
καὶ Βαρναβᾷ κοινωνίας, ἵνα ἡμεῖς εἰς τὰ
ἔθνη, αὐτοὶ δὲ εἰς τὴν περιτομήν

Gal 2:11–13

Ὅτε δὲ ἦλθεν Κηφᾶς εἰς Ἀντιόχειαν,
κατὰ πρόσωπον αὐτῷ ἀντέστην, ὅτι κα-
τεγνωσμένος ἦν. 12 πρὸ τοῦ γὰρ ἐλθεῖν
τινας ἀπὸ Ἰακώβου μετὰ τῶν ἐθνῶν
συνήσθιεν· ὅτε δὲ ἦλθον, ὑπέστελλεν
καὶ ἀφώριζεν ἑαυτὸν φοβούμενος τοὺς
ἐκ περιτομῆς. 13 καὶ συνυπεκρίθησαν
αὐτῷ [καὶ] οἱ λοιποὶ Ἰουδαῖοι, ὥστε
καὶ Βαρναβᾶς συναπήχθη αὐτῶν τῇ
ὑποκρίσει.

Col 4:10

Ἀσπάζεται ὑμᾶς Ἀρίσταρχος ὁ συναι-
χμάλωτός μου καὶ Μᾶρκος ὁ ἀνεψιὸς
Βαρναβᾶ (περὶ οὗ ἐλάβετε ἐντολάς, ἐὰν
ἔλθῃ πρὸς ὑμᾶς, δέξασθε αὐτόν)

Acts 4:32–37

Τοῦ δὲ πλήθους τῶν πιστευσάντων ἦν
καρδία καὶ ψυχὴ μία, καὶ οὐδὲ εἷς τι τῶν
ὑπαρχόντων αὐτῷ ἔλεγεν ἴδιον εἶναι
ἀλλ' ἦν αὐτοῖς ἅπαντα κοινά. 33 καὶ
δυνάμει μεγάλῃ ἀπεδίδουν τὸ μαρτύ-
ριον οἱ ἀπόστολοι τῆς ἀναστάσεως τοῦ
κυρίου Ἰησοῦ, χάρις τε μεγάλη ἦν ἐπὶ
πάντας αὐτούς. 34 οὐδὲ γὰρ ἐνδεής τις
ἦν ἐν αὐτοῖς· ὅσοι γὰρ κτήτορες χωρίων
ἢ οἰκιῶν ὑπῆρχον, πωλοῦντες ἔφερον
τὰς τιμὰς τῶν πιπρασκομένων 35 καὶ
ἐτίθουν παρὰ τοὺς πόδας τῶν ἀποστό-
λων, διεδίδετο δὲ ἑκάστῳ καθότι ἄν τις
χρείαν εἶχεν. 36 Ἰωσὴφ δὲ ὁ ἐπικληθεὶς
Βαρναβᾶς ἀπὸ τῶν ἀποστόλων, ὅ ἐστιν
μεθερμηνευόμενον υἱὸς παρακλήσεως,
Λευίτης, Κύπριος τῷ γένει, 37 ὑπάρχον-
τος αὐτῷ ἀγροῦ πωλήσας ἤνεγκεν τὸ
χρῆμα καὶ ἔθηκεν πρὸς τοὺς πόδας τῶν
ἀποστόλων.

Acts 9:26–27

Παραγενόμενος δὲ εἰς Ἰερουσαλὴμ ἐπεί-
ραζεν κολλᾶσθαι τοῖς μαθηταῖς, καὶ πάντες
ἐφοβοῦντο αὐτὸν μὴ πιστεύοντες ὅτι ἐστὶν
μαθητής. 27 Βαρναβᾶς δὲ ἐπιλαβόμενος
αὐτὸν ἤγαγεν πρὸς τοὺς ἀποστόλους καὶ
διηγήσατο αὐτοῖς πῶς ἐν τῇ ὁδῷ εἶδεν
τὸν κύριον καὶ ὅτι ἐλάλησεν αὐτῷ καὶ
πῶς ἐν Δαμασκῷ ἐπαρρησιάσατο ἐν τῷ
ὀνόματι τοῦ Ἰησοῦ.

Acts 11:22–26

Ἠκούσθη δὲ ὁ λόγος εἰς τὰ ὦτα τῆς
ἐκκλησίας τῆς οὔσης ἐν Ἰερουσαλὴμ
περὶ αὐτῶν καὶ ἐξαπέστειλαν Βαρνα-
βᾶν ⸀[διελθεῖν] ἕως Ἀντιοχείας. 23 ὃς
παραγενόμενος καὶ ἰδὼν τὴν χάριν [τὴν]
τοῦ θεοῦ, ἐχάρη καὶ παρεκάλει πάντας
τῇ προθέσει τῆς καρδίας προσμένειν
τῷ κυρίῳ, 24 ὅτι ἦν ἀνὴρ ἀγαθὸς καὶ
πλήρης πνεύματος ἁγίου καὶ πίστεως.
καὶ προσετέθη ὄχλος ἱκανὸς τῷ κυρίῳ.
25 ἐξῆλθεν δὲ εἰς Ταρσὸν ἀναζητῆσαι
Σαῦλον, 26 καὶ εὑρὼν ἤγαγεν εἰς Ἀντι-
όχειαν. ἐγένετο δὲ αὐτοῖς καὶ ἐνιαυ-
τὸν ὅλον συναχθῆναι ἐν τῇ ἐκκλησίᾳ
καὶ διδάξαι ὄχλον ἱκανόν, χρηματίσαι
τε πρώτως ἐν Ἀντιοχείᾳ τοὺς μαθητὰς
Χριστιανούς.

Acts 11:29–30

τῶν δὲ μαθητῶν, καθὼς εὐπορεῖτό τις,
ὥρισαν ἕκαστος αὐτῶν εἰς διακονίαν
πέμψαι τοῖς κατοικοῦσιν ἐν τῇ Ἰουδαίᾳ
ἀδελφοῖς· 30 ὃ καὶ ἐποίησαν ἀποστείλαν-
τες πρὸς τοὺς πρεσβυτέρους διὰ χειρὸς
Βαρναβᾶ καὶ Σαύλου.

Acts 12:25–13:3

Βαρναβᾶς δὲ καὶ Σαῦλος ὑπέστρεψαν
⸀εἰς Ἰερουσαλὴμ πληρώσαντες τὴν δια-
κονίαν, συμπαραλαβόντες Ἰωάννην τὸν
ἐπικληθέντα Μᾶρκον. **13** Ἦσαν δὲ ἐν
Ἀντιοχείᾳ κατὰ τὴν οὖσαν ἐκκλησίαν
προφῆται καὶ διδάσκαλοι ὅ τε Βαρναβᾶς
καὶ Συμεὼν ὁ καλούμενος Νίγερ καὶ Λού-
κιος ὁ Κυρηναῖος, Μαναήν τε Ἡρῴδου
τοῦ τετραάρχου σύντροφος καὶ Σαῦλος.
2 Λειτουργούντων δὲ αὐτῶν τῷ κυρίῳ
καὶ νηστευόντων εἶπεν τὸ πνεῦμα τὸ
ἅγιον· ἀφορίσατε δή μοι τὸν Βαρναβᾶν
καὶ Σαῦλον εἰς τὸ ἔργον ὃ προσκέκλη-
μαι αὐτούς. 3 τότε νηστεύσαντες καὶ
προσευξάμενοι καὶ ἐπιθέντες τὰς χεῖρας
αὐτοῖς ἀπέλυσαν.

Acts 15:1–2

Καί τινες κατελθόντες ἀπὸ τῆς Ἰουδαίας
ἐδίδασκον τοὺς ἀδελφοὺς ὅτι, ἐὰν μὴ
περιτμηθῆτε τῷ ἔθει τῷ Μωϋσέως, οὐ
δύνασθε σωθῆναι. 2 γενομένης δὲ στάσεως
καὶ ζητήσεως οὐκ ὀλίγης τῷ Παύλῳ καὶ
τῷ Βαρναβᾷ πρὸς αὐτούς, ἔταξαν ἀνα-
βαίνειν Παῦλον καὶ Βαρναβᾶν καί τινας
ἄλλους ἐξ αὐτῶν πρὸς τοὺς ἀποστόλους
καὶ πρεσβυτέρους εἰς Ἰερουσαλὴμ περὶ
τοῦ ζητήματος τούτου.

Acts 15:36–40

Μετὰ δέ τινας ἡμέρας εἶπεν πρὸς Βαρναβᾶν
Παῦλος· ἐπιστρέψαντες δὴ ἐπισκεψώμεθα
τοὺς ἀδελφοὺς κατὰ πόλιν πᾶσαν ἐν αἷς
κατηγγείλαμεν τὸν λόγον τοῦ κυρίου
πῶς ἔχουσιν. 37 Βαρναβᾶς δὲ ἐβούλετο
συμπαραλαβεῖν καὶ τὸν Ἰωάννην τὸν
καλούμενον Μᾶρκον· 38 Παῦλος δὲ ἠξίου,
τὸν ἀποστάντα ἀπ' αὐτῶν ἀπὸ Παμφυλίας
καὶ μὴ συνελθόντα αὐτοῖς εἰς τὸ ἔργον
μὴ συμπαραλαμβάνειν τοῦτον. 39 ἐγένετο
δὲ παροξυσμὸς ὥστε ἀποχωρισθῆναι
αὐτοὺς ἀπ' ἀλλήλων, τόν τε Βαρναβᾶν
παραλαβόντα τὸν Μᾶρκον ἐκπλεῦσαι
εἰς Κύπρον, 40 Παῦλος δὲ ἐπιλεξάμενος
Σιλᾶν ἐξῆλθεν παραδοθεὶς τῇ χάριτι τοῦ
κυρίου ὑπὸ τῶν ἀδελφῶν.

Cf. Acts' entire account of the events of Paul's second missionary journey and the Jerusalem council, throughout which Paul was accompanied by Barnabas, especially 13:6–12; 13:42–52; 14:8–13; 14:14–18; 14:19–28; 15:12; 15:22–29.

§ 168 **Acts 11:22** ***διελθειν*** D E 33 *Byz*] *om.* 𝔓74 ℵ A B 1739 **Acts 12:25** ***εις*** ℵ B *Byz*] εξ 𝔓74 A 33. 1739 ¦ απο D E

168. Paul's Co-worker Barnabas

1 Cor 9:6–7

Or is it only Barnabas and I who have no right to refrain from working for a living? 7 Who at any time pays the expenses for doing military service? Who plants a vineyard and does not eat any of its fruit? Or who tends a flock and does not get any of its milk?

Gal 2:1–2

Then after fourteen years I went up again to Jerusalem with Barnabas, taking Titus along with me. 2 I went up in response to a revelation. Then I laid before them (though only in a private meeting with the acknowledged leaders) the gospel that I proclaim among the Gentiles, in order to make sure that I was not running, or had not run, in vain.

Gal 2:9

and when James and Cephas and John, who were acknowledged pillars, recognized the grace that had been given to me, they gave to Barnabas and me the right hand of fellowship, agreeing that we should go to the Gentiles and they to the circumcised.

Gal 2:11–13

But when Cephas came to Antioch, I opposed him to his face, because he stood self-condemned; 12 for until certain people came from James, he used to eat with the Gentiles. But after they came, he drew back and kept himself separate for fear of the circumcision faction. 13 And the other Jews joined him in this hypocrisy, so that even Barnabas was led astray by their hypocrisy.

Col 4:10

Aristarchus my fellow prisoner greets you, as does Mark the cousin of Barnabas, concerning whom you have received instructions—if he comes to you, welcome him.

Acts 4:32–37

Now the whole group of those who believed were of one heart and soul, and no one claimed private ownership of any possessions, but everything they owned was held in common. 33 With great power the apostles gave their testimony to the resurrection of the Lord Jesus, and great grace was upon them all. 34 There was not a needy person among them, for as many as owned lands or houses sold them and brought the proceeds of what was sold. 35 They laid it at the apostles' feet, and it was distributed to each as any had need. 36 There was a Levite, a native of Cyprus, Joseph, to whom the apostles gave the name Barnabas (which means "son of encouragement"). 37 He sold a field that belonged to him, then brought the money, and laid it at the apostles' feet.

Acts 9:26–27

When he had come to Jerusalem, he attempted to join the disciples; and they were all afraid of him, for they did not believe that he was a disciple. 27 But Barnabas took him, brought him to the apostles, and described for them how on the road he had seen the Lord, who had spoken to him, and how in Damascus he had spoken boldly in the name of Jesus.

Acts 11:22–26

News of this came to the ears of the church in Jerusalem, and they sent Barnabas to Antioch.[a] 23 When he came and saw the grace of God, he rejoiced, and he exhorted them all to remain faithful to the Lord with steadfast devotion; 24 for he was a good man, full of the Holy Spirit and of faith. And a great many people were brought to the Lord. 25 Then Barnabas went to Tarsus to look for Saul, 26 and when he had found him, he brought him to Antioch. So it was that for an entire year they met with the church and taught a great many people, and it was in Antioch that the disciples were first called "Christians."

Acts 11:29–30

The disciples determined that according to their ability, each would send relief to the believers living in Judea; 30 this they did, sending it to the elders by Barnabas and Saul.

Acts 12:25–13:3

Then after completing their mission Barnabas and Saul returned to[b] Jerusalem and brought with them John, whose other name was Mark. **13** Now in the church at Antioch there were prophets and teachers: Barnabas, Simeon who was called Niger, Lucius of Cyrene, Manaen a member of the court of Herod the ruler, and Saul. 2 While they were worshiping the Lord and fasting, the Holy Spirit said, "Set apart for me Barnabas and Saul for the work to which I have called them." 3 Then after fasting and praying they laid their hands on them and sent them off.

Acts 15:1–2

Then certain individuals came down from Judea and were teaching the brothers, "Unless you are circumcised according to the custom of Moses, you cannot be saved." 2 And after Paul and Barnabas had no small dissension and debate with them, Paul and Barnabas and some of the others were appointed to go up to Jerusalem to discuss this question with the apostles and the elders.

Acts 15:36–40

After some days Paul said to Barnabas, "Come, let us return and visit the believers in every city where we proclaimed the word of the Lord and see how they are doing." 37 Barnabas wanted to take with them John called Mark. 38 But Paul decided not to take with them one who had deserted them in Pamphylia and had not accompanied them in the work. 39 The disagreement became so sharp that they parted company; Barnabas took Mark with him and sailed away to Cyprus. 40 But Paul chose Silas and set out, the believers commending him to the grace of the Lord.

Cf. Acts' entire account of the events of Paul's second missionary journey and the Jerusalem council, throughout which Paul was accompanied by Barnabas, especially 13:6–12; 13:42–52; 14:8–13; 14:14–18; 14:19–28; 15:12; 15:22–29.

§ 168 [a] **Acts 11:22** *to Antioch* Other ancient authorities read *to journey to Antioch* [b] **Acts 12:25** *to* Other ancient authorities read *from*

169. Paul's Co-worker Silvanus

2 Cor 1:19–20
ὁ τοῦ θεοῦ γὰρ υἱὸς Ἰησοῦς Χριστὸς ὁ ἐν ὑμῖν δι' ἡμῶν κηρυχθείς, δι' ἐμοῦ καὶ Σιλουανοῦ καὶ Τιμοθέου, οὐκ ἐγένετο ναὶ καὶ οὒ ἀλλὰ ναὶ ἐν αὐτῷ γέγονεν. **20** ὅσαι γὰρ ἐπαγγελίαι θεοῦ, ἐν αὐτῷ τὸ ναί· διὸ καὶ δι' αὐτοῦ τὸ ἀμὴν τῷ θεῷ πρὸς δόξαν δι' ἡμῶν.

1 Thess 1:1
Παῦλος καὶ Σιλουανὸς καὶ Τιμόθεος τῇ ἐκκλησίᾳ Θεσσαλονικέων ἐν θεῷ πατρὶ καὶ κυρίῳ Ἰησοῦ Χριστῷ, χάρις ὑμῖν καὶ ⸀εἰρήνη.

2 Thess 1:1
Παῦλος καὶ Σιλουανὸς καὶ Τιμόθεος τῇ ἐκκλησίᾳ Θεσσαλονικέων ἐν θεῷ πατρὶ ἡμῶν καὶ κυρίῳ Ἰησοῦ Χριστῷ

Acts 15:22
Τότε ἔδοξε τοῖς ἀποστόλοις καὶ τοῖς πρεσβυτέροις σὺν ὅλῃ τῇ ἐκκλησίᾳ ἐκλεξαμένους ἄνδρας ἐξ αὐτῶν πέμψαι εἰς Ἀντιόχειαν σὺν τῷ Παύλῳ καὶ Βαρναβᾷ, Ἰούδαν τὸν καλούμενον Βαρσαββᾶν καὶ Σιλᾶν, ἄνδρας ἡγουμένους ἐν τοῖς ἀδελφοῖς

Acts 15:27
ἀπεστάλκαμεν οὖν Ἰούδαν καὶ Σιλᾶν καὶ αὐτοὺς διὰ λόγου ἀπαγγέλλοντας τὰ αὐτά.

Acts 15:32–35
Ἰούδας τε καὶ Σιλᾶς καὶ αὐτοὶ προφῆται ὄντες διὰ λόγου πολλοῦ παρεκάλεσαν τοὺς ἀδελφοὺς καὶ ἐπεστήριξαν, **33** ποιήσαντες δὲ χρόνον ἀπελύθησαν μετ' εἰρήνης ἀπὸ τῶν ἀδελφῶν πρὸς τοὺς ἀποστείλαντας ⸀αὐτούς. **35** Παῦλος δὲ καὶ Βαρναβᾶς διέτριβον ἐν Ἀντιοχείᾳ διδάσκοντες καὶ εὐαγγελιζόμενοι μετὰ καὶ ἑτέρων πολλῶν τὸν λόγον τοῦ κυρίου.

Acts 15:36–41
Μετὰ δέ τινας ἡμέρας εἶπεν πρὸς Βαρναβᾶν Παῦλος· ἐπιστρέψαντες δὴ ἐπισκεψώμεθα τοὺς ἀδελφοὺς κατὰ πόλιν πᾶσαν ἐν αἷς κατηγγείλαμεν τὸν λόγον τοῦ κυρίου πῶς ἔχουσιν. **37** Βαρναβᾶς δὲ ἐβούλετο συμπαραλαβεῖν καὶ τὸν Ἰωάννην τὸν καλούμενον Μᾶρκον· **38** Παῦλος δὲ ἠξίου, τὸν ἀποστάντα ἀπ' αὐτῶν ἀπὸ Παμφυλίας καὶ μὴ συνελθόντα αὐτοῖς εἰς τὸ ἔργον μὴ συμπαραλαμβάνειν τοῦτον. **39** ἐγένετο δὲ παροξυσμὸς ὥστε ἀποχωρισθῆναι αὐτοὺς ἀπ' ἀλλήλων, τόν τε Βαρναβᾶν παραλαβόντα τὸν Μᾶρκον ἐκπλεῦσαι εἰς Κύπρον, **40** Παῦλος δὲ ἐπιλεξάμενος Σιλᾶν ἐξῆλθεν παραδοθεὶς τῇ χάριτι τοῦ κυρίου ὑπὸ τῶν ἀδελφῶν. **41** διήρχετο δὲ τὴν Συρίαν καὶ [τὴν] Κιλικίαν ἐπιστηρίζων τὰς ἐκκλησίας.

Acts 17:1–4
Διοδεύσαντες δὲ τὴν Ἀμφίπολιν καὶ τὴν Ἀπολλωνίαν ἦλθον εἰς Θεσσαλονίκην ὅπου ἦν συναγωγὴ τῶν Ἰουδαίων. **2** κατὰ δὲ τὸ εἰωθὸς τῷ Παύλῳ εἰσῆλθεν πρὸς αὐτοὺς καὶ ἐπὶ σάββατα τρία διελέξατο αὐτοῖς ἀπὸ τῶν γραφῶν, **3** διανοίγων καὶ παρατιθέμενος ὅτι τὸν χριστὸν ἔδει παθεῖν καὶ ἀναστῆναι ἐκ νεκρῶν καὶ ὅτι οὗτός ἐστιν ὁ χριστὸς [ὁ] Ἰησοῦς ὃν ἐγὼ καταγγέλλω ὑμῖν. **4** καί τινες ἐξ αὐτῶν ἐπείσθησαν καὶ προσεκληρώθησαν τῷ Παύλῳ καὶ τῷ Σιλᾷ, τῶν τε σεβομένων Ἑλλήνων πλῆθος πολύ, γυναικῶν τε τῶν πρώτων οὐκ ὀλίγαι.

Acts 17:10
Οἱ δὲ ἀδελφοὶ εὐθέως διὰ νυκτὸς ἐξέπεμψαν τόν τε Παῦλον καὶ τὸν Σιλᾶν εἰς Βέροιαν, οἵτινες παραγενόμενοι εἰς τὴν συναγωγὴν τῶν Ἰουδαίων ἀπῄεσαν.

Acts 17:13–15
Ὡς δὲ ἔγνωσαν οἱ ἀπὸ τῆς Θεσσαλονίκης Ἰουδαῖοι ὅτι καὶ ἐν τῇ Βεροίᾳ κατηγγέλη ὑπὸ τοῦ Παύλου ὁ λόγος τοῦ θεοῦ, ἦλθον κἀκεῖ σαλεύοντες καὶ ταράσσοντες τοὺς ὄχλους. **14** εὐθέως δὲ τότε τὸν Παῦλον ἐξαπέστειλαν οἱ ἀδελφοὶ πορεύεσθαι ἕως ἐπὶ τὴν θάλασσαν, ὑπέμεινάν τε ὅ τε Σιλᾶς καὶ ὁ Τιμόθεος ἐκεῖ. **15** οἱ δὲ καθιστάνοντες τὸν Παῦλον ἤγαγον ἕως Ἀθηνῶν, καὶ λαβόντες ἐντολὴν πρὸς τὸν Σιλᾶν καὶ τὸν Τιμόθεον ἵνα ὡς τάχιστα ἔλθωσιν πρὸς αὐτὸν ἐξῄεσαν.

Acts 18:5
Ὡς δὲ κατῆλθον ἀπὸ τῆς Μακεδονίας ὅ τε Σιλᾶς καὶ ὁ Τιμόθεος, συνείχετο τῷ λόγῳ ὁ Παῦλος διαμαρτυρόμενος τοῖς Ἰουδαίοις εἶναι τὸν χριστὸν Ἰησοῦν.

170. Paul's Co-workers Prisca and Aquila

Rom 16:3–5
Ἀσπάσασθε Πρίσκαν καὶ Ἀκύλαν τοὺς συνεργούς μου ἐν Χριστῷ Ἰησοῦ, **4** οἵτινες ὑπὲρ τῆς ψυχῆς μου τὸν ἑαυτῶν τράχηλον ὑπέθηκαν, οἷς οὐκ ἐγὼ μόνος εὐχαριστῶ ἀλλὰ καὶ πᾶσαι αἱ ἐκκλησίαι τῶν ἐθνῶν, **5** καὶ τὴν κατ' οἶκον αὐτῶν ἐκκλησίαν. ἀσπάσασθε Ἐπαίνετον τὸν ἀγαπητόν μου, ὅς ἐστιν ἀπαρχὴ τῆς Ἀσίας εἰς Χριστόν.

1 Cor 16:19
Ἀσπάζονται ὑμᾶς αἱ ἐκκλησίαι τῆς Ἀσίας. ἀσπάζεται ὑμᾶς ἐν κυρίῳ πολλὰ Ἀκύλας καὶ Πρίσκα σὺν τῇ κατ' οἶκον αὐτῶν ἐκκλησίᾳ.

2 Tim 4:19
Ἄσπασαι Πρίσκαν καὶ Ἀκύλαν καὶ τὸν Ὀνησιφόρου οἶκον.

Acts 18:1–3
Μετὰ ταῦτα χωρισθεὶς ἐκ τῶν Ἀθηνῶν ἦλθεν εἰς Κόρινθον. **2** καὶ εὑρών τινα Ἰουδαῖον ὀνόματι Ἀκύλαν, Ποντικὸν τῷ γένει προσφάτως ἐληλυθότα ἀπὸ τῆς Ἰταλίας καὶ Πρίσκιλλαν γυναῖκα αὐτοῦ, διὰ τὸ διατεταχέναι Κλαύδιον χωρίζεσθαι πάντας τοὺς Ἰουδαίους ἀπὸ τῆς Ῥώμης, προσῆλθεν αὐτοῖς **3** καὶ διὰ τὸ ὁμότεχνον εἶναι ἔμενεν παρ' αὐτοῖς, καὶ ἠργάζετο· ἦσαν γὰρ σκηνοποιοὶ τῇ τέχνῃ.

Acts 18:18–21
Ὁ δὲ Παῦλος ἔτι προσμείνας ἡμέρας ἱκανὰς τοῖς ἀδελφοῖς ἀποταξάμενος ἐξέπλει εἰς τὴν Συρίαν, καὶ σὺν αὐτῷ

§ 169 **1 Thess 1:1** ***ειρηνη*** B 1739. 1881] *add.* απο θεου πατρος ημων και κυριου Ιησου Χριστου ℵ A (D) I 33 *Byz* **Acts 15:33** ***αυτους*** $\mathfrak{P}^{74}$ ℵ A B E *Byz*] *add.* [v. 34] εδοξε δε τω Σιλα επιμειναι αυτου (C) 33. 1739 ¦ *add.* εδοξε δε τω Σιλα επιμειναι προς αυτους, μονος δε Ιουδας επορευθη D

169. Paul's Co-worker Silvanus

2 Cor 1:19–20
For the Son of God, Jesus Christ, whom we proclaimed among you, Silvanus and Timothy and I, was not "Yes and No"; but in him it is always "Yes." **20** For in him every one of God's promises is a "Yes." For this reason it is through him that we say the "Amen," to the glory of God.

1 Thess 1:1
Paul, Silvanus, and Timothy, To the church of the Thessalonians in God the Father and the Lord Jesus Christ: Grace to you and peace.[a]

2 Thess 1:1
Paul, Silvanus, and Timothy, To the church of the Thessalonians in God our Father and the Lord Jesus Christ

Acts 15:22
Then the apostles and the elders, with the consent of the whole church, decided to choose men from among their members and to send them to Antioch with Paul and Barnabas. They sent Judas called Barsabbas, and Silas, leaders among the brothers,

Acts 15:27
We have therefore sent Judas and Silas, who themselves will tell you the same things by word of mouth.

Acts 15:32–35
Judas and Silas, who were themselves prophets, said much to encourage and strengthen the believers. **33** After they had been there for some time, they were sent off in peace by the believers to those who had sent them.[b] **35** But Paul and Barnabas remained in Antioch, and there, with many others, they taught and proclaimed the word of the Lord.

Acts 15:36–41
After some days Paul said to Barnabas, "Come, let us return and visit the believers in every city where we proclaimed the word of the Lord and see how they are doing." **37** Barnabas wanted to take with them John called Mark. **38** But Paul decided not to take with them one who had deserted them in Pamphylia and had not accompanied them in the work. **39** The disagreement became so sharp that they parted company; Barnabas took Mark with him and sailed away to Cyprus. **40** But Paul chose Silas and set out, the believers commending him to the grace of the Lord. **41** He went through Syria and Cilicia, strengthening the churches.

Acts 17:1–4
After Paul and Silas had passed through Amphipolis and Apollonia, they came to Thessalonica, where there was a synagogue of the Jews. **2** And Paul went in, as was his custom, and on three sabbath days argued with them from the scriptures, **3** explaining and proving that it was necessary for the Messiah to suffer and to rise from the dead, and saying, "This is the Messiah, Jesus whom I am proclaiming to you." **4** Some of them were persuaded and joined Paul and Silas, as did a great many of the devout Greeks and not a few of the leading women.

Acts 17:10
That very night the believers sent Paul and Silas off to Beroea; and when they arrived, they went to the Jewish synagogue.

Acts 17:13–15
But when the Jews of Thessalonica learned that the word of God had been proclaimed by Paul in Beroea as well, they came there too, to stir up and incite the crowds. **14** Then the believers immediately sent Paul away to the coast, but Silas and Timothy remained behind. **15** Those who conducted Paul brought him as far as Athens; and after receiving instructions to have Silas and Timothy join him as soon as possible, they left him.

Acts 18:5
When Silas and Timothy arrived from Macedonia, Paul was occupied with proclaiming the word, testifying to the Jews that the Messiah was Jesus.

170. Paul's Co-workers Prisca and Aquila

Rom 16:3–5
Greet Prisca and Aquila, who work with me in Christ Jesus, **4** and who risked their necks for my life, to whom not only I give thanks, but also all the churches of the Gentiles. **5** Greet also the church in their house. Greet my beloved Epaenetus, who was the first convert in Asia for Christ.

1 Cor 16:19
The churches of Asia send greetings. Aquila and Prisca, together with the church in their house, greet you warmly in the Lord.

2 Tim 4:19
Greet Prisca and Aquila, and the household of Onesiphorus.

Acts 18:1–3
After this Paul left Athens and went to Corinth. **2** There he found a Jew named Aquila, a native of Pontus, who had recently come from Italy with his wife Priscilla, because Claudius had ordered all Jews to leave Rome. Paul went to see them, **3** and, because he was of the same trade, he stayed with them, and they worked together—by trade they were tentmakers.

Acts 18:18–21
After staying there for a considerable time, Paul said farewell to the believers and sailed for Syria, accompanied by

§ 169 [a] **1 Thess 1:1** *peace* Other ancient authorities add *from God our Father and the Lord Jesus Christ* [b] **Acts 15:33** *them* Other ancient authorities add verse 34, *But it seemed good to Silas to remain there*

Πρίσκιλλα καὶ Ἀκύλας, κειράμενος ἐν Κεγχρεαῖς τὴν κεφαλήν, εἶχεν γὰρ εὐχήν. 19 κατήντησαν δὲ εἰς Ἔφεσον κἀκείνους κατέλιπεν αὐτοῦ, αὐτὸς δὲ εἰσελθὼν εἰς τὴν συναγωγὴν διελέξατο τοῖς Ἰουδαίοις. 20 ἐρωτώντων δὲ αὐτῶν ἐπὶ πλείονα χρόνον μεῖναι οὐκ ἐπένευσεν, 21 ἀλλὰ ἀποταξάμενος καὶ ⸂εἰπών· πάλιν⸃ ἀνακάμψω πρὸς ὑμᾶς τοῦ θεοῦ θέλοντος, ἀνήχθη ἀπὸ τῆς Ἐφέσου

Acts 18:24–28

Ἰουδαῖος δέ τις Ἀπολλῶς ὀνόματι, Ἀλεξανδρεὺς τῷ γένει, ἀνὴρ λόγιος, κατήντησεν εἰς Ἔφεσον, δυνατὸς ὢν ἐν ταῖς γραφαῖς. 25 οὗτος ἦν κατηχημένος τὴν ὁδὸν τοῦ κυρίου καὶ ζέων τῷ πνεύματι ἐλάλει καὶ ἐδίδασκεν ἀκριβῶς τὰ περὶ τοῦ Ἰησοῦ, ἐπιστάμενος μόνον τὸ βάπτισμα Ἰωάννου· 26 οὗτός τε ἤρξατο παρρησιάζεσθαι ἐν τῇ συναγωγῇ. ἀκούσαντες δὲ αὐτοῦ Πρίσκιλλα καὶ Ἀκύλας προσελάβοντο αὐτὸν καὶ ἀκριβέστερον αὐτῷ ἐξέθεντο τὴν ὁδὸν [τοῦ θεοῦ]. 27 βουλομένου δὲ αὐτοῦ διελθεῖν εἰς τὴν Ἀχαΐαν, προτρεψάμενοι οἱ ἀδελφοὶ ἔγραψαν τοῖς μαθηταῖς ἀποδέξασθαι αὐτόν, ὃς παραγενόμενος συνεβάλετο πολὺ τοῖς πεπιστευκόσιν διὰ τῆς χάριτος· 28 εὐτόνως γὰρ τοῖς Ἰουδαίοις διακατηλέγχετο δημοσίᾳ ἐπιδεικνὺς διὰ τῶν γραφῶν εἶναι τὸν χριστὸν Ἰησοῦν.

171. Paul's Co-worker Apollos

1 Cor 1:12

λέγω δὲ τοῦτο ὅτι ἕκαστος ὑμῶν λέγει· ἐγὼ μέν εἰμι Παύλου, ἐγὼ δὲ Ἀπολλῶ, ἐγὼ δὲ Κηφᾶ, ἐγὼ δὲ Χριστοῦ.

1 Cor 3:4–6

ὅταν γὰρ λέγῃ τις· ἐγὼ μέν εἰμι Παύλου, ἕτερος δέ· ἐγὼ Ἀπολλῶ, οὐκ ἄνθρωποί ἐστε; 5 Τί οὖν ἐστιν Ἀπολλῶς; τί δέ ἐστιν Παῦλος; διάκονοι δι᾽ ὧν ἐπιστεύσατε, καὶ ἑκάστῳ ὡς ὁ κύριος ἔδωκεν. 6 ἐγὼ ἐφύτευσα, Ἀπολλῶς ἐπότισεν, ἀλλὰ ὁ θεὸς ηὔξανεν

1 Cor 3:21–23

ὥστε μηδεὶς καυχάσθω ἐν ἀνθρώποις· πάντα γὰρ ὑμῶν ἐστιν, 22 εἴτε Παῦλος εἴτε Ἀπολλῶς εἴτε Κηφᾶς, εἴτε κόσμος εἴτε ζωὴ εἴτε θάνατος, εἴτε ἐνεστῶτα εἴτε μέλλοντα· πάντα ὑμῶν, 23 ὑμεῖς δὲ Χριστοῦ, Χριστὸς δὲ θεοῦ.

1 Cor 4:6

Ταῦτα δέ, ἀδελφοί, μετεσχημάτισα εἰς ἐμαυτὸν καὶ Ἀπολλῶν δι᾽ ὑμᾶς, ἵνα ἐν ἡμῖν μάθητε τὸ μὴ ὑπὲρ ἃ γέγραπται, ἵνα μὴ εἷς ὑπὲρ τοῦ ἑνὸς φυσιοῦσθε κατὰ τοῦ ἑτέρου.

1 Cor 16:12

Περὶ δὲ Ἀπολλῶ τοῦ ἀδελφοῦ, πολλὰ παρεκάλεσα αὐτόν, ἵνα ἔλθῃ πρὸς ὑμᾶς μετὰ τῶν ἀδελφῶν· καὶ πάντως οὐκ ἦν θέλημα ἵνα νῦν ἔλθῃ· ἐλεύσεται δὲ ὅταν εὐκαιρήσῃ.

Titus 3:13

Ζηνᾶν τὸν νομικὸν καὶ Ἀπολλῶν σπουδαίως πρόπεμψον, ἵνα μηδὲν αὐτοῖς λείπῃ.

Acts 18:24–19:7

Ἰουδαῖος δέ τις Ἀπολλῶς ὀνόματι, Ἀλεξανδρεὺς τῷ γένει, ἀνὴρ λόγιος, κατήντησεν εἰς Ἔφεσον, δυνατὸς ὢν ἐν ταῖς γραφαῖς. 25 οὗτος ἦν κατηχημένος τὴν ὁδὸν τοῦ κυρίου καὶ ζέων τῷ πνεύματι ἐλάλει καὶ ἐδίδασκεν ἀκριβῶς τὰ περὶ τοῦ Ἰησοῦ, ἐπιστάμενος μόνον τὸ βάπτισμα Ἰωάννου· 26 οὗτός τε ἤρξατο παρρησιάζεσθαι ἐν τῇ συναγωγῇ. ἀκούσαντες δὲ αὐτοῦ Πρίσκιλλα καὶ Ἀκύλας προσελάβοντο αὐτὸν καὶ ἀκριβέστερον αὐτῷ ἐξέθεντο τὴν ὁδὸν [τοῦ θεοῦ]. 27 βουλομένου δὲ αὐτοῦ διελθεῖν εἰς τὴν Ἀχαΐαν, προτρεψάμενοι οἱ ἀδελφοὶ ἔγραψαν τοῖς μαθηταῖς ἀποδέξασθαι αὐτόν, ὃς παραγενόμενος συνεβάλετο πολὺ τοῖς πεπιστευκόσιν διὰ τῆς χάριτος· 28 εὐτόνως γὰρ τοῖς Ἰουδαίοις διακατηλέγχετο δημοσίᾳ ἐπιδεικνὺς διὰ τῶν γραφῶν εἶναι τὸν χριστὸν Ἰησοῦν. **19** Ἐγένετο δὲ ἐν τῷ τὸν Ἀπολλῶ εἶναι ἐν Κορίνθῳ Παῦλον διελθόντα τὰ ἀνωτερικὰ μέρη [κατ]ελθεῖν εἰς Ἔφεσον καὶ εὑρεῖν τινας μαθητὰς 2 εἶπέν τε πρὸς αὐτούς· εἰ πνεῦμα ἅγιον ἐλάβετε πιστεύσαντες; οἱ δὲ πρὸς αὐτόν· ἀλλ᾽ οὐδ᾽ εἰ πνεῦμα ἅγιον ἔστιν ἠκούσαμεν. 3 εἶπέν τε· εἰς τί οὖν ἐβαπτίσθητε; οἱ δὲ εἶπαν· εἰς τὸ Ἰωάννου βάπτισμα. 4 εἶπεν δὲ Παῦλος· Ἰωάννης ἐβάπτισεν βάπτισμα μετανοίας τῷ λαῷ λέγων εἰς τὸν ἐρχόμενον μετ᾽ αὐτὸν ἵνα πιστεύσωσιν, τοῦτ᾽ ἔστιν εἰς τὸν Ἰησοῦν. 5 ἀκούσαντες δὲ ἐβαπτίσθησαν εἰς τὸ ὄνομα τοῦ κυρίου Ἰησοῦ, 6 καὶ ἐπιθέντος αὐτοῖς τοῦ Παύλου [τὰς] χεῖρας ἦλθε τὸ πνεῦμα τὸ ἅγιον ἐπ᾽ αὐτούς, ἐλάλουν τε γλώσσαις καὶ ἐπροφήτευον. 7 ἦσαν δὲ οἱ πάντες ἄνδρες ὡσεὶ δώδεκα.

172. Paul's Co-worker Luke

Col 4:14

ἀσπάζεται ὑμᾶς Λουκᾶς ὁ ἰατρὸς ὁ ἀγαπητὸς καὶ Δημᾶς.

2 Tim 4:11

Λουκᾶς ἐστιν μόνος μετ᾽ ἐμοῦ. Μᾶρκον ἀναλαβὼν ἄγε μετὰ σεαυτοῦ, ἔστιν γάρ μοι εὔχρηστος εἰς διακονίαν.

Phlm 23–24

Ἀσπάζεταί σε Ἐπαφρᾶς ὁ συναιχμάλωτός μου ἐν Χριστῷ Ἰησοῦ, 24 Μᾶρκος, Ἀρίσταρχος, Δημᾶς, Λουκᾶς, οἱ συνεργοί μου.

Cf. the "we passages" of Acts: 16:6–15; 16:16–18; 20:1–16; 21:1–19; 27:1–38; 28:1–16.

§ 170 Acts 18:21 *ειπων· παλιν* 𝔓74 ℵ A B E 33. 1739] ειπων· δει με (δε D*) παντως την εορτην την (ημεραν D) ερχομενην ποιησαι εις Ιεροσολυμα· παλιν δε (*om.* παλιν δε D) D *Byz*

Priscilla and Aquila. At Cenchreae he had his hair cut, for he was under a vow. **19** When they reached Ephesus, he left them there, but first he himself went into the synagogue and had a discussion with the Jews. **20** When they asked him to stay longer, he declined; **21** but on taking leave of them, he said, "I will return[a] to you, if God wills." Then he set sail from Ephesus.

Acts 18:24–28

Now there came to Ephesus a Jew named Apollos, a native of Alexandria. He was an eloquent man, well-versed in the scriptures. **25** He had been instructed in the Way of the Lord; and he spoke with burning enthusiasm and taught accurately the things concerning Jesus, though he knew only the baptism of John. **26** He began to speak boldly in the synagogue; but when Priscilla and Aquila heard him, they took him aside and explained the Way of God to him more accurately. **27** And when he wished to cross over to Achaia, the believers encouraged him and wrote to the disciples to welcome him. On his arrival he greatly helped those who through grace had become believers, **28** for he powerfully refuted the Jews in public, showing by the scriptures that the Messiah is Jesus.

171. Paul's Co-worker Apollos

1 Cor 1:12

What I mean is that each of you says, "I belong to Paul," or "I belong to Apollos," or "I belong to Cephas," or "I belong to Christ."

1 Cor 3:4–6

For when one says, "I belong to Paul," and another, "I belong to Apollos," are you not merely human? **5** What then is Apollos? What is Paul? Servants through whom you came to believe, as the Lord assigned to each. **6** I planted, Apollos watered, but God gave the growth.

1 Cor 3:21–23

So let no one boast about human leaders. For all things are yours, **22** whether Paul or Apollos or Cephas or the world or life or death or the present or the future—all belong to you, **23** and you belong to Christ, and Christ belongs to God.

1 Cor 4:6

I have applied all this to Apollos and myself for your benefit, brothers and sisters, so that you may learn through us the meaning of the saying, "Nothing beyond what is written," so that none of you will be puffed up in favor of one against another.

1 Cor 16:12

Now concerning our brother Apollos, I strongly urged him to visit you with the other brothers, but he was not at all willing to come now. He will come when he has the opportunity.

Titus 3:13

Make every effort to send Zenas the lawyer and Apollos on their way, and see that they lack nothing.

Acts 18:24–19:7

Now there came to Ephesus a Jew named Apollos, a native of Alexandria. He was an eloquent man, well-versed in the scriptures. **25** He had been instructed in the Way of the Lord; and he spoke with burning enthusiasm and taught accurately the things concerning Jesus, though he knew only the baptism of John. **26** He began to speak boldly in the synagogue; but when Priscilla and Aquila heard him, they took him aside and explained the Way of God to him more accurately. **27** And when he wished to cross over to Achaia, the believers encouraged him and wrote to the disciples to welcome him. On his arrival he greatly helped those who through grace had become believers, **28** for he powerfully refuted the Jews in public, showing by the scriptures that the Messiah is Jesus. **19** While Apollos was in Corinth, Paul passed through the interior regions and came to Ephesus, where he found some disciples. **2** He said to them, "Did you receive the Holy Spirit when you became believers?" They replied, "No, we have not even heard that there is a Holy Spirit." **3** Then he said, "Into what then were you baptized?" They answered, "Into John's baptism." **4** Paul said, "John baptized with the baptism of repentance, telling the people to believe in the one who was to come after him, that is, in Jesus." **5** On hearing this, they were baptized in the name of the Lord Jesus. **6** When Paul had laid his hands on them, the Holy Spirit came upon them, and they spoke in tongues and prophesied— **7** altogether there were about twelve of them.

172. Paul's Co-worker Luke

Col 4:14

Luke, the beloved physician, and Demas greet you.

2 Tim 4:11

Only Luke is with me. Get Mark and bring him with you, for he is useful in my ministry.

Phlm 23–24

Epaphras, my fellow prisoner in Christ Jesus, sends greetings to you, **24** and so do Mark, Aristarchus, Demas, and Luke, my fellow workers.

Cf. the "we passages" of Acts: 16:6–15; 16:16–18; 20:1–16; 21:1–19; 27:1–38; 28:1–16.

§ 170 [a] **Acts 18:21** ***I will return*** Other ancient authorities read *I must at all costs keep the approaching festival in Jerusalem, but I will return*

173. Paul's Co-worker Mark

Col 4:10

Ἀσπάζεται ὑμᾶς Ἀρίσταρχος ὁ συναιχμάλωτός μου καὶ Μᾶρκος ὁ ἀνεψιὸς Βαρναβᾶ (περὶ οὗ ἐλάβετε ἐντολάς, ἐὰν ἔλθῃ πρὸς ὑμᾶς, δέξασθε αὐτόν)

2 Tim 4:11

Λουκᾶς ἐστιν μόνος μετ᾽ ἐμοῦ. Μᾶρκον ἀναλαβὼν ἄγε μετὰ σεαυτοῦ, ἔστιν γάρ μοι εὔχρηστος εἰς διακονίαν.

Phlm 23–24

Ἀσπάζεταί σε Ἐπαφρᾶς ὁ συναιχμάλωτός μου ἐν Χριστῷ Ἰησοῦ, **24** Μᾶρκος,
Ἀρίσταρχος, Δημᾶς, Λουκᾶς, οἱ συνεργοί μου.

Acts 12:11–12

Καὶ ὁ Πέτρος ἐν ἑαυτῷ γενόμενος εἶπεν· νῦν οἶδα ἀληθῶς ὅτι ἐξαπέστειλεν [ὁ] κύριος τὸν ἄγγελον αὐτοῦ καὶ ἐξείλατό με ἐκ χειρὸς Ἡρῴδου καὶ πάσης τῆς προσδοκίας τοῦ λαοῦ τῶν Ἰουδαίων.
12 συνιδών τε ἦλθεν ἐπὶ τὴν οἰκίαν τῆς Μαρίας τῆς μητρὸς Ἰωάννου τοῦ ἐπικαλουμένου Μάρκου, οὗ ἦσαν ἱκανοὶ συνηθροισμένοι καὶ προσευχόμενοι.

Acts 12:25

Βαρναβᾶς δὲ καὶ Σαῦλος ὑπέστρεψαν ⸀εἰς Ἰερουσαλὴμ πληρώσαντες τὴν διακονίαν, συμπαραλαβόντες Ἰωάννην τὸν ἐπικληθέντα Μᾶρκον.

Acts 13:4–5

Αὐτοὶ μὲν οὖν ἐκπεμφθέντες ὑπὸ τοῦ ἁγίου πνεύματος κατῆλθον εἰς Σελεύκειαν,
ἐκεῖθέν τε ἀπέπλευσαν εἰς Κύπρον **5** καὶ
γενόμενοι ἐν Σαλαμῖνι κατήγγελλον τὸν λόγον τοῦ θεοῦ ἐν ταῖς συναγωγαῖς τῶν Ἰουδαίων. εἶχον δὲ καὶ Ἰωάννην ὑπηρέτην.

Acts 13:13

Ἀναχθέντες δὲ ἀπὸ τῆς Πάφου οἱ περὶ Παῦλον ἦλθον εἰς Πέργην τῆς Παμφυλίας, Ἰωάννης δὲ ἀποχωρήσας ἀπ᾽ αὐτῶν ὑπέστρεψεν εἰς Ἱεροσόλυμα.

Acts 15:36–40

Μετὰ δέ τινας ἡμέρας εἶπεν πρὸς Βαρναβᾶν Παῦλος· ἐπιστρέψαντες δὴ ἐπισκεψώμεθα τοὺς ἀδελφοὺς κατὰ πόλιν πᾶσαν ἐν αἷς κατηγγείλαμεν τὸν λόγον τοῦ κυρίου
πῶς ἔχουσιν. **37** Βαρναβᾶς δὲ ἐβούλετο
συμπαραλαβεῖν καὶ τὸν Ἰωάννην τὸν
καλούμενον Μᾶρκον· **38** Παῦλος δὲ ἠξίου,
τὸν ἀποστάντα ἀπ᾽ αὐτῶν ἀπὸ Παμφυλίας καὶ μὴ συνελθόντα αὐτοῖς εἰς τὸ ἔργον
μὴ συμπαραλαμβάνειν τοῦτον. **39** ἐγένετο
δὲ παροξυσμὸς ὥστε ἀποχωρισθῆναι αὐτοὺς ἀπ᾽ ἀλλήλων, τόν τε Βαρναβᾶν παραλαβόντα τὸν Μᾶρκον ἐκπλεῦσαι
εἰς Κύπρον, **40** Παῦλος δὲ ἐπιλεξάμενος
Σιλᾶν ἐξῆλθεν παραδοθεὶς τῇ χάριτι τοῦ κυρίου ὑπὸ τῶν ἀδελφῶν.

174. Paul's Co-worker Titus

2 Cor 2:12–13

Ἐλθὼν δὲ εἰς τὴν Τρῳάδα εἰς τὸ εὐαγγέλιον τοῦ Χριστοῦ καὶ θύρας μοι ἀνεῳ-
γμένης ἐν κυρίῳ, **13** οὐκ ἔσχηκα ἄνεσιν
τῷ πνεύματί μου τῷ μὴ εὑρεῖν με Τίτον τὸν ἀδελφόν μου, ἀλλὰ ἀποταξάμενος αὐτοῖς ἐξῆλθον εἰς Μακεδονίαν.

2 Cor 7:6–7

ἀλλ᾽ ὁ παρακαλῶν τοὺς ταπεινοὺς παρεκάλεσεν ἡμᾶς ὁ θεὸς ἐν τῇ παρουσίᾳ
Τίτου, **7** οὐ μόνον δὲ ἐν τῇ παρουσίᾳ
αὐτοῦ ἀλλὰ καὶ ἐν τῇ παρακλήσει ᾗ παρεκλήθη ἐφ᾽ ὑμῖν, ἀναγγέλλων ἡμῖν τὴν ὑμῶν ἐπιπόθησιν, τὸν ὑμῶν ὀδυρμόν, τὸν ὑμῶν ζῆλον ὑπὲρ ἐμοῦ ὥστε με μᾶλλον χαρῆναι.

2 Cor 7:13–15

διὰ τοῦτο παρακεκλήμεθα. Ἐπὶ δὲ τῇ παρακλήσει ἡμῶν περισσοτέρως μᾶλλον ἐχάρημεν ἐπὶ τῇ χαρᾷ Τίτου, ὅτι ἀναπέπαυται τὸ πνεῦμα αὐτοῦ ἀπὸ
πάντων ὑμῶν· **14** ὅτι εἴ τι αὐτῷ ὑπὲρ
ὑμῶν κεκαύχημαι, οὐ κατῃσχύνθην, ἀλλ᾽ ὡς πάντα ἐν ἀληθείᾳ ἐλαλήσαμεν ὑμῖν, οὕτως καὶ ἡ καύχησις ἡμῶν ἡ ἐπὶ
Τίτου ἀλήθεια ἐγενήθη. **15** καὶ τὰ σπλά-
γχνα αὐτοῦ περισσοτέρως εἰς ὑμᾶς ἐστιν ἀναμιμνῃσκομένου τὴν πάντων ὑμῶν ὑπακοήν, ὡς μετὰ φόβου καὶ τρόμου ἐδέξασθε αὐτόν.

2 Cor 8:3–6

ὅτι κατὰ δύναμιν, μαρτυρῶ, καὶ παρὰ
δύναμιν, αὐθαίρετοι **4** μετὰ πολλῆς πα-
ρακλήσεως δεόμενοι ἡμῶν τὴν χάριν καὶ τὴν κοινωνίαν τῆς διακονίας τῆς εἰς
τοὺς ἁγίους, **5** καὶ οὐ καθὼς ἠλπίσαμεν
ἀλλὰ ἑαυτοὺς ἔδωκαν πρῶτον τῷ κυ-
ρίῳ καὶ ἡμῖν διὰ θελήματος θεοῦ **6** εἰς
τὸ παρακαλέσαι ἡμᾶς Τίτον, ἵνα καθὼς προενήρξατο οὕτως καὶ ἐπιτελέσῃ εἰς ὑμᾶς καὶ τὴν χάριν ταύτην.

2 Cor 8:16–17

Χάρις δὲ τῷ θεῷ τῷ ⸀δόντι τὴν αὐτὴν σπουδὴν ὑπὲρ ὑμῶν ἐν τῇ καρδίᾳ Τί-
του, **17** ὅτι τὴν μὲν παράκλησιν ἐδέξατο,
σπουδαιότερος δὲ ὑπάρχων αὐθαίρετος ἐξῆλθεν πρὸς ὑμᾶς.

2 Cor 8:23

εἴτε ὑπὲρ Τίτου, κοινωνὸς ἐμὸς καὶ εἰς ὑμᾶς συνεργός· εἴτε ἀδελφοὶ ἡμῶν, ἀπόστολοι ἐκκλησιῶν, δόξα Χριστοῦ.

2 Cor 12:16–18

Ἔστω δέ, ἐγὼ οὐ κατεβάρησα ὑμᾶς· ἀλλὰ
ὑπάρχων πανοῦργος δόλῳ ὑμᾶς ἔλαβον.
17 μή τινα ὧν ἀπέσταλκα πρὸς ὑμᾶς, δι᾽
αὐτοῦ ἐπλεονέκτησα ὑμᾶς; **18** παρεκάλεσα
Τίτον καὶ συναπέστειλα τὸν ἀδελφόν· μήτι ἐπλεονέκτησεν ὑμᾶς Τίτος; οὐ τῷ αὐτῷ πνεύματι περιεπατήσαμεν; οὐ τοῖς αὐτοῖς ἴχνεσιν;

Gal 2:1–5

Ἔπειτα διὰ δεκατεσσάρων ἐτῶν πάλιν ἀνέβην εἰς Ἱεροσόλυμα μετὰ Βαρναβᾶ
συμπαραλαβὼν καὶ Τίτον· **2** ἀνέβην δὲ
κατὰ ἀποκάλυψιν· καὶ ἀνεθέμην αὐτοῖς

§ 173 **Acts 12:25** ***εις*** ℵ B *Byz*] εξ 𝔓^{74} A 33. 1739 ¦ απο D E 1739. 1881 *Byz* **§ 174** **2 Cor 8:16** ***δοντι*** 𝔓^{46} ℵ^{2} D] διδοντι ℵ* B C I^{vid} (33).

173. Paul's Co-worker Mark

Col 4:10

Aristarchus my fellow prisoner greets you, as does Mark the cousin of Barnabas, concerning whom you have received instructions—if he comes to you, welcome him.

2 Tim 4:11

Only Luke is with me. Get Mark and bring him with you, for he is useful in my ministry.

Phlm 23–24

Epaphras, my fellow prisoner in Christ Jesus, sends greetings to you, **24** and so do Mark, Aristarchus, Demas, and Luke, my fellow workers.

Acts 12:11–12

Then Peter came to himself and said, "Now I am sure that the Lord has sent his angel and rescued me from the hands of Herod and from all that the Jewish people were expecting." **12** As soon as he realized this, he went to the house of Mary, the mother of John whose other name was Mark, where many had gathered and were praying.

Acts 12:25

Then after completing their mission Barnabas and Saul returned to[a] Jerusalem and brought with them John, whose other name was Mark.

Acts 13:4–5

So, being sent out by the Holy Spirit, they went down to Seleucia; and from there they sailed to Cyprus. **5** When they arrived at Salamis, they proclaimed the word of God in the synagogues of the Jews. And they had John also to assist them.

Acts 13:13

Then Paul and his companions set sail from Paphos and came to Perga in Pamphylia. John, however, left them and returned to Jerusalem

Acts 15:36–40

After some days Paul said to Barnabas, "Come, let us return and visit the believers in every city where we proclaimed the word of the Lord and see how they are doing." **37** Barnabas wanted to take with them John called Mark. **38** But Paul decided not to take with them one who had deserted them in Pamphylia and had not accompanied them in the work. **39** The disagreement became so sharp that they parted company; Barnabas took Mark with him and sailed away to Cyprus. **40** But Paul chose Silas and set out, the believers commending him to the grace of the Lord.

174. Paul's Co-worker Titus

2 Cor 2:12–13

When I came to Troas to proclaim the good news of Christ, a door was opened for me in the Lord; **13** but my mind could not rest because I did not find my brother Titus there. So I said farewell to them and went on to Macedonia.

2 Cor 7:6–7

But God, who consoles the downcast, consoled us by the arrival of Titus, **7** and not only by his coming, but also by the consolation with which he was consoled about you, as he told us of your longing, your mourning, your zeal for me, so that I rejoiced still more.

2 Cor 7:13–15

In this we find comfort. In addition to our own consolation, we rejoiced still more at the joy of Titus, because his mind has been set at rest by all of you. **14** For if I have been somewhat boastful about you to him, I was not disgraced; but just as everything we said to you was true, so our boasting to Titus has proved true as well. **15** And his heart goes out all the more to you, as he remembers the obedience of all of you, and how you welcomed him with fear and trembling.

2 Cor 8:3–6

For, as I can testify, they voluntarily gave according to their means, and even beyond their means, **4** begging us earnestly for the privilege of sharing in this ministry to the saints— **5** and this, not merely as we expected; they gave themselves first to the Lord and, by the will of God, to us, **6** so that we might urge Titus that, as he had already made a beginning, so he should also complete this generous undertaking among you.

2 Cor 8:16–17

But thanks be to God who put[a] in the heart of Titus the same eagerness for you that I myself have. **17** For he not only accepted our appeal, but since he is more eager than ever, he is going to you of his own accord.

2 Cor 8:23

As for Titus, he is my partner and co-worker in your service; as for our brothers, they are messengers of the churches, the glory of Christ.

2 Cor 12:16–18

Let it be assumed that I did not burden you. Nevertheless (you say) since I was crafty, I took you in by deceit. **17** Did I take advantage of you through any of those whom I sent to you? **18** I urged Titus to go, and sent the brother with him. Titus did not take advantage of you, did he? Did we not conduct ourselves with the same spirit? Did we not take the same steps?

Gal 2:1–5

Then after fourteen years I went up again to Jerusalem with Barnabas, taking Titus along with me. **2** I went up in response to a revelation. Then I laid

§ 173 [a] **Acts 12:25** *to* Other ancient authorities read *from* **§ 174** [a] **2 Cor 8:16** *put* Other ancient authorities read *puts*

τὸ εὐαγγέλιον ὃ κηρύσσω ἐν τοῖς ἔθνε-
σιν, κατ᾽ ἰδίαν δὲ τοῖς δοκοῦσιν, μή πως
εἰς κενὸν τρέχω ἢ ἔδραμον. 3 ἀλλ᾽ οὐδὲ
Τίτος ὁ σὺν ἐμοί, Ἕλλην ὤν, ἠναγκάσθη
περιτμηθῆναι· 4 διὰ δὲ τοὺς παρεισάκτους
ψευδαδέλφους, οἵτινες παρεισῆλθον
κατασκοπῆσαι τὴν ἐλευθερίαν ἡμῶν
ἣν ἔχομεν ἐν Χριστῷ Ἰησοῦ, ἵνα ἡμᾶς
καταδουλώσουσιν, 5 οἷς οὐδὲ πρὸς ὥραν
εἴξαμεν τῇ ὑποταγῇ, ἵνα ἡ ἀλήθεια τοῦ
εὐαγγελίου διαμείνῃ πρὸς ὑμᾶς.

2 Tim 4:9–10

Σπούδασον ἐλθεῖν πρός με ταχέως· 10 Δη-
μᾶς γάρ με ἐγκατέλιπεν ἀγαπήσας τὸν
νῦν αἰῶνα καὶ ἐπορεύθη εἰς Θεσσαλονί-
κην, Κρήσκης εἰς ⸀Γαλατίαν, Τίτος εἰς
Δαλματίαν

Cf. Titus, passim.

175. *Paul's Co-worker Tychicus*

Eph 6:21–22

Ἵνα δὲ εἰδῆτε καὶ ὑμεῖς τὰ κατ᾽ ἐμέ, τί
πράσσω, πάντα γνωρίσει ὑμῖν Τύχικος ὁ
ἀγαπητὸς ἀδελφὸς καὶ πιστὸς διάκονος
ἐν κυρίῳ, 22 ὃν ἔπεμψα πρὸς ὑμᾶς εἰς
αὐτὸ τοῦτο, ἵνα γνῶτε τὰ περὶ ἡμῶν καὶ
παρακαλέσῃ τὰς καρδίας ὑμῶν.

Col 4:7–9

Τὰ κατ᾽ ἐμὲ πάντα γνωρίσει ὑμῖν Τύχικος
ὁ ἀγαπητὸς ἀδελφὸς καὶ πιστὸς διάκονος
καὶ σύνδουλος ἐν κυρίῳ, 8 ὃν ἔπεμψα
πρὸς ὑμᾶς εἰς αὐτὸ τοῦτο, ἵνα ⸂γνῶτε τὰ
περὶ ἡμῶν⸃ καὶ παρακαλέσῃ τὰς καρδίας
ὑμῶν, 9 σὺν Ὀνησίμῳ τῷ πιστῷ καὶ ἀγα-
πητῷ ἀδελφῷ, ὅς ἐστιν ἐξ ὑμῶν· πάντα
ὑμῖν γνωρίσουσιν τὰ ὧδε.

2 Tim 4:12

Τύχικον δὲ ἀπέστειλα εἰς Ἔφεσον.

Titus 3:12

Ὅταν πέμψω Ἀρτεμᾶν πρὸς σὲ ἢ Τύχικον,
σπούδασον ἐλθεῖν πρός με εἰς Νικόπολιν,
ἐκεῖ γὰρ κέκρικα παραχειμάσαι.

Acts 20:4–6

συνείπετο δὲ αὐτῷ Σώπατρος Πύρρου
Βεροιαῖος, Θεσσαλονικέων δὲ Ἀρίσταρχος
καὶ Σεκοῦνδος, καὶ Γάϊος Δερβαῖος καὶ
Τιμόθεος, Ἀσιανοὶ δὲ Τύχικος καὶ Τρό-
φιμος. 5 οὗτοι δὲ ⸀προελθόντες ἔμενον
ἡμᾶς ἐν Τρῳάδι, 6 ἡμεῖς δὲ ἐξεπλεύσαμεν
μετὰ τὰς ἡμέρας τῶν ἀζύμων ἀπὸ Φι-
λίππων καὶ ἤλθομεν πρὸς αὐτοὺς εἰς
τὴν Τρῳάδα ἄχρι ἡμερῶν πέντε, ὅπου
διετρίψαμεν ἡμέρας ἑπτά.

176. *Paul's Co-worker Demas*

Col 4:14

ἀσπάζεται ὑμᾶς Λουκᾶς ὁ ἰατρὸς ὁ ἀγα-
πητὸς καὶ Δημᾶς.

2 Tim 4:9–10

Σπούδασον ἐλθεῖν πρός με ταχέως· 10 Δη-
μᾶς γάρ με ἐγκατέλιπεν ἀγαπήσας τὸν
νῦν αἰῶνα καὶ ἐπορεύθη εἰς Θεσσαλονί-
κην, Κρήσκης εἰς ⸀Γαλατίαν, Τίτος εἰς
Δαλματίαν

Phlm 23–24

Ἀσπάζεταί σε Ἐπαφρᾶς ὁ συναιχμά-
λωτός μου ἐν Χριστῷ Ἰησοῦ, 24 Μᾶρκος,
Ἀρίσταρχος, Δημᾶς, Λουκᾶς, οἱ συνερ-
γοί μου.

177. *Paul's Co-worker Aristarchus*

Col 4:10

Ἀσπάζεται ὑμᾶς Ἀρίσταρχος ὁ συναι-
χμάλωτός μου καὶ Μᾶρκος ὁ ἀνεψιὸς
Βαρναβᾶ (περὶ οὗ ἐλάβετε ἐντολάς, ἐὰν
ἔλθῃ πρὸς ὑμᾶς, δέξασθε αὐτόν)

Phlm 23–24

Ἀσπάζεταί σε Ἐπαφρᾶς ὁ συναιχμά-
λωτός μου ἐν Χριστῷ Ἰησοῦ, 24 Μᾶρκος,
Ἀρίσταρχος, Δημᾶς, Λουκᾶς, οἱ συνερ-
γοί μου.

Acts 19:29

καὶ ἐπλήσθη ἡ πόλις τῆς συγχύσεως,
ὥρμησάν τε ὁμοθυμαδὸν εἰς τὸ θέατρον
συναρπάσαντες Γάϊον καὶ Ἀρίσταρχον
Μακεδόνας, συνεκδήμους Παύλου.

Acts 20:4

συνείπετο δὲ αὐτῷ Σώπατρος Πύρρου
Βεροιαῖος, Θεσσαλονικέων δὲ Ἀρίσταρ-
χος καὶ Σεκοῦνδος, καὶ Γάϊος Δερβαῖος
καὶ Τιμόθεος, Ἀσιανοὶ δὲ Τύχικος καὶ
Τρόφιμος.

Acts 27:1–2

Ὡς δὲ ἐκρίθη τοῦ ἀποπλεῖν ἡμᾶς εἰς τὴν
Ἰταλίαν, παρεδίδουν τόν τε Παῦλον καί
τινας ἑτέρους δεσμώτας ἑκατοντάρχῃ
ὀνόματι Ἰουλίῳ σπείρης Σεβαστῆς. 2 ἐπι-
βάντες δὲ πλοίῳ Ἀδραμυττηνῷ μέλλοντι
πλεῖν εἰς τοὺς κατὰ τὴν Ἀσίαν τόπους
ἀνήχθημεν ὄντος σὺν ἡμῖν Ἀριστάρχου
Μακεδόνος Θεσσαλονικέως.

2 Tim 4:10 ***Γαλατιαν*** A D 33. 1739. 1881 *Byz*] Γαλλιαν א C **§ 175** **Col 4:8** ***γνωτε τα περι ημων*** (א*) A B D$^{*.c}$ 048. 33] γνω τα περι υμων 𝔓^{46} א$^{(2).c}$ C D^{1} 1739. 1881 *Byz* **Acts 20:5** ***προελθοντες*** 𝔓^{74} B^{2} D] προσελθοντες א A^{vid} B* E 1739 **§ 176** **2 Tim 4:10** ***Γαλατιαν*** A D 33. 1739. 1881 *Byz*] Γαλλιαν א C

before them (though only in a private meeting with the acknowledged leaders) the gospel that I proclaim among the Gentiles, in order to make sure that I was not running, or had not run, in vain. **3** But even Titus, who was with me, was not compelled to be circumcised, though he was a Greek. **4** But because of false believers secretly brought in, who slipped in to spy on the freedom we have in Christ Jesus, so that they might enslave us— **5** we did not submit to them even for a moment, so that the truth of the gospel might always remain with you.

2 Tim 4:9–10

Do your best to come to me soon, **10** for Demas, in love with this present world, has deserted me and gone to Thessalonica; Crescens has gone to Galatia,[b] Titus to Dalmatia.

Cf. Titus, passim.

175. Paul's Co-worker Tychicus

Eph 6:21–22

So that you also may know how I am and what I am doing, Tychicus will tell you everything. He is a dear brother and a faithful minister in the Lord. **22** I am sending him to you for this very purpose, to let you know how we are, and to encourage your hearts.

Col 4:7–9

Tychicus will tell you all the news about me; he is a beloved brother, a faithful minister, and a fellow servant in the Lord. **8** I have sent him to you for this very purpose, so that you may know how we are[a] and that he may encourage your hearts; **9** he is coming with Onesimus, the faithful and beloved brother, who is one of you. They will tell you about everything here.

2 Tim 4:12

I have sent Tychicus to Ephesus.

Titus 3:12

When I send Artemas to you, or Tychicus, do your best to come to me at Nicopolis, for I have decided to spend the winter there.

Acts 20:4–6

He was accompanied by Sopater son of Pyrrhus from Beroea, by Aristarchus and Secundus from Thessalonica, by Gaius from Derbe, and by Timothy, as well as by Tychicus and Trophimus from Asia. **5** They went ahead[b] and were waiting for us in Troas; **6** but we sailed from Philippi after the days of Unleavened Bread, and in five days we joined them in Troas, where we stayed for seven days.

176. Paul's Co-worker Demas

Col 4:14

Luke, the beloved physician, and Demas greet you.

2 Tim 4:9–10

Do your best to come to me soon, **10** for Demas, in love with this present world, has deserted me and gone to Thessalonica; Crescens has gone to Galatia,[a] Titus to Dalmatia.

Phlm 23–24

Epaphras, my fellow prisoner in Christ Jesus, sends greetings to you, **24** and so do Mark, Aristarchus, Demas, and Luke, my fellow workers.

177. Paul's Co-worker Aristarchus

Col 4:10

Aristarchus my fellow prisoner greets you, as does Mark the cousin of Barnabas, concerning whom you have received instructions—if he comes to you, welcome him.

Phlm 23–24

Epaphras, my fellow prisoner in Christ Jesus, sends greetings to you, **24** and so do Mark, Aristarchus, Demas, and Luke, my fellow workers.

Acts 19:29

The city was filled with the confusion; and people rushed together to the theater, dragging with them Gaius and Aristarchus, Macedonians who were Paul's travel companions.

Acts 20:4

He was accompanied by Sopater son of Pyrrhus from Beroea, by Aristarchus and Secundus from Thessalonica, by Gaius from Derbe, and by Timothy, as well as by Tychicus and Trophimus from Asia.

Acts 27:1–2

When it was decided that we were to sail for Italy, they transferred Paul and some other prisoners to a centurion of the Augustan Cohort, named Julius. **2** Embarking on a ship of Adramyttium that was about to set sail to the ports along the coast of Asia, we put to sea, accompanied by Aristarchus, a Macedonian from Thessalonica.

[b] **2 Tim 4:10** *Galatia* Other ancient authorities read *Gaul* **§ 175** [a] **Col 4:8** *that you may know how we are* Other ancient authorities read *that I may know how you are* [b] **Acts 20:5** *went ahead* Other ancient authorities read *came* **§ 176** [a] **2 Tim 4:10** *Galatia* Other ancient authorities read *Gaul*

Glossary

apostolic parousia a feature of Paul's letters in which Paul reminds his readers of the presence of his apostolic authority and power among them through his written letter, the sending of envoys, or his own coming visit

appeal a conventional element in Paul's letters in which Paul exhorts his readers, typically using the verb form *parakalō* ("I appeal")

blessing a segment of Paul's letters, similar in function to the Pauline thanksgiving, in which Paul gives praise to God for his activity in the lives of the apostle and his readers

closing of the body a segment of Paul's letters, the nature and extent of which is debated, which functions to close the main body of the epistle

collection for the saints the gathering of funds from Paul's converts among the gentiles in behalf of the poor among the faithful in Jerusalem, organized by Paul at the behest of Peter, James, and John and serving as a concrete token of unity in Christ among Jewish and gentile believers

commendation a conventional element in Paul's letters in which he commends the bearer(s) of the epistle to the recipients

creedal fragments proposed tacit quotations, full or partial, of early Christian creeds

doxology a short acclamation of praise to God

greetings a segment in the closing portion of Paul's letters in which Paul conveys expressions of endearment to and from fellow believers

hardship catalogue a list of sufferings, trials, and afflictions

household code moral teaching addressed to the various members of the family or household, usually including the following pairs of relationships: husband/wife, parents/children, and master/slave

hymn fragments proposed quotations, tacit or explicit, of early Christian hymns

intermediate state the mode of existence of believers after death but prior to the resurrection of the body at Christ's second coming

new exodus the Old Testament expectation of God's coming redemptive liberation of Israel from exile

opening of the body a segment of Paul's letters which functions to open the main section of the epistle. This segment often introduces the main theme of the letter.

participation in Christ the supernatural and transforming union of believers with Christ through the indwelling of God's Spirit

pattern of teaching the best-known of several Pauline designations for the body of core Christian beliefs, often referred to as the "rule of faith"

salutation the opening segment of Paul's letters, identifying the sender and intended recipients, and adding a prayer for grace and peace. This segment may foreshadow themes to be developed in the body of the epistle.

sanctification the transformation of believers into the image of Christ through the power of the Holy Spirit so that they may share in and reflect the holiness of God

signature a segment of Paul's letters in which the apostle, after dictating the bulk of the letter to an amanuensis or secretary, takes pen in hand to add his name and brief closing remarks

summaries of the faith brief confessional formulas encapsulating core Christian beliefs

thanksgiving a segment of Paul's letters in which Paul gives thanks to God for the recipients of the letter. This segment typically foreshadows themes to be developed in the body of the epistle.

Index of Subjects

Note: Numbers following Scripture references refer to section numbers within the synopsis and *not* to page numbers.